The Macdonald
GUIDE
to
French
WINES
1986

The Macdonald
GUIDE
to
French
WINES
1986

General Editor: André Vedel

Introduced by Jancis Robinson

Macdonald

A **Macdonald** BOOK

© Hachette 1985
© English translation and text Macdonald & Co (Publishers) 1985
First published in Great Britain in 1985
by Macdonald & Co (Publishers) Ltd
London & Sydney

A member of BPCC plc

British Library Cataloguing in Publication Data
    Macdonald guide to French wines.
    1. Wine and winemaking—France
    I. Vedel, André
    641. 2'2'0944 TP553

    ISBN 0–356–10566–0

Filmset by Tradespools Ltd, Frome, Somerset.

Printed and bound in Great Britain
by Purnell & Sons (Book Production) Ltd
Member of the BPCC Group, Paulton, Bristol

Consultant Editor: Simon Taylor-Gill

Editorial: Julie Dufour, Christopher Fagg, Victoria Funk,
Deirdre McGarry, Marie-Louise Taylor, Sara Wheeler

Macdonald & Co (Publishers) Ltd
Maxwell House
74 Worship Street
London EC2A 2EN

Hachette
Wine Consultant: André Vedel
Project Director: Adélaïde Barbey
Coordinating Editors: Patrice Milleron and Catherine Montalbetti
Cartography: René Pineau and Alain Mirande
Illustrations: Véronique Chappée

With the assistance of:

FRANCE:
Georges-Albert Aoust
Pierre Bedot
Michel Bettane
Pierre Bidan
Jean Bisson
Pierre Casamayor
Robert Cordonnier
Pierre Coste
Michel Dovaz
Michel Feuillat
Christian Flacelière
Michel Garat

Pierre Gresser
Roland-Louis Guépey
Pierre Huglin
Jacques de Lamy
André Lardon
Antoine Legègue
Max Léglise
Philippe Léglise
Jean-Marie Mas
Hubert Meyer
Hugues Puel
Jacques Puisais
Charles Quittanson

Pascal Ribéreau-Gayon
François Roboth
Alex Rychlewski
Steven Spurrier
Pierre Torres
Jules Tourmeau

UK:
John Bertaut
Michael Jacobson
J. Livingstone-Learmonth
Michael Schuster
David Zambra

4

CONTENTS

QUICK REFERENCE
FOR THE READER

To find value for money at a glance, check the price points printed in red.

NB Wine labels illustrated in this book represent particularly highly recommended wines.

TABLE OF SYMBOLS

***   Exceptional
**   Very good
*   Wines of special interest
☐ White wine   ○ Sparkling white
◩ Rosé wine   ◕ Sparkling rosé
■ Red wine   ● Sparkling red
50 000, 20 000 . . . Average annual production in bottles
4ha   Area of production in hectares (does not apply to shippers', blended or cooperative wines)
▮   Vinified in stainless steel vat
◖▮   Aged in wooden cask
⌁   Thermoregulation
▣   May be bought direct from the producer
(1982) Year or vintage tasted (does not apply to blended wines or wines for drinking within the year)
✔   Other wines from the same producer or shipper
⌖ᴛ   Address
Ⲩ   Open for visiting and wine-tasting
⌖ᴛ   Proprietor's name if different from that given in the address
NB   Where no information is given it was either not supplied to the editors or does not apply to the particular wine in question

PRICE GUIDE (average price per bottle of wine bought by the case)
FRENCH PRICES
For all wines except champagne   **1** under 10F   **2** 10–20F   **3** 20–30F
                                               4 30–50F   **5** 50–100F   **6** over 100F
For champagne   ❶ under 50F   ❷ 50–70F   ❸ 70–100F
                                              ❹ 100–150F   ❺ over 150F

UK EQUIVALENT PRICES (including UK Excise Duty and VAT)
For all wines except champagne   **1** under £3   **2** £3–£4   **3** £4–£5
                                             4 £5–£9   **5** £9–£12.50   **6** over £12.50
For champagne   ❶ under £7   ❷ £7–£8.50   ❸ £8.50–£15
                                              ❹ £15–£20   ❺ over £20
Price symbols printed in red indicate particularly good value for money.

KEY TO VINTAGES

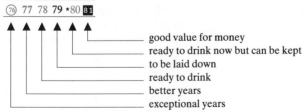

⑦⑥ 77 78 **79** *80 **81**

▲ ▲ ▲ ▲ ▲
                          good value for money
                      ready to drink now but can be kept
                  to be laid down
              ready to drink
          better years
      exceptional years

NB   No vintages are given for blended wines or wines intended for drinking within a year of the harvest.

ABOUT THIS BOOK

An Objective Guide
The *Macdonald Guide to French Wines* has been specially put together by over two hundred wine experts and professionals who have tasted wines throughout France and selected over five thousand for inclusion. The entries include wines of Appellation d'Origine Contrôlée, Vins Délimités de Qualité Supérieure and Vins de Pays. The sole aim of the book is to be a buyer's guide for wine-drinkers, and to ensure impartiality there has been no participation in the form of advertising by wine-producers, merchants or cooperatives. The quality ratings awarded by the tasters (0–3 stars for each wine) compare wines only within a single appellation, as it is impossible to judge wines of different appellations on the same scale.

Whenever a label is reproduced, that wine, in the estimation of the judges, is particularly worthy of recommendation. Both established and little-known wines have been singled out for this notice.

An Easy-to-Understand Classification System
The first part of the guide gives the background necessary to appreciate French wines, including historical and technical information, as well as advice on buying, keeping and serving. The wines are then listed:
– by region
– by appellation, arranged geographically within each region
– alphabetically within each appellation.
At the back of the book four indexes enable the reader to find appellations, wines, producers and communes, while 48 new maps show where all the French vineyards are situated.

Every effort has been made to include all French wines above a certain level of quality, but for several reasons this guide is not exhaustive. In some cases, wines were eliminated by the judges during tasting; in others, the producers refused to submit samples for tasting, or would not allow the publication of details about the wine. Likewise, some wines are listed without the full complement of background information. Absence of a year may mean (as with non-vintage champagnes) that the wine has been blended from the production of more than one vintage, or that (as with some Beaujolais wines) the wine is meant to be drunk as soon as possible or in the year it was produced. Shippers' blends or cooperative wines that are the product of more than one vineyard will not carry information about vineyard area.

A Buyer's Guide
The aim of the quide is to help the wine-drinker choose the most suitable wine at the best price. All the information is presented so as to make this process as simple and straightforward as possible. Before looking up a particular wine, it is important to read the general introductions and the introductions to each region and appellation, because certain information common to all the wines in that category is not repeated in each entry.
– The key to the symbols is given on page 7.
– The price categories (shown by the small numbers in black or red boxes) should be taken as general indications only. Because of local laws and taxes, wine prices vary widely and cannot be specified exactly.
– The technical terms used to describe the wines are explained in the Glossary.

8

INTRODUCTION

JANCIS ROBINSON MW

A CHASM yawns between Britain and France far deeper than the English Channel, and far deeper than the English like to admit. It has nothing to do with geography but concerns something much more important, our way of life. The French even manage to put it more elegantly. *'Façon de vivre'* is so much richer and more delicately nuanced than our blunt English phrase.

The poetry and measure of the French language is just one aspect of French culture that we envy. There are other more visible, yet no more attainable, symptoms of inherent superiority. Even the most fashion-conscious Londoner can see in the typical Parisienne a uniquely stylish way of dressing that is somehow quite inimitable. The Anglo-Saxon shopper in France feels cossetted by both presentation and packaging in a way that is quite unknown back home.

Of the several ways in which we British must admit the French are ahead of us, it is their gastronomy, and their attitude to it, that we find most exasperatingly covetable. For many of us, the mere sight of a French roadsign is enough to get the gastric juices flowing in free association with memories of glorious meals past. The Frenchman knows that food and wine are important and he knows, damn him, that he has access to the finest in the world. Not only that, he sees one as a necessary adjunct to and partner of the other. Whereas the Briton's wine connoisseurship consists so often in isolated and unnourished facts concerning vintages and classifications, the Frenchman's wine knowledge is made up of detailed local knowledge and specific experiences in matching the wine of a particular region with the appropriate regional dishes.

Now, at last, we are being given a chance to penetrate the Frenchman's world of wine. *The Macdonald Guide to French Wines 1986* is the first exciting attempt to bridge the chasm of ignorance that has kept the non-Gallic peoples from fully understanding those wines and producers considered best in France itself.

Translated from the first of a series of annual wine guides to be published simultaneously by Macdonald and the estimable French firm of Hachette, this book is the culmination of a daunting tasting exercise supervised throughout 1985 by André Vedel, recently retired Inspecteur Général of the official Institut National des Appellations d'Origine (INAO). It would be difficult to think of a less partial and more knowledgeable guide through France's *vignoble*.

After marshalling samples from producers all over the country, panels of distinguished and expert tasters (unidentified for the benefit of their own professional reputations) have chosen the 5000 current wines described so fully in this book. Here for the first time we have a book that describes exactly individual bottlings. Far more than a note on how Beaujolais in general tastes, much more than a description of the house style of Pasquier-Desvignes for instance, this unique new guide gives detailed notes on forty-one top quality different wines that qualify for the basic Beaujolais appellation, including Pasquier-Desvignes, 1984 bottling, as well as a further sixty 1983 and 1984 Beaujolais-Villages from a wide range of growers and *négociants*, and more than a hundred mouthwatering individual wines from the best *cru* villages.

The information given includes not just a detailed tasting note and assessment, but the full address of the producer, when he may be visited, which other vintages can be recommended, the size of the relevant vineyard, how much of the wine was produced and, in many cases, what sort of food it would partner particularly well. Inevitably, this first edition contains a tantalizing number of wines that are not yet commercially available in this country. (Just wait till our more energetic wine merchants get their hands on this book, however.) The sheer variety and range of the wines listed, in fact, is a positive temptation to transform your own next trip to France from mere holiday to a delightfully bibulous *voyage de dégustation*.

For me, one of the most useful aspects of the book is its accurate portrayal of the French winescape as it really is in the 1980s. The section on Vins de Pays, for instance, provides us with a uniquely useful and discerning guide to this recently established category, which can all too often blur into a succession of indistinguishable light red wines from the Midi. The Languedoc-Roussillon chapter likewise identifies the lifebouys in this wildly variable sea of vines. And in those corners of France such as Jura, Savoie and Corsica, about which we British are so shamefully ignorant, the guide's enlightenment must mark an English-language publishing first.

First things last, however. It is probably the general introductory chapters that provide us with the most concentrated information on how we are to acquire the *savoir faire* of the French in matters gastronomical. As suggested on page 67, I am already learning to distinguish between African and South American cocoa beans. Within these pages is the France that the French drink.

PREFACE

ANDRE VEDEL

Former Inspecteur Général, Institut National des Appellations d'Origine (INAO)

ONE OF the earliest records we have of the existence of *Vitis lambrusca*, the wild vine which all the so-called European varieties are descended from, is, by a strange coincidence, a grape pip which has been perfectly preserved for over a thousand years in the peat bogs of Beaune. But can it really be coincidence, or did the god of wine have a hand in this amusing connection between the capital of the Burgundy wine region and this humble relic of *Vitis vinifera*? Our distant ancestors, themselves descendants of the wild horse hunters of the Solutré area in the heart of Burgundy, were probably already enjoying, after their roast meat, an autumnal delicacy of grapes picked from the vine-branches climbing around the trees near the streams.

It would be misleading, however, to try to establish a continuity between the prehistoric lovers of the tiny, strong and bitter wild fruits and the knowledgeable and inspired vine-cultivators of today. For one thing, there cannot be a direct relationship between the indigenous *Vitis lambrusca* and vines such as the Pinot Noir in Burgundy, Cabernet-Franc in Bordeaux or Riesling in Alsace, as climatic conditions have on several occasions since driven certain vegetal species back into areas that were for a short time more favourable. Each time this happened, the vine had to wait for more temperate climes before recolonizing whole regions of France. For another thing, although some people think the first attempts at developing the vine took place in lakeside cities built on pilings, the evidence leads us to believe that vinification techniques were imported into France.

Wine and the Mediterranean are, after all, inextricably bound up together; it is one of the essential components of the civilization born on the banks of this inland sea. Cultivation of the vine and knowledge of vinification processes go far back into antiquity, to the first civilizations in the eastern basin of the Mediterranean and the neighbouring Asiatic countries: the best illustration of this are Egyptian wall-paintings showing the wine-harvest and grape-pressing.

There are two figures who show best to what extent wine dominates not only the material life of the Mediterranean peoples but also their spiritual life: Dionysus (the Roman Bacchus), and Jesus Christ. The first, the Greek god of wine and drunkenness, was always accompanied by his son Priapus and a wild procession of satyrs, silenuses and other scantily-clad bacchantes. But there was more to Dionysian revelries and Bacchanalian frolics than drinking sessions degenerating into wild orgies. The stimulating and intoxicating properties of wine enabled the reveller to shed his earthly fetters and become one with the divine. The major Dionysian spring festivities, at which poetry reading contests took place while the participants samples the new wine, mark the beginnings of Classical tragedy.

Any excuse to raise a glass or two, the sceptics may say. But the sacred nature of the holy drink is very much in evidence as far as Christianity is concerned: wine, the vine and the wine-grower are such apt metaphors for the human condition that they occur 441 times in the Bible. From Noah, whose first concern on leaving the ark was to plant a vine, to St Paul, who advised wine as a cure for stomach-ache, the list of Biblical names associated with wine includes Solomon,

11

David, Judith, Esther, Peter and many others. No coincidence, perhaps, that Christ's first miracle was to turn water into wine.

The digressions to ancient Greece and biblical Palestine do, in fact, partially explain why France has so many hundreds of thousands of hectares of vines. Followers of Dionysus introduced the cultivation of the vine, and then disciples of Jesus encouraged it. At the beginning of the sixth century BC the founders of the Phocaean colony Massila (now Marseilles) planted a vineyard in a rather wretched region where the benefits of wine were unknown. The vine did not spread beyond the shores of the Mediterranean until the Roman colonization of Gaul. It is uncertain whether the Gauls themselves initiated the techniques of vine development or whether their Italian masters taught them. Whichever it was, the result is undisputed: as soon as the grape-juice had passed their lips they were hooked. Wine production grew increasingly lucrative as trade developed, prospering so much to the detriment of wheat that in AD 92 Emperor Domitian had to pass measures limiting the trade's expansion in order to guarantee an adequate supply of bread! In fact, although bread and wine are so closely associated in the Eucharist, they were in fact great rivals in French economic history, representing solid necessity versus liquid luxury.

The Roman Empire in Europe crumbled in the fifth century. After the disasters of the barbarian invasions, the vine grew up again behind Attila and established itself in areas as far north as Normandy and Brittany, and even in what is now Belgium and southern England. The early medieval Church, whose influence was at that time decisive, was of course suspicious of the abuse of wine, which it claimed transformed men into beasts. But at the same time, it respected wine as a gift of God; it certainly contributed to the development of the vineyards for example. Medieval religious orders played a particularly large part in viticultural progress, and still today many crus, appellations and traditions bear witness to this action, which affected every wine-growing region of France for over a thousand years. We owe the perfecting of sparkling wine production, for example, to the famous Benedictine monk from Champagne, Dom Pérignon (1639–1715).

From the waning of the Middle Ages to the present day, we have witnessed the gradual disappearance of the vineyards of northern France, except those in Alsace and the east. There was little point in continuing the uphill struggle of producing wine in areas ill-suited to the task, since transportation, especially by train, was becoming increasingly fast, and one could easily bring wine up from the South of France. Thus Montmartre and Suresnes are the last remnants of one of the greatest vineyards (in quantity if not in quality) of the Middle Ages.

Where hail, drought, floods and Attila himself had failed, a minute aphid from America was about to succeed. From 1865 to 1895 *phylloxera vastatrix* destroyed virtually every vineyard in France. This was an unprecedented catastrophe and a scourge which affected many thousands of wine-growers, but, for all that, it did not break their spirit. After a good deal of trial and error it was realized that the only solution was to graft French vine strains onto American stocks that were resistant to the aphid. But the problem of phylloxera brought in its wake dire economic and social mutations. The vineyards of Bordeaux, Burgundy and Champagne recovered fairly quickly, but others took years to return to normal. What was more, many small wine-producers abandoned their work to migrate to the towns. Only those with the means and the foresight to carry out the necessary technical inventions survived.

Wine, then, is one of the essential components of French history, and, more generally, of the Mediterranean basin as a whole. But in certain regions it is even more than that: it directly determines the economy, traditions and attitudes – the civilization of entire communities. First and foremost, the vine dictates the yearly cycle of those who cultivate it. Between one harvest and the next, delicate operations such as pulling up the vine-props, earthing-up, replacing dead stocks, pruning, training the new shoots, chemical treatments and trimming, leave the wine-grower with precious little free time. Despite technical advances, viticulture demands constant care, far in excess of the work involved in mechanized cereal-growing or industrial stock-farming.

No one has demonstrated the truth of the adage 'strength through unity' better than the wine-grower. The amount of effort required, the need to keep the harvest as short as possible and the preservation of quality has led them to adopt community tactics. Until 1789 the guilds imposed very restrictive measures upon all agricultural work; for this reason the date the grape harvest began was collectively decided. This legacy has to a large degree been taken up by the *syndicats d'appellations* or by the *caves coopératives* which began in the Langue-doc at the beginning of the twentieth century and are now widespread in France.

This community organization goes beyond the strictly agricultural aspect. The medieval *confréries*, originally religious mutual aid groups, reappeared in the twentieth century and began to ally folklore or tradition with trade and promotion. Groups such as the Chevaliers du Sacavin, the Chevaliers du Tastevin, the Sorciers et Birettes de Bué-en-Sancerrois or the Fins Gosiers d'Anjou, all wine-lovers, make the most of St Vincent's day or St Vernier's day, or any other appropriate occasion, to show off the produce of their vineyards. Their insignias, costumes and high-flown titles call upon a glorious tradition; by claiming famous personalities, both French and foreign, as patrons in the name of public relations, these societies are doing no more than the religious communities of days gone by did in seeking the favour of eminent nobles for their wines. By their love of drinking, and their very names, these wine confréries consciously evoke a gustatory tradition going back to Ancient Greece and Rome.

The setting against which life unfolds is also shaped by the vine. The countryside of Champagne, the Gironde or Burgundy has for centuries fashioned itself around orderly rows of vine-stocks. Architecture is decisively influenced by it too, since in wine-growing areas the cellar is the most important part of a house. Often, the cellar is partially or completely underground, perhaps vaulted – and sometimes even hollowed into rock, as in the Loire valley or in the St-Emilion area – or, as in Bordeaux and the south-west, may constitute the entire ground floor of the house.

As well as being the undisputed master in areas where it is produced, wine also influences the life of regions where it is drunk. According to recent statistics, almost 80 per cent of French people over fourteen drink wine either regularly or occasionally. Only 20 per cent of the population do not drink it at all. In northern France, which had vineyards only briefly, and in all the beer-drinking nations, wine has been a welcome ray of sunshine ever since boats, lorries and trains have been able to transport it. It occupies the place of honour on dining-tables the world over, from Los Angeles and Stockholm to Tokyo and Sydney, and there are many foreigners, not least the English, who know as much about the great French wines as we French ourselves.

The success of French wines is clearly due to their quality, but in addition French writers have long been great ambassadors of wine. We French pride ourselves equally on our wine and our literature, and indeed the two go hand in hand, the first inspiring the second and the second in turn praising the first. Rabelais, the great sixteenth-century humanist and writer, whose father grew vines, wrote his magnum opus for a public who loved the 'sacred bottle'. One can hardly imagine Gargantua and Pantagruel without their local Chinon wine. '*Sus à ce vin, compaings! Enfants, beuvez à pleins guodetz*' writes Rabelais, and for him the sacred drink is the symbol of life and hidden truth: *in vino veritas*.

It is not possible here to list all the French authors who have written of wine, but we can at least note a keen interest in the subject in such varied a selection as Diderot, Voltaire, Baudelaire – who was highly suspicious of teetotallers – Huysmans, Barrès and Claudel. Some of them saw wine as a means of uniting men, others as a symbol of Mediterranean civilization, others again as a sort of quintessence of the French character. In a populist and humoristic vein, René Fallet, who wrote '*Le Beaujolais nouveau est arrivé*', takes up the themes of conviviality and national character. '*On ne trinque pas tout seul*' he writes in *La Soupe aux choux*, while one of his heroes declares '*Tu me fais offense! Tu es en France, mon gars, et en France on boit le coup quand on a quelqu'un à la maison, on n'est pas des sauvages!*'.

However, the sacred bottle has its opponents who see it as a poison to the body and a social scourge. But one should not confuse usage and excess. Their affirmations may be partly true, but they are often too dogmatic and should be qualified. It is absolutely indisputable that wine can be very good for the health. Consider its etymology: *vitis* (the vine) and *vita* (life) – wine is life. Its acidity is good for the digestion, and its relaxing properties benefit many bodily functions. Besides its therapeutic and constitutional qualities, which have been known for thousands of years, wine has properties which make it one of the most efficient ways of disinfecting polluted water, for the tannins it contains neutralize viruses and bacteria. Moreover, recent research has shown its effects on the cardio-vascular system: a public enquiry in *The Lancet* in 1979 revealed the inverse relationship between wine consumption and coronary death. The latter is three to five times less common in France and Italy than in Ireland and Scotland, where wine-drinking is not so widespread.

So perhaps one really can say 'Your health!' as one raises one's glass. One can go further and use particular wines as a cure for individual complaints. For example, light white wine is good for high blood pressure and obesity, sweet white for high blood pressure, champagne for convalescents, red Bordeaux for pregnant women and so on. Anyway, it's much more fun to go to the wine-seller than the chemist.

The correlation usually made between cirrhosis of the liver and wine may be unfounded. Anyone still sceptical should take note of Hippocrates, the father of medicine, whose opinion is quite clear-cut: 'Wine suits man marvellously well, if, in health as in illness, he uses it sensibly and in moderation, according to his individual constitution'.

The word moderation is essential. In fact wine is a good training in the exercise of moderation. Healthy in itself, it must be taken in reasonable proportion, as it is excess of it that justifiably invokes the doctors' anger. To moderation one can add the fundamental exercise of discernment, since through-out the history of vinification in France the quest for quality has mobilized the collective energy. Technical progress, restrictive laws, promotional activities by the wine confréries – all are different facets of the exclusive search for perfection.

Considering the question of exactly what constitutes quality in a wine, as early as 1600 Olivier de Serres concluded 'air, earth and the correct choice of vine'. This definition is in fact fairly unassailable, since the climate, the soil and the vine are always the three basic factors which determine the potential of a cru. They can be exploited to the full by a skilful wine-grower, but it is impossible to surpass them. In this sense, today's crus have not been 'created' by man; indeed, man's role has always been a humble one. The ideal combination of place and plant is found only through experience: in two thousand years of vine cultivation French wine-makers have accumulated a wealth of experience from which they have established an ecosystem. This is formed by the plant, the location and the techniques of cultivation, which vary from region to region, and give rise to the abundance of crus of which France is justifiably proud. There is no doubt that decisions such as that of Philippe le Hardi, who in 1395 passed an edict limiting the choice of vines and manures, have been positive ones. Nor is there any doubt that contemporary science has eliminated many of the accidents and diseases that have frequently caused vine defects in the past. But neither decisions at the highest level nor the findings of oenology can compare with the often faltering, sometimes even tortuous developments that have made French vineyards what they are today. The best wines are objects of great pride, and at the same time a lesson in patience and modesty.

One wonders if it is really possible to define the criteria for the quality of a wine. Taking gastronomic considerations alone, three elements stand out: the taste of the drinker, the suitability of a wine for any given occasion, and the class or hierarchical position it occupies. The first two are eminently subjective: taste is a function of personal preferences, habits and even prejudices; as for suitability, as anyone who has planned a meal knows, it depends upon many contradictory opinions, and the pairing of food and wine is often a terrible headache. Classification is more objective, as it depends on the 'length' of the wine, the yardstick of which is the aromatic persistence in the mouth, measured in seconds, after spitting out or swallowing.

To the eternal pessimists who claim that the quality of French wine is threatened, perhaps even mortally wounded, I would point out that we have nonetheless found five thousand different wines to recommended to our readers. From this wide range they may choose with confidence. When they have guests, the first thing they will do is go down to the cellar, choose a bottle to suit their guest's taste and the honour they wish to bestow upon him, then fill the glasses: wine, still a unique drink, remains for me the symbol of hospitality, friendship and *joie-de-vivre*.

AN INTRODUCTION TO WINE

WINE IS THE fermented juice – also called 'must' – of grapes, and occurs quite naturally. The pulp of the grape is composed of about 30 per cent sugar. When the skin of the grape is broken, natural yeasts on the skin begin to convert the sugar into alcohol – the process of fermentation.

Left to its own devices, the fermentation will continue until almost all the sugar is converted to alcohol – or until the alcohol is about 15 per cent of the total volume of wine. If the grapes are particularly rich in sugar, the wine will be sweet. Normally the sugar is consumed, so that, in general, wine can be said to be naturally dry.

The skills of the wine-maker shape the process of fermentation in a number of ways in order to produce different types and styles of wine. Fermentation can be stopped before all the sugar is used up by adding alcohol or sulphur, or by filtering out the yeast. This will produce a sweet wine. Or the fermentation can be left to run its course to produce a dry wine. Or the still-fermenting wine can be bottled and left to undergo secondary fermentation in the bottle. In this method, carbonic gases produced by fermentation dissolve into the wine to create sparkling wine. Moreover, depending on the variety of grapes used, the wine-maker can produce red, white or rosé wine. He can distil the wine to make brandy – or he can add distilled grape spirit to wine to make a fortified wine.

This brief summary gives some idea of what we mean by wine-making. Yet, within the last thirty years, wine-making (viniculture) has undergone a technical and conceptual revolution. Today's scientific methods underpin a multi-billion dollar international trade. Advances in knowledge and control have led to an overall improvement in quality in the technical sense that the customer is much less likely to buy a badly made or unstable product than was the case twenty years ago. Yet most wine drinkers would agree that the quality factor in wine runs far beyond the standardization of an industrial product. There is wine and wine. And it is no coincidence that those wines with the greatest reputations of a century ago, at the dawn of wine's Industrial Revolution, are still in the front rank of today's high-tech wine industry. The fact reminds us that wines of the first quality are the product of particularly favourable ecological and climatic circumstances combined with the highest standards of care in production.

THE CLASSIFICATION OF FRENCH WINES

France – which produces more wine of quality than any other nation in the world – was the first wine-growing country to begin the process of classification and regulation necessary to maintain and improve standards. The listing of the wine estates of Médoc, for example, completed in 1855, has been described as the most ambitious grading of the products of the soil ever attempted! The last forty years have seen France move towards its present integrated system of classification. At the top level are the wines permitted to use the classification Appellation d'Origine Controlée (AOC), in the second rank are the wines defined as Vins Delimités de Qualité Superieure (VDQS) and, since 1973, the table wines classified as Vins de Pays have formed a third category of their own.

Each category defines the criteria for inclusion – from where the wine may be grown, and the grape varieties which must be used, to the maximum permitted yield per hectare, the chemical composition of the wine, and the locations where the wine may be bottled. The bodies responsible for administering French wine law carry out a continuous programme of inspection, analysis and tasting, to ensure that the criteria are upheld, to advance deserving candidates from a lower to a higher rank – and, where necessary, to demote offenders.

The French system of classification has greatly influenced EEC wine law. The EEC classification Vins de Qualité Produits dans une Région Determiné (vqprd) includes both French aoc and vdqs wines. The vqprd category takes in the top 21 per cent of European wine production: the rest is classified as Vins de Table (66 per cent), with the remainder (13 per cent) kept for distillation.

TYPES OF WINE
French wines, whether red, white or rosé, can be divided into five main categories:

Dry Wines *(Vins secs)*
Wines in which nearly all the sugar in the grape must has been converted to alcohol, leaving less than 2 grams of sugar per litre.

Medium-Dry Wines *(Vins demi-secs)*
Wines in which the process of fermentation has been arrested to leave a residual amount of sugar, giving a shade of sweetness to the finished wine.

Sweet Wines *(Vins liquoreux)*
Wines produced from grapes that are very rich in sugar. When the natural process of fermentation has finished, the remaining sugar gives these wines their distinctive sweetness. The wines from Sauternes and Barsac are particularly rich. They are obtained from grapes not only naturally high in sugar but sweetened further by 'noble rot' *(pourriture noble)*. This is a fungus which, under the right conditions, softens the skin of the grape and lets the juice evaporate, concentrating the sugar and flavouring elements.

Sparkling Wines *(Vins mousseux)*
The sparkle in sparkling wine is created by the release of carbonic gas, a by-product of fermentation, dissolved in the wine. The classifications of French sparkling wines are:

Méthode Champenoise The legally prescribed method of producing champagne. The wine is allowed to undergo a secondary fermentation inside the specially strong and tightly sealed bottle. Under great pressure, the carbonic gas dissolves into the wine, giving champagne its uniquely vigorous and long-lasting sparkle.
Crémant A Méthode Champenoise wine, fermented so as to produce a carbonic gas content slightly lower than that of champagne.
Cuve close In this case, the secondary fermentation takes place in a sealed vat rather than the bottle. The method is used for producing a great deal of cheaper sparkling wine.
Other sparkling wines Industrially produced sparkling wine of modest quality is made by an artificial addition of carbonic gas using the cuve close method. This wine, 'fizzy' rather than sparkling, very quickly goes flat after being uncorked.
Pétillant wines Wines with a slight natural sparkle (defined as a pressure of between 1 and 2.5 bars). Their alcoholic content must exceed 7 per cent.

Fortified Wines *(Vins doux naturels)*
These are wines to which have been added neutral alcohol, wine-based alcohol
(such as brandy), concentrated grape must, or a combination of all three. The
additions may be made during or after fermentation. If made during fermentation, the addition of alcohol will prevent further fermentation.

VITICULTURE AND THE VINE

The vine belongs to the genera *Vitis*, a huge family of climbers which flourishes
throughout the world. Traditionally, wine has been produced from different
varieties of the species *Vitis vinifera*, cultivated in Greece from about 2000 BC, and
in Italy, Sicily and North Africa from about 1000 BC. Southern France received
the vine in about 600 BC; it was introduced by Greek or Phoenician traders. But
the real expansion of viticulture in Europe north of the Alps was the gift of the
Roman Empire. The Romans established what are still the most important
European vineyard regions, lying to the south of a line running from the German
Rhine valley to the estuary of the Loire.

In the ancient world, and through the Middle Ages, vines were cultivated by
the 'provignage' method. They were allowed to ramble unchecked, the woody
stems supported a small distance from the ground by little props, or trained up
trees or specially constructed pergolas – as still happens in Portugal today. As
time went by, however, growers learned to prune their vines right back to form
bushes: thus the yield was reduced in quantity, but more concentrated in sugar
and flavour. At the same time research went on to produce crossed varieties
specially suited to particular localities and micro-climates.

This process of refinement emphasized the vulnerability of *Vitis vinifera* to
fungal diseases such as oidium or mildew and insect pests such as the phylloxera
beetle. A century ago, phylloxera, imported from America, ravaged the European vines. Then it was discovered that American species of vine were immune to
phylloxera. The solution – to graft European vines onto a root-stock of a resistant
American variety – allowed for the re-establishment of the European vineyards.
With the trifling exceptions of very small plantings of 'pre-phylloxera' European
vines which still exist, all European wine is produced from vines grafted onto the
rootstocks of American varieties. Since the 1930s attempts have been made to
produce hybrids that would combine the disease-resistance of the American
varieties with the quality of wine produced by the true European vine. Such
hybrids have been grown experimentally outside the Appellation Contrôlée
areas. At best, they produce good rather than fine wine.

GRAPE VARIETIES

There are a number of varieties – often called 'varietals' – of the species *Vitis
vinifera*. Each wine-producing region has selected the varietal best suited to local
conditions, although economic factors and the development of the consumer's
taste may also influence this decision. Some vineyards produce wines from a
single type of vine (the Pinot Noir in Burgundy and the Riesling in Alsace). In
other regions (Champagne, Bordeaux) the greatest wines are produced from a
combination of several varietals with complementary qualities. Each varietal itself
represents a collection of individual elements (clones) which may vary considerably in growth rates, productivity and resistance to infection. The selection of the
best stocks has, therefore, always been a matter for careful research.

The conditions in which the vine is grown have a decisive influence on the
quality of the wine. Yields may be considerably altered according to fertilization,
the density of planting, the choice of root-stock and method of pruning. In
general, quality usually suffers when yields are increased. However, quality is not

19

Region	Grape Variety	Type of Wine
Burgundy red wines	Pinot Noir	Fine wines for long-term drinking
Burgundy white wines	Chardonnay	Fine wines for long-term drinking
Beaujolais	Gamay	Light wines for early drinking
Northern Rhône red wines	Syrah	Fine wines for long-term drinking
Northern Rhône white wines	Marsanne, Rousanne, Viognier	Fine wines for short- or long-term drinking
Southern Rhône, Languedoc, Côtes de Provence	Grenache, Cinsault, etc.	Soft wines for short- to medium-term drinking
Alsace (each grape variety is vinified alone and lends its name to the wine)	Riesling, Pinot Gris, Tokay, Gewürztraminer, Sylvaner, etc.	Aromatic wines for immediate drinking. The best may be laid down.
Champagne	Pinot, Chardonnay	For immediate drinking
Loire white wines	Sauvignon	Aromatic wines for immediate drinking
Loire white wines	Chenin	Improve with age
Loire white wines	Melon (Muscadet)	For immediate drinking
Loire red wines	Cabernet-Franc (Breton)	For short- or long-term drinking
Bordeaux red wines (Bergerac and the South-West)	Cabernet-Sauvignon, Cabernet-Franc and Merlot	Fine wines for long term drinking
Bordeaux white wines (Montravel, Monbazillac, Duras, etc.)	Sêmillon, Sauvignon, Muscadelle	Dry wines: short- to medium-term drinking Sweet wines: medium- to long-term drinking

affected when the increased quantity is obtained from favourable natural factors; certain very good years may also result from particularly large harvests. The increased yields, with no loss in quality, obtained over recent years are especially bound up with improved methods of cultivation. Maximum yield is now around 50–60 hectolitres per hectare for the better red wines and a little more for dry white wines. Yields for really great wines are much smaller, perhaps 30 hl/ha. This is because the vines from which they are produced must be mature – at least ten years old. By that age they have developed the root system essential to produce top-quality grapes.

WINE-GROWING REGIONS: SOIL AND CLIMATE

In its widest sense, the term 'wine-growing region' expresses a complex relationship between many natural factors. Particulars of geography, climate, fundamental geology, the composition of the topsoil, all bear on the question as to which type of vine will thrive under local conditions. However, historical, human and commercial factors must also be considered; it is clear, for example, that the existence of the port of Bordeaux and the great flow of trade with Europe to the north stimulated the Bordelais wine producers to improve the quality of their produce from the beginning of the eighteenth century.

The vine may be cultivated in the northern hemisphere between 35° and 50° latitude and is adaptable to a range of climates. The vine's greatest need is for water: its greatest enemies are cold and damp – its optimum ripening temperature is in the range 25°–28°C. These factors determine which types of vine can be grown where. The most northerly vineyards, for example, grow only white grapes, which ripen before the autumn cold. In warm climates, late-ripening vines are grown, in some cases allowing large-scale production.

Although ripe grapes are required to produce a good wine, they must not ripen too quickly or too completely since this would cause a loss of aromatic potential. For the great vineyards situated in 'marginal' climatic zones, the irregularity, from one year to another, of the climatic conditions during the ripening period is the major problem. These conditions may be exaggerated by being too dry or too wet.

The soils, both topsoil and subsoil, of the vineyard play a vital, if often misunderstood, role. Vines will grow on very poor soils and, indeed, the restricted yield of poor soils helps to concentrate flavour and richness in the grapes. However, drainage is a critical factor. At various times in the growing season conditions may be too dry or too wet. The soil must be able to supply enough water for the vines to grow, yet be able to drain off excess rainwater, especially during the ripening period. Well-drained soil is essential, too, to absorb and retain heat in vineyards with summer temperatures below the optimum 25°–28°C range. Chalky and gravelly soils are particularly favourable, although sandy and clay soils are also found in vineyards of repute. Artificial drainage may be used to improve local soil conditions.

The soil also contributes to the colour, aroma and flavour of the wine. The same grape variety, under the same climatic conditions, may produce wines of markedly different character according to the type of soil on which it is grown. For example, an increase in the proportion of clay in sand and gravel beds produces red wines that are more acid, more tannic and more vigorous, but with less finesse. Equally, white wine made with the Sauvignon Blanc is more aromatic when grown on limestone, less so on sand or gravel beds or on granite schists.

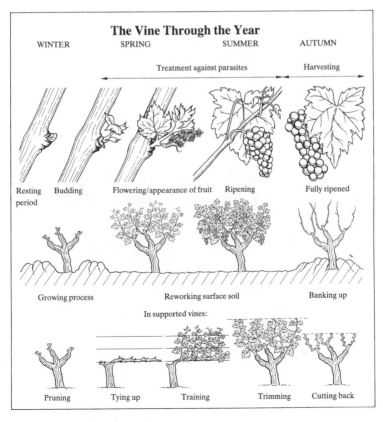

The Vine Through the Year

WINTER   SPRING   SUMMER   AUTUMN

Treatment against parasites   Harvesting

Resting period   Budding   Flowering/appearance of fruit   Ripening   Fully ripened

Growing process   Reworking surface soil   Banking up

In supported vines:

Pruning   Tying up   Training   Trimming   Cutting back

The Growers' Calendar

January

The best time for pruning is between December and March.

July

Treatment against parasites continues; the vine is regularly inspected during this period of large variations in temperature.

February

As the temperature drops, so the wine contracts. The casks are checked and topped up periodically throughout the year. The malo-lactic fermentation must now be stopped.

August

To work the soil would be harmful to the vine, but the grower must watch out for possible invasion by certain parasites. The vats are prepared in advanced regions.

March

The growing process starts. The final pruning is done. Wines that are to be drunk young are bottled.

September

A few grapes are picked regularly to check the ripening process so that a date can be fixed for the harvest. In the Mediterranean region the harvesting commences.

April

Before the phylloxera attacks, the vines are attached to poles with wire, except at Hermitage, Côte-Rôtie and Condrieu.

October

Harvesting is taking place in the majority of the vineyards. Wines that are to be laid down are put in casks to mature.

May

The vines are watched and protected against the spring frosts. The soil is treated for a second time.

November

The young wines are put in bottles. The development of the new wines is watched. The preparation for pruning begins.

June

The vines are tied up and the trimming of the young shoots begins. The flowering season will decide the size of the vintage.

December

The temperature in the cellars remain constant to ensure proper alcoholic and malo-lactic fermentation.

PROGRAMME FOR WORK ON THE VINE

The vine's growing season begins in mid-March, when the sap begins to rise. In early June, the vine flowers: when the grapes are set, the long period of ripening starts, culminating in the *vendange* or grape harvest in September (although late picking may go on into November). At every stage, the wine-grower has to devote great care to the present and future welfare of his vines.

Annual pruning is usually carried out between December and February, when the vine is dormant. The length of the branch on the vine directly controls the number of bunches of grapes produced, and must be regulated in line with the plant's strength.

Work carried out during the early spring exposes the base of the vine by raking the earth back towards the middle of the dividing rows, creating a loose, well-drained bed. The process of cleaning continues into the late spring: the vineyards are tidied up, and any soil remaining between the vines is removed.

May brings the danger of late frosts – to be protected against, in the most vulnerable zones, by keeping stoves burning in the vineyard overnight. The soil is re-worked to get rid of weeds, to allow correct drainage and prevent evaporation. Increasingly, weeds are controlled chemically by a single spraying at the end of winter at a considerable saving in labour costs. But May is still a busy month, time for first spraying against oidium and mildew – and for trimming extraneous growth.

In June the vines come into flower. Many of the greatest vintages have been early-flowering years, and most of the worst have been late-flowering years. The shoots are thinned out and, from now on, the vines must be sprayed regularly with powdered sulphur and Bordeaux mixture (copper sulphate, slaked lime and water). As the vines proliferate along their espaliers, they are clipped, trimmed and their leaves thinned to limit their growth and to allow more sunlight to reach the grapes. The work continues through July and August until the grapes are ready to be harvested.

The last task to be performed in autumn, after the harvest, is that of pushing the earth back towards the stocks in order to protect them from winter frosts; this leaves a channel in the middle of the rows between the vines, enabling surface water to be drained off. At the same time, fertilizer may be ploughed in to prepare for the next season.

GRAPES AND HARVESTS

The degree of ripeness of the grape is an essential factor in the quality of the wine. However, in a single region the weather conditions may vary from one year to the next, producing differences in the grapes which determine the individual characteristics of each vintage.

For a good maturation, long spells of hot, dry weather are generally necessary. The harvest date must be very carefully chosen, bearing in mind the ripeness and general health of the grapes. The balance between acid and sugar is the critical factor in measuring ripeness and making the decision to begin picking.

Picking by hand is increasingly giving way to mechanical harvesting. The machines, fitted with threshers, cause the grapes to fall on to a moving belt, while a fan removes most of the leaves. This rough handling of the grape does not, in principle, favour quality, especially for white wines. The most renowned vineyards will be perhaps the last to adopt this method of gathering, despite considerable progress made in refining the performance of mechanical grape-pickers.

Once gathered, the grapes are pressed, for white wines, or lightly crushed in the case of reds. They are then sent to the fermentation vat, the first stage in the process of vinification. The natural acidity level of the grapes may be corrected

23

upwards or downwards, according to the degree of ripeness, in order to provide a well-balanced flavour. Tartaric acid is used to correct low acidity, while calcium carbonate will reduce high acidity. The proportion of sugar in the must may also be adjusted, although in very precisely defined circumstances. The must may be concentrated further or, depending on the area, sucrose may be added – a process called 'chaptalization'.

THE MICROBIOLOGY OF WINE

The basic microbiological phenomenon that produces wine from grape must is the alcoholic fermentation. The fresh must is stored in a vat, where the evolution of a species of yeast (*Saccharomyces cerevisiae*), in the absence of air, breaks down the sugar in the must into alcohol and carbonic gas. During this process, a number of secondary products appear (glycerol, succinic acid, esters, etc.) which contribute to the wine's aroma and flavour. Fermentation releases calories that cause the vat to heat up, and artificial cooling may be necessary.

In certain cases, secondary or 'malo-lactic' fermentation may follow the alcoholic fermentation: malic acid – a constituent of the grape – is broken down into lactic acid and carbonic gas by the action of lactic bacteria. As a result the acidity level is lowered, the wine is softened and the aroma refined; this transformation gives the wine greater stability, and it may be cellared with confidence. While the effects of malo-lactic fermentation always improve red wine, only more complex white wines needing to mature in bottle benefit from it.

The yeasts and lactic bacteria responsible for the alcoholic and malo-lactic fermentations are naturally present on the grape. In some regions, the natural wine yeasts are sufficient to start the alcoholic fermentation. Other regions aid the process by adding a live yeast solution, or even commercially marketed dry yeasts. The possibility of altering the typicity and quality of wines by using selected micro-organisms during fermentation has often been discussed. However, it has never been proved beyond doubt: the wine's quality depends on the quality of the grape, and therefore on natural factors such as soil and climatic conditions.

Once the yeasts have stopped fermenting, care must be taken to eliminate elements which may contaminate the developing wine. These include toxic by-products of the yeasts themselves, together with bacteria which begin to grow as soon as the yeasts become inactive. A recently discovered process enables the toxic substances left behind by the yeasts to be removed. Different precautions must be taken against the bacteria which remain in the wine during conservation in vats or barrels. These may cause decomposition of certain of the wine's constituents, as well as oxidation and formation of acetic acid (the process by which vinegar is manufactured). These risks can, however, be avoided by modern methods of vinification.

DIFFERENT VINIFICATION PROCESSES

Vinification of Red Wine

In many cases the bunches of grapes are first de-stemmed; the stems contain an excess of tannin which may make the wine too hard. The grapes are then crushed and treated with a small amount of sulphur dioxide to ensure protection against oxidation and bacterial contamination. After this, the mixture of pulp, seeds and skins is transferred to the fermentation vat. From the moment fermentation begins, the carbon dioxide causes all the solid particles to rise and form a compact mass called the cap or 'marc' at the top of the vat or tank.

As alcoholic fermentation takes place in the vat, the grape skins macerate with the juice. Complete fermentation of the natural sugar generally takes from five to

The Vinification Process: Red Wine

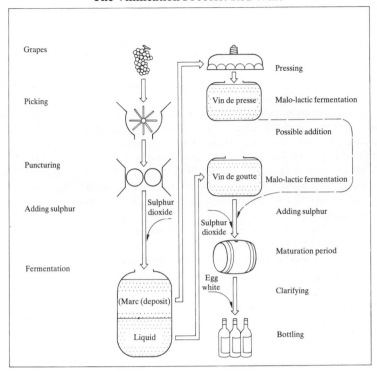

The Vinification Process: White Wine

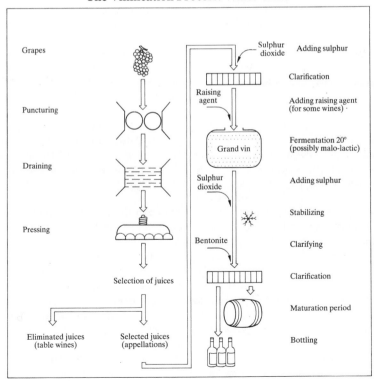

eight days; it is facilitated by aeration, which increases the growth of the yeast culture, and by temperature control (thermoregulation); the temperature must not exceed 35°C to avoid killing the yeasts. Maceration is essentially responsible for the colour and tannic structure of red wine. Wines which are to age for a long time must be rich in tannin and their period of maceration must be long, two to three weeks at 25–30°C. On the other hand, red wines for early consumption, of the light, 'primeur' type, must be fruity and contain little tannin; their period of maceration is therefore only a few days.

The next stage is racking, that is draining off the juice, called the 'vin de goutte' (free-run wine), from the marc. The marc is then pressed to give the 'vin de presse', a more concentrated wine. The free-run wine is blended with the 'vin de presse' in proportions based on taste and analytical criteria. The blended wine is now stored in oak casks for the final stage of the cycle, the malo-lactic fermentation. During the first year the wine is racked several times, each time into clean casks. Each time sulphur dioxide is added to prevent oxidation and decomposition.

This technique constitutes the basic method. There are however other modern modern fermentation processes which offer special advantages in different cases (high-temperature fermentation, continuous fermentation, carbonic maceration).

Vinification of Rosé Wines

The wide range of light red or rosé wines are obtained by maceration periods of varying lengths, and the grapes used may be either relatively pale in colour or very dark red. Most often they are vinified by pressing the red grapes gradually until the desired colour is obtained. In the less common 'saignée' process, the vat is filled with grapes to macerate as for a conventional red wine vinification; after several hours, the free-run juice is run off and fermented separately to produce a rosé wine.

Vinification of White Wine

There are many different types of white wine, each with its appropriate harvesting and vinification methods. Most often, white wine is the product of the fermentation of pure grape juice, in which case pressing takes place before fermentation. In some instances, however, the skins are macerated for a short period before fermentation in order to extract their aromas. This process requires perfectly ripe and healthy grapes in order to avoid contaminating the wine with a bitter aftertaste and sour aroma. The juice is extracted with the greatest care by lightly crushing the grapes. The white must, which is very vulnerable to oxidation, needs to be protected by the immediate addition of sulphur dioxide, and kept free from aeration. Once the juice has been extracted, it has to be clarified: this may happen naturally, or it may be necessary to use a centrifuge or a filtration system. Fermentation at low temperature is now common practice for white wine in order to extract and preserve the youthful aromas.

In many cases, white wines are prevented from going through the stage of malo-lactic fermentation. Such wines may need the freshness provided by acidity and, in addition, certain grape varieties lose their aromas in the course of secondary fermentation. However, malo-lactic fermentation is good for white wines that spend time in wood and are intended for a long period of ageing. White Burgundies are good examples of the extra roundness that the process can bring. Secondary fermentation is also the basis of the Méthode Champenoise: the process ensures biological stabilization of the wine, while the carbonic gas it produces gives champagne its sparkle.

Vinification of Sweet Wines

Sweet wines are made from grapes that are rich in sugar. By the end of the alcoholic fermentation only a proportion of the sugar has been converted into alcohol; the residual sugar gives the wine its sweetness. The finest sweet wines are made from grapes affected by 'noble rot' – a fungus (*Botrytis cinerea*) which attacks the skin of the grape and imparts a particular flavour. As the water content evaporates through the punctured skin, so the sugar and flavour become more concentrated. The top-quality wines of Barsac and Sauternes – 13–16 per cent alcohol, 50–100 g/l sugar – are produced in this way from carefully selected grapes of exceptional ripeness. After three pressings the must is fermented for anything from two to twelve weeks, depending on the sugar content, until alcoholic fermentation comes naturally to an end. In sweet wines of lesser quality, the alcoholic fermentation is stopped artificially by the addition of sulphur dioxide or by pasteurization; alternatively the wine yeasts may be eliminated by racking or the centrifuge method. To produce Château d'Yquem, the most famous of the Sauternes, the wine is racked off into new casks every three months for three and a half years before being filtered and bottled.

STABILIZATION AND CLARIFICATION

New wine is rough, cloudy and gassy: the 'growing-up' phase (clarification, stabilization, and refinement of the quality) lasts until bottling. Its duration according to the different types of wine. Wines for early consumption are bottled a few weeks, even a few days, after vinification has finished; wines destined for a long life spend more than two years in the cask or vat before being bottled.

Clarification may occur naturally, by the simple formation of a sediment; more often the wine is clarified by racking into new barrels, especially if the wine is stored in containers of small capacity (wooden casks). Where the wine is stored in a large vat, centrifugation or filtration will be necessary.

At any stage, the living, developing wine may become cloudy or produce sediment. These are natural occurrences with bacterial or chemical causes. Such accidents are extremely serious when they occur in the bottle and for this reason a measure of stabilization must take place before bottling.

There are various treatments to avoid bacterial contamination. The wine can be stored in a completely filled, airtight vat or tank; this must be topped up regularly. In addition, the wine can be treated with sulphur dioxide, which is both an antiseptic and an antioxidant. In the last resort, the effect of sulphur dioxide may be reinforced by the addition of sorbic acid (an antiseptic) or ascorbic acid (an antioxidant).

Other treatments are designed to eliminate deposits or suspended particles which would otherwise make the wine cloudy. One type of deposit is produced by the formation of tartaric crystals. These can be removed by sharply chilling the wine before it is bottled, or by the addition of metatartaric acid, which prevents crystallization.

The wine may also contain tiny particles – colouring matter in red wine or natural proteins in white – which will affect its appearance over the long term. These are dealt with by fining. Fining agents include egg white, gelatin, gum arabic, and bentonite, a colloidal clay. Essentially they work by forming a coating on the surface of the wine which slowly descends, gathering up the impurities on the way to the bottom of the vat or tank.

Finally, the wine may become cloudy because of an excess of certain metals, such as iron or copper. These traces can be removed with potassium iron-nitrate. All these methods are tried and tested remedies, evolved over many years. Nevertheless, the modern trend is to intervene as early as possible in the vinification stage so as to keep any subsequent treatment and handling to a minimum.

MATURING WINE

Wine is often matured, or 'aged', in wooden casks. The wine is transferred to small oak barrels which, when new, give the wine vanilla-scented aromas which combine perfectly with those of the fruit. This traditional aspect of making fine wine is labour-intensive and proportionately expensive: the wood, specially selected from top-quality forests, has to be dried in the open air for three years before it is ready to be made into casks. The casks themselves lose their specific character after a certain age, and may carry a risk of bacterial contamination to the wine they contain. Moreover a proportion of wine in cask is lost to evaporation. These cost factors are inevitably reflected in the price of the finished wine.

BOTTLING AND AGEING IN BOTTLE

After weeks, months or even years of storage, the wine is finally ready for bottling – an operation requiring great care and cleanliness. In bottle, the wine must be protected against oxygen in the air. Cork is still the best material for sealing bottles; its elasticity ensures an airtight seal good for twenty-five years at least. There are, however, two risks with the use of cork: faulty corks may allow the wine to leak and, occasionally, a diseased cork may impart an unpleasant taste to the wine.

Fine wines continue to improve in the bottle: great wines may continue to age in this way for decades. The changes that occur in the wine in the bottle are various and extremely complex, involving colour, taste and smell. First of all the colour is altered, a process perfectly demonstrated in the case of red wine: the bright red of young wine develops slightly yellow tinges resembling the colour of brick. Indeed, in very old wines – say fifty years in bottle – the red colouring tends to disappear completely and the dominant impression is of a mahogany or light brown hue. These changes are responsible for the deposits of colouring matter, known as sediment, in very old wines. They affect the taste of the tannins and produce a general softening in the wine's structure. Another vital transformation during the process of ageing in bottle affects the wine's aromas. As time goes on, the aromas evolve in complex ways to produce the 'bouquet' specific to old wine. The chemical basis of this aspect of ageing is still not fully understood.

QUALITY CONTROL

A good wine is not necessarily a great wine. When we speak of 'quality' wines we refer to the whole range from table wines to the great vintages. At any point in this range, a definition of quality reflects the distinction between the 'natural' and the 'human' factors involved. The wine-maker's knowledge, skill and attention to detail are essential to produce a good wine; a great wine requires, in addition, particular and very critical environmental conditions which lie beyond human control.

Defining quality in wine is much more a matter of judgement, comparison and experience than of scientific data. While chemical analysis enables anomalies to be detected and certain defects of the wine to be revealed, its influence on determining the standard of the wine is limited. Ultimately, only actual tasting can provide the essential criteria for assessment. Over the last twenty years or so considerable progress has been made in the techniques of such sensorial analysis, enabling the subjective aspects to be better controlled. This progress takes account of advances in understanding the psychology of taste and smell, and of the need to standardize the practical conditions in which tasting takes place.

In France and elsewhere, expert tasters are becoming more and more involved in quality control, whether in the approval of AOC wines or on expert judging panels. The quality of French wine has been legally controlled for a long time.

The French law of 1 August 1905, concerning the genuineness of goods in commercial transactions, is the first official text. The regulations have been progressively refined as scientific knowledge of wine has increased. Today, on the basis of chemical analysis, the French regulations define a minimum quality which must be free from certain common defects. They also stimulate techniques for improving this basic standard. In Paris, the official government body, the Direction de la Consommation et de la Répression des Fraudes, is responsible for the verification of the analytical standards established in this way.

This role is complemented by that of the Institut National des Appellations d'Origine (INAO), which, after consultation with the wine-growing associations involved, determines the conditions of production and ensures that these are checked. Such conditions include: the location of the vineyard, the choice of grape variety, planting and pruning methods, viticultural methods, vinification techniques, analysis of the musts and the wine, and yield. This body also ensures that AOC wines are protected in France and abroad.

Another body, L'Office National Interprofessional des Vins de Table (ONIVIT), is specifically responsible for intervening in and managing the market and promoting sales, both in France and abroad. It also initiates measures to rationalize production, vinification, stocking and distribution.

In each region the wine-growers' associations contribute to the protection of their members' interests. In particular, they are concerned with the local applications of the regional appellation laws. This action is often coordinated by interprofessional councils or committees, made up of representatives from the different wine-growers' associations and the wine trade in general, together with others from the professions and local government.

A Consumer's Guide to Buying French Wines

F RANCE is, by universal consent, the home of most of the world's great wines. Tens of thousands of worthwhile wines are produced there each year (at every conceivable price level), and even the local supermarket in a small provincial town may stock more than a hundred lines. It is hardly surprising, therefore, that visitors to France feel inclined to take some of these excellent wines back home. This chapter contains information on how, where, and under what conditions wine may be purchased in France, as well as general advice on buying, keeping, serving and enjoying wine.

THE LABEL

The European Common Market's wine laws are designed to protect the consumer by laying down the way that – in any case, within the EEC area – table wines and other still light wines should be described and presented on the bottle labels (and also in price lists, advertising, and so on). Some of the information is mandatory; other details are optional. Overall, the basic intention is to help ensure that customers get the exact wine they pay for and to provide information enabling them to ascertain the type of wine it is with considerable accuracy.

What the labels for all wines produced within the EEC *must* tell you is: the wine's country of origin; the nominal volume (i.e. the quantity in the bottle); the name and address of the bottler responsible; and either the expression 'table wine' or, for quality wines, the name of the specified region of origin.

Details that *may* be given are: the wine's colour or type; the grape variety (if a single type predominates); the alcohol content, expressed as a percentage of the whole; whether the wine is sweet or dry; the best way to serve it and the kind of food it goes well with; the name and address of the shipper, distributor or retailer, and any recognized citation with which one of these has been honoured (e.g. a royal warrant). The wine may have a brand name, too, provided this is not misleading, as well as showing the vintage (the year it was grown), either on the main label or on a neck label.

Putting the mandatory and the optional together, the kind of facts at your disposal might be that the bottle contains a 1983 dry white table wine from France, 75cl in nominal volume, was made principally from the Sauvignon grape variety, bottled by Messrs X at Bordeaux, should be served chilled and goes excellently with fish and shellfish, and has an alcohol content of 11 per cent. Even if labels are nothing like as comprehensive, merely confining themselves to the four facts it is obligatory for them to declare, they at least give would-be purchasers guidelines that are essential in helping them to decide which wines to buy. Of these pointers, none is more immediately helpful than the indication of the wine's official quality status. The main quality grades are listed below in descending order.

Appellation d'Origine Contrôlée

Often abbreviated to Appellation Contrôlée, and familiarly known just by the initials AOC or AC. A mark of status legally defined by French governmental decree, it is not a guarantee of high quality, as such, but it *does* confirm that the wine:

1 Comes from the particular area, town, or sometimes even an individual vineyard, stated on the label.

HOW TO READ A LABEL

Under French wine regulations, the wine label must allow for the identification of the wine and the person legally responsible for it. The last person to intervene in the process of production is the bottler, and his name must, by law, be present on the label. Each category of wine has its own specific set of regulations, and the first duty of the label is to inform the consumer as to which of four categories the wine falls into: Vin de Table; Vin de Pays; VDQS or AOC.

AOC **Alsace**

Green tax disc

Grape variety (permitted only when the wine is made from a single grape type)

Optional (but required for certain export markets)

Required information

AOC **Bordeaux**

Green tax disc

Château or brand name (optional)

Classification (optional)

Appellation (obligatory)

Name and address of bottler (obligatory). The word 'proprietaire' defines the legal status of the producer

Volume in centilitres (obligatory)

Required for certain export markets

Vintage (optional)

AOC **Burgundy**

Green tax disc

Appellation (obligatory)

Required for certain export markets

Vineyard name (optional). If this is in the same type size as the appellation, the wine is a Premier Cru

'Tête de Cuvée': mark of prestige referring to a former classification (optional)

'Monopole': indicates that the wine is the product of a single property (optional)

Name and address of bottler (obligatory). This also indicates whether the wine is estate-bottled. Shippers' and cooperatives' wines may not refer to themselves as estate-bottled

Volume (obligatory)

Vintage (optional) is often displayed on the neck label

31

AOC **Champagne**

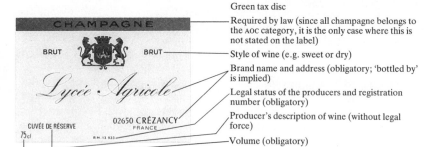

Green tax disc

Required by law (since all champagne belongs to the AOC category, it is the only case where this is not stated on the label)

Style of wine (e.g. sweet or dry)

Brand name and address (obligatory; 'bottled by' is implied)

Legal status of the producers and registration number (obligatory)

Producer's description of wine (without legal force)

Volume (obligatory)

VDQS

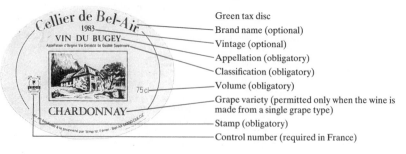

Green tax disc

Brand name (optional)

Vintage (optional)

Appellation (obligatory)

Classification (obligatory)

Volume (obligatory)

Grape variety (permitted only when the wine is made from a single grape type)

Stamp (obligatory)

Control number (required in France)

Vins de Pays

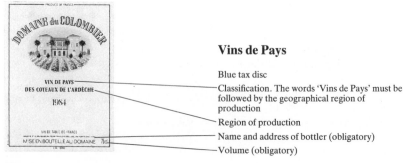

Blue tax disc

Classification. The words 'Vins de Pays' must be followed by the geographical region of production

Region of production

Name and address of bottler (obligatory)

Volume (obligatory)

2 Is produced only from the grape varieties specified for that wine, planted in approved kinds of soil, and in quantities which do not exceed the prescribed maximum yield per hectare.

3 Has been produced in accordance with local custom and the traditional practice of the district concerned.

Accordingly, while AOC does not explicitly promise top quality, you can take it that wines that meet the above requirements and receive an Appellation are certainly *likely* to be of above-average standards. Indeed, all of France's greatest wines belong to this category.

There are two ways in which the term normally appears on labels. Besides being shown directly below the name of the specified region, the expression Appellation ... Contrôlée may also be used – in this case, with the name of the specified region between the two words (for example: Appellation Saumur Contrôlée). In fact, whenever the name of a vineyard, grape variety or brand name is shown on a label, it is mandatory to repeat the specified region in this manner – for example, Château Latour, Appellation Pauillac Contrôlée.

Vin Délimité de Qualité Supérieure

Again, familiarly abbreviated to its initials VDQS. Like Appellation Contrôlée, it is an officially backed guarantee that the wine concerned comes from a specific area, is made only with the approved grape varieties, and meets the regulations regarding maximum yield per hectare, approved alcoholic strength, traditional local production methods, and so on.

Although VDQS is below AC in status, it is still a difficult distinction to obtain; before qualifying, wines in this category also have to be tasted and approved by an expert committee. In short, wines of VDQS status are anything but second-rate. As a general rule, however, while some of them do undoubtedly improve in the bottle, they are not wines to be laid down for a great many years.

Vins de Pays

At one time one of the soundest bits of wine advice given by knowledgeable friends to people touring France was that they should seek out some of the little-known 'country wines' which were produced in individual village vineyards, usually for local consumption alone, and rarely sold outside their own area. Many such wines, it was held, were positive bargains and would be in demand much farther afield if their volume of production was not too small to allow regular supply to other markets.

Be that as it may, regulations establishing a formal Vins de Pays category were brought into force in 1976 – part of the French authorities' efforts to solve the problem of the Wine Lake, caused by the over-abundant production (notably in the south of France) of wines that were of inferior quality and surplus to demand. Peasant growers were encouraged to replant with better vines and instructed in improved techniques and equipment. The idea was that, out of the untold thousands of ordinary Vins de Table, those able to climb out of the ruck would be distinguished by an added geographical attribution, confirming that they had gone up in life. Each would now be a Vin de Pays of, say, the Côtes du Tarn, the Agenais, or whatever the locality might be. (Under EEC regulations the label on a Vin de Pays bottle still has to bear the phrase Vin de Table as well – but this is only to confirm that it is a table wine, not a fortified wine.)

Such was the success of this scheme that by the early 1980s more than 90 production zones had already received recognition for their Vins de Pays. These zones, many of them very extensive, are found in nearly all of France's wine regions, covering at least 30 of the country's départements (counties), and the wines made are of almost every style from light to full and dry to medium-sweet. They, too, are subject to a range of quality controls, albeit somewhat less rigorous than those for AC and VDQS. However, while all can be relied on as 'honest bottles', they should be regarded as fresh young wines for rapid drinking. It would be pointless, even counter-productive, to lay them down for more than a year.

Other Distinguishing Marks

Below the three main quality grades, at the bottom end of the scale amid the host of ordinary Vins de Table and cheap-and-cheerful branded wines for everyday drinking purposes, one minor category you might encounter comprises the blends previously known as 'EEC wine' or 'two-country wine'. (You could come across some in France, but it is not likely – they are sold much more commonly in other European countries.) Under new Common Market regulations, table wines made in a country other than that in which the grapes were harvested must now be described on the label as 'Wine made in [for example] Germany from grapes harvested in [for example] Italy'. Table wines produced from a mixture of grapes or a blending of products originating in more than one country must be described as 'Blend of wines from different countries of the European Community'. All such expressions must be in English, whatever other language may be used for the rest of the label.

At the top end of the scale, of course, the best wines often have additional descriptions of distinction – for instance, the five Grands Crus, or 'classed growths', into which 62 of the best red wines of Bordeaux are divided. As well as these, there are about 28 classed growths for the superb sweet white wines of Sauternes, plus the 11 Premiers Grands Crus Classés and the 73 Grands Crus Classés of the reds of St-Emilion. Altogether, in fact, of the many thousands of vineyards in the Bordeaux region, fewer than 200 of those in the Médoc, Sauternes, St-Emilion and Graves rank officially as the aristocrats. Next in line behind them are the Crus Bourgeois – a growing number of which often have pretensions to quite as much character and finesse as some of the superior class of wines.

In each case, naturally, the extra distinction will assuredly be proclaimed on the label, as will the fact – ultimately the best guarantee of the product's authenticity – that the wine was bottled at or by the château, estate or domaine where it was grown. The phrase most commonly used in such cases, and applicable to many other wine regions besides Bordeaux, is 'Mis en bouteilles au château ...', or 'Mis en bouteilles à la propriété ...', or 'Mis en bouteilles au domaine'. A word of caution here: beware of any wording that does not convey a direct and close link between the precise place where the wine was made and where it was bottled. Expressions such as 'Mis en bouteilles dans la région de production', 'Mis en bouteilles par nos soins', 'Mis en bouteilles dans nos chais', 'Mis en bouteilles par X' may be used, meaning respectively: 'Bottled in the region where it was produced', 'Bottled by ourselves personally', 'Bottled in our wine stores', 'Bottled by Messrs X [some intermediary agent]'. However accurate these descriptions may be, they do *not* carry the guarantee of origin of château- or domaine-bottling.

All the labelling regulations and requirements outlined above have a dual purpose. In addition to providing the purchaser with information, they have a legal function. If at any time there are suspicions that all is not above board, the label details and accompanying trade documentation, as well as marks on the cork (and sometimes on the capsule), enable each stage of the wine's progress to be traced back – from retailer and point-of-sale to wholesaler or shipper, and from there to vinifier and grower.

Many producers of quality wine, instead of relying solely on the bottle labels, provide a further guarantee of their wine's authenticity by stamping its place of origin and vintage on the cork as well. This is not only a precaution against a label becoming ungummed and genuinely lost, but also serves as a deterrent to any tricksters who might think to remove the labels and replace them with fake ones, so as to present the wine as a more expensive type. It makes the swindle more costly and complex to stage if the corks have to be replaced too. However, it should be stressed that, despite the occasional horror story in the newspapers, serious fraud in the wine trade really is quite rare.

BUYING WINE IN FRANCE

Asking where one can buy wine in France may seem an all too obvious question, because the plain answer is 'almost anywhere' – from a vineyard proprietor, specialist vintner, cooperative winery, all the normal retail outlets, or even, perhaps, some local café owner who buys in bulk to bottle his own house wines.

Nevertheless, whatever your chosen source, there will be a number of different points to bear in mind. For a start, much will depend on whether you are buying wines for more or less immediate drinking or for laying down. If the former, they should be wines that will not benefit from being kept, so are likely to be wines of simple origin or from a modest vintage that has developed quickly. Or, of course, they could be fine vintages that have reached their peak (and are normally almost impossible to find on the open market).

On the other hand, if you are setting out to buy wines to lay down, you should always ensure that they are wines that will improve with age. Accordingly, it makes sense to buy them young – before their market price has started to soar – and also to spend as much on them as you can reasonably afford so as to get the best available vintages.

In Bulk or Bottle

The term 'bulk wine' may apply to wine contained in anything from a massive steel road tanker to a glass carboy or a 5-litre 'bag in the box'.

If you are in a position to arrange for the shipping of wine in cask – holding 225 litres if it's Bordeaux, for instance, or 228 litres if it's Burgundy – the chances are that you are already close to being a professional in the wine trade and have no need of a guide of this nature.

In contrast, many people touring France by car find it quite feasible to pop two or three carboys or plastic flagons in the boot before leaving. For these, the most important point to remember is that the contents are virtually certain to be ordinary wines of no more than average quality. It is only very rarely that you will be able to buy high-quality wine in bulk packs of this nature. Indeed, in some regions, for example the classified vineyards of Bordeaux, selling in such packs is actually prohibited.

The fact that a bulk wine is likely to be a run-of-the-mill product doesn't matter in the least if the visitors happen to have developed a fondness for the wine concerned during their holiday. The same applies to wines in bottle, of course, no matter whether you are buying a few individual bottles or by the caseload (normally 12 bottles per case). However, buying wine in bottle does have a number of particular advantages:

1 From a vineyard proprietor, it enables you to seek out 'unknown' wines, little distributed outside their own area.

2 From a cooperative, when collected direct, it enables you to avoid delivery charges, which are on the increase for small quantities.

3 From a specialist wine merchant, it can open the door to rarities to which you might not normally have access.

BOTTLES

Bordeaux

Champagne

Burgundy

Alsace

Côtes du Rhone

Clavelin (Jura)

Provence

On this last aspect, a word of explanation. Many of the best-known wine-growing estates (châteaux, domaines or whatever) will welcome visitors, but you may not be able to buy any of their wines on the spot – and even if you can, they will not be at bargain prices. Some of the top growers contract to sell almost all of their annual production solely to one, two or three négociants or shippers. But the main reason is that producers and négociants are restrained by law from competing unfairly with their distributors and therefore, for instance, must not try to sell bottled wine at less than retail prices.

Who to Buy From

Buying wine from the grower or producer affords pleasures quite distinct from the mere prospect of getting a good bargain. It is always worth visiting vineyards and getting to know as many producers as you can, because there is no better way of beginning to acquire a real understanding of the art of wine-making – and of coming to appreciate all the skills that go into the bottle.

Throughout France's wine regions, you will also come across cooperatives, producing wines from grapes supplied by a considerable number of peasant farmers. The pooling of resources has permitted the introduction of improved methods and equipment, beyond the reach of the individual small-scale grower, which have greatly raised the standard of cooperative wines over the past 20 years or so. As a general rule, the products of these rural wineries cost rather less than those of named estates in the region. While their wines are increasingly good, they tend to be of a standardized nature, with any marked characteristics ironed out. Equally, though, they rarely disappoint and many are of much higher quality than you might expect (to cite just one example, those of St-Emilion).

At a more specialized level, the négociant, or shipper, found in all the main wine regions, not only buys wine to sell on, but often owns vineyards as well. He may have an exclusive sales contract with a given producer. He may be a 'négociant-éleveur', denoting that he 'raises' wines in his own cellars by assembling different cuvées (blends) of the same appellation from different producers. Thereby, he is responsible for the resultant wine in two ways: through the choice of what he buys and through the way he combines the various cuvées – a function of crucial importance in such regions as Burgundy, for instance.

In the cities and large towns, good wine can be bought most readily from the specialist retailers, whether individual wine merchants or the branches of national liquor chains. In the past, oddly enough, high-level wine merchants' shops were less common in France than in many other European countries; over the last few years, however, there has been a marked increase in their number and you will find them extremely well qualified to advise you. A word of caution, though, about some of the wine shops in predominantly holiday areas, which set out to attract the passing tourist trade and are not always as expert as they may appear.

Towards the lower end of the retail ladder, it is as well to be clear-minded about wines sold in supermarkets. Many of France's supermarkets, particularly those getting on for hypermarket status, offer enormously wide selections of wine, often several hundred lines. But although the great majority of wines in any country's supermarkets are naturally intended for everyday drinking, there is one surprising way in which French self-service stores often differ from some of the better ones in, say, Britain or the United States. From time to time, if not always, these carry a small stock of high-quality estate-bottled wines, capable of further improvement if kept for a while. But France's supermarkets rarely if ever do. You may find the occasional exception, of course, and a few of them certainly carry some above-average wines which are ready for immediate drinking. In general, though, you would *not* go to a French supermarket to buy wines for laying down.

Three other very effective ways of acquiring good wines are buying 'en primeur', through wine clubs, or at auctions.

Buying 'en primeur' is a system developed some years ago by the Bordeaux wine trade which has proved increasingly popular. A better name for it would be 'buying by subscription', and the principle is simple: to put your name down for a wine before it is matured and bottled, at a price much lower than it will reach once it is ready for delivery.

Subscriptions, for a fixed volume, are open for a limited period, usually in the spring or early summer following the harvest. The purchaser pays at least half the agreed price with the order and undertakes to settle the remainder on delivery of the bottles, perhaps 12 or 15 months later. The system, therefore, has the twin advantage of helping the producer's immediate cash-flow, and of giving purchasers the prospect of a good deal, especially if prevailing wine prices subsequently rise.

Of course, this system of buying could come badly unstuck if prices collapse in the interim, when subscribers would end up paying more for the wine than non-subscribers. This has happened in the past and could do again – it is always risky 'going long' in a volatile market. But when all goes well, as it has for the last 10 years, the 'en primeur' method is without doubt the best way to buy wine for less than its retail price – usually, anything from 20 to 40 per cent less. The selling of wine in this manner is organized directly by individual vineyard proprietors, shippers, merchants and wine clubs.

In addition to arranging 'en primeur' purchases of fine wines, the growing number of wine clubs afford their members several benefits – from reliable, well-informed newsletters, up to regular offers of assorted wines, selected by experts and covering a fairly wide choice, sometimes including quite uncommon wines. Though you may need to exercise a little discrimination here and there, the prices charged are fair.

Buying wines at auction sales has also become increasingly popular in recent years – but it has to be stressed that France still does not have a particular tradition of fine-wine auctions and that most châteaux deciding to sell parcels of great old wines in this way would be more likely to do so in London rather than Paris. Even so, you *could* still find bargains at local auctions, particularly among less familiar appellations which did not attract the attention of restaurant owners and other professionals. If you do try your luck in this field, here are two tips which may be useful:

1 Probably the best way to land yourself a bargain is to form a syndicate or buying group with three or four friends or business associates. Your syndicate will then be able to bid for larger lots, which frequently sell at lower price levels, per bottle, than small ones do.
2 The size of lots varies greatly. Some salerooms offer lots of one or two dozen bottles, but most are of three, four or upwards, which can get expensive. Remember that, except for very small lots, bidding is normally conducted at the rate-per-case (i.e. a dozen bottles, six magnums or 24 half-bottles). So, if you were to buy a lot of three cases for a hammer price of 200 francs say, the actual purchase price would be 600 francs.

Among the various wine auctions held in France, by far the best known are the very specialized charity sales for the Hospices de Beaune each November. The proceeds of the Beaune auction go to the upkeep of the town's traditional hospital for old people. However, although the sale prices are a pointer to likely Burgundy prices for the ensuing year, they do tend to be inflated. The purchasers at these special charity sales are nearly always wine trade professionals, as the wines are sold in cask and it is the purchaser who has to finance the raising and bottling of the wine.

Export and Import

Apart from commercially organized vineyard tours, the names of châteaux and other estates willing to receive visitors can always be obtained from each wine region's Maison du Vin or equivalent – a central office and showroom customarily run by the Comité Interprofessionnel, which is the body uniting all the various interests (growers, cooperatives, négociants, and so on) involved in the local trade.

Likewise, the Comité's head offices are the best place to check about any specific export formalities to be observed. No French customs officer is going to be bothered if you are merely taking out a few bottles. Indeed, the capsules of any wine bottles you have bought from normal retail outlets are quite likely to bear a small tax disc, known as a 'vignette', showing that the relevant French duties have already been paid. But if you are exporting a case or more, especially wine you have bought direct rather than from a retailer, then you would be advised to obtain a receipt form known as an 'acquit' for it.

The 'acquit' shows such details as the name of the vendor, the nature and quantity of the wine, the name of the purchaser, the place to which the wine is being transported and the length of time the journey is expected to take. It is habitually issued by the tax office nearest the sales outlet, or by the vineyard proprietor or bottler, who may be empowered to fill in the form themselves whenever they make a sale. When buying your wine from the proprietor, therefore, you should make it clear that your purchase is for export, which can enable you to obtain exemption from VAT and freight tax. In this case, your wine must be accompanied by a freight movement permit (a green form, No. 8102, for Appellation wines, or a blue form, No. 8101, for ordinary table wines), which will be accepted by customs as granting tax-free status to the consignment when you leave the country with it. All such goods would then have to be declared, and relevant taxes and duties paid at the port of entry into the home country. To reiterate the essential point: such documentation will be necessary only if you are exporting appreciably more than a normal tourist quantity. Should the seller fail to supply it, or you have any other doubts on the matter, seek advice from the local Comité Interprofessionnel.

As for the precise legal formalities at journey's end, import regulations vary so much from one country to another that it would be impossible to list them all in this chapter.

To give an example of the complexities: if alcoholic drinks have been bought duty-free in an EEC country or aboard a ship or plane, or have been bought outside the EEC, the amount currently allowed in by the British customs without penalty comprises 1 litre of spirits (alcoholic drinks over 22 per cent volume – 38.8° proof), *or* 2 litres of fortified or sparkling wine not over 22 per cent volume (e.g. port, sherry, vermouth, champagne), *plus* 2 litres of still light wine (i.e. table wine). But if the bottles were bought from a normal retail outlet in an EEC country, the amount you can bring in without further duty rises to $1\frac{1}{2}$ litres of spirits or 3 litres of fortified or sparkling wine, plus 4 litres of table wine. If table wine *only* is shipped, the permitted amount is 7 litres.

In contrast, the United States customs allow in only 1 litre of *any* alcoholic beverage duty-free, and thereafter, depending on the point of entry, apply the liquor laws of the state concerned as regards how much extra may be brought in on payment of duty – allowances which range from unrestricted or quite generous in some states to nil in others!

In the light of such wide differences, the only advice that may safely be given to people wishing to import wine from France in above-average quantity is to consult their own local customs office about the procedures required.

BUYING WINE IN BRITAIN

Buying wine should be no more of a chore than drinking it. Fortunately, the wine buyer in Britain has the widest choice of wines at the most advantageous prices available. There are perhaps more impressive wine shops in New York and San Francisco, showing a range of fine wines that is impossible to conceive of on this side of the Atlantic; the French have the possibility of buying their wine direct at rock-bottom prices, yet, with the exception of Paris, are relatively badly served for retail shops; wine buying in the producing countries of Germany, Italy and Spain is regional and not international. Only Britain has the full range of the wines of the world at her disposal, offered by the different elements of the wine trade, and French wines still remain the basis of the selection. This book will tell you, chapter by chapter, what to buy, so we should look at *where* to buy French wines.

The choice is wide: supermarkets, off-licences or high-street shops, specialist wine merchants, wine warehouses, mail order, or auction. All have their advantages and their disadvantages, so let us take them in turn.

Supermarkets

The greatest change in the 1980s, compared to previous decades, has been the emergence of the supermarket as the most important market force in the UK. Today they control over 55 per cent of the wines sold, and expect this figure to rise. The buyers are amongst the most qualified in the country, the standards of quality control high, and the financial clout undeniable. Having begun by concentrating on the lower-priced wines, supermarkets are now turning to fine wines to complete their range. While their very size will make it unlikely that supermarkets will sell the gems of French wine, produced as they are in tiny quantities, they are now offering a wide range of well-chosen wines, often with full information on their origins and what food they should be drunk with, and fully justifying themselves as a serious place to buy wine.

Retail Shops

The high-street shops, of which the largest chain is Victoria Wine, have seen their market eroded by the supermarkets and are now fighting back. Shops are being redesigned to display wines more intelligently, and more information is being offered to the customers. Prices are in many cases competitive with the supermarkets, and buying will have been done by a team of highly qualified experts, many of them Masters of Wine. Certain chains are concentrating on a price war with the supermarkets, which they will surely lose. Their strength lies in a personalized service and perhaps a larger range of wines than supermarkets are prepared to sell.

Wine Merchants

Taking this position further is the specialist wine merchant. In a country where wine consumption is expanding, it is not surprising to see a proliferation of specialist wine companies. These are generally businesses with a single outlet, often owner-run. The person in charge of buying the wine will almost always be the owner, who will travel to France several times a year in addition to attending trade tastings. His selection will certainly be more individual than that of a supermarket or an off-licence, and the advice more knowledgeable. Such shops will also offer a series of services including delivery, hire of glasses, wine-storage and cellar management. The problem is that an independent wine merchant has to make a good profit margin to cover these services, as well as the investment in time and travel which underpins the interest of his range; as a result his wines may look expensive. In terms of quality this may be far from the case, and one of the most important things for someone really interested in wine is to make friends with a good wine merchant.

Wine Warehouses

Another recent trend has been the emergence of wine warehouses, mainly in cities or on the edge of heavily populated centres. They provide the link between the specialist wine merchant and the supermarket. Prices are kept low by buying direct from France in full truckloads, and unloading directly onto the warehouse floor. Apart from attractive prices, the more energetic companies, such as Majestic, offer a range of wines to taste before you buy, something that the supermarkets cannot do. The minimum purchase is a mixed case of 12 bottles.

Mail Order

One of the easiest ways of buying wine, and the most agreeable for many people, is by mail order. The great advantage is that the purchaser has the leisure to study a full list of wines before being committed to an order. The two major mail order merchants, the old established Wine Society and the Sunday Times Wine Club, both claim to have over 50 000 members and provide an excellent service. Most specialist wine merchants will have a well-written list that they mail to clients, and many of these are a pleasure to read for the descriptions of the wines listed. Selling by mail is costly for the merchant, so there will not be the bargains that are to be found in the High Street, except for special offers, but all respectable mail order houses will take back wine that is unsatisfactory, or that the client has over-ordered.

Buying at Auction

Perhaps the most risky, but also the most exciting way to buy wine is at auction. The risk is not so much in the quality, as the catalogue will give an indication of this, but in the final hammer price. Unless you are knowledgeable, it is better to have a wine merchant bid for you, or to put yourself in the hands of the auctioneers. For inexpensive wines, or wines selling in lots of over three or four cases, it is wise to group with friends to make a satisfactory purchase. Auction houses, of which Christie's and Sotheby's lead the field, are also the main way of disposing of wine.

LAYING DOWN WINE

Once you start to store wine, you already have, in wine jargon, a 'cellar'. Of course, if that really meant an underground, dark, cool wine-cellar, most of us would be put off from the start. But beginning a cellar means simply having a few more bottles in the house than you can drink at one time. Laying down wine is quite different. This means purchasing wine in advance of its drinkability and storing it, or having it stored for you, until it is at its best. The advantage of having a current drinking cellar is that you do not run out of wine, and you should have a type of wine to suit all occasions. The advantage of laying down wines is that you purchase them when they are young and available (and therefore much cheaper than when they are at their peak and are being drunk), and you always have something to look forward to.

The basic rule of laying down wine is to keep only those wines that will improve with age. These, for France, include all major red wines – their ageing potential being determined by the style of wine and the character of the vintage – top-class, sweet white wine, and some dry white wine that comes from the noble grape varieties, (Riesling, Chardonnay, Sémillon), especially those with some wood ageing. This might cover:

Red: Bordeaux (Claret) from the classic appellations; Burgundy from good vintages; the northern Rhône wines (Hermitage, Côte-Rôtie) and possibly some southern Rhônes (Châteauneuf-du-Pape); and some of the 'country' wines made with tannic grape varieties. Red wines that should not be kept are, in general, Beaujolais (with the exception of the finer crus from good vintages); any other wines from the Gamay grape; the reds from the Loire; light country reds and all rosés.

White: Burgundy, especially the Premier Crus and Grands Crus; the Cru Classé white Graves; Hermitage and the finer Rieslings from Alsace; Cru Classé Sauternes; and all sweet white wines made with botrytized grapes.

Fortified wines do not in general improve with age, as either they are made to be drunk young for their freshness (Beaumes de Venise, Muscat de Frontignan), or they have been aged in cask before bottling (Banyuls). There is no equivalent in France of early bottling of fortified wines such as exists for vintage port.

The length of time a wine can be kept is based on its character and the style of the vintage. Here are some guidelines, but it must be borne in mind that light vintages will mature sooner and great vintages must be kept longer, and that a lifespan of thirty years and more for such wines is not exceptional.

Bordeaux: St-Emilion, Pomerol and other Libournais wines, 5–7 years, Cru Classés 7–12; Médoc 6–8 years, Cru Classés 7–15; Graves, midway between these two. Sauternes 3–5 years, Cru Classés 5–10 and over.

Burgundy: Whites, Premier Cru Chablis and Premier Cru Côtes-de-Beaune 3–7 years, Grand Crus 4–10. Reds, Côte-de-Beaune 4–7 years, Côtes de Nuits 5–8 years, plus half as much again for the Grands Crus.

Rhône: Hermitage and Côte-Rôtie 5–10; Châteauneuf-du-Pape 3–8.

The key to ageing wine correctly is a good cellar. For those who have the money but not the space, all good wine merchants will store wines (usually) under good cellarage conditions, but you must make sure that title to the wines is yours, in case of the failure of the merchant.

Finally, there are some basic rules to buying wines to put in your cellar. Wines for everyday consumption, such as light reds, all rosés and most whites, should be bought on a month-to-month basis, and no more than three months in advance, as the climate has a distinct effect on one's drinking choices. However attractive they are in the summer, very dry wines, such as Muscadet, will not taste so appealing in the dead of winter. Wines to lay down, as we have seen, are the classic red and white wines from good years. The red wines will probably still be available near to their peak, but at a higher price, while the white wines will almost certainly be unavailable. If you are buying wines purely for investment, buy only the best, the highest-quality claret from the finest vintages, and buy in case lots and keep the wine in its original cases. If possible, buy magnums and never half-bottles. This advice seems easy to follow, but it need a well-furnished cheque book. Unless you have a very clear idea of what you are doing when buying wine to lay down (in which case you will not be reading this chapter), it is best, if not essential, to deal with a reputable wine merchant.

THREE SUGGESTIONS FOR YOUR CELLAR

Every individual stocks his cellar according to his or her own tastes. The combinations described opposite are only suggestions which you can interpret as you wish. Early-drinking wines, which gain nothing from being kept in a cellar, are not included amongst these suggestions. The fewer bottles you have, the more care you must take to replenish the cellar. The values given in brackets are, of course, only rough estimates.

CELLAR OF 50 BOTTLES (£250–£300 approx.)

20 Bordeaux	14 red Graves St-Emilion, Médoc, Pomerol, Fronsac) 6 white: 3 dry (Graves) 3 sweet (Sauternes-Barsac)
20 Burgundy	12 red (Côte-de-Nuits, Côte-de-Beaune) 8 white (Chablis, Meursault, Puligny)
10 Rhône	7 red (Côte-Crôtie, Hermitage, Châteauneuf-du-Pape 3 white (Hermitage, Condrieu)

CELLAR OF 150 BOTTLES (£1000 approx.)

Region		Red	White
35 Bordeaux	25 red 10 white	Fronsac Pomerol St-Émilion Graves Médoc (Crus Classés) (Crus Bourgeois)	3 Grands Secs (Graves) 7 { St-Croix-du-Mont Sauternes-Barsac
35 Burgundy	20 red 15 white	Côte-de-Nuits Côte-de-Beaune Côte Chalonnaise	Chablis Meursault Puligny-Montrachet
25 Rhône	19 red 6 white	Côtes-Rôties Hermitage rouge Cornas St-Joseph Châteauneuf-du-Pape Gigondas Côtes-du-Rhône Villages	Condrieu Hermitage Châteauneuf-du-Pape
15 Loire	8 red 7 white	Bourgueil Chinon Saumur-Champigny	Pouilly Fumé Vouvray Coteaux du Layon
10 South-West	7 red 3 white	Madiran Cahors	Jurançon (dry and sweet)
8 South-East	6 red 2 white	Bandol Palette	Cassis Palette
7 Alsace	(white)		Gewürztraminer Riesling Tokay
5 Jura	(white)		Vins Jaunes Côtes du Jura-Arbois

		10 Champagne and sparkling wines. (Worth having in store but do not all improve with keeping.)	Crémant de { Loire
			              Bourgogne
			              Alsace
			 Various types of champagnes

CELLAR OF 300 BOTTLES

This would cost approximately £2000 and could be arrived at by doubling the quantities of wines in the suggested 150-bottle cellar.

HOW TO KEEP WINE

Building up a good wine cellar is somewhat akin to doing a Chinese puzzle. A number of more detailed requirements must be added to the principles laid down above, such as:

1 You should try to acquire wines of the same usage and style but which do not develop at the same rate, so that they do not all reach their peaks at the same time.

2 Try to find wines which stay at their peak for the maximum possible period, so that you don't have to consume them all within a short space of time.

3 Vary them as much as possible, so that you don't always have to drink the same wines, no matter how good they are, and so that you will have a variety to hand for any occasion or type of food.

Finally, there are two parameters upon which the application of all these principles depends: your budget and the size of your cellar.

What Makes a Suitable Cellar?

A good cellar must be enclosed and well protected against burglars. It must be dark and sheltered from vibration and noise, free from smells and excessive draughts, but ventilated and not too dry or too damp, at about 75 per cent in degrees of humidity (as measured by a hygrometer) and, above all, kept at a stable temperature as near as possible to 11°C.

Cellars in town houses rarely have these features, and it may be necessary to effect improvements. Make the door and the lock stronger. Set up some ventilation if the cellar is stuffy, or block off the basement window if it is letting in too much air. Make the atmosphere more humid by putting out a bowl of water with some charcoal in it, or dry it out with gravel and an increase in ventilation. Try and stabilize the temperature with insulating panels. If possible, put the wine racks up on blocks of rubber to neutralize vibrations. If there is a boiler nearby or the smell of heating oil in the atmosphere, it might be better to abandon the project.

You may not have a cellar, or the one you do have may be unfit for use. There are two possible solutions: buy a cellar cabinet, a ready-made storage unit, holding between 50 and 500 bottles, in which the temperature and humidity are automatically maintained. Or you could construct your own storage area in a corner where the temperature can be made fairly stable and, if possible, rises no higher than 16°C. Note that the higher the temperature, the more rapidly the wine will develop. Do guard against one particularly common error; just because a wine reaches its peak quickly in bad storage conditions, this does not mean that it will compare in quality with the standard it would have reached more slowly in a cool cellar. Consequently, you should refrain from leaving good vintage wines, which develop slowly, to mature in a place or a cellar that is too warm. It is up to wine enthusiasts to adapt what they buy to the layout of their particular cellars.

The Right Layout

Experience has proven that a cellar is always too small. The arrangement of the bottles must therefore be logically worked out. Ready-made bottle racks have a lot to recommend them. They are inexpensive, can be installed instantly and provide easy access. Unfortunately, they waste a lot of space. The most economical use of space is to stack the bottles directly on top of each other. In order to gain access to the different wines, you will need to separate the stacks. The best way is to build (or have built), blockboard or plasterboard racks which will take 24, 36 or 48 bottles stacked in two rows.

If your cellar permits, you could have wooden wine racks made up. Make sure that the wood is sound, well-seasoned and treated against insect pests which may attack wine corks.

Two pieces of apparatus go to complete the equipment of a cellar: a maximum-and-minimum thermometer, and a hygrometer, which measures humidity. Regular readings will enable you to correct any variations in temperature or humidity.

The arrangement of the bottles in the cellar can be rather a headache. The following guidelines may be useful.

Keep whites near the ground and reds above. Wines being left to age should be laid on the back rows (or racks). Those ready for drinking should be towards the front.

Bottles which are bought or delivered in cardboard boxes, unlike those packed in wooden cases, must *not* be left in this type of packaging. Those thinking of reselling the wine will leave it in its case; ordinary wine drinkers will not, since cases take up a lot of room.

A system of notation will make it easier to locate racks and bottles. These notations can be used to further advantage in the cellar's most useful adjunct, namely the cellar book.

The Cellar Book

This is the wine-lover's memory, guide and the ultimate court of appeal. It ought to contain the following information: date of entry, number of bottles of each vintage, exact identification of the wines, price, the supposed time of each wine's peak, its location in the cellar and, if possible, what dish it ought ideally to accompany, and the taster's remarks.

Specialist bookshops and some wine merchants sell expensive cellar books, but a loose-leaf file would do just as well.

THE ART OF DRINKING WINE

If drinking is a physical necessity, drinking wine is a pleasure. This pleasure can be more or less intense depending on the wine, the circumstances of the tasting and the sensitivity of the taster.

Tasting Wine

There are several kinds of wine-tasting, each suited to a particular end. The technical, analytical and comparative type is the preserve of the professional. The wine-lover, however, will enjoy any wine-tasting which encourages him or her to appreciate the finer points of the wines, and to develop the sensitivity of nose and palate through discussion with fellow enthusiasts.

Tasting wine can not be undertaken anywhere or anyhow. The location must be pleasant, well-lit, preferably decorated in light colours, and free of all clinging odours such as perfume, smoke, cooking smells, or flowers and so on. The average temperature should be in the range 18–20°C.

The choice of an appropriate glass is important. The wines colour will be displayed to best advantage in plain glass or crystal. The classic wine glass is tulip-shaped, to enclose the wine's aromas, and the body of the glass should be separated from the base by a stem. The stem prevents the wine from becoming warm when the base of the glass is held in the hand and makes it easier to swirl the wine in the glass, a process which releases the aromas by contact with the air and intensifies the sensation by spreading the wine over a greater surface area of the glass.

The shape of the glass has such an influence on one's appreciation of the taste and bouquet of the wine that the French Standards Board (AFNOR, L'Association Française de Normalisation) and the International Standards Organization (ISO) have, following studies on the subject, chosen a glass which offers every guarantee of efficacy to the taster and consumer. This type of glass is not confined to professionals and is sold by some specialist shops.

The Sampling Technique

Sampling wine calls upon the senses of sight, smell, taste and even touch, in that the mouth is sensitive to the physical properties of wine, such as temperature, consistency, dissolved gas, and so on.

THE EYE

The taster's first contact with the wine is through the eyes. An examination of colour is extremely informative. Whatever its colour and shade, the wine must be clear, not turbid. Streaks or mistiness are signs that it is unhealthy, or should be rejected. You should not, however, worry about the presence of small bitartrate crystals (which are insoluble and tasteless) since they do not affect the quality of the wine itself.

You can examine the clarity of a wine by holding the glass horizontally against a light source. In the case of red wine, its transparency can be determined by examining the wine against a white background such as a tablecloth or a sheet of paper. In order to examine transparency you will have to tip the glass. The surface will then form an ellipse and should inform you about the age of the wine and how well it has been conserved. You should then examine the exact shade of colour. All young wines should be transparent, which is not always the case with old, quality wines.

The eye should also be concerned with the sparkle or brilliance of a wine. A wine which sparkles will probably have a fresh, lively character. A dull colour may indicate a lifeless wine.

This visual inspection of the colour should end up with a look at its intensity, which is not to be confused with its shade or hue. This, the most readily perceptible aspect of red wines, tells you most about them.

What Wine Colour Means:

Wine	Colour	Meaning
White	Almost colourless	Very young and closely protected against oxidation. Made by modern methods in a vat.
	Very pale yellow with green reflections	Young to very young. Made and raised in a vat.
	Straw or golden yellow	Mature. May have been raised in wood.
	Copper or golden-bronze	Already old.
	Amber to black	Oxidized. Too old.
Rosé	Flecked white, off white with pink reflections	Young rosé vinified according to white wine procedure.
	Salmon-pink to pure, very bright red	Young, fruity rosé ready to drink.
	Pink tinged with yellow or golden-yellow	Getting old for its type.
Red	Purplish	Very young. A good colour for Gamays and Beaujolais Nouveaux (6–18 months)
	Pure (cherry) red	Light red wines at their peak. Bigger red wines still immature.
	Red with bands of orange	The first signs of maturity in a big red wine.
	Brownish-red to brown	Only great wines will reach their maturity with this colour. For any others, it is too late.

The Relationship Between Wine Colour and Wine Quality:

Wine	Causes	Meaning
Too clear in colour	Insufficient extract A rainy year Excess yield Young vines Grapes not ripe enough Rotten grapes Not kept in the vat long enough Fermentation at a low temperature	Light wines not worth keeping long Wines of minor vintage
Dark colour	Well pressed Low yield Old vines Successful vinification	Good or great wines Good prospects for the future

By looking at the wine you may also discover 'legs', droplets formed on the side of the glass when you rotate the wine to sniff the bouquet (see below). They are an indication of the wine's alcoholic content

Some Words and Phrases used for Visual Examination:

Shades: purple, scarlet, garnet-coloured, ruby, violet, cherry, peony.
Intensity: light, strong, dark, deep, intense.
Brilliance: dull, lifeless, sad, sparkling, brilliant.
Clarity: opaque, murky, crystalline
Transparency: flawless, misty.

THE NOSE

Olfactory examination is the second test which the wine being sampled must undergo. Certain unpleasant odours eliminate everything else, for example vinegar smell, or the smell from contaminated cork. In most cases, however, the bouquet of wine offers a pleasurable experience, with something new to discover every time.

The aromatic components of the bouquet are expressed according to their volatility, or rate of evaporation, which is why the temperature at which wine is served is so important: if it is too cold there will be no bouquet at all, if it is too warm the bouquet will vaporize too quickly and combine with, oxidize and thus destroy any highly volatile fragrances, as well as bringing out any abnormal aromatic elements.

The bouquet of wine may therefore be thought of as a swarm of aromas which are constantly changing. They emerge in succession depending on the temperature and exposure to the air, which is why the way in which the glass is handled is so imortant. Begin by sniffing when the glass is held still, then rotate the wine inside the glass. As the air reaches the wine other aromas will emerge.

The quality of a wine is often shown by the intensity and complexity of its bouquet. Lesser wines offer little or no bouquet; what little they have is simple, even monotonous, and could easily be summed up in a single word. Great wines, on the other hand, are characterized by full, deep bouquets, constantly renewing their complexity. The vocabulary used to describe a bouquet is infinite, because analaogy is the only means of description available to the taster. Various systems for classifying aromas have been put forward. For the sake of simplicity let us keep to those which use the characteristics of flowers, fruit, vegetables, (herbs), spices, balsam, animals, wood, fire and chemicals.

Some Words and Phrases used for Olfactory Examination:

Flowers:	violet, lime, jasmine, elderflower, acacia, iris and peony.
Fruits:	raspberry, blackcurrant, cherry, Morello cherry, gooseberry, apple, apricot, banana and plum.
Vegetables:	herbs, fern, moss, undergrowth, wet earth, chalk, various mushrooms.
Spices:	all the spices, especially pepper, ginger, cloves and nutmeg.
Balsam:	resin, pine and turpentine tree.
Animal:	meat, 'hung' meat, game, musk and fur.
Fire:	burnt, grilled, toasted aromas; tobacco, dried hay, and all aromas relating to roasting (coffee, etc.).

THE MOUTH

Once it has passed the visual and olfactory tests, the wine undergoes a final test in the mouth.

A small quantity of wine is held in the mouth. Take in a little air so that it will circulate through the entire buccal cavity. The wine will warm up in the mouth and diffuse more aromas which are picked up at the rear of the nasal passage; the taste buds themselves are, of course, sensitive only to bitter, sharp, sweet and salty tastes; someone with a cold cannot fully taste wine or food, because the rear nasal passage is blocked.

The mouth is also sensitive to the temperature of wine, to its viscosity, to the presence, or absence, of carbon dioxide gas and to the wine's astringency. The last of these is a tactile effect, in which absence of lubricating saliva and contraction of the mucous membranes result from the action of tannin, an astringent compound found naturally in the stems and skins of the grape.

It is in the mouth that you will discover a wine's balance and harmony, or on the contrary, signs of a badly made wine which you should avoid buying.

A good wine lies at the point where the three components of smoothness, tannins and acidity are perfectly balanced. These structural elements support its aromatic richness. A great wine can be distinguished from a good one by its strong, powerful structure, even though it may be blended, and by the range and complexity of its aromas.

Examples of Vocabulary relating to Tasting:

Criticism:	shapeless, limp, flat, thin, aqueous, limited, transparent. poor, heavy, coarse, rough, thick and unbalanced.
Praise:	structured, well-constructed, balanced, full-bodied, complete, elegant, fine, flavoursome, rich.

After being analysed in the mouth, the wine is swallowed or spat out. The wine-lover then assesses the persistence of the aroma or aftertaste, often called 'length' of flavour. One method of measuring length is by units called 'caudalies', equivalent to one second of persistence. The longer the aroma lasts, so the theory runs, the better the wine. This length of flavour makes it possible to organize wines into a hierarchy of gustative length.

The Identification of a Wine

Sampling wine, or drinking it wisely, is a matter of appreciation, of tasting a wine fully and determining if it is great, average or minor. Very often, you may want to know if it conforms to its type or not, so that it also may be necesssary to clarify the wine's origin.

'Blind' tasting is a sport or parlour game. However, it is a game that cannot be played without a minimum of information. You may recognize a type of vine, a Cabernet-Sauvignon for example. But is it a Cabernet-Sauvignon from Italy, Languedoc, California, Chile, Argentina, Australia or South Africa?

If you confine yourself to France, the identification of the great regions is possible. If you wish to be more precise, however, some difficult problems arise. Faced with six glasses of wine, having been clearly told that they represent the six 'appellations' of Médoc (Listrac, Moulis, Margaux, St-Julien, Pauillac and St-Estèphe), how often will even a skilled taster get it completely right?

One classic experiment, which anyone can undertake, demonstrates the difficulty. The taster, with his eyes bandaged, tastes, in any order, red wines low in tannin and non-aromatic whites, perferably raised in wood. He has only to tell the white from the red, and vice versa, but it is extremely rare that no mistakes are made at all. Paradoxically, it is much easier to recognize a very specific type of wine having once tasted it.

Tasting Prior to Buying

When you go to a winery to buy wine, you will have to taste before you choose. Comparative sampling of two or three wines is easy. It becomes complicated only when you allow wine prices to interfere. If you are working within a fixed budget (which is unfortunately true for most people), certain purchases can easily be eliminated. Comparative tasting, which seems quite easy and simple to start with, becomes extremely tricky when the buyer has to presuppose the development of various wines, and to calculate the period when they will reach their peak. Even vineyard owners sometimes get it wrong when they try to imagine how their wine will develop in the future. Some owners have been known to buy back their own wine which they had sold off cheaply, having wrongly believed that it wouldn't improve.

Certain principles can, however, provide facts about the valuation of wine. If wines are to improve, they must have sufficient firmness and alcohol content. You must pay attention to acidity and tannins. An extremely supple wine, which may be very pleasant to drink, has low acidity, even too low, and so will be too delicate for its longevity to be guaranteed. Equally, a wine which is low in tannin will have a limited future.

These two components of wine – acidity and tannin – can be accurately measured, and will have been checked by a laboratory or oenologist at various stages before the wine was bottled.

The future of a wine with a low acidity cannot be guaranteed. Less critical is the tannin level, below which keeping wine for a long time becomes difficult. Nevertheless, it is useful to know about this indicator, because tannins which are very ripe, sweet or coated are sometimes underestimated in sampling.

You should always sample the wine under good conditions, and avoid being unduly influenced by the atmosphere of the vineyard owner's cellar. You will certainly find it hard to form an objective view if you sample wine just after a meal, after taking brandy, coffee, chocolate or mints, or even after smoking.

If the vineyard owner offers you nuts, beware! They improve the taste of all wines. Also beware of cheese, which modifies the sensitivity of the palate. If you really must eat something, have a piece of plain bread.

Practising Wine Tasting

Your ability to taste wine improves with practice. If you have a passion for it you can enrol on one of the increasing number of courses which are obtainable, whether on wine-tasting alone, food and wines, or even on a particular region or regions. Some of these courses take the form of study holidays in vineyard areas, taking in analysis of the influence of vine types, vintages, soils, the effects of vinification techniques, and visiting estates to taste the wines in the company of the vineyard owner.

SERVING WINES

In a restaurant serving wine is the prerogative of the wine waiter. At home, you must become your own wine waiter and must acquire the necessary skills, beginning by choosing the best type of wine for the dishes making up the meal and selecting those which have reached their peak.

Of course, individual choice will aways play an important role in choosing which wine for which food. Nevertheless, centuries of experience have made it possible to extract some general principles, ideal combinations and major incompatibilities.

The development of wines varies greatly form one to another. Their peak is all that interests the wine-lover, who wants the best. Depending on the appellation,

Guide to Development of Wine in Bottle:

Appellation or region	Peak (in years)	
	white	red
Alsace		within the year
Alsace Crus		within the year
Alsace late harvest – sweet	8–12	
Jura	4	8
Jura rosé		6
Vin Jaune	20	
Savoy	1–2	2–4
Burgundy	5	7
Burgundy	8–10	10–15
Mâcon	2–3	2–4
Beaujolais		within the year
Beaujolais Crus		3–4
North Rhône Valley	2–3	4–5
(Côte Rôtie, Hermitage etc.)	(8)	(8–15)
South Rhône Valley	2	4–8
Loire (including sparkling)	5–10	5–12
Loire mellow, sweet	10–15	
Perigord wines	2–3	3–4
Perigord sweet wines	6–8	
Bordeaux	2–3	6–8
Bordeaux Crus	8–10	10–15
Bordeaux, sweet	10–15	
Jurançon, dry	4–6	
Jurançon mellow, sweet	6–10	
Madiran		8–12
Cahors		5–10
Gaillac	3	5
Languedoc	1–2	2–4
Côtes de Provence	1–2	2–4
Corsica	1–4	2–4

Remarks

– Do not confuse peak with maximum longevity.

– A warm cellar or one in which the temperature varies accelerates the development of wines.

and therefore on the type of wine, soil and vinification, the peak could come within a period stretching from one to twenty years. Depending on the year shown on the bottle, a wine can develop two or three times more quickly. It is possible, however, to establish averages, which act as a base and which can be altered according to the cellar and the information on the vintage chart.

Methods of Serving

Every care should be taken in fetching the bottle, from taking it out of the cellar to the moment when the wine reaches the glass. The older a wine is the more care it requires. The bottle should be taken from the stack and gradually turned upright to be brought to its place of consumption, unless it is going to be put directly into a pouring basket.

Unpretentious wines can be served quite simply, but very old, and consequently very delicate wines, should be transferred from the rack to a pouring basket with as little change in position as possible. Young wines and robust wines should be opened in advance to start off some beneficial oxidation and stood upright to allow sediment, if any, to fall to the bottom of the bottle. In the case of marked sediment, the wine should be decanted with care, in front of a light source, so that clouded wine and solid matter can be easily seen and left in the bottle.

When to Uncork Wine and When to Serve It

Professor Emile Peynaud – France's leading scientific authority on wine-tasting – maintains that wine cannot 'breathe' in an open bottle, however long the cork has been drawn, as the surface area in contact with the air (at the neck of the bottle) is too small. However, the table given below provides a resumé of customs which, if they do not always improve the wine, certainly never do it any harm.

Aromatic whites 'Primeur' wines ⎫ Ordinary wines ⎬ R and W Rosés	Uncork and drink without delay and keep the bottle vertical.
White Loire wines ⎫ Sweet white wines ⎭	Uncork and wait an hour. Keep the bottle vertical.
Young red wines ⎫ Red wines at their peak ⎭	Decant half an hour to two hours before drinking.
Old, delicate red wines	Uncork in the pouring basket and serve without delay.

Uncorking

The cap must be cut below the ring or in the middle of the rim. The wine must not come into contact with the metal of the cap. In cases where the neck of the bottle is sealed with wax, make several little cuts so the wax will flake off. Better still try to get the wax off using a knife on the top of the neck, as this method has the advantage of not shaking the bottle or the wine.

The only satisfactory way to draw the cork is with a good-quality corkscrew. It is worth buying the best, as poor-quality corkscrews will simply tear and crumble the cork.

Theoretically, the corkscrew should not pierce the lower end of the cork. Once the cork has been drawn, it should be sniffed. It should not have any parasitic odours clinging to it nor should it smell of cork. The wine is then tasted to check it one last time, before being served to the guests.

Temperature

You can kill a wine by serving it at an incorrect temperature, or you can allow it to show its best by serving it at the right temperature. This is rarely achieved by guesswork, and so a wine thermometer is useful.

The temperature at which a wine is served depends on its appellation, age and, to a lesser degree, on the ambient temperature. Do not forget that wine served in a warm room will rise in temperature by several degrees in the glass.

Guide to Temperatures at which to Serve Wine:

	°C
Vintage Bordeaux reds	16–18
Vintage Burgundy reds	15–16
Quality red wines, vintage reds before their peak	15
Vintage dry whites	12–13
Light, fruity and young reds	11
Rosés, early whites	10
Dry whites, local reds	9
Lesser whites, local whites	8
Champagne, sparkling wines	7–8
Sweet wines	6

These temperatures should be raised by one or two degrees if the wine is old.

There is a tendency to serve wines slightly cooler if they are acting as an aperitif, and to drink the wine accompanying the meal slightly nearer to room temperature. All the same, the ambient temperature is critical. In scorching weather, a wine drunk at 11°C will seem frozen and it will be necessary to bring it up to 13°C or even 14°C.

Nevertheless, you should avoid going above 20°C, because beyond this point certain irreversible changes may take place which can spoil the qualities of the wine and any pleasure you might expect from it.

Glasses

Each region has its glass. In practice, unless you fall into obsessive pedantry, you should be content either with an all-purpose glass (of the style used in wine-tasting), or with one of the two commonest types, the Bordeaux glass and the Burgundy glass.

Whichever glass you choose, it should be moderately filled, between a third and a half.

At the Restaurant

Reading the wine list is informative, not just because it reveals the secrets of the cellar, which is what it is there for, but because it will enable you to assess the degree of competence of the wine waiter, or the proprietor.

A good list must include the following information for each wine: the appellation, the year, the place of bottling, and the name of the shipper or proprietor responsible for the wine. (This last piece of information is often omitted.)

A good list should offer a wide range of appellations and vintages. An intelligent wine list will be specially adapted to suit the style and specialities of the cuisine, or will make a feature of regional wines.

Wine Bars

In France, there have always been bistros and bars selling quality wine by the glass, quite often wines chosen by the owner during a visit to a vineyard. Selections of cold pork and cheeses are normally offered to customers at these establishments.

During the 1970s, a new generation of bistros, commonly known as wine bars, grew up. The perfecting of a dispensing machine, which protects wine by pumping

GLASSES

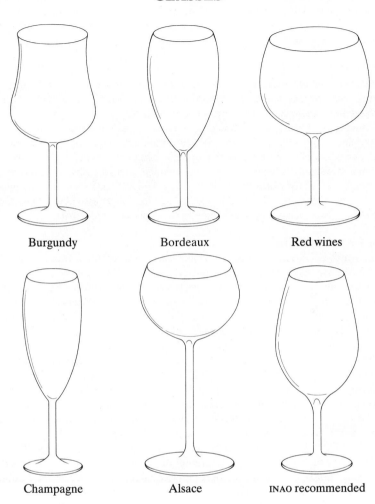

Burgundy   Bordeaux   Red wines

Champagne   Alsace   INAO recommended

Professional tasting glasses

Sparkling wines   White wines   Young red wines   Vintage red wines
                               and rosés

an inert gas into partly drunk bottles, keeping the contents at their vintage standard, has enabled these establishments to offer customers some very great wines of renowned vintages. At the same time, less rudimentary catering has made it possible for them to build up their menus.

VINTAGE

Almost all quality wines state the year that they were made. Only some wines and certain champagnes are an exception to this rule, and their particular type of development, the mixing of several years, justifies this.

Having said this, what should one think of a non-vintage bottle? Two situations are possible: either the vintage cannot even be admitted to because it has such a terrible reputation in that appellation, or it cannot be given a vintage because it contains a combination of assembled wines of several years, as the professional form of words has it. The quality depends on the talent of the person assembling the wine. Generally wine which has been assembled like this is superior to each of its components, but it is not advisable to keep it.

The Genesis of a Vintage

Wine which bears a great vintage is concentrated and balanced. It is generally but not necessarily made from an early-picked crop which is small in volume. In any case there are no great vintages which do not come from perfectly healthy grapes, completely devoid of rot. When it comes to obtaining a great vintage, the weather at the beginning of the vegetative cycle does not really matter. It could even be argued that some misadventures such as frost are favourable because they diminish the number of grapes per vine. The period from 15 August up to the harvest (end of September), on the other hand, is of crucial importance. A maximum of sun and heat is required. Nineteen sixty-one, which remains thus far 'the year of the century', is exemplary. Everything happened as described above. The years 1963, 1965 and 1968 were, on the other hand, disastrous. Combined cold and rain lead to lack of maturity and a poor yield, because grapes soak up too much water. Heat and rain are no better as tepid water favours rotting. This was the stumbling block of a potentially great vintage in the south-west in 1976. The advances made in the protective treatment of grapes, particularly those designed to counter grape worms and the development of rot, make it possible to obtain quality harvests which would once have been under threat. These treatments also make it possible to wait for the grape to ripen completely, even if the weather conditions at the time are not encouraging, a fact which has lead to a significant improvement in quality. As early as 1978, excellent last-harvested vintages began to be noted.

It is customary to summarize the quality of the vintages in valuation tables. These notes are only averages. They do not take into account specific local micro-climates, nor the heroic efforts made at vigorous selection of grapes during the harvest, nor vagaries and aberrations during the wine-making process. Chance and skill can confound all expectation; for example the Graves wine, Domaine de Chevalier 1965 – a frightful year – shows that you can develop a great wine even in a year registered zero!

Year-by-Year Vintage Chart for French Wines (20 points maximum)

	Bordeaux R	Bordeaux W (sweet)	Bordeaux W Dry	Burgundy R	Burgundy W	Champagne	Loire	Rhône	Alsace
1900	19	19	17	13		17			
1901	11	14							
1902									
1903	14	7	11						
1904	15	17		16		19		18	
1905	14	12							
1906	16	16		19	18				
1907	12	10		15					
1908	13	16							
1909	10	7							
1910									
1911	14	14		19	19	20	19	19	
1912	10	11							
1913	7	7							
1914	13	15				18			Under German rule
1915		16		16	15	15	12	15	
1916	15	15		13	11	12	11	10	
1917	14	16		11	11	13	12	9	
1918	16	12		13	12	12	11	14	
1919	15	10		18	18	15	18	15	15
1920	17	16		13	14	14	11	13	10
1921	16	20		16	20	20	20	13	20
1922	9	11		9	16	4	7	6	4
1923	12	13		16	18	17	18	18	14
1924	15	16		13	14	11	14	17	11
1925	6	11		6	5	3	4	8	6
1926	16	17		16	16	15	13	13	14
1927	7	14		7	5	5	3	4	
1928	19	17		18	20	20	17	17	17
1929	20	20		20	19	19	18	19	18
1930							3	4	3
1931	2	2		2	3		3	5	3
1932				2	3	3	3	3	7
1933	11	9		16	16	16	17	17	15

	Bordeaux R	Bordeaux W (sweet)	Bordeaux W Dry	Burgundy R	Burgundy W	Champagne	Loire	Rhône	Alsace
1934	17	17		17	18	17	16	17	16
1935	7	12		13	16	10	15	5	14
1936	7	11		9	10	9	12	13	9
1937	16	20		18	20	18	16	17	17
1938	8	12		14	10	10	12	8	9
1939	11	16		9	9	9	10	8	3
1940	13	12		12	8	8	11	5	10
1941	12	10		9	12	10	7	5	5
1942	12	16		14	12	16	11	14	14
1943	15	17		17	16	17	13	17	17
1944	13	11	12	10	10		6	8	4
1945	20	20	18	20	18	20	19	18	19
1946	14	9	10	10	13	10	12	17	9
1947	18	20	18	18	18	18	20	18	19
1948	16	16	16	10	14	11	12		15
1949	19	20	18	20	18	17	16	17	17
1950	13	18	16	11	15	16	14	15	14
1951	8	6	6	7	6	7	7	8	8
1952	16	16	16	16	18	16	15	16	14
1953	19	17	16	18	17	17	18	14	18
1954	10			14	11	15	9	13	9
1955	16	19	18	15	18	19	16	15	17
1956	5						9	12	9
1957	10	15		14	15		13	16	13
1958	14	14		10	9		12	14	12
1959	19	20	18	19	17	17	19	15	20
1960	11	10	10	10	7	14	9	12	12
1961	20	15	16	18	17	16	16	18	18
1962	16	16	16	17	19	17	15	16	14
1963					10				
1964	16	9	13	16	17	18	16	14	19
1965			12				8		
1966	17	15	16	18	18	17	15	16	12
1967	13	18	16	15	16		13	15	14
1968									

	Bordeaux R	Bordeaux W (sweet)	Bordeaux W Dry	Burgundy R	Burgundy W	Champagne	Loire	Rhône	Alsace
1969	9	13	12	19	18	16	15	16	13
1970	18	17	18	15	15	17	15	15	14
1971	16	17	19	18	20	16	17	15	19
1972	10		9	11	13		9	14	9
1973	14	12		12	16	16	16	13	16
1974	11	14		12	13	8	11	12	13
1975	19	17	18		11	18	15	10	16
1976	14	19	16	18	15	15	18	16	19
1977	12	7	14	11	12	10	11	11	12
1978	18	14	17	19	17	16	17	19	17
1979	17	18	18	15	16	15	14	16	15
1980	14	18	18	11	12	14	13	15	12
1981	17	17	17	12	15	16	15	14	17
1982	19	4/17	16	13	16	14	14	13	14
1983	18	13	16	14	13	12	12	16	20
1984	14	12	12	10	14	5	10	11	10

Red rules indicate wines for laying down.

Vintages to Drink Now

Wines develop differently according to whether the year was sunny or gloomy, and also according to their appellation, quality, vinification, how they were raised and the conditions under which they were stored. The table below indicates, by region, which high-quality wines of recent vintage are likely to be ready for drinking now. The column on the right shows other particularly fine years which are generally available and known to be already drinking well. The table does not deal with exceptional growths or legendary vintages.

Red Bordeaux	1979–83	1978
Bordeaux dry white	1983–84	1982
Bordeaux sweet	1978 (?), 1979–81	1975
Burgundy red	1979, 1980, 1983	1978
Burgundy white	1981, 1983	1982
Beaujolais	1984, 1985 (?)	
Beaujolais vintage	1981	1983
North Rhône Valley	1979, 1983	1978
South Rhône Valley	1979, 1981	1978
Provence, Corsica	1982, 1984	
Languedoc	1982, 1984	
South-West	1982	
Alsace		1983
Alsace late harvest		1971, 1983
Loire	1978, 1983	1976
Loire sweet	1981	1976
Champagne (vintage only)	1979	1981

FOOD AND WINE

A s soon as you begin to discuss which dish should be served with which wine, or which wine would go best with which dish, a stance has already been taken; the relative importance of one or the other has been established, which the second must then complement, or match. It might therefore be better to talk of a 'marriage' between these two individuals, thereby treating them as equals. So that readers may form their own opinions on this matter, there follows a discussion between two experts: André Vedel, an eminent oenologist, who speaks here in his capacity as wine-taster, and Alain Dutournier, one of the great chefs of French cuisine, known particularly for his ability to be creative and innovative while remaining true to his gastronomic roots – the traditional cuisine of south-west France. They are not stating rules or set traditions, customs or fashion, but rather offer advice that sometimes puts into question widely accepted notions about combining wine with food.

A.V. Although there are no strict rules about marrying wine with food, there are nevertheless two principles that always hold true: the less high-class a wine and the younger it is, the more easily it adapts to various types of food. Very old or very high-class wines are much more problematical, and need to be tasted with something quite simple and neutral, such as Dutch cheese and bread.

A.D. I agree. In order to appreciate an older wine fully, I often drink it an hour or so before the main meal, as a kind of aperitif, after which there should be a break before starting again – maybe with champagne.

SPARKLING WINES

A.V. I call sparkling wines 'detergent' wines, because they really prepare the mouth for what is to follow, cleaning and refreshing the palate. This applies to all sparkling wines, be they champagne, crémant, Blanquette de Limoux, or Mousseux de Jura, and some of them are of very good quality and exceptional value. To serve champagne throughout a meal, as many people do, seems a great pity to me – I feel sorry for the champagne! I have only ever found three dishes that do not spoil it; chicken, and even then only the white meat; fromage blanc made with goat's milk; and plain avocado with just salt and pepper. Contrary to popular practice, champagne should not be served as a dessert wine, but it makes an excellent aperitif and is a very pleasant way to quench a thirst. Or you could, I suppose, also serve it between two courses as a kind of transitional wine.

A.D. In practice, when I'm cooking a dish I always consider which wines would go well with it. Until recently most restaurants put their food first and wines second. This has never been my practice, and I agree wholeheartedly with those customers who decide on their wines first and then select a menu to complement their choice.

'GREAT' WINES VERSUS 'LESSER' WINES

A.V. In my opinion, if you have already planned a menu, do not serve a great wine. If you want to serve a great wine, choose that first and then plan your menu around it. Never assume that you have to serve an impressive wine with an impressive dish.

A.D. Absolutely. And I would go even further than that: I would say that if you are catering for lots of people, don't serve great wines; they should be saved for more intimate company. If there is a crowd, stick to simpler wines, especially if the dishes are at all complicated. To me, great wines should be served with a dish that is good, but not too demanding. In the case of a red wine, for example, this would be chicken, leg of lamb, or something similar.

A.V. Well, I would be even more specific than that. If you are serving up Poulet de Bresse you should not be drinking a Chambertin. But this dish would go very well with a small Burgundy or a young Brouilly, both relatively light wines. I believe there should always be relative equality between the type of wine and type of food, so that a sophisticated dish would be best served with a great wine. A plain Burgundy would go well with chicken and a Chambertin with pheasant or woodcock.

A.D. Indeed, what you have just suggested are perfect combinations, but let me explain myself more clearly. When I talk about great wines, I am referring to Grand Cru wines, but also to vintage wines. And I meant that if you want to drink a very special and very old bottle, it would probably be best to drink it at, say, 5 o'clock and have nothing to eat with it, rather than wait until the end of the meal to produce your treasure.

A.V. I agree with you there. I also feel it is a shame that so few chefs concern themselves with how to combine wine and food, particularly since this leads to the creation of fish or meat dishes including various fruits, for which it can be very difficult to find a suitable wine.

A.D. Yes. Any dish with mangoes in it, for example, can probably only be matched by a Condrieu.

A.V. Condrieu wines should always be drunk young, because although they gain in character as they age, they also lose the ability to stand up to more problematical dishes. I have established that a very young, high-class Condrieu goes as well with mint leaves as it does with plain Foie Gras de Canard. This would tend to support the notion that older wines are much more difficult to please, whatever their class.

BEAUJOLAIS

A.D. The success of Beaujolais can be attributed to the fact that most people who know nothing about wine are attracted to its colour and fragrance.

A.V. Yes. Beaujolais is a very seductive wine, but its taste hardly ever changes, even when it's served with very different dishes, from milky oysters to steak. Beaujolais is suitable for serving with almost anything. Although for me the Beaujolais wines obtained by carbonic maceration, as opposed to traditional methods, don't really go well with anything – not even charcuterie – they are too sweet.

A.D. By choosing Beaujolais you are really avoiding having to make a choice at all, and although it may be acceptable with almost anything, it does not complement anything particularly well. Unlike a Médoc, it does not demand any culinary skills; and very often Beaujolais is drunk because people do not dare to change their habits and try something new.

BORDEAUX, BURGUNDY AND COTES DU RHONE

A.V. That leads us now to Bordeaux wines, and I think it would be best if we first stuck to red wines, both Bordeaux and Burgundy. Within this vast range the main criterion for choice has to be aromatic strength. The most delicate aromatic wines are the Médocs, and at the opposite end of the scale we find the great Burgundy and St-Emilion wines. In between there are the Côtes du Rhône wines, especially Hermitage.

A.D. In fact, the best Côtes du Rhône are those produced in northern parts, which go very well with Gibier à Poil (that is, four-legged game).

A.V. Yes. And among the northern Côtes du Rhône one of the best value wines around is St-Joseph, which can reasonably stand comparison with a Graves. When matching wine with food, one of the most important elements is the grape variety – although it is not, of course, the only one. Let's take charcuterie as an example: a Cabernet loses all its character if served with rillettes, and Chinon, which is a Cabernet wine, should never be served with rillettes. However, a Burgundy wine produced in the same region will go very well with them, because it is made from Pinot grapes. As for the Chinon, it is very good for serving with liver, including liver pâté, because, in common with the great Médocs, it is a tannic wine. A Burgundy is no good because it is not sufficiently tannic.

ALSACE

A.V. Here are some combinations that I have found to be successful for Alsace wines, according to grape type. For dishes that come somewhere between fish and meat, such as Tripoux d'Auvergne (Auvergne tripe), a Tokay is best, but this totally contradicts local tradition. It is also very good with Petit Gris, the Mont Ventoux mushroom, which is in no way a native of Alsace!

A.D. Wouldn't snails go well with a Tokay?

A.V. Not really. You'd be better off with something a bit crisper. Snails usually have so much butter with them that you need something that will freshen the mouth; a Burgundy Aligoté would be much better. Riesling, on the other hand, is perfect for choucroute (sauerkraut). Beer may often be drunk with it, but physiologically that is not a good idea. Smoked meats are particularly indigestible, and beer does not aid digestion. White wine does, however, because it is acidic.

A.D. I agree with you completely. Riesling is not my favourite wine, but the one time I do drink it is with choucroute because it cuts through the grease, and also its acidity goes well with the cabbage.

THE LOIRE VALLEY

A.V. If we are going to talk about the Loire Valley, I would like to make the distinction between two interesting styles of wine here: Muscadet, which is ideal for all types of fish and seafood, on the one hand; and all the Breton or Cabernet red wines on the other. These are extremely interesting wines that have all the fruitiness of a Beaujolais or Rhône valley wine and yet still remain full-bodied, making them very easy to please. I am thinking particularly of Champigny in Anjou and of Chinon in Touraine, to mention but two of the principal styles. There are also all the Loire Valley Sauvignons. This would encompass the whole of the Loire basin, from the Haut-Poitou Sauvignons, which are quite crisp, through Pouilly, Touraine, and so on, to the most famous of all, those of Sancerre. These wines have the same good points as a Beaujolais: although they are very distinctive, they go well with all kinds of dishes. In fact, here as in Burgundy and in south-west France, Sauvignon is a grape variety that can almost always be served where other wines won't work. Anything smoked – for example, smoked sprats, duck breast or kippers – should be served with a Sauvignon. It is not by chance that the people of Pouilly-sur-Loire call their Sauvignon 'Blanc-Fumé'; because it has a certain smoky smell. A typical dish that I am trying at the moment is one that is also very problematical – egg pockets of smoked cod; it is guaranteed to spell death to any white wine in the world except a Sauvignon.

A.D. As far as I'm concerned, I can't really see much that one would serve with a Sauvignon, apart from smoked fish, as you have said – except maybe a salad. I certainly can't imagine turbot with Sauvignon.

THE VIN JAUNE, OR 'YELLOW WINE', OF JURA

A.V. There is a little-known wine that is, however, one of the greatest in the world, and which should really be more widely used not only to drink but also in cooking – Jura Vin Jaune. Try one day putting a soup spoon of Vin Jaune into a simple Blanquette de Veau five minutes before serving, just enough time to allow the alcohol to evaporate – you'll see that it is almost spicy, like pepper, and gives the dish a certain liveliness and class. Vin Jaune is really quite remarkable, and it has one great advantage for cooking: you can open a bottle, take out a glassful, recork it and leave it for a month. When you open it again, the wine will not have changed one bit. A good Vin Jaune can be kept for three to six months in a kitchen cupboard without spoiling – an almost unheard-of ability among French wines!

A.D. It is not very well known and, unfortunately, is also quite expensive. There is very little of it, and half of what there is is not perfect. Much of it already has a slight acetic acid or maderized flavour, but the genuine, well-made ones, are perfect, and, if so, they should really be drunk and not simply used in cooking. I cook prawns in court bouillon, or sautée prawns with lots of pepper, and at the last minute I make a very small amount of glaze with Vin Jaune. I then drink the same wine with them. Wild prawns have a very strong-flavoured section just above the coral, in the centre of the head. I've tried some of the great Burgundy wines with them, but only Vin Jaune is really right.

A.V. I must mention in passing that, apart from a very young Beaujolais, Vin Jaune is the only wine I know that can stand up to Sauce à l'Armoricaine, which is made with white wine, fish stock, shallots, tarragon and tomatoes etc.

A.D. Yes, it's the only contestant there is, apart from sweet wines.

A.V. The problem with Vin Jaune is that it tends to be served early-on in a meal, with fish, white meat dishes, and so on, and it is difficult to find another wine to follow it. This is where champagne can step in to make a 'champagne interlude' instead of the more usual 'Normandy interlude', or 'trou normand' (where Calvados or some other spirit is drunk between courses). You cannot drink Vin Jaune throughout a meal, for financial, gastronomic, and even physiological reasons! It is extremely rich and I fear you would have problems the next morning. But to go on to Roquefort: Vin Jaune and Roquefort is the most wonderful combination. They have a synergistic effect: the Roquefort becomes stronger and the Vin Jaune becomes richer as they mutually complement one another.

A.D. I love to create a meal around a wine like this. In the hunting season I sometimes prepare a meal consisting of a game dish followed by a chocolate dessert and I serve a Sauternes or a Vin Jaune throughout the whole meal. Admittedly, you have to be healthy to stand up to it!

The second half of this dialogue between André Vedel and Alain Dutournier is arranged according to types of dishes in the order that they would appear in a meal. Although it may seem obvious, it is not as simple as it first appears.

A.V. It was much simpler to match food and wines twenty or so years ago, when there were many different dishes but only a few basic ways of preparing them. Nowadays it is much more complicated. We mentioned turbot a little while ago; if you simply grill, poach, or bake it, that's simple enough, but as soon as you add for instance, all is changed. Modern cuisine has become rather too fussy.

APPETIZERS

A.V. Appetizers come at the beginning of the meal, and so go very well with champagne, provided anything sweet is avoided.

A.D. Yes. Although plums are grown where I come from, I discourage their use in appetizers because they are sweet, and the same goes for dates. I also detest the current trend of putting all kinds of fruit into savoury dishes, such as duck or liver. The resulting sweetness is an impossible combination for any good-quality wine. People should rather be encouraged towards simplicity – today they cook everything with cream, fruit or herbs. Fruit with fish is absolutely disastrous.

FOIE GRAS

A.V. The simplest way to prepare foie gras is with just salt and pepper, but in the south-west it is made with grapes. These are, however, green, unripe grapes, which have always been used to give acidity to the pâté and to counteract its richness.

A.D. Yes. You could also prepare foie gras with ver juice because the acidity, like the tannin in certain red wines, acts on the rich pâté to make it more digestible. But foie gras with grapes is something I used to watch being made at the inn by my mother or my grandmother, and they only ever used to make it in winter. At that time, the geese were force-fed in December and January, so the only grapes we could use were ones we had already – beautiful bunches of grapes that had been drying on reeds or bamboo in the hayloft and were therefore very sweet. The custom of using grapes in cooking probably dates from the time of the Moorish invasions, but I have to agree that it is a taste we have become used to, rather than something which aids digestion. Physiologically it doesn't make sense. It's fine to put sugar with spicy things, but with something as rich as this you need acidity. Traditionally, it is the fruity dessert wines that are enjoyed with foie gras; at home, for example, we always had a Sauternes or a Jurançon. However, it would probably make more sense to drink a very tannic red wine with it, especially if the pâté is served hot, to help digest it.

A.V. When asked, every French wine-maker claims that his or her wine is best with foie gras.

A.D. Yes. In their eyes it gives their wine more standing.

A.V. But if we conducted an experiment, first of all tasting the wine by itself and then tasting it after eating some foie gras to see if the taste has been changed, we would see that it doesn't improve the wine at all! If you take an Alsace Tokay, for example, I guarantee that it will be completely demolished by foie gras, despite all they say in Alsace; the only exception would be if the Tokay was sweet. A Gewürztraminer would hold its own a little better. People serve foie gras with red Burgundy, but again, this is the best way to destroy this wine, unless it is a really exceptional Burgundy, such as a very tannic, southern Nuits that is less than two years old and only just bottled. Foie gras needs a tannic wine, but there are other types of wine that go very well with it, too, and not always the ones that people think. Sweet wines go very well, at least with pâté that is served cold, but my favourite is a young, tannic red wine such as a Côtes-de-St-Mont, a Madiran or a Médoc.

A.D. I would also recommend a tannic wine for hot foie gras.

A.V. In France there are also some sweet wines, such as Banyuls, that would go very well, and it's a shame that people don't often think of these Vins Doux Naturels. Muscats would not be very good at all – they are too fragrant. They should rather be served with Roquefort; they are wonderful for that. Their fragrance changes but keeps its same high quality, distinction, and charm.

OYSTERS

A.V. Another problematical food to combine with wine, and one where current practice is not necessarily successful, is oysters. I have often demonstrated that you should never serve a Riesling with oysters, despite what certain labels may claim! Generally speaking, don't serve a great wine with oysters; a small, straightforward, simple and uncomplicated wine that is one of the best for oysters is Sylvaner, the most modest Alsace wine.

A.D. I really enjoy a Gros-Plant with oysters. With Colchesters, which are close to Belons in flavour, you need a dry, acidic wine. Other favourites are Cassis Blanc (white wine with blackcurrant liqueur) and Cassis Dur (the red-wine equivalent).

ENTREES

A.V. For entrées in general (vol-au-vents, charcuterie, sweetbreads, and so on), white wines are the most suitable; ones that are not too young and not too acidic, and that have had time to develop a certain amount of roundness and balance. If the entrée is made with cream, Muscadet or Burgundy Aligoté should be avoided because they are both too acidic. A better choice would be a warmer wine, such as a southern white Burgundy. For entrées that have mushrooms in them, Tokay d'Alsace is the best choice.

A.D. But customers are not usually attracted to Alsace wines...

A.V. Nevertheless, Muscat d'Alsace is perfect with asparagus.

A.D. When talking about mushrooms, I feel it is important to distinguish between sautéed mushrooms and mushrooms in cream sauce. The latter marry very well with white wines from Jura (Côtes du Jura, made with Savagnin grapes), Alsace (Tokay) and Burgundy (Givry Blanc and some of the rounder Mâcons). There are two wines apart from Vin Jaune that I like with truffles, the older Jurançons and some Pomerols.

A.V. For me, the choice would be a very good and very old white Burgundy, such as a Chassagne. But of course these are much more difficult to find.

A.D. As for charcuterie, I find that it can be divided into two types: some goes best with red wine; some with white. More acidic charcuterie, such as pork brawn or Burgundy-style ham, needs a dry white wine as an accompaniment. Some sausages, on the other hand, marry very well with a simple red wine, such as a young, fruity Languedoc-Roussillon, rather than any of the great wines.

FISH AND SEAFOOD

A.D. I have very fixed ideas about the central part of the meal, and I do not understand how anyone can eat fish and drink red wine. The tradition of serving white wine with fish is one that should be kept at all costs. For some fish – cod, for example – the only compatible wines are very dry, severe white wines, such as a Vin Jaune or some Jurançons. Even rosés are not tough enough.

A.V. The only other wines that can justifiably be served with fish, apart from white wines, are in fact rosés made from one of the tannic grape varieties, such as Cabernet (Val de Loire) or Mourvèdre (Provence). But I agree with you completely on the general principle of serving white wine with fish, and am totally against the snobbish trend that claims to match red wines with fish; a trend which is unfortunately being encouraged by certain gastronomic journalists. There is, however, an exception in the case of very spicy dishes, such as Dorade à l'Antillaise (fish in a spicy sauce). If it is accompanied by a St-Véran, the spiciness will stay in your mouth; serve a young southern Côtes du Rhône with it, even though it's red, and this wine will taste just as good as the St-Véran, but at the same time will remove the spiciness. Seafood needs a simple, not particularly high-class wine: lobster should not be served with a Sancerre, for example.

A.D. I love a white Burgundy with seafood.

A.V. I think it's better to serve good seafood with a stronger wine, such as a Meursault, or even certain Mâcons, rather than the more delicate Chablis.

A.D. It is in fact very difficult to find a good match for Chablis wines, particularly as they age. They are best served with grilled fish, rather than shellfish.

A.V. And the younger, smaller Chablis wines go very well with oysters.

OFFAL

A.V. I find that offal requires quite a young and fruity wine: Burgundy Aligoté or similar wines for tripes and sweetbreads, and young reds for veal kidneys.

A.D. In fact, offal dishes allow for some surprising combinations, since such dishes most drastically affect the taste of the wine.

A.V. Older Rieslings of five or six years of age become wonderfully transformed when served with sweetbreads.

POULTRY

A.V. There are subtle variations within the range of poultry. It can vary in texture from chicken through to duck, and in flavour from chicken to pheasant, and these variations should be taken into consideration when choosing a wine. For roast chicken, the best choice would be a small, light, not too tannic Burgundy, whereas for roast duck a more tannic, Médoc-style wine would be better. For canard à l'orange, providing the oranges are bitter ones, it is the Jura Vin Jaune again that provides the perfect match – something like a Château-Chalon. Some of the more acidic Jurançons would also be good, or a good-quality Quart-de-Chaume (Anjou), although admittedly these are becoming increasingly difficult to find.

A.D. A combination that I like very much is Poulet à l'Ail (chicken with garlic) washed down with a Sauternes.

GAME

A.V. I would very definitely like to challenge the custom of serving the same wine with a dish as has been used in making the sauce. A sauce needs a very tannic wine that is only slightly acidic; the wine that you drink needs to have a sufficiently expansive bouquet, but can be acidic and does not have to be particularly tannic. To make the sauce, then, a Côtes de St-Mont, a Madiran, a Provence red (Mouvèdre grape variety), or even certain southern Côtes du Rhône would be perfect, and to accompany the dish I would choose a Burgundy, a northern Côtes du Rhône or a Châteauneuf-style southern Côtes du Rhône, or even a St-Emilion.

A.D. At one time, Mascara was perfect for making jugged hare. Nowadays northern Côtes du Rhône wines would be fine, but they are too expensive to use in cooking. I try to import a wine from Spain to make my jugged hare with now, as it has very little acidity.

A.V. But there is a French wine that you would probably find suitable: the Vin Coeur that, as its name suggests, is becoming famous in Aude for guarding against coronary thrombosis. It is not very alcoholic but is very tannic.

ROASTS

A.V. I think everyone accepts the traditional combination of great red wines with roast meat. Leg of lamb is favourite with the French, and is the perfect food with which to appreciate the Médoc Grand Cru wines. Milk-fed lamb, on the other hand, is a white meat and therefore needs a much lighter, young and fruity red wine.

VEGETABLES

A.V. Some of the sweeter vegetables, such as carrots, peas, and turnips, should never be used in dishes that are going to require a red wine. Red wine with carrots is a particularly difficult combination, since carrots are not only sweet but also have an aniseed flavour. This is one of the problems with so-called 'modern' cuisine. There are other vegetables, such as artichokes, broccoli, and cauliflower that simply cannot be matched with a good-quality wine. By contrast, hotpot of cabbage goes very well with red wine.

A.D. It seems to me that combinations of vegetables are going to form the basis of a new style of cuisine to be eaten by vegetarians, who are in danger of being condemned to drinking nothing but water and fruit juice with their meals. But, fortunately, we have the potato, a vegetable that can be used in all manner of dishes, and other vegetables that go well with wine and which come into their own when providing support for various dishes.

A.V. Potatoes are the perfect vegetable. There is no problem at all as far as matching them with wine is concerned; they are completely neutral in this respect.

A.D. They are very amenable, and you can make any kind of dish with them.

A.V. Yes. The potato forces its personality onto a wine much less than even the country-style bread that is so often provided at wine tastings.

A.D. If I'm tasting a very good wine, I'll make a potato dish to go with it, such as a real Dauphinois, without cheese. Pastries also have the advantage of not changing the taste of the wine that is served with them, and they, too, are making a gastonomic comeback. But I do believe that we are going to see vegetables becoming predominant in cuisine, probably without any wines to go with them.

A.V. Although in general any sweet or aniseed-flavoured vegetables are a bad match for wine, it depends greatly on how they have been prepared. Spinach, for example, may or may not go well with wine, depending on whether or not it has been blanched. And if they are cooked alongside the meat, as often happens in home cooking, even carrots can be acceptable with wine.

SALADS

A.V. It is imperative to use only wine vinegar in salads, unless it is a soy salad, and one thing is strictly forbidden – mustard! A short while ago I was saying that you can recognize a good restaurant by the absence of mustard on the table. Mustard demolishes everything else.

A.D. Raw mustard is disastrous! It is made to be cooked, to use in cooking.

A.V. In my classes we always serve a salad with a meal, and there are some wines that go well with salads and some that don't. In the former category come what I call vigorous white or rosé wines, that is, ones that are quite lively quite acidic, I would also include some very young and fruity reds. Take a Beaujolais Primeur, for example: it goes very well with salad, much better than with carrots.

A.D. What I like to see is a very simple but quite sappy wine, like one of the smaller, vigorous white wines, which seem almost to slap the tongue. I would serve a simple wine, then, rather than an impressive wine with a salad.

CHEESE

A.V. For red wine, high-fat cheeses should be avoided, that is any with above 50 per cent fat. Even 45 per cent fat cheeses, such as Beaufort or Comté, present a problem for red wine, and the same is true of goat's cheese and strong blue cheeses, particularly Roquefort. These should all be served with white wine. If served with some wines (Sauternes, Rivesaltes Blanc, Muscat de Beaumes-de-Venise), Roquefort will weaken them and also be softened itself; but serve it with a Château-Chalon or another Jura Vin Jaune, and they will enhance each other marvellously.

A.D. I am convinced that it is wrong to bring out your oldest and best bottle of red wine at the end of the meal to serve it with cheese, which is probably going to detract from rather than enhance its flavour. It is true that as the meal progresses you serve ever more powerful wines, but an old wine is very often not strong enough to stand up to cheese, especially for those guests who insist on eating the skin, the mouldy part of their cheeses! In order to appreciate the complementary flavours of wine and cheese, the skin must be removed.

A.V. For Brie-style cheeses, the most suitable wines are smooth ones, for example Burgundies. Certain Burgundies can also be served with Pont-l'Evêque, provided they are young and therefore quite tannic; a Côtes de Nuit would be very good, as would a Cahors or even certain Bordeaux. By contrast, Burgundy wines are not at all suitable for Camembert, except maybe a small southern Nuits-St-Georges and, again, a very young one. What would go very well is a Côtes de St-Mont or a young Médoc, as well as any young Cabernet or a Bandol de Provence. Livarot and other 'smelly' cheeses, such as Maroilles or Munster, just kill red wines, and so need to be served with a Gewürztraminer – provided the Munster has no caraway in it. And for Comté or Gruyère you need a rich white wine: maybe a Meursault-Charmes, a Corton-Charlemagne, or even a Vin Jaune, but definitely not red wine. The same goes for Emmenthal and Beaufort. For goat's cheese, almost any white wine is suitable. Sheep's cheese, like Dutch cheese, is more universal, and goes well with white wines, such as Burgundy Aligoté or Jurançon, and also with reds, such as Madiran.

DESSERTS

A.V. It seems to me that the problem of choosing a suitable accompaniment still remains; it is very difficult indeed to find good wines to go with desserts. At the moment I am searching around for spirits and liqueurs that will do the job instead, and I have practically given up on wine – except for one or two particular desserts such as strawberries, with which I would serve a very young and very fruity Vin Doux Naturel – red, of course. I have been searching for a long time for 'the' chocolate gâteau that can be served with wine, because chocolate really presents a problem, and is particularly effective at killing any champagne! For a long time I have claimed that a Médoc wine goes well with chocolate, providing that it is bitter enough to neutralize the sweetness of the chocolate. I have now found a pâtissier who has made the perfect gâteau for me, but who refuses to sell it commercially because its consistency isn't right. It doesn't have much sugar in it, so it doesn't rise properly and is too dense. But it is marvellous with a Médoc.

A.D. I understand the problem. For a long time I have tried to make a sugarless gâteau that would go with red wine. But, deep down, what I prefer with chocolate is Armagnac.

A.V. I disagree with you there. I prefer Cognac; I find it goes much better with chocolate than Armagnac, which is good for soaking prunes in or for serving with Far Breton (flan, or custard tart containing prunes). That's when it really comes into its own.

A.D. I've detected a cocoa flavour in some Armagnacs, that's why . . .

A.V. No, there's much more often a cocoa flavour in Cognac! I don't know whether you've ever tasted Cognac as it comes out of the still – it always smells of cocoa, or cocoa beans. I used to have an office in Dijon next to Lanvin's place, and when the wind was blowing in the right direction I could smell cocoa beans, and it was exactly the same.

A.D. Yes, but that was African cocoa, not South American cocoa, and there is a difference. For South American cocoa I look to Médoc wines, to iodized wines. I would love to see a Bordeaux Mission-Haut-Brion, a wine with a marked inky, slightly iodized flavour, with cocoa. But on the whole, I agree with you; if I choose to have a rum baba for dessert, I like it to be soaked with rum, and then I don't need to drink anything with it.

A.V. Although in general champagne and other sparkling wines do not go well with desserts, you could serve a traditional-style Clairette de Die, which has a musky fragrance, is sweet, and can taste quite good with a dessert. For fruit tarts, spirits are again best: Calvados with apple tart, Kirsch with cherry tart, and Armagnac with plum tart. Lemon tart goes well with a Vin Doux Naturel, such as Rivesaltes.

While not solving the problem of what to drink with dessert, I would like to conclude by saying two things. On the one hand, there are dishes that are enjoyed for their own sake; on the other, there is the effect that a dish has on the wine served with it. A young wine from south-west France, for example, (Madiran or Côtes de St-Mont) is absolutely undrinkable while young, but drink it with a piece of foie gras and you will enjoy it as if it were a Beaujolais! This is a purely objective factor; there are always relationships between liquids and solids, which are obvious or not, as the case may be. Only by experience can you discover these principles and so be able to predict how a dish will modify a wine: whether it will increase or decrease its tannin, its bouquet, or its roundness. It is a true art to match a wine and a dish harmoniously, but a general principle is that a dish will modify a wine much more than a wine will change the character of a dish.

A.D. I would just like to add one thing to that: a subjective factor to take into account is enjoyment. On different days you might feel like drinking a red rather than a white wine, or vice versa, and in this case I would try to find a combination that would satisfy this requirement. If I then found that the wine and the dish that I had chosen matched each other well, I would consider the marriage to be a total success!

LOT Departments producing Vins de Pays
● Major wine localities
◉ Other major towns and cities

The Wines of France

0   50   100 km

Alsace (South)

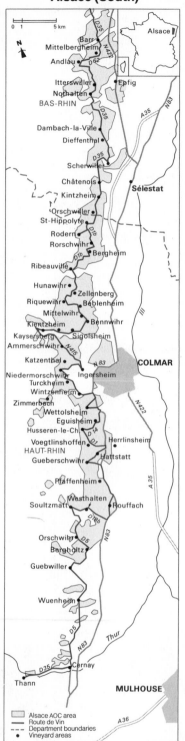

Alsace (North)

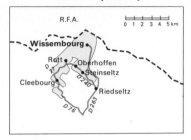

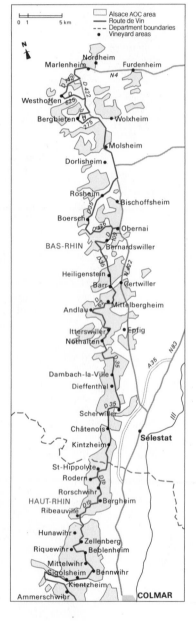

ALSACE

THE VINEYARDS of Alsace are concentrated in the foothills that flank the Vosges mountains on their eastern face and run down to the Rhine plain. The Vosges provide a mountainous barrier between this area and the rest of the country, protecting Alsace from the large amounts of rainfall that come from the ocean and giving the region as a whole its exceptionally dry climate. The average annual rainfall in the region of Colmar, less than 500 mm, is the lowest in the whole of France. However, the highly varied relief of these mountains results in a great diversity of micro-climates, and it is this factor that principally affects the quality of each individual vineyard.

Another characteristic of this region is the many different soil types. In what geologists would term the comparatively recent past – a mere fifty million years ago – the Vosges and the Black Forest formed a single mountainous area, created by successive earth movements and erosion. At the beginning of the third geological era, the centre of this mountain range began to subside, eventually becoming a plain. As a result, all the layers of earth that had accumulated during the different geological eras were exposed where the land had split. It is exactly here that the vineyards are located, which explains why most of the wine-growing communes are characterized by at least four or five different soil types.

The origins of wine-growing in Alsace are lost in the mists of time. Prehistoric man almost certainly used fruit from vines, although actual viticulture seems to have begun after the Roman conquest. The Germanic invasion in the fifth century AD resulted in a temporary lapse in viticulture, but documents show that the Alsace vineyards regained importance quite quickly under the influence of the abbeys, convents and episcopal estates. Even documents from before AD 900 mention more than 160 localities where vines were cultivated.

This expansion continued unbroken until the sixteenth century when it reached its peak. The magnificent Renaissance houses that are still to be found in several wine-growing communes are indisputable proof of the prosperity of the time when vast quantities of Alsace wine were already being exported to the rest of Europe. But the Thirty Years' War (1618–48) and the damage caused by pillage, famine and plagues had catastrophic consequences for French viticulture and commerce in general.

Once peace was restored, the cultivation of vines in Alsace began anew, but vineyards were being expanded mostly with low-quality grape varieties. In 1731, a royal edict attempted to rectify the situation but had little success. After the French Revolution (1789–99), vineyard planting continued and the registered wine-growing area grew from 23 000 hectares in 1808 to 30 000 hectares in 1828. This rapid expansion produced a glut of poor-quality wine at a time when the export trade had vanished completely and, in general, wine consumption was falling in favour of beer. These problems were exacerbated by competition from the cheaper wines of southern France, made more easily available by the advent of rail travel. A further threat arose from the appearance and spread of mysterious diseases such as phylloxera and other pests. Thus, from 1902 there was a gradual decline in the size of the vineyards which continued until 1948, leaving just 9500 hectares, 7500 of which had the right to the Alsace appellation.

The post-war economic boom, together with the huge efforts made by wine-makers themselves, have had a favourable influence on the development of viticulture in Alsace. At present, vines cover some 13000 hectares with a potential annual production averaging 900000 hectolitres. The wines are sold both in France and abroad, exports accounting for more than one-quarter of all current sales. This is the result of the combined energies of the entire Alsace wine trade, each part of which markets roughly similar amounts of wine. Growers, co-operatives and shippers (who are often growers, too) are all involved, the shippers buying large amounts of wine from those growers who do not vinify their crops themselves.

The trade as a whole works concertedly to maintain quality and promote the unique identity of Alsace wines. Throughout the year, for example, there are numerous wine festivals in various localities along the 'Route du Vin' in Alsace. These festivals are probably the major tourist and cultural attractions of the region, and culminate in the great Alsace wine fair, held every August in Colmar. Before this, however, one may attend other wine fairs in Guebwiller, Ammersch-wihr, Ribeauvillé, Barr and Molsheim. Special mention should be made of the wine festival organized by the Confrérie St-Etienne. The festival originated in the fourteenth century and was revived in 1947.

The most obvious characteristic of Alsace wine is its highly developed, strongly scented bouquet, a result of the cool, temperate growing climate, which tends to favour a long, slow ripening of the grape. The specific aromatic nature of the wine depends, of course, on the grape variety; a major peculiarity of this region is for wines to take the name of the grape variety from which they were produced. Other French AOC wines usually take their name from the region or smaller geographical location where they were grown.

Harvesting takes place in October and the bunches of grapes are cut, rapidly transported to the cuverie, and then pressed. The juice, or must, that is run off from the press contains minute particles of dirt or earth. These impurities have to be removed as quickly as possible, either by allowing them to sediment naturally in a collecting tank, or by the use of a centrifuge. The clarified must is then fermented, with regular temperature checks to avoid extremes of hot and cold. In the months after the fermentation, the young wine will require many further treatments from the wine-maker, including racking and topping up the wine, adding sulphur dioxide, clarifying and fining. The wine will be matured in vat or cask until about May, when it will be filtered and bottled. This wine-making process is used to obtain dry white wine, which in Alsace accounts for more than 90 per cent of total production.

Alsace also produces, in exceptional years, two special categories of wine called Vendanges Tardives and Sélection des Grains Nobles, which are made from late-picked grapes of extreme ripeness, often attacked by 'noble rot'. Official recognition, in the form of AOC status, was granted to these wines in 1984 and lays down stringent conditions concerning the minimum natural alcoholic degree. An even higher degree of natural alcohol is required for the Sélection des Grains Nobles than for the Vendanges Tardives. The only permitted grape varieties are Gewürztraminer, Pinot Gris, Riesling and, under certain conditions, Muscat. The special climatic conditions needed to produce such wines and the labour and expense involved in late harvesting help explain their rarity and high price.

Popular wine-drinking opinion holds that Alsace should be drunk young. This is mostly true for a Sylvaner, Chasselas, Pinot Blanc or an Edelzwicker, but a Riesling, Gewürztraminer or a Pinot Gris (Tokay d'Alsace) may be better left for two years or more. In practice there are no fixed rules for when to drink an Alsace wine, and great wines from years which produced exceptionally ripe grapes will keep much longer – even for decades.

Edelzwicker holds a special place among the wines of Alsace. The name means 'noble mixture', and designates the long-standing practice of making wines from a blend of approved grape types. It should be remembered that, a century ago, vineyards planted with a single grape variety were the exception rather than the rule in Alsace. The grapes used in Edelzwicker wine are, predominantly, Pinot Blanc, Sylvaner and Chasselas. Although there is certainly some rather dull Edelzwicker, the better wines are particularly popular with the local inhabitants, and most restaurants and cafés go to great lengths to find well-made examples. The wine really deserves a better reputation.

The Alsace appellation itself, which covers the 110 wine-growing areas in Alsace, takes second place to the seven major grape varieties that are used here: Gewürztraminer, Riesling, Muscat (including Muscat Blanc, Muscat Ottonel and Muscat Rosé à petits grains), Pinot Blanc (also known as Auxerrois or Klevner), Pinot Gris (or Tokay d'Alsace), Pinot Noir and Sylvaner. There is also a small amount of Chasselas Blanc and Chasselas Rosé, principally used in blended Edelzwicker wines.

In practice, the name 'Alsace' is rarely used alone. It is usually followed by the name of the grape variety, or the description 'Edelzwicker'. In all, there are eight types of wine, which will be described individually; nevertheless they have common characteristics, which may usefully be grouped together. For example, to have the right to the AOC 'Vin d'Alsace', the grapes or the wine they produce must meet certain requirements. The grapes should come from vines that have been pruned back to a maximum of twelve buds per square metre and should not be harvested before a certain date, which is fixed by a qualified commission. Wine production should not exceed – unless granted specific authorization – a yield of 100 hectolitres per hectare. The wines have to be made from must with a natural potential for at least 8.5 per cent alcohol. They have also to undergo an analysis and official tasting. Finally, all Alsace AOC wines must be bottled in Alsace.

Alsace Chasselas or Gutedel

Forty years ago this grape variety represented over 20 per cent of the total vineyard area. Today, this has fallen to 3 per cent. The wine is light and smooth with moderate acidity. It is mostly used in Edelzwicker wines, which are blends of more than one grape variety, so that the actual name has practically disappeared from the market.

ROBERT SCHOFFIT*

□		0.5 ha	4000	**2** **D** ◍ ↓

Typical firm aromas of a wine from clay-limestone soil, with, in addition, some varietal character. Light, easy flavour with reasonable length. A good quaffing wine for drinking at any time of day. (1983)
↜ Robert Schoffit, 27 Rue des Aubépines 96800 Colmar; tel. 89 41 69 45 ☎ By appt.

Alsace Sylvaner

The origin of the Sylvaner grape is unclear, but it seems to have fared particularly well in Germany and the Lower Rhine in France. In Alsace itself production of Sylvaner has declined, the vine occupying 27 per cent of the appellation ten years ago and only 20 per cent now. It is, however, an extremely useful varietal due to its consistent quality and high yield.

The wine that it produces is very fresh, with good acidity and a subtle fruitiness. There is a wide range of Sylvaners on the market with considerable variations in quality. The better wines come from well-exposed, low-yielding vineyard sites; others tend to be unpretentious wines with easy appeal. Sylvaner goes well with sauerkraut, hors d'oeuvres and first courses, as well as shellfish, especially oysters.

ANCIEN MOULIN DE L'ABBAYE***

□		2 ha	24000	**3** **D** ⬛

Beautiful colour and rich, firm bouquet with an immediately perceptible hint of over-ripeness in the grape. On the palate the wine is full-bodied, well-rounded, delightfully clean and very well made. (1983) ✔ The full range of Alsace wines.
↜ J.-P. Klein et Fils, 1 Rue de Maréchal Joffre, 67140 Andlau; tel. 88 08 93 03 ☎ No visitors.

73

CAVES JEAN-BAPTISTE ADAM★★★

| ☐ | 3.00ha 24000 | 3 D ▮ |

Bright gold appearance with unexpected fruit for this varietal. Round, harmonious flavour with complex hazelnut aromas – a well-known trait of many great white wines. A choice wine which may be drunk from now onwards, and an ideal accompaniment to seafood. (1981)
➥ Caves Jean-Baptiste Adam, 5 Rue de l'Aigle 68770 Ammerschwihr; tel. 89 78 23 21 ☏ No visitors.

ALSACE SELTZ *Zotzenberg*

| ☐ | 1.8ha 15600 | 2 D ⌼ |

The Zotzenberg vineyard produces celebrated and distinctive Sylvaners. This example is extremely well-made, with good varietal character enhanced by the special contribution of the terroir. Will make a very good bottle. (1983)
➥ Alsace Seltz, 67140 Mittelbergheim; tel. 88 08 91 77 ☏ By appt.

COOPERATIVE VINICOLE D'ANDLAU★★★

| ☐ | 9ha 72000 | 2 D ▮ ⌼ |

Lovely clear colour with a hint of lime. Full vinous character, with a light fruity note, and excellent balance make this a top-class Sylvaner. Its clean, mouthwatering flavours go equally well with seafood and fish. (1983) ✔ The full range of Alsace wines.
➥ Société Coop. Vinicole d'Andlau, 15 Avenue des Vosges, 67140 Barr; tel. 88 08 90 53 ☏ By appt.

PAUL BECK *Frankstein*★

| ☐ | 6ha 28800 | 2 D ⍾ ⌼ |

A classic example of this grape variety from the Frankstein vineyard. The wine is pleasant and easy to drink with some richness coming from the firm, sandy soil. Will continue to improve over the next few years. (1981) ✔ Pinot Blanc, Riesling, Muscat, Pinot Noir.

➥ Paul Beck, 1 Rue Clemenceau, 67650 Dambach; tel. 88 92 40 17 ☏ By appt.

PAUL BECK★

| ☐ | 6ha 54000 | 2 D ⍾ |

Originally located within the town's fortified walls, this vineyard moved in 1968 to the edge of the Route du Vin. A straightforward, light and very gulpable Sylvaner. Good varietal character with attractive fruit and delicate bouquet. (1983)
✔ Pinot Blanc, Muscat.
➥ Paul Beck, 1 Rue Clemenceau, 67650 Dambach-la-ville; tel. 88 92 41 07 ☏ By appt.

CLAUDE BLEGER

| ☐ | 1ha 12000 | 2 D ⍾ |

A rather indifferent vineyard site, discernible in the slightly harsh character of the wine. Its tannic flavour may be due to drought. Overall, a firm wine with clear varietal flavour. (1983)
➥ Claude Bleger, 23 Grand-Rue, 67600 Orschwiller;tel.88 92 32 56☏ By appt.,daily8.00–20.00.

RAYMOND ENGEL★★★

| ☐ | 1.7ha 21600 | 2 D ⍾ |

A distinguished wine with refined aromas, which exemplifies this grape variety and year. Robust, elegant and full-flavoured, it will age well and can already be drunk in place of a Riesling with fish or shellfish. (1983) ✔ Riesling, Gewürztraminer, Tokay (Pinot Gris), Muscat, Crémant.
➥ Raymond Engel Père et Fils, 1 Route du Vin, 67600 Orschwiller; tel. 88 92 01 38 ☏ By appt.

BERNARD HAEGI★★

| ☐ | 1.6ha 15600 | 2 D ⍾ |

This estate in the charming village Trois Montagnes has been in the Haegi family for several generations. The wine has refined, delicate aromas with firm, assertive acidity. The ripeness and balance of the wine would make it a perfect partner to many first courses and baekaoffa. (1983) ✔ Muscat, Pinot Noir, Crémant, Riesling.
➥ Bernard Haegi, 33 Rue de la Montagne, 67140 Mittelbergheim; tel. 88 08 95 80 ☏ By appt. Closed 25 Aug.–10 Sept.

ROBERT KARCHER★

| ☐ | 0.6ha 3600 | 2 D ⍾ |

Grown on sandy soil, this attractive, floral wine is well-balanced on the palate. An easy-going, thirst-quenching mouthful. (1983) ✔ Riesling, Sylvaner, Crémant.
➥ Robert Karcher, 11 Rue de l'Ours, 6800 Colmar; tel. 89 41 14 42 ☏ By appt.

PIERRE KIRSCHNER★★

| ☐ | 0.8ha 72000 | 2 D ⍾ |

A very well-made Sylvaner with a delicate bouquet. Good balance and subtle fruit, with a clear fresh taste benefiting from the granite sub-soil. (1983) ✔ Riesling, Tokay (Pinot Gris), Muscat, Gewürztraminer.
➥ Pierre Kirschner, 26 Rue Théophile Bader, 67650 Dambach-la-ville; tel. 88 92 40 55. ☏ Daily 8.00–12.00/13.00–19.00.

COOPERATIVE D'ORSCHWILLER-KINTZHEIM *Les Faîtières*★★

☐ 33 ha 237 600 | 3 D ▪ ⌀

Fine gold-green colour characteristic of the Sylvaner grape type. Well-developed aromas with a lingering floral scent. An elegant but delicate wine with excellent balance, proof of a well-ripened crop of grapes. (1983) ✔ Riesling.
➤ Coop. d'Orschwiller-Kintzheim, 67600 Sélestat; tel. 88 92 09 87 ☏ By appt.

OSTERTAG PERE ET FILS★★

☐ 1.5 ha 13 000 | 2 D ▪ ⌀

Excellent varietal character in a refined style with attractive floral bouquet. A very well-balanced wine which could be drunk with first courses or even between meals. The vineyard is situated near the charming Romanesque chapel of Ste Marguerite. (1983) ✔ Gewürztraminer, Sylvaner, Tokay, Pinot Noir, Crémant.
➤ Ostertag Père et Fils, 114 Rue Finkwiller, 67680 Epwig; tel. 88 85 51 34 ☏ By appt.

JOSEPH SCHAFFAR★

☐ 7 ha 6000 | 2 D ⌀

8Generous floral bouquet. Pleasant and smooth on the palate. A good thirst-quenching wine. (1983)
➤ Joseph Schaffar, 125 Rue Clémenceau, 68000 Wintzenheim; tel. 89 27 00 25 ☏ By appt.

F.-E. TRIMBACH★

☐ 3 ha 31 200 | 3 D ▪

A firm, rich wine with plenty of fruit and an excellent balance coming from the perfect ripeness of the grape. Clean flavours and refreshing acidity. Well worth keeping for a few years. (1983) ✔ Riesling, Gewürztraminer, Tokay (Pinot Gris), Pinot Blanc, Muscat.
➤ F.-E. Trimbach, 15 Route de Bergheim, 68150 Ribeauvillé; tel. 89 73 60 30 ☏ By appt. Closed during August.

CAVES ALFRED WANTZ *Zotzenberg*★

☐ 3 ha 24 000 | 2 D ⌀

A cellar dating from 1618 and hundred-year-old oak barrels are the setting for this noble wine which comes from the most famous vineyard for the Sylvaner varietal. Harmonious flavour and light, clean aromas, but a little more ageing will bring out its full character and bouquet. (1983) ✔ Riesling, Gewürztraminer, Pinot Noir, Crémant.
➤ Alfred Wantz, 3 Rue des Vosges, 67140 Mittelbergheim; tel. 88 08 91 43 ☏ By appt.

ALSACE WILLM★

☐ 3.5 ha 14 400 | 3 D ▪ ⌀ ⌀

Good varietal character with leafy, humus aromas. A well-balanced flavour, the richness of the vintage producing a robust pleasant wine with no excess acidity. It would go well with seafood, salads and fish of all kinds. (1983)
➤ Alsace Willm, 32 Rue du D-Sultzer, 67140 Barr; tel. 88 08 19 11 ☏ By appt.

ZEYSSOLTT★

☐ 2 ha 21 600 | 3 D ⌀

Slightly amber-edged colour. Floral aromas, strongly marked by the terroir, and a firm acid structure, with a clean, lightly scented finish. (1983) ✔ Pinot Blanc, Pinot Noir, Tokay (Pinot Gris), Muscat.
➤ Zeyssoltt, 156 Rue Principale, 67140 Gertwiller; tel. 88 08 90 08 ☏ By appt.

Alsace Pinot or Klevner

Referred to as either Pinot or Klevner – the latter being its traditional Alsace name – the wine may come from two grape types, the Pinot Blanc 'vrai' and the Auxerrois Blanc. Both are fairly hardy and capable of surprising results in very ordinary locations, producing well-rounded wine with a full, fresh flavour. In the last twelve years or so, the area of these vines has almost doubled, increasing from 10 per cent to 18 per cent of the total planting.

The Pinot Blanc stands very much in the middle of the range of Alsace wines, and it is often better than a modest Riesling. It goes with most food although it is less suitable for puddings or cheese.

COOPERATIVE VINICOLE D'ANDLAU★★★

☐ 4 ha 30 000 | 2 D ▪ ⌀

Firm structure and rich extract, with well-developed primary aromas and bouquet, complement the fine bright appearance of this pleasantly fruity wine. Good value for money. (1983) ✔ The full range of Alsace wines.
➤ Coop. Vinicole d'Andlau, 15 Avenue des Vosges, 67140 Barr; tel. 88 08 90 53 ☏ By appt.

COOPERATIVE D'ANDLAU★★★

☐ 1.5 ha 6000 | 2 D ▪ ⌀

This Klevner varietal from the Heileigstein vineyard is characterized by a deep amber-yellow colour and ripe, spicy nose. It has strong, full-bodied flavour and long finish. A perfect wine to lay down, it is ideal with foie gras. (1983) ✔ Sylvaner, Riesling, Muscat, Tokay (Pinot Gris), Gewürztraminer.
➤ Coop. Vinicole d'Andlau, 15 Avenue des Vosges, 67140 Barr; tel. 88 18 91 53 ☏ By appt., Mon.–Fri. 8.00–12.00/14.00–18.00.

JEAN-PIERRE BECHTOLD★★

☐ 1 ha 9000 | 2 D ⌀ ⌀

Easy and supple, with plenty of fruit. Perfectly vinified, light and pleasant on the palate. (1983)
➤ Jean-Pierre Bechtold, 49 Rue Principale, 67000 Dahlenheim; tel. 88 50 66 57 ☏ Daily by appt.

PAUL BECK*

☐ 0.45ha 2880 ③ Ⓓ ⦿ ↓

Characteristic and clean, but could be little crisper. From granite soil, and thus a little too dry on the palate, but easy to drink. Drink within two years. (1983)
☞ *Mme.* Paul Beck, 1 Rue Clémenceau, 67650 Dambach-la-Ville; tel. 88 92 41 17 ⅄ By appt.

LES VIGNERONS DE BENNWIHR*

☐ 30ha 288000 ③ Ⓓ ⓘ↓

The extreme ripeness of the grapes is immediately obvious on the palate. A late-picked wine from a great vintage with balance, structure and a smooth finish. (1983)
☞ Les Vignerons de Bennwihr, 3 Rue du Général-de-Gaulle, 68630 Bennwihr; tel. 89 47 90 27 ⅄ By appt.

CLAUDE BLEGER*

☐ 0.34ha 3600 ② Ⓓ ⦿

A good vineyard site complemented by meticulous vinification makes for an excellently-produced wine. Pure, clean taste but still rather young. The well-balanced acidity will allow it to develop favourably. (1983)
☞ Claude Bleger, 23 Grand-Rue, Orschwiller, 67600 Sélestat; tel. 88 92 32 56 ⅄ Daily 8.00–20.00.

COOPERATIVE VINICOLE DE CLEEBOURG***

☐ 38ha 366000 ② Ⓓ ▤ ↓

First-rate wine with excellent fruit and great finesse. Typical full body and weight are underlined by the extreme ripeness of the grapes. A very pleasant drink. (1983) ✔ Riesling, Sylvaner, Tokay (Pinot Gris), Gewürztraminer, Pinot Noir.
☞ Coop. Vinicole de Cleebourg, 67160 Cleebourg; tel. 88 94 50 33 ⅄ By appt.

COOPERATIVE DE DAMBACH-LA-VILLE*

☐ 19.8ha 194880 ③ Ⓓ ▤ ⦿ ↓

A mature yellow-gold colour signals a slightly heavy wine with hazelnut aroma. Sweet entry and full weight on the palate make it best suited to rich first courses. Ready to drink. (1983).
☞ Coop. de Dambach-la-Ville, 67650 Dambach-la-Ville; tel. 88 92 40 03 ⅄ By appt.

JEAN-PAUL ECKLE**

☐ 0.95ha 7200 ② Ⓓ ⦿ ↓

Good wine with pleasing nose. Good body and lovely bouquet. Very light, delicate and exceptional for Pinot Blanc. Deserves to be kept for a few years. (1983)
☞ Jean-Paul Eckle, 29 Grande Rue, 68230 Katzenthal; tel. 89 12 70 94 ⅄ Daily by appt.

CAVE VINICOLE D'EGUISHEIM

☐ 73ha ② Ⓓ ▤ ⦿ ↓

This wine is mid-yellow in colour, with golden hints. Already very well-developed, with low acidity, it has a rich, round flavour. Drink now. (1983)
☞ Cave Vinicole d'Eguisheim, 6 Grand-Rue, 68420 Eguisheim; tel. 89 41 11 06 ⅄ By appt.

WILLY GISSELBRECHT ET FILS*

☐ 3ha 27000 ② Ⓓ ⦿ ↓

Pale colour with light-green hints. Very typical, delicate fruit aromas and fine balance between the bouquet and the refreshing flavour. (1983)
☞ Willy Gisselbrecht et Fils, Route du Vin, 67650 Dambach-la-Ville; tel. 88 92 41 02 ⅄ By appt.

LOUIS HAULLER*

☐ 0.51ha 40000 ② Ⓓ ▤

Excellent colour and rich aromas with typical Pinot fruit. Although still rather young, this wine is fairly smooth and pleasant to drink and may still improve. (1982) ✔ Sylvaner, Riesling, Gewürztraminer, Tokay (Pinot Gris).
☞ Louis Hauller, 92 Rue du Maréchal Foch, 67650 Dambach-la-Ville; tel. 88 92 41 19. ⅄ Tues.–Sun. 8.00–11.45/14.00–18.00. Closed early September.

BRUNO HERTZ

☐ 1ha 7000 ② Ⓓ ▤

Fine colour and striking aromas. Light and refreshing on the palate, the wine appears to be fully mature and should be drunk from now onwards. (1982)
☞ Bruno Hertz, 9 Place de l'Eglise, 68420 Eguisheim; tel. 89 41 81 61 ⅄ By appt.

HUGEL ET FILS***

☐ 20ha 108000 ③ Ⓓ ▤ ↓

This shows just what a Pinot Blanc is capable of in a great year. A rich, powerful wine with fresh hazelnut aromas. As it ages, it will come to resemble a white Burgundy. Excellent balance and good long finish. A refreshing wine to be drunk at any time of day. (1983) ✔ The full range of Alsace wine.
☞ Hugel et Fils, 68340 Riquewihr; tel. 89 47 92 15 ⅄ By appt. Closed 1 Oct.–31 May.

CAVE VINICOLE DE HUNAWIHR***

☐ 36ha 360000 ③ Ⓓ ▤ ↓

Excellent colour and good fruit on the nose, very typical of the 1983 vintage. Great richness in bouquet and aroma and good structure, sustained by a pleasant acidity, makes it an exceptional wine. (1983)
☞ Cave Vinicole de Hunawihr, 68150 Hunawihr; tel. 89 73 61 67 ⅄ By appt.

COOPERATIVE VINICOLE D'INGERSHEIM*

☐ 50ha 407000 ③ Ⓓ ▤

This is one of the oldest cooperatives in Alsace and boasts the largest cask (370hl) still in use. Very characteristic Pinot Blanc nose, with plenty of finesse. On the palate, a well-balanced, light and very thirst-quenching wine. (1983)
☞ Coop. Vinicole d'Ingersheim, 1 Rue Clemenceau, 68000 Ingersheim; tel. 88 27 05 96 ⅄ By appt.

JOSMEYER ET FILS
*Pinot Auxerrois 'H' Vieilles Vignes****

☐ 1.5ha 7200 ④ Ⓓ ⦿ ↓

From 25-year-old vines grown on the Hengst hillsides, with their south-south-east exposure. Spirited and powerful Auxerrois which could certainly stand another three or four years in

bottle and can be kept for at least ten years. Resembles a Pinot Gris in character and will make a very great bottle. (1983) ✔ Pinot Les Lutins, Riesling Hengst Vendanges de Novembre, Gewürztraminer Les Archenets, Tokay (Pinot Gris) Cuvée du Centenaire.
🍷 Josmeyer, 76 Rue Clemenceau, Wintzenheim, 68000 Colmar; tel. 89 27 01 57 �️ By appt 🍷 Jean Meyer.

CAVE DE KIENTZHEIM-KAYSERSBERG*

☐	4 ha	4000	2 D 🎗 ⬇

The wines from this supplier come mainly from the well-exposed slopes which surround the little village of Kientzheim. This Pinot has excellent, clear colour with deep, ripe aromas. Smooth, well-made wine produced from very ripe grapes, typical of the 1983 vintage. It should be drunk from now onwards. (1982)
🍷 Cave de Kientzheim-Kaysersberg, 68240 Kientzheim; tel. 89 47 13 19 ⏤ By appt. Mon.–Thurs. 8.00–12.00/14.00–18.00.

KUENTZ-BAS***

☐	3 ha	36000	3 D 🎗

A firm of grower-shippers with 12 hectares of vines. Rich vinous aromas; a well-balanced wine with a firm structure, its residual sugar content and pleasant acidity giving it immediate appeal. It is very versatile, being particularly well suited to first courses. (1983)
🍷 Kuentz-Bas, Husseren-les-Châteaux, 68420 Herrlisheim-près-Colmar; tel. 89 49 30 24 ⏤ By appt.

COOPERATIVE D'ORSCHWILLER-KINTZHEIM

☐	13 ha	93600	3 D 🎗 ⬇

Bright appearance and mild fruit aromas with good varietal character. The aroma and bouquet are already well developed. A smooth, subtle, elegant wine which may be drunk from now onwards. (1983) ✔ Gewürztraminer Les Faîtières, Pinot Noir Les Faîtières.
🍷 Coop. d'Orschwiller-Kintzheim, 67600 Sélestat; tel. 88 92 09 87 ⏤ By appt.

RENE SCHAEFLE**

☐	0.8 ha	7200	2 D 🎗

Full, vinous character on the nose. A smooth, refreshing gulpable wine. On the palate the delicate bouquet is very characteristic of the grape variety. This wine can be drunk at any time of day and goes particularly well with first courses. (1982) ✔ Sylvaner, Tokay (Pinot Gris),

Pinot Noir, Riesling.
🍷 René Schaefle, 4 Rue de la Lauch, Pfaffenheim 68250, Rouffach; tel. 89 49 62 92 ⏤ By appt.

GENEVIEVE SCHWARTZ*

☐	1 ha	96000	2 D ⬤

Refined aromas but somewhat sharp flavour coming from the soil. Should round out with bottle age. A full-bodied, assertive wine which would go well with smoked pork or baekaoffa. (1983)
🍷 Geneviève Schwartz, 101 Rue Principale, 67650 Blienschwiller; tel. 88 92 41 73 ⏤ By appt.

COOPERATIVE VINICOLE DE SIGOLSHEIM**

☐	14 ha	720000	3 D 🎗 ⬇

Rich, mature aromas combined with delicate fruit. A powerful, firmly structured wine on the palate, with enough acidity to give it lovely harmony. A wine for keeping which could last ten years. (1983) ✔ Crémant, Riesling, Gewürztraminer, Pinot Noir.
🍷 Coop. Vinicole de Sigolsheim, 68240 Kaysersberg; tel. 89 47 12 55 ⏤ By appt.

CAVE VINICOLE DE TRAENHEIM*

☐	10 ha	550000	2 D 🎗

A well-made wine. Not typical Pinot character, but lovely vinous aromas. Pleasant freshness on the palate in a light style; still rather young, but should develop well. (1983)
🍷 Cave Vinicole de Traenheim, Route de Scharzachbergheim, 67310 Tràenheim; tel. 88 50 66 21 ⏤ By appt.

F.-E. TRIMBACH*

☐	2 ha	16000	3 D 🎗

A rich wine with a delicate bouquet and well-balanced flavour. Its young, firm yet smooth character makes it a pleasure to drink. (1983) ✔ The full range of Alsace wines.
🍷 F.-E. Trimbach, 68150 Ribeauvillé; tel. 89 73 60 30 ⏤ By appt. Closed during Aug. and grape harvest.

CAVE VINICOLE DE TURCKHEIM
Pinot Val St-Gregoire

☐	15 ha	108000	2 D 🎗 ⬇

A light but pleasant wine with a slightly sharp acidity which will disappear after a few months in the bottle. (1983)
🍷 Cave Vinicole de Turckheim, 68230 Turckheim; tel. 89 27 06 25 ⏤ Daily (except Sun.) 8.00–12.00/14.00–18.00.

CHARLES WANTZ
*Klevner de Heiligenstein***

☐	1.8 ha	8400	3 D ⬤ ⬇

Very floral; light in colour, with bouquet typical of the grape variety. Very aromatic and well made. A curiosity for lovers of Alsace wines. (1981)
🍷 Charles Wantz, 67140 Barr; tel. 88 08 90 44 ⏤ By appt., Mon.–Fri.

CAVE VINICOLE DE WESTHALTEN★★

| ☐ | | 22ha | 115000 | **2** **D** **▮** |

A refined, attractive bouquet introduces a refreshing wine with some structure, well-developed fruit aromas and pleasant acidity. Drink now. (1983) ♠ Cave Vinicole de Westhalten, 68111 Westhalten, tel. 89 47 01 27 ⌕ By appt.

ALSACE WILLM★

| ☐ | | 2.1ha | 8500 | **3** **D** **▮** **⦿** **⌙** |

Pleasant, yellowy colour. Easy to drink. Rich, with a bit of acidity that adds crispness. (1983) ♠ Alsace Willm, 32 Rue du Dr Sultzer, 67140 Barr; tel. 88 08 19 11 ⌕ By appt.

Alsace Riesling

The Riesling is the grape variety of the Rhine par excellence and the Rhine valley is universally recognized as its real home. It ripens quite late for the region, but production is consistent and good quality, accounting for almost 20 per cent of the Alsace crop.

Alsace Riesling is a dry wine, a fact that distinguishes it from the German wine of the same name. Its main virtue is to be found in the complex balance between refined bouquet, subtle fruit, firm body, and refreshing, gentle acidity found in Rieslings of the best quality. The Riesling vine has spread to other wine-growing areas, and the name Riesling cannot always be trusted, unless it is the true Rhine Riesling, since a dozen other grape varieties throughout the world have been given the same name. As far as food is concerned, Riesling goes especially well with fish, shellfish and of course sauerkraut à l'alsacienne and coq au Riesling. Of recent years, 1984 was of modest quality, 1983 was exceptional and 1982 good.

ANCIEN MOULIN DE L'ABBAYE★

| ☐ | | 2ha | 18000 | **3** **⦿** **▮** |

Attractive, well structured and elegant. Perhaps a little too supple for Riesling, but characteristic of its vintage. Perfect with choucroute, the regional speciality. (1983) ♠ J.-P. Klein et Fils, 1 Rue du Maréchal-Joffre, 67140 Andlau; tel. 88 08 93 03 ⌕ No visitors.

CAVES JEAN-BAPTISTE ADAM

| ☐ | | 5ha | 48000 | **3** **D** **▮** |

A pale-yellow wine still displaying its youth, with little developed aromas. Good, robust body on the palate. Pleasant, fresh acidity with a hint of residual sugar, typical of the 1983 vintage. This fine Riesling could easily take fifteen years to achieve its full potential as a great wine. (1983) ♠ Caves Jean-Baptiste Adam, 5 Rue de L'Aigle,

68770 Ammerschwihr; tel. 89 78 23 21. ⌕ Mon.–Sat. 8.00–12.00/14.00–18.00.

DOMAINE ARBOGAST *Rotheingrubler*

| ☐ | | 2.5ha | 19200 | **3** **D** **⦿** |

The property is situated above an old sandstone quarry originally used by Vauban to build the ramparts of Strasbourg. One of the wines grown here was among Napoleon's favourites. This Riesling has great finesse on the nose, and elegance on the palate. Good balance, but rather short finish. (1983) ✔ Tokay (Pinot Gris), Gewürztraminer, Sylvaner, Muscat. ♠ Vins d'Alsace Arbogast, 18 Route de Molsheim, 67120 Soultz-les-Bains; tel. 88 38 17 10 ⌕ By appt.

COOPERATIVE VINICOLE DE BEBLENHEIM★★

| ☐ | | 50ha | 600000 | **3** **D** **▮** **⦿** **⌙** |

A very typical 1983. Lovely pale-gold, nicely fruity nose, well-balanced scents and flavours. Worth keeping for a few years. (1983) ✔ Sylvaner, Pinot Blanc, Tokay (Pinot Gris), Muscat, Gewürztraminer. ♠ Coop. Vinicole de Beblenheim, 14 Rue Hoen, 68980 Beblenheim; tel. 89 47 90 02 ⌕ By appt. Closed Jan., Feb.

J.-P. BECHTOLD *Riesling Grand Cru*★

| ☐ | | 1ha | 7200 | **4** **D** **⦿** |

Very fruity. Earthy quality supported by typical Riesling characteristics. Pleasant on the palate, well balanced and long finishing. Will improve with age. (1981) ✔ Full range of Alsace wines. ♠ J.-P. Bechtold, 49 Rue Principale, 67310 Dablenheim; tel. 88 50 66 57 ⌕ By appt.

J.-P. BECHTOLD *Riesling Engelberg*★

| ☐ | | 1ha | 7200 | **3** **D** **⦿** |

Very delicate, pleasant nose but short on the palate. Will improve with age; drink in two or three years. (1983) ♠ Jean-Pierre Bechtold, 49a Rue Principale, 67310 Dahlenheim; tel. 88 50 66 57 ⌕ By appt.

PAUL BECK *Frankstein*

| ☐ | | 3ha | 8400 | **3** **D** **⌙** |

Traces of residual fermentation on the nose. Still unbalanced. Needs time to sort itself out. (1983) ✔ Full range of Alsatian wines. ♠ Paul Beck, 1 Rue Clémenceau, 67650 Dambach-la-Ville; tel. 88 92 40 17 ⌕ By appt.

J.-PH. ET M. BECKER *Lerchenberg*★

| ☐ | | 0.55ha | 5400 | **3** **D** **⦿** **⌙** |

Attractive pale-gold. Still rather reticent aromas, but fat, mouth-filling flavour. Full body and pleasant acidity give lingering finish. (1983) ✔ Pinot Noir, Gewürztraminer, Muscat, Sylvaner. ♠ M. et Mme. J.-Ph. et M. Becker, 2 Route d'Ostheim, Zellenberg, 68340 Riquewihr; tel. 89 47 90 16 ⌕ By appt.

J.-PH. ET M. BECKER *Hagenschlauf*★★

| ☐ | | 1.6ha | 15600 | **3** **D** **⦿** **⌙** |

Pale-gold with fleeting fragrance of delicate, musky fruit. Wonderfully elegant bouquet. Complex aromas and pleasant acidity give fine har-

mony on the palate. (1983) ✔ Tokay (Pinot Gris), Pinot Noir, Pinot Blanc, Sylvaner.
♠ *M. et Mme.* J.-Ph. et M. Becker, 2 Route d'Ostheim, Zellenberg, 68340 Riquewihr; tel. 89 47 90 16 ☎ By appt.

LES VIGNERONS DE BENNWIHR
Riesling Rebgarten★★

| ☐ | | 27 ha | 24 000 | 3 D ▮ ↓ |

Well-developed, slightly musky fruit on the nose and earthy taste from flinty-sandstone soil. Its balance and controlled acidity make this a great wine – dry, aristocratic, discreet and elegant. Perfect by itself or with Truite Bleu. (1983)
♠ Les Vignerons de Bennwihr, 3 Rue du Gal-de-Gaulle, 68630 Bennwihr; tel. 89 47 90 27 ☎ By appt.

LEON BEYER *Cuvée particulière*

| ☐ | | | 6000 | 5 D ⑪ ↓ |

A great wine, generous, full-bodied and very well balanced. It has a good structure and an excellent fruitiness. Should be drunk within the next two or three years. (1981)
♠ Léon Beyer, Eguisheim 68420, Herrlisheim-près-Colmar; tel. 89 41 41 05 ☎ Daily 9.00–13.00/14.00–19.00.

CLAUDE BLEGER *Réserve Particulière*★

| ☐ | 0.56 ha | 4800 | 3 D ⑪ |

The product of a light, sandy soil, and thus not particularly fruity. Low in alcohol content. Nicely rounded but a bit flat. (1983)
♠ Claude Bléger, 23 Grand-Rue, Orschwiller, 67600 Sélestat; tel. 88 92 32 56 ☎ Daily 8.00–20.00.

LEON BOESCH ET FILS *Sélection*

| ☐ | 0.6 ha | 4800 | 2 D ⑪ |

Grown on heavy soil. Dry but with attractive, fruity nose. Well developed and well made on the palate. (1983) ✔ Sylvaner, Pinot Blanc, Edel-zwicker, Tokay (Pinot Gris), Pinot Noir.
♠ Léon Boesch et Fils, 4 Rue du Bois, 68570 Soultzmatt; tel. 89 47 01 83 ☎ By appt. Daily 8.00–12.00/13.00–18.00.

PIERRE BOTT★

| ☐ | | 2 ha | 16 320 | 3 D ⑪ |

This wine combines great delicacy with a fullness that slightly reduces its direct appeal. Typical of its vintage, it will appeal to those who like a full-bodied Alsace to drink throughout a meal. (1983) ✔ Tokay (Pinot Gris), Pinot Noir, Gewürztra-miner, Muscat.
♠ Pierre Bott, 13 Avenue du Général de Gaulle, 68150 Ribeauvillé; tel. 89 73 60 48 ☎ By appt.

F. BRAUN ET FILS★

| ☐ | | 2 ha | 13 200 | 3 D ▮ |

Clear and well defined with attractive fruitiness. Easy to drink. (1983) ✔ Pinot Noir, Gewürztra-miner, Sylvaner, Tokay (Pinot Gris), Crémant.
♠ MM. Braun et Fils, 19–21 Grand-Rue, 68500 Orschwihr; tel. 89 76 95 13 ☎ By appt.

CAVE VINICOLE DE DAMBACH-LA-VILLE *Cuvée des Guillemettes*★★★

| ☐ | 155.1 ha | 1 726 000 | 3 D ▮ ⑪ ↓ |

A copy-book wine from this excellent vintage; well-developed, sweetly scented nose with a hint of acacia. Fat, long flavour which will allow it to keep for as long as twenty-five years. (1983)
♠ Cave Vinicole de Dambach-la-Ville, 67650 Dambach-la-Ville; tel. 88 92 40 03 ☎ By appt.

CAVE VINICOLE DE DAMBACH-LA-VILLE★

| ☐ | | 99 ha | 195 000 | 3 D ▮ ⑪ ↓ |

The Riesling grape, grown on the sandy and stony soils of Dambach-la-Ville and especially Scherwiller, produces a surprisingly light and fragrant wine with a very floral nose and a hint of lemon. Very pleasant in the mouth, with well-judged acidity and plenty of refinement. (1983) ✔ Sylvaner.
♠ Cave Vinicole de Dambach-la-Ville, 67650 Dambach-la-Ville; tel. 88 92 40 03 ☎ By appt.

MARCEL DEISS★

| ☐ | | 2 ha | 14 400 | 3 D ▮ |

A heavy wine, slightly lacking in freshness, but very rich and full-bodied. The typical aroma of the grape variety is still rather weak, but perceptible. Needs time to develop. To be drunk with fish. (1983) ✔ Gewürztraminer Grand Cru Altenberg, Gewürztraminer Vendanges Tardives, Pinot Noir, Muscat, Riesling Grand Cru Altenberg.
♠ Marcel Deiss et Fils, 15 Route du Vin, 68150 Bergheim; tel. 89 73 63 37 ☎ By appt., daily 9.00–12.00/13.30–19.00.

UNION VINICOLE DIVINAL★★

| ☐ | | 4 ha | 30 000 | 3 D ▮ ↓ |

Very delicate, elegant and well balanced, with good body. Hint of nutmeg in the bouquet. (1983) ✔ The whole range of Alsace wines.
♠ Union Vinicole Divinal, 30 Rue du Général Leclerc, 67210 Obernai; tel. 88 95 61 18 ☎ By appt.

DOMAINE EXPERIMENTAL VITICOLE★

| ☐ | | 10 ha | 72 000 | 4 D ▮ ⑪ |

This Riesling comes from a heavy, clay–limestone soil. Despite the distinctive fruitiness, it is still a little closed-up, but on the palate reveals excellent structure that promises to develop in quality. (1983) ✔ Sylvaner, Pinot Noir.
♠ Domaine Expérimental Viticole, 8 Rue Kléber, 68000 Colmar; tel. 89 41 16 50 ☎ By appt.

DOPFF *'Au Moulin'*

☐   8ha   57600   **4** **D** ▤ ↓

Discreet but refined nose and well-rounded, exciting flavour. Although elegant and very pure in taste, the wine nevertheless has a surprising softness which masks its acidity. Best as an aperitif. (1983)
� Dopff et Irion, 'Au Moulin', 68340 Riquewihr; tel. 89 47 92 23 ϒ By appt. Closed 1 Nov.–30 Mar.

DOPFF *'Au Moulin'*★

☐   3ha   19200   **4** **D** ◑ ↓

Pale-gold in colour with very refined fruit aromas typical of the Riesling variety. Pure, firm flavour with good body and pleasant acidity contributing to the excellent balance on the palate. Already well developed for a 1981. (1981)
� Dopff et Irion, 'Au Moulin', 68340 Riquewihr; tel. 89 47 92 23 ϒ By appt. Closed 1 Nov.–30 Mar.

DOPFF ET IRION *Les Murailles*★★★

☐   10ha   36000   **4** **D** ◑ ↓

An exceptional wine, with strong terroir character. Complex fruit fragrance on the nose and strongly scented flavour on the palate enhance typical Riesling bouquet. Firm structure and good acidity. Should make a great bottle. (1982)
� *MM.* Dopff et Irion, Château de Riquewihr, 68340 Riquewihr; tel. 89 47 92 51 ϒ By appt. Closed 1 Nov.–1 April.

ANDRE DURRMAN *Wieberlsberg*

☐   6ha   3600   **3** **D** ◑

Needs time to fulfil its potential. Strong gooseberry note on the palate; well-rounded flavour. (1982) ✔ Sylvaner, Tokay (Pinot Gris), Gewürztraminer, Pinot Noir, Crémant.
� André Durrman, 11 Route des Forgerons, 67140 Andlau; tel. 88 08 26 42 ϒ By appt. Mon.– Sat. 9.00–12.00/14.00–19.00. Closed second and third weeks May.

JEAN-PAUL ECKLE★

☐   0.2ha 1920   **3** **D** ▤

Beautifully coloured wine, combining enticing grapeyness with marvellous body and balance. A well-developed, high-class wine. Drink from now onwards. (1981)
� Jean-Paul Eckle, 29 Grand-Rue, 68230 Katzenthal; tel. 89 27 09 41 ϒ By appt.

CAVE VINCOLE D'EGUISHEIM
Cuvée des Seigneurs★

☐   68.8ha 602664   **3** **D** ▤ ◑ ↓

Very light, delicate bouquet that is seductive and very persistent. Slightly acid on first taste, but very clean. (1983) ✔ Rieslings Cuvées Spéciales.
� Cave Vinicole d'Eguisheim, 6 Grand-Rue, 68420 Eguisheim; tel. 89 41 11 06 ϒ By appt.

RAYMOND ENGEL ET FILS★★

☐   2.6ha 240000   **3** **D** ◑

Delicate, blackcurrant-leaf nose and well-balanced body. Residual sugar is not excessive. Typical of its year, this wine should be kept for some years before drinking. (1983) ✔ Sylvaner, Gewürztraminer, Tokay (Pinot Gris), Muscat, Crémant.
� Raymond Engel et Fils, 1 Route du Vin, Orsch-

willer, 67600 Orschwiller; tel. 88 92 01 83 ϒ By appt.

DAVID ERMEL ET FILS

☐   1ha   8000   **3** **D** ◑ ↓

Attractive, well-vinified wine with a light, smooth flavour. Well worth drinking now, but not a wine to lay down. (1983) ✔ Gewürztraminer, Muscat, Tokay (Pinot Gris).
� David Ermel et Fils, 5 Route de Ribeauvillé, 68150 Hunawihr; tel. 89 73 61 71 ϒ Daily 8.00– 12.00 Closed Oct.

JEAN FREYBURGER

☐   0.75ha 7200   **3** **D** ▤

A traditionally-made wine from an old (established 1653) family firm. The style is typical of the heavy, clay-limestone terroir. Attractive fruitiness on the nose, but rather harsh on the palate due to acidity. Very dry. (1983) ✔ Sylvaner, Muscat, Gewürztraminer, Pinot Noir.
� Jean Freyburger, 7 Place du Général-de-Gaulle, Wettolsheim, 68000 Colmar; tel. 89 41 39 15 ϒ Mon.–Sat. 8.00–12.00/14.00–18.30.

LOUIS FREYBURGER ET FILS

☐   0.3ha 2600   **3** **D** ◑

Good, clean flavour but surprisingly light for the vintage. Lovely, refreshing taste with balanced alcohol, acidity and fruit. A light, charming, thirst-quenching wine for immediate drinking. (1983) ✔ Tokay (Pinot Gris), Pinot Noir, Muscat.
� Louis Freyburger et Fils, 1 Rue du Maire-Witzig, 68750 Bergheim; tel. 89 73 66 10 ϒ By appt.

ROMAIN FRITSCH★★

☐   0.74ha 5000   **3** **D** ◑

This family concern is in the first wine-growing village on the Route du Vin. Marlenheim is famous for its annual festival, known as 'the marriage of L'Ami Fritz'. This typical, firm Riesling has a pleasant nose and long flavour. All in all, a wine with excellent fruit and considerable character – a tribute to the quality of the skills and ingredients which produced it. Worth stopping for. (1983)
� Romain Fritsch, 49 Rue du Général-de-Gaulle, 67520 Marlenheim; tel. 88 87 51 23 ϒ By appt.

JEROME GESCHICKT ET FILS★★

☐   0.5ha 4800   **3** **D** ◑

Beautifully fruity on the nose. Well made and worthy of the great 1983 vintage. Rather closed-up at present but lots of class. Promises to develop well and be at its best in about ten years. (1983) ✔ Sylvaner, Pinot Blanc, Tokay (Pinot Gris), Pinot Noir, Muscat.
� Jerôme Geschickt et Fils. 1 Place de la Sinne, 68770 Amerschwihr; tel. 89 47 12 54 ϒ By appt.

ROGER ET ROLAND GEYER★

☐   0.74ha 5000   **3** **D** ◑

Situated at the entrance to the village on the road from Barr, this estate boasts vineyards that were prepared and planted as far back as the twelfth century. The wine has excellent breeding and shows good sugar-acid balance on the palate. It can be kept, but not for too long. (1983) ✔ Sylvaner, Tokay (Pinot Gris), Gewürztraminer,

Pinot Noir, Pinot Blanc.
↬ Roger et Roland Geyer, 146 Route du Vin, 67680 Northalten; tel. 88 92 41 80 Ⴤ By appt., daily 11.30–13.30/17.00–20.00.

ARMAND GILG ET FILS
Zotzemberg★★

☐	1 ha	10 000	❸ D ▮

This firm, founded in 1572, is located in a village with striking Renaissance houses and cellars. The wine shows rich fruit and exceptionally good structure from the clay-limestone soil. Very powerful nose reminiscent of gooseberries. Well balanced and full bodied. Will age well and improve. (1983) ✔ Sylvaner, Muscat, Tokay (Pinot Gris4Gewürztraminer, Pinot Noir.
↬ Armand Gilg et Fils, 2 Rue Rotland, 67140 Mittelbergheim; tel. 88 08 92 76 Ⴤ By appt. Mon.–Sat. 8.00–12.00/Sun. 9.00–11.45/13.30–17.30.

PAUL GINGLINGER★★★

☐	2 ha	13 000	❸ D ▥ ⚓

The clay-limestone soil gives this wine a firm, scented nose and a subtle, slightly musky fruitiness. Fresh, attractive flavour with the smoothness characteristic of the 1983 vintage. This wine still has plenty in reserve and should be put aside for a few years, by which time it will make a connoisseur's bottle. (1983)
↬ Mme Paul Ginglinger, 8 Place Charles de Gaulle, 68420 Eguisheim; tel. 89 41 44 25 Ⴤ Daily except Sun. 8.00–12.00/14.00–18.00.

WILLY GISSELBRECHT ET FILS

☐	3 ha	32 000	❸ D ▮ ⚓

Clear and luminous with golden hints. Delicate fruit aromas and fine, elegant taste, with pleasant acidity. Worth keeping for a few years; should develop well. (1983)
↬ Willy Gisselbrecht et Fils, Route du Vin, 67650 Dambach-la-Ville; tel. 88 92 41 02 Ⴤ By appt.

PHILIPPE GOCKER★★

☐	1.5 ha	10 800	❸ D ▮

Subtle floral nose, with excellent Riesling character and flavour. Good body, clean aromas and pleasant acidity testify to its clay-limestone origin. (1983) ✔ Gewürztraminer, Tokay (Pinot Gris), Muscat, Sylvaner, Pinot Noir.
↬ Philippe Gocker, 24 Rue de Riquewihr, 68630 Mittelwihr; tel. 89 47 88 02 Ⴤ By appt. Closed Oct.

GREINER-SCHLERET *Côte des A.-M.*★

☐	0.25 ha	1920	❸ D ▥ ⚓

Lovely yellow-gold tinge allied with roundness and suppleness in the mouth. Very appealing. (1983) ✔ Sylvaner, Riesling, Tokay (Pinot Gris), Muscat, Pinot Noir.
↬ Pierre Greiner-Schleret, 68630 Mittelwihr; tel. 89 47 92 67 Ⴤ By appt.

BERNARD HAEGI *Brandluft*

☐	0.24 ha	2400	❸ D ▥

Ravishing greenish-yellow hue. Well forward on the palate. Drink now to enjoy its freshness and youth. (1983) ✔ Riesling, Crémant, Sylvaner, Muscat, Pinot Noir.
↬ Bernard Haegi, 33 Rue de la Montagne, Mittel-

bergheim, 67140 Barr; tel. 88 08 95 80 Ⴤ By appt. Closed 25 Aug.–10 Sept.

LOUIS HAULLER★★

☐	2 ha	20 000	❷ D ▥

Pale, green-gold colour. Delicate, tangy fruit aromas marked by the vineyard soil. Well built and robust with excellent balance due to perfect ripeness of the grapes. (1983)
↬ Louis Hauller, 92 Rue du Maréchal-Foch, 67650 Dambach-la-Ville; tel. 88 92 41 19 Ⴤ By appt. Tues.–Sun. 8.00–11.45/14.00–18.00. Closed beg. Sept.

HEITZMANN ET FILS *Cuvée Réservée*

☐	1.5 ha	10 800	❸ D ▥

Rather modest fruit aromas, but showing the character of the grape. Flavour is strongly marked by the clay-limestone soil. (1983)
↬ Heitzmann et Fils, 2 Grand Rue, 6877 Ammerschwihr; tel. 89 47 10 64 Ⴤ By appt.

BRUNO HERTZ

☐	1 ha	6000	❸ D ▮

Very fruity Riesling from a loess soil. Youthful on the palate, which, combined with pleasant acidity, means it will age well. (1983)
↬ Bruno Hertz, 1 Porte des Chevaliers, Eguisheim, 68420 Merrlisheim; tel. 89 41 81 61 Ⴤ By appt.

ERNEST HORCHER ET FILS★

☐	1 ha	8000	❸ D ▥

The wines produced on the clay-limestone Mandelberg slope need time to develop, and this wine's bouquet is still rather immature, although the flavour is pleasantly fresh. A well-balanced wine that will continue to improve for some time to come. (1983) ✔ Pinot Noir, Muscat, Sylvaner, Tokay (Pinot Gris), Edelzwicker.
↬ Ernest Horcher et Fils, 6 Rue du Vignoble, 68360 Mittelwihr; tel. 89 47 92 94 Ⴤ By appt.

HUGEL ET FILS *Réserve Personnelle*★

☐	3 ha	18 000	❺ D ▥

Both fruity and scented. Typical Riesling but fuller than usual. Exceptional balance and length of finish. To be kept. (1981)
↬ Hugel et Fils, 68340 Riquewihr; tel. 89 47 92 15 Ⴤ By appt. Closed 1 Nov.–31 May.

CAVE VINICOLE DE HUNAWIHR★★

☐	30 ha	360 000	❸ D ▮ ⚓

Beautiful yellow-green colour. Outstanding fruit on the nose. Well balanced, delicate and elegant. Good body. Typical of the grape variety and vintage. Worth keeping for a few years. (1983)
↬ Cave Vinicole de Hunawihr, 68150 Hunawihr; tel. 89 73 61 67 Ⴤ By appt.

ROGER JUNG

☐	1 ha	8400	❸ D ▮ ⚓

Very unusual character coming from the terroir, a particular area of clay-limestone soil known as Le Kleuper. This wine needs time for its scents and flavours to develop fully. (1983) ✔ Crémant, Pinot Blanc, Muscat, Tokay (Pinot Gris), Gewürztraminer.
↬ Roger Jung, 23 Rue de la Première Armée, 68340 Riquewihr; tel. 89 47 92 17 Ⴤ By appt.

PIERRE KIRSCHNER★★

☐ 0.9 ha 7200 3 D ▪

Grown on a clay-granite soil, the wine combines a fresh, crisp flavour with delicate fruitiness and a clean, sweet finish. Clear varietal character with the specific local flavour of a Riesling from Dambach, one of the top growing areas for this grape variety. (1983) ✔ Sylvaner, Tokay (Pinot Gris), Muscat, Gewürztraminer.
➻ Pierre Kirschner, 26 Rue Théophile-Bader, 67650 Dambach-la-Ville; tel. 88 92 40 50 ☎ By appt., daily 8.00–12.00/13.00–19.00.

VINS D'ALSACE KUEHN
Cuvée Reservée★★

☐ 2 ha 7900 4 D ▥ ♦

This Riesling has a very good, delicate, musky nose. Good body and flavour with a trace of residual sugar (typical of the year) and excellent length. With its firm structure and pleasant acidity, this wine should keep for years. (1983) ✔ Sylvaner, Pinot Blanc, Pinot Noir, Gewürztraminer.
➻ Vins d'Alsace Kuehn, 3 Grand-Rue, 68770 Ammerschwihr; tel. (89) 78 23 16 ☎ By appt., Mon.–Fri. 8.00–12.00/13.30–17.30, Sat. 9.00–12.45

KUENTZ-BAS★★

☐ 1 ha 13 200 3 D ▥

Bright colour with a lime-green tinge. The nose displays good fruit, strength and subtlety. An assertive wine of great class with a little residual sugar and good structure. Perfectly balanced on the palate. Although showing promise for the future it can be drunk from now onwards. Delightful by itself but even better with a good trout. (1982)
➻ Kuentz-Bas, 14 Route du Vin, 68420 Husseren-les-Châteaux; tel. 89 49 30 24 ☎ By appt.

MARCEL LEHMAN

☐ 0.59 ha 4680 3 D ▥

A very unusual wine, hard to compare with any other, but with plenty of personality of its own. Great aromatic richness, yet a surprising hint of acidity as well. Rather like a late-picked wine, but with less body. (1983) ✔ Gewürztraminer, Tokay (Pinot Gris), Sylvaner, Muscat, Pinot Noir.
➻ Jean Lehman et Fils, 2 Chemin de Beblenheim, 68340 Riquewihr; tel. 89 47 82 99 ☎ By appt.

DOMAINE DES COMTES DE LUPFEN *Furstentum*★

☐ 2.5 ha 6000 4 D ▪

Astonishing for its colour and star-bright clarity. Delicately fruity on the nose. On tasting, very typical of a 1983. Well made. Enough acidity to develop well over the next few years. (1983)
➻ Paul Blanck et Fils, Domaine des Comtes de Lupfen, Kientzheim, 68240 Kayersberg; tel. 89 78 23 56 ☎ Mon.–Sat. 9.00–12.00/14.00–19.00.

JEAN-PAUL MAULER★★

☐ 3 ha 27 600 3 D ▥

Very typical 1983. Full-bodied and well balanced with very elegant nose. Plenty of flavour and lasts well on the palate. Will fill out with age. (1983)

✔ Gewürztraminer, Tokay (Pinot Gris), Muscat, Sylvaner, Pinot Noir.
➻ Jean-Paul Mauler, 3 Place des Cogognes, 68630 Mittelwihr; tel. 89 47 93 23 ☎ By appt. Closed second fortnight in Sept.

FRANÇOIS MEYER★

☐ 1.5 ha 67 000 2 D ▥ ♦

Light, traditionally made Riesling with lovely opaline colour, beautiful nose, and fresh flavours that will last and improve. (1983) ✔ Sylvaner, Tokay (Pinot Gris), Gewürztraminer, Pinot Noir, Crémant.
➻ François Meyer, 55 Route du Vin, 67650 Blienschwiller; tel. 88 92 45 67 ☎ By appt. Mon.–Sat. 8.00–12.00/16.00–19.00.

JEAN MEYER *Les Pierrets*★

☐ 4.5 ha 12 000 4 D ▥

Made from selected grapes grown on the best soils of Wintzenheim and Turckheim, mainly alluvial gravel mixed with clay and limestone soil. This wine will age very well with its light, graceful body and firm acid structure, but patience is required! (1983) ✔ Pinot Auxerrois 'H' Vieilles Vignes, Riesling Hengst Vendanges de Novembre, Gewürztraminer Les Archenets, Tokay Cuvée du Centenaire.
➻ Jean Meyer et Fils, 76 Rue Clémenceau, Wintzenheim, 6800 Colmar; tel. 89 27 01 57 ☎ By appt.

MITTNACHT-KLACK★

☐ 1.2 ha 10 000 4 D ▪ ♦

A warm welcome awaits you at this typical cellar located amongst the vineyards overlooking the city walls. Rich, well-balanced wine of very sound everyday quality. (1983) ✔ Sylvaner, Muscat, Gewürztraminer, Tokay (Pinot Gris).
➻ Mittnacht-Klack, 8 Rue des Tuileries, 68340 Riquewihr; tel. 89 47 92 54 ☎ By appt.

FRANCOIS MUHLBERGER *Rothstein*★★

☐ 2 ha 13 200 2 D ▥

Napoleon's favourite Alsace wines came from Wolxheim and, judging by this example, it is easy to understand why. Grown on a light sandstone soil it has a very delicate but subtle bouquet. It is perfectly balanced and will mature well as both the nose and the palate open up. (1982)
➻ Françoise Muhlberger, 1 Rue de Strasbourg, 67120 Wolxheim; tel. 88 38 10 33 ☎ Daily 9.00–12.00/13.00–19.00.

M. MURE *Clos-Saint-Landelin*

☐ 2 ha 18 000 3 ▥ ▪

Green-coloured Riesling. Delicately fruity on the nose but still closed-up on the palate. Well balanced; shows its limestone origins. Dry, with enough acidity to improve and develop over the next ten years. (1983) ✔ Sylvaner, Gewürztraminer, Tokay (Pinot Gris), Muscat, Pinot Noir.
➻ M. Muré, Clos St-Landelin, Route du Vin, 68250 Rouffach; tel. 89 49 62 19 ☎ By appt. Mon.–Sat. 8.00–12.30/13.00–18.30.

MICHEL NARTZ★★★

☐ 1.7ha 10000 **2 D ◑**

From one of the most picturesque towns on the Route du Vin, this Riesling shows all the characteristics of the vintage. Obvious richness of the grapes, full of flavour yet with an attractive vivacity. Keep for special occasions. (1983) ✔ Sylvaner, Gewürztraminer, Muscat, Tokay (Pinot Gris), Pinot Noir.
☛ Michel Nartz, 40 Rue de la Paix, 67650 Dambach-la-Ville; tel. 88 92 41 11 ⊼ By appt.

COOPERATIVE D'ORSCHWILLER-KINTZHEIM★★ *Les Faîtières*

☐ 28ha 192000 **3 D ▮ ↓**

Lovely yellowish-green colour. Reserved but distinct fruitiness on the nose. Very typical varietal character, with unusually delicate fragrance. The combination of light acidity and inviting bouquet make this wine very easy to drink. (1983)
☛ Coop. d'Orschwiller-Kintzheim, Orschwiller, 67600, Sélestat; tel. 88 92 09 87 ⊼ By appt.

DOMAINE OSTERTAG *Noenchberg*★

☐ 1ha 8000 **3 D ▮ ↓**

This very elegant wine is produced on a hillside first farmed by monks in the 11th century. Its full character will not come through until the wine is more mature. Still very firm, it combines good depth and length of finish; a wine for special occasions. (1983) ✔ Gewürztraminer Vendanges Tardives, Sylvaner, Tokay (Pinot Gris), Pinot Noir, Crémant.
☛ Ostertag Père et Fils, 114 Rue Finkwiller, 67680 Epfig; tel. 88 85 51 34 ⊼ By appt.

CAVE VINICOLE DE PFAFFENHEIM★★

☐ 15ha 138000 **3 D ▮ ↓**

Beautiful to look at. Very delicate, elegant and slight musky fruitiness on the nose. On tasting the fruit comes out and engulfs the mouth. A very attractive wine. (1983) ✔ All Alsace grape varieties.
☛ Cave Vinicole de Pfaffenheim, N.83, 68250 Pfaffenheim; tel. 89 49 61 08 ⊼ By appt.

CAVE COOPERATIVE DE RIBEAUVILLE★★

☐ 40ha 360000 **3 D ▮ ↓**

Very good, classic Riesling. Wonderfully elegant and well balanced, with the earthy quality much sought after by connoisseurs. A wine with a great future. (1982) ✔ The full range of Alsace wines.
☛ Cave Coop. de Ribeauvillé, 22 Route de Colmar, 68150 Ribeauvillé; tel. 89 73 61 80 ⊼ By appt. Mon.–Sat. 8.00–12.30/13.30–17.30. Sun. 9.00–11.45.

JOSEPH RIEFLE ET FILS

☐ 1ha 8200 **3 D ▮**

Relatively undeveloped for 1982 vintage. Still developing and needs more time. Pleasant and elegant fruitiness on the palate promises well for the future (1982) ✔ The full range of Alsace wines.
☛ Joseph Riefle et Fils, 11 Place de la Mairie Pfaffenheim, 68250 Rouffach; tel. 89 49 62 82 ⊼ By appt.

PIERRE RIESTCH★★

☐ 1ha 6000 **3 D ▮**

A great Riesling. Nose still closed-up but full of promise. Plenty of character and depth. Excellent balance. A wine of great distinction, which will develop slowly to reach its peak in several years. (1983) ✔ Sylvaner, Gewürztraminer, Pinot Noir, Crémant.
☛ Pierre Riestch, 32 Rue Principale, 67140 Mittelbergheim; tel. 88 08 00 64 ⊼ By appt.

CHATEAU DE RIQUEWIHR
Les Murailles★★★

☐ 10ha 36000 **4 D ◑ ↓**

An exceptional wine, with strong terroir character. Complex fruit fragrance on the nose and strongly scented flavour on the palate enhance typical Riesling bouquet. Firm structure and good acidity. Should make a great bottle. (1982)
☛ MM. Dopff et Irion, Château de Riquewihr, 68340 Riquewihr; tel. 89 47 92 51 ⊼ By appt. Closed 1 Nov.–1 April.

WILLY ROLLI-EDEL★

☐ 1ha 9600 **4 D ◑**

Attractively robust, with subtlety and character provided by top-quality ingredients. Well balanced despite high alcohol level. Excellent in a few years (1983)
☛ Willy Rolli-Edel, 5 Rue de l'Eglise, 68590 Rorschwihr; tel. 89 73 63 26 ⊼ By appt. Closed during harvest.

CLOS SAINT-LANDELIN

☐ 3ha 24000 **4 D ◑ ↓**

Green-coloured Riesling. Delicately fruity on the nose but still closed-up on the palate. Well balanced; shows its limestone origins. Dry, with enough acidity to improve and develop over the next ten years. (1983) ✔ Sylvaner, Gewürztraminer, Tokay (Pinot Gris), Muscat, Pinot Noir.
☛ M. Muré, Clos St-Landelin, Route du Vin, 68250 Rouffach; tel. 89 49 62 19 ⊼ By appt. Mon.–Sat. 8.00–12.30/13.00–18.30.

DOMAINE SAINTE-GERTRUDE★★

☐ 2.5ha 12000 **3 D ◑**

A good example of this family firm's commitment to quality. Beautifully fruity nose but still young for 1983 vintage. Characteristic gun-flint taste. Keep for a few years to appreciate its true value. (1983)
☛ MM. Buecher et Fils, Domaine Ste-Gertrude, Wettolsheim, 68000 Colmar; tel. 89 41 04 73 ⊼ Daily 9.00–12.00/13.00–19.00.

CLOS SAINTE ODILE★★★

☐ 3.2ha 13000 **3 D ◑ ↓**

Great finesse on the nose. Full-bodied, smooth; firm taste, with plenty of character. Recommended for sea-food, fish, choucroute and smoked meats. (1983) ✔ Sylvaner, Pinot, Gewürztraminer.
☛ Soc. Vinicole Ste-Odile, 3 Rue de la Gare, 67210 Obernai; tel. 88 95 50 23 ⊼ By appt.

RENE SCHAEFLE***

| ☐ | 1 ha | 9000 | 3 D ⚭ |

A very good Riesling with pronounced fruity character and aromatic finesse. There is no mistaking the great quality of this 1982: magnificent, full flavour from perfectly ripe grapes. It seems to be at its peak now and should be drunk immediately. (1982) ✔ Sylvaner, Muscat, Tokay (Pinot Gris), Pinot Noir, Gewürztraminer.
🕭 René Schaefle, 4 Rue de la Lauch, Pfaffenheim, 68250 Rouffach; tel. 89 49 62 92 ✆ By appt.

JEAN SCHAETZEL**

| ☐ | 0.5 ha | 4000 | 3 D ⚭ |

A good example of the 1982 vintage, made in the traditional way. Lovely, star-bright colour. Delicate but typical fruit, already well forward. On the palate, a high-class, virile Riesling with good balance. Drink from now onwards. (1982) ✔ Gewürztraminer Kaeffernopp, Sylvaner, Pinot Noir.
🕭 Jean Schaetzel, 3 Rue de la 5ème DB, 68770 Ammerschwihr; tel. 89 47 11 39 ✆ By appt.

AIME SCHAFFAR

| ☐ | 1 ha | 8400 | 3 D ⚭ |

Gives little on the nose, but in tasting can appreciate its youth and freshness. Light residual sugar makes it slightly unbalanced. (1983) ✔ Sylvaner, Pinot Blanc, Gewürztraminer, Muscat, Edelzwicker.
🕭 Aimé Schaffar, 126 Rue Clémenceau, Winstzenheim, 68000 Colmar; tel. 89 27 02 12 ✆ By appt.

JOSEPH SCHAFFAR*

| ☐ | 7 ha | 7200 | 3 D ⚭ |

Good quality with lots of fruit and beautiful finish. Length of flavour and full body indicate first-rate quality of the grapes. The residual sugar works against its freshness, however. (1983)
🕭 Joseph Schaffar, 125 Rue Clémenceau, 68000 Wintzenheim; tel. 89 27 00 25 ✆ By appt.

EDGAR SCHALLER***

| ☐ | 2.5 ha | 67000 | 3 D ⚭ ⚑ |

A very great wine now at its best. Well made, with lovely scents and flavours, and very good balance. The slight taste of gun-flint emphasizes its breeding. (1982) ✔ Muscat, Tokay (Pinot Gris), Gewürztraminer, Crémant, Sylvaner.
🕭 Edgar Schaller et Fils, 1 Rue du Château, 68630 Mittelwihr; tel. 89 47 90 28 ✆ By appt. Mon.–Sat. 8.00–17.30. Sun 9.00–11.45.

CHARLES SCHLERET*

| ☐ | 1 ha | 8400 | 3 D ⚏ ⚑ |

From stony gravel soils near the Fecht river. Good, clear colour and delicate nose. Well balanced on the palate. Already fully developed; drink from now onwards. (1982)
🕭 Charles Schleret, 1–3 Route d'Ingersheim, 68230 Turckheim; tel. 89 27 06 09 ✆ By appt.

MAURICE SCHOECH**

| ☐ | 0.7 ha | 6000 | 3 D ⚭ |

Exceptional brightness and colour – sparkling yellow with green highlights. Good fruit on the nose but still very young. Real character on the palate, with outstandingly rich structured body and good, sustained acidity. A great wine, very refined, which will reach its peak a few years from now. (1983) ✔ Sylvaner, Muscat, Tokay (Pinot Gris), Gewürztraminer.
🕭 Maurice Schoech, 4 Route de Kientzheim, 68770 Ammerschwihr; tel. 89 78 25 78 ✆ By appt., Mon.–Sat. 9.00–12.00/14.00–18.00. Closed during winter months.

ROBERT SCHOFFIT***

| ☐ | 1 ha | 10800 | D ⚭ ⚑ |

Grown on sandy soil. Lovely yellow colour merging into green. Typically fruity on the nose. Both pleasant and delicate on the palate, proof of well-ripened grapes. Overall balance, body and attractive acidity means that this wine can be kept for several years. (1982)
🕭 Robert Schoffit, 27 Rue des Aubépines, 68000 Colmar; tel. 89 41 69 45 ✆ By appt.

PAUL SCHWACH *Cuvée Selectionnée**

| ☐ | 1.7 ha | 17000 | 3 D ⚏ |

Extremely full-bodied, heavy Riesling. Still very reserved. Shows potential for the future, but will not reach its peak for a year. (1983) ✔ Pinot Noir, Gewürztraminer, Tokay (Pinot Gris), Muscat, Pinot Blanc.
🕭 Paul Schwach, 32 Route de Bergheim, 68150 Ribeauvillé; tel. 88 73 62 73 ✆ By appt.

GENEVIEVE SCHWARTZ*

| ☐ | 1 ha | 9600 | 2 D ⚭ |

Grown on a sandy soil this wine has very well-developed aromas. Good, refreshing, fruity flavour with fine varietal character. Would go well with snails, pike in a cream sauce or coq au Riesling. The strength of the 1983 vintage will allow it to keep for a few more years. (1983) ✔ Sylvaner, Pinot Blanc, Gewürztraminer, Muscat, Tokay (Pinot Gris).
🕭 Oscar Schwartz, 107 Rue Principale, 67650 Blienschwiller; tel. 88 92 41 73 ✆ By appt.

ALSACE SELTZ *Brandluft***

| ☐ | 0.35 ha | 105000 | 3 D ⚭ ⚑ |

Bright, sparkling colour, typical Riesling fruit on the nose and elegant, refined flavour. Firm backbone and complex, fairly mature aromas give an exceptionally well-balanced wine: a very fine Riesling indeed. (1981)
🕭 Alsace Seltz, 67140 Mittelbergheim; tel. 88 08 91 77 ✆ By appt.

SICK ET DREYER *'Kaefferkopf'*

| ☐ | 3.5 ha | 22000 | 3 D ⚭ |

Bright colour and generous aromas. Good, firm flavour, certainly due to the clay-limestone soil. Nevertheless, some residual sugar, often found in the 1983s, upsets its balance somewhat and obscures its Riesling character. Even so, this is a good wine which can be kept for several years. (1983)
🕭 R. Sick et P. Dreyer, 68770 Ammerschwihr; tel. 89 47 11 31 ✆ By appt.

COOPERATIVE VINICOLE DE SIGOLSHEIM

☐	40ha	480000	**4** **D** **🖺** **🥄**

Good colour. Nose indicates restrained fruit flavours, but still closed-up. Taste typical of wines grown on clay-limestone soil. Full-bodied and powerful; slightly too high alcohol content. A young wine with a little too much acidity; will improve. (1983) ✔ All Alsace grape varieties.
🍴 Coop. Vinicole de Sigolsheim, Sigolshei868240 Kayersberg; tel. 89 47 12 55 ⚕ By appt.

J.-P. ET D. SPECHT★★

☐	0.4ha	3600	**3** **D** **🍶**

From the great 1983 vintage, this wine has a well-developed bouquet despite its youth. It promises a great future and is a typical 1983. Good varietal aromas with plenty of character coming from the excellent ripeness of the grapes. Would go well with fish casserole or other assertive fish dishes. (1983) ✔ The full range of Alsace wines. 🍴 Jean-Paul et Denis Specht, 2 Rue Des Eglises, 68630 Mittelwihr; tel. 89 47 90 85 ⚕ By appt.

BERNARD STAEHLE★

☐	0.5ha	4800	**3** **D** **🍶**

Good fruit on the nose but rather short. Good depth on the palate but slightly high alcohol content means some loss of finesse. (1983) ✔ All Alsace grape varieties.
🍴 Bernard Staehle, 15 Rue Clémenceau, Wintzenheim, 68000 Colmar; tel. 89 27 39 02 ⚕ By appt.

CAVE VINICOLE DE TRAENHEIM★

☐	15ha	570000	**2** **D** **🖺**

Good colour and rich, generous fruit aromas. Firm structure on the palate with a pleasant acidity. Still a little closed, this wine deserves laying down for a few years to bring out its potential. (1983)
🍴 Cave Vinicole de Traenhaim, Route de Scharrachbergheim, 67310 Traenheim; tel. 88 50 66 21 ⚕ By appt.

F.-E. TRIMBACH
Cuvée Frédéric Emile★

☐	4ha	36000	**4** **D** **🖺** **🥄**

A wine grower and shipper whose business dates from 1626. This flourishing firm has now maintained a solid tradition of quality for eleven generations. A beautifully coloured wine with delicate, mild aromas still a little unassertive for the vintage. Appears dry and elegant on the palate and yet surprisingly forceful. Well-filled out and sustained by pleasant acidity, a delight to lovers of good Riesling. (1981)
🍴 F.-E. Trimbach, 68150 Ribeauvillé; tel. 89 73 60 30 ⚕ No visitors. Closed August.

CAVE VINICOLE DE TURCKHEIM
Vendanges Tardives★

☐	2ha	12000	**5** **D** **🖺**

Very pronounced bouquet and lingering scent in the mouth; reasonable acidity in spite of a hint of sweetness. A wine to lay down. (1983)
🍴 Cave Vinicole de Turckheim, 68230 Turckheim; tel. 89 27 06 25 ⚕ Daily 8.00–12.00/14.00–18.00. Closed mornings in winter.

CAVE COOPERATIVE DE WESTHALTEN
Cuvée Particulière Les Comtes d'Alsace★★★

☐	7ha	130000	**3** **D** **🖺**

The product of a Mediterranean micro-climate in the southern part of the region. Fine, subtle fruit and warm, velvety character. A lively and aristocratic wine from this forward-looking cooperative. (1983)
🍴 Cave Coop. de Westhalten, 68111 Westhalten; tel. 89 47 01 27 ⚕ By appt.

CAVE COOPERATIVE DE WESTHALTEN★★

☐	4.1ha	52000	**3** **D** **🖺**

Good colour, with flowery fruitiness on the nose. Aromas and bouquet well developed for 1979 vintage. Well balanced with good acidity. A choice wine. (1979) ✔ Riesling.
🍴 Cave Coop. de Westhalten, 68111 Westhalten; tel. 89 47 01 27 ⚕ By appt.

ALSACE WILLM★

☐	55ha		**2** **D** **🖺** **🍶** **🥄**

Highly floral bouquet with a hint of new-mown hay. Surprisingly mature on the palate, a reflection of this great 1983 vintage. The generosity of this wine, which is ready to drink now, means that it is good with sauerkraut or fish, even if accompanied by a sauce. (1983)
🍴 Alsace Willm, 32 Rue du Dr-Sultzer, 67140 Barr; tel. 88 08 19 11 ⚕ By appt.

LOUIS WINTZER

☐	5ha	54000	**3** **D** **🍶**

High but not unpleasant acidity. Very dry. Could be kept. (1983) ✔ Sylvaner, Crémant, Pinot Noir, Gewürztraminer.
🍴 Louis Wintzer, 53 Rue du Mal.-de-Lattre-de-Tassigny, 68360 Soultz; tel. 89 76 80 79 ⚕ Daily 8.00–12.00/13.00–20.00.

FRANÇOIS WISCHLEN
Réserve Particulière★

☐	0.72ha	36000	**3** **D** **🍶**

Characterized by freshness and understated fruitiness. Very well constructed but needs time to develop to its best. (1983) ✔ Tokay (Pinot Gris), Gewürztraminer, Pinot Noir, Muscat, Crémant.
🍴 A. Wischlen, 4 Rue de Soultzmatt, 68111 Westhalten; tel. 89 47 01 24 ⚕ By appt. Mon.–Sat. 8.00–12.30/13.30–17.30. Sun. 9.00–11.45.

85

ZEYSSOLFF★

☐	2ha	18000	**3** **D** ◑

Good colour and delicate, musky fruit aromas. Well-balanced but still immature flavour. A young, healthy wine which will improve with keeping. (1983) ✔ Pinot Blanc, Pinot Noir, Tokay (Pinot Gris), Muscat.
☛ Zeyssolff, 156 Rue Principale, 67140 Gertwiller; tel. 88 08 90 08 ☥ By appt.

A. ZIMMERMANN ET FILS★★★

☐	0.5ha	6000	**3** **D** ◑

Shows its excellent origins to the full; the 1983 vintage has succeeded in bringing out all the aromas and fruits of the grape. Perfect balance of acidity, full body and alcohol content. Will improve and peak in two to three years. A delight for Riesling lovers. (1983)
☛ GAEC A. Zimmermann, 3 Grand-Rue, 67600 Orschwiller; tel. 88 92 08 49 ☥ By appt.

JULES ZIMMERMANN

☐	1ha	96000	**3** **D** ◑

Dry, with reserved nose that nevertheless develops an entrancing bouquet in the glass. Light and easy to drink. (1983) ✔ Gewürztraminer, Sylvaner, Pinot Noir, Muscat.
☛ Jules Zimmermann, 13 Rue des Prêtres, 68570 Soultzmatt; tel. 89 47 02 69 ☥ By appt.

DOMAINE ZIND-HUMBRECHT
Herrenweg★★

☐	5ha	8000	**4** **D** 🍸 ↓

Beautiful, pale, greeny-yellow. Fruity nose and agreeable, earthy character. Slight acidity; keep for three to five years. (1983)
☛ Dom. Zind-Humbrecht, Wintzenheim, 68000 Colmar; tel. 89 27 02 05 ☥ By appt.

Alsace Muscat

Two Muscat grape varieties are used to make this aromatic dry wine that has the sharp, refreshing flavour of fresh grapes. The first of these has always been known as Muscat d'Alsace, but is perhaps more correctly known as the Muscat de Frontignan. Since it is late maturing, it is only planted on the most favourable locations. The second variety, the Ottonel Muscat, ripens earlier and is much more common. The two grape varieties, however, make up less than 3 per cent of production. An Alsace Muscat is an agreeable and unusual local speciality that should be drunk as an aperitif before the main meal, or served at parties with canapés or pretzels.

LEON BOESCH ET FILS

☐	0.35ha	3000	**2** **D** ◑

A slightly clumsy first impression, but slowly reveals delicious bouquet. Attractive to taste. Recommended for asparagus and grilled andouillette sausages. (1983) ✔ Sylvaner, Pinot Blanc, Edelzwicker, Tokay (Pinot Gris), Pinot Noir.
☛ Léon Boesch et Fils, 4 Rue du Bois, 68570 Soultzmatt; tel. 89 47 01 83 ☥ By appt. Daily 8.00–12.00/13.00–20.00.

CAVE VINICOLE DE DAMBACH-LA-VILLE *Cuvée des Guillemettes*★

☐	3.3ha	32400	**3** **D** 🍸 ◑ ↓

Yellow-green with fine musky aromas. Typical, attractive, round-bodied flavour. May be drunk alone or as an aperitif or pudding wine. (1983) ✔ Muscat (medal).
☛ Cave Vinicole de Dambach-la-Ville, 67650 Dambach-la-Ville; tel. 88 92 40 03 ☥ By appt.

AVE VINICOLE DE DAMBACH-LA-VILLE

☐	3.3ha	32400	**3** **D** 🍸 ◑ ↓

Opens out into an attractive, easy wine. Typical of this vintage, with great richness and low acidity. (1983)
☛ Cave. Vinicole de Dambach-la-Ville, 67650 Dambach-la-Ville; tel. 88 92 40 03 ☥ By appt.

UNION VINICOLE DIVINAL★★

☐	1ha	6000	**3** **D** 🍸 ↓

Pretty, pale-gold colour. Typical fruity Muscat aromas. Clean, fresh grapey taste on the palate. Complete, elegant and refined, with very good balance. Ideal with plain white asparagus. (1983)
☛ Union Vinicole Divinal, 30 Rue du Général Leclerc, 67210 Obernai; tel. 88 95 61 18 ☥ By appt.

CAVE VINICOLE D'EGUISHEIM
Cuvée de la Comtesse Sigalle

☐	8.6ha	75936	**3** **D** 🍸 ◑ ↓

Rather raw, undeveloped aromas for a Muscat, but well rounded, generous flavour and very smooth on the palate. Will keep for three to five years. (1983) ✔ Muscat Médaillé, Muscat Cuvée de la Comtesse.
☛ Cave Vinicole d'Eguisheim, 6 Grand-Rue, 68420 Eguisheim; tel. 89 41 11 06 ☥ By appt.

R. ENGEL ET FILS

☐	0.8ha	4800	**3** **D** ◑

Delicious nose but still too closed. Well-bred Muscat that is like biting into the grapes themselves. Well balanced and easy on the palate. Good example of grape variety without overwhelming. Will please lovers of dry, easy-to-drink aperitifs. (1983) ✔ Sylvaner, Riesling, Gewürztraminer, Tokay (Pinot Gris), Crémant.
☛ R. Engel et Fils, 1 Route du Vin, 67600 Orschwiller; tel. 88 92 01 83 ☥ By appt.

PHILIPPE GOCKER

☐ 0.3 ha 2500 **3 D ▮**

Subtle, beautiful colour matched by delicate, but not too fruity, nose. Light and easy to drink by itself. (1983) ✔ Riesling, Gewürztraminer, Sylvaner, Tokay (Pinot Gris), Pinot Noir.
☛ Philippe Gocker, 24 Rue de Riquewihr, 68630 Mittelwihr; tel. 89 47 88 02 ☗ By appt.

COOPERATIVE VINICOLE D'INGERSHEIM*

☐ 4 ha 19000 **3 D ▮**

Lovely grapeyness on the nose backed by fullness on tasting, and held together by pleasant acidity. Bouquet typical of 1982 vintage. Dryness and refreshing fruitiness make this wine a perfect aperitif. Drink within two years. (1982)
☛ Coop. Vinicole d'Ingersheim, 1 Rue Clémenceau, 68000 Ingersheim; tel. 89 27 05 96 ☗ By appt.

ROBERT KARCHER

☐ 0.6 ha 3600 **3 D ◐**

Fruity, light and well balanced on the palate. Drink from now onwards. (1983) ✔ The whole range of Alsace wines.
☛ Robert Karcher, 11 Rue de l'Ours, 68000 Colmar; tel. 89 41 14 42 ☗ By appt.

DOMAINE DES COMTES DE LUPFEN*

☐ 1 ha 7200 **4 D ▮**

Good wine with very fruity, delicate nose. Light but well balanced on the palate. Freshness due to the pleasant acidity, surprising for this vintage. (1982)
☛ Paul Blanck et Fils, 32 Grande-Rue, 68240 Kientzheim; tel. 89 78 23 56. ☗ By appt. Mon.–Sat. 9.00–12.00/14.30–18.00. Sun. 10.30–12.00/14.30–18.00.

M. MURE *Clos Saint Landelin**

☐ 1 ha 6000 **4 D ◐ ⚘**

Lovely green colour with delicately fruity nose. Quite full bodied, but with subtle bouquet and flavour characteristic of Muscat. Well balanced and fresh for this year. An excellent aperitif. (1982)
☛ M. Mure, 68250 Rouffach; tel. 89 49 62 19 ☗ By appt. Mon.–Sat. 8.00–12.30/13.00–18.30. Sun. 10.30–12.00/14.30–18.00.

CAVE VINICOLE DE PFAFFENHEIM*

☐ 5 ha 42000 **3 D ◐**

Good wine with agreeably grapey nose. Well made and typical of the vintage. Despite being rather light, well balanced and easy to drink. (1983)
☛ Cave Vinicole de Pfaffenheim, 68250 Pfaffenheim; tel. 89 49 61 08 ☗ By appt.

CHARLES SCHLERET

☐ 0.5 ha 3600 **2 D ▮ ⚘**

Light, dry, fresh and typical of this vintage. Has developed good fruit and could get better. (1982)
☛ Charles Schleret, 1–3 Route d'Ingersheim, 68230 Turckheim; tel. 89 27 06 09 ☗ By appt.

COOPERATIVE VINICOLE DE SIGOLSHEIM

☐ 30 ha 60000 **4 D ◐ ⚘**

Good colour; good Muscat nose, but not overwhelming. Despite slight bitterness on the palate, dry and pleasantly drinkable. Good as an aperitif or with not-too-sweet puddings. (1983) ✔ Crémant, Pinot Blanc, Riesling, Gewürztraminer, Pinot Noir.
☛ Soc. Coop. Vinicole de Sigolsheim, Sigolsheim, 68240 Kaysersberg; tel. 89 47 12 55 ☗ By appt.

CAVE VINICOLE DE TRAENHEIM

☐ 8 ha 48000 **3 D ▮**

Lovely pale-gold colour. Typically 1983 in its grapeyness on the nose. On tasting, light and well balanced. Altogether an agreeable and refreshing wine. (1983)
☛ Cave Vinicole de Traenheim, Route de Scharrachbergheim, 67310 Traenheim; tel. 88 50 66 21 ☗ By appt.

CAVE VINICOLE DE TURCKHEIM

☐ 1.5 ha 12000 **D ▮**

Fine bouquet and refined flavour with a fresh, grapey character. A very well-balanced wine. (1983)
☛ Cave Vinicole de Turckheim, 68230 Turckheim; tel. 89 27 06 25 ☗ Mon.–Sat. 8.00–12.00/4.00–18.00, Sun. 10.30–12.00/14.00–18.00.

ALSACE WILLM

☐ 0.3 ha 1320 **3 D ▮ ◐ ⚘**

A very refined, delicate Muscat nose. Dry but pleasantly fruity flavour. An excellent aperitif. (1983) ✔ Muscat (medal), Muscat Cuvée Emile Willm.
☛ Alsace Willm, 32 Rue du Dr-Sultzer, 67140 Barr; tel. 88 08 19 11 ☗ By appt.

PIERRE WURTZ*

☐ 3 ha 3600 **3 D ◐**

Very pleasant nose with a pronounced bouquet. A Muscat which should be drunk immediately as this variety of grape needs no ageing. A light, fruity, rather feminine wine. It has great charm when served chilled as an aperitif. (1983)
☛ Pierre Wurtz, 21 Route du Vin, 68630. Mittelwihr; tel. 89 47 93 57 ☗ By appt.

A. ZIMMERMANN ET FILS

☐ 0.4 ha 6000 **3 D ◐**

At its peak. Very attractive, undemanding, soft; lovely gold colour. First-class aperitif. Drink within the year. (1979) ✔ Sylvaner, Pinot Noir, Tokay (Pinot Gris), Gewürztraminer.
☛ Jean-Pierre Zimmermann, 3 Grand-Rue, Orschwiller, 67600 Sélestat; tel. 88 92 08 49 ☗ By appt.

JULES ZIMMERMANN*

☐ 0.14 ha 1200 **3 D ◐**

Light, dry wine with delicate fruit and good balance of acidity. Tastes just like the grapes from which it is made. Mild and pleasant. (1983) ✔ Riesling, Gewürztraminer, Tokay (Pinot Gris), Sylvaner, Pinot Noir.
☛ J. Zimmermann, 13 Rue des Prêtres, 68570 Soultzmatt; tel. 89 47 02 69 ☗ By appt.

DOMAINE ZIND-HUMBRECHT★★

| ☐ | 0.9ha | 96000 | 4 D ▪ ↓ |

01∪∪Fruit that appears on the nose develops further on the palate. A very obvious wine which tastes exactly of the grapes from which it is made. Light, dry and good acidity. For lovers of good Muscat. (1983)
↬ Dom. Zind-Humbrecht, Wintzenheim, 68000 Colmar; tel. 89 27 02 05 ⵙ By appt.

Alsace Gewürztraminer

The grape from which this wine is made is a particularly aromatic variety of the traminer family. A treatise published as early as 1551 defined it as a typical Alsace grape variety. The truth of this statement has been proved over the centuries, almost certainly because the Alsace vineyard really does do justice to the grape, allowing it to show off its unique potential to the full.

The wine is robust, full-bodied and usually dry, though it may sometimes have some residual sweetness. Most of all, it has a marvellous bouquet, which is more or less pronounced according to location and vintage. The Gewürztraminer vine is relatively low-yielding, but the grapes ripen early and are rich in sugar. It is planted over some 2500 hectares, or about 20 per cent of the area under vine in Alsace. The wine may be served as an aperitif before a meal or as a pudding wine, but a rich Gewürztraminer also goes well with strongly flavoured cheeses such as Roquefort or Munster. The outstanding recent years were 1983 and 1971; 1976 was very successful; 1981, 1979 and 1978 all good, and 1984 and 1982 average.

CAVES JEAN-BAPTISTE ADAM
Réserve★

| ☐ | 2ha | 14400 | 4 D ▪ ↓ |

Golden-yellow with attractive, fruity Gewürztraminer nose. Immediately inviting, well made and typical of the soil and vintage. To keep for up to fifteen years. (1983)
↬ Jean-Baptiste Adam, 5 Rue de l'Aigle, 68770 Ammerschwihr; tel. 89 78 23 21 ⵙ No visitors.

PIERRE ADAM★

| ☐ | 1.2ha | 12000 | 3 D ◖ ↓ |

Lovely colour; easy and delicate nose. Well made, dry and slightly tough. Needs a few years to soften down. (1983)
↬ Pierre Adam, 2 Rue du Lieutenant-Mourier, 68770 Ammerschwihr; tel. 89 78 23 07 ⵙ By appt. Closed in winter.

DOMAINE ARBOGAST

| ☐ | 1.5ha | 9600 | 3 D ◖ ↓ |

Well made but only average character. Good balance of fruit, acidity and body. (1983)
✓ Tokay Pinot Gris, Riesling, Pinot Noir, Sylvaner, Muscat.
↬ Vins d'Alsace Arbogast, 28 Route de Soultz, 67120 Wolxheim; tel. 88 38 17 10 ⵙ Mon.–Fri. 9.00–12.00/13.30–18.00. Sat. 9.00–12.00.

BAUMANN ET FILS★★★

| ☐ | 1ha | 7200 | 4 D ◖ ↓ |

Very great wine from the famous 1981 vintage. Fragrance of peonies and roses lingering on the palate gives a spicy, rich, warm character. Will become even better with age. To fully appreciate this wine, drink it on its own, without food. (1981) ✓ Riesling, Tokay (Pinot Gris), Pinot Noir, Muscat.
↬ J.-J. Baumann et Fils, 43 Rue du Général-de-Gaulle, 68340 Riquewihr; tel. 89 47 92 47 ⵙ 9.00–12.00/14.00–18.00. Closed Aug.

JEAN-PIERRE BECHTOLD

| ☐ | 1.2ha | 7200 | 4 D ◖ |

Very delicate, floral nose. Spicy taste, excellent balance and long finish. Will improve. (1981)
↬ Jean-Pierre Bechtold, 49 Rue Principale, 67310 Dahlenheim; tel. 88 50 66 57 ⵙ By appt.

JEAN-PIERRE BECHTOLD

| ☐ | 1.5ha | ˙9600 | 3 D ◖ |

Grown on clay–limestone soil. Nose full of character. Full-bodied, well balanced and complete; very typical of the vintage. Will gain class with age. (1982)
↬ J.-P. Bechtold, 49 Rue Principale, 67310 Dahlenheim; tel. 88 50 66 57 ⵙ Daily 8.00–12.00/14.00–19.00.

PAUL BECK *Cuvée Frankstein★*

| ☐ | 6ha | 33600 | 4 D ◖ ↓ |

Earthy taste, strongly marked by the granite soil. Good varietal character, with very pronounced nose and lasting acidity. The flavour is still not revealed suggesting that the wine will age well. Light alcohol content will make it good aperitif – soft, rich and well balanced. (1981) ✓ Riesling, Muscat, Sylvaner, Pinot Blanc.
↬ Mme. Paul Beck, 1 Rue Clemenceau, 67650 Dambach-la-Ville; tel. 88 92 40 17 ⵙ Mon. 10.00–12.00/14.00–18.00.

J.-PH. ET M. BECKER *Froenreben*

| ☐ | 1ha | 10800 | 3 D ◖ ↓ |

Amber colour, with elegant, reserved nose. Unusual taste of Savagnin grape (used for Vin Jaune) and aroma of roses. Well made, clean but a bit closed up. Residual sugar makes it round and softens scents and bouquet. Will improve well. (1983) ✓ Riesling, Pinot, Tokay (Pinot Gris), Sylvaner, Muscat.
↬ J.-Ph. et M. Becker, 2 Route d'Ostheim, Zellenberg; 68340 Riquewihr; tel. 89 47 90 16 ⵙ By appt. Closed during harvest.

LES VIGNERONS DE BENNWIHR
Vendanges Tardives★★★

| ☐ | 28 ha | 31 000 | 5 D ⬛ ↓ |

From late-picked (early November) grapes. Immediately striking fruit and flavour, which go on to overwhelm the mouth. Full bodied and beautifully structured. Distinctive aroma reminiscent of the grapes themselves. A very great wine from the driest part of Alsace. (1983)
🍷 Les Vignerons de Bennwihr, 3 Rue du Général-de-Gaulle, 68630 Bennwihr; tel. 89 47 90 27 ⵏ By appt., daily 9.00–11.30/14.30–17.30.

LES VIGNERONS DE BENNWIHR
Réserve 1983★★

| ☐ | 10 ha | 48 000 | 4 D ⬛ ↓ |

Lovely amber colour. A strikingly fruity wine, very typical of this vintage. Well developed and aromatic; full-bodied, powerful and balanced by light acidity. First-class aperitif. (1983)
🍷 Les Vignerons de Bennwihr, 3 Rue du Général-de-Gaulle, 68630 Bennwihr; tel. 89 47 90 27 ⵏ By appt. Daily 9.00–11.30/14.30–17.30.

LEON BEYER
Cuvée des Comtes Eguisheim★★

| ☐ | | 12 000 | 5 ⬛ ⬛ ↓ |

Fine, balanced and full bodied. Characterized by great generosity. Drink immediately – has reached its peak. (1978)
🍷 Léon Beyer, Eguisheim 68420, Herrlisheim-prés-Colmar; tel. 89 41 41 05 ⵏ Daily 9.00–13.00/14.00–19.00.

LEON BOESCH ET FILS
Vendanges Tardives★

| ☐ | 80 ha | 38 400 | 4 D ⬛ ↓ |

A good wine, with a very easy, grapey character coming from fruit and balance. Well developed. Drink at once. (1983) 🍷 Sylvaner, Pinot Blanc, Edelzwicker, Tokay (Pinot Gris), Pinot Noir.
🍷 Léon Boesch et Fils, 4 Rue du Bois, 68570 Soultzmatt; tel. 89 47 01 83 ⵏ By appt., Tue.–Sun. 8.00–12.00/13.00–20.00.

LEON BOESCH ET FILS *Zinnkoepfle*★★

| ☐ | 70 ha | 29 000 | 3 D ⬛ ↓ |

A dry wine from a limestone soil; lots of fruit on the nose and good depth on the palate. Excellent balance and body indicate fine ageing potential. (1983)
🍷 Léon Boesch et Fils, 4 Rue du Bois, 68570 Soultzmatt; tel. 89 47 01 83 ⵏ By appt. Tue.–Sun. 8.00–12.00/13.00–20.00.

PIERRE BOTT

| ☐ | 3 ha | 21 600 | 4 D ⬛ ↓ |

Very easy on the nose; good accompaniment to sweets and desserts. Would benefit from a little more acidity. Drink now. (1983) 🍷 Tokay (Pinot Gris), Muscat, Riesling, Pinot Noir.
🍷 Pierre Bott, 13 Avenue du Général-de-Gaulle, 68150 Ribeauvillé; tel. 89 73 60 48 ⵏ By appt.

LUCIEN BRAND ET FILS *Kefferberg*

| ☐ | 3 ha | 12 000 | 3 D ⬛ ↓ |

Plenty of body and substance coming from grapes grown on marl-limestone soil. Still too young to show its true colours; reserved character will change with age. To drink in one or two years. (1983) 🍷 Riesling, Muscat, Tokay (Pinot Gris), Sylvaner, Crémant.
🍷 Lucien Brand et Fils, 71 Rue de Wolxheim, Ergersheim, 67120 Molsheim; tel. 88 38 17 71 ⵏ Daily 8.00–12.00/14.00–20.00.

CHARLES BRONNER-WEBER

| ☐ | 0.5 ha | 3800 | 3 D ⬛ ↓ |

Spicy, floral nose. Flavours still bit closed-up, but very mature for its vintage. Recommended for petits-fours and other sweet dishes. (1983) 🍷 Riesling, Muscat, Sylvaner, Pinot Blanc, Tokay (Pinot Gris).

🍷 Charles Bronner-Weber, 2 Rue Kilian, 68340 Riquewihr; tel. 89 47 94 82 ⵏ By appt.

THEO CATTIN ET FILS
Bollemberg Cuvée de l'Ours Noir★

| ☐ | 0.7 ha | 6000 | 4 D ⬛ |

Lovely yellow-green, indicating a wine still very young for the vintage. Well-developed floral nose typical of the region. Good balance and body, well developed with a hint of residual sugar. A good wine. (1981) 🍷 Riesling Cuvée de l'Ours Noir, Riesling, Muscat, Gewürztraminer, Pinot Noir.
🍷 Théo Cattin et Fils, 35 Rue Roger-Frémeaux, 68420 Voegtlinshoffen; tel. 89 49 30 43 ⵏ By appt. Closed 1–20 Aug.

THEO CATTIN ET FILS
Cuvée de l'Ours Noir★★

| ☐ | 6 ha | 38 400 | 4 D ⬛ |

Lovely golden-yellow colour; reserved and delicate fruit on the nose. Well balanced on the palate despite high alcohol content. Although well made and powerful, still a bit closed-up. Fresh, light acidity; easy to drink. Worth laying down for development. (1983) 🍷 Riesling, Tokay (Pinot Gris), Muscat, Gewürztraminer, Pinot Noir.
🍷 Théo Cattin et Fils, 35 Rue Roger-Frémeaux, 68420 Voegtlinshoffen; tel. 89 49 30 43 ⵏ By appt. Closed 1–20 Aug.

CAVE VINICOLE DE DAMBACH-LA-VILLE *Cuvée des Guillemettes*

| ☐ | 26.4 ha | 285 000 | 3 D ⬛ ⬛ ↓ |

Very mature. Demonstrates the powerful personality of the Gewürztraminer to the full. Round and held together by hint of residual sugar. Very distinctive character. (1983) 🍷 Gewürztraminer Médaille.
🍷 Cave Vinicole de Dambach-la-Ville, 67650

Dambach-la-Ville; tel. 88 92 40 03 ☿ By appt. Closed Sun.

UNION VINICOLE DIVINAL★★

| ☐ | 2ha 12500 | 3 D ☷ ↓ |

Great wine with very fruity nose and good body. Spicy flavours on the palate typical of the grape variety. Worth keeping for a few years. An excellent aperitif. (1983)
↬ Union Vinicole Divinal, 30 Rue du Général Leclerc, 67210 Obernai; tel. 88 95 61 18 ☿ By appt.

DOMAINE EXPERIMENTAL VITICOLE★★

| ☐ | 10ha 72000 | 4 D ☷ ⬤ |

A great wine: reserved, spicy and fruity on the nose; deliciously full-bodied, powerful and well made on the palate, with a hint of over-ripeness. Promises a lot in a few years. (1983) ✔ Tokay (Pinot Gris), Pinot Blanc, Sylvaner, Pinot Noir.
↬ Dom. Expérimental Viticole, 8 Rue Kléber, 68021 Colmar; tel. 89 41 16 50 ☿ By appt.

DOPFF *Au Moulin*

| ☐ | 4ha 22920 | 4 D ⬤ ↓ |

Despite the year, still closed-up on the nose. Well made and typical of the clay–limestone soil from which it comes. A soft and delicate wine which will develop well over next few years. (1981)
↬ Dopff 'Au Moulin', 68340 Riquewihr; tel. 89 47 92 23 ☿ By appt. Closed 1 Nov.–30 Mar.

JEAN-PAUL ECKLE

| ☐ | 11ha 9000 | 4 D ☷ ↓ |

Golden colour. Typical Gewürztraminer fruitiness on the nose. Excellent on the palate; dry and full-bodied. Pleasant acidity will allow it to be kept for several years. (1983) ✔ Sylvaner, Klevner, Riesling, Tokay (Pinot Gris), Muscat.
↬ Jean-Paul Eckle, 29 Grand-Rue, 68230 Katzenthal; tel. 89 27 09 41 ☿ Daily 8.00–12.00/13.00–19.00.

CAVE VINICOLE D'EGUISHEIM
Cuvée St-Léon-Vendanges Tardives★★

| ☐ | 116.10ha 65000 | 4 D ☷ ⬤ ↓ |

A Gewürztraminer that has already developed strong aromas and a large quantity of sugar with very little acidity. On the nose a hint of lemon. Relatively closed in, but sumptuously rich on the palate. Excellent for laying down. (1983)
↬ Cave Vinicole d'Eguisheim, 6 Grand-Rue, 68420 Eguisheim; tel. 89 41 11 06 ☿ By appt.

JEROME GESCHICKT ET FILS
Kaefferkopf★★★

| ☐ | 1ha 8400 | 3 D ⬤ ↓ |

Beautiful colour coming from the distinctive *kaefferkopf* soil. Masses of fruit on the nose; lovely balance on the palate. Full bodied, with alcohol content, acidity and bouquet making it a fine example of this exceptional vintage. Will age well and reach its peak in four to five years. (1983) ✔ Riesling, Tokay (Pinot Gris), Sylvaner, Pinot Noir.
↬ Jérome Geschickt et Fils, 1 Place de la Sinne,

68770 Ammerschwihr; tel. 89 47 12 54 ☿ By appt., daily 8.00–12.00/13.00–19.00.

WILLY GISSELBRECHT ET FILS★

| ☐ | 1.8ha 18000 | 4 D ☷ ↓ |

Lovely gold colour with attractive, spicy nose. The strength of the vintage and good body come through on tasting. Good balance between scents and flavours and hint of residual sugar. Worth waiting for; will become much more interesting. (1983) ✔ Sylvaner, Tokay (Pinot Gris), Pinot Noir, Riesling, Muscat.
↬ Willy Gisselbrecht et Fils, 20 Route du Vin 67650 Dambach-la-Ville; tel. 88 92 41 02 ☿ By appt.

GREINER-SCHLERET★

| ☐ | 1.7ha 11400 | 3 D ⬤ ↓ |

Good wine with lots of depth but not giving much at the moment. Well made, with an excellent future; to keep. Look forward to drinking it with foie gras, cheese and puddings. (1983) ✔ Sylvaner, Riesling, Tokay (Pinot Gris), Muscat.
↬ P. Greiner-Schleret et Fils, 22 Rue de Riquewihr, 68630 Mittelwihr; tel. 89 47 92 67 ☿ By appt.

DOMAINE ANDRE GRESSER *Kritt★*

| ☐ | 1ha 6000 | 3 D ⬤ ↓ |

Easy and generous. Delicate nose and open taste. Will appeal to light-wine lovers. (1983)
↬ André et Rémy Gresser, 2 Rue de l'Ecole, 67140 Andlau; tel. 88 08 95 88 ☿ Daily by appt., 11.00–12.00/13.00–19.00.

DOMAINE ANDRE GRESSER
Andlau★

| ☐ | 1ha 7200 | 4 D ⬤ ↓ |

Rich and spicy wine with a lovely amber colour, testifying to first-rate grapes. Strongly made and, coming from clay-limestone soil, will age well even though it is already at its best. Excellent aperitif. (1982) ✔ Edelzwicker, Riesling, Gewürztraminer, Pinot Noir.
↬ André et Rémy Gresser, 2 Rue de l'Ecole, 67140 Andlau; tel. 88 08 95 88. ☿ Daily bny appt. 11.00–12.00/13.00–19.00.

MARTIN HARTMANN★

| ☐ | 1.6ha 5000 | 3 D ⬤ ↓ |

Orschwihr is famous for its well-exposed slopes which produce celebrated wines. This example is dry, still very young but powerful. Bouquet developing well; still needs some ageing. (1983)
↬ Martin Hartmann, 1 Rue du Centre, Orschwihr 68000 Gebwiller; tel. 89 76 89 30 ☿ Daily 11.00–20.00.

H. ET J. HEITZMANN ET FILS
Estampille de Noblesse

| ☐ | 1ha | 7200 | **3** **D** ⏸ ⚲ |

Very good pale-gold. Typical fragrant fruitiness on the nose. Good balance of scents and flavours backed by firm yet flexible body. Residual sugar is natural and characteristic of this vintage. Excellent aperitif. (1983)
⮞ H. et J. Heitzmann et Fils, 2 Grand-Rue, 68770 Ammerschwihr; tel. 89 47 10 64 ☎ By appt, 8.00–12.00/14.00–20.00 daily.

ERNEST HORCHER ET FILS

| ☐ | 1.5ha | 9600 | **3** **D** ⏸ ⚲ |

Full bodied and well made. Will have lovely aromas after a little more bottle age. (1983) ✔ Riesling.
⮞ Ernest Horcher et Fils, 6 Rue du Vignoble 68630 Mittelwihr; tel. 89 47 92 94 ☎ By appt.

HUGEL ET FILS *Vendanges Tardives*★★★

| ☐ | 4ha | 19200 | **6** **D** ⏸ ⚲ |

Twelve generations of the Hugel family have produced top-quality Alsace wines for some 350 years. This exceptional example is elegant, with great finesse. Concentrated, luscious and rich in lemon and honey scents. Length on the palate continues with freshness and balance unusual for this grape variety. A great wine from a famous name. (1981) ✔ The whole range of Alsace wines.
⮞ Hugel et Fils, 68340 Riquewihr; tel. 89 47 92 15 ☎ By appt. Closed 1 Nov.–31 May.

SÉLECTIONNÉ PAR JEAN HUGEL

ALSACE
APPELLATION ALSACE CONTRÔLÉE

HVH

DEPUIS 1639

GEWURZTRAMINER "HUGEL"

VENDANGE TARDIVE 700 ml e

MISE EN BOUTEILLE PAR HUGEL ET FILS-RIQUEWIHR-ALSACE-FRANCE
PRODUCE OF FRANCE BOTTLED IN FRANCE

BERNARD HUMBRECHT

| ☐ | 0.8ha | 7800 | **3** **D** ⏸ ⚲ |

Character very marked by the rough clay–limestone vineyard soil; still closed-up despite the year. Fresh and firm on the palate. Well made; requires patience. (1981) ✔ Crémant, Pinot Noir.
⮞ Bernard Humbrecht, 9 Place de la Mairie, 68420 Gueberschwihr; tel. 89 49 31 42 ☎ By appt.

CAVE VINICOLE DE HUNAWIHR

| ☐ | 20ha | 132000 | **4** **D** ▮ ⚲ |

Lovely yellow-gold. Fruity and spicy nose. Scents and flavours combine with body to produce perfect balance. A well-made wine typical of the region and heavy clay soil. Keep to give of its best. (1983).
⮞ Cave Coop. de Hunawihr, 68150 Hunawihr; tel. 89 73 61 67 ☎ By appt.

COOPERATIVE VINICOLE D'INGERSHEIM

| ☐ | 60ha | 67000 | **3** **D** ▮ |

Amber colour with lovely, spicy fruitiness typical of Gewürztraminer. Well made from fully matured grapes. A well-developed wine to be drunk from now onwards. (1983) ✔ Riesling, Tokay (Pinot Gris), Muscat, Pinot Blanc, Pinot Noir.
⮞ Coop. Vinicole d'Ingersheim, 1 Rue Clémenceau, 68000 Ingersheim; tel. 89 27 05 96 ☎ By appt.

ROGER JUNG *Les Terres Blanches*★★

| ☐ | 0.6ha | 4800 | **5** **D** ▮ |

This 1983 still has a long way to go; full of promise but still far too young. (1983) ✔ Schoenenberg, Pinot Gris Schoenenberg, Riesling.
⮞ Roger Jung, 23 Rue de la 1ère Armée, 68340 Riquewihr; tel. 89 47 92 17 ☎ By appt.

ROGER JUNG
Les Terres Blanches – Vendanges Tardives★★

| ☐ | 1ha | 6000 | **5** **D** ▮ ⚲ |

Lovely pale-gold. Spicy aroma of cinnamon and nutmeg lingers on the palate. Will develop in the bottle, and may be drunk for many years to come. (1983) ✔ Crémant, Pinot Noir, Riesling, Muscat, Tokay (Pinot Gris).
⮞ Roger Jung, 23 Rue de la 1ère Armée, 68340 Riquewihr; tel. 89 47 92 17 ☎ By appt.

ROBERT KARCHER

| ☐ | 3.8ha | 24000 | **3** **D** ▮ ⚲ |

Good colour, backed up by delicate and spicy fruit. Well developed and typical of this vintage. Full bodied and powerful. (1983) ✔ The whole range of Alsace wines.
⮞ Robert Karcher, 11 Rue de l'Ours, 68000 Colmar; tel. 89 41 14 42 ☎ Daily by appt.

A. KIENTZLER

| ☐ | 1ha | 4200 | **5** **D** ⏸ ⚲ |

Generous wine made from very mature destemmed grapes. Nose needs to open out. Good example of this vintage, but too little tannin to give persistent flavour or good keeping properties. Drink in next three to four years. (1983)
⮞ M.A. Kientzler, Route du Vin, 68150 Ribeauvillé; tel. 89 73 67 10 ☎ By appt.

PIERRE KIRSCHNER

| ☐ | 1.5ha | 72000 | **3** **D** ⏸ ⚲ |

Very pleasant but quite dry. Will not improve, but good now with Munster cheese or fruit tart. (1983) ✔ Sylvaner, Riesling, Tokay, Muscat.
⮞ M. Pierre Kirschner, 26 Rue Théophile-Bader, 67650 Dambach-la-Ville; tel. 88 92 40 55 ☎ Daily 8.00–12.00/13.00–19.00.

JEAN PIERRE KLEIN ET FILS
Ancien Moulin de l'Abbaye★★

| ☐ | 1ha | 9600 | **4** **D** ▮ |

Lovely to look at; fruity fragrance on the nose. Obviously produced from fully ripe grapes because well developed and slightly too high in alcohol, but attractively supple. (1983)

↳ J.-P. Klein et Fils, 1 Rue du Maréchal Joffre, 67140 Andlau; tel. 88 08 93 03 ⏳ No visitors.

HUBERT KRICK

| ☐ | 2.5 ha | 90000 | **3** **D** **▪** **↓** |

Not very interesting, despite the vintage. Good body but tough. Needs a few more years to reach its peak. (1981) ✔ Sylvaner, Reisling, Muscat, Tokay (Pinot Gris).
↳ Hubert Krick, 93–95 Rue Clemenceau, Wintzenheim, 68000 Colmar; tel. 89 27 00 01 ⏳ No visitors.

VINS D'ALSACE KUEHN
Cuvée Saint-Hubert

| ☐ | 3 ha | 6000 | **4** **D** **▪** |

Lovely colour, but closed-up nose. Appears to have been bottled very recently; though robust is still a little tough and needs time to improve. Influence of clay-limestone soil is apparent. (1983)
↳ Vins d'Alsace Kuehn, 3 Grand-Rue, 68770 Ammerschwihr; tel. 89 78 23 16 ⏳ By appt. Mon.–Fri. 8.00–12.00/13.30–17.30.

KUENTZ-BAS *Réserve Personnelle*★★

| ☐ | 1 ha | 7800 | **4** **D** **◑** **↓** |

Amber colour. Fruity fragrance and typical Gewürztraminer nose. Well made, with a hint of residual sugar keeping it well balanced. Beautifully fresh for the year. Can be kept for a few years more. (1981)
↳ Kuentz-Bas SA 14, Route du Vin, 68420 Husseren-les-Châteaux; tel. 89 49 30 24 ⏳ By appt.

KUENTZ-BAS
Cuvée Caroline – Vendanges Tardives★★★

| ☐ | 1 ha | 3600 | **5** **D** **▪** **↓** |

Marvellous fruit on the nose and unmistakeable character of late-picked wine; 'noble rot' shows through on taste and smell. Full and powerful on the palate, soft and rich in style. A straightforward wine, perfect for formal drinks parties. (1982)
↳ Kuentz-Bas SA Husseren-les-Châteaux, 68420 Herrlisheim; tel. 89 49 30 24 ⏳ By appt.

GERARD LANDMAN★

| ☐ | 0.5 ha | 3600 | **3** **D** **◑** **↓** |

Immediately attractive on the nose. Agreeably fruity. Delicate fragrance of the grape variety melds well with alcohol content and acidity. (1983)
↳ Gerard Landman, 124 Route du Vin, 67680 Northalten; tel. 88 92 43 96 ⏳ By appt. Mon.–Sat. 8.00–19.00.

LANDMANN-OSTHOLT
Cave de la Vallis Praenobelis Zinkoepfle★

| ☐ | 0.6 ha | 2160 | **5** **D** **◑** **↓** |

Very characteristic Gewürztraminer from a sunny limestone vineyard. Elegant floral aromas. Harmonious but powerful flavour, with balance and crispness promising well for the future. (1982)
↳ M. Landmann-Ostholt, 20 Rue de la Vallée, 68570 Soultzmatt; tel. 89 47 09 33 ⏳ By appt. Mon.–Sat. 9.30–12.00/14.00–18.00. Sun. 10.30–13.00. Closed Jan.

JEAN LEHMAN ET FILS

| ☐ | 0.5 ha | 3720 | **3** **D** **◑** |

Nose still closed-up; the residual sugar on the palate hides the wine's true character. Will develop well with age. Good to lay down. (1983)
↳ Jean Lehman et Fils, 68340 Riquewihr; tel. 89 47 82 99 ⏳ By appt.

DOMAINE DES COMTES DE LUPFEN★

| ☐ | 5 ha | 26400 | **3** **D** **▪** **↓** |

Untypical 1982. Well-developed, fruity and spicy nose. Dry but well made. Drink from now onwards. (1982)
↳ Paul Blanck et Fils, 32 Grand-Rue, Kientzheim 68240 Kayserberg; tel. 89 78 23 56 ⏳ By appt. Mon.–Sat. 9.00–12.00/13.00–19.00.

JEAN-MEYER *Les Archenets*★★

| ☐ | 4.5 ha | 7200 | **4** **D** **◑** **↓** |

Made from a selection of grapes grown on gravelly clay-limestone soils in the best part of Wintzenheim and Turckheim. Will continue to improve for many years without losing its distinctive, elegant, floral character. (1979) ✔ Riesling les Pierrets, Pinot Auxerrois 'H' Vieilles Vignes, Riesling Hengst Vendanges du 28/11/1978, Tokay-(Pinot Gris) Cuvée du Centenaire.
↳ Jean Meyer et Fils, 76 Rue Clémenceau, Wintzenheim, 68000 Colmar; tel. 89 27 01 57 ⏳ By appt.

M. MURE *Clos Saint-Landelin*★★★

| ☐ | 4 ha | 30000 | **4** **D** **◑** **↓** |

Lovely gold, star-bright colour. Strikingly floral and delicate, fruity nose. Well made without being heavy. Still fresh for this vintage (1982). ✔ Sylvaner, Riesling, Tokay (Pinot Gris), Muscat, Pinot Noir.
↳ M. Muré, Clos St-Landelin, 68250 Rouffach; tel. 89 49 62 19 ⏳ By appt.

MICHEL NARTZ

| ☐ | 0.8 ha | 4000 | **3** **D** **◑** **↓** |

Mild bouquet but well balanced. Fine, structured, round flavour but not heavy. Will gain from laying down. A good aperitif and pudding wine. (1983)
↳ Michel Nartz, 40 Rue de la Paix, 67650 Dambach-la-Ville; tel. 88 92 41 11 ⏳ By appt.

COOPERATIVE D'ORSCHWILLER-KINTZHEIM *Les Faîteières*★

| ☐ | 14 ha | 67200 | **4** **D** **▪** **↓** |

Lovely amber colour and star-bright quality matched by spicy Gewürztraminer nose. Full body, well-developed scents and flavours – all proof of fully ripened grapes. Powerful yet easy to drink. (1983)
↳ Coop. d'Orschwiller-Kintzheim, 67600 Sélestat; tel. 88 92 09 87 ⏳ By appt.

DOMAINE OSTERTAG
Vendanges Tardives★

| ☐ | 1.5 ha | 4200 | **5** **D** **▪** **◑** **↓** |

Very complex wine. At present has a delicate nose, but no depth. This will develop in time into something more profound and spicy. Tastes very rich, luscious and well balanced. A fat and powerful wine which will remain so for many

years to come. (1983) ✔ Gewürztraminer, Sylvaner, Tokay (Pinot Gris), Pinot Noir, Crémant.
↜ Ostertag Père et Fils, 114 Rue Finkwiller, 67680 Epfig; tel. 88 85 51 34 ☒ By appt.

CAVE COOPERATIVE DE RIBEAUVILLE★★★

| ☐ | 30 ha | 24 000 | **3** **D** **▮** **↓** |

Very velvety Gewürztraminer character, aristocratic and full bodied. Fills the mouth but not overwhelmingly, due to exceptional strength and liveliness. A very fine wine. (1983)
↜ Cave Coop. de Ribeauvillé, 22 Route de Colmar, 68150 Ribeauvillé; tel. 89 73 61 80 ☒ Mon.–Fri. 8.00–12.00/14.00–18.00. Sat., Sun. 10.00–12.00/14.00–17.00. Closed Jan.–Mar.

JOSEPH RIEFLE ET FILS
Berg-Weingarten

| ☐ | 1 ha | 9000 | **3** **D** **◖** **↓** |

Characterized by assertiveness on the palate, delicate bouquet and relative youth. Sure to improve; worth waiting for. (1982) ✔ Crémant Riesling.
↜ J. Rieflé et Fils, 11 Place de la Mairie, 68250 Pfaffenheim; tel. 89 49 62 82 ☒ By appt. Mon.–Sat. 8.00–12.00/14.00–18.30. Sun. 14.00–18.30. Closed Jan., Feb.

PIERRE RIESTCH

| ☐ | 0.9 ha | 4200 | **3** **D** **▮** |

Made from the best and ripest grapes. Not much character, however, despite nice balance; should have more depth. Elegant, discreet nose. Good as an aperitif. (1982) ✔ Gewürztraminer, Riesling, Pinot Noir, Crémant.
↜ Pierre Riestch, 32 Rue Principale, 67140 Mittelbergheim; tel. 88 08 00 64 ☒ By appt.

CHATEAU DE RIQUEWIHR
Les Sorcières

| ☐ | 10 ha | 48 000 | **D** **▮** **↓** |

Sparkling gold colour. Strong character but delicate and reserved flavour. Still slightly closed-up but well made; will develop well. Excellent aperitif wine. (1983) ✔ Riesling, Muscat.
↜ Dopff et Irion, 68340 Riquewihr; tel. 89 47 92 51 ☒ By appt. Daily 9.00–12.00/13.00–19.00.

WILLY ROLLI-EDEL★

| ☐ | 2 ha | 10 800 | **4** **D** |

From a fine clay limestone soil giving strength and good body. Underdeveloped but promising nose; rich, generous flavour needing a few years to round out. Ideal with Munster cheese, fruit tart or kougelhopf pie (1983) ✔ Riesling.
↜ Willy Rolli-Edel, 5 Rue de l'Eglise, 68590 Roschwihr; tel. 89 73 63 26 ☒ By appt. Closed during harvest.

WILLY ROLLI-EDEL

| ☐ | 2 ha | 10 800 | **4** **D** **◖** |

Fairly delicate nose; in general, an obvious wine, robust and high in alcohol. A little more age will develop its character to the full. Look forward to drinking it with foie gras or strong cheeses. (1983)
↜ Willy Rolli-Edel, 5 Rue de l'Eglise, Rorsch-

wihr, 68590 St-Hippolyte; tel. 89 73 69 26 ☒ By appt. Closed during harvest.

CLOS SAINT-IMER

| ☐ | 1.5 ha | 12 000 | **3** **D** **◖** **↓** |

From an ancient (10th-century) vineyard. Colour rather too gold for the vintage. Not particularly fruity, but good Gewürztraminer taste. Drink within a year. (1983) ✔ Muscat, Riesling, Tokay (Pinot Gris).
↜ GAEC Ernest Burn, 14 Rue Basse, 68420 Gueberschwihr; tel. 89 49 31 41 ☒ By appt., daily 9.00–12.00/14.00–18.00.

DOMAINE SAINTE-GERTRUDE★★

| ☐ | 2 ha | 18 000 | **3** **D** **◖** **↓** |

A wine from a limestone soil; shows very good colour. Pleasantly fruity yet spicy nose with particularly grapey flavour. Still dry, it is very good for this year. (1982)
↜ Paul Buecher et Fils, Dom. Ste-Gertrude, Wettolsheim, 68000 Colmar; tel. 89 41 04 73 ☒ Mon.–Sat. 8.00–12.00/13.00–18.00. Sun. 14.00–18.00.

SOCIETE VINICOLE SAINTE-ODILE
Clos Ste-Odile★★

| ☐ | 3.5 ha | 18 000 | **3** **D** **◖** **↓** |

Beautiful colour, with lots of fruit on the nose. Delicate, spicy and typical of the grape variety. Strong terroir character. The combination of scents, flavours and pleasant acidity make for a great wine which will continue to develop in quality for a few years more. (1983) ✔ Sylvaner, Pinot Noir, Riesling Clos Ste-Odile.
↜ Ste Vinicole Ste-Odile, 3 Rue de la Gare, 67210 Obernai; tel. 88 95 50 23 ☒ By appt.

RENE SCHAEFLE★★★

| ☐ | 1 ha | 6000 | **4** **D** **◖** |

Very great wine from grapes picked at exactly the right moment. Tastes of young fruit with hint of honey. Robust and full-bodied, but well balanced. Exceptional flavour to be expected of a great Gewürztraminer. A pleasant wine to drink for many years to come. (1983) ✔ Sylvaner, Riesling, Pinot Noir.
↜ René Schaefle, 4 Rue de la Lauch, Pfaffenheim, 68250 Rouffach; tel. 89 49 62 92 ☒ By appt.

JEAN SCHAETZEL★★★

| ☐ | 0.6 ha | 5000 | **3** **D** **◖** |

A Gewürztraminer from clay-limestone soil. Well forward on the nose: spicy, with a dominant noTe of roses. On the palate develops attractive flavour of great richness and complexity. Good body combining light acidity and agreeable suppleness. Under good conditions could be kept for twenty years. (1983) ✔ All Alsace grape varieties. ♦ Jean Schaetzel, 3 Rue de la 53ème DB, 68770 Ammerschwihr; tel. 89 47 11 39 � By appt.

JOSEPH SCHAFFAR★

| ☐ | 7 ha | 5200 | **3** **D** ⦿ ↓ |

A little reserved on the nose but beautifully young on the palate. Full bodied and elegant. Will develop, but requires a little patience. (1983) ♦ Joseph Schaffar, 125 Rue Clemenceau, 68000 Wintzenheim; tel. 89 27 00 25 ☿ By appt.

CHARLES SCHLERET★

| ☐ | 1.8 ha | 15000 | **3** **D** ▮ ↓ |

Lovely golden colour with good, fruity nose. Well balanced but lightly built. Already well developed; drink now. (1982) ✔ Muscat, Riesling, Sylvaner, Pinot Noir. ♦ Charles Schleret, 1 Route d'Ingersheim, 68230 Turckheim; tel. 89 27 06 09 ☿ By appt.

ROBERT SCHOFFIT

| ☐ | 2 ha | 16800 | **3** **D** ⦿ ↓ |

Lovely gold colour. Attractive, grapey nose but still rather closed up. Well made but a bit tough, although scents and flavours are beginning to develop. Could keep for several years without difficulty. (1981) ♦ Robert Schoffit, 27 Rue des Aubépines, 68000 Colmar; tel. 89 41 69 45 ☿ By appt.

PAUL SCHWACH
Cuvée Selectionée

| ☐ | 1.8 ha | 13000 | **4** **D** ▮ |

Taste indicates ripe grapes, although scents are still underdeveloped. A good example of this vintage, but lack of tannin means that the wine has no keeping properties. (1983) ♦ Paul Schwach, 30–32 Route de Bergheim, 68150 Ribeauvillé; tel. 89 73 62 73 ☿ By appt.

LOUIS SIFFERT ET FILS
Praelatenberg★★

| ☐ | 0.5 ha | 2400 | **5** **D** ⦿ ↓ |

Rich aromas and sweetness from the overripe grapes finely balanced in the course of long and careful vinification. Exceptional wine which will long continue to delight with foie gras or lobster. To be kept with confidence. (1983) ✔ Riesling, Pinot Noir, Tokay (Pinot Gris), Crémant d'Alsace. ♦ Louis Siffert et Fils, 16 Rout du Vin, 67600 Orschwiller; tel. 88 92 02 77 ☿ Daily. Closed Jan.

COOPERATIVE VINICOLE DE SIGOLSHEIM
Sélection de Grains Nobles★★★

| ☐ | 2 ha | 3500 | **6** **D** ▮ ↓ |

The grapes were picked one at a time to select those with 'noble rot'. This wine is required to have a potential alcohol level of 279 g of sugar per litre. Very long-lasting on the nose. A great wine

for the real connoisseur. Worth keeping for a good fifteen years. (1983) ✔ Crémant, Pinot Blanc, Riesling, Gewürztraminer, Pinot Noir. ♦ Coop. Vinicole de Sigolsheim, Sigolsheim 68240 Kaysersberg; tel. 89 47 12 55 ☿ By appt.

PIERRE SPARR ET FILS
Mambourg Vendanges Tardives

| ☐ | 4 ha | 24000 | **5** **D** ▮ ↓ |

Beautiful colour; nose promises well, but still marked by rot on the late-picked grapes. Powerful in the mouth, with good balance of residual sugar and pleasant acidity. Put away for a while to allow the wine's quality to develop. (1981) ✔ Riesling Altenbourg, Tokay Cuvée Particulière-(Pinot Gris) 1982, Pinot Noir Cuvée Particulière. ♦ Pierre Sparr et Fils, 2 Rue de la Première Armée, 68240 Sigolsheim; tel. 89 78 24 22 ☿ By appt.

J.-P. ET D. SPECHT★

| ☐ | 0.6 ha | 5400 | **3** **D** ⦿ |

Dry, typical Gewürztraminer with well-developed nose, demonstrating excellent background. Well made, will be even better after two years in bottle. (1982) ✔ All the Alsace grape varieties and Crémant. ♦ Jean-Paul et Denis Specht, 2 Rue des Eglises, 68630 Mittelwihr; tel. 89 47 90 85 ☿ By appt.

BERNARD STAEHLE

| ☐ | 0.5 ha | 9800 | **3** **D** ⦿ ↓ |

Still closed in on the nose, and not much taste; grapes might have suffered from drought. Could still develop favourably. (1983) ♦ Bernard Staehle, 15 Rue Clemenceau, Wintzenheim, 68000 Colmar; tel. 89 27 39 02 ☿ By appt.

CAVE VINICOLE DE TRAENHEIM★

| ☐ | 70 ha | 72000 | **3** **D** ▮ ↓ |

Lovely colour. Good, lasting, spicy fruitiness on the nose. Good body with well-developed scents and bouquet. Light acidity and fullness; good, well balanced and promises to keep well. (1983) ♦ Cave Vinicole de Traenheim, Route de Scharrachbergheim, 67310 Traenheim; tel. 88 50 66 21 ☿ By appt.

F.-E. TRIMBACH
Cuvée des Seigneurs de Ribeaupierre

| ☐ | 3 ha | 2400 | **5** **D** ▮ |

Good colour and delicate, spicy fruit on the nose. Complex palate typical of this vintage. Perfectly balanced. Good body and lasting, light acidity, which will let it develop. (1981) ♦ F.-E. Trimbach, 68150 Ribeauvillé; tel. 89 73 60 30 ☿ No visitors.

CAVE VINICOLE DE TURCKHEIM
Baron de Turckheim★★

| ☐ | 12 ha | 108000 | **3** **D** ▮ ↓ |

Refined, elegant, fruity Gewürztraminer with smooth bouquet. (1983) ♦ Cave Vinicole de Turckheim, 68230 Turckheim; tel. 89 27 06 25 ☿ Daily 8.00–12.00/14.00–18.00.

DOMAINE AU VIEUX PRESSOIR

| ☐ | 3ha | 25000 | **3** **D** ⚲ |

Well developed and full bodied, very rich and high in alcohol. Fruit needs to open out; acidity hidden at present. (1983) ✔ Riesling Wiebelsberg, Sylvaner, Pinot Blanc, Pinot Noir.
↻ Marcel Schlosser, 5–7 Rue des Forgerons, 67140 Andlau; tel. 88 08 03 26 ⵣ By appt.

CHARLES WANTZ★★

| ☐ | 2ha | 10200 | **4** **D** ⊪ ⚲ |

Star-bright in the glass. Spicy fruitiness characteristic of a Gewürztraminer that has had a few years in bottle. Marvellous mouth-filling quality. Full body; strong and flexible. Very well-balanced. (1979) ✔ Sylvaner, Riesling, Tokay (Pinot Gris), Pinot Noir, Muscat.
↻ Charles Wantz, Vins d'Alsace, 67140 Barr; tel. 88 08 90 44 ⵣ Mon.–Fri. 8.00–12.00/14.00–18.00. Sat. 8.00–12.00.

COOPERATIVE VINICOLE DE WESTHALTEN *Vorburg*

| ☐ | 6ha | 85000 | **4** **D** ▮ |

Very good colour; easy, fruity, spicy nose. Flavours derive from the limestone soil. Well made with all elements combining well to make full-bodied, attractive wine. Drink from now onwards. (1983)
↻ Cave Coop. Vinicole de Westhalten, 68111 Westhalten; tel. 89 47 01 27 ⵣ By appt.

ALSACE WILLM *Clos Gaensbroennel*

| ☐ | 8.6ha | 36000 | **3** **D** ▮ ⊪ ⚲ |

Attractive gold colour and very inviting bouquet. Rich and clean tasting on the palate, with character and fruit. (1983) ✔ Gewürztraminer Médaillé, Gewürztraminer Cuvée Emile Willm, Gewürztraminer Clos Gaensbroennel.
↻ Alsace Willm, 32 Rue du Dr-Sultzer, 67140 Barr; tel. 88 08 19 11 ⵣ Mon–Sat. 8.00–12.00/ 14.00–18.00. Sun. 10.00–12.00/14.00–18.00.

FRANÇOIS WISCHLEN
Réserve Particulière

| ☐ | 60ha | 36000 | **4** **D** ⊪ |

Still young and closed-up, but will certainly improve as it develops. Clarity, body and fruit indicate it can be kept with confidence. (1983) ✔ Gewürztraminer.
↻ François Wschlen, 4 Rue de Soultzmatt, 68111 Westhalten; tel. 89 47 01 24 ⵣ By appt.

WUNSCH-MANN *Steingrubler*

| ☐ | 1ha | 6800 | **3** **D** ▮ ⚲ |

Straw-coloured wine. Good body and aromatic nose make it easy and charming. Reaching maturity in bottle; drink now. (1982)
↻ *MM.* Wunsch et Mann, 2 Rue des Clefs, 68920 Wettoslheim; tel. 89 41 39 63 ⵣ Mon.–Sat. 8.00– 12.00/13.30–18.00. Sun. 15.00–18.00.

ZEYSSOLFF★

| ☐ | 2ha | 24000 | **4** **D** ⊪ ⚲ |

Amber colour with delicate, elegant nose. Very typical varietal character. Fills the mouth with well-developed scents and flavours. Well balanced and straightforward. (1983) ✔ Pinot Blanc, Pinot Noir, Tokay (Pinot Gris), Muscat.

↻ Zeyssolff SA, 156 Rue Principale, 67140 Gertwiller; tel. 88 08 90 08 ⵣ By appt.

A. ZIMMERMAN ET FILS★★

| ☐ | 1ha | 6000 | **3** **D** ⊪ ⚲ |

Very good example of this vintage from a sandy soil. Delicate, aristocratic scents. Tastes delicious, with a firm grapey character and body. At its peak. Recommended for foie gras and Alsace-style fruit tarts. (1976) ✔ Sylvaner, Muscat, Pinot Noir, Tokay, Gewürztraminer.
↻ GAEC A. Zimmermann et Fils, 3 Grand'-Rue, Orschwiller, 67600 Sélestat; tel. 88 92 08 49 ⵣ By appt.

JULES ZIMMERMANN

| ☐ | 2ha | 7200 | **3** **D** ⊪ ⚲ |

Delicate, dry and developing a certain suppleness. Very good fruit on the nose. Well made with well-developed bouquet on the palate, confirming limestone soil origins. (1983) ✔ Riesling, Pinot Noir, Sylvaner, Muscat.
↻ Jules Zimmermann, 13 Rue des Prêtres, 68570 Soultzmatt; tel. 89 47 02 69 ⵣ By appt.

Alsace Tokay – Pinot Gris

Tokay d'Alsace, the local name for Pinot Gris for 400 years now, is often the cause of some surprise. In fact, this grape variety has nothing to do with the famous Tokay wines of Eastern Hungary. Legend has it that it was brought from Hungary by General L. de Schwendi, who owned many vineyards in Alsace. However, like all the Pinots, it probably originated from the lands once owned by the duchy of Burgundy.

Pinot Gris vines account for only 5 per cent of production but they can produce a heady and very full-bodied wine that is quite capable of accompanying meat dishes as an alternative to red wine. A sumptuous Alsace Tokay, such as the outstanding 1983, is one of the best partners of foie gras. Apart from the excellent 1983, recent vintages of note are the fine 1981 and good 1979.

CAVES JEAN-BAPTISTE ADAM★★

| ☐ | 2ha | 16800 | **4** **D** ▮ ⚲ |

Pale gold in colour with a mild, refined nose. Excellent bouquet and complex aromas on the palate. Wonderful velvet texture and good acidity create an impression of elegance and harmony. Plenty of life ahead. (1981)
↻ Les Caves Jean-Baptiste Adam, 5 Rue de l'Aigle, 68770 Ammerschwihr; tel. 89 78 23 21 ⵣ No visitors.

COOPERATIVE VINICOLE DE BEBLENHEIM★★

☐ 10ha 132000 **3 D ⬛ ↓**

A lovely, smooth wine with delicate and subtle fruitiness and fragrant Tokay aromas. Fine, rounded body, firm structure and real breeding. Excellent, refreshing acidity and youthful character. Would do credit to any table. (1983) ✔ Sylvaner, Pinot Blanc, Riesling, Muscat, Gewürztraminer.
� Coop. Vinicole de Beblenheim, 14 Rue de Hoen, 68980 Beblenheim; tel. 89 47 90 02 ☨ By appt. Closed Jan.–Feb.

PAUL BECK *Pinot Gris Schlossberg*

☐ 6ha 12960 **3 D ⬛ ↓**

Already very mature and extremely forward for the vintage. Full, robust flavour. Good with game birds, meat pie and foie gras. (1982) ✔ Sylvaner, Pinot Noir, Pinot Blanc, Muscat, Riesling.
➤ Paul Beck, 1 Rue Clemenceau, 67650 Dambach-la-Ville; tel. 88 92 41 17 ☨ By appt.

LES VIGNERONS DE BENNWIHR

☐ 4ha 28200 **3 D ⬛ ↓**

Flavour well-marked by the wine's clay-limestone origin. Mild, fruity nose with rich vinosity and Tokay fragrance. Well-structured on the palate, with a wonderful velvet texture and pleasant acidity. Would go well with foie gras and pâté de campagne. (1983)
➤ Les Vignerons de Bennwihr, 3 Rue de Général-de-Gaulle, 68630 Bennwihr; tel. 89 47 90 27 ☨ By appt.

ANDRE BLANCK ET FILS

☐ 0.5ha 4200 **3 D ⬛**

Deep, golden yellow with green highlights. Smoky Tokay fruit nose. Scented, mouth-filling flavour and good structure. Its strong alcohol content gives the wine a certain harshness which is characteristic of the 1983 vintage. (1983) ✔ Sylvaner, Pinot Blanc, Gewürztraminer Schlossberg Grand Cru, Riesling Schlossberg Grand Cru, Pinot Noir.
➤ Andre Blanck et Fils, Cour des Chevaliers de Malte, 68240 Kientzheim; tel. 89 78 24 72 ☨ By appt.

CLAUDE BLEGER

☐ 0.6ha 5400 **2 D ⬛**

Very undeveloped aromas with a hint of fruit and varietal character. Strong, robust flavour, however, well-suited to game pâté or foie gras. (1983)
➤ Claude Bleger, 23 Grand-Rue, Orschwiller, 67600 Selestat; tel. 88 92 32 56 ☨ Mon.–Sat. 8.00–12.00/14.00–20.00, Sun. 14.00–18.00.

CAVE VINICOLE DE DAMBACH-LA-VILLE *Cuvée les Guillemettes*

☐ 3.3ha 32400 **3 D ⬛ ⬛ ↓**

Spicy, fragrant note coming from the rocky sandstone soil. Smooth, fat flavour on the palate. Already quite mature because it has been aged in wood, but plenty of life ahead of it. (1983) ✔ Tokay (medal).
➤ Cave Vinicole de Dambach-la-Ville, 67650 Dambach-la-Ville; tel. 88 92 40 03 ☨ By appt.

UNION VINICOLE DIVINAL

☐ 2.5ha 16800 **3 D ⬛ ↓**

A beautifully coloured wine with sparkling highlights, revealing a very delicate typical Tokay fruitiness on the nose. Still rather reserved flavour in the mouth. (1983) ✔ All Alsace grape varieties.
➤ Union Vinicole Divinal, 30 Rue du Général Leclerc, 67210 Obernai; tel. 88 95 61 18 ☨ By appt.

JEAN-PAUL ECKLE★★

☐ 29ha 3600 **3 D ⬛ ↓**

Fine colour. Rich, smoky, fruity nose typical of the Tokay. Full-bodied yet elegant scented flavour. Good with white meat and foie gras. (1983)
➤ Jean-Paul Eckle, 29 Grand-Rue, 68230 Katzenthal; tel. 89 27 09 41 ☨ Mon.–Fri. 9.00–19.00, Sat. 9.00–18.00, Sun. 10.00–12.00/14.00–17.00.

CAVE VINICOLE D'EGUISHEIM *Cuvée du Schlossherr*★★

☐ 17.2ha 150000 **4 D ⬛ ⬛ ↓**

An extremely rich wine with a floral nose, and full, voluptuous flavour. Worthy of comparison with the greatest Pinot Gris from exceptional years. Exceptionally robust, and equally good with foie gras or white meat. Its balance will allow it to keep for several decades. (1983) ✔ Tokay (medal), Tokay Sigillé Confrérie-St-Etienne.
➤ Cave Vinicole d'Eguisheim, 6 Grand-Rue, 68420 Eguisheim; tel. 89 41 11 06 ☨ By appt.

JEAN FREYBURGER

☐ 0.35ha 2400 **3 D ⬛**

Typical Tokay fragrance. Firm, solid flavour, but decidedly lacking in roundness. These characteristics owe as much to the clay-limestone soil as to the vintage. (1982)
➤ Jean Freyburger, 7 Place du Général-de-Gaulle, Wettolsheim, 68000 Colmar; tel. 89 41 39 15 ☨ By appt.

ARMAND GILG ET FILS★

☐ 1.5ha 10000 **3 D ⬛ ⬛**

Very fruity and full-bodied, from a south-facing limestone slope. Delightful, opulent flavour. Already very good with foie gras, red meats and game, but will be even fuller in a few years. (1983) ✔ Sylvaner Zotzenberg, Riesling Zotzenberg, Muscat Klevner, Gewürztraminer, Pinot Noir.
➤ Armand Gilg et Fils, 2, Route Rotland (Route du Vin), 67140 Mittelbergheim; tel. 88 08 92 76 ☨ By appt., Mon.–Sat. 8.00–12.00/13.30–17.30, Sun. 10.00–12.00/14.00–17.00.

CAVE VINICOLE DE HUNAWIHR *Domaine de Windsbuhl*

☐ 5ha 48000 **4 D ⬛**

Brilliant, clear colour, and bouquet of light fruit, combining generous alcohol and a fragrance of Tokay grapes. Very rich in flavour, but still young and undeveloped. This wine has good acidity which will allow it to go on improving for some fifteen years. (1983) ✔ Riesling, Gewürztraminer, Domaine de Windsbuhl.
➤ Cave Vinicole de Hunawihr, 68150 Hunawihr; tel. (89) 73 61 67 ☨ By appt.

COOPERATIVE VINICOLE D'INGERSHEIM**

☐ 5ha 27000 `4 D `

Fine amber colour; delicate but rather undeveloped aromas. Good structure and rich, smooth flavour marked by the clay-limestone soil. Sustained but pleasant acidity. Should make an excellent bottle in a few years. (1983)
☛ Cooperative Vinicole d'Ingersheim, 1 Rue Clemenceau, 68000 Ingersheim; tel. 89 27 05 96 ☍ By appt.

CAMILLE KUBLER ET FILS

☐ 0.31ha 3000 `3 D `

This wine, coming from a well-exposed limestone vineyard, can be tasted in the estate's eighteenth-century cellar. Fine colour, but rather undeveloped bouquet. Similarly reserved flavour on the palate. However, good balance and body suggest it should develop well. (1982) ✔ Gewürztraminer, Pinot Noir, Riesling, Pinot Blanc, Sylvaner.
☛ Camille Kubler et Fils, 103 Rue de la Valle Vallée, 68570 Soultzmatt; tel. 89 47 00 75 ☍ By appt.

KUENTZ-BAS *Cuvée Caroline*

☐ 0.5ha 3600 `5 D `

A fine amber yellow in colour, this wine displays mild, soft fruit aromas, with the extra ripeness of the late-harvested grapes showing through. Rich, full-bodied flavour with a wonderful velvet texture. Ideal with foie gras. (1981) ✔ Crémant d'Alsace.
☛ Kuentz-Bas, 14 Route du Vin, Husseren-les-Châteaux, 68420 Herrlisheim; tel. 89 49 30 24 ☍ By appt.

JEAN-PAUL MAULER*

☐ 3ha 27600 `3 D `

Grown on clay-limestone soil, this wine has an authoritative, vigorous flavour. Should be kept. With further bottle age it would suit white meat and other full-flavoured dishes. A powerful, four-square wine. (1983) ✔ Sylvaner, Riesling, Muscat, Gewürztraminer, Pinot Noir.
☛ Jean-Paul Mauler, 3 Place des Cigognes, 68630 Mittelwihr; tel. 89 47 93 23 ☍ By appt. Closed second two weeks in Sept.

L. ET A. MITTNACHT*

☐ 0.38ha 3600 `4 D `

A well developed, highly distinctive nose, given its character by the vineyard soil. Robust, well-balanced flavour and fine acidity. Needs time to round out and develop the bouquet. A wine for special occasions. (1983) ✔ Crémant, Pinot Noir, Riesling, Gewürztraminer, Riesling.
☛ L. et A. Mittnacht, Hunawihr, 68130 Ribeauvillé; tel. 89 73 62 01 ☍ By appt.

M. MURE *Clos St-Landelin*

☐ 2ha 12000 `4 D `

Good colour for a 1982. Discreet nose with Tokay fragrance. Good structure, but the flavour is still rather undeveloped. Dry with slightly harsh acidity; needs to mature for a few years. (1982) ✔ Sylvaner, Gewürztraminer, Riesling, Muscat, Pinot Noir.
☛ Muré, Route du Vin, 68350 Rouffach; tel. 89 49 62 19 ☍ By appt.

COOPERATIVE D'ORSCHWILLER-KINTZHEIM *Les Faîtieres***

☐ 5ha 36000 `3 D `

Subtle, delicate fruitiness on the nose. Well-structured body on the palate. A full, rich wine with a marked flavour coming from its clay-limestone soil. Needs to age for a few years. (1983)
☛ Coop. d'Orschwiller-Kintzheim, 67600 Selestat; tel. 88 92 09 87 ☍ By appt.

CAVE VINICOLE DE PFAFFENHEIM
Steiner

☐ 10ha 108000 `3 D `

Very fine yellow-amber colour and notably smoky nose. Full bodied and admirably round on the palate. A very good bottle. (1983)
☛ Cave Vinicole de Pfaffenheim, RN 83, 68250 Pfaffenheim; tel. 89 49 61 08 ☍ By appt.

CAVE COOPERATIVE DE RIBEAUVILLE *Clos du Zannacker**

☐ 1ha 12000 `4 D `

An exceptional wine from a vineyard with a history going going back to the ninth century. Strongly marked by the vineyard soil and needs to be savoured slowly to show its full qualities – as it was for centuries in noble and princely courts throughout the Rhine valley. (1981)
☛ Cave Coop. de Ribeauvillé, 2 Route de Colmar, 68150 Ribeauvillé; tel. 89 73 61 80 ☍ By appt., Mon.-Fri. 8.00–12.00/14.00–18.00. Sat., Sun. 10.–12.00/14.00–17.00. Closed weekends Jan.–Mar.

CAVE COOPERATIVE DE RIBEAUVILLE

☐ 10ha 72000 `3 D `

Strong, rather 'hot' flavour despite the hint of acidity which gives it balance. Fruity and very typical of the grape variety; an ideal wine for buffet lunches, or parties. (1982)
☛ Cave Coop. de Ribeauvillé, 2 Route de Colmar, 68150 Ribeauvillé; tel. 89 73 61 80 ☍ By appt., Mon.-Fri. 8.00–12.00/14.00–18.00, Sat., Sun. 10.00–12.00/14.00–17.00. Closed weekends Jan.–Mar.

JOSEPH RIEFLE ET FILS
*Ambassadeur Rieflé***

☐ 1ha 9000 `3 D `

The heavy clay-limestone soil is perfectly apparent in this wine. Lovely, slightly golden-yellow colour. Robust, full-bodied, fat flavour. Lingering scented finish. An excellent choice for laying down for a few years. ✔ All Alsace wines. (1983)
☛ Joseph Rieflé et Fils, 11 Place de la Mairie, 68250 Pfaffenheim; tel. (89) 49 62 82 ☍ By appt. Mon.-Sat. 9.00–12.00/14.00–18.00, Sun. 10.00–12.00/14.00–17.00. Closed Jan.–Feb.

WILLY ROLLI-EDEL

☐ 1ha 9600 `3 D `

Lovely amber colour and taut, well-balanced flavour. Great finesse on the nose and very pleasant on the palate. Will develop well. Its delicate harmony would suit baekaoffa, meat pie or roast meats. (1983)

☞ Willy Rolli-Edel, 5 Rue de l'Eglise, 68590 Rorschwihr; tel. 89 73 63 26 ☎ By appt. Closed during grape harvest.

SOCIETE VINICOLE SAINTE-ODILE
Clos Sainte-Odile★

☐	2.04 ha	9600	🟦 D ⛁ ⬇

A beautifully coloured wine grown on the upper slopes of Obernai. Characteristic Tokay aromas of fruit and rich vinosity. Firm, round, mouth-filling flavour, and fine all-round balance. A splendidly supple and harmonious wine. (1983) ✔ Riesling, Gewürztraminer, Crémant.

☞ Société Vinicole Ste-Odile, 3 Rue de la Gare, 67210 Obernai; tel. 88 95 50 23 ☎ By appt.

RENE SCHAEFLE★

☐	0.34 ha	3600	🟦 D ⛁

Characteristic Tokay fragrance. Smooth and full-bodied with some acidity. May be kept for a few years. (1982) ✔ Sylvaner, Pinot Blanc, Muscat, Gewürztraminer, Pinot Noir.

☞ René Schaefle, 4 Rue de la Lauch, Pfaffenheim, 68250 Rouffach; tel. 89 49 62 92 ☎ By appt.

JEAN SCHAETZEL★

☐	0.3 ha	2400	🟦 D ⛁

Pretty colour with sustained bouquet marked by characteristic Tokay fragrance. Light-textured flavour with complex aromas and smooth finish due to the residual sugar content. A complete wine. (1983) ✔ Riesling, Gewürztraminer.

☞ Jean Schaetzel, 3 Rue de la 5ème DB, 68770 Ammerschwihr; tel. 89 47 11 39 ☎ By appt.

SICK ET DREYER★★

☐	0.8 ha	4800	🟦 D ⛁

Mild fruit aromas with rich alcoholic undertone. Good structure, with added roundness coming from the residual sugar but reasonable acid support. A wine which needs to age for a few years. (1983)

☞ R. Sick et P. Dreyer, 9 Route de Kientzheim, 68770 Ammerschwihr; tel. 89 47 11 31 ☎ By appt.

FERNAND SIEGLER-KUSTER★★

☐	5.5 ha	48000	🟦 D ▮

Still very young, this wine has a very delicate nose. Good structure but needs time to reach its full potential. (1983) ✔ Riesling, Muscat, Pinot Noir, Sylvaner, Pinot Blanc.

☞ Fernand Siegler-Kuster, 8 Rue des Merles, 68630 Mittelwihr; tel. (89) 47 93 07 ☎ By appt., Mon.–Sat. 9.00–12.00/14.00–18.00, Sun. 10.00–12.00/14.00–17.00.

CAVE VINICOLE DE TRAENHEIM★★

☐	15 ha	72000	🟦 D ⛁

Beautiful amber-yellow colour. Mild fruit aromas characteristic of the Tokay grape. Substantial, well-rounded flavour with a silky texture. Still seems very young. Needs time to reach its peak. (1983)

☞ Cave Vinicole de Traenheim, Route de Scharrachbergheim, 67310 Traenheim; tel. 88 50 66 21 ☎ By appt.

F.-E. TRIMBACH★

☐	0.5 ha	3600	🟦4 D ⛁ ⬇

Smart amber colour and fine, discreet fruit on the nose along with the typical smokiness of the Pinot Gris. Full bodied and without great length on the palate but supple and well balanced overall. Drink now. (1981) ✔ The full range of Alsace wines.

☞ F.-E. Trimbach, 68150 Ribeauvillé; tel. 89 73 60 30 ☎ No visitors.

CAVE VINICOLE DE TURCKHEIM
Brand

☐	0.5 ha	3600	🟦4 D ▮

Deep amber-gold in colour. Discreet fruity fragrance with a firm alcoholic note. Fat, heavy, perfumed flavour on the palate. Will keep for a very long time and improve in bottle. (1982)

☞ Cave Vinicole de Turckheim, 68230 Turckheim; tel. 89 27 06 25 ☎ Daily 8.00–12.00/14.00–18.00.

CAVE VINICOLE DE TURCKHEIM
Cuvée Prestige

☐	2 ha	14400	🟦 D ▮

A nice wine with pleasant, reserved aromas and silky, beautifully rounded flavour. An ideally versatile partner for any fine food. (1983)

☞ Cave Vinicole de Turckheim, 68230 Turckheim; tel. 89 27 06 25 ☎ Daily 8.00–12.00/14.00–18.00. Closed mornings in winter.

CAVE COOPERATIVE DE WESTHALTEN★

☐	11.5 ha	70500	🟦 D ▮

Fine, deep, golden colour and mild fruit bouquet. Strong, smooth taste with typical varietal aromas. Finely-tuned harmony with the potential to go on improving for up to twenty years. (1983)

☞ Cave Coop. de Westhalten, 68111 Westhalten; tel. 89 47 01 27 ☎ By appt.

FRANÇOIS WISCHLEN

☐	40 ha	36000	🟦 D ⛁

Still rather dumb; bouquet as yet undeveloped, but the class of the vineyard and the firm-structured flavour and underlying acidity should persuade one to be patient. (1983) ✔ Riesling, Gewürztraminer, Pinot Noir, Muscat, Crémant.

☞ François Wischlen, 4 Rue de Soutzmatt, 68111 Westhalten; tel. 88 47 01 24 ☎ By appt.

A. ZIMMERMANN ET FILS★★

☐	0.9 ha	8400	🟦 D ⛁

Although from the 1979 vintage, this Tokay is already beginning to develop a fine mature bouquet. Still very firm on the palate due to its acidity. A rich, full-bodied wine which can still be kept. (1979) ✔ The full range of Alsace wines.

☞ MM. Zimmermann et Fils, 3 Grand-Rue, 67600 Sélestat; tel. 88 92 08 49 ☎ By appt.

Alsace Pinot Noir

Alsace is known above all for its white wines, but few people realize that during the Middle Ages its red wines were also extremely important. After a period of near-total eclipse, the best red grape variety of the north, the Pinot Noir, is now being revived and already represents 6 per cent of the total Alsace crop.

At present it is the rosé wine made from this grape that is best known; it is dry and fruity and, like most rosé wines, good with a whole range of dishes. However, a true red Alsace wine made from Pinot Noir is beginning to gain the recognition it deserves.

CAVES JEAN-BAPTISTE ADAM*

■　　　　　6 ha　4800　　4 D 🛒 ⬇

Colour of faded tiles. Delicate, slightly woody nose reminiscent of raspberries. Well made, relatively easy to drink and well balanced. Has lasted well for a 1982. A high-class wine, perfect with beef. (1982)
🍷 Caves Jean-Baptiste Adam, 5 Rue de l'Aigle, 68770 Ammerschwihr; tel. 89 78 23 21 ⊻ No visitors.

COOPERATIVE VINICOLE D'ANDLAU *Rouge d'Ottrott*

■　　　　1.3 ha　8500　　3 D 🛒 ⬇

Strong red colour. Plenty of character; supple and full-bodied. Aromas of truffles and raspberries combine with light, pleasant acidity. Needs a few more years in bottle. (1983)
🍷 Coop. Vinicole d'Andlau, 15 Avenue des Vosges, 67140 Barr; tel. 88 08 90 53 ⊻ By appt. Mon.–Fri.

J.-PH. ET M. BECKER**

■　　　　1.2 ha　12000　　3 D ⬤ ⬇

Vermilion colour. Very attractive, grapey nose. Good body and just enough acidity. A seductive, well-made, clean and well balanced wine. (1983)
✔ Riesling, Tokay (Pinot Gris), Muscat, Gewürztraminer.
🍷 J.-Ph. and M. Becker, 2 Route d'Ostheim, Zellenberg, 68340 Riquwihr; tel. 89 47 90 16 ⊻ By appt. Closed during harvest.

LES VIGNERONS DE BENNWIHR*

■　　　　18 ha　96000　　3 D 🛒 ⬇

Lovely bright-red colour and good, grapey nose with hint of raspberries. Powerful, full bodied but slightly bitter; although full on the palate, still some way to go. Keep for a few years; will develop well. (1983)
🍷 Les Vignerons de Bennwihr, 3 Rue de Général-de-Gaulle, 68630 Bennwihr; tel. 89 47 90 27 ⊻ Daily 9.00–11.30/14.30–17.30.

CAVE VINICOLE DE DAMBACH-LA-VILLE*

▱　　　　9.9 ha　97584　　3 D 🛒 ⬤ ⬇

Good, bright colour. Pleasant nose and slight flavour of raspberries. Recommended for charcuterie and roast meats. (1983) ✔ Pinot Noir Médaillé, Pinot Noir Cuvée des Guillemettes.
🍷 Cave Vini. de Dambach-la-Ville 67650 Dambach-la-Ville; tel. 88 92 40 03 ⊻ By appt. Closed Sun.

JEAN-PIERRE DIRLER

■　　　　0.55 ha　4800　　3 D 🛒 ⬤ ⬇

Beautiful colour. Nose marked by delicacy, fruit and fragrance of the Alsace Pinot Noir. Well balanced but rather short in the finish. (1983)
🍷 Jean-Pierre Dirler, Bergholtz, 68500 Guebwiller; tel. 89 76 91 00 ⊻ By appt. Mon.–Fri. 8.00–12.00/14.00–18.00.

UNION VINICOLE DIVINAL
*Rouge d'Ottrott**

■　　　　1.5 ha　8400　　3 D 🛒 ⬇

Good, grapey nose with light hints of raspberries. Lovely deep-red colour. Nicely made with slight bitterness masked by touch of residual sugar, making a well-balanced wine overall. Will keep for many years. (1983)
🍷 Union Vinicole Divinal, 30 Rue du Général Leclerc, 67210 Obernai; tel. 88 95 61 18 ⊻ By appt. Mon.–Fri.

CAVE VINICOLE D'EGUISHEIM**

■　　　25.3 ha　216000　　3 D 🛒 ⬤ ⬇

From limestone soil, and made slowly over a ten to twelve-day period, which gives the dark colour. Eight to ten months' ageing in oak barrels ensures delicacy and subtlety. A very pleasant wine which will age well. (1983) ✔ Pinot Noir Médaillé, Pinot Noir Cuvée du Prince Hugo, Pinot Noir Sigillé Confrérie St-Etienne.
🍷 Cave Vinicole d'Eguisheim, 6 Grand'-Rue, 68420 Eguisheim; tel. 89 41 11 06 ⊻ By appt. Closed Sun.

ROMAIN FRITSCH *Steinklotzler*

▱　　　　3 ha　12000　　3 D 🛒 ⬤ ⬇

Light red, almost rosé, in colour, from a particular type of Pinot Noir related to the *vorloauf* rosé. Good nose; elegant and delicate on the palate. Finishes well. Worth trying for its curiosity value. (1983)
🍷 Romain Fritsch, 49 Rue du Général-de-Gaulle, 67520 Marlenheim; tel. 88 87 51 23 ⊻ By appt. Mon.–Sat. 8.00–12.00/13.00–17.00. Sun. 10.00–12.00.

DOMAINE ANDRE GRESSER
Andlau Brandhof

■　　　64 ha　202332　　4 D ⬤ ⬇

Strong colour and everything you could expect in a red wine. The tannic note on the palate suggests that it will keep very well to make a fine partner for red meat and game. (1983)
🍷 André et Remy Gresser, 2 Rue de l'Ecole, 67140 Andlau; tel. 88 08 95 88 ⊻ Daily 11.00–12.00/13.00–19.00.

LOUIS HAULLER**

▱　　　　0.4 ha　4000　　3 D ⬤ ⬇

Lovely colour, shading to deep red. Still reserved on the nose, but well balanced and typical of Pinot Noir. Powerful and long lasting; will develop into a good partner for game dishes. (1983) ✔ The whole range of Alsace wines.
🍷 Louis Hauller, 92 Rue du Maréchal-Foch, 67650 Dambach-la-Ville; tel. 88 92 41 19 ⊻ By appt., Tues.–Sun. 8.00–11.45/14.00–18.00. Closed beg. Sept.

COOPERATIVE VINICOLE D'INGERSHEIM

☑   8ha   81000   3 D ▄ ↓

Faded terracotta colour. Good on the nose, with delicate and well-developed scents and flavours. Good composition, typical of this vintage, with authentic Alsace character. Drink from now onwards. (1981)
➥ Coop. Vinicole d'Ingersheim, 1 Rue Clemenceau, 68000 Ingersheim; tel. 89 27 05 96 ⊺ By appt., daily 9.00–12.00/14.00–18.00.

ROBERT KARCHER*

■   0.48ha   4200   3 D ▄ ↓

Star-bright ruby red. Attractive, reserved fruitiness. Good body, elegance and delicacy typify the Alsace Pinot Noir. (1983)
➥ Robert Karcher, 11 Rue de l'Ours, 68000 Colmar; tel. 89 41 14 42 ⊺ By appt.

KUENTZ-BAS

■   1ha   6000   4 D ◑ ↓

Strikingly untypical, deep-red colour. Very good body on the palate but still closed up. Slightly bitter flavour and easy acidity mean it can be kept for ten years without difficulty; should improve. (1983)
➥ Kuentz-Bas, 14 Route du Vin, Husseren-les-Châteaux 68420 Herrlisheim-pres-Colmar; tel. 89 49 30 24 ⊺ By appt. Closed Sun.

LANDMANN-OSTHOLT*
Cave de la Vallis Praenobelis Pfingsthberg

■   0.35ha   3000   3 D ▄ ↓

Beautifully coloured, intense and full bodied. Nose still faint but certain to improve. (1982)
✔ Riesling, Gewürztraminer, Tokay (Pinot Gris), Crémant d'Alsace.
➥ M. et Mme. Landmann-Ostholt, 20 Rue de la Vallée, 68570 Soultzmatt; tel. 89 47 09 33 ⊺ By appt. Mon.–Sat. 9.30–12.00/14.00–18.00. Sun. 10.30–13.00. Closed Jan.

M. MURE *Clos Saint-Landelin**

■   2ha   12000   4 D ◑ ↓

Deep-red colour. Good, very typical grapey nose. Very well made, with strength and promise; requires few more years' ageing to mature. (1983)
➥ Muré, Route du Vin, 68250 Rouffach; tel 89 49 62 19 ⊺ By appt. Mon.–Sat.

CHATEAU D'ORSCHWIHR
*Rouge d'Alsace**

■   0.01ha   10000   3 D ◑ ↓

Ruby colour. Very good fruit on the nose. Straightforward, clean taste makes it easy to drink. A delicate and elegant wine. (1983)
✔ Riesling, Gewürztraminer, Muscat, Sylvaner.
➥ Martin Hartmann, 1 Rue du Centre, Orschwihr 68000 Gebwiller; tel. 89 76 89 30 ⊺ Daily 10.00–12.00/13.30–20.30.

COOPERATIVE D'ORSCHWILLER KINTZHEIM *Les Faitières**

■   5ha   33000   3 D ▄ ↓

Lovely ruby-red with easy, attractive nose. Flavour and aroma blend well. Made to last. (1983)
➥ Coop. d'Orschwiller-Kintzheim, 67600 Séles-

tat; tel. 88 92 09 87 ⊺ By appt. Mon.–Fri. 9.00–17.00.

CAVE COOPERATIVE DE RIBEAUVILLE *Rosé d'Alsace***

☑   12ha   96000   3 D ▄ ↓

From the choicest vineyards of Ribeauvillé comes a very great wine, more red than rosé. Full-bodied character, supremely Alsace, nevertheless recalls a very good Burgundy. Excellent with red meat. As a matter of interest, the cooperative at Ribeauvillé, founded in 1895, is the longest-established in France. (1983)
➥ Cave Coop. de Ribeauvillé, 22 Route de Colmar, 68150 Ribeauvillé; tel. 89 73 61 80 ⊺ By appt. Closed Sat., Sun. Jan.–Mar.

CHATEAU DE RIQUEWIHR

■   7ha   42000   3 D ◑ ↓

Very good ruby-red colour with typically grapey nose. Strong; high in alcohol. Good acidity and slight toughness due to tannin. Still young and worth keeping for a few years. (1983) ✔ Riesling, Gewürztraminer, Muscat, Tokay (Pinot Gris).
➥ Dopff et Irion, 68340 Riquewihr; tel. 89 47 92 51 ⊺ By appt. daily 9.00–12.00/13.00–19.00.

ROBERT SCHOFFIT**

■   0.3ha   3000   3 D ▄ ↓

Lovely colour. Attractive grapeyness on the nose. Well developed, easy to drink and finishes well with lingering flavours on the palate. Will please the most expert tasters. (1983)
➥ Robert Schoffit, 27 Rue des Aubépines, 68000 Colmar; tel. 89 41 69 45 ⊺ By appt., 8.00–12.00/14.00–19.00. Closed end of August.

PAUL SCHWACH *Cuvée Selectionée*

■   0.7ha   8000   3 D ▄ ↓

Lovely deep colour. Very attractive nose and easy on the palate, if a little too round. (1983)
➥ Paul Schwach, 30–32 Route de Bergheim, 68150 Ribeauvillé; tel. 89 73 62 73 ⊺ By appt. Closed Nov.–March.

DOMAINE AU VIEUX PRESSOIR

■   1ha   8400   3 D ◑ ↓

Fine strong colour and subtle bouquet. Very pleasant on the palate, but could do with a little more fullness. Will go well with white meat and cooked soft cheese. (1983)
➥ Marcel Schlosser, 5–7 Rue des Forgerons, 67140 Andlau; tel. 88 08 03 26 ⊺ By appt.

EDMOND VONVILLE★★

■	3.3 ha	30000	**3 D ▪ ↓**

This grower specializes in 'Rouge d'Ottrott', made expertly in oak barrels from excellent grapes. Good colour indicates the quality typical of the area (at the foot of Mont Ste-Odile). Powerful on the palate, with lots of staying power. Tannic character suggests that this wine should develop well. (1983) ✔ Riesling, Gewürztraminer, Sylvaner.
► E. Vonville et Fils, 4 Place des Tilleuls, 67530 Ottrott; tel. 89 95 80 25 ☂ By appt.

ALFRED WANTZ

■	1.5 ha	7800	**3 D ◑ ↓**

Pretty ruby colour. Full bodied on the palate, but short finish. Good, honest wine, even better after a year or two. (1983)
► Alfred Wantz, 3 Rue des Vosges, 67140 Mittelbergheim; tel. 88 08 91 43 ☂ By appt. Mon.–Sat. 9.00–12.00/14.00–18.00. Sun. 9.00–12.00.

ALSACE WILLM★

■	0.3 ha	1320	**3 D ▪ ◑ ↓**

Deep rosé type wine, with very subtle raspberry bouquet, giving great deal of quality. (1983)
► Alsace Willm, 32 Rue du Docteur Sultzer, 67140 Barr; tel. 88 08 19 11 ☂ By appt.

Alsace Grand Cru

In Alsace the notion of 'cru', or classification by vineyard, takes second place to the classification by grape variety. In this respect, Alsace wines differ from most other AOC regions. However, there have long been certain prestigious vineyards which seemed worthy of special mention. These include Rangen (Thann), Brand (Turckheim), Sporen (Riquewihr), Kirchberg de Barr and many others.

In an effort to promote the best vineyard sites the appellation Alsace Grand Cru was created in 1975. It is restricted to wines produced from the Gewürztraminer, Pinot Gris, Riesling and Muscat grapes and lays down very strict conditions concerning yield and minimum natural degree of alcohol. The final attributions of Grand Cru status have still to be completed, but the wines already produced under the new appellation are taking their place, alongside a small number of other prestige cuvées (such as those endorsed by the Confrérie St-Etienne), at the very pinnacle of Alsace wines.

Alsace Grand Cru Altenberg de Bergbieten

FREDERIC MOCHEL
Gewürztraminer★★

□	1.28 ha	8400	**3 D ◑**

The clay-limestone soil on which it is grown gives the wine an acidity which heightens its character. Attractive floral aromas, good balance, elegant style. Will age well, opening out further after a year in the bottle. (1983) ✔ Riesling, Muscat.
► Frédéric Mochel, 56 Rue Principale, Traenheim, 67310 Wasselonne; tel. 88 50 38 67 ☂ By appt.

FREDERIC MOCHEL *Riesling*★

□	2 ha	14400	**3 D ◑**

The old press dated 1669 is no longer in use, but wine still flows here. This Altenberg Riesling is grown on clay-limestone soil and has typically refined, if rather immature, aromas. Firm, fruity strike but a bit short; very good varietal character. (1983) ✔ Gewürztraminer, Muscat, Tokay (Pinot Gris).
► Frédéric Mochel, 56 Rue Principale, Traenheim, 67310 Wasselonne; tel. 88 50 38 67 ☂ By appt.

ROLAND SCHMITT *Riesling*

□	6 ha	48000	**3 D ◑**

Flowers bloom in a charming farmyard setting – a typical Alsace scene to be found at this friendly vineyard founded in 1610. The wine is particularly refined, with delicate aromas and fine assertive palate. Generous flavour, needing some bottle age to round out. (1983) ✔ Sylvaner, Muscat, Gewürztraminer, Pinot Noir, Edelzwicker.
► Roland Schmitt, 50 Rue des Vosges, 67130 Bergbieten; tel. 88 38 20 72 ☂ By appt. Closed 25 Aug.–10 Sept.

Alsace Grand Cru Altenberg de Bergheim

MARCEL DEISS ET FILS★★

□	1 ha	6000	**5 D ◑ ↓**

The Deiss family have long been vignerons (and, since 1774, have been bell founders too). Now they have vines in eight villages including the famous Grand Cru Altenberg vineyard with its very shallow pebbly alluvial soil. The wine it produces is markedly crisp and elegant, with a firm dry flavour very suitable for modern cuisine. Will keep well. (1982) ✔ Gewürztraminer Vendanges Tardives, Gewürztraminer Grand Cru Altenberg, Pinot Noir, Muscat.
► Deiss et Fils, 15 Route du Vin, 68150 Bergheim; tel. 89 73 63 37 ☂ Daily 9.00–12.00/13.30–19.00.

LOUIS FREYBURGER ET FILS
Gewürztraminer★

□	0.5 ha	3000	**3 D ◑**

Excellent grapes combining with a perfect terroir to make a great wine. Dry, very well-vinified and displaying fine varietal character. Made from destemmed grapes, the wine has good balance, although there is not much acidity. An enjoyable aperitif. (1983) ✔ Tokay (Pinot Gris), Pinot Noir, Muscat.
► Louis Freyburger et Fils, 1 Rue du Maire-Witzig, 68750 Bergheim; tel. 89 73 66 10 ☂ By appt.

CAVE DE KIENTZHEIM-KAYSERSBERG *Altenberg*★

| ☐ | 0.03 ha | 33 000 | **4** **D** **🍾** **❀** |

From well-exposed clay-limestone soil. Fine colour and pleasant nose showing well-developed Gewürztraminer fruit. Good structure on the palate with elegant aromas. Keep for a few years to let the wine improve still further. (1981)
❧ Cave de Kientzheim-Kaysersberg, 68240 Kientzheim; tel. 89 47 13 19; Mon.–Thur. 8.00–12.00/14.00–18.00; Fri. 8.00–12.00/14.00–17.00. 🍷 No visitors.

GUSTAVE LORENTZ
Gewürztraminer Vendanges Tardives★

| ☐ | 6 ha | 14 400 | **5** **D** **🍾** |

This late-picked wine is fairly high in alcohol but still preserves a floral, spicy, varietal bouquet, with a mineral note coming from the soil. A rich, fat wine, not unlike some great Sauternes. (1976)
✔ The full range of Alsace wines.
❧ Gustave Lorentz, 35 Grand Rue, 68750 Bergheim; tel. 89 73 63 08 🍷 By appt., Mon.–Sat. 7.30–12.00/13.30–17.00.

GUSTAVE LORENTZ *Riesling*★★★

| ☐ | 4 ha | 30 000 | **5** **D** **🍾** |

Three generations of the family manage this old-established property, founded in 1748. This wine is from an exceptional vintage and is impressively mature, with a very individual bouquet coming from the clay-limestone soil, which receives full sun. Rich, sustained flavour with the ripe sweetness and typical acidity of this varietal in finely-tuned balance. The 1983 will develop identically; the 1979 and 1981 vintages will have a broadly similar but less assertive character. (1976) ✔ The full range of Alsace wines.
❧ Gustave Lorentz, 35 Grand-Rue, 68750 Bergheim; tel. 89 73 63 08 🍷 Mon.–Sat. 7.30–12.00/13.30–17.00.

Alsace Grand Cru Altenberg de Wolxheim

FRANCOIS MUHLBERGER *Riesling*★★

| ☐ | 2 ha | 13 200 | **3** **D** **❀** |

Mature aromas somewhat lacking in character. Elegant, round flavour. However, this Riesling will not keep very long and should be drunk without further delay. (1982)
❧ François Muhlberger, 1 Rue de Strasbourg, 67120 Wolzheim; tel. 88 38 10 33 🍷 By appt., daily 9.00–12.00/13.00–19.00.

Alsace Grand Cru Brand

ALBERT BOXLER ET FILS
Gewürztraminer★★

| ☐ | 10 ha | 72 000 | **3** **D** **🍾** **❀** |

Fine, fruity nose. Very firm structure on the palate but very undeveloped taste. A wine to lay down for ten years or so. (1983)
❧ Albert Boxler et Fils, 78 Rue des Trois Epis, 68230 Niedermohrschwihr; tel. 89 27 11 32 🍷 By appt.

CAVE VINICOLE DE TURCKHEIM
Gewürztraminer★★★

| ☐ | 4.5 ha | 30 000 | n/a **D** **🍾** |

The initially reserved fruit aromas develop wonderfully as soon as the wine is allowed to breathe. Great elegance and distinctive character are the hallmarks of this fine vineyard. A first-class wine, ideal as an aperitif. (1981)
❧ Cave Vinicole de Turckheim, 68230 Turckheim; tel. 89 27 06 25 🍷 Daily 8.00–12.00/14.00–18.00. Closed mornings in winter.

CAVE VINICOLE DE TURCKHEIM
Riesling★

| ☐ | 4 ha | 21 600 | **4** **D** **♨** |

A Riesling from the Grand Cru Brand vineyard showing breeding, fruit and very sound acidity, factors which will allow the wine to keep its characteristic crispness for a long time. A marvellous bottle. (1983)
❧ Cave Vinicole de Turckheim, 68230 Turckheim; tel. 89 27 06 25. 🍷 Daily 8.00–12.00/14.00–18.00. Closed mornings in winter.

Alsace Grand Cru Eichberg

DOPFF *Au Moulin Gewürztraminer*★

| ☐ | 3 ha | 9000 | **5** **D** **❀** **♨** |

From a vineyard at Turckheim characterized by a sandy soil of eroded granite. Beautiful, glistening, amber-gold appearance. Well developed and persistent fruit on the nose, a feature it owes to the soil. Firm, delicate, elegant flavour. Lovely velvety bouquet and aromas. Excellent with foie gras, and puddings that are not too sweet. (1981) ✔ Sylvaner, Tokay (Pinot Gris), Pinot Noir.
❧ Dopff, Au Moulin, 68340 Riquewihr; tel. (89) 47 92 23 🍷 By appt. Closed Sat. and Sun. 1 Nov.–31 Mar.

PAUL GINGLINGER *Gewürztraminer★*

| □ | 1.5 ha | 13 000 | 3 D ◐ ↓ |

The wine comes from a clay-limestone vineyard with an excellent south-easterly aspect, and has good late-harvest character. Despite the vintage the nose is still undeveloped. Very young on the palate, but with excellent structure and balance. This wine still has all its crispness and should be laid down for a few years. (1983) ✔ Riesling, 16y (Pinot Gris), Muscat, Pinot Noir.
➟ Paul Ginglinger, 8 Place Charles-de-Gaulle, 68420 Eguisheim; tel. 89 41 44 25 ☎ Mon.–Sat., 8.00–12.00/14.00–18.00.

Alsace Grand Cru Geisberg

J.-B. FALLER *Riesling★*

| □ | 1.03 ha | 9000 | 5 D ◐ |

This is produced by a very old family firm, which owns vineyards on the slopes of Geisberg, Kirchberg and Trottacker. Pure, well-developed aromas. It is at its peak, and should be drunk now to catch its full flavour and richness. (1981) ✔ Gewürztraminer Kirchberg, Muscat Kirchberg.
➟ Robert Fuller et Fils, 36 Grand-Rue, 68150 Ribeauvillé; tel. 89 73 60 47 ☎ By appt.

A. KIENTZLER *Riesling★★*

| □ | 1.3 ha | 9000 | 4 D ◐ |

The wines made here come from the Geisberg vineyard, which is characterized by very stony clay soil and plenty of sun. This very firm soil produces powerful slow-maturing wines. This is an outstanding example which should develop magnificently. Well-structured, pleasant, balanced taste with alcohol, acidity and fruit in perfect proportion. Will improve with age and may be laid down for many years with confidence. (1983)
➟ A. Kientzler, Route du Vin, 68150 Ribeauvillé; tel. 89 73 67 10 ☎ By appt.

Alsace Grand Cru Goldert

CAVE VINICOLE DE PFAFFENHEIM
Gewürztraminer★★

| □ | 5 ha | 54 000 | 4 D ◐ |

From a limestone soil vineyard facing east-south-east. Lovely gold-tinted, yellowy-green appearance with spicy fruit on the nose. The soil, vintage and late harvest are all evident in the body and aroma. A choice wine. (1982)
➟ Cave Vinicole de Pfaffenheim, 68250 Pfaffenheim; tel. 89 49 61 08 ☎ By appt.

Alsace Grand Cru Hatschbourg

JOSEPH CATTIN ET FILS
Tokay (Pinot Gris)★★

| □ | 1 ha | 4800 | 5 D ◐ ↓ |

The name of this vineyard was already well-known in the Middle Ages. Its soil is rather heavy and deep but well drained. The wine has a very characteristic, elegant nose. On the palate it has firm but very smooth flavour. An extremely rich wine and a typical example of the 1983 vintage with its high alcohol content. (1983) ✔ Muscat, Gewürztraminer, Riesling, Pinot Noir, Crémant.
➟ Joseph Cattin et Fils, 18 Rue Roger Fremeaux, 68420 Voegtlinshoffen; tel. 89 49 30 21 ☎ By appt.

Alsace Grand Cru Hengst

JEAN MEYER *Riesling★★*

| □ | 1.5 ha | 6000 | 5 D ◐ |

This Riesling does not qualify for the Vendanges Tardives appellation, but the grapes were picked on 28 November to ensure optimum ripeness while keeping the firm, dry character of the varietal. The wine has all the nobility of a great Rhine Riesling. (1979) ✔ Riesling les Pierrots, Pinot Auxerrois, Riesling Hengst, Gewürztraminer, Tokay (Pinot Gris).
➟ Jean Meyer et Fils, 76 Rue Clemenceau, Wintzenheim, 68000 Colmar; tel. 89 27 01 57 ☎ By appt.

DOMAINE ZIND-HUMBRECHT
Gewürztraminer★

| □ | 1.38 ha | 9000 | 4 D ◐ ↓ |

From a vineyard facing south and south-east with very stony clay soil. Fine golden-yellow in appearance. Mild aromas of fruit and spice. Firm, ripe flavour in the mouth. Dry, but full-bodied with a long, rich finish. (1982)
➟ Léonard Humbrecht, Wintzenheim, 68000 Colmar; tel. 89 27 02 05 ☎ By appt.

Alsace Grand Cru Kastelberg

FERNAND GRESSER *Riesling★★*

| □ | 1 ha | 4800 | 4 D ◐ |

From the Steige vineyard which boasts a uniquely pure schist soil capable of producing the finest Rieslings. Floral primary aromas and the promise of a complex bouquet when mature. Lingering finish on the palate with a hint of gunflint, characteristic of wines from such soil. (1983)
✔ Tokay Moenchberg Grand Cru, Tokay Wiebelsberg Grand Cru, Klevner, Crémant.
➟ Marc Kreydenweiss, 12 Rue Deharbe, 67140 Andlau; tel. (88) 08 95 83 ☎ By appt.

Alsace Grand Cru Kirchberg de Barr

PIERRE HERING *Riesling★★*

| □ | 2 ha | 15 600 | 3 D ◐ |

Sixty per cent of the wines produced by this family estate come from Grand Cru Kirchberg vineyard. This Riesling has a delicately scented, elegant flavour. Not yet in balance, with surprising acidity and residual sugar. Needs bottle age to round out. (1983)
➟ Pierre Hering, 6 Rue du Dr-Sultzer, 67140 Barr; tel. 88 08 90 07 ☎ By appt.

PIERRE HERING
Gewürztraminer Gaensbrönnel★★

| □ | 3 ha | 25 000 | 4 D ▮ ↓ |

A thoroughbred wine. It is not yet possible to appreciate its full qualities, as the bouquet and flavour are still very closed up. It will gain balance with maturity. (1983)
➟ Pierre Hering, 6 Rue du Dr-Sultzer 67140 Barr; tel. 88 08 90 07 ☎ By appt.

103

ALSACE WILLM *Riesling*★★

| ☐ | 10 ha 42 000 | **4 D 📠 ↓** |

This carefully vinified Grand Cru Riesling has very rapidly acquired a lemony floral note, the sign of a very rich year. (In other vintages there is often a hint of broom flower). A particular crispness on the palate suggests a wine which will keep well. (1983) ✔ Riesling (medal), Riesling Cuvée Emile Willm, Riesling Kirchberg Grand Cru.
🕿 Alsace Willm, 32 Rue du Dr-Sultzer BP13, 67140 Barr; tel. 88 08 19 11 ⟡ By appt.

Alsace Grand Cru Kitterlé

DOMAINE SCHLUMBERGER
Gewürztraminer★

| ☐ | 7 ha 34 000 | **5 D 📠 ⑪** |

A smooth, elegant wine with a characteristic fruit bouquet. The vineyard's sandy, well-exposed slope certainly adds a note of finesse. (1981) ✔ Riesling, Gewürztraminer, Grands Crus.
🕿 Domaine Schlumberger, 68500 Guebwiller; tel. (89) 74 27 00 ⟡ Mon.–Fri. 8.00–12.00/13.00–18.00.

DOMAINE SCHLUMBERGER
Riesling★★

| ☐ | 6 ha 30 000 | **5 D ⑪** |

Klaus Schlumberger was growing vines at Guebwiller as early as 1540. After the French Revolution, Nicholas Schlumberger gave particular impetus to this well-exposed hillside vineyard – still the biggest in Alsace. This Grand Cru Kitterlé Riesling is a lovely, densely fruity wine, with good acidity and balance. A good prospect. (1982) ✔ Riesling, Gewürztraminer, Grands Crus.
🕿 Domaine Schlumberger, 68500 Guebwiller; tel. 89 74 27 00 ⟡ Mon.–Fri. 8.00–12.00/13.00–18.00.

Alsace Grand Cru Moenchberg

DOMAINE ANDRE GRESSER
Riesling★★

| ☐ | 0.6 ha 2600 | **4 D ⑪ ↓** |

The family have worked this estate since 1667. Their Moenchberg Riesling has a fruity, balanced nose and clean, ripe taste. A copybook Riesling which can be drunk now, but will gain in elegance and bouquet as it ages. (1983)
🕿 André et Rémy Gresser, 2 Rue de l'Ecole, 67140 Andlau; tel. 88 08 95 88 ⟡ By appt.

Alsace Grand Cru Rangen

BRUNO HERTZ *Gewürztraminer*★★

| ☐ | 0.38 ha 1800 | **3 D ⑪** |

A famous vineyard, already well-known in the twelfth century for its unique soil, made up of volcanic rocks and poor, shallow earth. Very steep south-facing slopes are another important quality factor. This particular wine has yet to open up fully, but shows good structure on the palate, with a rich alcohol presence and fine balance. (1983)
🕿 Bruno Hertz, 1 Porte des Chevaliers, Eguisheim, 68420 Henlisheim; tel. 89 41 81 61 ⟡ By appt.

Alsace Grand Cru Rosacker

CAVE VINICOLE D'HUNAWIHR
Riesling★★

| ☐ | 6 ha 39 000 | **5 D ↓** |

This vineyard was already known by name in 1483. The soil is heavy, pebbly limestone, and the exposure south-south-east. The wine has a light fruity fragrance very characteristic of the 1981 growths. Fine flavour gradually opening out on the palate with well-developed bouquet and aromas. May be drunk now. (1981) ✔ Gewürztraminer
🕿 Cave Vinicole de Hunawihr, 68150 Hunawihr; tel. 89 73 61 67 ⟡ By appt.

Alsace Grand Cru Saering

DOMAINE SCHLUMBERGER *Riesling*

| ☐ | 6 ha 42 000 | **4 D ⑪ ↓** |

Dry, masculine wine. Fruity and well-developed nose and taste. Short finish but easy to drink. (1982) ✔ Riesling, Gewürztraminer and Grands Crus.
🕿 Dom. Schlumberger, 68500 Guebwiller; tel. 89 74 27 00 ⟡ Mon.–Fri. 8.00–12.00/13.00–18.00.

Alsace Grand Cru Schlosberg

PAUL BECK *Tokay (Pinot Gris)*

| ☐ | 6 ha 12 900 | **3 D 📠 ↓** |

Already surprisingly mature and very forward for the vintage. Full, round, solid flavour. Would go well with game birds, pies or foie gras. (1982) ✔ Sylvaner, Muscat, Riesling, Pinot Noir.
🕿 Paul Beck, 1 Rue Clemenceau, 67650 Dambach-la-Ville; tel. 88 92 41 17 ⟡ By appt.

PAUL BLANCK ET FILS *Riesling*★

| ☐ | 2.5 ha 25 000 | **4 D 📠 ↓** |

Very pretty yellow-green. Fine characteristic grapeyness on the nose, albeit a little closed up. Dry, full-bodied with good, pleasant acidity. Still young; keep for a few years. (1983)
🕿 Paul Blanck et Fils, 32 Grand-Rue Kientzheim, 68240 Kaysersberg; tel. 89 78 23 56 ⟡ By appt.

CAVE DE KIENTZHEIM-KAISERSBERG *Riesling*★

| ☐ | 8 ha 67 000 | **3 D 📠 ↓** |

Beautiful yellow-green but very closed-up nose. Well made. Held together by pleasant acidity hidden by little residual sugar. Needs nothing more than age. (1983)
🕿 Cave de Kientzheim-Ka, 68240 Kientzheim; tel. 89 47 13 19 ⟡ Mon.–Thur. 8.00–12.00/14.00–18.00. Fri. 8.00–12.00/14.00–17.00.

COUR DES CHEVALIERS DE MALTE *Riesling*

| ☐ | 0.71 ha 4800 | **3 D ⑪ ↓** |

Beautiful colour and fine, fruity nose. Light but alert on the palate. Long finish held together by good acidity. Still very youthful; worth laying down for a few years. (1983)
🕿 André Blanck et Fils, 68240 Kientzheim; tel. 89 78 24 72 ⟡ By appt., daily 8.00–20.00.

COUR DES CHEVALIERS DE MALTE *Gewürztraminer*★

☐	0.17ha	1440	4 D ◑ ↓

Beautiful deep yellow colour. Masses of fruit on the nose–very typically Gewürztraminer. Well made with perfect blend of scent and flavour. Could be kept for at least ten years. Excellent aperitif. (1983). ✔ Sylvaner, Tokay (Pinot Gris), Pinot Blanc, Riesling Schlossberg.
➤ André Blanck et Fils, Cour des Chevaliers de Malte, 68240 Kientzheim; tel. 89 78 24 72 ⓘ Daily by appt.

Alsace Grand Cru Sommerberg

ALBERT BOXLER ET FILS *Riesling*★★★

☐	1ha	7200	3 D ▊ ◑

Beautifully fruity wine, with scent and flavour coming from the granite soil. Well balanced, with terrific potential. In three to five years will be a very great wine indeed. (1983) ✔ Riesling, Gewurztraminer Vendeanges Tardives, Gewurztraminer Brand, Tokay (Pinot Gris) Vendanges Tardives.
➤ Albert Boxler et fils, 78 Rue des Trois-Epis, 68230 Niedermorschwihr; tel. 89 27 11 32 ⓘ By appt.

Alsace Grand Cru Spiegel

JEAN-PIERRE DIRLER *Riesling*★★

☐	37ha	3 000	4 D ◑ ↓

Forty per cent of the area covered by this family estate is18ssified Grand Cru. Here is an attractive wine with long-lasting fruit. Freshness promises interesting development. Deserves to be laid down for a few years. (1983)
➤ Jean-Pierre Dirler, Bergholtz, 68500 Guebwiller; tel. 89 76 91 00 ⓘ Daily by appt. Closed Sun.

Alsace Grand Cru Wiebelsberg

DOMAINE ANDRE GRESSER *Riesling*★★

☐	1ha	6000	4 D ◑ ↓

Very delicate, elegant nose. Well made, with lasting appeal. Well balanced and fully matured. (1982)
➤ André et Remy Gresser, 2 Rue de l'école, 67140 Andlau; tel. 88 08 95 88 ⓘ By appt.

DOMAINE AU VIEUX PRESSOIR *Riesling*

☐	5ha	42000	3 D ◑ ↓

A magnificent 1814 wine press, to be seen in the courtyard, gives the estate its name. Typical Riesling from Wiebelsberg with strength and power. Will not improve with age; drink now. Recommended for fish and charcuterie. (1983)
➤ Marcel Schlosser, 5–7 Rue des Forgerons, 67140 Andlau; tel. 88 08 03 26 ⓘ By appt.

CHARLES WANTZ *Riesling*★

☐	0.5ha	42000	3 D ▊ ↓

Beautiful pale-yellow. Very delicate nose. Characteristic breeding and fullness on the palate. Pleasant hint of acidity. Already well developed

and full of flavour. (1983).
➤ Charles Wantz, Vins d'Alsace, 67140 Barr; tel. 88 08 90 44 ⓘ Mon.–Fri. 8.00–12.00/14.00–18.00. Sat. 8.00–12.00.

Crémant d'Alsace

This appellation, created in 1976, gave new life to the production of sparkling wines made by the Méthode Champenoise, which was already used in Alsace but on a much smaller scale. The grape varieties permitted in this wine, which has rapidly gained in popularity, are the Pinot Blanc, Auxerrois, Pinot Gris, Pinot Noir and Chardonnay.

CAVE COOPERATIVE DE BEBLENHEIM *Baron de Hoen*★★

○	30ha	360000	4 D ▊ ↓

Blanc de Blancs crémant of attractive amber-gold colour. Very delicate mousse that lasts. Elegant, light and easy to drink in spite of too much dosage. For special occasions. (1981)
➤ Coop. Vinicole de Beblenheim, 14 Rue de Hoen, 68980 Beblenheim; tel. 89 47 90 02 ⓘ By appt.

LES VIGNERONS DE BENNWIHR *Cuvée Hansi*★

○	15ha	180000	4 D ▊

Lovely green-gold colour, Long-lasting, delicate mousse. Blend of Pinot Blanc and Pinot Noir give elegance and body. A good party wine. (1983)
➤ Les Vignerons de Bennwihr, 3 Rue du Gal. de Gaulle, 68630 Bennwihr; tel. 89 47 90 27 ⓘ Daily 9.00–11.30/14.30–17.30.

LES VIGNERONS DE BENNWIHR★

○	7ha	60000	4 D ▊

The clear bottle highlights the strikingly beautiful pink colour. Elegant, grapey nose. Good mousse and inviting fruit on the palate. Unusual crémant. (1982)
➤ Les Vignerons de Bennwihr, 3 Rue du Gal. de Gaulle, 68630 Bennwihr; tel. 89 47 90 27 ⓘ Mon.–Sat. 9.00–11.30/14.00–17.30.

EMILE BOECKEL★

○	5ha	31000	4 D ◑

Beautiful pale golden colour and very light mousse; from Pinot Blanc and Chardonnay. Beautiful grapeyness on the nose combining with elegance and fruit. A joy to drink, and a match for any special occasion. (1982) ✔ Sylvaner, Riesling, Gewürztraminer, Pinot Blanc.
➤ Emile Boeckel, 2 Rue de la Montagne, Mittelbergheim, 67140 Barr; tel. 88 08 91 02 ⓘ By appt. Closed some Sundays and public holidays.

CAVE VINICOLE DE DAMBACH-LA-VILLE *Krossfelder*

○	13.2ha	129600	4 D ▊ ◑ ↓

Shows its origins – Pinot Blanc and Auxerrois – rather obviously. Two years being racked, plus high dosage, make it easy to drink; for aperitifs or cocktails.

105

⤙ Cave Vinicole de Dambach-la-Ville, 67650 Dambach-la-Ville; tel. 88 92 40 04 ☎ By appt.

UNION VINICOLE DIVINAL★

| ○ | | 10ha | 84000 | **4** D ▮ ↓ |

Beautiful, fruity nose. Good body and surprisingly vigorous on the palate for Pinot Blanc. Drink as an aperitif or to accompany a good meal. (1982)
⤙ Union Vinicole Divinal, 30 Rue du Général-Leclerc, 67210 Obernai; tel. 88 95 61 18 ☎ By appt.

DOPPF 'AU MOULIN' *Cuvée Julien*★

| ○ | | 40ha | 120000 | **4** D ▮ ↓ |

This producer has over 80 years' experience in making Méthode Champenoise wines. Pale golden colour; an elegant and taut wine showing full Pinot Blanc character. (1981)
⤙ Doppf 'Au Moulin', 68340 Riquewihr; tel. 89 47 92 23 ☎ By appt. Closed 1 Nov.–30 Mar.

CAVE VINICOLE D'EGUISHEIM
Wolfberger★

| ○ | | 50ha | | **4** D ▮ ⑴ ↓ |

Fruity, rather lemony nose and very delicate mousse. Riesling makes this wine fruity and characteristically Alsace, if a little crisper than those made with Pinot Blanc. Drink as an aperitif.
⤙ Cave Vinicole d'Eguisheim, 6 Grand-Rue, 68420 Eguisheim; tel. 89 41 11 06 ☎ By appt.

COOPERATIVE VINICOLE
D'EGUISHEIM *Wolfberger Brut*★★

| □ | | 60ha | 596000 | **4** D ⑴ ↓ |

Already fully developed and complete. Slight heaviness hidden by the grape variety used. Easy to drink, thanks to heavy dosage, low acidity and attractive scents and flavours. (1983)
⤙ Coop. Vinicole d'Eguisheim, 6 Grand-Rue, 68240 Eguisheim; tel. 89 41 11 06 ☎ By appt.

COOPERATIVE VINICOLE
D'EGUISHEIM *Wolfberger Prestige*★★

| ○ | | 60.2ha | 596000 | **4** D ⑴ ↓ |

Beautifully presented cremánt in old-style painted bottle. The wine is a blend of grape varieties and vintages. Rich, with high dosage; round and easy to drink. (1982)
⤙ Coop. Vinicole d'Eguisheim, 6 Grand-Rue, 68240 Eguisheim; tel. 89 41 11 06 ☎ By appt.

RAYMOND ENGEL

| □ | | 0.61ha | 12000 | **4** D ⑴ ↓ |

Good, clean and very dry. Not too obvious on the nose. If kept for another year will fill out and develop into a classic aperitif. (1982) ✔ Sylvaner, Gewürztraminer, Riesling, Tokay (Pinot Gris), Muscat.
⤙ Raymond Engel et Fils, 1 Route du Vin, 67600 Orschwiller; tel. 88 92 01 83 ☎ By appt.

BRUT FREYBURGER
Réserve Particulière★

| □ | | 1ha | 8400 | **4** D |

Very dry. Characterized by light, delicate and long-lasting mousse. Pinot Blanc and Pinot Noir give body and roundness in the blend. Riesling contributes crispness and grapeyness. (1982)
⤙ Jean Freyburger, 7 Place du Général de Gaulle,

Wettolsheim, 68000 Colmar; tel. 89 41 39 15 ☎ By appt.

JEROME GESCHICKT★

| ○ | | 1.5ha | 12000 | **4** D ▮ |

Beautiful colour; good mousse. Clean, characteristic and elegant. (1982) ✔ Sylvaner, Tokay-Pinot Gris, Gewürztraminer, Pinot Noir.
⤙ Jérôme Geschickt et Fils, 1 Place de la Sinne, 68770 Ammerschwihr; tel. 89 47 12 54 ☎ By appt.

H. ET J. HEIZMANN ET FILS

| ○ | | 1ha | 8400 | **4** D ⑴ |

Méthode Champenoise crémant that is very attractive to look at. Very light mousse. Light, easy to drink but lasts well on the palate. Well developed; ready to drink. (1982) ✔ Sylvaner, Gewürztraminer Kaefferkopk, Muscat, Pinot Noir.
⤙ H. et J. Heizmann et Fils, 2 Grand-Rue, 68770 Ammerschwihr; tel. 89 47 10 64 ☎ Daily 8.00–20.00.

CAVE VINICOLE DE HUNAWIHR
Cuveé Calixte II 1123★★

| ○ | | 10ha | 72000 | **4** D ▮ ↓ |

Delicate, pale-gold colour and good mousse. Unassertive nose which develops beautifully; light, crisp and elegant on the palate. Now at its peak and a delight to drink. (1983)
⤙ Cave Vinicole de Hunawihr, 68150 Hunawihr; tel. 89 73 61 67 ☎ By appt.

COOPERATIVE D'INGERSHEIM

| ○ | | 30ha | 63000 | **4** D ▮ |

Crémant of beautiful colour and fine, lasting mousse. Nose develops well in the glass. Easy to drink with elegant, but thoroughly Alsace, bouquet. Ready to drink as an aperitif. (1982)
⤙ Coop. Vinicole d'Ingersheim, 1 Rue Clémenceau, 68000 Ingersheim; tel. 89 27 05 96 ☎ By appt.

CAVE DE KIENTZHEIM-
KAYSERSBERG★★

| ○ | | 3ha | 26400 | **4** D ▮ |

Very dry champagne-method Blanc de Blancs based on the Pinot Blanc. Picking took place about ten days before the official harvest, giving the best possible balance, acidity and sugar. Very beautiful mousse, elegant and inviting. Shows promise. (1981)
⤙ Cave de Kientzheim-Kaysersberg, 68240 Kientzheim; tel. 89 47 13 19 ☎ Mon.–Thurs. 8.00–12.00/14.00–18.00. Fri. 8.00–12.00/14.00–17.00.

KUENTZ-BAS *Réserve Personnelle*★★

| ○ | | 2ha | 13200 | **4** D ▮ ↓ |

Excellent aperitif typified by lovely grapeyness and great elegance on the nose. Light, fine and persistent mousse. Still a little young; will improve. (1982)
⤙ Kuentz-Bas, 14 Route du Vin, 68420 Husseren-les-Châteaux; tel. 89 49 30 24 ☎ Mon.–Sat. 8.00–12.00/14.00–18.00.

LANDMANN-OSTHOLT

| □ | | 0.6ha | 4800 | **4** D ⑴ ↓ |

Brut de Brut with no added sugar. Clean, elegant, delicate and light to drink. Excellent aperitif, and perfect party wine. (1982)

➤ *M.* et *Mme.* Landmann-Ostholt, 20 Rue de la Vallée, 68570 Soultzmatt; tel. 89 47 09 33 ⏳ By appt.

DOMAINE DES COMTES DE LUPFEN★

☐   1 ha   10 800   4 D 🗑 ↓

Beautiful colour. Very delicate and persistent mousse and grapey, Pinot nose. Crisp and clean: attractive to drink. Not yet very complex but with a good future. (1982)
➤ Paul Blanck et Fils, 32 Grand-Rue, 68240 Kientzheim; tel. 89 78 23 56 ⏳ Mon.–Sat. 9.00–12.00/13.00–19.00.

CAVE VINICOLE DE PFAFFENHEIM★★

○   20 ha   202 000   4 D 🗑 ↓

Pale golden-yellow. Not too fruity; lightness and sparkle make it a good aperitif which could be drunk through the meal up until the sweet course. (1982)
➤ Cave Vinicole de Pfaffenheim, 68250 Pfaffenheim; tel. 89 49 61 08 ⏳ By appt.

CAVE COOPERATIVE DE RIBEAUVILLE *Giersberger*

☐   10 ha   24 000   4 D 🗑 ↓

Beautiful pale gold with delicate and lasting mousse. Beautifully grapey nose, characteristically Pinot, with plenty of length. Light and easy to drink. Very good balance. A fine aperitif wine. (1981)
➤ Cave Coop. de Ribeauvillé, 2 Route de Colmar 68500 Ribeauvillé; tel. 89 73 61 80 ⏳ Mon.–Fri. 8.00–12.00/14.00–18.00; Sat. and Sun. 10.00–12.00/14.00–17.00. Closed Sat. and Sun. in Jan., Feb. and March.

DOMAINE SAINTE-GERTRUDE

○   4 ha   36 000   4 D 🗑

Successful blend of Pinot and Riesling. Elegant and alive on the nose. Easy and soft to drink. (1982)
➤ Paul Buecher et Fils, Wettolsheim, 68000 Colmar; tel. 89 41 04 73 ⏳ Mon.–Sat. 8.00–12.00/13.00–18.00; Sun. 14.00–18.00.

SCHALLER ET FILS★

○   7 ha   60 000   3 D ⑪

Good example of crémant type from the 1982 vintage. Neutral nose; very clean, well balanced and dry on the palate. Excellent aperitif; will still be good in two or three years. (1982)
➤ Edgard Schaller et Fils, 1 Rue du Château, 68630 Mittelwihr; tel. 89 47 90 28 ⏳ Daily 8.00–20.00.

CAVE VINICOLE DE TRAENHEIM★★

○   10 ha   80 000   4 D 🗑

High-quality crémant with very delicate mousse. Beautifully grapey but not too obvious on the nose. Tasting reveals elegance and beautiful balance. Perfect. (1981)
➤ Cave vinicole de Traenheim, Route de Scharrachbergheim, 67310 Traenheim; tel. 88 50 66 21 ⏳ By appt.

ALSACE WILLM★★

○   1.9 ha   8 000   4 D 🗑 ⑪ ↓

Beautiful white mousse. Exquisite flavour – lightly fruity in character – from the blend of Pinot and Riesling. (1982) ✔ Crémants Cuvées Spéciales.
➤ Alsace Willm, 32 Rue du Dr-Sultzer, 67140 Barr; tel. 88 08 19 11 ⏳ By appt.

EASTERN FRANCE

THE COTES de Toul and the Moselle vineyards are the only remaining traces of the once-flourishing wine-making area of Lorraine. Not only was there a vast expanse of vines – more than 30000 hectares in 1890 – but the area also enjoyed a fine reputation. There was an occasional export market for the red wines from the region of Metz and part of the production of the Toul vineyard was sent out of the region to be made into Méthode Champenoise sparkling wine.

The two vineyard areas reached their peak at the end of the nineteenth-century; since then a number of unfortunate circumstances have contributed to their decline. The phylloxera epidemic forced the introduction of lower-quality hybrid grape varieties, while in 1907 wine producers suffered a severe economic crisis; later, the battlefields of World War I were not far away, and, finally, the increasing industrialization of the area brought about an exodus from the countryside. It was not until 1951 that the authorities concerned recognized the originality of these wines and classified Côtes de Toul and Moselle wines as VDQS, thus ranking them definitively amongst the better wines of France.

Côtes de Toul VDQS

The vineyards are situated to the west of Toul and cover eight communes strung out along a ridge formed by the erosion of the sedimentary layers of the Parisian basin. Soils from the Jurassic period are found here; clayey-limestone land that has good drainage and plenty of sunshine. The semi-continental climate gives high summer temperatures, although there is always the threat of spring frosts. Such facts explain the predominance of the Gamay grape, a hardier and more resistant variety that produces 'gris' (pale rosé) wines that are full of character, very fruity, with a lively finish. Pinot Noir is also grown, but only for red wine, which can be quite full bodied; the Auxerrois, too, is planted to produce delicate and fruity white wines.

At present, the vineyards cover 65 hectares, giving an average annual production of 3000 hectolitres. The potential for expansion is enormous, as one may discover when travelling along the Route du Vin and the Route de la Mirabelle, at the western exit of Toul.

LAROPPE FRERES *Vin Gris*★

☑ 7ha 90000 **2** **D** ▤ ↓

The only vineyard in the region that is both producer and négociant. Well-balanced, honest Vin Gris. Typical of its appellation but slightly understated for this vintage. (1983)
↦ Laroppe Frères, Bruley, 54200 Toul; tel. 08 34 31 10 ⟑ Daily 14.00–20.00. Closed Jan., Feb.

LAROPPE FRERES

▦ 7ha 90000 **3** **D** ▤ ↓

Vinified as a classic Pinot Noir red. Very intense red colour and the aromatic quality often found with this variety in northern France. Fully developed character gives very good structure. (1983)
↦ Laroppe Frères, Bruley, 54200 Toul; tel. 08 34 31 10 ⟑ Daily 14.00–20.00. Closed Jan., Feb.

YVES MASSON *Vin Gris*★★

☑ 2ha 15000 **2** **D** ▤ ↓

Typical example of Vin Gris, produced by a single, immediate pressing of black grapes. Light-pink colour, easy on the eye. Attractive, fruity nose allied with well-balanced crispness. Very drinkable. (1983)
↦ Yves Masson, Bulligny, 54710 Colombey-les-Belles; tel. 08 34 35 00 ⟑ By appt.

FERNAND POIRSON *Vin Gris*★★

☑ 3ha 20000 **2** **D** ▤ ↓

Very typical vin gris distinguished by exceptional fullness from excellent-quality vintage. Fruity, easy to drink and well balanced. (1983)
↦ Fernand Poirson, Bruley, 54200 Toul; tel. 08 34 31 11 7 ⟑ By appt.

MICHEL VOSGIEN *Vin Gris*★★

| ☑ | 5 ha | 30000 | 2 D ■ ↓ |

Pretty pink vin gris with deeper colour than usual due to strength and development of vintage. Elegant; very developed, fruity character. Excellent example of its type. (1983) ✔ Côtes de Toul Pinot Noir Rouge, Mousseux.
➡ Michel Vosgien, 24 Rue St-Vincent, Bulligny, 54170 Colombey-les-Belles; tel. 08 34 35 05 5 ⚲ By appt.

Vins de Moselle VDQS

The vineyards are planted on the hillsides of the Moselle valley on sedimentary layers that form the eastern border of the Parisian basin.

The VDQS area is concentrated around two main centres, south-west of Metz and near Sierck-les-Bains on the Luxembourg border. The soil is clayey-limestone with good drainage.

Around Metz viticultural practices have much in common with those of Burgundy, with low-trained, densely planted Pinot Noir vines. Around Sierck-les-Bains, by contrast, vine cultivation is influenced by the proximity of Luxembourg; high-trained and broadly spaced vines are planted producing predominantly dry and fruity whites.

The amount of wine produced under this VDQS appellation is still quite limited, a major constraint being the fragmented geography of the wine-growing area itself. Nevertheless the area has undoubted potential for the future.

CENTRE D'EXPLOITATION FRUITIERE

| □ | 1 ha | 7000 | 2 D ⑪ ↓ |

From a vineyard still using wooden barrels. This particular wine is made from the Auxerrois grape. Typically crisp and well balanced, with slightly woody note. (1983) ✔ Vin de Table Rouge, Vin Rosé VDQS.
➡ Centre d'Exploitation Fruitière, Laquenexy, 57530 Courcelles-Chaussy; tel. 08 76 44 01 ⚲ By appt. Closed 22 Dec.–2 Jan.➡ Département de la Moselle.

Beaujolais

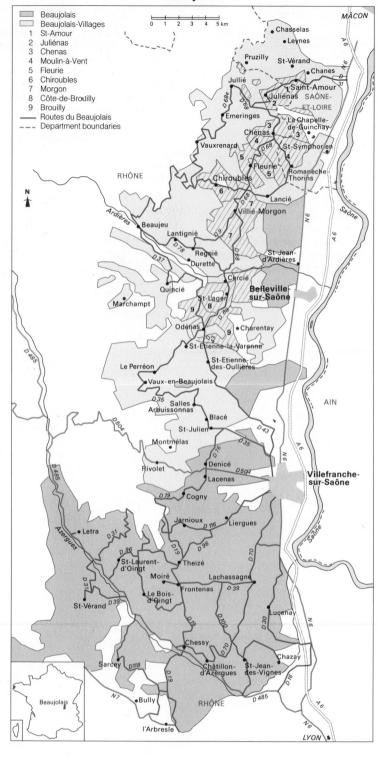

Légende :

- Beaujolais
- Beaujolais-Villages
- 1 St-Amour
- 2 Juliénas
- 3 Chenas
- 4 Moulin-à-Vent
- 5 Fleurie
- 6 Chiroubles
- 7 Morgon
- 8 Côte-de-Brouilly
- 9 Brouilly
- Routes du Beaujolais
- Department boundaries

0 1 2 3 4 5 km

MÂCON

Chasselas
Leynes
Pruzilly
St-Vérand
Chanes
Jullié
Saint-Amour
Juliénas   SAÔNE-ET-LOIRE
Emeringes
La Chapelle-de-Guinchay
Chénas
Vauxrenard
St-Symphorien
Fleurie
Chiroubles
Romanèche-Thorins
Lancié
Villié-Morgon

RHÔNE

N

Ardières
Beaujeu
Lantignié
Regnié
Durette
St-Jean-d'Ardières
Quincié
Cercié
Belleville-sur-Saône
Marchampt
St-Lager
Odénas
Charentay
St-Etienne-la-Varenne
Le Perréon
St-Etienne-des-Oullières
Vaux-en-Beaujolais
Salles-Arbuissonnas
Blacé
St-Julien
Montmélas
Rivolet
Denicé
Lacenas
Cogny
Villefranche-sur-Saône
Jarnioux
Liergues
Letra
St-Laurent-d'Oingt
Theizé
Moiré
Lachassagne
Le Bois-d'Oingt
Frontenas
St-Vérand
Lucenay
Chessy
Chazay
Sarcey
Châtillon-d'Azergues
St-Jean-des-Vignes
Bully
RHÔNE
l'Arbresle
LYON

Saône
AIN
Azergues

Beaujolais

BEAUJOLAIS

A CCORDING to the Institut National des Appellations d'Origine Contrôlée, the region of Beaujolais is officially and legally part of Burgundy. In practice, however, it is an area in itself, a concept which has been further reinforced by a passionate promotional campaign by the people who have made Beaujolais wine famous throughout the world, especially for the annual festivities, every 15 November, which mark the arrival of Beaujolais Nouveau. Even nature differentiates this vineyard from its famous neighbour; whereas Burgundy has relatively straight and regular rows of hillsides, Beaujolais is a tumble of hills and valleys with hundreds of scattered, sundrenched slopes.

Forming the southernmost part of the Burgundy region, Beaujolais already has a hint of the Midi about it. The region covers 22000 hectares and 96 communes in the departments of the Saône-et-Loire and Rhône. It is 50 km from north to south and an average of 15 km across, wider in the south than in the north. To the north there is no clear-cut or immediately apparent boundary to separate it from the Mâcon region. To the east, however, the border is clearly marked by the Saône plain, where the curves of the river sparkle in the sun. To the west, the Beaujolais hills are the first foothills of the Massif Central, and the highest peak – Mont St-Rigaux, at 1012 m – rises up like a giant milestone between the two areas of the Saône and the Loire. Finally, to the south, the Lyonnais vineyard takes over and runs as far as the metropolis of Lyons, where, as everyone knows, three rivers flow: the Rhône, the Saône, and. . . . Beaujolais!

There is no doubt that Beaujolais wines owe a lot to Lyons. Following the eighteenth-century expansion of the vineyard, they found a very favourable market there and, to this day, they still supply the famous 'bouchons' – local wine bars. The town of Beaujeu, which gave the area its name, was the cradle of the Beaujolais wine trade. Over many years, the medieval *seigneurs* of Beaujeu, modelling themselves on their powerful and illustrious neighbours – the Counts of Mâcon and Forez, abbots of Cluny and archbishops of Lyons – gradually consolidated and extended their domains. They ensured their future prosperity by having Beaujolais made part of the five extensive royal farms which did not have to pay transport tax in order to deliver to Paris (for a long time this was done via the Briare canal). This far-sightedness was a significant cause of the rapid expansion of the vineyards which later took place.

Today, Beaujolais produces on average one million hectolitres per year of its distinctive red wine. The amount of white wine produced is very small. The grape used – and this is the essential difference between Beaujolais and Burgundy – is almost exclusively the Gamay. The wine is produced under the appellations Beaujolais, Beaujolais Supérieur and Beaujolais-Villages, and the following nine prestige growths or 'crus': Brouilly, Côte de Brouilly, Chenas, Chiroubles, Fleurie, Morgon, Juliénas, Moulin-à-vent, and St-Amour. The first three appellations may be used for red, white, or rosé wines, the nine others only for reds which may also be declared AOC Bourgogne.

Geologically speaking, Beaujolais has been subjected to successive folding which eventually formed the relief that we see today. During the Quaternary Era, glaciers and rivers flowing from east to west scoured out the many valleys which separate the hillside vineyards. The vineyard slopes face due east and descend like a huge staircase to the Saône valley.

Northern and southern Beaujolais are traditionally divided by an imaginary line drawn through Villefranche-sur-Saône, now the regional capital. The scenery in the north is softer and rounder, with sand-filled valley floors. It is a region of very old rocks – granite, porphyry, schist, and diorite. The very slow process of granite decomposition produces clay-sand soils, the thickness of which can vary between a few centimetres and several metres of granite sand. This type of soil is acid, permeable, and not very fertile; it contains little organic matter and is consequently poor in nutrients. Although easy to work, it is a problem in dry weather. The north produces the best-quality Beaujolais, including both the Beaujolais-Villages and the nine Grand Cru appellations.

The southern half of Beaujolais is less hilly than the north, and characterized by a larger proportion of sedimentary and clay-limestone soils. This is also the area of 'pierres dorées', or 'golden stones'; the colour comes from the ferrous oxide they contain, and imparts a warm, golden glow to the buildings of the region. The nature of the soil – richer and more moist than in the north – makes this the main growing zone for AOC Beaujolais.

A third area, the Haut-Beaujolais, appears as a backdrop to the main appellations. Here the vines grow between the 140 m and 550 m contours on harder, metamorphic rocks which above 600 m are covered variously with bracken and forests of conifers and chestnut. The best growing conditions are found between 190 m and 350 m on south or south-east facing slopes.

The Beaujolais region as a whole enjoys a temperate climate as a result of three different climatic influences: continental, Atlantic, and Mediterranean. Each of these may predominate in a particular season, with sudden changes that can send the thermometer or barometer into a state of shock. The winter may be cold or wet; spring wet or dry. The months of July and August can be extremely hot when the drying wind blows from the Midi, but may also be very wet, with thunderstorms or hailstorms. Autumn, similarly, may be either hot or wet. Average annual rainfall is 750 mm, and the temperature can vary between −20°C and 38°C. These climatic factors are modified significantly by local micro-climates which allow vines to be planted in situations which would otherwise seem unfavourable. In general, however, the vineyards enjoy a good deal of sunshine and have the right conditions to aid the ripening of the grapes.

In Beaujolais, the choice of grape varieties is at its simplest – 99 per cent of all vines planted are Gamay, or more exactly Gamay Noir à jus blanc, commonly called Gamay Beaujolais. The grape was outlawed from the Côte d'Or by Philippe le Hardi, who in 1395 issued an edict to that effect, condemning it as a 'most disloyal plant' – probably in comparison with the more reliable Pinot. Despite this, the vine adapts well to many soil types, and indeed occupies more than 33 000 hectares throughout the wine regions of France. In Beaujolais soils, Gamay vines tend to droop and need to be staked during the first ten years of their life. The vine is quite susceptible to spring frosts, as well as to the usual vine diseases and pests. Buds sometimes appear early (late March) but more often can be seen around the second week in April. The vines usually flower during the first half of June, and the harvest begins in the middle of September.

There are other grape varieties which can be included in Beaujolais appellation wines: Pinot Noir and Pinot Gris for red and rosé wines, Chardonnay and Aligoté for white wine. In theory, it is still permitted to plant up to 15 per cent of Chardonnay, Aligoté or Gamay Blanc among the red vines, but the practice is now rare.

Two pruning methods are used in the Beaujolais region. The 'taille en gobelet', authorized throughout the whole region, produces a plant resembling a small bush: the vine is short-pruned and two vigorous young canes are tied down to form the 'gobelet' (literally, 'beaker') shape. The 'taille Guyot' leaves a single fruit-bearing cane trained horizontally some 45–60 cm above the ground: this is the Côte d'Or method, but in Beaujolais the resulting yield is too heavy. For this reason, the method is restricted to the simplest appellation, AOC Beaujolais.

The basic yields for AOC Beaujolais wines are 50–55 hl/ha for Beaujolais-Villages, and about 48 hl/ha for the growths, but these figures may be modified each year by the INAO in light of production conditions.

Red Beaujolais is most commonly made by a fermenting process known as carbonic maceration. The bunches of grapes, including stems, are sent straight to the fermentation vat without being crushed. The vat is sealed and filled with carbon dioxide gas. Under these conditions, fermentation takes place in each individual grape, drawing colour from the skin until the grape bursts open. The process produces the exuberant fruitiness and full aromas characteristic of Beaujolais wine: at the same time there is a significant reduction in the amount of malic acid, giving the wine a particular softness.

The precise composition and aroma of the wine obviously depends on the location where the grapes were grown. One difficulty with the carbonic maceration method is that the vigneron must choose his moment to intervene in the natural process of fermentation, given that the vat contains a constantly changing proportion of liquid must to solid matter as the grapes progressively liberate their juice. In general, Beaujolais wines are dry, not too tannic, smooth, refreshing and very aromatic, with an alcohol content of 12–13.5 per cent, and an acidity of 3.5 g per litre.

A special characteristic of the Beaujolais vineyard is the 'métayage' system, inherited from the past but still alive and strong today. Owner and grower share the harvest and also certain costs, the owner providing the land, somewhere to live, a cellar with all the basic wine-making equipment and chemicals, and the vines. The wine-grower, or 'métayer', supplies all his own tools, is responsible for any work that needs doing to keep the vines in perfect order, and also meets the expense of harvesting the grapes. Métayage contracts come into effect on St Martin's Day (11 November), and are used in almost 90 per cent of all cases in which the owner does not work his own land. Some 46 per cent of the vineyards are cultivated under this system; owner-growers account for another 46 per cent, while tenant-farming (in which the grower rents the land from the owner) comprises no more than 9 per cent. It is not unusual to find growers who own a few vines themselves and are also métayers.

A typical Beaujolais property is between 5 and 8 hectares, most of which would be vineyards. Properties tend to be smaller in the Beaujolais crus, where the vines are worked predominantly on the métayage system, and larger in the south where mixed farming is much more common. Eighteen cooperative cellars produce 30 per cent of the wine; local négociant-éleveurs buy and distribute 85 per cent of the crop, and the purchasing goes on steadily throughout the year. However, the main period of commercial activity is centred around the 'en primeur' sales at the beginning of the annual campaign. Almost 50 per cent of the young wine, the first of the harvest, is exported, chiefly to Switzerland, West Germany, Belgium, Luxembourg, the Netherlands, Great Britain, Denmark, the United States and Canada.

Only wines entitled to the appellations Beaujolais, Beaujolais Supérieur, or Beaujolais-Villages may be sold as vins primeurs. The grapes that go into these wines are harvested on granite-sand soils and the must is allowed to infuse for about four days, producing light, soft, refreshing wine with fruity, ripe banana aromas. Legislation controls the required analytical standards of the wine and its market release date. From mid-November, the wines are ready to be consumed throughout the world. The amount produced has risen from 13 000 hectolitres in

113

1956 to 100000 hectolitres in 1970, 200000 in 1976, 400000 in 1982, and continues to grow apace. From mid-December the Grand Cru wines are tasted and assessed and begin to appear on the market.

In general, Beaujolais wines are for drinking young in the first two years or so after the harvest – although there are exceptional bottles which may still be drinking well after ten years. However, the main attraction of the wines lies in their unique freshness and finesse, their lively notes of peony, violet and iris, and their heady aromas of apricot, cherry, peach, strawberry and raspberry.

Beaujolais

The Beaujolais appellation covers almost half of all the wine produced. The appellation area comprises 9650 hectares, the majority of which is to the south of Villefranche. Average annual production is 550000 hecto-litres of wine, 5000 of which are white. The white wine is made from Char-donnay grapes, two-thirds of which are harvested in the canton of Cha-pelle-de-Guinchay, a transitional zone between the silicious soils of the cru areas and the limestone soils of the Mâcon area. East of Bois d'Oignt and south of Villefranche, in the area known as 'les pierres dorées', the wines tend to have fruity rather than floral aromas, sometimes with a leafy or vegetable note; they are deeply coloured, full-bodied, country-style wines that will age quite well. In the western section of the region, in the higher parts of the Azergues valley, the crystalline rocks impart a more mineral-like quality to the wines, an indication of good keeping properties. Finally, the highest areas produce lively, light-coloured wines that are clean and crisp, especially in hot years. The nine cooperatives that have been established here produce almost 75 per cent of the Vins Primeurs, and play an important part in the local economy.

The appellation Beaujolais Supér-ieur is not limited to any specific area, but is used for wines which at the time of harvest have a potential alcohol content 0.5 per cent higher than the simple Beaujolais AOC wines. Some 10000 hectolitres of Beaujolais Supér-ieur are declared every year, coming mostly from AOC Beaujolais land.

Touring the countryside in the main AOC area, visitors can admire the distinctive vignerons' dwellings typical of the region. Built to a traditional pattern, they have their wine cellars on the ground floor, with an outside staircase leading to a covered balcony and the main living accommodation on the first floor. Towards the end of the eighteenth century it was common to build huge outdoor cellars separ-ated from the main house, and there is one such building at Lacenas, 6 km from Villefranche. This is part of the Château de Montauzan and houses the Confrérie des Compagnons du Beaujolais. Created in 1947 to pro-mote Beaujolais wine, the brother-hood now has a worldwide member-ship. A similar organization, Les Grapilleurs des Pierres Dorées, was founded in 1968.

If you feel inclined to taste a 'pot' of Beaujolais (the 46cl broad-based carafe that adorns bistro tables) then you should serve the wine with any kind of pork – including pork scratch-ings, tripe, boudin, saveloy, sausage – or pike in cream sauce, a famous Lyonnais dish. The vins primeurs go perfectly with artichokes or a gratin of potatoes with onions.

COOPERATIVE BEAUJOLAIS DE BULLY*

■   525ha   350000   2 D ▮ ↓

A colour with shades of violet and a powerful and earthy bouquet that reflects the qualities of the soil where the grapes were grown. Very smooth, this wine will be particularly attractive to those who dislike a wine high in acidity. (1984)
↠ Coop. Beaujolais de Bully, Bully, 69210 l'Ar-bresle; tel. 74 01 27 77 ᛏ By appt.

BERNARD CHAFFANJON**

■   13ha   108000   3 D ▮ ↓

Lively, beautiful red colour, and very expansive, fruity bouquet. Firmness and well-balanced, fat palate combine with distinguished aromas to produce an elegant wine. (1984)
↠ Bernard Chaffanjon, Les Rochons, St-Jean-d'Ardières, 69220 Belleville; tel. 74 66 12 18 ᛏ By appt.

CHATEAU DU CHATELARD★

☐Médaille d'Or   1.5 ha   10000   **3** ■ ↓
⑦⑨ 82 **83** **84**

Beautiful colour and classic nose. When tasted at six months the wine had not yet fully developed the attractive features of the nose and was rather unpolished on the palate. By the end of the year, however, it should be more refined and mature. (1984)
☛ Robert Grossot, Lancié, 69220 Belleville; tel. 74 04 12 99 ☿ By appt.

COLLIN ET BOURISSET★

■   50000   **3** ■ ↓
83 **84**

Beautiful and very intense colour with a powerful nose which is more vinous than fruity. Mellow and full bodied on the palate, this wine will suit those who prefer discretion to exuberance. (1984)
☛ *MM.* Collin et Bourisset, Rue de la Gare, 71680 Crêches-sur-Saône; tel. 85 37 11 15 ☿ No visitors.

GEORGES DUBOEUF★★

■   50 ha   60000   **3** **D** ◑ ↓
⑦⑥ **78** **81** *★83* **83** 84

A good wine, notable for its elegance, power and fruitiness. Its balance on the palate, enhanced by an excellent, full fragrance, compensates for its youth. (1984)
☛ Georges Duboeuf, Romanèche-Thorins, 71570 La Chapelle-de-Guinchay; tel. 85 35 51 13 ☿ Mon.–Fri. 8.00–12.00/14.00–17.00. Closed Aug.

PIERRE DURDILLY★★

■   15 ha   120000   **2** **D** ◑ ↓

Deep colour with a tinge of intense ruby, and a fruity bouquet with a hint of violets. Full and round on the palate, this is a wine with great aromatic qualities, and is an excellent Beaujolais. (1984)
☛ Pierre et Paul Durdilly, 69620 Le Bois-d'Oingt; tel. 74 71 65 11 ☿ By appt.

CHATEAU DE L'ECLAIR★★

■   3.5 ha   24000   **2** ■ ↓

Everything about this wine seems to be light, from its colour through to its balance on the palate. It has a forthcoming, fruity bouquet and great suppleness. A perfect example of a charming, eminently drinkable wine. (1984)
☛ Sicarex Beaujolais, Liergues, 69400 Ville-franches-sur-Saône; tel. 74 68 76 27 ☿ By appt.

DOMAINE DE L'ECLAIR★

☐   1.5 ha   8000   **2** **D** ■ ↓
80 83 84 **84**

Pretty colour; nose particularly well-developed and very pleasant. More fine qualities on the palate, but not everything that the nose promised. In this respect it will perhaps improve in months to come. (1984)
☛ Clément Antoine, Liergues, 69400 Ville-Franche-sur-Saône; tel. 74 68 08 64 ☿ By appt. Closed end Aug. to beg. Sept.

DOMAINE DE L'ECLAIR★★★

■   5 ha   30000   **2** **D** ◑ ↓
⑦⑥ **76** 80 **80** 81 83 84

A Beaujolais Supérieur which offers everything you could ask for: crimson, ruby colour, remarkable fruity nose, equally pleasant aromas on the palate, roundness and length. Fruity Beaujolais style at its best. (1984)
☛ Clémant Antoine, Liergues, 69400 Ville-Franche-sur-Saône; tel. 74 68 08 64 ☿ By appt. Closed end Aug. to beg. Sept.

DOMAINE DE L'ECLAIR★

◿   1.5 ha   8000   **2** **D** ◑ ↓
83 **83** 84

The beautiful colour and fine nose announce a classic Beaujolais rosé, an impression confirmed by the lingering taste on the palate. (1984)
☛ Clément Antoine, Liergues, 69400 Ville-Franche-sur-Saône; tel. 74 68 08 64 ☿ By appt. Closed end Aug. to beg. Sept.

HENRY FESSY★★

■   2 ha   12000   **3** ■ ↓

Fruity, well-developed nose; soft, full and fat on the palate and easy to drink, with a beautiful colour which emphasizes an expansive aroma. An excellent Beaujolais. (1984)
☛ Henry Fessy, Bel-Air, St-Jean-d'Ardières, 69220 Belleville; tel. 74 66 00 16 ☿ By appt.

DOMAINE DE FONDLENT★★

■   7 ha   50000   **2** **D** ■ ↓

Beautiful, strong colour tinged with deep purple. Fresh, light and very fruity nose, powerful and full-bodied on the palate with very good length. An excellent, well-balanced wine. (1984)
☛ Jean Pagnon, Morancé, 69480 Anse; tel. 74 84 36 62 ☿ By appt. Closed Aug.

CHATEAU DU GRAND-TALANCE★

■   35 ha   280000   **3** ■ ◑ ↓
76 **83** 83

Pretty colour and a pleasant but discreet nose which seems already mature. Classic Beaujolais palate, and certainly one of the better wines in its class. (1984)
☛ M.J. Pellerin, Le Moulin, 69830 St-Georges-de-Reneins; tel. 74 67 61 36 ☿ No visitors.

CHATEAU DES GRANGES★★

■   20 ha   160000   **3** ◑ ↓

Remarkably well preserved at 18 months and has retained its colour and other characteristics of youth. All the Beaujolais qualities – warmth, fruitiness and a good finish – come together in this delightful wine. (1983)
☛ SA Thorin, Pontanevaux, 71570 La Chapelle-de-Guinchay; tel. 85 36 70 43 ☿ No visitors.

VIGNOBLE DE LA GRENOUILLERE★

■   2 ha   15000   **2** **D** ◑ ↓
76 **84**

A rather modest, light colour, but the very full nose tells all. This is a powerful wine, supple and flowing on the palate. A very pleasant and extremely drinkable Beaujolais Supérieur. (1984)

♦ Charles Bréchard, Chamelet, 69620 Le Bois-d'Oingt; tel. 74 71 34 13 ⏳ By appt.

VIGNOBLE DE LA GRENOUILLERE*

■   3ha   24000   [2] [D] ◫ ⬇

㉖ 84 [84]

Over the last decade, 'Père' Bréchard, known as 'the old lion' has emerged as the greatest perso-nality among all the Beaujolais growers. The man and his wine share the same characteristics and qualities – both are expansive and light in spirit. (1984)
♦ Charles Bréchard, Chamelet, 69620 Le Bois-d'Oingt; tel. 74 71 34 13 ⏳ By appt.

PIERRE JOMARD*

■   5ha   31000   [2] [D] ◫ ⬇

A wine of intense colour, its powerful bouquet literally leaping up from the glass before delight-ing the palate with its fruitiness and light, agree-able nature. Impossible to be indifferent to this kind of wine. (1984) ✔ Coteaux du Lyonnais.
♦ Pierre Jomard, Le Morillon, 69210 Fleurieux; tel. 74 01 02 27 ⏳ By appt. Closed during harvest.

CAVES DES VIGNERONS DE LIERGUES**

☐   2ha   10000   [3] [D] ⬛ ⬇

㉘ [79] [81] 83 84

Beautiful bright colour with a full and very direct nose; very smooth, almost creamy on the palate. An easy-to-drink wine which makes a fine, very pleasant bottle. (1984)
♦ Cave des Vignerons des Liergues, Liergues, 69400 Villefranche-sur-Saône; tel. 74 68 07 94 ⏳ By appt. Closed Sept.–Nov.

CAVES DES VIGNERONS DE LIERGUES**

◪   5ha   5000   [2] [D] ⬛ ⬇

The colour is extremely light and brilliant and the bouquet is very pleasant. This wine has consider-able presence, combined with excellent balance and rather remarkable fruit on the palate. An excellent rosé. (1984)
♦ Cave des Vignerons de Liergues, Liergues, 69400 Villefranche-sur-Saône; tel. 74 68 07 94 ⏳ By appt. Closed Sept.–Nov.

CAVE DES VIGNERONS DE LIERGUES***

■   470ha   3600000   [3] [D] ⬛ ⬇

Pleasing in every aspect, from its colour right through to the long-lasting finish. The bouquet is powerful and very fruity; round, mature, and full bodied on the palate. A truly excellent Beaujo-lais. (1984)
♦ Cave des Vignerons de Liergues, Liergues, 69400 Villefranche-sur-Saône; tel. 74 68 07 94 ⏳ By appt. Closed Sept.–Nov.

LORON ET FILS

■   90000   [3] ⬛ ⬇

This average-quality Beaujolais has a tendency to develop quickly, making it ready to drink young. (1984)
♦ Ets Loron et Fils, Pontanevaux, 71570 La Chapelle-de-Guinchay; tel. 85 36 70 52 ⏳ No visitors.

DOMAINE DE MILHOMME**

■   10ha   72000   [2] [D] ◫ ⬇

Beautiful, very lively colour and light bouquet. Highly scented, quite lively and very pleasant on the palate; a very drinkable wine, and entirely satisfactory if well cooled. (1984)
♦ GAEC du Dom. de Milhomme, Ternand, 69620 Le Bois-d'Oingt; tel. 74 71 33 13 ⏳ By appt. Closed during harvest. ♦ L. J. and R. Per-rin.

PHILIBERT MOREAU**

☐   750000   [4] [D] ⬛ ◫ ⬇

*78 *79 *80 ㉜

Beautiful bright colour and well-developed nose. Very pleasant and smooth on the palate, sliding down easily. Note that this wine keeps remark-ably well. (1982)
♦ Philibert Moreau, 4 Rue Georges Lecomte, 71003 Mâcon; tel. 85 38 42 87 ⏳ By appt.

NICOLAS*

■   340000   [3] ⬛

Fruity and crisp but very light, ideal for a Beaujo-lais. It is a classic of its type and, like the others, should be consumed young, preferably before it is eighteen months old. (1984)
♦ Ets Nicolas, 2 Rue de Valmy, 94220 Charen-ton; tel. 01 37 59 20 ⏳ No visitors.

PASQUIER-DESVIGNES**

■   30000   [3] ⬛ ◫ ⬇

76 [76] *84

Beautiful colour, and a fine expansive nose. Well balanced on the palate, with fullness, smoothness and a lingering aroma. A very pleasant wine. (1984)
♦ Ets Pasquier-Desvignes, St-Lager, 69220 Belle-ville; tel. 74 66 14 20 ⏳ No visitors.

CHATEAU DE LA RIGODIERE*

■   30ha   240000   [3] ◫ ⬇

This wine was tasted at 18 months and has retained a great deal of crispness with a beautiful dark red colour. A fairly powerful bouquet and good varietal fruit on the palate combine to make a very easy-to-drink wine. Although it is still very good, it is advisable not to keep it much longer, or to opt for a more recent year. (1983)

⌐┬ SA Thorin, Pontanevaux, 71570 La Chapelle-de-Guinchay; tel. 85 36 70 43 ⍺ No visitors.

DOMAINE DE ROCHECORBIERE
■   ③ D 🍾 ⌕

Behind an attractive colour lies a complex, already quite well-developed, grapey nose, even though the wine is only six months old. It is light in the mouth and should be drunk young. Serve chilled. (1984)

⌐┬ Alain Bidon, Chessy-les-Mines, 69380 Lozanne; tel. 74 84 39 23 ⍺ By appt. Closed early Aug.

DOMAINE DE ROCHECORBIERE
□   12 ha   95 000   ③ D 🍾 ⌕

The lightness of the colour is reflected in the lightness of the very delicate bouquet which is followed by quite a crisp, clean finish. A modest white wine that should be served very cold. (1984) ✔ Beaujolais Blanc.

⌐┬ Alain Bidon, Chessy-les-Mines, 69380 Lozanne; tel. 74 84 39 23 ⍺ By appt. Closed early Aug.

DOMAINE DES SABLES D'OR★★
■   10 ha   72 000   ③ D 🍾 ⑪ ⌕

Beautiful, brilliant colour, and a well-developed, fruity nose dominated by banana. Full, round, rich, very aromatic and long on the palate. A very good Beaujolais. (1984) ✔ Beaujolais Gie de Roche-Cours.

⌐┬ Olivier Ravier, 'Descours', 69220 Belleville; tel. 74 66 12 66 ⍺ By appt.

CAVE COOPERATIVE DE SAINT-BEL★
■   59 ha   25 000   ② D 🍾 ⌕

Here is a prime example of a *petit Beaujolais* wine: brightly coloured, light, crisp and aromatic, with predominant fragrances of banana and soft fruit. A pleasant, refreshing wine that should be served between 10° and 12°C. (1984)

⌐┬ Cave Coop. de St-Bel, St-Bel, 69210 L'Arbresle; tel. 74 01 11 33 ⍺ By appt.

COOPERATIVE DE SAINT-VERAND★
■   320 ha   2 530 000   ③ D 🍾

Tasted in February 1985, this Primeur is typical of the Beaujolais Nouveaux, which are intended to be drunk while still young. Scented and fresh, this wine will adapt to all dishes and all occasions, provided it is drunk when in balance and very cool (12°C). (1984)

⌐┬ Coop. de St-Vérand, St-Vérand, 69620 Le Bois-d'Oingt; tel. 74 71 73 19 ⍺ By appt.

CELLIER DES SAMSONS★★
■   ④

Attractive colour and powerful nose confirmed on the palate where it is firm and balanced. Good structure for a Beaujolais.

⌐┬ Cellier des Samsons, Quincié-en-Beaujolais, 69430 Beaujeu; tel. 74 66 24 19 ⍺ No visitors.

DOMAINE DE SANDAR
Cuvée Prestige★
☑   2 ha   96 000   ③ D ⌕
⑦ *81 ⑧⑨ *82 *83

Very rich pink colour. A pleasant nose, confirmed on the palate, although one might have preferred the taste to have a little more persistence. A nice, agreeable rosé. (1983)

⌐┬ Vins Mathelin, BP 3, Châtillon-d'Azergues 69380 Lozanne; tel. 74 84 39 24 ⍺ By appt. Closed week of 15 Aug.

LES TOQUES GOURMANDES★
■   ③ D

Brilliant colour and a peppery nose reminiscent of peony. Initially lively and slightly acidic on the palate, it boasts a lingering elegance which comes from the aroma of well-matured red fruit. Selected by *Les Toques Gourmandes*.

⌐┬ Les Toques Gourmandes, 29 Bis, Route de Versailles, 78560 Port-Marly; tel. 01 91 61 17 ⍺ By appt.

CHARLES VIENOT★
■   ③ D 🍾 ⌕

Deep colour and powerful bouquet, typical of this particular vineyard. A very full-bodied wine that is closed-in at six months of age. Its toughness needs to round out a little to allow the fragrance to show through, and it will probably have achieved good balance by the summer. (1984) ✔ Bourgogne style wines.

⌐┬ Charles Vienot, 21700 Nuits-St-Georges; tel. 80 62 31 05.

GAEC VIVIER-MERLE
Coteaux Matiron★★
■   13 ha   8400   ③ D 🍾 ⌕

A very attractive and well-balanced Beaujolais. Its distinctive characteristics are a powerful and fruity nose and an elegant appearance. (1984)

⌐┬ GAEC Vivier-Merle Frères, Matiron, St-Vérnand, 69620 Le Bois-d'Oingt; tel. 74 71 73 06 ⍺ By appt.

Beaujolais-Villages

This classification covers wines with an extra degree of strength and character produced by 37 villages in the steep foothills of the Beaujolais mountains. In theory, each village can produce Beaujolais under its own name; in practice, most of the wine is marketed as Beaujolais-Villages. Seven of the villages, however, also produce Beaujolais Grand Cru wines, dealt with individually below.

All the wines from this area share the same qualities, derived from the granite sands on which the vines are grown. They are fruity, clean and lively, with a marvellous bright red colour – and make the best cuvées of the vins primeurs. The soils with the highest proportion of granite produce the bigger wines that keep longest. In general, the area offers a full range of wines, combining every nuance of aromas, finesse and body and capable of partnering an equally varied selection of dishes: pike in cream sauce, terrine, even a rump steak of Charollais beef.

The 6220 hectares of the AOC area produce on average 350000 hectolitres of wine per year. The regulations, which also cover the Grand Cru vineyards, specify that vines must be pruned en gobelet and that the minimum potential natural alcohol in the grapes must be 0.5 per cent higher than straight AOC Beaujolais.

PAUL BEAUDET

■ 150000 ③ D ■ ↓

Beautiful dark ruby colour, but all the signs of recent bottling in the nose and palate. Once it has recovered, however, this wine promises to become a classic bottle of the highest quality. (1984)

•┐ Paul Beaudet, Pontanevaux, 71570 La Chapelle-de-Guinchay; tel. 85 36 72 76 ⵏ By appt.

JEAN-PIERRE BELLEVILLE
Beaujolais-Regnié*

■ 3.7ha 24400 ② D ■ ↓

Attractive wine, light bouquet and correspondingly light palate. Bursting with young, refreshing acidity – and best appreciated by drinking within the year. (1984)

•┐ Jean-Pierre Belleville, Les Bruyères, Regnié-Durette, 69430 Beaujeu; tel. 74 04 32 78 ⵏ By appt.

JEAN BENON**

■ 0.85ha 6000 ③ D ■ ↓

With its colour of ripe cherries, and very intense, flowery nose, this wine has such remarkable steadiness and persistence that it can be classed among the best of its category. (1984)

•┐ Jean Benon, Les Blémonts, 71570 La Chapelle-de-Guinchay; tel. 85 36 71 92.

RENE BERROD***

■ 1ha 5000 ③ D ■ ↓
⑧ 82 83 84

Beautiful, intense colour – a deep, violet. The nose has an aroma of fresh fruit. Round and powerful on the palate, with a very good, lingering taste. An excellent wine! (1984)

•┐ René Berrod, 69820 Fleurie; tel. 74 04 13 63 ⵏ By appt.

CHATEAU DU CARRA*

■ 15ha ③ D ◑

Ruby-violet colour and warm, fruity nose. Rich and warm on the palate with a pleasing delicacy sustained by a strong, fleshy body. To be drunk immediately. (1983)

•┐ Guy Durieu, Le Carra, St-Etienne-la-Varenne, 69460 St-Etienne-des-Ouillières; tel. 74 03 20 01 ⵏ By appt.

JEAN-LOUIS CHANAY*

■ 5ha 36000 ③ D ■ ↓

Delicate, light, brilliant colour and a flowery nose with a predominant scent of lime blossom. Full on the palate, with a touch of firmness – a typical Beaujolais and a lovely bottle. (1984) ✔ Beaujolais Primeur.

•┐ Jean-Louis Chanay, Le Trêve, 69460 St-Etienne-des-Ouillières; tel. 74 03 43 65 ⵏ By appt.

DOMAINE DU CHAPITRE*

■ 23ha 168000 ③ D ◑ ↓

Lively, straightforward and well rounded. An attractive wine, with balanced fruit and a certain amount of power. (1984) ✔ Pommard Petit Clos, Aloxe-Corton, Beaune Clos du Roi, Clos de Vougeot.

•┐ SA Aujoux 20 Bvd Emile Guyot, 69830 St-Georges-de-Reneins; tel. 74 66 07 99 ⵏ By appt.

DOMAINE DU CHAPITRE*

■ 25ha 150000 ③ D ■ ↓

The fruity nose gives no clue to a surprising – and very pleasant – fleshiness on the palate. A wine with potential. (1984)

•┐ Ets Aujoux, 20 Bvd Emile Guyot, 69830 St-Georges-de-Reneins; tel. 74 66 07 99 ⵏ By appt.

CHATEAU DE CHATELARD

■ 6ha 42000 ② D ■ ↓

Light colour and very young, 'green' nose. Extremely light on the palate with a great deal of charm and should be drunk while still young. (1984)

•┐ Robert Grossot, Lancié, 69220 Belleville; tel. 74 04 12 99 ⵏ By appt.

PAUL CINQUIN***

■ 5ha 40000 ② D ■ ↓

Pleasing in every way, and even exceeds expectations, as some of the tasters rated it above its appellation, placing it with the crus and comparing it with a Morgon, although it lacks the character peculiar to that wine. Rich and fruity enough to be drinking well now, yet has sufficient quality to guarantee its longevity. Its lengthy finish is sensational. (1984)

•┐ Paul Cinquin, Les Braves, Régnié-Durette, 69430 Beaujeu; tel. 74 74 04 31.

LOUIS COILLARD

■ 8.05ha 4000 ② D ◑ ↓

This wine has a good deal of potential, which should develop quickly. Full bodied, with concentrated fruit, warm and full; a wine full of promise. (1984)

•┐ Louis Coillard, 69430 Beaujeu; tel. 74 04 35 37 ⵏ By appt.

COLLIN ET BOURISSET**

■ 80000 ④ ■ ↓
★83 ★84

Good appearance with the classic Beaujolais pink/purple colour (at ten months) and a well-developed bouquet. The aroma is quite fruity on the palate with considerable quality. Eminently drinkable. (1984)

↰ *MM*. Collin et Bourisset, Rue de la Gare, 71680 Crèches-sur-Saône; tel. 85 37 11 15 **Ⱦ** No visitors.

COLLIN ET BOURISSET
Cuvée Grange-Charton

■ 31 ha 96 000 [3] ■ ↓
⑧⑨ *83 83

Tasted at 18 months, this wine nevertheless still shows a very agreeable lightness and fragrance. A creditable performance. (1983)
↰ *MM*. Collin et Bourisset, Rue de la Gare, 71680 Crèches-sur-Saône; tel. 85 37 11 15 **Ⱦ** No visitors.

DOMAINE DU CRET-DES-BRUYERES★★

■ 8 ha 4970 [3] [D] ■ ↓

Light ruby colour, with a rather delicate nose. Supple, smooth and distinguished on the palate. Very good finish and very fruity overall,. A light and thoroughbred wine. (1984)
↰ René Desplace, Aux Bruyères, Regnié-Durette, 69430 Beaujeu; tel. 74 04 30 21 **Ⱦ** By appt.

CREUX-NOIR★

■ 5 ha 25 000 [3] [D] ◐ ↓
⑦⑨ 82 84

Attractive colour and fruity bouquet. On the palate it is very well-made, revealing considerable character and a highly individual *goût de terroir* which many will appreciate. (1984)
↰ *M*. Duperron, Leynes, 71570 La Chapelle-de-Guinchay; tel. 85 35 11 89.

PIERRE DESHAYES ET FILS

■ 8 ha 42 000 [3] [D] ■ ↓

Well-presented, classic Beaujolais-Villages with undeniable qualities but somewhat lacking in character; otherwise completely satisfactory. (1984)
↰ Pierre Deshayes et Fils, 69460 Le Perreon; tel. 74 03 21 31 **Ⱦ** Daily 9.00–20.00.

VINS DESSALLE★★

■ 150 000 [2] [D] ■ ↓
*⑧③ 84 84

Beautiful, deep, ruby-violet colour and richly fruity nose with aromas of stone-fruits such as cherry and prune, and, finally, a touch of banana. Well-developed fruit confirmed in the aroma on the palate, which is very fleshy and full. Good length, with a powerful and pleasant finish. (1984)
↰ Vins Dessalle, 42 Rue Marshal Foch, St-Jean-d'Ardières 69220 Belleville; tel. 74 66 00 16.

CAVEAU DES DEUX-CLOCHERS
Beaujolais Régnié★

■ 600 ha 55 000 [3] [D]
⑧③ 84

An extremely light and fruity wine, rather in the Primeur style, with much finesse. Real Beaujolais lovers will drink it well-chilled in the shade of the plane trees, between games of boules. (1984)
↰ Caveau des Deux-Clochers, Régnié-Durette,

69430 Beaujeu; tel. 74 04 36 50 **Ⱦ** By appt. Closed Wed.

JOSEPH DROUHIN★★

■ [3] ■ ↓

The colour is embellished with purplish glints; bouquet of ripe banana, along with hints of chocolate, is confirmed on the palate. A slight dash of Morello cherry also emerges, which all goes to make a pleasant wine. (1984)
↰ Joseph Drouhin, 7 Rue d'Enfer, 21200 Beaune; tel. 80 22 06 80 **Ⱦ** By appt.

GEORGES DUBOEUF
Cuvée Quincie Domaine de la Treille★

■ 10 ha 66 000 [2] [D] ■ ↓

Beautiful, lively colour, and good fruity, flowery bouquet. A very rounded and long Beaujolais with a very pleasant, fruity finish. (1984)
↰ Georges Duboeuf, Romanèche-Thorins, 71570 La Chapelle-de-Guinchay; tel. 85 35 51 13 **Ⱦ** Mon.–Sat. 8.00–12.00/14.00–17.00. Closed Aug.

GEORGES DUBOEUF★

■ 80 000 [2] [D] ■ ↓

A lovely red colour with purple glints, and a fragrant, spicy nose with hints of red fruits and nuts. It is very easy on the palate, showing balance and distinction. (1984)
↰ Georges Duboeuf, Romanèche-Thorins, 71570 La Chapelle-de-Guinchay; tel. 85 35 51 13 **Ⱦ** Mon.–Fri. 8.00–12.00/14.00–17.00. Closed Aug.

PIERRE DUPOND★

■ 250 000 [3] ■ ↓

Beautiful, strong colour, but light nose still not completely developed in February 1985, although promising. Full and young on the palate – a typical Beaujolais, ready to drink from about eight months on. (1984) ✔ Full range of Beaujolais wines.
↰ Pierre Dupond, 339 Rue de Thizy, 69653 Villefranche-en-Beaujolais; tel. 74 65 24 32 **Ⱦ** No visitors.

JEAN DURAND *Beaujolais Régnié★★★*

■ 10 ha 7000 [3] [D] ■ ↓

Fine colour and a good fruity nose are pointers to the remarkable qualities of this wine. A delight on the palate: class, fleshiness, fruit – everything one expects of a Beaujolais-Villages – as well as the stature which will allow it to keep its youth for a good while. (1984)
↰ Jean Durand, Ponchon, Régnié-Durette, 69430 Beaujeu; tel. 74 04 30 97 **Ⱦ** By appt.

DOMAINE DE L'ECUSSOL

■ 2 ha 12 000 [3] [D] ■ ◐ ↓

Light colour, and a beautiful nose; very supple and light on the palate. A very nice wine which was probably even better when younger. (1983)
↰ Ets Chevalier et Fils, Charnay, 71000 Mâcon; tel. 85 34 26 74.

119

PAUL GAUTHIER★★★

■ 10ha 60000 ② D ⬛ ↓

Exceptional finesse and elegance backed by outstanding class and excellent balance. Without doubt this is one of the best Beaujolais produced. (1984) ✔ Beaujolais-Villages Primeur, Beaujolais Primeur.
•┓ Paul Gauthier, 'Les Granges', Blacé, 69460 St-Etienne-des-Ouillières; tel. 74675355 ⦿ By appt.

DOMAINE DE LA GERARDE★★

■ 6ha 33000 ② D ⬛ ↓

Lovely colour and a well-developed, very fruity nose pave the way for the excellent qualities found on the palate. Full Gamay flavour, along with a great deal of elegance and characteristic Beaujolais style. (1984)
•┓ Roland Martin, Régnié-Durette, 69430 Beaujeu; tel. 74043037 ⦿ By appt.

GOBET *Les Quatre Clochers*★★

■ 20ha 96000 ③ ⬛ ↓

This wine has elegance, suppleness, fruitiness and a high level of quality. (1984) ✔ Beaujolais and other regional wines.
•┓ Vins Gobet, Cuvier Beaujolais, Blaceret, 69830 St-Georges-de-Reneins; tel. 74675457 ⦿ No visitors.

HENRI GRANDJEAN *Régnié*

■ 5ha 25000 ③ D ⬛ ↓

A very light and pleasant wine with a rather discreet nose. Ruby colour with purple tinges; very fruity on the palate. (1984)
•┓ Henri Grandjean, Vallière, Régnié-Durette, 69430 Beajeu; tel. 74048705 ⦿ By appt.

COOPERATIVE DES GRANDS VINS★★

■ 118ha 800000 ③ D ⬛

Bright, ruby-violet colour and a sustained, intense and richly fruity nose. A very full, rich wine with fruity aromas and a good, long finish. (1984)
•┓ Coop. des Grands Vins, Ch. du Bois de la Salle, 69840 Juliénas; tel. 74044261 ⦿ By appt. Closed 1 Aug.–30 Nov.

MARCEL JAMBON★

■ 6ha 8000 ② D ⬛ ↓

This wine is a delight to the eye and the nose. On the palate it proves robust and of good quality with a hint of warmth. Should be drunk very cool. (1984)
•┓ Marcel Jambon, Les Chastys, Régnié-Durette, 69430 Beaujeu; tel. 74043768.

CHATEAU DE LACARELLE★★

■ 100ha 300000 ③ D ⬛ ↓

76 78 81 ⑧³ **84** ⬛

Beautiful colour and well-developed, fruity nose. Delicately fleshy and round on the palate, with marked aromas. Very delicate, lingering finish. A Beaujolais of great charm. (1984)
•┓ Comte Durieu de Lacarelle, 69460 St-Etienne-des-Ouillères; tel. 74034080 ⦿ By appt.

CHATEAU DE LACARELLE★

■ 100ha 360000 ④ D ⬛ ↓

Refined colour tending towards purple, with a nose which is developing slowly. Round, supple and full-bodied, this is a wine which needs to mature for six to eight months. (1984)
•┓ Comte Durieu de Lacarelle, Lacarelle, 69460 St-Etienne-des-Ouillères; tel. 74034080 ⦿ By appt.

CAVE DES VIGNERONS DE LIERGUES★

■ ③ ⬛ ↓

A beautiful, eye-catching colour; very reserved nose, revealing the wine to be feeling the effects of its recent bottling. A good deal of fullness, substance and warmth on the palate, though not fully balanced at present. Needs only a short time to recover from its 'bottle sickness'. (1984)
•┓ Cave de Vignerons de Liergues, Liergues, 69400 Ville-Franche-sur-Saône; tel. 74680794 ⦿ By appt.

DOMAINE DE LA MADONE★★

■ 5ha 36000 ③ D ⬛ ↓

Very lively cherry colour, with a highly perfumed and pleasantly fruity nose. Warm, delicate, elegant and positive on the palate; a very attractive wine. (1984)
•┓ André Bererd, Le Trève, Le Perreon, 69460 St-Etienne-des-Ouillères; tel. 74032074 ⦿ By appt.

BERNARD MERA★★

■ 6ha 36000 ② D ⬛ ↓

A beautifully coloured Beaujolais-Villages. The nose is well developed but still needed to mature at the time of tasting (early 1985). On the palate it is quite sweet, soft, full and very refined. A

very complete wine which will keep its good qualities a little longer than is usual with this type. (1984) ✔ Beaujolais.
🕯 Bernard Mera, Marchampt, 69430 Beaujeu; tel. 74 04 32 94 ꭲ By appt.

RENE ET CHRISTIAN MIOLANE★★

| ■ | 16ha | 100000 | 3 D 🍾 ↓ |

Very lively, with a pleasant, clean bouquet and great character and originality. This is one for Beaujolais lovers and for all those who seek a little something extra. (1984) ✔ Beaujolais, Beaujolais-Villages 'Cuvée Cotabras', Marc de Beaujolais.
🕯 GAEC Miolane René et Christian, Le Cellier, Salles en Beaujolais, 69460 St-Etienne-des-Ouillières; tel. 74 67 52 67 ꭲ By appt.

CHATEAU DE MONTMELAS

| ■ | 90ha | 3 D 🍾 ◑ ↓ |

82 **83** 84

A rather seductive wine, with a promising ruby colour and fruity nose. On the palate it has substance and considerable warmth, but a necessarily rather short finish. (1984)
🕯 Ets Mommessin, Charnay-les-Mâcon, 7100 Mâcon; tel. 85 34 47 74 ꭲ By appt.

DOMAINE DES NUGUES★★

| ■ | 11ha | 72000 | 3 D 🍾 ↓ |

Very beautiful, strong colour, and expansive nose, with a good, harmonious blend of fruity tones, for this powerful, full-bodied wine. A superior Beaujolais-Villages. (1984) ✔ Beaujolais-Villages Primeur.
🕯 Gérard Gelin, Les Pasquiers, Lancié, 69220 Belleville; tel. 74 04 14 00 ꭲ By appt.

PASQUIER-DESVIGNES *Marquisat*★

| ■ | 40000 | 3 D |

⑦⑥ **83** 84

Good fruity colour and nose; finesse and warmth on the palate. Not quite ready when tasted in March but will soon round out. (1984)
🕯 Ets Pasquier-Desvignes, St-Lager, 69220 Belleville; tel. 74 66 14 20.

PASQUIER-DESVIGNES *Bérangère*★

| ■ | 60000 | 3 |

⑦⑥ **83** 84

Nice ruby colour with a touch of violet. Pleasantly light on the nose. Smooth on the palate with a slightly acidic aroma. The initial touch of acidity, supported by a touch of pétillance, quickly gives way to reveal a good, typical wine in the lighter style. (1984)
🕯 Ets Pasquier-Desvignes, St-Lager, 69220 Belleville; tel. 74 66 14 20 ꭲ No visitors.

PIAT PERE ET FILS

| ■ | 96ha | 706000 | 4 🍾 ↓ |

A beautiful colour and a good bouquet are followed by a subtle, pleasant flavour on the palate, although the body is rather harsh for a Beaujolais. It should be left to soften for a few months. (1984)
🕯 *MM*. Piat Père et Fils, 71570 La Chapelle-de-Guinchay; tel. 85 36 77 77 ꭲ By appt.

DOMAINE DU PY-DE-BULLIAT★

| ■ | 10ha | 600000 | 3 D 🍾 ↓ |

Splendid colour and fruity bouquet reminiscent of strawberries; the overall effect is rich and harmonious. Very young on the palate in its fifth month, but will be just right next summer. (1984)
🕯 R. Martin et Fils, Régnié-Durette, 69430 Beaujeu; tel. 74 04 20 17 ꭲ By appt.

DOMAINE DES QUARANTE ECUS★

| ■ | 5ha | 23000 | 3 D 🍾 ◑ |

A refreshing, pleasant wine with a light, pretty colour and a fruity nose evocative of grapes. It is very fresh and youthful on the palate and the Gamay aroma is highly developed. (1984)
🕯 Bernard Nesme, Les Vergers, Lantignié, 69340 Beaujeu; tel. 74 04 85 80 ꭲ By appt.

DOMAINE DES RAMPAUX *Régnié*★

| ■ | 3ha | 14000 | 2 D 🍾 ↓ |

Good colour and nose; equally pleasant on the palate; well balanced with powerful aromas. A very nice wine, to be drunk very cool within the year. (1984)
🕯 René Passot, Dom. des Rampaux Régnié-Durette, 69430 Beaujeu; tel. 74 04 35 68 ꭲ By appt.

CHATEAU DE LA ROCHE★

| ■ | 35ha | 216000 | 3 🍾 ↓ |

A lovely colour and a fine bouquet. Supple and fruity on the palate, this is the true Beaujolais-Villages, with everything as one would expect it to be. A classic. (1984)
🕯 Ets Loron et Fils, Pontanevaux, 71570 La Chapelle-de-Guinchay; tel. 85 36 70 52 ꭲ No visitors.

DOMAINE DE LA ROCHE★

| ■ | 3 ↓ |

A beautiful colour and fine nose, with a very pleasant roundness on the palate: the good bottle that one expects from this grower. (1984)
🕯 SA Thorins, Pontanevaux 71570 La Chapelle-de-Guinchay; tel. 75 36 70 43 ꭲ No visitors.

JOEL ROCHETTE★★★

| ■ | 1ha | 10000 | 2 D ◑ ↓ |

Glistening purple colour, subtle, distinguished bouquet – and sheer perfection on the palate. A full-bodied wine, with light, mouth-filling fruit and a smoothness which caresses the palate. A very fine bottle. (1984)
🕯 Joel Rochette, Le Chalet, Régnié-Durette, 69430 Beaujeu; tel. 74 04 35 78 ꭲ By appt.

CLAUDE ET BERNARD ROUX
Beaujolais-Régnié★★

■　　　　　7.5ha　4800　　[3] [D] 🍶 ↓

Lovely, light colour and very fruity bouquet. Light on the palate with considerable quality and freshness. This combination is typical of the region. (1984)
☛ Claude et Bernard Roux, La Haute-Ronze, Régnié-Durette, 69430 Beaujeu; tel. 74 69 22 58
☛ Héritiers Vernay.

DOMAINE DE LA ROUZE★

■　　　　　3.1ha　19000　　[2] [D] 🍶 ⑪ ↓

The very beautiful colour is indicative of a good constitution. This wine is extremely open, with depth and clarity in which many youthful qualities are retained. Consequently it can be left for a while to become perfectly balanced. (1984)
☛ G. Bernardo-Braillon, Régnié-Durette, 69430 Beaujeu; tel. 74 04 30 48 ⊻ By appt.

JEAN-MICHEL SAUZON★★

■　　　　　4ha　27600　　[3] [D] ⑪ ↓

A strong colour with purple reflections, a very fruity and expansive bouquet. Well balanced and full on the palate. A very good bottle. (1984)
☛ Jean-Michel Sauzon, Les Grandes Bruyères, 69460 St-Etienne-des-Ouillières; tel. 74 03 42 84 ⊻ Closed 1st fortnight in Aug.

DOMAINE DE LA SORBIERE★

■　　　　　12ha　90000　　[3] [D] 🍶 ↓

76 79 81 ★82 ★83 ★⑧④ [84]

A distinctive bottle for this wine whose structural qualities make it mature slower than the standard Beaujolais-Villages. Nice colour and pleasant, delicate nose; full and balanced on the palate with very fruity aromas. Keep for a while yet. (1984)
☛ Jean-Charles Pirot, Quincié-en-Beaujolais, 69430 Beaujeu; tel. 74 04 30 32 ⊻ By appt.

DOMAINE DE LA TEPPE★

■　　　　　24400　　[3] [D] 🍶 ↓

This wine was tasted at 18 months and still has a lovely, young colour, a great deal of fruitiness and also a youthful, pleasant nose. It is very pleasant on the palate and you can detect a lessening of acidity. A very attractive wine which has reached the end of its youth, by no means a disadvantage. (1983) ✔ Moulin à Vent.
☛ Philibert Moreau, 4 Rue Georges-Lecomte, 71003 Mâcon; tel. 85 38 42 87 ⊻ By appt ☛ Henri et Robert Bouzereau.

DOMAINE DES TERRES-DESSUS★

■　　　　　10ha　66000　　[2] [D] 🍶 ↓

Beautiful strong garnet colour and a pleasant nose with a somewhat original hint of Morello cherries. Full and fresh on the palate. (1984) ✔ Fleurie.
☛ Jean Floch, Les Terres-Dessus, Lancié, 69220 Belleville; tel. 74 04 13 85 ⊻ Daily 8.00–20.00.

LA TOUR BOURDON
Beaujolais-Régnié★

■　　　　　13ha　42000　　[3] [D] 🍶 ↓

The colour is something between ruby-red and a very ripe cherry shade. Ready for drinking, so one may open it immediately to enjoy the fruit, or postpone it for six months or a year, to let the body develop. (1984)
☛ *MM.* Rampon Frères, GAEC de la Tour Bourdon, Régnié-Durette, 69430 Beaujeu; tel. 74 04 32 15 ⊻ By appt.

GERARD ET JACQUELINE TRICHARD★

■　　　　　3ha　21600　　[3] [D] 🍶 ⑪ ↓

Seems to be going through a difficult age, which is unusual but not unpromising. Lively, full-bodied and long, it has good foundations and will develop its bouquet. It should be ready when a year old. (1984)
☛ G. et J. Trichard, Bel Avenir, 71570 La Chapelle-de-Guinchay; tel. 85 36 77 54 ⊻ By appt.

DOMAINE DES TROIS VOUTES★

■　　　　　7.5ha　55000　　[3]

76 [76] 81 83 84

The colour is a lovely light purple and the nose has an attractive, well-developed fruity quality. Well balanced, rounded and full-bodied, with a good, long finish. (1984)
☛ J. Pellerin, Le Moulin, 69830 St-Georges-de-Reneins; tel. 74 67 61 36 ⊻ No visitors.

Brouilly and Côte-de-Brouilly

From the summit of Mont Brouilly, 484 m high, the visitor can survey Beaujolais, the Mâconnais and Dombes as far as the Mont d'Or. The surrounding slopes are divided between the twin appellations Côte-de-Brouilly and Brouilly both producing rich, grapey Grand Cru wines. The AOC Côte-de-Brouilly vineyard is situated on the upper slopes of granite and extremely hard, blue-green schist. Some 16000 hectolitres of wine are produced from 3300 hectares of land, divided between the four communes of Odénas, St-Lager, Cercié, and Quincié.

The Brouilly AOC area covers the foothills to the east and south of Mont Brouilly, and produces 65000 hectolitres of wine from 12000 hectares of land. The appellation also extends into St-Etienne-la-Varenne and Charentay. In the commune of Cercié there is a famous vineyard called 'La Pisse-Vieille'.

Brouilly

CHATEAU D'ALEYRAC★★

■   7ha   45000   🔳4 D ⑪ ⌄

82 83 84

Beautiful, brilliant colour and good bouquet. On the palate an excellent balance and plenty of firmness. This bottle will drink well in its second year. (1984)
↪ Emil Chandesais, Ch. St-Nicolas, Fontaines, 71150 Chagny; tel. 85 91 41 77.

SCI VIGNOBLES DE BEL-AIR★★

■   5ha   36000   🔳3 D ▮ ⌄

★79 81 82

Beautiful, brilliant colour with a bouquet reminiscent of soft fruits, and hints of strawberries and raspberries in the powerful aroma. Well balanced on the palate and very good length. A pleasant wine. (1984) ✔ Beaujolais.
↪ SCI. Vignobles de Bel-Air, St-Jean-d'Ardières, 69220 Belleville; tel. 74 66 00 16 ☘ By appt ↪ M. Fessy.

CAVE BETHU★

■   6ha   20000   🔳4 D ▮ ⌄

Light colour and fruity nose announce an extremely supple wine with a well-defined, aromatic character, smooth and very pleasant on the palate. Best drunk in its first year. (1984)
↪ Paul Beaudet, Pontanevaux, 71570 La Chapelle-de-Guinchay; tel. 85 36 72 76 ☘ By appt.

COLLIN ET BOURISSET

■   30000   🔳4 ▮ ⌄

★83 83 ★84 84

Beautiful colour and full nose, confirmed by fine qualities on the palate. The overall effect is still a bit rough (at six months) but should become more rounded after a few months to make a perfect wine. (1984)
↪ MM. Collin et Bourisset, Rue de la Gare, 71680 Crêches-sur-Saône; tel. 85 37 11 15 ☘ No visitors.

ROBERT CONDEMINE *Pissevieille*★

■   6ha   10000   🔳3 D ▮ ⑪ ⌄

Good bright colour; a robust wine, fairly true to the Brouilly form. Should preferably be drunk young. (1984)
↪ Robert Condemine, Les Bruyères, Cercié, 69220 Belleville; tel. 74 66 19 45.

DOMAINE CRET DES GARANCHES★★★

■   7ha   42000   🔳3 D ▮ ⌄

55 59 62 80 ★81 82 ★83 ★(84) 84

This 1984 Brouilly is truly exceptional – the best you can find in this appellation. Deep colour and powerful and varied bouquet. Rounded and warm on the palate, a very long finish and perfect balance. A very refined wine. It can be drunk now or will keep a little longer; either way it will be excellent. (1984)
↪ Bernard Dufaitre, Dom. Crêt des Garanches, Odenay, 69460 St-Etienne-des-Ouillières; tel. 74 03 41 46 ☘ By appt. Closed 15 Aug.–15 Sept.

PIERRE DUPOND★

■   90000   🔳3 ▮ ⌄

79 ★81 ★82 83

Light in colour but with a very pleasant, fruity bouquet. Perfect for drinking young. (1984)
↪ Pierre Dupond, 339 Rue de Thizy, 69653 Villefranche-en-Beaujolais; tel. 74 65 24 32 ☘ No visitors.

DOMAINE DE LA FOLIE★★

■   5ha   18000   🔳3 ⑪ ⌄

A beautiful bottle: the fruity nose combining with fullness on the palate. A fine example of the appellation. (1984)
↪ Vins Gobet, Cuvier Beaujolais, Blaceret, 69830 St-Georges-de-Reneins; tel. 74 67 54 57 ☘ No visitors.

ALAIN MICHAUD★

■   6ha   18000   🔳3 D ⑪ ⌄

74 ★75 76 78 ★81 ★83 84

A beautiful colour, with a delicate nose little developed on the day after bottling, but which should become more evident during the year. It is marked by a fairly original *goût de terroir* and a full-bodied character, and has its own particular place in the appellation. (1984)
↪ Alain Michaud, Beauvoir, Cédex 1145, St-Lager, 69220 Belleville; tel. 74 66 29 49 ☘ By appt. Closed during harvest.

J. PELLERIN

■   11ha   66000   🔳4 ▮ ⑪

(76) ★83 84

Lightness is the main quality of this wine and shows itself in both the colour, the nose and on the palate, where it turns out to be fruity and very drinkable. (1984)
↪ J. Pellerin, Le Moulin, 69830 St-Georges-de-Reneins; tel. 74 67 61 36 ☘ No visitors.

PIAT PERE ET FILS

■   11ha   73000   🔳2 ▮ ⌄

84 84

Light colour and nose carry through to fruitiness, suppleness and charm on the palate. A Brouilly to be drunk in its first year. (1984)
↪ MM. Piat Père et Fils, BP 10, 71570 La Chapelle-de-Guinchay; tel. 85 36 77 77 ☘ No visitors.

JEAN-PAUL RUET★★★

■ 11ha 78000 3 D ▮ ↓

Beautiful, brilliant colour and fruity bouquet. Full and fat on the palate, this is a complete wine, true to form, and among the best of the growth. (1984) ✔ Beaujolais Primeur and Nouveau, Beaujolais-Villages, Brouilly Morgon.
↱ Jean-Paul Ruet, Voujon, Cercié, 69220 Belleville; tel. 74 66 35 45 ☌ By appt. Closed Sun.

DOMAINE DE SABURIN★

■ 16.5ha 96000 4 D ▮ ↓

83 83 84

Ruby colour and a hint of chocolate on the nose; it is also full-bodied and stylish, and has a lovely, silky finish. Should be served chilled (11°C.). (1983) ✔ Brouilly Dom. de Saburin, Juliénas, Beaujolais-Villages.
↱ *MM.* Bouchard Père et Fils, Au Château, 21200 Beaune; tel. 80 22 14 41 ☌ By appt. Closed Aug. and one week in Feb.

CHATEAU SAINT-LAGER★★

■ 15ha 30000 3 D

★⑧③ 83 ★84

A beautifully presented wine: pretty colour and remarkable nose. Full and round on the palate, perfectly balanced, fruity and characteristic. (1984)
↱ Jacques Depagneux, 69400 Ville-Franche-sur-Saône; tel. 74 65 42 60 ☌ By appt.

CELLIER DES SAMSONS★

■ 4

★⑧③ 83 ★84

Fresh and fruity wine; discreet nose, but smooth and pleasant on the palate. (1984)
↱ Cellier des Samsons, Quincié-en-Beaujolais, 69430 Beaujeu; tel. 74 66 24 19 ☌ No visitors.

CHATEAU DES TOURS★★

■ 46ha 300000 4 D ▮ ↓

81 83 84

Still closed up at six months, this wine is complex on the palate, showing that it will be an outstanding bottle in a few months' time. (1984)
↱ Dom. des Tours, St-Etienne-la-Varenne, 69830 St-Georges-de-Reneins; tel. 74 03 40 86 ☌ By appt.

Côte de Brouilly

PAUL BEAUDET★★

■ 12ha 20000 3 ▮ ↓

⑦⓪ 81 83 83 ★84

The colour indicates a robustness which will slow down the wine's development. At six months it is still immature, but full of promise for the future. Every chance of making a remarkable bottle in its second year, in line with the general character of this cru. (1984)
↱ Paul Beaudet, Pontanevaux, 71570 La Chapelle-de-Guinchay; tel. 85 36 72 76 ☌ No visitors.

ALAIN BERNILLON★★

■ 7ha 30000 3 D ▮ ⑾ ↓

76 78 81 82 83 ★84

Beautiful colour and full, complex bouquet with a hint of blackberries. Very well balanced and strong on the palate, with a fairly full-bodied finish. A marvellous wine which should preferably be left to improve for a while. It will go well with strongly flavoured dishes. (1984)
↱ Alain Bernillon, 'Godefroy', St-Lager, 69220 Belleville-sur-Saône; tel. 74 66 12 00 ☌ By appt.

COLLIN ET BOURISSET★

■ 10000 4 ▮ ↓

⑦⑨ 81 83 84

A handsome wine which was not yet fully in bloom at six months, but which showed a great deal of potential. Its beautiful colour and full body give promise of a very fine bottle at about 18 months. (1984)
↱ *MM.* Collin et Bourisset, Rue de la Gare, 71680 Crêches-sur-Saône; tel. 85 37 11 15 ☌ No visitors.

JACQUES DEPAGNEUX★★★

■ 25ha 30000 3 ⑾ ↓

⑧③ 83 84

Beautiful colour and fine bouquet; ideal balance on the palate. Its dominant tannin means it will be good this year, next year and perhaps even later. Among the best of its class. (1984)
↱ Jacques Depagneux, 69400 Ville-Franche-sur-Saône; tel. 74 65 42 60 ☌ No visitors.

GEORGES DUBOEUF★★

■ 10ha 30000 3 D ⑾ ↓

A pretty colour and a highly developed bouquet. Easy to drink, fragrant and extremely pleasant. This wine has some of the distinction of its growth but, as it is ready now, it needs to be drunk in its first year. (1984)
↱ Georges Duboeuf, Romanèche-Thorins, 71570

La Chapelle-de-Guinchay; tel. 85 35 51 13
Ⓧ Mon.–Fri. 8.00–12.00/14.00–17.00. Closed
Aug.

DOMAINE GRAND CUVAGE*

■ 15ha 50000 **4** **D** **◗** **⌄**
⑦ 83 *83

Rather more feminine than one expects of this
cru. Beautiful colour and delicate character; very
good first impression, but there is a risk that this
wine may mature very quickly. (1984)
◗ Pierre Ferraud et Fils, 69220 Belleville; tel.
74 66 08 05.

DOMAINE DES GRANDES VIGNES*

■ 6ha 40200 **4** **D** **◗** **⌄**
76 78 79 82 **83**

A beautiful colour and an expansive bouquet
with a fruity element dominated by banana. Still
a little tannic (just after bottling), it should
mature in a few months' time. (1984) ✔ Morgon,
Beaujolais-Villages, Brouilly.
◗ A. J.-C. et J. Nesme, Quincié-en-Beaujolais,
69430 Beaujeu; tel. 74 04 31 02 Ⓧ By appt. Closed
1 Jan., 25 Dec.

CLAUDIUS GUERIN*

■ 6ha 25000 **3** **D**
76 **83**

A fairly ordinary wine which has developed quite
quickly. At 18 months it has a light colour already
a little marked by age, but it still has plenty of
quality. A pleasant wine which should be drunk
young. (1983)
◗ Claudius Guérin, Odenas, 69460 St-Etienne-
des-Ouillières; tel. 74 03 41 63.

ETS LORON ET FILS**

■ 20000 **3** **◗** **⌄**
⑧③ **83** 84

Although still reserved on the nose, this wine
shows all the usual qualities of the 1984 on the
palate. Very full body and, considering a mere six
months bottle age, remarkably developed aromas. Will probably be at its peak at around 18
months, and will then be an excellent bottle.
(1984)
◗ Ets Loron et Fils, Pontanevaux, 71570 La
Chapelle-de-Guinchay; tel. 85 36 70 52 Ⓧ No
visitors.

MATHELIN*

■ 17ha 9000 **3** **D** **◗** **⌄**
82 ⑧③ 84 **84**

Béautiful colour and nose, but an over-mature
taste. This, while certainly very pleasant, generally indicates rapid – perhaps too rapid – future
development. A good bottle to be drunk fairly
young. (1984)
◗ Vins Mathelin, BP3, Châtillon-d'Azergues,
69380 Lozanne; tel. 74 84 39 24 Ⓧ Daily 8.30–
12.00/14.00–19.00. Closed week of 15 Aug.

J. PELLERIN**

■ 11.5ha 70000 **4** **◗** **◗** **⌄**
*83 **83** 84

Tasted at 18 months. A slow-maturing wine, full
bodied but not too powerful. Consistent balance,
from the colour to the final note of fruitiness. A
good example of the cru. (1983)
◗ J. Pellerin, Le Moulin, 69830 St-Georges-de-
Reneins; tel. 74 67 61 36 Ⓧ No visitors.

CELLIER DES SAMSONS**

■ **4**
⑧③ **83** **84**

Good colour and fruit on the nose. A medium-
bodied wine, with good aromatic development,
which will stay young at least until its second year
in bottle. Consistent quality overall. (1984)
◗ Cellier des Samsons, Quincié-en-Beaujolais,
69430 Beaujeu; tel. 74 66 24 19 Ⓧ No visitors.

SARRAU*

■ 20000 **4** **◗** **⌄**
⑦ 81 83 84

A fairly typical Côte de Brouilly, very characteristic of its vintage. An above average wine.
(1984)
◗ *M.* Sarrau, St-Jean-d'Ardières, 69220 Belleville; tel. 74 66 19 43 Ⓧ No visitors.

GILBERT THIVEND*

■ 4.2ha 15000 **3** **◗** **⌄**
76 79 81 *82 *84

A bright, beautiful colour like that of very ripe
cherries, and a bouquet with a hint of smoke. On
the palate it is very full of flavour, easy to drink
and fairly long. (1984)
◗ Gilbert Thivend, Brouilly, 69460 Odenas; tel.
74 03 45 13 Ⓧ By appt.

CHATEAU THIVIN**

■ 20ha 132000 **4** **D** **◗** **⌄**
76 79 81 83 **84**

Beautiful, intense ruby colour, and attractive,
fruity bouquet. On the palate this wine is of a
high standard, well balanced and mature with a
long finish. All this goes to make an excellent
wine from a charming old estate which belonged
to Humbert II, Lord of Beaujeu, in the 12th
century. (1984) ✔ Brouilly.
◗ Claude Geoffray, Ch. Thivin, Odenas, 69460
St-Etienne-des-Ouillières; tel. 74 03 40 15 Ⓧ By
appt. ◗ *Mme* Veuve Claude Geoffray.

Chenas

Chenas is one of the smallest Beaujolais appellations, covering a mere 250
hectares within the departments of the
Rhône and Saône-et-Loire. It produces 13000 hectolitres of wine in the
communes of Chenas and La Chapelle-de-Guinchay. The Chenas wines
that are grown on the steep granite
slopes in the west are brightly coloured, powerful, but not overly assertive. Their floral aromas of roses and

125

violets are reminiscent of Moulin-à-Vent – which in fact occupies most of the commune's land. The wines that come from the silty, less hilly area in the east are not quite so full-bodied. Although the appellation produces fine wines, its small size is a disadvantage, and Chenas tends to be seen as the poor relation of other Beaujolais growths. The cooperative in the Château produces 45 per cent of the appellation wines; a very attractive display of oak casks is to be seen in its medieval cellars.

PAUL BEAUDET★★

■   14ha   60000   3 D ⬛ ⬤ ↓

Good colour, and fruity, very expansive and seductive nose. On the palate, an excellent balance of body and lingering fruit. A wine with class and charm. (1984)
↜ Paul Beaudet, Pontanevaux, 71570 La Chapelle-de-Guinchay; tel. 85 36 72 76 ⍑ By appt.

JEAN BENON★

■   2ha   12000   4 D ⬛ ⬤ ↓
66 67   70 71   72 73   74 75 **76** 77 78 79

This 1984 is typical of the growth, with a beautiful ruby colour, and an exceptional nose. This wine is easy to drink, very round on the palate, warm and grapey. (1984) ✔ Juliénas 1983, Beaujolais-Villages 1984.
↜ Jean Benon, Les Blémonts, 71570 La Chapelle-de-Guinchay; tel. 85 36 71 92.

CHATEAU BONNET★

■   8ha   30000   3 D ⬛ ⬤
69 76 **81** 82 83

Colour still a touch purple. This very fresh wine, bottled at the end of the winter, is still a little clumsy and not yet in condition, but it is full and solid, and in a few months' time will have developed considerably. (1984) ✔ Juliénas, Moulin à Vent, Beaujolais Blanc.
↜ Pierre Perrachon, Ch. Bonnet, 71570 La Chapelle-de-Guinchay; tel. 85 36 70 41 ⍑ By appt.

UNION DES VITICULTEURS DU CRU CHENAS★★

■   60000   3 D ⬛ ⬤ ↓
★76 78 81 ★⑧³ ★83

The nose of this wine is rather closed in, but releases its qualities when it has been opened for a short time. It then appears light and quite long-lived on the palate. (1984)
↜ Cave du Ch. de Chenas, Chenas, 69840 Juliénas; tel. 74 04 11 91 ⍑ By appt.

COLLIN ET BOURISSET★★

■   30000   4 ⬛ ↓
83 84

A beautiful appearance with considerable fragrant quality and a most pleasant texture. This is a very warm wine. (1984)
↜ MM. Collin et Bourisset, Rue de la Gare, 71680 Crèches-sur-Saône; tel. 85 37 11 15 ⍑ No visitors.

GEORGES DUBOEUF★★

■   24000   3 D ⬤ ↓
⑦⑥ 81 ★83 83 ★84 ★ 84

A very pretty colour and an excellent, well-balanced wine overall. On the palate it is quite outstanding. A very good wine. (1984)
↜ Georges Duboeuf, 71720 Romanèche-Thorins; tel. 85 35 51 13 ⍑ Mon.–Fri. 8.00–12.00/14.00–17.00. Closed Aug.

LES GANDELINS★★

■   2ha   12000   3 D ⬛ ⬤ ↓

A beautiful, very intense ruby red, still with the fruitiness of the Primeur (in February 1985). It does not completely cover the variety of fragrances (fruity and spicy) which will develop during the next few months, but is well balanced on the palate, rich and strong, and is a wine which promises well. (1984) ✔ Moulin à Vent.
↜ Hubert Lapierre, 'Les Gandelins', 71570 La Chapelle-de-Guinchay; tel. 85 36 74 89 ⍑ Daily 9.00–19.00.

GERARD LAPIERRE

■   215ha   1320000   3 D ⬤ ↓
76 78 ★81 ★83 83 84

Youthful colour and fruitiness even at 18 months! Rather discreet on the nose, but full on the palate. A very appealing wine. (1983)
↜ Gérard Lapierre, Les Deschamps, Chenas, 69840 Juliénas; tel. 85 36 70 74 ⍑ By appt.

LORON ET FILS★

■   4ha   24000   3 ⬛ ↓
⑧³ 83 84

Very beautiful colour but, at six months, still a very discreet nose. Well balanced and pleasant on the palate. (1984)
↜ Ets Loron et Fils, Pontanevaux, 71570 La Chapelle-de-Guinchay; tel. 85 36 70 52 ⍑ No visitors.

MATHELIN★

■   10000   3 D ⬤ ↓

A pretty enough wine, but the bottle we tasted had sadly been affected by what the scientists call a 'reduction' in taste, revealed more on the nose than on the palate. Fortunately, when decanted, the wine recovered and showed its very considerable qualities to the full. (1984)
↜ Vins Mathelin, BP 3, Châtillon-d'Azergues, 69380 Lozanne; tel. 74 84 39 42 ⍑ Mon.–Sat. 8.30–12.00/14.00–19.00. Closed week of 15 Aug.

DOMAINE DES PINS★★

■   4.5ha   4 D
⑧³ 83 84

A beautiful appearance confirmed on the palate with an aromatic character strongly reminiscent of soft red fruit; perfect balance and remarkable length on the palate. (1984)
↜ M. Sarrau, St-Jean-d'Ardières, 69220 Belleville; tel. 74 66 19 43 ⍑ By appt.

SARRAU★★

■ 28 500 [4] [D] [▮] [⌁]

⑧ [83] [84]

Bright colour and masses of charm; intensely aromatic character of red fruit on the nose, well sustained by perfect balance and a remarkable lingering quality on the palate. (1984)
⊷ *M*. Sarrau, St-Jean-d'Ardières, 69220 Belleville; tel 74 66 19 43 ⍾ By appt.

CHARLES VIENOT★★

■ 12 000 [4] [D]

83 84

Tasted at 18 months, this wine had kept its youth and fullness without any signs of weakening. Beautiful colour, fine nose, lovely taste, perfectly balanced on the palate – a fruity wine of great character. (1983)
⊷ Ets Charles Vienot, 21700 Nuits-St-Georges; tel. 80 62 31 05 ⍾ By appt.

Chiroubles

This is the highest of all the Beaujolais crus, grown at an altitude of 400 m on 350 hectares of commune land forming a natural amphitheatre of vines. The soil is light, thin granite sand and produces about 18 000 hectolitres of wine each year. The cooperative at Chiroubles produces 15 per cent of the total. Chiroubles is a delicate, elegant wine, clean and charming, with a fragrance of violets, that can sometimes show a hint of its neighbours Morgon and Fleurie. The wine can be drunk very young, at any time of day – preferably with a plate of charcuterie. Visitors can try the combination themselves at the wine chalet high on the slopes of the Fut d'Avenas, rising 700 m above the village and easily accessible from it.

In April of each year, Chiroubles honours a famous son, nineteenth-century ampelographer (grape expert) Victor Pulliat. Born in 1827, Pulliat achieved an international reputation for his work on the ripening times of grapes and the grafting of vines. In the course of his studies he collected more than 2000 varieties at his Tempéré estate.

COLLIN ET BOURISSET★★

■ 4 000 [5] [⌁]

⑦ *81 *82 *[83] *84

A well-matured wine, the fruitiness of its first youth having faded to allow a harmonious overall effect with no real loss of stature. (1983)
⊷ *MM*. Collin et Bourisset, Rue de la Gare, 71680 Crêches-sur-Saône; tel. 85 37 11 15 ⍾ By appt.

JACQUES DEPAGNEUX★

■ [D]

[83] ⑭

The colour is light and the whole is a characteristic example of the growth. A classic Chiroubles. (1984)
⊷ Jacques Depagneux, 69400 Villefranche-sur-Saône; tel. 74 65 42 60 ⍾ By appt.

GEORGES DUBOEUF★★★

■ 30 000 [3] [D] [ⅲ] [⌁]

⑦ 78 [78] 81 *83 *[83] [84]

This 1984 is full of charm, from its vivid colour, delightfully fruity bouquet and perfect mature balance in the mouth, right through to a finish which leaves a good, long sensation on the palate. It has great finesse and is quite outstanding. (1984)
⊷ Georges Duboeuf, 71720 Romanèche-Thorins; tel. 85 35 51 13 ⍾ Mon.–Fri. 8.00–12.00/14.00–17.00. Closed Aug.

VIGNERONAGE DURAND★★

■ 30 000 [4] [D]

81 ⑧ [84]

A beautiful colour and a very fruity bouquet, which is prolonged on the palate by a distinguished aroma. This wine is easy, elegant and well made, with a great deal of charm. (1984)
⊷ Paul Beaudet, Pontenavaux, 71570 La Chapelle-de-Guinchay; tel. 85 36 72 76 ⍾ By appt.

MATHELIN★★★

■ 2 000 000 [3] [D] [⌁]

[83] [84]

The fruity bouquet introduces a wine which is light on the palate and enlivened by carbon dioxide bubbles, creating a refreshing effect overall. (1984)
⊷ Vins Mathelin, Châtillon-d'Azergues, 69380 Lozanne; tel. 74 84 39 24 ⍾ By appt.

DOMAINE DU MOULIN★★★

■ 6 ha [▮] [ⅲ] [⌁]

⑧ [84]

Remarkable in all its aspects, from its colour to its persistence on the palate. Appearance, nose, length and aroma all conform to the highest standards. (1984)
⊷ André Depré, Dom. du Moulin, 69115 Chiroubles; tel. 74 69 11 18 ⍾ By appt.

PIAT PERE ET FILS★★

■ 23 000 [3] [D]

83 84 [84]

A pleasant appearance and a liveliness on the palate, due to the acidity, give this wine a certain depth which makes it very agreeable. (1984)
⊷ *MM*. Piat Père et Fils, 71570 La Chapelle-de-Guinchay; tel. 85 36 77 77.

CELLIER DES SAMSONS★★

■ 320 ha [4]

⑧ [83] [84]

A wine which has kept its youthful suppleness and fruitiness. Simply begs to be drunk – the finest of compliments. (1984)

127

⚓ Cellier des Samsons, Quincié-en-Beaujolais, 69430 Beaujeu; tel. 74 66 24 19 ⊤ No visitors.

Fleurie

Fleurie is the third largest Beaujolais appellation after Brouilly and Morgon. The 780 hectares of the appellation area lie entirely within the communal boundaries; the local soil is quite homogenous, consisting mostly of large-crystal granite which gives the wine finesse and fleshiness. About 44 000 hectolitres are produced each year. Fleurie is a wine with all the exuberance of the countryside in spring; full of light and promise, and fragrant with aromas of iris and violet. Some people like to drink it chilled, others at room temperature, but both factions would enjoy the famous Beaujolais dish of andouillette cooked in Fleurie wine.

There are two tasting cellars in the heart of the village – one near the town hall, the other at the cooperative. Both offer a wide range of wines, all with evocative local names such as La Rochette, La Chapelle des Bois, Les Roches, Grille-Midi and La Joie du Palais.

RENE BERROD★

■	1.5 ha	7500	4 D 🏺 ↓

㊶ 82 83 84

Beautiful deep red colour with glints of violet. Typical Fleurie style, the nose reminiscent of iris and the palate of violets. Tannic, full and rich. (1983)
⚓ René Berrod, 69820 Fleurie; tel. 74 04 13 63 ⊤ By appt.

DOMAINE BOUCHARD PERE ET FILS

■	11.8 ha	68 400	4 D 🏺 ↓

76 ㊲ 81 82 83 84

A 1984 wine that is very, very light – a common characteristic of this estate's production. Its colour, bouquet and balance are all *finot* (clever), as the people of Haut-Beaujolais used to say. Although it is light-weight, it is an attractive wine with a bright colour and a fruity nose, and is immensely drinkable. (1984)
⚓ MM. Bouchard Père et Fils, Au Château, 21202 Beaune; tel. 80 22 14 41 ⊤ By appt. Closed Aug. and one week in Feb.

MICHEL CHIGNARD *Les Muriers*★

■	7 ha	42 000	4 D 🏺 ◗ ↓

76 ㊲ 81 83 84

A beautiful colour and bouquet give a foretaste of a wine which, on the palate, is very well balanced, somewhat full bodied, and already very successful. Will mature still further in the months to come. (1984)

⚓ Michel Chignard, Le Point-du-Jour, 69820 Fleurie; tel. 74 04 11 87 ⊤ By appt.

GEORGES DUBOEUF
Chateau des Déduits★★

■		7 ha	30 000	3 D ◗ ↓

82 ★83 ★83 84

Lovely, deep colour. It was tasted in 1985 and has a dominant dash of banana which is common in very young wines. It shows considerable promise of developing a fine complex nose in a few months, with an underlying crispness of positive acidity which ensures that it will keep perfectly. It has a lovely finish on the palate, a sign that it will soon become pleasantly well balanced. (1984)
⚓ Georges Duboeuf, 71720 Romanèche-Thorins; tel. 85 35 51 13 ⊤ Mon.–Fri. 8.00–12.00/14.00–17.00. Closed Aug.

PIERRE DUPOND★

■		75 000	3 🏺 ↓

76 ★78 ★81 ★83

Very pronounced, deep colour with, at present, a closed nose. However, it is very powerful and promises well. It is full on the palate, with a lingering touch of freshness, so that at the end of 1985 it may well start to develop its true qualities. (1984)
⚓ Pierre Dupond, 339 Rue de Thizy, 69653 Villefranche-en-Beaujolais; tel. 74 65 24 32 ⊤ No visitors.

COOPERATIVE DE FLEURIE
Cuvée du Cardinal Bienfaiteur★

■	390 ha	35 000	4 D 🏺 ↓

53 76 78 81 81 ★㊸

Cardinal's red suits this Fleurie well, and although Fleurie is sometimes thought of as the most 'feminine' of the Beaujolais crus, this wine has been judiciously blended to give a touch of something extra. (1983) ✔ Beaujolais, Beaujolais-Villages.
⚓ Coop. de Fleurie, Le Bourg, 69820 Fleurie; tel. 74 04 11 70 ⊤ By appt.

COOPERATIVE DE FLEURIE
Cuvée Présidente Marguerite★

■		50 000	4 D 🏺 ↓

㊸ 83

Thirty years ago, 'la Marguerite', the daughter of Chabert of Fleurie, owner of the best charcuterie in the Beaujolais, became Présidente of the Coopérative. Her name is remembered in this 1983, with its lovely colour, its original, rather spicy bouquet and its great finesse, suppleness and charm. A silky wine which matures quickly. (1983)
⚓ Coop. de Fleurie, Le Bourg, 69820 Fleurie; tel. 74 04 11 70 ⊤ By appt.

CHATEAU DE FLEURIE★

■	6 ha	32 000	3 🏺 ↓

㊸ 83 84

A characteristic Fleurie of high quality and good balance; all the signs are that it will keep for a while yet. (1984)
⚓ Ets Loron et Fils, Pontanevaux, 71570 La Chapelle-de-Guinchay; tel. 85 36 70 52 ⊤ No visitors.

MATHELIN*

■	8 000	4 D ◧ ↓

The beautiful colour is the clue to a wine of elegance and delicacy combined with a certain lightness. Overall, a feminine, flattering wine. (1984)
↬ Vins Mathelin, BP 3, Châtillon-d'Azergues, 69380 Lozanne; tel. 74 84 39 24 ℣ Daily 8.30–12.00/14.00–19.00.

VIGNERONNAGE MEZIAT*

■	4 ha	22 000	4 D ◾ ↓

A wine with considerable fullness and stature. Very promising at six months, it needs a bit more time to blossom and become more rounded, but will then make an excellent bottle. (1984)
↬ Paul Beaudet, Pontanevaux, 71570 La Chapelle-de-Guinchay; tel. 85 36 72 76 ℣ By appt.

Juliénas
The Grand Cru Juliénas lies in the north-east of the Beaujolais-Villages region. Four communes make up the geographical area of the appellation: Juliénas, Jullié, Emeringues and Pruzilly, which is in Saône-et-Loire. The Gamay vine is grown over 560 hectares, partly on the granite soils of the west and partly on the sedimentary soils of very old alluvium in the east. Annual production of AOC Juliénas is about 30 000 hectolitres. These are full-bodied wines with fine colour and a bright, lively style, to be enjoyed in the spring after just a few months of bottle age. Thirty per cent of the appellation wine is made by a cooperative located within the walls of the former priory of Château du Bois de la Salle at Juliénas. In an annual ceremony held in mid-November, the commune presents its Victor Peyret prize to the artist, writer or journalist who has proved the worthiest taster of the new vintage; the prize is the winner's own weight in wine.

DOMAINE DE BEAUVERNAY*

■	4 ha	27 000	4 D ◾ ↓

Good colour and fruity nose; light, supple and pleasant on the palate. A fully rounded wine. (1984)
↬ Piat Père et Fils, BP 10, 71570 La Chapelle-de-Guinchay; tel. 85 36 77 77 ℣ By appt.

DOMAINE DE BOISCHAMPT*

■	6 ha	32 400	4 ◾ ↓

⑦⑥ ⑦⑧ ⑦⑨ *⑧① 82

Tasted on the day after it was bottled, this wine already had remarkable qualities. The colour was beautiful and the fruity bouquet had hints of peaches and wild strawberries. Well balanced, with a youthfulness on the palate, this wine

promises to have character in the future. (1984)
✔ Beaujolais-Villages.
↬ Pierre Dupont, 339 Rue de Thizy, 69653 Villefranche; tel. 74 65 24 32 ℣ No visitors.

DOMAINE BOUCHARD PERE ET FILS

■	8.3 ha	48 000	4 D ◾ ↓

⑦⑨ ⑧⓪ 81 *82 83 ⑧④

This style of wine will be attractive to those who like lightness in their wines as well as early maturity. It is pleasant, but not really typical of a 1984. (1984)
↬ Bouchard Père et Fils, Au Château, 21202 Beaune; tel. 80 22 14 41 ℣ By appt. Closed Aug. and one week Feb.

DOMAINE DE LA CONSEILLERE*

■	6 ha	40 000	4 D ◧ ↓

⑧② *83 ⑧③ *84

An attractive wine, fruity and supple, which should probably be drunk young. (1984)
↬ Ets Mommessin, Charnay-les-Mâcon, 71000 Mâcon; tel. 85 34 47 74 ℣ By appt.

GEORGES DUBOEUF**

■	30 000	3 D ◧ ↓

This 1983 has kept its very strong ruby-red colour and the youthfulness of its bouquet, combining scents of soft fruits, peach and cinnamon, which together create great finesse. On the palate it is perfectly balanced and rich, with good fruit. Its long finish forms a fitting conclusion to a generally well-made wine. (1983)
↬ Georges Duboeuf, 71720 Romanèche-Thorins; tel. 85 35 51 13 ℣ Mon.–Fri. 8.00–12.00/14.00–17.00. Closed Aug.

COOPERATIVE DES GRANDS VINS ***

■	164 ha	1 000 000	4 D ◾

78 ⑦⑨ *⑧⓪ 81 ⑧② ⑧④ ⑧④ 85

A quite remarkable Juliénas wine with a lovely deep ruby colour and a powerful, fruity bouquet that has hints of pine forests. The forthcoming nose is confirmed in the mouth where it is full bodied and lingering, and where the fruitiness is accompanied by a slight woodiness. A very attractive wine which will improve for being laid down for a few more months. (1984) ✔ Beaujolais-Villages, St-Amour.
↬ Coop. des Grands Vins, Ch. du Bois de la Salle, 69840 Juliénas; tel. 74 04 42 61. ℣ By appt. Closed 1 Aug.–30 Nov.

CHATEAU DE JULIENAS

■	20 ha	25 000	3 D ◾ ↓

⑦⑥ 77 ⑦⑧ ⑦⑨ *⑧① 82

This 1983 has a beautiful, strong colour and a fruity bouquet of peaches and blackcurrants. It presents something of a contrast on the palate, with a fairly high level of tannins and acidity, which masks the nose somewhat. Time may make it more supple and, after maturing for a short while, it should reveal its qualities. (1983)
↬ François Condemine, Ch. de Juliénas, 69840 Juliénas; tel. 74 04 41 43.

MATHELIN *Cuvée Bouchy*★★

■   15 000   🔲3 D ⑪ ↓

Good colour; nice and steady on the palate. Characteristic of its type with a solid structure giving it body, as well as its very fruity aroma. A good wine to be drunk in its second year. (1984)
↖ Vins Mathelin, BP 3, Châtillon-d'Azerques, 69380 Lozanne; tel. 74 84 39 24 ❦ Daily 8.30–12.00/14.00–19.00. Closed week 15 Aug.

PHILIBERT MOREAU

■   13 000   🔲4 D ▮ ⑪ ↓

⑦⑥ 78 79 80 81 82 ⑧③

A wine which has matured well but which, at 18 months, has little hope of further improvement, and indeed may soon begin to fade. A good bottle for immediate drinking. (1983)
↖ Philibert Moreau, 4 Rue Georges Lecomte, 71003 Mâcon; tel. 85 38 42 87 ❦ By appt.

DOMAINE DES POUPETS★★

■   5 ha   24 000   🔲4 D ▮ ↓

A very supple and fruity wine which, tasted at six months, still showed the dominant nuance of banana found in the primeurs. Will probably be at its best at about ten or twelve months, when it should have achieved a charming roundness. (1984)
↖ Paul Beaudet, Pontanevaux, 71570 La Chapelle-de-Guinchay; tel. 85 36 72 76 ❦ By appt.

CELLIER DE LA VIEILLE EGLISE ★★

■   15 000   🔲4 D ▮ ↓

78 ⑦⑨ ★⑧⓪ 81 ⑧② **83** ⑧④

This cellar was opened in 1954, specializing in Juliénas wines, and the 1983 vintage was selected as characteristic of the appellation. It is of high quality and has all the characteristics of the growth: a beautiful colour, a powerful and fruity aroma, balance, roundness and fullness on the palate, while still remaining youthful. (1983)
↖ Ass. des Prod. du Cru Juliénas, Cellier de la Vieille Eglise, 69840 Juliénas; tel. 74 04 41 43 ❦ Daily 10.00–12.00/14.30–18.00. Closed Tues. 1 Nov.–30 Jun.

DOMAINE DE LA VIEILLE EGLISE★

■   7 ha   36 000   🔲3 ▮ ↓

⑧③ **83** 84

Despite a light colour this wine has a good fruity nose and is splendid on the palate. Excellent balance and good persistent aroma. A very nice wine which can be drunk young. (1984)
↖ Ets Loron et Fils, Pontanevaux, 71570 La Chapelle-de-Guinchay; tel. 85 36 70 52 ❦ No visitors.

Morgon

This cru is located entirely within the commune of Villié-Morgon. The 1030 hectares classified AOC produce on average 55 000 hectolitres per year of this full-bodied, generous and fruity wine. Its characteristic fragrances of cherry and apricot come from the vineyard soil, a particular form of non-silicious schist, impregnated with manganese and ferrous oxide, which the local wine-makers call 'terre pourrie' (literally 'rotten soil'). In general, soil and climate combine to produce a Gamay wine with some of the qualities of a Burgundy.

Villié-Morgon takes pride in having been the first prestige Beaujolais growth to cater for wine-loving visitors. An excursion to the hillside vineyards of Mont Py (300 m) will give visitors a fine view of the appellation land. The old Roman road linking Lyons and Autun runs quite close to this landmark. In addition, the village has spacious, traditional-style tasting cellars in the Château de Fontcrenne which can accommodate several hundred people.

DOMAINE DE L'ANCIENNE CURE★★

■   5 ha   31 500   🔲4 D ▮ ↓

78 **79** **83** **84**

A soft, light, distinguished wine which is extremely pleasant. It has a lovely colour and a bouquet of great finesse, which is confirmed on the palate in the continuing aroma of peach. (1984)
↖ M. Sarrau, St-Jean-d'Ardières, 69220 Belleville; tel. 74 66 19 43 ❦ By appt.

DOMAINE AUCOEUR★

■   7 ha   60 000   🔲3 D ⑪ ↓

76 78 ⑦⑨ ⑧① ★⑧② **★82** ★⑧③

Good, lively, strong colour, and a beautiful nose reminiscent of soft fruits. Excellent on the palate, full-bodied, with good alcohol, tannin and acidity, which should soon start to soften, allowing the body and fragrance to predominate. This wine should be kept for a little, or else drunk with game. (1983) ✔ Beaujolais-Villages Cuvée Particulière, Beaujolais-Villages, Beaujolais.
↖ Noël Aucoeur, 'La Rochaud', 69910 Villié-Morgon; tel. 74 04 22 10 ❦ By appt. Closed 15 Aug.–1 Sept.

THOMAS BASSOT★

■   3500   🔲4 D ▮ ⑪ ↓

83 84

An attractive colour and an alluring, grapey nose. On the palate it is light and soft and has a great deal of charm. Should be drunk fairly young. (1984)
↖ Thomas Bassot. 5 Quai Dumorey, 21700 Nuits-St-Georges; tel. 80 62 31 05.

BOUCHARD PERE ET FILS★

■   11 ha   62 000   🔲4 D ▮ ↓

⑦⑥ 77 ⑧① ⑧③ 84

The lightness that the Bouchard estate seems to strive for in its Beaujolais wines has perhaps been taken a little too far here. This 1984 Morgon is rather thin, but nevertheless is quite fruity and very attractive. (1984)

➥ *MM*. Bouchard Père et Fils, BP 70, Au Château, 21202 Beaune; tel. 80 22 14 41 ☖ By appt. Closed Aug. and one week in Feb.

DOMAINE DE LA CHANAISE★

■   13 ha   78 000   ⬛3 ◻D ◻■ ⬛◗ ⬛↓

㊌ ㊍ ㊐ 76 ⬛76 ㊒ 81 83

This 1984 has a strong colour and a nose not yet developed at the end of 1985. The warm taste with a touch of vanilla promises well, although it is still a little dry. It needs to mature and should be allowed to breathe for a short time before drinking. (1984)

➥ Dominique Piron, Morgon, 69910 Villié-Morgon; tel. 74 04 22 11.

COLLIN ET BOURISSET★★

■   4000   ⬛4 ⬛↓

78 79 ★81 ★82 ★⬛83 ⬛84

An attractive colour and an excellent nose are notable in this wine which is quite well constructed on the palate. It has a great deal of finesse in its highly-concentrated flavours. Kirsch predominates and it is a very lingering wine, beautiful, scented and subtle. (1984)

➥ *MM*. Collin et Bourisset, Rue de la Gare, 71680 Crèches-sur-Saône; tel. 85 37 11 15 ☖ By appt.

JACQUES DEPAGNEUX *Les Versauds*★

■   25 000   ⬛3 ◻D

83 ⬛83

Classic Morgon colour and nose. Lovely light harmonious quality on the palate, with a flavour of soft fruits which is pleasantly lingering. The overall result is a very attractive wine. (1984)

➥ Jacques Depagneux, 69400 Villefranche-sur-Saône; tel. 74 65 42 60 ☖ By appt.

GEORGES DUBOEUF★

■   24 000   ⬛3 ◻D ⬛◗ ⬛↓

76 ㊛ ⬛81 ★83

Strong ruby-red colour and a forthcoming nose, with a dash of blackcurrant and a hint of oak. Full bodied and alcoholic on the palate and will probably reach its peak at the end of 1985 or beginning of 1986. (1983) ✐ Beaujolais and Maconnais wines.

➥ Georges Duboeuf, 71720 Romanèche-Thorins; tel. 85 35 51 13 ☖ Mon.–Fri. 8.00–12.00/14.00–17.00. Closed Aug.

DOMAINE DE L'EVEQUE★★

■   6 ha   40 000   ⬛4 ◻D ⬛◗ ⬛↓

78 ⬛78 ⬛81 ⬛83 84

The colour is a very strong purplish red, and makes a good introduction to a full-bodied, well-constructed wine, rather closed-in at six months, but possessing qualities which will emerge in a few months' time. (1984)

➥ Pierre Ferraud et Fils, 69220 Belleville; tel. 74 66 08 05. ☖ By appt.

CHATEAU GAILLARD★

■   9 ha   48 000   ⬛3 ◻D ◻■ ⬛↓

83 ⬛83

This wine, tasted at 18 months, is just ready for drinking. It is fruity, with a cherry aroma, and is quite delightful on the palate, where it has a good finish. (1983)

➥ Vins Mathelins, Châtillon-d'Azergues, 69380 Lozanne; tel. 74 84 39 24 ☖ By appt. Closed week of 15 Aug.➥ GAEC Gutty.

CHATEAU GAILLARD★★★

■   9.5 ha   25 000   ⬛3 ◻D ⬛◗ ⬛↓

72 ㊅ ㊇ ㊑ 82 ㊓ ⬛84

A beautiful, brilliant, strong colour with purplish reflections, and a very intense and pleasant bouquet, very well structured on the palate, with plenty of roundness, flavour and alcohol. A tempting nose of apricots and peaches. This is a very big wine which should be left for a few months to reach its peak. (Tasted at six months.) (1984)

➥ Guy Père et Fils, 69910 Villié-Morgon; tel. 74 69 12 77 ☖ By appt.

VIGNERONNAGE JAMBON★★

■   5 ha   24 000   ⬛3 ◻D

㊛ ⬛82 ⬛83

Good cherry-red colour, with an aroma of kirsch which dominates the fruity nose and carries through onto the palate. Overall, a light, smooth and harmonious wine, with a good lingering quality. A very pleasant bottle. (1984)

➥ Paul Beaudet, Pontanevaux, 71570 La Chapelle-de-Guinchay; tel. 85 36 72 76 ☖ By appt.

DOMAINE DE LATHEVIEILLE★★

■   15 ha   80 000   ⬛3 ◻D ◻■ ⬛◗ ⬛↓

76 78 80 ㊓ ★84

Beautiful violet-red colour, with an aroma of kirsch on the nose. Supple on the palate, with a certain slenderness, this wine is a good representative of its vintage. (1984)

➥ Ets Mommessin, Charnay-les-Mâcon, 71000 Mâcon; tel. 85 34 47 74 ☖ By appt.

LORON ET FILS★★

■   300 000   ⬛3 ◻■ ⬛↓

★83 ★⬛83

Extremely fruity and supple. A very pleasant, subtle, eminently drinkable wine. (1984)

➥ Ets Loron et Fils, Pontanevaux, 71570 La Chapelle-de-Guinchay; tel. 85 36 70 52 ☖ No visitors.

NICOLAS★

■   100 000   ⬛4 ◻■

An attractive ruby-red colour and a beautiful nose which is distinguished, spicy and very attractive. The elegance and finesse of its aroma are confirmed on the palate. (1984)

➥ Ets Nicolas, 2 Rue de Valmy, 94220 Charenton; tel. 01 37 59 20 ☖ No visitors.

PASQUIER-DESVIGNES★★

■ 30000 ▨4

⑦⑥ 81 83 84

Lively, beautiful and intense colour. The overall effect is of finesse allied to fortitude, aromatic distinction and full body. A wine of class and stature, that will probably improve and certainly keep. (1983)
⊶ Ets Pasquier-Desvignes, St-Lager, 69220 Belleville; tel. 74 66 14 20 ⥷ No visitors.

J. PELLERIN★

■ 80000 ▨4

76 ★83 ★84

This is a classic of its growth, without any outstanding features; it comes up to standard in every respect, and is well made and pleasant. (1984)
⊶ J. Pellerin, Le Moulin, 69830 St-Georges-de-Reneins; tel. 74 67 61 36 ⥷ No visitors.

DOMAINE DES PILLETS★

■ 32ha 10800 ▨4 ▨D ▤ ◑ ⥯

⑥④ ⑦① ⑦③ ⑦⑥ 76 78 ★79 80 81 ★82 83

Vinified and looked after by an oenologist. The 1983 has the typical characteristics of the Morgon wines which need a little time to come round before reaching maturity. It should be tried in 1986. (1983) ✔ Beaujolais-Villages.
⊶ Gérard Brisson, GFA les Pillets, 69910 Villié-Morgon; tel. 74 04 21 60. ⥷ By appt. Closed first fortnight Aug.

CELLIER DES SAMSONS★

■ 66000 ▨4

81 ⑧③ 83 84

A Morgon of the old school, very fleshy, which, at six months, still needs the refining effects of time. Full of promise and worth waiting for. (1984)
⊶ Cellier des Samsons, Quincié-en-Beaujolais, 69430 Beaujeu; tel. 74 66 24 19 ⥷ By appt.

PIERRE SAVOYE *Côte de Py*★★★

■ 14ha ▨D ▤ ◑ ⥯

76 77 ⑦⑧ 81 83 84

A very beautiful wine with a bouquet characteristic of the growth. Full, rich and powerful, this wine is well balanced with plenty of flavour and a very persistent, big grapey nose. Very consistent overall, this is the top-quality wine of the growth. (1984)
⊶ Pierre Savoye, 69910 Villié-Morgon; tel. 74 04 21 92 ⥷ By appt.

CHARLES VIENOT★

■ ▨4 ▨D

79 80 ⑧③ 83 84

Well balanced and supple at 18 months, and still of a good standard. Fruity, with a dominant note of peach-stones on the nose, this is an excellent combination of taste and scent. (1983) ✔ All Burgundy wines.

⊶ Ets Charles Vienot, 21700 Nuits-St-Georges; tel. 80 62 31 05.

CAVEAU DE VILLIE-MORGON★★★

■ 60000 ▨4 ▨D

81 82 83 ⑧③ 84

A wine in which everything is of high standard, including the intense colour and the highly-concentrated bouquet. On the palate it is robust and yet has finesse in its overtones of fruit, cherry, peach and apricot. A very remarkable bottle of wine which will probably not fully develop until its second year. (1984)
⊶ Caveau de Villié-Morgon, Le Bourg, 69910 Villié-Morgon; tel. 74 04 20 99 ⥷ Daily 9.00–12.00/14.00–19.00.

LA VOUTE *Javernière*★★

■ 7ha 24000 ▨3 ▨D ▤ ◑ ⥯

70 ⑦① 72 73 74 76 76 79

Wine has been produced at Villié-Morgon since 1712. The 1984 is magnificent in every respect, with a beautiful, deep colour and alcoholic nose which will soon open out. Full, powerful and rich on the palate. (1984)
⊶ Louis-Claude Desvignes, La Voute, 69910 Villié-Morgon; tel. 74 04 23 35 ⥷ By appt.

Moulin-à-Vent

The sovereign of the Beaujolais crus spreads its 650 hectares over the commune of Chenas in the Rhone and Romanèche-Thorins in the Saône-et-Loire. The ancient windmill, now defunct, that gives the appellation its name, stands on top of a rounded, granite hill 240 m above the hamlet of Les Thorins. The vines grow in fairly shallow soil which is rich in manganese, producing a wine with a deep red colour, an iris-like fragrance, and a bouquet and body that recalls its Burgundy cousins of the Côte d'Or. It may be enjoyed very young, after just a few months in bottle, but it will also keep well for a few years. Annual production is about 35000 hectolitres.

Moulin-à-Vent was one of the first crus to be classified AOC in its own right. That was in 1936, but the wine has a much longer history: each year, in an age-old ritual, the new vintage is taken to be christened at the font of the parish church in Romanèche-Thorins and then paraded through all the villages of the region. Visitors can sample the wine at two tasting cellars – one at the foot of the windmill, the other by the RN 6 – which also serve light refreshments and snacks.

CHATEAU DE CHENAS★★

■	138ha 100000	4 D ▮ ↓

76 79 ⑧③ ⑧④

Beautiful deep ruby colour and a pronounced grapey nose. On the palate, this wine is full bodied, of a high standard and good rich taste. A wine of distinction in its youth, it will be delicious when it has reached maturity. (1984)
➻ Cave de Ch. de Chenas, Chenas, 69840 Juliénas; tel. 74 04 11 91 ♈ By appt. Closed 8–15 Aug.

DOMAINE DESVIGNES★★

■	3ha 13300	4 D ▮ ↓

76 78 ⑧③ ⑧④

This warm, fruity wine has a very beautiful colour and spicy nose, and will give a great deal of pleasure. (1984)
➻ Aimé Desvignes et Fils, Pontanevaux, 71570 La Chapelle-de-Guinchay; tel. 85 36 72 32.

GEORGES DUBOEUF★★★

■	20000	4 D ▮ ↓

⑦⑥ **78 ★81 ★**⑧③

Very fine colour, and the bouquet is well developed. On the palate it is balanced, well made and elegant and has a long finish with an outstanding fruitiness. An excellent bottle. (1983)
➻ Georges Duboeuf, 71720 Romanèche-Thorins; tel. 85 35 51 13 ♈ Mon.–Fri. 8.00–12.00/14.00–17.00. Closed Aug.

GERARD LAPIERRE★

■	4ha 2420	4 D ▮ ⑪ ↓

76 81 **★83** ⑧③ **★84**

Nice colour. The nose is still reserved, quite normal at this stage, but with lots of promise. Fleshy and rich on the palate. A serious wine worth waiting for. (1984) ✔ Chenas.
➻ Gérard Lapierre, Les Deschamps, Chenas, 69840 Juliénas; tel. 85 36 70 74 ♈ By appt.

DOMAINE LEMONON★

■	8ha 50000	③ ▮ ↓

83 ⑧③ 84

Good appearance and bouquet and very positive on the palate. The harsh complexity of tannins makes it rather closed in. It ought to be left for a few months to soften and not drunk before 1986 at the earliest. (1984)
➻ Ets Loron et Fils, Pontanevaux, 71570 La Chapelle-de-Guinchay; tel. 85 36 70 52 ♈ No visitors.

MAISON MACONNAISE DES VINS★

■	10000	4 D ▮ ⑪ ↓

59 ⑥⑨ **76 78** 81 82 83 ⑧④

La Maison Mâconnaise des Vins, situated just north of Mâcon, offers a chance to taste the wines of the Saône-et-Loire region. The Moulin-à-Vent 1983 is very representative of the appellation and is a well-presented bottle of a good standard which can either be drunk or kept to mature. (1983)
♈ Maison Mâconnaise des Vins, 484 Av. de Lattre-de-Tassigny, 71000 Mâcon; tel. 85 38 36 70. ♈ Daily 8.00–21.00. Closed 1 May, 25 Dec., first week Jan.

GFA DES MARQUISATS★★

■	14000	4 ⑪

⑧③ ⑧③ ⑧④ ⑧④

Beautiful colour and good nose for this very well-balanced wine, with good support on the palate and a slight woody tone which adds to the fruitiness. Not only a good example of its type, but an excellent wine which will gain by ageing a little. (1984)
➻ Pierre Ferraud et Fils, 69220 Belleville; tel. 74 66 08 05 ♈ No visitors.

JEAN MORTET *Les Rouchaux*★

■	9ha 30000	4 D ⑪ ↓

70 **71 ★76 78** 79 81 **★83** ⑧④ ⑧④

This is a lovely bottle with a beautiful, deep colour and fruity bouquet. Well balanced on the palate, this wine is well made and has a good grapey nose. (1984) ✔ Beaujolais-Villages.
➻ Jean Mortet, Romanèche-Thorins, 71570 La Chapelle-de-Guinchay; tel. 85 35 55 51 ♈ Daily 8.00–20.00. Closed 25 Dec.–1 Jan.

NICOLAS★

■	50000	4 ▮

A lovely wine, tasted at six months and still rather immature. Well balanced, with a complex though rather undeveloped nose, it shows great promise. It has some traces of youthful acidity which should become more refined with time. (1984)
➻ Ets Nicolas, 2 Rue de Valmy, 94220 Charenton; tel. 01 37 59 20 ♈ No visitors.

PASQUIER-DESVIGNES★

■	20000	4

⑦⑥ ⑧③ ⑧④

Despite a rather light colour, this wine, tasted at 18 months, is everything it should be. Definitely in the upper bracket of its cru. (1983)
➻ Ets Pasquier-Desvignes, St-Lager, 69220 Belleville; tel. 74 66 14 20 ♈ No visitors.

PIAT PERE ET FILS

■   12ha   90000   `4` ◻ ⌄

A good Moulin-à-Vent with the classic qualities of its cru, but which has yet to round out and fulfil its promise. (1984)
↜ Piat Père et Fils, BP 10, 71570 La Chapelle-de-Guinchay; tel. 85 36 77 77 ⟂ No visitors.

VIGNERONNAGE PICOLET★★

■   6ha   30000   `4` ◻ ◻ ⌄

Beautiful colour and fine bouquet. Well balanced on the palate with excellent aromas and a very good, fragrant finish. (1984)
↜ Paul Beaudet, Pontanevaux, 71570 La Chapelle-de-Guinchay; tel. 85 36 72 76 ⟂ By appt.

CHATEAU PORTIER★★

■   10ha   60000   `4` ◻ ◻ ◻ ⌄
67 69 71 74 76 ⑱ 81 *82 83 `84`

A beautiful, deep colour with a nose which is still developing. Very good flavour, with a hint of oakiness. It should be left to develop the balance of a mature wine, when it will make a beautiful bottle. (1984) ✔ Fleurie, Chiroubles, Beaujolais Supérieur Ch. Chassagne.
↜ Michel Gaidon, Romanèche-Thorins, 71570 La Chapelle-de-Guinchay; tel. 80 22 22 60 ⟂ By appt. Closed Sat. and Sun.

DOMAINE DU PRIEURE★

■   3ha   20000   `4` ◻ ⌄
*⑱ `78` *⑧③ `83`

Lightness is the theme: lightness of colour, lightness of nose, lightness on the palate. Lots of charm, then, but a wine which should not be left to grow too old. (1984)
↜ M. Sarrau, St-Jean-d'Ardières, 69220 Belleville; tel. 74 66 19 43 ⟂ No visitors.

DOMAINE DE LA ROCHELLE

■   26ha   60000   `4` ◻ ◻
76 78 80 81 82 *84

Tasted in March 1985, the 1978 vintage is still of excellent stature with good nose and fullness on the palate. A wine which upholds the reputation of Moulin-à-Vent as the Beaujolais cru most likely to age well. (1978)
↜ Ets Mommessin, Charnay-les-Mâcon, 71000 Mâcon; tel. 85 34 47 74 ⟂ By appt.

UV ROMANECHE ET CHENAS
Prestige 84★★

■   30000   ◻ ◻ ⌄
*⑯ 82 *83 `84`

This wine has an attractive appearance and great charm on the palate, with a mature and enduring quality and a very pleasant finish which leaves the palate eager for more. (1984)
↜ UV Romanèche-Thorins et Chenas, 71720 Romanèche-Thorins; tel. 85 35 51 03 ⟂ By appt.

HOSPICES DE ROMANECHE-THORINS

■   12ha   50000   `5` ◻ ◻ ⌄
*⑧③ `83` *⑧④ `84`

Slightly immature when tasted at six months, but, on this evidence, should blossom and become more refined within six months or a year. One to watch. (1983)
↜ MM. Collin et Bourisset, Rue de la Gare, 71680 Crêches-sur-Saône; tel. 85 37 11 15 ⟂ No visitors.

CELLIER DES SAMSONS★★

■   640ha   `4`
*⑧③ `83` *`84`

Handsome overall effect: strong colour; fullness and aromas of cherry on the palate. A quality wine. (1984)
↜ Cellier des Samsons, Quincié-en-Beaujolais, 69430 Beaujeu; tel. 74 66 24 19 ⟂ No visitors.

CLOS DU TREMBLAY★★★

■   5ha   25 000   `3` ◻ ◻ ⌄
74 76 79 81 83 ⑧④ `84`

A beautiful, intense colour and quite exceptional bouquet in terms of quality and expansiveness make this full, rich wine a beautiful bottle. It is big and powerful on the palate with an extraordinary, persistent fragrance. A great Moulin-à-Vent. (1984)
↜ Paul Janin, 71720 Romanèche-Thorins; tel. 85 35 52 80 ⟂ By appt.

BENOIT TRICHARD ET FILS
Mortperay★

■   6ha   36000   `4` ◻ ◻ ⌄
`80` *83 84

This is a classic Moulin-à-Vent with the colour and bouquet which are characteristic of the growth. Ready for drinking now. (1984) ✔ Brouilly, Côtes de Brouilly, Beaujolais.
↜ Benoît Trichard et Fils, Odenas, 69460 St-Etienne-des-Ouillières; tel. 74 03 40 87 ⟂ By appt. Closed during harvest and end Aug.

CHARLES VIENOT

■   3000   `4` ◻ ◻ ⌄
⑯ ⑲ *⑧③ `83` *84

A classic Moulin-à-Vent, characteristic in all but its rather light colour. Good Gamay character. (1983)
↜ Ets Charles Vienot, 21700 Nuits-St-Georges; tel. 80 62 31 05.

St-Amour

This is the most northerly of the Beaujolais Grand Cru villages, situated in a transitional zone between the granite sands of Beaujolais and the limestone terrain of the St-Véran and Mâcon appellations to the north. The St-Amour appellation covers 275 hectares and produces 15000 hectolitres of wine a year. The vines are grown on a mixture of sandstone and granite-based gravel, making a wine that is perhaps the lightest of the Beaujolais crus. There are two methods of vinification. The first means that the wine must spend a long time in the vat undergoing carbonic maceration to give it the necessary body and colour. Alternatively, a version of the vins primeurs procedure may be used to produce St-Amour that will be ready sooner, although it will not keep so well. Whichever method is used, St-Amour is delicious with snails, frogs' legs, mushrooms or poularde à la crème. The wine is now firmly established in foreign markets and a large proportion of the annual production is exported. Visitors who wish to catch a sense of the area should visit the tiny hamlet of Le Plâtre-Durand perched on top of a 309m hill offering fine views over the surrounding countryside. As well as its church and town hall, the village has a caveau, or tasting cellar, where St-Amour wines can be sampled.

THOMAS BASSOT★

■   2500   4 D ▤ ⑪ ↓

⑧² 83 84

This wine was tasted at 18 months, and shows good, youthful acidity, rich colour, and bouquet. The classic St-Amour. Needs some age, but not much. (1983)
↬ Thomas Bassot, 5 Quai Dumorey, 21700 Nuits-St-Georges; tel. 80 62 31 05 ⵏ No visitors.

PAUL BEAUDET★

■   40000   4 D ▤ ↓

Tasted at six months, this is a classic St-Amour which will grow in stature in the coming months. (1984)
↬ Paul Beaudet, Pontanevaux, 71570 La Chapelle-de-Guinchay; tel. 85 36 72 76 ⵏ By appt.

DOMAINE DES BILLARDS★★

■   6ha 35000   3 ▤ ↓

⑧³ 83 84

Nice colour and lovely nose. Full of promise, reflected on the palate by excellent aromas, suppleness and roundness, and a full body. An excellent St-Amour. (1984)
↬ Ets Loron et Fils, Pontanevaux, 71570 La Chapelle-de-Guinchay; tel. 85 36 70 52 ⵏ No visitors.

DOMAINE BOUCHARD PERE ET FILS★

■   4.8ha 28000   4 D ▤ ↓

82 83 *84

The Bouchards aim for a light, smooth and clean style, even in their Beaujolais Cru productions and this is exactly what is found here in this 1984 St-Amour that is delectably light and also very elegant. (1984)

↬ Bouchard Père et Fils, Au Château, 21202 Beaune; tel. 80 22 14 41 ⵏ By appt. Closed Aug. and one week Feb.

COLLIN ET BOURISSET

■   20000   4 ▤ ↓

*83 *84 84

Beautiful colour and fruity bouquet. Supple and pleasant on the palate. An honest wine which is very easy to drink. (1984)
↬ MM. Collin et Bourisset, Rue de la Gare, 71680 Crêches-sur-Saône; tel. 85 37 11 15 ⵏ No visitors.

GEORGES DUBOEUF★★★

■   10ha 18000   3 D ⑪ ↓

*83 83 84

Fruit and flowers on the nose; good balance on the palate, together with a warm, insistent note of coffee. A perfectly balanced one of exceptional quality. (1984)
↬ Georges Duboeuf, 71720 Romanèche-Thorins; tel. 85 35 51 13 ⵏ Daily 9.00–12.00/14.00–17.00. Closed Aug.

JACQUES DUC

■   8ha 48000   4 D ▤ ↓

78 79 81 *83 *84

Outstandingly attractive St-Amour, light, balanced with full Gamay character. Supple on the palate but nevertheless shows keeping potential. (1983) ✔ Beaujolais-Villages.
↬ Jacques Duc, St-Amour-Bellevue, 71570 La Chapelle-de-Guinchay; tel. 85 37 10 08 ⵏ By appt.

MATHELIN★★

■   6000   3 D ⑪ ↓

Light colour contrasts with a full nose; the same contrast is also found on the palate, where delicious fruity aromas are supported by a very light body. (1984)
↬ Vins Mathelin, BP 3, Châtillon-d'Azergues; 69380 Lozanne; tel. 74 84 39 24 ⵏ Mon.–Sat. 8.30–12.00/14.00–19.00. Closed week of 15 Aug.

PIAT PERE ET FILS★

■   5ha 33000   3 ▤ ↓

A good-looking wine with a nice fruitiness on the nose which is confirmed on the palate. Good tannic quality promises that it will age well. Some might like it as it is (at six months), others might prefer to wait a few months for it to round out. (1984)
↬ Piat Père et Fils, BP 10, 71570 La Chapelle-de-Guinchay; tel. 83 36 77 77 ⵏ No visitors.

135

THE LYONNAIS

THE PRODUCTION area of the Coteaux du Lyonnais appellation lies to the east of the Massif Central, and is bordered by the Rhône and Saône rivers on the east, and by the Lyonnais mountains on the west. The Beaujolais vineyards lie to the north and Côtes du Rhône to the south. The historic vineyard of Lyons dates from Roman times and enjoyed a period of prosperity during the Middle Ages under the influence of the monks and the rich city merchants who aided and encouraged the cultivation of vines. As recently as 1936 the register listed 13 500 hectares of vineyards. The phylloxera crisis and the urban expansion of Lyons have reduced the area to 350 hectares, divided between 49 communes that encircle the western side of the city from Mont d'Or in the north to the Gier valley in the south.

The area is 40 km long by 30 km wide, made up of a series of high valleys running south-west to north-west, alternating with hills which reach 500 m. The varied soil types include granite, metamorphic rock, sedimentary rock, silt, alluvium, and loess. Light, fairly shallow, permeable soils, are the common factor in the viticultural zone.

The three main Beaujolais climatic tendencies are present here. Although the Mediterranean influence tends to predominate, the higher slopes are more exposed to the hazards that the oceanic and continental influences bring. Vines are planted only below 500 m and not on north-facing slopes, the most favourable locations being on the plateaus. The main variety is the Gamay Noir à jus blanc which, when vinified in the traditional Beaujolais way, produces a most attractive wine much prized by the local clientèle. The white appellation wines are made from the Chardonnay and Aligoté varieties. The legal minimum density of planting is 6000 stocks per hectare, and the gobelet, cordon, and guyot pruning methods are authorized. The basic permitted yield is 60 hectolitres per hectare, and the authorized alcohol content is between 10–13 per cent for red wines, 9.5–12.5 per cent for whites. On average, 10000 hectolitres of red wine are produced each year and 300 hectolitres of white. In this region of mixed farming, where there are also many fruit orchards, the cooperative of St-Bel is the driving force behind local viticulture and processes three-quarters of the harvest.

Coteaux du Lyonnais

Coteaux du Lyonnais wines were granted AOC status in 1984; they are clean, fruity, rich, and fragrant, and are a simple but pleasant accompaniment to all kinds of Lyonnais pork dishes; saucisson, saveloy, *queue de cochon* (pig's tail), *petit salé* (bacon joint), *pieds de porc* (pig's trotters), and *jambonneau* (knuckle of ham) – as well as local goat's cheese.

LUCIEN BOULIEU*

■	10ha 60000	2 D ☗ ↓

78 81 82 83 **84**

Light colour with ruby tints. Very fruity nose with a markedly youthful character. Fresh and light on the palate; a refreshing wine that slips down very pleasantly. (1984)
↴ Lucien Boulieu, 69390 Millery; tel. 74 84 61 93
☖ By appt. Closed Sun.

CAVE COOPERATIVE COTEAUX-DU-LYONNAIS

■	115ha 20000	2 D ☗ ↓

83 **84**

A very pleasant, refreshing wine of a beautiful, brilliant colour: a combination of ruby and straw-

berry. The nose is fruity and fresh, and is still dominated by banana after six months. Good long finish. Should be served at 10–12°C. (1984)
✔ Beaujolais.
☛ Cave Coop. Coteaux-du-Lyonnais, St-Bel, 69210 L'Arbresle; tel. 74 01 11 33 ⟐ By appt.

ETIENNE DESCOTES ET FILS*

■   4 ha   15 000   **2** **D** ▮ ◧ ↓
(78) **81 82** 83 84

A very light burnt-ruby colour, and a fruity bouquet which improves on contact with the air. It is extremely light and easy to drink, and combines the typical balance of a white wine with the fruitiness of a red. (1984)
☛ Etienne Descotes et Fils, 69390 Millery; tel. 74 84 61 83. ⟐ By appt.

FRANÇOIS DESCOTES**

☐   1 ha   2500   **2** **D** ◧ ↓
78 (82) 83 *84

A beautiful, brilliant, light golden-green colour and a flowery, fruity, distinguished and light nose. On the palate, fresh and fruity, very fragrant, with a long finish. A very pleasant white wine for serving chilled. (1984)
☛ François Descotes, 69390 Millery; tel. 74 84 61 87 ⟐ By appt.

FRANÇOIS DESCOTES**

■   2.5 ha   4500   **2** **D** ▮ ↓
*(83) 84 84

A light reddish purple in colour, with the very forthcoming, fruity, fresh nose of youth. (Six months.) This freshness is also found on the palate, together with a very pleasant lightness and fruity aroma, which leave a magnificently scented finish. (1984)
☛ François Decotes, 69390 Millery; tel. 74 84 61 87.

PIERRE JOMARD**

■   0.5 ha   40 000   **2** **D** ◧ ↓
83 (84) 84

A very strong colour and expansive bouquet make this an excellent wine, and this is confirmed

on the palate by its fruitiness and distinction. A wine typical of the Coteaux du Lyonnais in the northern part of the area where this appellation is produced. (1984) ✔ Beaujolais.
☛ Pierre Jomard, Le Morillon, 69210 Fleuriex; tel. 74 01 02 27 ⟐ By appt. Closed during harvest.

GILBERT MAZILLE

■

Fuller and warmer than most of the appellation, in which freshness and lightness are usually dominant in the young wines. Deep ruby colour and slightly closed-in nose. Full bodied, well balanced, and high in alcohol and flavour, with a hint of vanilla. (1984)
☛ Gilbert Mazille, 69390 Millery; tel. 74 84 62 06

ROBERT THOLLET**

■   5 ha   8000   **2** **D** ▮ ↓
(82) 83 *84

Light ruby colour and extremely young nose, with the dominant note of pear drops typical of these six-month-old vins nouveaux. Excellent fruitiness with a soupçon of violets and spice. Fresh and light on the palate, yet very smooth, leaving a velvety and balmy persistence which is truly remarkable. (1984)
☛ Robert Thollet, 69390 Millery; tel. 74 84 62 43 ⟐ By appt. Closed Sun. and Mon.

GUIDE TO SYMBOLS

★★★	Exceptional
★★	Very good
★	Wines of special interest

□	White wine	○	Sparkling white
◪	Rose wine	◕	Sparkling rose
■	Red wine	●	Sparkling red

50 000, 20 000 . . . Average annual production in bottles

4ha   Area of production in hectares (does not apply to shipper's, blended or cooperative wines)

▮	Vinified in stainless steel vat
◀▮▶	Aged in wooden cask
♨	Thermoregulation
▣	May be bought direct from the producer
(1982)	Year or vintage tasted (does not apply to blended wines or wines for drinking within the year)
✔	Other wines from the same producer or shipper
⌐⊓	Address
Ⴤ	Open for visiting and wine-tasting
⌐⊓	Proprietor's name if different from that given in the address
NB	Where no information is given it was either not supplied to the editors or does not apply to the particular wine in question

PRICE GUIDE (average price per bottle of wine bought by the case)

FRENCH PRICES

For all wines except champagne	**1** under 10F	**2** 10–20F	**3** 20–30F
	4 30–50F	**5** 50–100F	**6** over 100F
For champagne	**❶** under 50F	**❷** 50–70F	**❸** 70–100F
	❹ 100–150F	**❺** over 150F	

UK EQUIVALENT PRICES (including UK Excise Duty and VAT)

For all wines except champagne	**1** under £3	**2** £3–£4	**3** £4–£5
	4 £5–£9	**5** £9–£12.50	**6** over £12.50
For champagne	**❶** under £7	**❷** £7–£8.50	**❸** £8.50–£15
	❹ £15–£20	**❺** over £20	

NB   UK duty is charged on all wines at the same rate. Thus the cheaper the wine at UK prices, the less wine value for money.

NB   Champagne prices. Pricing policy of individual champagne houses varies widely according to the market. Thus champagnes that sell for the same price in the French market may differ considerably in price in foreign (non-French) markets.

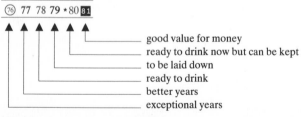

NB   No vintages are given for blended wines or wines intended to be drunk within a year of the harvest.

BORDEAUX

THE NAME Bordeaux has become synonymous with wine throughout the world and with good reason: it is, quite simply, the largest fine-wine region on earth. Bordeaux is the capital of the department of the Gironde, named after the great estuary produced by the confluence of two rivers, the Garonne and the Dordogne, as they flow into the Bay of Biscay. Almost all of the department is planted with vines: 80 per cent of the total production is AOC wine, in the proportion 70–80 per cent red and 20–30 per cent white.

It is possible to divide the Gironde into left-bank and right-bank regions. On the left bank, the major wine-producing areas skirt the Gironde estuary itself, continuing south of Bordeaux along the Garonne: from the Médoc in the north to Graves, Barsac and Sauternes. The other major red wine region, the Libournais, lies 25 km north-east of Bordeaux on the right bank of the Dordogne. Between the two rivers is the white-wine country of Entre-Deux-Mers, with a strip along the right bank of the Garonne making red wine under the appellation Premières Côtes de Bordeaux.

With the exception of the great sweet wines of Barsac and Sauternes, and a handful of dry Graves, all the fine wines of Bordeaux are red. The most famous are the Crus Classés (classed growths) of the Médoc, Graves and the Libournais: St-Estèphe, Pauillac, St-Julien, Margaux and Graves on the left bank, Pomerol and St-Emilion on the right bank.

Such a brief summary does scant justice to the complex interplay of historical, geographical and climatic factors which resulted in the pre-eminence of Bordeaux as a wine-making region. Indeed, Bordeaux's long involvement with wine predates not only the Roman conquest, but even the appearance of the vine itself. During the first half of the first century BC Bordeaux was already a wine port, buying Italian wine from Neapolitan merchants and distributing to the hinterland via the river routes. The first vines did not appear until almost a century later, after the Roman settlement of Aquitaine.

By the twelfth century vines had become widespread. In 1152 the marriage of Eleanor of Aquitaine to Henry Plantagenet, the future king of England, began a long association between Bordeaux and the English market. Bordeaux wines were called 'vins clairets' – literally, 'light-coloured wine' – to distinguish them from the darker wines imported to England from Spain and Portugal. Anglicized as 'claret', the name continues to be applied in English-speaking countries to Bordeaux red wine (although not to the light reds, between a red and a rosé, which the Bordelais today call 'vins clairets').

In medieval times, Bordeaux wines were made for rapid drinking. Exported in barrels just before Christmas, they were not intended to be kept beyond the end of the following year. The British attachment to claret survived not only competition from new beverages such as tea and coffee, and from richer wines from the Iberian peninsula, but even a ban on French wines imposed by the English government during the wars against Louis XIV of France.

Early in the eighteenth century, a few London shippers began to create a new, more refined style of wine which they called 'the new French Claret'. They bought the wine young and aged it themselves. To increase their profits further they had the idea of selling it in bottles. Corked and sealed, the wine now reached the

The Bordeaux Appellations

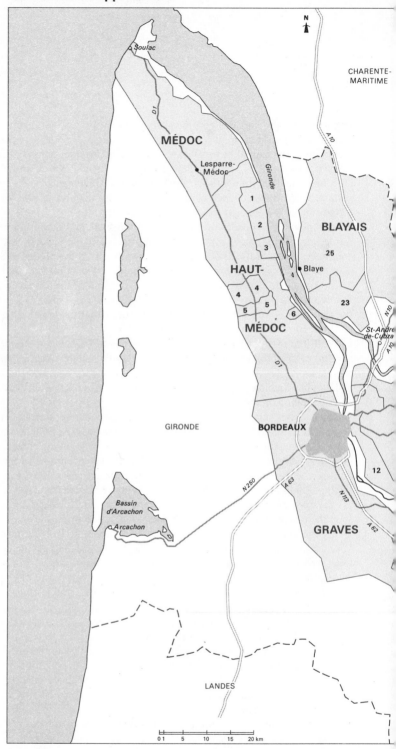

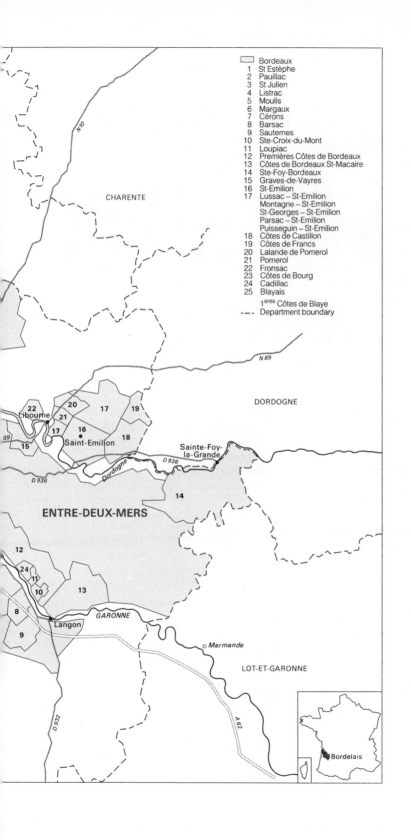

Bordeaux
1 St Estèphe
2 Pauillac
3 St Julien
4 Listrac
5 Moulis
6 Margaux
7 Cérons
8 Barsac
9 Sauternes
10 Ste-Croix-du-Mont
11 Loupiac
12 Premières Côtes de Bordeaux
13 Côtes de Bordeaux St-Macaire
14 Ste-Foy-Bordeaux
15 Graves-de-Vayres
16 St-Emilion
17 Lussac – St-Emilion
   Montagne – St-Emilion
   St-Georges – St-Emilion
   Parsac – St-Emilion
   Puisseguin – St-Emilion
18 Côtes de Castillon
19 Côtes de Francs
20 Lalande de Pomerol
21 Pomerol
22 Fronsac
23 Côtes de Bourg
24 Cadillac
25 Blayais
   1eres Côtes de Blaye
--- Department boundary

consumer with some guarantee of origin. Imperceptibly, the connection between a 'château', a particular vineyard and a particular quality of wine began to emerge as a market value. These circumstances encouraged the Bordeaux wine-growers to take special care to select prime vineyard sites, restrict the yield per hectare and age the wine in barrels to enable it to keep longer. In the process, many of the classic wine-making techniques, now standard, were developed: adding sulphur dioxide to allow the wine to age without spoiling; racking and fining to clear the wine of sediments and impurities.

The eighteenth century also saw the first attempts at a rough hierarchy of Bordeaux crus, or growths. Despite the Revolution and the Napoleonic Wars which followed, temporarily closing the English market, the prestige of great Bordeaux wines continued to grow. The famous classification of the Médoc growths was established in 1855 which, although perhaps needing some minor rectifications, still holds good today. Following this period of steady growth, Bordeaux experienced a number of crises: the vineyards were attacked by epidemics of mildew and phylloxera, while the trade suffered dislocation due to economic slumps and the effects of two world wars. Since 1960, however, Bordeaux wines have steadily advanced in quality and popularity. The hierarchy of classed growths and the notion of 'terroir' – the soils and micro-climates of a particular vineyard – have regained their original importance for the red wines. The whites, however, have not benefited from this renewal of interest to the same degree.

Climate and soil, as ever, are major factors influencing the quality of the wine produced. The Bordeaux vineyards are situated along three main waterways: the Garonne and Dordogne rivers and their common estuary, the Gironde. The position near the sea creates a temperate climate for the vines to grow on their gentle slopes. Further protection is given by the pine forests that lie between the wine-growing areas and the sea. Although winter frosts are unusual, cold weather in April and May can freeze the young buds, while cold and wet weather in June, the time of flowering, will inhibit pollination, thus preventing a proportion of the buds from developing into grapes, a condition known as 'coulure'. These problems of spring cold and coulure cause large losses, and explain why the size of the harvest can vary so greatly. Nevertheless, Bordeaux has a climatic trump card to play – its famous sunny autumns. It is the long, slow ripening period between July and October which finally determines the quality of the harvest, and many a potentially disastrous Bordeaux vintage has been saved by an Indian summer.

The soils of the Gironde differ widely in nature. Most of the Grands Crus grow on deep, east-facing gravel banks in the Médoc, but there are well-known red-wine vineyards with clay-limestone and sandy soils: the classic, sweet white wines of Sauternes and Barsac come from limestone or chalk under gravel. While research continues, notably at the University of Bordeaux, to determine the relationship between soil and wine quality in the Gironde, it is generally agreed that drainage – whether by the composition of the soil or by the many small streams of the region – is a crucial factor. The better-drained the land, the argument runs, the deeper the vine's roots must go for water, and the more complex the combination of minerals and trace elements the grapes contain, leading to the distinctive flavours and aromas of the wine made from them.

Today the Bordeaux vineyards cover about 100 000 hectares, only two-thirds of the total at the end of the nineteenth century. Gradually growers have abandoned the least favourable soils, while at the same time working to improve soils under cultivation. The total annual production of Bordeaux wines is now fairly constant at between three and six million hectolitres, depending on the vintage. The AOC vineyards cover 78 000 hectares under the ownership of 22 000 producers. The average size of a property is 5 hectares, but one or two growers own less than 2 hectares. Only 5 per cent of growers own more than 20 hectares, but they account for more than one-third of total AOC production. In addition there are 60 cooperatives, which process a little over one-quarter of the average harvest, including some of the most prestigious appellations. In 1983, a good year despite some variations in quality, AOC production was 4 107 323 hectolitres out of a total Bordeaux production of 5 100 000 hectolitres. AOC red wines accounted for 3 190 000 hectolitres.

Bordeaux wines – red, white and rosé – are made from several different grape varieties with complementary characteristics. For reds the main varieties in use are the Cabernet-Sauvignon, the Cabernet-Franc and the Merlot. The Cabernet grapes are rich in tannin, which allows the wines to age over many years in order to reach optimum quality. The Cabernet-Sauvignon in particular is a late-ripening variety which does not always reach full maturity: it is, however, highly resistant to rot, a common enemy in the frequently damp climate. The Merlot, with less tannin, produces a softer wine that develops more quickly in bottle. In all respects it is a more forward variety than Cabernet-Sauvignon, and ripens well, but has a correspondingly greater vulnerability to spring cold, coulure and rot. Experience has shown that the best results come from blending the two varieties in proportions that vary according to the soil and the type of wine – fast- or slow-maturing – required.

For dry white wines the main grape variety is the Sauvignon Blanc, blended with the Sémillon and Muscadelle, which have very distinctive aromas. The Sémillon is responsible for the great wines of Sauternes and Barsac because of its susceptibility to 'pourriture noble' ('noble rot') produced by the *Botrytis cinerea* fungus. In certain ideal autumn conditions, microscopic threads of the fungus soften and penetrate the skin, allowing the juices to evaporate and concentrating the flavour and extract of the grape to produce a unique combination of sweetness and flavour. Another white grape, the Ugni Blanc, is increasingly cultivated because of its high yield, but the wines it produces are lacking in finesse.

The vines are planted in trellissed rows and the density per hectare varies dramatically: 10 000 stocks in the Grand Cru vineyards of Médoc and Graves; 2000 stocks in a typical Entre-Deux-Mers vineyard; less than 1000 for high-trained vines planted in widely spaced rows. High-density planting means a lower yield, better ripeness and higher-quality fruit. However, it also means higher planting, growing and labour costs.

A long tradition of research and ingenuity has gone hand in hand with Bordeaux growers' efforts to establish and improve the quality of their wines. The famous 'Bordeaux mixture' (copper sulphate and lime) was developed locally to counter mildew, and growers have continued to take advantage of the latest developments of wine science. The fact that there have been more good-quality vintages than mediocre ones over recent years may well have been the result of progressive wine-making techniques on the part of the growers as much as of particularly favourable weather conditions. For red wines 1982, 1961 and 1959 were outstanding, while 1983, 1981, 1979, 1978, 1976, 1975, 1970 and 1966 were very good. Before them came the legendary vintages of 1955, 1949, 1947, 1945, 1929 and 1928

The Quality of Bordeaux Red Wines by Vintage

1983	Very good	1979	Good
1982	Outstanding	1978	Very good
1981	Good	1977	Average
1980	Fair	1976	Good

1975	Very good	**1966**	Very good
1974	Fair	**1965**	Poor
1973	Fair	**1964**	Very good
1972	Poor	**1963**	Poor
1971	Good	**1962**	Very good
1970	Very good	**1961**	Outstanding
1969	Average	**1960**	Fair
1968	Poor	**1959**	Outstanding
1967	Good	**1958**	Poor

Over the last twenty-five years, the major change in the trade itself has been the extent to which the grower has increasingly come to bottle his own wine. Estate bottling has been carried out on the Grand Cru estates for several decades, but in the case of the simpler generic appellations it was traditionally the négociant, or shipper, who took charge of raising, bottling and distributing the wine, rounding off any rough edges by careful blending. Today, advances in wine technology have made it possible for the growers themselves to produce good quality wines that can be drunk young, and thus offered directly to the consumer.

The cooperatives in particular have had a hand in this development by imposing standard regulations concerning the ageing and marketing of wine. Nevertheless the négociants still play an important part in distribution, especially in foreign markets, offering as they do a network of clients built up over many years. It is quite possible that there will be a resurgence of interest among the retail trade in shippers' blended wines.

Meanwhile all elements of the Bordeaux wine trade combine to coordinate a business totalling several billion francs a year, two billion of which stems from the export trade alone. Indeed, it is estimated that throughout the Gironde one person in six depends directly or indirectly on wine-making for his or her livelihood. The main organizations concerned are Le Conseil Interprofessionel des Vins de Bordeaux, the trade's general advisory body; the various 'syndicats viticoles' which supervise and regulate the appellation criteria, and the ten 'confréries', or wine brotherhoods, which organize events, fairs and exhibitions to promote Bordeaux wines. Their activities are coordinated by the Grand Conseil du Vin de Bordeaux.

All these organizations are very active. For example, the Conseil Interprofessionel has on occasion stepped into the market to maintain prices by establishing a buffer stock of generic and high-quality wines. Such intervention protects the trade against economic fluctuations, whether arising from trade conditions in general or from variations in the quality of the harvest. Very recently the Conseil has also introduced an engraved wine bottle, reserved exclusively for Bordeaux wines, in an attempt to counter competition from non-Bordeaux growers who bottle their wines in Bordeaux-style bottles. The Syndicats Viticoles hold tastings of all wines produced each year, and may deny the use of the appellation to wines which fail to reach the required standard.

Despite this ongoing programme of regulation, Bordeaux wines are very far from being a standardized product. From the great châteaus of the Médoc, to the less-exalted wines of the generic appellations, wine-making in Bordeaux is a cultural as much as an economic phenomenon, and all the wines, each in its own way, reflect the unique viticultural history, skills and tradition of the region as a whole.

The Classification of Bordeaux Wines

The Bordeaux system of classification is quite confusing to the non-Bordelais, and merits a word of explanation, as does the equally confusing practice of calling a wine estate a 'château', regardless of the size of the main residence. This may range from a comfortable, old-fashioned farmhouse to the grandest house, from eighteenth-century elegance to late nineteenth-century neo-Gothic.

There are nearly two thousand such châteaux in the Gironde, although only a few names are widely familiar, and they tend to be the greatest of all, such as Château Lafite, Château Margaux and Château Latour. These are all 'first growths' or Grands Crus, under the first and most comprehensive official classification of Bordeaux wines in 1855. Formalizing existing practice, the wine merchants and growers of Bordeaux agreed to recognize the price of a wine over a number of years as a measure of its quality. The 60 or so most expensive wines were then divided into five classes or 'crus'. The crus were the aristocrats of the Médoc and Sauternes, with Graves being represented only by Château Haut-Brion. Behind them came the Crus Bourgeois – the merchants' name for wines of good quality which nevertheless failed to be included in the 1855 classification.

In 1932 these Bourgeois growths received their own classification as Crus Exceptionnels, Crus Bourgeois Supérieurs and Cru Bourgeois. This created in turn a new class of nearly Cru Bourgeois, the Crus Artisans.

Meanwhile Graves, St-Emilion and Pomerol, which had been largely left out of the 1855 classification, instituted their own systems of ranking, each on a different basis. The ten best Graves wines are simply 'Crus Classés'; the wines of St-Emilion have undergone several changes in classification up to 1984; while Pomerol still relies on unofficial classification reflecting the broad agreement of the local wine trade. For the wine buyer this state of affairs can become something of a maze, and he or she is likely to rely on the advice of a reputable wine merchant or wine guide when choosing among the less well-known wines of Bordeaux.

The Regional Appellations of Bordeaux

It is sometimes difficult to grasp exactly what the Bordeaux appellation means. At first sight, the definition appears to be quite straightforward; any wine produced in the department of Gironde and conforming to certain clearly defined minimum standards has a right to use the appellation. Exceptions are those wines grown on the unsuitable sandy soils in the west and south, now largely given over to pine forests.

However, there is more to it than that. There are many different styles of wine, making it more sensible to consider 'Bordeaux' not as a single appellation but rather as a collection of appellations. These include red, rosé and clairet (light red) wines; also dry and sweet white wines – and white or rosé sparkling wines. All these wines have AOC status; there are no Bordeaux VDQS or Vins de Pays.

The vineyard areas for these appellations show a corresponding variety, although they can be divided into two main categories. First, there are the wines which come from different parts of the Gironde and which are only allowed to use the simple Bordeaux appellation. These would include the 'palus' regions (certain alluvial areas near rivers where the vines are grown on trellises), or some parts of the Libournais, such as the communes of St-André-de-Cubzac, Guitres, and Coutras. Secondly, there are the wines which are allowed to use a more specific appellation (Médoc, St-Emilion, Pomerol, etc.). Even in this case, the regional rather than the local appellation may sometimes be used if the latter is not well known. Instances of this are Bordeaux Côtes de Franc, Bordeaux Haut-Benauge, Bordeaux

145

St-Foy and Bordeaux St-Macaire. Thus, where the local appellation adds little or nothing in the consumer's mind, the growers prefer to settle for the plain AOC Bordeaux label.

Although Bordeaux is best known for its Grands Crus, the Bordeaux and Bordeaux Supérieur appellations produce the greatest volume of wine in the Gironde: 222 million bottles of red in 1982 and 86.3 million bottles of white; plus 2.1 million bottles of rosé and clairet and 2.5 million bottles of sparkling wines. Despite the scale and variety of this production, and the huge area (36650 hectares) covered by the vineyards themselves, some common factors emerge to make sense of the Bordeaux regional appellations.

In general, basic red Bordeaux wines are well balanced, harmonious, fruity but not too full, and may be drunk young. The higher category of Bordeaux Supérieur reds are fuller and more complex. They are made from the best grapes and may be kept longer.

Bordeaux Clairet and Rosé are made from red grapes, by allowing the juice to stay on the skins for a short time. The crisp and fruity clairet wines are rather deeper-coloured than the rosés, and are produced in much smaller quantities.

Bordeaux dry white wines are firm and fruity. Their quality has improved in recent years thanks to the progress made in wine-making technology, but the appellation has still failed to make the popular impact it deserves. Some of the wines, indeed, are declassified as table wines; the difference in price received for the grapes may be so small as to make it easier to sell table wine than Bordeaux Blanc. The white Bordeaux Supérieur wineš form a higher category; they are smooth and full, but production is small.

Finally, there are the two sparkling Bordeaux appellations, Bordeaux Mousseux Blanc and Bordeaux Mousseux Rosé. These Méthode Champenoise wines are made from grapes grown in the Bordeaux appellation area and must be bottled within the zone of AOC Bordeaux production.

Bordeaux

CHATEAU LES ARROMANS★★

■ 20ha 120000 **2** D ▪ ↓
⑦ 75 ⑦ 80 **82**

Sold under its own label for about fifteen years, this wine bears little relation to the mediocre product once marketed by this property. With its deep-ruby colour and pleasing nose, it is a satisfying wine with body, good structure and fine tannins, leading to a pleasing finish. An example of the beneficial effects of direct sales in Bordeaux. (1982) ✔ Entre-Deux-Mers Ch. les Arromans, Bordeaux Rosé Ch. les Arromans.
↪ Jean Duffau, Ch. les Arromans, Moulon, 33420 Branne; tel. 57 84 50 87 ☥ By appt.

DOMAINE DE LA BACONNE★

■ 3ha 19000 **2** D ▪ ↓
⑦ 75 76 **78** 79 80 81 ★**82 83**

A lively, dark colour. The nose, although floral and fruity, lacks fullness. On the palate a good structure supports solid tannins, leading to a pleasing finish. (1983)
↪ GAEC Faveraud Père et Fils, Ch. Tayat, Cézac, 33620 Cavignac; tel. 57 68 62 10 ☥ By appt.

CHATEAU BALLUE-MONDON

■ 7ha 48000 **3** D ▪ ↓
⑦ 80 81 ★**82** ★**82** ★83 ⑧

This wine comes from one of the highest slopes of the Gironde. Lively red colour, with a nose of discreet but pleasing floral perfumes and ripe fruit. Well structured, tannic, and with a long finish. (1982) ✔ Bordeaux Sauvignon Ch. Ballue-Mondon.
↪ Guy Ballue, Ch. Ballue-Mondon, 33890 Gensac; tel. 57 40 42 25 ☥ By appt. Closed 1–15 Sept.

CHATEAU BEAULIEU★

■ 7ha 40000 **3** ▪ ↓
★**82 82**

Intense, deep-red Bordeaux colour. Delicate, ripe-fruit nose. Quite powerful, robust, full bodied, spicy, clean and flowing. Ready to drink. (1982)
↪ Robert Bonneau 33540 Sauveterre-de-Guyenne; tel. 56 71 50 67 ☥ No visitors.

BEAU-MAYNE★

■ 800000 **3** D ⑪ ↓
★81 ⑧

Attractive appearance. Subtly but delicately fragrant, with a few shades of ripe fruit. Quite flavourful in the mouth, giving a pleasant character.
↪ MM. Dourthe Frères, Moulis, 33480 Castelnau-de-Médoc; tel. 56 35 84 64 ☥ By appt. Closed Sat. and Sun.

CHATEAU BEL AIR FONROQUE★

■ 9ha 48000 **3** D ▪ ↓
⑦ **81 82 82** 83

This highly coloured wine is solid, round and pleasantly tannic. (1982)

╺┱ Maison Daniel Querre SA, Place Guadet, 33500 Libourne; tel. 57 51 56 18 � By appt.

CHATEAU BELLEVUE-LA-MONGIE★

■		8 ha	46 000	2 D ■ ↓

★79 ★81 ⓐ 82 83

Deep-purple in colour, vigorous and attractively tannic on the palate. (1982) ✔ Bordeaux Clairet Ch. Bellevue-la-Mongie.
╺┱ C. Boyer, Ch. Bellevue-la-Mongie, Génissac, 33420 Branne; tel. 57 24 48 43 � Mon.–Sat. 8.00–12.00, 14.00–19.00, Sun. by appt.

DOMAINE DE BELLEVUE★★

■		4 ha	25 000	2 D ■ ↓

★⑧ ★81 ★82 ★83

A good and satisfying colour, and a delicate, subtle (though not very intense) nose. Attractive palate with well-matured tannin together make for a well-balanced wine. (1981)
╺┱ Hugues Barateau, 33240 St-André-de-Cubzac; tel. 57 43 02 98 � By appt ╺┱ M. Barateau.

LE BERGER BARON★

■		70 ha	450 000	3 ■ ↓

72 73 74 **75** 76 77 **78** 79 81 ⑧ **83** 83

From the same négociant as Mouton Cadet, this Berger Baron has a lovely dark ruby colour with slightly acidic, fruity and agreeable a46s on the nose. Good structure and harmony show that it has already matured and is enjoyable to drink. Nonetheless, the hint of tannin suggests that it will age well for a few years more. Overall, a good typical claret. (1983)
╺┱ Baron Philippe de Rothschild, La Baronnie, BP 2, 33250 Pauillac; tel. 56 59 20 20 � By appt. Closed Aug.

CHATEAU BERTINERIE★

■		8 ha	48 000	3 D ■ ↓

64 70 ⑦⑤ **75** 78 79 81 **82** 83

A good combination of substance and pleasing suppleness. The nose is still a little undeveloped, but will open out if the wine is allowed to breathe before serving. (1982)
╺┱ Daniel Bategnies, Ch. Bertinerie, Cubnezais, 33620 Cavignac; tel. 57 68 70 74 � By appt. Closed 24 Dec.–12 Jan.

CHATEAU DE BERTIN★★★

■		10 ha	40 000	2 ■ ↓

75 ★76 **78** ★79 **80 81 82** ⑧ **83**

Only 4000 bottles are produced per hectare. A wine with a powerful Cabernet-Sauvignon nose. Plenty of extract and a touch of youthful bitterness on the palate. Will certainly mature well. (1983) ✔ Bordeaux Ch. Haut-Tucaou Rouge, Bordeaux Ch. Josseme Rouge, Bordeaux Ch. Bertin Blanc Melleu, Bordeaux Ch. Bertin Mousseux, Bordeaux.
╺┱ Guy Ferran, 337600 Cantois 33760 Targon; tel. 56 23 93 61 � By appt.

CHATEAU LA BERTRANDE★

■		10 ha	54 000	3 D ■ ⅃ ↓

75 79 **80 81 81** ⑧ **82**

Attractive colour. Delicate bouquet, round and supple on the palate. Pleasing and agreeable. (1982) ✔ Bordeaux Dom. de Camelon Blanc Sec, Cadillac Ch. la Bertrande Blanc Liquoreux, Loupiac Ch. Grand Peyruchet Blanc Liquoreux, Premières Côtes de Bordeaux Dom. du Moulin Rouge.
╺┱ Henri Gillet, Ch. la Bertrande, Omet, 33410 Cadillac; tel. 56 62 97 16 � By appt.

CHATEAU BONNET★★

■			200 000	2 D ⅃ ↓

⑦⑧ 79 81 ★82 **83**

Although Château Bonnet is one of the best known Entre-Deux-Mers crus, it also produces this very pleasing red Bordeaux which is round, supple and long on the palate. (1982) ✔ Entre-Deux-Mers Ch. Bonnet, Graves Ch. Rochemorin, Graves Ch. Cruzeau Rouge et Blanc, Graves Ch. la Louvière Rouge et Blanc, Graves Ch. Couhins-Lurton.
╺┱ André Lurton, Ch. Bonnet, Grézillac, 33420 Branne; tel. 57 84 52 07 � By appt.

LA BORDELAISE★★

■			10 000	2

Lovely, velvety-red colour and a delicate, slightly woody, red-fruit nose. In the mouth, begins well, is smooth, round and balanced, and has a finish typical of a traditional Bordeaux.
╺┱ W. et A. Gilbey, St-Yzans-de-Médoc, 33340 Lesparre-Mèdoc; tel. 56 41 15 03 � No visitors.

CHAI DES BORDES★

■			1 000 000	3 D ■ ↓

★⑧

Pretty, ruby-red colour. Very fruity nose, pleasant start, and clean and flowing in the mouth. Already drinking well. (1982)
╺┱ Marcel Quancard et Fils, 33440 Arebarès-et-Lagrave; tel. 56 77 66 66 � By appt. Closed one fortnight in Aug.

CHATEAU LA BOTTE★★

■		8 ha	50 000	3 D ⅃ ↓

76 78 **79** 80 **81 82** 82

Deep colour beginning to turn brick-red at the rim. Nicely developed Merlot on the nose. Rich, fleshy, well balanced and softly tannic palate. (1982) ✔ Premières Côtes de Blaye Rouge, Côtes de Blaye Blanc Sec.
╺┱ René Blanchard, Ch. la Botte, 33920 St-Savin; tel. 57 58 90 03 � By appt. Closed Aug.

DOMAINE LE BOUILLEROT

■		5 ha	33 000	3 D ■

78 ⑦⑨ **79** 80 81 82 **83**

Its appearance is on the light side, but the wine is ready to drink. The nose, although somewhat thin, has finesse and a pleasing freshness. (1979) ✔ Bordeaux Dom. de Bouillerot Blanc Sec.
╺┱ Lucien Bos, Dom. de Bouillerot, Gironde-sur-

Dropt, 33190 La Réole; tel. 56 71 46 04 ☥ By appt.

CHATEAU LA BOURGUETTE*

■ 8 ha 50 000 **2** **D** ▤ ⤓
82 Ⓧ **83**

Attractive ruby colour. Nose full of rich aromas, especially of hot toast; smooth and easy to drink. (1983)
☙ Bertrand Lalande, Ch. la Bourguette, 33220 St-Philippe-du-Seignal; tel. 57 46 34 86 ☥ No visitors.

CHATEAU BRANDE-BERGERE

■ 1 ha 5 000 **2** **D** ⤧ ⤓
Ⓧ **83**

Rather severe in style, but pleasant nevertheless. Smooth and quite vigorous on the palate. (1983)
☙ Jacques Doussoux, Ch. Brande-Bergère, Les Eglisottes, 33230 Coutras; tel. 57 69 50 55 ☥ By appt.

CHATEAU DU BRU

■ 15 ha 8 000 **3** **D** ⤧ ⤓
78 79 81 Ⓧ **82** **83**

Bright, crimson robe; overall a little thin and short, but with complex aromas of red fruit and spices, and fairly supple tannins. (1983) ✔ Bordeaux Clairet Ch. du Bru Clairet, Bordeaux Dom. Ies Picadis Blanc Sec,, Bergerac Dom. de Lestignac Rouge.
☙ Guy Duchant, Ch. du Bru, St-Avit-St-Nazaire, 33220 St-Foy-La-Grande; tel. 57 46 12 71 ☥ By appt.

CHATEAU DES CABANNES

■ 17 ha 100 000 **2** **D** ▤ ⤓
Ⓧ *79 82 83 84

A wine of classic colour, with a certain acidity and a nose that is not very powerful but quite fruity, and quite long. A certain amount of tannn is detectable on the palate, but not too much. (1982)
☙ Patrice Baratin, Ch. des Cabannes, 33760 Targon; tel. 56 23 92 25 ☥ No visitors.

DOMAINE DES CAILLOUX*

■ 7 ha 45 000 **2** **D** ▤ ⤓

Fine colour and complex, ripe-fruit nose. Smooth and nicely tannic. (1983) ✔ Bordeaux Rosé, Entre-Deux-Mers, Bordeaux Blanc Moelleux,
☙ Nicole Legrand-Dupuy, Romagne, 33760 Targon; tel. 56 23 09 47 ☥ By appt.

CHATEAU DE CAPPES

■ 4 ha 25 000 **3** **D** ▤ ⤓
*79 **80** *81 *82 83

Although the colour is deep red, the nose is still a little closed-in and is therefore not very expressive. Easy to taste and, on the whole, a light and pleasant wine. (1981)
☙ Yves Boulin, St-André-du-Bois, 33490 St-Macaire; tel. 56 63 70 88 ☥ By appt.

CARAYON-LA-ROSE

■ 30 000 **2** ▤ ⤓
*Ⓧ **83**

The appearance is faultless, but the nose is still slightly reserved. Good, evident. (1982)
☙ M. Dulong, 33270 Floirac; tel. 56 86 51 15 ☥ By appt. Closed Christmas.

LE CARIBIER*

■ 500 000 **3** ▤ ⤓
Ⓧ

Red, with shades of brick. The nose is discreet, but has finesse. Harmonious, well-balanced, flowing and quite persistent.
☙ Adet Steward SA, 41 Rue Vergniaud, 33081 Bordeaux Cédex; tel. 56 44 90 90 ☥ By appt. Closed Aug.

CHATEAU CHAMPBRIN-CADET

■ 18 ha 120 000 **2** **D** ▤ ⤓
Ⓧ **81 82**

Although there is a hint of bitterness at the finish, this brightly coloured wine is nevertheless smooth and vigorous, especially at the beginning. (1983) ✔ Bordeaux Rouge, Premières Côtes-de-Blaye Rouge, Côtes de Blaye Blanc, Côtes de Bourg Rouge.
☙ Marc Cazaufranc, St-Vivien-de-Blaye, 33920 St-Savin; tel. 57 42 48 99 ☥ By appt. Closed 10 Aug.–10 Sept. and during harvest.

CHATEAU CHANET*

■ 15 ha 100 000 **2** **D** ▤ ⤓
Ⓧ **82** 83

Attractive ruby colour. Powerful Cabernet-Sauvignon nose. Firm attack, smooth and flowing overall. Drink soon. (1982)
☙ Jacques et Bernard Large, Guillac, 33420 Branne; tel. 57 84 52 08 ☥ By appt.

LE BORDEAUX DE CHANTECAILLE*

■ 250 000 **3** **D** ▤ ⤓
*83 84

Lovely, deep-red colour. Quite immature but clean and delicate nose. Very crisp and pleasant despite a certain tannic astringency that will soften in time. (1983)
☙ Maison Chantecaille et Cie, 127 Rue de Turenne, 33000 Bordeaux; tel. 56 48 04 54 ☥ By appt. Closed Aug.

CHATEAU CHANTELOISEAU

■ 20 ha **3** **D** ▤ ⤓
*Ⓧ *82 *83

Lacks a little body, but has an attractive colour. Quite aromatic with a pleasant fruitiness, and a certain roundness in the mouth. (1981)
☙ MM. Dulac et Séraphon, Verdelais, 33490 St-Macaire; tel. 56 62 02 08 ☥ By appt.

CHATEAU CHAVRIGNAC★★

■　　　　　　7ha　40000　　３ D ■ ↓

⑦⑤ 78 **82 83** 83

Rich, aromatic, smooth and well balanced. (1983)
↜ Paul Bouron, 'Charignac', Fosses-et-Baleyssac, 33190 La Réole; tel. 56 61 70 50 ⵏ By appt.

CHATEAU LA COMMANDERIE

■　　　　　12ha　90000　　３ D ■ ↓

*80 *81 ⑧② **82 83**

Bright colour and flowery nose. Best drunk young. (1982) ✔ Entre-Deux-Mers.
↜ Michel Raffin, Ch.-la-Commanderie, Martres, 33119 Frontenac; tel. 56 71 54 62 ⵏ By appt Sat. and Sun. Closed 15 Sept.–15 Nov.

CLOS LES CONFRERIES★

■　　　　　10ha　66000　　２ D ■ ↓

70 75 81 *⑧② *83

The deep bright colour suggests a well-made wine; a promising nose and nicely rounded and full-bodied on the palate.
↜ René Lafon, Clos les Confréries, 33750 St-Germain-du-Puch; tel. 57 24 52 53 ⵏ By appt.

CHATEAU LE CONSEILLER

■　　　　　35ha　200000　　３ D ⑪ ↓

79 81 *82 *82 *83 *83

Lovely colour showing some development. Mature nose with a hint of prune and coffee. Supple and pleasing palate; to be drunk very soon. (1982)
↜ Vignobles Liotard, Ch. de la Grande-Chapelle, Lugon, 33240 St-André-de-Cubzac; tel. 57 84 41 52 ⵏ By appt. ↜ Gérald Liotard.

LA COUR-PAVILLON★

■　　　　　　　2000000　　２ D

Lovely, bright red colour already with shades of brick-red. Subtly fragrant bouquet; harmonious and well balanced in the mouth, with a touch of dryness at the finish. (1982)
↜ W. et A. Gilbey, St-Yzans-de-Médoc, 33340 Lesparre-Médoc; tel. 56 41 15 03 ⵏ No visitors.

CHATEAU COURTEY★

■　　　　　3ha　26000　　２ D ■ ↓

*81 *⑧② 82 *83

Lovely brick-red, almost orangish colour; a subtle but delicate nose. A clean and flowing wine that should be drunk as soon as possible. (1982)
↜ Philippe Danies-Sauvestre, Ch. Courtey, 33490 St-Martial; tel. 56 63 71 97 ⵏ By appt.

DOMAINE DE CRANNE

■　　　　　10ha　60000　　２ D ■ ↓

75 76 79 **81** 83 84

This wine has a certain rustic quality but it is clean, straightforward, well balanced and has good tannin. (1983)
↜ Michel Lacoste, Dom. de Cranne, Donzac, 33410 Cadillac; tel. 56 62 10 50 ⵏ Daily 8.00–12.00/14.00–19.00.

DOMAINE DE LA CROIX-DE-MAILHE

■　　　　　10ha　60000　　２ D ■ ↓

⑧② **83**

Attractive, rater delicate red colour. Delicate, reserved bouquet. Light, with some tannin. (1982)
↜ J. Cailleux, Escoussans, 33760 Targon; tel. 56 23 63 23 ⵏ By appt.

CHATEAU DU CROS-LA-BARRAQUE

■　　　　　6ha　36000　　２ D ■ ↓

80 82

Young, lively colour perhaps lacks a little depth. Quite light, but firm attack on the palate. (1982)
↜ Michel Fournol, Ch. du Cros-la-Barraque, Virelade, 33720 Podensac; tel. 56 27 04 27 ⵏ By appt.

CUVEE DES 2 'R'★

■　　　　　10ha　15000　　２ D ■ ↓

75 *76 79 81 *82 *82 *⑧③

Bright red colour gives the wine a distinguished appearance. The nose has rich, elegant aromas; on the palate it lacks a little roundness but has a pleasing, full-bodied flavour. (1982)
↜ M. et Mme M.-T. et Y. Roumegous, Ch. Ginesta, Lignan-de-Bordeaux, 33360 Latresne; tel. 56 21 23 03 ⵏ By appt.

CHATEAU DUCLA

■　　　　　20ha　100000　　２ D ■ ↓

*⑧② 82 *83

A little short, but has good colour and a nose characterized by aromas of prune and chocolate. Quite tannic, with a slight woodiness. (1982)
↜ Michel Mau, Ch. Ducla, St-Exupéry, 33190 Gironde-sur-Dropt; tel. 56 71 11}11 ⵏ No visitors.

CHATEAU DUDON

■　　　　　23ha　140000　　２ D ■ ↓

79 79 80 ⑧① 82

Light colour. Has a certain subtlety in the nose that indicates finesse, with a slightly spicy note. Smooth and round. Ready to drink. (1982)
✔ Bordeaux Sec.
↜ Jean Merlaut, Ch. Dudon, Baurech, 33880 Cambes; tel. 56 21 31 51 ⵏ By appt.

CHATEAU DUFILHOT★

■　　　　　8ha　40000　　２ D ⑪ ↓

79 80 81 *⑧② *82 83

This small, family vineyard dating from 1932 has been painstakingly expanded over the years. It produces an aromatic, distinctive wine with a somewhat meaty flavour. (1983)
↜ Successeurs de M. Dufilhot, Ch. Dufilhot Verdelais, 33490 St-Macaire; tel. 56 96 23 06 ⵏ Fri.–Sun.

LE MAITRE D'ESTOURNEL★

■　　　　　　　750000　　３ D ■ ↓

⑧② *83 84

Lovely deep-red colour. Aromas of chocolate. Begins well but tannin betrays a certain immaturity. Needs to wait a while. (1983)

✦ *MM*. Mostermaes et Nas, 60 Bld Pierre 1er, 33000 Bordeaux; tel.56 52 53 06 ⟁ No visitors.
✦ GFA Dom. Prats.

CHATEAU FAUGAS

■	14 ha	84 000	2 D ▮ ↓

80 81 82

True finesse in the red-fruit nose, and beautifully smooth in the mouth. (1982) ✔ Premières Côtes de Bordeaux Blanc, other Bordeaux wines.
✦ Thial de Bordenave-Berckman, Ch. Faugas, Gabarnac, 33410 Cadillac; tel. 56 62 97 62 ⟁ Daily 9.00–12.00/1400–19.00.

CHATEAU FON-DE-SERGAY★

■	6 ha	48 000	3 D ▮ ↓

75 76 78 79 ⑧ 82 83 84

Bright red in colour, this is a typical Bordeaux. A pleasant nose, lively on the palate and still needing to age a bit. ✔ Bordeaux Ch. Queyréaud, Bordeaux Ch. Fon-de-Sergay.
✦ Pierre et Michel Aroldi, Ch. Fon-de-Sergay, St-Hilaire-du-Bois, 33540 Sauveterre-de-Guyenne; tel. 56 71 53 77 ⟁ Daily 8.00–12.30/14.00–20.00.

FONTAINE-SAINT-LUC

■	5 ha	27 000	3 D ▮ ⑾ ↓

79 80

Rather mature colour, indicative of a wine already a bit old. However, the nose is still very present. Clean and flowing in the mouth. (1980) ✔ Première Côtes de Bordeaux Rouge, Bordeaux Rouge.
✦ Alain Lajus, Fontaine-St-Luc, Yvrac, 33370 Tresses; tel. 56 06 70 02 ⟁ By appt.

CHATEAU FRONTENAC★

■	20 ha	150 000	2 D ▮ ↓

★79 ★80 ★81 ⑧ 82

Lovely Bordeaux colour. Fairly typical 1982, especially the slightly cooked finish with a hint of overripeness. Nose beginning to develop a bouquet; in the mouth, round and full bodied. (1982) ✔ Bordeaux Blanc.
✦ N. et R. Mésange, Ch. Frontenac, Pineuilh, 33220 Ste-Foy-la-Grande; tel. 57 46 09 82 ⟁ By appt.

GAMAGE★

■		80 000	2 D ▮ ↓

⑧ 82 83

Simple and pleasant wine, with a particularly good attack. (1982)
✦ Union St-Vincent, St-Vincent-de-Pertignas, 33420 Branne; tel. 57 84 13 66 ⟁ By appt. Closed Aug.

CLOS DE GARDE

■	12 ha	80 000	2 D ▮ ↓

⑦⑨ ★82

Although this subtly aromatic wine may not yet be asserting its true personality, it has a certain roundness and smoothness. (1982)
✦ Eric Duffau, Génissac, 33420 Branne; tel. 57 24 49 12 ⟁ Mon.–Sat. 8.00–12.00/14.00–19.00.

CHATEAU LA GRANDE-METAIRIE

■	8 ha	50 000	2 D ▮ ↓

★81 ★82 83

Perhaps a little too light, but has a lovely ruby colour, crisp and fruity nose, and is nicely smooth in the mouth. (1983) ✔ Entre-Deux-Mers.
✦ Jean-Pierre Buffeteau, Castelvieil, 33540 Sauveterre-de-Guyenne; tel. 56 61 97 59 ⟁ No visitors.

COOPERATIVE GRANGENEUVE★

■		150 000	2 D ▮ ↓

⑧⑧ ★83 84

Although the nose is not yet fully open, everything indicates a pleasant, mature wine; lovely red colour, kind 'attack', with an overall smoothness and roundness. (1983) ✔ Entre-Deux-Mers, Bordeaux Sec, Bordeaux Clairet, Bordeaux Supérieurs Rouge, and Blanc Moelleux.
✦ Cave Coop. de Romagne, Romagne, 33760 Targon; tel. 56 23 94 62 ⟁ Tue.–Sat. 8.00–12.00/14.00–17.00.

CHATEAU DE GUERIN★

■	3 ha	20 000	2 D ▮ ↓

★⑦⑤ ★76 ★78 ★82 ★83 ★83

The colour is beginning to develop towards tile-red. The nose is young, the palate supple, full and balanced. (1983)
✦ Léon Jaumain, Ch. de Guerin, Castelviel, 33540 Sauveterre-de-Guyenne; tel. 56 56 61 97 5.

CHATEAU HAUT-BAYLE★

■	5 ha	30 000	3 D ▮ ↓

★82 ★82

Lovely Bordeaux colour, already turning brick-red, and a delicate nose with an easy approach. In the mouth, there is a certain pepperiness and quite a long finish. (1982)
✦ Claude Renie, Blasimon, 33540 Sauveterre-de-Guyerre; tel. 56 71 55 01 ⟁ By appt.

DOMAINE DU HAUT-BONNEAU

■	6 ha	40 000	3 D ▮ ↓

82 ⑧

Slightly brick-red colour. Light bouquet, averagely intense, with a hint of fresh-cut grass. Smooth on the palate. (1983) ✔ Sauternes Haut-du-Grand-Carretey, Ste-Croix-du-Mont Ch. Crabitan.
✦ Vincent Labouille, Ch. de Crabitan, 33410 Ste-Croix-du-Mont; tel. 56 62 10 47 ⟁ By appt.

CHATEAU HAUT-CASTENET★

■	25 ha	80 000	3 D ▮ ↓

75 76 78 79 ★82

From the heart of Gironde, a wine which still bears a certain rustic stamp but which has good colour and a respectable amount of tannin. Its qualities suggest that over the years it will mature and mellow. (1982) ✔ Entre-Deux-Mers Ch. Launay, Bordeaux Rosé Champ-de-la-Rose.
✦ Rémy Greffier, Ch. Haut-Castenet, Soussac, 33790 Pellegrue; tel. 56 61 31 44 ⟁ No visitors.

CHATEAU HAUT-CATALOGNE★

■ 6ha 40000 ◼3 D ▮ ⬇
80 81 ⑧ ◼82 83 ⑧

This attractive, light-red wine's nose is modest but on the palate it is smooth, fruity and clean, flowing easily over the palate. (1982) ✔ Bordeaux Blanc Ch. Haut-Catalogne, Côtes de Bordeaux St-Macaire, Bordeaux Blanc Haut-Catalogne.
☛ Joël Bourgoint, Ch. Haut-Catalogne, St-Laurent-du-Bois, 33540 Sauveterre-de-Guyenne; tel. 56 63 70 72 ♈ By appt. Closed 20 Dec.–3 Jan. and school holidays in Feb.

CHATEAU HAUT LA PEYRERE★

■ 12ha 70000 ◼3 D ▮ ⬇
78 81 ★⑧ ★◼82 83

Attractive, deepish-red colour and quite a rich nose; it has good attack and is well made. The finish is a little dry, but on the whole the wine has aged well. (1982)
☛ J. Cailleux, Escoussans, 33760 Targou; tel. 56 23 63 23 ♈ By appt.

CHATEAU HOSTIN-LE-ROC★★

■ 7ha 8000 ◼2 D ▮ ⬇
67 70 75 79 ⑧ 82

An intense, bright red colour, with round, mature tannin on the palate. The wine is well structured and has good length. (1981) ✔ Entre-Deux-Mers, Bordeaux Rosé.
☛ André Boutinon, Ch. Hostin-le-Roc, St-Quentin-de-Baron, 33750 St-Germain-du-Puch; tel. 57 84 61 26 ♈ Daily.

CHATEAU DE JAYLE★

■ 25ha 140000 ◼2 D ▮ ⬇
81 ⑧ ◼82 83

Severe appearance due to the intensity and depth of its colour. Full bodied and rustic, almost rugged, character. Extremely strong personality that may still be a little harsh, but which is very promising. (1982)
☛ Michel Pelle, Ch. de Jayle, St-Martin-de-Sescas, 33490 St-Macaire; tel. 56 62 80 07 ♈ By appt.

CHATEAU LES JESUITES★

■ 3ha 25000 ◼2 D ▮ ⑩ ⬇
76 79 81 ◼82 83 84

A richly aromatic wine with flavourful tannin and a full body which suggest that it will develop well. (1982)
☛ Guy Lucmaret, Ch. les Jésuites, St-Maixant, 33490 St-Macaire; tel. 56 63 17 97 ♈ By appt.

KRESSMANN MONOPOLE★

■ 500000 ◼3 D ⑩ ⬇
81 ★⑧ ◼82

Lovely, clean and lively colour. Above all, a handsome nose combining grape and blackcurrant. In the mouth, the clean attack and solid tannin give the wine its typical Bordeaux character.
☛ Jean Kressmann, Parempuyre, 33290 Blanquefort; tel. 56 35 84 64 ♈ By appt. Closed Sat. and Sun.

LAMOTHE-PARROT★

■ 100000 ◼2 D ▮ ⬇
⑧ ◼82 ★83

Lovely shining red colour. Nose still inexpressive, although it shows signs of being delicate and persistent. Good attack on the palate. (1982)
☛ Ets Parrot, 33000 Bordeaux, tel. 56 39 45 87 ♈ By appt.

CHATEAU LA LANDE SAINT-JEAN★

■ 16ha 120000 ◼2 D ▮ ⬇
70 ⑦ 78 ⑦ 81 ⑧ ◼82 ★83

A classic wine, both in terms of nose and appearance. Fine colour, light, crisp and pleasing; easy to drink. (1982)
☛ Michel Manaud, Ch. Lalande St-Jean, 33450 St-Loubes; tel. 56 31 51 20 ♈ By appt.

CHATEAU LAPEYRERE★

■ 16ha 80000 ◼2 ▮ ⬇
◼80 82 83 84

An attractive wine with a delicate bouquet of Cabernet-Sauvignon. Fleshy on the palate, this is a good wine by 1980 standards. (1980) ✔ Bordeaux Ch. Lapeyrere Blanc Sec, Bordeaux Ch. Laronde Blanc Sec.
☛ *Mme* Catherine Yung, Ch. Lapeyrere, Béguey, 33410 Cadillac; tel. 56 62 95 49 ♈ No visitors.
☛ Charles et J.-P. Yung.

DOMAINE DE LAUBERTRIE★

■ 7ha 40000 ◼2 D ▮ ⬇
75 78 79 80 ◼81 82 83

Good colour, red with brick tints; pleasant nose, and appealing fruitiness. (1981) ✔ Bordeaux Sec Domaine de Laubertrie.
☛ Bernard Pontallier, Dom. de Laubertrie, Salignac, 33240 St-André-de-Cubzac; tel. 57 43 03 37 ♈ By appt.

CHATEAU DE LUGAGNAC★

■ 32ha 150000 ◼2 D ▮ ⬇
⑦ 76 79 80 81 ★82 ★◼82

The pedigree of this noble 15th-century residence is reflected in its wine: fine, lively red robe; pleasing, deep nose and solid, well-structured body. (1982)
☛ Maurice Bon, Ch. de Lugagnac, 33790 Pellegrue; tel. 56 61 30 60 ♈ By appt.

DOMAINE DE MALINEAU★

■ 11ha 70000 ◼2 D ⑩ ⬇
★75 ★76 ★78 79 80 ★82 ★83 ★◼83

Although the colour is a little weak, tending to tile-red, the nose is a complex mixture of red fruit and bread crust. In the mouth the wine is supple, rich and lingering. (1983)
☛ Henri Gardera, Dom. de Malineau, Saint-Martial, 33490 St-Macaire; tel. 56 63 70 58 ♈ By appt.

151

CHATEAU MAUTRET★

■ 12ha 80000 **3** **D** ▮ ⑪ ↓

★⑧ ★83 **84**

Attractive, quite light colour. Subtly fruity nose. Smooth, clean and flowing in the mouth. Slips down easily. (1982) ✔ Bordeaux AOC Blanc Sec Dom. de la Grave Marquis-de-Mautret, Côtes de Bordeaux Ste-Croix-du-Mont.
🕯 Jacques Mouras, Ch. Mautret, Semens, 33490 St-Macaire; tel. 56 62 05 27 ☿ By appt.

CHATEAU MONDETOUR

■ 20ha 100000 **2** ▮ ⑪ ↓

81 ⑧

Pleasant, delicate colour and discreet, subtle bouquet. Smooth, light and agreeable on the palate. (1982)
🕯 Yves Courpon, 33620 Cavignac; tel. 57 68 61 16 ☿ Daily 9.00–12.00/14.00–19.00.

CHATEAU MORILLON★★

■ 10ha 80000 **2** **D** ▮ ⑪

★79 ★80 ★82 **83** **83**

Brilliant in appearance. Complex blend of soft red fruit on the nose. Rich and supple with a well-balanced finish. (1983)
🕯 Olga Bagot, Ch. Morillon, Neuffons, 33580 Monsegur; tel. 56 71 42 26 ☿ By appt.

MOUTON CADET★★

■ 5 000 000 **4** ▮ ↓

72 73 74 75 **76** 77 78 79 **80** **81** ⑧ **82** 83

The nose is still a little closed-in, but has potential. Crisp attack and good structure. Rich, smooth tannin; could easily wait three or four years. (1982)
🕯 Baron Philippe. de Rothschild, La Baronnie, BP 2, 33250 Pauillac; 56 59 20 20 ☿ By appt. Closed Aug.

RESERVE DE LA MAISON NICOLAS★

■ **2** ▮

Rather a light colour for the vintage. The nose of soft fruits is still a little closed, and its astringency on the palate suggests one should wait another two or three years. Recommended for *foie gras* or duck. (1982)
🕯 Ets Nicolas, 2 Rue de Valmy, 94220 Charenton; tel. 01 37 59 20.

NICOLAS★

■ 1 500 000 **2** ▮

A contradiction between, on the one hand, the light colour and delicate nose of this wine, and, on the other, its hard finish on the palate.
🕯 Ets Nicolas, 2 Rue de Valmy, 94220 Charenton; tel. 01 37 59 20.

CHATEAU PASQUET★

■ 22ha 160000 **3** **D** ▮ ↓

75 79 **80** 81 82 **83**

Good colour. Bouquet is not yet fully developed, but already has the fresh aroma of red-fruit. Round and firm, with good body and pleasantly spicy finish. (1983) ✔ Bordeaux Ch. Pasquet Blanc Sec.

🕯 Georges Pernette, Ch. Pasquet, Escoussans, 33760 Targon; tel. 56 23 94 30 ☿ By appt.

CLOS DE PELIGON★★

■ 9ha 50000 **2** **D** ⑪ ↓

★81 ⑧ **82**

Beautiful red colour, deep and bright. Great finesse on the nose. The attack is delicate, with a slight oak-vanilla quality, and it is full-bodied and meaty on the palate. (1982)
🕯 Pierre Reynaud, 33450 St-Loubès; tel. 56 20 47 52 ☿ No visitors.

CHATEAU PERPONCHER

■ 6ha 30000 **3** **D** ▮ ↓

⑥ **64** **72** **74** **75** 78 79 ★81 ★82

A very dark colour giving a slightly sombre appearance. A slight touch of oxidation n the nose but the palate reveals solid tannins. (1982)
✔ Bordeaux Blanc, Entre-Deux-Mers.
🕯 G. Weisweller et M. Lemord, Ch. Perponcher, 33420 Naujan-de-Postiac; tel. 57 84 55 39 ☿ By appt.

CHATEAU DE PERRE★

■ 7ha 46000 **2** ▮

79 ★81 82 **82** 83 **83**

Watch this vineyard closely. The wine is already showing certain qualities: good colour and bite, suppleness and body. Still unsophisticated, but should develop well. (1982) ✔ Bordeaux Ch. de Perre Blanc Liquoreux, Bordeaux Cru de Perre Blanc Sec.
🕯 Claude Mayle, Ch. de Perre, St-Martin-de-Sescas, 33490 St-Macaire; tel. 56 62 83 31 ☿ By appt.

CHATEAU DU PETIT-PUCH★

■ 7ha 50000 **2** **D** ▮ ↓

⑧ **83**

Quite light-coloured and has a young, fruity, pleasantly crisp nose. Elegant, well-balanced and quite flowing. (1983)
🕯 *Mme* Méandre de Lapouyade, Ch. du Petit-Puch, 33750 St-Germain-du-Puch; tel. 57 24 52 36 ☿ By appt.

CHATEAU PHILIPPON★★

■ 18ha 110000 **2** **D** ▮ ↓

★78 ★79 ★80 ★81 **82**

Deep ruby-red colour and pleasant nose; charming attack on the palate, which is full-bodied, meaty, and robust, with an unusually long finish. (1982)
🕯 *MM.* Mariotto Père et Fils, Cleyrac, 33540 Sauveterre-de-Guyenne; tel. 56 71 51 45 ☿ By appt.

DOMAINE DE PILET★

■ 14ha 60000 **3** **D** ▮ ↓

⑧ **82** 83 **83**

Well structured and consistent. Crisp, clean appearance; straightforward vigorous nose; good balance, smooth and round on the palate. (1983)
🕯 Jean Queyrens, Dom. de Pilet, Donzac, 33410 Cadillac; tel. 56 62 97 42 ☿ By appt.

CHATEAU POUCHAUD-LARQUEY**

■ 5ha 30000 [2] [D] ■ ↓

*77 *78 *80 *82 *[83] *84

Lovely ruby colour; complex and subtle nose, richness, ripe-fruit arómas, and well-balanced finish. (1983) ✓ Entre-Deux-Mers Blanc Sec, Bordeaux Rouge.

⊶ René Piva et Fils, Morizes, 33190 La Réole; tel. 56 71 44 97 Ⲧ By appt.

DOMAINE DE POURQUEY*

■ 11ha 70000 [2] [D] ■ ↓

Attractive, intense ruby colour. Strong and fruity nose. In the mouth, smooth with just a hint of tannin. (1983) ✓ Entre-Deux-Mers Bordeaux Sec, Bordeaux Supérieurs Blanc Moelleux.

⊶ Roger Fouilhac et Fils, Castelvieil, 33540 Sauveterre-de-Guyenne; tel. 56 61 97 62 Ⲧ By appt.

CHATEAU LA PRIOULETTE

■ 10ha 55000 [3] [D] ■ ↓

75 79 **80** **81** (82) [82]

Despite a slight hint of bitterness in the finish, full and tannic. Agreeable bite slightly disguised by roundness. (1982) ✓ Premières Côtes de Bordeaux Ch. la Prioulette, Bordeaux Ch. la Prioulette.

⊶ François Bord, Ch. la Prioulette, St-Maixant, 33490 St-Macaire; tel. 56 62 01 97 Ⲧ By appt.

DOMAINE DES RAIGNEAUX**

■ 13ha 80000 [3] [D] ■ ↓

***81** *[81]

Lovely, attractive deep red colour and a discreet but delicate nose. A 'tasty' wine that is mature, well-balanced and serious. Likely to age well. (1981)

⊶ Jean Bustarret, Dom. des Raigneaux, Madirac, 33670 Crèon; tel. 56 23 03 49 Ⲧ By appt.

CHATEAU ROC-DE-CAYLA***

■ 7ha 42000 [3] [D] ■ ↓

*75 ***78** **79** **81** ***82** *[82] 83

Deeply coloured. Delicate and floral on the nose. Full, fleshy, harmonious and well balanced on the palate. (1982)

⊶ Jean-Marie Lanoue, Ch. Roc-de-Cayla, Soulignac, 33760 Targon; tel. 56 23 91 13 Ⲧ By appt.

CHATEAU LE RONDAILH*

■ 13ha 80000 [2] [D] ■ ↓

(82) [82] **83**

Fine, rather deep colour suggests an intense wine. Full, promising bouquet; great character and even a touch of aggression on the palate, especially on the attack. (1982)

⊶ *MM.* Pallaruelo et Fils, Le Rondailh, Ste-Foy-la-Longue, 33490 St-Macaire; tel. 56 63 70 54 Ⲧ No visitors.

DOMAINE DE LA SERIZIERE

■ 10ha 60000 [2] [D] ■ ↓

(82) [83] **84**

Slightly developed colour, hint of greenness in the nose, and round and smooth in the mouth. Drink while still quite young. (1983)

⊶ Gérard et Jean-Marc Lobre, Dom. de la Serizière, Ladaux, 33760 Targon; tel. 56 23 91 75 Ⲧ By appt.

MONSIEUR TAVERNIER*

■ 100000 [2] ■ ↓

*[81] ***82** **83**

Bright red colour and jammy nose. In the mouth there is a certain cooked quality, but good structure shows through. Already worth drinking. (1981)

⊶ André Quancard, 21 Rue Calvé, 33000 Bordeaux; tel. 56 52 95 95 Ⲧ No visitors.

CHATEAU TERTRE CABARON**

■ 13ha 80000 [4] [D] ■ ↓

78 79 81 (82) [82] **83**

Very deep red colour and a promising nose; the wine is full and meaty and really fills the mouth. Will keep well. (1982)

⊶ Michel Dugrand, St-Brice, 33540 Sauveterre-de-Guyenne; tel. 56 71 54 19 Ⲧ By appt.

CHATEAU THIEULEY**

■ 15ha 120000 [2] [D] ■ ⊕ ↓

81 (82) [82] [83]

Quite an elegant wine, the nose already refined, if a little discreet. On the palate it is round and tannic with a pleasant impression of vanilla, topped by a good finish. (1982) ✓ Entre-Deux-Mers Ch. Thieuley, Bordeaux Clairet Ch. Thieuley.

⊶ Francis Courselle, Ch. Thieuley, La Sauve-Majeur, 33670 Créon; tel. 56 23 00 01 Ⲧ By appt.

CHATEAU TIMBERLAY**

■ 110ha 730000 [3] ■ ⊕ ↓

*47 *59 ***78** ***79** ***81** ***82** *[82]

This wine has a lovely deep colour and a delicate nose. Full, rich, harmonious – very well made. (1982) ✓ Bordeaux Ch. de Cadillac, Bordeaux Ch. Haut-Fourat, St-Emilion Ch. Villemaurine.

⊶ Robert Giraud SA, Dom. de Loiseau, BP 31, 33240 St-André-de-Cubzac; tel. 57 43 01 44 Ⲧ By appt.

CHATEAU TOUR-DE-SARRAIL

■   16ha   8000   **2** **D** ■ ↓

75 **78** **81** *82 83

A wine that is perhaps a little short, but pleasantly light and smooth. (1982)
↠ Jean-Pierre Rivière, Ch. Tour-de-Sarrail, Pompignac, 33370 Tresses; tel. 56 30 96 47 ♈ By appt.

CHATEAU DE LA TOUR★★

■   24ha   140000   **3** **D** ■ ↓

80 **81** ▨▨ 82 ⑧▨ ▨▨

Lovely Bordeaux colour. Clean but still immature nose. Crisp but not harsh on the palate. Powerful and meaty, with a good future. (1983)
✔ Margaux Ch. Rausan-Segla Rouge.
↠ *MM.* Holt Frères, et Fils, Ch. Rausad Segla, 33460 Margaux; tel. 56 52 11 82 ♈ By appt. Closed Aug.

CHATEAU LE TREBUCHET★

■   14ha   80000   **2** **D** ■ ↓

*⑧▨ **83** ▨▨

Plenty of colour, powerful on the nose, well balanced in the mouth; overall a well-resolved wine despite a hint of acidity. Should age well. (1982)
↠ Bernard Berger, Ch. le Trébuchet, Les Esseintes, 33190 La Réole; tel. 56 71 42 28 ♈ By appt.

CHATEAU DES TROIS-TOURS★★

■   6ha   16000   **3** **D** ■

83 82

From this medieval château comes a wine with fine colour, attractively earthy on the nose and palate, with additional aromas of venison and leather. (1982) ✔ Bordeaux Ch. des Trois-Tours.
↠ Jean de la Blanchardière, Ch. des Trois-Tours, Caumont, 33540 Sauveterre-de-Guyenne; tel. 56 71 53 28 ♈ No visitors.

CHATEAU TURCAUD★

■   9ha   54000   **3** **D** ◧ ↓

78 *80 **81** 82 ▨▨ ⑧▨

Bright-red colour. An interesting blend of floral and vegetal characters on the nose. Round and supple in the mouth, but still somewhat closed. Will improve with age (1983)
↠ Robert Maurice 33670 Créon – La Sauve-Majeure; tel. 56 23 04 41 ♈ By appt.

CHATEAU DES VALLEES

■   6ha   33000   **2** **D** ■ ↓

75 78 79 ▧▨ ⑧▨ 83

This wine is pale Bordeaux-red with shades of copper, and has a nose rather rustic in character. (1982)
↠ Laurent Boudet, Ch. des Vallées, St-Laurent-du-Boix, 33540 Sauveterre-de-Guyerre; tel. 56 63 71 83 ♈ By appt.

Bordeaux Clairet

ALAIN BONNEAU★

Clairet   2ha   13000   **3** **D** ■ ↓

Rather pale red colour, but pleasingly fruity on the nose and supple on the palate. (1984)
↠ Alain Bonneau, 33420 Branne; tel. 57 84 50 01 ♈ By appt. Closed last weeks Dec.

DOMAINE DU BRU

Clairet   2.5ha   20000   **2** **D** ■ ↓

81 82 *83 *84

Typically pale-coloured clairet. A bit light on the nose but fresh and fruity to drink. (1982)
↠ Guy Duchant, Ch. du Bru, St-Avit-St-Nazaire, 33220 Ste-Foy-la-Grande; tel. 57 46 12 71 ♈ By appt.

COOPERATIVE DE GENISSAC

Clairet   4ha   25000   **2** **D** ■ ↓

⑧▨ 84

Rosé colour, red fruit nose, quite fruity and good for drinking now. (1984) ✔ Bordeaux Supérieur Celliers-de-la-Rafinette, Bordeaux Sec, Bordeaux Supérieur Blanc, Bordeaux Supérieur Rouge.
↠ Cave Coop. de Génissac, 33420 Génissac 33420 Brane; tel. 57 24 48 01 ♈ By appt.

GRANGENEUVE

Clairet   6ha   24000   **2** **D** ■ ↓

⑧▨

Light in colour, this wine has a rather floral nose with a certain finesse and is well balanced on the palate, though rather neutral. (1984)
↠ Coop. de Grangeneuve, Ramagne, 33760 Targon; tel. 56 23 94 6 ♈ By appt.

CAVE DE QUINSAC

Clairet   30ha   90000   **2** **D** ■ ↓

The colour of this wine is nearer a rosé than red. The nose is fairly discreet and it is very supple on the palate. (1984) ✔ Bordeaux Blanc et Mousseux, Premières Côtes de Bordeaux Rouge.
↠ Cave Coop. de Quinsac, Quinsac, 33360 Latresne; tel. 56 20 86 09 ♈ Tues.–Sat. 8.00–12.00/ 14.00–17.30.

CHATEAU ROLLET-SAUVIAC

Clairet   2ha   12000   **2** **D** ■ ↓

75 76 78 80 ⑧▨ 84

Good claret colour, slightly darker than that of a rosé. Although the nose is rather neutral, the wine is light, round and thirst-quenching on the palate. (1982) ✔ St-Emilion Ch. Vieux Guinot, St-Emilion Ch. Fourney, St-Emilion Ch. Roc-St-Michel, St-Emilion Ch. Gaillard de la Gorce.
↠ Jean-Pierre Rollet, Ch. Fourney, St-Pey d'Ar-

mens, 33330 St-Emilion; tel. 57 40 15 13 ☂ No visitors.

Bordeaux Sec

CLOS DE L'ANGE★

☐		8ha	50000	**3** D ▮ ⚲

Pale yellow colour with shades of light green, and mature, aromatic nose; a well-balanced wine that is crisp, pleasant, and fruity.
⚲ *MM*. Dulac et Séraphon, Verdelais, 33490 St-Macaire; tel. 56 62 02 08 ☂ By appt.

CHATEAU BALLUE-MONDON★★

☐		2ha	12000	**3** D ▮ ⚲
75 78 81 ★82 **83** 84				

A light Sauvignon, yellow-green in colour. Agreeably fruity bouquet; firmness and vigour on the palate. Well balanced with a long finish. (1983) ✔ Bordeaux Ch. Ballue-Mondon Rouge.
⚲ Guy Ballue, Ch. Ballue-Mondon, 33890 Gensac; tel. 57 40 42 25 ☂ By appt. Closed 1–15 Sept.

BEAU-MAYNE★

☐	410000	**2** D ⅷ ⚲

Straw-gold colour with shades of green. Exactly the right amount of acidity.
⚲ *MM*. Dourthe Frères, Moulis, 33480 Castelreau-de-Médoc; tel. 56 35 84 64 ☂ By appt. Closed Sat. and Sun.

CHATEAU DU BIAC

☐		5ha	31000	**2** D ▮ ⚲
81 82 ⑧③				

Classic but very clean straw-gold colour. Subtly aromatic and very sweet. Lacks crispness. (1982) ✔ Premières Côtes-de-Bordeaux Rouge, and Blanc Moelleux.
⚲ Nicole et Hélène Ducatez, Ch. du Biac, 33550 Langoiran; tel. 56 67 19 98 ☂ Daily.

CHATEAU DE BONHOSTE★

☐		2ha	5000	**2** D ▮ ⚲
82 ⑧③ **83** 84				

A small, family-run vineyard producing a good wine, with a lively colour and a pleasant bouquet. Delicate and well balanced on the palate. (1983)
⚲ Bernard Fournier, Ch. Bonhoste, St-Jean-de-Blaignac, 33420 Branne; tel. 57 84 12 18 ☂ Daily 7.00–21.00.

LA BORDELAISE★

☐	400000	**2** D ⅷ ⚲

Gleaming pale-yellow colour. Slightly fruity nose. Well balanced, smooth yet lively.
⚲ W. et A. Gilbey, St-Yzans-de-Médoc, 33340 Lesparre-Médoc; tel. 56 41 15 03 ☂ No visitors.

CHATEAU LA BOURGETTE

☐		4ha	15000	**2** D ▮ ⚲

Straw-gold and quite pale, but still attractive. Subtle, pleasant and delicate aromas. Serve very cold. (1984)
⚲ Bertrand Lalande, Ch. la Bourguette, 33220 St-Philippe-du-Seignal; tel. 57 46 34 86 ☂ No visitors.

DOMAINE DE CAMELON★

☐		8ha	20000	**3** D ▮ ⅷ ⚲
81 82 83 84				

Fine, pure, clear appearance. Highly aromatic, it has both finesse and elegance on the palate, despite a slightly acidic balance. (1983) ✔ Cadillac Ch. la Bertrande, Loupiac Ch. Grand-Peyruchet, Premières Côtes de Bordeaux Dom. du Moulin, Bordeaux Ch. la Bertrande.
⚲ Henri Gillet, Ch. la Bertrande, Omet, 33410 Cadillac; tel. 56 62 97 16 ☂ By appt.

CARAYON-LA-ROSE★

☐	40000	**6** ▮ ⚲
⑧③ 84		

Lovely, soft, pale-yellow colour and lightly flowery nose. Delicate and agreeable on the palate. (1983)
⚲ *M*. Dulong, 33270 Floirac; tel. 56 86 51 15 ☂ By appt. Closed Christmas.

CHATEAU CHAMPBRIN

☐		6ha	35000	**3** D ▮ ⚲

Quite intense, pale-yellow colour and aggressive, somewhat overripe nose. Smooth in the mouth, where it is extremely sweet, perhaps overly so. (1983)
⚲ Marc Cazaufranc, St-Vivien-de-Blaye, 33920 St-Savin; tel. 57 42 48 99 ☂ By appt.

LE BORDEAUX DE CHANTECAILLE

☐	10000	**2** D ▮ ⚲
⑧④		

Very clear. Nose still a little closed, but nicely fruity. Slightly oaky palate. (1984)
⚲ Maison Chantecaille et Cie, 127 Rue de Turenne, 33000 Bordeaux; tel. 56 48 04 54 ☂ By appt. Closed Aug.

CHEVALIER-DE-MALLE★

☐		27ha	30000	**4** D ▮ ⚲
⑦⑥ 78 ★80 ★81 ★82 **82**				

Pure, crystal-clear colour and typical Bordeaux Sec nose. Almost excessively warm and spirited attack on the palate. (1982)
⚲ Pierre de Bournazel, Ch. de Malle, Preignac, 33210 Langon; tel. 56 63 28 67 ☂ By appt.

LA COUR-PAVILLON★

☐	1200000	**2**

Lovely pale-yellow colour. Subtle but delicate nose. In the mouth, very smooth and distinctively long-lasting. (1983)
⚲ W. et A. Gilbey, St-Yzans-de-Médoc, 33340 Lesparre-Médoc; tel. 56 41 15 03 ☂ No visitors.

CHATEAU COURTEY★★

☐		4ha	30000	**2** D ▮ ⚲
83 84				

Rather sombre colour and remarkably intense bouquet with scents of lime blossom. Vigorous attack and great character on the palate. Really captures the imagination. (1983) ✔ Bordeaux Rouge, Bordeaux Supérierus Rouge.
⚲ Philippe Danies-Sauvestre, Ch. Courtey, St-

Martial, 33490 St-Macaire; tel. 56 63 71 97 ☛ By appt.

CHATEAU LA CROIX-DE-LAMOTHE★

☐	3 ha	18000	② D 🍾 ↓

Lovely straw-gold colour and extremely rich bouquet. On the palate it is not quite so perfect, but still very drinkable. (1984)
☛ Jean Renaud, St-Ciers-d'Abzac, 33230 Coutras; tel. 57 49 45 03 ☛ By appt.

CRU DE PERRE★★

☐	7 ha	45000	② ↓
78 79 81 **82** 83			

Fresh, bright colour and a pleasing, clear-cut floral rose. Nicely balanced, with good length. (1982) ✔ Bordeaux Ch. de Perre Rouge.
☛ Claude Mayle, Ch. de Perre, St-Martin-de-Sescas, 33490 St-Macaire; tel. 56 62 83 32 ☛ By appt.

CHATEAU DUDON★

☐	6 ha	25000	② D 🍾 ↓
⑦⑨ 81 *84			

Crystal-clear straw-gold colour is indicative of maturity. Will be enjoyed by those who like a really smooth wine.
☛ Jean Merlaut, Ch. Dudon, Baurech, 33880 Cambes; tel. 56 21 31 51 ☛ By appt.

MAITRE D'ESTOURNEL★★

☐	750000	② D ↓

Lovely, crystal-clear yellow colour. Typically Sauvignon nose, round and lively on the palate. (1984)
☛ MM. Mostermars et Mas, 60 Bld Pierre 1er, 33000 Bordeaux; tel. 56 52 53 06 ☛ By appt. Closed Aug. ☛ GFA Bruno Prats.

CHATEAU FON-DE-SERGAY★★

☐	4 ha	32000	② D 🍾 ↓
81 82 83 ⑧④ **84**			

Good colour, with a crisp, fruity nose, this wine has a vigorous attack on the palate and is then balanced and refined. (1984) ✔ Bordeaux Ch. Fon-de-Sergay, Bordeaux Ch. Queyréaud.
☛ Pierre et Michel Aroldi, Ch. Fon-de-Sergay, St-Hilaire-du-Bois, 33540 Sauveterre-de-Guyenne; tel. 56 71 53 77 ☛ Daily 8.00–12.30/14.00–20.00.

CHATEAU GINESTA

☐	1 ha	7000	② D 🍾 ↓
⑧③			

From a very small vineyard, this dry white wine has a limited production. The colour is straightforward, and the wine is very crisp but perhaps not yet quite mature. (1983)
☛ M. et Mme M.-T. et Y. Roumegous, Ch. Ginesta, Lignan-de-Bordeaux, 33360 Latresne; tel. 54 21 33 03 ☛ By appt.

CHATEAU DU GRAND CAMPSEC★

☐	1 ha	7000	② D 🍾 ↓

Clear yellow colour and a fragrance of very ripe grapes with a curious hint of garlic. Soft, easy to drink and vinous, with a pleasant, nutty flavour.
☛ MM. G. et P. Lesnier, St-Vincent-de-Paul,

33440 Ambarès-et-Lagrave; tel. 56 38 96 10 ☛ By appt.

GRANGENEUVE-SAUVIGNON★

☐	110000	② D 🍾 ↓
⑧④ 84		

Pale yellow colour; aromatic floral Sauvignon nose; fresh and lively on the palate. (1984)
☛ Coop. de Grangeneuve, Romagne, 33760 Targon; tel. 56 23 94 62 ☛ By appt. ☛ Mme Vve. Baluteau.

DOMAINE DE LA GRAVETTE

☐	12 ha	60000	② D 🍾 ↓
83 *84			

A light straw-yellow wine, with a nose which, while not particularly intense, nevertheless offers a clean Sauvignon fragrance. On the palate, a certain freshness with a slight touch of acidity. (1983)
☛ Jacques Mouras, Ch. Mautret, Semens, 33490 St-Macaire; tel. 56 62 05 27 ☛ By appt.

CHATEAU DE HAUX★★

☐	3 ha	20000	② D 🍾 ↓
75 79 *82 *83			

This elegant château produces a correspondingly elegant wine that is full but smooth, agreeable to both the nose and the palate. (1983)
☛ B. Pellegrin, 33550 Langoiran; tel. 56 67 09 06 ☛ Daily 9.00–12.00/14.00–19.00.

DOMAINE DE JUNIAC★★

☐	8 ha	26000	② D 🍾 ↓

A wine that goes against current trends, remaining staunchly faithful to ancient wine-making traditions: yellow to straw-gold in colour; well developed on the nose; smooth and round on the palate, perhaps a bit heavy overall.
☛ Jacques Boireau, Ch. Birot, Béguey, 33410 Cadillac; tel. 56 62 96 50 ☛ By appt.

KRESSMANN MONOPOLE★

☐	125000	② D ◑ ↓

Charming, straw-gold colour. Bouquet seduces the nose with a succession of fragrances: blossom, liquorice and cachou, along with an impression of crispness. In the mouth it begins well and has exactly the right amount of acidity. An agreeable wine.
☛ Jean Kressmann, Parempuyre, 33290 Blanqueort; tel. 56 35 84 64 ☛ By appt. Closed Sat. and Sun.

CHATEAU LABATUT★

☐	6 ha	45000	③ D 🍾 ↓
71 81 82 *83 *84			

Extremely attractive palest yellow colour and ripe-fruit scents on the nose. Light, crisp and clean, a very pleasant wine. (1983)
☛ Michel Bouchard, Ch. Labatut, St-Maixant, 33490 St-Macaire; tel. 56 62 02 44 ☛ By appt.

CHATEAU LAGUT★

☐	2 ha	15000	③ D 🍾 ↓

Pale-yellow colour and a subtle but clean and pleasant nose. Light, smooth and flowing overall. (1984)

♠ Alain Bonneau, 33420 Branne; tel. 57 84 50 01
Ⓨ By appt. Closed last week in Dec.

CHATEAU DE LARDILEY

☐	14ha	80000	3 D ▤ ↓

83 84

Pale colour and quite robust on the palate. Some flowery aromas. (1983) ✔ Première Côtes de Bordeaux Rouge, Bordeaux Supérieur Rouge.
♠ P. Lataste, Ch. de Lardiley, 33410 Cadillac; tel. 56 27 10 74 Ⓨ By appt. Closed 25 Dec.–1 Jan., May and Aug. ♠ Marthe Lataste.

DOMAINE DE LAUBERTRIE

☐	4ha	24000	2 D ▤ ↓

⑦⑦ ⑦⑨ *⑧② 83 *⑧④ *84

A well-presented wine with good balance on the palate. (1982)
♠ Bernard Pontallier, Dom. de Laubertrie, 33240 Salignac; tel. 57 43 03 37 Ⓨ By appt.

CHATEAU DE LOUDENNE★★

☐	12ha	80000	3 D ▤ ↓

Extremely crisp colour is so pale as to be practically clear. Interestingly complex nose with shades of pear, passion-fruit and grapefruit. Rich, full and very long. (1984)
♠ W. et A. Gilbey, St-Yzans-de-Médoc, 33340 Lesparre-Médoc; tel. 56 41 15 03 Ⓨ No visitors.

DOMAINE DE MALINEAU★★

☐	8ha	50000	6 D ▤ ↓

Pale straw yellow; pleasantly fuity nose, elegant and lingering to taste.
♠ Henri Gardera, Dom. de Malineau, St-Martial, 33490 St-Macaire; tel. 56 63 70 58. Ⓨ By appt.

CHATEAU MARAC★

☐	40ha	25000	2 D ▤ ↓

75 78 79 81 *82 83

Yellow-to-green colour. Delicate bouquet, and a fruity end-taste. (1982)
♠ Alain Bonville, Ch. Marac, Pujols, 33350 Castillon-la-Bataille; tel. 57 40 53 21 Ⓨ By appt.

CHATEAU LA MONGIE★

☐	9ha	70000	2 D ▤ ◑ ↓

79 79 81 81 83 83 ⑧④ 84

Straw-yellow colour with a hint of petillance. Floral and faintly musky nose. Lively, bone-dry flavour. Ideal with seafood. Should be drunk young. (1984)
♠ Pierre Blouin, Ch. la Mongie, Vérac 33240 St-André-de-Cubzac; tel. 57 84 37 08 Ⓨ By appt.

MOUTON-CADET★

☐	100ha	6000000	4 ▤ ↓

83 84 84

Pale-yellow with shades of green. Pleasant and fruity nose. Light and agreeable despite a touch of acidity at the finish. (1984)
♠ Baron Philippe de Rothschild, La Baronnie, BP 2, 33250 Pauillac; tel. 56 59 20 20 Ⓨ By appt. Closed Aug.

PAVILLON BLANC★★

☐			3 D ▤ ↓

Attractive whitish-yellow colour with some greenish shades. Floral nose; well balanced, delicate and aromatic on the palate. Blends well to provide a perfect balance. (1982)
♠ Sté. Civ. du Ch. Margaux, 33460 Margaux; tel. 56 88 70 28 Ⓨ No visitors.

DOMAINE DE PICADIS★★

☐	2.5ha	20000	2 D ▤ ↓

*81 *82 *83 *84

Pronounced, aromatic Sauvignon on the nose and the palate; a well-balanced wine with a lively acidity and a long, harmonious finish. (1983)
♠ Guy Duchant, Ch. du Bru, St-Avit-St-Nazaire, 33220 Ste-Foy-la-Grande; tel. 57 46 12 71 Ⓨ By appt.

DOMAINE DE PIN-FRANC-PILET

☐	0.5ha	4000	2 D ▤ ↓

Attractive colour with shades of green. Rather discreet aromas on the nose, but respectively vigorous on the palate.
♠ Jean Queyrens, Dom. de Pilet, Donzac, 33410 Cadillac; tel. 56 62 97 42 Ⓨ By appt.

CHATEAU DE PLASSANS

☐	8ha	106000	2 D ▤ ↓

70 ⑦⑤ 79 82 83 84

Straw-coloured wine with aromas of ripe fruit. Light and easy to drink. (1983)
♠ Jean Mercier, Cellier de Graman, 33550 Langoiran; tel. 56 67 09 06 Ⓨ Daily 9.00–12.00/14.00–19.00.

CHATEAU PONCET★★

☐	35ha	202000	2 D ▤ ↓

83 83 ⑧④

Bright, yellow-green colour, with a classic bouquet. On the palate, initially vigorous, then fresh and extremely agreeable. Excellent value for money. (1983) ✔ Bordeaux Supérieur Ch. Poncet.
♠ Jean-Luc David, Ch. Poncet, Omet, 33410 Cadillac; tel. 56 62 97 30 Ⓨ By appt.

RAYNE SEC★

☐	12ha	60000	3 ◑

⑧② 83 83 84

Distinctive golden colour. A bouquet of honey and flowers. Rich, lively and mouth-filling Semillon flavour. Note that from 1984 this wine will be called 'Sec de Rayne-Vigneau'. (1983)
♠ Sté. Civ. Ch. Rayne-Vigneau, 33720 Barsac; tel. 56 52 11 46 Ⓨ By appt.

CHATEAU RENON★★

☐	4ha	25000	2 D ▤ ↓

75 78 81 82 ⑧③ 84

Although it does not have quite the vigour that one expects from a dry white, this wine has a pleasing, fruity Sauvignon nose, well suited to the limpid amber-yellow colour. ✔ Bordeaux Ch. Renon Rouge.
♠ Jacques Boucherie, Ch. Renon, Tabanac, 33550 Langoiran; tel. 56 67 13 59 Ⓨ By appt.

CHATEAU REYNON★★★

☐	6ha	40000	3 D ▪ ↓

★80 ★81 ★83 ★83 84

An elegant dry white wine, with a real fireworks nose – explosive and flowery; on the palate it has a delicate balance between roundness and fullness on the one hand, finesse on the other. (1983) ♦ *M.* et *Mme* F. et D. Dubourdieu, Ch. Reynon, Béguey, 33410 Cadillac; tel. 56 62 96 51 ⊻ By appt.

DOMAINE DE LA REYRE *Sainte-Foy*★★

☐	2ha	12000	3 D ▪ ↓

83 83

Delicate but powerful nose. Well balanced and nicely vigorous in the mouth. (1983) ♦ Sylvie Ribaille, Dom. de la Reyre, 33790 Pellegrue; tel. 56 61 36 75 ⊻ No visitors.

CHATEAU DE RICAUD

☐	12ha	80000	2 D ▪ ↓

★82 83

Fresh colour; this wine should be drunk young, otherwise it becomes too heavy. (1982) ♦ Alain Thienot, Ch. de Ricaud, Loupiac, 33410 Cadillac; t5756 62 97 57 ⊻ By appt. Closed 1–20 Aug.

CHATEAU ROC-DE-CAYLA

☐	6ha	38000	2 D ▪ ↓

75 ⑧ 83 84

Straw-gold colour, an aromatic nose and a light palate – such, it seems, are the wine tastes of military men, since this wine is sold to the French air force, the *gendarmerie* and the police force. (1983) ✔ Bordeaux Ch. Roc-de-Cayla Rouge, Bordeaux Ch. Roc-de-Cayla Rosé. ♦ Jean-Marie Lanoue, Ch. Roc-de-Cayla, Soulignac, 33760 Argon; tel. 56 23 91 13 ⊻ Daily 8.00–12.00/14.00–18.00.

CHATEAU SALLE-D'ARCHES

☐	17ha	6000	2 D ▪ ↓

⑦⑨

This dry white wine has a classic colour and a discreet nose, and is slightly tart in the mouth. (1979) ♦ André Guiraud, Ch. Salle-d'Arches, St-André-du-Bois, 33490 St-Macaire; tel. 56 63 70 02 ⊻ Daily 8.00–12.00/14.00–18.00.

CHATEAU SARANSOT-DUPRE★

☐	1.5ha		3 D ▪ ↓

⑧③ 83 84

Attractive colour and pleasantly fruity nose. Good to drink now. (1983) ♦ P. et Y. Raymond, Ch. Saransot-Dupré, Listrac-Médoc, 33480 Castelnau-de-Médoc; tel. 56 58 03 02 ⊻ By appt.

DOMAINE DE LA SERIZIERE

☐	7ha	50000	2 D ▪ ↓

Yellow with shades of gold. Quite a contrast between the robust nose, and the pleasant smoothness on the palate. ✔ Bordeaux Rouge, Entre-Deux-Mers. ♦ Gérard et Jean-Marc Lobre, Dom. de la Serezière, Ladaux, 33760 Targon; tel. 56 23 91 75 ⊻ By appt.

CHATEAU THIEULEY★★★

☐	8ha	40000	2 D ▪ ↓

80 81 ★82 ★83 ★⑧④ ★84

Pale yellow; complex nose of citrus fruit, passion fruit and boxwood. On the palate it is full and vigorous. An exceptional wine, to be drunk within a year. (1984) ♦ François Courcelles, Ch. Thieuley, La Sauve-Majeure, 33670 Créon; tel. 56 56 23 00 0 ⊻ By appt.

LES TOQUES GOURMANDES★★

☐			2 D

Very light colour, with a flowery, well-developed nose, slightly acidic and fruity. This wine is very characteristic of the Sémillon-Sauvignon grape combination, and is the choice of Les Toques Gourmandes, a leading Parisian food-and-wine suppliers. (1984) ♦ Les Toques Gourmandes, 29 bis Route de Versailles, 78560 Port-Marly; tel. 01 91 61 17 ⊻ By appt.

TOUTON SAUVIGNON

☐	100000	1

⑧③ 84

Very clear colour, with no hint of yellow. Certain finesse is evident in the nose, and in the mouth it has distinct Sauvignon qualities. (1983) ♦ André Quancard, 21 Rue Calvé, 33000 Bordeaux; tel. 56 52 95 95 ⊻ No visitors.

Bordeaux Rosé

AGNEAU-ROSE★

◪	50ha	320000	4 ▪ ↓

Fruity nose. On the palate, smooth, rich and crisp. Clean, flowing and more like a clairet than a typical rosé. ♦ Baron Philippe de Rothschild, La Baronnie, BP 2, 33250 Pauillac; tel. 56 59 20 20 ⊻ By appt. Closed Aug.

CHATEAU LES ALBERTS

◪	0.2ha	12000	2 D ⑪

Bright slightly tile-red colour; a little heavy in the mouth, but otherwise classic. ♦ Bernard Paille, Ch. les Alberts, 33390 Mazion; tel. 57 42 18 13 ⊻ By appt.

CHATEAU LES ARROMANS★

☑	1 ha	10000	2 D ■ ↓

Possibly slightly lower quality than the same producer's red, but nonetheless a good wine with a nice bright colour, a fresh, well-structured palate, and some length. (1983)
↬ Jean Duffau, Ch. les Arromans, Moulon, 33420 Branne; tel. 57 84 50 87 ⟼ By appt.

CHATEAU BERTINERIE★★

☑	1 ha	6000	3 D ■ ↓

82 83 **83**

Good rosé. Almost tile-red in colour; agreeably fruity bouquet; full, balanced, and harmonious on the palate. (1982)
↬ Daniel Bantegnies, Cubnezais, 33620 Cavignac; tel. 57 68 70 74 ⟼ By appt.

DOMAINE DE BOUILLEROT

☑	1 ha	4000	3 D ■

Attractive red colour, with a touch of purple. On the palate a supple and lively attack is followed by a fine balance. (1982)
↬ Lucien Bos, Dom. de Bouillerot, Gironde-sur-Dropt, 33190 La Réole; tel. 56 71 46 04 ⟼ By appt.

DOMAINE DES CAILLOUX

☑	1 ha	6000	2 D ■ ↓

Attractive coppery cast to the colour. Light and delicate on the palate, with aromas of dried fruit.
↬ Nicole Legrand-Dupuy, Romagne, 33760 Targon; tel. 56 23 09 47 ⟼ By appt.

CHATEAU CHANET★★

☑	5 ha	30000	2 D ■ ↓

Lovely aromatic nose with shades of wild rose. Smooth and flavourful in the mouth. ✔ Bordeaux Sec, Entre-Deux-Mers.
↬ Jacques et Bernard Large, Guillac, 33420 Branne; tel. 57 84 52 08 ⟼ By appt.

CHATEAU CHARDAVOINE

☑	1 ha	5000	2 D ■ ↓

★⑧② ★83 ★84

Hearty and rustic in style with a good bouquet and smooth texture.
↬ Claude Paillet, Soulignac, 33760 Targon; tel. 56 23 94 09 ⟼ By appt.

CHATEAU LA CROIX-DE-MAILHE

☑	0.5 ha	4000	2 D ■ ↓

Salmon-pink wine with a bouquet of freshly baked bread. Smooth and fluid on the palate.
↬ Cailleux, Escoussans, 33760 Targon; tel. 56 23 63 23 ⟼ By appt.

CHATEAU LES GRANDS-JAY★

☑	0.5 ha	3400	3 D ■ ↓

Slightly tawny colour, consistent with a ripe-fruit nose that has a gamey quality about it. On the palate it is rich and round, with a long finish. It should be drunk fairly soon.
↬ Jean Boireau, Les Artigues-de-Lussac, 33570 Lussac; tel. 57 84 01 08 ⟼ By appt.

CHATEAU GRAND-VILLAGE★

☑	1 ha	6000	2 D ■ ↓

83 (84)

A very clear wine with a deep raspberry glint. Vinous nose with a smell of green peppers; slightly tannic on the palate, with a Clairet-style concentration in flavour. (1983)
↬ *Mme et M.* S. and J. Guinaudeau, Ch. Grand-Village. Mouillac, 33240 St-André Cubzac; tel. 57 84 44 03 ⟼ By appt.

DOMAINE DE GRANEY

☑	7 ha	36000	2 D ■ ◐ ↓

81 ★82 ★83 84

This wine has a bright attractive appearance. The nose and palate do not yet have a distinctive character, but still a well balanced and very drinkable bottle. (1982)
↬ Roland Rey, Dom. de Graney, Izon, 33450 St-Loubes; tel. 57 74 81 16 ⟼ By appt.

DOMAINE DE LADENAC

☑	1 ha	4500	3 D ■ ↓

(77) 80 80 (83)

Somewhat fleeting, but with an honest, clear appearance, a discreet nose, and a pleasant balance on the palate. (1983)
↬ Francis Boulière, Le Bergey, 33450 St-Loubès; tel. 56 20 42 00 ⟼ By appt. Closed Aug., 24 Dec.–2 Jan.

CHATEAU LAGARDE

☑	20 ha	130000	2 D ◐ ↓

(79) 84

Not particularly fruity, but pleasing to the eye and has some marked fig-like aromas. (1984)
✔ Entre-Deux-Mers Ch. de Lagarde.
↬ Norbert Raymond, Ch. Lagarde, St-Laurent-du-Bois, 33540 Sauveterre-de-Guyenne; tel. 56 63 70 63 ⟼ By appt.

CHATEAU LA MONGIE

☑	1 ha	6000	2 D ■ ↓

(83) **83** 84 **84**

The label is very 'strawberry ice' in character. The wine has a floral nose and pleasant, fruity flavours on the palate. (1983)
↬ Pierre Blouin, Ch. la Mongie, Vérac 33240 St-André-de-Cubzac; tel. 57 84 37 08 ⟼ By appt.

CHATEAU TERRE D'AGNES★

☑	2 ha	8000	2 D ■ ◐ ↓

Deep purple-hued rosé. Vinous nose with a hint of lime. Quite full on the palate; rich, round and warm but with a short finish. (1983)
↬ Edgar Marchan, Ch. Terres d'Agnes, Moulon, 33420 Branne; tel. 57 84 50 74 ⟼ By appt.

Bordeaux Supérieur

CHATEAU DE L'ABBAYE

■	15 ha	100000	3 ■

★75 ★76 78 79 ★81 ★(82) 83

The property lies around the Abbey of Saint-Ferme, its namesake. A supple, light and pleasing wine with a discreet bouquet. (1982) ✔ Entre-Deux-Mers.

159

☞ Claude de Raignac, Ch. de l'Abbaye, St-Ferme, 33580 Monségur; tel. 56 61 62 19 ☎ No visitors.

CHATEAU LES ALBERTS

■　　　　　6ha　33000　② D ▮ ⑪

71 75 76 79 ⑧ 83

Bright in appearance. Although the nose and attack lack vigour, the finish is delightful. Will please those fond of light wines. (1981) ✔ Bordeaux Rosé Ch. les Alberts, Blayais Blanc Ch. les Alberts.
☞ Bernard Paille, Ch. les Alberts, Mazion, 33390 Blaye; tel. 57 42 18 13 ☎ By appt.

CHATEAU ANGELIQUE

■　　　　13ha　85000　② D ▮ ⑪

79 80 81 *⑧ 83

A wine which has suffered slightly from poor storage (old casks?), nonetheless, the colour is pleasing and it is well structured on the palate. (1982)
☞ Denis Ardon, SA Ch. Plain-Point, St-Aignan, 33126 Fronsac; tel. 57 24 96 55 ☎ By appt.

CHATEAU DES ARRAS★★

■　　　　30ha　200000　② D ▮ ⑪ ♨

*⑦ 79 *80 *81 *82 82 *83 83

Quite aromatic, rich, fat and robust. Open two hours before tasting. (1982)
☞ M. Rozier, St-Gervais, 33240 St-André-de-Cubzac; tel. 57 43 00 35 ☎ By appt. ☞ J. Rozier.

CHATEAU BAUDUC★

■　　　　4ha　60000　③ D ▮ ♨

81 *82 *82 83

Fine colour and good nose, although still undeveloped. Well-structured on the palate. (1982) ✔ Entre-Deux-Mers Ch. Bauduc.
☞ Véronique Thomas, Ch. Bauduc, 33670 Créon; tel. 56 23 23 38 ☎ By appt.

CHATEAU BEAU-RIVAGE

■　　　　8ha　36000　③ D ▮ ⑪ ♨

70 75 *78 79 80 ⑧

A deeply coloured palus wine, solid and rather rustic. The nose is light but evokes red fruit and game; the palate is tannic and distinctive. (1982)
☞ André Barateau, Ch. Beau-Rivage, Macau, 33460 Margaux; tel. 56 30 45 93 ☎ By appt.

CHATEAU LES BEDATS-BOIS-MONTET★

■　　　　15ha　90000　③ D ▮ ♨

64 70 75 80 ⑧ 81 82 84

A deep, bright, ruby colour with a subtle nose suggesting red fruit. On the palate, round and supple, with a vigorous finish. (1981)
☞ Suzette Destouesse, Les Bédats-Bois-Montet, 33560 Ste-Eulalie; tel. 56 06 14 54 ☎ By appt. Closed during harvests.

CHATEAU BELLEVUE

■　　　　15ha　34000　③ D ▮ ⑪ ♨

*76 *77 *78 *79 *81 *⑧

This wine can only be tasted at La Sarthe (in Avoise), where the owner lives and the wine is marketed. Fine bright purple robe and nose of red fruit and green pepper. (1981) ✔ Entre-Deux Mers Ch. Bellevue, Bordeaux Ch. Bellevue Rosé.
☞ Bruno de Ponton d'Amécourt, Ch. Bellevue, Ch. de Pescheseul, Avoise, 72430 Noyen-sur-Sarthe; tel. 43 95 39 16 ☎ By appt.

CHATEAU LE BERGEY★

■　　　　13ha　86000　④ D ⑪ ♨

73 75 *78 79 81 82

A pleasant, light ruby colour. Although the nose is a little closed, it has an honest attack on the palate and a smooth, fluid, refreshing character. (1981) ✔ Bordeaux Dom. des Greseaux Rouge, Bordeaux Rosé Dom. de Ladenac, Bordeaux Ch. les Porcherons Rouge.
☞ Françis Boulière, Ch. Le Bergey, 33450 St-Loubès; tel. 56 20 42 00 ☎ By appt. Closed Aug., 24 Dec.–2 Jan.

CHATEAU DE BLASSAN

■　　　　25ha　150000　③ D ▮

70 75 *76 *⑦ 81 82

A fine colour and fruity nose followed by a palate with plenty of matter and body. The finish, is dry and coarsely herbaceous. (1982)
☞ MM. Boubou-Cénni, Ch. de Blassan, Lugon, 33240 St-André-de-Cubzac; tel. 57 84 40 91 ☎ Daily 9.00–12.00/14.00–19.00.

MARQUIS DE BOIRAC★

■　　　　3ha　18000　④ D ⑪ ♨

71 75 *76 *⑧ *82

Produced by the St-Pey-de-Castets cooperative, this wine has a fine red colour, a strongly oaky nose (vanilla-connoisseurs please note!) but needs at least five years to mellow and harmonize (1981) ✔ Entre-Deux-Mers, Bordeaux Rosé.
☞ Cave Coop. de St-Pey-de-Castets, 33350 Castillon-la-Bataille; tel. 57 40 52 07 ☎ Tues–Fri. 8.30–11.45/14.00–17.00, Sat. 8.30–11.45.

CHATEAU BOSQUET★

■　　　　10ha　60000　③ D ▮ ♨

78 79 *80 *⑧ 83

In contrast with the moderate colour, the nose is well developed, aromatic and intense. The supple attack is followed by very ripe tannins on the palate. (1982)
☞ A. Marquier, Ch. Bosquet, Gironde-sur-Dropt, 33190 La Réole; tel. 56 61 06 75 ☎ No visitors.

CHATEAU BOSSUET

■　　　　7ha　30000　② D ⑪ ♨

*75 *76 *78 *81 *⑧ 83

This vineyard does not use any chemical products. Despite a touch of oxidation, the wine is rich and tannic. (1979) ✔ Pomerol Ch. la Fleur-du-Roy, St-Emilion Vieux-Ch.-Carné, Lalande de Pomerol Ch. la Vallière, Bordeaux Clos-Paquerette Blanc.

↬ Exploitation Dubost, Catusseau, Pomerol, 33500 Libourne; tel. 57 51 76 57 ⟂ By appt.

CHATEAU DU BOUILH

■ 50ha 200000 **3** **D** ◑ ↓

79 81 *82 *83

Designed by Victor Louis (who built the Grand-Théâtre at Bordeaux), this is an impressive and beautiful house, despite the fact that it was originally intended to form only one wing of an enormous two-winged château. The wine, while not as impressive as the château is brick-red in colour, somewhat developed but still discreet on the nose, easy and flowing to drink. (1982) ✔ Bordeaux Supérieur Ch. Tour-Clariet Rouge, Bordeaux Blanc Sec.
↬ P. de Feuilhade de Chauvin, Ch. du Bouilh, 33240 St-André-de-Cubzac; tel. 57 43 01 45 ⟂ By appt.

CHATEAU LE BOURDIEU

■ 4ha 24000 **2** **D** ▤ ↓

*79 81 *82 83

Dull in appearance and on the nose, but better on the palate; supple and pleasing overall. (1982) ✔ Bordeaux Rosé, Entre-Deux-Mers, Bordeaux Mousseux.
↬ B. Daste et Dr Bordes, St-Radegonde, 33350 Castillon-la-Bataille; tel. 57 40 53 82 ⟂ Mon.–Sat. 8.30–12.30/14.00–18.00.

CHATEAU BOURDIEU-DE-L'HERMITAGE★

■ 8ha 54000 **2** **D** ◑

*76 *78 *⟨80⟩ *81 ⟨81⟩ *⟨82⟩ *⟨82⟩ *83

Despite looking a little too advanced for its age, the colour is a bright precursor to the wine's pleasant aromas. Straightforward and eminently drinkable. (1982)
↬ Raymond Savy, Ch. Bourdieu-de-l'Hermitage, Lugon, 33240 St-André-de-Cubzac; tel. 57 84 41 61 ⟂ By appt.

DOMAINE DE BOURGAT★

■ 9ha **3** **D** ▤ ↓

⟨75⟩ ⟨82⟩

Brightly coloured and aromatic. Good attack and full body on the palate. Agreeable, with good length. (1982)
↬ Jean-Christian Seyral, Beychac-et-Cailleau, 33750 St-Germain-du-Puch; tel. 56 30 97 73 ⟂ No visitors.

CLOS DE BRAGUE

■ 15ha 60000 **2** **D** ▤ ↓

74 75 76 *78 81 *82 *83

Deeply coloured wine with a particularly powerful nose, reminiscent of cooked fruit, and a supple attack. There is, however, a slight imbalance on the palate. (1982) ✔ Bordeaux Supérieur Ch. Courrèges Rouge, Bordeaux Supérieur Ch. Couréges Rosé.
↬ SCE du Clos de Bragou, 33240 St-André-de-Cubzac; tel. 57 84 41 70 ⟂ By appt ↬ Jack Pineaud.

CHATEAU BRONDEAU

■ 10ha 60000 **3** ▤ ↓

75 76 79 *82 *⟨83⟩

A fine, classical residence; large yet unpretentious. Its wine is similar: while lacking a particularly strong character, it is well made and pleasing. (1982) ✔ Pomerol Clos du Clocher.
↬ Jean Audy, 35, Quai du Priourat, Libourne, 33502 Libourne Cedex; tel. 57 51 62 17 ⟂ No visitors.

CHATEAU CAILLOU-DE-RENE

■ 10ha 40000 **3** **D** ▤ ◑ ↓

70 ⟨71⟩ 76 78 *79

Red to tile-red colour; a hint of bitterness in the mouth. Nevertheless, this wine has a lively attack and a full, warm palate. (1981)
↬ André Cassoulet, Ch. Caillou-de-René, St-Genès-de-Lombaud, 33670 Créon; tel. 56 21 34 31 ⟂ By appt.

CHATEAU CANDELEY★

■ 15ha 90000 **3** **D** ▤ ↓

⟨78⟩ 80 81 ⟨81⟩ 82 83 ⟨83⟩

Dark garnet colour and a well-structured palate. Still austere but with good length, this wine should develop elegantly given time. (1982) ✔ Entre-deux-Mers Ch. Candeley, Bordeaux Supérieur Ch. Candeley Blanc Moelleux.
↬ Henri Devillaire, Ch. Candeley, St-Antoine-du-Queyret, 33790 Pellegrue; tel. 56 61 31 46 ⟂ By appt. Closed Dec.

CHATEAU CAP-DE-MERLE

■ 8ha 28000 **3** **D** ▤ ↓

*78 *79 81 82

A deliberately light wine, in which more emphasis is placed on finesse than body. Fine colour and fruit. (1982) ✔ Puisseguin-St-Emilion Ch. Dur-and-Laplagne, Lussac-St-Emilion Ch. de Tabuteau.
↬ Jacques Bessou, Ch. Cap-de-Merle, LesArtigues-de-Lussac, 33570 Lussac; tel. 57 84 03 07 ⟂ By appt.

CHATEAU CASTAGNAC★★

■ 23ha 120000 **3** **D** ▤ ↓

67 70 75 76 78 *⟨82⟩ *⟨82⟩

With its attractive red colour, this is a pleasing, well-constructed wine with body and fruit. Perhaps still a little young; needs keeping. (1982) ✔ Other Bordeaux wines.
↬ Coudert Père et fils, Ch. Castagnac, 33141 Villegouge; tel. 57 84 44 07 ⟂ By appt.

CHATEAU DE CATHALOGNE

■ 6ha 20000 **2** **D** ▤

*75 *78 80 81 82

A pleasingly rustic, somewhat coarsely tannic wine. (1982) ✔ Bordeaux Ch. de Cathalogne Blanc Sec.
↬ *Mme* Marie-Josée Joubert, Ch. de Cathologne, St-Laurent-du-Bois, 33440 Sauveterre-de-Guyenne; tel. 56 63 71 92 ⟂ By appt.

CHATEAU DES CHARMILLES★

■ 7ha 42000 **3 D ▮ ↓**

73 *81 *82 *82 *83

Produced in the Médoc but outside the appellation, this wine is somewhat lacking in colour
but nevertheless supple and tannic on the palate,
with good length. (1982) ✔ Margaux Cru de
Castelbryck.
↳ Marc Raymond, Ch. des Charmilles, Le Tayet,
33460 Macau-en-Médoc; tel. 56304273 ☏ No
visitors.

CHATEAU DE CHELIVETTE

■ 10ha 47000 **3 D ▮ ⋔ ↓**

61 62 64 69 ⑦ 78 79 82 85

A well-made, typical Supérieur, at once light and
rustic, discreetly evocative of cherry (1982)
✔ Entre-Deux-Mers Dom. du Télégraphe.
↳ Jean-Louis Boulière, Ch. de Chelivette, St-
Eulalie, 33560 Carbon-Blanc; tel. 56061179
☏ By appt. Closed July or Aug.

CHEVALIERS-DE-BELLEVUE★

■ 30ha 18000 **3 D ▮ ↓**

75 *77 *78 *79 *81 *82 *83

This wine, produced by a consortium of growers,
has a lively appearance and a light but harmonious bouquet; initially supple on the palate but
with a rather hard finish. (1978) ✔ Bordeaux
Prestige des Chevaliers Rouge, Bordeaux Cheva-
liers-de-BellevueBlanc Sec, Bordeaux Chevaliers-de-Bellevue Blanc Moelleux, Bordeaux
Chaveliers-de-Bellevue Mousseux.
↳ SICA les Chevaliers-de-Bellevue, les Grézyx,
Lalande-de-Fronsac, 33240 St-André-de-Cubzac;
tel. 57581237 ☏ No visitors.

CHATEAU COMPASSANT★

■ 10ha 50000 **3 D ▮ ⋔ ↓**

70 75 79 80 ⑧ 83

Fine views from this property looking out over
the confluence of the Isle and Dordogne rivers. A
wine which is attractive to look at and has a
pleasing nose, with delicate flowery aromas. Supple, round, balanced and slightly woody, the
overall impression is of finesse and delicacy.
(1982) ✔ St-Emilion Dom. de Lagrezolle.
↳ Sté Vignobles Michel Decazes, Ch. Compas-
sant, Génissac, 33420 Branne; tel. 57244760
☏ By appt.

CHATEAU LE CONSEILLER★

■ 23ha 130000 **3 D ▮ ⋔ ↓**

75 *79 *81 *⑧ *83

Fine, bright-red colour and powerful, somewhat
alcoholic nose. This pleasantly aromatic wine is
smooth and flowing on the palate; very drinkable. (1982) ✔ Other Bordeaux wines.
↳ Vignobles Liotard, Ch. Le Conseiller, Lugon,
33240 St-André-de-Cubzac; tel. 57844456
☏ Daily 7.30–12.00/14.00–20.00.

CHATEAU COURSOU

■ 18ha 100000 **3 D ▮ ↓**

79 80 81 *⑧ 83 84

Bright, colourful wine with a nose of ripe fruit.
Although the attack is pleasantly supple, the
flavours on the palate are a little spoilt by a hint

of aggression. (1982) ✔ Other Bordeaux.
↳ M. Dupas, SCEA du Ch. Coursou, Pessac-sur-
Dordogne, 33890 Gensac; tel. 57404027 ☏ By
appt.

CHATEAU COURTEY★★

■ 2ha 12000 **3 D ▮**

80 *81 ⑧ 82

A fine wine from a little-known property. At-
tractive colour, a nose of small red fruit, pleasing
attack; round and powerful on the palate. (1982)
✔ Bordeaux Ch. Courtey Rouge, Bordeaux Ch.
Courtey Blanc Sec.
↳ Philippe Danies-Sauvestre, Ch. Courtey, St-
Martial 33490 St-Macaire; tel. 56637197 ☏ By
appt.

CHATEAU LA CROIX-BOUEY

■ 11ha 80000 **2 D ▮ ↓**

79 80 81 82

Unpretentious; classic colour; clean and flowing
in the mouth. (1982) ✔ Bordeaux Sec Ch. la
Croix- Bouey, Cadillac Ch. la Croix-Bouey
Blanc.
↳ SCA Vignobles Bouey, Ch. la Croix-Bouey, St-
Maixant, 33490 St-Macaire; tel. 56632578
☏ Daily 8.00–20.00. ↳ Maxime Bouey.

CHATEAU LA CROIX-DE-ROCHE

■ 7ha 42000 **3 D ▮ ↓**

*⑧ 82

Ruby-red in colour. A fine, vinous and fruity
nose with a slight touch of garlic that some people
may not enjoy. Good structure and relatively fine
on the palate. (1982) ✔ Other Bordeaux wine.
↳ Françiset Bernard Maurin, Ch. la Croix-de-
Roche, 33133 Galgon; tel. 57843852 ☏ By appt.

CHATEAU FAYAU★

■ 18ha 85000 **3 D ▮ ↓**

*79 *78 81 *⑧ 83

Aromatic, with floral touches, this wine is crisp,
round and delicate. Although it matures quickly,
it will please those who enjoy light wines without
too much tannin. (1982) ✔ Premieres Côtes de
Bordeaux Ch. Fayau Rouge, Premieres Côtes de
Bordeaux Ch. du Juge Rouge, Cadillac Ch.
Fayau, Graves Ch. Boyreim.
↳ Jean Madeville et Fils, Ch. Fayau, 33410 Cadillac; tel. 56270351 ☏ Mon.–Fri. 9.00–12.00/
14.00–18.00.

CHATEAU FONCHEREAU★★★

■ 23ha 105000 **2 D ▮ ⋔ ↓**

75 76 78 79 *80 *81 *82 *83

Although this 15th-century château has had a
troubled history, its wine can claim a more
peaceful existence. Rich aromas, frank attack
and fine tannins. A good future. (1982) ✔ Other
Bordeaux wines.
↳ Suzanne Vinot-Postry, Ch. Fonchereau Montussan, 33450 St-Loubés; tel. 56309612 By appt.

CHATEAU FOND-RONDES★★

■	2ha 12000	3 D 📄 ⏶

70 75 76 78 **79** ⑧2 **82** 83

Deep, clear, velvety robe; a scarcely developed nose with a touch a cooked prunes. On the palate, however, there is power, roundness and fine finish, blending tannins and ripe fruit. A wine to keep and to leave to age. (1982)
➥ Vignobles Fomperier, La Gaffelière, 33330 St-Emilion; tel. 57 24 74 48 ⵣ By appt.

DOMAINE DE FONTENILLE★

■	16ha 72000	2 D 📄 ⏷

78 ★79 ★ ⑧2 ★ **82** ★83 **84**

Fine colour; pleasing finesse on the nose and good structure on the palate. A fairly tannic wine, although some may consider this an advantage. (1982) ✔ Entre-Deux-Mers Dom. de Fontenille.
➥ SCA Dom. de Fontenille, La Sauve-Majeure, 33570 Créon; tel. 56 23 03 26 ⵣ By appt.

CHATEAU FOUCHE★★

■	9ha 50000	3 D 📄 ⏷

74 75 76 **78** ★79 81 ⑧2 **82** 83

Promising ruby colour; complex, jammy fruit nose. Supple and pleasantly tannic on the palate; finishes well. (1982) ✔ Blayais Ch. Fouché Blanc Sec, Bordeaux Supérieur Ch. Fouché Blanc Moelleux, Bordeaux Ch. Fouché Mousseux.
➥ Jean Bonnet, Ch. Haute-Guiraud, St-Ciers-de-Caresse, 33710 Bourg-sur-Gironde; tel. 57 42 17 39 ⵣ By appt.

CHATEAU GABACHOT

■	13ha 84000	2 D 📄 ⏷

75 79 80 ⑧2 ★83

Attractive dark red colour, but slightly disappointing nose. Nevertheless, A supple wine with a certain degree of acidity – just right for drinking with a rich sauce. (1982)
➥ Roger Fernandez, Rue Lafon 33540 Sauveterre-de-Guyenne; tel. 56 71 51 24 ⵣ No visitors.

CHATEAU GAURY-BALETTE★

■	27ha 162000	2 D 📄 ⏷

★76 ★78 ★81 ★82 83

A small estate full of rustic charm, as is its wine. This has a dark colour, a nose still a little closed-in, and a palate which is fleshy and substantial. (1982) ✔ Entre-Deux-Mers.
➥ Bernard Yon, Ch. Gaury-Balette, Mauriac,

33540 Sauveterre-de-Guyenne; tel. 57 40 52 82 ⵣ By appt.

CHATEAU DE GAUSSENS★★

■	20ha 75000	3 D 📄

71 74 75 ★76 ★ ⑦9 ★**79** ★81 ★82

Bright red in colour with a particularly appealing bouquet, subtle and floral in character; light, elegant and harmonious on the palate with nicely mellowed tannin. (1979)
➥ M. de Lambert des Granges, Ch. de Gaussens, Baurech, 33880 Cambes; tel. 56 21 31 43 ⵣ No visitors.

CHATEAU GAYON★★

■	15ha 72000	3 D 📄 ⏷ ⏶

★78 ★79 80 ★ ⑧2 **83** **883**

Good ruby-red colour, with a delicate vanilla nose. On the palate it is well structured, well made, and has a very pleasing finish. (1983)
➥ Jean Crampes, Ch. Gayon, Caudrot, 33490 St-Macaire; tel. 56 62 81 19 ⵣ Mon.–Sat. 9.00–19.00.

CHATEAU GINESTA

■	12ha 72 000	2 D 📄 ⏷

★82

Unpretentious, subtly aromatic and has a good, clean, flowing character. (1982)
➥ M.-Mme M.-T. et Y.Roumegous, Ch. Ginesta, Lignan-de-Bordeaux, 33360 Latresne; tel. 56 21 23 03 ⵣ By appt.

CHATEAU GOELANE

■	52ha 192000	3 D 📄 ⏷

⑦6 **79** 81 82 83 84

From a pretty little château, this wine is classic red in colour, and, although a little firm on the nose, is pleasantly supple in the mouth. (1982)
➥ Angel Castel, Ch. Goelane, Saint-Léon, 33670 Créon; tel. 56 23 05 48 ⵣ No visitors.

CHATEAU DU GRAND-CAMPSEC★

■	13ha 30000	3 D 📄 ⏷

⑧2 **83** **83**

On the palate this wine is round, with a taste of well-blended ripe fruit, powerful aromas and a pleasing finish. (1983) ✔ Bordeaux Ch. Grand-Campsec, Premières Côtes de Bordeaux Ch. Dintrans.
➥ Gérard et Philippe Lesnier, St-Vincent-de-Paul, 33440 Ambarès-et-Lagrave; tel. 56 38 96 10 ⵣ By appt.

CHATEAU GRAND-CANTELOUP★★

■	9ha 60000	2 D 📄 ⏷

70 71 ★75 79 ⑧2 **82**

A fine robe, delicate, crisp and fruity nose, and a full, harmonious structure on the palate. A noteworthy floral finish. (1982) ✔ Entre-Deux-Mers Ch. le Caillou, Bordeaux Blanc du Caillou.
➥ Charles Pasquiers, Ch. Grand-Canteloup, Nérigean, 33750 St-Germain-du-Puch; tel. 57 24 52 68 ⵣ By appt.

163

CHATEAU DE LA GRANDE-CHAPELLE★

■   17ha 122000 **3** **D** ▮ ⑪ ↓

75 *79 *81 *⑧② *83

Extremely attractive colour, somewhere between ruby and cherry-red, and an intense nose with shades of cooked fruit. A round and powerful wine, somewhat astringent on the finish but with good length nonetheless. (1981)
⊶ Vignobles Liotard, Ch. de la Grande-Chapelle, Lugon, 33240 St-André-de-Cubzac; tel. 57 84 41 52 ☎ By appt.

CHATEAU GRANDEFONT★★

■   20ha 120000 **2** **D** ▮ ↓

80 *81 *82 *⑧② *83

A fine, dark-red colour and aromas of red and blackcurrants; a full, fleshy, round and pleasantly tannic wine. Ready to drink. (1982)
⊶ GFA Dom. de Grandefont, Ch. Grandefont, St-Avit-St-Nazaire, 33220 Ste-Foy-la-Grande; tel. 57 46 12 67 ☎ By appt.

CHATEAU GRAND MONTEIL

■   70ha 420000 **3** **D** ⑪ ↓

75 76 77 *⑧⓪ *82 ⑧③

On this property is a cellar with iron girders, built by Gustave Eiffel, who owned vines in the region. The wine has a deep colour, a nose of ripe fruit and a pleasing attack to the palate, but the finish is a little short. (1982)
⊶ SC du Ch. du Grand Monteil, Sallebœuf, 33370 Tresses; tel. 56 21 29 70 ☎ By appt.

GRAND LAVERGNE

■   10ha 53000 **3** **D** ▮ ↓

70 71 75 76 79 ⑧⓪ 81 82 **82** 83 **83**

A well-developed colour, and nose evocative of dried fruit. To be drunk without delay. (1982)
⊶ Jean Boireau, Les Artigues-de-Lussac, 33570 Lussac; tel. 57 84 01 08 ☎ Daily 8.00–12.00/14.00–19.00.

CHATEAU LES GRANDS-JAYS

■   20ha 120000 **3** **D** ▮ ↓

70 71 ⑦⑤ 76 79 81 82 **82** 83 **83**

Dark ruby colour with an orange hue, suggesting that the wine is quite forward. Ripe-fruit nose with equal fruit on the palate and a supple tannin. Ready to drink. (1982) ✎ Lussac St-Emilion Haut-Milon, Bordeaux Supérieur Grand-Lavergne Rouge, Bordeaux Rosé les Grands-Jays.
⊶ Jean Boireau, Les Artigues-de-Lussac, 33570 Lussac; tel. 57 84 01 08 ☎ By appt.

CHATEAU GRAND VILLAGE★

■   12ha 18000 **2** **D** ⑪ ↓

80 *⑧① ***81** 82 83

Colour pleasing rather than striking, similarly with the fruity, fairly intense nose. Despite a touch of aggression, is a well-structured wine with good length on the palate; will certainly improve with age. (1981)

⊶ Sylvie et Jacques Guineadeau, Ch. Grand Village, Mouillac, 33240 St-André-de-Cubzac; tel. 57 84 44 03 ☎ By appt.

CHATEAU GRAVEYRON LA FRANCE

■   20ha 190000 **3** **D** ▮ ↓

79 80 81 *82 *83 84

Clear, bright red; fruity on the nose, tannic on the palate. A rustic wine which might gain a little refinement with time. (1982)
⊶ Jean-Claude Simon, Ch. Graveyron la France, 33126 Fronsac; tel. 57 51 45 02 ☎ No visitors.

DOMAINE GREYZEAU★

■   3ha 10000 **3** **D** ▮ ⑪ ↓

74 75 76 78 *79 81 82 83

Fine, delicate bouquet and good structure and balance on the palate. Limited production from this very small vineyard. (1981) ✎ Premières Côtes de Bordeaux Dom. le Greyzeau.
⊶ Roland Pestoury, Dom. le Greyzeau, Yvrac, 33370 Tresses; tel. 56 06 75 50 ☎ No visitors.

CELLIER DES GUINOTS★

■   120ha 700000 **2** **D** ▮ ↓

*75 76 *78 79 81 82 83

Aromatic and floral on the nose, supple and balanced on the palate, with a pleasing finish. Pleasant to drink now; not for keeping. (1982) ✎ Bordeaux Ch. Barbazan, Bordeaux Dom. des Hautes-Coutures.
⊶ UP Juillac et Flaujagues, Flaujagues, 33350 Castillon-la-Bataille; tel. 57 40 08 06 ☎ Tues.–Fri. 8.30–12.00/14.00–18.00. Sat. 8.30–12.00.

CHATEAU HAUT-BARDIN★

■   10ha 66000 **3** **D** ⑪ ↓

73 75 76 78 *79 *80 *81 *⑧② 83

A dark red robe and vinous nose. Full and fleshy on the palate. Its tannins, however, are a little coarse. (1982)
⊶ Yves Catherineau, Ch. Haut-Bardin, St-Martial, 33490 St-Macaire; tel. 56 63 71 32 ☎ By appt.

CHATEAU LES HAUTS-DE-GRANGE *Côtes de Castillon*★

■   6ha 40000 **3** **D** ▮ ⑪ ↓

⑦⑤ 76 **79** **81** 82

Fine ruby colour; vinous but closed on the nose; rather tough on the finish but with good keeping potential. For those who like an old-fashioned Bordeaux. (1982) ✎ Bordeaux Rosé les Hauts de Grange, Bordeaux Sec.
⊶ Yvon Castel, Ch. les Hauts-de-Grange, Les Salles-de-Castillon; 33350 Castillon-la-Bataille; tel. 53 57 22 23 ☎ By appt.

CHATEAU L'HERMITAGE

■   15ha 15000 **2** **D** ▮ ↓

75 76 79 82 83

Sold mainly in Germany, this wine has a fruity and peppery bouquet, but with a slight hint of oxidation. Firm on the palate, with a substantial tannic finish. (1982)
⊶ Jean Lopez, Ch. l'Hermitage, St-Martin-de-Puy, 33540 Sauveterre-de-Guyenne; tel. 56 71 52 82 ☎ By appt.

CHATEAU LA JOYE

■   12ha   72000   2 D 🍷 ⌷

*78 *79 80 *81 *82

Light, clear colour and discreet aromas. Despite a touch of astringency on the finish, it is smooth on the palate. (1981) ✔ Bordeaux Supérieur Ch. Croix-Beaurivage Rouge, Bordeaux Ch. la Joye Blanc Sec.
• Jean-Christian Donet, Ch. la Joye, 33240 St-André-de-Cubzac; tel. 57 43 18 93 ⌶ By appt.

CHATEAU LABORDE*

■   11ha   80000   2 D 🍷 ⌷

75 76 78 80 *81 *82

Intense red colour and a powerful nose, both floral and vegetal in character; warm and smooth in the mouth. (1982)
• Jean Borderie, Ch. Laborde, St-Médard-de-Cuizières, 33230 Coutras; tel. 57 69 61 33 ⌶ By appt.

CHATEAU LACOMBE-CADIOT***

■   3ha   24000   2 D ⑪ ⌷

*76 *78 81 **82** **83** **84**

A good example of a Palus wine, grown on the alluvial soils of the Garonne. A splendid colour precedes an aromatic and classy nose. In the mouth it is quite oaky (but not excessively so), fruity, tannic, full and long. (1982)
• Françis Guillaume, Ch. Lacombe-Cadiot, Ludon-Médoc, 33290 Blanquefort; tel. 56 30 43 54 ⌶ By appt.

Château Lacombe Cadiot
1982
BORDEAUX SUPERIEUR

CHATEAU LAGRANGE-LES-TOURS**

■   7ha   40000   2 D ⑪ ⌷

From a vineyard recently rescued from disuse comes a wine with an honest, fruity nose, suggesting a good balance. A frank attack, fine, powerful aromas and good length confirm this, and suggest the wine will age well. (1982)
• Paulette Laval, Ch. Lagrange-les-Tours, Cubzac-les-Ponts, 33240 St-André-de-Cubzac; tel. 57 43 04 96 ⌶ By appt.

CHATEAU LAGUT*

■   15ha   80000   4 D 🍷 ⌷

*75 *78 *79 80 81 **82**

Moderate ruby-red colour; good fruit on the nose, although still a little closed up. The attack is good and the wine is balanced, well structured and pleasing on the palate. (1983)
• Alain Bonneau, 33420 Branne; tel. 57 84 50 01 ⌶ By appt. Closed last weekend in Dec.

CHATEAU DE LA LAMBERTIE**

■   7ha   50000   3 D ⑪ ⌷

82 83 84

A pleasing wine in every way: for its colour; its fairly rich although still slightly closed nose; its body and its good tannic structure (a guarantee of a good future). (1982) ✔ Bordeaux Ch. de la Lambertie Rouge.
• *Mme* F. Hoarau-Marchand, Ch. de la Lambertie, 33220 Ste-Foy-la-Grande, tel. 57 46 40 14 ⌶ By appt. Closed end Aug.–early Sept. and during harvest.

CHATEAU LAMOTHE GAILLARD**

■   15ha   3 D 🍷 ⌷

Very deep, sustained colour and expressive, fruity nose. Firm on the palate, but with fine underlying structure. Exceptionally persistent flavour. (1982)
• Jean Renaud, St-Ciers-d'Abzac, 33230 Coutras; tel. 57 49 45 03 ⌶ No visitors.

CHATEAU LANDEREAU

■   43ha   250000   3 D 🍷 ⌷

*75 *78 81 *82 83

A light wine, perhaps a little lacking in character, but smooth and easy on the palate. (1982) ✔ Bordeaux Ch. Landereau Rosé.
• Michel Baylet, Ch. Landereau, Sadirac, 33670 Créon; tel. 56 23 02 40 ⌶ By appt. Closed Sun. and public holidays.

CHATEAU LARTEAU

■   18ha   72000   2 D 🍷 ⌷

79 **82** 83

Deep-coloured wine with pleasant, jammy aromas. In the mouth, a certain acidity and lots of tannin – maybe even too much. (1983)
• Paul Alla, Ch. Larteau, Arveyres, 33500 Libourne; tel. 57 24 80 04 ⌶ No visitors.

CHATEAU LATOUR**

■   18ha   98000   4 D 🍷

73 ⑦⑤ 76 **77** **78** 79 **82** **83**

Not the famous Château Latour in Pauillac, but a good Bordeaux Supérieur for all that. The old manor-house dates back to the 14th century and tradition has it that the ubiquitous Henri IV once stayed there. Gourmet that he was, Heri would certainly have appreciated the wine produced today. With its fine red colour and its pleasing nose, it is supple and round on the palate with a perfect tannic finish. Certainly a bottle to keep. (1983)
• Raymond Laguens, Ch. Latour, St-Martin-du-Puy, 33540 Sauveterre-de-Guyenne; tel. 66 71 53 15 ⌶ No visitors.

CLOS LAURIOLE*

■   9ha   60000   3 D 🍷 ⑪

75 76 77 78 79 80 81 ⑧② **82**

A lively red colour. Discreet nose, with delicate vinous and floral aromas. Warm, round and long on the palate. (1982)
• Jean-François Mauros, Clos Lauriole, Isle-St-Georges, 33640 Portets; tel. 56 67 15 45 ⌶ By appt. Closed during harvests (Oct.).

CHATEAU LAVILLE★★

■ 20ha 145000 **3** D ◑

64 66 70 ★79 ★81 ★82 83

This vineyard has just been re-established after thirty years of non-production following the frosts of 1956. Fortunately so, to judge by this vintage with its pronounced candied-fruit nose. Tannic, rich, full and powerful, it needs keeping for five to ten years. (1982) ✔ Bordeaux Ch. Moulin-de-Raymond Rouge, Bordeaux Clairet. ⚲ Claude Faye, Ch. Laville, St-Sulpice-et-Cameyrac, 33450 St-Loubés; tel. 56 30 84 19 ⏃ By appt. Closed Aug.

CHATEAU DE LA LIMAGERE★

■ 20ha 120000 **2** ■ ↓

Dark, attractive colour; the nose, in contrast, is like an escape into the countryside, with its shades of undergrowth and hay, and an overall impression of ripe fruit. Smooth, round and full, it is a pleasant, crisp wine. (1982) ✔ Graves Rouges from various châteaux. ⚲ Albert et Lucien Yung, Ch. de la Limagerie, Beautiran, 33640 Portets; tel. 56 67 05 25 ⏃ By appt. Closed Aug.

CHATEAU LOISEAU★

■ 22ha 130000 **3** D ■

★78 ★79 ★82 ★83

In contrast with the aristocratic air of the Renaissance-style château, the wine is nicely rustic, with a red-fruit nose; on the palate it is full bodied and robust. (1982) ⚲ Pierre Goujon, Ch. Loiseau, Lalande-de-Fronsac, 33240 St-André-de-Cubzac; tel. 57 58 14 02 ⏃ Mon.–Fri. 8.00–20.00.

CHATEAU LONGEREAU★

■ 10ha 67000 **3** D ■ ↓

64 ⑺⁰ ★75 ★78 ★79 ★81 ★82 ★83

Typical 1982 colour, but still somewhat closed on the nose. A lively attack, plenty of body and good length, but needs time to mellow. (1982) ⚲ Pierre Ballange, Ch. Longereau, 33240 St-André-de-Cubzac; tel. 57 43 11 97 ⏃ By appt.

CHATEAU MAINEDONT

■ 11ha 50000 **3** D ■ ◑ ↓

79 81 ⑻² **82** 83

Clear and bright in colour; light on the nose and similarly light – with some astringency – on the palate. (1982) ⚲ Jean-Marie Chaudet, Le Meyney, St-Germaine-la-Rivière, 33240 St-André-de-Cubzac; tel. 57 84 46 40 ⏃ By appt. Closed 15 Aug.– 1 Sept.

CHATEAU MARAC★

■ 15ha 90000 **3** D ■ ↓

★75 ★78 ★79 ★81 ★⑻² 83

An attractive wine characteristic of the vintage, with good colour and a classy nose, all resulting in a nicely balanced palate. (1982) ✔ Bordeaux Rosé. ⚲ Alain Bonville, Ch. Marac, Pujols, 33350 Castillon-la-Bataille; tel. 57 40 53 21 ⏃ By appt.

CLOS DE MAS

■ 3ha 17000 **3** D ■

74 75 76 **78** ★79 ⑻² 83

Lively red hue; nose has strong aromas of red fruit with touches of chocolate. Solid tannic structure on the palate, but the finish is a little hot and dry. (1982) ✔ Lussac St-Emilion Ch. Chouteau, Bordeaux Clos le Mas Blanc. ⚲ Michel Rougerie, Chouteau, Petit-Palais, 33570 Lussac; tel. 57 74 65 85 ⏃ By appt.

CHATEAU MEAUNE★★

■ 24ha 100000 **2** D ■ ↓

⑻¹ 82 **83**

A dark red wine, powerfully aromatic on the nose, well-constituted and very long on the palate. (1983) ⚲ Alan Johnson-Hill Ch. Meaune, Maransin, 33230 Coutras; tel. 57 49 41 04 ⏃ By appt. Closed Dec. and Jan.

CHATEAU MEILLAC★

■ 5ha 23000 **3** D ■ ◑ ↓

74 78 **80** **81** ⑻²

Good, bright colour. Flowery nose with a touch of oak, not yet fully developed. (1981) ⚲ Claude Bertrand, Ch. Meillac, St-Romain-la-Virvée, 33240 St-André-de-Cubzac; tel. 57 43 23 58 ⏃ By appt.

CHATEAU DU MERLE★

■ 10ha 60000 **2** D ↓

⑺⁰ **78** ★**79** 80 **81**

Magnificently deep colour and floral nose. On the palate a supple attack is followed by concentrated, soft tannins. Although still somewhat unrefined this wine will gain stature as it ages. (1982) ✔ Lalande du Pomerol Clos-des-Tuileries ⚲ Fernand et Francis Merlet, Goizet, St-Denis-de-Pile, 33230 Coutras; tel. 57 84 25 19 ⏃ No visitors.

CHATEAU LA MICHELIERE★★

■ 8ha 45000 **2** D ■ ↓

74 ★75 ★79 ★81 ⑻² **82**

A red colour with deep purple tinges and a fruity but still closed-up nose. Good balance and substance on the palate, leading to a very tannic finish, indicate clearly that this is a wine with a very fine future which must be left to mature. (1982) ✔ Bordeaux Ch. du Tertre-de-Cascard. ⚲ Michel Tobler, Ch. la Michelière, St-Romain-la-Virvée, 33240 St-André-de-Cubzac; tel. 57 58 16 39 ⏃ By appt. Closed Sept.–Nov.

CHATEAU LES MOINES-MARTIN★★

■ 6ha 24000 **2** D ■ ◑ ↓

75 79 81 **81** 82

Attractive in appearance; ripely aromatic on the nose; round and well structured on the palate – a fine and distinctive wine. (1982) ⚲ Jacques Boudin, Ch. Les Moines-Martin, 33133 Galgon; tel. 57 84 33 07 ⏃ By appt.

166

CHATEAU LA MONGIE★★

■   15ha   100000   3 D ▮ ⑾ ↓

70 **75 78** 81 82 ⑧③

This typical Bordeaux estate of woods, fields and vines makes a very pleasant wine that is smooth, round and long. (1981) ✔ Other Bordeaux wines. ☛ Pierre Blouin, Ch. la Mongie, Vérac, 33240 St-André-de-Cubzac; tel. 57 84 37 08. ⟰ By appt. Closed first fortnight in Aug.

CHATEAU MONTAIGNE★

■   20ha   130000   D ▮ ⑾ ↓

Pleasant bouquet and well balanced in the mouth. Drink now. (1983)
☛ Héritiers A. Sue, Ch. Montaigne, Quinsac, 33360 Latresne. ⟰ By appt.

CHATEAU MONTLAU★★

■   6ha   50000   3 D ▮ ↓

*⟨82⟩ **83**

Pleasing cherry-red colour with darker shades. Delicate, subtle and slightly fruity nose. On the palate, good substance and solid tannin, but not to the exclusion of roundness and smoothness. (1982)
☛ L. Schuster de Ballwill, Moulon, 33420 Branne; tel. 57 84 50 71 ⟰ By appt.

CHATEAU MORILLON

■   1ha   6000   3 D ▮ ⑾ ↓

79 **80** 81 82 **83**

According to tradition the north wall of the storehouse dates from the Gallo-Roman period. A fine ruby colour. Perhaps a little short on the palate; nonetheless, delicate and fruity. (1982)
☛ Olga Bagot, Ch. Morillon, Neuffons, 33580 Monségur; tel. 56 71 42 26 ⟰ By appt. Closed at harvest time.

CHATEAU DE MOUCHAC

■   30ha   n/a   2 D ▮

*⟨75⟩ 78 **79** 80 **81 82**

A dark but brilliant red wine; impressive and characterful, but rather raw on the finish. (1982)
☛ *M.* Du Serech de Saint-Avit, Ch. de Mouchac, Grézillac, 33420 Branne; tel. 57 84 52 10 ⟰ By appt.

CHATEAU MOUGNEAUX★★

■   27ha   170000   4 D ⑾ ↓

75 76 *78 *79 *80 *82 83

Produced not far from the famous abbey of St-Ferme, this wine is attractive and well coloured with a fine and fruity nose; round, supple and well structured on the palate, with a fairly long finish. (1983)
☛ Jean Bocquet, ch. Mongneaux, St-Ferme, 33580 Monségur; tel. 56 61 62 02 ⟰ By appt.

CHATEAU MOULIN-DE-SERRE

■   15ha   100000   2 D ▮ ↓

78 79 80 **81 82** 83

A pleasing ruby-amber colour. Although perhaps a little short on the palate, it has a nice, light blend of floral and herbal aromas. (1982)
☛ J.-F. et J.-J. Martinez, Ch. Moulin-de-Serre,

33230 St-Martin-de-Laye; tel. 5749 42 05 ⟰ By appt.

CAVE COOPERATIVE DE NERIGEAN

■   408ha   2200000   2 D ▮ ↓

75 *78 **79** 81 82

Attractive red colour, shading to cherry; smooth on the palate. A light wine, lovely to look at, but perhaps a little short on the finish. (1979)
☛ Cave Coop. de Nérigean, Nérigean, 33750 St-Germain-du-Puch; tel. 57 24 50 64 ⟰ Mon.–Fri. 8.30–12.30/14.00–18.00; Sat. 8.30–12.00.

NICOLAS★

■   476000   2 ▮

Good colour; discreet and elegant nose; harmonious on the palate. A good wine of its type.
☛ Ets Nicolas, 2 Rue de Valmy, 94220 Charenton; tel. 01 37 59 20 ⟰ No visitors.

CHATEAU L'ORTOLAN-GENISSAC★

■   6ha   33000   2 D ▮

73 81 **82**

An attractive wine that still needs to lose a little aggression; although tannic, it is already fairly rounded, and has potential. (1981)
☛ François Badard, Ch. L'Ortolan-Génissac, Génissac, 33420 Branne; tel. 57 24 48 05 ⟰ By appt.

CHATEAU DE LA PAILLETTE★

■   9ha   60000   2 D ▮ ⑾

70 71 75 *78 81 *⟨82⟩ 82 83

An aromatic, fruity and delicate wine, pleasant and round on the palate but perhaps lacking a little length. (1982) ✔ Bordeaux Supérieur Ch. Jean-Mathieu, Bordeaux Supérieur Ch. Jean-Fonval.
☛ Henri-Christian Brasseur, Ch. de la Paillette, 33500 Libourne; tel. 57 51 17 31 ⟰ Daily 10.00–13.00/14.00–19.00.

CHATEAU DU PALANQUEY★

■   13ha   65000   2 D ⑾ ↓

75 *79 81 **82 83**

Not quite bright in appearance; a warm supple attack is followed by a lean, tannic development. (1981) ✔ St-Emilion Grand Cru Ch. Haut-Bardoulet, Puisseguin St-Émilion Ch. Haut-Bernat, Entre-Deux-Mers Ch. Montfayet.
☛ Jacques Baraize, Ch. du Palanquey, Ste-Colombe, 33350 Castillon-la-Bataille; tel. 57 40 07 78 ⟰ By appt.

CHATEAU PALMERAIE

■   3ha   20000   3 D ▮ ↓

81 82

Despite having suffered a little from poor storage, this is an attractive bright red wine, and has a fairly strong flavour with a touch of smoke. (1982)
☛ Eric Bordas, Ch. Patarabert, Vignonet, 33330 St-Emilion; tel. 57 24 74 73 ⟰ By appt. Closed last week in Feb.

CHATEAU PASSE-CRABY*

■   15ha   90000   **2** **D** **ⅱ** ↓
*75 *78 ***81** ***82** *82 (83)

Dark red colour and intense, flowery nose. Despite the slightly short finish, the overall impression is good; a supple, rich and pleasing wine. (1982)
🍷 Vincent Boye, Ch. Passe-Craby, 33133 Galgon; tel. 57 74 32 58 ⵙ By appt. Closed Aug. 🍷 GFA Champ d'Auron.

DOMAINE DE PENETURE

■   3ha   20000   **2** **D** **ⅱ** ↓
70 75 *78 *81 *82 83

A light wine with a fairly deep colour and fine, delicately fruity aromas on the nose. (1981)
🍷 SDF Lagarde, Dom. de Peneture, 33240 St-André-de-Cubzac; tel. 57 43 16 53 ⵙ By appt.

CHATEAU PENIN*

■   11ha   67000   **3** **D** **ⅱ** ↓
80 (81) *82 (83) 83

An attractive dark ruby colour. The nose is perhaps a little too discreet but the wine is pleasant in the mouth: round, fruity and well constituted. (1982) ✔ Other Bordeaux wines.
🍷 Lucette Carteyron, Ch. Penin, Génissac, 33420 Branne; tel. 57 24 48 45 ⵙ By appt. Closed 15–31 Aug.

CHATEAU PEYMELON

■   13ha   80000   **3** **D** **ⅱ** ↓
76 78 82 82 83

At the moment this wine is a little rustic but has plenty of fruit on the nose and is very easy to drink, with a good balance of tannins. (1982)
🍷 *M.* et *Mme* Chapard-Truffaud, Dom. des Petits, Cars, 33390 Blaye; tel. 57 42 19 09 ⵙ By appt. Closed Aug.

CHATEAU PEYREBON*

■   15ha   67000   **2** **D** **ⅱ** ↓
75 75 *76 78 79 81 *82 (83)

Although it does not have a strong nose, this is a straightforward wine – full bodied, well balanced and pleasantly round. (1982) ✔ St-Emilion Grand Cru.
🍷 Jean-André Robineau, Ch. Peyrebon, Grezillac, 33420 Branne; tel. 57 84 52 26 ⵙ By appt.

CHATEAU PICON**

■   30ha   130000   **2** **D** **⑪** ↓
75 *78 79 80 *81 82 83 83

The nose is not yet fully open, but on the palate the wine has plenty of matter, good balance and length. Visitors should note the branding iron that was used in the 18th century to mark the barrels. (1983)
🍷 Jean-Claude Audry, Ch. Picon, Eynesse, 33220 St-Foy-la-Grande; tel. 57 46 41 91 ⵙ By appt.

CHATEAU DE LA PIERRE-BLANCHE*

■   2ha   10000   **2** **D** **ⅱ** ↓
75 78 79 **81** *(82) 82 83

Rich, black-cherry colour with purple edges. Fruity nose. Begins well in the mouth, has good composition and a tannic finish. Well balanced. (1982)
🍷 *Mme* Veuve Hervé, Ch. de la Pierre-Blanche, Izon, 33450 St-Loubès; tel. 57 74 86 67 ⵙ By appt.

CHATEAU DU PINTNEY

■   5ha   20000   **3** **D** **ⅱ** **⑪** ↓
76 78 82 82 83

This lovely, Regency-style property, with its water-mill and old dovecote, produces this fairly light wine that, in the case of this vintage, should not be kept for too long. (1979)
🍷 M. de Coninck-Horeau, Ch. du Pintney, 33500 Libourne; tel. 57 51 06 07 ⵙ By appt. 🍷 René de Coninck.

CHATEAU PUY-FAURE**

■   7ha   30000   **2** **D** **ⅱ** ↓
*75 76 **78** *79 *(82) *82 83

Very characteristic of the 1982 vintage; lovely colour, with a nose that is discreet yet fine. A well-made wine with a good balance on the palate. (1982)
🍷 Bernard Dublaix, Ch. Puy-Faure, Aubie-et-Espessas, 33240 St-André-de-Cubzac; tel. 57 43 19 44 ⵙ By appt. Closed Tues.–Fri. during July and Aug.

CHATEAU PUY-FAURE**

■   7ha   34000   **2** **D** **⑪** ↓
81 (82) 82 83 84

Brilliant appearance. Fine if rather delicate on the nose. Pleasing, well made and nicely balanced. At its best fairly soon. (1982)
🍷 Bernard Dublaix, Ch. Puy-Faure, 33240 Aubie-Espessas; tel. 57 43 19 44 ⵙ By appt.

CHATEAU PUYFROMAGE**

■   40ha   240000   **3** **D** **ⅱ** ↓
*70 75 (78) 79 80 81 82

This is a good château to visit, with a superb dovecote. Its wine is warm, elegant, likeable and harmonious; should age well. (1982)
🍷 Philippe Marque, Ch. Puyfromage, St-Gibard, 33570 Lussac; tel. 57 40 61 08 ⵙ Mon.–Fri. 9.00–12.00/14.00–17.00.

CHATEAU DU PUY*

■   8ha   42000   **3** **ⅱ** **⑪**
67 70 74 *75 76 78 **79** 80 81 (82) 82

This wine is already showing an orange tinge at the rim; light on the nose but remarkably well balanced on the palate – round, supple and good length. The property is situated on a slope that served as a campsite for the famous La Hire, Joan of Arc's companion, during the Hundred Years War. (1982)
🍷 Pierre-Robert Amoreau, Ch. du Puy, Saint-Cibard, 33570 Lussac; tel. 57 41 61 06 ⵙ By appt.

CHATEAU LES RAGOTTES★

■ 12ha 5400 ⬛3 Ⓓ 🖻 ↓

64 68 **75** ★⑧2

Behind the deep colour lies a charming flowery spicy nose. On the palate the wine is smooth and tannic. (1982) ✔ Bordeaux Les Ragottes Mousseux.

🖙 Daniel Orsini, Ch. Les Ragottes, 33790 Pellegrue; tel. 56 61 33 03 ♈ By appt.

DOMAINE DE RAIGNEAUX★★

■ 12ha 60000 ⬛2 Ⓓ 🖻 ↓

74 ★**75** 76 77 **78** ★**79** ★**81** ⑧2 **82**

According to tradition, this very old estate was established by monks in the Middle Ages. The wine is attractive to look at, while the nose is still closed up and rustic. On the palate it is well structured and should improve with age. (1982) ✔ Bordeaux Clairet Dom. des Raigneaux.

🖙 Jean Bustarret, Dom. des Raigneaux, Madirac, 33670 Créon; tel. 56 23 03 49 ♈ By appt.

CHATEAU LES RAMBEAUDS★

■ 7ha 46000 ⬛2 Ⓓ 🖻 ↓

⑦9 ★80 81 **82** **82** **83**

Pleasant if rustic, wine made in traditional fashion. A bouquet that is developing nicely, and a palate that is at once frank on the attack, supple and fairly tannic. (1983) ✔ Bordeaux Clairet Ch. les Rambeauds, Entre-Deux-Mers Ch. les Rambeauds.

🖙 Jean Cazade, Ch. les Rambeauds, Fosseset-et-Baleyssac, 33190 La Réole; tel. 56 61 72 72 ♈ By appt.

CHATEAU LE RELAIS-FONTENELLE★

■ 6ha 26000 ⬛3 Ⓓ 🖻

73 75 ★76 ★79 ★81 ⑧2 83

Made in a charming old coaching inn that is typical of the area, this is an intensely aromatic wine with a classic composition. Should age well. (1981) ✔ Entre-Deux-Mers.

🖙 Raymond Labounoux, Ch. le-Relais-Fontenelle, Montussan 33450 St-Loubès; tel. 56 30 92 45 ♈ By appt. Closed during harvest.

CHATEAU RIFFAUD★

■ 11ha 80000 ⬛2 Ⓓ 🖻 ↓

75 78 79 ⑧3 **83**

Deep purple to ruby in colour; underlying the red-fruit character the nose has a distinctly Cabernet aroma. A pleasant, well-balanced wine. (1983) ✔ Entre-Deux-Mers Petit-Mayne, Bordeaux Petit-Mayne Blanc Sec, Bordeaux Petit-Mayne Rosé.

🖙 Jaques Ballarin, Le Bourg, Castelvieil, 33540 Sauveterre-de-Guyenne; tel. 56 61 97 52 ♈ No visitors.

CHATEAU LA ROSE-LINAS

■ 22ha 150000 ⬛3 Ⓓ 🖻 ↓

★75 78 ★79 ★82 **83**

Very bright colour, although a little lacking in intensity, and a good nose; will please connoisseurs of light wines. (1982)

🖙 SC du Ch. la Rose-Linas, Arveyres, 33500 Libourne; tel. 57 51 57 72 ♈ By appt.

CHATEAU ROUQUETTE★

■ 22ha 120000 ⬛3 Ⓓ 🖻 ↓

⑧1 ★82 **83** 84

Overlooking the small Durèze valley, this charming rustic château produces an attractive wine that is well balanced on the palate. (1981)

🖙 A. et F. Collas, Ch. Rouquette, 33790 Pellegrue; tel. 56 61 35 59 ♈ No visitors.

CHATEAU LA SABLIERE FONGRAVE★★

■ 42ha 250000 ⬛3 Ⓓ 🖻 ↓

67 70 71 73 74 ⑦5 **75** ★76 78 81 82 83

Mature leathery bouquet, round and pleasing on the palate yet still fairly tannic. Will continue to please for a few years more. (1975)

🖙 Pierre Perromat, Dom. de Fongrave, Gornac, 33540 Sauveterre-de-Guyenne; tel. 56 61 97 64 ♈ By appt.

CHATEAU DES SABLONS

■ 20ha 50000 ⬛3 Ⓓ 🖻 ◑

70 75 ★⑦8 79 82

Although still rather young, there are aromas of red fruit both on the nose and on the palate, where it is supple and has good length. (1982) ✔ Entre-Deux-Mers.

🖙 Paul Frédefon, Ch. des Sablons, 33450 St-Loubès; tel. 56 20 40 94 ♈ No visitors.

CHATEAU SAINT-IGNAN★

■ 15ha 93000 ⬛2 Ⓓ 🖻 ↓

★79 ★80 ★81 ★82 **83**

A deep ruby wine with a powerful nose. Harmonious, despite a fairly short finish. (1981) ✔ Côtes de Bourg, Ch. les Rocques.

🖙 Feillon Père et Fils, Ch. St-Ignan, St-Gervais, 33240 St-André-de-Cubzac; tel. 57 68 42 82 ♈ By appt. 🖙 GAEC Feillon Frères.

CHATEAU SAINT-JACQUES★

■ 12ha 74000 ⬛3 Ⓓ ◑ ↓

75 ★78 80 ★81 ⑧2 **82**

An attractive garnet-coloured wine with an expressive nose and a frank attack to the palate, followed by a fairly full and pleasantly aromatic flavour. (1982)

🖙 W.A. Miailhe, Ch. St-Jacques, Labarde, 33460 Margaux; tel. 56 81 35 01 ♈ Mon.–Fri. 9.30–11.30/14.30–17.30. Open summer.

CHATEAU LA SALARGUE

■ 8ha 50000 ⬛3 Ⓓ 🖻 ↓

79 80 81 ★82 ★83 84

From an old estate, a pale red wine with an orange tint. The nose is undeveloped but gives an impression of warmth, with a slightly cooked scent mirrored by the faintly supple palate (1983) ✔ Bordeaux, Bordeaux Clairet.

🖙 Bruno Leroy, Ch. La Salargue, Moulon, 33420 Branne; tel. 57 24 48 44 ♈ By appt.

CHATEAU SARAIL-LA-GUILLAMERIE★★

■   10ha   67000   **3** D ▮ ↓

⑦ 79 80 **81** **82** **82**

In the spirit of *Clochemerle* this estate has heroically resisted the urbanization taking over the commune of Saint-Loubes. Its main defence must be the quality of its wine – ample, fleshy, supple and well balanced. (1981) ✔ Bordeaux Vieux-Guillaume Rosé.
☙ Michel Deguillaume, Ch. Sarail-la-Guillamerie, 33450 St-Loubes; tel. 56 20 40 14 ￥ Mon.–Sat. 9.00–12.00. Closed during the harvest.

CHATEAU HAUT-SORILLON★

■   10ha   96000   **3** D ▮

⑦ 78 **79** 80 **81** 82

If the colour is unremarkable, the bouquet compensates, being distinctly spicy. The palate is lively and tannic but a little short. (1982)
☙ M. Rosseau, Ch. Haut-Sorillon, Abac, 33230 Coutras; tel. 57 49 11 83 ￥ By appt.

CHATEAU TERRE FORT★

■   70ha   420000   **3** D ◫ ↓

75 78 80 **81** *82 **82**

Deeply coloured, velvety red. Nose is still closed-in but is pleasantly well balanced in the mouth. (1982)
☙ Marcel Quancard et Fils, Ch. Vernay-Bonfort, Montagne, 33570 Lussac; tel. 56 77 66 66 ￥ By appt.

DOMAINE DE TERREFORT★

■   10ha   55000   **3** D ▮ ↓

75 78 *79 *80 *81 82 **82**

Shows balance both in colour and on the nose, which has aromas of red fruit of some finesse. After a harmonious attack, it develops well on the palate and is fairly long. (1982) ✔ Entre-Deux-Mers Clos Lalaigune.
☙ F. Massé, Dom. de Queyssard, Pompignac, 33370 Tresses; tel. 56 30 51 38 ￥ By appt.

CHATEAU TOUR-CAILLET

■   25ha   130000   **2** D ▮

81 **81** 82 ⑧

From this elegant little château comes a wine that, despite an initial slightly vegetal impression on the nose, has a frank attack and tannic finish. (1982) ✔ Entre-Deux-Mers Ch. Tour Caillet, Bordeaux Ch. Tour Caillet.
☙ Denis Lecourt, Ch. Tour Caillet, 33420 Génissac; tel. 57 24 46 04 ￥ By appt.

CHATEAU LA TOUR DE GILET★★

■   4ha   18000   **3** D ▮ ◫ ↓

70 74 *75 *78 79 *⑧ *82

This is a typical 1982, a very elegant wine, with a truly splendid colour. (1982)
☙ Guy Bachelot, Cadiot, Ludon-Médoc, 33290 Blanquefort; tel. 56 30 32 95 ￥ By appt.

CHATEAU TOUR-DE-L'ESPERANCE★

■   35ha   240000   **2** D ▮

⑥ *⑦ *⑧ 83

The nose gives a subtle impression of ripe fruit, followed by the aromas of well-matured Merlot. On the palate the wine is smooth and refined. (1982)
☙ Robert Boye, Ch. Tour-de-l'Esperance, 33133 Galgon; tel. 57 74 30 02 ￥ By appt.

CHATEAU TOUR-PETIT-PUCH★★

■   15ha   106000   **2** D ▮ ↓

75 **75** ⑦ 80 *81 *82

A fresh, intense and complex nose, harmonizing with the deep ruby colour. Round, balanced and elegant on the palate. A fine wine. (1981) ✔ Entre-Deux-Mers Ch. Tour-Petit-Puch, Bordeaux Rosé Ch. Soulières.
☙ Elie Coudreau, Ch. Tour-Petit-Puch, 33750 St-Germain-du-Puch; tel. 57 24 59 13 ￥ By appt.

CHATEAU TROCARD★

■   30ha   150000   **3** D ▮ ↓

70 71 75 **75** 78 79 81 82 83

Already warm and round, with aromas of Merlot and violet, but needs to become more supple. (1982)
☙ GAEC Trocard, Ch. Trocard, Les Artigues-de-Lussac, 33570 Lussac; tel. 57 84 01 16 ￥ By appt. Closed Aug.

CHATEAU LA TUILERIE-DU-PUY★

■   26ha   120000   **2** D ▮ ↓

*81 82 *83

The name reflects the fact that one of the specialities of the Dropt valley is the manufacture of tiles. The other speciality is of course wine, like this one – slightly spicy, round, tannic, and fairly alcoholic on the finish. (1983) ✔ Entre-Deux-Mers.
☙ Jean-Pierre Regaud, Ch. la Tuilerie-du-Puy, Le Puy, 33580 Monségur; tel. 56 61 61 92 ￥ By appt.

CHATEAU TURON-LA-CROIX

■   25ha   132000   **4** D ▮ ↓

*⑧ *82 83

Moderate in colour, but the nose is clean and crisp, with a pleasing fruitiness. A good light wine. (1982)
☙ M.-H. Saric et Fils, Ch. Turon-la-Croix, Lugasson, 33119 Frontenac; tel. 56 24 05 55. ￥ By appt.

DOMAINE DE LA VALLEE★★

■ 4ha 24000 **2** D ▊ ⑪ ⌄

71 75 78 79 80 **81** ⑧ **82**

Attractive colour, ripe-fruit on the nose and a nicely balanced palate with some tannin. (1982) ✔ Lalande de Pomerol, Montagne St-Emilion. ⟊ Jean-Michel Bertrand, Dom. de la Vallée, 33570 Artigues-de-Lussac; tel. 57 84 01 22 ⟂ Mon.–Sat. 8.00–19.00.

VIEUX VAURE★

■ 103ha 100000 **2** D ▊ ⌄

79 80 ★⑧ ★**82**

Produced by the Ruch cooperative, this wine is bright in colour, aromatic on the nose; light, supple, well balanced and ready to drink. (1982) ✔ Entre-Deux-Mers, Bordeaux Ch. de Vaure Rouge, Bordeaux Ch. de Blaignac Rouge, Bordeaux Rosé. ⟊ Cave Coop. de R70 Ruch, 33350 Castillon-la-Bataille; tel. 57 40 54 09 ⟂ By appt.

CHATEAU DE LA VIEILLE-TOUR★★

■ 22ha 130000 **3** D ▊ ⌄

75 76 79 80 **81** ⑧

The first owner of this estate, about the year 1100, was a poet and teacher who would doubtless have appreciated this elegant, well-balanced wine. Long on the palate and with subtle but as yet undeveloped flavours, it needs keeping for a while. (1982) ⟊ *MM*. Boissonneau Père et Fils, Ch. de la Vieille-Tour, St-Michel-Lapujade, 33190 La Réole; tel. 56 61 72 14 ⟂ By appt.

CHATEAU VIEIL-ORME

■ 12ha 80000 **3** D ▊

75 ★**76** ★**79** ★**81** ★82

Lively red appearance; a nose which is faintly dusty but strongly red-fruit in character; nicely rounded palate. (1982) ✔ Bordeaux Côtes St-Macaire Ch. Vieil-Orme Blanc Moelleux, Bordeaux Dom. de Malineau Rouge, Bordeaux Ch. Vieil-Orme Rosé, Bordeaux Dom. Malineau Mousseux. ⟊ Henri Gardera, Ch. Vieil-Orme, St-Martial, 33490 St-Macaire; tel. 56 63 70 48 ⟂ By appt.

VIEUX CHATEAU DU COLOMBIER

■ 40ha 240000 **3** ▊ ⌄

★**70 75** ⑦ 79 **79** 80 81 82

With a castle keep and a dovecote both from the 12th century, this is a patrician setting for the wine, which is a little harsh on the nose but fruity, slightly peppery, and well balanced on the palate. (1982) ⟊ Philippe Marque, Ch. Puyfromage, St-Cobard, 33570 Lussac; tel. 57 40 61 08 ⟂ Mon.–Fri. 9.00–12.00/14.00–17.00 ⟊ SCE Ch. Puyfromage.

CHATEAU VIEUX-MANOIR-DE-BENAUGE

■ 28ha 170000 **2** ▊ ⌄

★**79** ★**82** ★**82** ★⑧

Despite a certain softness on the attack, this wine has an attractive colour, a fresh nose suggesting

cherries and violets, and roundness and elegance on the palate. The ancient château is still a family residence. (1983) ✔ Bordeaux Sec Ch. Lardiley, Premier Côtes de Bordeaux Ch. de Grand Loc, Bordeaux Rosé. ⟊ P. Lataste, Ch. Lardiley, 33410 Cadillac; tel. 56 27 10 74 ⟂ By appt. Closed 25 Dec.–1 Jan, and Aug.

CHATEAU VIEUX MOULIN★★

■ 25ha 90000 **3** D ▊ ⑪

⑥ **75 77** 78 79 80 81 **82** 83

A good all-round wine; fine, bright-red colour; lively aromas on the nose. Long, supple attack on the palate, with a solid structure and very ripe tannins. (1982) ⟊ C. Simon, Ch. Vieux Moulin, 33141 Villegouge; tel. 57 84 42 16 ⟂ By appt. Closed during harvest and first fortnight in March.

CHATEAU VIGNOL

■ 40ha 180000 **3** D ▊ ⌄

★**75** ★**78 79 81** ⑧

The bouquet of this wine is both discreet and refined, the palate fairly smooth. (1979) ⟊ Bernard Doublet, Ch. Vignol, St-Quentin-de-Baron, 33750 St-Germain-du-Puch; tel. 57 84 62 93 ⟂ By appt.

Bordeaux Côtes de Castillon

CHATEAU CASTEGENS

■ 12ha 75000 **3** D ▊

76 77 79 ★82 ⑧ **83**

An attractively coloured wine, well balanced and lightly fruity, but with a finish that is a little too short. (1981) ⟊ *Mme* de Fontenay, Ch. Castegens, Belves-de-Castillon, 33350 Castillon-la-Bataille; tel. 57 40 06 07 ⟂ By appt. Closed Aug. ⟊ Jean-Louis de Fontenay.

CHATEAU LA GASPARDE★

■ 12ha 60000 **3** D ⑪ ⌄

★**75** ★**76 82 82** ⑧ **83**

Light ruby in colour with hints of amber; very fruity bouquet. (1983) ⟊ SC Bosne et Fils, Ch. la Gasparde, Gardegan-et-Tourtirac, 33350 Castillon-la-Bataille; tel. 57 40 06 09 ⟂ Daily 9.00–12.00/14.00–18.00. Closed Aug.

CHATEAU DE PITRAY★★

■ 26ha 180000 **3** D ▊

★**79** 80 81 **81** ⑧ **82** 83

A quality wine, solid in structure with good tannin content due to a high proportion of Cabernet Sauvignon and old vines. (1982) ⟊ Ste Civile la Frérie, Gardegan et Tourtirac, 33350 Castillon-la-Bataille; tel. 57 40 63 38 ⟂ No visitors. ⟊ *Vicomte* Louis de Pitray.

Bordeaux Supérieur Côtes de Castillon

CHATEAU BEYNAT★

| ■ | | 15ha | 65000 | **3** ▮ ⌄ |

79 **80** **81** ⑧⑵

A fairly delicate colour with mauvish tints. Initially warm and smooth on the palate; there is also a hint of acidity before a tannic finish. (1982)
☞ Daniel Borliachon, Ch. Beynat, St-Magne-de-Castillon, 33350, Castillon-la-Bataille; tel. 57 40 01 14 ⍦ By appt.

CHATEAU DES DEMOISELLES

| ■ | | 32ha | 250000 | **3** **D** ▮ ⌄ |

76 77 79 ★⑧⑵ ★**82**

Garnet-red in colour and well balanced, but spoiled by a slightly stemmy flavour. (1982)
✔ Bordeaux Supérieur Rouge Ch. de Rhode, Entre-Deux-Mers Ch. des Rivaux, St-Emilion Ch. Jacques Noir.
☞ Rémy Daut, Ch. des Demoiselles, 33350 St-Magne-sur-Castillon; tel. 57 40 11 88 ⍦ By appt.

CHATEAU FONTBAUDE★

| ■ | | 15ha | 12000 | **2** **D** ▮ ⌄ |

80 81 ★⑧⑵ ★**82** **83 84**

A rustic wine with a lovely deep colour. The nose is initially a little closed-in, but opens up as the wine is allowed to breathe. Fairly solid on the palate and finishes well. (1982)
☞ Christian Sabaté, St-Magne-de-Castillon, 33350 Castillon-la-Bataille; tel. 57 40 06 58 ⍦ Daily 8.00–13.00/14.00–19.00 ☞ François Sabaté.

CHATEAU GRAND-TUILLAC★★

| ■ | | 20ha | 120000 | **3** **D** ▮ ⑾ ⌄ |

70 75 78 **79** **81** ★82

Deep red colour with hint of purple. Delicate, flowery nose. Full bodied, harmonious and pleasantly long on the palate. (1982) ✔ St-Emilion Ch. Grand Bert.
☞ Philippe Lavigne, Ch. Grand-Tuillac, St-Philippe-d'Aiguille, 33350 Castillon-la-Bataille; tel. 57 40 60 09 ⍦ Mon.–Sat. 9.00–12.00/14.00–18.00. Closed second fortnight in Feb.

DOMAINE DU HAUT-BEYNAC★

| ■ | | 3ha | 18000 | **2** **D** ▮ ⌄ |

75 76 79 80 81 ⑧⑵ **82**

Light wine with a nose recalling soft red-fruits, followed by a well-balanced palate with a touch of astringency. (1982)
☞ Michel Meynard, Dom. du Haut-Beynac,

33350 St-Magne-de-Castillon; tel. 57 40 05 36 ⍦ By appt.

CHATEAU MOULIN-NEUF

| ■ | | 6ha | 42000 | **3** **D** ▮ ⑾ ⌄ |

74 75 76 ⑺⑻ **80** 81 82

Ruby-red in colour with shades of garnet, and subtly aromatic on the nose. On the palate this wine is smooth at first but has a somewhat harsh, tannic finish. (1979)
☞ René Nicot, Ch. Moulin-Neuf, St-Gênès de Castillon, 33350 Castillon-la-Bataille; tel. 57 40 16 97 ⍦ By appt.

CHATEAU MOULIN-ROUGE★★

| ■ | | 20ha | 12000 | **3** **D** ▮ ⌄ |

80 81 ★⑧⑵ **83** **83** **84**

An attractive wine with subtle but delicate aromas of very ripe soft red fuit. Round, fleshy and well-made on the palate; leaves a pleasant impression and finishes well. (1983) ✔ Bordeaux Clairet, St-Emilion Grand Cru, Bordeaux Rosé.
☞ Jean-Claude Bassilicaux, Ch. Moulin-Rouge, St-Magne-de-Castillon, 33350 Castillon-la-Bataille; tel. 57 40 06 71 ⍦ No visitors.

CHATEAU PERVENCHE★

| ■ | | 5ha | 30000 | **2** **D** ▮ ⌄ |

The amber-ruby colour has a slightly veiled quality. The nose is quite flowery. Light and not too acidic on the palate; a pleasant wine overall. (1982) ✔ Bordeaux Côtes de Castillon Domaine de Lagardette, Montagne-St-Emilion Ch. Coucy.
☞ Dominique Maurèze, GFA de Puy-Arnaud, 33350 Belves-de-Castillon; tel. 57 40 06 10 ⍦ By appt. Closed 15–31 Aug.

CHATEAU LA PIERRIERE

| ■ | | | 132000 | **3** **D** ⑾ ⌄ |

75 78 79 **80** 81 ⑧⑵ 83

Lacks a little body, but has a deep colour, an honest nose, and, on the palate, some quite mature tannin. (1982)
☞ *MM.* Dourthe et Kressmann, 35 Rue de Bordeaux, Parempuyre, 33290 Blarquefort; tel. 56 35 84 64 ⍦ By appt.

CHATEAU LA TERRASSE

| ■ | | 16ha | 80000 | **2** **D** ▮ ⑾ |

80 **81**

Ruby-tinted purple in colour; firm on the attack, tannic on the finish with a slightly vegetal, grassy character.
☞ Bigarette Frères, Ch. la Terrasse, St-Magne-de-Castillon, 33350 Castillon-la-Bataille; tel. 57 40 08 86 ⍦ By appt.

CHATEAU TOUR-BIGORRE

| ■ | | 16ha | 70000 | **2** **D** ▮ ⑾ ⌄ |

64 67 72 78 **78** 79 82 83 84

The wine is crystal clear, and a beautiful amber-ruby colour; fragrant and flowery nose, followed by a good, solid, full-bodied palate. The only reservation is that it lacks fullness on the finish. (1979) ✔ St-Emilion Ch. Pistouley.
☞ Paul et J.-P. Fressineau, Ch. Tour-Bigorre, St-Gênès-de-Castillon, 33350 Castillon-La-Bataille; tel. 57 40 09 84 ⍦ By appt.

CHATEAU LA TREILLE-DES-GIRONDINS

| ■ | 12ha 75000 | ② Ⅾ ▣ |

▨76 80 ▨80 ▨81 ▨83

Not far from this vineyard three members of the Gironde party met their death during the French Revolution. Hence the name of this wine, which has a light oaky character. (1982)

↬ Alain Goumaud, Ch. La Treille-des-Girondins, St-Magne-de-Castillon, 33350 Castillon-la-Bataille; tel. 57 40 05 38 ☎ Mon.–Sat. 9.00–12.30/14.00–20.00. Sun. 9.30–12.00/15.00–18.00.

Bordeaux Côtes de Francs

CHATEAU PUYGUERAUD★★

| ■ | 20ha 110000 | ④ ▤ ⑪ ↓ |

⑦70 75 79 81 82 ▨83

Attractively coloured wine with a powerful nose and lots of charm; round and tannic. Should age well. (1983)

↬ Ets Thienpont de Berlaere, Ch. Puygueraud, St-Cibard, 33570 Lussac; tel. 57 40 61 04 ☎ By appt.

The Blayais and Bourgeais Appellations

The fortified port of Blaye lies opposite the Médoc on the other side of the Gironde Estuary in the Charentes region. Its hinterland, the Blayais, contains the smaller district of Bourg and together the two areas make up a charming and intimate landscape. Notable sights include the citadels at Blaye and Bourg, and important prehistoric carvings at the cave of Pair-Non-Pair, while the countryside, crisscrossed by little valleys, contains many small châteaux and hunting lodges. Sturgeon (and caviar) has always been a speciality of the region, along with a significant amount of white wine, much of it formerly distilled to make cognac. Today, however, white wine production is declining, since red wines are much more profitable. The

The Blayais and Bourgais Appellations

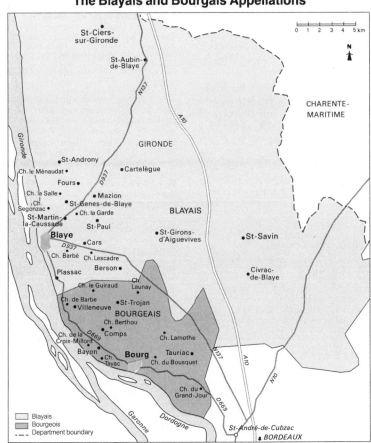

173

recent creation of a new Eau-de-Vie, 'Fine de Bordeaux', distilled from white wine, may help to stabilize the erosion of white wine's share of the local economy.

It can be something of a puzzle to sort out all the various appellations in this region; Blaye, Blayais, Premières Côtes de Blaye, Côtes de Blaye, Bourg, Bourgeais, or Côtes de Bourg, all producing red and white wines. The wines can, however, be divided into two main groups: those from Blaye, a region with many different soil types, and those from Bourg, which is geologically more homogenous.

Blaye, Côtes de Blaye and Premières Côtes de Blaye

Blaye's ancient citadel is attributed to the great military engineer Vauban. It surveys the surrounding vineyards, which cover approximately 2700 hectares and produce red and white wines.

The simple Blaye and Blayais appellations are becoming less common; most growers prefer to produce wines made from the better grape varieties, and thus claim the right to call them Côtes de Blaye or Premières Côtes de Blaye.

Red Premières Côtes de Blaye (16.5 million bottles a year) are good country wines with a full colour and powerful, fruity flavour. They go very well with meat or cheese. White Côtes de Blaye and Premières Côtes de Blaye usually have a pale colour and dry flavour, and would normally be served at the beginning of a meal.

Blaye

CHATEAU BERTINERIE

☐   3ha   19000   **2** **D** ▬ ⬙

62 64 70 75 ㉘ **82** **83**

The pale-yellow robe still has some hints of green. The fruit is fairly strong, both on the nose and palate, but has a slightly rancid note. (1982)
☙ Danile Bantegnies, Cubnezais, 33620 Cavignac; tel. 57 68 70 74 ⏱ By appt.

Côtes de Blaye

CHATEAU BERTHENON

☐   6ha   40000   **3** **D** ▬ ⬙

Straw-coloured, slightly golden colour. Light, subtly aromatic and predominantly acidic on the palate.
☙ Henri Ponz, Ch. Berthenon, St-Paul, 33390 Blaye; tel. 57 42 52 24 ⏱ By appt.

CHATEAU LA BOTTE

☐   2ha   12000   **2** **D** ▬ ⬥ ⬙

This vineyard was established soon after the Revolution. The wine is somewhere between yellow and white in colour and is developing a crisp, hay-like nose. In the mouth it has a classic quality with a touch of vivacity. ✔ Côtes de Blaye Cru Cazeaux la Botte Rouge, Bordeaux Ch. la Botte Rouge.
☙ René Blanchard, BP 3, 33920 St-Savin-de-Blaye; tel. 57 58 90 03 ⏱ By appt. Closed Aug.

CHATEAU LARDIERE

☐   5ha   30000   **2** **D** ▬ ⬙

This large house, belonging to a well-known local family, produces a wine whose nose is still a little closed-in but which is quite delicate and pleasantly crisp.
☙ René Bernard, Ch. Lardière, Marcillac, 33860 Reignac; tel. 57 32 14 38 ⏱ Mon.–Sat. 10.00–20.00. Closed Oct.

CHATEAU MARINIER★★

☐   2ha   12000   **2** **D** ▬ ⬙

An attractive, bright yellow colour. A light smell evocative of fresh bread. Both vigorous and delicate on the attack, this wine is well balanced with a pleasing, lively acidity. (1983) ✔ Premier Côtes-de-Blaye Ch. Marinier Rouge, Bordeaux Ch. Marinier Rouge, Bordeaux Ch. Marinier Rosé, Fine Bordeaux Dom. de Marinier.
☙ Thierry Cotet, Dom. Marinier, Cézac, 33620 Cavignac; tel. 57 68 63 13 ⏱ Daily 8.00–22.00.

RIOUCREUX-CHANTELOUP★

☐   3ha   20000   **2** **D** ▬ ⬙

83 **83** ⑧④

Very pale yellow colour with highlights of gold; the typically Sauvignon nose is followed by a clean and lively attack. A well-structured wine; should be drunk now. (1983) ✔ Côte de Bourg Ch. Tortais Rouge, Bordeaux Supérieur Ch. Rioucreaux-Chanteloup, Bordeaux Rosé Ch. Tortais, Bordeaux Sec Ch. Rioucreux-Chanteloup.
☙ Joël Grillet et *Mme* B. Joffre, Le Rioucreux, St-Christoly-de-Blaye, 33920 St-Savin; tel. 57 42 54 87 ⏱ No visitors.

Premières Côtes de Blaye

DOMAINE ARNAUD★

■   16ha   100000   **3** **D** ▬ ⬙

77 78 79 **81 82 83** **83**

Rather pale colour but sharply scented, gamey nose with a particular note of venison. The bouquet is confirmed on the palate, along with fairly full body and good tannin. Keep a little longer. (1982) ✔ Bordeaux Rouge and Rosé.
☙ Dominique Arnaud, Dom. Arnaud, St-Christoly-de-Blaye, 33920 St-Savin; tel. 57 42 48 24 ⏱ By appt.

CHATEAU BARBE★★

■   23ha   160000   **3** **D** ⬥ ⬙

75 76 79 80 81 **82** **82** 83

The nose is somewhat closed in, but this is a full, rich and satisfying wine that will age well. (1982) ✔ Bordeaux Sec Ch. Barbe, Premières Côtes-de-

Blaye Ch. Pardaillan, Côtes de Bourg Ch. Eyquem Rouge.
🕊 *MM.* Bayle-Carreau, Ch. Eyqueau, Bayon, 33710 Bourg-sur-Gironde; tel. 57 64 32 43 ⟆ Mon.–Fri. 8.00–12.00/14.00–18.00 🕊 GFA du Ch. Barbé.

CHATEAU BERTHENON★

■ 16ha 60000 ③ D ▮ ⬇

74 75 79 **80** **81** *82 ***82**

A discreet red colour, and a fresh nose recalling red fruit. On the palate, frank, full and unexciting, but well made. (1982) ✔ Bordeaux Ch. Berthenon Rosé, Côtes-de-Blaye Blanc Sec, Blaye ou Blayais Mousseux, Other Bordeaux wines.
🕊 Henri Fonz, Ch. Berthenon, 33390 St-Paul-de-Blaye; tel. 57 42 52 24 ⟆ By appt.

CHATEAU BERTINERIE

■ 9ha 55000 ③ D ▮ ⬙ ⬇

Has an appealing, predominantly ruby colour and fruity aromas. To taste it is light and quite easy to drink. (1983)
🕊 Daniel Bantignies, Cubnezais, 33620 Cavignac; tel. 57 68 70 74 ⟆ By appt.

CHATEAU LA BRAULTERIE-PEYRAULT★★

■ 8ha 35000 ③ ⬙

70 **75** 76 77 **78** 79 *█**81** *82 ***82**

A red wine with a hint of orange at the rim. Slightly oak-vanilla on the nose, but not too much. After a warm, round attack, a well-balanced wine. Already pleasant to drink but could take a few more years of bottle age. (1982) ✔ Bordeaux Rosé.
🕊 SCA La Braulterie-Morisset, Ch. La Braulterie, Berson, 33390 Blaye; tel. 57 64 39 51 ⟆ No visitors.

CHATEAU CAP-SAINT-MARTIN★

■ 10ha 60000 ③ D ⬙ ⬇

77 78 79 **81** **82** **82**

A wine which is developing warmth on the nose, with aromas of lightly stewed ripe fruit. (1982)
🕊 Laurent Ardoin, Ch. Cap-St-Martin, St-Martin-Lacaussade, 33390 Blaye; tel. 57 42 13 92 ⟆ Mon.–Fri. 9.00–12.00/15.00–19.00. Closed 23 Sept.–15 Oct.

CHATEAU CAPVILLE★

■ 10ha 60000 ③ D ▮ ⬙ ⬇

61 64 81 *82 ***82** 83

The nose is perhaps a little lacking, although refined and delicate, but the palate is pleasantly full-bodied. (1982)
🕊 *Mme* Janick Bénéteau, Ch. Capville, Cars, 33390 Blaye; tel. 57 42 15 24 ⟆ Daily 8.00–20.00.

CHATEAU LA CASSAGNE-BOUTET

■ 8ha 50000 ③ D ▮ ⬇

79 80 80 81 ⑧② **82**

Dating from the end of the 17th century, the château is built from rubble mixed with clay. The wine has a good red colour and an attractive attack but the finish is somewhat short. (1981)
🕊 *Mme* M.-L. Mirieu de Labarre, Ch. La Cas-

sagne, Cars, 33390 Blaye; tel. 57 42 80 84 ⟆ Tues.–Fri.

CHATEAU LES CHAUMES★

■ 20ha 120000 ③ D ⬙ ⬇

*77 *78 *79 81 **81** 82

A charming wine with a subtle and distinguished nose; round and pleasant in the mouth. Ready to drink now. (1981)
🕊 Robert Parmentier, Ch. les Chaumes, Fours, 33390 Blaye; tel. 57 42 18 44 ⟆ By appt. Closed Dec.

DOMAINE DU CHAY★

■ 14ha 75000 ③ D ▮ ⬙ ⬇

*81 ***81** *82 ***82** *83

A pleasant wine, round and well balanced, but it will age quite quickly. (1982)
🕊 Guy Bénéteau, Dom. du Chay, Cars, 33390 Blaye; tel. 57 42 15 24 ⟆ Daily 8.00–20.00.

CHATEAU CONE-TAILLASSON★★

■ 3ha 20000 ③ D ⬙ ⬇

64 76 80 81 ⑧② **82** 83

Pleasant colour, quite a delicate nose and good balance: the wine has both elegance and distinction. (1982)
🕊 *MM.* Sabourin Frères, Ch. Crusquet-Sabourin, Cars, 33390 Blaye; tel. 57 42 15 27 ⟆ Mon.–Fri. 9.00–12.00/14.00–19.00. Closed last week in Dec.

CHATEAU CRUSQUET DE LA GARCIE★★★

■ 20ha 120000 ③ D ⬙ ⬇

78 *⑧② ***82** 83

Deep red colour and refined, intense nose. A good bottle, full-bodied and round, with oak-vanilla and tannin harmoniously and elegantly balanced. (1982)
🕊 GFA des Vignobles de la Garcie, Ph. de Lagarcie, 33390 Blaye; tel. 57 42 15 21 ⟆ By appt.

CHATEAU CRUSQUET-SABOURIN★★

■ 7ha 45000 ③ D ⬙ ⬇

79 80 81 ⑧② **82**

Strong ruby colour and an intense, cooked nose; the first impressions on the palate are of warmth and fullness, followed by a slight bitterness which will mellow with time. Should age well. (1982) ✔ Côtes de Blaye Cône Taillasson Sabourin, Médoc Lemoine-Lafon-Rochet Rouge, Bordeaux Clairac Charmille Rosé.
🕊 Sté Sabourin Frères, Ch. Crusquet-Sabourin,

Cars, 33390 Blaye; tel. 57 42 15 27 ☎ Mon.–Fri. 9.00–12.00/14.00–19.00. Closed last week of the year.

CHATEAU L'ESCADRE★★

■   82ha   150 000   **3** D ❖ ⬇
77 79 81 ⑧② **82**

A dark ruby wine with deep purple tints and a nose that is delicate as well as warm and powerful, with a venison-like scent. On the palate, generous, full and fleshy. (1982)
🕯 Sté G. Carreau et Fils, Ch. L'Escadre, Cars, 33390 Blaye; tel. 57 42 15 18 ☎ Mon.–Sat. 8.00–12.00/14.30–19.30. Closed 15–31 Aug.

CHATEAU FOUCHE

□   2ha   15 000   **2** D ⬛ ⬇
82 *83 **83**

Pale yellow and crystal-clear. Subtle nose. In the mouth, quite round, with a touch of acidity. Perhaps a little old for a Blaye white, which should be drunk within a couple of years of harvest. (1982)
🕯 Jean Bonnet, Ch. Haut-Guiraud, St-Ciers-de-Caresse, 33710 Bourg-sur-Gironde; tel. 57 42 17 39 ☎ By appt.

CHATEAU GARDUT-HAUT-CLUZEAU

■   13.5ha   60 000   **3** D ⬛ ❖ ⬇
77 78 79 **81 82 82 83** 83

Attractive colour but the nose is still closed-in. Slight harshness on the palate due to tannin that needs time to soften. (1981) ✔ Bordeaux Rosé Ch. Gardut, other Côtes de Blaye wines.
🕯 J.-A. and J.-C. Revaire, Ch. Gardut, Cars, 33390 Blaye; tel. 57 42 30 35 ☎ By appt.

CHATEAU GARDUT★

■   13ha   90 000   **2** D ❖ ⬇
66 70 75 78 81 ⑧② **82** 83

A vineyard that has been selling directly to the consumer since before 1940. An attractive wine with a flowery nose and complex flavour. (1982)
🕯 J.-A. et J.-C. Revaire, Ch. Gardut, Cars, 33390 Blaye; tel. 57 42 20 35 ☎ Daily 8.00–13.00/14.00–20.00.

CHATEAU LE GRAND MAZEROLLES★

■   10ha   70 000   **3** D ⬛ ❖ ⬇
82 **82** 83

A cherry-red colour of medium intensity and a discreet but detectable nose for this agreeable, easy-to-drink wine. (1982)
🕯 Claude Rigal, Ch. le Grand Mazerolles, Cars, 33390 Blayes; tel. 57 42 86 68 ☎ By appt.

CHATEAU GRILLET-BEAUSEJOUR

■   8ha   40 000   **3** D ⬛ ⬇
76 80 81 82 **82** 83

Dark ruby-red in colour. A tannic attack followed by a well-balanced and fairly round palate. (1982) ✔ Blayais Ch. Grillet-Beausejour Blanc Sec, Blayais Clos de Belle Brune Mousseux.
🕯 Jean-Jacques Jullion, Ch. Grillet-Beausejour, Berson, 33390 Blaye; tel. 57 42 52 16 ☎ By appt. Closed during harvests.

CHATEAU HAUT-NODEAU★

■   11ha   70 000   **2** D ⬛ ⬇
75 79 81 **82 82**

This medium-red wine may still lack a little fullness, but it has a subtle nose and is lightly tannic in the mouth. (1982) ✔ Bordeaux Rosé.
🕯 M. et *Mme* N. et *M.* Grillet, Ch. Haut-Nodeau, Cars, 33390 Blaye; tel. 57 42 25 59 ☎ No visitors.

CHATEAU LARDIERE★

■   10ha   60 000   **2** D ⬛ ⬇
⑦⑤ 77 79 *81 **82** 83

Good, red colour with orange edges. Nose displays the characteristics of the Cabernet-Sauvignon grape (artichoke followed by roast coffee). In the mouth, it is tannic and solid. Needs to wait a few years more. (1982)
🕯 René Bernard, Ch. Lardière, Marcillac, 33860 Reignac; tel. 57 32 41 38 ☎ By appt. Closed Oct.

CHATEAU LOUMEDE★

■   10ha   60 000   **2** D ⬛ ❖ ⬇
76 78 80 81 *82 *82 *83 84

Produced by a château that is really a small hamlet, this wine has a somewhat dry finish but a deep colour, and a well-balanced, round and smooth palate. (1982)
🕯 Louis Raynaud, 33390 Blaye; tel. 57 42 16 39 ☎ By appt.

CHATEAU MARINIER★

■   15ha   90 000   **2** D ⬛ ⬇
74 75 79 ⑧② **82** 83

Garnet-red colour showing little age yet; very smooth palate, but lacking a little in body. Should make pleasant drinking for the next three years. (1982)
🕯 Thierry Cotet, Dom. Marinier, Cezac, 33620 Cavignac; tel. 57 68 63 13 ☎ Daily 8.00–19.00.

CHATEAU LES MOINES★★

■   21ha   190 000   **3** D ❖ ⬇
76 78 **78** *82 *82 **83**

Attractive ruby colour; the nose still a little closed in; on the palate smooth, well balanced – better still, well resolved – with a lasting finish. (1982)
🕯 Jean et Alain Carreau, Ch. les Moines, 33390 Blaye: tel. 57 42 12 91 ☎ By appt.

CHATEAU DES MONTS

■   6ha   40 000   **3** D ⬛ ❖ ⬇
⑧③

Although it is somewhat dried-out on the palate, one cannot fail to appreciate its attractive, promising colour, and its ripe, fruit aromas. (1981) ✔ Côtes de Bourg Ch. Donis.
🕯 Michel Bertin, Ch. Donis, Lansac, 33710 Bourg-sur-Gironde; tel. 57 68 41 04 ☎ No visitors.

CHATEAU PENAUD★★

■   6ha   32 500   **3** D ⬛ ❖ ⬇
77 78 79 **80 82 82 83**

Lovely red colour, followed by a pleasantly fruity nose that is quite firm and high in alcohol. The whole blends together well and is well-balanced despite a somewhat austere finish. A wine to be

laid down. (1983) ✔ Other Côtes de Blaye wines
⊶ Sergé Pénaud, La Lande, St-Aubin-de-Blaye, 33820 St-Ciers-sur-Gironde; tel. 57 64 71 70 ♈ By appt.

CHATEAU PERENNE OUDINOT★

■		35ha	200000		**3**	■ ↓
★80	★81	★81	★82	★82	83	83

Light, fruity bouquet. Well balanced and consistent, with a long finish. (1982)
⊶ M. et P. Oudinot, Ch. Perenne Oudinot, St-Gênes-de-Blaye, 33390 Blaye; tel. 57 42 18 25 ♈ By appt. Closed Sun.

DOMAINE DES PETITS

■		20ha	40000		**3**	D ■ ↓
77	78	79	80	82		

This vineyard has been cultivated by the same family since at least 1750, and produces a light coloured, almost ethereal wine with a cinnamon and spice nose; should be drunk very soon. (1979) ✔ Bordeaux Sec. Ch. Lussier.
⊶ M. et Mme. Chapard-Truffeau, Dom. des Petits, Cars, 33390 Blaye; tel. 57 42 19 09. ♈ By appt.

CHATEAU LES PETITS ARNAUDS★★

■		23ha	110000		**3**	D ⑾ ↓
73	77	79	79	81	83	

A warm, round, delicate and fruitily aromatic wine. Pleasant drinking now, it should not be kept waiting too long. (1982) ✔ Blayais Ch. les Petits Arnauds Blanc Sec, Bordeaux Ch. les Petits Arnauds Blanc Moelleux.
⊶ Sté G. Carreau et Fils, Ch. l'Escadre, Cars, 33390 Blaye; tel. 57 42 15 18 ♈ Mon.–Sat. 8.00–12.30/14.30–19.30. Closed 15–31 Aug.

CHATEAU PEYREYRE★★

■		18ha	100000		**3**	D ⑾ ↓
79	80	81	82	82		

A classy but unpretentious wine with a full, intense nose; quite smooth, fleshy and delicately woody on the palate. Already pleasant to drink. (1982) ✔ Bordeaux Ch. Peyreyre Rosé.
⊶ Michel Trinque, Ch. Peyreyre, St-Martin La Caussade, 33390 Blaye; tel. 57 42 18 57 ♈ Mon.–Fri. 9.00–12.00/14.00–18.00.

CHATEAU DE REBOUQUET-LA-ROUQUETTE★

■		10ha	45000		**3**	D ■ ↓
81	82	83	83			

An as yet undeveloped nose and somewhat rough attack are followed by a full body and plenty of tannin, both characteristics of a wine that will age and develop well. (1982)
⊶ J.-F. Braud, Ch. Rebouquet-la-Rouquette, Berson, 33390 Blaye; tel. 57 64 35 06 ♈ Mon.–Sat. 9.00–12.00/14.00– 19.00.

CHATEAU LA RIVALERIE★

■		27ha	200000		**3**	■ ⑾ ↓
★82	★82	★83				

Although the wine has a delicate nose of strawberries and raspberries, the palate is a little austere. But the vineyard is being totally replanted and the wine is worth watching. (1982)

⊶ SCEA La Rivalérie, St-Paul, 33390 Blaye; tel. 57 42 18 84 ♈ By appt.

CHATEAU LES ROCHES

■		8ha	50000		**2**	D ■ ↓
79	80	80	81	81	82	82	★83

The nose is as yet only partially developed, but the wine is light and tannic, and represents good value for money. (1980)
⊶ Jean-Michel Roche, Le Thil, Cars, 33390 Blaye; tel. 57 42 03 37 ♈ No visitors.

CHATEAU ROLAND LA GARDE★

■		20ha	120000		**3**	D ■ ↓
76	★81	★81	★82	82		

Beautiful red colour; warm and round on the palate; is a powerful wine with a good future. It owes its name to the legend of Roland, who is supposed to have thrown his sword, Durandal, into the River Gironde from this spot. (1982)
⊶ Olivier Martin, Ch. Roland La Garde, St-Seurin-de-Cursac, 33390 Blaye; tel. 57 42 18 04 ♈ Daily 9.00–19.00.

CHATEAU SOCIONDO★

■		9ha	60000		**3**	D ■ ⑾ ↓
★81	★82	★82				

Dating from the Middle Ages, this estate offers a garnet-red wine as yet somewhat unresolved, but basically well constituted. (1982)
⊶ Michel Elie, Av. de Ferrard, Berson, 33390 Blaye; tel. 57 64 33 61 ♈ By appt.

CHATEAU TAYAT★

■		6ha	40000		**3**	D ■ ↓
75	76	78	79	81	82	83

A well-balanced brick-red wine, despite some rather predominant earthy flavours that should mellow with age. (1982) ✔ Côtes de Blaye Blanc Sec.
⊶ Guy et Bernard Favereaud, Ch. Tayat, Cezac, 33620 Cavignac; tel. 57 68 62 10 ♈ Mon.–Sat. 9.00–19.00.

CHATEAU LE VIROU★

□		4ha	12000		**3**	■ ↓
77	78	79	82	83	84	

Pale colour with just a few hints of brightness; pleasant grapey aromas on the nose and holds together well in the mouth. In all a very distinctive wine of its type. (1984) ✔ Côtes de Blaye Ch. le Virou Rouge.
⊶ GFA du Ch. du Virou, St-Girons-d'Aiguevives, 33920 St-Savin; tel. 56 88 34 02 ♈ No visitors.

Côtes de Bourg

The village of Bourg-sur-Gironde is the centre of the Côtes de Bourg appellation. The high clay content of the vineyard area – resulting in clay-limestone and clay-gravel soils – gives wines of marked local character.

The red wines have a high proportion of Merlot grapes, giving their characteristic colour and red-fruit nose, with enough tannin to age well. The few white wines that are produced under this appellation are in general dry, with a bouquet strongly marked by the soil.

CHATEAU DE BARBE*

■		58 ha	300 000	4 D ■ ↓

⑦⑤ 76 79 *80 81 *82 83

A harmonious and distinctive wine, whose discreet nose is evocative of cooked fruit, almost of jam. The palate is warm, tannic and has plenty of matter. (1982)
•┑ Savary de Beauregard, Ch. de Barbe, Villeneuve-de-Blaye, 33710 Bourg-sur-Gironde; tel. 57 64 80 51 ☨ By appt.

CHATEAU BEGOT★★

■		11 ha	60 000	2 D ■

78 79 80 81 ⑧② 83

A deep purple-red wine with a powerfully ripe-fruit nose. Fleshy, fat and quite long, it will improve further with age. (1981)
•┑ Alain Gracia, Ch. Bégot, Lansac, 33710 Bourg-sur-Gironde; tel. 57 68 42 14 ☨ By appt.

DOMAINE DE BOUCHE

■		6 ha	36 000	3 D ◫ ↓

77 78 81 82 83

The wine has a good colour, if a little overdeveloped. Woody and vinous and fresh on the palate; finish is a little dry. (1982)
•┑ Marc Robert, Tauriac, 33710 Bourg-sur-Gironde; tel. 57 68 41 12 ☨ Tues.–Sat. 8.00–12.00/14.00–18.00. Closed on public holidays.

CHATEAU DU BOUSQUET*

■		55 ha	143 000	3 D ◫ ↓

70 75 78 81 *82 *83

Good, red-colour edged with the slightest deep-purple border. Smooth, round, well balanced and slightly tannic, with a delicate woodiness. Already very pleasant, and needs to be drunk young. (1983)
•┑ M. Lacoste, Sté Civile du Ch. du Bousquet, 33710 Bourg-sur-Gironde; tel. 56 95 29 92 ☨ By appt.

CHATEAU BRULESCAILLE★★★

■		15 ha	75 000	3 D ■ ↓

75 78 81 81 *⑧② 82 83

Exceptional finesse. Progresses well towards a firework display of smooth and flowery tannins. (1982)
•┑ MM. Rodet et Recapet, Ch. Brulescaille, Tauriac, 33710 Bourg-sur-Gironde; tel. 57 68 40 31 ☨ By appt. Closed 15–28 Aug. •┑ Jacques Rodet.

CHATEAU CIVRAC

■		15 ha	75 000	3 D ■ ↓

70 75 78 *79 ⑧① 81 *82

An attractive 16th-century residence where traditional methods of production are followed. The wine has a pretty colour and a delicate nose but is possibly a little short. (1981) ✔ Bordeaux Ch. Lacroix-de-Millorit Rosé.
•┑ GFA Lacroix-de-Millorit, Bayon, 33710 Bourg-sur-Gironde; tel. 57 64 84 13 ☨ By appt.

CHATEAU DE LA CLOTTE-BLANCHE

■		11 ha	60 000	3 D ■ ◫ ↓

75 78 79 *80 *81 *82

Supple and round, this wine has some tannin, but should nevertheless be drunk while fairly young. (1981)
•┑ Gérard Bergeon, Ch. de la Clotte-Blanche, 33710 Bourg-sur-Gironde; tel. 57 68 47 67 ☨ By appt.

CHATEAU CONILH-LIBARDE★★

■		5 ha	23 000	3 D ■ ↓

75 78 79 *81 ⑧② 82

Lovely, bright red colour; a smooth wine with a flowery and fruity nose and a promising flavour. (1982)
•┑ Mme Bernier et Fils, Ch. Conilh, 33710 Bourg-sur-Gironde; tel. 57 68 30 10 ☨ Tues.–Sat. 9.00–12.30/15.00–19.00.

CHATEAU CROUTE-COURPON★★

■		8 ha	40 000	3 D ■ ↓

*73 *73 *74 75 78 *⑧② *82

Rustic and solid, this is a wine with a distinctive, earthy, redcurrant nose. Pleasantly smooth on the palate with a faint taste of cooked prunes. (1982) ✔ Bordeaux Supérieur Ch. Croute-Courpon Rouge.
•┑ Jean-Paul Morin, Ch. Croute-Courpon, 33710 Bourg-sur-Gironde; tel. 57 68 42 81 ☨ By appt. Closed 15 Aug.–15 Sept.

CHATEAU CROUTE-MALLARD

■		4 ha	3 000	2 D ■ ◫ ↓

⑦⓪ 73 75 78 79 81 82

This estate is next to Ch. Gros Moulin, and shares the same owner. The wine is discreetly aromatic and will be enjoyed by those who like a very light style. (1979)

♠ Pierre-Max Eymas, Ch. Croute-Mallard, 33710 Bourg-sur-Gironde; tel. 57 68 41 56 ⍨ By appt.

CHATEAU DONIS★

| ■ | | 14ha | 42000 | 3 D ⬛ ⬛ ↧ |

⑦ 78 79 81 82

Although the wine's colour is still bright, it is beginning to show some age. Should not be kept waiting too long if its present qualities are not to disappear. (1979)
♠ Michel Bertin. Ch. Donis, Lansac, 33710 Bourg-sur-Gironde; tel. 57 68 41 04 ⍨ By appt.

CHATEAU EYQUEM★

| ■ | | 28ha | 190000 | 3 D ⬛ ↧ |

75 76 79 80 81 **82** 82 83

A wine with a strawberry-raspberry nose and a pleasing palate. (1981) ✔ Premières Côtes de Blaye Ch. Barbé Rouge, Premières Côtes de Blaye Ch. Pardaillan Rouge, Premières Côtes de Blaye Ch. la Carelle Rouge, Bordeaux Ch. Barbé Blanc Sec.
♠ *MM.* Bayle-Carreau, Ch. Eyquem, Bayon, 33710 Bourg-sur-Gironde; tel. 57 64 32 43 ⍨ By appt. ♠ *M.* et *Mme* Claude Carreau.

CHATEAU FOUGAS★

| ■ | | 11ha | 63000 | 3 D ⬛ ↧ |

★77 78 79 80 81 ⑧ **82** 83

The owners of this château caused a stir by initiating the idea of 'vines to rent'; their wine possesses a quite delicate though somewhat closed-in nose, a rough attack and good balance and finish. (1982)
♠ Jean-Yves Béchet, Ch. Fougas, Lansac, 33710 Bourg-sur-Gironde; tel. 57 68 42 15 ⍨ Mon.–Sat. 8.00–12.00/14.00–20.00.

CHATEAU GENIBON★★

| ■ | | 4ha | 23000 | 3 ⬛ ↧ |

75 78 79 ★83

A small family vineyard typical of the Côtes de Bourg. The wine lacks a little strength, but has a delicate bouquet and is forthright, quite round and rich on the palate. (1983) ✔ Bordeaux Supérieur Ch. Haute-Sauvetat Rouge.
♠ Yves Arnaud, Av. Daléau, 33710 Bourg-sur-Gironde; tel. 57 68 45 89 ⍨ No visitors.

CHATEAU DE LA GRAVE★★★

| ■ | | 40ha | 239976 | 3 D ⬛ ↧ |

79 81 ⑧ **82** 83

Restored during the 19th century in the style of Louis XIII, this château is one of the most beautiful in the Bourg region. The wine is worthy of the estate: its bouquet, already well balanced, will develop further; on the palate tannic, closed and perhaps somewhat angular – a wine with a great future. (1982)
♠ *M.* Bassereau, Ch. de la Grave, 33710 Bourg-sur-Gironde; tel. 57 68 41 49 ⍨ Mon.–Fri. 9.00–19.00. Closed 10–31 Aug.

CHATEAU GROS-MOULIN

| ■ | | 24ha | 150000 | 4 D ⬛ ↧ |

75 78 79 **81** ★⑧ ★**82**

A light colour and subtle aromas both suggest a wine that is still young. (1981)
♠ P.-M. et J. Eymas, Ch. Gros-Moulin, 33710 Bourg-sur-Gironde; tel. 57 68 41 56 ⍨ By appt.

CHATEAU GUERRY★★

| ■ | | 22ha | 100000 | 3 D ⬛ ↧ |

75 78 80 81 ⑧ 83

A typical Bordeaux; solid yet easy to drink that deserves some bottle age.
♠ SC du Ch. Guerry, Dom. du Ribet, Tauriac, 33710 Bourg-sur-Gironde; tel. 57 68 41 31 ⍨ By appt.

CHATEAU GUIRAUD-CHEVAL-BLANC

| ■ | | 13ha | 100000 | 3 D ⬛ ↧ |

70 72 75 78 79 ⑧ 81 ★82

Clear Bordeaux colour; the nose, with its aromas of spices and cocoa, proves that finesse can be combined with a certain richness. A light yet tannic wine on the palate. (1983) ✔ Côtes-de-Bourg, Ch. Nicoleau.
⍨ Bernard Deliaune, Dom. de Nicoleau, St-Ciers-de-Canesse, 33710 Bourg-sur-Gironde; tel. 57 42 03 00 ⍨ By appt.

CHATEAU HAUT-CASTENET

| ■ | | 9ha | 50000 | 3 D ⬛ ↧ |

70 72 75 78 79 80 81 ★82

Clear red in colour: a good bottle for those fond of a lighter style of wine. Drink now. (1981)
♠ Pierre Audouin, Ch. Haut-Castenet, Samonac, 33710 Bourg-sur-Gironde; tel. 57 64 36 15 ⍨ By appt.

179

CHATEAU HAUT-GUIRAUD★★

■   24ha   150000   **3** D ▯ ◫ ⬛

70 75 79 ★81 ⑧② ▨ 83

A large vineyard for the Bourg appellation; the wine has a good red colour, a subtle nose and a good attack. Smooth, round, rich and harmonious, it should age well. (1982)
⟟ Jean Bonnet, Ch. Haut-Guiraud, St-Ciers-de-Canesse, 33710 Bourg-sur-Gironde; tel. 57 42 17 39 ☖ Mon.–Fri. 9.00–11.00/14.00–18.00.

CHATEAU HAUT-MACO★★

■   25ha   125000   **3** D ▯ ⬛

75 78 79 ⑧② ▨ 83

Orange shades in the colour suggest that this wine is developing quickly. It has a berry nose (especially reminiscent of blackcurrants) and is smooth at first then long, soft and delightfully drinkable. (1982) ✔ Bordeaux Dom. de Lilotte Rouge.
⟟ GAEC Mallet Frères, Tauriac, 33710 Bourg-sur-Gironde; tel. 57 68 81 26 ☖ By appt.

CHATEAU LACROIX-DAVIDS★

■   30ha   190000   **2** D ▯ ◫ ⬛

79 81 ★82 ★▨ ★83 ★84

Attractive red colour, with an already well-developed bouquet, but still has a faint bitterness, as one would expect from a young wine. It is pleasing now but needs to mellow further. (1982)
⟟ André Birot, 55 Rue Valentin-Bernard, 33710 Bourg-sur-Gironde; tel. 57 68 40 05 ☖ By appt.

CHATEAU LAMOTHE

■   20ha   110000   **3** D ◫ ⬛

78 ⑦⑨ 81 82

Refined and delicate bouquet but modest on the palate. Drink now. (1982)
⟟ Pierre Pessonnier, Ch. Lamothe, Lansac, Bourg-sur-Gironde 33710; tel. 57 68 41 07 ☖ By appt.

CHATEAU LIDONNE★★★

■   18ha   110000   **3** D ▯ ⬛

75 78 79 ▨⓪ 81 ⑧② 83

The monks who once owned this inn on the road to Compostelle and put a shell (the symbol of St-Jacques de Compostelle), carved out of a barrel, on the door. With intense ripe fruit on the nose, this is nicely robust, well balanced, solid and very long on the palate. (1982)
⟟ Roger Audoire, Ch. de Lidonne, 33710 Bourg-sur-Gironde; tel. 57 68 47 52 ☖ Daily 8.00–20.00.

CHATEAU LION-NOIR★★

■   6ha   32000   **3** D ▯ ◫

70 75 81 ▨

Attractively ruby-red, this wine gives off a pleasant and powerful aroma. Well balanced and lightly woody; a good wine but one that will not benefit much from being laid down. (1981)
⟟ Michel Cosyns, Ch. Grand-Launay, Teuillac, 33710 Bourg-sur-Gironde; tel. 57 64 39 03 ☖ By appt. Closed Aug.

CHATEAU LA MONGE★

■   12ha   80000   **3** D ▯ ⬛

74 75 76 78 81 **82** ⑧③

Cherry-coloured wine, with a nose of red fruit blended with a strong gamey aroma. The palate is similar in flavour, combined with a slight hint of truffle. A direct, tannic wine with a fine attack. (1980) ✔ AOC Côtes de Bourg Ch. le Mayne Rouge, Bordeaux Supérieur AOC Ch. Beausoleil Rouge.
⟟ GAEC Bourdillas, Tauriac, 33710 Bourg-sur-Gironde; tel. 57 68 22 46 ☖ By appt.

CHATEAU MONTAIGUT★

■   15ha   90000   **3** D ▯ ⬛

75 78 80 ⑧① ★82 ★▨ 83

An intensely coloured wine that is easy to drink. Fruity nose; smooth and light. (1982)
⟟ François de Pardieu, St-Ciers-de-Canesse, 33410 Bourg-sur-Gironde; tel. 57 42 17 49 ☖ By appt.

CHATEAU MOULIN-DES-GRAVES

□   2ha   12000   **2** D ▯ ⬛

A moderately Sauvignon nose, but a bit short on the palate; an impression of fluidity despite a slightly acidic feel.
⟟ Robert Bost, Ch. Moulin-des-Graves, Teuillac, 33710 Bourg-sur-Gironde; tel. 57 64 39 41 ☖ By appt.

CHATEAU NODOZ-MAGDELEINE★

■   15ha   92000   **3** D ▯ ◫ ⬛

75 78 ★81 ★82 ★▨

Made at the Tauriac cooperative, this wine is dark red with a concentrated, grapey and somewhat cooked nose and a nicely balanced palate. (1982)
⟟ Cave Coop. de Tauriac, Tauriac, 33310 Bourg-sur-Gironde; tel. 57 68 41 12 ☖ By appt.

LE CLOS DU NOTAIRE★

■   13ha   68000   **3** D ▯ ◫ ⬛

78 79 81 ★⑧② ★▨ ★83

Overlooking the confluence of the rivers Dordogne and Garonne, this property produces a wine with a fairly powerful and spicy nose, while on the palate it is round, supple and agreeable. (1982) ✔ Côtes de Bourg Ch. le Croix-de-Bel-Air Rouge.
⟟ Roland Charbonnier, Clos du Notaire, 33710 Bourg-sur-Gironde; tel. 57 68 44 36 ☖ By appt. Closed second fortnight in Aug.

CHATEAU DE PIAT★

■   7ha   42000   **3** D ▯ ◫ ⬛

75 78 ★81 ★82 ★▨

A fine, deep red colour and a nose with rich perfumes of red fruit. Although it may be a little hard on the palate, this wine has a pleasing attack, good tannin and some length. (1982)
⟟ François Lisse, Ch. de Tauriac, Tauriac, 33370 Bourg-sur-Gironde; tel. 57 68 41 12 ☖ By appt.

CHATEAU POYANNE

■   17ha 100000   **3** **D** ▪ ⌄

78 79 81 82 83

Although this wine is slightly inferior to the Château de Thau, produced by the same grower, it has a delicate and discreet bouquet and is round and warm on the palate. (1982)
➦ Léopold Schweitzer et Fils, Ch. de Thau, Gauriac, 33710 Bourg-sur-Gironde; tel. 57 64 80 79 ⍭ By appt.

CHATEAU LES ROCQUES*

■   14ha 65000   **3** **D** ▪ ⌄

81 *(82)* *82* 83

Brick-red colour; the nose is maybe a little thin, but pleasant, and the palate is quite clean with a hint of astringency. (1981) ✔ Bordeaux Supérieur St-Ignan, Bordeaux Supérieur Blanc Moelleux, Bordeaux Blanc Sec.
➦ *MM.* Feillon Frères, St-Seurin-de-Bourg, 33710 Bourg-sur-Gironde; tel. 57 68 42 82 ⍭ Daily 9.00–19.00.

CHATEAU ROUSSET**

■   23ha 150000   **3** **D** ▪ ⌄

(79) 80 81 82 83

The house itself, formerly the property of a noble family, is of interest. Its wine has an attractive colour, a powerful nose and considerable finesse; to be laid down. (1982)
⍭ Jean Tesseire, Ch. Rousset, Samonac, 33710 Bourg; tel. 57 68 46 34 ⍭ By appt. Closed 15 Aug.–15 Sept.; 24 Dec.–2 Jan.

CHATEAU SAUMAN*

■   22ha 132000   **3** **D** ◖ ⌄

79 **80** (82) 83

Rustic but honest, creating a good first impression with its deep, clear colour. The nose is a little farmyardy, but the wine is well made with clean, straightforward tannin. It will reach its peak in two or three years. (1981)
➦ Jean Kressmann, 35 Rue de Bordeaux, Parempuyre, 33290 Blanquefort; tel. 56 35 84 64 ⍭ By appt.

CHATEAU TAYAC*

■   20ha 120000   **4** **D** ▪ ◖ ⌄

75 78 **78** (82)

Despite a still-delicate bouquet, this vintage is already old and a little tired, and should be drunk soon. Hardly representative of the usual quality of this property. (1971)
➦ Pierre Saturny, SC du Ch.Tayac, St-Seurin-de-Bourg, 33710 Bourg-sur-Gironde; tel. 57 68 40 60 ⍭ Mon.–Sat. 9.00–12.30/14.30–20.00. Closed Sun. and holidays except by appt.

CHATEAU DE THAU*

▪   41ha 130000   **3** **D** ▪ ⌄

78 79 *81 *82 *82

Dating from the Middle Ages, this château is said to be haunted at night by a werewolf! Fortunately the wine is friendlier, with a bouquet of cooked fruit and a round and supple palate. (1982)
➦ Léopold Schweitzer et Fils, Ch. du Thau, Gauriac, 33710 Bourg-sur Gironde; tel. 57 64 80 79 ⍭ By appt.

The Libournais Appellations

Although there is no Libourne appellation as such, the Libournais is a real area, with Libourne at its centre and the River Dordogne running through it. It is quite different from the rest of the Gironde, depending less directly on the metropolitan centre, Bordeaux. Significantly, the adjective 'Libournais', as distinct from 'Bordelais', is often used to describe the less ostentatious architecture of the local wine as well as the inhabitants of chateaux, Corrèze (the department to the east of Bordeaux) and their role in the Libourne wine trade.

But what really makes the Libournais vineyards different is the sheer density of planting. Beginning right outside the town, they extend almost without a break over several very famous communes, such as Fronsac, Pomerol and St-Emilion. The area is divided up into hundreds of fairly small properties, a far cry from the large estates of Médoc or the wide expanses of Aquitaine.

The individuality of the Libournais also extends to the choice of grape varieties used. Merlot is the most common grape variety, giving the wines their richness and warmth. These wines, however, mature more rapidly than those which have a predominance of Cabernet-Sauvignon. They do, of course, have the advantage that they can be drunk a little younger. They also go well with many different foods – red or white meat, cheese, and some fish, such as lamprey.

Fronsac and Canon-Fronsac

Bordered by the Dordogne and Isle rivers, the area around Fronsac offers beautiful scenery, fine churches and châteaus, a rich and fascinating history – and a distinctive style in wine. The old-established vineyards of the Fronsadais produce rich, fruity, full-bodied reds with a characteristic edge. Six villages are allowed to use the Fronsac appellation, but only the hillsides of Fronsac itself and St-Michel-de-Fronsac may produce Canon-Fronsac,

The Libournais Appellations

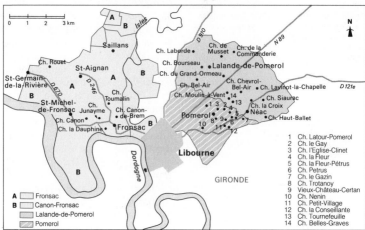

grown in clay-limestone soils on a bed of star limestone. Total annual production of Fronsac is 5.4 million bottles, that of Canon-Fronsac 2 million.

Canon-Fronsac

CHATEAU CANON*

■   10ha   48000   ▣ Ⓓ ▮ ⑪ ↓
⑲ ⑲ 83

A wine with a straightforward style and a nose reminiscent of pebbles; warm and tannic on the palate. (1979)
↱ René de Coninck, Ch. Canon, 33145 St-Michel-de-Fronsac; tel. 57 51 06 07 Ⴤ By appt. ↱ *Mlle* Henriette Horeau.

CHATEAU CANON-DE-BREM***

■   10ha   104000   ▣ Ⓓ ⑪ ↓
66 70 71 **75** 76 **78 81** ⑧ ⑧ **83**

A superb colour – sombre, deep yet brilliant. The bouquet is powerful and subtly complex; smoky and spicy with a hint of tobacco. To taste it has attractive depth, and is meaty and full-bodied. Should age very well; in a few years you will uncork a quite remarkable bottle. (1982) ✔ Fronsac, other Canon-Fronsac wines.
↱ SCEA du la Ch. Dauphine, 33216 Fronsac; tel. 57 52 64 44 Ⴤ By appt.

CHATEAU CAP-ET-BEGAUD*

■   4ha   13000   ▣ Ⓓ ⑪ ↓
75 76 77 80 *⑧* ⑧ 82 83

A solid but rather tough wine, with a rich, honest colour. Has a rather difficult nose, and to taste, a good, solid attack; well-made and quite tannic.

(1981) ✔ Fronsac Ch. Bourdieu-Lavalade, other Canon-Fronsac wines.
↱ Alain Roux, Ch. Coustolle, 33126 Fronsac; tel. 57 51 31 25 Ⴤ By appt.

CHATEAU CASSAGNE-HAUT-CANON**

■   9ha   48000   ▣ Ⓓ ⑪ ↓
79 ⑧ 81 ⑧

With an aroma of dried fruit and almonds, this wine has an attractive attack to the palate, where it is generous and lingering. Should age well. (1981) ✔ Pomerol Ch. La Ganne.
↱ Jean-Jacques Dubois, Ch. Cassagne-Haut-Canon, 33145 St-Michel-de-Fronsac; tel. 57 51 63 98 Ⴤ By appt. Closed Aug.

CHATEAU COUSTOLLE**

■   20ha   120000   ▣ Ⓓ ⑪ ↓
70 **75** ⑧ ⑧

This tannic, warm and well-balanced wine has a strikingly clear, bright colour followed by a nose that is both delicate and powerful with a distinct oakiness. ✔ Canon-Fronsac Ch. Capet-Bégaud Rouge, Fronsac Ch. Bourdieu-Lavalade Rouge, Canon-Fronsac Ch. Chêne-de-Gombeau Rouge.
↱ Alain Roux, Ch. Coustolle, 33126 Fronsac; tel. 57 51 31 25 Ⴤ By appt.

CHATEAU GRAND-RENOUIL**

■   7ha   26000   ▣ Ⓓ ▮ ↓
⑲ 80 ⑧

Situated in beautiful rolling country, the château is a little inaccessible; the wine however, is welcoming enough with its 'breakfast' nose (hot toast and coffee . . .). The attack is good, and the finish full. A wine that deserves a few more years' patience. (1982) ✔ Canon-Fronsac.
↱ *M.* Ponty et fils, Ch. du Pavillon, 33126 Fronsac; tel. 57 51 29 57 Ⴤ By appt.

CHATEAU JUNAYME★

■ 16ha 110000 **3** **D** ▮ ◗ ⬥
77 **80** **81** ⑧ **83**

Cherry-red in colour, this wine is light, round and smooth; to be enjoyed while young. (1981)
🕿 René de Coninck, Ch. du Pintey, 33500 Libourne; tel. 57 51 06 07 Ⓨ By appt.

CHATEAU LAFLEUR-CAILLEAU

■ 3ha 18000 **5** **D** ▮ ◗ ⬥
★⑧ ★83

Good colour. Powerful and concentrated nose. Very rich and full-bodied. The finish is a little overpowering. (1982) ✔ Fronsac la Grave.
🕿 Paul Barre, Ch. la Grave, 33126 Fronsac; tel. 57 51 64 95 Ⓨ By appt.

CHATEAU MAZERIS★★★

■ 14ha 72000 **5** **D** ▮ ⬥
59 64 67 70 **79** **81** 82 83

A beautiful, classic-style château and an attractive wine with an extremely powerful nose. Fat and full on the palate; the tannin that is apparent on the attack remains at the finish but is never aggressive. Definitely needs some bottle age.
🕿 Christian de Cournuaud, Ch. Mazeris, 33145 St-Michel-de-Fronsac; tel. 57 51 37 03 Ⓨ By appt.

Produce of France
CHATEAU MAZERIS
CANON FRONSAC
Appellation Canon Fronsac Contrôlée

1979

CHRISTIAN DE COURNUAUD
Propriétaire à Saint-Michel-de-Fronsac (Gironde) France

MIS EN BOUTEILLES AU CHATEAU 75cl.

CHATEAU DU PAVILLON★

■ 4ha 19200 **4** **D** ◗ ⬥
79 80 ⑧

Lovely garnet-red colour, followed by a subtle, ripe-fruit nose. On the palate, the wine has a good attack and is quite well resolved. (1982) ✔ Canon-Fronsac Ch. Grand-Renouil, Bordeaux Supérieur Dom. de l'Esperance Rouge.
🕿 *MM.*Jean Ponty et Fils, Ch. du Pavillon, 33126 Fronsac; tel. 57 51 29 57 Ⓨ By appt. Mon.–Fri.

Fronsac

CHATEAU LES ABORIES-DE-MEYNEY

■ 3ha 20000 **3** **D** ▮ ◗ ⬥
79 **80** 82 83

Dark ruby-red; rich, intense and complex on the nose, with touches of mint and hay. The attack is supple, the palate smooth and lightly tannic. (1982)

Ⓨ Jean-Marie Chaudet, Le Meyney, St-Germain-la-Rivière, 33240 St-André-de-Cubzac; tel. 57 84 46 40 Ⓨ By appt. Closed 15 Aug.–15 Sept.

CHATEAU LA BRANDE

■ 2ha 12000 **3** **D** ▮ ◗ ⬥
⑦ 79 **80** 81 82 83

A very rustic wine with a bright red colour. So tannic that it is almost rough, but it does have a certain strength. (1979) ✔ Bordeaux Supérieur Ch. la Brande Rouge.
🕿 Pierre Beraud, GAEC de la Brande, Saillans, 33141 Villegouge; tel. 57 84 32 88 Ⓨ Mon.–Sat. 8.00–12.00/14.00–18.00.

CHATEAU CARDENEAU★★

■ 13ha 65000 **4** ▮ ⬥
78 81 ★⑧ **83**

Behind a deep and lively colour is a wine with a slightly woody nose; initially tannic, then rich and long on the palate. (1982)
🕿 Jean-Noël Hervé, Ch. Cardeneau, Saillans, 33141 Villegouge; tel. 57 84 32 07 Ⓨ By appt. Closed Oct. and Nov.

CHATEAU CHADENNE★

■ 2ha 12000 **3** **D** ▮
★79 ★81 ★82 ★83

Average colour and nose, but much more pleasant to taste, being rich and meaty with a good balance of tannin. (1982) ✔ Other Fronsac wines.
🕿 Marc Allard, Ch. Haut-Ferrand, St- Aignan, 33126 Fronsac; tel. 57 24 98 62 Ⓨ By appt.

CHATEAU DALEM★

■ 8ha 50000 **4** **D** ▮ ◗
64 67 73 74 75 76 77 78 79 ⑧ **80** 81 82

A wine with an attractive topaz colour and berry nose. Pleasing and delicate initially, it has a full, tannic finish. Should be laid down for a few years. (1979) ✔ Fronsac Ch. de la Huste.
🕿 Michel Rullier, Ch. Dalem, Saillans, 33141 Villegouge; tel. 57 84 34 18 Ⓨ By appt.

CHATEAU LA DAUPHINE★★

■ 20ha 184000 **4** **D** ◗
★79 ★81 ★⑧ ★**82** 83

Attractive colour and powerful nose. Full of character, body, meatiness, and quite full tannin. (1982) ✔ Other Fronsac wines.
🕿 SCEA du Ch. la Dauphine, 33126 Fronsac; tel. 57 51 26 44 Ⓨ By appt.

CHATEAU HAUT-FERRAND★

■ 9ha 50000 **3** ▮
★79 ★81 ★⑧ 83

Medium red colour; bouquet still somewhat closed-in, but an immediately luscious character on the palate, with a tannin background. (1982)
🕿 Marc Allard, Ch. Haut-Ferrand, St-Aignan, 33126 Fronsac; tel. 57 24 98 62 Ⓨ No visitors.

CHATEAU DE LA HUSTE

| ■ | 12 ha | 6500 | 🖩 D ▮ |

64 67 73 74 75 76 77 78 `79` `80` (82) 83

The honest, red colour is quite lively, the nose still a little weak, but to taste the wine is warm and round. Needs to be drunk soon. (1979)
🐦 Michel Rullier, Ch. Dalem, Saillans, 33141 Villegouge; tel. 57 84 34 18 ⏻ By appt.

CHATEAU JEANDEMAN*

| ■ | 22 ha | 143 000 | 🖩 D ▮ ⑪ 🔱 |

*79 *`81` (82) 83

This vineyard is located on one of the highest hills in the region. Rich nose, at first underdeveloped, but which opens up to be heady and quite intense; more richness on the palate, where the wine is quite big, well-made, and finishes well with a light tannin. (1981)
🐦 Roy Trocard, Ch. Jeandeman, St-Aignan, 33126 Fronsac; tel. 57 74 30 52 ⏻ By appt. Closed first fortnight in Aug. and weekends in summer.

CHATEAU MAGONDEAU-BEAUSITE*

| ■ | 2 ha | 20 000 | 🖪 D ▮ ⑪ 🔱 |

75 76 78 79 81 82 83

Deep, brilliant colour; a little too much alcohol on the nose, but not enough to spoil the fine vanilla aromas. Well-made and pleasantly round on the palate, with a slight acidity in the finish which indicates that it will age well. (1982)
🐦 André Goujon, Ch. Magondeau, 33141 Saillans; tel. 57 84 32 02 ⏻ By appt. Closed Sun. during summer.

CHATEAU MAGONDEAU*

| ■ | 14 ha | 100 000 | 🖪 D ▮ ⑪ |

*76 *79 *81 82 83

This brilliant ruby-coloured wine is discreetly aromatic. A certain softness on the palate and finishes with a slightly 'rancio' hint of stewed fruit. Ready to drink now. (1982)
🐦 André Goujon, Ch. Magondeau, 33141 Saillans; tel. 57 84 32 02 ⏻ By appt. Closed Sun. during summer.

CHATEAU MAYNE-VIEIL

| ■ | 24 ha | 140 000 | 🖩 D ▮ 🔱 |

79 80 81 (83)

This estate is unusual; a 16th-century country house with a 17th-century cellar. The ruby-red wine has a cooked fragrance on the nose; on the palate there is a taste of prunes. Should be drunk fairly soon. (1979) ✔ Haut-Médoc Ch. Charmail Cru Bourgeois.
🐦 Roger Sèze, Ch. Mayne-Vieil, 33133 Galgon; tel. 57 74 30 06 ⏻ By appt. Closed second fortnight in Aug.

CHATEAU DU MOULIN-HAUT-LAROQUE★★

| ■ | 13 ha | 80 000 | 🖪 ▮ ⑪ 🔱 |

75 `76` `77` `78` 79 (81) `81` `82` `83`

This estate was ruined by phylloxera in the 19th century, but its owners, the Olier family, worked as coopers and so managed to rebuild it. The wine offered by their successors keeps well, has a powerful nose, and is tannic and well balanced on the palate. (1981)
🐦 Jean-Noël Hervé, Ch. Carderau, Saillans, 33141 Villegouge; tel. 57 84 32 07 ⏻ By appt. Closed Oct. and Nov.

CHATEAU MOULIN-HAUT-VILLARS*

| ■ | 8 ha | 50 000 | 🖪 ▮ 🔱 |

79 `80` (82) 83

A clear, bright colour precedes a flowery, delicate but quite intense nose. Very smooth, perhaps a little flabby on the attack, but this does not spoil the wine's charm. Should be drunk soon. (1982)
🐦 J.-C. Gaudrie, Ch. Moulin-Haut-Villars, Saillans, 33141 Villegouge; tel. 57 84 32 17 ⏻ By appt.

CHATEAU DU MOULIN-MEYNEY*

| ■ | 1 ha | 6000 | 🖩 D ▮ 🔱 |

75 76 *81 *`82` *`83` 84

Although the colour shows some age, the nose is simple and delicate, the palate supple and fine. To drink fairly soon. (1981)
🐦 Jean-Pierre Gazeau, Château du Moulin-Meyney, Saillans, 33141 Villegouge; tel. 57 84 45 11 ⏻ By appt.

CHATEAU PLAIN-POINT*

| ■ | 13 ha | 8400 | 🖪 D ▮ ⑪ 🔱 |

69 70 77 78 `81` 82 83

From a château that retains its feudal towers and chapel comes a pleasing wine that is neither young Nor old but at a delicate age, with a pleasantly vinous nose and an ample palate. (1978)
🐦 Denis Ardon, Château Plain-Point, St-Aignan, 33126 Fronsac; tel. 67 24 96 55 ⏻ Mon.–Fri. 9.00–12.00/14.00–18.00. Closed Aug.

CHATEAU DE LA RIVIERE★★

■   40 ha   180 000   **5** **D** ◖ ⚓

74 78 79 80 **81** 82 ⑧⑨

A Loire-style château perched on the slopes of the Dordogne, La Rivière produces an authentic Gironde wine, with a woody vanilla nose; it has a smooth attack and a development that is round, warm and pleasing. (1979)
↜ J. Borie, Ch. de la Rivière, 33145 St-Michel-de-Fronsac; tel. 57 24 98 01 ⏋ Mon.–Fri. 8.00–11.00/14.00–17.00.

CHATEAU LES ROCHES-DE-FERRAND

■   11 ha   65 000   **3** **D** ▮ ◖ ⚓

*78 *78 *79 *79 *81 *81 *⑧② *82

An attractive deep red. The nose reveals a certain rustic strength and on the palate the wine is warm and tannic. Unfortunately the finish is a little tart. (1982) ✔ Lalande-de-Pomerol Dom. Pont-de-Guestres.
↜ Jean Rousselot et Fils, Dom. du Pont de Guestres; St-Aignan, 33126 Fronsac; tel. 57 24 95 16 ⏋ By appt.

CHATEAU LES TROIS-CROIX★

■   12 ha   65 000   **3** **D** ◖ ⚓

70 75 78 79 80 **81** ⑧②

Both delicate and intense, the nose is typically Merlot, with perfumes of red fruit. If tannin dominates the attack, there is sufficient fruit to support it, but the wine needs ageing. (1982) ✔ Fronsac la Babionne.
↜ Bernard Guillou-Kérédan, Ch. Trois-Croix, 33126 Fronsac; tel. 57 84 32 09 ⏋ By appt. Closed second fortnight in Aug.

CHATEAU LA VIEILLE CURE★★

■   100 000   **4** ▮ ⚓

Fronsac is an appellation which is being deservedly rediscovered. La Vieille Curé 1982 is a crimson garnet in colour with a full, fruity nose, and its good structure suggests that in about four years' time it will have plenty to offer. Nicolas have reserved this wine solely for export to the USA. (1982)
↜ Ets Nicolas, 2 Rue de Valmy, 94220 Charenton; tel. 01 37 59 20 ⏋ No visitors.

CHATEAU VILLARS★★

■   8 ha   50 000   **4** ◖ ⚓

80 81 ⑧② 83

The clear, bright colour of the wine makes a good first impression that is followed by a predominantly oaky nose. On the palate it is enriched but not smothered by a hint of vanilla, and has a good finish, worthy of this long-lasting wine. (1982)
↜ J.-C. Gaudrie, Ch. Moulin-Haut-Villars, Saillans, 33141 Villegouge; tel. 57 84 32 17 ⏋ By appt.

Pomerol

The gentle vineyard slopes of Pomerol run down to the Isle, a tributary of the Dordogne. The vineyards are very old indeed, although for a long time they remained quite small. Vines flourished in the twelfth century, thanks to the Knights of St John who maintained a large residence there, but the vineyards were almost completely destroyed during the Hundred Years' War. Re-established during the fifteenth and sixteenth centuries, they did not really flourish again until the nineteenth century, their fortunes being restored by the Golden Age of viticulture in the Gironde during the third quarter of the last century. Vines now cover 734 hectares and produce more than five million bottles per year.

The range of grape varieties is fairly limited, with a predominance of Merlot (70 per cent) complemented by Bouchet (30 per cent). The incomparable Château Petrus is exceptional in harvesting nearly 100 per cent Merlot. There are several different types of soils, including the clay plateau where some Graves de Vayres is grown, and sandy soils to the west. Nevertheless the wines show an overall similarity of style; warm and powerful bouquets, round and smooth in the mouth, but also full bodied – good wines to lay down. The fuller Pomerols can be very tannic when young.

CHATEAU BEAUREGARD★★

■   13 ha   70 000   **6** **D** ◖ ⚓

77 *78 *80 *81 ⑧②

Slightly minty nose, and harmonious blend of ripe fruit and new wood in the mouth. A delicate, pleasant bottle. (1981)
↜ Héritiers Clauzel, Ch. Beauregard, 33500 Pomerol; tel. 57 51 13 36 ⏋ By appt. Closed July.

185

CHATEAU BELLE-BRISE

■ 3 ha 10000 5 D ▤ ⑴ ↓

70 **75 79** 80 **81** ⑧ **82**

A deep red colour is followed by a pleasant, flowery nose. The wine is tannic and perhaps a little aggressive. (1981)
☛ Michel Lafage, Ch. Belle-Brise, Pomerol, 33500 Libourne; tel. 57 51 16 82 ☎ By appt.

CHATEAU BONALGUE*

■ 5 ha 750000 5 D ▤ ↓

74 75 **76 78** 79 80 81 **82 82 83** 84

Arms, flags and other military paraphernalia adorn the facade of this château, built by an officer in Napoleon's army. The wine is very round and smooth. (1982) ✔ Lalande-Pomerol Ch. Hauts-Conseil, Lussac-St-Emilion Ch. Courlat.
☛ Pierre Bourotte, 28 Rue Trocard, 33500 Libourne; tel. 57 51 20 56 ☎ By appt. Closed 15 July–15 Aug.

CHATEAU LE BON-PASTEUR★★★

■ 8 ha 30000 5 D ⑴ ↓

75 **76 78** 79 80 **81** 82 ⑧ **83**

Very pleasing to the eye, this wine has a generous bouquet with aromas of berries and new wood; on the palate it is fleshy, well balanced and harmonious. (1981)
☛ *Mme* Geneviève Rolland, Maillet, Pomerol, 33500 Libourne; tel. 57 51 10 94 ☎ By appt.

CHATEAU BOURGNEUF-VAYRON★★

■ 9 ha 50000 5 D ▤ ⑴ ↓

79 **79** 80 **81 81** ⑧ **82**

Deep red colour, and gives off ripe fruit aromas that are as complex as they are powerful. On the palate it is well rounded and has good length. (1981)
☛ *MM.* Vayron Père et Fils, Pomerol, 33500 Libourne; tel. 57 51 42 03 ☎ No visitors.

CHATEAU LA CABANNE

■ 10 ha 60000 5 D ⑴ ↓

70 **75 76** 78 **81 82 82**

A wine with an attractive colour and a heavy bouquet; with very little help it could become a great bottle. (1982) ✔ Pomerol Ch. Ht Maillet Rouge, Lalande-de-Pomerol Dom. de Gachet Rouge, St-Emilion Dom. des Gourdins Rouge, Montagne St-Emilion Ch. la Papeterie.
☛ Jean-Pierre Estager, 33–41 Rue de Montau-

don, 33500 Libourne; tel. 57 51 04 09 ☎ By appt. Closed Aug.

CHATEAU CERTAN
De May-de-Certan★★

■ 5 ha 20000 6 D ▤ ↓

80 **80** ⑧

This property was established nearly four centuries ago by a family of Scottish origin. The wine, with aromas of vanilla and liquorice, and fine tannins, leaves an impression of great harmony on the palate. Needs more bottle age. (1982)
✔ Lussac St-Emilion Ch. Poitou.
☛ *Mme* Barreau-Badar, Ch. Certan, Pomerol, 33500 Libourne; tel. 57 51 41 53 ☎ By appt.

CHATEAU GOMBAUDE-GUILLOT*

■ 7 ha 30000 5 D ▤ ↓

69 72 74 76 77 80 **81** ⑧ 83

A straightforward, classic wine with an intense red colour and a warm bouquet. (1982)
☛ S. H. Laval et Filles, Pomerol, 33500 Libourne; tel. 57 51 17 40 ☎ Mon.–Wed. 10.30–16.30.

CLOS DU CLOCHER★★★

■ 6 ha 30000 5 ⑴ ↓

★79 **80** ★81 ⑧ **83**

A lovely ruby-coloured wine with pleasantly pronounced aromas of new wood and a good depth of fruit; eminently likeable. (1981) ✔ Bordeaux Supérieur Rouge.
☛ Jean Audy, 35 Quai du Priouzat, BP 79, 33500 Libourne; tel. 57 51 62 17 ☎ No visitors.

VIEUX CHATEAU CLOQUET★★

■ 2 ha 12000 4 D ⑴ ↓

75 76 78 79 82

Deep ruby in colour, this wine is bright and clear. Its nose is pleasant and elegant; on the palate it has both body and substance. It should age happily and beautifully. (1981)
☛ Pierre Boyer, Vieux-Ch. Cloquet, Pomerol, 33500 Libourne; tel. 57 51 31 41 ☎ No visitors.

CHATEAU CLOS-RENE★★

■ 12 ha 60000 5 D ▤ ↓

72 73 74 **75 76** 77 79 80 **81 82 83** 84

A lovely deep colour introduces this robust and concentrated wine. Has good tannin, ensuring that it will age well. (1982)
☛ P. Lasserre, Ch. Clos-René, Pomerol, 33500 Libourne; tel. 57 51 10 41 ☎ By appt.

CHATEAU LA CONSEILLANTE★

■	12ha	30000	**6** ⅏ ⌶

76 77 **78** 80 **81** 82 **83** **83** 84

Bright colour, a powerful nose with a hint of mushrooms; warm and attractive to drink with a long finish. (1981)
↜ Héritiers Nicolas, Ch. la Conseillante, Pomerol, 33500 Libourne; tel. 57 51 15 32 ⌶ By appt.

CHATEAU LA CROIX★★

■	12ha	70000	**5** D ⅏ ⌶

75 **76** 77 78 79 **80** **81** ⑧② 83

The owner of the estate has a real passion for wine: this one has good colour, a fine nose and is round and well balanced on the palate, with marked ripe tannin. (1982)
↜ Joseph Janoueix, Ch. Haut-Sarpe, 33330 St-Emilion; tel. 57 51 41 86 ⌶ By appt.

CHATEAU LA CROIX TOULIFAUT★★

■	2ha	10000	**5** D ⅏ ⌶

⑦⑤ 76 77 79 **80** 81 82 83

Deep red in colour, a heavy, fragrant, berry-like aroma on the nose; rich in tannin on the palate and with a mellowness typical of the Merlot grape. Unfortunately a bit short on the finish. (1982)
↜ Jean-Francois Janoueix, Ch. La Croix-Toulifaut, Pomerol, 33500 Libourne; tel. 57 51 41 86 ⌶ By appt. Closed Sun.

CHATEAU LA CROIX-DE-GAY

■	15ha	75000	**5** D ⅏ ⌶

70 **72** 75 76 **76** 80 **81** 82 ⑧③

Deep red colour, very ripe tannin and maybe even a little too rich. For those who love a big, aristocratic wine for keeping. (1979) ✔ Montagne-St-Emilion Ch. Faizeau.
↜ M. Raynaud, Ch. la Croix-de-Gay, Pomerol, 33500 Libourne; tel. 57 51 19 05 ⌶ By appt.

CHATEAU LA CROIX-DE-GAY★★

■	15ha	90000	**5** D ▮ ⌶

72 73 74 **75** 76 77 79 80 **81** 82 **83** **83** 84

A lovely deep colour and a nose that is clean, easy and has a hint of fresh fruit. A smooth wine that begins richly and finishes with ripe fruit and liquorice flavours. (1983)
↜ Raymond Ardurats, Pomerol, 33500 Libourne; tel. 57 51 19 50 ⌶ By appt.

CHATEAU L'EGLISE-CLINET★★

■	5.5ha	24000	**5** D ⅏ ⌶

72 74 **75** 76 77 79 ★80 **81** **82** **83** 84

This deep-coloured wine has plenty of depth on the palate, good tannin content, and lots of potential for the future. (1982)
↜ Denis Durantou, GFA Ch. l'Eglise-Clinet, Pomerol, 33500 Libourne; tel. 57 51 79 83 ⌶ No visitors.

CLOS DE L'EGLISE★★

■	6ha	25000	**4** ⅏ ⌶

66 **75** 76 77 **78** 79 80 **81** **82** **83** 84

Bright colour. Rich and complex but clearly harmonious nose. Well made. In the mouth it is still young, vigorous and tannic, full and meaty, and finishes with aromas of ripe fruit, vanilla, and cocoa. (1966)
↜ Michel et Francis Moreau, Ch. Plincé, Pomerol, 33500 Libourne; tel. 57 51 20 24 ⌶ No visitors.

CHATEAU L'ENCLOS★★

■	9ha	40000	**5** D ⅏ ⌶

75 76 **78** **79** 80 81 ⑧②

A wine that looks good and has a rich bouquet. (1982) ✔ Lalande-de-Pomerol Dom. du Chapelain.
↜ SC du Ch. l'Enclos, Pomerol, 33500 Libourne; tel. 57 51 04 62 ⌶ By appt.

CHATEAU L'EVANGILE★★★

■	13ha	60000	**6** ⅏ ⌶

75 77 ★**78** ★79 **82** **82** 83 84

A fine wine. Fragrant, spicy bouquet; remarkably vigorous on the palate. The fine balance between the tannins from the oak barrels and those from the wine itself combine to create a discreetly woody mellowness which brings out the character of the wine. (1978)
↜ SC du Ch. l'Evangile, Pomerol, 33500 Libourne; tel. 57 51 15 30 ⌶ By appt. ↜ MM. Ducasse.

CHATEAU LA FLEUR-PETRUS★★

■	8ha	32000	**5** D ▮ ⌶

72 73 **74** 75 **75** 76 **76** **77** 79 80 **81** **82** 83 84

A fruity, round, easy to drink, warm and pleasantly unctuous wine that is at the same time tannic and robust. Needs to be kept. (1982)
↜ SC Ch. la Fleur-Pétrus, Pomerol, 33500 Libourne; tel. 57 51 17 96 ⌶ By appt.

CHATEAU LA GANNE★★

■	4ha	15000	**4** D ⅏ ⌶

80 81 ⑧②

From the planting of vines to the final stages of wine-making, everything here is done traditionally. The result is a wine with an attractive red colour, a pleasing bouquet and a richly tannic palate. (1981) ✔ Canon Fronsac.
↜ Dubois Lachaud, 222 Av. Foch, Pomerol, 33500 Libourne; tel. 57 51 18 24 ⌶ Mon.–Sat. 8.30–12.00/14.30–19.00. Closed Aug.

187

CHATEAU GAZIN★★

■   23 ha 120 000   5 ◗ ↓

75 76 77 **78** 79 *80 81 82 ⑧ **83** 84

Good colour; the nose reflects the general style, with an impression of warmth from the vinous aromas. In the mouth it begins well and is nicely round. Overall, a charming wine. (1976)
•⊣ Etienne de Baillencourt, Ch. Gazin, Pomerol, 33500 Libourne; tel. 57 51 88 66 ⌾ By appt.

CHATEAU LES GRAVES-GUILLOT★

■   2 ha 12 000   5 D ◗ ↓

76 78 ⑧ **83** **83** 84

Red colour with deeper shades. The nose and palate confirms the first impressions of strength and vigour, fading a little towards the finish. (1982)
•⊣ Paul Clauzel, Ch. les Graves-Guillot, Pomerol, 33500 Libourne; tel. 57 51 13 36 ⌾ By appt.

CHATEAU LA GRAVE-TRIGNAN-DE-BOISSE★★

■   8 ha 36 000   5 D ▤

73 74 **75 76** 77 79 *80 **81** **82** **83** 84

Good, flowery nose and a very well-balanced taste. Deserves to be laid down. (1982)
•⊣ Christian Moueix, Ch. la Croix-Trignan-de-Boisse, Pomerol, 33500 Libourne; tel. 57 51 78 96 ⌾ By appt.

CHATEAU LAFLEUR★★

■   4 ha 12 000   D ◗ ↓

59 **61** 64 66 75 80 *81 82 83

A deeply coloured wine that is quite forceful to taste, but also has good balance and genuine finesse. Distributed by Moueix at Libourne. (1982)
•⊣ *Mlles* Robin, Ch. Lafleur, 33500 Libourne; tel. 57 51 78 96 ⌾ No visitors.

CHATEAU MAZEYRES★

■   10 ha 50 000   4 ▤ ◗ ↓

80 **81** ⑧ **83**

A classic Pomerol wine with a fruity nose that is typical of the Merlot grown on this estate. (1982) ✔ St-Emilion.
•⊣ M. Querre, Pomerol, 33500 Libourne; tel. 57 51 00 40 ⌾ Mon.–Fri. 9.00–12.00/14.00–18.00.
•⊣ Sté Civile Ch. Mazeyres.

CHATEAU MOULINET

■   18 ha 60 000   5 ▤ ↓

75 **76** 77 **78** *80 81 82 **83** **83** 84

This ancient estate is very proud of the boundary stone marking the entrance, stamped with the cross of the Knights Hospitallers. The wine has quite a mature colour, is fragrant, and has a certain amount of tannin. (1981) ✔ St-Emilion la Tour-du-Pin, St-Emilion Fonplégade, Lalande-Pomerol Ch. Croix-Bellevue.
•⊣ Sté Civile *Mme* Langlet-Rietsch, Ch. Moulinet, Pomerol, 33500 Libourne; tel. 57 51 50 63 ⌾ Weekends 8.00–12.00/14.00–18.00.

CHATEAU PETIT-VILLAGE★★

■   11 ha 50 000   6 ◗ ↓

76 **78** 79 80 **81** **81** 82 **83** 84

Fine colour and typical nose, with aromas of prunes and roasted almonds. A well-made wine, rich and silky on the palate. (1981) ✔ St-Estèphe, St-Emilion, Bordeaux Rouge and Blanc.
•⊣ Bruno Prats, Ch. Petit-Village, Pomerol, 33500 Libourne; tel. 56 44 11 37 ⌾ By appt.

CHATEAU PETRUS★★★

■   11 ha   6 ◗ ↓

61 66 71 72 73 74 78 79 **80** **81** **82** **83**

Beautiful bright, shimmering colour. An aromatic nose that has a thousand different nuances; undergrowth, prune, vanilla, and so on. Good attack, a full, round body, richness and smoothness and remarkably delicate tannin, which is very unusual for this year. A wine of great class. (1980)
•⊣ *Mme* L.-P. Lacoste-Loubat, Ch. Pétrus, Pomerol, 33500 Libourne; tel. 57 51 17 96 ⌾ By appt.

BARON PHILIPPE★★

■   2 ha 24 000   5 ▤ ↓

73 74 **75 76** 77 **78** 79 80 81 *⑧ *82 **83**

Attractive to look at and has a nose with plenty of finesse, with a hint of dead leaves. Round, rich, and meaty to taste, with an attractive and well-balanced finish. (1982)
•⊣ Baron Philippe de Rothschild, La Baronnie, BP 2, 33250 Pauillac; tel. 56 59 20 20 ⌾ By appt. Closed Aug.

CHATEAU PLINCETTE

■   2 ha 10 000   5 D ◗ ↓

*80 *81 ⑧

Attractive colour, but somewhat disappointing in the mouth. (1982) ✔ Lalande-de-Pomerol Domaine de Gachet Rouge, St-Emilion Domaine des Gourdins Rouge, Montagne-St-Emilion Ch. la Papeterie.
•⊣ Jean-Pierre Estager, 33–41 Rue de Montaudon, 33500 Libourne; tel. 57 51 04 09 ⌾ By appt. Closed 1–31 Aug. •⊣ Héntiers Coudreau.

CHATEAU PLINCE★

■   8 ha 35 000   4 ◗ ↓

74 75 **76** **78** 79 *80 81 82 **83** 84

Good colour and a charming nose; well balanced and harmonious in the mouth. Pleasant to drink now. (1981)

↱ Michel et Francis Moreau, Ch. Plincé, Pomerol, 33500 Libourne; tel. 57 51 20 24 ⏧ No visitors.

CHATEAU LA POINTE★★

■   20 ha   100000   **5** D 🍷 ⬟ ⚲

79 80 81 **82** ⑧③

Lively colour, and a warm, intense nose with a predominantly liquorice scent. A rounded and powerful wine. ✔ GCO St-Emilion Ch. la Serre Rouge, Canon Fronsac Ch. Toumalin Rouge, Fronsac Ch. Tessendey Rouge.
↱ M. d'Arfeuille, Ch. la Pointe, Pomerol, 33500 Libourne; tel. 57 51 02 11 ⏧ By appt.

CHATEAU LA RENAISSANCE★

■   3 ha   15000   **4** D 🍷 ⬟ ⚲

61 **75** 78 **81** ⑧② **82** 83

With a nose that is already developed, this wine is still distinctly oaky. On the whole it should not age too badly. (1981)
↱ François de Lavaux, Ch. Martinet, Pomerol, 33500 Libourne; tel. 57 91 17 29 ⏧ By appt.

CHATEAU RENE★

■   4 ha   30000   **4** D ⬟ ⚲

66 70 74 76 **78** 79 *81 *82

Also sold under the label Château La Bassonerie; thus the producer of this wine combines his two passions: wine-growing and . . . the bassoon! This wine is still a little immature to the nose, but it opens up when swirled in the glass. Firm on the palate. Should be left a few years to open up fully and become completely rounded. (1982)
↱ Gérard Faisandier, Ch. de René, Pomerol, 33500 Libourne; tel. 57 51 20 79 ⏧ No visitors.

CHATEAU REVE-D'OR

■   7 ha   40000   **4** D 🍷 ⬟ ⚲

⑦⑤ 76 78 79 *81 ***81** 82

After the purplish-red colour, the nose is still thin and closed. Not yet very expressive, this wine cannot really be properly judged at present. (1982) ✔ Pomerol Ch. du Mayne Rouge, Lalande-de-Pomerol Ch. la Croix Blanche.
↱ M. Vigier, Ch. Rêve-d'Or, Pomerol, 33500 Libourne; tel. 57 51 11 92 ⏧ By appt.

CHATEAU ROCHER-BEAUREGARD★

■   3 ha   16000   **4** D 🍷 ⬟ ⚲

67 **70** 71 73 **75** 76 78 79 81 ⑧②

A powerful Pomerol from a sandy soil; thick, perhaps a bit rustic. (1982) ✔ St-Emilion Ch. Rocher-Figeac.
↱ Max Tournier et Fils, Thaihas, Pomerol, 33500 Libourne; tel. 57 51 36 49 ⏧ By appt.

CHATEAU DE SALES★

■   45 ha   150000   **5** 🍷 ⬟ ⚲

74 **75** 76 77 **78** *79 80 **81** 82 **83** **83** 84

Has a certain simplicity that shines through its roundness, smoothness, and balance. (1978)
↱ Bruno de Lambert, Ch. de Sales, Pomerol, 33500 Libourne; tel. 57 51 04 92 ⏧ By appt.

CHATEAU LES GRANDS-SILLONS-GABACHOT

■   3 ha   17000   **4** ⬟ ⚲

81 ⑧② **82**

The intensity, colour, nose and taste of this wine are not yet fully developed; it needs to wait. (1982) ✔ Lalande-de-Pomerol, Montagne-St-Emilion.
↱ François Janoueix, 20 Quai du Priourat, BP 135, 33500 Libourne; tel. 57 51 55 44 ⏧ By appt. Closed Christmas–1 Jan., Aug.

CHATEAU TAILLEFER

■   22 ha   120000   **5** 🍷 ⚲

75 76 77 **78** 79 *80 81 82 **83** **83** 84

An attractively coloured, clean red wine which is well put together and ready to drink now. (1981) ✔ St-Emilion, Lalande-Pomerol.
↱ Marcel Moueix, Ch. Taillefer, Pomerol, 33500 Libourne; tel. 57 51 50 63 ⏧ Weekends 8.00–12.00/14.00–18.00 ↱ Héritiers Marcel Moueix.

CHATEAU TRISTAN★★

■   3 ha   12000   **5** D 🍷 ⬟ ⚲

69 72 73 76 ⑦⑧ **79** 80 81 **82**

A wine that is at present somewhat austere but also refined, elegant and robust; it will develop well as it ages. (1981) ✔ Lalande-de-Pomerol Ch. la Gravière Rouge.
↱ Simone Cascarret, Ch. Tristan, Pomerol, 33500 Libourne; tel. 57 51 04 54 ⏧ No visitors. ↱ See Cascarret.

CHATEAU TROTANOY★★★

■   7 ha   36000   **5** ⬟ ⚲

69 72 73 74 76 **77** 78 **79** **80** **81** ⑧② **83**

A perfect example of this appellation: a lovely, deep-red colour; a delicate, warm, and concentrated nose; real fullness in the mouth, and wonderful aromatic intensity at the finish. (1982)
↱ SC du Ch. Trotanoy, Pomerol, 33500 Libourne ⏧ By appt.

CHATEAU VALOIS★

■   8 ha   35000   **4** D 🍷 ⬟ ⚲

75 **76** 77 **78** 79 *80 81 82 **83** **83** 84

Behind a somewhat neutral colour this wine is discreetly but delicately fragrant, with hints of ripe fruit, vanilla and blossom. Full-bodied and easy to drink. Good tannin balance. (1982) ✔ St-Emilion Grand Cru, St-Emilion Clos Valentin.
↱ SC des Vignobles Leydet, Ch. Valois, Pomerol, 33500 Libourne; tel. 57 51 19 77 ⏧ Mon.–Sat. 9.00–12.00/14.00–19.00.

CHATEAU VIEUX-CERTAN★★

■   13 ha   60000   **6** ⬟ ⚲

*⑧②

Attractive ruby colour and fragrance of strawberries and raspberries with a hint of vanilla. Full and harmonious on the palate. (1982)
↱ SC du Ch. Vieux-Certan, Pomerol, 33500 Libourne; tel. 57 51 17 33 ⏧ Daily 9.00–12.00/14.00–17.00.. Closed during harvest.

CHATEAU VRAYE-CROIX-DE-GAY*

■   3 ha   13 000   ▌5▐ D ◑ ↓

64 ⑧② ▌82▐ ▌83▐

Intensely red, clear and bright; a heady wine, rich in tannin and marked by oak. Unfortunately the finish is a little dry. (1982) ✔ Lalande-de-Pomerol Ch. Siaurac Rouge, St-Emilion le Prieuré Rouge. ↔ *Mme* Guichard, Néac, 33500 Libourne; tel. 57 51 64 58 ⊤ No visitors. ↔ *Mme* la Baronne Guichard.

Lalande de Pomerol

Like its neighbour Pomerol, these vineyards were established by the Order of St John, also responsible for the beautiful twelfth-century church in Lalande. Vivid red wines are produced here from the classic Bordeaux grape varieties; powerful and fragrant, they have established a well-deserved reputation. The best can almost rival a Pomerol or a St-Emilion. The AOC area of 896 hectares produces 6.1 million bottles.

CHATEAU BECHEREAU*

■   5 ha   25 000   ▌4▐ D ▮ ↓

80 *81 *▌81▐ ⑧② ▌82▐ 83

A simple wine with a clear red colour; perhaps slightly lacking in body but with a delicate fruity nose (a hint of grapeyness) and a very pleasant palate. (1982) ✔ Bordeaux Supérieur Dom. de la Vallée Rouge, Montagne-St-Emilion Ch. Bechereau Rouge. ↔ Jean-Michel Bertrand, 33570 Les Artigues-de-Lussac; tel. 57 84 01 22 ⊤ By appt.

CHATEAU BEL-AIR*

■   13 ha   50 000   ▌5▐ D ◑ ↓

76 79 ▌79▐ 80 ▌80▐ ⑧① ▌81▐ 82 ▌82▐

Beautiful dark red colour and distinctive nose. Fleshy and tannic on the palate – but needs more bottle age. (1981) ↔ *MM.* Musset, Lalande de Pomerol, 33500 Libourne; tel. 57 51 40 07 ⊤ Mon.–Fri.

CHATEAU BELLES-GRAVES*

■   12 ha   50 000   ▌4▐ D ◑ ↓

80 81 ▌81▐ ⑧② ▌82▐ 83

With a nose reminiscent of ripe fruit, this wine is round and warm in the mouth. (1982) ↔ Hermine Théallet, Ch. Belles-Graves, Néac, 33500 Libourne; tel. 57 51 09 61 ⊤ By appt.

CHATEAU BERTINEAU-SAINT-VINCENT*

■   5 ha   25 000   ▌4▐ D ▮ ◑ ↓

75 76 78 79 80 *▌81▐ ⑧② ▌82▐ ▌83▐

Youthful garnet-red in colour, discreet and undeveloped on the nose. Tannic and well balanced, but needs time to mature. (1981) ↔ Geneviève Rolland, Maillet, Pomerol, 33500 Libourne; tel. 57 51 10 94 ⊤ Mon.–Sat.

CHATEAU LA BORDERIE MONDESIR**

■   2 ha   20 000   ▌4▐ D ◑ ↓

79 80 81 ⑧② ▌82▐

Attractive, intensely coloured wine that has a pleasant nose, with aromas of jam and ripe fruit. Good balance in the mouth and a slight taste of aniseed and overripe grapes. The finish is still a little austere. Will improve with a little more age. (1982) ↔ J.M. et R. Rousseau, Ch. Haut-Sorillon, Abzac, 33230 Coutras; tel. 57 49 06 10 ⊤ By appt.

CHATEAU BROUARD**

■   1 ha   5000   ▌4▐ D ◑ ↓

75 *78 *79 ⑧① ▌81▐ 82 83

Still developing; the nose had only ripe fruit aromas but is beginning to take on more complex ones of hay and earth. To taste, it progresses from fruit to vanilla. Full bodied, round and well balanced, with a good finish. Not widely distributed. (1982) ↔ Claude Bonhomme, Brouard, Lalande-de-Pomerol, 33500 Libourne; tel. 57 51 17 75 ⊤ By appt.

CHATEAU CANON CHAIGNEAU

■   18 ha   100 000   ▌4▐ ▮ ◑ ↓

⑧② ▌83▐

A light, medium-coloured wine. Quite easy to drink. (1983) ✔ St-Emilion Ch. Graves Chantecaille, Lussac St-Emilion Ch. la Claymore, Montagen St-Emilion, Bordeaux Supérieur. ↔ SA du Ch. le Claymore, Ch. Canon-Chaigneau, 33570 Lussac; tel. 57 74 60 44 ⊤ By appt. ↔ Famille Marin-Audra.

CHATEAU CHAMPS DE LALANDE

■   25 000   ▌4▐ D ▮ ↓

*⑧② *▌82▐ 83

Behind a clean, ruby-red colour and a candied-fruit nose, the palate is warm, round and straightforward. (1982) ↔ Marcel Audubert, Lalande-de-Pomerol, 33500 Libourne; tel. 57 51 24 63 ⊤ No visitors.

CHATEAU CHEVROL-BEL-AIR**

■   14 ha   60 000   ▌4▐ D ▮ ↓

*⑧②

The nose is still somewhat closed, but there is already a hint of very ripe grapes. A complex, round and well-balanced wine with great potential. (1982) ↔ Guy Pradier, Néac 33500 Libourne; tel. 57 51 10 23 ⊤ Daily.

CHATEAU LA CROIX

■   8 ha   30 000   ▌4▐ D ▮

61 64 ▌80▐ ⑧② ▌82▐

This wine has a slightly autumnal air, with its colour turning brick at the rim and its scent of dead leaves. Smooth on the palate; at its peak now. (1980) ✔ Montagne Ch. Vieux-Palon. ↔ P. Colombel, Ch. la Croix, Néac, 33500 Libourne; tel. 57 51 37 86 ⊤ By appt.

CHATEAU LA FLEUR-GALVESSE

■   3 ha   14 000   🔳3 D ▮ ◑ ↓

*82 **83

Unpretentious, with an intense colour and a full nose reminiscent of cooked Merlot. A simple but sound wine. (1982) ✔ Pomerol Ch. Vieux-Tressac Rouge.

🕐 Jean-Louis Hollet, 118 Av. de la Roudet, 33500 Libourne; tel. 57 51 08 46 ☥ No visitors.

CHATEAU LA FLEUR SAINT-GEORGES

■   6 ha   36 000   🔳4 ▮ ◑ ↓

77 **81 82**

Pretty, quite deep colour. A nose of soft red fruits; in the mouth, good balance initially and a dry finish. (1979)

🕐 Jean de Robillard, Ch. La Fleur-St.-Georges, Gelos, 64110 Jurançon; tel. 59 06 05 34 ☥ By appt.

CHATEAU GRAVES-DES-ANNEREAUX*

■   5 ha   32 000   🔳4 D ◑ ↓

*81 *(82) **82

An intense red colour and a well-developed faintly cooked nose. Round and complex, this wine has character and will develop quickly. (1982)

🕐 Paul Boujut, Ch. Graves-des-Annereaux, Lalande-de-Pomerol, 33500 Libourne; tel. 57 51 22 45 ☥ Daily.

CHATEAU HAUT-CHATAIN**

■   14 ha   63 000   🔳4 D ▮ ◑ ↓

*75 *76 *79 **80** **81 82** (83)

Full, rich and pleasing – a good example of a Lalande-de-Pomerol. Fine bright ruby colour and a generous, fruity aroma evocative of vanilla and undergrowth. (1982)

☥ A. Rivière et P. Junquas, Ch. Haut-Chatain, Néac, 33500 Libourne; tel. 57 51 51 02 ☥ By appt.

CHATEAU HAUTS-CONSEILLANTS**

■   9 ha   48 000   🔳4 D ↓

(82) **82** (83)

Not yet finished developing although it has quite a deep colour and some good, fruity fragrances. Full, round and well-balanced to taste, with a good, quite strong body. (1982) ✔ Pomerol Ch. Bonalogue, St-Emilion Ch.-du-Courlat.

🕐 Pierre Bourotte, 28 Rue Trocard, 33500 Libourne; tel. 57 51 20 56 ☥ By appt. Closed 15 July–15 Aug.

CHATEAU HAUT-SURGET*

■   16 ha   75 000   🔳4 D ◑ ↓

81 **81** (82) **82** 83

Bright cherry-red in colour. The nose is a blend of floral and berry scents and, after a smooth attack, the wine is full bodied on the palate with a long finish. (1981)

🕐 M. Ollet-Fourreau, Néac 33500 Libourne; tel. 57 51 28 68 ☥ Mon.–Sat.

CHATEAU LABORDE*

■   13 ha   82 000   🔳4 D ▮ ◑ ↓

*80 ***80** 81 **81** (82) **82**

This estate has almost always been passed on from mother to daughter. The wine is typically Bordeaux in its balance. The nose is pronounced without being intense; the palate is full and round, if a little rustic. (1982) ✔ Fronsac Ch. Jeandeman.

🕐 Jean-Marie Trocard, Lalande-de-Pomerol, 33500 Libourne; tel. 57 74 30 52 ☥ Mon.–Fri.

CHATEAU LACROIX-DES-MOINES

■   9 ha   50 000   🔳4 D ◑ ↓

76 **78** 79 81 (82) **82**

An elegant, dark ruby colour; nose and palate both very oaky. (1982)

🕐 GAEC Trocard, 33570 Artigues-de-Lussac; tel. 57 84 01 16 ☥ By appt. Closed Aug.

CHATEAU LAGRAVIERE*

■   6 ha   28 000   🔳4 D ▮ ◑ ↓

80 **80** *81 ***81** 82 **82**

A fairly deep colour and a discreetly flowery nose. Initially somewhat rounded on the palate, and lacking a little in weight, but overall quite pleasant. (1981) ✔ Pomerol Ch. Tristan Rouge.

🕐 *Mme.* Cascarret Ch. Lagravière, 33500 Libourne; tel. 57 51 04 54 ☥ No visitors.

CHATEAU MARCHESSEAU*

■   8 ha   35 000   🔳4 D ▮ ◑ ↓

70 74 80 **80** *81 ***81** (82) **82** **83**

The colour is only moderate, but the nose is strong, warm, and reminiscent of ripe fruit. On the palate it is round and powerful. Should develop well. (1982) ✔ Pomerol Clos St-Yves Rouge, Bordeaux Ch. Haut-Pigeonnier Rouge.

🕐 Christian Renie, Néac 33500 Libourne; tel. 57 51 40 32 ☥ Mon.–Fri. 8.00–12.00/14.00–18.00.

CHATEAU MONCETS

■   18 ha   100 000   🔳4 D ▮ ◑ ↓

79 80 **80** 81 (82)

Light and discreetly aromatic; quite easy to drink. (1982) ✔ Ch. la Bastidette.

🕐 M. de Jerphanion, Ch. Moncets, Néac, 33500 Libourne; tel. 57 51 19 33 ☥ By appt.

DOMAINE DU PONT DE GUESTRES***

■   2 ha   10 000   🔳4 D ▮ ◑ ↓

*75 *78 *79 *81 ***81** (82)

An attractive ruby colour, and full evidence of a ripe harvest, both on the nose and on the palate. Still a slightly tannic bitterness which should disappear with age. (1982) ✔ Fronsac Ch. les Roches-de-Ferrand.

🕐 Jean Rousselot et Fils, Dom. du Pont de Guestres, St-Aignan, 33126 Fronsac; tel. 57 24 95 16 ☥ By appt.

CHATEAU SIAURAC★★

◼   25ha   125000   4 D ◉ ⌣

80 80 *81 *81 82 82 83

This château, which also produces a Pomerol, offers a deep-red wine with a powerful, complex nose. Fat and well balanced, it is certain to age well. (1982) ✔ St-Emilion Ch. Le Prieuré GCC Rouge.
◆ᵼ *Mme.* Guichard, Néac, 33500 Libourne; tel. 57 51 64 58 ⊥ Mon.–Fri.

CHATEAU DES TOURELLES★★★

◼   17ha   75000   4 D ▮ ◉ ⌣

78 78 *79 *79 81 81 82

Well-balanced, rich and aromatic, with a subtle vanilla flavour, the wine is made to age beautifully. (1982) ✔ Pomerol Ch. Grands-Sillons-Gabachot Rouge.
◆ᵼ François Janoueix, 20 Quai du Priourat, BP 135, 33500 Libourne; tel. 57 51 55 44 ⊥ Mon.–Fri. Closed 24 Dec.–2 Jan., Aug.

CHATEAU TOURNEFEUILLE★

◼   14ha   85000   5 D ◉ ⌣

78 78 *79 *79 ⑧⑴ 81 82 83

Quite a flowery nose, reminiscent of lime blossom. A nice attack on the palate, which shows harmony and finesse. (1981).
◆ᵼ Sautarel et Fils, Néac 33500 Libourne; tel. 57 51 18 61 ⊥ Mon.–Sat.

CLOS DES TUILERIES★

◼   1.5ha   8000   3 D ▮ ◉ ⌣

64 66 *70 78 *79 80 81 ⑧⑵

A wine of varying impressions; a fine nose followed by a palate that is coarsely tannic to start with, rather silkier on the finish (1982)
◆ᵼ Fernand et François Merlet, Goizet, St-Denis-de-Pile, 33230 Coutras; tel. 57 84 25 19 ⊥ By appt.

CHATEAU LA VALLIERE

◼   1ha   3500   4 D ◉ ⌣

79 80 81 ⑧⑵ 82 83

A beautiful garnet colour, brick-red at the rim; Extremely complex nose reminiscent of fudge and crystallized fruit, but old wood is also too much in evidence. (1979) ✔ Pomerol Ch. La Fleur du Roy Rouge, St-Emilion Vieux Ch. Carré Rouge, Bordeaux Supérieur Ch. de Bossuet Rouge, Bordeaux Clos Pâquerette Blanc Sec.
◆ᵼ Yvon Dubost, Catusseau-Pomerol, Ch. La Vallière, Catusseau-Pomerol, 33500 Libourne; tel. 57 51 74 57 ⊥ Mon.–Fri.

CHATEAU DU VIEUX DUCHE★

◼   6000   5 D

*83

Good, brilliant colour and a slightly fruity, delicate nose. Initially pleasant on the palate, this wine is still far from fulfilling its promise. (1983)
◆ᵼ Robert Giraud SA, Dom. de L'Oiseau, BP 31, 33240 St-André-de-Cubzac; tel. 57 43 01 44 ⊥ By appt ◆ᵼ Gérard Chanet.

CHATEAU VIEUX-CHEVROL★

◼   20ha   125000   4 D ◉ ⌣

75 75 80 80 81 81 ⑧⑵ 82 83

Clear and bright in colour, with some development. The nose recalls flowers and ripe fruit, and on the palate the wine is round and fleshy. (1982)
◆ᵼ Champseix, Néac 33500 Libourne; tel. 57 51 09 80 ⊥ Daily.

St-Emilion and St-Emilion Grand Cru

St-Emilion is a charming and historic small town on the slopes of a hill overlooking the Dordogne valley. It was a stage on the pilgrims' route to the shrine of St-Jacques de Compostelle (Santiago de Compostela), and a fortress town during the Hundred Years' War: during the Revolution it became a refuge for the deputies of the Gironde who were outlawed under the Convention.

According to legend the vineyards date from Roman times, but it seems that they only began to be of any significant size in the thirteenth cen-

St-Emilion

tury. Whatever the truth of the matter, St-Emilion is today at the centre of some of the most famous vineyards in the world.

Spanning nine communes, the vineyards include a whole range of soil types; surrounding the town itself is a limestone plateau and clay-limestone ridge – the latter occupied by several classed growths. The wines grown in this area have a fine, deep colour, indicative of robust, full-bodied wines. The gravel soils of Pomerol produce some outstanding wines of great finesse; this region also has a number of Grands Crus. However, most of the generic St-Emilion appellation area is on sandy alluvium soils that run down towards the Dordogne.

Among the grape varieties used, there is a noticeable predominance of Merlot, complemented by Cabernet-Franc (called Bouchet here), and to a lesser degree by Cabernet-Sauvignon.

One of the unusual features of the St-Emilion region is its classification system. Dating only from 1955, it is nonetheless reviewed regularly and systematically; the first revision was in 1958, the last in 1985. The current situation is that there are now two official AOC classifications: AOC St-Emilion Grand Cru Classé, and AOC St-Emilion. The latter can be claimed by all wines produced in St-Emilion itself and the eight communes that surround it. AOC St-Emilion Grand Cru Classé, on the other hand, is reserved for specially designated estates; the wines are subjected to a further tasting just before they are bottled.

This new classification simplifies the previous state of affairs whereby St-Emilion was divided into four appellations. As well as the two mentioned above there was an AOC Grand Cru and an AOC Premier Grand Cru. Wine buyers are likely to find these classifications on labels for some time to come, but should note that the old four-level classification has now been superseded.

In 1982 St-Emilion AOC production reached 38.6 million bottles. The Producers' Union in St-Emilion (Union des Producteurs de St-Emilion) is the largest Cave-Coopérative in any French fine wine area.

St-Emilion

BARONNAT★

| ■ | 50ha | 333324 | 5 ▪ ↓ |

72 73 74 **75 76** 77 **78** 79 80 81 **82 83 83**

A rich, clean colour, but still closed-in and young. Not particularly full bodied on the palate, but delicate and with a certain fullness, and a good, lightly tannic finish. (1983)
↬ Baron Philippe de Rothschild, La Baronnie, BP 2, 33250 Pauillac; tel. 56 59 20 20 ⏣ By appt.

CHATEAU BARRAIL DES GRAVES★

| ■ | 16ha | 85000 | 4 D ▪ ⑾ ↓ |

75 77 78 ★79 ⑧② **82**

A very dark ruby colour, with ripe fruit both on the nose and on the palate. Tannic, needs keeping. (1982) ✔ Bordeaux Château Renaissance.
↬ Ch. et G. Descrambe, Ch. Barrail-des-Graves, St-Sulpice de Faleyrens, 33330 St-Emilion; tel. 57 84 51 54 ⏣ By appt.

CHATEAU BERTINAT-LARTIGUE★

| ■ | 5ha | 19000 | 3 D ▪ ↓ |

79 ⑧② **82** 83

A pleasing colour of average intensity, an expressive nose, good balance and good length in the mouth – already attractive, and should last for a few years yet. (1982)
↬ J. et R. Dubois, 'Lartigue', St-Sulpice-de-Faleyrens; 33330 St-Emilion; tel. 57 24 72 75 ⏣ By appt.

CHATEAU BRUN★

| ■ | 5ha | 25000 | 3 D ▪ |

71 **75 78** 79 81 ⑧② **82**

A handsome ruby wine. Its nose is still underdeveloped undoubtedly due to an over-dominant extract. (1982)
↬ GFA du Ch. Brun, Ch. Brun-Beauvallon, 33330 St-Emilion; tel. 57 24 77 06 ⏣ By appt.

CHATEAU CROIX-DE-FIGEAC

| ■ | 3.5ha | 15000 | 4 D ▪ ↓ |

66 70 74 ★**75** ★79 80 81

An unassuming wine with a good red colour, a fruity nose and, in the mouth, just the right amount of taste. (1982)
↬ Georges Meunier, Ch. Croix-de-Figeac, 33330 St-Emilion; tel. 57 24 67 58 ⏣ No visitors.

CHATEAU GRAND-BERT★

| ■ | 8ha | 50000 | 4 D ▪ ⑾ ↓ |

70 ★**75** ★81 ★**82** ★**82**

Very deep in colour; still closed but promising on the nose, and plenty of matter on the palate. Should not be drunk straight away. ✔ Côtes-de-Castillon Ch. Grand Tuillac.
↬ Philippe Lavigne, Ch. Grand-Bert, St-Philippe-d'Aguille, 33350 Castillon-la-Bataille; tel. 57 40 60 09 ⏣ Mon.–Sat. 9.00–12.00/14.00–18.00.

193

CHATEAU HAUT-BADETTE★

■   4.5 ha   33 000   ④ Ⓓ ▮ ⑩ ⌁

75 ⑦⑧ 80 81 **82** 🄸🄸 83

A wine with a fine bright colour. The nose has powerful and complex aromas, reflected on the palate, which is also fairly tannic. (1982)
🗣 Jean-François Janoueix, Le Castelot, 33330 St-Emilion; tel. 57 51 41 86 ☖ By appt. Closed Sun.

CHATEAU HAUT-BRULY

■   8 ha   50 000   ④ Ⓓ ▮ ⌁

61 64 79 80 **81** 🄸🄸 ⑧⑨

Although this wine is certainly a little short on the palate, it has an attractive colour, good bouquet and pleasing flavour. (1982)
MM. Cante, Ch. Haut-Bruly, 33330 St-Emilion; tel. 57 24 70 71 ☖ By appt.

CHATEAU HAUT-GROS-CAILLOU

■   6 ha   30 000   ④ Ⓓ ⑩ ⌁

79 80 **81 82** 83

Here it is not the residence but the huge rock, weighing 500 kilos, that gives the estate its name. The wine is powerful but well balanced. Should be allowed to breathe for a long time. (1982)
🗣 Paul Lafaye, Ch. Haut-Gros-Caillou, St-Sulpice-de-Faleyrens, 33330 St-Emilion; tel. 54 24 75 75 ☖ By appt. Closed Aug.

CHATEAU JACQUES-NOIR★

■   10 ha   35 000   ③ Ⓓ ▮ ⌁

76 77 78 79 ⑧⑨ 🄸🄸 82

A moderate, mid-red colour; the nose is not yet fully open but is nevertheless quite strong. Well balanced on the palate. (1982)
🗣 Rémy Daut, Ch. des Demoiselles, St-Magne-sur-Castillon, 33350 Castillon-la-Bataille; tel. 57 40 11 88 ☖ By appt.

JEAN-SANS-TERRE★

■   60 000   ③

Behind the wine's good colour the nose is subtly fruity and well balanced, qualities rediscovered on tasting. (1982)
🗣 W. et A. Gilbey, St-Yzans-de-Médoc, 33340 Lesparre-Médoc; tel. 56 41 15 03 ☖ No visitors.

CHATEAU MARTINET

■   17 ha   100 000   ④ Ⓓ ▮ ⑩ ⌁

61 71 75 76 🄸🄸 81 82 83

Rather feeble in the mouth, but compensates with other qualities such as an intense colour, and a pleasing nose. Perhaps a little over-developed. (1980)
🗣 François de Lavaux, Ch. Martinet, Pomerol, 33500 Libourne; tel. 57 91 17 29 ☖ By appt.

CHATEAU PATARBET★★

■   7 ha   40 000   ④ Ⓓ ▮ ⑩ ⌁

★⑦⑤ 78 79 80 81 **82** 🄸🄸 83

Fine, dark appearance. Burnt nose with a touch of prunes, followed by a full, fleshy, well-balanced palate. (1982)
🗣 Eric Bordas, Ch. Patarbet, 33330 St-Emilion; tel. 57 24 74 73 ☖ Closed one week in late Feb.

CHATEAU PETIT-GARDEROSE

■   4 ha   20 000   ④ Ⓓ ⑩

70 72 74 ★⑦⑤ 78 79 **81** 82

The first signs of fading can be detected in this already mature vintage; the wine is light but it still has a pleasant colour and a reasonable bouquet. (1979)
🗣 Jacques Henocque, 94 Bd Garderose, 33500 Libourne; tel. 57 51 58 84 ☖ By appt. Closed 25 Aug.–10 Sept.

DOMAINE DE PEYRELONGUE★

■   12 ha   70 000   ⑤ Ⓓ ▮ ⑩ ⌁

⑦⓪ 🄸🄸 78 **82**

A well-aged wine of deep amber colour, having a complex bouquet that blends shades of venison, plum brandy and roast coffee. On the palate, plenty of extract and a long finish. (1975) ✔ St-Emilion Ch. Mauvezin Grand Cru Classé, St-Emilion Ch. Grand Gueyrot Grand Cru.
🗣 Pierre Cassat et Fils, BP 44, 33330 St-Emilion; tel. 57 24 72 36 ☖ By appt.

CHATEAU PEYROUQUET★

■   20 ha   125 000   ④ ▮ ⌁

61 66 ★⑦⓪ **71** ⑧⑨ 🄸🄸

A dark, lively red colour; fairly attractive nose, evocative of ripe fruit; the palate gives pleasing impression of well-resolved tannins. (1982)
🗣 Maurice Chéminade, Ch. Peyrouquet, 33330 St-Emilion; tel. 57 24 70 71 ☖ By appt.

CLOS-LA-PIGNONNE

■   3 ha   18 000   ④ Ⓓ ⑩ ⌁

64 ★⑥⑦ 70 **74** ★⑦⑤ **76** ★78 ★**79** 80 81 82

Produced under the Saint-Emilion appellation. Clear ruby colour; perhaps a little short overall, but with a pleasant bouquet and a light but pleasing flavour on the palate. (1981) ✔ Roussillon, Vin de Pays.
🗣 Denis Pueyo, 15 Av. du Gourinat, 33500 Libourne; tel. 57 51 13 26 ☖ By appt.

CHATEAU ROCHER FIGEAC★

■   4 ha   24 000   ④ Ⓓ ⑩

75 76 80 **81** 🄸🄸 82 🄸🄸 🄸🄸

Bright, medium colour. The sappy, fragrant character of the nose is reflected on the finish. A pleasing wine with some potential. (1982)
🗣 Max Tournier, 'Tailhas', 33330 St-Emilion; tel. 57 51 36 49 ☖ By appt.

CHATEAU TOUR-DE-PEYREAU

■   25 ha   130 000   ④ Ⓓ ▮ ⑩ ⌁

79 80 **81** 🄸🄸 ⑧⑨

The quite light colour is indicative of its style: smooth and easy to drink. The reserved but pleasant nose is allied to a very unaggressive attack. (1981)
🗣 Adet Steward SA, 41 Rue Vergniaud, 33081 Bordeaux Cédex; tel. 56 44 90 90 ☖ By appt.

CLOS VALENTIN★★

■　　　　　5ha　26000　**4** **D** ▮ ◍ ⬇

75 76 ★78 ★**78** ★⑦ ★**79** 81 **82**

Bright mahogany-red. A subtle bouquet of black-currant, plum and mint. Supple, well-constituted palate. A promising St-Emilion from an estate that has been in local hands for at least ten generations. (1979)
⬧ Bernard Leydet, Ch. Leydet-Valentin, 33330 St-Emilion; tel. 57 24 73 05 ⵏ By appt.

CHATEAU VIEILLE-TOUR-LA-ROSE★

■　　　　　5ha　25000　**3** **D** ▮ ◍ ⬇

70 75 78 79 81 ⑧ **82**

Attractive, deep ruby colour. A wine with delicate aromas, mellowed tannin and good length. (1982)
⬧ *MM*. Ybert et Fils, Ch. Vieille-Tour-La-Rose, 33330 St-Emilion; tel. 57 24 73 41 ⵏ By appt.
⬧ Daniel Ybert.

CHATEAU LES VIEUX MAURINS★

■　　　　　8ha　75000　**3** **D** ▮ ⬇

A lovely deep-red colour and quite a rich nose with a hint of chocolate. Good attack, but the tannin is a little too obvious. Needs time to develop. (1982)
⬧ *MM*. Goudal Père et Fils, Les Maurins, St-Sulpice-de-Faleyrens, 33330 St-Emilion; tel. 57 24 62 96 ⵏ By appt.

St-Emilion Grand Cru

CHATEAU L'ANGELUS★

■Gd Cru　　28ha　144000　**6** ◍ ⬇

70 71 77 **78 80 81 81 82**

An elegant, attractive wine with good balance and a firm aptitude for ageing. The fine tasting cellars are worth a visit. (1981)
⬧ *MM*. de Bouard de Laforest, Ch. L'Angelus, 33330 St-Emilion; tel. 57 24 71 39 ⵏ By appt.

CHATEAU D'ARCIE★★

■　　　　　7ha　20000　**4** ▮ ⬇

70 ★75 76 77 **78** 79 80 81 ⑧ **82** 83

Attractive wine with a fine colour. The nose is still closed-up but promises well. Good structure on the palate, and all the signs of a successful maturity to come. (1982)
⬧ J.-A. Baugier, Ch. d'Arcie, 33330 St-Emilion; tel. 57 24 07 71 ⵏ By appt.

CHATEAU AUSONE★★★

■1er Gd Cru　7ha　21000　**6** ◍ ⬇

61　62　64 70 71 ★⑦ **77** 78 **79** **80** **81 82 82** 83

A vineyard of great character, surrounded by rocks which protect it from the north winds. It produces a wine with splendid colour and a nose both complex and rich. Well blended and warm on the palate, it has achieved a perfect balance between new wood and rich, noble tannins. An exceptional wine which should be kept before drinking. (1982)
⬧ *Mme* Dubois-Challon, *M*. Vauthier, Ch. Ausone, 33330 St-Emilion; tel. 57 24 70 26 ⵏ By appt.

CHATEAU BALESTARD LA TONNELLE★★★

■Gd Cru　　11ha　55000　**5** **D** ▮ ◍ ⬇

70 71 **76** 78 **79** ★**81 82** 83

Beautiful colour, with a delicate and subtle nose; harmony and balance on the palate. A very fine bottle with a good future. (1981)
⬧ Jacques Capdemourlin, Ch. Capdemourlin, 33330 St-Emilion; tel. 57 84 02 06 ⵏ By appt.

CHATEAU DU BASQUE★

■　　　　　10ha　75000　**4** ▮ ⬇

70 ★75 **76** 77 **78** 79 80 **81** ⑧ **82** 83

Deep cherry-red colour. The nose is still a little undeveloped, but the tannin on the palate is of high quality, suggesting it will age well. (1982)
⬧ Elie Lafaye, Ch. du Basque, 33330 St-Emilion; tel. 57 24 70 71 ⵏ By appt.

CHATEAU BEAU-SEJOUR-BELOT★★

■1er Gd Cru　18ha　00000　**6** ▮

71 75 ★78 **79** ★80 **81 82 82**

Magnificent colour and rich aromas suggest that this wine has a good future, although it is still a little dominated by the wood. Should be kept. (1982)
⬧ Michel Bécot et Fils, Ch. Beau-Séjour-Bécot, 33330 St-Emilion; tel. 57 74 46 87 ⵏ By appt.

CHATEAU BEL-AIR-OUY

■　　　　　6ha　35000　**4** ▮ ⬇

70 ★75 76 **77 78** 79 80 **81 82 82** 83

Lively, deep ruby colour; nose evocative of over-ripe fruit and full, if coarse, tannin on the palate. (1982)
⬧ Gellie, Ch. Bel-Air-Ouy, 33330 St-Emilion; tel. 57 24 70 71 ⵏ By appt.

CHATEAU BELFONT-BELCIER★★

■   13ha 85000   4 D ▬

71 75 ⑦ **77 78 79** 80 81 82

Ruby colour with shades of brick-red; elegant, lively, rather subtle nose; refined and pleasing on the palate. A good representative of its appellation. (1982)

☛ *M.* et *Mmes* Labusquière, Ch. Belfont-Belcier, St-Laurent des Combes 33330, St-Emilion; tel. 57 24 72 16 ⟊ By appt.

CHATEAU BELLEVUE★

■Gd Cru   6ha 30000   4 D ▬ ◑ ↓

70 **75 79 81 82** 83

Attractive colour and pleasant fruit on the nose. Not much length on the palate but the attack has appeal. The house has associations with the Gironde insurrection of 1793, during the revolution. (1981)

☛ Sté Civ. de Conink, Ch. Bellevue, 33330 St-Emilion; tel. 57 51 06 07 ⟊ By appt.

CHATEAU BERLIQUET★★

■Gd Cru   8ha 40000   4 D ◑ ↓

77 79 80 **81** ⑧ 82

Solid, bright-red colour; well-harmonized notes of fruit and vanilla on the nose, with surprisingly round tannins and finish on the palate. (1982)

☛ *M.* et *Mme* De Lesquen, BP 27, 33330 St-Emilion; tel. 57 24 70 71 ⟊ By appt.

CHATEAU BILLEROND

■   10ha 65000   4 D ▬ ↓

70 75 76 77 *78 79 80 **81** 81 ⑧ 83

A fairly standard colour and an agreeable bouquet. Although the finish is a little short, the attack is pleasing. (1982)

☛ A. Martin et A. Robin, Ch. Billerond, 33330 St-Emilion; tel. 57 24 70 71 ⟊ By appt.

CHATEAU JACQUES BLANC

■   20ha 120000   4 D ▬ ◑ ↓

74 ⑦ 77 *79 **81** 82

Supple and light wine, though the nose is still somewhat closed. (1982)

☛ GFA du Ch. Jacques Blanc, Ch. Jacques Blanc, 33330 St-Emilion; tel. 57 40 18 01 ⟊ By appt.
☛ Chouet Consorts.

CHATEAU LA BOISSERIE★

■   6ha 35000   4 ▬ ↓

70 *75 76 77 **78 79** 80 **81** ⑧ 82 83

A rustic wine, deep in colour with aromas of cooked prunes and abundant, slightly harsh tannins on the palate. Should not be kept too long. (1982)

☛ Louis Boisserie, Ch. La Boisserie, 33330 St-Emilion; tel. 57 24 70 71 ⟊ By appt.

CHATEAU LA BONNELLE★

■   6.5ha 43200   4 D ▬ ↓

Colour shading from red to deep ruby; powerful nose and well structured on the palate. Solid. Promises an interesting future if left to develop. (1982)

☛ François Sulzer, Ch. La Bonnelle, 33330 St-Emilion; tel. 57 24 70 71 ⟊ By appt.

CHATEAU BONNET

■   23ha 100000   5 D ◑ ↓

75 76 **79** 80 **81 82 83**

A large property producing an attractive wine, fairly well balanced on the palate, despite a slightly abrupt finish. (1982) ✔ St-Emilion Grand Cru la Fleur-Bonnet, St-Emilion Grand Cru Ch. d'Armens.

☛ Roger Bonnet, Père et Fils, Ch. Bonnet, 33330 St-Emilion; tel. 57 47 15 23 ⟊ By appt.

CHATEAU LA BOUTISSE★

■   10ha 50000   4 D ▬ ◑ ↓

⑦ 79 80 81 **82** 82 **83**

The building is more like a country railway station than a 'château', but the wine is certainly worthy of its appellation. A lovely, clear red colour, though light for the vintage. The nose is discreet, and pleasantly perfumed, recalling redcurrants especially. In the mouth, harmony and elegance. (1982)

☛ Jean-François Carrille, Ch. Cardinal-Villemaurine, 33330 St-Emilion; tel. 57 24 74 46 ⟊ By appt.

CHATEAU BRAGARD

■   11ha 20000   4 ▬ ◑ ↓

76 77 78 **79** 80 81 82

The colour, not yet fully developed, has some coppery highlights, but is generally clear. Flows easily on the palate and has a fruity aroma enhanced by a hint of wood. (1979)

☛ *Mme*. Petitguillaume-Sauvaitre, Ch. Bragard, Loiseau, 33126 Fronsac; tel. 57 51 17 16 ⟊ By appt.

CHATEAU CADET BON★

■   5ha 20000   5 D ▬ ◑ ↓

⑥⑥ **70** 74 **75** 76 **78 79** 80 81 82

According to tradition, this growth dates back to the early 17th century. An intense and complex nose. Drink now. (1980)

☛ François Gradatour, Ch. Cadet Bon, 33330 St-Emilion; tel. 57 24 72 19 ⟊ By appt.

CHATEAU CADET-PIOLA★★

■Gd Cru   82ha 30000   5 D ▬ ◑ ↓

77 80 **82** 82 **83** 83

Already well developed, with an attractive bouquet, forthcoming and complex. Generous and full bodied on the palate. ✔ St-Emilion Grand Cru Dom. Casquette. (1982)

☛ Alain Jabiol, Ch. Cadet-Piola, 33330 St-Emilion; tel. 57 24 70 67 ⟊ Mon.–Fri. 10.00–11.30/ 14.00–17.30.

CHATEAU CANON LA GAFFELIERE★★★

■Gd Cru   19ha 110000   5 D ◑ ↓

76 ⑦ 79 80 81 82

A distinguished wine, with a delicate aroma and a charming, mellow bouquet. Well balanced and full bodied on the palate, with a hint of wood. A fine bottle from a great year. (1979)

☛ SCEV des Comtes de Neipperg, Ch. Canon la Gaffelière, 33330 St-Emilion; tel. 57 24 71 33 ⟊ Daily 8.00–12.00/14.00–18.00. Closed Aug.

CHATEAU CANON★★

■1er Gd Cru   18ha   80000   **6** ⅷ ↓

61 64 71 75 76 **78** 79 80 81 **82** 83

This vintage fully justifies Château Canon's high reputation. Attractive cherry-red colour; nose still rather discreet but promising riches to come, with notes of wood, chocolate and vanilla in particular. The palate is dense, rich and well structured, with soft, ripe tannins and long concentrated fruit and oak finish. A wine with a great future. (1982)
➤ SEV Fournier, Ch. Canon, 33330 St-Emilion; tel. 57 24 70 79 ⅎ By appt.

CHATEAU CANTENAC

■   14ha   65000   **4** D ⅷ ↓
⑲ 80 81 82

From a château with a neo-Tudor air, this wine is light in colour, with a firm nose and a tannic palate. (1982) ✔ St-Emilion Ch. Piganeau.
➤ Héritiers Brunot, Ch. Cantenac, 33330 St-Emilion; tel. 57 51 35 22 ⅎ By appt.

CHATEAU CAPDEMOURLIN★★

■Gd Cru   14ha   68000   **5** D ■ ⅷ ↓

70 71 **75** 76 78 79 ★**81** ⑧ 83

Traditional style but nonetheless fine quality. Complex aromas, and great balance between fruit and tannin. A wine to keep. (1981)
➤ Jacques Capdemourlin, Ch. Capdemourlin, 33330 St-Emilion; tel. 57 84 02 06 ⅎ By appt.

CHATEAU CAPET-GUILLIER★★

■   15ha   75000   **4** D ■ ⅷ ↓
⑺ 77 78 79 **79** 80 81 **82**

Attractive, lively and vigorous, with an aroma of ripe fruit mingling harmoniously with the tannins. (1979)
➤ Sté Capet-Guillier, 33330 St-Emilion; tel. 57 24 70 21 ⅎ By appt.

CHATEAU CARTEAU-COTES-DAUGAY★★

■   12ha   75000   **4** D ⅷ ↓
71 72 73 74 75 **76** 77 78 **79** 80 **81 82** **82**

This wine already has good depth of colour, powerful bouquet of ripe fruit and is very tannic on the palate. Will improve with age. (1982)
➤ Jacques Bertrand, Ch. Carteau-Côtes-Daugay, 33330 St-Emilion; tel. 57 24 73 94 ⅎ By appt.

CHATEAU LE CASTELOT★★

■   5.5ha   30000   **5** D ⅷ ↓

78 79 **79 80** 81 **82** 83

The estate owes its existence to Henry IV's munificence. The royal *bon vivant*, impressed by the standard of food and service encountered on a flying visit to the local inn, granted the innkeeper and his wife permission to build this small château ('castelot' in Gascon). The wine is typical of the region: aromas of ripe fruit with a touch of toast; round, with a good overall balance, on the palate. (1982)
➤ Jean-François Janoueix, Le Castelot, 33330 St-Emilion; tel. 57 51 41 86 ⅎ By appt. Closed Sun.

DOMAINE CHANTE ALOUETTE CORMEIL

■   8ha   30000   **4** D ⅷ
75 78 **79** 80 81 ⑧ 83

A pastoral name for this wine, from a vintage that is already tiring a little. Although not long on the palate, it has a warm and subtle aroma. For those who like a light but mature wine. (1979)
✔ St-Emilion Ch. Gueyrosse.
➤ Yves Delol, Ch. Gueyrosse, 33500 Libourne; tel. 57 51 02 63 ⅎ By appt.

CHATEAU CHAUVIN★★

■Gd Cru   13ha   80000   **5** D ■ ⅷ ↓
⑺ **76** 78 ★**79** 81 **82**

A lovely, deep-red wine made from grapes still harvested by hand. The nose is delicate, flowery and woody, but still somewhat closed. On the palate there is a rapid attack and an attractive development. Overall, a well-structured wine. (1982)
➤ Henri Ondet, 137 Rue du President-Doumer, 33500 Libourne; tel. 57 51 33 76 ⅎ By appt.

CHATEAU CHEVAL-BLANC★★★

■1er Gd Cru, A   36ha   150000   **6** ⅷ ↓
★61 64 72 73 **75** 76 77 **78** 82

The most famous of the St-Emilion growths. This classic example has a deep colour, fading to orange at the edges, and a pleasantly fragrant nose. On the palate, harmonious attack is followed by a firmly tannic development. A great wine from a great vintage. (1978)
➤ SA Cheval-Blanc, 33330 St-Emilion; tel. 57 24 70 70 ⅎ By appt. Closed 15 July–31 Aug. and public holidays.

CHATEAU LA CLOTTE★

■   24000   **5** D ⅷ ↓
76 77 78 79 80 81 ⑧

May sometimes seem a little austere but it is

basically well made and well balanced, with plenty of depth. (1982)
↬ *M.* Chailleau, Ch. la Clotte, 33330 St-Emilion ⟁ By appt.

CHATEAU LA CLUSIERE★

■ Gd Cru	2.75 ha	11 000	5 ⅏ ⚲

72 73 74 76 77 **79** ★ 80 **81 82 83**

Despite its age, this wine has maintained freshness and lightness; this; an aroma of dead leaves is apparent. Drink now. (1972) ✔ St-Emilion Ch. Pavie, St-Emilion Ch. Pavie Décesse.
↬ Consorts Valette, Ch. Pavie, 33330 St-Emilion; tel. 57 24 72 02 ⟁ By appt ↬ Jean-Paul Valette.

CHATEAU CORBIN-MICHOTTE★

■ Gd Cru	7 ha	32 000	5 D ⅏ ⚲

71 73 74 77 78 **79 80** 80 **81 82**

Fine ruby colour, with tawny hues. The nose is delicate and fine; the palate, by contrast, full and velvety. (1980) ✔ St-Georges-St-Emilion, Montagne-St-Emilion.
↬ J.-N. Boidron, Ch. Corbin-Michotte, 33330 St-Emilion; tel. 57 96 28 57 ⟁ By appt.

CHATEAU CORMEIL FIGEAC★★

■	25 ha	110 000	4 D ▮ ⅏ ⚲

74 ⑦⑤ **78** 78 **79** 80 81 **82**

Already mature vintage that has developed well. Deep ruby colour with a few hints of amber. Powerful and elegant bouquet, aromatic and well balanced. Definite quality on the palate, with a positive tannic character. Most agreeable. (1978)
↬ R. et L. Moreaud, 33330 St-Emilion; tel. 57 24 70 53 ⟁ By appt.

COTES-ROCHEUSES★

■	70 ha	500 000	4 D ▮ ⚲

70 71 ★**75** 76 77 78 79 80 81 ⑧② 82 83

Darkish red colour, with a rather straightforward nose and palate. The overall balance, however, is good, with round, pleasant tannins which suggest this wine will age well. (1982)
↬ Union des Producteurs, Ch. Côtes-Rocheuses, 33330 St-Emilion; tel. 57 24 70 71 ⟁ By appt.

CHATEAU COUDERT-PELLETAN★

■	6 ha	30 000	4 D ▮ ⅏ ⚲

★**75** ★**76 78** 79 80 81 ⑧② 82

Deep ruby colour and a nose with aromas evocative of ripe fruit. Honest, warm attack and a good impression on the palate. To be drunk fairly soon. (1982) ✔ Bordeaux Supérieur Dom. la Tuque Bel Air Rouge, Bordeaux Côtes de Castillon Ch. Terrasson.
↬ GAEC Jean Lavau et Fils, Ch. Coudert-Pelletan, St-Cristophe-de-Bardes, 33330 St-Emilion; tel. 57 24 77 30 ⟁ By appt.

CHATEAU COUTET

■	11 ha	43 000	5 D ▮ ⅏

⑥① 62 **64** 67 **71** 72 74 76 **78** 79 81 83

This graceful country house overlooking the Dordogne Valley has an equally attractive *chai* where wine is stored. The wine is light, smooth and flowing, although the nose is slightly closed-in. (1981)
↬ Jean David-Beaulieu, Ch. Coutet, 33330 St-Emilion; tel. 57 24 72 27 ⟁ No visitors.

CHATEAU DASSAULT★★

■ Gd Cru	22 ha	96 000	5 D ⅏

75 76 ⑦⑦ **78 79** 80 **81** 82

Delightful ruby colour. Subtle shades of roasted cereal, vanilla and roasted almonds on the nose; complex, predominantly floral aromas on the palate. Generally, a robust and well-balanced wine. (1982) ✔ St-Emilion Ch. Mérissac.
↬ Ch. Dassault, 33330 St-Emilion; tel. 57 24 71 30 ⟁ By appt.

CHATEAU DESTIEUX-BERGER★

■	10 ha	45 000	4 D ▮ ⚲

70 ★**75** 76 77 **78** 79 80 **81** ⑧② 82 83

Bright and youthful in appearance, somewhat vegetal on the nose, but fairly concentrated on the palate. (1982)
↬ Claude Tribaudeau, Ch. Destieux-Berger, 33330 St-Emilion; tel. 57 24 70 71 ⟁ By appt ↬ Alain Cazenave.

CHATEAU FAURIE DE SOUCHARD★★

■	11 ha	40 000	5 ▮ ⅏ ⚲

66 72 74 **76** 77 ★**78** 79 80 **81 82** 82 83

Very deep colour; delicate yet clear-cut aromas on the nose. There is a good balance on the palate between oak and tannin, and a subtle but persistent finish. (1982) ✔ St-Emilion.
↬ *Mme* Françoise Sciard-Jabiol, Ch. Faurie-de-Souchard, 33330 St-Emilion; tel. 57 24 70 67 ⟁ By appt.

CHATEAU DE FERRAND★★★

■	24 ha	150 000	4 D ⅏ ⚲

71 75 76 78 **79** ★80 81 ⑧② 82

Owned by the celebrated Baron Bich, this estate deserves to be recognized both for its distinguished architecture and the quality of its wine. The latter is brilliant red in colour and has a powerful, well-developed bouquet. Powerful, elegant and well balanced on the palate, with a slightly velvety texture. A promising wine. (1982)
↬ *M.* le Baron Bich, Ch. de Ferrand, 33330 St-Emilion; tel. 57 24 77 07 ⟁ By appt.

CHATEAU DE LA FLEUR-PICON★★

■   5 ha   30 000   4 D ▮ ❶ ♦

75 76 **79** 80 ★**81** ★⑧ 82

Good colour with a good strong bouquet. Fat and well balanced on the palate. A most agreeable wine. (1982)
❧ Christian Lassegues, La Fleur-Picon, 33330 St-Emilion; tel. 57 24 70 60 ☙ By appt.

LA FLEUR-POURRET★★

■   7 ha   36 000   5 ❶ ♦

⑥ **75** 78 79 80 81 **82 83**

PE0070A rather undistinguished colour despite a touch of brightness, but the nose is beautifully full and quite woody. Good subtance in the mouth, very definite aromas and good balance. A typically Merlot wine, round and full but not at all harsh. (1980) ✔ St-Estèphe, St-Emilion, Pomerol, Bordeaux Rouge.
❧ SA Dom. Prats, Ch. La Fleur-Pourret, 33330 St-Emilion; tel. 56 44 11 37 ☙ No visitors.

CHATEAU FOMBRAUGE★

■   49 ha   300 000   5 D ❶ ♦

75 76 77 **78** 79 81

A wine of consistent quality from a large estate; the château itself is a fine country house. Firmly structured and fairly tannic on the palate, but a wine which mellows with age. (1982)
❧ Sté Civile de Fombrauge, St-Christophe-des-Bardes, 33330 St-Emilion; tel. 57 24 77 12 ☙ By appt. ❧ M. Charles Bigodt.

CHATEAU FONPLEGADE

■Gd Cru   18 ha   100 000   5 ▮

55 ⑥ **64 66 70** 78 79 80 **81** 82

A good colour. The nose is still somewhat closed but the wine should improve with age. (1979)
✔ Pomerol Ch. Taillefert, Pomerol Ch. Moulinet, St-Emilion Ch. Tour du Pin Figeac, Lalande de Pomerol Ch. Criox Bellevue.
❧ Armand Mueix, Ch. Fonplegade, 33330 St-Emilion; tel. 57 51 50 63 ☙ Mon.–Fri. 8.00–12.00/14.00–18.00.

CHATEAU FRANC BIGAROUX★★

■   9 ha   50 000   4 D ❶ ♦

67 69 71 76 78 ⑦ **79** 80 81 **82 83**

Very attractive colour. Powerful and complex bouquet, with good balance and length on the palate. Already well developed, but will continue to mature. (1979)
❧ Yves Blanc, Ch. Haut-Brisson, 33330 St-Emilion; tel. 57 51 54 73 ☙ By appt.

CHATEAU FRANC GRACE-DIEU★

■   8 ha   40 000   4 ▮ ❶ ♦

61 64 71 75 76 **78** 79 80 **81** ⑧ 83

At first rather spring-like, with cherry colour and raspberry bouquet, this wine becomes autumnal on the nose, with shades of leather, venison and undergrowth. On the palate it is as fleshy as a good mushroom, and develops from a creamy beginning to a somewhat dry tannic texture, upsetting the balance a little but suggesting that it should age well. (1981)
❧ SEV Fournier, Ch. Franc Grace-Dieu, 33330 St-Emilion; tel. 57 24 70 79 ☙ By appt.

CHATEAU FRANC-MAYNE★

■Gd Cru   7 ha   37 000   5 D ▮ ❶ ♦

70 75 78 79 ★**80** 81 ⑧ **82** 83

The nose, in contrast with the deep colour, is still undeveloped, but aromas of ripe fruit can already be detected, prolonged on the palate by a good and pleasing structure. A wine that certainly has a fine future.
❧ SCA Ch. Franc-Mayne, 33330 St-Emilion; tel. 57 24 62 61 ☙ By appt.

CHATEAU FRANC-PIPEAU★

■   4.5 ha   25 000   4 D ❶ ♦

★75 76 ★**79 79** 80 **81** 82 **82**

Dark in colour, with a nose that is still to develop. Despite a slight tannic astringency, the balance on the palate is good. (1982)
❧ *Mme* Jacqueline Bertrand, Ch. Franc-Pipeau, 33330 St-Emilion; tel. 57 24 73 94 ☙ No visitors. ❧ *M.* et *Mme* Descombes.

CHATEAU LA GAFFELIERE★

■1er Gd Cru B   22 ha   100 000   6 D ❶ ♦

61 ⑥ ★**70 75** 76 77 **78** 79 **82 82**

Half English manor, half chapel, the appearance of this château is somewhat eclectic, but not without distinction. The wine reflects some of this character, too: a lovely deep red, it has a complex nose that is both flowery, woody and faintly gamey. On the palate it is a little short, but well balanced delicate and elegant. (1982) ✔ St-Emilion Clos la Gaffelière.
❧ *Comte* Léo Malet de Roquefort, La Gaffelière, 33330 St-Emilion; tel. 57 24 72 15 ☙ By appt.

CHATEAU GAILLARD DE LA GORCE

■   8 ha   45 000   4 D ▮ ♦

74 **75** 76 77 **78** 79 80 ⑧

Bright amber-red wine; a little short, but pleasantly supple on the palate. (1982) ✔ Other St-Emilions, Bordeaux Côtes de Castillon Ch. Grand-Tertre, Bordeaux Supérieur Ch. Pinasse Rouge, Bordeaux Supérieur Ch. Pinasse Clairet, Entre-Deux-Mers Ch. Pinasse.
❧ Jean-Pierre Rollet, Ch. Fourney, St-Pey-d'Armens, 33330 St-Emilion; tel. 57 40 15 13 ☙ No visitors.

CHATEAU GAILLARD★★

■   18 ha   85 000   4 D ❶

64 70 **75** ★**78** ★**79 81 81**

This is a property where visitors are enthusiastically welcomed, on condition that they do not smoke. The wine has a powerful nose and palate, tasting complex and very full bodied. Already pleasing but far from its peak. (1981) ✔ St-Emilion Grand Cru Clos St-Julien.
❧ Jean-Jacques Nouvel, ch. Gaillard, 33330 St-Emilion; tel. 57 24 72 05 ☙ By appt. Closed part of Aug.

CUVEE GALIUS★

■   7 ha   35 000   4 D ❶ ♦

★**82** ★**82**

A newish (1982) brand from this cave-cooperative. Fine colour; nose slightly marked by the wood but still undeveloped. Overall, the wine is

pleasantly fruity and should mature well. (1982)
•ᴛ Uni. Prod. de St-Emilion, BP 27, 33330 St-
Emilion; tel. 57 24 70 71 ⲧ By appt.

CHATEAU GESSAN*

■   8ha   45000   🄴 Ⓓ ⛁ ↓
81 82

This wine has a fine appearance and a nose with a
few vegetal nuances; plenty of flavour on the
palate, but needs keeping. (1982) ✔ Champagne
Philippe-de-Langoz.
•ᴛ M. B. Gonzalez, Ch. Gessan, St-Sulpice-de-
Faleyrens, 33330 St-Emilion; tel. 57 74 44 04
ⲧ Mon–Fri. 9.00–12.00/14.00–19.00.

CHATEAU LA GRACE-DIEU-LES-MENUTS**

■   13ha   60000   🄴 Ⓓ ⑪ ↓
74 75 **78 79 80** 🄼 **81 82** 🄼

Beautiful colour, although the bouquet has yet to
develop fully. Ample promise, of a generous and
elegant wine ready to drink in a few years' time.
(1982)
•ᴛ H. Xans et M. Pilotte, Ch. la Grace-Dieu-les-
Menuts, 33330 St-Emilion; tel. 57 24 73 10 ⲧ By
appt.

CHATEAU GRAND CORBIN DESPAGNE**

■Gd Cru   25ha   120000   🄴 Ⓓ ⛁ ⑪ ↓
⑦⓪ 71 **75** *76 *78 79 80 81 **82** 🄼

Lovely, dark colour. A nose that is remarkable
for its combination of vigour and delicacy. On the
palate, a supple attack is followed by a fleshy fruit
and rich, ripe tannins. Exceptionally well-
rounded finish. (1982) ✔ St-Emilion Ch. de la
Reine Blanche.
•ᴛ Consorts Despagne, Ch. Grand Corbin Despagne, 33330 St-Emilion; tel. 57 51 74 04 ⲧ No
visitors.

CHATEAU GRAND-MAYNE*

■Gd Cru   19ha   110000   🄳 Ⓓ ⑪ ↓
70 ⑦① **76** 78 🄼 81 **82**

A pretty colour and good presence. Very delicate
nose, followed by an honest attack, nicely prolonged by a well-balanced palate. (1982)
•ᴛ Jean-Pierre Nony, Ch. Grand-Mayne, 33330
St-Emilion; tel. 57 74 42 50 ⲧ By appt.

CHATEAU GRANGEY*

■   6ha   30000   🄴 Ⓓ ⛁ ↓
70 *75 76 77 **78** 79 80 **81** ⑧② 🄼 83

Elegant colour, solid and bright. The nose has
not yet fully developed, but the wine already has
good balance and length on the palate. (1982)
•ᴛ Félix Araoz, Ch. Grangey, 33330 St-Emilion;
tel. 57 24 70 71 ⲧ By appt.

CHATEAU GRAVET*

■   11ha   50000   🄴 Ⓓ ⛁ ↓
69 71 76 78 79 80 🄼 **82** 🄼 83

Fine colour. If left to breathe will take an aroma
of ripe fruit, also reflected in the mouth, where it
mingles with already developed tannins. (1982)
•ᴛ Jean Faure, Ch. Gravet, St-Sulpice-de-Faleyrens, 33330 St-Emilion; tel. 56 24 47 68 ⲧ By
appt. Closed Jun.–Sept.; Sat.–Mon.

CHATEAU DES GRAVIERS D'ELLIES

■   7ha   40000   🄴 Ⓓ ⛁ ↓
76 ⑦⑧ 79 80 *81 **82** 🄼 **83**

Slightly severe because of its dark colour, but an
agreeable, unsophisticated wine that is fairly
aromatic, with hints of meatiness. (1982)
✔ Côtes-de-Castillon Ch. du Tertre Rouge,
Côtes-de-Castillod Ch. la Fourquerie Rouge,
Bordeaux Supérieur Ch. Pinasse, Bordeaux
Supérieur Clairet Ch. Pinasse.
•ᴛ Jean-Pierre Rollet, Ch. des Graviers d'Elliès,
St-Sulpice-de-Faleyrans, 33330 St-Emilion; tel.
57 40 15 13 ⲧ No visitors. •ᴛ Max Elliès.

CHATEAU GUADET-SAINT-JULIEN**

■Gd Cru   6ha   24000   🄵 Ⓓ ⑪ ↓
*70 71 74 *75 77 *⑦⑧ 79 🄼 82

As fine in appearance as in bouquet; this wine is
long and aromatic on the palate. The label and
name pay homage to Guadet, the Girondin revolutionary (guillotined in 1794), whose family
owned this property. (1981)
•ᴛ Robert Lignac, Ch. Guadet-Saint-Julien, 33330
St-Emilion; tel. 57 74 40 04 ⲧ By appt.

CHATEAU GUEYROT*

■   9ha   40000   🄴 Ⓓ ⑪ ↓
78 79 🄹 ⑧②

Attractive; still intensely coloured, although
verging on tile-red. Substantial and full bodied on
the palate. (1979) ✔ Fronsac Ch. Beau-Site-de-
la-Tour.
•ᴛ M. De La Tour Du Fayet, Ch. Gueyrot, 33330
St-Emilion; tel. 57 24 72 08 ⲧ By appt.

CHATEAU GRAND GUEYROT

■   12ha   70000   🄵 Ⓓ ⑪ ↓
⑦⓪ 74 **75** 76 78 🄼 80 **82**

A red colour with some development precedes a
subtle but delicate bouquet. Clean, flowing and
easy to drink. Ready now. (1978) ✔ St-Emilion
Ch. Mauvezin, St-Emilion Dom. de Peyrelongue.
•ᴛ GFA Cassat Père et Fils, BP 44, 33330 St-
Emilion; tel. 57 24 72 36 ⲧ By appt.

CHATEAU GUILLEMIN-LA-GAFFELIERE**

■   12ha   80000   🄴 Ⓓ ⛁ ⑪ ↓
78 79 **81 82** 🄼 **83**

A pleasing, dark ruby colour and a fine, delicate
nose. Round, supple, well-balanced and delicately woody on the palate. (1982) ✔ Bordeaux
Supérieur, Côtes de Castillon ch. Fonds Rondes.
•ᴛ Vignobles Fomperier, La Gaffelière, 33330 St-
Emilion; tel. 57 24 74 48 ⲧ By appt.

CHATEAU HAUT BARDOULET*

■   4ha   20000   🄳 Ⓓ ⑪ ↓
75 **78** *79 🄼 **82**

A lively attack and good rich tannins on the
palate. Unpretentious and typical of its appellation. (1981)
•ᴛ Jacques Baraize, Ch. Haut Bardoulet, St-
Etienne-de-Lisse, 33350 St Emilion; tel.
57 40 07 78 ⲧ No visitors.

CHATEAU HAUT-BRISSON

■ 13ha 75000 **4** **D** ◫ ↓
78 79 80 81 ⑧

An attractively coloured wine with an honest, country style and a subtle but very pleasant nose. Originally made by the cooperative, for the past ten years it has been made separately here. (1979)
↜ Yves Blanc, Ch. Haut-Brisson, 33330 St-Emilion; tel. 57 51 54 73 ⅄ By appt.

CHATEAU HAUTE-NAUVE★

■ 6ha 35000 **4** **D** ▤ ↓
70 ★75 76 77 **78 79 80 81 82** ⑧ 83

Produced by a cooperative, this wine shows a typical ruby-red colour; rather distinctive nose with aromas of candied fruit. The palate is fairly tannic. (1982)
↜ Raymond Reynier, Ch. Haute-Nauve, 33330 St-Emilion; tel. 57 24 70 71 ⅄ By appt.

CHATEAU HAUT-LAVALLADE★★★

■ 12ha 60000 **4** **D** ▤ ◫ ↓
66 ★70 71 ★75 76 78 79 81 ⑧ ⑧

Superbly attractive wine, with a magnificent dark red colour. The nose is still a little undeveloped, but is already very promising. After a good attack, rich, harmonious and elegant flavours develop on the palate. A fine wine which should be kept. (1982)
↜ J.-P. Chagneau et Fils, Ch. Haut-Lavallade, St-Christophe-des-Bardes, 33330 St-Emilion; tel. 57 24 77 47 ⅄ Mon.–Sat. 9.00–12.00/14.00–18.00, Sun. by appt.

CHATEAU HAUT-MOUREAUX

■ 9ha 60000 **3** **D** ▤ ↓
⑦ ⑦ 75 76 **78 81** ⑧ 82

The clear, bright colour and bouquet are immediately attractive, although the wine is a little short on the palate. (1982)
↜ Christian Courrèche, BP 27, 33330 St-Emilion; tel. 57 24 70 71 ⅄ By appt.

CHATEAU HAUT-PLANTEY★

■ 9ha 50000 **5** **D** ◫
70 74 ★75 78 ⑦ 79 ★80 81 82

Colour shading into brick-red; well-developed nose with a smoky touch, and very aromatic. After a slightly sharp attack, the palate, too, is aromatic. Drink now. (1978)
↜ Michel Boutet, Haut-Plantey, 33330 St-Emilion; tel. 57 24 70 86 ⅄ By appt. Closed Aug.

CHATEAU HAUT-SARPE★

■Gd Cru 11ha 65000 **5** **D** ◫ ↓
78 79 ⑦ ⑧ 81 ⑧ 83

An aristocratic château, modelled after the famous Trianon at Versailles. The wine, too, shows distinction, with strong colour and plenty of flavour on the palate. (1982)
↜ Joseph Janoueix, Ch. Haut-Sarpe, 33330 St-Emilion; tel. 57 51 41 86 ⅄ By appt. Closed Sun.

CLOS DES JACOBINS★★

■Gd Cru 8ha 50000 **6** ◫ ↓
★78 ★79 ★⑧ ★⑧ 81 ★82 ⑧

This very fine wine, still a little difficult to assess, is certainly assured of a very good future. (1983)
✔ St-Estèphe Ch. Meyney, Sauternes Ch. Lafaurie-Peyraguey, Médoc Ch. Plagnac, Bordeaux Ch. Le Gardera-Ch. Tanesse Rouge et Blanc, St-Julien Ch. Talbot.
↜ Dom. Cordier, Ch. Clos des Jacobins, 33330 St-Emilion; tel. 57 24 70 14 ⅄ By appt. Closed end Aug.–beginning Sept.

CHATEAU JEAN FAURE★

■ 18ha 96000 **5** **D** ◫ ↓
★⑦ ★79 ★⑦ ★80 ★⑧ ★81 82 83

A rather light wine, despite a dark colour. Nevertheless round, supple and of good quality. (1978) ✔ Montagne-St-Emilion Ch. Montaiguillon, Pineau-des-Charentes Blanc Dom. de Lizet, Pineau-des-Charentes Rouge Dom. de Lizet.
↜ Michel Amart, Ch. Jean Faure, 33330 St-Emilion; tel. 57 51 49 36 ⅄ By appt.

CLOS LABARDE★

■ 4.5ha 20000 **4** **D** ▤ ◫ ↓
66 70 75 77 **78 79** ⑦ ⑧ **81 82** 83

A good colour and a pleasantly aromatic nose. Overall, pleasing and well balanced on the palate. (1979) This property will shortly have an apartment available for visitors who wish to stay in St-Emilion in order to discover its wines. ✔ St-Emilion Grand Cru Ch. Tour-de-Bardes.
↜ Jacques Bailly, Clos Labarde, 33330 St-Emilion; tel. 57 74 40 26 ⅄ By appt. Closed 12–18 Aug.

CHATEAU LAMARTRE★

■ 11ha 80000 **4** **D** ▤ ↓
⑦ ⑧ ⑧ ⑧ 82

Fine bright ruby colour; natural scent of ripe fruit on the nose, followed by body and suppleness on the palate. (1982)
↜ *MM.* Vialard, Lamartre, 33330 St-Emilion; tel. 57 24 70 71 ⅄ By appt.

CHATEAU LAPELLETRIE★

■ 12ha 62000 **4** **D** ▤ ↓
76 77 79 ⑦ 80 ⑧ ⑧ ⑧ 83

Aged underground in a former quarry, now converted into a cellar, this wine has a very pleasant spicy bouquet. First impressions are of finesse, but the tannin becomes too apparent. (1979) ✔ St-Emilion Grand Cru Ch. Trimoulet, Montagne St-Emilion Vieux Ch. Négrit.
↜ Pierre Jean, Lapelletrie, 33330 St-Emilion; tel. 57 24 77 54 ⅄ By appt. Closed Aug. ↜ GFA du Ch. Lapelletrie.

CHATEAU LARCIS-DUCASSE★★

■Gd Cru 10ha 36000 ⑤ D ⬙
㊹ 64 75 78 ▓78 80 81 82

A 1978 wine with an intense colour and pleasantly complex nose, recalling fruit and wood especially. Smooth and harmonious in the mouth, with a long, tannic finish. A good future. (1978)
➼ *Mme* Gratiot, Ch. Larcis-Ducasse, 33330 St-Emilion; tel. 57 24 70 84 ☂ By appt.

CHATEAU LARMANDE★★★

■Gd Cru 19ha 100000 ⑤ ⬙ ⬙
71 75 76 78 79 80 81 82 ▓82 83

A rich wine with good colour. Powerful bouquet, with a hint of vanilla and spices; full, ample and well balanced on the palate. (1982) ✔ St-Emilion Grand Cru Ch. des Templiers.
➼ SCE Vig. Méneret-Capdemoulin, Ch. Larmande, 33330 St-Emilion; tel. 57 24 71 41 ☂ By appt.

Saint-Emilion Grand Cru Classé

CHATEAU LARMANDE

APPELLATION SAINT-EMILION GRAND CRU CLASSE CONTROLEE

1982

SOCIETE CIVILE D'EXPLOITATION DES VIGNOBLES MENERET-CAPDEMOULIN
A SAINT-EMILION - GIRONDE - FRANCE

MIS EN BOUTEILLE AU CHATEAU 75cl

CHATEAU LAROQUE★

■ 44ha 240000 ⑤ D ⬙ ⬙
76 77 78 ★79 80 81 ㊷ ▓82 83

This lovely château has a vineyard whose products have a silky appearance, a heady soft fruit bouquet, and a well-structured, tannic palate. (1982)
➼ Sté Civ. du Ch. Laroque, St-Christophe-de-Bardes, 33330 St-Emilion; tel. 57 24 77 28 ☂ By appt.

⚡CHATEAU LAROZE

■Gd Cru 30ha 140000 D ⬙ ⬙
75 78 81 82 83 *8o*

A 19th-century château is the centrepiece for this sandy-soiled vineyard which produces a pleasant wine. Warm, supple yet fairly tannic. (1982)
➼ Héritiers Meslin-Gurch, Ch. Lagorce, 33330 St-Emilion; tel. 57 24 72 10 ☂ By appt.

CHATEAU LASSEGUE★★

■ 23ha 130000 ④ ⬙ ⬙
64 66 70 75 77 78 79 ▓79 80 81 82 ▓82 83

This elegant 18th-century residence surrounded by greenery produces an equally charming and elegant wine. The robe is a fine, dark red, while the nose, although a little discreet, has very delicate aromas. Round, supple and harmonious on the palate. (1982)
➼ J.-P. Freylon, Lassègue-St-Hippolyte, 33330 St-Emilion; tel. 57 24 72 83 ☂ By appt.

CLOS LA MADELEINE★

■Gd Cru 2ha 12000 ⑤ D ⬙ ⬙ ⬙
Pretty ruby colour, with a strong, fruity nose, followed on the palate by a well-rounded attack. (1981)
➼ M.H.Pistouley,LaGaffelière,3330St-Emilion; tel. 57 24 71 50 ☂ No visitors.

CHATEAU MAGNAN LA GAFFELIERE★★

■ 8ha 35000 ④ D ⬙ ⬙ ⬙
★75 77 79 80 81 ▓81 82

Fine ruby colour with hints of orange. The nose is also pleasing: powerful and warm. Promising tannin, some finesse and good length on the palate. (1981) ✔ St-Emilion Grand Cru Classé Clos la Madeleine.
➼ Hubert Pistouley, Magnan la Gaffelière, 33330 St-Emilion; tel. 57 24 71 50 ☂ No visitors.

CHATEAU ROLLAND MAILLET★

■ 4ha 18000 ④ D ⬙ ⬙ ⬙
75 76 78 79 80 ★▓81 ㊻ ▓82 ▓83

The aromas of overripe fruit blend harmoniously with one another, as do the tannins. Barrel age has given the wine a pleasing oaky flavour, and its long finish is particularly pleasant. (1981)
➼ Geneviève Rolland, Maillet, Pomerol, 33500 Libourne tel. 57 51 10 94 ☂ By appt.

CHATEAU LA MARZELLE

■ 14ha 69800 ⑤ D ⬙ ⬙
㊶ 73 75 78 79 80 81 82 83

Ruby turning brick-red at the rim. Closed on the nose. Fairly tannic, roasted and aromatic fruit character on the palate. (1981)
➼ GAEC Carrère, 33330 St-Emilion; tel. 57 24 71 43 ☂ No visitors.

CHATEAU MATRAS

■Gd Cru 10ha 60000 ⑤ D ⬙ ⬙ ⬙
66 67 74 75 76 77 78 79 ▓80 81 ▓81 82 ▓82 83 ▓83

A little short, but a fine appearance and a pleasing nose. (1982) ✔ St-Emilion, Jean Voisin Grand Cru, St-Emilion l'Hermtage Grand Cru.
➼ Jean Bernard, Ch. de Matras, Loiseau, 33126 Fronsac; tel. 57 51 52 39 ☂ By appt.

CHATEAU MAUVEZIN★

■ 4ha 14500 ⑥ D ⬙ ⬙ ⬙
㊀ 74 75 76 78 ▓78 80 82

This pleasant château produces a wine which, though a little heady, has good colour, a finely aromatic nose and supple balance in the mouth. Ready to drink from now on. (1978) ✔ St-Emilion Dom. de Peyrelongue, St-Emilion Grand Cru Ch. Gueyrot.
➼ Pierre Cassat et Fils, B.P. 44, 33330 St-Emilion; tel. 57 24 72 36 ☂ By appt.

CHATEAU MAUVINON★

■ 13ha 65000 ④ D ⬙ ⬙
60 66 70 71 ▓81 ㊷ 83

A fine purple wine with a powerful nose, evocative of ripe fruit. The tannins are noticeable on the palate, although perhaps already a little mellowed. (1982)

↰ Claude Tribaudeau, BP 27, 33330 St-Emilion; tel. 57 24 70 71 ⍩ By appt.

CHATEAU MONBOUSQUET

■		45ha	160000	5 D 🍾 ⑪

66 70 73 74 75 76 77 ⑦⑧ **79** 80 82

Dark ruby in colour. Aromatic but closed on the nose; similarly undeveloped on the palate. (1982)
↰ Daniel Querre, BP 140, 33500 Libourne; tel. 57 51 56 18 ⍩ By appt.

CHATEAU LA MONDOTTE★

■		4.16ha	20000	4 D ⑪ ↓

70 71 72 **75** 78 79 ★80 ⑧① **81 82**

Raised in the same cellars as its famous brother, Canon la Gaffelière, this is a classic wine. It has a fine, lively ruby robe and fruity, pleasing aromas. The palate is fairly tannic – the guarantee of a good future. (1981)
↰ SCEV des Comtes de Naipperg, Ch. Canon la Gaffelière, 33330 St-Emilion; tel. 57 24 71 33 ⍩ No visitors.

CHATEAU MONTLABERT★

■		15ha	70000	4 D 🍾 ⑪ ↓

69 71 73 74 ⑦⑤ 76 77 **78** 79 81 82 83

A pale, youthful colour and delicate, grassy nose. Supple and refined, but on the whole lacking a little body. A pleasing wine, ready to drink now. (1979) ✔ Graves.
↰ SC du Ch. Montlabert, 33330 St-Emilion; tel. 56 39 59 86 ⍩ By appt. Closed weekends and public holidays.

CHATEAU MOULIN-BELLEGRAVE★

■		14ha	65000	4 🍾 ↓

70 72 73 75 ⑦⑨ 79 80 81

Already a mature vintage, but one which has aged well. An agreeable nose; still smooth and pleasing to drink. (1979) ✔ St-Emilion Ch. des Graves.
↰ Max Perier, Moulin-Bellegrave, Vignonet, 33330 St-Emilion; tel. 57 84 53 28 ⍩ No visitors.

CHATEAU MOULIN SAINT-GEORGES★★★

■		6ha	25000	5 D 🍾 ⑪ ↓

70 70 **75** 75 77 77 79 82 82

A deep ruby colour; the nose is still closed but suggests plenty of class; a crisp attack is followed by a full-bodied, well-balanced palate and good length. It would be a pity to drink this too young. (1982)
↰ Alain Vauthier, Moulin St-Georges, 33330 St-Emilion; tel. 57 24 70 26 ⍩ By appt.

CHATEAU DE NAUDE★

■		6ha	35000	5 D 🍾 ↓

76 78 ★**79** 80 81 82 82

Velvety deep-red appearance; very ripe-fruit nose; rich, round and supple on the palate. Pleasing wine for drinking now. (1982)
↰ Alain Bonneau, 33420 Branne; tel. 57 84 50 01 ⍩ By appt.

CLOS DE L'ORATOIRE★

■Gd Cru		9.45ha	50000	5 D ⑪ ↓

71 74 **75** 76 ★78 ★⑦⑨ ★79 80 81 82

In spite of a slightly short finish, this wine has a fine bouquet, with a strong and supple palate. (1979)
↰ SC du Ch. Peyreau, 33330 St-Emilion; tel. 57 24 70 86 ⍩ By appt. Closed Aug.

CHATEAU PALAIS-CARDINAL-LA-FUIE★

■		13ha	70000	4 D 🍾 ↓

62 64 66 71 77 79 80 81 ⑧② 82

A striking deep ruby colour, the wine has a clean bouquet and a pleasant, moderately rich, mature taste. Should be drunk soon. (1982)
↰ Gérard Fretier, St-Sulpice-de-Taleyrens, 33330 St-Emilion; tel. 57 24 75 91 ⍩ By appt. Closed Tues. and Fri.

CHATEAU PAVIE DECESSE★★

■Gd Cru		9.5ha	80000	5 ⑪ ↓

75 76 77 **78** ★⑦⑨ ★79 80 **81**

Dark ruby colour; a bouquet that is still very strong, even rich and powerful, and a palate to match. (1979) ✔ St-Emilion 1er Grand Cru Classé Ch. Pavite, St-Emilion Grand Cru Classé Ch. la Clusière.
↰ SCA Les Consorts Valette, Ch. Pavie, 33330 St-Emilion; tel. 57 24 72 02 ⍩ By appt. ↰ Jean-Paul Valette.

CHATEAU PAVIE★★

■1er Gd Cru		37ha	185000	6 ⑪ ↓

67 71 72 73 74 **76** 77 **79** 79 80 **81** ⑧② **83**

Has a beautiful colour, and is balanced enough on the palate to fulfil the finesse and complexity promised by the nose, if left to age a little. (1979)
↰ Consorts Valette, Ch. Pavie, 33330 St-Emilion; tel. 57 24 72 02 ⍩ By appt. ↰ Jean-Paul Vallette.

CHATEAU PETIE-FAURIE DE-SOUTARD★

■Gd Cru		8ha	40000	5 D 🍾 ↓

77 ★78 **79** 79 80 81 ⑧②

Colour shading to garnet; warm, powerful aromas; is somewhat heavy. This is a wine that has reached its peak. Drink now. (1979)
↰ Françoise Capdemoulin, Ch. Petit-Faurie de-Soutard, 33330 St-Emilion; tel. 57 74 62 06 ⍩ By appt.

CHATEAU PETIT VAL

■		6.11ha	30000	4 D ⑪ ↓

74 76 77 ★**79** 80 **81** 82

Typical St-Emilion, deep ruby in colour with tinges of violet. The nose, which is still very closed up, has a slight woody character with a pleasing touch of fruit. (1981)
↰ Michel Boutet, Haut-Plantey, 33330 St-Emilion; tel. 57 24 70 86 ⍩ By appt.

CHATEAU PETIT-GRAVET★

■   5ha   25000   4 D ◑ ⌄

64 66 70 71 ⑦⑤ 77 78 79 *⑧① *82

Intense ruby-coloured wine from a small family estate that has been handed down through several generations. It has a powerful, fruity nose, and is full in the mouth. Still a bit hard and tannic, perhaps, but should mellow in time. (1981)
↜ *Mme* L. Nouvel, Petit-Gravet, 33330 St-Emilion; tel. 57 24 72 34 ⼻ By appt.

CHATEAU PEYREAU★★

■   13ha   75000   4 D ◑ ⌄

*75 76 **78** *79 *⑦⑨ *80 **81 82**

Pleasing, with lively floral aromas and a frank attack. Finesse and length on the palate. Ready to drink, but may be kept. (1979)
↜ SC du Ch. Peyreau, 33330 St-Emilion; tel. 57 24 70 86 ⼻ By appt. Closed Aug.

CHATEAU HAUT-PEYROUTAS★★

■   8ha   35000   4 D ⼿ ⌄

68 72 **75** 79 80 ⑧② ⑧②

A smart wine with fine red colour and plenty of character, despite a slight touch of aggression on the nose (due to the time spent in cask). Needs keeping. (1982) ✔ Bordeaux Labécot Rouge.
↜ Labécot et Fils, Haut-Peyroutas, Vignonnet, 33330 St-Emilion; tel. 57 84 53 31 ⼻ By appt. Closed Nov.

CHATEAU PINDEFLEURS★

■   8.5ha   33000   4 ⼿ ◑ ⌄

78 ⑧① **82 83**

An attractive wine with an elegant and delicate nose, shades of linden blossom, undergrowth and cocoa. On the palate, it displays a certain breeding, with good attack and very good balance (1982)
↜ Micheline Dior, Ch. Pindefleurs, 33330 St-Emilion; tel. 57 24 72 04 ⼻ No visitors.

CHATEAU PINEY★

■   9ha   60000   4 D ⼿ ⌄

78 ⑦⑨ ⑧⓪ *⑧① *⑧②

A wine that is ready to drink now, with a straightforward and typical Merlot nose. Elegant, pleasing and smooth on the palate. (1982)
↜ Union des Prod. Jean Catusseau, Ch. Piney, 33330 St-Emilion; tel. 57 24 70 71 ⼻ By appt.

CHATEAU LE PRIEURE★

■Gd Cru   5ha   20000   5 D ◑ ⌄

70 71 **75 78** 79 80 81 ⑧② ⑧② 83

This property came into being as a result of the breaking-up of the famous Cordeliers vineyard. It produces a wine deep in colour and pronounced on the nose, with tannins and good length on the palate. It should still be kept for some time. (1982) ✔ Pomerol Ch. Vraye Croix de Gay, Lalande-de-Pomerol Ch. Siaurac.
↜ Baronne Guichard, Néac, 33500 Libourne; tel. 57 51 64 58 ⼻ No visitors.

CHATEAU PUYBLANQUET-CARRILLE

■   14ha   70000   4 D ⼿ ◑ ⌄

75 ⑦⑥ 79 **82 83**

A lovely cherry red, tinged with amber. Despite a somewhat weak nose, it should appeal to those who enjoy mature wines. (1979) ✔ St-Emilion Rouge, Bordeaux Supérieur Rouge.
↜ Jean-François Carrille, Ch. Cardinal-Villemaurine, 33330 St-Emilion; tel. 57 24 74 46 ⼻ By appt.

CHATEAU PUY-RAZAC★

■   7ha   36000   5 D ⼿ ⌄

⑦⓪ ⑦① 73 74 75 ⑦⑤ 76 ⑦⑥ ⑦⑧ ⑦⑨ 80 ⑧① 82 ⑧① 82

The owners of this château are as proud of the ham, mushrooms and baby eels prepared by the mistress of the house, as of the wine itself. This has a good colour, is pleasantly fresh and fruity, but should be given time to develop. (1982)
↜ Daniel Querre, BP 140, Place Guadet, 33500 Libourne; tel. 57 51 56 18 ⼻ By appt. ↜ Guy Thoilliez.

HAUT-QUERCUS★

■   5ha   30000   4 D ◑ ⌄

71 76 78 **79** **81 82** ⑧②

Fine, deep colour. Still dominated by the flavour of new wood, which means a certain lack of sophistication. Good body, with a marked degree of tannin. (1982)
↜ Union des Producteurs, de St-Emilion, 33330 St-Emilion; tel. 57 24 70 71 ⼻ By appt.

CHATEAU QUINAULT★

■   11ha   62000   4 D ⼿ ◑ ⌄

⑧⓪ 81 ⑧② ⑧②

Once a country estate in the middle of nowhere, this pleasant little château is now trapped within the urban area of Libourne. The vine does not seem to have suffered, however, as the 1982 vintage shows; a charming wine with a delicate bouquet; supple and rich. (1982)
↜ Henri Maleret, Av. du Parc-des-Sports, 33502 Libourne Cedex; tel. 57 51 13 39 ⼻ By appt. Closed Aug. and during harvest.

CHATEAU ROC ST-MICHEL

■   4ha   25000   4 D ⼿ ⌄

70 71 73 74 **75** 76 77 ⑦⑧ 79 81 82

Pleasing colour, and 'toasted' aromas on the nose. Tannins still a little harsh, but fairly dense on the palate. (1982) ✔ Other St-Emilions, Bordeaux Côtes de Castillon Ch. Grand-Tertre, Bordeaux Supérieur Ch. Pinasse Rouge, Bordeaux Supérieur Ch. Pinasse Clairet, Entre-Deux-Mers Ch. Pinasse.
↜ J.-P. Rollet, Ch. Fourney, St-Pey d'Armens, 33330 St-Emilion; tel. 57 40 15 13 ⼻ No visitors.

CHATEAU DU ROCHER★

■   14ha   75000   4 D ⼿

79 81 ⑧②

The estate has been in the same family since the 15th century. A wine that is light in appearance; similarly light and supple on the palate. (1979)
↜ Baron Stanislas de Montfort, Ch. du Rocher, 33330 St-Emilion; tel. 57 40 18 20 ⼻ By appt.

CHATEAU LA ROSE-COTES-ROL★★

■   8ha 45000 4 D ▪ ◫↓

⑦⑨ ⁊⁹ 80 81 **82**

A wine of quality that is ageing well. Its colour is still very fresh and strong, and a fine, powerful nose is followed by a crisp attack and delicate palate. (1979)
☞ Yves Mirande, La Rose-Côtes-Rol, 33330 St-Emilion; tel. 57 24 71 28 ⏀ By appt.

CHATEAU LA ROSE-POURRET

■   6ha 36000 4 D ▪ ◫ ↓

67 *⑦ 71 ⁊⁊ 79 81 82

Possibly past its best, and beginning to show its age, but pleasing and generously supple none the less. Drink soon. (1979)
☞ Bernard Warion, La Rose-Pourret, 33330 St-Emilion; tel. 57 24 71 13 ⏀ By appt.

ROYAL-ST-EMILION★

■   60ha 350000 4 D ▪ ↓

78 79 ⑧⁰ ⁸⁰ ⁸¹ **82** ⁸²

At 350 000 bottles a year, this is a large-scale production, but a high-quality one. Witness its amber-hued red, with a delicate, faintly roasted nose, and warmth and roundness on the palate. (1982)
☞ Union des Prod. de St-Emilion, 33330 St-Emilion; tel. 57 24 70 71 ⏀ By appt.

SAINT-GEORGES-COTES-PAVIE★

■Gd Cru   20000 5 ◫ ↓

71 75 76 **79** 80 **81** *82 83

A well-made wine; pleasing in appearance with an appealing nose and a well-balanced palate. (1982)
☞ Jacques Masson, 33330 St-Emilion; tel. 57 74 44 23 ⏀ No visitors.

CLOS SAINT-JULIEN★★★

■   2ha 60000 4 D ◫

64 **70** 71 73 75 78 ⑦⁹ ⁊⁹

A good wine with a fine appearance and good tannin on the palate. ✔ St-Emilion Ch. Gaillard.
☞ Jean-Jacques Nouvel, Clos St-Julien, 33330 St-Emilion; tel. 57 24 72 05 ⏀ By appt.

CHATEAU DE SAINT-PEY★

■   16ha 90000 4 D ◫ ↓

⑦⁵ 79 81 *⁸²

Fine ruby colour. Warmly aromatic. Clean, fresh flavour with an interesting finish. Good to drink now. (1982)
☞ Maurice Musset, Ch. de St-Pey, St-Pey d'Armens, 33330 St-Emilion; tel. 57 40 15 25 ⏀ Mon.–Sat. 9.00–19.00.

CHATEAU SANSONNET

■Gd Cru   7ha 40000 5 D ◫ ↓

⑦⁵ 78 **79** 80 81 ⁸¹ 82 83

At present a little austere, the wine has an attractive red colour and combines a certain finesse with a light fruity flavour. (1981) ✔ St-Emilion Ch. Doumayne.
☞ Françis Robin, Ch. Sansonnet, 33330 St-Emilion; tel. 57 51 03 65 ⏀ No visitors.

CHATEAU DE LA SEIGNURIE★

■   10ha 50000 4 ▪ ↓

*79 80 81 ⑧² ⁸² **83**

Lively ruby colour. Somewhat closed on the nose, though ripe fruit certainly present. Soft attack, well-constituted development, but fairly tannic on the finish. Needs keeping for a while. (1982) ✔ Montagne St-Emilion les Tours de Bayard, Montagne St Emilion les Tuileries de Bayard.
☞ Bayard Laporte, Montagne, 33570 Lussac; tel. 57 74 62 47 ⏀ By appt.

CHATEAU LA SERRE★★

■Gd Cru   7ha 40000 5 D ▪ ◫ ↓

66 75 **81 82** ⁸³

A wine combining beautiful deep-ruby colour with a fine nose (spices, vanilla and woodiness). Very powerful on the palate, with superb presence. Needs to be left for some time. (1983)
☞ M. d'Arfeuille, Ch. La Pointe, Pomerol, 33500 Libourne; tel. 57 51 02 11 ⏀ By appt.

CHATEAU TERTE DAUGAY★★
Grand Cru Classé

■   16ha 60000 5 D ◫ ↓

61 ⑥⁴ *70 **75** 76 77 **78** 80 **82** ⁸²

Situated on a hilltop that used to be a lookout point, the estate belongs to one of the oldest and most famous St-Emilion families that consistently produces good wine, of which this 1982 is a fine example. A delicate, ripe fruit bouquet. Harmonious, well balanced and long on the palate. (1982) ✔ St-Emilion Ch. de Roquefort.
☞ Comté Léo Malet de Roquefort, Tertre Daugay, 33330 St-Emilion; tel. 57 24 72 15 ⏀ By appt.

CHATEAU LE TERTRE-ROTEBOEUF★★

■Gd Cru   4ha 15000 4 D ◫ ↓

71 76 79 80 *81 ⑧² ⁸²

Good colour with aromas of ripe fruit. Well-balanced, round and supple palate with marked finesse and good length. (1982)
☞ MM. F. and E. Mitjaville, Ch. Le Tertre-Roteboeuf, 33330 St-Emilion; tel. 57 24 70 57 ⏀ Daily 10.00–12.00/15.00–19.00.

CHATEAU TEYSSIER★

■   15ha 90000 4 ◫ ↓

76 77 **78 79** 80 **81** ⁸¹ **82** 83

Attractive looking, with a pretty, intense ruby colour allied to quite a fruity nose. Unaggressive to taste; pleasant and easy to drink. (1981)
☞ MM. Dourthe Frères, 35 Rue de Bordeaux, Parempuyre, 33290 Blanquefort; tel. 56 35 84 64 ⏀ No visitors.

CHATEAU TOUR-SAINT-CHRISTOPHE★★

■   17ha 85000 4 ◫ ↓

75 78 80 81 **82** ⁸² **83**

Distinguished less by its bright, garnet colour than by its aroma, which has distinctive hints of spices and liquorice. Most agreeable on the palate; round, with an excellent finish. (1982)
✔ Montagne-St-Emilion.

☙ Henri Guiter, Tour St-Christophe, 33330 St-Emilion; tel. 57 24 77 15 ☿ By appt. Closed Aug.

CHATEAU LA TOUR-FIGEAC★

■Grand Cru	13ha 75000	5 D ⚭ ⚓

71 **75** 76 77 ⑦⑧ **78** 79 80 81 82

The nose seems a little weak, given the fine ruby colour, but after a frank attack one discovers a supple roundness on the palate. (1978)
☙ SC du Ch. la Tour-Figeac, 33330 St-Emilion; tel. 57 24 70 86 ☿ By appt. Closed August.

CHATEAU TRAPAUD★

■	14ha 75000	4 D ⚓ ⚭ ⚓

⑦⑤ **79** **81** **82**

Shading from red to garnet in colour, the wine is still a little closed, but straightforward and tannic. It will benefit from being laid down. (1982)
✔ St-Emilion Grand Cru.
☙ André Larribière, Ch. Trapaud St-Etienne-de-Lisse, 33330 St-Emilion; tel. 57 40 18 08 ☿ Mon.–Fri. 8.00–12.00/14.00–19.00.

CHATEAU TRIMOULET★

■Gd Cru	16ha 75000	5 ⚓ ⚭ ⚓

76 78 **79** 80 **81** **81** 82

Makes a very good impression; aromas and taste are 'country-style' with conspicuous tannin. (1981)
☙ Michel Jean, Ch. Trimoulet, 33330 St-Emilion; tel. 57 24 70 56 ☿ By appt. Closed August.

CLOS-TRIMOULET★★

■	7ha 40000	4 D ⚓ ⚭ ⚓

79 **80** **81** **81** **82** 82

A well-balanced wine, dark red in colour, with a positive soft fruit bouquet, and a pleasing and fairly tannic palate. (1981) ✔ Montagne St-Emilion Rouge.
☙ Guy Appollot, Clos-Trimoulet, 33330 St-Emilion; tel. 57 24 71 96 ☿ By appt.

LES TROIS COURONNES

■	60ha 120000	3 ⚭ ⚓

⑥① **66** 70 71 **75** 81 **82** **82**

There is undoubtedly a delicate side to this wine, but the colour is strong and the palate rounded with nicely resolved tannins. (1982)
☙ P. Salin et Fils âiné, 67 Rue Prunier, 33300 Bordeaux; tel. 56 39 67 32.

CHATEAU TROPLONG-MONDOT★

■Gd Cru	29ha 120000	5 ⚭ ⚓

★70 **71** 76 79 80 81 **82** 83

This estate originally belonged to the influential Sèze family, one of whom defended Louis XVI before the Revolutionary Court. The wine has a fine colour, but the nose is still undeveloped. The solid structure on the palate suggests that it will age well. (1979)
☙ Claude Valette, Ch. Troplong-Mondot, 33330 St-Emilion; tel. 57 24 70 72 ☿ Mon.–Fri. 8.00–18.00. Closed Aug.

CHATEAU VIEUX GUINOT

■	10ha 60000	4 D ⚓ ⚓

74 **75** 76 77 **78** 79 80 ⑧②

This property has belonged to the same family since at least the beginning of the 18th century. Its light, crisp and pleasant wine is amber-red in colour, warm and easy to drink. (1982) ✔ Other St-Emilions, Bordeaux Côtes de Castillon Ch. Grand-Tertre, Bordeaux Supérieur Ch. Pinasse Rouge, Bordeaux Supérieur Ch. Pinasse Clairet, Entre-Deux-Mers Ch. Pinasse.
☙ Jean-Pierre Rollet, Ch. Fourney, St-Pey-d'Armens, 33330 St-Emilion; tel. 57 40 15 13 ☿ No visitors.

CHATEAU DU VIEUX-POURRET★

■	4ha 20000	4 D ⚭ ⚓

80 **80** **81** **82** **82**

A somewhat unusual wine that cleverly combines finesse with a certain rustic style. Lively and straightforward at first, it is round on the palate but a little too harshly tannic on the finish. (1981)
☙ Michel Boutet, Haut-Plantey, 33330 St-Emilion; tel. 57 24 70 86 ☿ By appt. Closed Aug.

CHATEAU VIEUX-SARPE★

■	6.5ha 35000	5 D ⚭ ⚓

70 78 ⑦⑨ **79** 81 **82**

Legend has it that this vineyard was established by soldiers of the Emperor Probus. Their labours were fruitful if judged by this country-style wine that is rounded and full of character. Needs to be laid down for a while. (1982)
☙ Jean-François Janoueix,Le Castelot, 33330 St-Emilion; tel. 57 51 41 86 ☿ By appt. Closed Sun.

CHATEAU VILLEMAURINE★★★

■Gd Cru	8ha 50000	5 D ⚓ ⚭ ⚓

62 **64** 69 70 73 74 **75** 76 77 78 ⑦⑨ 80 81

Aged in casks in a most impressive underground cellar, this wine is moderate in colour, but has a fine oaky nose, and an attractive palate, with marked ripe fruit, excellent balance and a long, aromatic finish. (1981)
☙ Robert Giraud, SA, Dom. de l'Oiseau, BP 31, 33240 St-André-de-Cubzac; tel. 57 43 01 44 ☿ By appt. Closed Mon.

CHATEAU CARDINAL VILLEMAURINE★★★

■	10ha 50000	4 D ⚓ ⚭ ⚓

70 **75** ⑦⑥ 78 79 81 **82** **82** 83

A classy, well-coloured wine, with a complex nose (roasted almonds and cocoa), and a full, rich palate. (1982)
☙ Jean-François Carrille, Ch. Cardinal-Villemaurine, 33330 St-Emilion; tel. 57 24 74 46 ☿ By appt.

CHÂTEAU
CARDINAL-VILLEMAURINE
S'Emilion Grand Cru
APPELLATION ST-EMILION GRAND CRU CONTROLÉE
1981
P. CARRILLE
PROPRIÉTAIRE A S'EMILION . GIRONDE
MIS EN BOUTEILLE AU CHATEAU

The St-Emilion Regional Appellations

Several communes bordering St-Emilion, and formerly under its jurisdiction, are allowed to add the name of their famous neighbour. These are Montagne St-Emilion, Lussac St-Emilion, Puisseguin St-Emilion, St-Georges St-Emilion and Parsac St-Emilion. The last two appellations refer to communes that today are part of Montagne.

All of these lie to the north of the town, in hilly country dotted with many fine châteaux. The soils are very varied, but the same grape varieties are used as for St-Emilion, producing wines with a marked family resemblance. In 1982, 24 million bottles of wine were produced.

Lussac St-Emilion

CHÂTEAU BELLEVUE D'ESPY★

■　　　　　3ha　20000　**3** **D** **▐** ↓

Light red; very agreeable fruity nose; quite rich and round to drink, and at its best now. (1981) ✔ Bordeaux Supérieur Ch. Bellevue d'Espy Rouge.
➤ Yvan Lajarthe, Ch. Bellevue-d'Espy, Abzac, 33230 Coutras; tel. 57 49 05 1 ☎ Mon.–06 8.00–12.00/14.00–19.00.

CHÂTEAU DE BELLEVUE★★

■　　　　11.5ha　70000　**4** **D** **▐** ⑩ ↓
81 ⑧② **82** **83**

This wine has a spicy nose suggesting fruit brandy, and well-resolved tannin on the palate. It shows nothing of the dryness which can mark wines from limestone soils. (1982)
➤ Charles Chatenoud, Ch. de Bellevue, 33570 Lussac; tel. 57 84 00 25 ☎ By appt.

CHÂTEAU LE BOURDIL★

■　　　　8.6ha　57000　**4** **D** **▐** ↓

A handsome wine with an honest, clear red colour. Finesse and distinction on the palate, but a finish which needs time to smooth out. (1982)
➤ Claude Bonhomme, Brouard, Lalande-de-Pomerol, 33500 Libourne; tel. 57 51 17 75 ☎ Daily 9.00–18.00.

CHÂTEAU BRANDA★★

■　　　　14ha　78000　**3** **D** **▐** ⑩ ↓
★79 80 **84** ⑧② 83

The carmine-red colour is pleasing, as is the ripe, concentrated and complex nose. On the palate the wine is well balanced; full, rich, tannic and with good potential. (1982)
➤ Paul Bordes, Ch. Branda, Puisseguin, 33570 Lussac; tel. 57 84 02 55 ☎ By appt.

CHÂTEAU DU COURLAT★

■　　　　13ha　72000　　**4** **▐** ↓

Noticeably deep-red colour; somewhat reserved on the nose, but full, mellow and nicely balanced on the palate. Already good to drink. (1983)
➤ Pierre Bourotte, 28 Rue Trocard, 33500 Libourne; tel. 57 51 20 56 ☎ By appt. Closed 15 Jul.–15 Aug.

CHÂTEAU CROIX-DE-RAMBEAU★★

■　　　　5ha　30000　**3** **D** **▐** ↓
70 75 ⑦⑧ 79 81 **82**

The wine's colour is attractive, and the nose both intense and delicate. In the mouth it is powerful and well balanced. A wine that will age well. (1982)
➤ GAEC Trocard, Ch. Trocard, Les Artigues-de-Lussac, 33570 Lussac; tel. 57 84 01 16 ☎ By appt.

CHÂTEAU LA FRANCE DE ROQUES

■　　　　6ha　30000　**3** **D** **▐** ⑩ ↓
73 75 **76** 78 79 80 ★⑧① **82** **83**

Bright, solid colour and delicate, if slightly vegetal, nose. Frank and quite refined on the palate (1982)
➤ Michel Chassagne, Ch. la France de Roques, 33570 Lussac; tel. 57 74 63 74 ☎ By appt.

CHÂTEAU DE LA GRENIERE★★

■　　　　7ha　40000　**4** **D** **▐** ↓
70 ⑦⑤ 76 **78** ★80 **82** **82**

The château is rustic enough, but with a touch which indicates something more than a simple country house. The same could be said of the wine, undeveloped as yet, but rich and full of promise. Deep colour, delicate nose of wild, burnt aromas and richly concentrated flavour. (1982)
➤ Jean-Paul Dubreuil, Ch. de la Grenière, 33570 Lussac; tel. 57 74 64 96 ☎ No visitors.

CHÂTEAU HAUT-MILON★★★

■　　　　5ha　30000　**4** **D** **▐** ⑩
75 **76** 78 **79** 81 82

Deep red colour; complex, flowery and fruity nose. Well-balanced on the palate, with good quality tannins. A wine of some distinction. (1982)
➤ Jean Boireau, Les Artigues-de-Lussac, 33570 Lussac; tel. 57 84 01 08 ☎ By appt.

CHATEAU MAYNE-BLANC★★

■   14ha 90000 4 D ■ ◑ ↓
81 ⑧ 82 83 84

A good combination of dark colour, a powerful, ripe-fruited nose, and a palate rich in substance and ripe, soft tannin. A touch of youthful bitterness, but a promising future. (1982)
🕭 Jean Boncheau, Ch. Mayne-Blanc, 33570 Lussac; tel. 57 74 60 56 ⵂ Daily 9.00–21.00.

CHATEAU TABUTEAU★

■   7ha 40000 3 D ■ ↓
75 76 78 79 81 ⑧ 82 83

A small criticism of this wine would be the hint of earthiness, almost garlic-flavoured, revealed on swirling the glass. Nevertheless it has good colour, quite pleasant aromas when the wine is at rest, and is well balanced in the mouth. (1982)
✔ Bordeaux Supérieur Ch. Cap-de-Merle Rouge, Puisseguin-St-Emilion Ch. Durand-Laplagne.
🕭 Jacques Bessou, Ch. Cap-de-Merle, 33570 Les Artigues-de-Lussac, 33570 Lussac; tel. 57 84 03 07 ⵂ By appt.

CHATEAU TOUR DE GRENET★★

■   28ha 100000 3 D ■ ◑ ↓

The vineyard takes its name from the tall square tower, formerly a windmill, that stands isolated among the vines. This wine has good colour and a nose that is delicate, refined and distinguished. Well balanced on the palate. (1982)
🕭 Jean-Baptiste Brunot, Ch. Tour-de-Grenet, 33570 Lussac; tel. 57 51 35 22 ⵂ Mon.–Fri.

Montagne St-Emilion

VIEUX CHATEAU BAYARD★

■   8ha 50000 3 D ■ ↓
⑦ 83

An attractively coloured wine with a delicate nose, and marked with a certain richness of tannin. (1982)
🕭 Jeanine Latorre, Montagne, 33570 Lussac; tel. 56 71 54 51 ⵂ By appt. Closed 15–31 Aug.

CHATEAU BECHEREAU★

■   6ha 30000 3 D ■ ↓
80 81 ⑧ 82 83

Bright and clear in appearance. Nose of leather with a slightly roasted quality. Smooth at the outset and well constituted on the palate. Should age well despite an as yet somewhat harsh finish.
✔ Bordeaux Supérieur Dom. de la Vallée Rouge, Lalande de Pomerol Ch. Bèchereau Rouge.

🕭 Michel Bertrand, 33570 Les Artigues-de-Lussac; tel. 57 84 01 22 ⵂ Mon.–Sat. 8.00–19.00.

CHATEAU CALON★★

■   30ha 150000 4 D ■ ↓
73 74 76 79 81 ⑧ 83

Grown at the feet of three huge windmills; aged in a cellar hollowed out of rock. Complex nose that is both flowery and spicy. Begins well. Smooth and tannic. Should be very good in a few years' time. (1979) ✔ St-Emilion Grand Cru, St-Georges-St-Emilion.
🕭 Jean-Noel Boidron, Ch. Calon, Montagne, 33570 Lussac; tel. 56 96 28 57 ⵂ By appt. Closed 1 Nov.–30 Jun.

CHATEAU CAZELON★

■   3ha 20000 4 D ◑ ↓
70 75 ★76 ★78 79 80 81 ⑧

Garnet-red with silky address; velvety on the palate, despite a somewhat hollow finish.
🕭 Jean Fourloubey, Ch. Cazelon, Montagne, 33570 Lussac; tel. 57 84 02 75 ⵂ By appt.

CHATEAU LA CHAPELLE★

■   10ha 60000 3 D ■ ◑ ↓
78 79 79 80 ⑧ 83

Brick-red colour turning yellowish at the rim; cooked, roasted nose, followed in the mouth by a smooth beginning and good development. A wine to keep, but already drinking well. (1979)
🕭 G. et T. Demur, Ch. la Chapelle, Montagne, 33570 Lussac; tel. 57 24 78 33 ⵂ By appt.

CHATEAU COUCY★

■   18ha 120000 3 D ■ ↓
71 73 75 80 81 82 82 83

Cherry-red wine that should be nosed very gently; bouquet a little closed at first, but then opens up with a red-fruit fragrance. (1982)
✔ Bordeaux Côtes Castillon Ch. Pervenche, Bordeaux. Côtes Castillon Dom. de Lagardette.
🕭 Maureze et Fils GAEC, Ch. Coucy, Montagne, 33570 Lussac; tel. 57 74 62 14 ⵂ By appt. Closed 15–31 Aug.

CHATEAU FAIZEAU★

■   9ha 55000 3 D ■ ◑ ↓
82 ★⑧ 84

The colour is a lively brick-red; the nose recalls lily-of-the-valley and lilac; frank, smooth and full on the palate. Drink now. ✔ Pomerol Ch. la Croix-de-Gay Rouge.
🕭 G. Raynaud, SC du Ch. Faizeau, Montagne, 33570 Lussac; tel. 57 51 19 05 ⵂ No visitors. 🕭 Sté Civile du Ch. Faizeau.

CHATEAU FARQUET

■   5ha 25000 3 D ■ ↓
75 78 82 ★83

Light colour with fine, attractive nose. Supple on the palate, and slips down comfortably. Best drunk fairly soon. (1982)
🕭 Ets Dulon, 29 Rue J. Guesde, 33270 Floirac; tel. 56 86 51 15 ⵂ No visitors.

CHATEAU GRAND-BARIL★★★

■ 22ha 110000 **3 D ▣ ↓**
75 **81** ★ ⑧ ★ **82 83**

Excellent wine made by the Agricultural Lycée of Montagne. Lovely cherry-red colour. Full, fine and very fruity nose enhanced by a touch of venison. Frank address to the palate. A good future. (1982)
◆┐ Lycée Agricole de Montagne, Ch. Grand-Baril, Montagne, 33570 Lussac, tel. 57 51 01 75 ▼ By appt.

CHATEAU HAUT-BERTIN★

■ 2ha 12000 **3 D ▣ ◫ ↓**
Deep cherry-red; somewhat vegetal on the nose, and overall rather rustic in quality. (1982)
◆┐ Sté Fortin et Fils, Montagne, 33570 Lussac; tel. 57 84 04 99 ▼ By appt. ◆┐ GFA Fortin Belot.

CHATEAU JURA PLAISANCE★★

■ 8ha 40000 **4 D ▣ ↓**
64 71 74 77 78 79 ⑧

A tile-red wine with a well-developed, particularly prune-like nose. Initially supple on the palate, it becomes full bodied, tannic and well balanced, with plenty of presence. (1979)
◆┐ Bernard Delol, Ch. Jura Plaisance, Montagne, 33570 Lussac; tel. 57 51 88 92 ▼ By appt.

CHATEAU LANGLADE★

■ 6ha 35000 **3 D ▣ ◫ ↓**
79 ⑧ **82**

Bright ruby colour. Meaty nose, silky attack and moderately tannic development on the palate. Straightforward and well balanced. (1982)
◆┐ François Bodet, Ch. Langlade, Montagne, 33570 Lussac; tel. 57 84 02 13 ▼ By Appt.

CHATEAU DES LAURETS★★

■ 60ha 375000 **3 D ◫ ↓**
71 73 78 79 **81 81** ⑧ 83

Attractive colour. Rich, complex, and subtly oaky nose. On the palate, well balanced and well constituted.
◆┐ SC des Laurets et Malengin, Ch. des Laurets, Puisseguin, 33570 Lussac; tel. 57 84 03 03 ▼ By appt.

CHATEAU DE MAISON-NEUVE★

■ 40ha 225000 **3 D ▣**
79 **81** ⑧ 83 **83**

This authentic wine-maker's house belongs to a family who have been growing vines here since the 16th century. Even the wine, a red colour with brick shades, possesses the sort of balance and stability that is the strength of rural life.
✔ Lalande de Pomerol la Faurie Maison-Neuve Rouge, Bordeaux St-Pierre Maison-Neuve Rouge.
◆┐ Michel Coudroy, Ch. de Maison-Neuve, Montagne, 33570 Lussac; tel. 57 74 62 23 ▼ Daily 9.00–19.00.

CHATEAU MONTAIGUILLON★★

■ 30ha 230000 **3 ▣ ↓**
80 **81** ⑧ **82**

Very appealing red colour with golden highlights, and a charming nose of very ripe red fruits. To taste, the first impression indicates a smooth, round wine that already makes very pleasant drinking. Should not be kept too long. (1982)
◆┐ Sté Viti. Montagne-St-Emilion, Montagne, 33570 Lussac; tel. 57 84 02 34 ▼ By appt.

CHATEAU LA PAPETERIE★★★

■ 9ha 55000 **4 D ◫ ↓**
73 74 75 78 79 ㉛ **81 82**

Brick-red with shades of topaz. Strong but fine nose with toast-like fragrance. On the palate, rich, full, thick and long-lasting. Leave for a few years. (1982) ✔ Pomerol Ch. la Cabanne Rouge, Pomerol ch. Haut-Maillet Rouge, Pomerol Ch. Plincette Rouge, St-Emilion, Lalande de Pomerol.
◆┐ Jen-Pierre Estager, 35 Rue de Montaudon, 33500 Libourne; tel. 57 51 04 09 ▼ By appt. Closed Aug.

CHATEAU PETIT-CLOS-DU-ROY★★

■ 20ha 85000 **4 D ▣ ◫ ↓**
75 78 79 80 ⑧ **82**

Simple and elegant. Very attractive dark red. Lime-blossom and tobacco-leaf aromas. Rapid tannin and fullness of flavour on the palate. Well-balanced. (1982) ✔ Montagne-St-Emilion Ch. la Bastienne.
◆┐ SC Entente Janqueix, Ch. Petit-Clos-du-Roy, Montagne, 33570 Lussac; tel. 57 51 55 44 ▼ By appt. Closed Christmas–New Year, Aug.

CHATEAU PUYNORMOND★★

■ 4ha 27000 **2 D ◫**
79 ⑧ **82** 83

Youthful garnet-red appearance; hints of venison on the nose. On the palate, after a supple attack, the wine is well balanced, fleshy and tannic. (1982)
◆┐ Paul Massoudre, Ch. Puynormond, Montagne, 33570 Lussac; tel. 57 84 71 74 ▼ By appt.

209

CHATEAU ROUDIER★★

■   30ha   160 000   **4** **D** ▤ ⑴ ↓

79 **80** 81 ⑧ **83**

Bright red with tannin that is still a little harsh; but will improve dramatically with age. Leave for a while. (1982)
↬ Jacques Cademourlin, 33330 St-Emilion; tel. 57 84 02 06 ☎ By appt.

VIEUX CHATEU SAINT-ANDRE★★★

■   5ha   26 000   **4** **D** ▤

★79 81 82 **82** **83**

Lovely, long-lasting and has intense colour. Very fine nose reminiscent of cherry, vanilla and liquorice, with an overall fragrance of candy; on the palate it is soft, complex, satisfying and lastingly aromatic. Should be left for ten or twenty years. (1982)
↬ Jean-Claude Berrouet, Vieux Ch.-St-André, Montagne, 33570 Lussac; tel. 57 51 75 55 ☎ No visitors.

CHATEAU SAINT-JACQUES CALON★

■   9ha   50 000   **3** **D** ▤ ↓

70 75 76 ★**78** 79 80 81 82 **82** 83

Deep purple with bouquet reminiscent of tea and mushrooms. (1982)
↬ Paul Maule, Bertin, Montagne, 33570 Lussac; tel. 57 76 62 43 ☎ By appt.

CHATEAU TOUR-CALON

■   20ha   120 000   **4** **D** ⑴ ↓

61 70 71 **75** 76 ⑧ **82** 83

Almost tile-red in colour, with hints of cocoa and roast coffee in the bouquet. A little mushroomy on the palate. (1982)
↬ Claude Lateyron, Ch. Tour-Calon, Montagne, 33570 Lussac; tel. 57 84 02 04 ☎ By appt.

CHATEAU TOUR-MUSSET★★

■   35ha   150 000   **4** ▤ ↓

79 80 ⑧ **82** 83

The vineyard was already established by the 18th century. An unusual colour to this wine, with salmon tints at the rim. The nose has an aroma of apricot jam, very slightly flowery; on the palate the wine is full bodied, smooth and fleshy, and in time should develop well. (1982) ✔ St-Emilion Grand Cru.
↬ Henri Guiter, Montagne, 33570 Lussac; tel. 57 24 77 15 ☎ By appt.

CHATEAU LES TUILERIES-DE-BAYARD★★

■   17ha   950 000   **4** **D** ▤ ↓

⑦⑤ **82** 83

The colour is not exceptional, but it has a lovely, gamey and spicy nose. In all, a well-balanced wine that is developing well and whose tannin has already softened down. (1982)
↬ SCE Laporte-Bayard, Bayard, Montagne, 33570 Lussac; tel. 57 74 62 47 ☎ No visitors.

CHATEAU VERNAY-BONFORT★

■   4ha   18 000   **3** ▤ ↓

78 79 80 **81** ⑧ **82** 83

A nicely presented wine, with an eye-catching Japanese paper label. Deep red colour, berry-like nose, but a short finish in the mouth. (1981)
✔ Lalande de Pomerol Ch. Vieux-Cardinal.
↬ Marcel Quancard, Ch. Vernay-Bonfort, Montagne, 33570 Lussac; tel. 56 81 76 50 ☎ No visitors.

Puisseguin St-Emilion

CHATEAU LE BERNAT★

■   6ha   40 000   **4** **D** ▤ ↓

75 76 78 79 80 **81** ⑧ **83**

A mediocre colour, redressed by the nose, which carries a pleasant note of red fruit and ripe raspberry. Good concentration on the palate, rich and well integrated. (1982)
↬ SCE Laporte-Bayard, Bayard, Montagne, 33750 Lussac; tel. 57 74 62 47 ☎ By appt.

CHATEAU COTES DU FAYAN★

■   6ha   35 000   **3** **D** ▤ ↓

79 80 81 **82** **82** 83

An enticingly bright, clear wine. The nose has a floral character, and on the palate is smooth and fruity, the only problem being a rather hollow finish. (1981)
↬ Guy Poitou, Ch. Côtes-du-Fayan, Puisseguin, 33570 Lussac; tel. 57 84 07 38 ☎ By appt.

CHATEAU DURAND-LA-PLAGNE★

■   12ha   78 000   **3** **D** ▤ ↓

⑦⑤ ★**78** ★79 ★80 ★81 ★**82** 83

Intense, saturated red colour, and rather vinous nose. The attack is handsome, and leads to fullness on the palate. (1982)
↬ Jacques Besson, Ch. Durand-la-Plagne, Puisseguin, 33570 Lussac; tel. 57 74 63 07 ☎ By appt.

CHATEAU GUIBEAU

■   40ha   250 000   **3** **D** ▤ ⑴ ↓

64 66 67 70 **80** **81** ⑧ **82**

Attractive, deep-coloured wine. The nose is still a little closed but the bottle will probably develop satisfactorily. (1982) ✔ Puisseguin-St-Emilion Ch. la Fourvieille, St-Emilion Ch. Guibeau.
↬ Henri Bourlon, Ch. Guibeau-la-Fourvieille, Puisseguin, 33570 Lussac; tel. 57 74 63 29 ☎ By appt.

CHATEAU MOULINS-LISTRAC★

■ 10ha 60000 **3** D ☗ ⬇
62 64 66 70 71 ★75 ★**76** ★⑦⑨ ★**79** 82

Listrac is a Médoc name, but is used here for a château in the Libournais. The wine, although on the fruity side, is firm and well balanced.
☙ Jean-Charles Lalande, Ch. Piada, Barsac, 33720 Podenscac; tel. 57 74 69 56. ☙ Daily 8.00–20.00.

CHATEAU DE ROQUES

■ 20ha 120000 **4** D ⬙ ⬇
61 ★**70** ★**75** ★76 ★77 ★**78** ★79 ★81

Behind a red already brick at the rim lies a wine that, although lacking a little in fullness, makes up for it in finesse. According to tradition, Henry IV – a famous gourmet – came here to dine well with his friend, Jean de Roques, then lord of the manor. (1982)
☙ Michel Sublett, Puisseguin, 33570 Lussac; tel. 57 74 69 56 ☗ Daily 8.00–20.00.

CHATEAU SOLEIL★

■ 15ha 80000 **4** D ☗ ⬙ ⬇
76 78 79 81 ⑧②

Red with hints of orange. The nose has a slightly cooked quality. On the palate it tastes well made and well constituted. (1982)
☙ Jean Soleil, Ch. Soleil, Puisseguin, 33570 Lussac; tel. 57 74 63 46 ☗ Mon.–Fri, 8.00–12.30/14.00–18.00, Sat. 8.00–12.30.

CHATEAU VAISINERIE

■ 11ha 70000 **3** D ☗ ⬇
66 67 75 76 77 79 80 **81** ⑧②

Attractive colour – a clear, bright red – and an intense nose. Unfortunately there is a little too much acidity on the palate. (1981)
☙ Michel Sinet, Ch. Vaisinerie, Puisseguin, 33570 Lussac; tel. 57 84 03 48 ☗ By appt. Closed for two weeks Aug.

St-Georges St-Emilion

CHATEAU BELLONE SAINT-GEORGES★

■ 30ha 190000 **4** D ☗ ⬙ ⬇
75 78 ⑦⑨ 81 82

Pleasantly aromatic; vinous and spicy on the nose and developing well on the palate. Could do with a little more body. (1979) ✔ St-Georges-St-Emilion Ch. Macquin.
☙ Denis Corre-Macquin, Ch. Maissonneuve, Montagne-St-Georges, 33570 Lussac; tel. 57 74 64 66 ☗ By appt. Closed Aug.

CHATEAU CALON★★

■ 6ha 25000 **4** D ☗ ⬇
74 76 ★**79** ★81 **82** 83

Ruby-red with a ripe, almost jammy nose. Warm, round and powerful to taste, with a good finish. Needs ten years or so to open out. (1982)

☙ J.-N. Boidron, Ch. Calon, Montagne, 33570 Lussac; tel. 56 96 28 57 ☗ By appt. Closed 1 Nov.–30 Jun.

CHATEAU LA CROIX-DE-SAINT-GEORGES★

■ 7ha 40000 **3** D ☗ ⬇
75 ⑦⑧ **78** ★79 80 ★81 82

Still undeveloped, but warm, round and supple on the palate. (1981)
☙ Jean de Coninck, Montagne, 33570 Lussac; tel. 57 51 06 07 ☗ By appt.

CHATEAU SAINT-GEORGES★

■ 50ha 300000 **5** D ☗ ⬇
79 **79** 81 ⑧② 83

Despite being raised in the sumptuous surroundings of a vast and majestic Louis XVI chateau, this wine will perhaps not bowl you over. All the same, it is very pleasant, with characteristic Merlot aromas, fruitiness and a certain smoothness balanced by a distinctive tannin taste. (1981)
☙ *M*. Desbois-Petrus, Ch. St-Georges, Montagne, 33570 Lussac; tel. 57 74 62 11 ☗ By appt.

The Appellations between Garonne and Dordogne

Entre-Deux-Mers forms a huge triangle bounded by the rivers Garonne, Dordogne, and the south-west border of the Gironde. It must be one of the most charming areas in the whole of Bordeaux, with splendid views over the green countryside, and many picturesque buildings – fortified manors, small châteaux and stone windmills – all typical of the region. This is the Gironde that everyone imagines, steeped in immemorial beliefs and traditions. Primarily white-wine country, the region also produces red Premières Côtes de Bordeaux along the eastern bank of the Garonne river.

Entre-Deux-Mers

The Entre-Deux-Mers appellation covers white wines, for which the conditions are not really much stricter than for the Bordeaux appellation in general. In practice, however, growers tend to reserve it for their better white wines. The amount produced is deliberately small – 20 million bottles in 1982 – and the compulsory tastings to which all wines are submitted before the appellation is granted are particularly demanding. The predominant grape variety is the Sauvignon, which gives Entre-Deux-Mers wine its distinctive sharp, fresh aroma, which is at its best while the wine is young.

Between the Dordogne and the Garonne

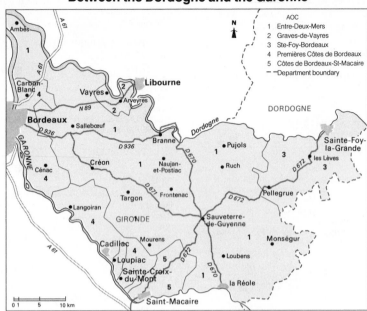

CHATEAU LES ARROMANS*

□   3.5ha   20000   **2 D ⬛ ⬇**

82 83 84

An old-established Bordelais family produce this wine, with its fine, lively and translucent colour. Residual carbon dioxide can be detected on the nose, but the palate is fresh and pleasant. (1984)
☙ Jean Duffau, Ch. les Arromans, Moulon, 33420 Branne; tel. 57 84 50 87 ⦑ By appt.

BARON D'ESPIET

□   6ha   30000   **2 D ⬛ ⬇**

Deep yellow hue, strange and faintly resinous nose, but a palate not without character. (1984)
☙ Coop. d'Espiet, 33420 Branne; tel. 57 24 24 08 ⦑ Mon.–Fri. 8.30–12.30/14.30–18.30.

CHATEAU BAUDUC*

□   8ha   60000   **2 D ⬛ ⬇**

82 ⑧₃ **83** 84

Bright yellow, fruity on the nose, with a hint of Sauvignon. Quite round on the palate and not too acidic. (1983) ✔ Bordeaux Supérieurs Ch. Bauduc.
☙ Véronique Thomas, Ch. Bauduc, 33670 Créon; tel. 56 23 23 58 ⦑ By appt. ☙ David Thomas.

CHATEAU BELLEVUE*

□   8ha   50000   **3 D ⬛**

Behind a greenish-white colour lies a clean and delicate aroma, with a palate characterized by a slightly aggressive finish. (1983)
☙ Bruno de Ponton d'Amecourt, Ch. Bellevue, 33540 Sauveterre-De-Guyenne; tel. 56 71 54 56 ⦑ By appt.

CHATEAU BERNOT*

□   3ha   20000   **3 D ⬛ ⬇**

78 81 ⑧₂ 83 84 **84**

Clear, yellow colour; cool-fermentation Sémillon on the nose. Rather neutral on the palate, freshness notwithstanding. (1984)
☙ Les Vignerons de Guyenne, Union de Coopératives Agricole Blasimon, 33540 Sauveterre-de-Guyenne; tel. 56 71 55 28 ⦑ By appt. ☙ Marcel Bernard.

CHATEAU LA BLANQUERIE**

□   10ha   70000   **2 D ⬛ ⬇**

81 82 83 ⑧₄ **84**

A delicate yet intense and distinctively Sauvignon nose; aromatic, full, round and long on the palate. (1984)
☙ GAEC Rougier, Ch. la Blanquerie, Mérignas, 33350 Castillon-la-Bataille; tel. 57 84 10 35 ⦑ No visitors.

CHATEAU BONNET**

□   30ha   150000   **2 D ⬛ ⬇**

83 84

Attractive 18th-century château, elegant and not overly grand. The wine is similar: lively, aromatic, intense and well balanced; neither too soft, nor too acidic. It too has a sense of moderation. (1983) ✔ Graves Rosé, Graves Blanc.
☙ André Lurton, Ch. Bonnet, Grézillac, 33420 Branne; tel. 56 84 52 07 ⦑ By appt.

CHATEAU BUSQUEYRON*

□   6ha   40000   **2 D ⬛ ⦿ ⬇**

From a 14th-century residence. Pale-gold with an unusual nose of complex aromas not typical of the appellation. With both presence and persistence on the palate, it should age quite well. (1982)

☛ René Maugey, Ch. Busqueyron, 33750 St-Germain-du-Puch; tel. 56 24 55 34 ℑ By appt.

CHATEAU DES CABANNES

☐	7ha	45 000	**2** ▮ ♨

Attractive green-yellow. Subtly aromatic, with touch of greenness and slightly herbaceous finish. (1983)

☛ Patrice Baratin, Ch. des Cabannes, 33760 Targon; tel. 56 23 90 25 ℑ No visitors.

DOMAINE DES CAILLOUX

☐	6ha	35 000	**2** **D** ▮ ♨

Quite feminine. Flowery colour. Harmonious and balanced on the palate with good length. (1983) ✔ Bordeaux Rosé.

☛ Nicole Lagrand, Dom. des Cailloux, Romagne, 33760 Targon; tel. 56 23 09 47 ℑ By appt.

CHATEAU CANDELEY

☐	7ha	47 000	**2** **D** ▮ ♨
80 ⋆(82) ⋆83 84			

Classic colour (pale yellow with green highlights) and particularly flowery nose. This wine is remarkable for its pronounced aromatic character – recalling roses especially. (1984) ✔ Bordeaux Supérieur Rouge et Blanc.

☛ Henry Devillaire, Ch. Candeley, St-Antoine-du-Queyret, 33790 Pellegrue; tel. 56 61 31 46 ℑ By appt. Closed Dec.

CHATEAU CANET⋆⋆

☐	20ha	35 000	**2** **D** ▮ ♨

Pleasing to the eye, with highlights of gold. Delicate, floral nose. The clean attack in the mouth leads to a well-balanced wine to taste. (1983)

☛ Bernard et Jacques Large, Guillac, 33420 Branne; tel. 57 84 52 08 ℑ By appt.

CHATEAU DE CHARDAVOINE

☐	4ha	12 000	**2** **D** ▮ ♨
83 84			

Although a little lacking in personality, this is a well-made wine, prettily coloured with discreet but pleasant nose and a well-balanced, supple palate. (1983)

☛ Claude Paillet, Soulignac, 33760 Targon; tel. 56 23 94 09 ℑ By appt.

CHATEAU DE CRAIN⋆

☐	13ha	10 000	**2** **D** ▮ ♨

A discreetly fruity nose with subtle, floral scents of garden and wild roses. To taste, has good attack and appears quite important. In all, a pleasant wine that needs to be served chilled. (1984)

☛ SCA de Crain, Baron, 33750 St-Germain-du-Puch; tel. 57 24 50 66 ℑ By appt. Closed end Aug.
☛ *Mme* Marie Barber.

DOMAINE LA CROIX DE MIAILLE

☐	3ha	4 500	**2** **D** ▮ ♨

An attractive wine. Clear, straw gold colour; subtly aromatic, good balance in the mouth with a slightly sugary background. (1983)

☛ J. Cailleux, Escoussans, 33760 Targon; tel. 56 23 63 23 ℑ By appt.

CHATEAU DUCLA⋆

☐	12ha	80 000	**2** ▮ ♨
81 82 (83) **83**			

Attractively presented wine with fine colour (clear, bright yellow), and flowery aromas. Drink now. (1983)

☛ Michel Mau, Ch. Ducla, Saint-Exupéry, 33190 Gironde-sur-Dropt; tel. 56 71 11 11 ℑ No visitors.

CHATEAU FARIZEAU⋆

☐	1.6ha	14 040	**D** ▮ ♨
82 83 ⋆(84) ⋆**84**			

Unassuming pale-yellow colour with hints of green. Subtle floral nose that is almost timid, were it not the for little hint of the country which makes the wine rather original. (1984)

☛ Max Moreau, Ch. Farizeau, Sadirac, 33670 Créon; tel. 56 23 09 24 ℑ No visitors.

CHATEAU FILLON⋆

☐	10ha	70 000	**2** **D** ▮ ♨
81 82 (83) **83**			

Without doubt the best time to visit is in February or March, when the vineyard is covered with wild daffodils and tulips. But choose any time to drink this lovely straw-yellow wine with its powerful flowery nose, and round, well-balanced palate. (1983)

☛ Serge Laguens, Ch. Fillon, Cazaugitat, 33790 Felleme; tel. 56 61 32 40 ℑ By appt. Closed Aug.

CHATEAU FONGRAVE⋆⋆

☐	18ha	110 000	**2** **D** ▮ ♨
81 **82** (83) **83** ⋆84			

Outstandingly well-balanced wine. The nose is discreet but characteristic and very refined. Fine and lingering on the palate with a hint of acidity which gives the wine an agreeable freshness. (1983)

☛ Pierre Perromat, Dom. de Fongrave, Gornac, 33540 Sauveterre-de-Guyenne; tel. 56 61 97 64 ℑ Mon.–Sat. 9.00–12.30/14.30–19.00.

CHATEAU GABACHOT

☐	4ha	8 400	**2** **D** ▮ ♨

Although the golden colour of this wine displays a certain amount of vigour, the discreetly aromatic nose has nowhere near the same strength. On the palate it has a light character but is well-balanced. (1983)

☛ Roger Fernandez, Rue Lafon, 33450 Sauveterre-de-Guyenne; tel. 56 71 51 24 ℑ By appt.

LA GAMAGE⋆

☐		400 000	**2** **D**
83 84			

Clear, bright yellow colour, rather pleasant, with a slightly sharp and spicy nose. Fresh and fragrant on the palate, with good balance. (1983

☛ Union St-Vincent, St-Vincent-de-Pertignas, 33420 Branne; tel. 57 84 13 66 ℑ By appt.

213

CHATEAU GAURY-BALETTE

| □ | | 6ha | 35 000 | **2** **D** **🍷** ↓ |

75 82 83 84

Although this wine is in reasonable condition, it is certainly inferior to more recent vintages; the wines of the Entre-Deux-Mers do not usually keep well. (1981)
↬ Yvon Bernard, Ch. Gaury-Balette, 33540 Mauriac; tel. 57 40 52 82 ☎ By appt.

CHATEAU GRAND-MONTEIL★★

| □ | | 25ha | 100 000 | **2** **D** **🍷** ↓ |

81 82 83 ⑧④ **84**

A pretty, clear yellow colour, with green highlights. Powerful, flowery nose lacking nothing in charm; round and balanced in the mouth. All in all, a very pleasant wine, to be drunk within the year. (1984)
↬ Sté. Civile Ch. Grand-Monteil, Salleboeuf, 33370 Tresses; tel. 56 21 29 70 ☎ Daily 8.00–12.00/14.00–18.00.

CHATEAU DE GUERIN

| □ | | 10ha | 70 000 | **2** **D** **🍷** ↓ |

81 82 83 ⑧④ **84**

Golden yellow colour; solid on the nose, soft on the palate overall, but not without quality. (1983)
✔ Bordeaux Rouge.
↬ Léon Jaumain, Ch. de Guerin, Castelvieil, 33540 Sauveterre-de-Guyenne; tel. 56 61 97 58 ☎ No visitors.

CHATEAU HAUT-BROUSQUET

| □ | | | 24 000 | **3** **🍷** ↓ |

83 84

Despite a rather unassertive personality, this is a serious showing many good qualities; a markedly limpid colour, rather an impressive nose, with a hint of lime, and charm on the palate. (1984)
↬ Robert Giraud SA, Dom. de l'Oiseau, BP 31 33240 St-André-de-Cubzac; tel. 57 43 01 44 ☎ By appt ↬ *Mme* Lherme-Bisson.

CHATEAU LES HAUT-DE-FONTANEAU★

| □ | | 5ha | 35 000 | **2** **D** **🍷** ◐ ↓ |

Pleasant, flowery and fruity. (1984)
↬ Coop. de Grange-Neuve, Ramagne, 33760 Targon; tel. 56 23 94 62 ☎ By appt. Closed Aug.
↬ *Mme* Baluteau.

LES HAUTS-DE-SAINTE-MARIE★

| □ | | 7.5ha | 7 000 | **2** **D** **🍷** ↓ |

⑧② 83 **84**

A subtle and attractive pale-yellow colour and a delicately flowery bouquet. To taste, it has the same qualities of subtlety and finesse, together with fruitiness, smoothness and good length. (1984)
↬ *M*. Mondon-Dupuch, 33760 Targon; tel. 56 23 64 30 ☎ By appt.

COOPERATIVE DE JUILLAC-FLAUJAGUES★

| □ | | 23ha | 117 600 | **2** **D** **🍷** ↓ |

Moderate colour; clear, light, well-developed nose. A straightforward and pleasing wine at the time of tasting, typical of its appellation.

↬ U.P. de Juillac et Flaujagues, Flaujagues, 33350 Castillon-la-Bataille; tel. 57 40 08 06 ☎ By appt.

CHATEAU DE LAGARDE★

| □ | | 10ha | 60 000 | **2** **D** **🍷** |

81 82 83 84

Flows well and is classic in colour. Perhaps a little thin, but has a pleasant aromatic character. (1983)
↬ Norbert Raymond, Ch. de Lagarde, St-Layrent-du-Bois 33540; tel. 56 63 73 63 ☎ By appt.

CHATEAU LAUNAY★

| □ | | 60ha | 42 000 | **2** **🍷** ↓ |

★⑧③ ★**84**

Clear, bright-yellow wine, with green highlights; the nose is unobtrusive, but pleasant and refined. A harmonious impression on the palate, despite the hint of acidity. (1984) ✔ Other Entre-deux-Mers.
↬ SCEA Claude-Bernard Greffier, Ch. Moulin-de-Launay, Soussac, 33790 Pellegrue; tel. 56 61 31 51 ☎ Daily 9.00–12.00/14.30–19.00.

CHATEAU MOUGNEAUX

| □ | | 10ha | 85 000 | **2** **D** **🍷** ◐ ↓ |

Pale, quite immature colour, followed by a rather reserved but slightly uninteresting nose with a slight hint of fresh fruit. In the mouth it is inviting and warm. (1983)
↬ Jean Bocquet, Ch. Mougneaux, Ste-Ferme 33580 Monségur; tel. 56 61 62 02 ☎ By appt.

CHATEAU HAUT-MOUSSEAU

| ■ | | 12ha | 75 000 | **2** **D** **🍷** ↓ |

Although lacking a little substance and fullness, a delicate and pleasant, almost sweet, aromatic character. (1982)
↬ Dominique Briolais, Château Haut-Mousseau, Teuillac, 33710 Bourg-sur-Gironde; tel. 56 64 34 38 ☎ No visitors.

CHATEAU LA NARDIQUE-LA-GRAVIERE★

| □Sec | | 11ha | 70 000 | **2** **D** **🍷** ↓ |

★**80** 81 82 **83**

Elegant, pale green. Aromas perhaps a little too fully developed, but rich and persistent. Its firmness, balance and structure are equally attractive. (1983)
↬ GAEC Thérèse et Fils, Ch. la Nardique-la-Gravière, St-Genès-de-Lombaud, 33570 Créon; tel. 56 23 01 37 ☎ By appt. Closed public holidays and last two weeks Aug. unless visit prearranged.

CAVE DE NERIGEAN★

| □ | | 120ha | 30 000 | **2** **D** ◐ ↓ |

81 82 ⑧③ **83**

A deep yellow wine, consistent throughout; delicately fruity nose, vigorous attack, and good finish. (1983)
↬ Cave Coop. de Nérigean, Nérigean, 33750 St-Germain-du-Puch; tel. 57 24 50 64 ☎ By appt.
↬ Cave Coop. Vinicole.

NICOLAS★

□ 　　　　　　　　　　　 2 ∎

An elegant, light wine, very discreet both on the nose and on the palate. (1984)
↬ ETS. Nicolas, 2 Rue de Valmy, 94220 Charenton; tel. 01 37 59 20 ⟙ No visitors.

CHATEAU PETIT-FREYLON

□ 　　　　4 ha　35000　　2 D ∎ ⌣

⑧⑴ 83 84

Both the pale green colour and the lightly spicy nose have much charm, while the palate is crisp, with plenty of flavour. (1983)
↬ Jean-Michel Lagrange, Ch. Petit-Freylon, St-Genis-du-Bois, 33119 Frontenac; tel. 56 71 54 79 ⟙ By appt.

CHATEAU DU PETIT-PUCH★

□ 　　　　2 ha　12000　　2 D ∎ ⌣

81 82 ⑧⑶ 83

A rather pale colour for its quality, but the nose retrieves the situation with lovely aromas of flowers and classic Sauvignon style. A vigorous first impression on the palate leads to a round and pleasing development. (1983) ✔ Bordeaux Blanc Moelleux, Bordeaux Rouge, Bordeaux Clairet, Graves de Vayres Blanc Sec.
↬ *Mme* Ch. Méandre-de-Lapouyade, Ch. du Petit-Puch, 33750 St-Germain-du-Puch; tel. 57 24 52 36 ⟙ By appt.

CHATEAU PEYREBON★★

□ 　　　　6 ha　25000　　2 D ∎ ⌣

⑧⑵ 83 ⑧⑷

Clear yellow colour and a varietal nose which combines freshness and a certain intensity. Long, rich and quite elegant on the palate.
↬ Jean-André Robineau, Ch. Peyrebnon, Grézillac 33420 Branne; tel. 57 84 52 26 ⟙ By appt.

CHATEAU POUCHAUD-LARQUEY★

□ 　　　　3 ha　3000　　2 D ∎ ⌣

82 83 ⑧⑷

A wine with all the exuberance of youth: brilliant colour; full, crisp nose and lively on the palate. A very pleasing wine, to be drunk straightaway. (1984)
↬ René Piva Père et Fils, Morizes, 33190 La Réole; tel. 56 71 44 97 ⟙ No visitors.

DOMAINE DE POURQUEY★

□ 　　　10 ha　7000　　1 D ∎ ⌣

80 82 84 84

A deep-coloured, almost brilliant, wine with plenty of character, especially in its rather spicy nose. Has both power and refinement.
↬ Roger Fouilhac et Fils, Castelviel, 33540 Sauveterre-de-Guyenne; tel. 56 61 97 62 ⟙ By appt.

CHATEAU PUDRIS

□ 　　　15 ha　40000　　2 D ∎ ⌣

*82 *82 84

A lovely greenish-tinged yellow colour, and a fairly powerful aroma of new-mown hay. Rich on the palate – alost too rich for a dry white wine. (1982)
↬ François Dupeyron, Ch. Pudris, Casseuil, 33190 La Réole; tel. 56 71 11 99 ⟙ By appt.

CHATEAU LES RAMBEAUDS★

□ 　　　6 ha　3000　　2 D ∎ ⌣

82 83 84

A clear wine with an elegant and delicately balanced nose. Vigorous on the palate, although perhaps a little short; should be drunk soon. (1983)
↬ Jean Cazade, Ch. les Rambeauds, Fosses-et-Baleyssac 33190 La Réole; tel. 56 61 72 72 ⟙ By appt.

CHATEAU REBULLIDE★

□ 　　　16 ha　40000　　2 D ∎ ⌣

81 82 ⑧⑶ 83 84

The golden highlights in the yellow indicate that this wine has reached maturity. On the nose scents of wild flowers accompany a hint of sweetness (very ripe fruit?) also found on the palate. (1983)
↬ Jacqueline Grasset, Ch. Rebullide, Guillac, 33420 Branne; tel. 57 84 52 23 ⟙ By appt.

CHATEAU REYNIER

□ 　　　20 ha　100000　　2 D ∎ ⌣

This fine château, with medieval ruins in its park, has a long and fascinating history. The wine has an elegant nose and initial roundness on the palate. Slightly acid finish. (1984)
↬ Dominique Lurton, Ch. Reynier, Grézillac, 33420 Branne; tel. 56 24 50 02 ⟙ No visitors. Closed Aug.

CLOS DE LA ROSE★

□ 　　　15 ha　　　　2 D ∎ ⌣

81 82 83 ⑧⑷ 84

Clear bright-yellow wine with a fine aromatic nose reflected on the palate. Overall, needs to lose a little youthful tartness. (1984)
↬ Jean Faure, Clos-de-la-Rose, Guillac, 33420 Branne; tel. 57 84 52 22 ⟙ By appt.

CHATEAU TOUR-DE-MIRAMBEAU★

□ 　　　40 ha　27000　　2 ∎ ⌣

Attractive pale-yellow colour and lightly floral nose. In the mouth it is quite vigorous and slightly aggressive, making it an excellent wine for seafood. (1984)
↬ M. Despagne 'Le Touyre', Naujan-et-Postiac, 33420 Branne; tel. 57 84 52 58 ⟙ By appt.

TUQUE DE L'ANE CROIX-DU-MOULIN

□ 　　　19 ha　144000　　2 ⌣

Mainly white with hints of yellow. Discreetly intense nose and slightly astringent on the palate. (1983)
↬ Jean Goulpier, Ch. La-Croix-du-Moulin, Soussac, 33790 Pellegrue; tel. 56 61 32 30 ⟙ No visitors.

CHATEAU TURCAUD★

□ 　　　9 ha　40000　　2 D ⌣

A good example of its type: pale-yellow colour, a distinctive Sauvignon nose, a good attack, floral aromas and average acidity to give it a certain lightness. (1984)

╺┱ Maurice Robert, La Sauve-Majeure, 33670 Créon; tel. 56 23 04 41 ⅄ Mon.–Sat. 9.00–12.00/ 14.00–19.00.

CHATEAU TURON-LA-CROIX*

□	6ha	35000	2 D 📑 ↓

*82 83 83

Pale yellow colour; very delicate varietal nose. Lively and fairly long on the palate. (1983)
╺┱ *Mme* M.-H. Saric et Fils, Lugasson, 33119 Frontenac; tel. 56 24 05 55 ⅄ By appt.

Premières Côtes de Bordeaux

The Premières Côtes de Bordeaux region runs for some 60km along the eastern bank of the Garonne from the outskirts of Bordeaux as far as Cadillac. The vines are planted on fine slopes high above the river, commanding superb views. The land is very varied here, and along the Garonne there are young alluvial soils which can produce good red wine; the hills are made up of gravelly or limestone soils, shading into clay as one moves away from the river.

The grape varieties used, the growing conditions and the wine-making process are all classically Bordelais. The appellation area covers 3660 hectares for red wines and 2700 for white. Much of the wine produced, especially the white, is marketed under the regional appellations of Bordeaux.

The red wines have a well-established reputation, and deservedly so. They are deeply coloured, fruity wines, not particularly tannic, and for relatively early consumption. Those from the slopes have greater finesse.

Since 1981 only dry white wines have taken this appellation, sweet wines appearing under the Cadillac appellation instead.

DOMAINE DES AUGUSTINS

■	5ha	28000	3 D 📑 ↓

82 83 84

Behind a colour neither pale nor dark, pleasant wine. The nose is definitely mute, but the wine is light and drinkable. (1982) ✔ Bordeaux Supérieur Rouge.
╺┱ M.-T. et M.Y. Roumegous, Ch. Ginesta, Lignan de Bordeaux, 33360 Latresne; tel. 56 21 23 03 ⅄ By appt.

CHATEAU BARREYRE*

■	10ha	55000	3 D 📑 ◁◀ ↓

66 70 75 77 (78) 79 81 82 83

Clear, bright, dark red. The nose is reminiscent of warm, concentrated grapes. On the palate a round, powerful attack is followed by a nicely textured tannin. (1982)

╺┱ Lucien Viollet, Ch. Barreyre, 33550 Langoiran; tel. 56 67 20 52 ⅄ By appt.

CHATEAU BEAU SITE*

□	2ha	6000	3 D 📑 ↓

Lovely gold colour. Distinctive nose, combining flowers and wax. Smooth and round on the palate. (1982)
╺┱ Yvan Reglat, Ch. Balot, Monprimblanc, 33410 Cadillac; tel. 56 62 98 96. ⅄ By appt.

CHATEAU DU BIAC

□	2ha	10000	3 D 📑 ◁◀

Following the straw-gold colour, a slightly vegetal bouquet. On the palate the flavours are exotic and slightly tart. The finish is a little short. (1979)
✔ Premières Côtes-de-Bordeaux Rouge, Bordeaux Blanc Sec.
╺┱ Nicole et Helene Ducatez, Ch. du Biac, 33550 Langoiran; tel. 56 67 19 98 ⅄ Daily 9.00–12.00/ 14.00–18.00.

CHATEAU DU BIAC

■	6ha	48000	3 D 📑 ◁◀ ↓

* 79 * 80 * 80 81 82

From this beautiful residence overlooking the Garonne valley comes a fragrant wine with spicy flavours. (1982)
╺┱ Nicole et Helene Ducatez, Ch. du Biac, 33550 Langoiran; tel. 56 67 19 98.

CHATEAU BRETHOUS***

■	13ha	n/a	3 D 📑 ↓

76 78 79 81 (82) 83

Charming with warm, intense and vigorous nose. On the palate a frank attack, with a nice ripe tannin; overall, delicate and well balanced. (1982) ✔ Bordeaux Clairet.
╺┱ François Verdier, Camblanes, 33360 Latresne; tel. 56 20 77 76 ⅄ Daily, all year 8.30–12.00/ 14.00–20.00.

DOMAINE DE BROUSSEY*

□	2ha	45000	2 D 📑 ↓

75 (76) 82 82 83

Brilliant, intense yellow colour; a delicate nose with flowery, acacia aromas. Good attack and perfect balance in the mouth. (1982)
╺┱ J. Cailleux, Escoussans, 33760 Targon; tel. 56 23 63 23 ⅄ By appt.

CHATEAU DE CAILLEVET★

■ 41ha 250000 **3** D ▪ ↓
77 ⑦ 79 80 81 ▪82 83

An elegant little château that used to be visited by Anatole France. Delicately shaded wine. The nose is perhaps a little discreet, but the palate is fruity and tannic. (1982)
➤ SCEA MAAF, Ch. de Caillevet, Capian, 33550 Langoir16tel. 56 67 20 58 ϒ By appt.

CHATEAU CASTAGNON★

■ 8ha 42000 **3** D ⦿ ↓
64 75 76 **78** ▪82 83

Good Gascon name for a wine with a subtle, refined bouquet with a hint of vanilla. Little woody in the mouth. Needs time. (1982)
➤ Charly Estansan, La Pergola, Quinsac, 33360 Latresne; tel. 56 20 86 90 ϒ Daily 9.00–19.00.

CHATEAU CHANTE L'OISEAU

□ 10ha 8000 **2** D ▪ ↓
⑦ **73 75 78 82**

Deep yellow wine with a powerful nose; rich and heady, perhaps a little too forceful. (1978)
➤ M. Mallié et fils, Pian-sur-Garonne, 33490 St-Macaire; tel. 56 63 21 15 ϒ No visitors.

DOMAINE DE CHASTELET★★

■ 7ha 15000 D ⦿ ↓
▪79 ▪80 *81 *82 ⑧3

The clean, deep colour indicates plenty of richness and substance. Very delicate already complex nose with pleasant vanilla flavour. Meaty, well-balanced taste with good tannin, which augurs well for the future. (1982)
➤ Jean Estansan, Dom. de Chastelet, Quinsac, 33360 Latresne; tel. 56 20 86 02 ϒ By appt.

CHATEAU LA CLYDE★★

□ 3ha 15000 **3** D ▪
Along with its red, the estate produces a white wine. A pleasant, bright, straw-gold. Finish a little short, but the roasted, honeyed flavour is refined and intense. Well balanced. (1983) ✔ Premières Côtes-de-Bordeaux Rouge, Bordeaux Blanc Sec.
➤ Jacqueline Cathala, Ch. la Clyde, Tabanac, 33550 Langoiran; tel. 56 37 47 78 ϒ By appt.

CHATEAU LA CLYDE★★

■ 12ha 80000 **4** D ▪ ⦿ ↓
70 75 78 82 *83

The vineyard is situated at the centre of the Premières Côtes. Intense, ruby colour, red-fruit nose and roundness on the palate, and slightly spicy flavour. (1983) ✔ Premières Côtes-de-Bordeaux Ch. la Clyde Blanc Moelleux, Bordeaux Blanc Sec, Bordeaux Rosé.
➤ Jacqueline Cathala, Ch. la Clyde, Tabanac, 33550 Langoiran; tel. 56 37 41 78 ϒ By appt.

CHATEAU CONSTANTIN

■ 7ha 40000 **3** D ▪ ↓
▪81 ⑧2 83

Tannic, nicely full wine with an aromatic character that is floral and lime scented. (1982)
➤ Claude Modet, 33880 Baudrech; tel. 56 21 34 71 ϒ By appt.

CHATEAU DINTRANS★★

■ 8ha 40000
A brilliant ruby-red wine with a charming nose. Harmonious palate with good, mature tannins, and some length. (1983)
➤ G. et P. Lesnier, St-Vincent-de-Paul, 33440 Ambarès-et-Lagrave; tel. 56 38 96 10 ϒ By appt.

CHATEAU FAYAU★

■ 10ha 60000 **2** D ▪ ↓
*81 *81 ▪82

Moderate colour, but very clear. The nose is aromatic, fine and rather discreet, the palate clean, light, flowing and straightforward. (1982)
✔ Cadillac, Bordeaux Blanc, Graves Rouge.
➤ Jean Médeville et Fils, Ch. Fayau, 33410 Cadillac; tel. 56 27 03 51. ϒ Mon.–Fri. 9.00–12.00/14.00–18.30.

CHATEAU GALLAND-DAST★

■ 2.5ha 15000 **3** D ⦿ ↓
76 78 79 80 **81** ▪81 82

A wine of character from this small vineyard. The colour is correct, the nose fine but discreet. On the palate, the tannin shows a touch of aggression, but this, mingling with a suggestion of oak, is what gives it personality. (1981)
➤ Léon Petit-Galland, Ch. Galland-Dast, 33880 Cambes; tel. 56 20 87 54 ϒ By appt.

CHATEAU DE GORCE★★

■ 3ha 18000 **3** D ⦿ ↓
81 ⑧2 ▪82

Pleasant, deep ruby colour with shades of purple. Good beginning and long finish. On the nose and palate it seems a bit over-oaked, but should pass with three to four years of bottle age. (1982)
➤ Charly Estansan, Chemin de Bichoulin, Quinsac, 33360 Latresne; tel. 56 20 86 90 ϒ By appt.

CHATEAU DU GRAND MOUEYS★

■ 27ha 125000 **3** D ▪ ↓
82 ⑧3 ▪83

Not much length, but an attractive colour, with a pleasant, flowing quality on the palate. (1982)
✔ Bordeaux Ch. du Piras Blanc.
➤ SCA du Ch. du Grand-Moueys, Capian, 33550 Langoiran; tel. 56 67 29 53 ϒ By appt.

DOMAINE LE GREYZEAU★

■ 2ha 10000 **3** D ▪ ⦿ ↓
76 78 79 80 81 **82** ▪82 83 ▪83

A little austere, but has an attractive, bright ruby colour and quite marked tannin on the nose and in the mouth. (1982) ✔ Bordeaux Supérieur Rouge.
➤ Roland Pestoury, Dom. le Greyzeau, Yvrac, 33370 Tresses; tel. 56 06 75 50 ϒ No visitors.

CHATEAU GUILLEMET★

■   3ha   15000   3 D 🍷 ⚓

78 79 ★80 ★81 82 82 83 84

A not particularly distinctive colour, but delicate and spicy nose. The good attack fits in well with an overall good impression. (1982)
☛ Francis Bordeneuve, Ch. Guillemet, St-Germain-de-Grave, 33490 St-Macaire; tel. 56 63 71 14 ☗ By appt.

CHATEAU DE HAUX

□   17ha   100000   3 D 🍷 ⚓

Pale-yellow. Perhaps lacks a little roundness, but has delicate nose. The château is a lovely 19th-century residence. (1982)
☛ Le Cellier de Graman, Haux, 33550 Langoiran, tel. 56 23 05 06 ☗ Daily 9.00–12.00/14.00–19.00.

CHATEAU LABATUT

■   30ha   190000   3 D 🍷 ⚓

78 ⑦ 80 81 82

Lacking a little fullness for the year; nevertheless light, bright and subtly aromatic. (1982) ✔ Cadillac Blanc Liquoreux.
☛ Michel Bouchard, Ch. Labatut, St-Maixant, 33490 St-Macaire; tel. 56 62 02 44 ☗ By appt.

CHATEAU LAFITTE★★

■   20ha   110000   3 D 🍷 ⚓

70 71 75 78 79 80 ⑧ 81 82 83

Combines attractive, ruby-raspberry colour with red-fruit nose. Long and smooth on the palate. (1982)
☛ J. Mengin et *M*. Larregieu, Ch. Lafitte, Camblanes, 33360 Latresne; tel. 56 20 77 19 ☗ By appt.

CHATEAU MADRAC★★

■   7ha   36000   3 D 🍷 ⚓

78 79 81 82 82 83

Pale red and pleasant. The nose is perhaps a little discreet weak, but on the palate agreeable, light and drinkable. (1982)
☛ Cellier de Graman, SICA de Vinification Graman, Tabanac, 33550 Langoiran; tel. 56 67 09 06 ☗ Mon.–Fri. 9.00–12.00/14.00–19.00.

CHATEAU MALAGAR★

□   14ha   50000   3 D ⚓

A lovely, golden coloured wine that has an unusual feeling of being both light and rich, giving it a rich, slightly sweet flavour. (1981)
☛ SCA du Dom. Dubourg, Ch. Gravelines, Semens-Verdelais, 33490 St-Macaire; tel. 56 62 02 01 ☗ By appt ☛ *M*. Dubourg.

CHATEAU MELIN★

■   5ha   30000   3 D 🍷 ⚓

70 75 78 80 81 82

Classic-coloured wine. Clean, crisp nose. On the palate, quite robust, with a hint of wood. (1981)
✔ Bordeaux Ch. Melin Blanc Sc, Bordeaux Clairet Ch. Melin, Premières Côtes-de-Bordeaux Ch. Melin Blanc Moelleux, Bordeaux Duc-de-Melin Mousseux.
☛ Claude Modet, Constantin, Baurech, 33880 Cambes; tel. 56 21 34 71 ☗ By appt.

DOMAINE DU MOULIN

■   5ha   23000   2 D 🍷 ⑪ ⚓

★81

Very well balanced with a little spicy touch. As yet not much to say for itself; it needs time to bring it out. (1981)
☛ Henri Gillet, Ch. Bertrande, Omet, 33410 Cadillac; tel. 56 62 97 16 ☗ By appt.

CHATEAU DE PAILLET★

■   35ha   150000   3 D ⑪ ⚓

79 80 ★81 ★82 ⑧

Pleasant, fruity and well-balanced wine. (1982)
☛ Marcel Quancard et Fils, Ch. Vernay-Bonfort, Montagne, 33570 Lussac; tel. 56 77 66 66 ☗ By appt.

CHATEAU LE PARVIS DE DOM TAPIA★★

■   7ha   35000   3 D ⑪

80 81 ⑧ 83

Made in a cellar attractive enough to appear on the Premières Côtes union's brochure. Delicate bouquet. Round and satisfying. Somewhat harsh finish, but a guarantee of good ageing. (1981)
☛ Pierre Reumaux Camblanes, 33360 Latresne; tel. 56 20 72 10 ☗ By appt.

CHATEAU DU PAYRE

■   15ha   6000   D 🍷 ⑪ ⚓

64 66 69 70 73 75 77 ⑦ 82 83

Slightly pale, suggesting a light wine, round, easy drinking. Candied-fruit aroma is typical of a 1982 wine. (1982) ✔ Cadillac Dom. du Vic Blanc Moelleux, Bordeaux Dom. de la Fontanille Rouge.
☛ *MM*. Arnaud et Marcuzzi, Ch. du Payre, Cardan, 33410 Cadillac; tel. 56 62 60 91 ☗ By appt. Closed Aug.

CHATEAU PEYRAT★★

□   5ha   25000   2 D 🍷 ⚓

The château dates from the 16th and 17th centuries and once belonged to a prominent Bordeaux family. Attractive golden colour. Intense bouquet, hints of honey and good balance. (1982)
☛ J.-C. de Biras, 33550 Langoiran; tel. 56 67 09 06 ☗ Daily 9.00–12.00/14.00–19.00

CHATEAU PEYRAT★

■   8ha   35000   3 D 🍷 ⚓

78 79 81 82 83

Shades of crimson enhance the ruby-red colour. Warm and meaty nose. Round, pleasing and well balanced on the palate. (1982)
☛ J.C. de Biras, Le Cellier de Graman, Cambes, 33550 Langoiran; tel. 56 67 09 06.

CHATEAU PONCET

■   5ha   28000   3 D 🍷 ⚓

★70 ★75 ★78 ★79 82 ★83

From a vineyard overlooking the River Garonne, an unusual wine with a nose reminiscent of boiled sweets. Will please those who like their wines old and light. (1979)
☛ Jean-Luc David, Ch. Poncet, Omet, 33410 Cadillac; tel. 56 62 97 30 ☗ By appt.

CHATEAU LA PRIOULETTE

□	1 ha 6000	3 D ■ ↓

82 83

Bright golden colour. Slightly lacking in personality, but pleasant. (1982)
⊷ François Bord, Ch. la Prioulette, St-Maixant, 33490 St-Macaire; tel. 56 62 01 97 ⊠ By appt.

CAVES DE QUINSAC*

■	11 ha 60 000	3 D ■ ↓

70 ⑦ 75 78 ⑧ ⑧ ⑧

Already showing hints of age in the deep ruby colour, this wine has a discreet bouquet and is well balanced on the palate with a slightly baked character. (1982)
⊷ Cave coop. de Quinsac, Quinsac, 33360 Latresne; tel. 56 20 86 09 ⊠ Mon.–Sat. 8.00–12.00/14.00–17.20.

CHATEAU RENOM*

■	3 ha 17 000	3 D ■ ⅰ

81 ⑧

Bright red colour. Aromas include subtle blend of overripe Merlot, venison, and burnt fragrance. Smooth and round on the palate. (1982)
⊷ Jacques Boucherie, Tabanac, 33550 Langoiran; tel. 56 67 13 59 ⊠ No visitors.

CHATEAU REYNON***

■	10 ha 60 000	3 D ⅰ ↓

79 81 82 82 83 83

The château is majestic, and so is the wine. Fresh nose with shades of mint and vanilla. On the palate, powerful, tannic, well balanced and with good length. (1982) ✔ Graves Blanc Sec, Bordeaux Rosé.
⊷ M. et *Mme* Dubourdieu, Ch. Reynon, Béguey, 33410 Cadillac; tel. 56 62 96 51 ⊠ By appt.

CHATEAU DE RICAUD*

■	40 ha 190 000	3 D ⅰ ↓

75 ★ ⑧ ★ 81 ★ 82 83

A huge estate in Loupiac, producing a sweet white wine and a crisp-coloured, bright red that has a berry-like bouquet and a clean, frank palate. (1981) ✔ Loupiac Ch. de Ricaud Blanc Liquoreux, Bordeaux Ch. de Ricaud Blanc Sec.
⊷ Alain Thienot, Loupiac, 33410 Cadillac; tel. 56 51 62 74 ⊠ By appt. Closed 1–20 Aug.

Graves de Vayres

Despite its name, this wine-growing area has nothing to do with the region of Graves. It is, in fact, situated on the west bank of the Dordogne near Libourne, forming a small enclave of gravelly terrain quite different from that of the rest of Entre-Deux-Mers. The appellation has been used since the nineteenth century, but was officially recognized in 1931. At first it applied to white wine, both sweet and dry, but the current trend, as elsewhere, is to increase the production of red wine, which may also use the appellation.

The vineyard, cover about 650 hectares of red vines and 350 hectares of white. A significant proportion of the red wine is marketed under the regional appellations of Bordeaux.

CHATEAU BACCHUS*

■	13 ha 85 000	3 D ⅰ ↓

81 ★ 82 ★ 83

Not a particularly well-chosen name, sounding more like a commercial brand than a real wine château! Nevertheless, this is a good, typical appellation wine, well-rounded and supple, with particular appeal for those fond of light wines. (1982) ✔ Bordeaux Ch. Lacrompe, Bordeaux Supérieur.
⊷ Jean-Paul Grimal, Ch. Bacchus, 33870 Vayres; tel. 57 74 74 61 ⊠ By appt ⊷ GFA Ch. Bacchus.

CHATEAU BARRE-GENTILLOT

■	20 ha 90 000	3 D ⅰ ⅰ

71 75 79 80 ⑧ 81 82

Quite well-developed light-red colour. Delicate and refined. Tobacco-like fragrance. Drink without delay. (1981) ✔ Bordeaux Supérieur.
⊷ GFA Cazenave-Mahé, Ch. Barre-Gentillot, Arveyres, 33500 Libourne; tel. 57 24 80 26 ⊠ By appt.

CHATEAU LA CROIX-DE-BAYLE*

■	6 ha 35 000	2 D ■ ↓

★81 ★82 ⑧

A deep-red, almost purple wine with an intense nose. On the palate, a flavour of cooked tannins makes for a somewhat leathery taste. (1982)
⊷ Philippe Battle-Simon, Ch. La Croix-de-Bayle, 33870 Vayres; tel. 57 24 57 95 ⊠ By appt.

CHATEAU LA CROIX-DE-BAYLE

□	10 ha 60 000	2 D ■ ↓

81 ⑧ ★83 ★84

Although perhaps a little short on the palate, this wine has a good, clear colour and a lively, fresh quality on the palate. (1982)
⊷ Philippe Battle-Simon, Ch. La Croix-de-Bayle, 33870 Vayres; tel. 57 24 57 95 ⊠ By appt.

CHATEAU JUNCARRET*

□	10 ha 45 000	2 D ■ ↓

★81 ★82 ★83 ★84

Buttercup-yellow colour; refined, distinct and pleasantly aromatic nose. A well-balanced wine with a fairly long finish. (1983)
⊷ Antoine Rouquette, Ch. Juncarret, 33870 Vayres; tel. 57 74 85 23 ⊠ By appt.

CHATEAU JUNCARRET

■	15 ha 75 000	3 D ■ ↓

66 67 70 76 81 ★ ⑧ ★ 82 83

Delicate and subtle flavours, but perhaps a little thin. (1982) ✔ Graves Blanc Sec, Bordeaux.
⊷ Antoine Rouquette, Ch. Juncarret, 33870 Vayres; tel. 57 74 85 23 ⊠ By appt.

CHATEAU PICHON-BELLEVUE★★

□ 11ha 75000 **2 D ▪ ↓**

Delicate and crystal-clear, with a fine nose and a frank attack, followed by a well-balanced palate. ✓ Graves de Vayres Ch. Pichon-Bellevue, Bordeaux Supérieur Ch. Pichon Bellevue, Bordeaux Clairet Ch. Pichon Bellevue.
↪ Daniel Reclus, Ch. Pichon-Bellevue, 33870 Vayres; tel. 57 74 84 08 **☎** By appt.

CHATEAU PICHON-BELLEVUE★

■ 19ha 75000 **2 D ▪ ↓**

70 75 79 81 ◆82 ⑧③

Subtle, almost fragile colour and delicate nose followed by full, warm attack. The cooked flavour is typical of this vintage. (1982) ✓ Graves de Vayres Blanc Sec, Bordeaux Supérieur Rouge.
↪ Daniel Reclus, Ch. Pichon-Bellevue, 33870 Vayres; tel. 57 74 84 08 **☎** By appt.

CHATEAU PONTETE-BELLEGRAVE★★

□ 8ha 50000 **2 D ▪ ↓**

79 80 81 82 ⑧③ 84

A distinctive wine. Clear colour and characteristically mellow Sémillon nose. Clear-cut and well balanced on the palate. (1983)
↪ Jean et Bernard Fièvre, Ch. Pontete-Bellegrave, 33870 Vayres; tel. 57 74 83 45 **☎** By appt.

CHATEAU LE TERTRE★

■ 11ha 60000 **2 D ▪ ↓**

70 75 76 79 80 ◆⑧② ◆82 83

A wine of medium colour with a pleasing nose of red fruit. On the palate, an agreeable attack is followed by a good overall balance; a slight hint of old wood provides a certain amount of character. (1982)
↪ René et Christian Labeille, Ch. le Tertre, 33870 Vayres; tel. 57 74 76 91 **☎** By appt.

THE GRAVES APPELLATIONS

These classic Bordeaux vineyards are also among the oldest; since Roman times there have been rows of vines around the city of Bordeaux producing, according to the agronomist Columelle (*fl.* first century AD), 'A wine for laying down which needs several years to reach its peak'.

The name Graves appeared during the Middle Ages, when it referred to the whole area on the west bank of the Garonne upstream of Bordeaux between the river and the Landes plateau. Today, however, the appellation area is cut in two by the sweet white wine appellations Sauternes, Cérons and Barsac.

Graves and Graves Supérieurs

Except for Graves de Vayres, Graves is the only appellation to carry the name of the soil that characterizes its vineyards, gravel slopes originally laid down by the floodwaters of the Garonne in distant geological eras. These deposited a great variety of pebbly debris (shingle and gravel) transported from the Pyrenees and the southern Massif Central.

The Graves du Nord – the northern vineyard area on the outskirts of Bordeaux surrounding the communes of Pessac and Léognan – has long had an unchallengeable reputation. All of the Graves Crus Classés are in this region, and the red and white wine areas are clearly differentiated. These circumstances led the Graves winegrowers, inspired by the example of the Médoc, to request two communal appellations, Pessac and Léognan. However, they were permitted only to add the name Pessac or Léognan to the Graves appellation and no new appellations were awarded.

Some of the more famous estates (including Haut-Brion) have become enclaves of vines within the town, a situation which is not without its problems for the growers. Urban development has reduced the size of the vineyard: in 1928 there were 287 separate holdings, but in 1981 the figure had dropped to 49.

The Graves du Sud does not have the same reputation as the north. The wines fetch much lower prices, and the same vineyards may be planted with red or white grapes, depending on market demand. There are, however, some very good sites which have not really been fully exploited – around Portets and Podensac, for example – and this is probably one where it would still be possible to create a new, top-quality vineyard.

One unusual feature of Graves wines is their classification system, which was established in two stages – 1855 for Haut-Brion and 1959 for the other growths – and includes both red and white wines.

The red wines are quite similar to those of the Médoc; they have the same full-bodied yet elegant structure which allows them to age well. Their delicate, smoky bouquet is particularly distinctive.

Graves

AOC Graves and
Graves Supérieurs

0 1 2 3 4 5km

The dry white wines are among the best in the Gironde; fragrant, refined and firmly flavoured. The best of all are aged in casks and improve in richness and complexity after a few years of bottle age.

A few of the once very popular white wines are still made today in the region; they too have their admirers.

Graves

CHATEAU ARCHAMBEAU*

	9ha	3	D	▮	◐	↓

76 79 ⑧ *83

Beautiful, deep ruby colour. Very aromatic and quite fruity in fragrance and taste. Unusual and not at all characteristic of the area; fruit and charm. (1983)
↪ Jean-Philippe Dubourdieu, Ch. Archambeau, Illats, 33720 Podensac; tel. 56 62 51 46 ☎ By appt.

CHATEAU D'ARRICAUD*

	6ha	30000	4	D	▮	↓

⑦⑤ 79 ⑧⑴ *82 83

Moderate colour and a soft, floral nose contrast with the vigorous attack – but, overall, a rounded and complete wine. (1981)
↪ A.-J. Bouyx, Landiras, 33720 Podensac; tel. 56 62 51 29 ☎ By appt.

CHATEAU LA BLANCHERIE**

☐	11ha	72000	2	D	▮	↓

66 70 74 75 ⑧⑵ ⑧⑶ 84

Pale golden-yellow wine with a pronounced and well-developed floral bouquet and a good balance on the palate. (1983) ✎ Graves Rouge Ch. Blancherie-Peyret.
↪ *Mme* Françoise Braud, Ch. La Blancherie, 33650 La Brède; tel. 56 20 20 39 ☎ By appt. Closed Sun. during Aug.

CHATEAU BOURDILLOT*

▦	4ha	18000	4	D	◐	↓

*78 *79 *80 *81 ⑧⑵ *⑧⑵

An attractive colour introduces a pleasant wine with a powerful but refined nose. A hint of bitterness on the attack, but the wine is full, well balanced, with an attractive tannin and plenty of character. (1982)
↪ *M.* Haverlans, 33640 Portets; tel. 56 67 11 32 ☎ By appt.

CHATEAU BOUSCAUT*

▦Gd Cru	32ha	100000	5	D	◐	↓

76 79 80 ⑧⑴

Fairly full-bodied, with aromas combining venison and fruit. (1982)
↪ Ste Civile Ch. Bouscaut, Cadaujac, 33140 Pont-de-la-Maye; tel. 56 30 72 40 ☎ By appt.

CHATEAU BOUSCAUT★★

		6.8ha	50000	**5** **D** 🍷 ◑ ↓

⑦ 73 78 80 82 ⑧

A genuine, wine with a rich and aromatic character. Best drunk young. (1983)
↜ Sté Civile, Ch. Bouscaut, Cadaujac, 33140 Pont-de-la-Maye; tel. 56 30 72 40 ⊤ By appt.

CHATEAU BROCHON

■		4ha	18000	**4** **D** 🍷 ◑ ↓

75 78 80 81 ⑧

An old estate with a few 17th-century remains. A wine with an intense nose and colour, definitely a bit vegetal but fragrant, too. (1981) ✔ Bordeaux Blanc Sec, Bordeaux Supérieur Rouge, Bordeaux Rosé.
↜ André Laulan, Château St-Marc, Barsac, 33720 Podensac; tel. 56 27 16 81 ⊤ By appt.

CHATEAU BRONDELLE★

■		8ha	48000	**4** **D** 🍷 ↓

75 78 79 ★⑧ ★82 83

The bright red colour is immediately apparent, but the subtle nuances of the nose – spicy and flowery tones with a hint of leather – require closer attention. Well balanced, tannic and long on the palate. (1983) ✔ Bordeaux Rouge Ch. Mayne-de-la-Cour, other Graves wines.
↜ Roland Belloc, Ch. Brondelle, 33210 Langon; tel. 56 65 42 32 ⊤ By appt.

CHATEAU BROWN *Léognan*★

■		11ha	45000	**4** **D** 🍷 ↓

78 ⑦ 81 ★82

Pleasing, if light, colour. The nose is unobtrusive but definite, and the palate particularly well rounded and supple. (1982)
↜ Jean-Claude Bonnel, 33850 Léognan; tel. 56 87 11 74 ⊤ By appt.

CHATEAU CABANNIEUX★★

■		21ha	12000	**4** **D** 🍷 ◑ ↓

★75 ★76 ★78 ★79 ★82 ★83

This pleasant wine is a lovely colour, and has a powerful aromatic character that is a blend of oak and fruit with a hint of liquorice on the palate. Full and well balanced, it should develop very well indeed. (1982) ✔ St-Emilion Grand Cru Ch. Montlanert.
↜ A. et R. Barrière, Ch. Cabannieux, 33640 Portets; tel. 56 67 22 01 ⊤ By appt ↜ R. Barrière et R. Dudignac.

CHATEAU CAMUS★

■		3ha	18000	**3** 🍷

★⑧ ★82 ★83

Delightful raspberry colour. The nose is delicately perfumed, and the palate firm and fairly tannic. (1982)
↜ Jean-Pierre Larriaut, Ch. Camus, 33210 Langon; tel. 56 63 13 29 ⊤ By appt.

CHATEAU CARBONNIEUX★

☐Cru Classé	37ha	200000	**4** **D** 🍷 ◑ ↓

75 78 82 ⑧ 83 84

A curious fact about this wine is that it was originally sold as 'mineral water' to the Muslim Sultan of Turkey. This was sound marketing by the Benedictine monks who used to own the château. The officially teetotal Sultan was able to drink his tipple with a clear conscience. Despite a light colour, the nose and palate leave no doubt as to the growth's true identity: a well-balanced wine that is developing well. (1983) ✔ Graves-Léognan Ch. La Tour-Léognan.
↜ Sté Civ. des Grandes Graves, 33850 Léognan; tel. 56 87 08 28 ⊤ By appt.

CHATEAU CARBONNIEUX★★

■Cru Classé	40ha	250000	**5** **D** 🍷 ◑ ↓

61 66 70 ⑦ 78 79 81

Like its white counterpart from the same estate, this attractive red is a Cru Classé, and probably an even better wine. Elegant and distinguished bouquet, with a fine oaky character. Typical Graves on the palate. Well balanced, with good-quality tannin, but needs a little more bottle age. (1981)
↜ Sté Civ. des Grandes Graves, 33850 Léognan; tel. 56 87 08 28 ⊤ By appt.

CHATEAU DE CARDAILLAN★

■		20ha	100000	**4** 🍷 ◑ ↓

75 79 81 82 83

Lovely deep-red colour, with a slightly burnt, overripe character to the bouquet. Rich and full on the palate, confirming the impression given by colour and nose. (1983)
↜ Pierre de Bournazel, Ch. de Malle, Preignac, 33210 Langon; tel. 56 63 28 67 ⊤ By appt.

CHATEAU LES CARMES-HAUT-BRION★

■		3ha	15000	**5** **D** ◑ ↓

78 79 80 82 83

A small château, but surrounded by one of the finest parks of the region. This 1983, with its rich crimson colour has a particular leafy quality on the palate, notably at the finish. (1983)
↜ Maison Chautecaille, 127 Rue de Turenne, 33000 Bordeaux; tel. 56 48 04 54 ⊤ No visitors.

CHATEAU CAZEBONNE★

☐		5ha	30000	**2** **D** 🍷

⑦ 78 79

Almost garnet in colour. Quite an intense bouquet, supple and at its best on the palate. (1979)
↜ Marc Bridet, Ch. Cazebonne, St-Pierre-de-Mons, 33210 Langon; tel. 56 63 17 13 ⊤ By appt.

CHATEAU CAZEBONNE★

☐		5ha	30000	**2** **D** 🍷

80 ⑧ 82

A particularly expressive Sauvignon-character bouquet precedes a palate that is light, fine and attractively fresh. To drink now. (1982)
↜ Marc Bridet, Ch. Cazebonne, St-Pierre-de-Mons, 33210 Langon; tel. 56 63 17 13 ⊤ By appt.

CHANTECAILLE★

🔲 18 000 **3** **D**

Produced by a wine merchant with an extensive knowledge of Graves wines, this particular wine is bright in colour, with a discreet yet grapey nose and fairly fat, supple feel on the palate. (1983)
🖝 Maison Chantecaille et Cie, 127 Rue de Turenne, 33000 Bordeaux; tel. 56 48 04 54 ⊤ No visitors.

CHATEAU DE CHANTEGRIVE★★

🔲 22 ha 360 000 **4** **D** ◗ ↓

71 75 76 78 ⑲ **79** 82

Poetically named wine. Highly aromatic; shades of cherry and liquorice mixed with touch of new wood. Full bodied, with good, long-lasting finish. (1982) ✔ Graves Ch. Bon-Dieu-des-Vignes Rouge et Blanc, Graves Ch. Mayne-Levêque Rouge et Blanc, Graves Ch, d'Anice Rouge et Blanc.
🖝 Henri Levêque, Ch. de Chantegrive, 33720 Podensac; tel. 56 27 17 38 ⊤ By appt.

CHANTELOISEAU-CHATEAU L'ETOILE★

🔲 22 ha 84 000 **3** **D** 🍶 ↓

82 83 ⑭ **84**

Two labels and two names for one wine. A pale but bright colour. Aromas of flowers and honey. Well balanced on the palate, despite a hint of acidity on the finish. (1983)
🖝 *MM.* Bonnin-Latrille, Petit, Mazères, 33210 Langon; tel. 56 63 41 70 ⊤ By appt.

LA CHANTELOISEAU★

🔲 22 ha 84 000 **3** **D** 🍶 ↓

73 ★**75** ★**76** ★**78** ★**79** ★82 ★**83**

Although the nose does not quite live up to the colour, the impression on the palate more than makes amends: full, found, generous and flattering. (1983)
🖝 SCA Dom. Bonnin-Latrille, Petit, 33210 Mazères; tel. 56 63 41 70 ⊤ By appt.

CHATEAU CHERET-PITRES

🔲 12 ha 50 000 **4** **D** 🍶 ◗ ↓

75 ★**76** ★**78** 79 ★**82**

Attractive garnet colour; a bit closed on the nose, but light and easy drinking. (1982)
🖝 Jean Boulanger, Ch. Chéret-Pitres, 33640 Portets; tel. 56 67 06 26 ⊤ By appt.

DOMAINE DE CHEVALIER★★

☐Cru Classé 2.5 ha 9000 **6** ◗ ↓

71 72 73 74 76 77 ★**78** ⑧ **80** 81 **82** 83 84

A classified wine, like the red from the same estate, this white Graves has a strong personality; intense on the nose and with real finesse on the palate. A wine to be kept a long while. (1982)
🖝 Claude Ricard, Dom. de Chevalier, 33850 Léognan; tel. 56 21 75 27 ⊤ By appt.

DOMAINE DE CHEVALIER★★

🔲 15 ha 60 000 **6** ◗ ↓

79 **80 81 82 83**

Plenty of body and excellent ageing potential as is generally the case for wines from this estate. (1982)
🖝 Sté Civile Dom. de Chevalier, 33850 Léognan; tel. 56 21 75 27 ⊤ By appt.

CHATEAU CHICANE★

🔲 80 000 **4**

Rather deep colour; typical nose with a note of violets. Warm, round, supple and fine on the palate, but also rather tannic. Not yet fully matured, this is certainly a wine to lay down. (1982)
🖝 Sté Coste-Capdeville, Ch. Chicane, Toulenne, 33210 Langon; tel. 56 63 50 52 ⊤ No visitors.

CUVEE PIERRE COSTE★★

🔲 25 ha 200 000 **3** **D** 🍶 ◗ ↓

75 **78 79 81** ⑧ **82 83**

Beautiful deep red colour. Tannic on the palate, but not excessively so, and with a pleasing impression of elegance and fruit harmoniously combined. A rich, ripe wine. (1983)
🖝 Pierre Coste, 8 Rue de la Poste, 33210 Langon; tel. 56 63 50 52 ⊤ By appt. Closed Aug. and Christmas.

CHATEAU COUHINS-LURTON★★

☐Cru Classé 6 ha **4**

★**81 82** ★**83**

This little vineyard arose from a division of the Coulins estate. Its wine has a yellow colour tending towards pale green, with quite intense but balanced aromas on the nose. Typical Graves palate, with a long, rich finish. (1983)
🖝 André Lurton, Ch. Bonnet, Grézillac, 33420 Branne; tel. 57 84 52 07 ⊤ No visitors.

CHATEAU DU CROS-DE-LA-GRAVIERE★

🔲 2 ha 12 000 **3** **D** 🍶 ↓

75 76 ★⑧ ★**82** 83

Fruity nose and a slightly aggressive attack. For those who like a light wine. (1982) ✔ Bordeaux Ch. du Cros-la-Barraque, Bordeaux Cuvée de-la-Gravière, Première Côtes-de-Bordeaux Ch. du Cros-les-Roches, Graves Ch. du Cros-la-Gravière.
🖝 Michel Fournol, Ch. du Cros-la-Barraque, Virelade, 33720 Podensac; tel. 56 27 04 27 ⊤ By appt.

CHATEAU DE CRUZEAU *Léognan*★

□	9ha	50000	**3** D ▤ ⬇

'81 '82 '83

A good all-round wine; sustained yellow colour, fine, delicate nose, and round, supple palate. (1983)
🍇 André Lurton, Ch. Bonnet, Grézillac, 33420 Branne; tel. 57 84 52 07 ☿ No visitors.

CHATEAU DE CRUZEAU *Léognan*★★

■	41ha	15000	**3** D ⬤ ⬇

78 *'79* 80 **'81** 82 **82** 83

Although the château itself is fairly modern (1912), certain of the estate buildings date from the 18th century. This 1983 offers a beautiful colour, fine perfume of ripe fruit, supported by a woody note, with plenty of flesh, vinosity, and good balance on the palate. (1982)
🍇 André Lurton, Ch. Bonnet, Grézillac, 33420 Branne; tel. 57 84 52 07 ☿ No visitors.

CHATEAU DOMS★★

■	8ha	48000	**3** D ▤ ⬤ ⬇

'75 *'78* *'79* 80 **81** *★**82*** ★⑧③

Once a royal hunting lodge, this elegant 18th-century manor house has a romantic past, while the wine it produces promises well for the future. Attractive colour, and delicate bouquet; well rounded and very pleasing on the palate, particularly on the attack. (1982)
🍇 Lucien Parage, Ch. Coms, 33640 Portets; tel. 56 67 20 12 ☿ By appt.

CHATEAU DOMS★

□	10ha	30000	**2** D ▤ ⬇

70 *'73* 78 **79** 80

Light and fruity white wine which has a pleasantly fresh character. (1983)
🍇 Duvigneau et Parage, Ch. Doms, 33640 Portets; tel. 56 67 20 12 ☿ By appt.

CHATEAU L'ETOILE★

■		40000	**3**

Very pretty deep red colour; the nose is already quite developed, with a hint of leather, but the taste is not yet fully formed. However, the qualities that one detects at this stage – both in the attack and the generous structure – promise good future development. (1982)
🍇 Héritiers Latrille, 33210 Langon; tel. 56 63 50 52. ☿ No visitors.

CHATEAU FERNON★

■	8ha	48000	**3** D ▤ ⬇

72 75 80 81 ★⑧ ★**82** 83

This wine has a slightly wild air about it, which you will either like or dislike. A very dark colour and a marked character, but with a certain lightness overall. (1982)
🍇 Jacques Girard de Langlade, Ch. Fernon, 33210 Langon; tel. 56 63 38 93 ☿ Mon.–Sat. 9.00–12.00/14.00–18.00.

CHATEAU FERRANDE★

□	10ha	60000	**4** D ▤ ⬤ ⬇

83 **84**

Interesting white Graves, with a lovely pale-yellow hue, a fine and lingering citrus fruit nose, and a rich, round palate with a good aromatic finish. (1984)
🍇 Castel SA, Castres, 33640 Portets; tel. 56 41 02 19 ☿ No visitors. 🍇 SCE du Ch. Ferrande.

CHATEAU FERRANDE★★

■	33ha	140000	**4** D ▤ ⬤ ⬇

75 *'78* 79 80 **'81** *★82* **83** **83**

A good red Graves from an estate better known for its white wine. Dark colour and rich, spicy nose. Fat and creamy on the palate, which is well structured. (1983)
🍇 Castel SA, Castres, 33640 Portets; tel. 56 41 02 19 ☿ No visitors 🍇 SCE du Ch. Ferrande.

CLOS FLORIDENE★★

□	2ha		**3**

A tiny property (two hectares) with an original *encépagement* (varietal planting) that is half Sémillon, half Muscadelle. This is a mature wine, full, fleshy and very aromatic, recalling banana, peach-stone and mint. A great success that deserves a wider distribution. (1982)
🍇 *M. et Mme* F. et D. Dubourdieu, Ch. Reynon, Beguey, 33410 Cadillac; tel. 56 62 96 51 ☿ No visitors.

CHATEAU DE FRANCE *Léognan*★★

■	23ha	140000	**5** D ⬤ ⬇

⑦⑤ **78** 81 82

Attractive colour. Rich, mature and powerful nose with a slightly smoky note. Very elegant flavour; pleasing, round and tasty, with a good finish. (1978)
🍇 Bernard Thomassin, Ch. de France, 33850 Léognan; tel. 56 21 75 39 ☿ By appt. Closed Christmas and New Year's Day.

DOMAINE DE GAILLET★

■		80000	**4**

Quite an intense colour, shading from red to ruby, and an equally intense nose, with a flowery perfume. On the palate, a pleasant roundness and some flesh, with good balance and length. (1982)
🍇 SA Coste et Fils, 26 Rue de la Poste, 33210 Langon; tel. 56 63 50 52 ☿ No visitors.

CHATEAU LA GARDE★

■	37ha	300000	**4** D ▤

75 78 **81** 82 ⑧③

The estate, apart from its elegant 18th-century house, is now owned by a large firm of wine merchants. The wine has a pleasing colour, preceding a powerful bouquet and well-balanced, fleshy palate. The finish is somewhat short. (1981) 🍷 Graves Ch. La Garde Blanc, Graves Smith Haut-Lafitte Rouge, Graves Smith Haut-Lafitte Blanc.
🍇 SCE Eschenauer, Ch. La Garde, Martillac,

33650 La Brède; tel. 56 81 58 90 **Y** By appt. Closed Aug.

CHATEAU GRAND-ABORD

■	15 ha	24 000	③ D ⏸ ♪

64 66 70 75 ⑧② 82 83

At one time the River Garonne flowed past this estate, and the barges used to berth here. Hence the name of this very smooth wine with its pleasant, mature aromas. Should be drunk soon. (1982) ✔ Bordeaux Supérieur.
• Ch. Grand-Abord, 33640 Portets; tel. 56 67 22 79 **Y** By appt. Closed Aug.

DOMAINE LA GRAVE

■	6 ha	30 000	⑤ ⏸ ♪

79 82 83

Beginning to show quite a personality. A property worth watching. (1982)
• Peter Vinding-Diers, Dom. la Grave, 33640 Portets; tel. 56 67 01 12 **Y** By appt.

CHATEAU HAUT-BAILLAN

☐	5 ha	28 000	③ D ⏸ ♪

78 79 81 83

A good-quality wine, discreetly and elegantly presented. Light and supple on the palate, with a flawless finish. An easy-to-drink bottle. (1984)
• Michel Dugoua, St-André-de-Cubzac, 33640 Portets; tel. 57 43 01 44 **Y** No visitors.

CHATEAU HAUT-BAILLY★★★

■ Cru Classé	22 ha	130 000	⑥ ⏸ ♪

★64 ★66 ★78 ⑦⑨ 79

Youthful colour and an undeveloped nose, dominated by Cabernet at present. On the palate, full and rich, with a fine, rapid tannin. Plenty to offer, but needs time. Its development will be worth following. (1979)
• J. Sanders, SA, Ch. Haut-Bailly, 33850 Léognan; tel. 56 27 16 07 **Y** By appt.

CHATEAU HAUT-BERGEY
Léognan★★

■	13 ha	80 000	⑤ D ⏸ ♪

⑦⑨ 79 80 81 82 83

The wine produced at this striking château is very pleasant; the nose is vanilla-scented, the palate richly flavoured. It is worth waiting a while to let the tannin mellow. (1979)
• Jacques Deschamps, Ch. Haut-Bergey, 33850 Léognan; tel. 56 21 75 02 **Y** By appt. Closed Aug.

CHATEAU HAUT-BRION *Pessac*★★★

■ 1er Cr Classé	40 ha	180 000	⑥ ⏸ ♪

64 75 76 78 **79** 80 ⑧① 83

A jewel, with its crystal-clear appearance, complex, aromatic, oak-scented nose, and fine balance between suppleness and tannin. (1983)
• Sté C. du Ch. Haut-Brion, 33600 Pessac; tel. 56 98 33 73 **Y** By appt.

CHATEAU HAUT-BRION *Pessac*★★★

☐	4 ha	16 000	⑥ ⏸ ♪

79 80 81 ⑧② 83 84

Lovely lemon-tinted colour, pleasant citrus-fruit aromas (orange and mandarin), and, after an initial warmth on the palate, full-bodied roundness and exceptional length on the finish. (1984)
• Sté Civ. du Ch. Haut-Brion, 33600 Pessac; tel. 56 98 33 73 **Y** By appt.

CHATEAU HILLOT★

■	3 ha	18 000	④ D 🍾 ⏸

★⑦⑤ ★76 ★79 ★82

The charming simplicity of the château is reflected in its attractive garnet-red wine. The nose is subtle, suggesting soft red fruit, followed by a frank attack and nice balance on the palate. (1979)
• Sté Bernard Leppert, Ch. Hillot, 33720 Illats; tel. 56 62 53 38 **Y** By appt.

CHATEAU HILLOT

☐	20 ha	48 000	⑤ D 🍾 ⏸

③④ 75 76 80 82

Less well known than the Cérons produced on this estate, this wine has a surprising, somewhat musky nose. On the palate it has a pleasing weight and a not unpleasant suggestion of resin in the flavour. (1982)
• Sté Bernard Leppert, Ch. Hillot, 33720 Illats; tel. 56 62 53 38 **Y** By appt.

CHATEAU LAGRANGE★

☐	4.32 ha	30 000	③ D 🍾 ⏸

82 83 83

Clear, pale, yellow colour, with a delicate, flowery bouquet. Round and full-bodied on the palate, although the finish is a little acidic. (1983)
✔ Bordeaux Dom. de Meychon Rouge.
• Hubert Dozier, Ch. Lagrange, Arbanats, 33640 Portets; tel. 56 67 21 35 **Y** By appt.

CHATEAU LAGRANGE

■	5.32 ha	35 000	③ D 🍾 ⏸ ♪

75 78 79 79 80 80 81 ⑧② 82

Well-presented, with a beautiful, dark ruby colour and a delightful bouquet of ripe fruit. A little less generous on the palate. Should be drunk young. (1982)
• Hubert Dozier, Ch. Lagrange, Arbanats, 33640 Portets; tel. 56 67 21 35 **Y** By appt.

CHATEAU LARRIVET-HAUT-BRION *Léognan*★★

■ 16ha 100000 4 D ▤ ⑪ ⌄

⑦⑤ 76 78 81

Pleasing red colour and a delicate, elegant, lightly oaky nose precede a palate with nice, ripe tannins, plenty of body and a very well-made character. (1981)
☛ Mme Guillemaud, Ch. Larrivet-Haut-Brion, 33850 Léognan; tel. 56 21 75 51 � By appt.

CHATEAU LAVILLE-HAUT-BRION *Pessac*★★

☐Cru Classé 6ha 26000 6 ⑪ ⌄

80 81 82 83 ⑧④

Lovely, clear yellow wine with aromas of honey, acacia and pollen. Supple, round and with the charm of a slightly oaky flavour. A fine, traditional Graves, with a breadth to the finish. (1984)
☛ Dom. Clarence Dillon SA, Ch. La Mission-Haut-Brion, 33400 Talence; tel. 56 98 11 85 � By appt.

CHATEAU LEHOUL★

■ 3ha 18000 3 D ⑪

75 76 78 81 ⑧② *83

Strikingly lively colour and an intense, complex nose, predominantly of flowers, strawberries and red currants. An extremely attractive wine, with a firm attack preceding a round texture and supple tannin. (1982) ✔ Graves Ch. Léhoul Blanc.
☛ Sergé Fonta, Route d'Auros, 33210 Langon; tel. 56 81 17 74 � By appt.

CHATEAU LA LOUVIERE★

☐ 15ha 100000 4 D ▤ ⌄

*82 *⑧③ *83

Although not in the same class as the estate's red, this is still an attractive wine, with a bright, lively colour, delicate, pleasantly fruity nose and round, supple palate. A well-balanced white that almost certainly has some ageing potential. (1983) ✔ Bordeaux Château Bonnet Rouge, Entre-Deux-Mers Ch. Bonnet, Graves Ch. Cruzeau Rouge et Blanc, Graves Ch. de Rochemorin Rouge et Blanc, Graves Ch. Couhins-Lurton Blanc.
☛ André Lurton, Ch. la Louvière, 33850 Léognan; tel. 57 84 52 07 � By appt. Closed Aug.

CHATEAU LA LOUVIERE★★★

■ 30ha 200000 4 D ⑪ ⌄

*76 *⑦⑧ *81 *83

A lovely, deep-red colour is followed by a ripe, cedary nose. After a sure attack the wine is supple, round, well balanced and not without elegance. Deserves to be given some time. (1981)
✔ Entre-Deux-Mers Ch. Bonnet, Bordeaux Ch. Bonnet Rouge, Graves Ch. Cruzeau Rouge et Blanc, Graves Ch. Rochemorin Rouge et Blanc, Graves Ch. Couhins-Lurton Blanc.
☛ André Lurton, Ch. Bonnet, Grézillac, 33420 Branne; tel. 57 84 52 07 � By appt. Closed Aug.

GRAND VIN DE GRAVES

1981
CHÂTEAU
LA LOUVIÈRE
MIS EN BOUTEILLE AU CHÂTEAU
GRAVES
LÉOGNAN
APPELLATION GRAVES CONTRÔLÉE 75cl
ANDRÉ LURTON
PROPRIÉTAIRE-VITICULTEUR À LÉOGNAN (GIRONDE)

CHATEAU MADELIS

☐ 3ha 96000 4 D ▤ ⌄

*⑦⓪ *⑦⓪ *76 *82

Although not up to the red from the same estate, this is a good wine. While perhaps a little too discreet on the nose, it is pleasantly smooth and supple on the attack, and agreeably round in the mouth. (1981)
☛ Jean Courbin, Ch. Madelis, Grand-Abord, 33640 Portets; tel. 56 67 22 03 � By appt.

CHATEAU MADELIS★★

■ 8ha 36000 4 D ⑪ ⌄

*75 *78 *81 *81 *82

Bright-red colour. Attractive violet-like fragrance on the nose although in the mouth more reminiscent of bitter almonds and roast peanuts. An especially pleasant roundness and good length. (1981)
☛ Jean Courbin. Ch. Madelis, Grand-Abord, 33640 Portets; tel. 56 67 22 03 � By appt.

CHATEAU MAGENCE★

☐ 12ha 72000 3 D ▤ ⌄

*70 *73 *78 *⑧⓪ *82

Pale-yellow in colour, with a mature Sauvignon nose that has subtle flowery overtones. Even better on the palate, which is rich and supple. (1982)
☛ D. Guillot de Suiduiraut, Ch. Magence, St-Pierre-de-Mons, 33210 Langon; tel. 56 63 07 05 � By appt.

CHATEAU MAGNEAU

☐ 15ha 120000 3 D ▤ ⌄

*⑧② *82 *83 *84

The family has managed this vineyard at La brède, not far from Montesquieu's château, since the 17th century. The wine is pleasing in appearance, light on the nose, delicate and ready to drink. (1983). ✔ Graves Ch. Magneau, Graves Ch. Guiravon.
☛ Henri et J.-L. Ardurats, Ch. Magneau, 33650 Labrède; tel. 56 20 20 57 ⦌ Daily 9.00–19.00.

CLOS DES MAJUREAUX★

■ 3ha 25000 4 ▤

*73 *75 *78 ⑦⑨ 81 *82

Light ruby colour. Fruity nose, and very smooth and light on the palate. When young it must have made an excellent *vin primeur*, but has aged well, too. (1981)
☛ M. Chaloupin, Clos des Majureaux, 33210 Langon; tel. 56 63 07 15 ⦌ No visitors.

CHATEAU MALARTIC-LAGRAVIERE★★

□Cru Classé	2ha	15000	4 ⏁ ↓
⑧ 84			

The whole of the production of this wine is sold to the trade. It is a clear, pale-yellow gold, intense, grapey and flowery (rose and honeysuckle) on the nose, and rich, unctuous and oaky on the palae. A fine wine which will appeal to lovers of 'waxy' Graves. (1983)
➤ GFA Marly-Ridoret, 39 Av. de Mont-de-Marsan, 33850 Léognan; tel. 56 21 75 08 ☎ By appt. Closed Aug.

CHATEAU MALARTIC-LAGRAVIERE★★

■Cru Classé	14ha	100000	5 ⏁ ↓
78 *79 ⑦ 81 83			

With its youthful colour this wine displays a complex, well-rounded bouquet. In the mouth it is vigorous, rich and subtle and particularly fine on the finish. (1979)
➤ GFA Marly-Ridoret, 39 Av. de Mont-de-Marsan, 33850 Léognan; tel. 56 21 75 08 ☎ By appt. Closed Aug.

CHATEAU DU MARAIS★

■	3ha	12000	3 D ⏁ ↓
79 82 83			

Dark colour, with depth, good tannins, and a slight vanilla aroma. It should age well. (1983)
➤ Patrick Bernard, Dom. de Maron, Landiras, 33720 Podensac; tel. 85 62 55 30 ☎ By appt.

CLOS LA MAURASSE★

□	8ha	24000	4 D ◼ ↓
70 76 78 ⑧ 82 83			

Made from organically grown grapes. Pale-yellow with an elegant, floral bouquet. On the palate, fine but perhaps a bit tart. (1983)
➤ R. Sessacq, Clos la Maurasse, 33210 Langon; tel. 56 63 20 24 ☎ By appt.

CHATEAU DES MAUVES

□	15ha	60000	3 D ◼ ↓
75 81 82 ⑧ 83			

A fresh-looking label for a fresh-tasting wine. Pale in colour, floral on the nose and smooth, though fairly thin in flavour. (1982)
➤ Bernard Bouche, Ch. des Maures, 33720 Podensac; tel. 56 27 17 05 ☎ By appt. Closed Aug.

CHATEAU DU MAYNE

■	10ha	54000	4 D ⏁
*75 *76 *78 *79 *82 *83			

'Mayne' is an old Gascon word meaning 'hamlet', and as the name implies, this wine is rustic in character: full bodied, robust and tannic. (1982)
✔ Graves Ch. le Maine, Graves Ch. du Barrail.
➤ J.-P. Duprat, 140 bis Cours du XIV Juillet, 33210 Langon; tel. 56 63 52 26 ☎ By appt. Closed Aug.

CHATEAU LA MISSION-HAUT-BRION *Pessac*★★★

■Cru Classé.	18ha	120000	6 ⏁ ↓
77 78 79 80 82 ⑧ 84			

Deep red in colour that with a well-developed nose, gives an impression of mature tannins. Weighty presence on the palate. Distinctive for its richness, elegance, finesse and breeding. (1983)
➤ Dom. Clarence Dillon SA, Ch. la Mission-Haut-Brion, 33400 Talence; tel. 56 98 11 85 ☎ By appt.

CHATEAU MONTALIVET★

■			4

A representative white wine with an aroma of violets, characteristic of Graves soil. Supple attack on the palate, fine and well balanced overall. (1982)
➤ Sté Coste-Dubourdieu, Pujols-sur-Ciron, 33210 Langon; tel. 56 63 50 52 ☎ No visitors.

CHATEAU MONTALIVET★★

□		100000	4

Beautiful colour, intense bouquet, mingled aroma of fruit and fruit stones. Rich and complete, the wine leaves a fine sense of harmony on the palate. (1983)
➤ Sté Coste-Dubourdieu, Pujols-sur-Ciron, 33210 Langon; tel. 56 63 50 52 ☎ No visitors.

CHATEAU MOULIN-DE-MARC★

□	6ha	6000	3 D ◼ ↓
83 ⑧			

A lovely limpid buttercup-yellow wine which creates a forceful impression. The nose has an intense bouquet of dried fruit with a hint of lime.
✔ Graves Ch. Moulin-de-Marc Rouge.
➤ Mme. Ch. Pauly, 21 Cours Xavier-Moreau, 33720 Podensac; tel. 56 27 07 33 ☎ By appt. Closed Aug. ➤ GFA Ch. Moulin-de-Marc.

CHATEAU MOULIN-DE-MARC★

■	8ha	36000	4 D ◼ ↓
75 *76 *78 *81 *82 83			

A wine produced at Cérons (a commune entitled to its own appellation for sweet wines but only the appellation Graves for other types), characteristic of the marvellous 1978 vintage. It is good for drinking now, with a crisp and interesting nose. (1978) ✔ Graves Ch. Moulin-de-Marc Blanc Sec.
➤ Mme Ch. Pauly, 21 Cours Xavier-Moreau, 33720 Podensac; tel. 56 27 07 33 ☎ By appt. Closed Aug. ➤ GFA Ch. Moulin-de-Marc.

CHATEAU OLIVIER★★

■Cru Classé	17ha	120000	5 D ◼ ⏁ ↓
64 66 78 79 80 81 82 ⑧			

Promises some very good vintages in future, when the vines are a little older. (1982)
➤ P. de Bethmann, Ch. Olivier, 33850 Léognan, tel. 56 21 75 16 ☎ By appt.

CHATEAU OLIVIER*

□Cru Classé	17ha	120000	
70 *73 *78 *80 82 ⑧⑧			

Light, aromatic, pleasant and easy to drink. Should be drunk sooner rather than later. (1983) ↳ P. de Bethmann, Ch. Olivier, 33850 Léognan; tel. 56 21 75 16 ⊤ By appt.

✕CHATEAU PAPE-CLEMENT**

■	23ha	150000	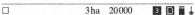
*75 *78 *79 *⑧⑧ *⑧⑧ *82			

The château might or might not have belonged to Pope Clement V; certainly, however, the wine is extremely fragrant, evoking autumnal undergrowth, with a predominant scent of mushrooms. On the palate it is quite solid. Already pleasant to drink, it could also wait a while. (1979) ↳ Montagne et Cie, Ch. Pape-Clement, 33600 Pessac; tel. 56 07 04 77 ⊤ By appt. Closed Aug.

CHATEAU PESSAN

□	3ha	20000	⬛ ⬛ ⬛ ⬛

Fine colour, but a certain contrast between the nose, fresh and fruity, and the palate, which is slightly more stuffy, approaching firmness at the finish. (1983) ↳ Jean Medeville et Fils, Ch. Fayau, 33410 Cadillac; tel. 56 27 03 51 ⊤ No visitors ↳ *Mme* Bitot-Bordessoules.

CHATEAU PICQUE-CAILLOU*

■	14ha	72000	⬛ ⬛ ⬛ ⬛
*78 *79 *80 *⑧⑧ *⑧⑧ *83			

One of the few remaining vineyards in the commune of Mérignac, the location of Bordeaux's airport; expanding urbanization has not affected its wine. A distinctive nose evokes cedarwood and pine. It has a wonderful structure; refined and delicate, with a lightly oaky definition. (1981) ↳ Alphonse Denis, Ch. Piacque-Caillou, 33700 Merignac; tel. 56 47 37 98 ⊤ By appt., SCI Picque-Caillou.

CHATEAU DE PINGOY

□	4ha	20000	⬛ ⬛ ⬛ ⬛
81 *82 *83 ·			

The distinguishing feature of this wine is its honey- and wax-scented nose; rich and sweet to taste. (1983) ↳ *Mme* Vve Simone Dozier et Fils, Ch. de Pingoy, 33640 Portets; tel. 56 67 22 78.

CHATEAU DE PINGOY*

■	7ha	32100	⬛ ⬛ ⬛
64 67 75 ⑧⑧ ⑧⑧ 82 ⑧⑧			

Lacking a little fullness, but has fine colour, a fruity and charming nose, and attractive balance on the palate. (1982) ✔ Other Graves wines, Bordeaux Supérieur, Bordeaux. ↳ *Mme*. Vve. Simone Dozier et Fils, Ch. de Pingoy, 33640 Portets; tel. 56 67 22 78 ⊤ No visitors.

CHATEAU PIRON**

□	20ha	116000	⬛ ⬛
61 76 81 82 83			

Fresh and fruity, with a lime flavour; pleasant and well made. (1982) ↳ André Boyreau, Ch. Piron, St-Morillon, 33650 Labrède; tel. 56 20 25 61 ⊤ By appt.

CHATEAU PONTAC-MONPLAISIR**

□	6ha	32400	⬛ ⬛
⑧⑧ 84			

A lively colour and appropriately vigorous palate, with a marked citrus character on the nose. (1984) ↳ Jean Maufras, Ch. Pontac-Monplaisir, Villenave-d'Ornon, 33140 Pont-de-la-Maye; tel. 56 87 08 21 ⊤ By appt.

CHATEAU RAHOUL

■	13ha	70000	⬛ ⬛ ⬛ ⬛
76 80 81 82 83			

A well-made wine. Among its other good features is a very pleasant bouquet. (1982) ↳ Lothardt Dahl, Ch. Rahoul, 33640 Portets, te. 56 67 01 12 ⊤ By appt.

CHATEAU DE ROCHEMORIN**

□	2ha	12000	⬛ ⬛ ⬛ ⬛
*78 *82 *⑧⑧ *⑧⑧			

Every bit the equal of its red brother. Good colour, a straightforward but flowery nose, and a smooth, rich palate with a suggestion of wax and honey. A typical traditional white Graves. (1983) ✔ Entre-Deux-Mers Ch. Bonnet, Bordeaux Ch. Bonnet Rouge, Graves Ch. la Louvière Rouge et Blanc, Graves Ch. de Cruzeau Rouge et Blanc, Graves Ch. Couhins-Lurton Blanc. ↳ André Lurton, Ch. la Louvière, 33850 Léognan; tel. 57 84 52 07 ⊤ No visitors.

CHATEAU ROCHEMORIN**

■	20ha	130000	⬛ ⬛ ⬛ ⬛
*⑦⑧ *79 *⑧⑧			

From one of Montesquieu's estates. this 1982 wine, with its attractive colour, powerful but delicate nose, shows elegance, body, fleshy fruit and ripe tannins. (1982) ✔ Entre-Deux-Mers Ch. Bonnet, Bordeaux Ch. Bonnet Rouge, Graves Ch. la Louvière Rouge et Blanc, Graves Ch. Couhins-Lurton Blancs, Graves Ch. de Cruzeau Rouge et Blanc. ↳ André Lurton, Ch. Bonnet, Grézillac, 33420 Branne; tel. 57 84 52 07 ⊤ No visitors. Closed Aug.

CHATEAU ROQUETAILLADE-LA-GRANGE*

■	36ha	129600	⬛ ⬛ ⬛ ⬛ ⬛
78 79 80 ⑧⑧ ⑧⑧			

The vineyard lies east of the famous fortress of Roquetaillade. Good, deep colour; well balanced in the mouth. (1982) ✔ Graves Roquetaillade-la-Grange. ↳ Pierre et Jean Guignard, Mazeres, 33210 Langon; tel. 56 63 24 23 ⊤ No visitors.

CHATEAU ROUSSEAU*

■ 1 ha 7200 **4** ▬

*81 *82 *⑧③ *⑧③ *84

A wine called Rousseau in Montesquieu country may sound strange, but this is a pleasantly aromatic wine that is fairly fruity and full 'bodied without being harsh, and with a good, long finish. (1983)
↬ Jean-Marie Duviella, St-Pierre-de-Mons, 33210 Langon; tel. 56 63 52 36 ☖ No visitors.

CHATEAU SAINT-GEROME

■ 15 000 **3**

Beautiful ruby colour. A little faded on the nose, but good structure on the palate, as well as pleasantly fruity aromas. (1982)
↬ M. Seiglan, 33640 Portets; tel. 56 63 50 52 ☖ No visitors.

CHATEAU SAINT-JEAN*

□ 14 ha 78 000 **3** D ▬ ↓

*78 *81 *⑧② *⑧③

Deep yellow in colour with a pronounced nose of flowers, resin, ripe peach and pineapple. On the palate the wine is full, round, smooth and nicely balanced. (1983) ✔ Barsac Ch. Liot.
↬ Jean-Gérard David, Ch. Liot, Barsac, 33720 Podensac; tel. 56 27 15 31 ☖ By appt. Closed Aug.

CHATEAU SAINT-ROBERT*

□ 10 ha 48 000 **2** D ⑴ ↓

67 ⑦⑥ 79 **81** **81** 82 83

Attractive pale-yellow with a touch of gold. Despite a faint hint of oxidation, a good wine with a powerful and well-developed bouquet. (1982) ✔ Graves Ch. St-Robert, Graves Supérieurs Ch. St-Robert, Sauternes Ch. Bastor-Lamontagne.
↬ Credit Foncier de France, Ch. St-Robert, Pujols-sur-Ciron, 33210 Langon; tel. 56 63 27 66 ☖ Daily 8.30–12.30/14.00–18.00.

CHATEAU SAINT-ROBERT**

■ 25 ha 108 000 **3** D ⑴ ↓

*75 ⑦⑥ *78 *81 *⑧②

An attractive, bright-red wine that is full, fruity and fine; lightly tannic with good length. (1982)
↬ CFF de Langon, Ch. St-Robert, Pujols-sur-Giron, 33210 Langon; tel. 56 63 63 36 ☖ By appt.

CHATEAU DE SAINTE-HELENE*

□ 25 ha 25 000 **4** D ▬ ↓

81 **81** 83

Produced by the owner of the Château de Malle, this wine is a green-tinted, pale-gold in colour. Its pretty bouquet smells of crystallized apricots, and the palate is rich, round and long. (1981)
↬ Pierre de Bournazel, Ch. de Malle, Preignac 33210 Langon; tel. 56 63 28 67 ☖ By appt.

CHATEAU SEGALIER*

■ 20 000 **4** ⑴

82 **83**

A classic touch in the colour, and a good, characteristic nose. On the palate, after a good attack, the wine shows roundness and balance. (1983)

↬ Mme Villard et Fils, Ch. Tour-Carelot, 33480 Castelnau-de-Médoc; tel. 56 41 14 86 ☖ No visitors.

CHATEAU SMITH HAUT-LAFITTE*

■Cru Classé 51 ha 250 000 **5** D ⑴ ↓

*75 *79 *80 ⑧① **1** *82

Pleasantly smooth and not without finesse. (1981)
✔ Graves Ch. Smith Haut-Lafitte Blanc, Graves Ch. La Garde Rouge, Graves Ch. La Garde Blanc.
↬ SCE Eschenauer, Martillac, 33650 La Brede; tel. 56 81 58 90 ☖ By appt. Closed Aug.

DOMAINE DE LA SOLITUDE

■ 19 ha 84 000 **4** D ▬ ↓

*77 78 *⑦⑨ *80 *81 *⑧① ⑧② 83

An interesting wine, produced by nuns. Pleasing if light appearance. Characteristic Graves nose, and a delicate, moderately rich palate. A great success. (1982) ✔ Graves Dom. de la Solitude.
↬ Dom. de la Solitude, Communauté Réligieuse, 33650 Martillac; tel. 56 23 74 08 ☖ By appt.

LES TOQUES-GOURMANDES***

■ **3** D

Good ruby colour, and a nose, already developed, reminicent of red fruits with a hint of spice. Fresh, fruity and well-structured on the palate: a perfect example of the appellation. (1983)
↬ Les Toques-Gourmandes, 29 Bis Route de Versailles, 78560 Port-Marly; tel. 01 91 61 17 ☖ By appt.

CLOS TOUMILON

■ **3**

Beautiful deep red colour, and nose recalling small red fruit, with a light 'cooked' touch. Round on the palate, with a noble attack. (1978)
↬ M. Aubric, 33210 Langon; tel. 56 63 50 52 ☖ No visitors.

CHATEAU TOUMILON

□ 6 ha 36 000 **3** D ▬ ↓

75 78 *⑧②

Not quite as good as the estate's red. An attractive, clear colour. Should be drunk young. (1983)
↬ J. Sevenet, St-Pierre-de-Mons, 33210 Langon; tel. 56 63 07 24 ☖ By appt.

CHATEAU TOUMILON*

■ 6 ha 36 000 **4** D ▬ ↓

75 78 *⑧② ⑧②

This pretty little château has been in the family since 1783. Attractive, ruby-coloured wine with refined nose. Develops nicely in the mouth. (1982)
↬ J. Sevenet, St-Pierre-de-Mons, 33210 Langon; tel. 56 63 07 24 ☖ By appt.

CHATEAU LA TOUR-BICHEAU*

■ 17 ha 60 000 **3** D ▬ ↓

75 76 78 *79 *80 81 82 83

Typical wine with aromas of violets blending with a fruity Merlot scent. A rather fine bottle. (1982)
↬ Daubas et Fils, Ch. la Tour-Bicheau, 33640

Portets; tel. 56 67 17 78 ℐ No visitors.

CHATEAU LA TOUR-MARTILLAC★★

☐Cru Classé   5 ha   30000   5 ⬛ ⑪ ↓

82 83 *⟨84⟩

Every bit as good as the red from the same estate. Attractive, pale-yellow colour; discreet nose, perhaps overly so, but a frank attack to the palate, followed by an abundance of vanilla flavour with a hint of coffee on the finish. A well balanced, attractive and delicate wine, with a touch of softness. (1982)
⊶ Jean Kressman, Ch. la Tour-Martillac, 33850 Martillac; tel. 56 35 89 64 ℐ By appt.

CHATEAU LA TOUR-MARTILLAC★★

■Cru Classé   20 ha   90000   5 ⑪ ↓

81 ⟨82⟩

Originally a medieval fort, the château was later Montesquieu's country house – although only fragments of the earlier buildings now remain. The wine has immediate appeal, wit delicate, cherry-like aromas on the nose. On the palate it is well balanced, with a firm acidity that renders it rather hard at present, but augurs well for the future. (1981)
⊶ Jean Kressmann, Ch. la Tour-Martillac, 33850 Martillac; tel. 56 35 89 64 ℐ By appt.

CLOS TOURMILLOT★

■   10000   3

Handsome, dark ruby colour; very powerful aromas and pleasant taste, with roundness, flesh and tannin. (1983)
⊶ *M.* Bellis, 33210 Langon; tel. 56 63 02 52 ℐ No visitors.

CHATEAU TOURTEAU-CHOLLET

☐   15 ha   100000   3 ⬛ ↓

*83 *⟨84⟩ *84

Not quite of the same standard as its red partner; a clear, bright wine that will probably not improve further. (1983)
⊶ SC Cle Ch. Tourteau-Chollet, 17 Cours de la Martinique, 33000 Bordeaux; tel. 56 52 11 46 ℐ No visitors.

CHATEAU TOURTEAU-CHOLLET★

■   20 ha   120000   4 ⬛ ↓

*⟨82⟩ *82 *83 *84

Unremarkable colour, but the nose compensates for this with a certain finesse also apparent on the palate. A smooth and pleasant wine that is quite ready for drinking. (1982)
⊶ SC Cle Ch. ourteau-Chollet, 17 Cours de la Martinique, 33000 Bordeaux; tel. 56 52 11 46 ℐ No visitors.

CHATEAU LA VIEILLE-FRANCE

■   4 ha   25000   3 D ⬛ ↓

75 79 81 82 83

Under the same ownership as the better-known Château Grand-Abord. Pleasantly supple wine. (1982)
⊶ Michel Dugoua, St-André-de-Cubzac, 33640 Portets; tel. 56 67 19 11 ℐ By appt.

CHATEAU VILLEFRANCHE

☐   7 ha   20000   4 D ⬛ ⑪ ↓

*75 81 *82 82

This wine does not have the fullness one might expect from a sweet wine, but on the other hand it is easy to drink. (1981) ✔ Bordeaux Dom. Mingets Rouge et Blanc, Graves Rouge.
⊶ Henri Guinabert et Fils, Ch. Villefranche, Barsac, 33720 Podensac; tel. 56 27 16 39 ℐ By appt.

Graves Supérieurs

CHATEAU D'ARRICAUD★

☐   12 ha   57600   4 D ⬛ ⑪ ↓

75 *⟨83⟩ *83 *84

A colourful, dry white wine with a spirited attack, roundness, richness and length. ✔ Graves Ch. d'Arricaud, Graves Supérieures Ch. d'Arricaud.
⊶ A.-J. Bouyx, Landiras, 33720 Podensac; tel. 56 62 51 29 ℐ By appt.

CHATEAU D'ARRICAUD

☐   12 ha   57600   4 D ⬛ ↓

76 * 81 83

This wine has a good golden yellow colour and a well-developed nose, and is agreeably fresh. ✔ Graves Ch. d'Arricaud, Graves Supérieures Ch. d'Arricaud.
⊶ A.-J. Bouyx, Landiras, 33720 Podensac; tel. 56 62 51 29 ℐ By appt.

DOMAINE DE MARON★

☐   6 ha   15000   3 D ⬛ ↓

83 84

The family house here is charming, incorporating the original 18th-century farmhouse. A magnificent collection of horse-drawn carriages is an added attraction. The wine itself is appropriately elegant – aromatic, fresh, fairly rounded and fine. (1984)
⊶ Patrick Bernard, Dom. de Maron, Landiras, 33720 Podensac; tel. 85 62 55 30 ℐ By appt.

The Médoc Appellations

The Médoc occupies a special place in the range of wines from the Gironde. Confined to its own little peninsula, yet at the same time open to the world through the seaway of the Gironde estuary, the Médoc and its people perfectly illustrate the introspective yet ambitious Aquitaine temperament. It is not surprising, therefore, to find practically unknown, small family concerns alongside the larger, world-famous estates belonging to powerful French or foreign companies.

Although the Médoc vineyard itself is over 80 km long and 10 km wide, it is only a part of the region as a whole. Off the beaten track, the

Médoc has quite a few surprises in store for the visitor, from the watery horizons of Margaux to the richly varied coastal landscapes of Bas (Lower) Médoc. But its greatest glory lies in the gentle gravel slopes that run down to the Gironde estuary. The combination of poor soil and excellent drainage helps to produce wines of outstanding quality.

It is common to make the distinction between Haut-Médoc, (from Blanquefort to St-Seurin de Car-

dourne) and Bas-Médoc (from St-Germain d'Esteuil to Soulac). At the heart of the Haut-Médoc area are the six communal appellations which produce its most famous wines. All of the 62 Crus Classés, except Haut-Brion, are planted within these appellation areas; however, five of them have only the Haut-Médoc appellation. The classed growths account for approximately 25 per cent of the total surface area of Médoc vines, 20 per cent of the volume of wine produced, and 40 per

Médoc and The Haut-Médoc

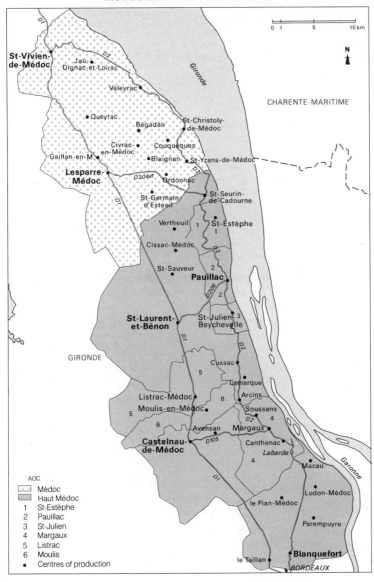

cent of the region's turnover. Apart from the Crus Classés, Médoc produces many reputed Crus Bourgeois which must be château-bottled. There are several cooperatives within the Médoc and Haut-Médoc appellations, as well as in three of the communal appellations.

A significant proportion of Médoc and Haut-Médoc appellation wine is sold in bulk to shippers who then market the wines under their own brand names.

The traditional Médoc grape variety is Cabernet-Sauvignon, although it is perhaps less universal than it once was. Even so, it covers 52 per cent of the total area; Merlot comes second with 34 per cent. Merlot makes characteristically smooth, round wines which develop fairly quickly and may therefore be drunk younger. Cabernet Franc, which gives the wines structure and finesse, makes up 10 per cent of the vines. Finally, there is a small amount of Petit-Verdot and Malbec.

Médoc wines have an enviable reputation and are universally recognized as the most prestigious red wines in the world. They are characterized by an attractive ruby colour, shading to brick-red as the wine ages, and a fruity fragrance in which the spiciness of the Cabernet-Sauvignon often blends with the vanilla of new oak casks. Their firm tannic structure matures into a smooth, elegant flavour, and their fine balance allows them to age harmoniously.

Médoc

All the vineyards in the Médoc have the right to use the Médoc appellation, although in practice it is only used in Bas-Médoc (the northern part of the peninsula near Lesparre); the communes that lie between Blanquefort and St-Seurin de Cadourne use the Haut-Médoc appellation instead. Production of the Médoc appellation is, however, substantial; 23 million bottles in 1982 from an area of 2976 hectares.

The wines have an attractive, often deep, colour. With a higher proportion of Merlot than the Haut-Médoc and communal appellations, they possess a typical fruity bouquet and roundness.

BARON PHILIPPE★★

■	400ha 480000	4 ■ ↓

73 74 **75** 76 77 ★78 79 80 **81** ⑧ **82** 83

Lovely deep colour. A fine, well-balanced and elegant wine which will develop well during the next four or five years. (1982)
↑↑ Baron Philippe de Rothschild, La Baronnie, BP 2, 33250 Pauillac; tel. 56 59 20 20 ☎ By appt. Closed Aug.

CHATEAU BELLERIVE★★

■Cru Bourg.	12ha 60000	3 D ■ ◑ ↓

78 79 80 81 **81** ⑧

The vineyard looks out over the Gironde estuary; it produces deeply coloured wines, this example showing itself to be well balanced on the palate with plenty of tannin, and an overall impression of quality. (1982)
↑↑ Guy Perrin, Ch. Bellerive, Valeyrac, 33340 Lesparre-Médoc; tel. 56 41 52 13 ☎ By appt. Closed 15 Sept.–15 June.

CHATEAU BELLEVUE★

■	13ha 70000	4 D ■

74 75 76 78 **79** 80 **81** 82

A wine with a fine colour and some character on the palate. (1982)
↑↑ Yves Lassalle, Ch. Bellevue, Valeyrac, Lesparre-Médoc; tel. 56 41 52 17 ☎ By appt.

CHATEAU DE BENSSE

▥	8ha 30000	3 D ■ ↓

75 78 80 81 ⑧ **83**

The château houses the Prignac cooperative which produces a wine with a fine colour but has still to open up. (1982) ✔ Médoc Vieux Colombier.
↑↑ Sté de Vinification de Prignac, Les Vieux Colombiers, Prignac, 33340 Lesparre-Médoc; tel. 56 41 01 02 ☎ Mon.–Sat. 9.00–12.30/14.00–18.00.

CHATEAU BOIS-DE-ROC

■	20ha 150000	3 D ■ ↓

75 80 **81 82 83**

This stone house, probably built during the 17th century, simple but elegant, produces a wine of a lovely deep colour, quite fine, with an individual character coming from the little-known Carmemère grape. (1982)
↑↑ Philippe Cazenave, St-Yzans de Médoc, 33340 Lesparre-Médoc; tel. 56 41 09 79. ☎ By appt.

CHATEAU BOURNAC★

■Cru Bourg.	7.5ha 50000	4 D ■ ◑ ↓

80 **82** 82 **83** 83

Entirely destroyed by phylloxera at the end of the last century, this vineyard was re-established about 15 years ago. The result is successful: a wine with aromas of slightly candied red fruit and liquorice. Warm, powerful and tannic, it has all the ingredients for good ageing. (1982)
↑↑ Pierre Secret, Ch. Bournac, Civrac, 33340 Lesparre-Médoc; tel. 56 41 51 24 ☎ By appt.

CHATEAU CASTERA*

■ 45ha 15000 ▣4 ▣D ▤ ◑ ↓
81 **81** 82 **82**

Parts of this well-built château date from the Middle Ages; the wine, too, has a fairly solid structure, with good balance and well-blended tannins. (1982)
↜ SA Alexis-Lichine, 109 Rue Achard, 33000 Bordeaux; tel. 56 50 84 85 ¶ By appt.

CHATEAU LA TOUR-HAUT-CAUSSAN***

■Cru Bourg. 10ha 60000 ▣4 ▣D ◑ ↓
79 80 **80** 81 **81** 82 **82** 83 **83**

A very attractive and complex nose, dominated by blackcurrant, vanilla and undergrowth. On the palate the attractive and very ripe tannins reveal this wine's fine future. (1982) ✔ Médoc Ch. la Landotte.
↜ Philippe Courrian, Ch. La Tour-Haut-Caussan, Blaignan, 33340 Lesparre-Médoc; tel. 56 41 04 77 ¶ By appt.

CHANTECAILLE

■ 18000 ▣3 ▣D ▤ ↓
81 82 **83**

Orange-hued ruby-red, with a discreetly aromatic nose, and a straightforward, well-flavoured palate. For drinking now. (1983)
↜ Maison Chantecaille et Cie, 127 Rue de Turenne, 33000 Bordeaux; tel. 56 48 04 54.

CHATEAU CHANTELYS**

■ 5.5ha 10000 ▣3 ▣D ▤ ↓
*82 *83 *84

A fairly typical Médoc with a deep colour, generosity and elegance. This wine could be laid down but it also makes very pleasant drinking relatively young. (1982)
↜ Villard et Fils 33480 Castelnau-de-Médoc; tel. 56 41 14 86 ¶ No visitors.

CHATEAU LA CLARE**

■Cru Bourg. 20ha 120000 ▣4 ▣D ▤ ↓
79 **79** **80** 81 **81** 82 **82** 83

A fine, deeply coloured wine. The nose is closed but promising, and the palate oaky and well balanced. (1981)
↜ Paul de Rozières, Ch. la Clare, Bégadan, 33340 Lesparre-Médoc; tel. 56 41 50 61 ¶ By appt.

CHATEAU DAVID*

■ 7ha 40000 ▣3 ▣D ▤ ↓

Lovely red colour with a violet tinge. Prune-scented, fruity nose, and plenty of concentration on the palate. (1982)
↜ Henri Coutreau, Ch. David, Vensac, 33590 St-Vivien-de-Médoc; tel. 56 41 44 62 ¶ Daily 9.00–12.00/14.00–18.00.

GILBEY'S*

■ 15ha 40000 ▣3 ▣D ▤ ◑ ↓
*76 *81 *82 83

A well-made wine whose bouquet is pleasant, blending the scents of crystallized fruit with wood. Almost too supple on the palate, but with a very ripe, quality tannin. (1981)
↜ W. et A. Gilbey's IDV, 33340 St-Ysans-de-Médoc; tel. 56 41 15 03 ¶ By appt.

CHATEAU GREYSSAC**

■Cru Gd Bourg. 60ha 300000 ▣4 ▣D ▤ ↓
70 71 75 76 79 **81** 82 83

The house here is very fine. Intense red wine with a delicately woody nose, round and charming attack and a tannic palate. All promise a fine future. (1982)
↜ Dom. Codem, Ch. Greyssac, Bégadan, 33340 Lesparre-Médoc; tel. 56 41 50 29 ¶ By appt. Closed Aug., Christmas week and New Year's Day.

CHATEAU GRIVIERE*

■Cru Bourg. 20ha 120000 ▣3 ▣D ▤ ↓
(81) **81** 82 **82** 83 **83**

This property disappeared after the frosts of 1956, and was replanted a decade or so later. It produces a very tannic wine which is a little slow to mature. (1982)
↜ François de Rozières, La Rivière, Blaignan, 33340 Lesparre-Médoc; tel. 56 41 04 46 ¶ By appt.

CHATEAU HAUT-CANTELOUP*

Cru Bourg. 18ha 100000 ▤ ◑ ↓ ▣3
64 66 69 75 76 78 79 (82) 83 84

Produced from a vineyard overlooking the Gironde estuary, this wine has an intense colour, and a pleasant, slightly spicy nose. The palate is an attractive blend of spicy, roasted flavours. (1982)
↜ M. Vilas-Samiac, Ch. Haut-Canteloup, St-Christoly 33340 Lesparre-Médoc; tel. 56 41 51 86 ¶07 No visitors.

CHATEAU HAUT-GRAVAT***

■ 5ha 5000 ▣3 ▣D ▤ ↓
(82) 83

A wine of some class; deep purple-red; elegant and minty on the nose, with a palate marked by flavours of prune, liquorice, vanilla and venison. (1982)
↜ Jean-Louis Lanneau, Ch. Haut-Gravat, Jau-Dignac et Loirac, 33590 St-Vivien-de-Médoc; tel. 56 41 41 20.

CHATEAU LACOMBE-NOAILLAC★★

■   18ha   100000   **3** D ▮ ↓

⑧ **82** 83

This vineyard has just been replanted and is still rather young, but the selection of grape varieties is really excellent, with Cabernet-Sauvignon accounting for 70 per cent of the vines. Fruity nose and an elegant palate, from the gravelly soil, well balanced by a substantial structure. (1982)
⊶ GFA Ch. Lacombe-Noaillac, Jau-Dignac-et-Loirac, 33590 St-Vivien-de-Médoc; tel. 56414255 ¥ By appt ⊶ Jean-Michel Lapalu.

CHATEAU LAGORCE

■Cru Bourg.   20ha   130000   **4** D ▮ ↓

78 **82** 84

From a pretty country house and recently reconstituted vineyard, belonging again to just one owner, the wine is a good colour, fairly tannic and should keep well. (1982)
⊶ Henri Fabre, Ch. Lagorce, Blaignan, 33340 Lesparre-Médoc; tel. 56412142 ¥ Mon.–Fri. 9.00–12.00/13.00–17.00.

CHATEAU LAUJAC★★

■Cru Bourg.   35ha   180000   **4** D ▮ ⑪ ↓

70 75 76 78 **81 82 82** 83

The wine from this huge estate, with its gravel slopes and neoclassical château, combines finesse and a certain tannic strength, very close to a Haut-Médoc in style. Needs to be left for a while. (1982)
⊶ Bernard Cruse, Ch. Laujac, Bégadan, 33340 Lesparre-Médoc; tel. 56 41 50 12 ¥ By appt.

CHATEAU LESTRUELLE

■Cru Bourg.   21ha   60000   **3** D ▮ ⑪ ↓

70 75 76 78 81 82 83

Produced by a cooperative until recently, this wine has just reappeared on the market. It is well-made and sufficiently tannic to age for several years. (1982)
⊶ GFA Labra, Lestruelle, St-Yzans-de-Médoc, 33340 Lesparre-Médoc; tel. 56411501 ¥ By appt.

CHATEAU LOUDENNE★

■Cru Bourg.   52ha   180000   **5** D ▮ ↓

66 **70** 71 **75** 76 **78** ⑲ 81 **82** 83

This elegant 18th-century château has a museum of wine-growers' tools. The wine is attractive, combining aromas of wood and vanilla. There is still a slight astringency but this should disappear as the wine ages. (1981)
⊶ W. et A. Gilbey, Ch. Loudenne, St-Yzans-de-

Médoc, 33340 Lesparre-Médoc; tel. 56411503 ¥ By appt.

CHATEAU MAZAILS★

■Cru Bourg.   21ha   50000   **3** D ⑪ ↓

75 76 77 78 81

The fine soil of this vineyard produces a pretty wine combining good colour, rather a powerful bouquet and real finesse.
⊶ Sté Civile du Ch. Haut-Marac, Ch. Mazails, St-Yzans-de-Médoc, 33340 Lesparre-Médoc; tel. 56411537 ¥ By appt. Closed Sun.

CHATEAU LES MOINES★

■   22ha   150000   **2** ▮

⑦⑤ 76 ★78 79 **82** **83**

Deep red colour, fruity scents on the nose and a good balance on the palate. (1983)
⊶ Claude Pourreau, Les Moines, Couquèques, 33340 Lesparre-Médoc; tel. 56415370 ¥ No visitors.

CHATEAU DU MONTHIL★

■Cru Bourg.   20ha   120000   **4** D ▮ ⑪ ↓

78 79 **80** ★81 ★**81 82** 83 **83**

A classic wine, very tannic, with a nose that is just beginning to develop. The unusually high proportion of Cabernet Franc (30%) is partly responsible for the character. (1981)
⊶ Jean Gabas, Ch. du Monthil, Bégadan, 33340 Lesparre-Médoc; tel. 56 41 50 73 ¥ By appt.

CHATEAU MOULIN DE BEL AIR★

■   27000   **4** ▮ ⑪

76 77 78 80 **81 82 82** 83

Moderate colour, but intense nose showing real finesse with its aromas of candied fruit. Light on the palate, but well balanced nonetheless. (1983)
⊶ Gilbert Dartiguenave, St-Yzans-de-Médoc, 33340 Lesparre-Médoc; tel. 56411531 ¥ By appt.

CHATEAU MOULIN-DE-CASTILLON★

■   12ha   6000   **3** D ▮ ↓

70 72 73 **75** 79 **82 82** 83

Still rather closed-in, but showing the fullness, strength and concentration that should allow it to age well. (1982)
⊶ Pierre Moriau, Le Bourg, St-Christoly, 33340 Lesparre-Médoc; tel. 56 41 53 01 ¥ No visitors.

CHATEAU MOULIN DE FERREGRAVE★★

■   5ha   20000   **3** D ▮ ⑪

⑧⑴ **82** **82**

This wine has only recently begun to be produced independently. Its intense colour suggests hidden promise. The nose is pleasantly fragrant and slightly fruity; the palate is robust and concentrated, refined and long. (1982)
⊶ Francis Ducos, Le Broustera, Jau-Dignac-et-Loirac, 33590 St-Vivien-de-Médoc; tel. 56 41 42 37 ¥ By appt.

CHATEAU MOULIN-TAFFARD

■ 5ha 15000 **3** **D** ▮ ◫ ⬤

78 *79 81 **82**

Very tannic and so has good ageing potential – hardly surprising, being made exclusively from Cabernet-Sauvignon grapes; nevertheless, it is also pleasantly smooth. (1982)
⬅ Pierre Peyruse, Ch. Moulin-Taffard, St-Christoly, 33340 Lesparre-Médoc; tel. 56 41 54 98 ⏃ By appt.

NICOLAS*

■ 102000 **3** ▮

An attractive wine with a good, typically 1983 colour, and 'baked' nose. Good structure on the palate but the finish could be more aromatic. (1983)
⬅ ETS Nicolas, 2 Rue de Valmy, 94220 Charenton; tel. 01 37 59 200.

CHATEAU LES ORMES-SORBET**

■Gd Cru Bourg. 20ha 110000 **4** **D** ◫ ⬤

78 79 80 **81** 81 ⑧⑧ ⑧⑧ 83 ⑧⑧

Red fruit and new wood on the nose; fine, balanced tannins and good length on the palate. This 1982 wine is in the top flight of its vintage. (1982) ✔ Médoc Ch. de Conques Rouges.
⬅ Jean Boivert, Ch. les Ormes-Sorbet, 33340 Lesparre-Médoc; tel. 56 41 53 78 ⏃ By appt.

CHATEAU PATACHE D'AUX**

■Cru Bourg. 38ha 125000 **4** **D** ◫ ⬤

78 79 80 **81** **81** **82** **82** 83 **83**

A closed but quite dense nose; this wine is well balanced with superb tannins, a good guarantee for the future. (1983) ✔ Médoc Ch. le Boscq Rouge.
⬅ SC Ch. Patache d'Aux, Bégadan, 33340 Lesparre-Médoc; tel. 56 41 50 18 ⏃ Mon.–Thurs. 8.00–12.00/14.00–17.00.

PAVILLON DE BELLEVUE

■ 24400 **4** **D** ◫ ⬤

79 80 81 ⑧⑧ **82**

This wine is produced by the Cave d'Ordonnac which will celebrate its golden jubilee in 1986. Plenty of tannin and definitely a wine for keeping. (1982)
⬅ Coop. d'Ordonnac, 'Plantignan', Ordonnac, 33340 Lesparre-Médoc; tel. 56 41 14 13 ⏃ By appt.

CHATEAU PEY-MARTIN*

■ 9ha 55000 **3** **D** ▮ ◫ ⬤

75 76 **78** 81 **82** 83

Deep cherry in colour; on the palate round and with some length though the tannin is a little vegetal in quality. (1982)
⬅ Jean Signoret, Ch. Pey-Martin, Ordonnac, 33340 Lesparre-Médoc; tel. 56 41 14 08 ⏃ By appt.

CHATEAU LA PIROUETTE**

■ 10ha 9600 **3** **D** ▮ ◫ ⬤

Deep, dark colour and bouquet of ripe fruit, prunes included, refined by a subtle cedar character. Wonderful balance between richness and finesse on the palate, leading to a good, long finish. (1982)
⬅ Yves Roux, Jau-Dignac-et-Loirac, 33590 St-Vivien-de-Médoc; tel. 56 41 42 02 ⏃ No visitors.

CHATEAU PLAGNAC**

■Cru Bourg. 28ha 180000 **3** ◫ ⬤

78 **78** 79 80 81 **81** **82** **82** 83 **83**

A remarkable 1983, a vintage that has still to be fully appreciated. The nose is not fully developed, but the wine is elegant, well balanced and delicate on the palate. A very well-bred bottle. (1983) ✔ St-Julien Ch. Talbot Rouge, St-Julien Ch. Gruaud Larose Rouge, St-Estèphe Ch. Meyney Rouge, Sauternes Ch. Lafaurie Peyraguey Blanc Liquoreux.
⬅ Dom. Cordier, 10, Quai de Paludate, 33800 Bordeaux; tel. 56 41 54 34 ⏃ By appt. Closed end Aug.–beginning Sept.

CHATEAU PONTET*

■ 11ha 70000 **3** ▮ ◫ ⬤

80 81 **81** ⑧⑧ **82** 83 **83**

A rather light, clear wine; straightforward and very fruity. (1981)
⬅ Emile Courrian, Ch. Pontet, Blaignan, 33340 Lesparre-Médoc; tel. 56 41 19 19 ⏃ By appt. Closed Aug.

CHATEAU POTENSAC**

■Cru Bourg. 40ha 460000 **4** ◫ ⬤

78 **78** 79 81 **81** 82 **82**

A plain and simple bourgeois house, but a beautiful vineyard on a gravelly slope which explains the beautiful colour and elegance of this wine. It is fine, rich, and similar in many ways to a Haut-Médoc. (1982) ✔ Médoc Ch. Lassalle, Médoc Ch. Goudy-la-Cardonne, Médoc Ch. Gallais-Bellevue.
⬅ Paul Delon, Ch. Potensac, Ordonnac, 33340 Lesparre-Médoc; tel. 56 59 25 26 ⏃ By appt. Closed Aug.

PRESTIGE-MEDOC*

■ 400ha 1900000 **3** **D** ▮ ⬤

78 ⑧⓪ 81 **82** **82**

This wine is a lovely dark red colour and has a delicate, refined nose of crystallized soft fruit. On the palate, this is still harshly tannic and needs time to develop. (1982)
⬅ Uni-Médoc, Gaillan 33340; tel. 56 42 03 12 ⏃ By appt.

CHATEAU PREUILLAC*

■Cru Bourg. 20ha 140000 **4** ◫ ⬤

*77 *79 *79 *80 *81 *81 83

Deep-coloured 1983; round, tannic and well structured. Should age well. (1983)
⬅ ETS. Thienpont de Berlaere, Ch. Puygeraud, St-Cibard, 33570 Lussac; tel. 57 40 61 04 ⏃ By appt ⬅ Raymond Bouet.

CHATEAU ROLLAN-DE-BY★

◼ 1.65ha 12000 ▣ D ▮ ⅻ ⤓
82 ⑭

Deep purple-red; cinammon and spice bouquet, and a velvety texture on the palate. (1982)
⤙ M. Malcore, Ch. Rollan-de-By, Bégadan, 33340 Lesparre-Médoc; tel. 56 41 52 21 � By appt.

CHATEAU ROQUEGRAVE

◼Cru Bourg. 26ha 100000 ▣ D ▮ ⤓
77 ⑦ 80 81 82 83

Classic Médoc colour enhanced by a few hints of brightness. A little light, but a very vinous bouquet and soft on the palate. (1982) ✔ Médoc AOC Ch. les Granges-d'Or Rouge.
⤙ MM. Joannon et LLeu, Ch. Roquegrave, Valeyrac, 33340 Lesparre-Médoc; tel. 56 41 52 02 � Daily 9.00–12.00/14.00/17.00.

CHATEAU SAINT-AUBIN★★

◼ 12ha 100000 ▣ D ▮ ⅻ ⤓
82 83

Produced independently for only a short while, this is a wine with a good, very dense colour. Ripe fruit on the nose, and solidly built on the palate, adding up to a good overall balance. (1982)
⤙ M. Monnier and J. Peduzzi, Jan-Dignac-et-Loirac, 33590 St-Vivien-de-Médoc; tel. 56 47 39 69 � By appt.

SAINT-BRICE★

◼ 120ha 110000 ▣ D ▮ ⤓
⑦ 75 79 81 82 83

Produced by the Cave Coopérative de St-Yzans. Characteristic Médoc with dark colour and round, full palate.
⤙ Coop. de Brice, St-Yzans-de-Médoc, 33340 Lesparre Médoc; tel. 56 41 15 46 � By appt.

CHATEAU SAINT-CHRISTOLY

◼Cru Bourg. 20ha 100000 ▣ D ▮ ⅻ ⤓
70 71 73 75 ⑦ 82 83

A true Médoc wine with plenty of character. Aromas that are both fruity and meaty, and especially reminiscent of venison. (1982) ✔ Médoc Ch. La Rose St-Bonnet, Médoc Ch. La Fleur St-Bonnet.
⤙ Paul Héraud, St-Christoly, 33340 Lesparre-Médoc; tel. 56 41 52 95 � By appt.

CAVE SAINT-JEAN★★

◼ 550ha 2000000 ▣ D ▮ ⤓
79 80 ⑧ 82 83

The lovely dark-red colour and rich, meaty nose give way to a fairly complex and tannic palate, which is still closed in and needs time to soften before drinking. (1982)
⤙ Cave Coop. de St-Jean, Bégadan, 33340 Lesparre-Médoc; tel. 56 41 50 13 � By appt.

CHATEAU SAINT-SATURNIN

◼Cru Bourg. 21ha 150000 ▣ D ▮ ⤓
70 71 75 76 78 79 81 82

Adrien Tramier is not afraid to harvest his grapes later than some of the other Sauternes châteaux. An unusual wine; very fragrant, with a slightly overripe taste. It is worth chancing a visit; depending on this colourful poet's mood, you will either be shown the door or offered a bottle of the best. (1982)
⤙ Adrien Tramier, Ch. St-Saturnin, 33340 Bégadan Lesparre; tel. 56 41 50 82 � By appt.

CHATEAU SESTIGNAN★★

◼Cru Bourg. 10ha 60000 ▣ D ⅻ ⤓
79 80 81 81 82 82 83 83

A few cable-lengths from the sea, this is the most northern of the Médoc châteaux. A fruity wine with nuances of cocoa beans, well balanced on the palate, with fine tannins and good length. (1982)
⤙ Bertrand de Rozières, Ch. Sestignan, Jau-Dignac-Loirac, 33590 St-Vivien-de-Médoc; tel. 56 41 43 06 � By appt.

CHATEAU SIGOGNAC★

◼Cru Bourg. 45ha 250000 ▣ D ▮ ⅻ ⤓
70 75 78 81 82 83

From a noble old house which may have inspired Théophile Gauthier's novel *le Captain Fracasse*. This wine is deeply coloured, elegant, fine, supple and yet not without tannin. (1982)
⤙ M. Bonny-Grasset, Ch. Sigognac, St-Yzans-de-Medoc, 33340 Lesparre-Médoc; tel. 56 41 15 04 � By appt.⤙ Colette Bonny.

CHATEAU TAFFARD★★

◼ 50ha 92000 ▣ D ▮ ⤓
80 81 82

Good Médoc colour, pleasantly forthcoming and fine nose. Full, rich and flowing on the palate. (1982)
⤙ Coop. de St-Brice, St-Yzans-de-Médoc, 33340 Lesparre-Médoc; tel. 56 15 41 46 � Mon.–Sat. 8.30–12.00/14.00–18.00.⤙ Paul Mottes.

CHATEAU LA TOUR BLANCHE★

◼Cru Bourg. 27ha 110000 ▣ D ▮ ⤓
78 80 81 81 82 83 83

The nose of undergrowth, mushrooms and coffee is already developed. This wine is warm on the palate, high in alcohol and has a marked astringency on the finish. Must not be drunk for six or eight years. (1982) ✔ Moulis Ch. Moulin-à-Vent Rouge.
⤙ SCA La Tour Blanche, St-Christoly-Médoc, 33340 Lesparre-Médoc; tel. 56 41 53 13 � By appt. Closed Aug.

CHATEAU LA TOUR DE BY★★★

◼Cru Bourg. 69ha 450000 ▣ D ▮ ⅻ ⤓
78 79 80 81 81 82 82 83 83

A wine with an attractive nose of slightly woody red fruit. Full bodied, exceptionally good quality tannins and fine length on the palate. This will develop into a great bottle. ✔ Médoc Moulin-de-la-Roque Rouge, Médoc la Roque-de-By Rouge, Médoc Cailloux-de-By Rouge.

➤ Marc Pages, Ch. La Tour de By, Bégadan, 33340 Lesparre-Médoc; tel. 56 41 50 03 ⟁ Mon.–Fri. 8.00–12.00/14.00–18.00, Sat. 9.00–12.00.
➤ *MM.* Cailloux, Lapalu et Pages.

TOUR PRIGNAC★

■Cru Bourg.　　139 ha　720000　③ D ▤ ⑪ ↓
★78 ★79 81 83

Overlooking its superb estate, this beautiful château produces a lively red wine whose nose has a certain finesse, marked by the scent of soft fruits. It has good weight on the palate, but perhaps, a slight lack of roundness. (1983)
➤ Castel SA, Castres, 33640 Portets; tel. 56 41 02 19 ⟁ By appt.

CHATEAU DES TOURELLES★

■Cru Bourg.　　25 ha　80000　③ D ▤ ⑪ ↓
79 80 81 82

This vineyard was classified as a Cru Bourgeois in 1969. It produces a nicely coloured wine with fruit on both nose and palate; ripe and concentrated. (1982)
➤ Fernand Miquau, Ch. des Tourelles, Blaignan, 33340 Lesparre-Médoc; tel. 56 41 14 88 ⟁ By appt.

TOUR-SAINT-VINCENT★★

■　　　　50 ha　75000　④ D ▤ ↓
80 81 82 82 (83)

Typically deep Médoc colour, and a nose with pronounced aromas of meat and venison. Round, warm, fat and elegant, this wine should age a good ten years. (1982)
➤ Jean-Louis Arnaud, St-Christoly-Médoc, 33340 Lesparre-Médoc; tel. 56 41 15 05 ⟁ By appt.

UNI-MEDOC★

■　　　　500 ha　200000　③ ▤ ↓
62 70 75 78 79 81 82 83 84

Beautiful mature red colour, and fine bouquet. A certain tannic note is discovered on the palate, especially in the rather imposing attack. (1982)
➤ Cave Coop. de Blaignan, Gaillan, 33340 Lesparre-Médoc; tel. 56 41 03 12 ⟁ By appt.

VIEUX CHATEAU LANDON★

■Cru Bourg.　　24 ha　13000　③ D ⑪ ↓
★80 ★81 ★81 ★82 83

This simple house boasts a splendid cellar and a powerful, vividly coloured wine with plenty of body and tannin.
➤ Philippe Gillet, Bégadan, 33340 Lesparre-Médoc; tel. 56 41 50 42 ⟁ By appt.

CHATEAU VIEUX ROBIN★

■Cru Bourg.　　12 ha　85000　④ D ⑪ ↓
79 80 81 81 (82) 82 83 83

This property has been run by the same family for six generations. Its wine is fairly tannic, warm, and gives a slightly baked impression. Moderately long. (1982) ✦ Médoc Dom. des Anguilleys Rouge.
➤ François Dufau, Ch. Vieux Robin, Bégadan, 33340 Lesparre-Médoc; tel. 56 41 50 64 ⟁ By appt.

Haut-Médoc

With the same production as Médoc, Haut-Médoc is generally rather better known, due mostly to the presence of its five first-growth wines. The famous village appellations contained within the Haut-Médoc area boast their own Crus Classés.

A typical Haut-Médoc is generous but not over-powerful. The nose usually has considerable finesse, and in general the wines age well. When mature they should be drunk at a moderate room temperature, and go very well with white meat, poultry, or light game. The lighter wines, however, can be drunk younger, in which case they are best served at a slightly cooler temperature: in France the young wines may even be drunk with fish or seafood.

CHATEAU D'AGASSAC

■Cru Bourg. Sup. 35 ha　120000　④ ⑪ ↓
70 71 75 76 **78 79 81 82**

This fourteenth-century fortified manor is surrounded by moats and towers. The wine, of a rather traditional sort, displays a touch of severity, but has a pleasant enough nose and palate. (1982)
➤ Sté Civile du Ch. d'Agassac, Ludon-Médoc, 33290 Blanquefort; tel. 56 30 44 44 ⟁ By appt.

CHATEAU D'ARCINS

■Cru Bourg.　　100 ha　650000　③ D ▤ ⑪ ↓
75 78 79 ★81 (82)

Lightly chocolate nose; the tannins on the palate might perhaps gain a little in maturity. (1982)
➤ Sté Civile du Ch. d'Arcins, Arcins, 33460 Margaux; tel. 56 58 91 29 ⟁ By appt.

CHATEAU BALAC★

■　　　　14 ha　95000　④ D ⑪ ↓
77 78 79 80 81 81 (82) 82 83 83

The 19th-century château was designed by Victor Louis, architect of the famous Grand-Théâtre in Bordeaux. Unusually, in the vineyard the three main grape varieties – Cabernet Sauvignon–Cabernet, Franc and Merlot – are grown in equal proportions. The wine is delicate and refined. Not very powerful, but well balanced with a particularly mellow tannin. (1982)
➤ Luc Touchais, Ch. Balac, 33112 St-Laurent-de-Benon; tel. 56 59 41 76 ⟁ Mon.–Fri. 10.00–12.00/14.00–18.00.

CHATEAU BARREYRES★

■Cru Bourg.　　100 ha　650000　③ D ▤ ⑪ ↓
75 78 79 ★81 (82)

In contrast with the château, which is architecturally rather heavy-handed, this wine displays an agreeable suppleness allied with good concentrated flavour on the palate. It is fairly tannic and

will make a good wine to lay down. (1982)
↖ Sté Civile du Ch. Barreyres, Arcins, 33460 Margaux; tel. 56 58 91 61 ☏ Mon.–Sat. 8.00–12.00/14.00–18.00.

CHATEAU BEAUMONT★★

■Cru Bourg. Sup. 80ha   360000   ▣ D ⑪ ↓
75 80 **81** 81 **82** 82 ⑧⑧ 83

A striking 19th-century château. A powerful wine; bouquet of red-fruit and fresh coffee. Full-bodied and tannic in the mouth. To be kept. (1982)
↖ Bernard Soulas, Ch. Beaumont, Cussac-Fort-Médoc, 33460 Margaux; tel. 56 28 15 53 ☏ By appt. Closed mid Aug.–early Sept., 20 Dec.–early Jan.

CHATEAU BELGRAVE★★

■5 Cru Classé   50ha   220000   ▣ D ⑪ ↓
77 79 80 ⑧① **81** 81 **82** 82 **83** 83

An attractive 1981, with full, complex, vanilla nose from the 18 months spent in new oak (50 per cent new casks each year). A rich wine, well balanced with tannin and acidity, and showing good length; ready to drink in three or four years. (1981) ✦ St-Emilion Grand Cru Ch. Teyssier.
↖ SCF Ch. Belgrave, 33112 St-Laurent-de-Benon; tel. 56 59 40 20 ☏ By appt.

CHATEAU BONNEAU-LIVRAN★

■Cru Bourg.   6ha   38000   ▣ D ⑪ ↓
78 79 80 ⑧① **81** 81 **82** 82 **83** 83

The estate was established in 1760; the Chinese-style dovecote in the courtyard is an unusual feature. This well-made Pauillac is still rather closed-in on the nose. A full, tannic wine with quite a harsh finish that will soften in two to three years. (1981)
↖ MM. Micalaudy-Millon, St-Seurin-de-Cadourne, 33250 Pauillac; tel. 56 59 31 26 ☏ Daily 9.00–12.00/14.00–20.00

CHATEAU BONNEAU

■   5ha   35000   ▣ D ▤ ↓
★**81** 81 ★⑧② 83 84

Deep colour; the nose is pleasant, spicy and roasted. On the palate the tannin is still rather hard. Patience required. (1981)
↖ Lucien Eyquem, Avensan, 33480 Castelnau-de-Médoc; tel. 55 58 20 56 ☏ No visitors.

CHATEAU LE BORDIEU★★

■Cru Bourg.   55ha   240000   ▣ D ▤ ⑪ ↓
61 78 80 81 ⑧① ⑧② 82 83 83

In the Middle Ages a *bourdieu* was land reclaimed from the forest for agriculture. At that time 'Le Bourdieu' was cultivated by Augustine monks, who also built Vertheuil Abbey. The wine is attractive, powerful, atomatic, very tannic and needs time to mellow. (1982) ✦ Haut-Médoc Ch. Victoria, Haut-Médoc Ch. Picourneau.
↖ Monique Barbe, Château le Bourdieu, Vertheuil-en-Médoc, 33250 Pauillac; tel. 56 41 98 01 ☏ By appt.

CHATEAU DU BREUIL★

■Cru Bourg.   15ha   120000   ▣ D ▤ ↓
79 81 **82** 83 84

The wine from this romantically mysterious estate is rather inconsistent, but has occasional successes like this elegant 1981. ✦ Haut-Médoc Ch. le Gat Rouge, Haut-Médoc Ch. Lanoette Rouge.
↖ M. et Mme. Germain, Ch. du Breuil, Cissac-Médoc, 33250 Pauillac; tel. 56 59 58 22 ☏ Daily 14.00–19.00. Closed Oct.

CHATEAU CANTEMERLE★★★

■   53ha   240000   ⑤ ⑪ ↓
80 **81** 82 **82** ⑧③ 83

Rich, full nose, very fruity with delicate oaky notes. Round and fleshy on the palate, with good-quality tannin and a very long finish. A beautiful wine from this château, with its enchanting wooded grounds. (1983) ✦ St-Julien, St-Estèphe, Sauternes.
↖ SC du Ch. Cantemerle, Macau, 33460 Margaux; tel. 56 30 30 63 ☏ By appt.

CANTERAYNE

■   102ha   600000   ③ D ▤ ↓
★79 ★80 ★80 ★81 ★82

Although this grower is a member of a cooperative, like many others he is concerned to preserve the individual character of his wine. It is a lovely red with a fine, though slightly closed, nose, and a firmly tannic, substantial palate. (1982) ✦ Haut-Médoc Les Gravilles.
↖ Cave Coop. de St-Sauveur, St-Sauveur, 33250 Pauillac; tel. 56 59 57 11 ☏ Mon.–Sat. 8.00–12.00/14.00–18.00.

CHATEAU CAPERANS★

■   4ha   20000   ③ D ▤ ↓
75 76 78 79 81 82

A wine of classic style, with a splendidly deep, dark red colour. Delicate nose, and frank attack on the palate with solid support. (1982)
↖ SICA Fort Médoc, Cussac, 33460 Margaux; tel. 56 58 92 85 ☏ Daily 14.00–19.00. Closed 15 Jun.–15 Sept.

CHATEAU CARONNE-SAINTE-GEMME★

■   43ha   220000   ▣ D ⑪ ↓
75 78 80 81 81 ⑧② 82 83 83

The château stands in what used to be the 12th-century parish of Saint-Gemme (Saint Jacques), which gives the wine its name. A well-balanced 1982, whose tannins should develop well. (1982)
↖ Veuve A. Nony-Borie, Ch. Caronne-Ste-

Gemme, 33112 St-Laurent-de-Benon; tel. 56
59 41 45 ☿ By appt. Closed Aug.

CHATEAU CHARMAIL★

■Cru Bourg.   18ha   110000   3 D ■ ↓
79 80 **81** 81 ⑧ 82 **83** 83

An unusual choice of vines for Médoc (50 per
cent Merlot) producing a supple and nicely
balanced wine. (1982) ✔ Fronsac Ch. Mayne-
Vieil.
↑ Roger Sèze, Ch. Charmail, St-Seurin-de-
Cadourne, 33250 Pauillac; tel. 56 59 30 62
☿ Mon.–Fri. 9.00–12.00/14.00–19.00; Sat. 9.00–
12.00. Closed second fortnight in Aug.

LES CHEVALIERS-DU-ROI-SOLEIL★

■   45ha   200000   3 D ■ ↓
75 78 80 81 ⑧ 82 83

Complete but still youthful, this wine needs
keeping for a few years to show really well.
(1982) ✔ Haut Médoc Ch. le Neurin.
↑ SICA des Viti. du Fort-Médoc, Les Chevaliers-
du-Roi-Soleil, Cussac, 33460 Margaux; tel. 56
58 92 85 ☿ By appt.

CHATEAU CISSAC

■Gd Cru Bourg.   45ha   240000   6 D ⑪ ↓
75 78 79 80 ⑧ 81 82 83

At present dominated by oak, the wine is closed
and needs time. The château, an elegant country
house, is one of the few in Gironde sharing the
name of the commune. (1981)
↑ GFA des Dom. Vialard, Ch. Cissac, Cissac-
Médoc, 33250 Pauillac; tel. 56 59 58 13 ☿ By
appt.

CHATEAU CITRAN★

■Cru Bourg. Sup. 85ha   450000   5 D ⑪ ↓
62 64 66 67 70 ★75 **78 79 81 82**

The vineyard of this old château produces a
pleasant, aromatic wine with charming fruity
flavours and good supple qualities in the mouth.
(1982)
↑ Cesselin, Sté Civ. du Ch. Citran, Avesan, 33480
Castelnau-de-Médoc; tel. 56 58 21 01 ☿ By appt.

CHATEAU CLOS DU MOULIN★★

■   2.5ha   17900   4 D ■ ↓
★82 ★82 83

A wine with a vigorous personality. It has a deep,
dark-red hue, a fine, spicy nose and a rich, well-
balanced palate. Typical of its vintage, and worth
waiting for. (1982)
↑ Villard et Fils, Ch. Clos du Moulin, Avensan,
33480 Castelnau-de-Médoc; tel. 56 39 20 21 ☿ By
appt. Closed Aug.

CHATEAU COUFRAN★★

■Cru Bourg.   50ha   400000   4 D ⑪
76 77 ★79 80 81 ⑧ 82

Satin appearance, and a powerful nose typical of
overripe Merlot (very ripe soft red-fruit). On the
palate it is warm, heady, and not without a
certain elegance. (1982)
↑ SCA du Ch. Coufran, St-Seurin-de-Cadourne,
33250 Pauillac; tel. 56 44 90 84 ☿ By appt.

CHATEAU DECORDE★

■   15ha   12000   3 ■ ↓
★⑧ 83 **84**

This château belongs to the owner of the Château
Séméillan-Mazau, and the estate produces an
attractive, bright-red wine with plenty of tannin.
Wait a while before drinking. (1983)
↑ GFA Séméillan-Mazau, Ch. Decorde, 33460
Listrac-Médoc, 33460 Castelnau-de-Médoc; tel.
56 58 01 12 ☿ By appt.

CHATEAU DILLON★★

■Cru Bourg.   32ha   150000   6 ⑪ ↓
Produced by the local agricultural college, the
wine is on the light side with an unobtrusive
bouquet, but it is an authentic Haut-Médoc wine
with all the good qualities that implies. A white
'Appellation Bordeaux' wine is also produced
here. (1982)
↑ Lycée Agricole de Blanquefort, 33290 Blanquefort; tel. 56 35 02 27 ☿ By appt.

CHATEAU FORT-LIGNAC★

■   4.5ha   30000   4 D ■ ⑪ ↓
75 75 ★79 81 81 82 83

A pretty shade of red; nose fine but barely
developed. All in all, an elegant, well-balanced
and pleasing wine. Good to drink from now on.
(1981)
↑ A. Fort et H. Pradère, Ch. Terrey-Gros-Cailloux, St-Julien-Beychevelle, 33250 Pauillac; tel.
56 59 06 27 ☿ By appt. Closed Sun.

CHATEAU GRAND-MOULIN★

■   20ha   120000   4 D ■ ↓
78 79 80 81 81 82 82 83 83

A light but well-developed nose characterized by
a berry fragrance. Despite the high proportion of
Cabernet-Sauvignon grapes, and thanks to care-
ful winemaking, round and already agreeable.
Can usually be drunk quickly, but will also
improve with age. (1982) ✔ Haut-Médoc Ch.
Lamothe.
↑ Robert Gonzalves, Ch. Grand-Moulin, St-
Seurin-de-Cadourne, 33250 Pauillac; tel. 56
59 35 95 ☿ By appt. Closed Oct.–Nov.

CHATEAU LES GRAVILLES★

■   4ha   25000   4 D ■ ↓
★81 ★82

Quite an aromatic wine, made at the Cave de St-
Sauveur. Well-balanced on the palate with some
pleasant coffee and caramel flavours. (1982)
✔ Haut-Médoc Canterayne.
↑ Cave Coop. de St-Sauveur, St-Sauveur, 33250
Pauillac; tel. 56 59 57 11   ☿ Mon.–Sat. 8.00–
12.00/14.00 18.00.

CHATEAU HANTEILLAN★★

■*Cru Bourg.*   70ha   360000   4 D ⑪ ↓
76 79 80 81 81 82 82 ⑧ 83

The nose is a blend of spicy (pepper and cinnamon) and vanilla aromas, the latter coming from
long ageing in oak. On the palate it is powerful
and youthfully tannic. (1982)
↑ Ch. Hanteillan, Cissac-Médoc, 33250 Pauillac;
tel.   56 59 35 31   ☿ Mon.–Thurs.   8.00–12.00/
13.30–17.30.

239

CHATEAU HAUT-LOGNAT★★

■   15ha   80000   ☐4☐ ◗

*82 83

Better on the nose than to the eye, although the dark red colour is good enough. Complex bouquet, already showing that lingering, oaky note. A balanced and elegant wine. (1982)
❧ M. et C. Quancard, Clissac-Medoc, 33250 Pauillac; tel. 56 77 66 66 ⏳ By appt.

CHATEAU DU JUNCA★

■   8ha   60000   ☐3☐ ☐D☐ ☐ ◗ ↓

75 79 80 **81** 81 ⑧2 **82** **83** 83

Attractive 1982 with light aromas of ripe, red fruit and nice, well-rounded tannin. Good balance and clean finish. An example of a well-made wine from a year that was not as easy to make as its reputation suggests. Good value for money, too, for this sought-after vintage. (1982)
❧ Sergé Tiffon, Ch. du Junca, St-Saveur, 33250 Pauillac; tel. 56 59 56 35 ⏳ By appt.

CHATEAU LACHESNAYE★

■Cru Bourg. Sup. 18ha 110000   ☐D☐ ☐ ↓

⑦9 80 **81 82 83** 83

Good dark colour; nose of raspberry. Full-bodied and rich in the mouth with spicy overtones of venison and leather. (1981) ✔ Bordeaux Supérieur.
❧ Hubert Bouteiller, Ch. Lachesnaye, Cussac-Fort-Médoc, 33460 Margaux; tel. 56 58 94 80 ⏳ By appt.

CHATEAU LA LAGUNE★★★

■3 Cru Classé   70ha   300000   ☐6☐ ◗ ↓

67 70 71 74 75 **78** 78 **79** 80 81 **81** 82 83

A well-balanced wine; rich, elegant and still distinctly oaky, with a palate marked by vanilla, liquorice and other spices. An excellent 1978, still a long way from its prime. (1978)
❧ Jean-Michel Ducellier, Ch. la Lagune, Ludon, 33290 Blanquefort; tel. 56 30 44 07 ⏳ By appt. Closed Aug.

GRAND CRU CLASSÉ

CHATEAU LA LAGUNE
HAUT·MÉDOC
APPELLATION HAUT-MÉDOC CONTROLÉE
1978
SOCIÉTÉ CIVILE AGRICOLE DU CHÂTEAU LA LAGUNE
PROPRIÉTAIRE A LUDON (GIRONDE) FRANCE
MIS EN BOUTEILLE AU CHÂTEAU
PRODUCE OF FRANCE   75cl

CHATEAU DE LAMARQUE★

■   47ha   275000   ☐6☐ ☐D☐ ◗ ↓

78 79 80 **81** 81 ⑧2 ⑧2 **83** 83

Lamarque is one of the most historic Haut-Médoc estates. Faithful to its aristocratic tradition, it continues to play host to distinguished visitors from all over the world. A delicate and rather light wine with attractive floral aromas, especially violets, and red fruit. (1982)

❧ Roger Gromand d'Evry, Ch. de Lamarque, 33460 Margaux; tel. 56 58 90 03 ⏳ By appt.

CHATEAU LAMOTHE★

■   16ha   100000   ☐4☐ ☐D☐ ☐ ↓

75 78 79 80 81 81⑧2 **82** 83

Fruity aromas, predominantly blackcurrant. A nice balance overall, despite a light style. Could benefit from another year or two in bottle age. (1982) ✔ Haut-Médoc Ch. Grand-Moulin.
❧ SC des Ch. Lamothe et Grand-Moulin, St-Seurin-de-Cadourne, 33250 Pauillac; tel. 56 59 35 95 ⏳ By appt. Closed Oct.–Nov.

CHATEAU LAMOTHE-BERGERON★★

■Cru Bourg.   50ha   300000   ☐4☐ ◗ ↓

78 79 80 **81 82 83**

This typical 19th-century wine château is rather lacking in character, but its wine is another matter. It is a lovely dark red with a discreet but clean and oaky nose. Its richness on the palate promises well for the future. (1982) ✔ Haut-Médoc Ch. Romefort Cru Bourgeois
❧ SC du Ch. Grand-Puy-Ducasse, 33250 Pauillac; tel. 56 52 00 40 ⏳ By appt. Closed Jul.–Sept. and during the grape harvest.

CHATEAU LAMOTHE-CISSAC★

■Cru Bourg.   45ha   250000   ☐4☐ ☐D☐ ◗ ↓

75 78 81 **82** 83

This well-appointed château produces a wine which is of a moderate colour and displays a supple and pleasing nature on the palate. (1982)
❧ M. Fabre, SC du Ch. Lamothe-Cissac, Cissac-Médoc, 33250 Pauillac; tel. 56 59 58 16 ⏳ By appt.

CHATEAU LANESSAN★★

■Cru Bourg. Sup. 40ha 190000   ☐5☐ ☐D☐ ◗ ↓

79 ⑧0 80 81 **81** 82 **82** 83 83

An old-established family estate. The château has fine cellars, and a museum in the stables. Lovely, sustained colour evoking a nose of venison with aromas of leather, almonds and liquorice. (1982)
❧ Hubert Bouteiller, Ch. Lanessan, Cussac-Fort-Médoc, 33460 Margaux; tel. 56 58 94 80 ⏳ By appt.

CHATEAU MALESCASSE★★

■   28ha   168000   ☐3☐ ☐D☐ ◗ ↓

79 80 **81** 81 ⑧2 **82** 83 83

A well-cut 1982 with a powerful, gamey nose. Attractive tannin and good length. Despite a long time in vat and two years ageing in casks, quite well rounded. Cellars typically Bordeaux in style. (1982) ✔ Bordeaux Supérieur Ch. Cadillon.
❧ Guy et Alfred Tesseron, Ch. Malescasse, Lamarque, 33460 Margaux; tel. 56 52 15 71 ⏳ By appt.

CHATEAU MAUCAMPS★★★

■Cru Bourg. Sup. 15ha   75000   ☐4☐ ☐D☐ ☐ ↓

79 *81 *82

This estate no longer has a château since the family holdings were split up, but it is getting its revenge with the indisputable breeding of this splendid wine. It is a lovely, deep, rich and concentrated colour, and its strong personality is confirmed by flavours of liquorice and almond from the new oak. (1982)

🕊 Indivision Tessandier, Ch. Maucamps, Macau, 33460 Margaux; tel. 58 30 42 04 ⚑ By appt.

LE MEYNIEU★

■Gd Cru Bourg.	15 ha	45 000	4 D ⑪ 🌡
75 76 77 78 79 80			

Pretty colour, slightly biscuit, and rather distinctive nose, a mixture of fruitiness and a grilled, 'cooked' quality. Good-quality tannins on the palate, but they still need time to become more refined. (1979)

🕊 Jack Pedro, Ch. Meynieu, Vertheuil, 33250 Pauillac; tel. 56 41 98 17 ⚑ By appt. Closed 1 Aug.–15 Aug.

CHATEAU MIGUEU★★

■	7 ha	3100	4 ▮ 🌡
⑦⑨ 80 81 82 83			

Lovely dark-red, with a nose of soft fruit, leather and mint. The palate is full of flavour, with hints of roasted coffee, liquorice and mint. (1982)

🕊 *M.* Bertin, Ch. Migueu, Vertheuil, 33250 Pauillac; tel. 56 41 96 11 ⚑ By appt. Closed June–Sept.

CHATEAU DU MOULIN ROUGE★★

■	15 ha	85 000	4 D ▮ ⑪ 🌡
78 79 80 81 81 82 82 83 83			

The château has been in the same family for 300 years. An attractive 1982, typical of the vintage: clean, well balanced, powerful and refined, with some nicely matured tannins. (1982)

🕊 *MM.* Veyries et Pelon, Ch. du Moulin Rouge, Cussac-Fort-Médoc, 33460 Margaux; tel. 56 58 91 13 ⚑ By appt. Closed Sun. during the summer.

CHATEAU MOULIN-D'ARVIGNY★★

■	30 ha	100 000	3 D ▮ 🌡
⑧② 83 84			

Fine colour and absolutely entrancing aromas of great finesse and variety. The palate is mellow, harmonious and lingering. A wine best drunk young, with a delicately flavoured dish. (1981)

🕊 *M.* Soulas, Ch. Beaumont, Cussac-Fort-Médoc, 33460 Margaux; tel. 56 58 92 29 ⚑ By appt. Closed end Aug.–8 Sept. 🕊 *MM.* Soulas et Paradivin.

CHATEAU PEYRABON

■Cru Bourg.	53 ha	240 000	4 D ⑪ 🌡
75 79 80 81 82 83			

The first known owner of the Château was one of Napoleon's departmental governors, but the most famous visitor was Queen Victoria, in whose honour the music room was decorated. Unfortunately, the harsh tannins of this wine do not do justice to the 1982 vintage. (1982)

🕊 Jacques Babeau, Ch. Peyrabon, St-Sauveur, 33250 Pauillac; tel. 56 59 57 10 ⚑ By appt.

CHATEAU PUY-CASTERA★

■	25 ha	180 000	3 D ▮ ⑪ 🌡
78 79 80 81 81 ⑧② 82 83 83			

A light, smooth 1982 with pleasant, red-fruit aromas. The vines are planted on a hill ('puy') that once had a Roman camp ('castrum') at the top. (1982)

🕊 SCE Ch. Puy-Castera, Cissac-Médoc, 33250 Pauillac; tel. 56 59 58 80 ⚑ By appt.

CHATEAU RAMAGE LA BATISSE★★

■Cru Bourg.	45 ha	240 000	4 D ⑪ 🌡
75 80 81 82 ⑧③			

Attractive, lively appearance and fine, typically Cabernet–Sauvignon nose. A wine with a frank attack, a rich, round development and distinctive flavours of raspberry and blackcurrant. (1981)

✔ Bordeaux Supérieur, Côtes de Castillon, Ch. de Belcier.

🕊 SA Ch. Ramage la Batisse, 33250 St-Sauveur; tel. 56 59 57 24 ⚑ Mon.–Fri. 8.00–12.00/14.00–18.00.

CHATEAU REYSSON★

■Cru Bourg.	56 ha	330 000	4 ⑪ 🌡
⑦⑤ 78 79 80 81 82 83			

A well-constituted wine whose deep colour already shows some maturity; the nose, however, still has some way to develop. (1982)

🕊 Sté. Civ. du Ch. de Reysson, 17 Cours de la Martinique, 33000 Bordeaux; tel. 56 52 11 46 ⚑ By appt.

CHATEAU ROMEFORT★

■Cru Bourg.	50 ha	325 000	4 ▮ 🌡
★78 ★79 ★80 ★81 ★82 ★83			

Clean appearance and bouquet. Moderately full and moderately tannic, but easy to drink nonetheless. (1982) ✔ Haut-Médoc Ch. Romefort.

🕊 SC Ch. Grand-Puy-Ducasse, 33250 Pauillac; tel. 56 59 00 40 ⚑ Closed July.–Sept. and grape harvest. 🕊 Sté Civ. Grand-Puy-Ducasse.

CHATEAU SAINT-PAUL★★

■	20 ha	110 000	3 D ▮ ⑪
78 79 79 80 81 81 82 82 ⑧③			

Attractive 1982, with a still somewhat closed-in nose. On the palate it begins boldly but smoothly, thanks to its good quality tannin. The finish is pleasant, with shades of undergrowth, spice and dried fruit. Excellent value for money. (1982)

🕊 Sté. Civ. du Ch. St-Paul, St-Seurin de Cadourne, 33250 Pauillac; tel. 56 02 68 30 ⚑ By appt.

241

CHATEAU SEGUR★★

◼Cru Bourg. Sup. 35ha   180000   4 D ▮ ⑪
75 80 ★82 82 83

An evocative name in Bordeaux history is today a wine with plenty of colour, closed on the nose, but full and richly tannic. (1982) ✔ Haut Médoc Ch. Ségur-Fillon.
⊶ J. et J.-P. Grazioli, Ch. Ségur, 33290 Parempuyre; tel. 56 35 28 25 ⵛ By appt.

CHATEAU SENEJAC★

◼   17ha   85000   4 D ⑪ ↓
79 79 80 80 81 82

A New Zealander is in charge of the wine cellar here. A wine with lovely spice scents including, cinammon and raspberry and very fine tannins on the palate. (1982)
⊶ Charles de Guigné, Ch. Sénéjac, Le Pian-Médoc, 33290 Blanquefort; tel. 56 72 00 11 ⵛ By appt.

CHATEAU SENILHAC★

◼Cru Bourg.   11ha   65000   4 D ▮ ⑪
75 78 79 80 81 (82) 83 84

This delightful country estate is lived in year-round by its owners – something of a rarity in the Médoc. The wine shows fine, attractive colour, very appealing to the eye; delicate fragrance on the nose and a characteristic Médoc earthiness on the palate. (1982)
⊶ Michel Grassin, Ch. Senilhac, St-Seurin-de-Cadourne, 33250 Pauillac; tel. 56 59 31 41 ⵛ By appt.

CHATEAU SOCIANDO-MALLET★★★

◼Cru Bourg.   30ha   150000   5 D ▮ ↓
70 71 76 78 80 81 82

Less than twenty years ago this estate was in a pitiable condition, but now everything has been renewed and a fine wine is being produced, with a delicate bouquet of liquorice, spices and vanilla. Round and full on the palate, it leaves a wonderful impression of ripe fruit. This wine has class! (1981)
⊶ M. M.-J. Gautreau, Ch. Sociando-Mallet, St-Seurin-de-Cadourne, 33250 Pauillac; tel. 56 59 36 57 ⵛ By appt.

CHATEAU SOUDARS★★

◼Cru Bourg.   15ha   130000   5 D ⑪ ↓

This estate was only established in 1973 but the wine has a sustained colour, a pleasant ripe-fruit flavour and plenty of texture. (1982)
⊶ Eric Miailhe, St-Seurin-de-Cadourne, 33250 Pauillac; tel. 56 59 31 52 ⵛ No visitors.

CHATEAU SOULEY-SAINTE-CROIX

◼Cru Bourg.   18ha   70000   3 D ▮ ↓
70 71 73 75 76 78 79 81 81 83

This wine is characteristic of its commune (Vertheuil); it may gain a little in finesse, but it is already light, clean, and very easy to drink. (1982)
⊶ M. Riffaud, Ch. Le Souley, 33250 Vertheuil; tel. 56 41 98 54 ⵛ By appt.

CHATEAU DU TAILLAN★

◼Cru Bourg.   5ha   30000   4 D ⑪ ↓
78 79 80 81 82 83

Fine and well-structured, attractive rather than serious, but very characteristic of this frontier zone between Graves and Médoc. (1982)
⊶ M. Cruse, Ch. du Taillan, Le Taillan-Médoc, 33320 Eysiness; tel. 56 39 26 04 ⵛ By appt.

CHATEAU TOUR SAINT-JOSEPH★★

◼Cru Bourg.   10ha   55000   4 ⑪
80 81 82 83

Handsome red colour, and clean flowery nose, with a pleasant touch of vanilla. Roundness and smoothness on the palate with an oaky quality providing a certain elegance. A wine of very pleasant character. (1982)
⊶ Marcel Quancard et Fils, 33440 Ambarès et Lagrave; tel. 56 77 66 66 ⵛ No visitors.

CHATEAU TOUR-CARELOT★★

◼   8ha   30000   4 D ⑪ ↓
★80 ★80 81 81 82 82

From a wide range of good wines produced by this firm, this is a fruity, nicely scented wine which will keep well. Can be drunk between one and five years from now. (1982)
⊶ Villard et Fils, Ch. Tour-Carelot, Avensan, 33480 Castelnau-de-Médoc; tel. 56 41 14 86 ⵛ By appt.

CHATEAU VERDUS★

◼Cru Bourg.   5ha   25000   4 D ▮ ⑪ ↓
75 78 (82)

From this château, part of the Bardis estate, comes a wine with a fine bouquet and toasted flavour. A very pleasant drink. (1982)
⊶ M. Dailledouze, Ch. Verdus, St-Seurin-de-Cadourne, 33250 Pauillac; tel. 56 59 31 59 ⵛ By appt.

Listrac

The appellation area lies entirely within the boundaries of the commune itself, on three gravelly hilltops. The wines (4.2 million bottles in 1982) are robustly fruity and full-bodied, with a firm, meaty flavour and fine, ruby colour. Their solidity makes them particularly attractive in years where some of the other appellations lack a little body.

CHATEAU CAP-LEON-VEYRIN★

◼Cru Bourg.   10ha   4800   4 D ⑪ ↓
★75 ★78 ★79 81 (82) 82 83

The estate, with its woods, fields and vines, is characteristic of the region. The wine, too, is typical, with good length and plenty of tannin to keep it well. (1982)
⊶ Alain Meyre, Ch. Cap-Leon-Veyrin, Litrac-Médoc, 33480 Castelnau-de-Médoc; tel. 56 58 07 28 ⵛ By appt.

CHATEAU CLARKE★★

■Cru Bourg.   105ha   520000   **5** **D** **ⓘ** **↓**

78 79 80 **81** 81 82 83

Since Edmond de Rothschild bought it a dozen years ago, the château and its wine have been given their second youth. A fine bouquet, with soft fruit aromas enhanced by roasted and oaky overtones; round and lingering on the palate. (1982)
➤ Sté Listrac-Moulis, Ch. Clarke, Listrac-Médoc, 33480 Castelnau-de-Médoc; tel. 56 88 88 00 ☎ By appt ➤*M. le Bar.* Edmond de Rothschild.

CLOS DES DEMOISELLES★

■   4.5ha   15000   **4** **D** **ⓘ** **↓**

★⑦ ★80 ★81 82

Consistent throughout: bright-red colour, aromatic nose, agreeable palate with tannins that are nonetheless slightly harsh at present. (1982)
➤ Jacques de Pourquery, Ch. Branas-Grand-Poujeaux, Moulis-en-Médoc, 33480 Castelnau-de-Médoc; tel. 65 58 22 42 ☎ No visitors.

CHATEAU DUCLUZEAU★

■Cru Bourg.   4ha   20000   **3** **D** **ⓘ** **↓**

82 **83**

With 90 per cent Merlot vines, this vineyard is unique in the Médoc. Light, smooth and fruity wine with remarkable finesse and balance. (1979)
➤ *Mme* Jean-Eugène Borie, Ch. Ducluzeau, Listrac-Médoc, 33480 Castelnau-de-Médoc; tel. 56 59 05 20 ☎ No visitors.

CHATEAU FONREAUD★

■Cru Bourg.   43ha   220000   **3** **D** **ⓘ** **↓**

70 **71** **75** 77 78 80 ⑧ **81** **82**

Powerful, alcoholic wine with stewed-prune nose and quite supple tannin, despite high proportion of Cabernet Sauvignon. (1981) ✔ Moulis Ch. du Chemin-Royal.
➤ SCI Ch. Fonreaud, Listrac-Médoc, 33480 Castelnau-de-Médoc; tel. 56 58 02 43 ☎ Mon.– Fri. 9.00–12.00/14.00–18.00.

CHATEAU FOURCAS DUPRE★

■Gd Bourg. Sup. 40ha   266000   **4** **D** **ⓘ** **↓**

⑦ 77 ⑦ 79 80 **81** **81** ⑧ **82** ⑧ **83**

Distinctively Médoc wine. Tannin still a little harsh, but will mellow nicely in time. Long-lasting wine that needs ageing. Quality a little below the estate's reputation. (1982) ✔ Moulis.
➤ SC Ch. Fourcas-Médoc, Listrac-Médoc, 33480 Castelnau de Médoc; tel. 56 58 01 07 ☎ By appt.

CHATEAU FOURCAS-HOSTEN★★

■   40ha   200000   **4** **D** **ⓘ** **↓**

70 71 74 75 76 77 78 ⑦ **79** 80 **81** **81** ⑧ **82** ⑧ **83**

Dense and concentrated, combining finesse and power. Could easily last for fifteen years or so. (1982)
➤ SC Ch. Fourcas-Hosten, Listrac, 33480 Castelnau-de-Médoc; tel. 56 58 01 15 ☎ Mon.–Fri. 8.00–12.00/14.00–18.00.

CHATEAU FOURCAS-LOUBANEY★★

■   4ha   200000   **4** **D** **ⓘ** **↓**

76 77 78 **79** 80 81 **81** ⑧ **82**

Small estate of old vines producing an attractively coloured wine that is delicate and well balanced. Will keep well. (1981)
➤ Michel Hostens, Ch. Fourcas Loubaney, Listrac-Médoc, 33480 Castelnau-de-Médoc; tel. 56 58 03 83 ☎ Mon.–Fri. 8.00–20.00.

GRAND-LISTRAC

■   150ha   850000   **3** **D** **ⓘ** **↓**

64 66 ⑦ 78 **79** 80 **81** 82

Proves that large-scale production and quality are not incompatible. Ready to drink in a year or two. (1981) ✔ Listrac Ch. Vieux Moulin, Moulis Ch. Guitignan.
➤ Cave Coop. de Listrac, Listrac-Médoc, 33480 Castelnau-de-Médoc; tel. 56 58 03 19 ☎ Mon.– Sat. 9.30–12.00/15.00–18.00, Sun. 8.00–12.00/ 14.00–18.00.

CHATEAU LALANDE

■   12ha   60000   **4** **D** **ⓘ** **↓**

★70 ⑧

A light, ruby-red wine with a discreetly fruity nose and an even, delicate palate. (1982)
➤ Dubosc et Darriet, Ch. Lalande, 33480 Listrac-Médoc,   33480   Castelnau-de-Médoc;   tel. 56 58 07 28 ☎ Mon.–Fri. 8.00–12.00/14.00–19.00.

CHATEAU LESTAGE★

■Cru Bourg.   54ha   266000   **3** **D** **ⓘ** **↓**

70 75 76 77 **78** 79 80 **89** ⑧

Still a little closed for the year; but fruity and pleasing on the palate, and slightly herbaceous in aroma on the finish. (1982)
➤ SCI Ch. Lestage, Listrac-Médoc, 33480 Castelnau-de-Médoc; tel. 56 58 02 43 ☎ Mon.– Fri. 9.00–12.00/14.00–18.00.

CHATEAU LIOUNER★★

■   15ha   80000   **4** **D** **ⓘ** **↓**

75 **76** 78 **78** 80 **81** ⑧ **82**

Deep ruby colour; powerful on the nose; firmly tannic, but well-constituted and well-balanced on the palate. (1982)
➤ Pierre Bosq, Ch. Liouner, 33480 Listrac-Médoc,   33480   Castelnau-de-Médoc;   tel. 56 58 04 38 ☎ By appt.

CHATEAU MAYNE-LALANDE★★★

■   10ha   25000   **4** **D** **ⓘ** **↓**

75 ★78 ★79 ★80 ⑧ 83

Wonderfully deep colour and a fine, powerful nose which blends almonds and coffee with leather and liquorice. All wrapped up in a rich tannic cloak. (1982)
➤ Bernard Lartigue, Ch. Mayne-Lalande, Listrac-Médoc, 33480 Castelnau-de-Médoc; tel. 56 58 14 74 ☎ By appt.

CHATEAU MOULIN-DE-LABORDE★

■　　　　　9ha　55000　　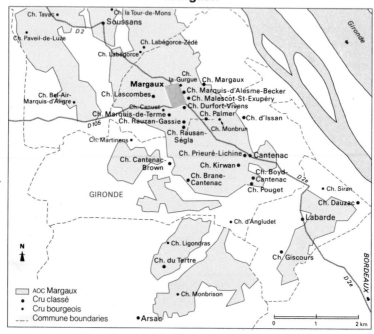

76 77 **78 79 80 81** 🎀 ⑧ 🎀

Warm and powerful, marked by aromas of black-currant and leather. (1982)
↬ Michel Hostens, Ch. Moulin de Laborde, Listrac-Médoc, 33480 Castelnau-de-Médoc; tel. 56 58 03 83 ⊤ By appt.

CHATEAU REVERDI★★

■　　　　　8ha　50000　　

69 70 75 **79** 80 **81 82** 🎀 **83**

A well-coloured wine whose nose is full of finesse, with a pleasant vanilla scent which reappears on the palate where it is blended with rich flavours of spice, prunes, liquorice and leather. (1982)
↬ Christian Thomas, Ch. Reverdi, Listrac-Médoc, 33480 Castelnau-de-Médoc; tel. 56 58 02 25 ⊤ By appt.

CHATEAU SARANSOT-DUPRE

■　　　　　10ha　60000　　

⑦⑤ 78 ＊81 ＊82 **83**

Despite a slight imbalance in the mouth, this is a pleasant wine, notably because of its redcurrants and raspberries nose, and its pleasant roundness on the palate. (1982)
↬ P. et Y. Raymond, Ch. Saransot-Dupré, Listrac-Médoc 33480 Castelnau-de-Médoc; tel. 56 58 03 02 ⊤ By appt.

Margaux

Famous the world over, the name Margaux refers to a village, an appellation, a splendid château and a Premier Grand Cru wine. Well-known it may be, but also misunderstood. It is all too easy to forget that this appellation includes five comunes, but grants the appellation only to the best soils in each of them – some 1150 hectares in all. The quality of the soils – some of the finest in the whole of the Gironde – explain why the appellation contains one-third of all the growths classified in 1855. In 1982, it produced 6.8 million bottles.

Margaux wines – with their high percentage of Carbernet-Sauvignon – share finesse, distinction, smoothness and a remarkable ability to age. However, there is a world of subtle differences between the various individual wines, most easily perceived when it comes to combining the wines with food. In general they go well with white meat, but each one has its own preferred partner; thus it would be quite easy to serve one growth with a steak, another with mushrooms or leg of lamb. The most important thing is not to serve them with anything too sweet or too spicy.

Margaux

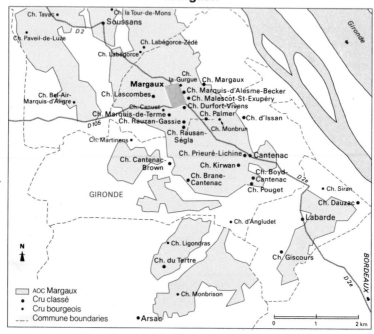

CHATEAU D'ANGLUDET*

■Cru Bourg. Exc. 30ha 150000 [5] [D] ◍ ⫰

73 74 75 77 **78 79** 80 **81 82** (83) [83]

Powerful and tannic, despite the immaturity of the vines (only fifteen years old, on average) and the high percentage of Merlot grapes. (1982)

🗝 *M.* et *Mme.* Peter Sichel, Ch. d'Angludet, Cantenac, 33460 Margaux; tel. 56 88 71 41 Ῡ By appt.

LES BARAILLOTS*

■ 5ha 25000 [4] [D] ▮ ⫰

75 76 **81 82** [82] 83

An unobtrusive vineyard made up in part by slopes that have in the past produced some top growths. No surprise, then, to find a complete, refined and tannic wine. (1982)

🗝 Michel Brunet, 2 Rue Corneillan, 33460 Margaux; tel. 56 83 33 56 Ῡ By appt.

CHATEAU LA BEGORCE*

■Cru Bourg. Sup. 30ha 150000 [5] [D] ⫰

70 75 78 79 80 81 (82) 83

Attractive colour and a pleasing bouquet. The palate is still a little marked by the wood, but it has good potential and is worth laying down for a few years. (1981)

🗝 Jean-Robert Condom, Ch. la Bégorce, 33460 Margaux; tel. 56 88 71 32 Ῡ By appt. Closed Sat., Sun.

CHATEAU BOYD-CANTENAC**

■3 Cru Classé 18ha 80000 [5] [D] ◍ ⫰

70 74 **75 76** *78 **80** 81 *82

Beautiful colour, with a bouquet that still needs time to develop fully. Agreeably round, full, well balanced and vinous on the palate. Its future is assured. (1982)

🗝 Pierre Guillemet, Ch. Pouget, Cantenac, 33460 Margaux; tel. 56 88 30 58 Ῡ By appt. Closed last fortnight of Aug.

CHATEAU BRANE-CANTENAC**

■2 Cru Classé 60ha 360000 [5] [D] ◍ ⫰

64 66 **67 70 71** *75 78 (80) 81 82 83

Great depth of colour. Very promising bouquet, and rich and full bodied on the palate. Will improve with age. (1978) ✔ Haut-Médoc.

🗝 Lucien Lurton, Ch. Brane-Cantenac, 33460 Margaux; tel. 56 88 70 20 Ῡ By appt. Closed Aug.

CHATEAU CANTENAC-BROWN*

■3 Cru Classé 32ha 180000 [5] [D] ◍ ⫰

75 76 **78** 79 80 **81** (82) [82]

Cantenac-Brown is a solid Margaux with definite substance: it needs to age. The 1982 is an imposing wine, entirely in keeping with the character of the year. Its serious style, dominated by Cabernet-Sauvignon, owes nothing to chance. (1982)

Ῡ Sté. Civ. du Ch. Cantenac-Brown, Cantenac, 33460 Margaux; tel. 56 88 30 07 Ῡ By appt 🗝 *M.* du Vivier.

CHATEAU CANUET*

■ 11ha 50000 [3] [D] ◍ ⫰

67 67 75 76 77 79 81 (82) **83**

A likeable country cottage that could have disappeared had the present owners not renewed the vineyard. The vines are a little young, but the wine is rich and has good tannin, suggesting it should age well. (1983)

🗝 J. et S. Rooryck, Ch. Canuet, 33460 Margaux; tel. 56 88 70 21 Ῡ By appt.

CHATEAU DAUZAC**

■5 Cru Classé 45ha 300000 [6] ◍ ⫰

73 74 75 76 77 **78 79 80** [80] **81** (82) [82] 83

A fine-looking wine. Although the bouquet needs to develop further, the bite and the good balance between delicacy and richness augur well for the future. (1982)

🗝 François Chatelier, Ch. Dauzac, Labarde, 33460 Margaux; tel. 56 88 32 10 Ῡ By appt.

CHATEAU DESMIRAIL**

■3 Cru Classé 18ha 68000 [4] ◍ ⫰

81 82 [82] **83**

A classic Cantenac wine with a lovely bouquet of mingled soft fruits, floral notes and the very special magic of Margaux wines. On the palate it has elegance coupled with delicacy. Limited production only. (1982) ✔ Margaux Dom. de Fontarney.

🗝 Lucien Lurton, Ch. Brane-Cantenac, 33460 Margaux; tel. 56 88 70 20 Ῡ By appt. Closed Aug.

CHATEAU DEYREM VALENTIN*

■Cru Bourg. [5] [D] ▮ ◍ ⫰

73 75 **77 78** 79 [80] **81** [81] (82) ***83**

A fine, elegant, well-balanced wine. The 1982 is already very promising, and will be even better in four years' time. (1982)

🗝 Jean Sorge, Ch. Deyrem Valentin, Soussans, 33460 Margaux; tel. 56 88 35 70 Ῡ By appt.

CHATEAU DURFORT VIVENS***

■2 Cru Classé 20ha 60000 [5] ◍ ⫰

64 **66 70 71** *75 *(78) [81] 82 83

Superbly bright in colour. Very fruity bouquet. Well balanced, rich, flavoursome and very smooth on the palate, with a delightful finish. (1981)

🗝 Lucien Lurton, Ch. Brane-Canterac, 33460 Margaux; tel. 56 88 70 20 Ῡ By appt.

CHATEAU FERRIERE★

■3 Cru Classé   4ha   12000   ⑤ Ⓓ ⊞ ⌘

70 75 76 77 **78** 79 80 **81** 81 ⑧ 82

The property is managed by the same company that runs Château Lascombes. The Château Ferrière is fermented, aged in cask and bottled at Lascombes, so it is no great surprise that there is a marked family resemblance between the second-growth Ch. Lascombes and the third-growth Ch. Ferrière. (1982)
↬ André Durand, Ch. Ferrière, 33460 Margaux; tel. 56 88 70 66 ⟁ By appt.

CHATEAU GISCOURS★★

■3 Cru Classé   71ha   240000   ⑥ Ⓓ ⊞ ⌘

66 **70** 71 75 *78 79 80 81 82 83

Beautiful colour, and a bouquet that combines vanilla and wood with a note of leather. Rich, well balanced and remarkably powerful for the vintage. Already drinking well and should develop still further. (1980)
↬ SA du Ch. Giscours, 33460 Margaux; tel. 56 88 34 02 ⟁ By appt.

CHATEAU LA GURGUE★★

■Cru Bourg. Sup.   12ha   55000   ④ ⊞ ⌘

81 82 ⑧ 83

Nestled between two Grand Cru Classé vineyards, this property produces a well-balanced wine with remarkably fine tannin and plenty of aromatic flavour. (1981) ✔ Pauillac Ch. Haut-Bages-Libéral, Moulis Ch. Chasse-Spleen, Haut-Médoc l'Hermitage de Chasse-Spleen.
↬ Ch. la Gurgue, 33460 Margaux; tel. 56 58 17 54 ⟁ By appt.

CHATEAU D'ISSAN★★★

■3 Cru Classé   28ha   120000   ⑤ Ⓓ ⊞ ⌘

73 75 76 77 78 79 80 **81** 82 83

Shows a youthful intensity of colour. On the nose, the aroma of Cabernet grape is enhanced by a discreet hint of new wood. Silky, fat, tannic and full on the palate, with a remarkably long finish. A very distinguished wine. (1979)
↬ SFV du Ch. d'Issan, Cantenac, 33460 Margaux; tel. 56 88 70 72 ⟁ By appt.

CHATEAU KIRWAN★★

■3 Cru Classé   32ha   140000   ⑥ ⊞ ⌘

66 71 75 77 78 ⑦⑨ 80 **81** 82 83

Beautiful, youthful colour. Delicate hint of vanilla in the bouquet and suppleness on the palate. A richly flavoured wine. (1979) ✔ Margaux Générique.
↬ MM. Schroder et Schyler, Ch. Kirwan Cante-

nac, 33460 Margaux; tel. 56 81 24 10 ⟁ By appt. Closed Aug. ↬ M. Schyler.

CHATEAU LABEGORCE-ZEDE★

■Cru. Bourg. Sup.   25ha   120000   ⑤ ⊞ ⌘

*79 80 81 ⑧ 82 83

Characterized by grace and delicacy; well balanced and long in the mouth. (1982) ✔ Margaux Ch. L'Amiral.
↬ GFA du Ch. Labegorce-Zédé, Soussans, 33460 Margaux; tel. 56 88 71 31 ⟁ Mon.–Fri. 9.00–12.00/14.00–19.00.

CHATEAU LARRUAU★

■   3ha   18000   ④ Ⓓ ⊟ ⌘

64 66 **70** 75 76 *78 81 82 83

Good colour and a fine bouquet. Fruity, round and supple on the palate, with a pleasant hint of wood. (1983)
↬ Bernard Château, Ch. Larruau, 33460 Margaux; tel. 56 88 35 50 ⟁ By appt.

CHATEAU LASCOMBES★★★

■2 Cru Classé   98ha   420000   ⑥ Ⓓ ⊞ ⌘

69 **70** 75 76 76 77 78 **81** 81 ⑧ 82 **83** 83

The château has Neo-Gothic-style gardens and a Californian winery-style courtyard. A superb 1982 wine combining strength with good-quality tannin. The nose already has cooked aromas of toast and liquorice, and on the finish a suggestion of faded roses and peonies. (1982) ✔ Margaux Ch. Segonnes, Bordeaux Supérieur Rosé de Lascombes.
↬ Sté Viticole Ch. Lascombes, 33460 Margaux; tel. 56 88 70 66 ⟁ By appt. Closed Aug.

CHATEAU MALESCOT-SAINT-EXUPERY★★

■3 Cru Classé   30ha   180000   ⑥ ⊞ ⌘

73 74 75 76 77 77 78 79 80 **81** 81 ⑧ 83 83

Shows its breeding in the beautiful ruby colour. Full, yet delicate on the palate: well balanced, supple and stylishly tannic. (1982) ✔ Margaux Ch. Loyac.
↬ SCA Ch. Malescot-St-Exupery, 33460 Margaux; tel. 56 88 70 68 ⟁ By appt. Closed Aug. ↬ Roger Zuger.

CHATEAU MARGAUX★★★

■1er Cru Classé   68ha   300000   ⑥ Ⓓ ⊞ ⌘

80 81 ⑧ 82 83 83 84

The deep red colour is the first indication of character, and if the oaky nose is somewhat closed, on the palate its full glory is revealed in a blend of suppleness and power, abundant charm and finesse. A great bottle of wine with an excellent future. (1983)

➥ Sté Civ. du Ch. Margaux, 33460 Margaux; tel. 56 88 70 28 ⟨ By appt. Closed Aug.

CHATEAU MARQUIS D'ALESME★★

■3 Cru Classé   9ha   60000   5 D ⦀ ⌀

71 75 76 **77** 78 79 80 **81** ⟨82⟩ 82 83

A rich, powerful, well-balanced and forthcoming wine. Will improve with age. (1982)

➥ Jean-Claude Zuger, Ch. d'Alesme, 33460 Margaux; tel. 56 98 70 27 ⟨ Mon.–Fri. 8.00–12.00/14.00–18.00. Closed Aug.

CHATEAU MARQUIS DE TERME★

■4 Cru Classé   30ha   140000   5 D ⦀ ⌀

⟨61⟩ **75 78** 79 80 **81 82** 82

The wines of this estate are concentrated, due to the high density of growth in the vineyard, and the long fermentation. The deep purple 1982 stands out because of the perfect maturity of its tannins. Despite 46 present soft appeal (35 per cent Merlot), it could do with waiting five to six years. (1982)

➥ Pierre Sénéclauze, Ch. Marquis de Terme, 33460 Margaux; tel. 56 88 30 01 ⟨ By appt.

CHATEAU MARSAC-SEGUINEAU

■Cru Bourg.   10ha   60000   4 D ⦀ ⌀

77 78 79 **81 82 83**

Classic colour. Clean and easy to drink. (1982)

➥ SC du Ch. Marsac-Séguineau, 33460 Margaux; tel. 56 52 11 46 ⟨ No visitors.

CHATEAU MARTINENS★

■Cru Bourg. Sup.   30ha   80000   5 D ⦀

73 75 **78** 79 81 82 83

The 1928 and 1929 produced by this property are considered to be two of the finest wines produced by the Médoc region. This 1982 shows a good deal of class. The very fine, dark colour is followed by a still discreet, but promising, nose. A well-structured wine which needs keeping. (1982)

✔ Haut-Médoc Ch. Bois-de-Monteil.

➥ M. et *Mme* Dulos-Seynat, Ch. Martinens, 33460 Margaux; tel. 56 88 71 37 ⟨ Daily 9.00–12.00/14.00–18.00.

CHATEAU MONBRISON★

■Cru Bourg. Sup.   15ha   90000   5 D ⦀ ⌀

74 **75** 76 77 **78** 79 80 81 82 83

Beautiful garnet colour. Powerful bouquet of ripe, red fruit (raspberries, cherries and blackcurrants) and cocoa. Powerful and well balanced on the palate. By the 1990s it should have developed

into a very fine bottle. (1982) ✔ Margaux Ch. Cordet.

➥ Elisabeth Davies, Ch. Monbrison, Arsac, 33460 Margaux; tel. 56 88 34 52 ⟨ By appt. Closed during harvest.

CHATEAU PALMER★★★

■3 Cru Classé   120000   6 ⦀ ⌀

73 74 75 77 **78 79** 80 81 82 ⟨83⟩ 83

This fine bottle, with its delicate, complex nose, its well balanced, supple and full palate and ripe, round tannins, should not be opened for at least five years. (1981)

➥ SCI Ch. Palmer, 33460 Margaux; tel. 56 88 72 72 ⟨ By appt. Closed weekends.

CHATEAU PAVEIL-DE-LUZE★

■Bourg. Sup. Exc. 28ha   120000   5 ▮ ⦀ ⌀

78 79 80 81 81 ⟨82⟩ 83

A light, delicate and not very vigorous wine. Will be enjoyed by those liking a wine light in tannin. (1982)

➥ Geoffroy de Luze, Soussans, 33460 Margaux; tel. 56 88 30 03 ⟨ No visitors.   •

PAVILLON ROUGE★★

■   ha   100000   6 D ⦀ ⌀

77 ⟨79⟩ 81 **82 83** 84

The second wine from the Château Margaux, this has its own attractive personality. Lovely, bright and distinct colour; fine, elegant nose reminiscent of toasted almonds and ripe grapes. A stylish, richly tannic, well-balanced wine, with a fine finish. (1979)

➥ Sté Civ. du Ch. Margaux, 33480 Margaux; tel. 56 88 70 28 ⟨ By appt.

CHATEAU PONTAC-LYNCH★

■Cru Bourg.   7ha   24000   6

A pretty, slender and refined wine, distinctly raspberry in its aromas. Given a little more breadth and depth it could become a great bottle. (1981)

➥ GFA du Ch. de Pontac-Lynch, Cantenac, 33460 Margaux ⟨ By appt ➥R. Bondon

CHATEAU POUGET

■4 Cru Classé   10ha   45000   5 D ⦀ ⌀

74 **75** 76 ★78 79 ★80 **81** 82

Unassuming. Colour and bouquet are delicate and pleasing, if a little light. (1980)

➥ Pierre Guillemet, Ch. Pouget, Cantenac, 33460 Margaux; tel. 56 88 30 58 ⟨ Mon.–Fri. 10.00–12.00/14.00–18.00.

CHATEAU PRIEURE-LICHINE★

■4 Cru Classé   45ha   240000   **5** **D** ◑

73 74 75 76 ★**77** ★**78** **79** 80 81 ⑧ **83**

The château, once a priory, nestles against the beautiful Church at Cantenac. The wine is deep in colour, somewhat closed on the nose as yet, bt rich and oaky on the palate. (1982)
➹ A. Lichine, Ch. Prieuré-Lichine, 33460 Cantenac; tel. 56 88 36 28 ✠ Mon.–Sat. 9.00–18.00.

CHATEAU RAUSAN SEGLA★

■2 Cru Classé   43ha   170000   **5** **D** ◑ ♨

70 71 **75** ★**78** **79** **80** **81** 82 ⑧

The elegance of this 17th-century manor house is matched by the delicate wine produced here. (1981)
➹ *MM*. Holt Frères et Fils, Ch. Rausan Segla, 33460 Margaux; tel. 56 52 11 82 ✠ By appt. Closed Aug.

CHATEAU RAUZAN-GASSIES★★

■2 Cru Classé   30ha   120000   **6** **D** ◑ ♨

70 71 **75** 76 77 78 79 **80** **81** ⑧ **82**

Fine, well-balanced, characteristic Margaux. Dark in colour, soft and subtle in the mouth. Can be compared to the 1970 and 1975 vintages, which were great successes for this particular grower. (1982)
➹ Sté Civ. du Ch. Rauzan-Gassies, 33460 Margaux; tel. 56 88 70 30 ✠ By appt.

CHATEAU SAINT-MARC★

■   7ha   20000   **4** ▤ ♨

80 81 82 83

A small family vineyard produces this pretty Margaux wine which is sound, clean and typical of its kind. (1982)
➹ Marc Faure, Ch. St-Marc, Soussans, 33460 Margaux; tel. 56 88 30 67 ✠ By appt.

CHATEAU SEGONNES★★

■   100000   **6** **D** ◑ ♨

82 **82**

Rich, dark colour and fine, strong nose. A certain tannic strength on the palate and aromas reminiscent of Toulouse violets, all pleasantly rounded. (1982)
➹ SA Alexis-Lichine, 109 Rue Achard, 33000 Bordeaux; tel. 56 50 84 85 ✠ By appt.

CHATEAU SIRAN★★

■Cru Bourg. Sup. 25ha   120000   **5** **D** ◑ ♨

70 71 73 75 76 77 78 **79** **79** **80** **80** **81** ⑧ **82** **83**

Powerful, aromatic and long in the mouth, with a tannic finish. Certain to age well. (1982)
➹ William Alain Miailhe, Ch. Siran, Labarde, 33460 Margaux; tel. 56 81 35 01 ✠ Mon.–Fri. 9.30–11.30/14.30–17.30. Closed in winter.

CHATEAU TAYAC★★

■Cru Bourg.   34ha   200000   **4** **D** ▤ ♨

75 76 78 **79** **81 82 83**

A typical, well-made Margaux; supple, round and warm with good quality tannin. (1982)
➹ André Favin, Ch. Tayac, Tayac-Soussans,

33460 Margaux; tel. 56 88 33 06 ✠ Mon.–Fri. 10.00–12.00/14.00–18.00.

CHATEAU DU TERTRE★★

■5 Cru Classé   50ha   120000   **5** **D** ◑ ♨

75 76 **78 79** **80** **81** ⑧ **82**

Dark colour, fruity bouquet and very concentrated. Richness and length on the palate mark this 90 per cent Cabernet wine, which has good ageing potential. (1982)
➹ SCA du Ch. du Tertre, Arsac, 33460 Margaux; tel. 56 88 34 61 ✠ By appt ➹ Philippe Gasqueton.

CHATEAU LA TOUR DE MONS★

■Bourg. Sup.   110ha   12000   **4** **D** ▮ ◑ ♨

⑦ 76 **78** 79 80 **81** ★**82** ★**82** **83**

This impressive property, part of it from the Middle Ages, produces a wine which is sometimes inconsistent but is more often worthy of its setting. This 1980, a difficult vintage, combines a pleasing suppleness with a lovely bouquet. (1980)
➹ P.-J. Dubos, Ch. de la Tour de Mons, 33460 Soussans, 33460 Margaux; tel. 56 88 33 03 ✠ By appt.

CHATEAU DES TROIS-CHARDONS★★

■   2.3ha   6000   **5** **D** ▮ ♨

70 75 76 **78** **79** **81** **82** ⑧

The 'Three Chardons' are *M*. Chardon and his sons, but 'chardon' is the French word for 'thistle'. The wine itself is serious even if its name is a play on words, and has plenty of quality, good colour and excellent length. (1983)
➹ Sté Chardon Père et Fils, Cantenac, 33460 Margaux; tel. 56 88 72 72 ✠ No visitors.

CHATEAU VINCENT★★

■Cru Bourg.   5ha   7000   **4** **D** ▮ ♨

61 64 70 71 75 ★**76** ★**78** ⑧ **81 82**

This estate produces high-quality wine even in reputedly difficult years, such as 1980. This classy example is fine, elegant and distinguished. (1980)
➹ *Mme* Martine Domec, Ch. Vincent, Cantenac, 33460 Margaux; tel. 56 88 30 12 ✠ No visitors.

Moulis

Moulis is a small ribbon of land 12 km long and 300–400 m wide, and is the smallest of the Médoc communal appellations. It does, however, have a wide range of soil types including gravel and clay-limestone hilltops. The wines (2.7 million bottles in 1982) have a lovely smooth flavour and a characteristically fruity bouquet.

CHATEAU ANTHONIC★

■Cru Bourg. Sup. 14ha   84000   **4** ◑ ♨

75 76 78 79 80 **81** **81** ⑧ **82**

Tannic and well balanced. Will keep well. (1982)
➹ Pierre Cordonnier, Ch. Anthonic, Moulis-en-Médoc, 33480 Castelnau-de-Médoc; tel. 56 88 84 60.

Moulis and Listrac

CHATEAU BISTON-BRILLETTE★★

| ■Cru Bourg. | 18ha | 85000 | 4 D ⦿ ↓ |

76 77 78 79 80 81 **81** 82 83 **83**

The richness is characteristic of the appellation. Still a little closed, with a flavour of strawberries and lots of tannin, which will mellow in a few years. Worth waiting for.
↜ Michel Barbarin, Ch. Biston-Brillette, Moulis-en-Médoc, 33480 Castelnau-de-Médoc; tel. 56 58 22 86 ⓨ By appt. Closed Feb.

CHATEAU BRANAS-GRAND-POUJEAUX★

| ■ | 5ha | 30000 | 4 ⦿ ↓ |

79 ★81 ★⑧² ★**82** 83

Intense colour marked by an intense nose with rich perfumes of ripe fruit, and a pleasing palate marked by soft, ripe tannins. (1982)
↜ Moulis-en-Médoc, 33480 Castelnau-de-Médoc Ch. Branas-Grand-Poujeaux, 33480 Moulis; tel. 56 58 22 42 ⓨ Daily 8.00–12.00/14.00–20.00.

CHATEAU BRILLETTE★★★

| ■Cru Bourg. Sup. | 30ha | 170000 | 4 D ⦿ ↓ |

75 **75** 76 ★78 ★**78** 79 **79** 80 ⑧¹ **81** 82

Attractive, rich and powerful, with a fine nose suggesting ripe plums, soft red fruit and vanilla. Needs keeping for a while. (1981)
↜ *Mme* Monique Berthault, Ch. Brillette, Moulis-en-Médoc, 33480 Castelnau-de-Médoc; tel. 56 58 22 09 ⓨ Mon.–Fri. 8.00–12.00/14.00–18.00. Closed Nov.–May.

CHATEAU CHASSE-SPLEEN★★★

| ■Bourg. Exc. | 66ha | 350000 | 5 D ↓ D |

70 71 72 74 75 76 78 **78** 79 81 **81** 82 83 **83**

Baudelaire cured his melancholy by drinking this wine. Royal ruby colour and nose that takes you into the undergrowth. A good wine that will keep well. Should have been included in the 1855 classification. (1978) ✔ Margaux Ch. la Gurgue Rouge, Haut-Médoc l'Hermitage-de-Chasse-Spleen Rouge, Pauillac Ch. Haut-Bages-Liberac Rouge.
↜ Bernadette Villars, Ch. Chasse-Spleen, Moulis-de-Médoc, 33480 Castelnau-de-Médoc; tel. 56 58 17 54 ⓨ By appt. Closed Aug.

CHATEAU DUPLESSIS-FABRE★

| ■Cru Bourg. | 12ha | 60000 | 4 D ⦿ ↓ |

79 80 81 **81** ⑧² 83 **83**

The wines here are quite round, like this fine and flattering 1982, not at all spoilt by its markedly high alcohol level. (1982)
↜ Guy Pages, Ch. Fourcas-Dupré, 33480 Listrac-Médoc; tel. 56 58 01 07 ⓨ By appt.

CHATEAU MAUCAILLOU★

| ■ | 55ha | 400000 | 5 D ⦿ ↓ |

76 77 79 80 ⑧²

This distinctive château produces a light wine with an expressive floral nose and vanilla and liquorice flavours. Already drinking well. (1981)
↜ Dourthe Frères, Moulis-en-Médoc; 33480 Castelnau-de-Médoc; tel. 56 56 35 846 ⓨ By appt.

CHATEAU MOULIN-A-VENT★

| ■Cru Bourg. Sup. | 23ha | 110000 | 4 D ⦿ ↓ |

70 75 79 80 81 **81** ⑧² **82** 83

Slightly hard on the nose, recalling fur and leather. Full and long on the palate. Ready to drink in about five years. (1982) ✔ Moulis Ch. Moulin-de-St-Vincent, Médoc Ch. la Tour Blanche.
↜ M. Dominique Hessel, Moulis-en-Médoc, 33280 Castelnau-de-Médoc; tel. 56 58 15 79 ⓨ By appt.

CHATEAU LA MOULINE★

| ■Cru Bourg. | 13ha | 33300 | 5 D █ ⦿ |

79 ★81 ★⑧² **82**

This deeply coloured wine, with its ripe-fruit nose, is very characteristic of the vintage. On the palate it is lively, fleshy and long. (1982)
↜ Jean Coubris, Ch. La Mouline, 33480 Moulis-en-Médoc; tel. 56 45 07 89 ⓨ By appt.

CHATEAU POUJEAUX★★

| ■ | 42ha | 200000 | 4 D █ ↓ |

75 76 ⑦⑦ 78

If the château is simple in style, the wine makes a contrast in its richness. The nose, which is quite refined, is still unobtrusive, but the palate is round and supple with a harmonious balance between the wine and wood, all leading to a long finish. (1982)
↜ GFA Jean Theil, Ch. Poujeaux, Moulis-en-Médoc, 33480 Castelnau-de-Médoc; tel. 56 58 22 58 ⓨ By appt.

Pauillac

With scarcely more inhabitants than a largish village, Pauillac is, in fact, a town in its own right, made even more attractive by the addition of a small marina along the Canal du Midi. But it is also, even more importantly, the wine-growing capital of the Médoc, as much by its central position as by the fact that it is the home of three first growths: Lafite-Rothschild, Latour and Mouton-Rothschild. Apart from these aristocrats, there is a cooperative which produces 5000 hectolitres of wine a year, and in 1982 total Pauillac AOC production was 5.9 million bottles.

Coming from hilltops composed of almost pure gravel, Pauillac wines manage to be full-bodied and robust, yet refined. They age superbly, although they demand patience. When mature they can stand up to quite solid dishes, such as mushrooms, red meat, dark game or foie gras.

Pauillac

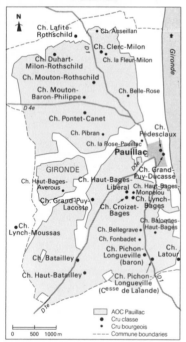

Map legend:
- AOC Pauillac
- ● Cru classe
- ● Cru bourgeois
- --- Commune boundaries

0   500   1000 m

CHATEAU ARTIGUES-ARNAUD★

■   10ha   18000   4 ⑪ ⌄
82 83 84

An intense, pretty red wine with a peach-like bouquet, still a little closed-in. It is quite supple and well balanced, with good vinosity on the palate. (1983)

250

↰ SC Ch. Grand-Puy-Ducasse, 33250 Pauillac; tel. 56 59 00 40.

CHATEAU LA BECASSE★

■5 Cru Classé   5ha   25000   4 D ⑪ ⌄
68 72 78 78 ⑧²

Although comparatively unknown, this little vineyard produces a well-made wine with good body and solid tannin content. (1982)
↰ Georges Fonteneau, 19 Rue Edouard-de-Pontet, 33250 Pauillac; tel. 56 59 07 14 ⵏ By appt.

CHATEAU CLERC-MILON★★

■5 Cru Classé   27ha   100000   6 ⑪
72 73 74 75 76 77 78 79 80 81 ⑧² 82 83

Wonderful deep-red colour, with a bouquet which, although still undeveloped, already shows signs of richness and finesse. On the palate, body, breadth and richness. A wine to wait for. (1982)
↰ Baron Ph. de Rothschild La Baronnie, BP 2, 33250 Pauillac; tel. 56 59 20 20 ⵏ Mon.–Thurs. 9.30–11.30/14.30–16.30, Fri. 9.30–15.00. Closed Aug.

CHATEAU CLOMBIER-MONPELOU★

■Cru Boug. Sup.   16ha   80000   5 D ⑪ ⌄
70 75 78 80

Grown in a vineyard situated on the plateau overlooking Pauillac, and aged in an underground cellar, this is a typical, classic Pauillac. (1982)
↰ Bernard Jucla, 33250 Pauillac; tel. 56 59 01 48 ⵏ By appt.

CHATEAU DE COUBERSANT★

■   16ha   100000   4 D ⌄
75 ⑦⁸ 81 ★82 ★82 83

An attractive red colour; fruity, yet still a little closed-in on the nose. Round and warm in the mouth, where the taste is still dominated by oak. It will need several years before fulfilling the promise held in its good, tannic finish. (1982)
↰ Bernard Jugla, 33250 Pauillac; tel. 56 59 01 48 ⵏ By appt. Closed 15 Aug.–5 Sept.

CHATEAU CROIZET-BAGES★

■5 Cru Classé   21ha   100000   5 ⑪ ⌄
64 70 75 76 78 79 80 81 81 ⑧² 82

The 1982 vintage shows what the producers are trying to achieve by means of a medium-length maceration and ageing in casks, which does not render the wine too 'woody'. In short, it has more charm and roundness than substance. (1982)
↰ M. Quié, Ch. Croizet-Bages 33250 Pauillac; ⵏ By appt.

CHATEAU DUHART-MILON-ROTHSCHILD★★

■4 Cru Classé   40ha   125000   5 ⑪ ⌄
61 70 75 76 79 80 81 ⑧² 82

This vast vineyard is located west of the properties of the Rothschild cousins Lafite and Mouton. The relative youth of the vineyard is compensated by the degree of pruning, which explains the small yields and typical concentration of this Pauillac. (1982)

━┓ Sté Duhart-Milon-Rothschild, 33250 Pauillac; tel. 56 59 22 97 ☿ By appt.

CHATEAU FONBADET*

| ■Cru Bourg. Sup. | 15ha | 70000 | 4 | D | ▤ | ⑪ | ⚓ |

70 72 73 74 **75** 76 **78** 78 79 80 **81** 81 ⑧ 82 83

A fragrance of violets in this rich, round, well-balanced wine, whose tannin will mellow with age. (1981) ✔ Pauillac Ch. Haut-Pauillac Rouge, Pauillac Ch. Pardanac Rouge, Pauillac Ch. Tour-du-Roc-Milon Rouge, Pauillac Ch. Monterand-Milon Rouge.
━┓ Pierre Peyronie, Ch. Fonbadet, 33250 Pauillac; tel. 56 59 02 11 ☿ By appt. Closed Aug.

LES FORTS-DE-LATOUR**

| ■ | | 50ha | 120000 | 5 | ⑪ | ⚓ |

73 74 75 76 77 **78 79** 80 81 ⑧ **83**

The second wine of a great name, Latour, and already a great wine itself. The colour is a lovely garnet red, the bouquet scented with ripe grapes and blended with aromas of new wood and liquorice. On the palate, richness, tannn, and a balance between power and elegance, show that this young wine has great potential. (1982)
━┓ Sté Civ. du Ch. Latour, 33250 Pauillac; tel. 56 59 00 51 ☿ By appt. Closed Aug.

CHATEAU GRAND-PUY-DUCASSE

| ■5 Cru Classé | 35ha | 150000 | 5 | ⑪ | ⚓ |

⑧

A beautiful 18th-century town-house, the home of the Bontemps wine brotherhood and its wine museum. The wine itself has a lovely deep red colour, good tannic structure and promises well several years hence. (1982)
━┓ S.C. du Ch. Grand-Puy-Ducasse, 33250 Pauillac; tel. 56 59 00 40 ☿ By appt. Closed Jul.–Sept. and harvest time ━┓ S.C. Grand-Puy-Ducasse.

CHATEAU-GRAND-PUY-LACOSTE**

| ■5 Cru Classé | 45ha | 200000 | 5 | ⑪ | ⚓ |

⑦⑨ 79

Fine, aromatic nose and a tannic but harmonious palate. Looks good for the future. (1979)
━┓ SC du Ch. Grand-Puy-Lacoste, 33250 Pauillac; tel. 56 59 06 66 ☿ By appt.

CHATEAU HAUT-BAGES-AVEROUS**

| ■Cru Bourg. | 12ha | 60000 | 5 | ⑪ | ⚓ |

75 78 79 80 **81** 81 ⑧ 82 **83** 83

Blended with the second wine from Lynch-Bages. Well structured with length, fullness and attractive aromas of liquorice and vanilla. (1981)
✔ Pauillac Ch. Lynch-Bages Rouge, St-Estèphe les Ormes-de-Pez Rouge.
━┓ A. et J.-M. Cazes, Ch. Lynch-Bages, 33250 Pauillac; tel. 56 59 19 19 ☿ By appt. Closed second fortnight in Aug.

CHATEAU HAUT-BAGES-LIBERAL*

| ■5 Cru Classé | 25ha | 110000 | 5 | ⑪ | ⚓ |

78 79 80 **81** 81 ⑧ 82 **83** 83

Tannic but a little harsh. Not a good example of this estate's production. (1979) ✔ Margaux Ch. la Gurgue Rouge, Moulis Ch. Chasse-Spleen Rouge, Haut-Médoc l'Hermitage de Chasse-Spleen Rouge.
━┓ Ch. Haut-Bages-Liberal, 33250 Pauillac; tel. 56 58 17 54 ☿ By appt. Closed Aug.

CHATEAU HAUT-BATAILLEY**

| ■5 Cru Classé | 20ha | 100000 | 5 | ⑪ | ⚓ |

75 76 77 78 **79** 80 **81** 81 ⑧ 82 83

Lacks a little length but is full, satisfying and well balanced. Some charm, if not yet fully open. (1978)
━┓ F. de Brest-Borie, Ch. Haut-Batailley, 33250 Pauillac; tel. 56 59 05 20 ☿ By appt.

CHATEAU HAUT-SAINT-LAMBERT

| ■ | 10ha | 40000 | 4 | ▤ | ⚓ |

An average, well-made wine, pleasant on nose and palate. (1982)
━┓ J.-P. Lambert, 33250 Pauillac; tel. 56 59 26 00 ☿ Mon.–Sat. 9.00–12.00/14.00–18.00. Closed Sun. in winter ━┓ M. Rambau.

CHATEAU LAFITE-ROTHSCHILD***

| ■1er Cru Classé | 90ha | 26600 | 6 | ⑪ | ⚓ |

59 ⑥① 62 **64** 66 69 70 **75 78** 79 **80** 81 82

Particularly noteworthy for its perfumed bouquet, lending it an air of grace and distinction. A great bottle, which needs keeping. (1981)
✔ Pauillac Moulin des Carruades, Pauillac Duhart-Milon-Rothschild, Médoc Ch. la Cardonne, Sauternes Ch. Rieussec.
━┓ Sté Ch. Lafite-Rothschild, 33250 Pauillac; tel. 56 59 01 74 ☿ By appt. Closed 15 Sept.–15 Nov.
━┓ Barons de Rothschild.

CHATEAU LATOUR***

| ■1er Cru Classé | 60ha | 180000 | 6 | ⑪ | ⚓ |

⑥① 73 74 75 **76** 77 **78** 79 81 **82**

Magnificent. The shade of red so dark as to be almost black, and on the palate an explosion of warmth, body and deliciously well-blended tannins. (1982)
━┓ Sté Civ. du Ch. Latour, 33250 Pauillac; tel. 56 59 00 51 ☿ By appt.

251

CHATEAU LYNCH-BAGES★★★

■5 Gd Cru Classé 68ha 300000 6 ⑪ ♂

75 76 77 **78 79** 80 **81** 81 ⑧ 82 **83** 83

The 1979 vintage does not yet have the full, dense bouquet characteristic of the estate, but certainly has promise. Robust and classy wine that will keep well. (1979) ✔ Pauillac Ch. Haut-Bages-Averous Rouge, St-Estèphe Ch. les Ormes-de-Pez Rouge.
↬ A. et J.-M. Cazes, Ch. Lynch-Bages, 33250 Pauillac; tel. 56 59 19 19 ⵊ By appt. Closed second fortnight in Aug.

CHATEAU LYNCH-MOUSSAS★

■5 Cru 25ha 100000 5 ⑪ ♂

75 78 79 80 **81** ⑧ 82

Despite a large percentage of Cabernet-Sauvignon grapes this wine is not particularly hard, nor for long-keeping. The 1982 vintage shows a pleasant and supple roundness which makes it thoroughly agreeable. (1982)
↬ M. Casteja, Ch. de Lynch-Moussas, 33250 Pauillac; tel. 56 59 57 14 ⵊ By appt.

CHATEAU MOUTON BARONNE PHILIPPE★★

■5 Cru Classé 50ha 150000 6 ⑪

72 73 74 75 76 77 78 **79** 80 81 ⑧ 82 83

Combines pretty colour with a very fine, lightly oaky, nose, and a palate which is rich, harmonious, elegant and long, with a good future. (1982)
↬ Baron Ph. de Rothschild La Baronnie, BP2, 33250 Pauillac; tel. 56 59 20 20. ⵊ Mon.–Thurs. 9.30–14.30; Fri. 9.30–15.00. Closed Aug.

CHATEAU MOUTON ROTHSCHILD★★★

■1er Cru Classé 80ha 200000 6 ⑪

72 73 74 **75** 76 77 **78** 79 80 81 ⑧ 82 83

Strong colour, an intense and refined nose with a hint of truffles and, on the palate, a lovely complex and balanced richness. (1982)
ⵊ Baron Philippe de Rothschild La Baronnie, BP 2, 33250 Pauillac; tel. 56 59 20 20 ⵊ By appt. Closed Fri. 15th Aug.

CHATEAU PEDESCLAUX

■5 Cru Classé 20ha 100000 5 Ⓓ ⑪ ♂

⑦ **75** 78 79 80 81 82

Undoubtedly the least known of the classical growths, as it is not sold through the trade or even through specialist wine merchants. It can, however, be ordered and bought directly from Château Pédesclaux at Pauillac. The 1982 vintage is warm and solid. (1982)
↬ SC du Ch. Pédesclaux, 33250 Pauillac; tel. 56 59 22 59 ⵊ By appt.

CHATEAU PICHON-LONGUEVILLE-BARON★★

■2 Cru Classé 30ha 130000 5 Ⓓ ⑪ ♂

64 75 76 77 78 ⑦ 80 **81** 81 82 82 **83** 83

Dense, full and very long on the finish; a good 1979; also well balanced. (1979)
↬ Bertrand Bouteiller, Ch. Pichon-Longueville-Baron, 33250 Pauillac; tel. 56 58 94 80 ⵊ By appt. Closed Aug. and last week in Dec.

CHATEAU PICHON-LONGUEVILLE COMTESSE-DE-LALANDE★★★

■2 Cru Classé 65ha 400000 6 Ⓓ ⑪ ♂

⑦ 76 **77** 78 79 80 81 ★**82** ★82 83

Beautiful, dense, dark wine with a fine bouquet of oak and real fruit. Elegant, full-bodied, delightfully expansive and voluptuous, with an unaggressive finish. (1982)
↬ Ch. Pichon-Longueville, 33250 Pauillac; tel. 56 59 19 40 ⵊ By appt. Closed Aug., Christmas, New Year ↬ *Mme* de Lencquesaing.

duced from vineyards with an average altitude of 40 metres on gravel soil, with a slightly higher clay content than in the other communal appellations.

The wines produced here (7.7 million bottles) tend to be more acidic, more deeply coloured and more tannic than other Médocs. They are very powerful wines, excellent for laying down.

CHATEAU PONTET-CANET★★

| ■5 Cru Classe | 72ha | 380000 | 6 | D | ⑪ | ↓ |
| 76 77 **78 79** 80 **81** 81 ⑧ 82 **83** 83 |

Made in one of the most attractive cellar wineries in Médoc. Nose of ripe fruit and a fair amount of tannin, a guarantee that it will age well, despite slight predominance of new wood. Should be left for about a dozen years. (1982)
↦ Guy et Alfred Tesseron, Ch. Pontet-Canet, 33250 Pauillac; tel. 56 52 15 71 ☎ By appt.

GRAND VIN DU PRELAT★★

| ■ | | 160ha | 720000 | 4 | ▮ | ↓ |

Lovely strong colour; nose somewhat reserved but promising. Good tannic structure, typically Pauillac, and everything about it indicates it will keep well. Wait at least four years. (1982)
↦ Baron Philippe de Rothschild, La Baronnie BP 2, 33250 Pauillac; tel. 56 59 20 20 ☎ By appt.

St-Estèphe

This appellation covers the commune of St-Estèphe (1089 hectares) and is the northern-most appellation in the Haut-Médoc. The St-Estèphes have a quite distinctive character, being pro-

St-Estèphe

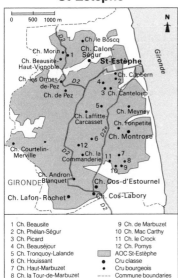

1 Ch. Beausite	9 Ch. de Marbuzet
2 Ch. Phélan-Ségur	10 Ch. Mac Carthy
3 Ch. Picard	11 Ch. le Crock
4 Ch. Beauséjour	12 Ch. Pomys
5 Ch. Tronquoy-Lalande	▨ AOC St-Estèphe
6 Ch. Houissant	● Cru classe
7 Ch. Haut-Marbuzet	● Cru bourgeois
8 Ch. la Tour-de-Marbuzet	---- Commune boundaries

CHATEAU ANDRON BLANQUET★

| ■Gd Bourg. Exc. | 16ha | 75000 | 4 | D | ⑪ | ↓ |
| 76 77 **78 79** 79 80 **81** 81 ⑧ |

An unpretentious 17th-century building, one of the oldest properties in St-Estèphe. The vineyard is planted with an unusual balance of vines for the Médoc: equal proportions of Cabernet-Franc, Cabernet-Sauvignon and Merlot. The wine is smooth and elegant, with mellow tannin and a peppery nose. (1982)
↦ Bernard Audoy, St-Estèphe, 33250 Pauillac; tel. 56 59 30 22 ☎ By appt.

BARON PHILIPPE★★

| ■ | | 1ha | 12000 | 4 | ▮ | ↓ |
| 72 73 74 75 76 77 78 79 80 81 ⑧ 82 83 |

A beautiful, brilliant red colour; intense rich nose; a full, powerful, roundness on the palate, as well as a final touch of tannin which augurs well for the future. (1982)
↦ Baron Philippe de Rothschild, La Baronnie, BP2, 33250 Pauillac; tel. 56 59 20 20 ☎ Mon.–Thurs. 9.30–11.30/14.30–16.30. Fri. 14.30–15.00. Closed Aug.

CHATEAU BEAU-SITE HAUT-VIGNOBLE★

| ■Cru Bourg. | 21ha | 85000 | 4 | D | ⑪ | ↓ |
| ⑦ 78 79 80 **81 82** 82 **83** |

Fruity, with a hint of oak, this delicate and subtle wine is charming, elegant, and has a very long finish. (1982)
↦ *MM.* Villard et Fils, Ch. Tour-Carelot, 33480 Castelrau-de-Médoc; tel. 56 41 14 86 ☎ Mon.–Fri.

CHATEAU LE BOSCQ★★★

| ■Cru Bourg. Sup. | 14ha | 90000 | 4 | D | ▮ | ⑪ | ↓ |
| 78 79 81 ⑧ 82 83 |

A great success for this young winemaker's first year. Powerful aromas that begin with strawberry and blackcurrant and finish with vanilla; the wine is full bodied and long on the palate. It will definitely age well. (1982)
↦ Philippe Durand, Ch. le Boscq, St-Estèphe, 33250 Pauillac; tel. 56 59 38 44 ☎ By appt.

CHATEAU CALON-SEGUR★★

■3 Cru Classé   69ha   240000   6 D ⑪ ⌄

61 75 76 78 79 80 81 82 82

A particularly successful wine, the like of which has not been produced on this estate for a quarter of a century. It has a great depth of colour, a distinctive wild-fruit-flavoured bouquet, and a sensation of depth, balance and great length on the palate. (1982)
↱ *MM*. Gasqueton et Peyrelonges, St-Estèphe, 33250 Pauillac, tel. 56 59 30 27.

CHATEAU COS-D'ESTOURNEL★★★

■2 Cru Classé   60ha   280000   6 D ⑪ ⌄

62 64 66 70 71 ⑦⑤ 76 78 80 ⑧① 81

There is no actual château here, but the famous pagoda-roofed tasting cellars combine Oriental exoticism (from Zanzibar to China) with European classicism. Something of the same blend may be found in the wine, in which the subtleness of the fine aroma of vanilla and coffee contrasts with the strength of the deep ruby colour, the generous attack and the fullness on the palate. What a wine! (1981) ✔ St-Estèphe Ch. de Marbuzet, St-Emilion Ch. Petit Figeac, St-Emilion Ch. La Fleur Pouret, Bordeaux Maître d'Estournel.
↱ Dom. Prats SA, Ch. Cos d'Estournel, St-Estèphe, 33250 Pauillac; tel. 56 44 11 37 ⫶ Mon.–Fri. 10.00–12.00/14.00–17.00.

CHATEAU COS-LABORY★★

■5 Cru Classé   13ha   80000   5 D ⑪ ⌄

76 77 78 78 79 79 81 81 ⑧②

A well-made wine, discreet and pretty, with a ruby-red colour and subtle, elegant aromas reminiscent of candied fruit. On the palate it is smooth and well balanced. (1981) ✔ St-Estèphe Ch. Andron-Blanquet.

↱ Bernard Audoy, St-Estèphe, 33250 Pauillac; tel. 56 59 30 22 ⫶ By appt.

CHATEAU DOMEYNE★★

■   3ha   20000   4 D ⑪ ⌄

⑦⑨ 82 82 83

An intense colour, and a powerful, grapey and oaky bouquet. On the palate you will find a rich, round wine with ripe and well-integrated tannin. (1983)
↱ *Mme*. Franchini, Ch. Domeyne, 33250 St-Estèphe; tel. 56 59 30 21 ⫶ No visitors ↱ GFA Château Domeyne.

CHATEAU HAUT-MARBUZET★★

■Cru Bourg.   40ha   220000   5 D ⑪ ⌄

76 78 79 80 81 82 82 ⑧③ 83

A striking, charming wine. Aged in casks of new oak, it is very smooth for a St-Estèphe; full and with rich, round tannins. (1982)
↱ *MM*. Dubosq et Fils, Ch. Haut-Marbuzet, St-Estèphe, 33250 Pauillac; tel. 56 59 30 54 ⫶ Mon.–Fri.

CHATEAU LAFON-ROCHET★★

■4 Cru Classé   27ha   160000   6 D ▮ ⑪ ⌄

76 77 78 81 82 82 83 83

Typical of the appellation: a wine with high tannin content, power and fine structure – characteristics enhanced by long ageing in cask. This wine could well last into the 21st century. (1982)
↱ Guy Tesseron, Ch. Lafon-Rochet, St-Estèphe, 33250 Pauillac; tel. 56 52 15 71 ⫶ Mon.–Fri.

CHATEAU MAC CARTHY★

■Cru Bourg.   7ha   25000   4 D ▮ ⌄

61 64 66 67 70 75 78 79 81 ⑧② 83

Shows aristocratic manners in its deep, almost black, colour, its richness, tannin and extreme concentration. (1982)
↱ *M*. Raymond, Ch. MacCarthy, 33340 Lesparre-Médoc; tel. 56 59 30 25

CHATEAU MEYNEY★★

■Gd Bourg. Sup.   50ha   270000   5 ⑪ ⌄

79 80 81 ⑧② 83 83

A wine with a good future: rich, fat and solid, it will keep for a very long time. (1983) ✔ St-Julien Ch. Talbot, St-Julien Ch. Gruaud Larose, St-Emilion Clos des Jacobins, Sauternes Lafaurie Peyraguey.
↱ Dom. Cordier, 10 Quai de Paludate, 33800 Bordeaux; tel. 56 59 30 01 ⫶ Mon.–Fri. Closed late Aug.–early Sept.

CHATEAU MONTROSE★★★

■2 Cru Classé   67ha   280000   6 ⑪ ⌄

78 81 82 82 83

A full, intense wine with exceptional length that will not be ready to drink for at least 12 years. (1982)
↱ Jean-Louis Charmolue, Ch. Montrose, St-Estèphe, 33250 Pauillac; tel. 56 59 30 12 ⫶ Mon.–Fri. 9.00–12.00/14.00–18.00.

CHATEAU LES ORMES-DE-PEZ

■Gd Cru Bourg. 30ha 145000 5 D ◧ ⬩
70 78 79 80 **81** 81 82 **83** 83

The first thing one notices is the depth of colour. This wine is full, robust and tannic – made to age, it will not be ready to drink for another couple of years. (1979) ✓ Pauillac Ch. Lynch-Bages, Pauillac Ch. Haut-Bages-Averous.
↬ A. et J.-M. Cazès, Ch. de Lynch-Bages, 33250 Pauillac; tel. 56 59 19 19 ⌶ By appt. Closed second fortnight Aug.

CHATEAU DE PEZ★★

■Cru Bourg. 25ha 130000 5 D ◧ ◧ ⬩
76 **78 79 81** 81 82 83

Consistent throughout. The colour is deep, the nose fruity; the palate round, balanced and oaky, all enhanced by a hint of liquorice and cocoa. (1981)
↬ M. Bernard SC Ch. de Pez, St-Estèphe 33250 Pauillac; tel. 56 59 30 07 ⌶ By appt.

CHATEAU PHELAN-SEGUR★

■Cru Bourg. Sup. 50ha 270000 4 D ◧ ⬩
78 79 80 **81** 81 82 82 83

This imposing château is on one of the largest estates in the Médoc. Its wine is perhaps a little light for a St-Estèphe, but it is smooth, elegant and pleasant to drink. (1981)
↬ SC du Ch. Phélan-Ségur, St-Estèphe, 33250 Pauillac; tel. 56 59 30 09 ⌶ Mon.–Fri. 9.00–12.00/ 14.00–17.30. Closed Aug. ↬ Roger Delon.

CHATEAU PLANTIER ROSE★

■Cru Bourg. 30000 4 ◧ ⬩
82 82 83

A keeping wine that needs to age perhaps ten years before yielding all it promises. Lovely dark colour; fine, delicate black- and redcurrant bouquet; round and grapey palate, with good structure and still very firm tannin. (1982)
↬ Mme Villard et Fils, Ch. Tour-Carelot, 33480 Castelnau-de-Médoc; tel. 56 41 14 86 ↬M. R.

CHATEAU TOUR DES TERMES

■Cru Bourg. 30ha 150000 4 D ◧ ◧ ⬩
79 81 **82** 83

Deep colour and almost violent bouquet, but supple and well-balanced. Perhaps not quite ready yet. (1979) ✓ St-Estèphe Ch. St-Corbian.
↬ Jean Anney, Ch. Tour des Termes, 33250 St-Estèphe; Pauillac; tel. 56 59 32 89 ⌶ Mon.–Fri. 8.00–12.30/14.00–17.30.

St-Julien

Lying in the exact centre of the Haut-Médoc, on gravelly hillocks (in Beychevelle and St-Julien), the 757 hectares of this appellation are best described as a harmonious blend of the Margaux and Pauillac soils. It is, therefore, hardly surprising to find eleven Crus Classés, no less than five of which are second growths. The wines, too, offer a good balance between the lightness and fragrance of Margaux and the more robust intensity of Pauillac; they have an attractive colour, a delicate but distinctive bouquet, and are rich, full-bodied and attractively sappy. Some 5.4 million bottles were produced in 1982.

St-Julien

CHATEAU BEYCHEVELLE★★

■4 Cru Classé 50ha 300000 5 D ◧ ⬩
76 **78** 79 80 80 **81 82 83** 83

The name of the château comes from the Gascon dialect for 'to lower sail' ('baisser le voile' in French). The site, once occupied by a formidable keep, served as a strongpoint from which to exact tolls from passing shipping, which had to lower sail in tribute. The splendid and elegant château now standing dates from the 18th century. This 1979 is a supple and elegant wine which is drinking well, but has many years ahead of it. (1979) ✓ Haut-Médoc les Brulières.
↬ Achille Fould, SC Ch. Beychevelle, St-Julien-Beychevelle, 33250 Pauillac; tel. 56 59 23 00 ⌶ By appt.

CHATEAU BRANAIRE-DUCRU★

■4 Cru Classé 50ha 400000 6 D ◧ ⬩
76 77 **78 79** 80 81 **82 83**

This straightforward wine has a fine, deep colour and a nose powerful almost to the point of pungency, with a few hints of musk, which may also be detected on the palate beneath supple, flavoursome tannins. (1983)
↬ MM. Tari et Tapie, Ch. Branaire-Ducru, St-Julien-Beychevelle, 33250 Pauillac; tel.

56 59 25 86 ⊤ Mon.–Fri. 10.00–17.00. Closed Aug.

CHATEAU LA BRIDANE★

■Cru Bourg.	17ha	65000	4 D ⦀ ↓

74 ★78 ★79 80 81 **82** 82 83

From a typical Haut-Médoc small family property, a wine which is simple and light, but attractively made and well structured. (1982)
↬ *Mme* Pierre Saintout, Ch. la Bridane, 33112 St-Laurent-et-Benon; tel. 56 59 41 28 ⊤ Mon.–Sun.

CHATEAU DUCRU-BEAUCAILLOU★★★

■2 Cru Classé	50ha	230000	4 ⦀ ↓

77 78 79 80 (81) 81 82 83 83

The advantage of the gravelly soil of Médoc is evident in quality wines such as this. Although the wood and tannins are still dominant, a superb balance will be achieved in eight to ten years. (1981)
↬ *Mme* Jean-Eugène Borie, Ch. Ducluzeau, Listrac-Médoc, 33480 Castelrau-de-Médoc; tel. 56 59 05 20 ⊤ By appt.

CHATEAU DU GLANA★

■Cru Bourg. Sup.	42ha	240000	⦀

★75 ★78 ★(82)

This wine passes too often unnoticed in the St-Julien repertoire. Yet it is pretty and colourful, with a simple, pleasant bouquet, and an unexpectedly rich suppleness on the palate, which allows it to be drunk fairly young. (1982)
↬ *M. G.* Meffre, Ch. du Glana, St-Julien-Beychevelle, 33250 Pauillac; tel. 56 59 19 75 ⊤ By appt.

CHATEAU GLORIA★

■Cru Bourg.	45ha	225000	5 D ⦀ ↓

★78 ★79 80 81 **82** 83

Extremely dark, almost black wine. Although the nose is still a little closed up, aromas of red fruit may be detected. These are also present on the palate, together with a slight gamey flavour. Overall, a tannic, well-balanced wine. (1982)
✔ St-Julien Ch. Haut-Beychevelle, St-Julien Ch. Peymartin, St-Julien Ch. St-Pierre, Haut-Médoc Ch. Bel-Air.
↬ Henri Martin, Ch. Gloria, St-Julien-Beychevelle, 33250 Pauillac; tel. 56 59 08 18 ⊤ By appt.

✗ CHATEAU GRUAUD-LAROSE

■2 Cru Classé	82ha	38500	5 ⦀ ↓

77 78 **80** **81** 82 83

The property, which bears the name of the first two owners, was re-established after the First World War. This wine is supple and fruity, with a good balance and structure on the palate. (1983)

✔ St-Julien Sarget de Gruaud-Larose, St-Estèphe Ch. Meyney, St-Julien Ch. Talbot, Médoc Ch. Plagnac.
↬ Sté du Ch. Gruaud-Larose, St-Julien-Beychevelle, 33250 Pauillac; tel. 56 59 27 00 ⊤ Mon.–Fri. 8.00–12.00/14.00–18.00. Closed end Aug.–beg. Sept.

CHATEAU LAGRANGE★★

■3 Cru Classé	80ha	480000	5 ⦀ ↓

★81 ★82 ★83 ★84

The elegance found in this wine's colour is present again on the nose, with a bouquet smelling quite strongly of fresh bread. In the mouth there is weight, roundness, warmth and definite strength, which lead neatly to a long and complex finish. (1984)
↬ SARL Ch. Lagrange, St-Julien-Beychevelle 33250 Pauillac; tel. 56 59 23 63 ⊤ By appt.

CHATEAU LALANDE-BORIE★

■Cru Bourg. Sup.	18ha	90000	4 ⦀ ↓

78 79 80 80 81 (82) 83

This château, which belongs to the owner of Ducru-Beaucaillou, was established in 1970. It produces a balanced and harmonious wine with light, well-blended tannins. (1981)
↬ *Mme* Jean-Eugène Borie, Ch. Ducluzeau, Listrac-Médoc, 33480 Castelrau-de-Médoc; tel. 56 59 05 20 ⊤ By appt ↬S.-F. Borie.

CHATEAU LANGOA-BARTON★★

■3 Cru Classé	15ha	50000	D ⦀ ↓

70 (71) 75 78 ★81 82 83

This wine is distinguished by a fine colour, with a promising, although still slightly closed bouquet. The palate is rich and smooth with flavours very characteristic of a St-Julien. (1978)
↬ SA des Ch. Langoa-Barton, St-Julien-Beychevelle, 33250 Pauillac; tel. 56 59 28 89 ⊤ By appt.

CHATEAU LEOVILLE-BARTON★★

■2 Cru Classé	40ha	200000	6 D ⦀ ↓

70 (71) 75 78 ★81 82 **82** 83 84

This property, owned by the same family as Château Langoa, has no buildings, the wine being vinified in the cellars of the Langoa property, although the wines from the two properties are vinified separately. The Léoville-Barton has a gamey nose with hints of cooked fruit on the palate; a tannic wine, very characteristic of St-Julien, which needs ageing. (1982)
↬ SA des Ch. Léoville-las-Cases St-Julien-Beychevelle, 33250 Pauillac; tel. 56 59 06 05 ⊤ By appt.

CHATEAU LEOVILLE-LAS-CASES★★★

■2 Cru Classé	80ha	480000	6 ⦀ ↓

70 71 73 (75) 76 78 ★79 80 81 82 **83**

The wine has a dark colour and a fine, elegant bouquet of vanilla and liquorice. It has an impressive flavour, with an exceptionally fine balance of rich fruit, tannin and alcohol. (1983)
↬ SA Ch. Léoville-Las-Cases, St-Julien-Beychevelle, 33250 Pauillac; tel. 56 59 25 26 ⊤ By appt.

CHATEAU LEOVILLE-POYFERRE★★

■2 Cru Classé   61 ha   300 000   `6` ▥ ↓

`77` `78` `79` `80` `81` `82` `83`

The property came into being during the 19th century, when the huge Léoville estate was divided up. The old château still stands. The 1982 is a very flattering, fine wine; delicate rather than powerful. (1982) ✔ St-Julien Ch. Moulin-Riche. ↱ SF du Ch. Léoville-Poyferré, St-Julien-Beychevelle, 33250 Pauillac; tel. 56 59 08 30 ☎ By appt. Closed Aug.

CLOS DU MARQUIS★★

■   `6` ▥ ↓

`75` `79` `80` `82` `83`

Produced on the Leoville-las-Cases estate, this wine is dark-red with a fine nose. Rich, smooth, well-structured and appealling on the palate. A distinguished wine. (1983) ↱ SA Ch. Léoville-las-Cases, St-Julien-Beychevelle, 33250 Pauillac; tel. 56 59 25 26 ☎ By appt.

CHATEAU MOULIN DE LA ROSE

■Cru Bourg.   4 ha   20 000   `4` `D` ▥ ↓

`78` `79` `79` `80` `81` `82` `83`

A tiny property, made up of a great many parcels of land scattered among the extensive St-Julien vineyards. The supple, delicate wine is unfortunately spoilt by a slight imbalance due to a small excess of alcohol. (1981) ↱ Guy Delon, St-Julien-Beychevelle, 33250 Pauillac; tel. 56 59 08 45 ☎ Mon.–Sat. 9.00–12.00/14.00–19.00; Sun. 9.00–12.00.

CHATEAU SAINT-PIERRE★★★

■4 Cru Classé   20 ha   45 000   `6` `D` ▥ ↓

`82` `82` `83`

Established in the 17th century, this property has had a chequered history. The present owner has successfully restored it to its former glory. This 1982 is delicately woody, velvety and warm, with a delicate, smooth attack and a nice long finish. The overall impression is of harmony, elegance and class. (1982) ✔ St-Julien Ch. Gloria, St-Julien Ch. Haut-Beychevelle, St-Julien Ch. Peymartin, Haut-Médoc Ch. Bel-Air. ↱ Henri Martin, Ch. Gloria, St-Julien-Beychevelle, 33250 Pouillac; tel. 56 59 01 18 ☎ By appt.

CHATEAU TALBOT★★

■4 Cru Classé   100 ha   500 000   `5` ▥ ↓

`77` `78` `80` `81` `82` `83`

A huge vineyard producing a fine wine: powerful on the nose, rich and ripely tannic on the palate. Will keep well. Five hectares of this property are planted with white grapes, sold (under the Bordeaux appellation) as 'Caillou Blanc'. (1983) ✔ St-Julien Connetable Talbot, Bordeaux Caillou-Blanc-de-Talbot, St-Julien Ch. Gruaud-Larose, Sauternes Ch. Lafaurie-Peyraguey. ↱ Jean Cordier, Ch. Talbot, St-Julien-Beychevelle, 33250 Pauillac; tel. 56 59 06 06 ☎ Mon.–Fri. 8.00–12.00/14.00–18.00. Closed end Aug.–beg. Sept.

CHATEAU TERREY-GROS-CAILLOUX★

■Cru Bourg.   24 ha   75 000   `5` `D` ▮ ▥ ↓

`78` `79` `80` `81` `82` `83`

A nicely coloured wine. Although the nose is still closed up it nevertheless suggests ripe fruit, while the impression on the palate is of good balance and structure. (1982) ✔ St-Julien Ch. Hortenie, Haut-Médoc Ch. Fort-Lignac. ↱ A. Fort et H. Pradère, Ch. Terrey-Gros-Cailloux, 33250 St-Julien-Beychevelle; tel. 56 59 06 27 ☎ Mon.–Sat. 9.00–12.00.

BORDEAUX SWEET WHITE WINES

The sweet wine appellations of the Gironde are gathered in a small area on either side of the river Garonne, near its confluence with the Ciron. Pure chance? Not really, since it is the meeting here with the cold waters of the little River Ciron, sliding through its tunnel of undergrowth, that gives rise to the special climatic conditions that favour the development of *Botrytis cinerea*, or 'noble rot'. The damp, misty autumn mornings, and hot, sunny afternoons allow the rot to develop on the perfectly ripe grapes. Minute threads of the botrytis fungus penetrate the grape skins, and water evaporates from the grape pulp, concentrating the juices and 'extract' to produce a very high sugar content.

257

The Sweet Wines of Bordeaux

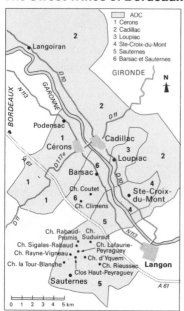

Even when conditions are right, enormous care has to be taken with the harvest. Noble rot does not develop at the same rate on each individual bunch of grapes, so that – for the finest wines – the grapes are gathered in successive stages, and only those which have reached the optimum are harvested at each stage. Furthermore, the permitted yield per acre is low (in Sauternes and Barsac the maximum allowed is 25 hectolitres per hectare). Finally, the whole painstaking process is fraught with risk because of the unpredictability of the weather. As a result, vintage years are rarer for these wines than for the red wines.

Cadillac

This walled town, with its magnificent seventeenth-century château, is often seen as the capital of the Premières Côtes region. In 1980, however, it received its own appellation for sweet white wines. As yet the appellation vineyards cover only some 80 hectares, and the characteristics of this wine have still to be definitively established.

CHATEAU LA BERTRANDE

☐ 5ha 8000 **3 D** ▊

71 73 ⑦⑤ 79 80 81 82 83 84

Bright gold in appearance, light in bouquet, firm but well balanced on the palate. (1981)
☙ GAEC Vignobles Gillet, Ch. La Bertrande, Omet, 33410 Cadillac; tel. 56 62 97 16 ♈ No visitors.

CHATEAU LA CROIX BOUEY

☐ 1ha 3800 **D** ▊ ↓

81 *82 *82 83

Deep buttercup-yellow in colour with an aroma of fresh straw; very sweet in the mouth.
☙ SCA La Croix Bouey, St-Maixant, 33490 St-Macaire; tel. 56 63 25 78 ♈ No visitors.

CHATEAU LABATUT★

☐ 10ha 50000 **3 D** ▊

78 79 81 *82 83

This is an almost excessively sweet wine, with a fine golden-yellow appearance. The nose is evocative and delicately floral. (1981)
☙ Michel Bouchard, Ch. Labatut, St-Maixant, 33490 St-Macaire; tel. 56 62 02 44 ♈ By appt.

Loupiac

The existence of vineyards at Loupiac has been attested since the thirteenth century. The appellation resembles Ste-Croix du Mont with respect to vineyard exposure, soil type, and grape varieties used, but, as on the west bank, the wines seem to grow progressively less rich as one follows the vineyards northwards.

CHATEAU DU CROS★★

☐ 24ha 75000 **4 D** ◉ ↓

70 71 73 ⑧① 82

A sweet wine, fat and round behind its golden-yellow colour and bouquet of toast and almonds, touched with acacia. (1981)
☙ Michel Boyer, Ch. du Cros, Loupiac, 33410 Cadillac; tel. 56 62 99 31 ♈ By appt Thurs., Sat., Sun.

CLOS JEAN★★

☐ 18ha 75000 **2 D** ▊ ↓

⑦⑧ 79 81 82

A beautiful amber-yellow, this wine has a light nose, delicate and subtle, but with a pineapple character that is also apparent on the palate. (1981)
☙ Henry Bord, Clos Jean, 33410 Cadillac; tel. 56 62 99 83 ♈ By appt.

CHATEAU LOUPIAC-GAUDIET★

☐ 25ha 100000 **3 D** ▊ ↓

76 78 ⑦⑨ 79

This wine is a pure, clear yellow colour, with a honeyed nose, and a rich, well-constituted palate. (1979)
☙ Marc Ducau, Loupiac, 33410 Cadillac; tel. 56 62 99 88 ♈ No visitors.

CHATEAU LA NERE

☐ 20ha 70000 **3** **D** ▪ ♦

75 ⑲ *81 *82 **83**

A slightly surprising colour with a few dark tinges. On the palate, however, this wine is round and well balanced. (1979) ✔ Ste-Croix-du-Mont Dom. Roustit Blanc Liquoreux, Bordeaux Clos de l'Ange Blanc Sec, Bordeaux Ch. Chanteloiseau Rosé, Bordeaux Ch. Chanteloiseau Rouge. ⊶ *MM.* Dulac et Séraphon, Verdelais, 33490 St-Macaire; tel. 56 62 02 08 ☿ By appt.

CHATEAU GRAND PEYRUCHET★

☐ 8ha 25000 **3** **D** ▪ ♦

An attractive pale yellow colour, and a nose that is not yet well developed but has shades of fruits and flowers, with a hint of overripeness; sweet and pleasantly refined on the palate. (1982) ⊶ Henri Gillet, Ch. La Bertrande, Omet, 33410 Cadillac; tel. 56 62 97 16 ☿ By appt.

CHATEAU DE RICAUD★

☐ 13ha 30000 **3** **D** ◍ ♦

In a neo-Gothic setting, this is a mischievous little wine that seems almost to play hide-and-seek behind its golden nuances and fleeting aromas. It is, however, well balanced. (1981) ⊶ Alain Thienot, Ch. de Ricaud, Loupiac, 33410 Cadillac; tel. 56 62 97 57 ☿ By appt. Closed first fortnight Aug.

Ste-Croix-du-Mont

This is a very little-known area, despite the obvious charm of its steep hillsides overlooking the River Garonne. Like other sweet white wine appellations on the east bank, its wine has suffered too long from the reputation of being no more than a good, cheap wine for banquets or wedding parties.

Nevertheless, this appellation, situated opposite Sauternes, deserves better; it has some fine vineyard land – predominantly limestone, with a few gravelly areas – and a micro-climate which encourages the development of noble rot. The grape varieties used, and the wine-making methods are very similar to those of Sauternes, and the wines, which are not overly sweet, leave a pleasant impression of fruitiness. Best drunk young, they are usually served in the same way as their west-bank equivalents, but their more affordable price allows one to be more adventurous.

CHATEAU BEL-AIR

☐ 10ha 38000 **3** **D** ▪ ◍ ♦

66 69 73 **76 78** 79 81 ⑧ 83

Bright, green-tinted yellow; the flowery nose is not yet very intense, but the wine is rich and sweet on the finish. (1979) ✔ Bordeaux Sec Bel-Air, Bordeaux Rouge Dom. du Pradey. ⊶ Michel Méric, Ste-Croix-du-Mont, 33410 Cadillac; tel. 56 62 01 19 ☿ Mon.–Sat. 8.00–20.00.

CHATEAU DE BERTRANON

☐ 7ha 40000 **3** **D** ▪ ♦

70 75 **76** ⑧ **80**

A slight bitter taste undermines this wine's harmony, but its lightness makes it pleasant enough on the palate. (1982) ⊶ André Remaut, Ch. de Bertranon, Ste-Croix-du-Mont, 33410 Cadillac; tel. 56 62 01 71 ☿ Daily 8.00–20.00.

CHATEAU LE GALLION

☐ 8ha 40000 **3** **D** ▪ ◍ ♦

⑦ 76 **82 83**

A deep yellow wine whose bouquet is quite original but whose palate is almost over-soft and rich. (1978) ✔ Barsac Plateau du Roc d'Or. ⊶ Jacqueline Larrue, St-Croix-du-Mont, 33410 Cadillac; tel. 56 62 01 23 ☿ No visitors.

CHATEAU GRAND COUSTIN★

☐ 7ha 30000 **3** **D** ▪

75 79 81 ⑧

Despite attractive shades of gold, the colour lacks depth. The nose is very flowery, and on the palate the wine is sweet, smooth, round and well balanced. (1982) ✔ Bordeaux Ch. Grand-Coustin Blanc Sec. ⊶ Camille Pourgaton, Ste-Croix-du-Mont, 33410 Cadillac; tel. 56 62 01 90 ☿ By appt.

DOMAINE DES GRAVES-DU-TICH

☐ 4ha 15000 **2** **D** ◍ ♦

79 81 *82 *82

Green-tinted straw-yellow; aromatic on the nose, rich and smooth on the palate. (1982) ⊶ Fonteyreau, Dom. du Tich, Ste-Croix-du-Mont, 33490 Verdelais-St-Macaire; tel. 56 56 62 054 ☿ No visitors.

CHATEAU LOUBENS★★

☐ 15ha 20000 **4** **D** ▪ ♦

37 42 55 59 ⑦ 78 **79**

A lovely 17th-century château in an exceptionally beautiful location, with cellars hewn out of a bed of fossilized oyster shells. Pierre de Lancre, the famous witch-hunter, was master of the châteawu in the time of Louis XIII. The wine has an attractive, bronzed, yellow colour, soft aromas of honey and Spanish broom, and fine balance on the palate. (1971) ⊶ Sté Civile du Ch. Loubens, Ste-Croix-du-Mont, 33410 Cadillac; tel. 56 62 01 25 ☿ By appt.

CHATEAU LOUSTEAU-VIEIL*

☐	10ha	45000	**4** **D** ▬ ⑪ ↓

(75) 76 **82** **83**

A sweet wine with a refined and well-developed nose; richness and length on the palate suggest that it will age well. (1982) ✔ Graves Clos la Maurasse.
↜ Roland Sessacq, Ch. Lousteau-Vieil, Ste-Croix-du-Mont, 33410 Cadillac; tel. 56 62 01 41
☵ Daily 9.00–12.00/14.00–19.00.

CHATEAU DU MONT*

☐	15ha	45000	**3** **D** ▬ ↓

80 (81)

Fine, sparkling golden-yellow colour. Delicate, refined nose and a good balance on the palate; will age well. (1981)
↜ Paul Chouvac, Ste-Croix-du-Mont, 33410 Cadillac; tel. 56 63 21 53 ☵ By appt.

DOMAINE DE MORANGE*

☐	15ha	50000	**3** **D** ▬ ↓

Maybe a little light on the finish, but this wine has a good, deep colour, a powerful nose with aromas of well-ripened grapes, and a sweet, smooth palate. (1982)
↜ Frédéric Durr, Ste-Croix-du-Mont, 33410 Cadillac; tel. 56 63 35 92 ☵ By appt.

CHATEAU LA RAME**

☐	17ha	65000	**3** **D** ▬ ⑪ ↓

71 73 (75) **78** 80 **82** 83

A clear golden-yellow colour, with a full, round nose; a pleasant, sweet wine that is almost creamy in texture. (1982)
↜ C. Armand, Ch. la Rame, Ste-Croix-du-Mont, 33410 Cadillac; tel. 56 63 20 33 ☵ Mon.–Sat. 8.30–13.00/14.30–19.00. Closed Oct.

Cérons

Tucked in among the Graves vineyards, Cérons provides a link between Barsac and the sweet type of Graves Supérieurs; unlike Sauternes and Barsac its wines may use the Graves appellation. Their fine character is expressed by a very distinctive sappiness and great finesse.

CHATEAU D'ARCHAMBEAU

☐	8ha	40000	**3** **D** ⑪ ↓

A wine of pleasant appearance, with a clean and distinct yellow hue; it is moderately sweet, discreetly scented, and agreeably fresh. (1980)
↜ D. Dubourdieu, Ch. Reynon, Beguey, 33410 Cadillac; tel. 56 62 96 51. ☵ By appt.

CHATEAU CERONS*

☐	6ha	16000	**5** **D** ⑪ ↓

55 62 67 73 75 79 (81) **82**

From a beautiful 17th-century château whose noble origins can be seen in its elegant aspects, this wine is made within the classic tradition, typical of its appellation, (1982)
↜ Jean Perromat, Ch. de Cérons, Cérons, 33720 Podcnsac; tel. 56 27 03 48 ☵ By appt.

GRAND ENCLOS DU CHATEAU DE CERONS***

☐		25000	**3** **D** ▬ ⑪ ↓

70 75 76 79 *81 *83

Beautiful golden colour and a fine, characteristically 'roasted' nose, rather like marmalade, and very full. Very smooth on the palate where the characteristic aromas of Vins Liquoreux blooms forth. Length and a good finish complete the picture of high quality. An exceptional wine for its appellation and price. (1982)
↜ Pierre et Olivier Lastate, Grand Enclos du Ch. de Cérons, Cérons, 33720 Podensac; tel. 56 27 01 53
☵ By appt.

CÉRONS
GRAND ENCLOS
DU
Château de Cérons
APPELLATION CÉRONS CONTRÔLÉE
1981
LATASTE FRÈRES PROPRIÉTAIRES A CÉRONS (GIRONDE) · FRANCE
75cl
MIS EN BOUTEILLES AU CHATEAU

CHATEAU HAURA*

☐	15ha	40000	**4** **D** ▬

81 82 **82** 83

This estate, in the same hands as the Château Hillot, produces an attractive straw-yellow wine. An elegant bouquet with a hint of honey; full and rich on the palate, with flavours reminiscent of dried fruit, particularly apricot. (1982)
↜ M. et *Mme* Leppert, Ch. Hillot, 33720 Illats; tel. 56 62 33 38 ☵ By appt.

Barsac

Although it has the right to use the Sauternes appellation, Barsac stands apart from the other communes, which more properly belong to Sauternes. The difference is reflected in Barsac's flatter countryside and stone-walled estates as well as in its wines, which are less forcefully sweet. Like Sauternes, however, Barsac may be served in the classic way, with dessert, or – and this is becoming increasingly popular – with an entrée such as foie gras, as well as with certain strong-flavoured cheeses, such as Roquefort.

CHATEAU BROUSTET

☐2 Cru Classé	14ha	40000	**5** ⑪ ↓

67 71 **81** 83 **83**

A clear golden-yellow wine with a definite presence on the palate. Good for drinking now. (1981) ✔ Bordeaux Blanc Sec.
↜ Sté Exploit. Vini. Fournier, Ch. Broustet, 33210 Barsac; tel. 57 24 70 79 ☵ By appt.

CHATEAU CAILLOU★★

| □2 Cru Classé | 20ha | 55000 | 5 D ▮ |

59 64 66 67 ⑦ 73 75 76 77 78 79 81

The grower of this wine is such a jazz fan that he started a 'Sauternes Jazz-Quartet', but he is a wine-grower first and foremost. His 1981 combines a clear yellow colour with an intense, honeyed bouquet and a beautifully rich palate. (1981) ✔ Bordeaux Blanc Ch. du Caillou, Bordeaux Blanc Dom. Sarraute.

⊷ Joseph Bravo, Barsac, 33720 Podensac; tel. 56 56 27 163 ⵏ By appt.

CHATEAU CANTEGRIL★★

| □ | 17ha | 3000 | 5 D ◐ ↓ |

*82

Good colour indicates a wine worthy of interest, the bouquet mingling orange, acacia and crystallized fruits. Fine, mellow, smooth and long, the palate has good botrytis flavour. (1982)

⊷ M. Dubourdieu, Ch. Cantegril, 33210 Sauternes; tel. 56 27 15 84 ⵏ By appt.

CHATEAU COUTET★★★

| □1er Cru Classé | 38ha | 68000 | 5 D ◐ |

76 77 78 79 80 81 82 ⑧

A château that has both charm and refinement, just like the delicately fragrant wine with its roasted scents. Warm, round and powerful on the attack; fullness and finesse on the palate. Very well made. (1981) ✔ Graves Ch. Coutet.

⊷ Sté Civ. du Ch. Coutet, Barsac, 33720 Podensac; tel. 56 27 15 46 ⵏ Mon.–Fri. 9.00–12.00/14.00–18.00.

CHATEAU DOISY-DAENE★★★

| □2 Cru Classé | 16ha | 40000 | 5 D ◐ ↓ |

82 83

Intense floral bouquet of exotic fruits (mango), apricot and peach, with a hint of citronnella. Very fresh, very long, this is a well-balanced wine, with nuances of fruit and flowers. In all respects, a very feminine and gracious wine. (1982)

⊷ M. Dubourdieu, Ch. Cantegril, 33210 Sauternes; tel. 56 26 15 84 ⵏ By appt.

CHATEAU DOISY-DUBROCA★

| □2 Cru Classé | 5ha | 7000 | 5 ◐ |

* 71 ⑦ 76 80 80 81 83

This amber-hued, yellow-gold wine is characteristic of Barsac, with its fine, flowery and complex bouquet. In the mouth, good balance and lightness make it easy to drink. (1978)

Lucien Lurton, Barsac, 33720 Podensac; tel. 53 66 22 9 ⵏ No visitors.

CHATEAU FARLURET★★

| □ | 10ha | 30000 | 4 D ▮ ◐ ↓ |

80 81 *82 *82

This wine shares its grower with the Château Haut-Bergeron and is equally successful, though different in style. The nose is very individual, with a characteristic over-ripe bouquet and aromas of toasted almonds and honey. Will be a very fine bottle. (1982) ✔ Sauternes Ch. Haut-Bergeron Blanc.

⊷ Robert Lamothe, Haut-Bergeron, Preignac, 33720 Langon; tel. 56 56 63 247 ⵏ By appt.

CHATEAU LIOT★

| □ | 30ha | 100000 | 4 D ▮ ↓ |

⑦ 76 *78 79 81 81 *82 83

This Haut-Barsac wine is a lovely golden yellow. The bouquet is fine with an individual note reminiscent of lime, and the palate quite rich with a suggestion of oak. (1981)

⊷ J.-G. David, Ch. Liot, Barsac, 33720 Podensac; tel. 56 27 15 31 ⵏ By appt.

CHATEAU MENOTA★★

| □ | 30ha | 90000 | 4 D ▮ ↓ |

⑦ 78 79 80 81 82

This small fort looks very theatrical, almost like a set in a Hollywood Western. The wine is certainly original: the nose pleasantly floral, the palate sweet, rich and creamy with a pleasing finish. (1981)

⊷ SCEA du Ch. Menota, Barsac, 33720 Podensac; tel. 56 27 15 80 ⵏ By appt.

CLOS MERCIER★★

| □ | 3ha | 6000 | 4 D ▮ ◐ ↓ |

70 71 ⑦ *79 *81

This vineyard is not very well known, but the wine is good. It has an attractive colour, with a honeyed nose, full; rich and lively on the palate with a nice, lingering finish. (1981)

⊷ Mme Pauly, Clos-Mercier, 33720 Barsac Podensac; tel. 56 27 16 17.

CHATEAU MONT-JOIE

| □ | 12ha | 36000 | 4 D ▮ ◐ ↓ |

67 70 75 80 *81 82 ⑧ 83

The wine is smooth, with a soft, straw-yellow colour and light, flowing texture. (1982)

⊷ Franck Glaunés, Cassoil Barsac, 33720 Podensac; tel. 56 71 12 73 ⵏ By appt.

CHATEAU NAIRAC★

| □Cru Cl. | 16ha | 50000 | 5 D ◐ ↓ |

*74 *76 *79 *80 *80 81

The wine is as elegant as the château itself. The golden-yellow colour belies the rich and complex nose with its hints of apricot and oak. In the mouth both structure and balance are good; fine and distinguished throughout. (1980)

⊷ Thomas Heeter-Tari, 33720 Barsac, Podensac; tel. 56 27 16 16 ⵏ By appt.

CHATEAU PIADA★★

| ☐ | 10ha | 30000 | 4 D |

70 71 ⑧

From a vineyard dating back to the Middle Ages, the wine has shades of green and a delicately toasted fragrance. Pleasing, rich round and promising. (1982) Bordeaux Clos du Roy Blanc Sec.
⌘ Jean Lalande, Ch. Piada, Barsac, 33720 Podensac; tel. 56 27 16 13 ⵏ By appt.

CHATEAU PIOT-DAVID★★

| ☐ | 8ha | 22000 | 4 D ▮ ⌄ |

A wine from one of the rare walled Gironde vineyards. A pleasant caramel scent with a hint of jam. Ready to drink. (1970)
⌘ Jean-Luc David, Dom. de Poncet, 33410 Omet; tel. 56 62 97 30 ⵏ By appt. '

CHATEAU DE ROLLAND

| ☐ | 16ha | 45000 | 4 D ⑪ ⌄ |

80 81 ⑧

Tourists may sample this lemon-coloured wine in a small tasting pavillion at the roadside. It is light, with floral and fruit aromas. (1981) ✔ Bordeaux.
⌘ Jean et Pierre Guignard, Château de Rolland, Barsac, 33720 Podensac; tel. 56 27 15 02 ⵏ By appt.

CHATEAU SAINT-MARC

| ☐ | 15ha | 45000 | 4 D ▮ ⑪ ⌄ |

64 70 76 80 81 82 ⑧

In spite of a little vegetal note in the finish, this discreetly aromatic wine has an appreciably flowing character on the palate. (1981) ✔ Bordeaux Vin Sec du Ch. St-Marc, Graves Ch. Brochon Blanc Sec et Rouge, Bordeaux Supérieur Ch. de Roux Rouge, Bordeaux Rosé Clos St-Marc.
⌘ André Laulan, Ch. St-Marc, Barsac, 33720 Podensac; tel. 56 27 16 81 ⵏ By appt.

CHATEAU SUAU★

| ☐2 Cru Classé | 10ha | 25000 | 4 D ⌄ |

75 79 80 81 ⑧

Appealing bright-yellow. Balance and richness on the palate. Slight bitterness on the finish. (1979) ✔ Sauternes Dom. du Coy Blanc Liquoreux, Ch. de Navarro Blanc Sec, Ch. de Navarro Rouge.
⌘ Roger Biarnes, Illats, 33720 Podensac; tel. 56 27 20 27 ⵏ By appt.

CHATEAU TUCAU

| ☐ | 6ha | 18000 | 4 D ▮ ⌄ |

75 76 79 ⑧

A golden-tinted, straw-yellow wine with a discreet nose. In the mouth it is light and nicely supple. Allow it to breathe before tasting. (1979)
⌘ Bernard Leppert, SCE du Ch. Hillot, 33720 Illats; tel. 56 62 53 38 ⵏ By appt.

Sauternes

Every tourist visiting a Sauternes château is told about the former owner who one year arrived late for his harvest, but had the bright idea – probably through stubbornness – of harvesting the overripe grapes anyway. In fact, no one really knows when, where, or by whom Sauternes was invented.

If the origins of Sauternes are shrouded in legend, scientific research has revealed the true story. Soil specimens from each of the five communes that make up the appellation, including Barsac, which has its own separate appellation, have been recorded and analysed into their smallest constituents. Science confirms that it is the great variety of soil types (gravelly, clay-limestone, or limestone) that gives each wine its personality. Sauternes is made from three grape varieties, Sémillon (70–80 per cent), Sauvignon (20–30 per cent) and minute quantities of Muscadelle. The wines have a rich, golden colour with a fine, subtle bouquet – often described as having a 'roasted' character – which matures excellently, becoming rich and complex and developing notes of honey, hazelnut, and spiced orange. It is worth noting that Sauternes was the only Bordeaux white wine to be classified in 1855.

CHATEAU D'ARCHE★★

| ☐2 Cru | 30ha | 60000 | 5 D ⑪ ⌄ |

70 71 75 76 ⑧ ⑧

A lovely, clear golden-yellow wine whose nose has the elegant scent of 'noble rot'. In the mouth, after a very rich attack, the wine is full, round and lingering. (1981)
⌘ Pierre Perromat, Dom. de Fongrave, Gornac, 33540 Sauveterre-de Guyenne; tel. 56 61 97 64 ⵏ By appt.

BARON PHILIPPE★★

| ☐ | 2ha | 26664 | 5 ▮ ⌄ |

72 73 74 75 *76 78 79 *81 *82 ⑧ ⑧

Bright golden yellow, this wine has an enchanting appearance. The nose is a little restrained, but nonetheless harmonious and on the palate there is balance, finesse and a roasted character on the finish. (1983)
⌘ Baron Philippe de Rothschild, la Baronnie, BP 2, 33250 Pauillac, tel. 56 59 20 20 ⵏ Mon.–Thurs. 9.30–11.30/14.30–167.30; Fri. 14.30–15.00. Closed Aug.

CHATEAU BASTOR LA MONTAGNE★★

| ☐ | 40ha | 100000 | 4 D ⑪ ⌄ |

⑦ ⑧

Characteristic bouquet, reminiscent of the neighbouring pine forest. Warm, round and well balanced. (1983)
⌘ Crédit Foncier de France, 33210 Preignac; tel. 56 63 27 66.

CHATEAU BECHEREAU*

☐   7ha   22000   🔳4 🅳 📦 ⬇

Despite a faint, almost burnt note on the finish, round and pleasant with some delicate aromas. (1981) ✔ Graves Domaine Terrefort Rouge, Graves Blanc Domaine Terrefort, Graves Sup. Blanc Domaine Terrefort.
🍴 Franck Deloubes, Cha. Berchereau, Bommes, 33210 Langon; tel. 56 63 61 73 ⍾ By appt. Closed Aug.

CHATEAU BERGERON

☐   8ha   21000   🔳4 🅳 📦 ⬥ ⬇
61 75 *78 *79 80 *81 🔳82 83

This estate near the River Ciron produces a lovely clear golden-yellow wine with a faint touch of citrus on the nose and nicely textured palate. (1981)
🍴 M. Laurans, Ch. Bergeron, Bommes, 33210 Langon; tel. 56 63 60 17 ⍾ By appt.

CHATEAU BOUYOT

☐   13ha   23000   🔳4 🅳 📦 ⬥
61 67 *75 *⑲ *81 *82 83

Lovely, bright-yellow wine. Despite a hint of dryness, evokes springtime with its floral fragrances – broom, among others. (1979)
🍴 Bertrand Jammy-Fonbeney, Le Bouyot, 33210 Barsac; tel. 56 27 19 46 ⍾ By appt.

CHATEAU CAMERON

☐   9ha   22000   🔳5 🅳 📦 ⬥ ⬇

Buttercup-yellow colour, with powerful aromas that are a bit stolid. Distinctive, gentle attack and suggestion of mint in the flavour. (1981) ✔ Graves Ch. Villefranche Rouge, Bordeaux Ch. Cameron Rouge.
🍴 Pierre Guinabert, Cha. Cameron, Bommes, 33210 Langon; tel. 56 27 16 39 ⍾ By appt.

PHILIPPE CHANTECAILLE*

☐   3.5ha   18000 🔳5   🅳 📦 ⬥ ⬇
75 76 77 78 79 🔳83

This is a wine-merchant's 'own-brand' wine, bearing the signature of its grower. It is a golden yellow with green tints. Very pleasing and well-balanced on the palate, reminiscent of candied fruits and honey. (1983)
🍴 Maison Chantecaille et Cie, 127 Rue de Turenne, 33000 Bordeaux; tel. 56 48 04 54 ⍾ No visitors.

CHATEAU CLIMENS**

☐1er Cru Classé   25ha   50000   🔳6 ⬥ ⬇
76 80 🔳81 83 🔳83

A fine, sweet bottle from an estate with an established reputation. (1980)
🍴 Lucien Lurton, Ch. Brane-Cantenac, 33460 Margaux; tel. 56 88 70 20 ⍾ By appt.

CHATEAU CLOS HAUT-PEYRAGUEY**

■1er Cru Classé   15ha   40000   🔳5 🅳 📦 ⬥ ⬇
67 70 71 75 ⑦6 81 🔳82 83

An extremely attractive, lively yellow wine with a fine powerful nose and a round, supple and rich palate. (1982)

🍴 Jacques Pauly, GFA du Clos Haut-Peyraguey, Bommes 33210, Langon; tel. 56 63 61 53 ⍾ By appt.

J.P. DANEY *Cru d'Arche Pugneau*

☐   12ha   22000   🔳5 🅳 ⬥ ⬇

Deep-yellow colour and sweet, rich flavour for this rather rustic Sauternes. The finish is slightly hard. (1982)
🍴 Jean-Pierre Daney et fils, Dom. d'Arche-Pugneau, Preignac, 33210 Langon; tel. 56 63 24 84 ⍾ By appt.

CHATEAU DOISY-VEDRINES*

☐2 Cru Classé   20ha   45000   🔳5 ⬥ ⬇
㊳

Attractive straw colour. Delicate bouquet of coffee and vanilla. (1982)
🍴 Pierre Casteja, Cha. Doisy-Vedrines, Barsac, 33720 Podensac; tel. 56 27 15 13 ⍾ By appt.

CHATEAU FILHOT**

☐2 Cru Classé   🔳5 🅳 📦 ⬥ ⬇
70 *71 74 75 76 🔳76 78 *79 *80 81 *82

The late-18th-century house was once known as the Château de Sauternes. This 1976 is an outstanding example of the vintage – a beautiful, intense, amber wine with the typical rich, dense and spicy bouquet of Sauternes. (1976)
🍴 GFA du Ch. Filhot, Sauternes, 33210 Langon; tel. 56 63 61 09 ⍾ By appt. 🍴 M.H. de Vaucelles.

CHATEAU GILETTE**

☐   3.5ha   8400   🔳6 🅳 📦

An unusual wine, being offered for sale after 35 years of ageing! Deep-yellow with a bouquet of fruits preserved in alcohol. Delicate address to the palate. Will be rejected by some, but received enthusiastically by others. A curiosity. (1950)
✔ Sauternes, Graves, Bordeaux Supérieur.
🍴 Christian Medeville, Ch. les Justices, Preignac, 33210 Langon; tel. 56 63 27 59 ⍾ By appt. Closed Aug.

CHATEAU GRAVAS**

☐   10ha   35000   🔳4 🅳 ⬥ ⬇
79 81 82 83

Has a particularly full bouquet. Beautiful golden colour; rich and smooth on the palate, but at the same time delicate and distinguished, with complex aromas. (1982)
🍴 Famille Perre Bernard, Ch. Gravas, Barsac, 33720 Podensac; tel. 56 27 15 20 ⍾ By appt.

CHATEAU HAUT-BERGERON**

☐   14ha   40000   🔳4 🅳 📦 ⬥ ⬇
*㊳ *75 *78 81 🔳82

Golden wine with a wonderful banana and pineapple bouquet. A striking palate; rich, aromatic, and well-balanced. (1982) ✔
🍴 Robert Lamothe, Ch. Haut-Bergeron, Preignac, 33210 Langon; tel. 56 63 24 76 ⍾ By appt.

CHATEAU HAUT-BOMMES★★★

☐   6ha   15000   **4** **D** **⠏** **↓**

⑧²

Bright-coloured wine with intense and pleasing nose. Rich and long on the palate. Made to age well. (1982)
↶ Jacques Pauly, GFA du Cha. Haut-Peyraguey, Bommes, 33210 Langon; tel. 56 63 61 53 **⟊** No visitors.

DOMAINE DU HAUT-CLAVERIE★

☐   10ha   30000   **3** **D** **▮** **⠏**

Pale-yellow with a touch of old copper. Delicate, roasted bouquet. On the palate a little short, but pleasant and smooth. (1982) **✔** Bordeaux Le Pouys Domaine Haut-Claverie.
↶ GAEC Sendrey Frères et Fils, Domaine du Haut-Claverie, Fargues-de-Langon, 33210 Langon; tel. 56 63 12 65 **↶** GFA Dom. de Haut-Claverie.

CHATEAU CLOS HAUT-PEYRAGUEY★★

☐1er Cru Classé   15ha   40000   **5** **D** **⠏** **↓**

⑧²

Lovely golden-yellow colour and pleasantly crisp, floral nose. Full and long on the palate, with plenty of character. Assured of a good future. (1981) **✔** Blanc Sec, Cerons.
↶ Jacques Pauly GFA, Cha. Haut-Peyraguey, Bommes, 33210 Langon; tel. 56 63 61 53 **⟊** By appt.

CHATEAU LAFAURIE PEYRAGUEY★★

☐1er Cru Classé   22ha   40000   **6** **▮**

77 **78** **80** 81 ⑧² 83

An ideal Sauternes, with its pear bouquet enhanced by a hint of spice. Well balanced on the palate with a suggestion of raspberry liqueur. Needs just a little more age. (1983) **✔** St-Julien Ch. Talbot Rouge, St-Julien Ch. Graud Larose Rouge, St-Estèphe Ch. Meyney Rouge, St-Emilion Ch. Clos des Jacobins Rouge, Bordeaux Ch. Gardère-Tanesse Rouge.
↶ Domaine Cordier, Ch. Lafaurie Peyraguey, 33210 Bommes; tel. 56 63 60 54 **⟊** Mon.–Fri. 8.00–12.00/14.00–18.00. Closed late Aug.–early Sept.

CHATEAU LAFON

☐   7ha   18000   **5** **D** **⠏**

62 70 71 75 79 **81** ⑧² **82**

Lovely bourgeois residence producing classic, fruity Sauternes. Benefits from being allowed to breathe before tasting. (1981)
↶ J.-P. Dufour, Cha. Lafon, Sauternes, 33210 Langon; tel. 56 63 30 82 **⟊** Daily 8.30–13.00/14.00–19.00. Closed 10–25 Aug., 15 Sept.–1 Nov.

CHATEAU LAMARINGUE★

☐   2ha   6000   **5** **D** **▮** **⠏**

Behind the deep-yellow colour a delicate nose. Smooth on the attack, harmonious and well balanced on the palate. Ready to drink in about four years. (1982) **✔** Graves Clos-la-Maurasse Rouge.
↶ Roland Sessacq, Ste Croix du Mont, 33410 Cadillac; tel. 56 62 01 41 **⟊** No visitors.

CHATEAU LAMOTHE★★

☐2 Cru Classé   8ha   22000   **4** **D** **▮** **⠏**

Lovely golden-yellow colour. Delicate, roasted and powerful nose. Good balance.
↶ Jean Despujols, Cha. Lamothe, Sauternes, 33210 Langon; tel. 56 63 61 22 **⟊** By appt.

CHATEAU LAMOTHE-GUIGNARD★

☐2 Cru Classé   13ha   26000   **5** **D** **▮**

Bright, clear yellow colour. The nose has a certain amount of oak. (1981)
↶ P. et J. Guignard, Ch. Lamothe, Sauternes, 33210 Langon; tel. 56 27 15 20 **⟊** No visitors.

CHATEAU LATREZOTTE★

☐   7ha   20000   **4** **D** **▮**

A wine some would say smelt like a vestry; others might suggest an Oriental fragrance. Sweet and well balanced on the palate. (1979)
↶ *Mlle* Marie-Pierre Badoures, Cha. Latrezotte, Barsac, 33720 Podensac; tel. 56 27 16 50 **⟊** By appt.

CHATEAU DE MALLE★

☐2 Cru Classé   25ha   42000   **6** **D** **▮** **⠏** **↓**

★71 ★75 ★76 ★81 **81**

This wine has a green-tinted, yellow-gold appearance. The nose is fine, with the roasted flavour so typical of Sauternes, and in the mouth it is fat, well-balanced and beautifully aromatic on the finish. (1981)
↶ Pierre de Bournazel, Ch. de Malle, Preignac, 33210 Langon; tel. 56 63 28 67 **⟊** By appt.

CRU PEYRAGUEY

☐   6ha   14400   **4** **▮** **⠏** **↓**

★75 ★76 **79** ★80 81

This wine is a lovely golden colour, sometimes a little surprising on the nose; the palate is sweet but not excessively so. (1979)
↶ Hubert Mussotte, Dom. Peyraguey, Preignac, 33210 Langon; tel. 56 44 43 48 **⟊** By appt.

CHATEAU RABAUD-PROMIS★

☐1er Cru Classé 30ha 63000 **5** **D** 🍾 ⦿ ⬇

71 ★75 76 **77** ★78 **81**

This wine has the lovely roasted attack so typical of a Sauternes. On the palate it is rich and nicely rounded. (1979)
🍷 *Mme* Dejeans, GFA Ch. Rabaud-Promis, Bommes, 33210 Langon; tel. 56 63 60 52 ⵣ By appt.

CHATEAU RAYNE-VIGNEAU★

☐1er Cru Classé 65ha 160000 **5** ⦿ ⬇

★76 77 ★78 **80** **81** **82** ★83

Light golden wine with its agreeably refreshing scent and flavour. (1982) ✔ Bordeaux Blanc.
🍷 Sté Civ du ch. Rayne-Vigneau, 33210 Bommes; tel. 56 52 11 46 ⵣ By appt. Closed July–Sept. and grape harvest.

CHATEAU ROMER-DU-HAYOT★★

☐2 Cru Classé 20ha 25000 **4** **D** 🍾 ⬇

★75 76 ★79 81 **82** 83

A lovely clear yellow wine with a pleasantly spring-like floral bouquet. (1982)
🍷 André Du Hayot, Bommes, 33210 Langon; tel. 56 27 15 37 ⵣ By appt. Closed Aug.

CHATEAU SAINT-AMAND★★

☐ 20ha 60000 **4** **D** 🍾 ⦿ ⬇

81 ⑧②

Fine complex of aromas. Rich, creamy and roasted on the palate. (1981) ✔ Sauternes Ch. la Chartreuse.
🍷 Louis Ricard, Cha. St-Amand, Preignac, 33210 Langon; tel. 56 63 27 28 ⵣ By appt. Closed 1 Aug.–10 Sept.

CHATEAU SIGALAS-RABAUD★★★

☐1er Cru Classé 14ha 40000 **5** **D** 🍾 ⦿

Superb golden colour, and lovely 'roasted' bouquet on the nose. On the palate, harmonious, well resolved, round and pleasing; an exceptional wine. (1976) ✔ Bordeaux Supérieur Ch. Gaussens Baurech Rouge, Bordeaux Supérieur Ch. Mirail Brouqueyra Rouge.
🍷 *Mme* de Lambert des Granges, Bommes, 33210 Langon; tel. 56 63 60 62 ⵣ By appt.

CHATEAU SIMON★

☐ 7ha 17000 **4** **D** ⦿ ⬇

Very light colour, but an honest wine with quite a flowery nose. Subtle and well balanced on the palate. (1982) ✔ Graves Ch. Simon Rouge, Bordeaux Rosé Rosegay.
🍷 Gaec Dufour, Cha. Simon, 33210 Barsac; tel. 56 27 15 35 ⵣ By appt.

CHATEAU SUDUIRAUT★★

☐1er Cru Classé 100ha 300000 **D** 🍾 ⬇

78 79 **79** 83

From this superb 17th-century château comes a golden-yellow wine elegant in appearance with a developed nose On the palate the wine is full, mellow and fine. (1979)
🍷 Léopold Fonquernie, Preignac, 33210 Langon; tel. 56 63 27 29

CHATEAU LA TOUR BLANCHE★★

☐1er Cru Classé 27ha 60000 **5** ⦿ ⬇

★⑦⑨ 80 ★81 82 83

Lovely, straw-coloured wine. Fine and powerful nose. Rich and well balanced on the palate. Needs some time. (1981) ✔ Sauternes Cru St Marc, Sauvignon Chevalier de Thinoy Bordeaux Blanc Sec.
🍷 Ministère de l'Agriculture, Ch. La Tour Blanche, Bommes, 33210 Langon; tel. 56 63 61 55 ⵣ By appt.

CHATEAU D'YQUEM★★★

☐1er Cru Sup. 90ha 66000 **6** ⦿

37 42 45 53 55 59 ⑥⑦ 70 75 76 78 79

It is said that each vine planted beside this 12th-century fortress produces only one glass of wine, a wine that is drunk anywhere between 15 and 150 years old. With age, the colour acquires shades of burnt topaz; and the palate develops an unrivalled smoothness, with a perfect balance of faintly bitter acidity and aromatic richness. Once tried, never forgotten. (1981) ✔ Bordeaux Supérieur.
🍷 Comté de Lur-Saluces. Ch. d'Yquem, Sauternes, 33210 Langorce; tel. 56 63 21 05 ⵣ By appt.

265

BURGUNDY

' A IMABLE ET vineuse Bourgogne'. So wrote the great French historian Michelet (1798–1874), and what wine lover would disagree with him? With Bordeaux and Champagne, Burgundy is synonymous with French wine at its greatest, but carries with it a particular reputation for richness and diversity. Such qualities are matched equally by Burgundian cuisine, varied enough to suit every taste and capable of partnering any of the wines.

In Burgundy, more than in any other viticultural region, wine is very much a part of everyday existence. From Auxerre to the Beaujolais, along the whole length of the region that links Paris with Lyon, the rhythm of life has been governed by the vine since ancient times. According to Gaston Roupnel, a Burgundian writer and wine-maker in Gevrey-Chambertin, the vine was intro-duced into Gaul during the sixth century BC via Switzerland and the Jura, and cultivated soon after on the slopes of the Saône and Rhône valleys. Even if, as others believe, it was the Greeks who were responsible for bringing vines from the Midi, there is no doubt that they reached Burgundy soil at a very early stage in French wine-making history, as is proved by some of the archaeological remains in the museum in Dijon. In his address to Emperor Constantine (274–337) at Autun, Eumene speaks highly of the vines cultivated in the region of Beaune, and already describes them as 'ancient and admirable'.

During the Middle Ages, the Church – notably the foundations of Cluny and Citéaux – played a very important part in maintaining and improving Burgundy's reputation for fine wines. The viticultural skills of the monks established vineyard sites that are still famous for their wines, and the names of the monastic 'clos', or walled vineyards, are familiar to every wine drinker. Yet the large Church estates were an exception to the ancient Burgundian tradition of small individually-owned vineyards, which even today rarely exceed 10 hectares. Many of these sites have been owned and worked by the same families for centuries. Undoubtedly this sturdy individualism has made a major contribution to the diversity of wines to be found within the hundred or so appellations of Burgundy.

Along with diversity there is complexity: the classification of Burgundy's great wines is perhaps the most complicated on earth. But the intricate weave of geological, geographical, climatic and human factors that underlies Burgundy's reputation rewards the time and patience necessary to understand it.

The main wine-growing regions of Burgundy are Chablis, the Côte d'Or (made up of the Côte de Beaune and the Côte de Nuits), the Côte Chalonnaise and the Mâconnais. A glance at the map shows that the Burgundy region as a whole is fragmented: more than 150 km separate Chablis in the north-west from the Mâconnais in the south. The officially delimited area of Burgundy extends as far south as the Beaujolais in the Rhône, where some wines may be sold under the regional appellation of Bourgogne. In practice, however, the Beaujolais is an autonomous wine region, distinguished by the use of a particular grape variety, and has been treated as such by this Guide.

With the exception, then, of Beaujolais, which is planted with the Gamay Noir à jus blanc, Burgundy's two great vines are Chardonnay for white wines and Pinot Noir for reds. There are, however, a few additional varieties, some the survivors of outdated agricultural practices, others specific adaptations to particular pieces of land. The best-known of these are as follows:

Aligoté A white variety from which the famous Bourgogne-Aligoté is made. This is often used in 'kir' or 'blanc-cassis', a mixture of white wine and blackcurrant liqueur. The Aligoté reaches its greatest potential in the small area of Bouzeron, near Chagny in Saône-et-Loire.

César This red variety used to be grown mostly around Auxerre, but is now increasingly rare.

Sacy A white wine grape variety which produces Bourgogne Grand Ordinaire in the Yonne, especially at Chitry.

Gamay Used alone, this grape produces Bourgogne Grand Ordinaire or, blended with Pinot Noir, may make Bourgogne Passe-tout-grain.

Sauvignon This famous aromatic variety of the Sancerre and Pouilly-sur-Loire vineyards is grown in Saint-Bris-le-Vineux in the department of the Yonne.

The climate is broadly the same throughout the region, being semi-continental in type; the Atlantic influence reaches its easternmost limits here. It is to the profusion of different soil types that we must look to explain the sheer variety of the wines of Burgundy. These soils, occurring side by side even in the tiniest vineyard, contribute the distinctive fragrances and flavours of the individual Burgundy 'crus'.

The soil factor is responsible for the complexity of the classification system for top-quality Burgundy wines. From medieval times it was known that some fields consistently produced better wines than others. By the eighteenth century, a system of classification was in use whereby the name of a vineyard – La Renarde, Les Cailles, Genevrières, Clos-de-la-Maréchale – was applied to a small area (called a 'climat') which produced a distinctive style of wine. The area might be a few hectares or even a few 'ouvrées' (an ancient measure roughly equal to 0.04 hectares).

The patient work of classification over two centuries, now reinforced by scientific research, forms the basis of modern Burgundy wine law. There are four levels of appellation: in ascending order of quality they are: regional appellation, communal (or village) appellation, Premier Cru and Grand Cru. Strict rules apply to the way the wines are represented on the label. The Grand Cru wines use only the name of the vineyard – Musigny, Chambertin, La Romanée are examples. The Premier Cru wines use the name of the commune followed by the name of the vineyard, as in Santenay La Comme. Some Premier Crus are produced from more than one vineyard: in this case the name of the commune is followed simply by the designation Premier Cru.

The third rank, Appellation Communale, is designated by the name of the village, although, if the wine comes exclusively from a single vineyard, that name may also appear on the label in small type size.

Finally, there are the vineyards of more modest quality, even within great wine-producing villages, which have the right only to call their wines Bourgogne.

Apart from these classifications which apply in their most developed form to the Côte d'Or, there are a number of other generic appellations, dealt with in detail on pages 279–92.

In a much more general way, it is usual to consider the viticultural area of Burgundy as four large regions. From north to south they are: the Yonne, Côte d'Or (Côte de Nuits and Côte de Beaune), Côte Chalonnaise and Mâconnais.

THE YONNE

Chablis is the most famous of the Yonne vineyards, collectively known as la Basse Bourgogne (lower Burgundy), which enjoyed a considerable reputation at the

Burgundy (Bourgogne)

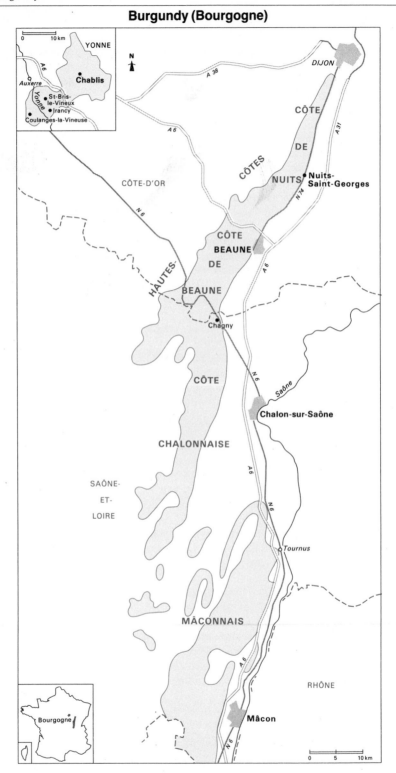

Parisian court throughout the Middle Ages. Arriving by the direct river route to the capital, Yonne wines were long known simply as 'les Bourgognes'.

Nestling in the charming Serein valley, near the beautiful medieval town of Noyers, the Chablis vineyard area is isolated more than 100 km north-west of the heart of wine-growing Burgundy. It is somewhat scattered and covers some 2500 hectares of hills with slopes that face in all directions, on which, according to one writer, 'a constellation of hamlets and a host of owners share the harvest of this dry, delicately fragrant, light wine which delights the eye with its surprising clarity and hint of greenish-gold'. South of Auxerre, we find white wines, predominantly from the Sauvignon grape, at St-Bris-le-Vineux and Chitry, and reds from the expanding vineyards of Irancy and Coulanges-la-Vineuse. A trace of the once-famous Auxerre vineyard still remains within the town walls – the Clos de la Chaînette.

There are three more vineyard areas in the Yonne that were almost completely destroyed by phylloxera but which today are being brought to life again. The Joigny vineyards, in the far north-west of Burgundy, cover scarcely five hectares of sunny slopes surrounding the town of Joigny above the river Yonne. The appellation Bourgogne Vin Gris (or pale rosé) is produced here, mostly for local consumption. The Tonnerre vineyards, which were once as famous as those of Auxerre, are also re-emerging today on the outskirts of Epineul, where thirty or so hectares have been replanted and are entitled to the Bourgogne-Epineul appellation. Finally, there is the famous slope of Vézelay, overlooking the Morvan, where the Dukes of Burgundy once owned a walled vineyard. A small vineyard started up on this very site has been producing wine since 1979. These are Burgundy regional appellation wines that will no doubt benefit from the vigorous tourist industry of the area.

THE CÔTE d'OR
The arid Langres plateau, the traditional invasion route, separates the Chablis, Auxerre, and Tonnerre areas from the incomparable Côte d'Or – poetically described as 'the slope of gold and purple', but more often referred to simply as 'La Côte'. It is impossible to understand the importance of this area without understanding something of the geological factors involved.

The Côte is the edge of a plateau made up of layers of sandy limestone. The formation of the Alps resulted in folding and faulting which disrupted the layers. Glaciation, which took place 18 000 years ago, and subsequent erosion by weather and cultivation, have broken the layers down into soil. Rubble and scree washed down the slope from the limestone and marl layers above have produced an almost incredible diversity of well-drained soils. Where hard limestone predominates – as in Meursault – the soil is excellent for white wines: where rich marl is mixed with limestone and scree, as in the Côte de Nuits, conditions favour red wines. The range of soil types and mixtures, and their distribution, accounts for the diversity and precision of the appellation system.

Geographically, the Côte extends for approximately 50 km from Dijon to Dezize-les-Maranges, in the northern part of the Saône-et-Loire. It is fairly straight, giving it a very favourable east-south-easterly exposure. The best wines – the Grands Crus – are produced on the slopes that receive the most of the morning sun. Above them, towards the crest of the escarpment, are the Haut-Côtes vineyards. Below them stretches the Saône plain.

From the point of view of its wines, the Côte d'Or is divided into several sections, the first of which, in the north, has been largely swallowed up by the urban expansion of Dijon. In the interests of tradition, however, the Dijon municipality has had a small area of vines replanted right in the middle of the town.

The Côte de Nuits begins in Marsannay and extends south as far as the Clos de Langres, in Corgoloin. It is a narrow ridge, only a few hundred metres wide, punctuated by alpine-style combes and covered with rocks and trees, and is subject to cool, dry winds. The Côte has 29 appellations up to Grand Cru level, and among its villages are such famous names as Gevrey-Chambertin, Chambolle-Musigny, Vosne-Romanée and Nuits-Saint-Georges. The Premiers Crus and the Grands Crus (Chambertin, Clos de la Roche, Musigny, Clos de Vougeot), are at an altitude of between 240 m and 320 m, where most of the outcrops of limestone marl are found among the varied scree. The best-structured – and longest-lasting – red wines in the whole of Burgundy are made here.

South of Prémeaux, the Montagne 69orton marks the beginning of the Côte de Beaune. Here the ridge is one or two kilometres wide, wider therefore than the Côte de Nuits. Its climate, too, is more temperate, with wetter winds, so that the grapes tend to ripen more quickly. Geologically, the Côte de Beaune is also more of a piece; at its base lies an almost horizontal plateau made of layers from the upper Bathonian covered with rich-coloured soils. The soil is quite deep, and it is here that the great red wines (Beaune-Grèves, Pommard-Epenots) are harvested. In the southern Côte de Beaune are benches of oolithic limestone over middle Bathonian marl, covered with more limestone scree. This provides good, pebbly, gravelly vine-growing land, where some of the most prestigious white wines are produced, particularly the Premiers Crus and Grands Crus of the communes of Meursault, Puligny-Montrachet, and Chassagne-Montrachet.

Vines are grown at a higher altitude on the Côte de Beaune than on the Côte de Nuits; 400 m or sometimes above. The hillside is carved into wide combes, one of which – Pernand-Vergelesses – seems almost to separate the Montagne de Corton from the rest of the Côte. For about fifty years now growers have been replanting the Hautes-Côtes region, where the regional appellations Bourgogne Hautes-Côtes de Nuits and Bourgogne Hautes-Côtes de Beaune are grown. The Aligoté grape finds its true home here, on soil that really does bring out its potential crispness. A few areas produce excellent Pinot Noir reds, with typical Burgundy aromas of raspberries and blackcurrants.

THE CÔTE CHALONNAISE

With the Côte Chalonnaise, the countryside opens up a little as the single vineyard ridge of the Côte d'Or widens into low hills that stretch farther west of the Saône valley. Geologically, it differs from the Côte d'Or; the soils lie on Jurassic limestone, but also Jurassic or older, Triassic or Liassic, marl. The communes of Mercurey, Givry and Rully produce red wines from the Pinot Noir, and whites from the Chardonnay, as does Montagny. Bouzeron is also situated in this area and has a fine reputation for its Aligoté wine. Finally, there is a good vineyard on the outskirts of Couches, watched over by its medieval château. There are many Romanesque churches and ancient châteaux in the region, and virtually any tourist route has the picturesque character of a 'route des vins'.

THE MÂCONNAIS

As the river Saône flows south from Chalon, it skirts the Mâconnais to the west, a broad range of hills that offer fine panoramic views of wooded slopes and lush grazing pastures. The Mâconnais is geologically simpler than the Chalonnais region, with Triassic or Liassic sedimentary land slashed through by east-west faults. The brown limestone soils produce Chardonnay whites, the best coming from the sunniest slopes of Pouilly, Solutré, and Vergisson. These wines are remarkable for their brilliant colour and their ability to age. The appellation Bourgogne reds and rosés are made from Pinot Noir, the Mâcon appellation wines from the Gamay Noir à jus blanc. The latter are grown at a lower altitude, on less favourable land, and on soils which are often alluvial but with some sand to improve drainage. Taking Beaujolais as a separate region, the Mâconnais represents the most southerly area of Burgundy wine.

THE WINE TRADE IN BURGUNDY

As we have seen, wine-growing in Burgundy is characterized by a large number of independent growers owning and working small vineyard sites. The famous Clos de Vougeot, 70 hectares in area, has more than 60 owners. This pattern has given rise to the distinctive Burgundian figure, the négociant-éleveur, or shipper. The négociant buys the young wine from individual growers, blending the different lots purchased to form a single, large cuvée to be sold under a particular appellation. The 'éleveur' refers to the practice whereby négociants 'raise' (élever) the wine, that is, age it in oak casks in their own cellars.

The négociant is the link between grower and the market. Yet he is more than a middleman. Many négociants are growers themselves. Moreover, through trade associations and organizations, such as the Confrérie des Chevaliers du Tastevin and the Fédération des Interprofessions Viticoles de la Grand Bourgogne, négociants join with growers to promote the traditions, quality and reputation of Burgundy wines. There are also strong links with the University of Dijon, which, in 1934, became the first university in France to offer a diploma course in wine studies.

The highlight of the year, each November, is the great wine auction and accompanying celebrations known as 'Les Trois Glorieuses'. At this sale the value of the vintage – sold in barrels at this stage – is established. The wines auctioned at the Hospices de Beaune sale come from vineyards donated to the famous medieval hospital in the centre of Beaune that has been serving the sick and needy since 1443. The wine sale is the occasion for celebration and tastings throughout the whole of Burgundy. Not that any special occasion is required to appreciate Burgundy and its wines. They have their own quite inimitable charm: above all other wines, to hold a glass of Burgundy is truly to hold a region in the palm of your hand.

The Regional Appellations of Burgundy

The generic appellations Bourgogne and Bourgogne Grand Ordinaire, and their variants, represent the largest part of the vineyard area of Burgundy. The wines come from traditional wine-making villages in the departments of the Yonne, Côte d'Or, Saône-et-Loire and the northern most part of the Rhône. Bourgogne Grand Ordinaire is the most general appellation, and the one which covers the largest growing area. Depending on which grape types are used, the wines may be subclassified into such categories as Bourgogne Aligoté or Bourgogne Passe-tout-grain.

Bourgogne

This catch-all appellation is both extensive and very diverse, if one counts the various sub-regions (Hautes-Côtes) and villages (Irancy, Marsannay) that may be incorporated into it. Each sub-region, however, is an area in its own right, and is dealt with individually below. Given the huge area involved, it is hardly surprising that producers have attempted to personalize their wines and persuade the law-making body to allow them a local appellation. As yet, only some of these micro-regions enjoy this right, one example being Epineuil, near Tonnerre in the Yonne. Here, the vineyards, once quite widespread, are now being replanted. In the Chatillon area, in Côte d'Or, the name Massigny was once used in the same way, but the vineyard has now practically disappeared. More recently, the growers of the Yonne hillsides have been adding their village names to the

Bourgogne appellation; two examples are St-Bris and Coulanges-la-Vineuse.

The Bourgogne appellation produces in an average year about 100 000 hectolitres of wine. Ten per cent of this production is white wine, which comes almost entirely from the Chardonnay grape (still called Beaunois in the Yonne). Although the Pinot Beurot is mentioned in lists of grape varieties, and indeed used to be more common in the Hautes-Côtes region of Burgundy, it is now rarely grown. The remaining 90 000 hectolitres are of red and rosé wine made from Pinot Noir grapes.

In some years the Bourgogne appellation includes surplus production from the Beaujolais crus: Brouilly; Côte de Brouilly; Chenas; Chiroubles; Fleurie; Juliénas; Morgon; Moulin-à-Vent and St-Amour. These wines are made exclusively from the Gamay Noir à jus blanc and have their own individual character (see the Beaujolais section).

Rosé wine may be encountered under one of two appellations: Bourgogne Rosé or Bourgogne Clairet. Rather more of it is made in bad years than good.

Finally, there are wine labels nowadays that specify not only the Bourgogne appellation, but also the vineyard name where the wine was produced. A few old and famous vineyards may deserve such an honour, Le Clos du Roy in Chenove, for example, or Les Montreculs, one of the last remaining vineyard traces amid the urban sprawl of Dijon. Less justifiably, many other vineyards have also adopted this practice, which may easily lead to confusion with Premier Cru vineyard names.

THOMAS BASSOT★

| □ | | 1500 | 4 D |

82

Pale, honey-tinged colour. Persistent aromas with notes of acacia and a trace of mint. Rich, fat flavour. Suitable with snails or richly sauced dishes. (1982)
➡ Thomas Bassot, 5 Quai Dumorey 21700 Nuits-St-Georges; tel. 80 62 31 05 ʇ By appt.

THOMAS BASSOT★

| ■ | | 6000 | 4 D |

71 74 76 78 79 81 82 83

A later-released 1979 now showing attractive maturity, with typical blackcurrant and vanilla aromas and a reasonable weight on the palate. (1979)
➡ Thomas Bassot, 5 Quai Dumorey 21700 Nuits-St-Georges; tel. 80 62 31 05 ʇ By appt.

PAUL BEAUDET

| ■ | 3ha | 10000 | 3 D ⅲ ↓ |

76 78 81 83

Marked Pinot Noir character; tannic, but a little dry, with good length. (1983) ✔ Pouilly Fuissé, St-Véran, Passe-tout-grain.
➡ Paul Beaudet, Pontanevaux, 71570 La Chapelle-de-Guinchay; tel. 85 36 27 76 ʇ By appt. Closed 15 July–20 Aug.; 22 Dec.–2 Jan.

MICHEL BERNARD *Clos du Roi*★

| ■ | 6ha | 30000 | 3 D ⅲ ↓ |

76 78 79 80 81 ⑧⑨

Impressively deep colour and powerful, heavy aromas. Good overall balance, with plenty of body and tannic support and high alcohol content. Should be laid down for two to three years to develop fully. Well-vinified wine. (1982)
➡ Michel Bernard, 17 Rue André-Vildieu, 89580 Coulanges-la-Vineuse; tel. 86 42 25 72 ʇ By appt.

PIERRE BERNOLLIN★

| ■ | 2ha | 13000 | 3 D ⅲ ↓ |

78 79 80 ★81 ★82 ★82

Fine floral aromas and elegant flavour. Aged in oak casks. Very good quality, still needing two years to reach its peak. (1982) ✔ Crémant de Bourgogne, Montagny Premier Cru 1983, Bourgogne Aligoté 1983.
➡ Pierre Bernollin, Jully-les-Buxy, 71390 Buxy; tel. 85 42 12 19 ʇ By appt.

ALAIN BERTHAULT *Pinot Noir*★

| ■ | 2ha | 96000 | 2 D ⅲ ↓ |

81 82 ⑧③

This wine has an immediate, fresh appeal. Bright colour and pleasant flavour but lacking aromatic character. Drink now. (1981) ✔ Bourgogne Passe-tout-grain, Bourgogne Aligoté, Crémant de Bourgogne.
➡ Alain Berthault, Cercot-Moroges, 71390 Buxy; tel. 85 47 91 03 ʇ By appt.

ALAIN BERTHAULT
Pinot Noir Chante-fluté★★

| ■ | 2ha | 96000 | 3 D ⅲ ↓ |

82 ⑧③

An extremely good wine with a subtle, pleasant flavour offering fine value for money. Selected by the local confrérie. (1982) ✔ Bourgogne Passe-tout-grain, Bourgogne Aligoté, Crémant.
➡ Alain Berthault, Cercot-Moroges, 71390 Buxy; tel. 85 47 91 03 ʇ By appt.

LEONCE BOCQUET *Pinot Noir*★

■ 10000 ▣ 🇩 ⑪ ↓

★59 ★⑥⑨ ★78 ★81 **81** ★82

Many generic Burgundies now indicate on the label the grape variety – Pinot Noir – from which they are made, in the manner of New World Wines. It is a good way to educate the consumer and promote a clear recognition of the wine's origins. (1982)
♁ Petit-Fils de Léonce Bocquet, 29 Blvd Clemenceau, 21200 Beaune; tel. 80 22 28 49 ⊥ Mon.–Fri. 9.30–11.30/14.00–17.30. Closed Dec. to Feb.

LEONCE BOCQUET★★

□ 10000 ▣ 🇩 ⑪

71 78 79 ★81 ★82 ★⑧③ **83**

The firm, rich qualities of the vintage transform this generic wine into the equivalent of a village appellation. Ripe aromas of cooked fruits and well-developed flavour with good acidity. Keep for several years. (1983)
♁ Petit-Fils de Léonce Bocquet, 29 Blvd Clemenceau, 21200 Beaune; tel. 80 22 28 49 ⊥ Mon.–Fri. 9.30–11.30/14.00–17.30. Closed Dec. to Feb.

GERARD BORGNAT★★

■ 2ha 9000 ▣ 🇩 ⑪ ↓

79 82 ★83 ★ **83**

Light colour shading to orange-brown, characteristic of this vintage. Delicate, smoky, cherry aromas. Smooth flavour without undue alcohol. Now ready. Drink cool. (1983) ◢ Bourgogne Rosé, Bourgogne Aligoté, Bourgogne Passetout-grain, Bourgogne Grand Ordinaire.
♁ Gérard Borgnat, 1 Rue de l'Eglise, Escolives-Ste-Camille, 89290 Champs-sur-Yonne; tel. 86 53 35 28 ⊥ Mon.–Sat. 9.00–12.00/14.00–20.00.

DOMAINE BOUCHARD PERE ET FILS *La Vignée*★★

■ 48ha 28800 ▣ 🇩 ⑪ ↓

An attractive wine with aromas of pepper and crushed red berries. Elegant refreshing flavour with notes of white peach and green coffee beans.
♁ Bouchard Père et Fils, Au Château, 21200 Beaune; tel. 80 22 14 41 ⊥ By appt. Closed Aug and 1 week in Feb.

DOMAINE PIERRE BOUTHENET ET FILS★★

◪ 5000 ▣ 🇩 ⑪ ↓

A rosé with crisp but well-rounded flavour, and an easy, thirst-quenching appeal. Pale-red colour with persistent, leafy aromas. (1983)
♁ Pierre Bouthenet et Fils, La Creuse, 71490 Couches; tel. 85 49 63 72 ⊥ By appt.

DOMAINE PIERRE BOUTHENET ET FILS★★

□ 2ha 5000 ▣ 🇩 ⑪ ↓

This typical 1983 has a clear, bright colour and round, full-bodied flavour. Very good with pike, trout or fish stew. (1983)
♁ Pierre Bouthenet, La Creuse, 71490 Couches; tel. 85 49 63 72 ⊥ By appt.

GEORGES BOUTHENET★

■ 4ha 20000 ▣ 🇩 ▮ ↓

Fine colour and, no doubt, a good vinification although our sample was slightly corked. Would suit goats' cheese and game. (1982) ◢ Bourgogne Aligoté, Bourgogne Rosé, Bourgogne Passetout-grain.
♁ Georges Bouthenet, Eguilly, 71490 Couches; tel. 85 49 66 65 ⊥ Daily 9.00–18.00.

CLOS DE LA CARBONNADE★★

■ 1ha 5000 ▣ 🇩 ⑪ ↓

This wine undergoes a long fermentation and is raised in oak casks. Brilliant red colour and robust structure which will allow it to age well and further develop its raspberry–blackcurrant aromas. Good with game dishes. (1982)
♁ André Lhéritier, 4 Blvd de la Liberté, 71150 Chagny; tel. 85 87 00 09 ⊥ By appt.

MICHEL CHAMPION
Pinot Noir Chante-fluté★

■ 2ha 11000 ▣ 🇩 ⑪ ↓

82 ⑧③

Clear ruby colour with aromas of blackcurrants and cherries. A long flavour still rather marked by its tannins; should be left for a couple of years. Best with game. Selected by the local Confrérie. (1980)
♁ Michel Champion, Cercot-Moroges, 71390 Buxy; tel. 85 47 90 94 ⊥ By appt.

EMILE CHANDESAIS★

□ 15000 ▣ ▮ ↓

66 73 **78** **82** ⑧③ **83**

Strong colour with grassy aromas. Strong flavour. (1982)
♁ Emile Chandesais, Ch. St-Nicholas, Fontaines, 71150 Chagny; tel. 85 91 41 77 ⊥ Tues.–Sat. 8.00–12.00–14.00–18.00. Closed July and Aug.

GUY CHAUMONT★★

□ 3ha 15000 ▣ 🇩 ▮ ↓

76 78 **78** **79** ⑧③

Clean, typical Chardonnay aromas. Round flavour, perhaps lacking persistence. (1982)
♁ Guy Chaumont, Le Treuil, St-Désert, 71390 Buxy; tel. 89 47 92 31 ⊥ Daily.

MICHEL COLBOIS★

□ 5ha 25000 ▣ 🇩 ▮ ↓

76 78 ★82 ★**82** 83

Light colour with greenish tints. delicate floral and mineral aromas, not unlike those of Chablis. Ripe, sweet acacia bouquet and reasonably crisp flavour. (1982) ◢ Chablis Grand Cru, Chablis, Bourgogne, Crémant.
♁ Michel Colbois, 15 Route de Montalery, Chitry-le-Fort, 89530 St-Bris-le-Vineux; tel. 86 41 40 23 ⊥ By appt.

CHATEAU CORTON-ANDRE
*Bourgogne Pinot***

■   7ha   35000   5 D ⑪ ↓

71 76 77 *78 *79 80 81 82 ⑧ 83

Great deal of character, an intense colour and very floral aroma. The 1983 vintage should guarantee it a long life. (1983)
☛ Pierre André, Ch. Corton-André, Aloxe-Corton, 21420 Savigny-lès-Beaune; tel. 80 26 44 25 ☓ By appt. ☛ Gabriel Liogier-d'Ardhuy.

LES VIGNES DE LA CROIX*

■   110ha   100000   3 D ⑪ ↓

Characteristic Pinot Noir red-fruit aromas, still rather enclosed in tannin, due to being raised in oak. Short in the mouth, but should age without problems. (1982) ✔ Montagny Premier Cru, Bourgogne Aligoté, Bourgogne Passe-tout-grain.
☛ Coop. des Vignerons de Buxy, Les Vignes-de-la-Croix, 71390 Buxy; tel. 85 92 03 03 ☓ By appt.

BERNARD ET ODILE CROS
*Pinot Noir**

■   2ha   10000   3 D ■ ⑪ ↓

80 82 ⑧ 83

Attractively coloured wine from a beautiful domaine. The present house was completed in 1700 but it was already a vigneron's home in the glorious days of Cluny Abbey. Persistent blackcurrant aromas and clean flavour, which would go well with a grilled rib of Charolais. (1981)
✔ Bourgogne Passe-tout-grain, Bourgogne Blanc, Bourgogne Aligoté, Crémant de Bourgogne.
☛ M et Mme Cros, Cercot-Moroges, 71390 Buxy; tel. 85 47 92 52 ☓ By appt. Closed Jan.

BERTRAND DARVIOT-SIMARD*

■   3ha   13000   3 D ⑪ ↓

80 82 ⑧

This generic red Burgundy is a good introduction to the other wines from this producer. Typical 1982 with light, smooth flavour. Can be drunk now and for several years to come. (1982)
✔ Meursault, Beaune, Savigny-lès-Beaune, Beaune Grèves.
☛ Bertrand Darviot-Simard, 17 Rue de la Velle, 21190 Meursault; tel. 80 21 22 83 ☓ By appt.

LUCIEN DENIZOT**

□   5ha   5000   4 D ■ ⑪ ↓
⑧

Rich, golden-yellow colour, strong, fruity aromas and a firm acid strike on the palate. Long, full-bodied flavour. Will keep well. (1982)
☛ GAEC Denizot Père et Fils, Les Moirots, Bissey-sous-Cruchaud, 71390 Buxy; tel. 85 42 16 93 ☓ By appt.

JEAN DERAIN*

■   1.50ha   9000   3 D ■ ⑪ ↓

80 81 82 ⑧

Flattering 1981 with pleasant colour; open one or two hours before drinking to release the aromas. (1981)
☛ Jean Derain, Bissey-sur-Cruchaud, 71390 Buxy; tel. 85 42 10 94 ☓ By appt. Closed end Aug.–beg. Sept.

JEAN DERAIN*

□   1.50ha   9000   3 D ■ ↓

81 82 83 84

Slightly astringent; will improve once it has aged for one or two years. (1982).
☛ Jean Derain, Bissey-sur-Cruchaud, 71390 Buxy; tel. 85 42 10 94 ☓ By appt. Closed end Aug.–beg. Sept.

BERNARD DESERTAUX *Pinot Noir**

■   3ha   12000   3 ■ ↓

79 83

All the natural harshness of its vintage. Nose of resin and bark with a characteristic burnt note: needs time to soften and mature. Nevertheless, good structure, with some ageing potential. (1983)
☛ Bernard Désertaux, Corgoloin, 21700 Nuits-St-Georges; tel. 80 62 98 40 ☓ By appt.

BERNARD DESERTAUX**

□   0.75ha   6500   3 ■ ↓

80 82 83

The colour and floral, fruity aromas of this 1982 have none of the sharpness of some generic white burgundies. Ideal to drink with cured ham and light party entrées such as vol-au-vent. (1982)
☛ Bernard Désertaux, Corgoloin, 21700 Nuits-St-Georges; tel. 80 62 98 40 ☓ By appt.

JEAN-CLAUDE DESRAYAUD***

□   0.37ha   7200   3 D ⑪ ↓

Fine clear golden colour. Rich, very flowery nose and harmonious palate with a hint of oak. A bottle with a great future. (1983)
☛ Jean-Claude Desrayaud, Solutré, 71960 Pierreclos; tel. 85 37 84 60 ☓ By appt.

ROGER DESSENDRE
*Pinot Noir Chante-flute***

■   8ha   18000   3 D ■ ⑪ ↓

⑲ 79 82

The Dessendre family have been tending their vines, a few miles from the Château de Marguerite de Bourgogne, since 1742. This wine, selected by the local Confrérie, will last for ten years without losing its ruby colour, red berry aromas, or its power, fullness and balance. (1979)
☛ Roger Dessendre, St-Maurice-les-Couches, 71490 Couches; tel. 85 49 67 60 ☓ By appt. Closed Sun.

ROGER DESSENDRE★★

■ 6ha 42000 **3** D ⬛ ⅰ⅃ ↓

76 79 82 82

The Dessendre family are very successful wine-makers and have won plenty of medals to prove the point. This wine has clean raspberry aromas, and enough tannin to age well. Good value for money. (1982) ✔ Bourgogne Blanc, Bourgogne Aligoté, Bourgogne Passe-tout-grain, Bourgogne Rosé.
↬ Roger Dessendre, St-Maurice-les-Couches, 71490 Couches; tel. 85 49 67 60 ⅰ By appt. Closed Sun.

ROGER DESSENDRE★

◪ 2500 **3** D ⬛ ⅰ⅃ ↓

A light, softly flavoured wine, with attractive, fresh aromas. Ideal for summer drinking around the barbecue. Ready to drink. (1979)
↬ Roger Dessendre, St-Maurice-les-Couches, 71490 Couches; tel. 85 49 67 60 ⅰ By appt. Closed Sun.

ROBERT DUCHESNE *Pinot Noir*★

■ 3ha 10000 **3** ⬛ ↓

⑦⑧

Good wine produced from the classic red burgundy vine; the Pinot Noir. Rather light for its age. (1979) ✔ Bourgogne Aligoté.
↬ Robert Duchesne, St-Denis-de-Vaux, 71640 Givry; tel. 85 44 38 81 ⅰ By appt.

RAYMOND DUPUIS
Coulanges-la-Vineuse★

■ 6ha 40000 **2** D ⬛ ↓

78 79 80 82 83

Little depth of colour, and an orange-pink rim, suggesting an already mature wine. Pleasant, rustic nose evocative of the farmyard. Very smooth, deliciously fruity and ready to drink. Typical of the Coulanges-la-Vineuse wines. (1982)
↬ Raymond Dupuis, 17 Rue des Dames, 89580 Coulanges-la-Vineuse; tel. 86 42 25 20 ⅰ By appt.

LOUIS DUSSORT★★

■ 0.5ha 3000 **3** D ⅰ⅃ ↓

82 **83 84**

Given long fermentation to compensate for the natural lightness of its colour. Acquired a strong, bright colour, persistent, fruity quality and good length on the palate. Will keep for several years. (1982) ✔ Meursault, Bourgogne Aligoté, Beaune, Chorey-les-Beaune.
↬ Louis Dussort 12 Rue Charles-Giraud 21190 Meursault; tel. 80 21 21 21 ⅰ Daily 9.00–18.00.

JEAN FOURNIER *Clos du Roy*★★

■ 1.75ha 9500 **4** D ⅰ⅃ ↓

★**78** ★**79 81** 81 **83**

Plenty of finesse, although the wine is still slightly hard. Will keep well. (1981) ✔ Bourgogne Marsannay Rouge
↬ Jean Fournier, 39 Rue du Château, 21160 Marsannay-la-Côte; tel. 80 52 24 38 ⅰ By appt.

DOMAINE MICHEL GAUNOUX★

■ 0.95ha 4500 **4** D ⬛ ↓

77 78 79 ⑧① 81 **82**

Ruby colour and fine Pinot fruit; aromas need time to develop. Elegant clean flavours of pepper and mint. Drink in three years' time. (1981)
↬ Michel Gaunoux, 21630 Pommard; tel. 80 22 18 52 ⅰ By appt.

JEAN-HUGHES GOISOT★

◪ 8ha 40000 **2** D ⅰ⅃ ↓

⑧② 82 **83**

Technically perfect, with a pale golden colour. The nose, in contrast, is classic, pure and fresh. Refined and more subtle than an Aligoté. Drink at once. (1983) ✔ Bourgogne Blanc.
↬ Jean-Hughes Goisot, 30 Rue Bienvenu-Martin, 89530 St-Bris-le-Vineux; tel. 86 53 35 15 ⅰ Mon.–Sat. 8.00–20.00.

JEAN-HUGHES GOISOT★

■ 8ha 55000 **2** D ⅰ⅃ ↓

82 82 83

Clear, pure colour. Clean fruit-drop aromas, and distinctive flavour quite free of the stalky taste of the vintage. Powerful, straightforward wine particularly suitable to drink with charcuterie. (1983)
↬ Jean-Hughes Goisot, 30 Rue Bienvenu-Martin, 89530 St-Bris-le-Vineux; tel. 86 53 35 15 ⅰ Mon.–Sat. 8.00–20.00.

MICHEL GOUBARD★

◪ 1ha 6000 **3** D ⬛ ↓

82 82 83

Attractive, thirst-quenching wine with a floral nose and fruity palate. Would go well with a picnic or a spicy grill. (1983) ✔ Bourgogne Passe-tout-grain, Bourgogne Aligoté, Bourgogne Blanc and Rosé, Bourgogne Pinot Noir.
↬ Michel Goubard, St-Désert, 71390 Buxy; tel. 86 47 91 06 ⅰ Daily 8.00–19.00. Closed sun. afternoon.

MICHEL GOUBARD★★

■ 10ha 60000 **3** D ⬛ ⅰ⅃ ↓

78 79 81 82 83

Do not worry if you find some sediment in the bottom of the bottle – this is quite natural. Lovely ruby-red colour and, although balanced and pleasant to drink straight away, it will continue to improve for four to five years. (1983)
↬ Michel Goubard, St-Désert, 71390 Buxy; tel. 85 47 91 06 ⅰ Daily 8.00–19.00. Closed Sun. afternoon.

SERGE GROFFIER★

■ 1ha 6000 **3** D ⬛ ↓

⑥④ **76 82** 82

All the freshness of the 1982 vintage. Once the wine has breathed it shows fine, soft aromas and flavour. Ready to drink. Serve with grilled meats. (1982)
↬ Serge Groffier, Morey-St-Denis, 21220 Gevrey-Chambertin; tel. 80 34 31 53.

L'HÉRITIER-GUYOT★

■ 50000 3 D ◗ ↓

⑦⑥ 78 79 80 82 83

Still very bright without any sign of age. Floral, fruity aromas of peony and elderberry. Firm, smooth flavour. (1982)
↖ L'Héritier-Guyot, Rue de Champ-aux-Prêtres, 21006 Dijon Cedex; tel. 80 72 16 14 ⲧ By appt.

DOMAINE JACQUES PRIEUR
Le Bourgogne du Prieur★★

■ 0.5ha 3000 3 D ◗ ↓

⑦⑨ 82

Vinified to compensate for the natural lightness of the vintage. Sustained, deep colour and a solid fruity structure. Will keep well. (1982) ✔ Chambertin, Musigny, Clos-Vougeot, Montrachet.
↖ Jacques Prieur, 2 Rue des Santenots, 21190 Meursault; tel. 80 21 23 85 ⲧ By appt.

LOUIS JADOT★★

■ 132000 3 D ◗ ↓

71 76 **78** 82 ⑧⑧

Deep ruby colour with aromas of spices and coffee beans and blackcurrant fruit. In the mouth, noble permeation of wood due to six months in cask. Bitter almond emerges at the finish. High standard despite its humble origins. (1982)
↖ Louis Jadot, 5 Rue Samuel-Legay, 21200 Beaune; tel. 80 22 10 57 ⲧ By appt.

LOUIS JADOT★

□ 30000 4 D ◗ ↓

★⑧⑧

Straw-yellow with a delicate but still rather inexpressive bouquet. Firm, ripe fruity flavour still needing to recover from its very recent bottling. (1983)
↖ Louis Jadot, 5 Rue Samuel-Legay, 21200 Beaune, tel. 80 22 10 82 ⲧ By appt. Closed Aug.

JEAN-NOEL JEANNET★★

■ 4ha 20000 3 D ▮ ↓

Luminous red colour but rather subdued bouquet. Attractive, but still rather astringent; needing a few more years in bottle. When mature the wine would suit roast meat and game. (1982)
↖ Jean-Noel Jeannet, Mazenay, 71510 St-Léger-sur-Dhenne; tel. 85 49 63 51 ⲧ By appt.

JEAN-LUC JOILLOT★

■ 3ha 20000 4 D ↓

70 71 72 74 76 78 ⑦⑨ 80

Very successful 1982 Burgundy with a full fruity flavour of cherry and vanilla. Well-balanced on the palate; should last several years. (1982)
↖ Jean-Luc Joillot, 21630 Pommard; tel. 80 22 10 82 ⲧ By appt.

HENRI JOUSSIER★★

■ 3ha 20000 3 D ▮ ↓

A young wine with plenty of promise. Good fruit and tannin, and enough richness to last four or five years. Ideal with red meat or game, perhaps venison. Selected by the local Confrérie. (1983)
✔ Bourgogne, Bourgogne Aligoté, Bourgogne

Passe-tout-grain.
↖ Henri Joussier, St-Denis-de-Vaux, 71640 Givry; tel. 85 44 32 42 ⲧ By appt.

MARC LABORDE *Pinot Noir*★★

■ 2ha 10000 3 D ◗ ↓

⑦⑥ 78 79 82 83

Richly coloured, good structure, with raspberry aromas. Should last well. (1982) ✔ Bourgogne Chardonnay, Bourgogne Aligoté, Mercurey.
↖ Marc Laborde, St-Jean-de-Vaux, 71640 Givry; tel. 85 47 20 10 ⲧ By appt. Closed 20 Sept.–20 Oct.

FRANÇOIS LAUGEROTTE
Pinot Noir Chante-fluté★

■ 1ha 6000 4 D ▮ ◗ ↓

81 82 ⑧⑧

Its strongly marked tannin is too dominant and obscures the aromas. Best stored away in the cellar and brought out again in a few years' time. Selected by the Confrérie. (1981) ✔ Bourgogne Passe-tout-grain, Bourgogne, Crémant de Bourgogne.
↖ François Laugerotte, St-Denis-de-Vaux, 71640 Givry; tel. 85 44 36 35 ⲧ By appt.

LEROY★

■ 30000 4 ◗ ↓

71 74 76 78 79

Bright colour with a copper hue. This seven-year-old wine is now displaying a mature, smoky bouquet with notes of blackcurrant and vanilla. Well-judged weight and texture on the palate. Still seems full of life. (1983)
↖ SA Leroy, Dom. de la Romanée-Conti, Vosne-Romanée, 21700 Nuits-St-Georges; tel. 80 61 04 57 ⲧ By appt.

LEROY★★

□ 40000 4 ◗ ↓

This 1983 has a deep, smooth colour with a pink tinge. Rich, warm aromas with complex notes of almonds, hazelnuts, cocoa and vanilla. Still rather sharp on the palate, but there is plenty of richness to offset the acidity. (1983)
↖ SA Leroy, Dom. de la Romanée-Conti, vosne-Romanée, 21700 Nuits-St-Georges; tel. 80 61 04 57 ⲧ By appt.

PRODUCTEURS DE LUGNY-SAINT-GENGOUX

■ 120ha 130000 3 D ▮ ↓

78 79 **82** 83

Cherry-red colour with a hint of orange; fruity and robust, but still lacking body. (1982)
↖ Producteurs de Lugny-St-Gengoux, Lugny-St-Gengoux, 71260 Lugny; tel. 85 33 22 85 ⲧ By appt.

BERNARD MARMAGNE★

□ 1ha 7000 3 D ▮ ↓

79 82 82 83 83 84

Bright greenish-gold; delicate floral nose with interesting hints of marshmallow and vanilla. Long and harmonious flavour, with intense aromatic persistence, not lacking acidity. (1982)
✔ Bourgogne Aligoté, Bourgogne Rouge, Rosé

and Sauvignon.
➤ Bernard Marmagne, 11 Rue Haute, 89530 St-Bris-le-Vineux; tel. 86 53 31 24 ☎ By appt.

MICHEL MARTIN
Coulanges-la-Vineuse★★

| ■ | 8ha | 20000 | 2 | D | ■ | ↓ |

⑦⑧ 79 80 81 **82** 83

Attractive delicate, clear colour. Very fruity but little-developed aromas. Long, complex, balanced flavour making it a magnificent example of this appellation. Lacking a little acidity, like many a 1982! (1982)
➤ Michel Martin, 89580 Coulanges-la-Vineuse; tel. 86 42 22 73 ☎ By appt.

RENE MARTIN★

| □ | 1ha | 5000 | 3 | D | ⑪ | ↓ |

76 79 **79** 82 (83)

A traditional family domaine which keeps faith with the practices of previous generations. Lovely colour and a distinctive truffle aroma. The palate, unfortunately, appears rather plain in comparison. Serve with fish and white meats. (1982) ✔ Sampigny-les-Maranges Côte-de-Beaune, Hautes-Côtes-de-Beaune, Bourgogne Hautes Côtes de Beaune, Crémant de Bourgogne, Bourgogne.
➤ René Martin. Cheilly-les-Maranges, 71150 Chagny; tel. 85 87 04 37 ☎ By appt.

DOMAINE DES VIGNES MARTIN★

| ■ | 5ha | 30000 | 3 | D | ■ | ⑪ | ↓ |

81 **82 83** 83

From the Couchois slopes behind the Côte de Beaune. A single, well-structured Bourgogne with a peony-red colour and good ageing potential. (1982) ✔ Bourgogne Aligoté, Bourgogne Passe-tout-grain.
➤ Jean Gaudet, St-Germain-du-Plain, 71310; tel. 85 49 62 12 ☎ Daily 830–12.00/14.00–20.00.

ALAIN MELLENOTTE★

| ■ | 3ha | 130000 | 3 | D | ■ | ⑪ | ↓ |

80 **80** 81 **81** ★**82** ★**83**

Pleasant but slightly thin flavour. Wait two or three years before drinking. (1982) Bourgogne Aligoté, Mercurey, Bourgogne Passe-Tout-grain, Crémant de Bourgogne.
➤ M. Mellenotte-Drillien, Mellecey, 71640 Givry; tel. 85 47 10 98 ☎ By appt.

DOMAINE DU CHATEAU DE MEURSAULT
Clos du Ch. de Meursault★★

| □ | 8ha | 6000 | 5 | D | ⑪ | ↓ |

79 81 (82) **82**

Pale-yellow colour with nose of citronella and golden butter. Thick, rich flavour with an elegant 'grilled' aroma. Rather alcoholic finish. (1982)
➤ Sté du Ch. de Meursault, 21190 Meursault; tel. 80 21 22 98 ☎ No visitors.

SCEA DES COTEAUX DE MONTBOGRE★★

| ■ | 10ha | 10000 | 2 | D | ■ | ⑪ | ↓ |

78 79 **82** **82** 83

The greater part of this vineyard is situated on well-exposed, south-easterly slopes. The wines from this soil are, like this 1982, of high quality. Refined bouquet but powerful, well-structured flavour. A lovely bottle of wine under twenty francs which will age well. A Confrérie selection. (1982) ✔ Bourgogne Blanc, Bourgogne Aligoté, Bourgogne Passe-tout-grain, Mercurey.
➤ Patrick Mazoyer, Place Romaine, St-Désert, 71390 Buxy; tel. 85 47 91 41 ☎ By appt.

MICHEL MORIN *Coteaux de Chitry*★★

| □ | 3ha | 1800 | 3 | D | ■ | ↓ |

80 81 **82** **82** **83**

Everything about this wine recalls nearby Chablis – the colour, aromatic notes of honey and mineral and light, refreshing flavour. The taste of the terroir is apparent at the finish, however, with rather less finesse than a good Premier Cru. Nonetheless, a wine of real individual character which has been superbly vinified. (1983) ✔ Bourgogne Aligoté, Pinot Noir.
➤ Michel Morin, 17 Rue du Ruisseau, Chitry-le-Fort, 89530 St-Bris-le-Vineux; tel. 86 41 41 61 ☎ By appt. Closed Sept.

NOEL PERRIN *Clos de Chenoves*★★★

| ■ | 3ha | 12000 | 3 | D | ⑪ | ↓ |

Before the French Revolution, the Clos de Chenoves belonged to the Bishops of Autun, who kept a fine table and cellar! Today, Noel Perrin works this estate with uncommon ability. This red wine, from an excellent vintage, is quite simply outstanding. Well-developed aromas and a round, balanced flavour at a bargain price. (1983) ✔ Bourgogne Clos de Chenoves Blanc, Bourgogne Aligoté, Mâcon Supérieur.
➤ Noël Perrin, Culles-les-Roches, 71460 St-Gengoux-le-National; tel. 85 44 04 25 ☎ By appt. Closed during grape harvest.

ROBERT PERRIN ET FILS★★

| ■ | 1.5ha | 3000 | 3 | D | ⑪ | ↓ |

(82) **82** 83

A rather woody flavour conceals this wine's character at present. Best drunk with a meal. (1982) ✔ Bourgogne Passe-tout-grain.
➤ Robert Perrin, Dennevy, 71510 St-Léger-sur-Dhenne; tel. 85 45 35 58 ☎ By appt.

LA PETITE MOTTE★

| ■ | 5ha | 30000 | 3 D ▮ ⑪ ↓ |

⑲ 83

A simple quaffing wine for modest occasions. Light colour and body, with a short but attractive flavour. Drink within the year. (1982) ✔ Bourgogne Passe-tout-grain.
•↴ René Gougler, Dennevy, 71510 St-Léger-sur-Dhenne; tel. 85 45 36 17 ▼ Daily 8.00–12.00/13.00–20.00 •↴ Marc Gougler.

DOMAINE DU PRIEURE★★

| ■ | 8ha | 40000 | 3 D ⑪ ↓ |

83

A young wine with a powerful, warm, oaky flavour and a lovely colour, which should acquire a more complex character in four to five years. (1983)
•↴ Fabien et Louis Saier, Mercurey, 71640 Givry; tel. 85 45 22 11 ▼ By appt.

CHARLES QUILLARDET *Montreuil*★

| ■ | 3ha | 20000 | 4 D ⑪ ↓ |

69 71 77 78 79 ★81 82 ⑧ 🅱

Beautiful deep red colour and nose of bitter almonds and crushed red fruit. Solid, well-constructed wine with a finish which is still rather harsh as the tannins need to dissolve. Has a good future (three or four years). (1983)
•↴ Charles Quillardet, 18 Route de Dijon, 21220 Gevrey-Chambertin; tel. 80 34 10 26 ▼ By appt. Closed Jan.

ANTONIN RODET *Rodet Chardonnay*★

| □ | | 65000 | 4 D ▮ ⑪ ↓ |

Bright, golden-green colour. Sweet, persistent, fruity aromas which can even stand up to Burgundy snails; should be served chilled. (1982)
•↴ Antonin Rodet, Mercurey, 71340 Givry; tel. 85 45 22 22 ▼ By appt. Closed Aug.

ANTONIN RODET *Pinot Noir*★

| ■ | 00ha | 145000 | 4 D ⑪ ↓ |

79 82

One, clear ruby colour, red-berry bouquet and long, balanced flavour. Would suit roast meats and fresh cheeses. (1982)
•↴ Antonin Rodet, Mercurey, 71340 Givry; tel. 85 45 22 22 ▼ By appt. Closed Aug.

DOMAINE ROUGEOT★★

| ■ | 2ha | 12000 | 3 D ▮ ⑪ ↓ |

⑲ 🅰 82

Well vinified and characterized by good extract and aromas of blackcurrant and truffle, a common feature of mature red Burgundy. Ready for drinking. (1980) ✔ Meursault, Meursault, Volnay, Pommard, Ladoix.
•↴ Marc Rougeot, 6 Rue André-Ropiteau, 21190 Meursault tel. 80 21 02 59 ▼ By appt.

PIERRE SAINT-ARROMAN★

| ■ | 5ha | 30000 | 3 D ▮ ↓ |

⑦ **73 76 78** 🔲 **79 81** 🅱

Straightforward generic Burgundy with a fine colour and pleasant, thirst-quenching flavour. (1981) ✔ Mercurey, Bourgogne Aligoté, Crémant de Bourgogne.
•↴ Pierre Saint-Arroman, St-Denis-de-Vaux, 71640 Givry; tel. 85 44 34 33 ▼ No visitors.

PAUL ET PHILIBERT TALMARD★

| ■ | 3.8ha | 20000 | 3 D ⑪ ↓ |

⑧

Typical clear-red Pinot colour and attractive aromas of crushed red fruit. However, rather light and short in the mouth. (1983)
•↴ Paul et Philibert Talmard, Uchizy, 71700 Tournus; tel. 85 51 10 37 ▼ By appt.

GERARD THOMAS★★

| ■ | 1ha | 6000 | 3 D ▮ ↓ |

79 81 ★82 ★⑧ ★🅱

This 1983, a good example of the vintage, has intense aromas and plenty of weight on the palate; a very fine bottle. (1983)
•↴ Gérard Thomas, St-Aubin, 21190 Meursault; tel. 80 21 32 57 ▼ By appt.

LES TOQUES GOURMANDES★

| ■ | | | 4 D |

Light, clear colour typical of the vintage. Rich flavour with spicy Côtes de Beaune aromas. (1982)
•↴ Les toques Gourmandes, 29 Bis, Route de Versailles, 78560 Port-Marly; tel. 01 91 61 17 ▼ By appt.

TURMEL-MORIZOT★

| ■ | 0.15ha | 1200 | 3 D ▮ ↓ |

79 80 81 ⑧ 83

This 1979 was vinified with the stalks to bring some tannic firmness to a rather soft vintage. Has the slightly gamey nose of a mature Burgundy, but the flavour is still pleasantly fresh. (1979) ✔ Nuits-St-Georges, Bourgogne Grand Ordinaire, Bourgogne Aligoté.
•↴ M. Turmel-Morizot, Place de la Mairie, Premeaux-Prissey, 21700 Nuits-St-Georges; tel. 80 62 30 70 ▼ No visitors.

FRANÇOISE ET PIERRE VICARD
Pinot Noir★

| ■ | 2ha | 76000 | 3 D ▮ ⑪ ↓ |

A young but very attractive wine from a small traditional Burgundy village. This enterprising young grower has already won several medals. (1983) ✔ Bourgogne Aligoté, Bourgogne Passe-tout-grain.
•↴ Pierre Vicard, St-Maurice-les-Couches, 71490 Couches; tel. 85 45 52 53 ▼ By appt •↴ Georges Constant.

CHARLES VIENOT★

| ■ | | 13000 | 4 D |

71 74 76 78 79 81 82 83

This cuvée is a good example of the vintage, with its bright colour and fresh, fruity character. Brisk, light flavour. (1982)
•↴ Ets Charles Vienot, 21700 Nuits-St-Georges; tel. 80 62 31 05 ▼ By appt.

CHARLES VIENOT★★

☐ 2800 **4 D**

82

A very attractive Bourgogne Blanc: pale colour with a hint of grey, clean, floral aromas and a light refreshing flavour which finishes well. (1982)
☙ Ets Charles Vienot, 21700 Nuits-St-Georges; tel. 80 62 31 05 ☥ By appt.

JACQUES VIGNOT
Côté Saint-Jacques★★

◪ 1 ha 7500 **3 D ∎ ♨**

78 79 ⑧ 83

Light, onion-skin colour, decidedly pale for a red wine. Delicate, smoky aromas with considerable finesse. Clean, fragrant, thirst-quenching Pinot flavour. (1983)
☙ Jacques Vignot, 22 Chemin Gravons, Paroy-sur-Tholon, 89300 Joigny; tel. 86 62 23 73 ☥ By appt.

Bourgogne Grand Ordinaire
The form Bourgogne Grand Ordinaire is preferred to Bourgogne Ordinaire on the rare occasions when the appellation is used. This is understandable, since the adjective 'ordinaire' is hardly encouraging. Some growing areas adjacent to the main vineyards may nonetheless produce excellent wines at very reasonable prices. Almost any approved Burgundy grape variety may be included in the production of this wine, which may be red, rosé, white or clairet.

The grape variety synonymous with Burgundy's finest white wines is the Chardonnay. However, there are other less familiar varietals which also have their role to play. The Melon (or Muscadet), once used extensively, has now virtually died out in Burgundy, although the varietal has fared much better in western France, where it is used to produce the well-known Muscadet in the Nantes region. Other white wine grape types are the Aligoté, which is almost always marketed under the Bourgogne-Aligoté appellation, and the Sacy (only in the Yonne department). This grape used to be grown throughout the Chablis area and in the Yonne valley to make sparkling wines for export; since the creation of the Crémant de Bourgogne appellation (*q.v.*), the grapes have also been used in this appellation.

The principal grape varieties used in red wines are the traditional Burgundy ones: the Gamay Noir à Jus Blanc and Pinot Noir. In the Yonne the César is also permitted, but in practice it is only used, and even then very rarely, in the Appellation Bourgogne Irancy. The Tressot, another permitted variety, is no longer grown. It is in the Yonne, in particular in Coulanges-la-Vineuse, that the best Gamay wines are found. The production of red AOC wines in the Yonne is between 15000 and 20000 hectolitres per year.

D'HEILLY ET HUBERDEAU★

■ 0.5 ha 5000 **2 D ◑ ♨**

Characteristic Gamay colour and aromas. Although it cannot be compared to red wines produced from the Pinot Noir, it is an attractive bottle at a reasonable price. (1982)
☙ *MM.* d'Heilly et Huberdeau, Cercot-Moroges, 71390 Buxy; tel. 85 47 95 27 ☥ No visitors.

Bourgogne Aligoté
Often called 'the Muscadet of Burgundy', this is an excellent jug wine, characterized by clean varietal aromas and a lively acidity. It should be drunk young. Until comparatively recently it was grown on good hillside vineyards, but the Chardonnay has gradually replaced it, especially in the better sites, and it is now confined to the plain. The Aligoté wines of Pernand-Vergelesses were also once well-known, but they, too, have largely given way to Chardonnay. Several villages – including Magny, Villers and Mary in the Hautes-Côtes de Nuits, and Chitry and St-Bris in the Yonne valley – have specialized in the production of Aligoté wines. However, the most famous Aligoté comes from Bouzeron, in the Chalonnais, and is sold as Bourgogne Aligoté-Bouzeron.

CIE DES VINS-D'AUTREFOIS★★

☐ **3 ∎ ♨**

1983 was an exceptional year for Aligoté, producing rich highly aromatic wines. Complex aromas, of honey, elderflower and hazelnut blend with the new oak; fresh flavour with good acidity. A rare Aligoté which could be kept for ten years without losing its clean flavour. (1983)
☙ Cie des Vins d'Autrefois 9 Rue Celer, 21200 Beaune; tel. 80 22 21 31.

DOMAINE GOUD DE BEAUPUIS★★

☐ 1 ha 6000 **3 D ◑ ♨**

The domaine still uses a traditional seven-tonne stone press which must be centuries old. This Aligoté is the domaine's only white wine. Brilliant golden-green colour with a lovely bouquet of acacia and honeysuckle, and a note of amber.

Solid, fat flavour. (1983) ✔ Aloxe Corton les Valozières, Savigny Vergelesses, Chorey Côtes-de-Beaune Villages, Bourgogne Ch. des Moutots.
➤ Goud de Beaupuis, Ch. des Moutots, Chorey-les-Beaune, 21200 Beaune; tel. 80 22 20 63 ☲ Daily 9.00–19.00.

ALAIN BERTHAULT*

☐		1 ha	5000	2 D ⏹ ↓

Good acidity making it very suitable for Kir. Pleasant but lacking character; surprisingly deep colour for an Aligoté. (1983) ✔ Bourgogne Pinot Noir, Crémant Bourgogne, Passe-tout-grain.
➤ Alain Berthault, Cercot, 71390 Moroges; tel. 85 47 91 03 ☲ By appt.

JEAN-CLAUDE BIOT *Côtes de Chitry**

☐		6 ha	40000	2 D ⏹ ⏹ ↓

69 76 78 80 81 82 ⑧ 83 84

A smooth, well-made wine clearly marked by its Chablis-character *terroir*. Almost colourless appearance with a subtle nose of apricot and honey, but a rather stiff, acid flavour. It is a shame that the bottle labels are so singularly unattractive; particularly as the village of Chitry, with its fine towers, offers the label designers excellent inspiration. (1983) ✔ Bourgogne, Bourgogne Aligoté, Bourgogne Blanc, Chablis.
➤ Jean-Claude Biot, 5 Chemin des Fossés, Chitry-le-Fort, 89530 St-Bris-le-Vineux; tel. 86 41 42 79 ☲ By appt.

DOMAINE BOUCHARD PERE ET FILS**

☐		11 ha	57600	4 D ⏹ ↓

Straw-yellow colour and floral nose with a hint of lime. Deep, fat flavour with acceptable acidity. Slight touch of honey at the finish. (1983)
➤ Bouchard Père et Fils, Au Château, 21200 Beaune; tel. 80 22 14 41 ☲ By appt. Closed Aug. and 1st week in Feb.

MICHEL CHAMPION**

☐		1 ha	6000	2 D ⏹ ↓

83 83

Fresh cherry and blackcurrant aromas, but sufficient tannin to last well. Long on the palate and would go well with game. (1983)
➤ Michel Champion, Cercot-Moroges, 71390 Buxy; tel. 85 47 90 94 ☲ By appt. Closed Sat., Sun.

CHANSON PERE ET FILS*

☐				3 D ⏹ ↓

78 79 80 ⑧ 83

Selected from various sources and blended to produce a harmonious, characteristic cuvée, this 1982 Aligoté has the fresh aromas typical of the grape variety. The vintage contributes a ripe fullness to the nose and the careful blend results in a pleasantly smooth flavour. (1982)
➤ Chanson Père et Fils, 10–12 Rue Paul-Chanson, 21200 Beaune; tel. 80 22 33 00 ☲ No visitors.

CLAUDE CORNU**

☐		1 ha	6000	3 D ⏹ ↓

⑦⑥ 80 81 ⑧2 83 83

Brightly-coloured, cleanly-flavoured wine with characteristic hazelnut, butter and vanilla aromas. Some complexity on the palate. Should be served cool. Drink now. (1983) ✔ Bourgogne Hautes-Côtes-de-Beaune Rouge, Bourgogne Hautes-Côtes de Nuits, Bourgogne Hautes-Côtes-de-Beaune, Bourgogne Passe-tout-grain.
➤ Claude Cornu, Magny-lès-Villers, 21700 Nuits-St-Georges; tel. 80 62 92 05 ☲ By appt.

ROBERT DEFRANCE
*Coteaux de Saint-Bris***

☐		4 ha	15000	2 D ⏹ ↓

Light golden-green, and floral bouquet with fair acidity for its age. Pleasant on the palate with a subtle persistent aroma. A fine Aligoté from the Yonne best drunk young. (1983)
➤ Robert Defrance, 5 Rue du Four, 89530 St-Bris-le-Vineux; tel. 86 53 33 82 ☲ By appt.

LUCIEN DENIZOT*

☐		3 ha	4500	3 D ⏹ ⏹ ↓

⑦⑥ 78 81 82 83

Attractive golden colour; rather immature aromas and fairly dry, sharp flavour typical of the appellation. Drink as an aperitif. (1982)
➤ GAEC Denizot Père et Fils, Les Moirots, Bissey-sous-Cruchaud, Buxy 71390; tel. 85 42 16 92 ☲ By appt. Closed end Aug.–beg. Sept.

ROGER DESSENDRE*

☐		0.7 ha	4200	3 D ⏹ ↓

An Aligoté with light-greenish hints showing good varietal character. Dry, firm, full flavour. Ready to drink; would suit pork dishes, fried fish and even certain cheeses. (1982)
➤ Roger Dessendre, St-Maurice-les-Couches, 71490 Couches; tel. 85 49 67 60 ☲ Mon.–Sat. 9.00–12.00/14.00–20.00.

DOMAINE FRIBOURG**

☐		4 ha	24000	2 D ⏹ ↓

82 ⑧ 83

Deep, attractive colour with a heavily-scented elderflower bouquet. (1983) ✔ Bourgogne Hautes-Côtes-de Nuits Rouge, Bourgogne Hautes-Côtes de Nuits Blanc, Côtes de Nuits Villages, Bourgogne Passe-tout-grain.
➤ Marcel et Bernard Fribourg, Dom. Fribourg, Villers-la-Faye, 21700 Nuits-St-Georges; tel. 80 62 91 74 ☲ By appt.

GILLES GAUDET**

☐		0.5 ha	54000	3 D ⏹ ↓

This typical Aligoté has the rich, fruity appeal of the 1983 vintage. Its complex bouquet will stand up well to simple charcuterie and pork dishes. (1983) ✔ Bourgogne Passe-tout-grain.
➤ Giles Gaudet, St-Germain-du-Plain, 71310 St-Germain-du-Plain; tel. 85 49 62 12 ☲ Daily 9.00–12.00/14.00–20.00.

CAVES DES HAUTES-COTES★★

☐	60ha	120000	**3** **D** ■ ↓

Pale colour, fruity nose and strong but quite elegant flavour. (1982)
➴ Caves des Hautes-Côtes, Route de Pommard, 21200 Beaune; tel. 80 24 63 12 ⊻ By appt.

L'HERITIER-GUYOT★

☐	75ha	50000	**3** **D** ■ ↓

82 83 84

Very ripe, well-developed wine, with a deep colour and classic aromas of mint, honeysuckle, vanilla and apple. Shows similarities to the 1983, and could equally well be served with a rich dish such as snails. (1984)
➴ L'Héritier-Guyot, Rue de Champ-aux-Prêtres, 21006 Dijon Cedex; tel. 80 72 16 14 ⊻ By appt.

MAURICE JOUBY
Coteaux-de-Saint-Bris★

☐	5ha	25000	**3** ■ ↓

Brilliant golden green colour. Although more than two years old the wine still has some positive qualities but it has lost much of its freshness. If you choose a more recent vintage you will find the hallmark qualities of an Aligoté: crispness, lightness and charm. (1982) ✔ Bourgogne.
➴ Maurice Jouby, 89530 St-Bris-le-Vineux; tel. 86 53 30 76 ⊻ By appt.

DOMAINE A ET B LABRY

☐	3ha	21600	**3** **D** ■ ↓

76 78 79 82 ⑧ **83** 84

Pale yellow colour with green glints. Fruity nose and strong acidity on the palate. Thirst-quenching. (1983)
➴ André et Bernard Labry, Melin-Auxey-Duresses, 21190 Meursault; tel. 80 21 21 60 ⊻ Daily.

ANDRE LHERITIER★★

☐	0.5ha	2500	**3** **D** ■ ↓

⑧ **82**

A very well-made wine which could age for up to five years without losing any of its fullness or attractive nutty flavour. High quality. (1982)
➴ André Lheritier, 4 Bld de la Liberté, 71150 Chagny; tel. 85 87 00 09 ⊻ By appt.

HENRI NAUDIN-FERRAND★★

☐	4.50ha	27000	**3** **D** ■ ↓

⑧ **83**

Golden yellow with a dry, flinty character and smooth flavour. Serve with a fairly rich first course. (1983) ✔ Bourgogne Haute-Côtes-de-Beaune Blanc. Bourgogne Passe-tout-grain, Bourgogne Haute-Côtes-de-Beaune Rouge, Bourgogne Haute-Côtes-de-Nuits Rouge.
➴ Henri Naudin-Ferrand, Magny-lès-Ferrand, 21700 Nuits-St-Georges; tel. 80 62 91 50 ⊻ By appt.

CHATEAU DE LA SAULE★

☐	1ha	6000	**3** **D** ■ ↓

76 78 79 **82** ⑧ **83**

Well-vinified Aligoté with brisk acidity and good varietal character. Makes a delicious kir, with one part blackcurrant to five parts wine. (1982)

✔ Montagny, Bourgogne Passe-tout-grain.
➴ Marcel Roy-Thevenin, Ch. de la Saule, 71390 Montagny-les-Buxy; tel. 85 42 11 83 ⊻ By appt. Closed 15–30 Aug.

JEAN-PIERRE SORIN
Côteaux de Saint Bris★

☐	3ha	17000	**3** **D** ■ ↓

75 76 **76** 78 80 81 82 **82** ⑧

Strong green reflections in the limpid colour. Heavy, expressive aromas of honey and lime. Striking roundness, but a lack of acidity and length. (1983) ✔ Bourgogne, Sauvignon de St-Bris.
➴ Jean-Pierre Sorin, 6 Rue de Grisy, 89530 St-Bris-le-Vineux; tel. 86 53 32 44 ⊻ By appt.

LUC SORIN *Coteaux de Saint-Bris★*

☐	5ha	38000	**2** **D** ■ ↓

75 76 78 80 81 82 ⑧

Pale colour with straightforward, slightly sharp floral aromas; good acidity and long, fruity flavour. Bottle age will soften it. (1983) ✔ Sauvignon de St-Bris, Bourgogne Rosé, Bourgogne Passe-tout-grain, Bourgogne.
➴ Luc Sorin, 13 bis, Rue de Paris, 89530 St-Bris-le-Vineux; tel. 86 53 36 87 ⊻ By appt.

DOMAINE THEVENOT-LEBRUN★★

☐	45ha	20000	**3** **D** ■ ↓

76 78 79 ⑧ **82** 83

A sur-lie wine with a fresh nose and pleasant spritz, making it very original and thirst-quenching. A 'modern', refreshing burgundy Aligoté. (1982)
➴ *MM*. Dom. Thévenot-Lebrun et Fils, Marey-les-Fussey, 21700 Nuits-St-Georges; tel. 80 62 91 64 ⊻ Mon.–Sat. 8.00–13.00/14.00–19.00.

Bourgogne Passe-tout-grains

The name is reserved for red and rosé wines which may be made from a blend of Pinot Noir and Gamay grapes. Officially, Pinot Noir should make up at least one-third of the wine, but it is generally agreed that the best wines contain 50 per cent or more Pinot Noir.

Rosé wines must be produced by the saignée method. These are true rosés, as opposed to the 'gris' (grey) wines obtained by pressing black grapes and processing the must as a white wine. In the saignée method the grapes macerate briefly in the fermenting tank, and the juice is drawn off when the colour is exactly as the wine-maker wants it. Inevitably, this is a very labour-intensive process and, in fact, very little Passe-tout-grain rosé is made. The appellation is known mainly for its red wine. About two-thirds of the Passe-tout-grain appellation is produced in Saône-et-Loire; most of the remainder comes from the Côte d'Or, with a small amount from the Yonne valley. Production ranges between 50000 and 60000 hectolitres per year. The wines are light and lively and should be drunk young.

DOMAINE ARNOUX PERE ET FILS★★

■   1 ha   6000   **3** **D** 🎍 💧 ⬤
81 ⑧② **82** 83

This Passe-tout-grain might be taken for a Bourgogne Rouge with its soft, smooth flavour and pronounced bouquet of crushed red fruit. Ready to drink. (1982) ✔ Aloxe-Corton Rouge, Savigny-lès-Beaunes et Premier Cru Rouge, Beaune Premier Cru Rouge, Bourgogne Aligoté. ↜ Dom. Arnoux Père et Fils, Chorey-les-Beaunes, 21200 Beaune; tel. 80 22 09 93 ⅄ By appt.

NICOLE BOUIN ET BERNARD PERRAUD★

■   4 ha   30000   **3** **D** ⬤ 💧
With its crimson colour, fruity aromas and lightly floral flavour this is a typical Passe-tout-grain in the classic proportions of two-thirds Gamay, one-third Pinot Noir. Would go equally well with cold pork meats or cheese, and should last for at least another two years. (1982) ✔ Bourgogne, Bourgogne Aligoté, Montagny. ↜ GAEC Dionysos, Culles-les-Roches, 71460 St-Gengouxe-le-National; tel. 85 44 01 59 ⅄ By appt. ↜ N. Bouin et B. Perraud.

CAVES DES HAUTES-COTES
Rose d'Orches★★

☑   40 ha   10000   **3** **D** 🎍 💧
Salmon pink colour with a faint orange rim. Pronounced ripe strawberry and spice aromas but a rather mild flavour. This wine is over three years old but it is still pleasantly fresh. Very reasonable value. (1981) ↜ Cave des Hautes-Cotes, Route de Pommard, 21200 Beaune; tel. 80 24 63 12 ⅄ By appt.

D'HEILLY-HUBERDEAU★

■   1 ha   4000   **2** **D** ⬤ 💧
82 ⑧③

A typical soft, open-flavoured Passe-tout-grain. Unpretentious, mouthfilling flavour. Should be drunk within the year. Try it with the local speciality, *œufs en meurette*. (1982) ✔ Bourgogne Pinot Noir, Bourgogne Grand Ordinaire Gamay, Bourgogne Aligoté. ↜ *M.* and *Mmm* D'Heilly-Huberdeau. Cercot-Moroges, 71390 Buxy; tel. 85 47 95 27 ⅄ By appt.

L'HERITIER-GUYOT★

■   75 ha   50000   **2** **D**
81 82 ⑧③

The typical, fruity charm of a Passe-tout-grain, with an expressive bouquet of raspberries and cherries and a slightly peppery note. A harmoniously-blended cuvée, but rather too strong in alcohol. (1983)

↜ L'Héritier-Guyot, Rue du Champ-aux-Prêtres, 21006 Dijon Cedex; tel. 80 72 16 14 ⅄ By appt.

LUGNY-SAINT-GENGOUX

■   30 ha   75000   **3** **D** 🎍 💧
76 *78 *79 *82 *⑧③

Not all blends of Pinot Noir and Gamay are equally successful. This is a good compromise, combining the fruit and freshness of the Beaujolais grape with the body of the Bourgogne grape. A light, refreshing, successful wine. (1983) ↜ Prod. Lugny-St-Gengoux, Lugny-St-Gengoux, 71260 Lugny; tel. 85 33 22 85 ⅄ By appt.

PIERRE MAHUET★

■   1 ha   5000   **3** **D** ⬤ 💧
⑧③ **83**

Attractive, quite mature red colour with an oaky Burgundy note and the fruitiness of a Beaujolais. Warm, full bodied and aromatic on the palate. Drink now. (1983) ↜ Pierre Mahuet, La Roche-Vineuse, 71960 Pierreclos; tel. 85 37 70 82 ⅄ By appt.

MELLENOTTE-DRILLIEN★

■   3 ha   20000   **2** **D** 🎍 💧
82 83

For light summer drinking. Soft, aromatic, quite long on the palate but a distinct whiff of sulphur dioxide. (1982) ✔ Mercurey Rouge, Bourgogne Rouge, Blanc; Bourgogne Aligoté. ↜ *M.* Melenotte-Drillien, Mellecey, 71460 Givry; tel. 85 47 10 98 ⅄ Mon.–Sat. 9.00–12.00/14.00–18.00.

GAEC DE PERCHERANGES★

☑   1 ha   5000   **2** **D** 🎍 💧
⑧② **82** 83 84

Try this straighforward, refreshing rosé with a summer meal out in the garden. Bright colour, fruity, open-knit aromas and thirst-quenching flavour. (1982) ✔ Mercurey Rouge, Bourgogne Rouge. ↜ Michel Bourgeon, GAEC de Percheranges, St-Denis-de-Vaux, 71640 Givry; tel. 85 44 30 75 ⅄ No visitors.

Bourgogne Irancy

This small vineyard, which lies about 50 kilometres to the south of Auxerre, had its fame assured in 1977 when the name Irancy was officially added to the Bourgogne appellation.

Irancy is best known for its red wines. The main grape of the appellation is the Pinot Noir, but at least part of Irancy's reputation is due to its historic local variety, the César, or Romain, which probably dates back to the time of the Gauls. Unfortunately, this grape variety is rather fickle. When the yield is low to normal the wine it produces has a distinctive character with a high tannin content which allows it to keep well. However, if the yield is too high, quality declines. As a result the César is not often encountered in this appellation.

The Pinot Noir thrives on the Irancy hills, producing a high-quality wine with good colour and fruit. The vineyards are mainly planted on slopes rising sharply above the village and surrounding it on three sides. The vineyard area formerly extended into the villages of Vincelottes and Gravant, where the Côte de Palette wines were once particularly well known. According to the year, production of Bourgogne-Irancy varies between 1500 and 2000 hectolitres, although this figure was higher in 1982 and 1983.

LEON BIENVENU★★

■		4 ha	25 000	3 D ◗ ⚭
73	76 **78** 79 80 81 **82** 82 83			

Deep, concentrated colour. Powerful nose of gooseberry and bark typical of the terroir. Firm, tannic structure; will keep well. Fine wine from the best red wine appellation of the Yonne. (1983)
🖝 Léon Bienvenu, Irancy, 89290 Champs-sur-Yonne; tel. 86 42 22 51 ☎ By appt. Mon.–Sat.

ROBERT MESLIN★

■		5 ha	25 000	3 D ▮ ◗ ⚭
69 73 76 77 **78** 79 80 81		82 ⑧		

Very dark colour, characteristic of Irancy and of the vintage. Powerful nose of roasted raisins; good structure and texture and strong, concentrated flavour. May seem rather rough at present, but should age magnificently. ✔ Bourgogne Aligoté.
🖝 Robert Meslin, Irancy, 89290 Champs-sur-Yonne; tel. 86 42 31 43 ☎ Daily.

LUC SORIN★

■		1.4 ha	9000	3 D ◗ ⚭
76 78 80 81 82 ⑧ 83 84				

Pink-edged rim. Moderately deep colour with leathery shade. Still very firm and harsh on the palate, with pronounced, fairly hard tannins. Needs to be left to soften in the bottle. (1983) ✔ Bourgogne Passe-Tout-Grains, Bourgogne Aligoté, Sauvignon de St-Bris.
🖝 Luc Sorin, 13 bis, Rue de Paris, 89530 St-Bris-le-Vineux; tel. 86 53 36 87 ☎ By appt.

Bourgogne Marsannay

Despite the ever-increasing expansion of Dijon, Marsannay-la-Côte remains essentially a wine-making village – but its proximity to Dijon has not helped the wine-makers. At the end of the last century, vineyards extended north of the city as far as the villages of Daix, Plombières and Malain. Today not a single vine-stock remains there. Traditionally the wines from these villages found a ready sale, at good prices, in Dijon. With a strong local market, producers were under less pressure to meet the higher standards of the AOC regulations than their neighbours further south on the Grande Côte.

Towards the beginning of this century, Monsieur Clair, a fine wine-maker, developed a rosé wine made by the saignée process and called it Rosé de Marsannay. However, despite repeated requests, the wine-makers in Marsannay-la-Côte, and those in Couchey, a small neighbouring commune, have yet to be granted a village appellation for red wines. In the meantime they are allowed to add the designation Marsannay or Marsannay-la-Côte to the Bourgogne appellation. The classification covers red and rosé wines harvested within the Bourgogne production area of these two communes.

Nevertheless, the appellation contains some excellent red wines, especially those grown next to the appellation area slopes of Fixin. The total amount declared is in the region of 1500 hectolitres per year, mostly rosé. A cooperative has been established here, a rare practice in northern Burgundy. It specializes in the production of rosé wine and has earned a well-deserved reputation.

CHARLES AUDOIN★

■		1 ha	7200	3 D ◗ ⚭
66 69 71 76 ⑦⑧ 79 ⋆82 83 84				

Well-vinified Bourgogne Marsannay Rouge that can equal wines of neighbouring villages. Full of charm on the nose, with aromas of rose and hyacinth. Flavours of fruit (blackcurrant, raspberry), vanilla and liquorice. Smooth, elegant but quite firm on the palate. (1982)
🖝 Charles Audoin, 7 Rue de la Boulotte, 21160 Marsannay-la-Côte; tel. 80 52 34 24 ☎ By appt.

Côte Dijonnaise

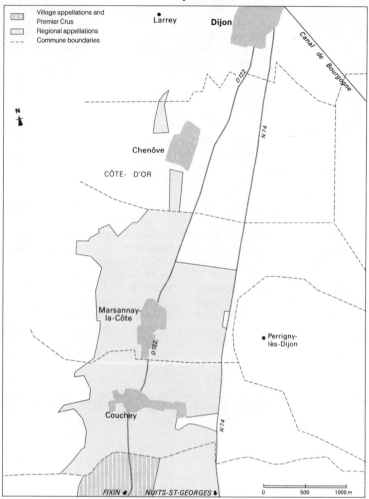

ANDRE BART★★

■   3 ha   18 000   🔳 🄳 ⑪ 🍷

★⑧⓪ 🟥 **81 83**

Fine, bright colour and choice aromas with notes of oats, cherries, coffee and Havana cigars. Full, sustained flavour. Drink now or keep. (1980)
🍷 André Bart, 24 Rue de Mazy, 21160 Marsannay-la-Côte; tel. 80 52 12 09 🍸 By appt.

RENE BOUVIER★

▨   1 ha   10 000   🔳 🍷 🄳

78 80 82 ⑧② 🟥

Powerful aromas of banana, elder-blossom, rose and balm. A bit less alcohol would have given it even more panache. (1983) 🍷 Bourgogne Marsannay Rouge.
🍷 René Bouvier, 2 Rue Neuve, 21160 Marsannay-la-Côte; tel. 80 52 21 37 🍸 By appt.

REGIS BOUVIER★

■   5 ha   24 000   🔳 🄳 ⑪ 🍷

78 80 ⑧② 83

At present very much an *enfant sauvage*, with a bitter, untamed character. The harsh tannins need to soften before it can be drunk with pleasure. (1983) 🍷 Bourgogne Marsannay Rosé.
🍷 Régis Bouvier, 52 Rue de Mazy, 21160 Marsannay-la-Côte; tel. 80 52 21 37 🍸 By appt.

RENE BOUVIER★★

■   5 ha   45 000   🔳 🄳 ⑪ 🍷

78 ★79 **80** ⑧② 🟥 83

Dull, copper-tinged colour suggesting a mature wine; aromas of cooked peach, cherry and liquorice. Full, round flavour. Drink new. (1982)
🍷 Bourgogne Marsannay Rosé.
🍷 René Bouvier, 2 Rue Neuve, 21160 Marsannay-la-Côte; tel. 80 52 21 37 🍸 By appt.

BRUNO CLAIR*

☑   1ha   7200   4 D ⑪ ↓

80 *83

Richness of the 1983 vintage is apparent with a fresh, fluid flavour and well-balanced acidity and sweetness. Rose and vanilla aromas. (1983) ✔ Bourgogne Marsannay Rouge, Fixin La Croix Blanche.
↦ Bruno Clair, 3 Rue de la Maladière, 21160 Marsannay-la-Côte; tel. 80 52 28 95 ⵣ By appt.

BRUNO CLAIR*

■   3ha   15000   3 D ⑪ ↓

61 69 70 71 80 82 83

Has reached maturity. Bright copper-tinged colour, with dry, slightly 'cooked' aromas. Good tannin and some richness on the palate. (1982) ✔ Bourgogne Marsannay Rosé, Fixin la Croix-Blanche Rouge.
↦ Bruno Clair, 3 Rue de la Maladière, 21160 Marsannay-la-Côte; tel. 80 52 28 95 ⵣ No visitors.

DOMAINE CLAIR-DAU**

☑   6ha   36000   3 D ■ ↓

Charming rosé, not without force, showing a striking orange colour with a hint of reddish-brown. Slightly roasted, orange-peel aromas, and complex flavours of banana and cocoa. Good acidity gives refreshing balance and elegance. (1983)
↦ Dom. Clair-Dau, 5 Rue du Vieux-Collège, 21160 Marsannay-la-Côte, tel. 80 52 15 58 ⵣ Mon.–Fri. 9.00–12.00/14.00–18.00.

DOMAINE FOUGERAY**

☑   2ha   12000   3 D ■ ↓

78 80 ⑧ 83

Already characterised by 'ripe', smooth flavours, has aromas of cut hay, faded roses and vanilla. (1983) ✔ Bourgogne Marsannay Rouge, Bourgogne Passe-tout-grain Rouge, Savigny-les-Beaune Rouge, Gevrey-Chambertin.
↦ Jean-Claude Fougeray, 44 Rue de Mazy, 21160 Marsannay-la-Côte; tel. 80 52 21 12 ⵣ By appt.

DOMAINE FOUGERAY*

■   4ha   24000   4 D ■ ⑪ ↓

78 80 ⑧ 83

Harshness of the 1983 vintage very apparent. The aromas are still undeveloped and the flavour lacks charm. To be laid down until it softens. (1983) ✔ Bourgogne Marsannay Rosé, Bourgogne Passe-tout-grain Rouge, Savigny-les-Beaune Les Gollardes Rouge, Gevrey-Chambertin.
↦ Jean-Claude Fougeray, 44 Rue de Mazy, 21160 Marsannay-la-Côte; tel. 80 52 21 12 ⵣ By appt.

COOPERATIVE DES GRAND VINS*

■   8ha   72000   3 D ⑪ ↓

⑦ 80 82 83

Pleasant, strongly fruity aromas. Slightly bitter, 'tarry' finish lending complexity. Good, firm flavour for a 1982. (1982) ✔ Bourgogne Marsannay Rosé.
↦ Coop. des Grands Vins, 21 Rue de Mazy, 21160 Marsannay-la-Côte; tel. 80 52 15 14 ⵣ No visitors.

LUCIEN GUYARD*

■   2ha   10800   3 D ⑪ ↓

76 78 79 82 83

Very much a 1982, with attractive, expressive aromas of peony, raspberry, redcurrant and pepper and a faint animal note. Fresh, fluid flavour. Will develop slowly. (1982) ✔ Fixin.
↦ Lucien Guyard, 10 Rue du Puits-de-Têt, 21160 Marsannay-la-Côte; tel. 80 52 14 46 ⵣ By appt.

Bourgogne Hautes-Côtes de Nuits

This is the name most commonly used for wines grown on the upper slopes above the main Côtes de Nuits appellation vineyards. Some sixteen hillside villages are involved in wine-making. The appellation produces between 5000 and 10000 hectolitres of wine annually, 95 per cent of which is red. The amount produced has increased significantly since 1970; before then production was concentrated on generic wines, especially Bourgogne Aligoté. Today vineyards are being steadily replanted, and land that was under vine in the pre-phylloxera era is being worked anew.

The best-exposed slopes may, on occasion, produce wines that rival those from more famous vineyards on the Côte; white wines, too, have often been very successful. Perhaps, for even better results, more Chardonnay should be planted here. Meanwhile strenuous efforts are being made to develop a tourist trade alongside the resurgent vineyard. In particular the recently-built Maison des Hautes-Côtes offers a display of local wines which can be tasted along with the regional cuisine.

CIE DES VINS D'AUTREFOIS*

■   4 ■ ↓

Intense, deep purple colopur and bouquet reminiscent of blackcurrant. Has all the characteristics of the Hautes-Côtes de Nuits and firmness of the 1983 vintage. Should keep well. (1983)
↦ Cie des Vins d'Autrefois, 9 Rue Celer, 21200 Beaune; tel. 80 22 21 31 ⵣ By appt.

LEONCE BOCQUET*

■   6000   4 D ⑪ ↓

*59 *69 *⑦ *81 *82

Still very young and fruity. Very typical of its vintage with plenty of life ahead. (1982)
↦ Petits-Fils de Léonce Bocquet, 29 Bvd Clemenceau, 21200 Beaune; tel. 80 22 28 49 ⵣ Mon.–Fri. 9.30–11.30/14.00–17.30. Closed Dec. to Feb.

HENRI FELETTIG★★

■ 1 ha 6000 ▨ D ◫ ↓
★76 ★⑦⑧ **82 83** ▨

The vintage transforms this Hautes-Côtes into something nearer a 'Village' appellation. Fresh, fruity aromas with a full firm presence in the mouth and prolonged finish. Should be laid down for a year or two before drinking. (1983)
☛ Henri Felettig, Chambolle-Musigny, 21220 Gevrey-Chambertin; tel. 80 62 85 09 ☎ By appt.

DOMAINE FRIBOURG★★

□ 2 ha 12000 ▨ D ▪ ↓
76 78 79 81 ★**82** ★83 ★▨

Rich, smooth, character is fully brought out by the 1983 vintage. Good floral aromas dominated by honeysuckle, and clean fresh flavour. Already very pleasing to drink. (1983)
☛ Marcel et Bernard Fribourg, Dom. Fribourg, Villers-la-Faye, 21700 Nuits-St-Georges; tel. 80 62 91 74 ☎ By appt.

DOMAINE FRIBOURG★

■ 8 ha 30000 ▨ D ▪ ↓
76 78 79 81 **82** ⑧③ ▨

Received very short fermentation to compensate for natural harshness. Clear, bright colour; pronounced fruit; fairly long on the palate, without being excessively tannic. Should keep for several years. (1983) ✔ Bourgogne Aligoté, Bourgogne Hautes-Côtes de Nuits Blanc, Bourgogne Passe-tout-grain.
☛ Marcel et Bernard Fribourg, Dom. Fribourg, Villers-la-Faye, 21700 Nuits-St-Georges; tel. 80 62 91 74 ☎ By appt.

DOMAINE FRANÇOIS GERBET★★

▨ 10 ha 60000 ▨ D ▪ ◫ ↓
76 77 ★⑦⑧ 79 80 ▨① 82 83

Good quality vintage of considerable finesse. Delicate aromas of blackberries and wild fruit. Balanced, restrained flavour. Long finish. Should keep several years. (1981)
☛ François Gerbet, Vosne-Romanée, 21700 Nuits-St-Georges; tel. 80 61 07 85 ☎ By appt.

PATRICK HUDELOT *Les Genevrières*★

□ 1 ha 12000 ▨ D ▪ ◫ ↓
78 ⑦⑨ **81** ▨② **83 84**

Strongly marked by new oak casks, which have given it an amber colour, woody, resinous and balsamy aromas, and a slightly mordant flavour. With age, these will be transformed into noble, fine aromas of great distinction. (1982)
☛ Patrick Hudelot, Villars-Fontaine, 21700 Nuits-St-Georges; tel. 80 61 06 38 ☎ By appt.

HENRI HUDELOT★★★

▨ 4 ha 20000 ▨ D ▪ ◫ ↓
76 78 ⑦⑨ **81 82** ▨

Vinified with great skill; a splendid wine. Tannic and powerful on the palate with good length; on the nose, aromas of fine wood with nuances of fruit and musk. Selected at the Tastevinage in 1985. (1983) ✔ Bourgogne Aligoté, Nuits-St-Georges.
☛ Henri Hudelot, Villars-Fontaine, 21700 Nuits-St-Georges; tel. 80 61 06 38 ☎ By appt.

1982

Bourgogne
Hautes Côtes de Nuits
APPELLATION CONTROLÉE

"LES GENEVRIÈRES"

MIS EN BOUTEILLE PAR
Domaine Bernard HUDELOT-VERDEL
Propriétaire-récoltant
à VILLARS-FONTAINE par NUITS-St-GEORGES (CÔTE-D'OR)
Produit de France

ROBERT JAYER-GILLES★★★

□ 6000 ▨ D ▪
Typical Meursault nose with toasty-smoky aromas evoking honey, white truffle. Has developed in a very interesting fashion from a modest beginning. Impossible to buy this vintage any more, so look out for more recent years. (1969)
☛ Robert Jayer-Gilles, Magny-les-Villers, 21700 Nuits-St-Georges, tel. 80 62 91 79 ☎ By appt.

MOILLARD★

■ 240000 ▨ ◫ ↓
78 ▨⑧ 83

Selected from among the most developed of the 1983 cuvées. Pleasing fruit and good quality on the palate. Already drinkable. (1983)
☛ SARL Moillard, 5 Rue F. Mignotte, 21700 Nuits-St-Georges; tel. 80 61 03 34 ☎ No visitors.

DOMAINE MONTMAIN
Les Genevrières★★

■ 4 ha 24000 ▨ D ◫ ↓
73 76 77 **78 79** 80 81 ⑧② ▨② 83

Has all the charm of the 1982 vintage, with its aromas of small fruit and subtle oak. Should reach its peak in five or six years' time. (1982)
☛ Bernard Hudelot, Dom. Montmain, Villars-Fontaine, 21700 Nuits-St-Georges; tel. 80 62 31 94 ☎ By appt.

DOMAINE MONTMAIN
Les Genèvrières★★

■ 6.5 ha 29000 ▨ D ◫ ↓
73 ★76 78 81 ★82 ★83

Ripe, plummy, gamey aromas. A rather rustic wine with a refreshing, fruity finish. Still very young, needing time to round out.
☛ Bernard Hudelot, Dom. Montmain, Villars-Fontaine, 21700 Nuits-St-Georges; tel. 80 62 31 94 ☎ By appt.

DOMAINE MONTMAIN★

■ 10 ha 48000 ▨ D ▪ ◫ ↓
⑦③ ★78 ▨⑨ ▨②

Fairly pale colour with spicy nose. Aromas of black pepper and carnation are confirmed in the mouth. Subtle, with a good length. (1982) ✔ Bourgogne Aligoté, Bourgogne Passe-tout-grain.
☛ Bernard Hudelot, Dom. Montmain, Villars-Fontaine, 21700 Nuits-St-Georges; tel. 80 62 31 94 ☎ Daily. Closed occasionally in Aug.

286

HENRI NAUDIN-FERRAND★★

■   1.28ha   9500   ▣ ▣ ▮ ⑪ ⬇
76 78 79 81 **82** ⑧ ▨

Has the strong, bright colour of its vintage. Pleasing fruit and a balanced structure of richness and tannin. May be kept for between five and ten years. (1983) ✔ Bourgogne Aligoté.
↷ Henri Naudin-Ferrand, Magny-les-Ferrand, 21700 Nuits-St-Georges; tel. 80 62 91 50 ⵫ By appt.

SIMON ET FILS

■   3ha   18000   ▣ ▣ ▮ ⑪ ⬇
73 76 78 79 81 **82** ▨ ⑧

Characterized by the finesse and delicacy of its vintage. Already quite mature, with a fruity bouquet and smooth flavour. Ready to drink. (1982) ✔ Bourgogne Aligoté, Bourgogne 'les Dames Huguette' Rouge.
↷ MM. Simon et Fils, Marey-les-Fussey, 21700 Nuits-St-Georges; tel. 80 62 91 85 ⵫ By appt.

DOMAINE THEVENOT-LEBRUN
Clos-du-Vignon★

☐   1ha   5400   ▤ ▣ ▮ ⑪ ⬇
73 76 78 79 81 82 ▨

Highly scented nose of butter and vanilla. The taste reveals more complex, spicy aromas and good acid support. (1980)
↷ MM. Thévenot-Lebrun et Fils, Marey-les-Fussey, 21700 Nuits-St-Georges; tel. 80 62 91 64 ⵫ Mon.–Sat. 8.00–12.00/14.00–19.00.

DOMAINE THEVENOT-LEBRUN
Clos-du-Vignon★★

■   5ha   21600   ▤ ▣ ▮ ⑪ ⬇
73 76 78 79 81 82 ▨

Dark colour and elegant nose marked by the smell of new oak. Spicy in the mouth, with sharp flavours of pepper mingled with small red fruits. Pronounced aroma of sloes at the finish. Good jug Burgundy. (1982)
↷ MM. Thévenot-Lebrun et Fils, Marey-les-Fussey 21700 Nuits-St-Georges; tel. 80 62 91 64 ⵫ Mon.–Sat. 8.00–12.00/14.00–19.00.

Bourgogne Hautes-Côtes de Beaune

More wine is produced under the appellation Bourgogne Hautes-Côtes de Beaune than Hautes-Côtes de Nuits. The production area is larger, comprising 20 or so communes, and overflows into the northern part of Saône-et-Loire. The vineyard sites, too, are more varied, including large areas planted with Aligoté and Gamay.

The Hautes-Côtes cooperative, which started up in Orches, a hamlet of Baubigny, has now moved to the south of Beaune, at the crossroads of the RN 73 and the RN 74. A significant amount of Bourgogne Hautes-Côtes de Beaune is made here. In general, a great expansion in vineyard planting has taken place since the early 1970s. The picturesque countryside has many beauty spots worth visiting, including Orches itself, La Rochepot with its castle, and Nolay, an attractive Burgundy village. Finally, it should be added that the entire Hautes-Côtes region still produces the berry crops, such as blackcurrants and raspberries, that supply the liqueur-makers of Nuits-St-Georges and Dijon: delicious liqueurs and Eau-de-Vie are a local speciality. Particularly worth noting is l'Eau-de-Vie de Poire (pear) from Monts-de-Côte-d'Or, which has its own appellation and is actually produced in the Hautes-Côtes region.

CIE DES VINS D'AUTREFOIS★

■   ▤ ▣ ⑪ ⬇
★83 ★ ▨

Attractive, bright colour. Warm and rich in alcohol. Aroma of red fruit, and solid structure on the palate. Drink from now on, but will gain nuances in a few years' time. (1983)
↷ Cie des Vins d'Autrefois, 9 Rue Celer, 21200 Beaune; tel. 80 22 21 31 ⵫ By appt.

JEAN-NOEL BAZIN★

■   4ha   18000   ▣ ▣ ▮ ⬇

Fully opened up. Attractive aromas in a fine, elegant bouquet, and very soft flavours. Can be drunk now and will certainly prove satisfying. (1982) ✔ Bourgogne Aligoté, Bourgogne Passetout-grain.
↷ Jean-Noel Bazin, La Rochepot, 21340 Nolay; tel. 80 21 75 49 ⵫ By appt.

LEONCE BOCQUET★

■   6000   ▤ ▣ ⑪ ⬇
★59 ★⑥ ▨ ★78 ★81 ★82

Finesse and elegance characterize this Hautes-Côtes de Beaune. The vintage adds typical deep colour and pronounced aromas of wild red fruit. (1981)
↷ Petits-Fils de Léonce Bocquet, 29 Bvd Clemenceau, 21200 Beaune; tel. 80 22 28 49 ⵫ Mon.–Fri. 9.30–11.30/14.00–17.30. Closed Dec. to Feb.

JEAN-CLAUDE BOULEY
Hautes-Côtes de Beaune★★

■   6ha   30000   ▢ ▣ ⑪ ⬇
61 78 ▨ ⑦ ▨ **81** ▨ 82 83

Smooth, fruity and well made. The grower claims to export it world-wide. (1982) ✔ Hautes-Côtes de Beaune, Bourgogne Passe-tout-grain, Crémant de Bourgogne.
↷ Jean-Claude Bouley, Changé, 21340 Nolay; tel. 85 87 11 57 ⵫ By appt.

287

DENIS CARRE★★

■   3ha   18000   3 ■ ⦿

76 78 ⑦ **81 82** 83

Although the colour has matured the aromas are still undeveloped; powerful on the palate, with well-balanced ingredients and plenty of promise. (1983)
↬ Denis Carre, Meloisey, 21190 Meursault; tel. 80 26 02 21 ⊤ By appt.

FRANÇOIS CHARLES★★

■   3ha   18000   4 D ■ ⦿

74 76 78 79 81 ⑧ 82 83

Considerable firmness. Still very young, with aromas of fresh, small fruit and good length on the palate. Leave it to open up for several years before drinking. (1982) ✦ Bourgogne Aligoté, Bourgogne Passe-tout-grain, Volnay, Pommard.
↬ François Charles, Nantoux, 21190 Meursault; tel. 80 26 01 20 ⊤ By appt.

DOMAINE PAUL CHEVROT★

■   4ha   20000   3 D ⦿ ⤓

73 76 79 82 83

Very dark ruby with heavy, slightly smoky, thickset aromas. Needs to age but would go well, when mature, with rabbit. (1982) ✦ Cheilly-lès-Moranges Côtes-de-Beaune, Santenay Premier Cru Clos Mousseau, Bourgogne Aligoté, Crémant de Bourgogne.
↬ Fernand Chevrot, Cheilly-lès-Maranges, 71150 Chagny; tel. 88 38 70 9 15 ⊤ By appt.

YVON ET CHANTAL CONTAT-GRANGE★

■   1.5ha   12000   3 D ■ ⤓

★81 ★82 ★⑧

From Décize-lès-Maranges, a small village at the southern tip of the Côte de Beaune, overshadowed by the Montagne des Trois Croix. This young, enthusiastic grower has only been making wine since 1980. He can, therefore, offer only very recent vintages but his wines are well made and have a firmly scented bouquet which is typical of the *terroir*. This 1983 still tastes very young but is sufficiently well constructed to age without any problem (1983) ✦ Bourgogne, Bourgogne Hautes-Côtes-de-Beaune, Crémant de Bourgogne, Côtes-de-Beaune, Cheilly-lès-Maranges.
↬ *M.* et *Mme* Contat-Grangé, Décize-lès-Maranges, 71150 Chagny; tel. 85 87 24 39 ⊤ By appt.

CLAUDE CORNU★

□   0.5ha   1320   3 D ⦿

79 81 82 ⑧ 83

In Burgundy, the Pinot Blanc gives a fairly rich but smooth white wine sometimes noticeably high in alcohol. Maurice Chevalier was apparently a great fan of this wine. The 1983, has been well vinified and shows attractive aromas of vanilla and roses. (1983) ✦ Bourgogne Aligoté, Bourgogne Passe-tout-grain, Bourgogne Hautes-Côtes de Beaune Rouge, Hautes-Côtes de Nuits.
↬ Claude Cornu, Magny-les-Villers, 21700 Nuits-St-Georges; tel. 80 62 92 05 ⊤ By appt.

COLETTE CORNU★★

■   0.38ha   1950   4 D ■ ⤓

76 ⑦ ★82 83

A keeping wine with all the characteristics of its vintage. Intense, dark-velvet colour; deep, firm aromas and robust but well-balanced flavours. (1983)
↬ Colette Cornu, Magny-les-Villers, 21700 Nuits-St-Georges; tel. 80 62 92 05 ⊤ By appt.

STEPHANE DEMANGEOT★★★

■   7ha   25000   3 D ■ ⦿ ⤓

81 82 ★83

A fine, open wine with a lovely dark colour. Aromas of flowers and wild berries. Solid, very tannic flavour which will allow it to keep for up to ten years. Canon Kir, who gave his name to the famous Aligoté and blackcurrant liqueur aperitif, was a close friend of the Demangeot family and would have enjoyed this very good-value bottle. (1981) ✦ Côtes-de-Beaune, Bourgogne, Bourgogne Passe-tout-grain. Bourgogne Aligoté.
↬ Stéphane Demangeot, Changé, 21340 Nolay; tel. 85 87 13 18 ⊤ By appt.

DOMAINE VIGNES DES DEMOISELLES★★★

■   7ha   35000   3 D ■ ⦿ ⤓

81 82 ⑧

Very fine 1983. Powerful and has body, although its bouquet is still undeveloped. Exceptional structure makes it a great wine for keeping, which will reach fullness in ten to twelve years' time. (1983)
↬ Jean-Luc Demangeot, Dom. Vignes des Demoiselles, Changé, 21340 Nolay; tel. 85 87 13 18 ⊤ By appt.

GUILLEMARD-DUPONT ET FILS★

■   2ha   10500   3 D ⦿

76 78 79 **80 81** ★82 ★⑧

Good example of the appellation, with deep colour and fine aromas, which is already showing well. (1983) ✦ Bourgogne Passe-tout-grain Rouge, Bourgogne-Hautes Côtes de Beaune Blanc.
↬ *MM.* Guillemard-Dupont et Fils, Meloisey, 21190 Meursault; tel. 80 26 01 11 ⊤ By appt.

DOMAINE LUCIEN JACOB★

■   10ha   60000   3 D ⦿ ⤓

76 78 79 81 ★⑧ ★82 83

Vinified to produce a keeping wine, with a body and tannin content guaranteed to last. (1982)
✦ Savigny-les-Beaune Blanc et Rouge.

🐌 Lucien Jacob, Echevronne, 21420 Savigny-les-Beaune; tel. 80 21 52 15 ⍾ By appt.

JEAN JOLIOT ET FILS★★★

■	6ha	24000	4 D ⑪ ↓

76 78 79 81 ★82 ⑧ 83

Splendid colour. Arouses enthusiasm with its aromas of fine wood and Morello cherries, harmony and distinction of its flavours. Worth waiting four or five years until it peaks. (1983)
✔ Pommard, Bourgogne Passe-tout-grain, Meursault, Bourgogne Aligoté.
🐌 Jean Joliot et Fils, Nantoux, 21190 Meursault; tel. 80 26 01 44 ⍾ By appt.

MIS EN BOUTEILLE A LA PROPRIÉTÉ

1983

Bourgogne
Hautes Côtes de Beaune

Appellation Bourgogne Hautes Côtes de Beaune Contrôlée

JEAN JOLIOT & FILS
PROPRIÉTAIRES-RÉCOLTANTS A NANTOUX, COTE-D'OR
75 cl
PRODUCE OF FRANCE

JOSEPH LAFOUGE
Hautes Côtes de Beaune★★

■	3ha	15000	3 D ▮ ↓

61 66 73 76 ⑲ 82 83

Velvety garnet colour; robust, clean flavour perhaps lacking persistence. Drink within three years. (1983) ✔ Côtes de Beaune-Village, Bourgogne Passe-tout-grain and Blanc, Bourgogne Rosé, Bourgogne Aligoté.
🐌 Joseph Lafouge, Marchezeuil-Change, 21340 Nolay; tel. 85 87 19 09 ⍾ By appt.

MARCEL LAFOUGE
Hautes Côtes de Beaune★★

■	4ha	14000	3 D ▮ ⑪ ↓

69 73 76 78 79 81 82 ⑧ 84

Pleasant nose and good balance in the mouth. Slightly short finish but should keep well. (1981)
🐌 Marcel Lafouge, Paris-l'Hôpital, 71150 Chagny; tel. 85 87 21 68 ⍾ By appt.

RENE MARTIN★

■	4ha	30000	3 D ⑪ ↓

⑯ 78 81 81 83

A light open-knit, carefully made wine for immediate drinking, perhaps with red meat or game. From an old family domaine which has been making wine for ten generations. (1981) ✔ Sampigny-les-Maranges, Côtes-de-Beaune, Bourgogne, Crémant de Bourgogne, Bourgogne Aligoté.
🐌 René Martin, Cheilly-les-Maranges, 71150 Chagny; tel. 85 87 04 34 ⍾ By appt.

MAZILLY PERE ET FILS★★

■	6ha	25000	4 D ⑪

76 ⑱ 79 81 82 83

Purple tinge in the colour is a sign of slow development; it will keep for a long time. With clear, direct flavours, it promises to open up well as it ages. Will repay patient keeping. (1983)
✔ Bourgogne Passe-tout-grain, Meursault, Pommard.
🐌 *MM.* Mazilly Père et Fils, Meloisey, 21190 Meursault; tel. 80 26 01 34 ⍾ By appt.

CHATEAU DE MERCEY★★

□	4ha	16000	3 D ▮ ↓

78 79 81 82 ★⑧ ★83

Delicate, fruity nose. Bottled six months after the harvest to capture the wine's freshness. May be left to age. (1983)
🐌 Jacques Berger, Ch. de Mercey, Cheilly-les-Maranges, 71150 Chagny; tel. 85 87 17 10 ⍾ Daily. Closed 20 Dec.–20 Jan.

CHATEAU DE MERCEY★

■	20ha	120000	3 D ▮ ⑪ ↓

63 64 66 **69** 76 78 79 82 ⑧

Pleasing to the eye and nose but rather heavy on the palate. Drink at once (1982) ✔ Santenay, Mercurey, Bourgogne Aligoté.
🐌 Jacques Berger, Ch. de Mercey, Cheilly-les-Maranges, 71150 Chagny; tel. 85 87 17 10 ⍾ Daily. Closed 20 Dec.–20 Jan.

BERNARD MONDANGE★★

■	5ha	18000	4 D ▮ ⑪ ↓

76 78 79 81 82 ⑧ 83

Vinified for long-term keeping. Still rather closed. Within five or six years will have developed a fine range of aromas, over a solid, well-balanced base. (1983) ✔ Bourgogne Rouge, Bourgogne Aligoté, Bourgogne Passe-tout-grain.
🐌 Bernard Mondange, L'Etang-Vergy, 21220 Gevrey-Chambertin; tel. 80 61 41 59 ⍾ No visitors.

HENRI NAUDIN-FERRAND★★

■	4.8ha	19000	3 D ▮ ⑪ ↓

74 76 78 79 81 82 ⑧ 83

Powerful body, and very firm, if reticent, bouquet. Needs to be kept for several years. (1983)
✔ Bourgogne Aligoté, Bourgogne Passe-tout-grain, Hautes-Côtes de Nuits Rouge, Bourgogne Hautes Côtes de Beaune Blanc.
🐌 Henri Naudin-Ferrand, Magny-les-Ferrand, 21700 Nuits-St-Georges; tel. 80 62 91 50 ⍾ By appt.

HENRI NAUDIN-FERRAND★★

□	0.85ha	4800	3 D ▮ ↓

73 76 78 79 81 ★⑧ ★82 **83**

Very flattering smoothly flavoured wine, with aromas of amber and broom flowers. (1982)
✔ Bourgogne Aligoté, Bourgogne Passe-tout-grain, Bourgogne Hautes-Côtes de Beaune, Bourgogne Hautes-Côtes de Nuits.
🐌 Henri Naudin-Ferrand, Magny-les-Ferrand, 21700 Nuits-St-Georges; tel. 80 62 91 50 ⍾ By appt.

289

CHARLES ET CLAUDE NOUVEAU*

| ■ | 2ha | 12000 | 3 D 🍾 ↓ |

73 76 **78** 79 81 **82 83**

An attractive colour with pleasant, leafy aromas, but a disappointing sharp flavour with too much acidity. (1981) ✦ Bourgogne Aligoté, Santenay Blanc, Côtes-de-Beaune Villages, Santenay.
•┐ Charles et Claude Nouveau, Marchezeuil-Change, 21340 Nolay; tel. 85 87 26 47 ⵑ By appt.

PARIGOT PERE ET FILS**

| ■ | 4ha | 21500 | 4 D ⦀ ↓ |

74 76 78 79 81 ★82 ⑧ 83

At present has a dark colour, dumb nose and harsh, teeth-clenching flavour. Will soften. (1983) ✦ Bourgogne Aligoté, Bourgogne Passe-tout-grain, Pommard, Meursault.
•┐ *MM.* Parigot Père et Fils, Meloisey, 21190 Meursault; tel. 80 26 01 70 ⵑ By appt.

DOMAINE SAINT-MARC**

| ■ | 1ha | 7000 | 3 D ⦀ |

82 ★83 83

A fine bottle for short- to medium-term drinking. Brilliant red with powerful red-berry aromas and a refined flavour of vanilla and new oak. (1983) ✦ Burgundy Passe-tout-Grain.
•┐ GFA La Comme, Dom. St-Marc, 71150 Paris-l'Hôpital 71150, Chagny; tel. 85 87 24 47 ⵑ By appt.

Crémant de Bourgogne

Like most viticultural regions of France, Burgundy, too, had a sparkling wine appellation covering the whole geographical area. Unfortunately, the quality of these wines was far from consistent and in general reflected little credit on the region. To be fair, this was probably because sparkling wines were being made from wines that were too heavy.

In 1975 Burgundy vignerons and wine-makers created a new appellation, Crémant de Bourgogne, a wine of completely different quality. Today this most recent of the Burgundy appellations has established an identity of its own. The current annual production is in the order of three million bottles.

PIERRE BERNOLLIN**

| ○ | 1ha | 9000 | 3 D |

A crémant from Pinot, Aligoté and Gamay grapes. Fine, long-lasting bubbles and well-married flavour, perhaps a trifle short. A very good aperitif.
•┐ Pierre Bernollin, Jully-les-Buxy, 71390 Buxy; tel. 85 42 12 19 ⵑ By appt.

ALAIN BERTHAULT**

| ○ | 0.2ha | 1800 | 3 D 🍾 ⦀ ↓ |

Fine, light mousse; pleasant, persistent flavour but lacking a little finesse. Nonetheless, a well-made, good-value wine. ✦ Aligoté, Passe-tout-grain, Bourgogne Pinot Noir.
•┐ Alain Berthault, Cercot-Moroges, 71390 Buxy; tel. 85 47 91 03 ⵑ By appt.

CAVE COOPERATIVE DE CHARDONNAY

| ○ | 45000 | 3 D 🍾 ↓ |

Would make a good aperitif with its elegant, refined nose. Lacking structure in the mouth, however.
•┐ Cave Coop. de Chardonnay, Chardonnay, 71700 Tournus; tel. 85 51 06 49 ⵑ By appt.

CAVE COOPERATIVE DE CHARNAY***

| ○ | 15000 | 3 D 🍾 ↓ |

Light golden-green colour and all finesse and elegance. Fine bubbles; long, satisfying palate.
•┐ Cave Coop. de Charnay, Charnay-les-Mâcon, 71000 Mâcon; tel. 85 34 54 24 ⵑ By appt.

CHEVALIER ET FILS*

| ○ | 150000 | 3 D 🍾 ⦀ ↓ |

Crémant with an elegant nose, crisp, light palate and excellent mousse. (1979)
•┐ Ets Chevalier et Fils, les Tournons, Charnay-les-Mâcon, 71000 Mâcon; tel. 85 34 26 74 ⵑ By appt.

MARCEL DELIANCE**

| ○ | 7ha | 35000 | 3 D 🍾 ⦀ D |

An attractive, pale-rose crémant with a crisp, satisfying flavour. A fine aperitif.
•┐ Marcel Deliance, Cidex 213, Dracy-le-Fort, 71640 Givry; tel. 85 47 13 43 ⵑ By appt.

CAVES DELORME-MEULIEN*

| ○ | 200000 | 4 D 🍾 ↓ |

One of the most famous Burgundy crémants from specially selected grapes. Lovely, delicate mousse and refined aromas of sweetness and fruit. Worth trying as a Kir Royal with blackcurrant, strawberry or raspberry liqueur, or better still, blackberry.
•┐ Les Caves Delorme-Meulien, Rue de la République, Rully, 71150 Chagny; tel. 85 87 10 12 ⵑ Daily. Closed Aug.

DENIZOT PERE ET FILS**

| ○ | 3ha | 5000 | 4 D 🍾 ⦀ ↓ |

⑦⑧ 79 81 82 83

Pale colour with delicate bubbles, good mouth and persistent aromas, full of fruit with a smooth, clear flavour.
•┐ GAEC Denizot Père et Fils, Les Moirots, Bissey-sous-Cruchaud, 13790 Buxy; tel. 85 42 16 93 ⵑ By appt.

LUCIEN DENIZOT*

| ○ | 3ha | 30000 | 3 D 🍾 ⦀ ↓ |

Well balanced and very rich. Paradoxically, its style is much more that of a Blanc de Noirs. (1982)

↱ GAEC Denizot Père et Fils, Les Moirots, Bissey-sous-Cruchaud, 71390 Buxy; tel. 85 42 16 93 ⵟ By appt.

CAVE COOPERATIVE D'IGE★★

○ 100000 **3** **D** ⵟ ↓

Green-gold crémant with fine bubbles and attractive mousse. Fruity, flowery nose and crisp, light palate. Ideal aperitif.
↱ Cave Coop. d'Igé, Igé, 71960 Pierreclos; tel. 85 33 33 56 ⵟ By appt.

ROBERT ET MICHEL ISAIE★

○ 3 ha 20000 **4** **D** ⵟ ⵑ ↓

The mousse fades rather fast and, despite a good clean finish, the flavour is a bit soft and flat. Drink soon. ✓ Bourgogne, Mercurey.
↱ Michel et Robert Isaie, St-Jean-de-Vaux, 71640 Givry; tel. 85 47 11 14 ⵟ By appt.

LUGNY SAINT-GENGOUX★★

○ 40 ha 400000 **4** **D** ⵟ ↓
76 78 79 82 ⑧③

A Méthode Champenoise vinification from Pinot Noir and Chardonnay grapes. A well-made, smooth, light crémant with fine bubbles and attractive floral aromas. Would make a good aperitif.
↱ Group. des Prod. Lugny-St-Gengoux, 71260 Lugny; tel. 85 32 22 85 ⵟ By appt.

DOMAINE MARLY-ROSE★★★

○ **4** **D**

Clear, pink-tinged colour; delicate, persistent mousse and fresh, elegant aromas. Subtle, concentrated flavour showing Pinot Noir character and fine texture and length. A marvellous bottle.
↱ Les Toques Gourmandes, 29 Bis Route de Versailles, 78560 Port-Marly; tel. 01 91 61 17 ⵟ By appt.

ARMAND MONASSIER★★★

○ 2 ha 13000 **4** **D** ⵟ ↓

Lovely golden colOur with very fine bubbles, and a fresh, light nose. Drink on its own, or as an aperitif with raspberry liqueur. (1982)
↱ Armand Monassier, Dom. du Prieuré, Rully, 71150 Chagny; tel. 85 87 13 57 ⵟ By appt.

DOMAINE ROUX PERE ET FILS★★

○ 5 ha 35000 **4** **D** ⵟ

As a result of skilful mixing of vines this one has considerable finesse, combining the fruitiness of the Gamay with the crispness of the Aligoté and the class of the Chardonnay. ✓ Bourgogne Aligoté, Bourgogne, St-Aubin, Chassagne Montrachet.
↱ *MM.* Roux Père et Fils, St-Aubin 21190 Meursault; tel. 80 21 32 92 ⵟ By appt.

COOPERATIVE DE VIRE★★

○ 500000 **3** **D**

A high-class crémant distinguished by its light golden-green colour and stream of very fine bubbles. Fruity, elegant nose and aromatic palate. Ideal aperitif.
↱ Coop. de Viré, 71260 Lugny; tel. 85 33 12 64 ⵟ By appt.

VITTEAUT-ALBERTI★

○ 4 ha 25000 **4** **D** ⵟ **D**

Crémant wines have been made at this property since 1951, when the father of the present owners settled here. An elegant wine with fine, light bubbles but it would be even more enjoyable if it were fruitier. Clean, crisp finish. Try it with blackberry liqueur. (1983) ✓ Vin Mousseux Blanc de Blanc, Rosé Vin Mousseux, Rosé Crémant Burgundy, Red Burgundy.
↱ L. Vitteaut-Alberti, Rue du Pont d'Arrot, Rully, 71150 Chagny; tel. 85 87 23 97 ⵟ By appt.
↱ Gérard Vitteaut.

CHABLIS

Despite its worldwide fame, true Chablis very nearly went out of existence altogether after two late, catastrophic frosts in May 1957 and 1961. These, added to the difficulties of working vineyards on very steep, rocky slopes, led growers gradually to abandon the cultivation of the vine. The price of Grand Cru land reached derisory levels, and the people who bought at this time were very shrewd. New methods of protecting against frost have appeared, and with increasing mechanization of work in the vineyards, the Chablis appellation has been given a new lease of life.

The appellation area covers 6834 hectares of land in and around the commune of Chablis, less than half of which is actually planted. The vines cover the steep slopes of the hills that run along both banks of the Serein, a small tributary of the Yonne. A south or south-easterly exposure encourages the grapes to ripen but some 'opposite' (north-facing) slopes are also planted on certain favourably exposed sites. The ground is made up of Jurassic marl, admirably well-suited to growing white grape varieties. This potential was first realized by the twelfth-century Cistercian monks of the abbey close to Pontigny. They almost certainly planted Chardonnay

291

Chablis

vines, called Beaunois locally. This grape variety expresses its subtlety and elegance better here perhaps than in any other region.

Petit Chablis
Produced from vines planted on land with the least favourable exposure, this wine is low in potential alcohol (a minimum of 9.5 per cent) but often high in acidity. As a result, it tends towards greenness and, more importantly, is less aromatic and less complex. Traditionally made as a jug wine to be drunk within the year, it cannot be expected to improve in bottle. Exceptions are a few cuvées from very old vines planted next to the Premier Cru vineyards.

LA CHABLISIENNE★★

□	50 ha	26 400	3 D 🖺 ↓

76 78 79 81 83 84

Slight golden colour indicates the maturity of the grapes. A pure nose consisting of peach/pear aromas and a deep bouquet of honey. Weak finish with a slight after taste of bitterness. (1983)

↤ Cave Coop. la Chablisienne, 8 Bld Pasteur, BP 14, 89800 Chablis; tel. 86 42 11 24 ⏱ Mon.–Sat. 8.00–12.00/14.00–18.00.

Chablis
Chablis wine takes its inimitable qualities of freshness and lightness from the soil. It is not good in cold and rainy years, when its acidity becomes excessive. In a hot year, on the other hand, it keeps a thirst-quenching quality that the Côte d'Or wines do not, even though they too are made from the Chardonnay grape. Usually drunk young, from one to three years old, it also ages well up to ten years or longer, its bouquet increasing in complexity and richness.

CHRISTIAN ADINE★

□	3.5 ha	10 000	3 D 🖺 ↓

81 ⑧ 83

Bright colour with powerful aromas of honey and peach typical of its vintage. Full-bodied flavour; should age well. Still a little short; needs another year to develop some finesse. (1983)
↤ Christian Adine, Rue Restif-de-la-Bretonne, Courgis, 89800 Chablis; tel. 86 41 40 28 ⏱ By appt.

LA CHABLISIENNE★★

☐	315ha	1800000	4 D ∎ ↓

69 71 75 76 ⑦⑧ **83** 84

Pale with green highlights. Clean, characteristic floral, honeyed aromas. Striking fat, round flavour but not flabby; still very young and lacking complexity at the finish. Wait two more years. The vintage should allow it to keep much longer. (1983)
➧ Cave Coop. la Chablisienne, 8 Bld Pasteur BP 14, 89800 Chablis; tel. 86 42 11 24 ϒ Mon.–Sat. 8.00–12.00/14.00–18.00.

CHANSON PERE ET FILS★

☐		5 D ∎ ↓

78 ⑦⑨ ⑧① **82** **82** 83

Aromas of flint sparks, new wax and broom flowers combine to give classic character. Very high quality; will long be remembered as a firm, rich white wine. (1983)
➧ *MM*. Chanson Père et Fils, 10–12 Rue Paul-Chanson, 21200 Beaune; tel. 80 22 23 00 ϒ No visitors.

DOMAINE DES COURTIS★

☐	10ha	75000	3 ⑾ ↓

79 80 81 ⑧② 83

Light, clear colour and reserved aromas marked by high alcohol content. Straightforward, perhaps lacking finesse. Should keep well. (1983)
➧ Frédéric Prain, Dom des Courtis, Milly, 89800 Chablis; tel. 86 42 40 82 ϒ By appt.

DOMAINE JEAN-PAUL DROIN
Valmur★★

☐ Gd Cru	1ha	6000	4 D ∎ ↓

69 75 76 78 80 81 ⑧② **82** 83

Although the colour may be a little pale, the nose is typical of Chardonnay grown in chalky soil. The bouquet is floral and mineral, and gives promise of a great wine in five years' time. Excellent, but would be even better if raised in wood. (1983) ✔ Chablis Premier Cru Vaillon et Montmain, Montmain-Montée-de-Tonnerre, Chablis Grand Cru Vaudesir-les-Clos, Grenouille.
➧ Jean-Paul Droin, 14 bis, Rue Jean-Jaurès, 89800 Chablis; tel. 86 42 16 78 ϒ By appt. Closed 1–25 Aug.

JOSEPH DROUHIN★★★

☐		4 ⑾ ↓

76 77 78 79 80 81 ★82 ⑧③

Straw-yellow chablis with attractive floral aromas with a touch of fresh mint. A delicate hazelnut flavour, well-judged acidity and a firm, rich flavour. (1983)
➧ Joseph Drouhin, 7 Rue d'Enfer, 21200 Beaune; tel. 80 22 06 80 ϒ By appt. Closed Aug., and Dec.

DOMAINE DE L'EGLANTIERE★★

☐	90ha	560000	4 D ∎ ↓

71 74 75 76 **78** 80 81 ⑧② **82** 83

Pale colour and great aromatic purity. Long honey-sweet flavour of great delicacy – a con-siderable wine-making achievement in this vintage characterized more by power than finesse. (1983)
➧ Jean Durup, 4 Grande Rue, Maligny, 89800 Chablis; tel. 86 47 44 49 ϒ By appt. Closed Aug. weekends and public holidays.

DOMAINE LAROCHE★

☐	47ha	300000	4 D ∎ ↓

71 75 76 78 79 80 81 ⑧② **82** **83**

Straw-yellow colour of this wine is a prelude to a very fruity nose, with an elegant hint of vine flower. Good, sappy flavour but a bit short. Traces of carbon dioxide that are still present should disappear after a year. (1983)
➧ Dom. Laroche, 10 Rue Auxerroise, 89800 Chablis; tel. 86 42 14 30 ϒ Mon.–Sat. 8.30–12.00/13.30–18.00.

DOMAINE LE VERGER★

☐	15ha	100000	3 D ∎ ↓

73 78 79 81 ⑧② **83**

Clear colour with characteristic green reflections. Subtle, refined aromas with hints of minerals and iodine, which make it ideal to drink with oysters. Will retain its fruity quality and acidity for several years. (1983)
ϒ Alain Geoffroy, 4 Rue de l'Equerre, Beines, 89800 Chablis; tel. 86 43 43 76 ϒ By appt.

NOEMIE VERNAUX★★

☐		8000	5 D ∎ ↓

★83

The rich vintage shows its character in the full, expressive aromas and fat flavour of this Chablis. Would suit fairly strong sauced dishes. (1983)
➧ Ets Noémie Vernaux, Rue des Vérottes, 21200 Beaune; tel. 80 22 28 50 ϒ By appt. Closed 15 Dec.–end Feb.

Chablis Premier Cru

This appellation comes from about thirty specific parts of the vineyard selected for their high-quality production. The wine differs from plain Chablis not so much by a better ripening of the grapes but by its more complex and persistent bouquet where various aromas mingle; honey and acacia, a trace of iodine and a suggestion of leafiness. All wine-makers agree that it reaches its peak at about five years when it acquires a certain nuttiness. The climats that produce the fullest wines are La Montée de Tonnerre, Fourchaume, Mont de Milieu, Forêt (or Butteaux) and Lechet.

LA CHABLISIENNE *Fourchaume*★

☐	28ha	240000	4 D ∎ ↓

69 71 75 76 ⑦⑧ **83** 84

Pale colour. The honey nose is very discreet and subtle. Great finesse of the aromas. While no richer than a plain Chablis, its flavour is decidedly more persistent. A hint of carbon dioxide, which appears if the serving temperature is rapidly cooled, makes it harsh. Leave to mature further. (1983)

🕶 Cave Coop. la Chablisienne, 8 Bld Pasteur, BP 14, 89800 Chablis; tel. 86 42 11 24 ☂ Mon.–Sat. 8.00–12.00/14.00–18.00

LA CHABLISIENNE *Mont-de-Milieu**

□		10 ha	72000	4 D ▮ ↓
69 71 75 76 ⑦⑧ 83 84				

Clear colour and characteristic aromas of honey and mineral salt. On the palate, lacks some force and acidity, but softness means it is almost ready to drink. Long refined finish. (1983)

🕶 Cave. Coop. la Chablisienne, 8 Bld Pasteur, BP 14, 89800 Chablis; tel. 86 42 11 24 ☂ Mon.–Sat. 8.00–12.00/14.00–18.00.

JEAN COLLET *Vaillons**

□		6 ha	48000	4 D ⑪ ↓
76 78 79 80 81 ⑧② 82 83				

Pale colour with green tints: immature aromas marked by a strong grassy character. Needs to age but will always perhaps lack finesse. A vigorous, slightly earthy flavour reminiscent of the Chablis of old, made by a producer descended from the aptly named Pinot family, which can be traced back as far as 1792. (1983) ✔ Chablis Premier Cru Montmains/Montée, Chablis Grand Cru Valmur, Chablis AOC.

🕶 Jean Collet et Fils, 1 Rue du Panonceau, 89800 Chablis; tel. 86 42 11 93 ☂ Mon.–Sat. 8.00–12.00/13.30–19.00. Closed 15 Aug.–31 Aug.

DOMAINE DE LA COUR DU ROY *Vaillons**

□		3 ha	19000	4 D ▮ ⑪
75 *79 *79 *81 ⑧② 83				

Unforthcoming nose, testifying to the recent bottling. Powerful flavour but short of acidity. Round and smooth but not very subtle. (1982) ✔ Chablis Grand Cru.

🕶 Christian Mignard, 40 Rue Auxerroise, 89800 Chablis; tel. 86 42 12 27 ☂ Daily 9.00–12.00/1500–20.00.

RENE DAUVISSAT *Forêt**

□		3.8 ha	23000	5 ⑪ D
*75 76 78 79 81 ⑧② 82 83				

This wine had just been bottled when it was tasted, and still had a slightly yeasty flavour. Deep, lustrous yellow colour coming from the new oak in which the wine was raised. Fat, round, very long flavour with a hint of new wood. Will be a fine, characterful bottle of wine in three years' time. (1983)

🕶 René Dauvissat, 8 Rue Emile Zola, 89800 Chablis; tel. 86 52 11 58 ☂ By appt.

JEAN DAUVISSAT *Vaillons****

□		4 ha	25000	4 D ⑪ ↓
*75 *76 78 79 80 81 ⑧② 83				

Uncommon bouquet and taste. Pronounced aromas of pineapple drops and hint of tobacco as the bouquet develops. Persistent flavour. Leave for two or three years. (1983)

🕶 Jean Dauvissat, 3 Rue de Chichée, 89800 Chablis; tel. 86 42 14 62 ☂ By appt. Closed Christmas and New Year.

DANIEL DEFAIX *Les Lys***

□		1 ha	6000	4 D ⑪ ↓
71 75 76 78 79 80 ⑧① 82 83				

Pale with green highlights. A bouquet of great finesse, with notes of honey and gunflint, due to its fine vineyard site on the left bank of the river Serein. Smooth deep flavour and unctuous finish. May be kept three to six years. (1983) ✔ Chablis.

🕶 Daniel Defaix, 23 Rue de Champlain, Milly 89800 Chablis; tel. 86 42 42 05 ☂ By appt Mon.–Sat. Closed Aug. and during harvest.

DOMAINE DEFAIX *Côte de Lechet***

□		1.5 ha	6000	4 D ▮ ↓
71 75 76 78 79 80 ⑧① 82 83				

The Côte de Lechet vineyard gives a very pronounced terroir character, showing itself here in the remarkably full, complex mineral-saline aromas which develop, on contact with the air, a distinctive note of nougatine. Considerable finesse but perhaps slightly lacking in concentration. (1983) ✔ Chablis.

🕶 Daniel Defaix, 23 Rue de Champlain, Milly, 89800 Chablis; tel. 86 42 42 05 ☂ By appt Mon.–Sat. Closed Aug. and during harvest.

DOMAINE J.-P. DROIN *Montmains**

□		0.71 ha	4500	4 D ▮ ↓
76 78 80 81 ⑧② 82 83				

Crisp, fresh wine; almost colourless. Nose characterized by aromas of honey and gunflint. Allow two or three years before this wine becomes more expressive. ✔ Chablis Premier Cru Vaillons, Montée-de-Tonnerre, Chablis Grand Cru Valmur et Vaudesir, Grenouille-les-Clos.

🕶 Jean-Paul Droin, 14 bis, Rue Jean-Jaurès, 89800 Chablis; tel. 86 42 16 78 ☂ By appt. Closed 1–25 Aug.

DOMAINE J.-P. DROIN *Vaillons***

□		2.6 ha	14000	4 D ▮ ↓
75 76 78 80 *81 ⑧② 83				

Very pale colour. Fine and subtle nose with hints of aniseed and honey. Suitable for keeping ten years, at least. (1983)

🕶 Jean-Paul Droin, 14 bis, Jean-Jaurès, 89800 Chablis; tel. 86 42 16 78 ☂ By appt.

MARCEL DUPLESSIS *Montée de Tonnerre**

□		5 ha	37000	4 D ▮ ⑪ ↓
76 78 79 81 82 82 83				

Typical slow-developing cru. Pale colour and austere, rather closed nose. Considerable acidity for a vintage that normally lacks it. Needs several years to develop its aromas. (1982) ✔ Chablis Grand Cru.

🕶 Marcel Duplessis, 5 Quai de Reugny, 89800 Chablis; tel. 86 42 10 75 ☂ No visitors.

ALAIN GEOFFROY *Fourchaume★*

☐	8.5ha	55000	4 D ▮ ↓

75 76 78 79 80 81 ⑧② 83

Characteristic green highlights and discreet, honeyed aromas. Smooth and pleasant on the palate, with a hint of carbon dioxide, which should disappear in a year. Length of flavour is worthy of a Premier Cru. (1983)
➤ Alain Geoffroy, 4 Rue de l'Equerre, Beines, 89800 Chablis; tel. 86 42 43 76 ☎ By appt.

ALAIN GEOFFROY *Beauroy★*

☐	8.5ha	55000	4 D ▮ ↓

73 78 79 80 81 ⑧② 83

Pale, classic colour with flashes of green. Needs to breathe, to bring out the bouquet of bush peach with a hint of iodine. Smooth, elusive flavour. Residual carbon dioxide will disappear after a few years in bottle. (1983)
➤ Alain Geoffroy, 4 Rue de l'Equerre, Beines, 89800 Chablis; tel. 86 42 43 76 ☎ By appt.

LAMBLIN ET FILS *Mont-de-Milieu★★*

☐	2ha	12000	4 D ▮ ◑ ↓

66 71 78 81 ⑧② 83

Pale colour and an intense, richly expressive nose. Honey, gunflint and dashes of rose and peony give a certain elegance. Fat, well rounded, attractive flavour; worth keeping for a long time.
➤ *MM.* Lamblin et Fils, Maligny, 89800 Chablis; tel. 86 47 40 85 ☎ Mon.–Fri. 8.00–12.00/14.00–17.00. Sat. 8.00–12.00.

DOMAINE LAROCHE *Vaillons★★*

☐	6ha	33000	5 D ◑ ↓

78 79 81 ⑧② 83

Pale colour and a subtle bouquet with a hint of smokiness. Good length and texture with the advantage of some barrel ageing. Above average. (1983)
➤ Dom. Laroche, 10 Rue Auxerroise, 89800 Chablis; tel. 86 42 14 30 ☎ Mon.–Sat. 8.30–12.00/13.30–18.00.

DOMAINE LAROCHE *Vaudeveys★★*

☐	11ha	65000	5 D ▮ ↓

78 79 ⑧② 82 83

Attractive, light colour and considerable aromatic finesse coming from the chalky vineyard soil. Fat, sappy flavour with good acidity, making it an excellent partner to seafood. This wine is made from young vines from a very well-situated vineyard which has only recently been replanted after a long period of neglect, due to the difficul-

ties of cultivation posed by the very steep slopes. (1983)
➤ Dom. Laroche, 10 Rue Auxerroise, 89800 Chablis; tel. 86 42 14 30 ☎ Mon.–Sat. 8.30–12.00/13.30–18.00.

DOMAINE LAROCHE
Fourchaume Vieilles Vignes★★★

☐1er Cru	7ha	40000	5 D ◑ ↓

78 79 80 81 ⑧② 83

Fuller colour than usual, with refined aromas of white peach and vanilla. Rich, full-bodied, smooth flavour, with well-knit new oak character. Produced from a selection of old vines. Outstanding. (1983)
➤ Dom. Laroche, 10 Rue Auxerroise, 89800 Chablis; tel. 86 42 14 30 ☎ Daily 8.30–12.00/13.30–18.00. Closed Sun.

J.-M. RAVENEAU
Montée-de-Tonnerre★★★

☐	1ha	5000	4 D ◑ ↓

⑦⑧ 79 80 81 82

Pale colour with green reflections, subtle nose with hints of acacia honey. Extreme concentration and astonishing vigour and fine, clean finish. Among the very top Chablis. (1983)
➤ Jean-Marie Raveneau, 9 Rue Chichée, 89800 Chablis; tel. 86 42 17 46 ☎ Closed July–Aug.

A. REGNARD *Fourchaume★★★*

☐	1 000 000	4 ▮ ↓

78 79 81 81 82 83 84

Unfortunately this wine is no longer on sale, but look out for it in a friend's cellar! Exceptionally rich aromas and perfectly balanced, rich flavour. A fine example of this vineyard with all the complexity one would expect from very old vines and excellent vinification. (1981)
➤ A. Regnard, Blvd Tacussel, 89800 Chablis; tel. 86 42 10 45 ☎ By appt.

A. REGNARD *Mont-de-Milieu★*

☐	1 000 000	4 D

78 79 81 82 83 83 84

An already mature colour; rich characteristic aromas of truffle and iodine. A finely balanced wine of great promise, although it is still n83ready. A very good bottle.
➤ A. Regnard, Blvd Tacussel, 89800 Chablis; tel. 86 42 10 45.

Chablis Grand Cru

Chablis Grand Cru is made from grapes grown on the best exposed slopes of the east bank of the Serein. The 90 hectares of Grand Cru vines are divided into seven sections: Blanchot, Bougros, Les Clos, Grenouilles, Preuses, Valmur and Vaudésir. Chablis Grand Cru possesses an intensity that is markedly superior to all other Chablis wines, for the vine feeds on a soil enriched by clay and stone alluvium. If well-made, a Chablis Grand

Cru is a full, round wine that has a long-lasting aroma with a certain firmness, distinguishing it from its rivals in the more southern parts of Burgundy. The greatest wines have been known to age for more than ten years in bottle.

LA CHABLISIENNE *Grenouilles*★★

☐	7ha	50400	5 D ▪ ↓

69 71 75 76 ⑦⑧ 83 84

Similar colour to the Preuses, but a much more expansive fruity character. Multi-layered bouquet of inimitable Grand Cru class. Rich, fat flavour of great concentration allowing the wine to be drunk now or kept for several years. One's only regret is the absence of new wood. (1983)
☙ Cave Coop. la Chablisienne, 8 Bld Pasteur, BP 14, 89800 Chablis; tel. 86 42 11 24 ☈ Mon.–Sat. 8.00–12.00/14.00–18.00.

LA CHABLISIENNE *Vaudésir*★★★

☐	0.5ha	3600	5 D ▪ ↓

69 71 75 76 ⑦⑧ 83 84

Pale colour and discreet aromas, but it is difficult to remain insensitive to the tremendous breeding and exquisite finesse of its touches of iodine and gunflint. It would be a crime to consume it too quickly. (1983)
☙ Cave Coop. la Chablisienne, 8 Bld Pasteur, BP 14, 89800 Chablis; tel. 86 42 11 24 ☈ Mon.–Sat. 8.00–12.00/14.00–18.00.

LA CHABLISIENNE *Les Clos*★★

☐	1ha	7200	5 D ▪ ↓

69 71 75 76 ⑦⑧ 83 ⑧③ 84

Pale colour and very dumb nose. More volume and concentration than the Vaudésir, but less finesse. Of all the Grands Crus, Les Clos is the most structured and the slowest to develop. This *cuvée* however, although rich and concentrated, seems to lack acid support. Things may change with a few more years' bottle age. Generally considered one of la Chablisienne's finest cuvées. (1983)
☙ Cave Coop. la Chablisienne, 8 Bld Pasteur, BP 14, 89800 Chablis; tel. 86 42 11 24 ☈ Mon.–Sat. 8.00–12.00/14.00–18.00.

LA CHABLISIENNE *Les Preuses*★★

☐	3ha	21600	5 D ▪ ↓

69 71 75 76 ⑦⑧ 83 84

Pale with green highlights. The nose is striking for its purity and strongly mineral nature. The bouquet has not yet blossomed, but there is a subtle scent of fresh hazelnuts characteristic of the soil. Excellently vinified, but would perhaps have benefited from a few months in new wood to give it more structure. Wait five years. (1983)
☙ Cave Coop. la Chablisienne, 8 Bld Pasteur, BP 14, 89800 Chablis; tel. 86 42 11 24 ☈ Mon.–Sat. 8.00–12.00/14.00–18.00.

LA CHABLISIENNE *Bougros*★

☐	1ha	7200	5 D ▪ ↓

69 71 75 76 ⑦⑧ 83 84

Very pale, clear colour. The class of this Grand Cru is expressed in a slight intensification of the aroma of honey and fruits, and, above all, by a note of flint. Extreme purity of taste, refreshing acidity and length. Clear Chardonnay character but less complex than the other Grand Crus from la Chablisienne. Its lifespan should well exceed ten years. (1983)
☙ Cave Coop. la Chablisienne, 8 Bld Pasteur, BP 14, 89800 Chablis; tel. 86 42 11 24 ☈ Mon.–Sat. 8.00–12.00/14.00–18.00.

JEAN DAUVISSAT *Les Preuses*★

☐	4ha	20000	4 D ◫ ↓

75 ★76 78 79 80 ⑧① 82 83 ⑧③

Attractive waxy, almond nose but a little upset by recent bottling. Palate requires more time to develop. Well constructed with sufficient acidity to age well; needs five years. (1983)
☙ Jean Dauvissat, 3 Rue de Chichée, 89800 Chablis; tel. 86 42 14 62 ☈ By appt. Closed 25 Dec., 1 Jan.

RENE DAUVISSAT *Les Preuses*★★

☐	1ha	6000	5 ◫ ↓

76 78 79 80 **81** ⑧② ⑧② 83

Light golden colour and powerful oaky nose with a hint of gunflint. Strikingly fat, smooth flavour giving an impression almost of fresh cream. Very complex flavours on the palate but already quite open and soft. An excellent bottle to drink with delicate fish dishes. (1982)
☙ René Dauvissat, 8 Rue Emile Zola, 89800 Chablis; tel. 86 52 11 58 ☈ By appt.

RENE DAUVISSAT *Les Clos*★★★

☐	1.7ha	10000	4 ◫ ↓

76 78 79 80 **81** ⑧② ⑧②

Brilliant, luminous colour and exceptionally refined smoky, mineral nose. Deep, firm flavour combined with a delicate yet persistent bouquet – a tribute to the vineyard and the meticulous vinification of this grower. A classic bottle which will keep on improving over the next decade. (1983)
☙ René Dauvissat, 8 Rue Emile-Zola, 89800 Chablis; tel. 86 52 11 58 ☈ By appt.

DOMAINE J.P. DROIN *Vaudésir*★★

☐	1.15ha	6000	4 D ▪ ↓

75 76 78 79 **81** ⑧② 83

Green glints form the introduction to a delightful bouquet which combines honey sweetness with a mineral note typical of the Chablis grand cru vineyards. Vigorous, fine, characterful, and worth keeping for ten years. (1983)
☙ Jean-Paul Droin, 14 bis, Rue Jean-Jaurès, 89800 Chablis; tel. 86 42 16 78 ☈ By appt.

DOMAINE LAROCHE
Les Blanchots★★★

| □Gd Cru | 4ha | 20000 | 5 D ◗ ↓ |

71 78 79 80 81 ⑧ 83

Fine colour and refined aromas. Characteristic nuances of sweetly-scented flowers and gunflint, and delicate smokiness coming from the new oak. Round, aristocratic flavour; already pleasant, but may be kept. (1983)
➸ Dom. Laroche, 10 Rue Auxerroise, 89800 Chablis; tel. 86 42 14 30 ☎ Daily 8.30–12.00/13.30–18.00. Closed Sun.

DOMAINE LAROCHE
Blanchot Vieilles Vignes★★★

| □ | 4ha | 20000 | 5 D ◗ ↓ |

78 79 80 81 ⑧ 83

Delicate golden colour with light pink highlights. Fruity (peach, pear) and the nose is very discreet and oaky. The old vines make up in refinement and subtlety what they lack in acidity and vigour. (1983)
➸ Dom. Laroche, 10 Rue Auxerroise, 89800 Chablis; tel. 86 42 14 30 ☎ Mon.–Sat. 8.30–12.00/13.30–18.00.

DOMAINE LAROCHE
Les Clos Vieilles Vignes★★

| □Gd Cru | 1ha | 5000 | 5 D ◗ ↓ |

71 ★79 81 ⑧ 82

Exceptional with light, clear, colour and delicate bouquet suggesting hazelnut and sweet acacia. Great but very firm Chablis quite unlike many softer, more immediately appealing white wines. (1983)
➸ Dom. Laroche, 10 Rue Auxerroise, 89800 Chablis; tel. 86 42 14 30 ☎ Daily 8.30–12.00/13.30–18.00. Closed Sun.

DOMAINE DE LA MALADIERE
Les Clos★★

| □Gd Cru | 4ha | 25000 | 5 ▮ ◗ ↓ |

68 76 78 79 80 81 81 ⑧ 82 83

Aromas of honey, acacia, vine blossom and vanilla mingle together in a delicate nose, which is not yet completely knit. The soft, easy 1982 vintage already gives the wine a smooth, pleasant flavour but the reserved aromas remind one that les Clos is the slowest developing Grand Cru; leave for five years. (1982)
➸ William Fèvre, 14 Rue Jules-Rathier, 89800 Chablis; tel. 86 42 12 51 ☎ Tues.–Sun. 9.00–12.00/14.00–18.00

J.-M. RAVENEAU *Valmur*★★★

| □ | 0.75ha | 4500 | 4 D ◗ ↓ |

⑦⑧ 79 80 81 82

Notable for the brightness and finesse of its honey scent, with dashes of mineral and iodine. Rare, creamy richness and penetrating flavour with an excellent acid structure. A perfect example of the appellation. (1983)
➸ Jean-Marie Raveneau, 9 Rue Chichée, 89800 Chablis; tel. 86 42 17 46 ☎ By appt.

A. REGNARD *Blanchot*★★★

| □ | 1000000 | 4 ◗ ↓ |

78 78 79 81 82 83 84

Yet another very attractive wine already sold out at the property. Those lucky enough to find it will discover the firm, refinement of a first-rate Chablis Grand Cru. Elegant aromas with a hint of iodine; finely judged acidity, and, finally, the distinctive contribution of the soil all add up to a remarkable bottle from an outstanding year. (1983)
➸ A. Regnard, Blvd Tacussel, 89800 Chablis; tel. 86 42 10 45.

A. REGNARD *Bougros*★★

| □ | | 5 |

A very attractive wine with a bright colour and clearly etched aromas of flowers, cork, bark and iodine. The finesse of the bouquet is matched by a rich, harmonious flavour. Ready to drink but will improve. (1983)
➸ A. Regnard, Blvd Tacussel, 89800 Chablis; tel. 86 42 10 45.

Sauvignon de Saint-Bris vDQS

PHILIPPE DEFRANCE★

| □ | 2ha | 12000 | 3 D ▮ ↓ |

Bright gold colour and a nose with the full aromas of ripe Sauvignon. Rich with character and a balanced flavour combining finesse and length. Ready to drink. (1982) ✔ Bourgogne Aligoté, Bourgogne Rouge.
➸ Philippe Defrance, 5 Rue du Four, 89530 St-Bris-le-Vineux; tel. 86 53 33 82 ☎ By appt. Closed 1 week beginning of Jan.

CLAUDE SEGUIN★

| □ | 0.75ha | 4800 | 3 D ▮ ↓ |

Very light golden green colour with some sharp Sauvignon varietal character. Complex bouquet now rather tired. Drink now. Younger vintages from this producer may be recommended. (1982)
✔ Bourgogne Aligoté.
➸ Claude Seguin, 3 Bis Rue Haute, 89530 St-Bris-le-Vineux; tel. 86 53 37 39 ☎ By appt.

JEAN-PAUL TABIT★

| □ | 2ha | 12000 | 3 D ▮ ↓ |

76 79 82 82 83 83

The chalky soil of Saint-Bris softens the very sharp fruitiness of the Sauvignon grape. This is a good example with its clear colour with green highlights, raspberry-leaf aromas and soft, honeyed flavour. Some residual carbon dioxide rather shortens the finish. (1983) ✔ Bourgogne Aligoté, Bourgogne Rouge, Bourgogne Passe-

tout-grain.
🍷 Jean-Paul Tabit, 2 Rue Dorée, 89530 St-Bis-le-
Vineux; tel. 86 53 33 83 ⏳ By appt.

THE COTE DE NUITS

Fixin

South of the vineyards of Marsannay-
la-Côte and Couchey is Fixin with 150
hectares – the first of a series of
communes for which the appellations
are simply designated by the commune or village name itself. Fixin
makes solid, robust red wines that are
often high in tannin and keep well.
The grower also has the option of
using, in place of the appellation
Fixin, the appellation Côte-de-Nuits-
Villages, but the declaration must be
made at harvest time.

Hervelets, Arvelets, Clos du Chapitre and Clos Napoléon are fine 'climats' (vineyard sites) which are all
classed as Premiers Crus. But perhaps
the most famous vineyard is Clos de la
Perrière, which has been described as
outstanding by several Burgundian
writers, and has even been compared
to a Chambertin. This clos extends
slightly into the neighbouring commune of Brochon. Another vineyard
of note is Meix-Bas.

CIE DES VINS D'AUTREFOIS★★

■1er Cru   5 D 🍴 ↓
*83 83

Already displays characteristics of a very good
wine. Intense, slightly bronzed colour; aromas of
blackcurrant, cooked peaches and fruit stones,
and a well-judged balance between tannin, acidity and sweetness on the palate. Drink in several
years' time. (1983)
🍷 Cie des Vins d'Autrefois, 9 Rue Celer, 21200
Beaune; tel. 80 22 21 31 ⏳ No visitors.

ANDRE BART *Hervelets*★

■1er Cru   1.25ha   2750   4 D 🍶 ↓
76 77 **78** *79 80 **81** 82

The power of the 1983 vintage and the all-
pervasive aroma of new wood make it harsh at
present. Needs to soften and should be kept.
(1983) ✔ Bourgogne Marsannay Rouge, Côtes de
Nuits-Villages.
🍷 André Bart, 24 Rue de Mazy, 21160 Marsannay-la-Côte; tel. 80 52 12 09 ⏳ By appt.

DOMAINE BERTHAUT *Les Crais*★★★

■   1ha   5500   4 D 🍶 ↓
76 *79 *⟨82⟩ *82

This small enclave produces an outstanding
cuvée; a fifteen-day fermentation is followed by
two years in cask. A wine to be laid down. (1982)
🍷 Dom. Berthaut, 9 Rue Noisot, Fixin, 21220
Gevrey-Chambertin; tel. 80 52 45 48 ⏳ By appt.

DOMAINE BERTHAUT *Les Arvelets*★★

■1er Cru   1ha   5500   5 D 🍶 ↓
76 79 ⟨82⟩ 82

One of the six Fixin Premier Crus. Has great
finesse while retaining the firmness characteristic
of its soil. (1982)
🍷 Dom. Berthaut, 9 Rue Noisot, Fixin, 21220
Gevrey-Chambertin; tel. 80 52 45 48 ⏳ By appt.

DOMAINE BERTHAUT★★

■   8ha   48000   4 D 🍶 ↓
76 *79 **80 81** *⟨82⟩ *82

The wines from this domaine are of a high quality
and this 1982 has several years ahead of it. A
perfect bottle to drink with coq au vin (cooked in
Fixin, obviously . . .) (1982) ✔ Fixin les Crais,
Fixin le Arvelets Premier Cru.
🍷 Dom. Berthaut, 9 Rue Noisot, Fixin, 21220
Gevrey-Chambertin; tel. 80 52 45 48 ⏳ By appt.

BRUNO CLAIR *La Croix-Blanche*★★

■   1ha   5400   4 D 🍶 ↓
82 *⟨83⟩

Fine wine with pleasantly structured flavours,
although the nose is still a little masked by the
strong scent of new oak casks. Length on the
palate promises a fine future. (1982) ✔ Bourgogne Marsannay Rouge et Rosé.
🍷 Bruno Clair, 3 Rue de la Maladière, 21160
Marsannay-la-Côte; tel. 80 52 28 95 ⏳ By appt.

GELIN ET MOLIN *Clos du Châpitre*★★

■1er Cru   4.78ha   27000   5 D 🍶 ↓
78 *79 81 ⟨82⟩ 82

This vineyard adjoined a chapter house and its
wines were no doubt used for the celebration of
the services. These good fathers, leaving the
humbler Aligotés and Gamays to the country
priests, must have felt that to do the Lord – and
their own tastebuds – justice required nothing
less than a premier cru. This 1982, has a firm
powerful flavour and needs to be laid down for
several years. (1982)
🍷 MM. Gelin et Molin, 62 Route des Grands-
Crus, Fixin, 21220 Gevrey-Chambertin; tel.
80 52 45 24 ⏳ By appt.

DOMAINE PIERRE GELIN
Clos Napoléon★★

■1er Cru   1.83ha   10000   5 D 🍶 ↓
78 *79 81 *⟨82⟩ *82

The 1982 has already acquired a complex bouquet and rich, full-bodied flavour, which will
allow it to keep well. (1982)

र Dom. Pierre Gelin, 62 Route des Grands-Crus, Fixin, 21220 Gevrey-Chambertin; tel. 80 52 45 24 ⚌ By appt.

DOMAINE PIERRE GELIN
Les Hervelets★★

| ■1er Cru | 0.6ha | 3300 | 5 D ⚏ ⚒ |

Combines subtlety and finesse with a solid structure and good length on the palate. A good bottle to lay down. (1982)
र Dom. Pierre Gelin, 62 Routes des Grands-Crus, Fixin, 21220 Gevrey-Chambertin; tel. 80 52 45 24 ⚌ By appt.

DOMAINE PIERRE GELIN★★

| ■ | 2ha | 10500 | 5 D ⚏ ⚒ |

78 ★**79 81** ★⑧② ★82

Firm, well-balanced 1982 Fixin produced from 25-year-old vines. Fine, bright colour and fruity aromas that are just beginning to open out. A good example of the Fixin 'terroir' with earthy, mineral-rich flavours, typical of this Northern Côte de Nuits vineyard land. May be drunk now or laid down. (1982)
र Dom. Pierre Gelin, 62 Route des Grands-Crus, Fixin, 21220 Gevrey-Chambertin; tel. 80 52 45 24 ⚌ By appt.

JEAN-PIERRE GUYARD★★

| ■ | 1ha | 4200 | 4 D ⚏ ⚒ |

★76 77 ★78 81 82

A fairly soft wine, typical of the 1982 vintage, but showing good depth of flavour and attractive cooked cherry aromas. Ready to drink but may be kept. (1982) ✔ Bourgogne Marsannay Rouge.
र Jean-Pierre Guyard, 4 Rue du Vieux-Collège, 21160 Marsannay-la-Côte; tel. 80 52 12 43 ⚌ By appt.

ALAIN GUYARD★★

| ■ | 1.8ha | 9000 | 4 D ⚒ |

77 **78 79** ★**80 81** 82 ⑧③

Aromas of candied fruit with a touch of oak, and refined flavours on the palate, make this Fixin at least the equal of the best Côte de Nuits-Villages. Although it may be drunk now, better to keep. (1982)
र Alain Guyard, 10 Rue du Puits-de-Têt, 21160 Marsannay-la-Côte; tel. 80 52 14 46 ⚌ By appt.

DOMAINE DR MARION *La Mazière*★★

| ■ | 0.88ha | 42000 | 5 D ⚏ ⚒ |

A well-vinified wine with a long life ahead of it. Elegant, well-rounded flavour with still youthful aromas. (1980)
र Bouchard Père et Fils, Au Château, 21200 Beaune; tel. 80 22 14 41 ⚌ By appt. Closed Aug.

DOMAINE DE LA PERRIERE
Clos de la Perrière★★★

| ■1er Cru | 5ha | 27000 | 5 D ⚍ ⚏ ⚒ |

75 **76** 77 **78** 79 80 **81 82** ⑧③ 83

The 1983 is particularly powerful, fullbodied and long on the palate. Should be a very good wine by the end of the century. (1983)
र Philippe Joliet, Manoir de la Perrière, Fixin, 21220 Gevrey-Chambertin; tel. 80 52 47 85 ⚌ By appt.

Gevrey-Chambertin

In Brochon, between Fixin and Gevrey, wines are entitled to one of three following appellations, according to the vineyard site: Fixin, a small area of Clos de la Perrière; Côtes de Nuits-Villages, for wines from the northern side of the village (including the vineyards of Préau and Queue-de-Hareng) and Gevrey-Chambertin, for wines from the south.

The vineyards of Gevrey were famous in the thirteenth century, when it was largely owned by the Abbey of Cluny. Today, as well as being the largest communal appellation (more than 10000 hectolitres), Gevrey-Chambertin is home to several prestigious classed-growth vineyards. To the north of the Combe de Lavaux, which divides the commune in two, lie the climats of Les Evocelles (in Brochon), Les Champeaux, La Combe aux Moines, Les Cazetiers, Le Clos-St-Jacques, and Les Varoilles. There are fewer Premiers Crus on the southern slopes – almost all the hillside is taken up with Grand Crus – but the Premiers Crus Fonteny, Petite-Chapelle and Clos-Prieur are all worth mentioning.

The hillside vineyards of this appellation produce full-bodied and powerful wines. The vineyards on the plain give wines that are less forceful but which may be elegant and refined. In passing one should correct the false belief that the Gevrey-Chambertin appellation stretches as far as the Dijon-Beaune railway line, that is, onto land that does not deserve this classification. In fact, limestone gravel soils similar to those in the hills fan out from the Combe de Lavaux, deposited during the Ice Age, when the Combe was the channel for glacial material. It is simply that, on the plain, these soils

299

Côte de Nuits (North)

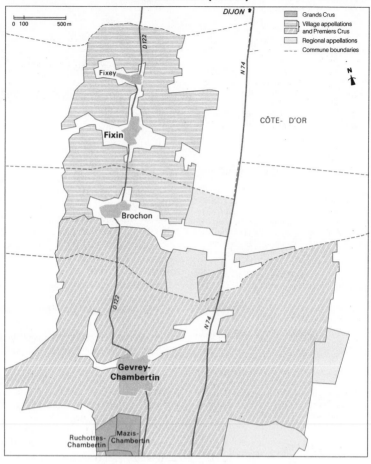

are deeper, giving the wines finesse without any loss of generic style.

THOMAS BASSOT
Lavaux-Saint-Jacques★

■1er Cru	300	6 D ⦿ ↓
71 74 78 ★79 81 82 83		

Still remarkably young for a 1979, with a fine bouquet of vanilla, pistachio and liquorice. Still needs several years to round out on the palate. (1979)
☞ Thomas Bassot, 5 Quai Dumorey, 21700 Nuits-St-Georges; tel. 80 62 31 05 ⵑ By appt.

THOMAS BASSOT★

■	3000	5 D ⦿ ↓
71 74 76 78 79 81 82 83		

A well-balanced, fairly firm 1982 with intense fruity flavours and enough tannin to be left for several years. (1982)

☞ Thomas Bassot, 5 Quai Dumorey, 21700 Nuits-St-Georges; tel. 80 62 31 05 ⵑ By appt.

PIERRE BERNOLLIN★★

■	3.5ha	6500	5 D ⦿ ↓
★76 ★78 ★82 83			

This 1982, which is beginning to mature, won full marks for its full, rich flavour, yet pleasing finesse. The aromas are still young and should become even richer with age. (1982)
☞ Pierre Bernollin, 29 Route de Dijon, 21220 Gevrey-Chambertin; tel. 80 34 36 12 ⵑ By appt.

300

ALAIN BURGUET★

| ■ | 4ha | 5 D ⅷ ⌁ |

78 ★79 ★80 **81 82** 83

Good, classic 1982 with a fresh, fruity flavour still appearing very young. (1982)
⌁ Alain Burguet, 18 Rue de l'Eglise, 21220 Gevrey-Chambertin; tel. 80 34 36 35 ☎ No visitors.

DOMAINE CLAIR-DAU
Clos-Saint-Jacques★

| ■ | 2ha | 9600 | 5 D ⅷ ⌁ |

69 71 ★72 ★73 79 ⑧ ★82

· Tasted from the cask; deep, dark cherry-red. Strong new oak aromas with a hint of liquorice. Harsh, very aggressive new-wood flavour but ripe, subdued tannins. Retaste in three years' time. (1983)
⌁ Dom. Clair-Dau, 5 Rue du Vieux-Collège, 21160 Marsannay-la-Côte; tel. 80 52 15 58 ☎ By appt.

DOMAINE DROUHIN-LAROZE
Lavaux-Saint-Jacques★★

| ■ | 20000 | 6 D ⅷ ⌁ |

74 76 77 ★⑦ 79 80 81 **82** 83 85

Picked at the beginning of the 1983 harvest and free of the harshness which marked the later-picked cuvées. Fresh, fruity character of cherry and redcurrant with round, ripe tannins. Keep for at least five years. (1983)
⌁ Dom. Drouhin-Laroze, 20 Rue du Gaizot, 21220 Gevrey-Chambertin; tel. 80 34 31 49 ☎ By appt. Closed Aug. and Oct.

DOMAINE DROUHIN-LAROZE★

| ■ | 20000 | 5 D ⅷ ⌁ |

74 76 77 ★78 ⑦ 80 81 **82** 83

Skilful vinification has produced a smooth, balanced wine from the rugged 1983 vintage. Aromas of conifer and vanilla blend with a rich, cherry-fruit flavour. Well-judged acidity and tannin will ensure a long life. (1983)
⌁ Dom. Drouhin-Laroze, 20 Rue du Gaizot, 21220 Gevrey-Chambertin; tel. 80 34 31 49 ☎ By appt. Closed Aug. and Oct.

DOMAINE DUJAC *Aux Combottes*★★

| ■1er Cru | 1.15ha | 4200 | 6 ⅷ ⌁ |

★76 **78** 79 80 81 82 ㊳

Light colour and rich, soft animal aromas. On the palate, strongly tannic and a discernible beeswax aroma. Distinguished with a great future, tasted two months after bottling. (1983) ✔ Morey-St-Denis, Clos St-Denis, Clos la Roche, Charmes Chambertin.
⌁ Dom. Dujac, Morey-St-Denis, 21220 Gevrey-Chambertin; tel. 80 31 32 58 ☎ By appt. ⌁ Jacques Seysses.

DOMAINE GREY-SERVOZ★

| ■ | 2.3ha | 4000 | 5 D ⅷ ⌁ |

73 ★76 78 81 82 83 84

Clear, bright colour. Typical aromas of coffee, fruit stones and fine wood. Both are characteristic of the vintage. Still very young. (1982)
⌁ Dom. Grey-Servoz, 21220 Gevrey-Chambertin; tel. 80 34 31 66 ☎ By appt.

SERGE GROFFIER★★

| ■ | 0.75ha | 3600 | 5 D ⅷ ⌁ |

79 ⑧ 80

Characteristic of a mature Gevrey-Chambertin. Firm, expressive flavour. Should be laid down for three years when it will be at its peak. (1980)
⌁ Serge Groffier, Morey-St-Denis, 21220 Gevrey-Chambertin; tel. 80 34 31 53 ☎ No visitors.

PHILIPPE LECLERC *La Combe-aux-Moines*★

| ◪1er Cru | 0.7ha | 3000 | 5 D ⅷ ⌁ |

⑦ 78 79 **81** 82

Strongly marked by its vintage. Plenty of finesse and a slight sharpness. Typical aromas of fruit stones and coffee and a light, brisk flavour. (1981)
⌁ Philippe Leclerc, Rue des Halles, 21220 Gevrey-Chambertin; tel. 80 34 30 72 ☎ Daily 9.00–12.00/14.00–19.00.

PHILIPPE LECLERC *Les Cazetiers*★★

| ■1er Cru | 0.5ha | 2400 | 5 D ⅷ ⌁ |

⑦ 78 79 81 **82**

Bottled after two years in cask. Quite open, with a bouquet of coffee, dry fruit and Morello cherries. Sharp tannic edges have been rounded off by the richness of the flavour. Leave to mature a little before drinking. (1982)
⌁ Philippe Leclerc, Rue des Halles, 21220 Gevrey-Chambertin; tel. 80 34 30 72 ☎ Daily 9.00–12.00/14.00–19.00.

DOMAINE MARCHAND-GRILLOT
Petite Chapelle★

| ■1er Cru | 0.8ha | 3850 | 5 D ⅷ ⌁ |

63 65 ⑦ 79 **81 82** 83

Skilfully vinified to compensate for the abundance of the 1982 vintage. Clean, rather severe character but with class. Refined aromas of oak, pepper and liquorice. Will improve with keeping. (1982)
⌁ Dom. Marchand-Grillot et Fils, 23 Rue Aquatique, 21220 Gevrey-Chambertin; tel. 80 34 33 98 ☎ By appt.

MOILLARD★

| ■ | 60000 | 5 ⅷ ⌁ |

78 ⑦ 82

The vintage provides a combination of good tannin and rich smoothness, giving an overall impression of a wine still very young. (1983)
⌁ SARL Moillard, 5 Rue F. Mignotte, 21700 Nuits-St-Georges; tel. 80 61 03 34 ☎ No visitors.

DOMAINE PERNOT-FOURRIER
Clos Saint-Jacques★★★

| ■ | 7.87ha | 30000 | 6 D ⅷ ⌁ |

★⑥ ★71 ★72 ★78 ★79 ★82

Very dark, almost black colour. Nose is still undeveloped although there is already a slightly spicey note. Firm, cherry flavour and elegant structure. The finish is fairly peppery, with a note of liquorice. Very 'masculine' wine and should be tasted around 1988–90. (1982) ✔ Chambolle-Musigny, Vougeot Premier Cru, Griottes Chambertin.
⌁ Dom. Pernot-Fourrier, 7 Route de Dijon,

21220 Gevrey-Chambertin; tel. 80 34 33 99 ♈ By appt.

CHARLES QUILLARDET*

| ■ | | 5 ha | 30000 | 5 D ⦿ ♨ |

*76 *78 79 80 81 *82 **83**

Cherry-red colour and the nose evokes Morello cherries with a hint of kirsch. On the palate, fairly smooth and full-bodied; soft, round finish. (1982) ✔ Chambertin, Fixin, Côtes de Nuits-Villages, Bourgogne Marsannay.
🍷 Charles Quillardet, 18 Route de Dijon, 21220 Gevrey-Chambertin; tel. 80 34 10 26 ♈ By appt. Closed Jan.

JEAN RAPHET*

| ■ | | 4 ha | 19000 | 5 D ⦿ ♨ |

76 *⑦⑧ 79 *⑧② 83

Good example of the type of wine produced in Gevrey in 1982. Perceptible fruit, with strong aromas of cherry and liquorice. Fresh and fairly firm palate. Will stay young for quite a long time. Well suited to grilled red meats. (1982) ✔ Charmes-Chambertin.
🍷 Jean Raphet, Morey-St-Denis, 21220 Gevrey-Chambertin; tel. 80 34 31 67 ♈ By appt.

DOMAINE HENRI REBOURSEAU*

| ■ | | 13 ha | 42000 | 5 D ⦿ ♨ |

76 78 80 82 84

Light, cherry-red colour and a nose strongly marked by oak. Fine, quality wine with very limited commercial distribution. Fat, full-bodied and elegant on the palate. The finish still rather tannic; needs to age at least three years. (1983) ✔ Chambertin Clos-Vougeot, Mazis-Chambertin, Charmes Chambertin.
🍷 Henri Rebourseau, 10 Place du Monument, 21220 Gevrey-Chambertin; tel. 80 34 30 46 ♈ By appt.

HENRI RICHARD**

| ■ | | 2 ha | 9600 | 6 D ⦿ ♨ |

69 71 73 74 76 78 79 81 ⑧② 83

Complex fruity, meaty aromas although the finish is still a little rough. Leave for several years. (1982)
🍷 Henri Richard, 21220 Gevrey-Chambertin; tel. 80 34 31 37 ♈ By appt.

DOMAINE LOUIS TRAPET
*Petite Chapelle**

| ■ | | 1.30 ha | 3600 | 5 D ⦿ ♨ |

76 ⑦⑧ 79 *80 *81 **82 83**

A reminder of the quality of the underrated 1980 vintage. Attractive fruity aromas of dry apricot and apple with a hint of violets. Surprising finesse and remarkable balance. Drink from now on. (1980)
🍷 Dom. Louis Trapet, Route Nationale, 21220 Gevrey-Chambertin; tel. 80 34 30 40 ♈ By appt 🍷 M et Mme Jean Trapet.

DOMAINE LOUIS TRAPET**

| ■ | | 7 ha | 25000 | 5 D ⦿ ♨ |

76 78 79 80 **81** 82 83

A very solid wine with a deep dark colour typical of the 1983 vintage. Complex but immature aromas of cloves, liquorice, fruit stone, almond and thyme. Rich but not harsh on the palate. Leave for a few years. (1983)
🍷 Dom. Louis Trapet, Route Nationale, 21220 Gevrey-Chambertin; tel. 80 34 30 40 ♈ By appt 🍷 M et Mme Jean Trapet.

GEORGES VACHET
*Lavaux-Saint-Jacques**

| ■ 1er Cru | | 7 ha | | 5 ⦿ ♨ |

75 **76** *78 79 80 ⑧② **83** ⑧③

Displays all the sustained power of its vintage, although smoothness and ripe tannins contribute a note of elegance. Fine bottle to keep until the end of the century. (1983)
🍷 Georges Vachet, 15 Rue de Paris, 21220 Gevrey-Chambertin; tel. 80 34 32 03 ♈ By appt.

DOMAINE DES VAROILLES
*Champonnet**

| ■ 1er Cru | | 0.7 ha | 2800 | 5 D ⦿ ♨ |

⑦⑥ **78** 80 **82** ⑧③

Fine 1980 with a musky, gamey nose and smooth flavour; good richness and density for the vintage. (1980).
🍷 Dom. des Varoilles, 11 Rue de l'Ancien Hôpital, 21220 Gevrey-Chambertin; tel. 80 34 32 34 ♈ By appt. Closed Aug. 🍷 Jean-Pierre Naigeon.

DOMAINE DES VAROILLES *Clos du Meix des Ouches**

| ■ | | 1 ha | 5900 | 5 D ⦿ ♨ |

76 78 79 80 82 83

Distinguished by its harmonious structure and light, well-knit flavour. Still not fully matured, and should get richer with some bottle age. (1982)
🍷 Dom. des Varoilles, 11 Rue de l'Ancien-Hôpital, 21220 Gevrey-Chambertin; tel. 80 34 32 34 ♈ By appt. Closed Aug. 🍷 Jean-Pierre Naigeon.

DOMAINE DES VAROILLES
La Romanée

| ■ 1er Cru | | 1.05 ha | 4500 | 6 D ⦿ ♨ |

⑦⑥ **78** 80 **83** ⑧③

Powerful 1983. Colour of blackcurrant liqueur; aromas of new wood with notes of flint stones and vanilla. Leave at the back of the cellar for a decade. (1983)
🍷 Dom. des Varoilles, 11 Rue de l'Ancien Hôpi-

tal, 21220 Gevrey-Chambertin; tel. 80 34 32 34
♀ By appt. Closed Aug. ♠ Jean-Pierre Naigeon.

DOMAINE DES VAROILLES
Clos des Varoilles★★

■1er Cru	6ha	19 000	6 D Ⅱ 〡
⑦⑥ **78** 80 ⑧③ 🔲			

Extremely aromatic 1976. Hard balsamy, resin aromas with hint of toast. Tannin is still very dense, and the flavours firm, direct and elegant. (1976)
♠ Dom. des Varoilles, 11 Rue de l'Ancien Hôpital, 21220 Gevrey-Chambertin; tel. 80 34 32 34
♀ By appt. Closed Aug. ♠ Jean-Pierre Naigeon.

DOMAINE DES VAROILLES★★

■	9.07ha	5 D Ⅱ 〡
76 78 79 80 *82 83		

Deep, bright-red colour and pleasing structure characterize this 1982. The aromas are still very flowery and have not begun to age. Needs to mature.
♠ Dom. des Varoilles, 11 Rue de l'Ancien-Hôpital, 21220 Gevrey-Chambertin; tel. 80 34 32 34
♀ By appt. Closed Aug. ♠ Jean-Pierre Naigeon.

Chambertin and Chambertin-Clos de Bèze

In AD 630 monks from the abbey of Bèze planted vines on a piece of land, with superlative results. This was the origin of the appellation Chambertin-Clos de Bèze (about 15 hectares); the wines may also be sold under the Chambertin appellation.

Bertin was a wine-maker in Gevrey who had land next to Clos de Bèze. Learning from the monks' experience, he planted the same vines in his vineyard, and obtained a wine of similarly good quality. This was Bertin's Field, or Champ de Bertin, from which the name Chambertin comes. The wines from this vineyard, which covers an area of about 12 hectares, are not entitled to the appellation Chambertin-Clos de Bèze.

Chambertin

DOMAINE HUBERT CAMUS★★

■Gd Cru	4ha	10 000	6 D Ⅱ 〡
⑦⑨ 🔲 81 82 83 84			

The difficulties of the vintage have been overcome by the skilful vinification. Displays all the splendid qualities of a mature Chambertin: fine aromas of fruit stones, balsamic resin, coffee and incense. Remarkable delicacy on the palate without appearing thin or dry. Enjoy from now on. (1980)
♠ Hubert Camus, 38 Rue de l'Eglise, 21220 Gevrey-Chambertin; tel. 80 34 31 70 ♀ By appt. Closed during harvest.

DOMAINE HENRI REBOURSEAU★★

■Gd Cru	1ha	1000	6 D Ⅱ 〡
*78 *79 81 *83 🔲			

While still very immature, it nevertheless has the potential roundness and full body that will make it a great wine. (1984)
♠ Dom. Henri Rebourseau, 10 Place du Monument, 21220 Gevrey-Chambertin; tel. 80 34 30 46
♀ By appt. ♠ Pierre Rebourseau et Fils.

DOMAINE LOUIS TRAPET★★

■Gd Cru	3.80ha	12 000	6 D Ⅱ 〡
76 78 ⑦⑨ 81 82 83			

The combined power of the 1983 vintage and the Chambertin vineyard gives this wine an unbelievable richness which almost overpowers the senses. Aromas of truffle, fruit stone and mocha offset the warm, enveloping flavour. Wait for a long, long, time! (1983)
♠ Dom. Louis Trapet, Route Nationale, 21220 Gevrey-Chambertin; tel. 80 34 30 40 ♀ By appt
♠ *M et Mme* Jean Trapet.

Chambertin-Clos de Bèze

CHANSON PERE ET FILS★★

■	6 D Ⅱ 〡
69 76 🔲 81 82	

Pronounced aromas of new oak over a background of vanilla and liquorice with a scent of fruit stones. Fine, keeping structure. (1982)
♠ *MM.* Chanson Père et Fils, 10–12 Rue Paul-Chanson, 21200 Beaune; tel. 80 22 33 00 ♀ No visitors.

DOMAINE DROUHIN-LAROZE★★★

■Gd Cru	20 000	6 D Ⅱ 〡
74 76 77 *⑦⑧ 79 80 81 82 83		

The domaine's top cuvée. Expressive, dry aromas of hay and parched land recalling the torrid 1983 weather. Powerful but refined on the palate with exceptional length. Ready in fifteen years. (1983)
♠ Dom. Drouhin-Laroze, 20 Rue du Gaizot, 21220 Gevrey-Chambertin; tel. 80 34 31 49 ♀ By appt. Closed Aug. and Oct.

DOMAINE DR MARION★★★

■Gd Cru	1.93ha	7000	6 D Ⅱ 〡

The power of a Grand Cru combines with the natural delicacy of the vintage to make a very elegant wine. Should be left to mature. (1982)
♠ Bouchard Père et Fils, Au Château, 21200 Beaune; tel. 80 22 14 41 ♀ By appt. Closed Aug.

303

DOMAINE LOUIS TRAPET★★

■Gd Cru   1.50ha   4800   ⑥ Ⓓ ⑪ ⬇

76 ⑦⑧ 79 *80 *81 **82** 83

Pronounced leafy, gamey aromas suggesting that, despite the vintage, this wine may mature more quickly than some of its peers. Well structured but not too harsh on the palate. Should reach maturity in five or ten years. (1983)

☛ Dom. Louis Trapet, Route Nationale, 21220 Gevrey-Chambertin; tel. 80 34 30 40 ☥ By appt
☛ M et Mme Jean Trapet.

Other Chambertin Appellations

In the same area as the previous two growths is a cluster of other Grand Cru vineyards which, although less exceptional, nevertheless belong recognizably to the same family. The wines still have the various characteristics that distinguish a Gevrey wine from its neighbours: solidity, power and full flavour, with a hint of liquorice. The vineyards include: Les Latricières, (about 7 hectares); Les Charmes (31 hectares); Les Mazoyères, which may also take the name of Charmes (but not vice versa); Les Mazis, comprising Les Mazis-Hauts (about 8 hectares), and Les Mazis-Bas (4.5 hectares). Les Ruchottes, a name derived from the word 'roichot', meaning 'rocky soil', is a very small vineyard. It comprises Les Ruchottes-du-Dessus (1.9 hectares) and Les Ruchottes-du-Bas (1.2 hectares). Wild cherries are said to have once grown in Les Groittes (5.4 hectares). Lastly, Les Chapelle (5.3 hectares) takes its name from a chapel built in 1155 by the brothers from Bèze abbey; the chapel itself was destroyed during the French Revolution.

Latricières-Chambertin

DOMAINE HUBERT CAMUS★

■Gd Cru   4ha   1000   ⑤ Ⓓ ⑪ ⬇

⑦⑨ 80 **81** 81 82

Has retained all the severity of the 1981 vintage, without so far showing the slightest sign of softening. However, age should make it more supple. Good aromas of blackcurrant and peppermint will continue to develop. Taste again in five years' time. (1981)

☛ Hubert Camus, 38 Rue de l'Eglise, 21220 Gevrey-Chambertin; tel. 80 34 31 70 ☥ By appt. Closed during harvest.

Chapelle-Chambertin

DOMAINE DROUHIN-LAROZE

■Gd Cru   5000   ⑥ Ⓓ ⑪ ⬇

74 76 77 **78** ⑦⑨ 80 81 **82** 83

The extreme ripeness of the 1983 vintage is evident here in the aromas of apple sauce, peach stone and cooked cherry. Firm tannin presence and rich flavour. Lay down. (1983)

☛ Dom. Drouhin-Laroze, 20 Rue du Gaizot, 21220 Gevrey-Chambertin; tel. 80 34 31 49 ☥ By appt. Closed Aug. and Oct.

DOMAINE LOUIS TRAPET★★

■Gd Cru   1.20ha   3600   ⑥ Ⓓ ⑪ ⬇

An unmistakeable Grand Cru from Gevrey-Chambertin with its wafting musky smell. Dense aromas of animal fur and wet leaves enlivened by a floral note. Warm, full-bodied flavours with distinct cherry fruit and a dash of tannin; a substantial 1982 but it should be consumed in the near future. (1982)

☛ Dom. Louis Trapet, Route Nationale, 21220 Gevrey-Chambertin; tel. 80 34 30 40 ☥ By appt
☛ M et Mme Jean Trapet.

Charmes-Chambertin

DOMAIN HUBERT CAMUS★★

■Gd Cru   4ha   10000   ⑤ Ⓓ ⑪ ⬇

⑦⑨ 80 81 82

Long and soft on the palate. Colour still bright. Gamey aromas of maturing Chambertin. Already drinkable, but may be kept. (1980)

☛ Hubert Camus, 38 Rue de l'Eglise, 21220 Gevrey-Chambertin; tel. 80 34 31 70 ☥ By appt. Closed during harvest.

CHANSON PERE ET FILS★★

■Gd Cru   ⑥ Ⓓ ⑪ ⬇

69 71 76 *79 **82** 82

Delicately coloured. Very aromatic nose. Leaves a soft and delicate impression on the palate. Drink soon. (1982)

☛ MM. Chanson Père et Fils, 10–12 Rue Paul-Chanson, 21200 Beaune; tel. 80 22 33 00 ☥ By appt.

DESVIGNES AINE ET FILS★

■Gd Cru	900	5 D ◉

★83

A fairly light 1982 which should mature into a charming, subtle wine. Lacking some structure but this is more than compensated for by its finesse. (1982) ✔ Clos-Vougeot, Nuits-St-Georges.
➥ *MM.* Desvignes Ainé et Fils, Pontanevaux, 71570, La Chapelle-de-Guinchay; tel. 85 36 72 32 ☎ By appt. Closed Aug.

PATRIARCHE PERE ET FILS★★

■Gd Cru	2200	6 ◉ ⚲

73 ⑲ 79

Displays all the charm of the 1979 vintage, with typical Côtes du Nuits aromas. Perfectly round smooth flavour. (1979)
➥ *MM.* Patriarche Père et Fils, 7 Rue du Collège, 21200 Beaune; tel. 80 22 23 20 ☎ By appt. Closed Jan.

JEAN RAPHET★★★

■Gd Cru	8ha	3000	6 D ◉ ⚲

76 ★78 79 ★82 83

Sumptuous aromas of resin, incense, candied cherry and fruit stones. Perfect smoothness on the palate, with a long, unctuous finish. (1979) ✔ Gevrey Chambertin.
➥ Jean Raphet, Morey-St-Denis, 21220 Gevrey-Chambertin; tel. 80 34 31 67 ☎ By appt.

DOMAINE HENRI REBOURSEAU★★

■Gd Cru	2ha	2000	5 D ⊟ ⚲

★⑦⑧ ★79 ★80 ★81 83 84

The aromas and fruit are still those of a new wine, but their power and character of Morello cherries and liquorice are already those of a Grand Cru. On the palate, there is a strong impression of finesse and suppleness. In due course, this 'Charmes' will have charm. (1984)
➥ Henri Rebourseau, 10 Place du Monument, 21220 Gevrey-Chambertin; tel. 80 34 30 46 ☎ By appt ➥ Pierre Rebourseau et Fils.

HENRI RICHARD★★

■Gd Cru	11ha	3000	4 D ◉ ⚲

76 78 79 81 ⑧② 82

A well-vinified 1982 with a solid texture and pleasant richness. Attractive aromas of fruit stones, resin and liquorice. Should be left for ten years. (1982)
➥ Henri Richard, 21220 Gevrey-Chambertin; tel. 80 34 31 37 ☎ By appt.

DOMAINE TAUPENOT-MERME★★

■Gd Cru	7800	6 D ◉ ⚲

⑦⑥ 78 81 83

The 1981 vintage gives this wine an expressive character but also a lack of maturity. Refined aromas of resin and wood with a firm, but not harsh flavour. Typical liquorice-scented finish. Should be ready in five years. (1981)
➥ Dom. Taupenot-Merme, Morey-St-Denis, 21220 Gevrey-Chambertin; tel. 80 34 35 24 ☎ By appt.

DOMAINE DES VAROILLES★

■G Cru	0.78ha	2800	6 D ◉ ⚲

⑦⑥ 78 82 83

Displays surprising power for its vintage, although not fully knit. Very young aromas of blackcurrant, raspberry and bitter cherry. Rich thick tannins, crisp acidity and full flavour. Leave to mature (1980)
➥ Dom. des Varoilles, 11 Rue de l'Ancien-Hôpital, 21220 Gevrey-Chambertin; tel. 80 34 32 34 ☎ By appt. Closed Aug. ➥ Jean-Pierre Naigeon.

Griottes-Chambertin

JOSEPH DROUHIN★★★

■Gd Cru	6 ◉ ⚲

72 74 76 77 78 79 80 81 ★82 83

No trace of age in the dark colour. Subtle nose of small, red fruit, undergrowth and tobacco. On the palate, very spicy aromas are dominated by cherry. Full and elegant, but with the alcohol still perceptible in the finish. Still not at its peak. (1978)
➥ Joseph Drouhin, 7 Rue d'Enfer, 21200 Beaune; tel. 80 22 06 80 ☎ By appt.

Mazis-Chambertin

HOSPICES DE BEAUNE
Cuvée Madeleine Colignon★★

■Gd Cru	1.74ha	3780	6 ◉ ⚲

A recent addition to the Hospices de Beaune vineyards and now, as befits a Côtes de Nuits Grand Cru, regularly the most expensive red wine at the auction fetching 36,000 to 36,500 F. in 1984. The 1984 was still very reserved at the pre-auction tasting but showed a solid, harmonious structure and good potential. (1984)
➥ Dom. Viti. Hospices de Beaune, Rue de L'Hôtel-Dieu, 21200 Beaune; tel. 80 24 75 75 ☎ No visitors.

DOMAINE HENRI REBOURSEAU**

■Gd Cru   1 ha   1000   5 D ↓

★⑦⑧ ★**79 80 81 83** 84

Has the class of a Grand Cru. Aromas of cherry, raspberry and liquorice. The solid structure guarantees it will keep for many years. Harmonious, well-balanced flavour. Leave to mature. (1984) ♠┐Henri Rebourseau, 10 Place du Monument, 21220 Gevrey-Chambertin; tel. 80 34 30 46 ☎ By appt ♠┐Pierre Rebourseau et Fils.

Mazoyères-Chambertin

DOMAINE HUBERT CAMUS*

■Gd Cru   4 ha   10000   5 D ❶ ↓

⑦⑨   80 **81** 82 **82**

This Grand Cru has developed fairly quickly showing a soft, round flavour. Notes of fruit and new oak on the nose. Ready to drink. (1982) ♠┐Hubert Camus, 38 Rue de L'Eglise, 21220 Gevrey-Chambertin; tel. 80 34 31 70 ☎ By appt. Closed during harvest.

Morey-St-Denis

A little over 100 hectares in area, Morey-St-Denis is one of the smallest communal appellations of the Côte de Nuits. Total annual production is between 2000 and 3000 hectolitres. There are some excellent Premiers Crus, and five Grands Crus: Clos de Tart, Clos-St-Denis. Bonnes-Mares (part), Clos de la Roche and Clos des Lambrays.

This area, wedged between Gevrey and Chambolle, has its own style, somewhere between the strength of the former and the subtlety of the latter. In March, the Morey-St-Denis wine-makers hold their Fête du Dionyse to present their wines to the public. This occasion takes place in the second week of March on the Friday before the Hospices de Nuits sale.

DOMAINE PIERRE AMIOT ET FILS**

■   1.5 ha   7200   5 D ❶ ↓

⑦⑥   **78** 79 80 **82** 83

Still very discreet aromas with fleeting notes of vanilla, blackcurrant and cherry. Round, open flavour without any bitterness. Drink in three years. (1982) ♠┐GAEC du Dom. Pierre Amiot, 27 Grande-Rue, Morey-St-Denis, 21220 Gevrey-Chambertin; tel. 80 34 34 28 ☎ By appt. Closed 15–30 Aug.

DOMAINE GEORGES BRYCZEK ET FILS *Cuvée du Pâpe Jean-Paul II***

■   0.4 ha   1900   6 D ❶ ↓

78 **80** 82 **83**

Nose of dried leaves and compost·with a gamey note. Aromas of prune and peppermint predominate on the palate. Still quite young for its vintage. A very complete, well-structured wine. (1980) ✔ Morey-St-Denis, Gevrey-Chambertin, Chambolle-Musigny. ♠┐Georges Bryczek et Fils, 14 Rue Ribordoc, Moray-St-Denis, 21220 Gevrey-Chambertin; tel. 80 34 34 17 ☎ No visitors.

GEORGES BRYCZEK PERE ET FILS*

■   1 ha   4200   6 D ❶

76 78 **83** 84

The deep colour almost reminds one of a Banyuls. Complex, slightly burnt aromas of liquorice, leather and Morello cherries. Sweet flavour of mint and candied orange. An extremely appealing wine, which is still exceptionally young. (1969) ♠┐Georges Bryczek Père et Fils, 14 Rue Ribordoc, Morey-St-Denis, 21220 Gevrey-Chambertin; tel. 80 34 34 17.

ANDRE COQUARD-CHAUVENET*

■   1.7 ha   8150   4 D ❶ ↓

⑦⑥   **78** 80 **82**

Very attractive aromas of oak bark and lichen with a complex flavour of cherries, fruit stones and a touch of new oak. Harmonious, long flavour. Ready in two or three years. (1982) ♠┐André Coquard-Chauvenet, Morey-St-Denis, 21220 Gevrey-Chambertin; tel. 80 34 38 43 ☎ No visitors.

GEORGES LIGNIER ET FILS*

■   1.5 ha   7200   5 D ❶ ↓

69 71 **76** 77 ★**78** 79 81 **82**

A well-proportioned wine near its peak. Subtle fruit character and full, quite deep flavour for a 1982. Ready to drink soon. (1982) ✔ Chambolle-Musigny, Clos de la Roche, Clos de St-Denis. ♠┐Georges Lignier et Fils, Morey-St-Denis, 21220 Gevrey-Chambertin; tel. 80 34 32 55 ☎ By appt. Closed Sat., Sun. and public holidays.

MAURICE LIGNIER-MICHELOT*

■   4 ha   14500   5 D ❶ ↓

76 ⑦⑧   82 **83**

Tasted shortly after bottling, needed a little time to recover its balance. Structure and texture guarantee a long future, and the aromas should open out with bottle age. (1983) ♠┐Maurice Lignier-Michelot, Morey-St-Denis, 21220 Gevrey-Chambertin; tel. 80 34 31 13 ☎ By appt.

DOMAINE FELIX MAGNIEN**

■   2 ha   8500   5 D ❶ ↓

⑦⑧   **81** 83

Expressive aromas of violet, resin, tobacco and incense and refined delicate flavour. An excellent 1981 which may be drunk in three or four years with plain roast beef or roast game. Avoid with

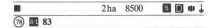

sauces. (1981)

↦ Jean-Paul Magnien, 5 Ruelle de L'Eglise, Morey-St-Denis, 21220 Gevrey-Chambertin; tel. 80 51 83 10 ☖ By appt. Closed 15–30 Aug.

CLAUDE MARCHAND*

■		6.3 ha	22 500	4 D Ⅲ ↓

76 *78 82 83

Attractively made, but needs five or six years to become more refined. Typical aromas of cherry liqueur, resin and liquorice, and a lovely, firm flavour that should open out after ageing. (1983)

↦ Claude Marchand, 17 Grande Rue, Morey-St-Denis, 21220 Gevrey-Chambertin; tel. 80 34 33 15 ☖ By appt.

MOILLARD*

■		18 000	5 Ⅲ ↓

74 79 81 83

Needs to be kept for a long time. From a soft vintage; has already matured considerably and lost all harshness. Good length on the palate. (1982)

↦ SARL Moillard, 5 Rue F.-Mignotte, 21700 Nuits-St-Georges; tel. 80 61 03 34 ☖ No visitors.

BERNARD SERVEAU ET FILS
*Les Sorbets**

■1er Cru	1.5 ha	5500	4 D Ⅲ ↓

⑦⑧ 80 81 82 83

Still remarkably young. Good length of flavour and firm texture. Should last well. Serve with plain grilled meats. (1981) ✔ Chambolle-Musigny les Chabrots Rouge.

↦ Bernard Serveau et Fils, 37 Grande-Rue, Morey-St-Denis, 21220 Gevrey-Chambertin; tel. 80 34 33 07 ☖ No visitors.

JEAN TARDY*

■		3 ha	14 500	4 D Ⅲ ↓

⑥⑨ 71 73 74 75 76 77 78 80 81 82

This wine still has a slight acid edge which should disappear in three or four years' time. (1982)

↦ Jean Tardy, Morey-St-Denis, 21220 Gevrey-Chambertin; tel. 80 34 35 28 ☖ By appt. Closed 15–30 Aug.

DOMAINE TAUPENOT-MERME**

■		1 ha	6000	5 D Ⅲ ↓

⑦⑥ 78 82 83

Expressive aromas characteristic of a Morey-Saint-Denis with notes of cherry and resin. Full, round flavour. Drink soon. (1982)

↦ Dom. Taupenot-Merme, Morey-St-Denis, 21220 Gevrey-Chambertin; tel. 80 34 35 24 ☖ By appt. Closed Aug.

Clos de la Roche, Clos de St-Denis, Clos de Tart, Clos des Lambrays

Clos de la Roche is the largest of this group – about 16 hectares – taking in several smaller holdings. Clos St-Denis (about 6.5 hectares) also combines several smaller vineyard sites. These two growths are made up of several different pieces of land, and

are cultivated by many different owners. Despite the designation clos, both these vineyards are in fact unwalled. Clos de Tart, on the other hand, is totally enclosed by walls and is in the hands of a single owner. It is a little over 7 hectares and the wines are made and aged on the property; the split-level cellars are worth a visit. Clos des Lambrays is also a monopoly, regrouping several smaller named vineyards: Les Buchots, Les Larrets (or Clos des Lambrays), and Le Meix Rentier. It covers just under 9 hectares, of which all but 0.5 hectares are cultivated by the same owner. Clos des Lambrays is the most recent appointment to Grand Cru status in Burgundy.

Clos de la Roche

DOMAINE PIERRE AMIOT ET FILS

■Gd Cru	1 ha	3850	5 D Ⅲ ↓

⑧② 83

Still extremely young, with an intense colour, fruity aromas of small berries and very harmonious palate with well balanced richness and tannin. Needs to age. (1982)

↦ GAEC du Dom. Pierre Amiot, 27 Grande Rue, Morey-St-Denis, 21220 Gevrey-Chambertin; tel. 80 34 34 28 ☖ By appt.

CHANSON PERE ET FILS*

■Gd Cru			6 D Ⅲ ↓

71 76 77 79 ⑧⓪ 80 81 82

Displays the classic characteristics of its terroir: distinction and delicacy on the nose, finesse of texture and roundness on the palate. Leave to mature. (1982)

↦ MM. Chanson Père et Fils, 10 –12 Rue Paul-Chanson, 21200 Beaune; tel. 80 22 33 00 ☖ No visitors.

DOMAINE DUJAC**

■Gd Cru	1.8 ha	7800	6 Ⅲ ↓

69 72 76 78 80 83

Robust, fairly masculine wine, with aromas of cocoa. Tasted just one month after bottling, it showed little character on the palate. However, its firm structure will, no doubt, allow it to mature well. (1983)

↦ Jacques Seysses, Dom. Dujac, Moray-St-Denis, 21220 Gevrey-Chambertin; tel. 80 34 32 58 ☖ By appt. Closed during school hols.

GEORGES LIGNIER ET FILS

■Gd Cru	1 ha	3850	6 D Ⅲ ↓

82 ⑧③

Vinified to last, and still has all the characteristics of a young wine: bright colour, fresh aromas and strong acidity. Needs a few more years for the flavours to mature and soften. (1982)

Côte de Nuits (Centre)

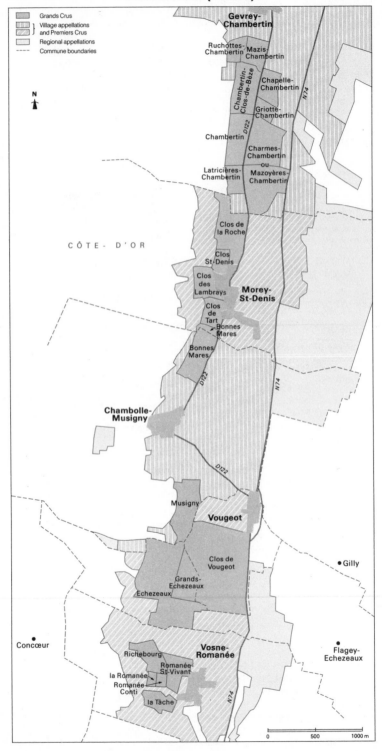

Grands Crus

Village appellations
and Premiers Crus

Regional appellations

Commune boundaries

N

CÔTE- D'OR

**Gevrey-
Chambertin**

Ruchottes-
Chambertin

Mazis-
Chambertin

Chambertin-
Clos-de-Bèze

Chapelle-
Chambertin

Griotte-
Chambertin

Chambertin

Charmes-
Chambertin
ou
Mazoyères-
Chambertin

Latricières-
Chambertin

Clos de
la Roche

Clos
St-Denis

Clos
des
Lambrays

**Morey-
St-Denis**

Clos
de
Tart

Bonnes
Mares

Bonnes
Mares

**Chambolle-
Musigny**

Musigny

Vougeot

Clos de
Vougeot

• Gilly

Grands-
Echezeaux

Echezeaux

• Concœur

**Vosne-
Romanée**

•Flagey-
Echezeaux

Richebourg

Romanée-
St-Vivant

la Romanée

Romanée-
Conti

la Tâche

0   500   1000 m

♠ Georges Lignier et Fils, Morey-St-Denis, 21220 Gevrey-Chambertin; tel. 80 34 32 55 ☌ By appt.

DOMAINE LOUIS REMY

■Gd Cru	0.6ha	2600	6	D	⑪	↓
⑦ 72 73 74 76 82						

Everything about this wine is evocative of raspberry: the bright colour, the red-fruit aromas and the fresh, clean flavour on the palate. Almost a shame that its marvellous freshness will give way to the maturity of a Grand Cru. (1982)
♠ Dom. Louis Rémy, Place du Monument, Morey-St-Denis, 21220 Gevrey-Chambertin; tel. 80 34 32 59 ☌ By appt.

Clos St-Denis

DOMAINE DUJAC★★★

■Gd Cru	1.5ha	6000	6	⑪	↓
69 72 76 78 80 83					

Highly concentrated, with a deep colour and aromas of kirsch. Elegantly proportioned, rich flavour. Will make a very good bottle. (1983)
♠ Jacques Seysses, Dom. Dujac, Morey-St-Denis, 21220 Gevrey-Chambertin; tel. 80 34 32 58 ☌ By appt. Closed during school hols.

GEORGES LIGNIER ET FILS

■Gd Cru	1.5ha	5500	6	D	⑪	↓
82 ⑧③						

Vinified for keeping, this 1982 is rather severe for its vintage, with strong tannin and a dense texture. Needs many years of bottle age. (1982)
♠ Georges Lignier et Fils, Place du Monument, Morey-St-Denis, 21220 Gevrey-Chambertin; tel. 80 34 32 59 ☌ By appt.

Clos de Tart

MOMMESSIN★

■Gd Cru	27ha	35000	5	D	⑪	↓

Young fresh flavours of fruit and new oak characterize this 1982 which will need several years to mature. (1982)
♠ Ets Mommessin Clos, de Tart, Morey-St-Denis, 21220 Gevrey-Chambertin; tel. 80 34 30 91 ☌ By appt.

Clos des Lambrays

DOMAINE DES LAMBRAYS★

■Gd Cru	8.7ha	34000	6	D	⑪	↓
71 78 79 82 82						

Fairly light ruby colour with trace of oak on the nose and strong smell of wild cherries. Light,

silky flavour and slightly warm finish. A bottle with some future which should be tasted in two years' time. (1982) ✔ Morey-St-Denis, Morey-St-Denis Premier Cru.
♠ Dom. des Lambrays, Morey-St-Denis, 21220 Gevrey-Chambertin; tel. 80 51 84 33 ☌ By appt.

Chambolle-Musigny

This tiny commune owes its reputation to the superb quality of its Grand Cru Musigny and to its Premiers Crus, the most famous of the latter being Les Amoureuses. However, there are many others, including Les Charmes, Les Chabiots, Les Cras, Les Foussottes, Les Groseilles and Les Laurottes. The village itself, with its narrow streets and century-old trees, boasts some magnificent cellars.

Chambolle wines are often said to be feminine, elegant and subtle: they combine strength of a Bonnes-Mares with the finesse of a Musigny. When well made, however, they last just as long as the more overtly rugged, tannic red Burgundies.

GASTON BARTHOD★★★

■	3.8ha	17000	5	D	⑪	↓
78 82 82						

This skilful producer is President of the Chambolle Wine Growers Association. His 1982 is a fine wine with a deep red colour, complex light aromas of violets, red fruit and precious wood, and firm, well-defined flavours. Still needs several years. (1982)
♠ Gaston Barthod, Chambolle-Musigny, 21220 Gevrey-Chambertin; tel. 80 62 85 95 ☌ No visitors.

DOMAINE BERTHEAU★

■	3ha	13500	5	D	⑪	↓
71 76 ⑦⑧ 82 83 83						

Rich tannic, oaky character with a flavour of roast chestnuts. Clean, fruity presence and good finish. (1982)
♠ Pierre Bertheau, Chambolle-Musigny, 21220 Gevrey-Chambertin; tel. 80 62 85 73 ☌ No visitors.

DOMAINE CLAIR-DAU★

■	0.27ha	1500	5	D	⑪	↓
68 69 71 73 ★79 80 81 ⑧② 82 83						

Only a small amount of this wine is produced. Bright colour and floral, fruity aromas of blackcurrant, iris and violet. Fresh, elegant flavour with a nose of black cherry, but rather short of body. (1982)
♠ Dom. Clair-Dau, 5 Rue du Vieux-Collège, 21160 Marsannay-la-Côte; tel. 80 52 15 58 ☌ By appt.

ANDRE COCQUARD-CHAUVENET*

■　　　　　0.8ha　4800　⑤ Ⅾ ⑪ ⌷

⑦⑥ **78 80** ⁸²

A typical refreshing 1982 with good acidity and attractive aromas of redcurrant and grenadine. Fairly strong note of alcohol on the palate. Drink soon. (1982)

☙ André Cocquard-Chauvenet, Route des Grands-Crus, Morey-St-Denis, 21220 Gevrey-Chambertin; tel. 80 34 38 43 ⵟ No visitors.

JOSEPH DROUHIN**

■1er Cru　　　　　　　⑤ ⑪ ⌷

72 74 **76** 77 **78** 79　80 81 *82 83

Delicate colour. Scent of new wood and bitter aromas of cherry, liquorice and betelnut. Elegant, mild flavour and finish, with a note of kirsch. Taste again in three years' time. (1982)

☙ Joseph Drouhin, 7 Rue d'Enfer, 21200 Beaune; tel. 80 22 06 80 ⵟ By appt.

HENRI FELETTIG*

■　　　　　2ha　9500　⑤ Ⅾ ⑪ ⌷

76 ⑦⑧ ⑧² ⁸³

The force of the 1983 vintage is felt in the strong warm flavours and 'roasted' aromas of tobacco, liquorice and toast. Full of potential. (1983)

☙ Henri Felettig, Chambolle-Musigny, 21220 Gevrey-Chambertin; tel. 80 62 85 09 ⵟ By appt.

DANIEL FUNES**

■　　　　　1.5ha　7200　⑤ Ⅾ ⑪ ⌷

69 **76** ⑦⑧ **79** ⁸² **83**

All the customary finesse of a Chambolle-Musigny with the fresh, fruity character of the 1982 vintage. Aromas of wild cherries and strawberries and soft, light flavour. Drink with plain grilled meats. (1982)

☙ Daniel Funès, Chambolle-Musigny, 21220 Gevrey-Chambertin; tel. 80 62 85 96 ⵟ By appt. Closed 1–15 Aug.

GEORGES LIGNIER ET FILS**

■　　　　0.75ha　4500　⑤ Ⅾ ⑪ ⌷

69 71 **76** 77 *⑦⑧ 79 81 ⁸²

A well-vinified 1982 with good structure and substance. Slightly 'animal' bouquet with notes of wood, cherry, vanilla and liquorice. Round but not too soft on the palate. Leave to mature further. (1982)

☙ Georges Lignier et Fils, Morey-St-Denis, 21220 Gevrey-Chambertin; tel. 80 34 32 55 ⵟ By appt. Closed during harvest.

MOILLARD*

■　　　　　　18000　⑤ ⑪ ⌷

71 ⑦⑨ **83**

Tenderness and freshness have combined to produce a harmonious, refreshing wine, with an aroma of raspberry. Already pleasing to drink, but may be kept for a good few years. (1982)

☙ SARL Moillard, 5 Rue F.-Mignotte, 21700 Nuits-St-Georges; tel. 80 61 03 34 ⵟ No visitors.

DOMAINE PERNOT-FOURRIER**

■　　　　0.67ha　4200　⑤ Ⅾ ⑪ ⌷

64 66 **72** 76 **78** *80 ⑧² ⁸² ⁸³

Very bright ruby-red, but the nose is still firmly closed. Long, elegant flavour, but lacking depth (a common failing of many 1982s from this appellation). Amply compensated, however, by its very appealing, velvety texture. (1982) ✔ Gevrey-Chambertin, Gevrey-Chambertin Premier Cru, Morey-St-Denis, Clos-Vougeot Premier Cru.

☙ Jean-Claude Fourrier, 7 Route de Dijon, 21220 Gevrey-Chambertin; tel. 80 34 33 95 ⵟ By appt. Closed Oct.

DOMAINE BERNARD SERVEAU ET FILS *Les Chabrots**

■1er Cru　　0.8ha　3850　⑤ Ⅾ ⑪ ⌷

78 80 ⁸² **83**

Chambolle is best known for its Grand Cru and Village wines but there are also several fine Premiers Crus, including this one. Still very young with good fruit and aromas. Will keep for many years. (1982) ✔ Morey-St-Denis Premier Crus.

☙ Bernard Serveau et Fils, 37 Grande-Rue, Morey-St-Denis, 21220 Gevrey-Chambertin; tel. 80 34 33 07 ⵟ No visitors.

DOMAINE SERVELLE-TACHOT *Les Charmes**

■1er Cru　　0.8ha　3850　⑤ Ⅾ ⑪ ⌷

64 66 ⑥⑨　71 72 *80 *⁸² 83

'Les Charmes' is a common vineyard name designating former arable land. This wine shows attractive fruit aromas but a slightly acid palate. Should be left two or three years to soften. (1982)

☙ Dom. Servelle-Tachot, Chamballe-Musigny, 21220 Gevrey-Chambertin; tel. 80 62 86 91 ⵟ By appt.

DOMAINE SERVELLE-TACHOT**

■　　　　　2ha　9500　⑤ Ⅾ ⑪ ⌷

Everyone's idea of Chambolle-Musigny with raspberry fruitiness and a touch of violet. Refined, gentle flavour but not oversoft. (1982)

☙ Dom. Servelle-Tachot, Chambolle-Musigny, 21220 Gevrey-Chambertin; tel. 80 62 86 91 ⵟ By appt.

ROBERT SIRUGUE**

■　　　　0.2ha　1200　⑤ Ⅾ ⑪ ⌷

70 ⑦⑥ **78 81** ⁸²

A good 1982 with typical raspberry and violet aromas and a fresh, firm flavour. Will mature slowly. (1982)

☙ Robert Sirugue, Vosne-Romanée, 21700 Nuits-St-Georges; tel. 80 61 00 64 ⵟ By appt.

Bonnes-Mares

This appellation of 15.55 hectares actually extends into the commune of Morey-St Denis up to the wall of the Clos de Tart. It is a perfect Grand Cru, producing wines that are full-bodied, sappy, rich and keep well; after a few years of bottle age they go very well with jugged hare or woodcock.

PIERRE BERTHEAU

■Gd Cru   0.34ha   1800   🔟 Ⓓ ⑪ 🍷
76 ⑦⑧ 82 **82** 83

Displays remarkable finesse, with fruity aromas and a firm flavour, which needs time to soften. (1982)
🍾 Pierre Bertheau, Chambolle-Musigny, 21220 Gevrey-Chambertin; tel. 80 62 85 73 ✗

DOMAINE CLAIR-DAU★★

■Gd Cru   2.5ha   9600   🔟 Ⓓ ⑪ 🍷
� **68** 69 71 72 73 *79 80 81 82 **83**

Bright, shimmering red with spicy red fruit aromas. Complex bouquet of blackcurrant and dried leaves. On the palate, a full, fleshy, solid flavour but rather a harsh finish. Enough structure and tannin to keep for a long time. (1981)
🍾 Dom. Clair-Dau, 5 Rue du Vieux-Collège, 21160 Marsannay-la-Côte; tel. 80 52 15 58 ✗ By appt.

DOMAINE DROUHIN-LAROZE★★

■Gd Cru   20000   🔟 Ⓓ ⑪ 🍷
74 76   77 *⑦⑧   79 80 *81 82 83

All the finesse and elegance of this Chambolle Grand Cru in a firm rich tannic structure typical of the vintage. Needs many years. (1983)
🍾 Dom. Drouhin-Laroze, 20 Rue de Gaizot, 21220 Gevrey-Chambertin; tel. 80 34 31 49 ✗ By appt. Closed Aug. and Oct.

ROBERT GROFFIER★★

■Gd Cru   1ha   3600   🔟 Ⓓ ⑪ 🍷
㊀⑦⑨ 80 81 83 84

High-quality 1980 with wealth of aromas (violet, ivy leaves, coffee, leather, liquorice), and a perfectly smooth roundness on the palate, without a trace of heaviness. Drink now and. (1980)
🍾 Robert Groffier, Morey-St-Denis, 21220 Gevrey-Chambertin; tel. 80 34 31 53 ✗ By appt.

DOMAINE DES VAROILLES★★★

■Gd Cru   0.5ha   1500   🔟 Ⓓ ⑪ 🍷
㊀⑦⑥ 78 **82** 83

Exceptional, displaying all the splendid qualities of a Grand Cru. Magnificent colour and intense aromas, with nuances of fruit stones and pepper over a background of blackcurrant and liquorice. The palate is all harmony and perfect balance, with a long finish. (1982)
🍾 Dom. des Varoilles, 11 Rue de l'Ancien-Hôpital, 21220 Gevrey-Chambertin; tel. 80 34 32 34 ✗ By appt 🍾Jean-Pierre Naigeon.

Musigny

The Musigny vineyard overlooks the Clos de Vougeot and, on its southern boundary, meets the Echézeaux appellation in the commune of Flagey-Echézeaux. The red wines here combine a certain strength with great refinement. Several owners share the 10 hectares or so that the appellation includes. A few hectolitres of white wine are also produced.

CHANSON PERE ET FILS★★

■Gd Cru   🔟 Ⓓ ⑪ 🍷
71 **77** 78 ⑦⑨ 81 82

The most complex and refined Grand Cru of Burgundy. Displays all the finesse, delicacy and persistence one would expect from such a great wine.
🍾 *MM.* Chanson Père et Fils, 10–12 Rue Paul-Chanson, 21200 Beaune; tel. 80 22 33 00 ✗ No visitors.

JOSEPH DROUHIN
Récolte du Domaine★★

■Gd Cru   🔟 ⑪ 🍷
72 74 **76** 77 **78** 79 80 81 **82** 83

Fairly deep colour, with ample body and a slightly bitter hint of fruit stones. Still fairly undeveloped. (1982)
🍾 Joseph Drouhin, 7 Rue d'Enfer, 21200 Beaune; tel. 80 22 06 80 ✗ By appt.

DOMAINE JACQUES PRIEUR★★

■   0.8ha   1200   🔟 Ⓓ ⑪ 🍷
76 78 80 **82** 83

Still gives an overall impression of youth, but is already showing characteristics of finesse, the first signs of rare aromas and the general harmony that will make it a great bottle of wine around 1990. (1982) ✦ Meursault Clos de Mazeray, Volnay Clos des Santenots Premier Cru, Beaune Clos de la Féguine Premier Cru, Montrachet Grand Cru.
🍾 Jacques Prieur, 2 Rue des Santenots 21190 Meursault; tel. 80 21 23 85 ✗ By appt. Closed Aug.

MUSIGNY

APPELLATION MUSIGNY CONTROLÉE

Domaine Jacques Prieur

Propriétaire à Meursault (Côte-d'Or)

FRANCE   750 ml

Vougeot

This is the smallest commune in the whole wine-growing area of the Côte – only 80 hectares. Indeed, if you take away the 50 hectares taken up by the Clos, the houses and the roads, there are only a few hectares left in Vougeot for the vines. There are several Premiers Crus, the most famous being Le Clos Blanc (which makes white wine) and Le Clos de la Perrière.

GRIVELET PERE ET FILS★

| □1er Cru | 2.28ha | 2500 | 5 D ◖ ↓ |

In the 18th century there was extensive planting of Pinot Blanc to soften the otherwise rugged cuvées of red wine. A handful of these vines remain. This 1983 is very rich with slightly burnt aromas and a well-judged blend of sweetness and acidity. (1983)
◖ *MM.* Grivelet Père et Fils, 21640 Vougeot; tel. 80 72 42 72 � By appt.

Clos de Vougeot

More than 70 owners share the 50 hectares of this world-famous vineyard. The land is so good for wine-growing that competition for ownership has always been fierce. The precise vineyard area was chosen with great care by the monks of Citéaux Abbey when they erected the surrounding wall. They blended wines from the upper, middle and lower parts of the slope to make a legendary wine. Today each section continues to produce wines of different but complementary character.

The Clos was established at the beginning of the thirteenth century, reaching its present size before the fifteenth century. For the visitor, the castle offers more interest than the Clos itself, where the attraction really lies only in the wine that it produces. The castle was built during the twelfth and sixteenth centuries, the oldest part being the cellar. Today this is

under the charge of the present owners, the Confrérie des Chevaliers du Tastevin. The cuverie has four magnificent antique wine presses, one in each corner.

CIE DES VINS D'AUTREFOIS★

| ■Gd Cru | | 6 ◖ ↓ |

Full of power and body, yet it does not seem to be ageing rapidly, and still shows no signs of development. (1983)
◖ Cie des Vins d'Autrefois, 9 Rue Celer, 21200 Beaune; tel. 80 22 21 31 � No visitors.

LEONCE BOQUET★

| ■Gd Cru | | 1000 | 6 D ◖ ↓ |

75 76 77 78 ★79 ★82

Rich aromas and densely structured palate. (1982)
◖ Petits-Fils de Léonce Boquet, 29 Bld Clemenceau, 21200 Beaune; tel. 80 22 28 49 � By appt.

CHANSON PERE ET FILS★

| ■Gd Cru | | 6 D ◖ ↓ |

71 72 76 **77** ⑦⑨ **82** **82** 83

The best 'Clos Vougeot' is often a skilful blend from different parts of the Clos, which has a relatively varied micro-climate. Such is the case with this 1982 selected by Chanson Père et Fils, which has a fine, delicate bouquet over a vigorous, but balanced, flavour. (1982)
◖ *MM.* Chanson Père et Fils, 10–12 Rue Paul-Chanson, 21200 Beaune; tel. 80 22 33 00 � No visitors.

CHATEAU CORTON-ANDRE★

| ■Gd Cru | | 1.10ha | 2700 | 6 D ◖ ↓ |

71 **76** 77 ★78 ★79 **80** **81** 82 ⑧③

Superlative colour, fruitiness and body. All it needs is the time to marry the various elements and gain some depth. Patience required. (1983)
◖ Pierre André, Ch. Corton-André, Aloxe-Corton, 21420 Savigny-lès-Beaune, tel. 80 26 44 25 � By appt.

JOSEPH DROUHIN★★

| ■Gd Cru | | 6 ◖ ↓ |

72 74 **76** 77 **78** 79 80 81 **82** 83

Great and full of promise, but still in its infancy. Dark red colour, and predominant aromas of new oak. Spicy palate with hints of blackcurrant and black cherry. Solidity, power, and a fairly masculine character. (1982)
◖ Joseph Drouhin, 7 Rue de l'Enfer, 21200 Beaune; tel. 80 22 06 80 � By appt.

DOMAINE DROUHIN-LAROZE★★★

| ■Gd Cru | | 15000 | 6 D ◖ ↓ |

72 74 **76** 77 **78** 79 80 81 **82** 83

A very well-vinified 1983 with classic Clos de Vougeot aromas of cherry and liquorice and a remarkable full, rich body. An outstanding success. (1983)
◖ Dom. Drouhin-Laroze, 20 Rue de Gaizot, 212200 Gevrey-Chambertin; tel. 80 34 31 49 � By appt. Closed Aug. and Oct.

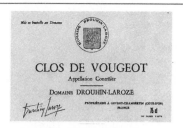

CLOS DE VOUGEOT
Appellation Contrôlée

DOMAINE DROUHIN-LAROZE

PROPRIÉTAIRE À GEVREY-CHAMBERTIN (CÔTE-D'OR)
FRANCE

DOMAINE ENGEL★★

■		1.37ha 5000	6 D ⑪ ↓
71 72 74 77 *78 82 83			

Very promising and still has all the freshness of a new wine, with an intense fruit of blackcurrant and cherry and notes of morels and cloves. Well vinified and without the roughness of so many 1983s; very full, rounded flavour. Leave to mature. (1983)
↑ René Engel, Vosne-Romanée, 21700 Nuits-St-Georges; tel. 80 61 10 54 ☂ By appt.

GRIVELET PÈRE ET FILS★

■Gd Cru	1 ha 500	5 D ⑪ ↓

From a light vintage but showing plenty of elegance. Mold, refined aromas with spices and liquorice over a background of resin and tar. Lean but attractive flavour. Keep for several years. (1981)
↑ *MM.* Grivelet Père et Fils, 21640 Vougeot; tel. 80 72 42 72 ☂ By appt.

JEAN GRIVOT

■Gd Cru	1.9ha 8800	6 D ⑪ ↓
80 81 ⑧² 82		

Complex aromas of cherry, peach, blackcurrant and vanilla, and hints of coffee and oak. Very fine, light, elegant flavour.
↑ SC Jean Grivot, Vosne-Romanée, 21700 Nuits-St-Georges; tel. 80 61 05 95 ☂ No visitors.

DOMAINE MOILLARD★★

■Gd Cru	1.2ha 6000	6 ⑪ ↓
71 73 83		

Manages to combine a rich, vigorous flavour and good extract with smoothness and balance. Leave to mature. (1983)
↑ SARL Moillard, 5 Rue F.-Mignotte, 21700 Nuits- St Georges; tel. 80 61 03 34 ☂ No visitors.
↑ Yves et Henri-Noel Thomas.

DOMAINE CHARLES NOELLAT★★

■Gd Cru	1.70ha 5400	6 D ▮ ↓
76 *78 79 *81 82 83		

The 1979 vintage contributes its aromatic richness to this wine and the Grand Cru vineyard brings body and extract. Complex, mature aromas of cut hay, privet, tobacco and pepper. Well-rounded and soft attractive flavour. Ready to drink but will keep. (1979)
↑ Sté. Charles Noellat, Les Genevrières, Vosne-Romanée, 21700 Nuits-St-Georges; tel. 80 61 10 82 ☂ By appt ↑ Famille Moreau.

NOEMIE-VERNAUX★★

■Gd Cru	2000	6 D ⑪

Grand Cru from a good vintage displaying all the harmony you could ask for, with very stylish aromas. May be drunk now. (1979)
↑ Ets Noémie Vernaux, Rue des Vérottes, 21200 Beaune; tel. 80 22 28 50 ☂ No visitors.

DOMAINE HENRI REBOURSEAU★★

■		2.5ha 2500	5 D ▮ ↓
⑦⑧ *79 *80 81 **83** 84			

Less rich than the 1983, it nevertheless boasts greater aromatic finesse. Persistent nose of coffee and almonds combined with cherry fruit and a silky texture on the palate. (1984)
↑ Henri Rebourseau, 10 Place du Monument, 21220 Gevrey-Chambertin; tel. 80 34 30 46 ☂ By appt.

RION PÈRE ET FILS★

■Gd Cru	0.37ha 1330	6 D ⑪ ↓
74 76 78 **79** 80 82		

Light colour. Has taken on the musky aromas of ageing Grands Crus, but still has good length and richness, and a firm tannic support. Drink within the next five years. (1979) ✔ Vosne-Romanée Premier Cru, Nuits-St-Georges Premier Cru.
↑ *MM.* Rion Père et Fils, Route Nationale, Vosne-Romanée, 21700 Nuits-St-Georges; tel. 80 61 05 31 ☂ By appt.

DOMAINE SERVELLE-TACHOT★

■Gd Cru	0.8ha 2850	6 D ⑪ ↓
64 66 ⑥⑨ **70** 71 72 *80 82 83		

Full of charm, this almost mature 1980 still has a firm red colour, a complex gamey nose and a firm, ripe flavour. Will last several years. (1980)
↑ Dom. Servelle-Tachot, Chambolle-Musigny, 21220 Gevrey-Chambertin; tel. 80 62 86 91 ☂ By appt.

CHATEAU DE LA TOUR★

■Gd Cru	5.6ha 22200	5 D ⑪ ↓
74 77 *78 *79 **80** *81 ⑧²		

Deep colour and nose of blackberries and wild cherries. Fruity palate, with touch of oak and pleasant finish. May be drunk now, but would be best kept for two years. (1980)
↑ *Mmes* Labet et Dechelette, Dom. du Ch. de la Tour, Clos-Vougeot, 21640 Vougeot; tel. 80 62 86 13 ☂ By appt. 10.00–12.30/13.30–19.00. Closed Nov.–Mar.

DOMAINE DES VAROILLES★★

■Gd Cru	2ha 7000	6 D ⑪ ↓
⑦⑥ 78 **80** 82 83		

Attractive, sweet aromas of marshmallow, grenadine, raspberry and vanilla. Finesse and roundness on the palate. (1982)
↑ Dom. des Varoilles, 11 Rue de l'Ancien-Hôpital, 21220 Gevrey-Chambertin; tel. 80 34 32 34 ☂ By appt. Closed Aug. ↑ Jean-Pierre Naigeon.

Echezeaux

The commune of Flagey-Echézeaux runs along the southern wall of the Clos de Vougeot, rising up into the vineyard area, although the main town is on the plain. The flat land has the appellation Vosne-Romanée; the hillside has two Grands Crus: Grands-Echézeaux and Echézeaux. The former is only about 9 hectares, whereas the latter is more than 30 hectares, and contains several separate holdings.

The wines from these two growths, the most prestigious of which is Grands-Echézeaux, are typical Burgundies: solid, robust and vigorous. They are mainly cultivated by winemakers from Vosne and Flagey.

JACQUES ET PATRICE CACHEUX★★★

■Gd Cru	0.5ha	3250	⑤ Ⓓ ⑪ ↓

⑦⑥ 78 **81** 82 83

Smooth flavour and powerful aromas are unexpected in this modest vintage. Splendid quality bottle selected at the Tastevinage in 1984.
❦ Jacques et Patrice Cacheux, Vosne-Romanée, 21700 Nuits-St-Georges; tel. 80 61 24 79 ☏ By appt.

CHANSON PERE ET FILS★★

■Gd Cru			⑥ Ⓓ ⑪ ↓

71 76 77 **77** ⑦⑨ 81 82

Characterized by aromas and flavours reminiscent of the best Vosne crus. The 1982 has a strong fruity presence with aromas of cherry and strawberry, and a solid structure that will allow it to keep for many years. (1982)
❦ MM. Chanson Père et Fils, 10–12 Rue Paul-Chanson, 21200 Beaune; tel. 80 22 33 00 ☏ No visitors.

DESVIGNES AINE ET FILS★★★

■Gd Cru	600		⑥ Ⓓ ⑪

82 ★83

Rich sustained colour, still very deep red, with a magnificent bouquet of new oak, leather, black pepper and cherry stones. Firm, expansive flavour still marked by the new oak barrels. Lay down. (1982)
❦ MM. Desvignes Ainé et Fils, Pontanevaux, 71570 La Chapelle-de-Guinchay; tel. 85 36 72 32 ☏ By appt.

J. FAIVELEY★★

■Gd Cru	1ha	3000	⑥ ⑪ ↓

59 64 ★66 71 ⑦④ 76 78 **80**

Full, fat flavour beneath its dark robe and fruity blackberry aromas. Compact yet elegant taste marked by strong aromas of prune and fruit stones. Very appealing. (1980)
❦ Maison Faiveley, 8 Rue de Tribourg, 21700 Nuits-St-George; tel. 80 61 04 55 ☏ By appt. Closed Aug.

HENRI JAYER★★★

■Gd Cru	1.2ha	5000	⑥ ⑪

59 64 ★66 69 71 ⑦④ ★76 78

Lustrous dark red. Immature nose with aromas of green tobacco. Very solid body, but still a little severe, on the palate. Prolonged finish. The empty glass reveals aromas of green nuts and Banyuls. Keep for five to eight years before drinking. (1982)
❦ Henri Jayer, Vosne-Romanée, 21700 Nuits-St-Georges; tel. 80 61 03 84 ☏ No visitors.

ROBERT JAYER-GILLES★★★

■Gd Cru	0.53ha	2400	⑥ Ⓓ ⑪ ↓

76 78 79 ★80 82 83

Almost ink-black, with a spicy nose. Pepper aroma is confirmed on the palate, with additional touches of violet and cherry stones. Overall balance is good, although the finish is still a little warm and dominated by the alcohol. Very fine bottle. No longer available from the producer, but a must if you have the opportunity to buy one. (1980)
❦ Robert Jayer-Gilles, Magny-les-Villers, 21700 Nuits-St-Georges; tel. 80 62 91 79 ☏ By appt.

ALFRED MARTIN★

■Gd Cru	1.5ha	7200	⑤ Ⓓ ⑪ ↓

74 76 78 80 ★⑧② **82**

Remarkable finesse on the nose and palate. Already at its peak. Drink now. (1982) ✦ Vosne-Romanée Rouge.
❦ Alfred Martin, Vosne-Romanée, 21700 Nuits-St-Georges, tel. 80 61 05 17 ☏ By appt.

DOMAINE MONGEARD-MUGNERET★★

■Gd Cru	4ha	21000	③ Ⓓ ⑪ ↓

76 ★79 ★80 ★81 ★82 ★**82** 83 **83**

Deep leafy, mushroom aromas intensified by age, together with the round, smooth flavours, make this an extremely good wine. (1980)
❦ Dom. Mongeard-Mugneret, Rue de Boncourt,

Vosne-Romanée, 21700 Nuits-St-Georges; tel. 80 61 11 95 �ோ By appt.

Vosne-Romanée

In line with local practice, the commune of Vosne has coupled its name with that of its most famous vineyard. Like Gevrey-Chambertin, this commune is home to a multitude of Grands Crus, but there are also some other well-known climats, among them Les Suchots, Les Beaux-Monts and Les Malconsorts. The Vosne-Romanée appellation covers about 250 hectares and produces only red wine, on average 5000 hectolitres per year.

JACQUES CACHEUX *Les Suchots*★★★

| ■1er Cru | 0.23ha | 1450 | 5 D ⑪ ↓ |

Already beginning to show maturity in the developing bouquet with gamey, animal nuances. Good structure and fine ageing potential. (1982).
� Jacques et Patrice Cacheux, Vosne-Romanée, 21700 Nuits-St-Georges; tel. 80 61 24 79 ☄ No visitors.

JACQUES CACHEUX★

| ■ | 1.3ha | 7800 | 5 D ⑪ ↓ |

Intense fruity character and youthful flavour with well-balanced acidity and richness. Will develop slowly. (1982)
� Jacques et Patrice Cacheux, Vosne-Romanée, 21700 Nuits-St-Georges; tel. 80 61 24 79 ☄ No visitors.

DOMAINE FRANÇOIS GERBET
Aux Réas★

| ■ | 2ha | 9600 | 5 D ⓘ ⑪ ↓ |

74 76 *78 79 81 82

Pale strawberry colour with aromas of raspberry liqueur and aniseed. Reasonable body, but short, slightly hot alcoholic flavour. (1982)
� Dom. François Gerbet, Vosne-Romanée, 21700 Nuits-St-Georges; tel. 80 61 07 85 ☄ By appt.

DOMAINE FRANCOIS GERBET
Les Petits-Monts★★

| ■1er Cru | 3ha | 2000 | 5 D ⑪ ↓ |

72 76 78 79 82 83

Intense fruity character strongly marked by new wood. An open, attractive wine for medium-term drinking. (1982)
� Dom. François Gerbet, Vosne-Romanée, 21700 Nuits-St-Georges; tel. 80 61 07 85 ☄ By appt.

JEAN GRIVOT★★

| ■ | 2.8ha | 16800 | 5 D ⑪ ↓ |

71 ⑯ 78 82

Good colour, harmonious, fruity but fairly soft on the nose and palate. May be kept for a short time. (1982)

➤ SC Jean Grivot, Vosne-Romanée, 21700 Nuits-St-Georges; tel. 80 61 05 95 ☄ No visitors.

LOUIS JADOT★

| ■1er Cru | 3200 | 6 D ⑪ ↓ |

71 72 73 74 **76 78** 79 82 **83**

Although the nose is still unforthcoming, this wine with its dark, rather intense colour, is already showing itself to be rich, full bodied and very tannic. Should be tasted again in two to three years. (1982)
➤ Louis Jadot, 5 Rue Samuel-Legay, 21200 Beaune; tel. 80 22 10 57 ☄ By appt. Closed Aug.

HENRI JAYER *Cros Parantoux*★★★

| ■1er Cru | 1ha | 3000 | 5 ⓘ ⑪ |

74 76 78 79 81 82

An exceptional wine, tasted from the wood, but which will not be available at the domaine when this guide appears; it will be found in some good restaurants. Almost black in colour, it is a very fatty wine with a complex nose with notes of cassis. On the palate the wood is dominated by the strong structure of the wine. A great wine but you will have to wait ten years before fully enjoying it. (1983)
➤ Henri Jayer, Vosne-Romanée, 21700 Nuits-St-Georges; tel. 80 61 03 84 ☄ No visitors.

HENRI JAYER★★

| ■ | 3ha | 1500 | 5 ⓘ ⑪ |

74 76 *78 79 81 82

Clear red colour and extraordinarily rich flavour showing wonderful aromas of strawberry, blackberry and bramble. Look out for this wine in France's top restaurants. (1982)
➤ Henri Jayer, Vosne-Romanée, 21700 Nuits-St-Georges; tel. 80 61 03 84 ☄ No visitors.

LEROY★★

| ■ | 3000 | 6 ⑪ ↓ |

72 74 76 *78 82

This firm, the co-proprietor of the Domaine de la Romanée-Conti, can be relied on for its other wines from Vosne-Romanée. Plenty of finesse with an attractive, copper-tinged colour and subtle aromas of wild cherry, resin, vanilla and angelica root. Still firm on the palate and very elegant. (1972)
➤ SA Leroy, Dom. de la Romanée-Conti, Vosne-Romanée, 21700 Nuits-St-Georges; tel. 80 61 04 57 ☄ No visitors.

BERNARD MARTIN-NOBLET★★

■   1 ha   3850   5 D ⑪ ↓
⑦⑥ **78 79** *80 *81 82 83

The finesse of the 1981 vintage with a delicate, fresh bouquet and a well-balanced, long flavour. Will reach its peak in five years. (1981)
↱ Bernard Martin-Noblet, Vosne-Romanée, 21700 Nuits-St-Georges; tel. 80 61 27 84 ⵑ No visitors.

1982
VOSNE-ROMANÉE
APPELLATION CONTROLÉE
Mis en bouteille au Domaine   75 d
MONGEARD-MUGNERET
PROPRIÉTAIRE-RÉCOLTANT A VOSNE-ROMANÉE (CÔTE-D'OR)
PRODUCE OF FRANCE

ALFRED MARTIN★★

■   2 ha   10800   5 D ⑪ ↓
⑦⑥ **78 79 80 81 82** 82 **83**

A well-made, fairly dense 1982 with firm tannic support and good acidity. Will develop slowly. (1982)
↱ Alfred Martin, Vosne-Romanée, 21700 Nuits-St-Georges; tel. 80 61 05 17 ⵑ By appt.

DOMAINE MOILLARD-GRIVOT
Malconsorts★

■1er Cru   3 ha   10800   6 ▤ ↓
76 78 80 81 82 **83**

Slight copper hue and nose of humus and autumn leaves. Elegant, tannic-backed flavour. Persistent aftertaste, but lacking acidity and extract. (1981)
✓ Beaune Grèves, Nuits-St-Georges Clos de Thorey Rouge, Nuits-St-Georges Clos des Grandes Vignes, Nuits-St-Georges Clos des Corvées Rouge.
↱ SARL Moillard, 5 Rue Mignotte, 21700 Nuits-St-George; tel. 80 61 03 34 ⵑ Weekends 9.00–11.00/14.00–17.00. Closed Aug.

MOILLARD★

■   72000   5 ⑪ ↓
78 ⑦⑨ **81 82**

The classic Vosne aromas of undergrowth, humus and game have not yet pierced the tough skin of this 1983. Patience will be required, but after a few years of bottle age the characteristic bouquet and flavour should emerge. Wait for it to soften. (1983)
↱ SARL Moillard, 5 Rue F.-Mignotte, 21700 Nuits-St-Georges; tel. 80 61 03 34 ⵑ No visitors.

DOMAINE MONGEARD-MUGNERET★★★

■   3 ha   16000   5 D ⑪ ↓
69 71 72 76 78 ⑧② 82

A model rich, full-flavoured wine. Exceptionally refined aromas with subtle floral nuances. Sustained, velvety flavour which will go on acquiring depth and complexity as it ages. (1982)
↱ Dom. Mongeard-Mugneret, Rue de Boncourt, Vosne-Romanée, 21700 Nuits-St-Georges; tel. 80 61 11 95 ⵑ By appt.

RENE MUGNERET★★

■   1 ha   7000   5 D ⑪ ↓
⑦⑧ **80** 82 **83**

Fine bouquet with notes of oak and moss and a fleeting musky aroma. Pronounced blackcurrant and gingerbread flavour. Will mature well. (1982)
↱ René Mugneret, Vosne-Romanée, 21700 Nuits-St-Georges; tel. 80 61 09 95 ⵑ By appt. Closed week of 15 Aug.

GERARD MUGNERET★★★

■   1 ha   7200   5 D ⑪ ↓
⑦⑧ **80** 82 **83**

Deep, lustrous red with exceptional fruit. Rich, full-bodied wine with very good potential. (1982)
↱ Gérard Mugneret, Vosne-Romanée, 21700 Nuits-St-Georges; tel. 80 61 09 95 ⵑ By appt. Closed week of 15 Aug.

ANDRE NOBLET-ADNOT★★

■   1.5 ha   7200   5 D ⑪ ↓
⑦⑦ **78 79 80 81** 82

Intense fruity character and firm presence on the palate. Enough structure to keep for a long time. (1982)
↱ André Noblet-Adnot, Vosne-Romanée, 21700 Nuits-St-Georges; tel. 80 61 03 11 ⵑ No visitors.

MICHEL NOELLAT *Les Beaumonts*★★

■1er Cru   2 ha   7500   5 D ⑪ ↓
⑦⑥ **78** 80

A good Vosne-Romanée Premier Cru with maturing aromas marked by a slightly 'animal' note. Round, delicate, persistent flavour. (1980)
↱ Michel Noellat, Vosne-Romanée, 21700 Nuits-St-Georges; tel. 80 61 12 79 ⵑ By appt.

DOMAINE CHARLES NOELLAT
Les Beaumonts★

■1er Cru   2.90 ha   9000   6 D ▤ ↓
⑦⑥ *78 *79 *81 *82 83

Slight 'reduction' smell of flour and ivy leaves characterizes this Vosne-Romanée Premier Cru. A rich, very refined flavour not unlike that of the 1978. Drink from now on. (1978)
↱ Sté. Charles Noellat, Les Genevrières, Vosne-Romanée, 21700 Nuits-St-Georges; tel. 80 61 10 82 ⵑ By appt.

RION PERE ET FILS *Les Chaumes*★

| ■ | 0.5 ha | 2250 | 5 D ⑪ ⌟ |

74 76 78 79 80 **82**

Aromas of cut hay over a background of musk and dried-fruit flavours. Firm, almost pinched on the palate. Has reached the limit of its development; drink soon. (1976)
➼ *MM.* Rion Père et Fils, Route Nationale, Vosne-Romanée, 21700 Nuits-St-Georges; tel. 80 61 05 31 ⍭ By appt.

ROBERT SIRUGUE★★

| ■ | 2 ha | 9500 | 5 D ⑪ ⌟ |

76 78 **81** 82

Luckily, not all wines need to be kept for years before drinking. This well-made 1982 is already good to drink with its delicate fruity bouquet and soft, refreshing flavour. (1982)
➼ Robert Sirugue, Vosne-Romanée, 21700 Nuits-St-Georges; tel. 80 61 00 64 ⍭ By appt.

Richebourg, La Romanée, Romanée-Conti, Romanée-St-Vivant, La Tâche

These growths are the crown jewels of Burgundy, and are among the most expensive wines in the world. Under the circumstances, comment seems superfluous. All authorities agree that the vineyards, totalling some 25 hectares, produce wines of unparalleled opulence and finesse. Romanée-Conti is certainly the most famous, possibly by association with the Domaine de la Romanée-Conti which owns and manages substantial holdings in four of these five vineyards. However, it would be invidious to single out any one wine as the best. For the record, Romanée-Conti covers 1.8 hectares, while La Romanée takes up an area of 0.83 hectares. Richebourg has 8 hectares Romanée-St- Vivant has 9.5 hectares and La Tâche a little more than 6 hectares. As with all the Grand Crus, the yield is of the order of 20 to 30 hectolitres per hectare, depending on the year.

Richebourg

JEAN GROS★★

| ■Gd Cru | 0.5 ha | 1920 | 6 D ⑪ ⌟ |

64 71 72 **76** 78 ⑧ 82

Light ruby colour. Nose of vanilla, soft butter and candied fruit. On the palate a dominant note of oak, but the overall impression is of elegance and good structure. Sweet but rather short finish. (1982) ✔ Vosne-Romanée, Vosne Clos des Réas, Clos-Vougeot, Nuits-St-Georges.
➼ Jean Gros, 21700 Vosne-Romanée, 21700 Nuits-St-Georges; tel. 80 61 04 69 ⍭ By appt.

DOMAINE DE LA ROMANEE-CONTI★★

| ■Gd Cru | 3.51 ha | 15000 | 6 D ⑪ ⌟ |

64 66 67 71 72 73 74 **78** ⑲ 81 82

Beautiful orange and copper-tinged colour, still quite deep. Aromas of oak bark, lichen and undergrowth with slightly bitter notes of Armagnac and wild cherry. Finesse and structure on the palate. An excellent wine from a modest vintage. (1967) ✔ La Tâche, Romanée-Conti, Richebourg, Romanée-St-Vivant.
➼ SA Leroy, Dom. de la Romanée-Conti, Vosne-Romanée, 21700 Nuits-St-Georges; tel. 80 61 04 57 ⍭ No visitors.

La Romanée

DOMAINE BOUCHARD PERE ET FILS★★★

| ■Gd Cru | 0.85 ha | 3000 | 6 D ⑪ ⌟ |

76 78 ⑲ 82

Deep colour and complex aromas of candied fruit, dates, figs, and game. Very dense and superbly elegant, with an attractive finish. Unforgettable and marvellous. (1979)
➼ *MM.* Bouchard Père et Fils, Au Château, 21200 Beaune; tel. 80 22 14 41 ⍭ By appt. Closed Aug., one week in Feb. ➼ *M. le Comte* Liger-Belhir.

Romanée-Conti

DOMAINE DE LA ROMANEE-CONTI★★★

| ■Gd Cru | 1.8 ha | 6500 | 6 ⑪ ⌟ |

An exceptional wine only sold by the Domaine as part of a mixed case and only then to a lucky few. One of the most expensive red wines in the world from a small vineyard in the heart of the appellation. In style and geographical location it is close to La Tâche – another of the Domaine's top wines – although it is generally regarded as being even finer.
➼ SA Leroy, Dom. de la Romanée-Conti, Vosne-Romanée, 21700 Nuits-St-Georges; tel. 80 61 04 57 ⍭ No visitors.

Romanée-St-Vivant

DOMAINE DE LA ROMANEE-CONTI★★★

■Gd Cru	5.28ha	20 000	6 D ⦀ ↓

67 71 72 73 74 75 ⑦⑧ 79 80 81 82

Lustrous colour with copper and bronze highlights. The hot, dry aromas of resin, incense and coffee recall the torrid summer of 1976. The complex bouquet and flavour also reveal a slight animal note and nuances of peppermint, vanilla and pistachio. Very clear, well-defined taste of great elegance. (1976)
➤ SA Leroy, Dom. de la Romanée-Conti, Vosne-Romanée, 21700 Nuits-St-Georges; tel. 80 61 04 57 ⊤ No visitors..

La Tâche

DOMAINE DE LA ROMANEE-CONTI★★

■	6ha	25 000	6 D ⦀ ↓

67 72 73 *74 75 78 ⑦⑨ 80 81 82

Still a very youthful colour showing little sign of maturity. Highly distinguished fleeting aromas of amber, resin and roses. Fine fruit on the palate and the fresh, balanced flavour of the vintage. Needs to age. (1982) ✔ Romanée-Conti, Richebourg, Romanée-St-Vivant.
➤ SA Leroy, Dom. de la Romanée-Conti, Vosne-Romanée, 21700 Nuits-St-Georges; tel. 80 61 04 57 ⊤ No visitors.

Nuits-St-Georges

This small town of 5000 inhabitants, unlike its neighbours to the north, has no Grand Cru vineyards. The appellation extends into the commune of Prémeaux, which borders it to the south. The very many Premier Crus enjoy a deservedly high reputation – Nuits-St-Georges is the southernmost communal appellation of the Côte de Nuits, and produces its own distinctive style of wine. Each climat has its own pronounced character; generally, the wines are high in tannin and therefore keep for a long time.

The best-known Nuits-St-Georges Premier Cru vineyards include Les St-Georges, said to have been already under vine in the year AD 1000; Les Vaucrains, which produces robust wines; Les Cailles and Les Champs-Perdrix, whose names, meaning respectively 'quail' and 'partridge', suggest an origin as game coverts. Les Porets, on the other hand, was once an orchard of wild pears, and indeed one may not too fancifully detect a wild pear flavour in its wine. All these are in Nuits-St-Georges. Prémeaux claims Le Clos de la Marechale, Les Argillières, Forêts-St-Georges, Corvées and Le Clos de L'Arlot: these growths are all marketed as Nuits-St-Georges. Altogether there are some 400 hectares of vineyards, producing almost 10000 hectolitres per year.

Nuits-St-Georges has its own Hospices – or charitable hospital – a smaller affair than the famous Hospices at Beaune. The Hospices de Nuits annual sale takes place on the Sunday before Palm Sunday, when the town auctions wine from the Hospices de Nuits vineyards to support the charitable foundation. Within the town are the main offices of a number of négociants, along with makers of Cassis de Bourgogne, the famous blackcurrant liqueur of the region. Sparkling Burgundy is also produced here, especially in years when less appellation wine can be made. Finally, Nuits-St-Georges is the administrative headquarters of the Confrérie des Chevaliers du Tastevin.

BERTRAND AMBROISE★★

■	0.5ha	2500	5 D ⦀ ↓

78 *79 *82 83

All the classic qualities of a Nuits-St-Georges here amplified by the outstanding 1983 vintage: colour, aromatic finesse and rich tannins. Should make a fine bottle in about ten years' time. (1983)
➤ Bertrand Ambroise, Prémeaux-Prissey, 21700 Nuits-St-Georges; tel. 80 62 30 18 ⊤ By appt.

CIE DES VINS D'AUTREFOIS
Les Rues-de-Chaux★

■1er Cru		5 ▮ ↓

Nuits-St-Georges wines are among the slowest developers in Burgundy. This powerful, full-bodied 1983 will be no excepton, lasting several decades. Typical, already expressive aromas of raspberry, kirsch and coffee. (1983)
➤ Cie des Vins d'Autrefois, 9 Rue Celer, 21200 Beaune; tel. 80 22 21 31 ⊤ No visitors.

JACQUES CACHEUX★

■	0.7ha	4000	5 D ⦀ ↓

Rich, expressive aromas of blackcurrant, coffee and oak with an unexpectedly fat, almost soft flavour. Already quite developed for the appellation and ready to drink in the near future.(1982)

� Jacques et Patrice Cacheux, Vosne-Romanée, 21700 Nuits-St-Georges; tel. 80 61 24 79 **Υ** No visitors.

J.-J. CONFURON *Les Chabœufs*★★

■1er Cru 0.5ha 2000 **5 D ⑪**

74 *76 **77** *78 79 **79** ⑧2 **82** 84

Although Les Chabœufs vineyard touches Les Vaucrains, the wines are not as firm and can be drunk younger. This is a typically light 1982 with a fruity *terroir* flavour and fair length on the palate which should allow it to age well. (1982)
✔ Clos-Vougeot, Chambolle-Musigny, Côtes-de-Nuits-Villages, Nuits-St-Georges.
� J.-J. Confuron, Prémeaux-Prissey, 21700 Nuits-St-Georges; tel. 80 62 31 08.

DOMAINE ROBERT DUBOIS ET FILS *Clos des Argillières*★

■1er Cru 0.42ha 3600 **5 D ⑪ ↓**

69 72 76 ⑦8 79 80 *81 82

Still rather inexpressive nose with a predominantly floral note. Palate of candied cherry and bitter almond with a sharp, menthol finish. Rather lacking in weight and complexity due, perhaps, to the vintage. (1982)
� Robert Dubois et Fils, Prémeaux-Prissey, 21700 Nuits-St-Georges; tel. 80 62 30 61 **Υ** By appt.

DOMAINE ROBERT DUBOIS ET FILS★★

■ 3ha 15000 **5 D ▮ ⑪ ↓**

76 77 78 ⑦9 80 **81 82 83 84**

A fine 1980. Deep colour and a powerful gamey nose; firm, subtle, well-balanced flavour. An ideal wine to drink with game birds. (1980)
✔ Bourgogne, Côtes-de-Nuits-Villages, Nuits-St-Georges, Nuits-St-Georges Premier Cru.
� Robert Dubois et Fils, Prémeaux-Prissey, 21700 Nuits-St-Georges; tel. 80 62 30 61 **Υ** By appt.

DOMAINE ROBERT DUBOIS ET FILS★

■ 3ha 24000 **5 D ▮ ⑪ ↓**

69 72 76 ⑦8 79 80 81 82

Light smooth with clear colour. Fruity but fairly light flavour. Firm slightly alcoholic finish. (1982)
✔ Nuits-St-Georges, Passe-tout-grain, Bourgogne Aligoté.

� Robert Dubois et Fils, Prémeaux-Prissey, 21700 Nuits-St-Georges; tel. 80 62 30 61 **Υ** By appt.

ROGER DUPASQUIER ET FILS★★

■ 5ha 25000 **5 D ⑪ ↓**

66 69 71 **76 78** 79 80 81 ⑧2 **82 83 84**

Surprisingly intense, dark colour for a 1982 with characteristic aromas of kirsch and coffee, and a solid structure which will enable it to keep. (1982)
� Roger Dupasquier et Fils, Prémeaux-Prissey, 21700 Nuits-St-Georges; tel. 80 62 31 19 **Υ** By appt.

ROGER DUPASQUIER ET FILS *Les Chaines Carteaux*★★

■1er Cru 1ha 5000 **5 D ⑪ ↓**

66 69 71 **76 78** ⑦9 80 *81 **82 83**

In 1981, the Nuits-St Georges Premiers Crus gave wines of remarkable finesse. This one is now at its peak, with a delicate bitter-sweet bouquet of coffee and fruit stones, and a long, silky flavour. Ready to drink. (1981) ✔ Bourgogne Rouge, Côtes de Nuits-Villages, Nuits-St-Georges Premier Cru, Nuits-St-Georges les Vaucrains.
� Roger Dupasquier et Fils, Prémeaux-Prissey, 21700 Nuits-St-Georges; tel. 80 62 31 19 **Υ** By appt.

MICHEL DUPASQUIER *Les Vaucrains*★★

■1er Cru 0.50ha 2000 **5 D ⑪ ↓**

66 69 **76 78** *79 80 **81** ⑧2 **82** ⑧3

Deep colour with classic aromas of lichen and Morello cherry and pronounced tannin which still needs to soften. Will develop slowly. (1982)
✔ Corton, Nuits-St-Georges, Bourgogne Rouge, Bourgogne Aligoté.
� Michel Dupasquier, Prémeaux-Prissey, 21700 Nuits-St-Georges; tel. 80 62 31 19 **Υ** By appt.

MICHEL DUPASQUIER★★

■ 2ha 10000 **5 D ⑪ ↓**

Bright colour and harmonious, mature bouquet with notes of fruit (Morello cherries) and musk typical of the appellation. Strong enough to be left to age. (1982) ✔ Corton, Nuits-St-Georges, Bourgogne Rouge, Bourgogne Aligoté.
� Michel Dupasquier, Prémeaux-Prissey, 21700 Nuits-St-Georges; tel. 80 62 31 19 **Υ** By appt.

MAISON J. FAIVELEY *Clos de la Maréchale*★★★

■1er Cru 10ha 36000 **6 ⑪ D**

59 64 *66 **69** 71 76 78

A slight orange hue and strong, spicy aromas with a distinct gamey nose. Robust, peppery flavour with a fruity aftertaste of myrtle. A somewhat unbalanced wine with plenty of future promise, but already sold out on this négociant's catalogue. Worth seeking out, however. (1969)
� M. J. Faiveley, 8 Rue du Tribourg, 21700 Nuits-St-Georges; tel. 80 61 04 55 **Υ** By appt. Closed Aug.

JEAN GRIVOT *Les Boudots*★★

■1er Cru	0.84ha	4800	6 D ◐ ↓

71 ⑦ 78 82

Bright colour with a violet tinge. Still very young but showing attractive aromas of fruit stones and resin and a fine rich presence on the palate. Needs several years. (1982)
◆┑ SC Jean Grivot, Vosne-Romanée, 21700 Nuits-St-Georges; tel. 80 61 05 95 ✕ No visitors.

LOUIS JADOT *Clos des Corvées*★★★

■	2ha	6000	6 D ◐ ↓

69 72 76 ⑦ 79 80 ★81 82

Very dark colour and nose of truffle, pepper and cloves lending it a rather oriental character. Fine flavour with notes of laurel and rum adding a fabulous aromatic complexity. Very great wine. Ready to drink but could be kept for two to three years. (1979)
◆┑ Louis Jadot, 5 Rue Samuel-Legay, 21200 Beaune; tel. 80 22 10 57 ✕ By appt. Closed Aug.

JACQUELINE JAYER★★

■	0.34ha	1900	5 D ◐ ↓

★76 ★78 82 82

Intense violet colour and refined aromas of coffee, resin and blackcurrant cordial. Full round flavour. A first-class wine. (1982)
◆┑ Jacqueline Jayer, Route de Concoeur, Vosne-Romanée, 21700 Nuits-St-Georges; tel. 80 61 23 06 ✕ No visitors.

MOILLARD★★

■		72000	5 ◐ ↓

⑦ 79 81 82

From a fine Premier Cru vineyard owned by Moillard. A skilfully vinified 1983 that will need at least ten years to peak. (1983)
◆┑ SARL Moillard, 5 Rue F.-Mignotte, 21700 Nuits-St-Georges; tel. 80 61 03 34 ✕ No visitors.

MUGNERET *Les Chaignots*★★

■1er Cru	1.3ha	8500	5 D ◐ ↓

★76 77 78 80 ★⑧ 82 83

'Les Chaignots', or variants, occurs several times as a vineyard name in Burgundy designating the oak trees which no doubt once occupied the vineyard land. This wine is aptly named, showing pronounced aromas of oak bark and a firm, elegant flavour. A very good bottle. (1982)
◆┑ Gérard Mugneret, Vosne-Romanée, 21700 Nuits-St-Georges; tel. 80 61 09 95 ✕ By appt.

DOMAINE CHARLES NOELLAT
Boudots★

■1er Cru	1.50ha	4800	5 D ▬ ↓

76 ★⑦ ★79 ★82 83

Light but brilliant colour, with fresh aromas of cut hay, elderflower, thyme and laurel. Dry, rusk-like flavour with a peppery finish. Firm, subtle balance on the palate. (1980)
◆┑ Sté Charles Noellat, Les Genevrières, Vosne-Romanée, 21700 Nuits-St-Georges; tel. 80 61 10 82 ✕ By appt ◆┑ Famille Moreau.

ALAIN PELLETIER ET FILS★★

■	2.5ha	4000	D ▬ ◐ ↓

78 79 ⑧ 83

This wine has been vinified to bring out all its substance. A long, slow vinification has brought out a strong colour, intense bouquet, rich extract and full-bodied power. Will age well. (1982)
◆┑ Alain Pelletier et Fils, Rue Moulin, Prémeaux-Prissey, 21700 Nuits-St-Georges; tel. 80 62 30 24.

HENRI REMORIQUET *Les Damodes*★★

■1er Cru	0.5ha	2400	3 D ◐ ↓

69 ★72 ⑦ 78 82

Bright red with slightly orange tints. A complete, very fleshy wine, with a complex acid structure and highly elegant finish. Will be at its peak in four years' time. (1982)
◆┑ Henri Remoriquet, 25–27 Rue de Charmois, 21700 Nuits-St-Georges; tel. 80 61 08 17 ✕ By appt.

HENRI REMORIQUET *Rue de Chaux*★

■	0.4ha	3840	5 D ◐ ↓

69 ★72 76 ⑦ 82

A rich, deeply coloured wine with complex fruit aromas of cherries and wild plums. Persistent, scented flavour which would suit coq au vin. (1982) ✔ Nuits-St-Georges Premier Cru.
◆┑ Henri Remoriquet, 25–27 Rue de Charmois, 21700 Nuits-St-Georges; tel. 80 61 08 17 ✕ By appt.

HENRI REMORIQUET *Les Allots*★★

■	0.73ha	3600	5 D ◐ ↓

69 72 73 76 ⑦ 82

An attractively coloured wine with orange hints and a nose of dried apricots. Strong, fruity presence on the palate – peach, cherry plum and apricot – and a very smooth, persistent flavour. Good finish. (1980) ✔ Nuits-St-Georges Rouge, Bourgogne Hautes-Côtes-de-Nuits Rouge, Bourgogne Passe-tout-grain, Bourgogne Aligoté.
◆┑ Henri Remoriquet, 25–27 Rue de Charmois, 21700 Nuits-St-Georges; tel. 80 61 08 17 ✕ By appt.

TURMEL-MORIZOT★

■	0.1ha	600	5 D ▬ ↓

71 72 ★76 ★78 ⑧ 83

Already mature colour with a brownish tinge and well-developed 'animal' bouquet. May be drunk now but is rich enough to age for a year or two. (1982) ✔ Bourgogne, Bourgogne Grand Ordinaire, Bourgogne Aligoté.
◆┑ M. Turmel-Morizot, Place de la Mairie, Pré-

Côte de Nuits (South)

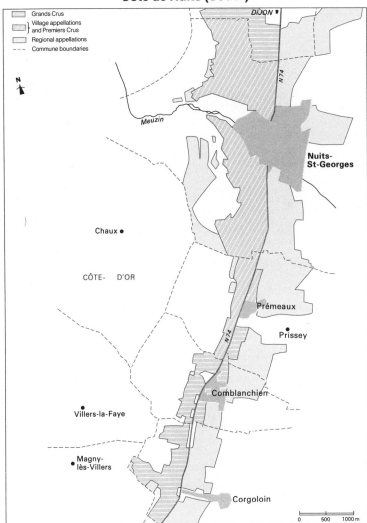

Grands Crus
Village appellations and Premiers Crus
Regional appellations
Commune boundaries

N

DIJON
N 74
Meuzin
Nuits-St-Georges
Chaux
CÔTE- D'OR
Prémeaux
Prissey
Comblanchien
Villers-la-Faye
Magny-lès-Villers
Corgoloin

0   500   1000 m

meaux-Prissey, 21700 Nuits-St-Georges; tel. 80 62 30 70 ⵢ By appt.

CHARLES VIENOT
Clos des Corvées-Paget*

■1er Cru	0.8 ha	600	6	D	ⵜ	ⵗ
71 74 **76** 78 79 **82** 82						

A typical 1982 with its pronounced fruity character and relatively light structure. The new oak barrels in which it was raised lend some firmness to the taste. Ready in three or four years. (1982) ⵜ Ets Charles Vienot, 5 Quai Dumorey, 21700 Nuits-St-Georges; tel. 80 62 31 05 ⵢ By appt.

Côtes de Nuits-Villages

Beyond Prémeaux the vineyard area gradually contracts. At Corgoloin it is a mere strip, only 200 metres wide, marking the narrowest part of the Côte. The hills fall away and the Côte de Nuits-Villages appellation (formerly known as Vins Fins de la Côte de Nuits) officially stops at Le Clos des Langres, in Corgoloin. Between these two are the villages of Prissey, adjoining Prémeaux, and Comblanchien, known for its limestone quarries. The quality of land in these villages would certainly entitle them to their own appellation were not the areas involved too small. They therefore combine with two other communes, Fixin and Brochon, and share a single appellation, Côtes de Nuits-Villages, whose annual production approaches 5000 hectolitres. Some very good wines are to be found here at a reasonable price.

BERTRAND AMBROISE★★

| ■ | 1.5ha | 4000 | 4 D ⦿ ⸖ |

*78 *79 *82 83

This 1983 has the typical, well-defined aromas of its vintage – dried fruits, toast and gingerbread. Rich enough in tannin to be left to age for several years. (1983) ✔ Bourgogne Rouge et Blanc, Nuits-St-Georges, Bourgogne Aligoté.
⊷ Bertrand Ambroise, Prémeaux-Prissey, 21700 Nuits-St-Georges; tel. 80 62 30 19 ⲧ By appt.

ANDRE BART★★

| ■ | 0.5ha | 1900 | 4 D ⦿ ⸖ |

64 66 76 78 79 80 82 ⑧₃

Marked by aromas of liquorice root, and showing good fruit. Vinification has succeeded in tempering some of the excesses of the vintage, and has produced a harmonious cuvée. Will be a fine bottle in a few years' time. (1983)
⊷ André Bart, 24 Rue de Mazy, 21160 Marsannay-la-Côte; tel. 80 52 12 09 ⲧ By appt.

JULES BELIN *Clos du Chapeau*

| ■ | 1.5ha | 6000 | 4 ⦿ ⸖ |

78 79 80 82 ⑧₃

Dark colour and a deep fruity nose of prunes and blackcurrants. Rich, fruity flavour. Marked by a rather hot finish owing to the dominance of the alcohol, which is not yet fully integrated. (1983)
⊷ Jules Belin, Clos du Chapeau, Premeaux, 21700 Nuits-St-Georges; tel. 80 62 30 98 ⲧ Mon.–Fri. 8.00–11.30/13.30–18.00. ⊷ SCI de l'Arlot.

MAURICE CHAUDAT★★

| ■ | 1.2ha | 6000 | 4 D ▤ ⦿ ⸖ |

*69 *71 *72 78

An attractive 1982 with a bright colour and fruity aromas. It still has all the characteristic freshness of its vintage, together with a great deal of finesse. Pleasant to drink, but will also keep well. (1982) ✔ Bourgogne Rouge, Bourgogne Aligoté.
⊷ Maurice Chaudat, Voie Romaine, Corgoloin, 21700 Nuits-St-Georges; tel. 80 62 92 85.

BERNARD CHEVILLON★★

| ■ | 3ha | 15000 | 4 D ▤ ⸖ |

71 72 74 76 78 79 80 81 82 83

A vintage for long-term keeping. Still very young with intense colour, tannin, and a lot of body; the bouquet is still immature. Drink in fifteen years' time. (1983) ✔ Bourgogne, Passe-tout-grain, Bourgogne Aligoté.
⊷ Bernard Chevillon, Voie Romaine, Corgoloin, 21700 Nuits-St-Georges; tel. 80 62 98 79 ⲧ By appt.

BERNARD DESERTAUX★

| ■ | 7ha | 30000 | 4 ⦿ ⸖ |

80 81 82

A good example of the village appellation: fresh aromas of blackcurrant, raspberry and vanilla with a note of new oak. Subtle but not oversoft flavour. The wine is firm enough to age well. (1982)

⊷ Bernard Désertaux, Corgoloin, 21700 Nuits-St-Georges; tel. 80 62 98 40 ⲧ By appt.

ROBERT DUBOIS ET FILS
Les Argillières★★

| ■ | 0.5ha | 2500 | 5 D ▤ ⦿ ⸖ |

76 77 78 79 80 83 84

An energetic wine grower, who is also president of his local syndicat. This well-vinified wine has an intense bouquet and a finely balanced flavour, neither too tannic nor too soft. A wine to buy now and drink in 1990. (1982) ✔ Passe-tout-grain, Côtes-de-Nuits-Villages, Nuits-St-Georges, Nuits-St-Georges Premier Cru.
⊷ Robert Dubois et Fils, Prémeaux-Prissey, 21700 Nuits-St-Georges; tel. 80 62 30 61 ⲧ By appt.

FORNEROL-VACHEROT★★

| ■ | 3ha | 15000 | 4 D ▤ ⦿ ⸖ |

76 78 79 *81 82 83

This 1982 is nicely mature and ready to drink. Classic Côtes de Nuits aromas of truffle and musk overlaid with a floral bouquet of peaches and cherries. Soft, well-matured flavour. A perfect wine with 'jambon persillé' or pork pâté. (1982)
⊷ MM. Fornerol-Vacherot, Corgoloin, 21700 Nuits-St-Georges; tel. 80 62 98 50 ⲧ By appt.

GACHOT-MONOT★★

| ■ | 3ha | 15000 | 4 D ⦿ ⸖ |

A well constructed, surprisingly powerful 1982; intense peony-red colour with sweetly scented aromas of blackcurrant and vanilla with a hint of coffee. Will keep for at least ten years. (1982)
⊷ M. Gachot-Monot, Gerland, 21700 Nuits-St-Georges; tel. 80 62 50 95 ⲧ By appt.

L'HERITIER-GUYOT★

| ■ | 190ha | 5000 | 4 D ⦿ ⸖ |

71 72 76 78 79 82 83

A fairly mature Côtes de Nuits-Villages 1982 with well-developed aromas of oak bark, gingerbread and liquorice. Fat but quite firm flavour which would suit game, boeuf bourguignon or jugged hare. (1982)
⊷ L'Héritier-Guyot, Rue du Champ-aux-Prêtres, 21006 Dijon Cedex; tel. 80 72 16 14 ⲧ By appt.

HUGUENOT PERE ET FILS★★

| ■ | 4ha | 19200 | 4 D ⦿ ⸖ |

76 77 ⑦₈ 79 ⑧₀ 81 82 83

All the charm of a mature 1980 with an attractive coppery colour, aromas of fresh red fruit, and a well rounded, smooth palate. (1980)
⊷ MM. Huguenot Père et Fils, 9 Ruelle Carron, 21160 Marsannay-la-Côte; tel. 80 51 11 56 ⲧ By appt.

ROBERT JAYER-GILLES★★

| ■ | 0.89ha | 4700 | 4 D ⦿ ⸖ |

64 66 76 ⑦₈ 79 *⑧₂ 83

Robert Gilles-Jayer supplies many of France's top restaurants. This wine has great finesse with a beautiful dark colour and light, subtle flavour. Still very young and should be left for at least three years. (1982) ✔ Echezeaux, Hautes-Côtes-de-Nuits, Passe-tout-grain. Hautes-Côtes-de

Nuits.
🔹 Robert Jayer-Gilles, Magny-les-Villers, 21700 Nuits-St-Georges; tel. 80 62 91 79 ⊺ By appt.

JEAN JOURDAN★★

■		2.2ha	10000	4 D ◫ 占

76 78 ⑦ *80 *81 82 83

This 1982 combines a fine colour with a lightly scented bouquet, and a well-balanced palate with good tannic support. Finesse as well as richness. (1982) ✔ Bourgogne Rouge, Bourgogne Aligoté.
🔹 Jean Jourdan, Corgoloin, 21700 Nuits-St-Georges; tel. 80 62 98 55.

DOMAINE DR MARION★

■		3.1ha	12000	5 D ◫ 占

Finesse but also depth of flavour in this 1982 combined with a long, fruity finish. Selected at the Tastevinage in 1984. (1982)
🔹 *MM.* Bouchard Père et Fils, 36 Rue Ste-Marguerite, 21203 Beaune; tel. 80 22 14 41 ⊺ By appt.

ALAIN PELLETIER ET FILS★

■		1.6ha	4000	4 D ▮ ◫ 占

This wine grower has managed to avoid the excesses of the 1983 vintage; a balanced and pleasing cuvée, with refreshing fruity notes of raspberry, blackcurrant and peach, and a light smooth flavour. Soft enough to drink now, although it could be left for a year or two. (1982)
🔹 Alain Pelletier et Fils, Prémeaux-Prissey, 21700 Nuits-St-Georges; tel. 80 62 30 24 ⊺ By appt.

JEAN PETITOT★

■		2.96ha	13500	4 D ◫ 占

47 54 57 59 69 71 78 82 ⑧

Vinified for ageing, this 1982 still has rather reserved aromas with a certain firmness on the palate. A long spell in the cellar should soften and mellow the wine. (1982)
🔹 Jean Petitot, Corgoloin, 21700 Nuits-St-Georges; tel. 80 62 98 21 ⊺ By appt.

CHARLES QUILLARDET★★

■		7ha	35000	4 D ◫ 占

*76 78 79 *81 83

Mature brick-red with ripe, pheasant aromas. Smooth flavour, lacking fullness, though, and not quite equal to the remarkable nose.
🔹 Charles Quillardet, 18 Route de Dijon, 21220 Gevrey-Chambertin; tel. 80 34 10 26 ⊺ By appt.

CAVE DE LA REINE PEDAUQUE
Clos des Langres★

■		3.50ha	15000	5 ◫ 占

64 66 69 71 76 78 79 80 81 82 ⑧

Subtle, well-developed 1982 with an attractive, round flavour and remarkable persistence. (1982)
🔹 Cave de la Reine Pédauque, Aloxe-Corton, 21420 Savigny-lès-Beaune; tel. 80 26 40 00 ⊺ By appt.

CHARLES VIENOT★

■	2400	5 D

71 74 76 78 79 81 82 83

Fresh, round flavour with more solidity than one often finds in this vintage. Subtle red fruit aromas and satisfying finish. (1982)
🔹 Ets Charles Vienot, 5 Quai Dumorey, 21700 Nuits-St-Georges; tel. 80 62 31 05 ⊺ By appt.

Ladoix

Three hamlets make up the commune of Ladoix-Serrigny: Serrigny, by the railway line, Ladoix on the RN 74, and Buisson, which is at the end of the Côte de Nuits. The communal appellation is Ladoix. Buisson is situated exactly at the geographical intersection of the Côte de Nuits and Côte de Beaune and, although for administrative purposes the Côte de Nuits stops at Corgoloin, the actual slope continues a little further. The division is made more obvious by the Combe de Magny, beyond which rise the steep Corton slopes. Their marl ridges, and varied exposures – east, south and west – provide one of the best wine-growing areas of the whole Côte.

These various geographical situations result in a wide range of red wine styles in the Ladoix appellation. There is also some distinctive white wine made which is well suited to the marl soil, to be found, for example, at Les Grechons, which is on the same geological level as Corton-Charlemagne to the south, but has a less favourable exposure. The volume of Ladoix produced rarely exceeds 2000 hectolitres of red and 200 hectolitres of white, and the wines deserve to be better known.

Another odd fact is that Ladoix used to have no Premiers Crus, despite its excellent classification from the Comité de Viticulture de Beaune in 1860. This omission has now been put right by the INAO (Institut National des Appellations d'Origine des Vins), and the principal Premiers Crus are La Corvée and Le Clou d'Orge, both with Côtes de Nuits character; Les Mourottes (Basses and Hautes), with a pronounced gamey style; Le Bois-Roussot, a very delicate wine grown on volcanic rock, and Les Joyeuses.

EDMOND CORNU★

■ 1 ha 6000 ▦ D ▯ ↓
76 78 ⑲ 80 **81** ▩ **83**

This wine has developed fairly quickly and already shows the character of a mature burgundy. At its peak. Drink now. (1982) ✔ Chorey-les-Beaune, Savigny-les-Beaune, Aloxe-Corton, Corton.
↦ Edmond Cornu, Le Meix-Gobillon, 21550 Ladoix-Sérrigny; tel. 80 26 40 79 ⊻ By appt.

CHATEAU CORTON-ANDRE
Clos des Chagnots★

■ 2.5 ha 10000 ▦ D ⑪ ↓
71 **76** 77 78 ★79 **80 81** 82 ㊊ ▩

Fine, young fruity character with enough structure and body to mature into a great wine. (1983)
↦ Pierre André, Ch. de Corton-André, Aloxe-Corton, 21420 Savigny-les24une; tel. 80 26 44 25 ⊻ By appt ↦Gabriel Liogier-d'Ardhuy.

CHRISTIAN GROS★★

■ 2 ha 10500 ▦ D ⑪ ↓

Clean, robust aromas of new oak, crushed red fruit and a hint of pepper, full but firm flavour. Still seems very young, and will become richer with age. (1982) ✔ Aloxe-Corton 1er Cru.
↦ Christian Gros, Prémeaux-Prissey, 21700 Nuits-St-Georges; tel. 80 62 31 06 ⊻ By appt.

JEAN GUITON

■ 1.5 ha 6000 ▦ D ▯ ⑪ ↓
73 78 **79 80** 81 **82** ▨ **84**

This 1983 Ladoix already has a highly developed nose with aromas of musk and oak. On the palate it is subtle, soft and delicate. It should be drunk at once. (1983) ✔ Bourgogne Passe-tout-grain, Bourgogne Rouge et Rosé, Aloxe-Corton, Bourgogne Aligoté.
↦ Jean Guiton, Route de Pommard, Bligny-les-Beaune, 21200 Beaune; tel. 80 26 82 88 ⊻ By appt.

MICHEL MALLARD★★

■ 4.5 ha 20000 ▦ D ⑪ ↓
78 ★⑲ ★81 ★▩ **83**

This wine has a very pleasing bouquet, is well balanced on the palate and excellent value. (1982)
↦ Michel Mallard, 21550 Ladoix-Sérrigny; tel. 80 26 41 59 ⊻ By appt.

PRINCE FLORENT DE MERODE★

■ 2.16 ha 10000 ▦ ⑪ ↓
76 ⑱ 79 ㉒ **83**

Intense bright colour, but undeveloped light, clean flavour. Needs three years. (1981) ✔ Corton Clos-du-Roi, Corton Bressandes, Corton Renardes, Aloxe-Corton Premier Cru.
↦ M. Florent de Mérode, Dom. de Sérrigny 21550 Ladoix-Sérrigny; tel. 80 26 40 80 ⊻ No visitors.

DOMAINE MESTRE PERE ET FILS

■ 2 ha 12000 ▦ D ▯ ⑪ ↓
80 82

Elegant. Fairly open on the palate and already beginning to show well. Well balanced with a pronounced note of sloes, but still rather lacking in aromatic complexity at this stage in its development. Retaste in three years' time. (1982)
↦ Dom. Mestre Père et Fils, 21590 Santenay; tel. 80 20 60 11 ⊻ By appt.

DOMAINE ANDRE NUDANT ET FILS *Les Gréchans★*

□ 0.6 ha 3500 ▦ D ⑪ ↓
⑲ 80 81 82 **83**

Bright and refreshing. Best drunk young to savour its fruity charm. (1982) ✔ Ladoix Premier Cru, Savigny-les-Beaune, Aloxe-Corton, Corton Bressandes.
↦ Dom. André Nudant et Fils, Cidex 24, No. 4, 21550, Ladoix-Sérrigny; tel. 80 26 40 82 ⊻ By appt.

DOMAINE ANDRE NUDANT ET FILS *La Corvée★★*

■1er Cru 3 ha 18000 ▦ D ⑪ ↓
78 79 80 81 ▩ **83**

A slow developer, keeping its youthful character for several years. The 1982 vintage still tastes of young fruit and is very immature. Keep. (1982)
✔ Chorey-les-Beaune, Savigny-les-Beaune, Aloxe-Corton, Corton Bressandes.
↦ Dom. André Nudant et Fils, Cidex 24 No. 4, 215500 Ladoix-Sérrigny; tel. 80 26 40 82 ⊻ By appt.

GASTON ET PIERRE RAVAUT *Les Corvées★★*

■1er Cru 1.67 ha 9500 ▦ D ▯ ⑪ ↓
78 ⑲ 81 ▩ **83**

Firmness and solidity are typical of the Ladoix premier crus, and make these wines similar to those of Aloxe. A keeping wine, of very good quality and a fine example of the appellation. (1982) ✔ Ladoix, Ladoix Premier Cru, Aloxe-Corton, Corton Bressandes.
↦ GAEC Gaston et Pierre Ravaut, Buisson, 21550 Ladoix-Sérrigny; tel. 80 26 41 94 ⊻ By appt.

DOMAINE ROUGEOT *Côtes de Beaune★*

■ 3 ha 16500 ▦ D ▯ ⑪ ↓
⑲ 80 ▧ 81 82 ▩ **83**

A red 1979 wine at its peak. A colour turning bronze, nose of candied fruits and vanilla, fullness on the palate and a certain firmness. Suitable with coq au vin and full fat cheeses. (1979) ✔ Meursault, Meursault Charmes, Volnay Santenots, Pommard.
↦ Marc Rougeot, 6 Rue André Ropiteau, 21190 Meursault; tel. 80 21 20 59 ⊻ By appt.

Côte de Beaune (North)

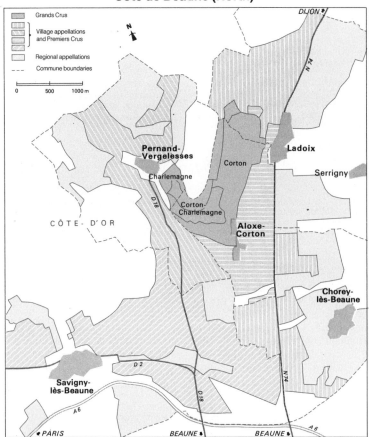

Grands Crus

Village appellations and Premiers Crus

Regional appellations

--- **Commune boundaries**

0   500   1000 m

DIJON

Pernand-Vergelesses

Ladoix

Corton

Serrigny

Charlemagne

Corton-Charlemagne

CÔTE- D'OR

Aloxe-Corton

Chorey-lès-Beaune

Savigny-lès-Beaune

PARIS

BEAUNE

BEAUNE

DOMAINE CACHAT-OCQUIDANT*

■   1 ha   5400   [4] [D] ⑪ ↓

73 76 77 **78*** 79* 80* 81⑧² ⑧³ 84

A lovely wine with a deep, bright colour and
well-defined aromas. For long-term keeping.
(1983) ✔ Bourgogne, Bourgogne la Chapelle-
Notre-Dame, Côtes-de-Beaune Villages, Aloxe-
Corton.
🕭 Cachat-Ocquidant et Fils, 21550 Ladoix-
Sérrigny; tel. 80 26 41 27 ☌ Daily 8.00–12.00/
14.00–18.00.

CAPITAIN-GAGNEROT *La Micaude**

■   1.4 ha   5000   [4] [D] ⑪ ↓

78 79 81 *⑧² **83**

Nose of blackcurrants with typical Côte de
Beaune aromas. Vinified to keep, but already
very pleasant to drink. (1982) ✔ Ladoix, Aloxe-
Corton, Corton. Corton Charlemagne.
🕭 Dom. François Capitain et Fils, 21550 Ladoix-
Sérrigny; tel. 80 26 41 36 ☌ By appt.

CAPITAIN-GAGNEROT**

□   0.8 ha   5000   [4] [D] ⑪ ↓

⑦⁶ **78** 79 81 *82 ⑧³

Fat, full-bodied flavour and should keep well.
(1983) ✔ Ladoix Premier Cru, Corton, Corton
Charlemagne, Aloxe-Corton Premier Cru.
🕭 Dom. François Capitain et Fils, 21550 Ladoix-
Sérrigny; tel. 80 26 41 36 ☌ By appt.

CHEVALIER ET FILS*

■   2 ha   10000   [4] [D] ⑪

75 76 77 **78** ⑦⁹ 80 **81** ⑧² **83**

A domaine characterized by long vatting times
and 'vins de garde'. The 1982 vintage is just
starting to open out but will not reach its peak for
several years yet. (1982) ✔ Bourgogne Aligoté,
Ladoix, Corton Charlemagne, Côtes-de-Nuits-
Villages.
🕭 GAEC Chevalier Père et Fils, Buisson, 21550
Ladoix-Sérrigny; tel. 80 26 46 30 ☌ By appt.

325

LES TERRES VINEUSES★★

■	15ha	90000	5 ◗ ◖ ↓

78 ⑦ 80 81 **82** 83 84

Highly scented wine with plenty of flavour, vinified for early drinking. A good, straightforward bottle. Distributed by the Société Pierre André in Aloxe-Corton. (1982) ✔ Corton Charlemagne, Corton Clos du Roi, Corton Renarde, Aloxe-Corton.
✦ SARL Les Terres Vineuses, Clos de Langres Corgoloin, 21700 Nuits-St-Georges; tel. 80 62 98 73 ⵎ Daily 9.00–12.00/14.00–18.00.

LES TERRES VINEUSES★★

□	1ha	6000	5 ▣ ◗ ◖ ↓

77 80 81 **82** 83 84

Remarkably fruity with good acidity and a smooth texture on the palate. Attractive. (1982)
✦ SARL les Terres Vineuses, Corgoloin, 21700 Nuits-St-Georges; tel. 80 62 98 73 ⵎ Mon.–Sat. 9.00–12.00/14.00–18.00.✦ *M.* Liogier-d'Ardfuy.

Aloxe-Corton

Only a small part of the Corton and Corton-Chalemagne vineyards are actually located within Aloxe-Corton, the smallest commune of the Côte de Beaune. The Corton and Corton-Charlemagne appellation extends into the communes of Ladoix and Pernand. Some 4000 hectolitres are produced annually. Its Premiers Crus are well-known, notable examples are Les Maréchaudes, Les Valozierès, Les Lolierès Grandes and Les Lolières Petites. The commune is the base of several busy shippers and there are some fine châteaux with their magnificently polished tiles. The Latour family owns a wonderful estate here, and a visit to their nineteenth-century cuverie, still a model of its kind for Burgundy wine-making, is an absolute must.

DOMAINE DES PIERRES BLANCHES★

■	0.50ha	600	5 ▣ ◗ ◖ ↓

76 78 ★79 ★81 82 83

Deep colour. Nose of crushed strawberry, fresh mint and blackberry. Lack of weight on the palate is disguised by good acidity, and elegant flavour, but the finish is rather harsh. (1982)
✦ Maurice Joliette, Dom. des Pierres Blanches, 21200 Beaune; tel. 80 22 26 45 ⵎ By appt.

CAPITAIN-GAGNEROT
Les Moutottes★★

■	1.5ha	4500	5 ▣ ◗ ◖ ↓

69 71 72 76 78 **79** 80 **82** 83

The rather severe, closed flavour of young Aloxe-Corton is especially evident in this wine. One of the best cuvées of the Société Capitain-Cagnerot, which also sells a wide range of other wines from this area. (1982)
✦ François Capitain et Fils, 21550 Ladoix-Sérrigny; tel. 80 26 41 36 ⵎ By appt.

CHANSON PERE ET FILS★

■			5 ▣ ◗ ◖ ↓

71 76 79 **80** ⑧⑴ 82

Fruity, rich and refined. 'Softer' and less severe than many of its appellation and may be drunk from now on. (1982)
✦ *MM.* Chanson Père et Fils, 10–12 Rue Paul-Chanson, 21200 Beaune; tel. 80 22 33 00 ⵎ No visitors.

LOUIS CHAPUIS★★

■1er Cru	1.25ha	6700	5 ▣ ◗ ◖ ↓

71 72 74 **76 78 79** 81 ⑧② **82**

Has enough structure to age well, and a bouquet that is beginning to open out. Good bottle for the future. (1982) ✔ Cortons.
✦ Louis Chapuis, Aloxe-Corton, 21420 Savigny-les-Beaune; tel. 80 26 40 99 ⵎ By appt. Closed Aug.

CHEVALIER PERE ET FILS★★

■	1.8ha	10000	5 ▣ ◗ ◖ ↓

75 **76** 77 78 ⑧⓪ 81 ★**82** 83

The wines of Aloxe-Corton remain young for a long time and are among the slowest developers of the Côte de Beaune. This bottle has good young fruit but should be kept for some time. (1982)
✦ GAEC Chevalier Père et Fils, Buisson, 21550 Ladoix-Sérrigny; tel. 80 26 46 30 ⵎ By appt.

DOMAINE ANTONIN GUYON
Les Fournières★

■	2.5ha	12000	5 ◗ ◖ ↓

79 80 ⑧⑴ 82 **82** 83

A very mature wine with complex aromas of damson fruit and animal hide and fur. Full flavour with a long, dry finish of bitter almonds. (1981)
✦ Antonin Guyon, 21420 Savigny-lès-Beaune; tel. 80 67 13 24 ⵎ By appt. Closed Aug.

DOMAINE DE LA JUVINIERE★★★

■	2ha	12500	5 ◗ ◖ ↓

64 66 69 71 **76** 78 79 **79** 80 81 82 83

Deep rich colour and a fine bouquet similar to a Corton. Very smooth, round flavour. Ready to drink although it will still improve. (1979)
✦ SC du Dom. de la Juvinière. Clos des Langres, Corgoloin, 21700 Nuits-St-Georges; tel 80 62 98 73 ⵎ By appt. ✦ Gabriel Liogier-d'Ardhuy.

ANDRE MASSON *Clos du Chapitre*★★

■1er Cru 1.5ha 6000 🔲 Ⓓ ▬ ⬇

71 72 73 74 76 ⑦⑧ **80 81 82** 🔲

Has been vinified to last ten years. The bouquet has, however, already opened out and is very attractive. (1982) ✔ Aloxe-Corton, Pernand-Vergelesses.
↬ André Masson, Aloxe-Corton, 21420 Savigny-les-Beaune; tel. 80 26 40 77 ⵉ No visitors.

DIDIER MEUNEVAUX★★

■1er Cru 1ha 5500 🔲 Ⓓ ⑪ ⬇

72 ⑦⑥ **78 79** 🔲

Already has a fruity persistent flavour. Wait several years. (1983) ✔ Aloxe-Corton, Corton Perrières, Beaune Premier Cru.
↬ Didier Meunevaux, Aloxe-Corton, 21420 Savigny-les-Beaune; tel. 80 26 42 33 ⵉ By appt.

DOMAINE ANDRE NUDANT ET FILS *La Couttière*★★

■ 1ha 6000 🔲 Ⓓ ⑪ ⬇

71 72 73 74 **76** 77 ⑦⑧ **79 81** 🔲 83

A firm, balanced wine with a slight tannic edge. A good Aloxe-Corton Premier Cru. (1982) ✔ Ladoix Premier Cru Savigny-les-Beaune, Aloxe-Corton, Corton Bressandes, Corton.
↬ André Nudant et Fils, Cidex 24 no. 4, 21550 Ladoix-Sérrigny; tel. 80 26 40 82 ⵉ By appt.

MAX QUENOT ET MEUNEVAUX★★

■ 2ha 10500 🔲 Ⓓ ⑪ ⬇

72 ⑦⑥ **78 79 81 82** 🔲

Very firm and tannic. Intense red colour. Will develop slowly and may be left for fifteen years before drinking. (1983) ✔ Corton Bressandes, Corton Perrières.
↬ *MM*. Max Quenot et Meunevaux, Aloxe-Corton, 21420 Savigny-les-Beaune; tel. 80 26 41 54 ⵉ By appt.

GASTON ET PIERRE RAVAUT★★

■ 2.5ha 9000 🔲 Ⓓ ▬ ⑪ ⬇

76 78 ⑦⑨ **81** 🔲 83

Solid and well constructed, with strong, fruity aromas. Will remain young for a long time. Good example of its appellation. (1982)
↬ GAEC Gaston et Pierre Ravaut, Buisson, 21550 Ladoix-Sérrigny; tel. 80 26 41 94 ⵉ By appt.

DOMAINE LES TERRES-VINEUSES★

■Premier Cru 1.20ha 5000 🔲 ⑪ ⬇

64 66 69 **71 76 78 79** 80 81 82 ⑧③

Has all the characteristics of a young wine with its intense colour, dense fruitiness and complex flavours. Needs several years. (1983) ✔ Ladoix Clos des Chagnots, Corton Renardes.
↬ SARL Les Terres Vineuses, Clos des Langres, Corgoloin, 21700 Nuits-St-Georges; tel. 80 62 98 73 ⵉ By appt. ↬ Gabriel Liogier d'Ardhuy.

MICHEL VOARICK★★

■ 3.5ha 20000 🔲 Ⓓ ⑪ ⬇

69 72 **76 78** 79 80 81 ★82 ★🔲 ★⑧③

All the firmness and elegance of a 1981 and is beginning to develop complex aromas. Has been vinified to last a long time. (1981) ✔ Pernand-Vergelesses, Cortons, Romanée-St-Vivant.
↬ Michel Voarick, Aloxe-Corton 21420 Savigny-les-Beaune; tel. 80 26 40 44 ⵉ No visitors.

Pernand-Vergelesses

Situated at the meeting place of two valleys, Pernand is a picturesque, traditional wine village. Its narrow streets, deep cellars, sunny hillside vineyards and subtle wines have all contributed to the village's solid reputation, built up over many years. About 2500 hectolitres of red wine are produced, and the best-known Premier Cru is the very delicate Ile de Vergelesses. Some excellent white wines are also produced here – about 400 hectolitres.

HOSPICES DE BEAUNE *Cuvée Rameau-Lamarosse*★

■ 0.7ha 2430 🔲 ⑪ ⬇

Only a minute amount of this wine is produced: (a mere nine burgundy casks, or 2700 bottles), but this cuvée certainly has its connoisseurs and followers. The 1984 was undergoing malolactic fermentation at the time of the auction, but a month later it was smooth and quite soft. (1984)
↬ Dom. Viti. Hospices de Beaune, Rue de l'Hotel-Dieu, 21200 Beaune; tel. 80 24 75 75 ⵉ No visitors.

CHANSON PERE ET FILS *Les Vergelesses*★

■1er Cru 4.6ha 16000 🔲 Ⓓ ⑪ ⬇

70 ⑦① **79** ★80 81 82 **83**

Pernand Premier Cru always produces intense, delicate fruit over a fairly firm body. This has been vinified accordingly and has enough structure to age a little. (1982)
↬ *MM*. Chanson Père et Fils, 10–12 Rue Paul-Chanson, 21200 Beaune; tel. 80 22 33 00 ⵉ No visitors.

MARIUS DELARCHE PERE ET FILS★★

■ 2ha 10500 🔲 Ⓓ ⑪ ⬇

76 78 ★79 80 81 🔲

The bouquet remains firmly shut even after the wine has been allowed to breathe. This, together with the full-bodied flavour indicate it will certainly keep well. (1982) ✔ Pernand-Vergelesses, Corton-Charlemagne, Corton-Renardes, Pernand-Vergelesses Ile des Vergelesses.
↬ Marius Delarche et Fils, Pernand-Vergelesses, 21420 Savigny-les-Beaune; tel. 80 21 50 53 ⵉ By appt.

DENIS PERE ET FILS★★

| ■ | | 3ha | 13000 | 4 D ⏶ |

71 72 73 **76 78** ★79 80 81 ⟨82⟩

Bright and still fruity. Firm, refreshing flavour has considerable elegance. (1981) ✔ Bourgogne Passe-tout-grain, Bourgogne Rouge, Savigny-les-Beaune, Bourgogne Aligoté.
☞ GAEC Denis Père et Fils, Pernand-Vergelesses, 21420 Savigny-les-Beaune; tel. 80 21 50 91 ⏴ By appt.

DOMAINE P. DUBREUIL-FONTAINE *Côte de Beaune*★

| ■ | | 2ha | 9600 | 4 D ⏶ ⏷ |

71 72 73 **76 78** ★79 80 ⟨82⟩

This 1980 is an eloquent rebuttal of the criticisms that have been made of the vintage; drink now. (1980) ✔ Savigny27-Beaune les Vergelesses, Aloxe-Corton, Corton-Bressandes, Corton Clos du Roi.
☞ Dom. P. Dubreuil-Fontaine, Pernand-Vergelesses, 21420 Savigny-les-Beaune; tel. 80 21 51 67 ⏴ By appt. Closed Sun., public hols.

DOMAINE JACQUES GERMAIN★

| ☐ | | 2.75ha | 12000 | 5 D ⏶ ⏷ |

78 79 82 82 83

From the Château de Chorey-les-Beaune, the domaine of Jacques Germain. Pale, straw-coloured wine with roasted almond aromas and soft lemony flavour. Smooth finish but rather lacking in vigour. (1982)
☞ Jacques Germain, Ch. de Chorey-les-Beaune, 21200 Beaune; tel. 80 22 06 05 ⏴ By appt. Closed 15 July–15 Aug.

L'HERITIER-GUYOT★

| ■ | | 7ha | 2000 | 4 D |

78 81 82 83 84

All the concentration of the 1983 vintage with a deep, violet colour, intense, scorched aromas and hard, uncompromising flavours. Leave to mature and soften. (1983)
☞ L'Héritier-Guyot, Rue du Champ-aux-Prêtres, 21006 Dijon Cedex; tel. 80 72 16 14 ⏴ By appt.

DOMAINE LALEURE-PIOT *Les Vergelesses*★★

| ■1er Cru | | 2ha | 12000 | 4 D ⏶ ⏷ |

72 **76 78** 81 82 83

Bright, intensely coloured 1982 with a bouquet that is already heavy with fruity aromas. Will be at its peak in five years. (1982)
☞ Jean-Marie Laleure, Pernand-Vergelesses, 21420 Savigny-les-Beaune; tel. 80 21 52 37 ⏴ By appt.

DOMAINE LOUIS LATOUR *Ile-des-Vergelesses*★★

| ■1er Cru | | 0.75ha | 3000 | 5 D ⏶ ⏷ |

66 69 78 81 ⟨82⟩ 82

Ruby-red with orange tints. Expressive bouquet of mint and cherry and spicy flavour, again with a hint of Morello cherry. Long, elegant finish. (1981)
☞ Louis Latour, 18 Rue des Tonneliers, 21200 Beaune; tel. 80 22 31 20 ⏴ By appt.

DOMAINE RAPET ET FILS *Les Vergelesses*★★

| ■1er Cru | | 1.5ha | 9000 | 4 D ⏸ ⏶ ⏷ |

76 78 79 **80** 81 82 83

Open-knit bouquet, and round, harmonious flavour that will peak in five to eight years' time. (1982) ✔ Pernand-Vergelesses, Corton-Charlemagne, Pernand-Vergelesses Côtes de Beaune, Aloxe-Corton.
☞ Dom. Rapet Père et Fils, Pernand-Vergelesses, 21420 Savigny-les-Beaune; tel. 80 21 50 05 ⏴ By appt.

ROLLIN PERE ET FILS★★

| ■ | | 3ha | 18000 | 4 D ⏶ |

76 78 79 80 82

Well vinified with a smooth fruity flavour; already attractive to drink. (1982) ✔ Bourgogne Aligoté, Pernand-Vergelesses Blanc, Bourgogne Hautes Côtes de Beaune.
☞ MM. Rollin Père et Fils, Pernand-Vergelesses, 21420 Savigny-les-Beaune; tel. 80 21 50 35 ⏴ By appt.

Corton

Dominating the Pernand-Vergelesses valley is the Montagne de Corton, which produces two Grand Cru appellations, the white Corton-Charlemagne and the red Le Corton. Woods crown the hard limestone crest of the mountain: on the upper slopes – the home of Corton-Charlemagne – the marl is whitened with limestone debris washed down from the summit. Below, the marl shows deeper brown on the red wine vineyards which produce Le Corton and, further down still, the Premier Cru Aloxe-Corton.

The Corton appellation may be used for white or red wines, although most people associate it with the reds. Here, as elsewhere, the name of the vineyard may be added to the appellation, reflecting the particular character of the wine. The grapes from Les Bressandes, for example, produce red wines that combine the inherent strength of the grape variety with a delicate quality taken from the soil. On the other hand, the lighter soil, in the upper part of Les Renardes, Les Languettes and Le Clos du Roy, gives full-bodied red wines that acquire distinctively gamey qualities as they age. This is true of Les Mourottes in Ladoix, the largest Grand Cru by volume – 2500 hectolitres.

HOSPICES DE BEAUNE
Cuvée Charlotte Dumay★★

■Gd Cru   3.5ha   8100   [6] ⦿ ↓

Classic aromas of liquorice, fruit stones and leather, with a very full, firm backbone of flavour. (1984)
↜ Dom. Viti. Hospices de Beaune, Rue de l'Hôtel-Dieu, 21200 Beaune; tel. 80 24 75 75 ⵀ No visitors.

HOSPICES DE BEAUNE
Cuvée Docteur Peste★★

■Gd Cru   2.6ha   8100   [6] ⦿ ↓

This *cuvée* rivals the cuvée Charlotte Dumay, being less immediately seductive but keeping better in the long term. The 1984 was still too immature to taste properly at the time of the auction but it had the structure of a keeping wine. (1984)
↜ Dom. Viti. Hospices de Beaune, Rue de l'Hôtel-Dieu, 21200 Beaune; tel. 80 24 75 75 ⵀ No visitors.

HOSPICES DE BEAUNE
Cuvée Paul Chanson★★★

□   0.32ha   540   [6] ⦿ ↓

In 1984 the wine was fragrant with honey, new wax and bergamot orange. The two hogsheads fetched 70000 francs apiece at the auction. (1984)
↜ Dom. Viti. Hospices de Beaune, Rue de l'Hôtel-Dieu, 21200 Beaune; tel. 80 24 75 75 ⵀ No visitors.

DOMAINE BONNEAU-DU-MARTRAY★★★

■Gd Cru   2ha   10000   [6] ▮ ↓

*71 76 *78 *⑧⓪ 81 82

Bright, cherry-red without any sign of the customary orange rim found in older wines. Aromas of carnation and pepper. Very appealing wine with attractive 'oriental', spicy flavour. Should make a great bottle. (1980)
↜ Dom. Bonneau-du-Martray, Pernand-Vergelesses, 21420 Savigny-les-Beaune; tel. 80 21 50 64 ⵀ By appt ↜ M.-A. Le Bault de la Dorinière.

CORTON
APPELLATION CONTRÔLÉE
Bonneau du Martray
DOMAINE A PERNAND-VERGELESSES & ALOXE-CORTON (CÔTE-D'OR)
Bouteille   1971
Mis en bouteille à la Propriété

DOMAINE CACHAT-OCQUIDANT
Clos de Vergennes★★

■   1.43ha   6000   [5] Ⓓ ⦿ ↓

76 ⑦⑧ *79 *80 ⑧⑶

Solid, vital flavour. The 1983 vintage, still tasting very young, is destined for long ageing. (1983)
✒ Bourgogne Rouge, Bourgogne la Chapelle Notre-Dame, Côte de Beaune-Villages, Aloxe-Corton.
↜ MM. Cachat-Ocquidant et Fils, 21550 Ladoix-

Sérrigny; tel. 80 26 41 27 ⵀ Daily 8.00–12.00/14.00–18.00.

CAPITAIN-GAGNEROT★★

■   2.21ha   5000   [5] Ⓓ ⦿ ↓

⑥⑴ 76 78 79 81 ⑧⑵ 83

Beginning to give pleasure, and the 1983 seems set to become a great wine. (1982) ✒ Ladoix Blanc, Ladoix Rouge Premier Cru, Corton-Charlemagne, Clos de Vougeot.
↜ Dom. François Capitain et Fils, 21550 Ladoix-Sérrigny; tel. 80 26 41 36 ⵀ By appt.

CHEVALIER PERE ET FILS
Le Rognet★★

■   1ha   5000   [5] Ⓓ ⦿ ↓

75 **76** 77 78 ⑦⑼ 80 **81** ⑧⑵ 83

A wine with body and good acidity, produced from the only red grand cru vineyard of the Côte de Beaune. Leave it to age. (1982)
↜ GAEC Chevalier Père et Fils, Buisson, 21550 Ladoix-Sérrigny; tel. 80 26 46 30 ⵀ By appt.

COLETTE CORNU★

■Gd Cru   0.61ha   1500   [5] Ⓓ ⦿ ↓

76 ⑦⑻ ⑺⑻ *82 83

Fine, subtle wine, with a light colour and smooth flavour. (1983)
↜ *Mme* Colette Cornu, Magny-les-Villers, 21700 Nuits-St-Georges; tel. 80 62 92 05 ⵀ By appt.

CHATEAU DE CORTON-ANDRE★★

■Gd Cru   0.33ha   1200   [6] Ⓓ ⦿ ↓

71 **76** 77 *78 *79 80 ⑻⓪ **81** 82 ⑻⑶

Bright, clear red colour. slightly musky nose, typical of a wine of this age, and bouquet of blackcurrant and liquorice. On the palate, its structure is a fine balance between finesse and solidity. Not yet at its peak. (1980)
↜ Pierre André, Ch. Corton-André, Aloxe-Corton, 21240 Savigny-les-Beaune; tel. 80 26 44 25 ⵀ By appt ↜ Gabriel Liogier d'Ardhuy.

J. FAIVELEY *Clos des Cortons★*

■Gd Cru   2.5ha   13200   [6] ⦿ Ⓓ

*69 *71 *78

A superbly coloured Corton with a nose of ripe fruits and spices. A well-constructed wine with a great future. (1980)
↜ M. J. Faiveley, 8 Rue du Tribourg, 21700 Nuits-St-Georges; tel. 80 61 04 55 ⵀ By appt.

DOMAINE MICHEL GAUNOUX
Rénardes 1981★★

■Gd Cru   1.5ha   4800   [5] Ⓓ ⦿ ↓

71 72 74 *76 *78 79 **81** 82

Very tannic on the palate, and more extract than fruit. In view of its concentration and structure, it is worth keeping for at least six years before drinking. (1981)
↜ Michel Gaunoux, 21630 Pommard; tel. 80 22 18 52 ⵀ By appt.

329

DOMAINE ANTONIN GUYON
Bressandes★★

■Gd Cru	1 ha	4200	6 ⑪ ↓

71 **78** ⑦ 80 81 **82** 🟦 **83**

Dark colour with clean aromas of crushed red fruit. Elegant leafy, peppermint flavour. Slightly harsh finish, but a good bottle. (1979)
🐦 Dom. Antonin Guyon, 21420 Savigny-lès-Beaune; tel. 80 67 13 24 ⵜ By appt.

DOMAINE DE LA JUVINIERE
Corton-Combes★★

■	0.6 ha	1800	6 ⑪ ↓

64 66 69 **71 76 78** 79 80 81 🟦 ⑧⑬

Fine dark-red colour. Delicate, developed bouquet, with the typical aroma of fine leather which rises from the glass. Openness enables it to be drunk now, but it will be much subtler in a few years' time. (1982)
🐦 SC du Dom. de la Juvinière, Clos des Langres Corgoloin, 21700 Nuits-St-Georges; tel. 80 62 98 73 ⵜ By appt 🐦 Gabriel Liogier d'Ardhuy.

DOMAINE LOUIS LATOUR
Château Corton-Grancey★★

■	17 ha	54 000	6 ⑪ ↓

78 ★⑦ 🟦 81 82

Fine brick-red colour but rather mute nose. Well-developed, subtle, balanced flavour. Should get even better with keeping. (1979) ✔ Corton Charlemagne Blanc, Corton Clos-de-la-Vigne au St, Beaune Vignes Franches Rouge, Pommard Epènots Rouge.
🐦 Louis Latour, 18 Rue des Tonneliers, 21204 Beaune; tel. 80 22 31 20 ⵜ By appt.

Château
1749
Année   1979

Corton Grancey
APPELLATION CORTON CONTROLÉE
Mis en bouteille par LOUIS LATOUR, Négociant à Beaune (Côte-d'Or)

DOMAINE ANDRE NUDANT ET FILS *Bressandes*★

■	0.6 ha	3500	5 D ⑪ ↓

⑦⑧ ★79 ★81 🟦 83

Good example of its appellation and the pride of the Nudant family, whose ancestors grew vines at Ladoix in 1760. (1982) ✔ Ladoix Premier Cru, Savigny-les-Beaune, Aloxe-Corton, Corton-Charlemagne.
🐦 Dom. André Nudant et Fils, Cidex 24 No. 4, 21550 Ladoix-Sérrigny; tel. 80 26 40 82 ⵜ Mon.–Sat. 8.00–12.00/14.00–19.00.

CAVES DE LA REINE PEDAUQUE
Renardes★★

■Gd Cru	2.1 ha	7200	6 ⑪ ↓

64 66 69 **71** 76 78 **79** 80 🟦 **82** ⑧⑬

Has all the finesse of its vintage, with fruity aromas beginning to develop a more mature note. Also has the structure and solidity expected of this grand cru, which will enable it to age well. (1981)
🐦 Caves de la Reine Pédauque, Aloxe-Corton, 21420 Savigny-les-Beaune; tel. 80 26 40 00 ⵜ By appt.

DOMAINE DANIEL SENARD★★

■	1 ha	5500	5 D ⑪ ↓

76 78 80 81 🟦 ⑧⑬

A particular success. Fine, bright colour. Beginning its long development, which will bring it to maturity in a decade, although it may be tempting to drink it before. (1982) ✔ Corton Clos du Roi, Corton-Bressandes, Corton Clos Desmeix, Aloxe-Corton Premier Cru.
🐦 SCE du Dom. Daniel Senard, Aloxe-Corton, 21420 Savigny-les-Beaune; tel. 80 26 41 65 ⵜ By appt.

DOMAINE LES TERRES-VINEUSES
Clos du Roi★★

■	1 ha	3300	6 ⑪ ↓

64 66 69 71 76 **78** 79 80 81 **82** ⑧⑬ 🟦

Still very young, with aromas just beginning to open up. On the palate, length and power, and promise a fine future. (1983)
🐦 SARL les Terres-Vineuses, Clos des Langres, Corgoloin, 21700 Nuits-St-Georges; tel. 80 62 98 73 ⵜ By appt. 🐦 Gabriel Liogier d'Ardhuy.

Corton-Charlemagne

Until 1948, Aligoté grapes were allowed to contribute to a Charlemagne appellation wine; however, this appellation is no longer used. A little more than 1000 hectolitres of Corton-Charlemagne is produced, mostly in the communes of Pernand-Vergelesses and Aloxe-Corton. These wines are named after the Emperor Charlemagne who is said to have had white vines planted rather than red so that the wine did not stain his beard! Today, they are among the most famous of Burgundy's white wines, big, mouth-filling, with a beautiful greeny-gold colour. They reach their full potential only after five to ten years in bottle.

HOSPICES DE BEAUNE
Cuvée Francois de Salins★★★

□	0.50 ha	945	6 ⑪ ↓

Francois de Salins was a descendant of the Guigone family; to perpetuate his keen involvement with the Hôtel-Dieu in Beaune, he bequeathed his vineyards in Aloxe-Corton to the Hospices in

1745. His plot of Corton-Charlemagne vines produces three and a half hogsheads (less than 1000 bottles) of outstanding and very expensive wine. The 1984 Corton Charlemagne was still undergoing fermentation when tasted but the aromas already provided a feast of exotic fruits and the flavour had a fine rounded sweetness. It sold for 105,000 francs per hogshead at the auction (1984).
➼ Dom. Viti. Hospices de Beaune, Rue de l'Hôtel-Dieu, 21200 Beaune ⟂ No visitors.

CAPITAIN-GAGNEROT★★★

	34ha	2000	⑤ D ⑾ ⌞
⑺③ 76 78 79 80 **81 82 83** 84			

The celebrated Corton-Charlemagne vineyard, once the property of the great Emperor himself. The wine's nut-and-cinnamon bouquet, and richly sustained, firm flavour give it a unique identity among the world's white wines. (1981)
✔ Ladoix Rouge, Ladoix Blanc Clos de Vougeot, Aloxe-Corton.
➼ François Capitain et Fils, 21550 La doix-Sérrigny; tel. 80 26 41 36 ⟂ By appt.

DOMAINE BONNEAU DU MARTRAY★★★

□Gd Cru	9ha	40000	⑥ ⑾ ⌞
52 **73** 76 78 **79 79 81** 82 83			

Straw yellow with a slight reduction smell giving way to light lemony aromas. Clean flavours on the palate, with a slight note of lime. Full and very refined, with a deep finish, and lingering taste of wild sloes and plums. Will continue to develop positively for several years. (1979)
➼ Dom. Bonneau du Martray, Pernand-Vergelesses 21420 Savigny-les-Beaune; tel. 80 21 50 64 ⟂ By appt. ➼ A. le Bault de la Morinière.

DOMAINE BOUCHARD PERE ET FILS★★★

■Gd Cru	3ha	12600	⑥ D ⑾ ⌞
76 78 **79** 80 81 **82 83** 84			

Straw-yellow colour and vanilla-scented bouquet with aromas of grilled orange peel and honey. Still rather heavy on the palate, even a bit harsh, but these characteristics will diminish with age, and a great bottle of wine will emerge. (1982)
➼ Bouchard Père et fils, BP 70, Au Château, 21200 Beaune; tel. 80 22 14 41 ⟂ By appt. Closed Aug. and 1 week in Feb.

CHANSON PERE ET FILS★★

□Gd Cru			⑥ D ⑾ ⌞
73 78 79 81 **82 82** ⑻③			

The aromas have not yet developed, but the body already has all the power and warmth that will with time make a great bottle. (1983)
➼ *MM.* Chanson Père et Fils, 10–12 Rue Paul-Chanson, 21200 Beaune; tel. 80 22 33 00 ⟂ No visitors.

CHATEAU CORTON-ANDRE★★

□Gd Cru	2.50ha	8200	⑥ D ⑾ ⌞
71 **76** 77 ★78 ★79 **80 81 82 82** ⑻③			

Lovely golden green colour and characteristic strongly scented bouquet of cinnamon, reinette apples and vanilla. Smooth but robust flavour which will go on improving for several years. (1982)
➼ Pierre André, Ch. Corton-André, Aloxe-Corton, 21420 Savigny-lès-Beaune; tel. 80 26 44 25 ⟂ By appt.

DOMAINE LOUIS LATOUR★★

□Grand Cru	8ha	30000	⑥ ⑾
71 73 79 **82**			

Straw-gold colour, with refined grilled aromas and taut flavour with excellent acidity. All in all, a very deep and concentrated wine which still needs five years. Serve at cellar temperature (13°C). (1982) ✔ Ch. Corton Grancey, Corton Clos de la Vigne au Saint.
➼ Louis Latour, 18 Rue des Tonneliers, 21200 Beaune; tel. 80 22 31 20 ⟂ By appt.

Savigny-Lès-Beaune

Set back into the hills to the west of Aloxe-Corton, Savigny is a typical French wine-making village. The local spirit is still strong and the tradition of Burgundian hospitality is vigorously promoted by the 'Cousinerie de Bourgogne.' Savigny wines are smooth, delicate and fruity; they are pleasant to drink when young, but will also age well. The average annual production is 9000 hectolitres.

ROBERT AMPEAU★★

■   1ha   4200   5 D ⦂ ↓

74 77 ⑦⑧ **79** *80 *81 *82 **84**

Lets hope all the younger vintages turn out as well as this splendid 1979! A very concentrated deep colour, intense nose and fruity vanilla quality of Savigny, with a full, fluid flavour. Will keep for at least another ten years. (1979) ✔ Puligny-Montrachet Combettes, Volnay Santenots, Pommard, Auxey-Duresses les Ecusseaux. ↬ Robert Ampeau, Rue du Cronin 21190, Meursault; tel. 80 21 20 35 ⋎ By appt.

HOSPICES DE BEAUNE
Cuvée Fouquerand★

■   1.96ha   6480   6 ⦂ ↓

High marks for freshness, smoothness and complex aromas of violets and fruit stones, and its clean smell of new oak. (1984) ↬ Dom. Viti. Hospices de Beaune, Rue de l'Hôtel Dieu, 21200 Beaune; tel. 80 24 75 75 ⋎ No visitors.

HOSPICES DE BEAUNE
Cuvée Arthur Girard★

■   2.5ha   5940   6 ⦂ ↓

Still very young, with aromas of violet and ripe banana, this smooth, fresh Savigny 1984 delighted tasters at the Hospices auction. (1984) ↬ Dom. Viti. Hospices de Beaune, Rue de l'Hôtel-Dieu, 21200 Beaune; tel. 80 24 75 75 ⋎ No visitors.

DOMAINE SIMON BIZE
Les Vergelesses★★

■1er Cru   3ha   12000   5 D ↓ ⦂

72 ⑦⑧ 79 *83 *84

Perfect autumnal wine, with its firm, red colour and complex aromas of dry leaves, humus and fruit stones. Rich, fat flavour with long finish marked by note of kirsch. (1977) ↬ Simon Bize et Fils, 21420 Savigny-les-Beaune; tel. 80 21 50 57 ⋎ By appt.

DOMAINE SIMON BIZE★

■   5ha   21000   4 D ⦂ ↓

65 71 79 **79** 81 **82** **82** 83

Light cherry red with undeveloped aromas. Still very marked by new wood. Good extract but needing another two years. (1982) ✔ Bourgogne Rouge Les Perrières. ↬ Simon Bize et Fils, 21420 Savigny-les-Beaune; tel. 80 21 50 57 ⋎ By appt. Closed 1–15 Jan.

VALENTIN BOUCHOTTE
Les Hauts-Jarrons★★

■1er Cru   1.76ha   12000   4 D ⦂ ↓

76 78 79 82 **82**

Deep colour and thickly-textured, full-bodied flavour. Well constituted but very immature demanding patience. Striking finish, not unlike a

bas-Armagnac. (1982) ✔ Savigny-les-Beaune les Peuillets, Pernand-Vergelesses, Beaune les Sizies. ↬ Valentin Bouchotte, Ave. des Combattants, 21420 Savigny-les-Beaune; tel. 80 21 50 93 ⋎ By appt.

VALENTIN BOUCHOTTE★

■   2ha   12000   4 D ⦂ ↓

76 78 *79 ***79** 82

Dark ruby. Although the nose is still closed, aromas of wild cherry and plum develop on the palate. Velvety finish. (1979) ↬ Valentin Bouchotte, Ave. des Combattants, 21420 Savigny-les-Beaune; tel. 80 21 50 93 ⋎ By appt.

N. ET J.-M. CAPRON-MANIEUX
Les Peuillets★★

■1er Cru   0.26ha   1500   4 D ⦂ ↓

76 78 79 81 *82 83

A game wine par excellence, partially raised in new casks, smooth and long on the palate. Drink with hare or woodcock. (1982) ↬ Savigny-les-Beaune Rouge and Blanc, Bourgogne Aligoté. ↬ M. et *Mme* Capron-Manieux, Rue de Bourgogne, 21420 Savigny-les-Beaune; tel. 80 21 55 37 ⋎ By appt.

DOMAINE CHANSON *Dominode*★

■   1.29ha   7500   5 D ⦂ ↓

71 ⑦⑧ 79 **80** 81 **82** 83

Very balanced, and has a charming aroma of new oak, which suggests it should keep for some time. (1982) ↬ MM. Chanson Père et Fils, 10–12 Rue Paul-Chanson, 21200 Beaune; tel. 80 22 33 00 ⋎ No visitors.

DOMAINE CHANSON *Marconnets*★

■1er Cru   2.6ha   8000   5 D ⦂ ↓

⑦ 76 78 79 **80** 81 **81** 82 **82** 83

Typical Savigny character. Fruity, fresh, clean and appetizing. Drink young. (1982) ↬ MM. Chanson Père et Fils, 10–12 Rue Paul-Chanson, 21200 Beaune; tel. 80 22 33 00 ⋎ No visitors.

CHATEAU DE CORTON-ANDRE
Clos des Guettes★

■1er Cru   2.35ha   10000   5 D ⦂ ↓

71 **76** 77 78 *79 *80 **81** 82 ⑧ **83**

'Les Guettes' is the highest point in Savigny, and is at the same stratum as Corton. Although this 1983 is still young and rather undeveloped, it reveals finesse, and has enough solid flavour in reserve to ensure a good future. (1983) ↬ Pierre André, Ch. de Corton-André, Aloxe-Corton, 21420 Savigny-les-Beaune; tel. 80 26 44 25 ⋎ By appt.

BERTRAND DARVIOT★★

■   0.5ha   2700   5 D ⦂ ↓

78 ⑧ **82** **83** 84

This wine has undergone a long vinification to compensate for the lightness of this abundant 1982 vintage, giving a balanced firm expressive flavour. (1982) ✔ Meursault, Bourgogne Rouge,

Beaune, Beaune Grèves.

ᐁ Bertrand Darviot, 17 Rue de la Velle, 21190 Meursault; tel. 80 21 22 83 ⏳ Mon.–Sat. 9.00–12.00/14.00–18.00.

MAURICE ECARD *Les Serpentières*★★

■1er Cru	2ha	8400	4 D ◑ ↓

76 78 ⑲ 81 82 83

Fine, bright ruby colour. This 1982 bears its title of premier cru majestically. Powerful and long on the palate, and its fruity aromas have opened up well. A wine for keeping. (1982) ✔ Savigny-les-Beaune Narbentons, Savigny-les-beaune Peuillets, Savigny-les-beaune Premier Cru, Bourgogne Blanc.

ᐁ Maurice Ecard, Rue Chanson-Maldant, 21420 Savigny-les-beaune; tel. 80 21 50 61 ⏳ By appt.

DOMAINE FOUGERAY
Les Golardes★★

■	2ha	4 D ▮ ◑ ↓

68 71 76 78 79 ★81 ★82 83

Skilfully vinified, with an attractive colour and rich, fruity bouquet, in which violet and passionfruit combine with aromas of banana and blackcurrant. The palate is round, with good length. Ready to drink soon. (1983)

ᐁ Jean-Claude Fougeray, 44 Rue de Mazy, 21160 Marsannay-la-Côte; 80 52 21 12 ⏳ No visitors.

M. ET J.-M. GIBOULOT★★

■	7ha	26000	5 D ▮ ◑ ↓

76 78 ⑲ 81 82 83

Has a good structure but is still very young. A good example of the appellation, with a long future ahead of it. (1982) ✔ SavignyPremier Cru les Serpentières, Savigny Premier Cru, Savigny Bourgogne Aligoté.

ᐁ SCE M. et J.-M. Rue du Général-Leclerc, 21420 Savigny-les-beaune; tel. 80 21 52 30 ⏳ By appt.

M. ET J.-M. GIBOULOT★★

□	0.65ha	4000	4 D ◑ ↓

76 78 ⑲ 81 82 83 83

Fine, little Chardonnay cuvée in the middle of an ocean of Pinot Noir. The 1983 is firm and rich with powerful aromas of butter, hazelnut, honey, ferns and cinnamon. Should be even better in two or three years. (1983) ✔ Bourgogne Aligoté, Bourgogne, Savigny, Savigny Premier Cru, Savigny Premier Cru les Serpentières.

ᐁ SCE M. et J.-M. Giboulot, Rue du Général-Leclerc, 21420 Savigny-les-beaune; tel. 80 21 52 30 ⏳ By appt.

GIRARD-VOLLOT★

■	1ha	6000	4 D ◑ ↓

76 78 79 80 ★82 83

Very enjoyable when tasted with some strong smelling cheeses and showed warmth, robust body and very firm finish. (1982) ✔ Savigny Premier Cru, Pernand-Vergelesses, Aloxe-Corton, Savigny-les-Beaune.

ᐁ *M.* Girard-Vollot, 21420 Savigny-les-Beaune; tel. 80 21 53 45 ⏳ By appt.

PIERRE GUILLEMOT *Les Serpentières*★★

■1er Cru	1.5ha	5000	4 D ▮ ◑ ↓

74 76 78 79 ★80 ★81 82 83

Has good structure and mouth-filling flavour but needs to soften and the aromas are still undeveloped. (1982)

ᐁ Pierre Guillemot, Rue Boulanger-et-Vallée, 21420 Savigny-les-beaune; tel. 80 21 50 40 ⏳ By appt. Closed during harvest.

ANNE-MARIE GUILLEMOT
Les Jarrons★★

■	0.28ha	1000	4 D ▮ ◑ ↓

74 76 78 79 ★80 ★81 ★82 83

Densely packed aromas of fruit and is warming enough to treat any ailments. A keeping wine; will reach its best in five years' time. (1982)

ᐁ Anne-Marie Guillemot, Rue Boulanger-et-Vallée, 21420 Savigny-les-beaune; tel. 80 21 50 40 ⏳ By appt. Closed during harvest.

PIERRE GUILLEMOT★★

□	2ha	7000	4 D ▮ ◑ ↓

74 76 78 79 ★80 ★⑧1 82 83

Offered by Pierre Guillemot, president of the Wine Growers' Union and one of the pillars of the association La Cousinerie de Bourgogne. Superb toasted hazel and vanilla aromas. Ready to drink. (1982) ✔ Savigny-les-beaune Rouge, Savigny-les-beaune Serpentières.

ᐁ Pierre Guillemot, Rue Boulanger-et-Vallée 21420 Savigny-les-beaune; tel. 80 21 50 40 ⏳ By appt. Closed during harvest.

DOMAINE LUCIEN JACOB
Vergelesses★★

■1er Cru	3ha	18000	4 D ◑ ↓

76 78 81 ⑧2 82

Very fine Savigny Premier Cru, with more substance than the average 1982. Captivating aromas, with a slight scent of wildfowl and truffle over a background of blackcurrant and well-balanced flavour. ✔ Bourgogne Hautes-Côtes de Beaune, Savigny-les-beaune, Pernand-Vergelesses.

ᐁ Lucien Jacob, Echevronne, 21420 Savigny-les-Beaune; tel. 80 21 52 15 ⏳ By appt.

DOMAINE LUCIEN JACOB★

■	7ha	42000	4 D ◑ ↓

69 ★71 ★⑦6 ★78 ★82 ★83

Displays all the fruity, flowery character of Savigny and, despite being three years old, has lost none of its freshness. Ready to drink. (1982) ✔ Bourgogne Hautes-Côtes de Beaune, Savigny-Vergelesses Premier Cru, Pernand-Vergelesses.

ᐁ Lucien Jacob, Echevronne, 21420 Savigny-les-Beaune; tel. 80 21 52 15 ⏳ By appt.

DOMAINE DE LA JUVINIERE
Les Godeaux★★

■	1ha	7000	5 ◑ ↓

64 66 69 71 76 78 79 80 ★⑧1 82 83

This 1982 is very characteristic of this vineyard with its clear colour, refined, mature aromas and soft flavour which tempts one to drink it now. (1982)

◆┓ SC du Dom. de la Juvinière, Clos des Langres, Corgoloin, 21700 Nuits-St-Georges; tel. 80 62 98 73 ⟙ By appt ◆┓ Gabriel Liogier d'Ard-huy.

LEROY*

■	2500	6 ⑪ ↓

72 74 76 78 79 **82**

Deep, fairly dark colour and characteristic Savigny fruitiness. Still very fresh and young on the palate. Would suit rare red meats and lightly spiced dishes. (1979)
◆┓ SA Leroy, Dom. de la Romanée-Conti, Vosne-Romanée 21700 Nuits-St-Georges; tel. 80 61 04 57 ⟙ No visitors.

MOILLARD*

■	60000	5 ⑪ ↓

73 **82 83**

The 1983 vintage provides this robust Savigny with an extra guarantee of long life. Leave for several years. (1983)
◆┓ SARL Moillard, 5 Rue F.-Mignotte, 21700 Nuits-St-Georges; tel. 80 61 03 34 ⟙ No visitors.

DOMAINE JEAN-MARC PAVELOT
Les Guettes*

■1er Cru	1.43ha	60000	4 D ⑪ ↓

74 76 78 79 **80 81 82 83** 83

Dark colour and rich nose of ripe fruit; despite its full body, still very woody and the aromas par-ticularly reserved. Will show much better in four to six years' time. (1983) ✔ Savigny-les-Beaune, Savigny-les-Beaune la Dominode, Savigny-les-Beaune les Narbontons, Pernand-Vergelesses les Vergelesses.
◆┓ Jean-Marc Pavelot, 21420 Savigny-les-Beaune; tel. 80 21 55 21 ⟙ By appt.

DOMAINE JEAN-MARC PAVELOT

■	4.5ha	20400	4 D ⑪ ↓

74 76 78 **79 81 82 83** 83

Bright, clear, colour and nose of crushed red berries. Still strongly marked by wood but plenty of body. Drink in four years' time. (1983) ✔ Savigny-les-Beaune les Guettes, Savigny-les-Beaune la Dominode, Savigny-les-Beaune les Narbontons, Pernand-Vergelesses les Verge-lesses.
◆┓ Jean-Marc Pavelot, 21420 Savigny-les-Beaune; tel. 80 21 55 21 ⟙ By appt.

CAVES DE LA REINE PEDAUQUE
Les Peuillets*

■	4.5ha	20000	5 ⑪ ↓

66 69 71 **76** 78 79 **80** *81 **83**

This 1982 is all finesse, with a well developed nose and palate, and a suppleness and roundness which make it good to drink now. (1982)
◆┓ Caves de la Reine Pédau33 Aloxe-Corton, 21420 Savigny-les-Beaune; tel. 80 26 40 00 ⟙ By appt.

DOMAINE DU PRIEURE
Les Hauts Jarrons**

■	0.30ha	1800	4 D ⑪ ↓

78 79 82 83

This 1982, with a firm flavour and long finish, has been vinified for keeping. Still has all the fruity qualities of youth and is slow to develop. Pro-duced in minute quantities, best not to waste it by drinking too soon. (1982)
◆┓ Jean-Michel Maurice, Dom. du Prieuré, 21420 Savigny-lès-Beaune; tel. 80 21 54 27 ⟙ By appt.

DOMAINE DU PRIEURE**

■	4.50ha	27000	4 D ⑪ ↓

78 79 *82 83

A 1982 Savigny that already has a very open oaky, berry-scented nose and a full rich flavour. Ideal for drinking now, although it can keep. (1982) ✔ Savigny Premier Cru les Lavières, Savigny Premier Cru les Hauts Jarrons, Savigny, Bourgogne Rouge.
◆┓ Jean-Michel Maurice, Dom. du Prieuré, 21420 Savigny-lès-Beaune; tel. 80 21 54 27. ⟙ By appt.

MANUEL SEGUIN *Les Lavières**

■1er Cru	5000	5 D ⑪ ↓

*83 84

This firm always takes great trouble to produce a fine cuvée from the village where it is based. Still very young, showing good fruit and depth of flavour. (1982)
◆┓ Manuel Seguin, Rue Paul Maldaut, 21420 Savigny-lès-Beaune; tel. 80 21 50 42 ⟙ By appt.

DOMAINE LES TERREGELESSES
Les Vergelesses**

□	0.5ha	3500	4 D ⑪ ↓

Benefits greatly from its vintage, which gives intense aromas and a pleasant mellowness that will increase with age. (1983)
◆┓ Dom. de Terregelesses, 25 Rue Pierre-Joig-neaux, 21200 Beaune; tel. 80 22 62 27 ⟙ By appt.

DOMAINE DES TERREGELESSES
Les Vergelesses*

□1er Cru	1ha	6000	4 D ⑪ ↓

Very representative of its vintage, with a firm long flavour and good fruit which will, in time, give a powerful bouquet. Leave to age. (1983) ✔ Aloxe-Corton Clos de la Boulette, Clorey-Côte-de-Beaune Rouge.
◆┓ Dom. des Terregelesses, 25 Rue Pierre-Joig-neaux, 21200 Beaune; tel. 80 22 32 27 ⟙ By appt.

Chorey-Lès-Beaune

Situated on the plain opposite the Combe de Bouilland, this village pos-sesses several vineyards bordering Savigny. Approximately 400 hecto-litres of red wine is produced with the communal appellation, most of which is sold as Côte de Beaune-Villages.

DOMAINE ARNOUX PERE ET FILS★★

■   9ha 55000 [4] [D] ▮ ⑾ ⌄

79 [80] (82) [82] 83

Fine, lively red-fruit colour and developed aromas of Morello cherry. Smooth, round and well balanced with good length on the palate. (1982) ✓ Aloxe-Corton, Savigny-les-Beaune Les Guettes, Beaune Premier Cru, Côte de Beaune-Villages.
↪ Dom. Arnoux Père et Fils, Chorey-les-Beaune, 21200 Beaune; tel. 80 22 09 93 ☎ By appt.

GAY PERE ET FILS★★

■   12ha 72000   [4] [D] ⑾ ⌄

78 79 80 **81** (82)

Fruity and still fairly closed up. Solid tannic flavour and bright, concentrated colour. Will keep well. (1982) ✓ Beaune Premier Cru, Savigny-les-Beaune Vergelesses, Savigny-les-Beaune Serpentières, Aloxe-Corton.
↪ *MM.*Gay Père et Fils, Chorey-les-Beaune, 21200 Beaune; tel. 80 22 22 73 ☎ By appt.

DOMAINE MAILLARD PERE ET FILS★★

■   14ha 85000   [4] [D] ⑾ ⌄

78 79 **80 81** (82) [82] 83

This 1982 with its strong, cherry colour was kept in oak casks for two years. Will fill out with age. (1982) ✓ Corton, Beaune, Côtes de Beaune, Bourgogne Aligoté, Aloxe-Corton.
↪ SARL Dom. Maillard Père et Fils, Chorey-les-Beaune, 21200 Beaune; tel. 80 22 10 67 ☎ By appt.

MAURICE MARTIN ET FILS★★

■   6.83ha 50000   [4] [D] ▮ ⑾ ⌄

78 (82) [82]

Recommended that this wine be served with coq au vin or game, at 16°F–18°C. At this temperature it exhales fresh aromas of oak and blackcurrant, over a firm, slightly tannic base. Will keep for a long time. (1982) ✓ Savigny-les-Beaune, Aloxe-Corton, Bourgogne Rouge, Bourgogne Aligoté.
↪ GAEC Maurice Martin et Fils, Chorey-les-Beaune, 21200 Beaune; tel. 80 22 07 17. ☎ By appt.

DOMAINE RENE PODECHARD★★

■   11ha 65000   [4] [D] ⑾ ⌄

76 78 79 80 **82** [82] 83 84

Strong colour, aromatic bouquet and persistence on the palate that reveals a balance between good tannin and fine mellowness. To keep. (1982) ✓ Savigny-les-Beaune, Aloxe-Corton, Beaune Cent Vignes, Bourgogne Passe-tout-grain.
↪ René Podechard, Chorey-les-Beaune, 21200 Beaune; tel. 80 22 21 76 ☎ By appt.

TOLLOT-BEAULT ET FILS★★

■   8ha 50000   [4] [D] ⑾ ⌄

75 76 77 (78) **79 ★80** 81 [82] **83** 84

Very well-balanced, an excellent example of the finesse achieved by the Pinot Noir on clay-limestone soil. Expressive, fruity aromas and rich flavour with a well-judged tannin/acid balance.

Ready to drink but may be kept. (1982) ✓ Corton, Aloxe-Corton, Beaune Clos du Roi, Savigny-les-Beaune.
↪ GAEC Tollot-Beault et Fils, Chorey-les-Beaune, 21200 Beaune; tel. 80 22 16 54 ☎ By appt.

Beaune

The Beaune appellation area (450 hectares) is one of the largest of the Côte. However Beaune itself, a town of about 20000 inhabitants, is first and foremost the wine-growing and wine-making capital of Burgundy. As well as being the headquarters of a large wine trade, it is also a major French tourist centre. The sale of the 'vins des Hospices' – held in aid of the ancient hospital – has become an international event and must be one of the biggest charity sales in the world. Since Beaune has now become the centre of a very important motorway network, tourism will obviously continue to grow.

The wines, almost all red, are powerful and distinctive. The favourable location means that most of the vineyard has been classed Premier Cru, the following being among the most prestigious: Les Bressandes, Le Clos du Roi, Les Grèves, Les Teurons, and Les Champimonts.

DOMAINE JEAN ALLEXANT *Grèves*★

■1er Cru   0.35ha 1920   [5] [D] ⑾

76 **77 78** 81 82 83

Dark colour with some tinges of orange, and aromas of crushed leaves and game. Elegant palate with a fruity note of cooked prunes. The finish is still a little too alcoholic. Nonetheless some delicacy. (1978) ✓ Côtes de Beaune Rouge and Blanc, Corton Vergennes, Santenay, Pommard.
↪ Jean Allexant, Ste-Marie-la-Blanche, 21200 Beaune; tel. 80 26 60 77 ☎ By appt.

DOMAINE JEAN ALLEXANT
Clos des Rouarts

■   2ha 7200   [5] [D] ⑾ ⌄

76 **78** 79 80 81 82

Despite a slightly thin finish, this is an attractive wine, with a slightly orangey colour and a nose of wild cherry and blackcurrant. (1982) ✓ Côtes de Beaune, Corton Vergennes, Santenay, Pommard.
↪ Jean Allexant, Ste-Marie-la-Blancne, 21200 Beaune; tel. 80 26 60 77 ☎ By appt.

CIE DES VINS D'AUTREFOIS
Les Tuvilains★★

1er Cru	4800	5 ▬ ⌄

Typical Beaune character present right from the outset, with gamey and slightly burnt aromas. Intense, dark, almost black colour, and long, vigorous flavours on the palate. (1983)
✦ Cie des Vins d'Autrefois, 9 Rue Celer, 21200 Beaune; tel. 80 22 21 31 ⟁ No visitors.

HOSPICES DE BEAUNE
Cuvée Clos-des-Avaux★

■1er Cru	2.16ha	5670	6 ⑪ ⌄

The only Hospices cuvée to bear the actual vineyard name rather than that of the benefactor. At the pre-auction tasting it seemed to be the least developed 1984, requiring several more weeks before an initial judgement could be made. (1984)
✦ Dom. Viti Hospices de Beaune, Rue de l'Hôtel-Dieu, 21200 Beaune; tel. 80 24 75 75 ⟁ No visitors.

HOSPICES DE BEAUNE
Cuvée Rousseau-Deslandes★

■	2.48ha	7290	6 ⑪ ⌄

Much appreciated, with its fruit stone and spice aromas, and its balanced, oaky flavour. (1984)
✦ Dom. Viti. Hospices de Beaune, Rue de l'Hôtel-Dieu, 21200 Beaune ⟁ No visitors.

HOSPICES DE BEAUNE
Cuvée Nicolas Rollin★★

■	2.77ha	8640	6 ⑪ ⌄

Very characteristic Beaune with flavours of spices and candied fruit typical of this vintage, and a strong taste of new oak. (1984)
✦ Dom. Viti. Hospices de Beaune, Rue de l'Hôtel-Dieu, 21200 Beaune ⟁ No visitors.

HOSPICES DE BEAUNE
Cuvée Maurice Drouhin★

■	2.69ha	7830	6 ⑪ ⌄

Maurice Drouhin demonstrated his affection for the Hospices by bequeathing a plot of Beaune vines, which are clearly holding their own against the traditional cuvées. The 1984 was the most forward of all the Hospices cuvées at the pre-auction tasting. (1984)
✦ Dom. Viti. Hospices de Beaune, Rue de l'Hôtel-Dieu, 21200 Beaune ⟁ No visitors.

HOSPICES DE BEAUNE
Cuvée Guigone de Salins★★

■	2.97ha	8640	6 ⑪ ⌄

One of the best Beaune vintages bears the name Guigone de Salins, the wife of the Chancellor Nicolas Rollin, and is made from selected old vines. The 1984 was much praised and fetched between 25000 and 27000 francs per hogshead at the Hospices auction. (1984)
✦ Dom. Viti. Hospices de Beaune, Rue de l'Hôtel-Dieu, 21200 Beaune ⟁ No visitors.

HOSPICES DE BEAUNE
Cuvée des Dames Hospitalières★★

■	2.58ha	8100	6 ⑪ ⌄

The lady hospitallers are the small community of nuns who have kept the Hôtel-Dieu for five centuries. Their name has been given to one of the best Hospice de Beaune cuvées. In 1984 one cask was singled out of the cuvée to be sold alone as the very first lot in aid of a charity. It was bought by the Beaune négociants Patriarche for 200000 francs! This gave a boost to the rest of the cuvée which fetched higher prices than any other Beaune cuvées. (1984)
✦ Dom. Viti. Hospices de Beaune, Rue de l'Hôtel-Dieu, 21200 Beaune ⟁ No visitors.

HOSPICES DE BEAUNE
Cuvée Cyrot-Chaudron★

■	1ha	4050	6 ⑪ ⌄

One hectare of Beaune vines was donated in 1979, by Monsieur and Madame Cyrot-Chaudron in aid of the Hôtel-Dieu. The vineyard has been carefully worked by the régisseur of the Hospices estate and the wine is beginning to acquire the house 'style', strongly coloured, with dense aromas and a good underlying structure. It fetched 20000 francs a hogshead in the November 1984 Hospice auctions. (1984)
✦ Dom. Viti. Hospices de Beaune, Rue de l'Hôtel-Dieu, 21200 Beaune ⟁ No visitors.

HOSPICES DE BEAUNE
Cuvée Brunet★

■	2.56ha	8640	6 ⑪ ⌄

The Brunet family in Beaune have made bequests to the Hôtel-Dieu on five different occasions. In recognition of this, their name has been given to a Beaune cuvée. The 1984 had a brilliant clear colour on the day of the sale and enchanted the buyers with its soft flavours and characteristic smoky bouquet. It fetched 20000 to 21000 francs a hogshead at the Hospice Auction. (1984)
✦ Dom. Viti. Hospices de Beaune, Rue de l'Hôtel-Dieu, 21200 Beaune ⟁ No visitors.

HOSPICES DE BEAUNE
Cuvée Betault★

■	2.67ha	8640	6 ⑪ ⌄

Hugues Betault, a counsellor to King Louis 13th, and his brother Louis expanded the Hôtel-Dieu in 1615 and added the Salle Saint-Louis and the women's infirmary. In commemoration of their contributions a Hospices de Beaune vintage has been named after them. The 1984 had a classic, clean-flavoured attractively fruity character. It made 19500 francs a hogshead at the Hospices auction in November 1984. (1984)
✦ Dom. Viti. Hospices de Beaune, Rue de l'Hôtel-Dieu, 21200 Beaune ⟁ No visitors.

LYCEE VITICOLE DE BEAUNE
Champimonts★

■1er Cru		3ha	4800	5 Ⓓ ⑪ ⌄
69 71 73 74 ★81 ⑧⑧ ⑧⑧ 83				

Similarly light colour but a much less developed nose than their AOC Beaune. Plenty of body, with an elegant, slightly bitter cherry stone flavour. (1982) ✔ Puligny-Montrachet, Beaune Bressandes, Beaune Perrières.

☀ Lycée Agricole et Viticole de Beaune, 21200 Beaune; tel. 80 22 27 45 ✕ By appt. Closed Aug.

LYCEE VITICOLE DE BEAUNE*

▧	1 ha	4900	6 ⏸ ⬥

Would satisfy even the most critical of examiners. Light colour and well-developed nose of exotic, burnt aromas reminiscent of incense. Elegant but full flavour with pronounced fruity finish. (1982) ✔ Beaune Premier Cru, Bourgogne Rouge and Blanc, Puligny-Montrachet.
☀ Lycée Agricole et Viticole de Beaune, 21200 Beaune; tel. 80 22 27 45 ✕ By appt. Closed Aug.

LEONCE BOCQUET**

▧		4000	5 D ⏸ ⬥

*69 *78 *81 *⑧② 82

A touch of new oak, a note of blackcurrant, a whiff of soot – a typical Beaune still retaining plenty of freshness. Suitable with cooked charcuterie dishes such as pâté or jambon persillé. (1982)
☀ Petits-Fils de Léonce Bocquet, 29 Bvd Clemenceau, 21200 Beaune; tel. 80 22 28 49 ✕ Mon.–Fri. 9.30–11.30/14.00–17.30. Closed Dec. to Feb.

DOMAINE BOUCHARD PERE ET FILS *Clos Saint-Landry***

☐	1.98 ha	20 200	6 D ⏸ ⬥

*78 79 80 81 82 83

Lemon-yellow colour and a nose of acacia and honeysuckle. Very elegant flavour with a dash of honey, almond and fine slightly 'roasted' aromas. Long finish. (1982)
☀ Bouchard Père et Fils, Au Château, 21200 Beaune; tel. 80 22 14 41 ✕ By appt. Closed Aug. and 1 week in Feb.

DOMAINE BOUCHARD PERE ET FILS *Beaune du Château**

☐	3.89 ha	17 000	5 D ▤ ⬥

Dark golden colour and lemon bouquet. Fragrant flavours on the palate of lemon, toffee and honeysuckle. A very fat, robust wine with an elegant finish which should be served no cooler than cellar temperature. (1982)
☀ Bouchard Père et fils, Au Château, 21200 Beaune; tel. 80 22 14 41 ✕ B83ppt. Closed Aug. and 1 week in Feb.

DOMAINE BOUCHARD PERE ET FILS *Les Marconnets***

▧1er Cru	2.32 ha	9600	5 D ⏸ ⬥

*⑦⑨ 80 81 82

Good colour with orange highlights. Complex bouquet of peppermint, mushroom and dry leaves with a peppery, spicy fragrance on the palate. Rich and full bodied with a smooth finish strongly marked by kirsch. Could wait another four years. (1979) ✔ Volnay-Fremiets, Pommard, Chambolle-Musigny, Nuits-St-Georges Clos-St-Marc.
☀ Bouchard Père et Fils, Au Château, 21200 Beaune; tel. 80 22 14 41 ✕ By appt. Closed Aug. and 1 week in Feb.

DOMAINE BOUCHARD AINE ET FILS *Les Sceaux***

▧	1.19 ha	4200	5 D ⏸ ⬥

From one of Beaune's best vineyards. This 1982 is still very young and seems best suited, with its elegant but delicate character, to a light game bird such as quail. (1982)
☀ MM. Bouchard Père et Fils, Au Château, 21200 Beaune; tel. 80 22 14 41 ✕ By appt. Closed Aug.

DOMAINE CHANSON *Clos des Fèves**

▧1er Cru	4 ha		D ⏸ ⬥

⑧⓪ 80 81 81 82 83

Dark colour shading towards orange. Aromas of fruit stones and dried leaves. Striking fruity flavour of blackcurrants and morello cherries, but lacking body. (1980)
☀ MM. Chanson Père et Fils, 10–12 Rue Paul-Chanson, 21200 Beaune; tel. 80 22 33 00 ✕ By appt. Closed Aug.

DOMAINE CHANSON *Teurons***

▧1er Cru	5 ha	19 000	4 D ⏸ ⬥

70 74 76 77 ⑦⑧ 79 80 82 83

Vinified in the 'Chanson style', it has kept its 1982 fruit, with a firmness that saves it from becoming soft. (1982)
☀ MM. Chanson Père et Fils, 10–12 Rue Paul-Chanson, 21200 Beaune; tel. 80 22 33 00 ✕ No visitors.

DOMAINE CHANSON *Grèves***

▧1er Cru	2.16 ha	10 000	5 D ⏸ ⬥

71 76 77 ⑦⑧ 79 80 81 82 82 83

Has all the firm's customary finesse, with intense fruit and a fine ruby colour. (1982)
☀ MM. Chanson Père et Fils, 10–12 Rue Paul-Chanson, 21200 Beaune; tel. 80 22 33 00 ✕ No visitors.

DOMAINE CHANSON *Clos du Roi***

▧1er Cru	2.4 ha	13 000	5 D ⏸ ⬥

71 ⑦② 76 77 78 79 80 81 83

Very smooth and flattering with charming colour and fruit. (1982)
☀ MM. Chanson Père et Fils, 10–12 Rue Paul-Chanson, 21200 Beaune; tel. 80 22 33 00 ✕ No visitors.

DOMAINE CHANSON *Bressandes***

▧1er Cru	1.57 ha	6000	5 D ⏸ ⬥

71 76 ⑦⑨ 80 81 82 83

Vinified to bring out all its vigour. Combines fruit that is still fresh with a fine, fleshy body. (1982)
☀ MM. Chanson Père et Fils, 10–12 Rue Paul-Chanson, 21200 Beaune; tel. 80 22 33 00 ✕ No visitors.

DOMAINE CHANSON *Clos des Marconnets**

▧	3.77 ha	12 000	5 D ⏸ ⬥

73 77 77 79 ⑧⓪ 80 81 81 82 82 83

Darker colour than the Marconnets 1982. Dense, composty nose. Meaty flavour and soft lingering finish. (1980)
☀ MM. Chanson Père et Fils, 10–12 Rue Paul-

Chanson, 21200 Beaune; tel. 80 22 33 00 ☎ By appt. Closed Aug.

DOMAINE CHANSON
Clos des Mouches★★

■1er Cru	4.42ha	19 000	5 D ⑪ ↓

71 76 **77 78** 79 **80** 81 83

Has more body and roundness than the wines produced to the north of Beaune. Vinified to develop its body and bouquet. (1982)
➦ *MM.* Chanson Père et Fils, 10–12 Rue Paul-Chanson, 21200 Beaune; tel. 80 22 33 00 ☎ No visitors.

BERTRAND DARVIOT★★

■	1ha	3500	5 D ⑪ ↓

80 81 ⑧ ★**83** 84

This 1983 Beaune shows all the vigour of the vintage with its intense colour, slightly burnt aromas and rich tannic flavour. Needs several years. (1983) ✔ Bourgogne Rouge, Meursault, Savigny-les-Beaune, Beaune Grèves.
➦ Bertrand Darviot, 17 Rue de la Velle, 21190 Meursault; tel. 80 21 22 83 ☎ By appt.

JOSEPH DROUHIN *Clos des Mouches*★★

■1er Cru			5 ⑪ ↓

72 74 **76** 77 **78** 79 80 81 ★**82** 83

The nose of this dark red wine is strongly marked by the wood, but swirling the glass releases attractive spicy aromas. Elegant structure on the palate and prolonged tannic finish. Fine bottle with a great future. (1983)
➦ Joseph Drouhin, 7 Rue d'Enfer, 21200 Beaune; tel. 80 22 06 80 ☎ No visitors.

JOSEPH DROUHIN★★

■1er Cru			⑪ ↓

72 74 **76** 77 **78** 79 80 81 ★**82** 83

Light cherry colour and reserved nose; fruity palate with a bitter note of fruit stones. Slightly thin texture compensated for by a great deal of elegance and charm, opening out into a 37tering finish. (1982)
➦ Joseph Drouhin, 7 Rue d'Enfer, 21200 Beaune; tel. 80 22 06 80 ☎ By appt.

DOMAINE JACQUES GERMAIN
Les Theurons

■1er Cru	2ha	7200	5 D ▮ ↓

71 72 73 74 76 77 **78 79 79** ⑧ 81 82 **83**

Partly raised in new casks, this deeply-coloured Beaune has elegant aromas still marked by the wood. Flavour not yet properly knit; will require another four years to reach its best. (1980)
➦ Jacques Germain, Ch. de Chorey-les-Beaune, 21200 Beaune; tel. 80 22 06 05 ☎ By appt. Closed 15 July–15 Aug.

EDMOND GIRARDIN
Clos des Mouches★★

■1er Cru	1ha	3000	5 D ▮ ⑪ ↓

Despite the firmness of the vintage there are already well-developed aromas of vanilla and allspice. Clean but still very robust flavour which should mature well. (1983)
➦ Edmond Girardin, 21630 Pommard; tel. 80 22 32 57 ☎ By appt.

LOUIS JADOT *Clos des Couchereaux*★★

■	2ha	7000	5 D ⑪ ↓

Good colour with pale orange highlights but a rather inexpressive nose. Vigorous swirling of the glass releases the heavier less volatile aromas of leather, pear and red fruits. On the palate, good extract but as yet little balance. Wait four years. (1978)
➦ Louis Jadot, 5 Rue Samuel-Legay, 21200 Beaune; tel. 80 22 10 57 ☎ By appt.

LOUIS JADOT *Clos des Ursules*★★★

■	2.50ha	12 000	6 D ⑪ ↓

76 ⑦⑧ 79 80 ★81 **82 83**

Very dark colour with 'singed' aromas of black-currant and orange peel. Spicy palate but still rather tannic at the finish; should last well and develop into a most attractive wine. (1981)
✔ Beaune Clos de Couchereaux, Beaune Boucherottes, Corton Charlemagne, Chevalier Montrachet les Demoiselles.
➦ Louis Jadot, 5 Rue Samuel-Legay, 21200 Beaune; tel. 80 22 10 57 ☎ By appt. Closed Aug.

DOMAINE MOILLARD-GRIVOT
Grèves★

■1er Cru	2ha	7200	5 ▮ ↓

66 69 **69** 71 76 78 **79** ⑧ **83**

Dark red colour and bitter, leafy aromas of quinine and sage. Surprising, exotic taste of orange peel on the palate. Light structure and finish rather dominated by the alcohol. ✔ Vosne-Romanée Malconsorts, Nuits Clos des Corvées, Nuits-St-Georges Clos des Grandes Vignes, Nuits-St-George Clos de Thorey.
➦ SARL Moillard, 5 Rue F.-Mignotte, 21700 Nuits-St-Georges; tel. 80 61 03 34 ☎ Weekends 9.00–11.00/14.00–17.00. Closed Aug.

PATRIARCHE PERE ET FILS
Réserve Barrique Frémiot★

■		8000	6

The soft, round contours of this wine are sure to please even if the smooth flavour is somewhat lacking in relief. Nonetheless a well-made 1979. (1979)
➦ *MM.* Patriarche Père et Fils, Rue de Collège, 21200 Beaune; tel. 80 22 23 20 ☎ By appt. Closed 15 Dec. to end Feb.

DOMAINE DES PIERRES BLANCHES★

□	8ha	36 000	5 D ⑪ ↓

72 ★75 76 ★79 81 83

Yellow-gold with brisk acidity but slightly thin finish. Fairly complex nose, suggesting honey-suckle, lime and toasted almonds. Fat but slightly sharp flavour, marked by the 'grilled' aromas of an older Chardonnay. (1981)
➦ Maurice Joliette, Dom. des Pierres Blanches, 21200 Beaune; tel. 80 22 26 45 ☎ By appt.

DOMAINE PRIEUR-BRUNET
Clos du Roy★★

■1er Cru   0.5ha   3000   ⑤ Ⅾ ⑪ ⌀

★76 78 79 ★81 ⑧② 83 84

There are numerous 'Clos du Roy' vineyards in Burgundy, former parts of ducal property which reverted to the crown. This 1982 has the classic characteristics of this premier cru; a bright, deep purple colour, aromas of cherry and toast and generous length on the palate. It is still young and ageing slowly. (1982) ✔ Santenay Commes Premier Cru, Santenay Foulut.
⊶ Dom. Prieur-Brunet, 21590 Santenay; tel. 80 20 60 56 �Ⲧ Daily 10.00–12.00/14.00–19.00.

DOMAINE PRIEUR ET CHATEAU HERBEUX
Clos de la Féguine★

■1er Cru   2ha   8500   ⑤ Ⅾ ⑪ ⌀

⑦⑧ 80 82 83

This 1982 is smooth with a good bouquet and is ready to drink. (1982) ✔ Montrachet Grand Cru, Chambertin Clos de Beze Grand Cru, Volnay Santenots Premier Cru, Puligny-Montrachet.
⊶ Dom. Jacques Prieur, 2 Rue des Santenots, 21190 Meursault; tel. 80 21 23 85 �Ⲧ By appt. Closed Aug.

ROSSIGNOL *Les Theurons*★

■1er Cru   1.23ha   6480   ⑤ Ⅾ ⑪ ⌀

76 ⑦⑧ 79 80 81 82 83

Light red, with delicate aromas of fruit and jam. Pleasantly full on the palate, though rather a disappointing finish. Should mature well. (1982) ✔ Volnay Premier Cru Les Pitures, Pommard Monthelie Premier Cru, Bourgogne.
⊶ Michel et Yves Rossignol, Rue de l'Abreuvoir, 21190 Volnay; tel. 80 22 30 41 �Ⲧ By appt. Closed second fortnight July.

DOMAINE VOIRET *Les Grèves*★★

■   0.45ha   2500   ⑤ Ⅾ ⑪ ⌀

⑦⑨ 83 84

The St-Martin area of Beaune lies next to fine premier cru vineyards. The name 'Grèves', denoting gravelly soil, almost always indicates a top rank vineyard – in this case one of the very best in Beaune. This 1983 is powerful, long and tannic, and the aromas are still closed up. It will keep for two decades. (1983) ✔ Beaune Premier Cru les Pertuisots, Beaune Premier Cru les Cras, Beaune Premier Cru Clos des Avaux, Beaune Premier Cru les Thuvilains.
⊶ GAEC Dom. Voiret, 48 Rue Faubourg St-Martin, 21200 Beaune; tel. 80 22 24 05 �Ⲧ By appt.

DOMAINE VOIRET *Les Cras*★★

■1er Cru   0.33ha   2000   ⑤ Ⅾ ⑪ ⌀

79 82 83 84

Cras or its variants, meaning stony soil, is a frequent vineyard name in Burgundy. This 1982, typical of its vintage, has very strong fruit and is still young. Its vinification has given it a tannin that will enable it to age. The Voiret property specializes in producing wines that keep for a long time. (1982) ✔ Beaune Premier Cru les Pertuisots, Beaune Premier Cru Clos des Avaux, Beaune Premier Cru les Tuvilains, Beaune Premier Cru les Grèves.

⊶ GAEC Dom. Voiret, 48 Rue Faubourg St-Martin, 21200 Beaune; tel. 80 22 24 05 �Ⲧ By appt.

DOMAINE VOIRET *Les Pertuisots*★★

■   1.28ha   7000   ④ Ⅾ ⑪ ⌀

77 ⑦⑨ 80 82 83 84

Give or take an acre all the vineyard land at the foot of the Montagne de Beaune is classified premier cru. This wine is made in very limited quantities, available only to a few regular customers. The 1982 still has a very young grapey flavour and has been vinified for long keeping. (1982)
⊶ GAEC Dom. Voiret, 48 Rue Faubourg St-Martin, 21200 Beaune; tel. 80 22 24 05 ⲦⲦ By appt.

DOMAINE VOIRET *Clos dex Avaux*★★

■1er Cru   0.46ha   2500   ⑤ Ⅾ ⑪ ⌀

⑦⑨ 82 ★83 84

Les Avaux is one of the finest Beaune premiers crus. This small piece of land is divided between ten owners, who each make only a few barrels. This 1983 has power and the customary solidity of the Voiret property's wines, and should reach its peak within two or three years. (1983).
⊶ GAEC Dom. Voiret, 48 Rue Faubourg St-Martin, 21200 Beaune; tel. 80 22 24 05 ⲦⲦ By appt.

Côtes de Beaune

Not to be confused with Côte de Beaune-Villages, the appellation Côte de Beaune may only be applied to wine produced in a few small areas on the Montagne de Beaune.

GRIVELET PERE ET FILS
Cuvée Saint-Vincent★★

■   6000   ④ Ⅾ ⑪ ⌀

78 81 82 83

Each year on 22 January the Burgundians celebrate St-Vincent the patron saint of wine in colourful local pageants. The Confrérie du Tastevin arranges a magnificent procession in a different village each year and wine flows liberally. In 1982 the festivities took place in Vougeot and this cuvée was used for several tastings. Still an extremely fresh and young wine. (1982)
⊶ *MM.* Grivelet Père et Fils, 21640 Vougeot; tel. 80 72 42 72 ⲦⲦ By appt.

ALAIN MITANCHEY★★

■   2ha   3000   ③ Ⅾ 🖻 ⌀

73 76 78 79 80 82 ⑧③ 83

In the 12th century, Paris-l'Hôpital was the site of a hostel of the Knights Hospitallers. The house dates from that period. This wine, with its bright, strong colour, powerful aromas and elegance should age well. (1982) ✔ Bourgogne Aligoté, Bourgogne Hautes-Côtes de Beaune, Côtes de Beaune-Villages, Santenay.
⊶ Alain Mitanchey, Paris l'Hôpital, 71150 Chagney; tel. 85 87 16 38 ⲦⲦ By appt.

MOILLARD★★

■ 120000 　4　⧉ ⌖

78 ⑧₂ **83**

The mature orange-tinged colour and aromas of ripe fruit suggest it will soon peak. This is confirmed by the soft, smooth palate. (1982)
↬ SARL Moillard, 5 Rue F.-Mignotte, 21700 Nuits-St-Georges; tel. 80 61 03 34 ⵣ No visitors.

MICHEL ARCELAIN★★

■ 1ha 5500 　5　D ⧉ ⌖

72 73 **76 78** 79 **81** 82

All the finesse of the 1981 vintage. Lustrous red colour and fine aromas of resin, vanilla, oak bark, strawberry and dried fig. Fairly long on the palate, with a delicate texture. Plenty of finesse, but not thin. Should keep for several years. (1981)
↬ Michel Arcelain, 21630 Pommard; tel. 80 22 13 50 ⵣ By appt.

Pommard

Of all the Burgundy appellations, this one is the best-known abroad; probably because the name is so easy to pronounce! The appellation covers more than 300 hectares, producing about 9000 hectolitres annually. The marl soil gives way here to soft limestone, and the wines are robust, tannic and long-lasting. The best 'climats' are classified Premier Cru, the most famous being Les Rugiens and Les Epenots.

DOMAINE DU COMTE ARMAND
Clos des Epeneaux★★

■ 5ha 5000 　5　D ⧉ ⌖

76 78 79 81 **82** ⑧₃ **83**

Solid, with powerful aromas of oak and pepper and a fruity note of cherry. Full, firm structure suggesting that this bottle will keep well. (1982)
↬ M. le Comte Armand, Dom. des Epeneaux, 21630 Pommard; tel. 80 24 71 50 ⵣ By appt.

Côte de Beaune (North Central Region)

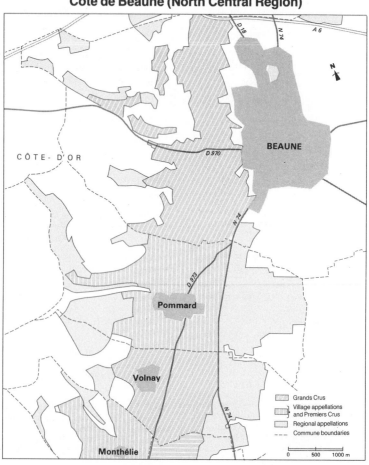

340

HOSPICES DE BEAUNE
Cuvée Cyrot-Chaudron★

| ■ | | 3ha | 12150 | 6 ◖ ↓ |

This 1984 cuvée had a clear colour and was one of the most advanced at the time of the sale. However, the relatively large quantity offered, (45 hogshead) kept bids fairly low. (1984)
↦ Dom. Viti. Hospices de Beaune, Rue de l'Hôtel-Dieu, 21200 Beaune; tel. 80 24 75 75 ☎ No visitors.

HOSPICES DE BEAUNE
Cuvée Billardet★

| ■ | | 2.10ha | 6480 | 6 ◖ ↓ |

Showed fruit, good persistence and a strongly marked new oak character which will diminish as the wine matures. (1984)
↦ Dom. Viti. Hospices de Beaune, Rue de l'Hôtel-Dieu, 21200 Beaune; tel. 80 24 75 75 ☎ No visitors.

DOMAINE GOUD DE BEAUPUIS
Epenots★★

| ■ | | 1ha | 5500 | 5 D ◖ ↓ |

78 79 **80 81 82** ⑧ **83**

Deeply coloured with violet hues in which sloe and pepper aromas are already emerging. Full bodied with remarkably long flavour. Will keep several decades. (1983) ✔ Pommard la Chanière, Beaune Grèves, Beaune Clos des Vignes Franches, Beaune Clos Ste-Anne des Theurons.
↦ Goud de Beaupuis, Ch. des Moutots, Chorey-les-Beaune, 21200 Beaune; tel. 80 22 20 63 ☎ Daily 9.00–19.00.

GABRIEL BILLARD★

| ■ | | 1.5ha | 3000 | 5 D ◖ ↓ |

74 **76 78** 79 ⑧

An appealing wine, already quite mature. Expressive aromas of fruit, coffee and spices and a smooth, fine flavour. Drink soon. (1982)
↦ Gabriel Billard, 21630 Pommard; tel. 80 22 27 82 ☎ By appt.

DOMAINE BILLARD-GONNET
Les Charmots★★

| ■1er Cru | | 0.45ha | 14440 | 5 D ◖ ↓ |

64 **66 69** 71 75 76 **78** 79 80 81 ★⑧ **82**

A dark colour and nose of cherry are followed by great elegance and body on the palate. This wine is well balanced but needs to mature for its aromas to be fully expressed. A delicate finish, hinting of bitter almond. (1982)
↦ Dom. Billard-Gonnet, Route d'Ivry, 21630 Pommard; tel. 80 22 17 33 ☎ By appt. Closed end Dec.–beg. Jan.

DOMAINE BILLARD-GONNET
Les Chaponnières★★

| ■1er Cru | | 8ha | 26400 | 5 D ◖ ↓ |

64 **66 69** 71 75 76 **78** 79 ⑧ **80** 81

A colour enriched by hints of orange; the nose combines aromas of dried leaves, eucalyptus and pine. A touch of sloe on the palate compensates for the light structure of this wine, making it delicate and smooth. A fine, silky Pommard. (1980) ✔ Pommard Premier Cru Rugiens, Pommard Premier Cru Charmots, Pommard Premier Cru Bertins, Pommard Premier Cru Pezerolles.
↦ Dom. Billard-Gonnet, Route d'Ivry, 21630 Pommard; tel. 80 22 17 33 ☎ By appt. Closed end Dec.–Jan.

DOMAINE BILLARD-GONNET
Rugiens★★★

| ■1er Cru | | 0.35ha | 1200 | 5 D ◖ ↓ |

64 **66 69 71** 75 76 **78** 79 80 81 ⑧ **82**

The dark colour reveals an under-developed nose that only continual swirling of the glass released aromas of sloe and blackcurrant. The wine is well balanced on the palate, with a good tannic base and a finish of kirsch. Must be kept for at least eight years. (1982) ✔ Pommard Premier Cru Clos de Verger, Pommard Premier Cru Chaponnières, Pommard Premier Cru Pezerolles, Pommard Premier Cru Bertins.
↦ Dom. Billard-Gonnet, Route d'Ivry, 21630 Pommard; tel. 80 22 17 33 ☎ By appt. Closed end of Dec.–beg. Jan.

POMMARD-RUGIENS
APPELLATION POMMARD CONTROLÉE
Domaine BILLARD-GONNET
PROPRIÉTAIRE A POMMARD, CÔTE-D'OR, FRANCE
MIS EN BOUTEILLE AU DOMAINE
75 cl

BERNARD CAILLET★

| ■ | | 0.5ha | 3000 | 5 D ◖ ↓ |

⑥ 74 **76 78** 79 80 81 **82**

Mature colour and fine aromas of mocha and cognac. Very smooth flavour. Should be drunk soon. (1982)
↦ Bernard Caillet, 21630 Pommard; tel. 80 22 59 90 ☎ By appt.

DOMAINE FELIX CLERGET
Les Petits Noizons★★

| ■ | | | | 5 ◖ |

75

An attractive sweet flavour and complex aromas, still with a bit of acidity to lose. Pale colour but clear Pinot flavour which will still develop further with age. (1975)
↦ Félix Clerget, 21630 Pommard; tel. 80 22 16 07 ☎ No visitors.

DOMAINE DE COURCEL *Epenots★★*

| ■1er Cru | | 7ha | 42000 | 5 D ◖ ↓ |

76 **78** 79 81 82

Vinified to keep for a long time. Still has very young character, with fruit of a new wine, good, rich tannin and appreciable length on the palate. (1982)
↦ Dom. de Courcel, 21630 Pommard; tel. 80 22 11 70 ☎ By appt.

ARMANDE DOUHAIRET *Chanlins*★★

■		0.5ha	2000	5 D ⦀ ↓

71 74 **76 78** ★**79** 80 **81 82** 83

This cuvée received a very long fermentation to compensate for the general lightness of the 1982 vintage. It has the peppery smell typical of Pommard and a bouquet of vanilla, blackcurrant and new oak. The impression on the palate is still tannic and vigorous. Keep. (1982) ✔ Volnay Champans, Meursault Santenots, Monthélie.
↱ *Mlle* Armande Douhairet, Monthélie, 21190 Meursault; tel. 80 21 21 01 ✗ By appt.

JEAN GARAUDET★★

■		2ha	12000	5 D ⦀ ↓

75 76 77 78 ⑦⑨ 82

A long vinification to compensate for the lightness of the vintage. Solid flavour with firm tannins and classic aromas which are beginning to appear beneath the strong scent of new wood. Leave it to age. (1982)
↱ Jean Garaudet, 21630 Pommard; tel. 80 22 59 77 ✗ By appt.

DOMAINE MICHEL GAUNOX
Grands Epenots★★

■1er Cru		2.9ha	15000	5 D ⦀ ↓

61 62 64 **66** 71 72 76 ★**78** 79 81 83

Deep, firm colour and still very closed aromas of balsam and herbs. Excellent presence on the palate and long, distinguished flavour with the fruity finesse of the 1981 vintage. (1981)
↱ Michel Gaunoux, 21630 Pommard; tel. 80 22 18 52 ✗ By appt.

Mis en bouteilles
au Domaine

POMMARD GRANDS ÉPENOTS

Appellation POMMARD GRANDS ÉPENOTS Contrôlée

MICHEL GAUNOUX
PROPRIÉTAIRE - VITICULTEUR
à POMMARD (COTE-D'OR)   75 cl

EDMOND GIRARDIN★

■		2ha	9000	5 D ▤ ⦀ ↓

82

Strongly marked by the vintage with a deep red colour and relatively undeveloped aromas. Firm, tannin-encased flavour and very full body. Leave for several years. (1983)
↱ *MM.* Edmond Girardin, 21630 Pommard; tel. 80 22 32 57 ✗ By appt.

JEAN-LUC JOILLOT★★

■		3ha	18000	5 D ⦀ ↓

71 72 74 76 79 80 ⑧② 82

Fine aromas of blackcurrant, fruit stones, pepper and oak bark, with a long, well-knit flavour. (1982)
↱ Jean-Luc Joillot, 21630 Pommard; tel. 80 22 10 82 ✗ By appt.

JEAN JOLIOT ET FILS★★

■		1ha	3000	5 D ▤ ↓

★76 ⑦⑧ ★80 81 82 ★83

Strongly marked by the vintage, this Pommard will be a splendid wine by the end of the century. A few bottles might, nevertheless, be tasted in five or six years' time, just to keep an eye on how the wine develops. (1983) ✔ Beaune Boucherottes Premier Cru, Bourgogne Hautes-Côtes de Beaune Rouge, Bourgogne Passe-tout-grain, Meursault.
↱ Jean Joliot et Fils, Nantoux, 21190 Meursault; tel. 80 26 01 44 ✗ No visitors.

DOMAINE LAHAYE PERE ET FILS★

■		0.75ha	4500	5 D ⦀ ↓

74 ★76 78 79 81 ⑧② 82

Complex aromas with notes of strawberry, pepper, oak bark and lichen. On the palate, well structured and harmonious. Soon ready to drink. (1982)
↱ Dom. Lahaye Père et Fils, 21630 Pommard; tel. 80 22 52 22 ✗ By appt.

DOMAINE RAYMOND LAUNAY
Les Perrières★

■		2.5ha	12000	5 D ⦀ ↓

64 66 69 71 72 **74** 76 78 79 ★82

Dark velvety colour and round flavours marked by blackberries, bilberries and blackcurrant with a note of pepper. Drink soon. (1982) ✔ Other Pommard wines, Bourgogne Pinot Noir, Santenay.
↱ Dom. Raymond Launay, 21630 Pommard; tel. 80 22 12 23 ✗ By appt.

DOMAINE LEJEUNE *Les Argillières*★★

■1er Cru		1.33ha	4800	5 D ⦀ ↓

74 76 78 79 80 ⑧② **83**

Well-vinified with a mature bouquet of pepper over a background of vanilla. Firm, balanced flavour which will age well. (1982) ✔ Pommard Rugiens, Pommard Poutures, Pommard, Bourgogne Rouge.
↱ Famille Jullien de Pommerol, 25 Rue Thiers, 21200 Beaune; tel. 80 22 10 28 ✗ By appt.

DOMAINE RAOUL LENEUF★★

■		1.2ha	7200	5 D ⦀ ↓

74 76 ★78 ★79 ★81 ⑧② 82

Rich, with a deep colour and intense aromas of pepper, resin, dry fruit and new wood. Long, rich and solid on the palate; should age very well. (1982)
↱ Héritiers Dom. Raoul Leneuf, 21630 Pommard; tel. 80 22 09 43 ✗ By appt.

MAZILLY ET FILS *Les Poutures*★★

■		0.8ha	2900	5 D ⦀ ↓

⑦⑧ ★83 ★83

Produced from old vines this Pommard comes from Les Poutures vineyard which gives firm wines. Full-bodied, with good extract; needs to be laid down. (1982) ✔ Bourgogne Passe-tout-grain, Bourgogne Hautes-Côtes de Beaune, Meursault, Beaune Premier Cru les Vignes Franches.

↞ *MM.* Mazilly Père et Fils, Meloisey, 21190 Meursault; tel. 80 26 01 34 ⅂ By appt.

MOILLARD★

■		72 000	5 ⅏ ↓
74 79 82 83			

This full-bodied, well structured 1983 Pommard, is a slow developer. Leave for a decade. (1983)
↞ SARL Moillard, 5 Rue F.-Pérazols, 21700 Nuits St-Georges; tel. 80 61 03 34 ⅂ No visitors.

HUBERT DE MONTILLE *Rugiens*★★

■1er Cru	1 ha	3600	6 Ⓓ ⅏ ↓
⑥④ 69 **72 76 78 82** 82			

A remarkable success bearing in mind the 1983 vintage. Harvested at the optimum moment and very skilfully vinified it now displays uncommon finesse and balance. Should begin to open up more quickly than some 1983s but will not reach its peak for many years. (1983) ✔ Pommard Grands Epenots Rouge, Volnay Pérazols/Champans/Mitans Rouge, Volnay Premier Cru Rouge, Bourgogne Rouge.
↞ Hubert de Montille, Volnay, 21190 Meursault; tel. 80 22 27 72 ⅂ By appt.

DOMAINE PARENT *Epenots*★★

■1er Cru	10 ha	40 000	5 Ⓓ ⅏ ↓
78 79 80 81 82 83			

Rich in aromas, with nuances of new wood, cherry and pepper, over a firm and very full body, with a deep colour. Should keep well. (1982)
↞ Dom. Parent, 21630 Pommard; tel. 80 22 15 08 ⅂ By appt.

CHATEAU DE POMMARD★★

■	20 ha	65 000	6 Ⓓ ⅏ ↓
★76 ⑦⑧ **79 80 81** ★82 83			

Dark velvet colour; firm aromas of resin, leather, fruit stones, laurel and pepper. Smooth and very distinguished on the palate. Beginning to open out. (1979)
↞ Jean-Louis Laplanche, 21630 Pommard; tel. 80 22 07 99 ⅂ By appt.

MICHEL REBOURGEON★

■	0.7 ha	4300	5 Ⓓ ⅏ ↓
★76 78 79 ⑧② 82			

Rugged; vinified from grapes which were not de-stemmed. Fairly mature, slightly musky nose. Still a little astringency on the palate, which tempts one to leave it to age. (1982)
↞ Daniel Rebourgeon, 21630 Pommard; tel. 80 22 75 39 ⅂ By appt.

DANIEL REBOURGEON★

■	1.4 ha	8400	5 Ⓓ ⅏ ↓
73 74 75 76 78 ⑦⑨ 80			

A very appealing wine, already drinkable, smooth and round on the palate, despite its firm tannin. Fruity aromas of bush peach, fruit stones and raspberry over a background of vanilla, wth a peppery finish. This bottle was selected at the Tastevinage in 1984. (1982)
↞ Daniel Rebourgeon, 21630 Pommard; tel. 80 22 75 39 ⅂ By appt.

JEAN TARTOIS★★

■	2 ha	12 000	5 Ⓓ ⅏ ↓
76 79 ⑧② 83			

Deep colour and rich aromas of soft new oak, cherry, vanilla and pepper. Very pleasing on the palate, with good balance between richness and tannin. Will improve even further with time. (1982)
↞ Jean Tartois, 21630 Pommard; tel. 80 22 11 70 ⅂ By appt.

DOMAINE DE VAUX *Clos Micault*★

■1er Cru	2.17 ha	14 000	5 Ⓓ ⅏ ↓
59 76 78 79 82			

Has already developed considerably and is drinking well now. Woody aromas, with notes of pistachio and pepper, and a soft, smooth, well-balanced flavour. (1982)
↞ Dom. de Vaux, 21630 Pommard; tel. 80 21 11 08 ⅂ By appt.

NOEMIE VERNAUX★

■		5000	6
★79 ★81			

A full, soft fruity wine with clean aromas and flavour and a reasonable finish. (1979)
↞ Ets Noémie Vernaux, Rue de Vérottes, 21200 Beaune; tel. 80 22 28 50 ⅂ By appt. Closed 15 Dec. to end Feb.

GILBERT VIOLOT★

■	0.35 ha	2400	5 Ⓓ ⅏ ↓

The purple flush of youth is still clearly apparent in the colour of this wine. Intense, fruity aromas of redcurrant, wild cherry and raspberry and clean but still undeveloped flavours. Should be left several years. (1982)
↞ Gilbert Violot, 21630 Pommard; tel. 80 22 03 49 ⅂ By appt. Closed Sun.

RENE VIRELY-ARCELAIN
Clos des Arvelets★★

■1er Cru	0.88 ha	5500	5 Ⓓ ⅏ ↓
64 66 69 71 72 73 76 78 ⑦⑨ 79 82 83			

Characterized by a round, smooth flavour, with delicate, mature aromas of raisins and bran, and a trace of musk. (1979)
↞ René Virely-Arcelain, 21630 Pommard; tel. 80 22 19 71 ⅂ By appt.

BERNARD VIRELY-ROUGEOT★

■	1.08 ha	6500	5 Ⓓ ⅏ ↓
★76 78 ★79 82 83			

This 1982 has matured quickly and is now ready to drink. Complex animal and fruit aromas with notes of cherry and vanilla over a background of oak. On the palate it shows the freshness and lightness of its vintage. (1982)
↞ Bernard Virely-Rougeot, 21630 Pommard; tel. 80 22 34 34 ⅂ By appt.

Volnay

Barely a kilometer to the south of Pommard, tucked into the crook of a hill, Volnay is one of Burgundy's picture-postcard villages. Less well-known than its neighbour, the standard of its extremely refined appellation wines is just as high, varying between the lightness of a Santenots in the neighbouring commune of Meursault, to the solidity and strength of a Clos des Chênes or a Champans. The Clos des Soixante Ouvrées is also very famous, and this gives us the opportunity to give the derivation of the 'ouvrée' (4.28 ares), the unit used to define the price of vine-growing land. This ancient measure, dating from the Middle Ages, corresponds to the area that could be worked by one man in a day.

DOMAINE R. ET M. AMPEAU
Santenots★★

■1er Cru	1.5 ha	8000	5 ⊪ ↓

*73 *76 77 **78** 79 *80 80

An interesting, even surprising wine with a rather severe character, dark colour and, after being allowed to breathe in the glass, heavy scents of roast coffee and burning. Complex palate of black cherries mingled with pepper and spices. Full-bodied flavour. (1980).
➦ R. et M. Ampeau, 21190 Meursault; tel. 80 21 20 35 ☎ By appt.

DOMAINE MARQUIS
D'ANGERVILLE *Clos des Ducs*★★★

■1er Cru

Dark colour and a very reserved nose hinting at spices and vanilla. Full on the palate, although the flavours are still not fully knit. In three or four years' time it should develop marvellously. (1982)
➦ M. le Marquis d'Angerville, Volnay, 21190 Meursault; tel. 80 22 07 53 ☎ No visitors.

DOMAINE MARQUIS
D'ANGERVILLE *Champans*★★

■1er Cru

Ruby-red colour and an undeveloped bouquet with aromas of small soft fruit, dominated by cherry and blackcurrant. On the palate, it has body and a certain fullness for its vintage, with a very fresh, kirsch-flavoured finish. Elegant, rather feminine; will improve further with bottle age. (1982)
➦ M. le Marquis d'Angerville, Volnay, 21190 Meursault; tel. 80 22 07 53 ☎ No visitors.

HOSPICES DE BEAUNE
Cuvée Jehan de Massol★

■1er Cru	1.54 ha	4590	6 ⊪ ↓

In 1669 the king's councillor, Jehan de Massol, left all his possessions to the Hôtel-Dieu, for the succour of the poor. This cuvée which bears his name is a typical Volnay, much sought-after by connoisseurs. The 1984, with a strong flavour of new oak, will need a long time to reach its peak. (1984)
➦ Dom. Viti. Hospices de Beaune, Rue de l'Hôtel-Dieu, 21200 Beaune; tel. 80 24 75 75 ☎ No visitors.

HOSPICES DE BEAUNE
Cuvée Général Muteau★★

■	1.72 ha	4050	6 ⊪ ↓

One of the generals of the notorious Muteau family who preferred the glory of wine growing to that of the battlefield, left a large property to the Hospices de Beaune. The 1984 cuvée which bears his name won unanimous approval, even though it was the most expensive at the annual auction, fetching 31000 francs a hogshead. Scents of violet, cherry, spices and new wood, with full body. (1984)
➦ Dom. Viti. Hospices de Beaune, Rue de l'Hôtel-Dieu, 21200 Beaune; tel. 80 24 75 75 ☎ No visitors.

HOSPICES DE BEAUNE
Cuvée Blondeau★★

■	2.54 ha	4860	6 ⊪ ↓

Among the first to be harvested, and already bright by the time of the auction, this 1984 cuvée had the perfumed charm and customary soft flavours of a Volnay. (1984)
➦ Dom. Viti. Hospices de Beaune, Rue de l'Hôtel-Dieu, 21200 Beaune; tel. 80 24 75 75 ☎ No visitors.

HOSPICES DE BEAUNE
Cuvée Gauvin★

■1er Cru	1.4 ha	5940	6 ⊪ ↓

The finesse of this 1984 Volnay-Santenots cuvée was remarked upon at the pre-auction tasting. It had all the customary freshness of its *terroir* and a very long flavour. Should keep well. (1984)
➦ Dom. Viti. Hospices de Beaune, Rue de l'Hôtel-Dieu, 21200 Beaune; tel. 80 24 75 75 ☎ No visitors.

DOMAINE BOUCHARD PERE ET
FILS *Ancienne Cuvée Carnot*★

■1er Cru	3.72 ha	15600	6 D ⊪ ↓

76 78 79 80 82

Dark red with a bouquet of new oak and vanilla. Predominantly oaky flavour marked by a tannic note at the finish. Fine balance. (1979)
➦ Bouchard Père et fils, Au Château, 21200 Beaune; tel. 80 22 14 41 ☎ By appt. Closed Aug. and 1 week in Feb.

CHANSON PERE ET FILS★

■	5 D ⊪ ↓

71 78 ⑦⑨ 80 81 82 83

Firm structure which will enable it to keep. It still has a raw, cherry flavour, and the bouquet has scarcely begun to open out. Keep for a long time. (1982)
➦ MM. Chanson Père et Fils, 10–12 Rue Paul-Chanson, 21200 Beaune; tel. 80 22 33 00 ☎ No visitors.

DOMAINE FELIX CLERGET
Le Clos Martin★★

■	5 ⊪ ↓

74

An attractive wine with animal aromas of fur and hide. Elegant, balanced flavour. (1974)
➦ Félix Clerget, 21630 Pommard; tel. 80 22 16 07 ☎ No visitors.

ARMANDE DOUHAIRET *Champans*★

■1er Cru   0.9ha 3500 ⑤ Ⓓ ⬤ ↓

71 74 **76** *78 *79 80 **81** ⑧② 83

Has been given a long fermentation to offset the general lightness of the vintage. Refined violet aroma typical of the *terroir* with a note of new oak; the palate is still tannic and vigorous. A bottle to be left to age. (1982) ✔ Pommard Premier Cru, Meursault Santenots.
◕┐ *Mlle* Armande Douhairet, Monthélie, 21190 Meursault; tel. 80 21 21 01 ☎ By appt.

DOMAINE GLANTENAY *Brouillards*★

■1er Cru   1.2ha 1000 ⑤ Ⓓ ⬤ ↓

*76 *78 *82 *83

Typical of its vintage; has an intense colour of blackcurrant juice, a nose of dried fruits and a harsh tannic impression on the palate. Patience is required, as it should be left for a decade. (1983)
◕┐ SC *MM*. Glantenay et Fils, Volnay, 21190 Meursault; tel. 80 22 08 44 ☎ By appt.

GRIVELET PERE ET FILS★

■   500 ④ Ⓓ ⬤ ↓

Typical Volnay aromas of violet and oak combine with fresh butter and notes of blackcurrant and pepper. Firmer in the mouth than most 1982s and able to age well. (1982)
◕┐ *MM*. Grivelet Père et Fils, 21640 Vougeot; tel. 80 72 42 72 ☎ By appt.

DOMAINE MICHEL LAFARGE★★

■   3ha 15000 ⑤ Ⓓ ⬤

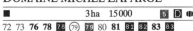

72 73 **76 78** ⁷⁸ ⑦⑨ ⁷⁹ 80 **81** ⁸¹ ⁸² **83** ⁸³

This 1982 is fuller and more deeply coloured than most wines of this vintage. Dense fruity character with a long fragrant flavour of flowers and crushed red fruit. (1982) ✔ Bourgogne Aligoté. Bourgogne Passe-tout-grain, Volnay Premier Cru.
◕┐ Michel Lafarge, Volnay, 21190 Meursault; tel. 80 22 04 70 ☎ By appt.

MOILLARD★★

■   48000 ⑤ ⬤ ↓

⑦⑨ **80 81 82 83**

Showing the finesse of a mature wine with initial aromas of musk and a trace of candied fruit and dried flowers. A good bottle to drink with game birds or stews. (1980)
◕┐ SARL Moillard, 5 Rue F.-Mignotte, 21700 Nuits-St-Georges; tel. 80 61 03 34 ☎ No visitors.

HUBERT DE MONTILLE *Champans*★

■1er Cru   0.75ha 2000 ⑤ Ⓓ ⬤ ↓

⑥④ 69 72 **76 78 82** ⁸²

Still a very firm red colour; well-developed nose of crushed red fruit with a round, smooth flavour. Already beginning to drink well but will not reach its peak for another five years. (1979)
◕┐ Hubert de Montille, Volnay, 21190 Meursault; tel. 80 22 27 72 ☎ By appt.

PATRIARCHE PERE ET FILS★

■   3000 ⑤ Ⓓ

All the freshness of the 1982 vintage and retains its original fruity character. Finishes with great finesse. (1982)
◕┐ Patriarche Père et Fils, Rue du Collège, 21200 Beaune; tel. 80 22 23 20 ☎ By appt. Closed 15 Dec. to end Feb.

DOMAINE DE LA POUSSE-D'OR
Clos de la Pousse d'Or★★

■1er Cru   2.2ha 9000 ⑤ Ⓓ ⬤ ↓

72 *76 *78 *81 *82

Vinified with consummate skill ,this wine has acquired an international following. The 1982 shows complex animal and game aromas with notes of truffle and vanilla. Still very young on the palate with a clean fruity strike. (1982)
✔ Volnay Premier Cru en Caillerets, Pommard Premier Cru les Jarollières Santenay Premier Cru Clos Tavannes.
◕┐ C Dom. de la Pousse d'Or, Volnay, 21190 Meursault; tel. 80 22 10 73 ☎ By appt. ◕┐ Gérard Potel (manager).

DOMAINE PRIEUR BRUNET
Santenots★★

■1er Cru   0.50ha 3000 ⑤ Ⓓ ⬤ ↓

78 79 **81** ⑧② **83 84**

The characteristic Volnay violet scent is opening out in this wine, which has an appealing, clear red colour. Ought to retain its fresh, fruity character for several years. (1982)
◕┐ Dom. Prieur-Brunet, 21590 Santenay; tel. 80 20 60 56 ☎ Daily 10.00–12.00/14.00–19.00.

DOMAINE JACQUES PRIEUR
Clos des Santenots★★

■1er Cru   1ha 5000 ⑤ Ⓓ ⬤ ↓

76 ⑦⑧ *80 81 ⁸² 83

Volnay-Santenots is traditionally harvested within the parish of Meursault but is every bit as good as the other Volnay Premiers Crus. This 1982 should last twenty years, according to expert tasting opinion. (1982) ✔ Chevalier Montrachet Grand Cru, Volnay Champans Premier Cru, Musigny, Beaune Clos de la Feguine Premier Cru.
◕┐ Jacques Prieur, 2 Rue des Santenots, 21190 Meursault; tel. 80 21 23 85 ☎ By appt. Closed Aug.

REGIS ROSSIGNOL *Les Brouillards*★

■1er Cru   0.4ha 1000 ⑤ Ⓓ ⬤ ↓

*76 *78 ⑦⑨ ⁷⁹ 80 **81 82 83**

This 1980 premier cru, which has now fully opened up, is a clear bright red, with musky, spicy aromas and a refined but not overthin flavour. An ideal wine to drink with game birds. (1980) ✔ Bourgogne Rouge, Bourgogne Passe-tout-grain, Beaune Premier Cru, Savigny-les-Beaune.
◕┐ Régis Rossignol, Volnay, 21190 Meursault; tel. 80 22 24 71 ☎ By appt.

DOMAINE MICHEL ET YVES ROSSIGNOL★

■	3ha	14440	5 D ⑪ ↓

76 ⑦⑧ ★80 81 82 83

An appealing wine with a light red colour and aromas of blackberries. The acidity is good, but lacks body on the palate. It may be drunk now, but will improve if kept for at least two years. (1982) ✔ Beaune Premier Cru Les Theurons, Côtes de Beaune Clos de Pierres Blanches, Bourgogne Rouge, Monthélie Les Champs Fuillot. ♠ Michel et Yves Rossignol, Rue de l'Aubrevoir, 21190 Meursault; tel. 80 22 30 41 ☎ By appt. Closed second fortnight in July.

JOSEPH VOILLOT★★

■1er Cru	0.75ha	3600	5 D ⑪ ↓

This fine Premier Cru comes from the 1978 vintage – one of the best recent years in Burgundy. Refined bouquet of musk and leather with notes of pepper and vanilla. Smooth, balanced flavour with pronounced raspberry fruitiness. Not yet at its peak and should be kept. (1978) ✔ Volnay and Volnay Champans, Pommard and Pommard Premier Cru, Meursault Premier Cru, Bourgogne Rouge. ♠ Joseph Voillot, Volnay, 21190 Meursault; tel. 80 22 24 30 ☎ By appt ♠Joseph et Maurius Voillot.

Monthélie

The deep Combe de St-Romain marks the southern boundary of the major red-wine area of the Côte de Beaune. The small village of Monthélie, on the south-facing slope, produces red and white wines of a very high standard at extremely reasonable prices.

HOSPICES DE BEAUNE
Cuvée Lébelin★

■	0.88ha	4050	6 ⑪ ↓

Very typical Monthélie with pronounced fruit and a harmonious structure. (1984) ♠ Dom. Viti. Hospices de Beaune, Rue de l'Hôtel-Dieu, 21200 Beaune; tel. 80 24 75 75 ☎ No visitors.

ERIC BOUSSEY★★★

■	1ha	5000	4 D ⑪ ↓

79 81 ★82 82 83 83

A 1983 *cuvée* of exceptional quality, which expresses to the full, the rich, intense character of its vintage. (1983) ✔ Pommard, Monthélie Premier Cru, Puligny-Montrachet Premier Cru.

♠ Eric Boussey, Monthélie, 21190 Meursault; tel. 80 21 60 70 ☎ By appt.

XAVIER BOUZERAND★★★

■	3ha	7000	4 D ⑪ ↓

76 78 79 ⑧⓪ 81 ★82

This wine grower is also a sculptor and his 1980 Monthélie deserves praise for its exceptional quality. Delightful aromas of musk, blackcurrant, fruit stones and pear with real finesse and roundness on the palate. (1980) ✔ Meursault, Auxey-Duresses, Monthélie Premier Cru, Bourgogne Passe-tout-grain. ♠ Xavier Bouzerand, Monthélie, 21190 Meursault; tel. 80 21 20 08 ☎ By appt.

JEHAN CHANGARNIER★★

■	4ha	11000	4 D ⑪ ↓

76 78 79 82 83

Firm structure and will undoubtedly keep for a long time. (1983) ✔ Monthélie Champs-Fulliots Premier Cru, Meursault, Auxey-Duresses Premier Cru. ♠ Jehan Changarnier, Monthélie, 21190 Meursault; tel. 80 21 22 18 ☎ By appt.

MARCEL ET MICHEL DESCHAMPS★★

■	5ha	20000	5 D ⑪ ↓

78 ★79 83

Very concentrated, with aromas of grapes and figs and a note of almond shells. Should be laid down for ten years. (1983) ♠ Marcel et Michel Deschamps, Monthélie, 21190 Meursault; tel. 80 21 28 60 ☎ By appt.

ARMANDE DOUHAIRET★★

■	1.9ha	8500	4 D ⑪ ↓

71 74 76 78 79 80 81 ⑧② 83

This 1981 displays all the qualities of its vintage; great finesse and delicacy, without too much softness. Striking flavours of blackcurrant and violet; has already developed good texture on the palate. A delight now, but may be kept for a long

Côte de Beaune (South Central Region)

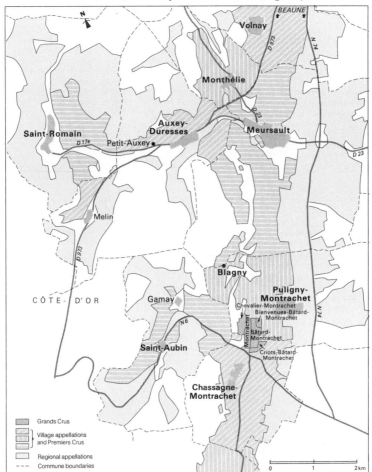

Grands Crus

Village appellations
and Premiers Crus

Regional appellations

--- Commune boundaries

0   1   2 km

time. (1981) ✔ Pommard Premier Cru, Volnay Champans, Meursault Santenots.
↦ *Mlle* Armande Douhairet, Monthélie, 21190 Meursault; tel. 80 21 21 01 ⲇ By appt.

CHATEAU DE MONTHELIE★★

	5 ha	3000	4 D ⦿ ↓
59 **61 62 64** ★66 ★71 ★72 ★73			

A skilful blend of quality vines, long vinification and new oak casks, have given this 1982 a deep purple colour, an aroma of oak and vanilla and a nice full palate, with a great deal of finesse. Will keep for a long time. (1982)
↦ Robert de Suremain, Monthélie, 21190 Meursault; tel. 80 21 23 32 ⲇ By appt.

MAURICE PINQUIER★★

	2 ha	3500	4 D ▤ ⦿ ↓
78 ★**79** **81** ★**82 83**			

This wine, which is keeping well, has all the freshness of its vintage on the nose and palate. Although it may be enjoyed already this is a bottle which will last and age further. (1982) ✔ Meursault, Bourgogne Aligoté, Bourgogne Rouge.

↦ Maurice Pinquier, Monthélie, 21190 Meursault; tel. 80 21 22 78 ⲇ Daily 8.00–20.00.

MAISON PIERRE PORROT★★

■1er Cru	2 ha	300	4 ⦿ ↓
79 80 ★**81 82 83**			

Has spicy aromas and a fine colour which make it tempting to drink. It should not, however, be opened too soon as it is capable of ageing. If you cannot resist open for at least three hours before serving. (1982)
↦ Pierre Porrot, Monthélie, 21190 Meursault; tel. 80 21 22 63 ⲇ By appt.

HENRI POTINET-AMPEAU★★

	2 ha	15000	4 D ▤ ⦿ ↓
★72 ★73 74 76 **78** ⑦⑨ ★**82** ★**83**			

Well matured; just ready for drinking. Fine colour of autumn vine leaves and still has its classic aromas of small red fruit. On the palate, pleasing, soft and easy to drink. (1980) ✔ Volnay Clos-de-Chênes, Pommard Pezerolles, Auxey-Duresses, Meursault Perrières, Meursault Charmes.

↦ Henri Potinet-Ampeau, Monthélie, 21190 Meursault; tel. 80 21 23 50 **Ŧ** No visitors.

DOMAINE ROPITEAU-MIGNON
Clos des Champs-Fulliot★★

| ■ | | 1 ha | 5500 | 5 ⦀ ⬇ |

The wines of Monthélie deserve to be better known. Once sold under the Volnay appellation, this is a fairly strong 1982 in terms of both colour and flavour with an aroma which has remained young and fruity. It possesses an overall harmony which makes it ready for drinking. (1982)
↦ *MM.* Ropiteau-Mignon, 21190 Meursault; tel. 80 21 23 94 **Ŧ** Daily 9.00–19.30. Closed winter.

CHARLES VIENOT★★

| ☐ | | | 600 | 4 D |
| 80 | | | | |

Very little white Monthelie is produced but it is worth getting to know for its honey and vanilla bouquet and rich full-bodied flavour. This example still appears very young without the cloying heaviness which frequently marks these wines. (1980)
↦ Ets Charles Vienot, 5 Quai Dumorey, 21700 Nuits-St-Georges; tel. 80 62 31 05 **Ŧ** By appt.

Auxey-Duresses

Auxey, on the southern flank of the Combe de St-Romain, has vineyards on two slopes. The Premier Cru red wines Les Duresses and Le Val are perhaps the most famous of the wines grown there. Some excellent white wines are produced on the Meursault slope; although lesser known than those from the larger appellations, they are just as worthy of interest. Annual production is 1000 hectolitres of white wine and 3000 of red.

CIE DES VINS D'AUTREFOIS★★

| ☐ | | | | 5 ⦀ ⬇ |

The 1984 vintage was successful for white wines, here giving an attractive golden-green colour and aromas of mint, honeysuckle and green pasture. Good acidity on the palate, with enough body to keep for a long time. (1984)
↦ Cie des Vins d'Autrefois, 9 Rue Celer, 21200 Beaune; tel. 80 22 21 31 **Ŧ** No visitors.

HOSPICES DE BEAUNE *Cuvée Boillot*★

| ■ | | 0.66 ha | 1080 | 6 ⦀ ⬇ |

Very much enjoyed by the tasters for its fruitiness and fullness, this cuvée, which is produced in tiny quantities (four barrels), set the Hospices auction alight and, sold for more than most of the Beaune and Pommard wines.
↦ Dom. Viti. Hospices de Beaune, Rue de l'Hôtel-Dieu, 21200 Beaune; tel. 80 24 75 75 **Ŧ** No visitors.

JULIEN COCHE-DEBORD ET FILS★★

| ■ | | 0.5 ha | 2700 | 4 D ⦀ ⬇ |
| 71 *76 **78** 79 82 **83 84** | | | | |

Long vatting has made this 1982 into a solidly structured wine with plenty of extract. It has acquired a deep, bright colour, full aromas and flavour. Should keep well. (1982) ✓ Bourgogne Rouge, Meursault, Monthélie.
↦ *MM.* J. Coche-Debord et Fils, 5 Rue de Mazeray, 21190 Meursault; tel. 80 21 22 38 **Ŧ** By apt.

ANDRE ET BERNARD LABRY★

| ■ | | 4 ha | 9000 | 4 D ⬛ ⦀ ⬇ |
| *76 **78** *⑧⓪ **80** *81 82 83 | | | | |

Light orange hints enrich the colour of this wine with a plummy nose and aromas of kirsch and fruit stones on the palate. A very mature wine with a fairly tannic edge; should age well. (1980) ✓ Crémant de Bourgogne, Bourgogne Passetout-grain, Bourgogne Hautes-Côtes de Beaune Blanc and Rouge, Bourgogne Aligoté.
↦ André et Bernard Labry, Melin-Auxey-Duresses, 21190 Meursault; tel. 80 21 21 60 **Ŧ** By appt.

CLAUDE MARECHAL★★

| ☐ | | 1 ha | 6000 | 3 D ⬛ ⬇ |
| 76 **78** 79 82 **83** 83 | | | | |

The Southern slopes of Auxey-Duresses, on which white grapes are grown, are similar to those of Meursault, whereas the red wine production area borders Monthélie. This white 1983 does indeed have something of a Meursault about it with its delightful aromas of honey and mild spices, and its refreshing acidity on the palate, with a rich alcoholic support. (1983)
↦ Claude Maréchal, Bligny-les-Beaune, 21200 Beaune; 80 21 44 37 **Ŧ** By appt.

CLAUDE MARECHAL★★

| ■ | | 2 ha | 10500 | 4 D ⬛ ⦀ ⬇ |
| ⑦③ 76 **78** 79 82 **83** 83 | | | | |

Before the introduction of 'appellations d'origine', the red wines of Auxey-Duresses were often sold as Volnay, without the latter's reputation suffering as a result. This 1983 has a very fine, intense, cherry-red colour and the bouquet of a great wine combining spices, fruit stones and liquorice. Its power on the palate needs to be toned down by ageing. (1983) ✓ Auxey-les-Beaune, Savigny-les-Beaune, Ladoix, Bourgogne Rouge.
↦ Claude Maréchal, Bligny-les-Beaune, 21200 Beaune; tel. 80 21 44 37 **Ŧ** By appt.

MICHEL PRUNIER★

| ■ | | 2 ha | 10800 | 4 D ⦀ ⬇ |
| 76 **78** 79 81 82 | | | | |

An honest colour and rustic nose, with a pronounced redcurrant aroma. The grapes are not destemmed here which gives this wine a good firm structure. Although the finish is a little harsh, everything points to this bottle having a fine future. To be drunk in two years' time. (1982) ✓ Côtes de Beaune-Villages.
↦ Michel Prunier, Route Nationale, Auxey-Duresses, 21190 Meursault; tel. 80 21 21 05 **Ŧ** By appt. Closed Christmas and New Year.

MICHEL PRUNIER★

□	0.5 ha	6000	4 D ⑪ ⚲

74 **78** 82 83

Green-gold colour and an undeveloped nose. Brisk, elegant flavour with aromas of small green pears. Good acidity and plenty of fat. (1983)
↘ Michel Prunier, Route Nationale, Auxey-Duresses, 21190 Meursault; tel. 80 21 21 05 ⟄ By appt. Closed Christmas and New Year.

St-Romain

These vineyards are located between the Côte and the Hautes-Côtes. St-Romain wines, especially the whites, are, according to the growers, 'always clean and fruity, with a promise of hidden charm'. The location is magnificent and well worth a visit.

DOMAINE GERMAIN PERE ET FILS★

□	1.5 ha	6000	4 D ▮ ⑪ ⚲

73 74 ★**76** 78 79 **81 82 83**

Straw-yellow colour; still somewhat dumb on the nose but sharp, clean flavours of honey, lime and grilled almonds. Slightly alcoholic finish. Needs two years before the full qualities will reveal themselves. (1979) ✔ Beaune, St-Romain Blanc, Bourgogne Aligoté.
↘ Dom. Germain Père et Fils, St-Romain, 21190 Meursault; tel. 80 21 22 11 ⟄ By appt.

DOMAINE GERMAIN PERE ET FILS★

■	6 ha	21 600	4 D ▮ ⑪ ⚲

★76 **78 79** ★**81** 82 ⑧③

Slightly orange hue and a nose of dried leaves and damp earth. Fleshy and full-bodied on the palate, with a touch of bitter almond in the finish. A rather rustic wine that goes well with everyday fare. (1981) ✔ Beaune, St-Romain Blanc, Bourgogne Aligoté.
↘ Dom. Germain Père et Fils, St-Romain, 21190 Meursault; tel. 80 21 22 11 ⟄ By appt.

Meursault

Meursault is the largest village of the Côte de Beaune and the point at which white wine production really begins. More than 15 000 hectolitres are made a year, including some world-famous Premiers Crus: Les Perrières, Les Charmes, Les Poruzots, Les Genevrières and La Goutte d'Or. All of them combine seemingly contradictory qualities; subtlety and strength, a bouquet of fern and roasted almonds, the ability to be drunk young and yet also to be laid down for some years.

The small chateaux that are still to be found in Meursault are evidence of former prosperity and bear witness to the fame that these wines have always enjoyed. The traditional celebration of La Paulée, which began as a communal meal taken at the end of the harvest, has now grown into a great event, which takes place on the third day of the Hospices de Beaune wine sales.

ROBERT AMPEAU
La Pièce Sous le Bois★★

□	0.8 ha	3500	5 D ⑪ ⚲

71 ★⑦⑥ **77** ★78 79 **80 81 82** 83

Intense aroma of ambergris and truffles against a vanilla background, and strong, firm flavour. (1977) ✔ Puligny-Montrachet Combettes, Volnay Santenots, Pommard, Savigny-les-Beaune.
↘ Robert Ampeau, Rue du Cromin, 21190 Meursault; tel. 80 21 20 35 ⟄ By appt.

CIE DES VINS D'AUTREFOIS★

□		5 ⑪ ⚲

Pronounced classic Meursault aromas of acacia, honey, Cox's orange pippin and ripe banana. Attractive, delicate colour, and smooth, harmonious flavour. (1984)
↘ Cie des Vins d'Autrefois, 9 Rue Celer, 21200 Beaune; tel. 80 22 21 31 ⟄ No visitors.

CIE DES VINS D'AUTREFOIS
Perrières★

□1er Cru		6 ⑪ ⚲

Complex aromas of hazel and toasted almond, with notes of privet and ivy leaves, indicate that this wine will develop an exceptional bouquet when mature. Smooth, with a young fruity flavour on the palate. Should open out beautifully in five years time. (1984)
↘ Cie des Vins d'Autrefois, 9 Rue Celer, 21200 Beaune; tel. 80 22 21 31 ⟄ No visitors.

CIE DES VINS D'AUTREFOIS
Genevrières★★

□1er Cru		6 ⑪ ⚲

This Meursault premier cru is considered by many to be the equal of a grand cru. Its long, deep flavours are intensified by this great vintage; rich and persistent enough to be served with all fish sauces. Will be even better if kept for a few years. (1983)
↘ Cie des Vins d'Autrefois, 9 Rue Celer, 21200 Beaune; tel. 80 22 21 31 ⟄ No visitors.

HOSPICES DE BEAUNE
Cuvée Philippe le Bon★★★

□1er Cru	0.57 ha	1350	6 ⑪ ⚲

The name of the third Grand Duke of Burgundy, the protector of Nicolas Rollin, has been given to one of the most prestigious Meursault *cuvées* produced by the Hospices. This small lot of five casks was already showing well at the pre-auction tasting in 1984. (1984)
↘ Dom. Viti. Hospices de Beaune, Rue de l'Hôtel-Dieu, 21200 Beaune; tel. 80 24 75 75 ⟄ No visitors.

HOSPICES DE BEAUNE
Cuvée Baudot★★

| ☐1er Cru | 1.48ha | 4590 | 🔲6 ⑪ ↓ |

Although it had barely begun to develop at the time of the November 1984 sale, this fine Meursault nonetheless gave a glimpse of its future qualities; its rich aromas and subtle flavours. By December the wine was starting to come out of its shell. (1984)
🕯 Dom. Viti. Hospices de Beaune, Rue de l'Hôtel-Dieu, 21200 Beaune; tel. 80 24 75 75 ⏳ No visitors.

HOSPICES DE BEAUNE
Cuvée Bahèzre de Lanlay★★

| ☐1er Cru | 0.9ha | 3870 | 🔲6 ⑪ ↓ |

Richer and already further advanced than the village Meursault wines at the time of the sale, this wine won favourable comment for its bouquet of acacia, revette apples and honey. (1984)
🕯 Dom. Viti. Hospices de Beaune, Rue de l'Hôtel-Dieu, 21200 Beaune; tel. 80 24 75 75 ⏳ No visitors.

HOSPICES DE BEAUNE
Cuvée Albert Grivault★★★

| ☐1er Cru | 0.55ha | 1350 | 🔲6 ⑪ ↓ |

The Hospices Meursault-Charmes are always exceptionally subtle wines with considerable aromatic finesse. The 1984 Grivault cuvée – a mere five hogshead – soared to a price of 50000 francs a hogshead at the auction. (1984)
🕯 Dom. Viti. Hospices de Beaune, Rue de l'Hôtel-Dieu, 21200 Beaune; tel. 80 24 75 75 ⏳ No visitors.

HOSPICES DE BEAUNE
Cuvée Loppin★★

| ☐ | 0.73ha | 1350 | 🔲6 ⑪ ↓ |

This 1984 cuvée was further advanced than its peers at the time of the sale and delighted the tasters with its intensely fruity qualities, fine-grained texture and length on the palate. (1984)
🕯 Dom. Viti. Hospices de Beaune, Rue de l'Hôtel Dieu, 21200 Beaune; tel. 80 24 75 75 ⏳ No visitors.

HOSPICES DE BEAUNE
Cuvée Jéhan Humblot★★

| ☐ | 0.6ha | 1160 | 🔲6 🄳 ↓ |

When tasted in November 1984 this cuvée was still undergoing fermentation. By the end of December, however, the fermentation was completed and the wine's fine golden tint and complex aromas of grilled almond, vanilla and grapefruit began to emerge. Very promising. (1984)
🕯 Dom. Viti. Hospices de Beaune, Rue de l'Hôtel-Dieu, 21200 Beaune; tel. 80 24 75 75 ⏳ No visitors.

HOSPICES DE BEAUNE
Cuvée Goureau★★

| ☐ | 0.5ha | 1620 | 🔲6 ⑪ ↓ |

Still clouded and gassy at tasting and in the middle of fermentation. One month later, however the wines began to clarify, and became easier to taste. This cuvée had a finely tuned flavour with good acidity and a most attractive bouquet of flowers, fruits and spices. (1984)

🕯 Dom. Viti. Hospices de Beaune, Rue de l'Hôtel-Dieu, 21200 Beaune; tel. 80 24 75 75 ⏳ No visitors.

LEONCE BOCQUET★★

| ☐ | | 3000 | 🔲5 🄳 ⑪ ↓ |

71 78 79 ★81 ★82 ⑧⑤ 🔲83

Strongly flavoured, highly aromatic and rather rich in alcohol. Clearly marked by the vintage and the terrain. Needs to be left to settle down for several years. (1983)
🕯 Petits-Fils de Léonce Bocquet, 29 Bvd Clemenceau, 21200 Beaune; tel. 80 22 28 49 ⏳ Mon.–Fri. 9.30–11.30/14.00–17.30. Closed Dec. to end Feb.

HUBERT BOUZEREAU-GRUERE
Le Limozin★★

| ☐ | 10ha | 48000 | 🔲4 🄳 ⑪ ↓ |

79 82 🔲83 84

The strong gold colour of generous wine, aromas of hazelnut and honey with a most warming flavour – Qualities which together add up to a wine that will keep for many years. (1983)
✔ Meursault Charmes, Bourgogne Aligoté, Chassagne-Montrachet, Corton Bressandes.
🕯 Hubert Bouzereau-Gruère, 22A Rue de la Velle, 21190 Meursault; tel. 80 21 20 05 ⏳ By appt.

PHILIPPE BOUZEREAU★★

| ☐ | | 2ha | 🔲5 🄳 ⑪ ↓ |

73 76 78 80 🔲83

After you have admired the green-gold colour, you will enjoy a nose of lime. This Meursault is a little harsh on the palate and not fully developed but with its excellent ingredients will become a great bottle. (1983) ✔ Puligny-Montrachet Premier Cru, Bourgogne Pinot Chardonnay, Chassagne-Montrachet, Corton Bressandes, Bourgogne.
🕯 Philippe Bouzereau, 15 Place de l'Europe, 21190 Meursault; tel. 80 21 20 32 ⏳ By appt. Closed end Aug.

YVES BOYER-MARTENOT
Les Narvaux★

| ☐ | 1ha | 3300 | 🔲4 🄳 ⑪ ↓ |

78 79 82 ★🔲83

A warm, mouth-filling 1983 which will need some ageing to acquire more finesse. (1983) ✔ Meursault Perrières, Meursault Charmes, Meursault Genevrières, Meursault l'Ormeau.
🕯 Yves Boyer-Martenot, 17 Rue Mazeray, 21190 Meursault; tel. 80 21 26 25 ⏳ No visitors.

MICHEL BUISSON-CHARLES★

| ☐ | 2ha | 11000 | 🔲4 🄳 ⑪ ↓ |

76 79 81 82 ⑧ 🔲83

This 1983 has avoided the excesses of its vintage. It is fruity, balanced and although pleasant to drink now, will also keep well. (1983)
🕯 Michel Buisson-Charles, 3 Rue de la Velle, 21190 Meursault; tel. 80 21 22 32 ⏳ By appt.

CHANSON PERE ET FILS★★

☐   5 D ⋒ 🍷

66 73 78 79 80 ⑧② 8̲2̲ 83

Intense aromas and a satisfying roundness on the palate. Leave it to age a little. (1983).
⌐ *MM.* Chanson Père et Fils, 10–12 Rue Paul-Chanson, 21200 Beaune; tel. 80 22 33 00 ☓ No visitors.

CHANSON PERE ET FILS★★

☐1er Cru   D ⋒ 🍷

70 78 79 ⑧② 8̲2̲ 83

Plenty of substance revealed in the intense, fluid aromas and the warm, smooth palate. Avoid temptation: do not drink it too soon. (1983)
⌐ *MM.* Chanson Père et Fils, 10–12 Rue Paul-Chanson, 21200 Beaune; tel. 80 22 33 00 ☓ No visitors.

JULIEN COCHE-DEBORD ET FILS★

☐   1 ha   5500   4 D ⋒ 🍷

71 ★76 ★78 79 8̲2̲ 83 84

This bright, clear 1982 has been vinified to avoid the excessive flabbiness which characterizes many wines of this vintage. Its bouquet is already quite open but firm enough to keep well. (1982)
✔ Bourgogne Blanc, Auxey-Duresses, Meursault Premier Cru.
⌐ Coche-Debord et Fils, 5 Rue de Mazeray, 21190 Meursault; tel. 80 21 22 38 ☓ By appt.

BERTRAND DARVIOT★

☐   0.5 ha   3 600   5 D ⋒ 🍷

78 79 82 ★83 ★⑧④

Strongly flavoured and sufficiently firm to last two decades, although it lacks a bit of finesse. (1982) ✔ Bourgogne Rouge, Beaune, Savigny-les-Beaune, Beaune Grèves.
⌐ Bertrand Darviot, 17 Rue de la Velle, 21190 Meursault; tel. 80 21 22 83 ☓ By appt.

LOUIS DUSSORT★

☐   0.5 ha   2700   4 D ⋒ 🍷

76 79 81 8̲2̲ 83

A fair 1982 Meursault, good bouquet, and soft on the palate, can be drunk almost immediately. (1982) ✔ Bourgogne Aligoté, Bourgogne Rouge, Beaune, Chorey-les-Beaune.
⌐ Louis Dussort, 12 Rue Charles-Giraud, 21190 Meursault; tel. 80 21 21 21 ☓ No visitors.

GABRIEL FOURNIER★★★

☐   1 ha   4 D ⋒ 🍷

⑧③ 8̲3̲ 84

A truly exceptional wine in every way. Marvellous green-gold colour; bouquet offers a succession of intense aromas (oak, vanilla, cinnamon), while the palate shows freshness and finesse. Already a dazzling bottle but will also keep well. Gabriel Fournier's excellence as a wine-maker has been noted elsewhere in this guide. (1983) ✔ Bourgogne Rouge, Bourgogne Aligoté.
⌐ Gabriel Fournier, Tailly, 21190 Meursault; tel. 80 21 46 50 ☓ By appt.

CHATEAU DE MEURSAULT

☐   8 ha   6 D ⋒ 🍷

73 76 78 ★79★ 80 ⑧②

A golden colour and rich nose though not fully developed. Full bodied flavour with good acidity. Wait a few years before drinking until the wine has softened and matured. (1982) ✔ Bourgogne Clos du Château, Pommard Clos des Epenots, Volnay Clos des Chênes, Beaune Cent Vignes.
⌐ Sté du Ch. de Meursault, 21190 Meursault; tel. 80 21 22 98 ☓ By appt. Closed 1 Nov.; Dec.–Jan.

DOMAINE MICHELOT-BUISSON
Limozin★★

☐   0.65 ha   3500   5 D ⋒ 🍷

73 74 76 78 79 80 82 8̲2̲ 83

Remarkably smooth and well-balanced with an attractive floral bouquet. (1982) ✔ Meursault, Bourgogne Chardonnay, Bourgogne Aligoté, Bourgogne Pinot Noir.
⌐ Bernard Michelot, Rue de la Velle, 21190 Meursault; tel. 80 21 23 17 ☓ No visitors.

GENEVIEVE MICHELOT
Clos du Cromin★★

☐   1 ha   5400   5 D ⋒ 🍷

73 74 76 78 79 80 81 8̲2̲

Pale, lustrous colour and clean fruity strike typical of the 1982 vintage. Fine, smooth flavour with good length suggesting that it will keep well. (1982) ✔ Meursault, Bourgogne Chardonnay.
⌐ Geneviève Michelot, Rue de la Velle, 21190 Meursault; tel. 80 21 24 32 ☓ By appt.

RAYMOND MILLOT★

☐   2 ha   2500   4 D ⋒ 🍷

76 77 79 82 ⑧③

Very successful 1983 in which the alcohol, sweetness and acidity combine harmoniously. Leave to age so the aromas will improve and it will acquire finesse. (1983) ✔ Meursault Goutte d'Or, Meursault Perrières, Puligny-Montrachet, Meursault, Rouge.
⌐ GAEC Raymond Millot, 12 Rue de la Velle, 21190 Meursault; tel. 80 21 23 48 ☓ By appt.

DOMAINE JEAN MONNIER ET FILS
Clos du Cromin★

☐   1.25 ha   7500   5 D ⋒ 🍷

71 73 74 ⑦⑨ ★81 ★8̲3̲ ★83

A brightly coloured 1982 with rather mute aromas and very soft, open flavour. This family have been producing successful wines since 1721. (1982) ✔ Meursault, Bourgogne, Beaune, Pommard.

351

Jean Monnier et Fils, 20 Rue du 11 Novembre, 21190 Meursault; tel. 80 21 22 56 ☎ By appt. Closed Aug.

PATRIARCHE PERE ET FILS
*Réserve Sainte-Anne**

□	5000	5 ⑪
*79 81		

Sustained golden colour and well-developed bouquet of dried fruit and resin. Will keep on improving. A good 1979. (1979)
MM. Patriarche Père et Fils, Rue de Collège, 21200 Beaune; tel. 80 22 23 20 ☎ By appt. Closed 15 Dec. to end Feb.

DOMAINE PRIEUR-BRUNET
*Charmes**

□1er Cru	1.5ha	6000	5 D ⑪ ↓
80 81 82 ⑧ 84			

Particularly successful in 1983, this strongly flavoured and scented wine with aromas of broom flower and hazelnut, broad mouthfilling taste and firm structure augurs well for keeping. (1983)
✔ Chassagne-Montrachet, Batard-Montrachet, Meursault Chevalières, Santenay Clos Rousseau.
Dom. Prieur-Brunet, 21590 Santenay; tel. 80 20 60 56 ☎ Daily 10.00–12.00/14.00–19.00.

DOMAINE JACQUES PRIEUR
Clos de Mazeray

■	1.5ha	8500	4 D ⑪ ↓
71 *76 *⑦ 79 *82 83			

The 'Clos de Mazeray' vineyard has a long-established reputation for its red wine. Currently planted with 50 per cent Chardonnay, to give a strong fruity flavour which comes out very well in this 1982. It also has a touch of firmness ensuring its conservation. (1982) ✔ Montrachet Grand Cru, Puligny-Montrachet, Chambertin Grand Cru, Clos Vougeot Grand Cru.
Jacques Prieur, 2 Rue des Santenots, 21190 Meursault; tel. 80 21 23 85 ☎ By appt. Closed Aug.

DOMAINE ROPITEAU-MIGNON*

■	3ha	14 500	5 D ⑪ ↓
78 82 ⑧			

Comparable to a Volnay, this red Meursault made from the Pinot Noir is deeply coloured and well constructed with good body. Still coarse and not fully open, definitely needs to age. (1982)
MM. Ropiteau-Mignon, 21190 Meursault; tel. 80 21 23 94 ☎ Daily 9.00–19.30. Closed winter.

DOMAINE ROPITEAU-MIGNON**

□	12ha	72 000	5 ⑪ ↓
78 82 *⑧			

Do not be put off by the dull colour often found in wines which are oversoft and low in acidity. Full bodied flavour with a bouquet of broom flowers and almonds; this wine is pleasantly long on the palate. (1983)
MM. Ropiteau-Mignon, 21190 Meursault; tel. 80 21 23 94 ☎ Daily 9.00–19.30. Closed winter.

DOMAINE ROUGEOT*

□	4ha	24 000	5 D 🍾 ⑪ ↓
76 79 82 ⑧ 83			

The lovely balance of this still immature 1983 comes from its finely tuned, sweet but firm flavour. You will need to wait a few years before it really opens out. (1983) ✔ Meursault Charmes, Meursault Perrières, Pommard, Volnay Santenots.
Marc Rougeot, 6 Rue André-Ropiteau, 21190 Meursault; tel. 80 21 20 59 ☎ By appt.

DOMAINE GUY ROULOT
*Les Luchet**

□	2.5ha	4800	5 D ⑪ ↓
*71 75 *78 80 82 82 83			

Pale-gold colour with refined aromas of hazelnut, caramel and fern. Smooth texture and fat, complex flavour which will improve with keeping. Still rather firm at the finish. (1982) ✔ Beaune, Auxey-Duresses, Bourgogne Rouge, Meursault.
SC Dom. Guy Roulot, 1 Rue Charles-Giraud, 21190 Meursault; tel. 80 21 21 65 ☎ By appt.

DOMAINE GUY ROULOT
*Meix-Chavaux**

□	1.5ha	8000	5 D ⑪ ↓
71 75 *78 79 80 82 ⑧			

This well-balanced 1983 Meursault with an attractive refined flavour comes from a domaine with an outstanding reputation for white wine vinification. (1983) ✔ Bourgogne Pinot Rouge, Beaune les Prevolles, Auxey-Duresses.
SC Dom. Guy Roulot, 1 Rue Charles-Giraud, 21190 Meursault; tel. 80 21 21 65 ☎ By appt.

NOEMIE VERNAUX**

□	5000	5
*79 *81		

All the finesse and subtlety of the 1981 vintage with good acidity and a well-developed bouquet. (1981)
Ets Noémie Vernaux, Rue de Vérottes, 21200 Beaune; tel. 80 22 28 50 ☎ By appt.

Blagny

Blagny is a small hamlet, partly in Meursault and partly in Puligny, which enjoys its own appellation, reserved for red wines. All the wines are of high quality and several estates are classed Premier Cru.

DOMAINE R. ET M. AMPEAU
*La Piece sous le Bois***

■	0.80ha	3600	5 D ⑪ ↓
69 73 76 77 78 80			

If left to breathe in a glass for ten minutes, the aromas of pepper and animal of this deep-coloured wine will be replaced by that of cherry brandy. On the palate this substantial wine is rich, full and even slightly harsh at the finish. (1973)
MM. R. and M. Ampeau, 21190 Meursault; tel. 80 21 20 35 ☎ By appt.

Puligny-Montrachet

André Vedel describes Puligny's situation as follows: 'If Meursault is the white wine capital of Burgundy, then Puligny, along with neighbouring Chassagne, is the royal residence of its king: Le Montrachet.' But Puligny is also a general appellation that applies to about 9000 hectolitres of wine, among which are several well-known Premiers Crus. Worth mentioning are Les Pucelles, Les Caillerets, and Les Combettes. The wines produced here have a flowery, fresh quality, lighter and more delicate than Meursault.

DOMAINE R. ET M. AMPEAU
Les Combettes★★★

□1er Cru	1ha	5400	5 ◐ ↓

72 73 *76 *77 78 80

Fine golden colour, with rich bouquet of toast and almond and touch of black truffle. Great wine that is both warm and soft on the palate. Still has a future (at least four years). Great finesse. (1972)
☛ R. et M. Ampeau, 21190 Meursault; tel. 80 21 20 35 ☓ By appt.

CIE DES VINS D'AUTREFOIS★

□			5 ◐

Classic Puigny aromas of amber, fern and ripe banana. Attractive gold-green colour and clean well-defined flavours. Should age well. (1984)
☛ Cie des Vins d'Autrefois, 9 Rue Celer, 21200 Beaune; tel. 80 22 21 31 ☓ By appt. Closed Aug.

LYCEE VITICOLE DE BEAUNE★

□	1ha	3000	5 ◐ ↓

73 75 77 79 *80 (83)

Straw-yellow colour and rather mute aromas. Sharp, slightly harsh acidity with notes of almond and melted butter. (1983)
☛ Lycée Agri. et Viti. de Beaune, 21200 Beaune; tel. 80 22 27 45 ☓ By appt.

PHILIPPE BOUZEREAU
Les Champs-Gains★★

□1er Cru		3500	5 D ◐ ↓

78 79 80 (82) *83

The lemon-yellow colour can almost be forgotten when it reveals its magnificent nose of moss, white truffle and classic grilled Chardonnay aromas. Very crisp on the palate, although slightly lacking in vigour. Long, unctuous finish.

☛ Philippe Bouzereau, 15 Place de l'Europe, 21190 Meursault; tel. 80 21 20 32 ☓ By appt. Closed end Aug.

CHANSON PERE ET FILS★★

□			5 D ◐ ↓

73 78 79 82 82 (83)

This 1983 has characteristic Puligny aromas of green fern and stock with a slight note of flint coming from the vintage. It is also more luxuriously smooth than in a normal year – it has a long future. (1983)
☛ MM. Chanson Père et Fils, 10–12 Rue Paul-Chanson, 21200 Beaune; tel. 80 22 33 00 ☓ No visitors.

JOSEPH DROUHIN *Les Folatières*★★★

□1er Cru			6 ◐ ↓

76 77 78 79 80 81 (82) 82

A pale golden colour and floral toasty nose. Solid, expansive, fat flavour on the palate, with excellent balance. A very delicate finish and the prospect of a great future. (1982)
☛ Joseph Drouhin, 7 Rue d'Enfer, 21200 Beaune; tel. 80 22 06 80 ☓ By appt.

PATRIARCHE PERE ET FILS★★

□		2500	6 D

*79 *81

The flavour is still slightly sharp but the acidity will certainly soften. Attractive colour and expressive aromas. (1981)
☛ MM. Patriarche Père et Fils, Rue de Collège, 21200 Beaune; tel. 80 22 23 20 ☓ By appt.

DOMAINE ETIENNE SAUZET
La Truffière★★★

□	0.25ha	1800	5 D ◐ ↓

78 79 81 82 (83)

Tasted in cask. Golden-green colour and reserved aromas strongly marked by new oak. Good lemony acidity on the palate and subtle flavours of mango and pineapple. An unusual wine of very high quality. (1983)
☛ Etienne Sauzet, Puligny-Montrachet, 21190 Meursault; tel. 80 21 32 10 ☓ By appt.

DOMAINE ETIENNE SAUZET
Les Perrières★★★

□1er Cru	0.7ha	3500	5 D ◐ ↓

78 79 81 82 (83)

Tasted in cask, a fine wine of the very highest quality. Golden-green colour with a nose, of toasted almonds. Rich, powerful, complex flavour of great resource. (1983)
☛ Etienne Sauzet, Puligny-Montrachet, 21190 Meursault; tel. 80 21 32 10 ☓ By appt.

DOMAINE ETIENNE SAUZET★★

□	4ha	14000	5 D ◐ ↓

78 79 81 82 (83)

Although the alcohol was still apparent when this wine was tasted, immediately after bottling, all the signs of a great future are here: bright straw-yellow with ripe pumpkin aromas and a fat compact flavour with a lingering honeysuckle scent. (1983)
☛ Etienne Sauzet, Puligny-Montrachet 21190

Meursault; tel. 80 21 32 10 ☎ By appt.

Montrachet, Chevalier-Montrachet, Bâtard-Montrachet, Criots-Bâtard-Montrachet

To do full justice to these wines, we can do no better than to quote André Vedel once again: 'With no false modesty, it could be said that Montrachet is the greatest dry white wine in the world. Of his many neighbours, the lords who are his subjects, you may well ask which has the noblest blood; Chevalier-Montrachet, Bâtard Montrachet, Criots or Bienvenues. They have a totally different character from a Meursault, and are easily distinguished from it. As one buyer once said, a Meursault is more in the Romanesque style, whereas a Montrachet would be better described as high Gothic.'

Chevalier-Montrachet

LOUIS JADOT *Les Demoiselles*★★★

☐Gd Cru		4ha	1500	6	D	⏷	⬇
70 71 73 **76** 78 **79** 81 **82 83** 83							

Full of future and with surprising power lurking behind a rare elegance. Golden-green colour, floral, lemony nose and a very clear note of honey on the palate. The most surprising feature, however, is that although this wine has an alcohol content of 14.6°, it is virtually imperceptible. A very great bottle, with a very fine future in prospect. (1983)
➼ Louis Jadot, 5 Rue Samuel-Legay, 21200 Beaune; tel. 80 22 10 57 ☎ By appt. Closed Aug.

Bâtard-Montrachet

DOMAINE ETIENNE SAUZET★★★

☐Gd Cru		0.40ha	2000	6	D	⏷	⬇
78 79 81 ★**82 83**							

Quite outstanding wine, with a golden-green colour and a surprisingly pronounced scent of truffle. Complex palate marked by aromatic herbs and perfect overall balance. A masculine wine with a great future. (1983)

➼ Etienne Sauzet, Puligny-Montrachet, 21190 Meursault; tel. 80 21 32 10 ☎ By appt.

Criots-Bâtard-Montrachet

DOMAINE JOSEPH BELLAND★★

☐Gd Cru		0.64ha	3000	6	D	▤	⏷	⬇
73 78 79 **81** 82 ⑧3								

A fine, subtle, pale golden colour and a nose which is still fairly closed; vigorous swirling of the glass releases aromas of aniseed and peppermint. Solid, firmly structured flavour with a good balance of sweetness and acidity and a full finish. A wine that will keep for several years. (1982)
➼ Joseph Belland, 21590 Santenay; tel. 80 20 61 13 ☎ By appt.

Chassagne-Montrachet

At St-Aubin, the cutting made for the new N6 road is the approximate southern border of the white wine area, Les Ruchottes marking the end. The most famous of the Chassagne red wines are Clos-St-Jean and Morgeot, both firm and full-flavoured. About 7000 hectolitres of red wine are produced, but less than 5000 hectolitres of white.

THOMAS BASSOT★★

■			240	5	D
71 74 76 78 79 81 83					

Mature colour and distinguished aromas of oak bark, resin, blackcurrant and fruit stones. Lean, elegant flavour. A well-made 1980. (1980)
➼ Thomas Bassot, 5 Quai Dumorey, 21700 Nuits-St-Georges; tel. 80 62 31 05 ☎ By appt.

ROGER BELLAND *Clos Pitois*★★

■1er Cru		2.5ha	15000	4	D	▤	⬇
69 71 76 78 ⑦9 81 ★82 **83 84**							

The fame of Chassagne-Montrachet rests not only on its white wines but also on its reds. The Clos Pitois dates back to 1481 and was the exclusive property of the lords of Chassagne. Like the other Premier Cru vineyards it is situated on the Santenay side of Chassagne. The 1982 is relatively light with an open-knit bouquet, making it suitable for immediate drinking. (1982)
✓ Santenay Beauregard Premier Cru, Santenay Comme Premier Cru, Pommard, Puligny-Montrachet les Champs Gains.
➼ M. Roger Belland, Rue de la Chapelle, 21590 Santenay; tel. 80 20 60 95 ☎ By appt.

DOMAINE JOSEPH BELLAND
*Clos Pitois**★★*

■1er Cru	4ha	12000	5 D ◗

61 62 64 66 73 76 78 79 80 ⑧ 82

Brick-red colour with orange highlights and strong aromas of quinine and grilled orange on the nose and palate. Complex finish reminiscent of a mature Banyuls. An attractive, if rather curious, wine. (1973)
❧ Joseph Belland, 21590 Santenay; tel. 80 20 61 13 ⵣ By appt.

MARC COLIN *Cailleret****

☐1er Cru	0.73ha	3600	5 D ◗

73 74 **76** ⑦ 79 81 **82** ⑧ 83

A superb cuvée, from a superb vintage! This premier cru draws its great aromatic finesse and exceptionally strong aromas from the fine chalky soil. An excellent wine in prospect. (1983)
❧ Marc Colin, Gamay-sur-St-Aubin, 21190 Meursault; tel. 80 21 30 43 ⵣ By appt.

MARC COLIN★★

■	2.5ha	15000	4 D ▮ ◗

73 74 **76** ⑦ 79 81 **82** 83

Chassagne-Montrachet, known especially for its white wines, also produces very worthwhile reds, from its vineyards on the Santenay border. This 1983 is powerful and strongly coloured. It should keep for a long time. (1983)
❧ Marc Colin, Gamay-sur-St-Aubin, 21190 Meursault; tel. 80 21 30 43 ⵣ By appt.

GEORGES DELEGER★★

■	2ha		4 D ◗

73 78 79 80 81 **82 83**

This 1980 red Chassagne is remarkably successful, and has all the characteristics of a wine of substance that will keep well. (1980) ✔ Chassagne-Montrachet Premier Cru, Chevalier-Montrachet Grand Cru, Bourgogne Aligoté.
❧ Georges Deleger, Place de l'Eglise, Chassagne-Montrachet, 21190 Meursault; tel. 80 21 32 56 ⵣ By appt. Closed 20–30 Jan. and Sundays.

DOMAINE FLEUROT-LAROSE
*Abbaye de Morgeot**

■1er Cru	6.5ha	40000	5 D ◗

71 **76 78 79** 80 *81 *82 **83 84**

During the Middle Ages, the Abbaye de Morgeot was the wine-growing centre of the southern Côte de Beaune. This wine, from the original vineyard area, is still very young, with a crisp, fruity flavour. It could be drunk now to capture its freshness. (1982)
❧ Dom. Fleurot-Larose, Ch. du Passe-Temps, 21590 Santenay; tel. 80 20 61 15 ⵣ By appt.

L'HERITIER-GUYOT★★

■	400ha	10000	3 D ◗

78 79 80 **81 82**

A very good 1982 Chassagne, with a bright colour and intense fruity aromas of blackcurrant, peach and vanilla offset by a flavour of wild fowl. Still light and fresh on the palate. Would go well with cooked meats and pâtés. (1982)
❧ L'Héritier-Guyot, Rue du Champ-aux-Prêtres, 21006 Dijon Cedex; tel. 80 72 16 14 ⵣ By appt.

LOUIS JADOT★★

☐	3ha	10000	5 D ◗

78 80 81 *82 83

Pure, elegant and airy. Deep golden colour, and nose of lime and honeysuckle. On the palate roasted Chardonnay flavour with a note of white almonds (1982)
❧ Louis Jadot, 5 Rue Samuel-Legay, 21200 Beaune; tel. 80 22 10 57 ⵣ By appt. Closed Aug.

RENE LAMY *Boudriotte**

■1er Cru	0.50ha	2700	4 D ◗

82 83 83

This 1983 Premier Cru Boudriotte is already well developed and reminiscent of a good 1971. Its aromas are already delightful, but has sufficient body to keep well. (1983) ✔ Chassagne-Montrachet Clos St-Jean, Chassagne-Montrachet Morgeot, Santenay, St-Aubin les Pucelles.
❧ René Lamy, Route de Santenay, Chassagne-Montrachet, 21190 Meursault; tel. 80 21 30 52 ⵣ By appt. Closed Feb. and when work being done on the vines.

LEROY★★

■	3000		5 D ◗

76 78 *79

Deep, velvety red wth attractive aromas of oak, resin and blackcurrant. The ripe, round tannins are typical of the vintage. Well-balanced acidity and sweetness and sufficiently soft flavour to drink now. (1979)
❧ SA Leroy, Dom. de la Romanée-Conti, Vosne-Romanée, 21700 Nuits-St-Georges; tel. 80 61 04 57 ⵣ No visitors.

MOILLARD

■	40000		5 ◗

78 82 ⑧

Despite a microclimate and *terroir* closely resembling those of Santenay the red wines of Chassagne-Montrachet are nevertheless different, generally showing a fuller body and richer tannins. This 1983 looks set to mature excellently. (1983)
❧ SARL Moillard, 5 Rue F.-Mignotte, 21700 Nuits-St-Georges; tel. 80 61 03 34 ⵣ No visitors.

JEAN-MARC MOREY *Champs-Gains**

■1er Cru	1ha	5500	5 D ◗

73 76 78 79 82 83 84

A 1982 premier cru *Champs Gains* that is still very youthful with a good, bright colour, fruity aromas and firm body. May be laid down for several years. (1982) ✔ Chassagne-Montrachet Rouge, Chassagne-Montrachet Caillerets, Chassagne-Montrachet Caillerets, Chassagne Montra-

chet Blanc, Santenay Grand-Clos Rousseau.
☛ Jean-Marc Morey, Chassagne-Montrachet 21190 Meursault; tel. 80 21 32 62 �YBy appt. Closed Feb., Aug., Sept., Oct.

JEAN-MARC MOREY★★

☐		1 ha	5500	⑤ Ⅾ ⑪ ↓
73 76 78 79 ㊃ ⑧ **84**				

Combines fine, bright colour with a rich, very open-knit aroma and full-bodied character, which should allow it to keep at least ten years. (1982)
☛ Jean-Marc Morey, Chassagne-Montrachet 21190 Meursault; tel. 80 21 32 62 ☛By appt. Closed Feb., Aug., Sept., Oct.

BERNARD MOREY★★

■		4 ha	25 000	④ Ⅾ ⑪
㊉ 76 78 79 81 ㊂ **83**				

Coming from near the heavy vineyard soil of Santenay this is fuller than the average 1982. Young colour and aromas with sufficient tannin to allow it to keep. Should be good in five years time, better in ten, and at its peak by the year 2000 (1982) ✔ Chassagne-Montrachet, Chassagne-Montrachet Premier Cru, Santenay Cru Grand-Clos Rousseau, Beaune Grèves Premier Cru.
☛ Bernard Morey, Chassagne-Montrachet, 21190, Meursault; tel. 80 21 31 13 ☛By appt.

DOMAINE PRIEUR-BRUNET
Morgeot★★

■1er Cru		0.75 ha	4500	⑤ Ⅾ ⑪ ↓
★76 ★78 79 ★81 ㊂ ⑧ **84**				

This Premier Cru vineyard traditionally produces strongly flavoured, long-lasting wines. The 1982 has refined fruit-stone aromas with a hint of sloes. Its solid, full-bodied taste suggests it will keep well. (1982)
☛ Dom. Prieur-Brunet, 21590 Santenay; tel. 80 20 60 56 ☛

DOMAINE ANDRE RAMONET
Morgeot★★

☐1er Cru		5 ha	20 000	⑥ ⑪ ↓
76 78 **79** 81 82 **83**				

Lemon-yellow colour and floral nose with a touch of acacia honey, toast and wild mint. Palate full and rich, with undertones of toast and lemon. A powerful and very satisfying wine with good acidity. Will keep well for at least five years. (1982)
☛ André Ramonet, Chassagne-Montrachet, 21190 Meursault ☛ No visitors.

DOMAINE ANDRE RAMONET
Clos Saint-Jean★★★

■		1 ha	3500	⑤ ⑪
㊉ 76 78 **79** 81 82 **83**				

Very dark ruby colour with a nose of cocoa and small red fruit. Substantial flavour on the palate, with a note of oak. Aromas of wild blackberry and bilberry. Very spicy, flavoury finish and an astonishing aroma of cherry brandy in the empty glass. This very promising wine already tastes good, but should be kept several years. Not for sale, but it can be found in several top French restaurants. (1982)
☛ André Ramonet, Chassagne-Montrachet, 21190 Meursault ☛ No visitors.

ROUX PERE ET FILS *Clos Saint-Jean*★★

■		0.5 ha	3000	⑤ Ⅾ ⑪ ↓
73 74 76 **78** 79 81 **82** ㊌				

The Knights Hospitallers owned several properties in this area which still bear their name and which occupy – clearly – the best soils. This 1983 has a solid, tannic base and is developing rich aromas overlaid with the scent of new oak. A keeping wine. (1983) ✔ St-Aubin, Chassagne-Montrachet, Puligny-Montrachet, Meursault.
☛ *MM.* Roux Père et Fils, St-Aubin, 21190 Meursault; tel. 80 21 32 92 ☛By appt.

St-Aubin

The commune of St-Aubin is situated in the Hautes-Côtes, but part of it borders Chassagne in the south and Puligny and Blagny to the east. St-Aubin's Premier Cru, Les Murgers des Dents de Chien, is not very far from Chevalier-Montrachet and Les Caillerets, and it should be said that the wine is of a particularly high standard. There is some red wine but the whites are best.

JEAN-CLAUDE BACHELET★★

☐		7 ha	42 000	④ Ⅾ ⑪ ↓
79 81 ㊃ ⑧				

The fresh flavour comes from the use of only whole, uncrushed grapes for pressing; 12 to 18 months in casks completes the process. Pleasantly soft and already good to drink. (1982) ✔ Bourgogne Aligoté, Chassagne-Montrachet Blanc et Rouge, Puligny-Montrachet Premier Cru Sous le Puits, Bienvenues Batard Montrachet, Côtes de Beaune-Villages.
☛ Jean-Claude Bachelet, St-Aubin, 21190 Meursault; tel. 80 21 31 01 ☛By appt.

MARC COLIN *La Chatenière*★★

☐1er Cru		0.25 ha	1500	④ Ⅾ ⑪ ↓
73 74 76 78 79 81 **82** ⑧ ㊌				

Clean, firm natural flavour and pleasant hint of oak. Will reach its peak in 10 years. (1983)
☛ Marc Colin, Gamay-sur-St-Aubin, 21190 Meursault; tel. 80 21 30 43 ☛By appt.

DOMAINE HUBERT LAMY
Les Castets★★

■1er Cru		4 ha	18 000	④ Ⅾ ⑪ ↓
76 78 79 80 81 **82** ㊌				

Dark colour, a nose of Morello cherries and a distinct taste of new wood on the palate. This is still a bit tannic but there is plenty of extract and it will be a lovely bottle in four years time. (1983) ✔ St-Aubin Premier Cru les Frionnes, Chassagne-Montrachet, Puligny-Montrachet, Bourgogne Rouge.
☛ Hubert Lamy, St-Aubin, 21190 Meursault; tel. 80 21 32 55 ☛By appt.

DOMAINE HUBERT LAMY *Les Frionnes**

□1er Cru 1ha 5000 4 D ◖◗ ⫰

76 78 79 80 81 **82**

Seventeenth-century methods are still used to produce this white wine. Golden yellow colour with an interesting pear aroma. Good acidity on the palate which enhances its grilled almond and hazelnut aromas. (1983) ⊶ Hubert Lamy, St-Aubin, 21190 Meursault; tel. 80 21 32 55 Y By appt.

DOMAINE AIME LANGOUREAU *En Rémilly***

□ 1ha 6500 4 D ▮ ⫰

79 82 83

Crisp and highly scented, with a brisk acidity, which suits it to seafood. (1982) ✔ St-Aubin Premier Cru Blanc, St-Aubin Premier Cru Rouge, Puligny-Montrachet Premier Cru, Chassagne-Montrachet.
⊶ Gilles Bouton, Gamay-sur-St-Aubin, 21190 Meursault; tel. 80 21 32 63 Y By appt.

DOMAINE AIME LANGOUREAU**

■ 2ha 11500 4 D ◖◗ ⫰

76 78 79 **80** **81** 82

A promising 1982, only just beginning to open out, and still far from its peak. (1982) ✔ St-Aubin Premier Cru Blanc, St-Aubin Premier Cru Rouge, Puligny-Montrachet Premier Cru, Chassagne-Montrachet.
⊶ Gilles Bouton, Gamay-sur-St-Aubin, 21190 Meursault; tel. 80 21 32 63 Y By appt.

HENRI PRUDHON ET FILS *Les Frionnes***

■1er Cru 0.5ha 3500 4 D ◖◗ ⫰

79 80

Fine 1983 Premier Cru with refined aromas and a good acid structure, which should allow it to keep. This vineyard deserves to be better known. (1983) ✔ Chassagne-Montrachet Blanc, Chassagne-Montrachet Rouge, St-Aubin, Bourgogne Aligoté.
⊶ Henri Prudhon et Fils, St-Aubin, 21190 Meursault; tel. 80 21 36 70 Y By appt.

HENRI PRUDHON ET FILS**

□ 0.75ha 5000 4 D ◖◗ ⫰

*79 *82 83

Varied aromas of dry fruits and oak characterize. Typically vigorous 1983, long on the palate and with fair acidity. Will keep well. (1983)
⊶ Henri Prudhon et Fils, St-Aubin, 21190 Meursault; tel. 80 21 36 70 Y By appt.

DOMAINE ROUX PERE ET FILS *La Chatenière***

□1er Cru 0.7ha 2000 5 D ◖◗ ⫰

73 74 76 77 78 79 81 **82** (83) 83

Complex hazelnut and vanilla, which will develop further with age. This Premier Cru already has a powerful flavour and astonishing aftertaste of sugared almonds. (1983)
⊶ *MM.* Roux Père et Fils, St-Aubin, 21990 Meursault; tel. 80 21 32 92 Y By appt.

GERARD THOMAS *Les Frionnes***

■1er Cru 1ha 5400 4 D ▮ ◖◗ ⫰

69 73 *76 *78 **79** **81** **82** **83** 83

This little known Premier Cru is transformed by the 1983 vintage into a remarkable wine. Strong colour and structure with a persistent flavour of cherry stones. Elegant finish. (1983)
⊶ Gerard Thomas, St-Aubin, 21190 Meursault; tel. 80 21 32 57 Y By appt.

Santenay

The village of Santenay, in the shadow of Mount Trois-Croix, has become famous for its mineral water, said to have the highest lithium salt content of any water in Europe. Some excellent red wines are produced here, the most famous growths being Les Gravières, La Comme, and Beauregard. As in Chassagne, the vines are often trained and pruned in the 'Cordon de Royat' style, a significant factor in determining the quality of the wine. Both the Chassagne and Santenay appellation areas extend slightly into the commune of Remigny (Saône-et-Loire).

ADRIEN BELLAND*

■ 4ha 7200 4 D ◖◗

78 **79** **81** 82 **83**

Ruby-red colour and nose of cooked prunes. Blackcurrant predominant on the palate. Thick, fleshy wine with a finish that is still rather alcoholic. (1979) ✔ Santenay Clos des Gravières, Santenay Premier Cru Commes, Aloxe-Corton, Corton Grèves Grand Cru.
⊶ Adrien Belland, Place du Jet-d'Eau, 21590 Santenay; tel. 80 20 61 90 Y By appt.

ADRIEN BELLAND *Commes**

■1er Cru 1ha 4200 4 D ◖◗ ⫰

79 *80 81 **82** **83**

With its light ruby colour this is a pleasing, slightly rustic wine which is already surprisingly mature. Slightly hot alcoholic finish. Drink now. (1980) ✔ Santenay, Santenay Clos des Gravières, Chassagne-Montrachet Clos Charreau, Corton Clos de la Vigne au Fine.
⊶ Adrien Belland, Place du Jet d'Eau, 21590 Santenay; tel. 80 20 61 90 Y By appt.

ADRIEN BELLAND *Clos Genet**

■ 11ha 60000 4 D ◖◗ ⫰

79 **80** **81** (82) **83** **84**

Lovely dark colour and firmness in the mouth, typical of the 1983 vintage. Rather dumb aromas needing time to develop. To be laid down. (1983)
⊶ Adrien Belland, Place du Jet d'Eau, 21590 Santenay; tel. 80 20 61 90 Y By appt. Closed 15–25 Aug.

Côte de Beaune (South)

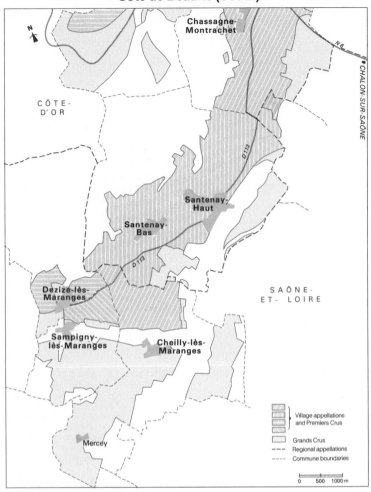

Chassagne-Montrachet

N 6

CHALON-SUR-SAÔNE

CÔTE-D'OR

D 113

Santenay-Haut

Santenay-Bas

D 113

Dézize-lès-Maranges

SAÔNE-ET- LOIRE

Sampigny-lès-Maranges

Cheilly-lès-Maranges

Mercey

	Village appellations and Premiers Crus
	Grands Crus
- - -	Regional appellations
- - - -	Commune boundaries

0   500   1000 m

ROGER BELLAND *Beauregard★*

■1er Cru		2 ha	10 500	4 D ⑩ ⬇
69 71 76 ★78 ⑦⑨ **81** ★**82 83 84**				

This wine-growing family has carefully maintained traditional customs. This 1982 is bright and fruity but still seems very young and far from its peak. Vinified to last. (1982) ✔ Santenay Premier Cru Gravières, Chassagne-Montrachet Premier Cru Morgeot, Pommard, Santenay Premier Cru Santenay.
✦┑ Roger Belland, Rue de la Chapelle, 21590 Santenay; tel. 80 20 60 95 ⲧ By appt.

ROGER BELLAND
Santenay-Commes★★

■1er Cru		2 ha	10 500	3 D ▤ ⬇
69 71 76 ★78 ⑦⑨ **81** ★**82** 8̲2̲**83 84**				

This cuvée is, according to the grower, always vigorous and powerful and the 1982 still seems very young. Complex aromas worthy of a prem-

ier cru, but simple, immature flavour; needs several years to reach its peak. (1982).
✦┑ Roger Belland, Route de la Chapelle, 21590 Santenay; tel. 80 20 60 95 ⲧ By appt.

DOMAINE DE LA BUISSIERE
Clos des Mouches★★

■1er Cru		1 ha	5500	5 D ⑩ ⬇
79 80 8̲1̲ 82 83				

Several vineyard names in Burgundy allude to beekeeping – as does this 'Clos des Mouches'. Keeping bees ('mouches à miel') was a widespread activity in earlier days. These warm, well-sheltered vineyards bring the grapes to excellent maturity. This 1981 is very refined, with subtle fruit and oak aromas. On the palate it is solid and rather firm with a long finish. (1981)
✦┑ Jean Moreau, 21590 Santenay; tel. 80 20 61 79 ⲧ Daily.

MICHEL ET DENIS CLAIR
Clos de la Comme★★

■1er Cru   0.5ha   6000   `4` `D` `▮` `◑` `⌟`
*76 79 82 `82` 83 84

Ths Clos de la Comme is one of Santenay's top three vineyards. This 1982 is just beginning to mature and mellow. Its colour is still bright red, but its fruity aromas have already opened out and there is a round, harmonious and persistent flavour. (1982) ✔ Santenay Clos de Tavannes, Santenay Gravières.
↬ Michel et Denis Clair, 21590 Santenay; tel. 80 20 62 55 ⟟ By appt.

MICHEL DELORME★

■   6.5ha   8000   `5` `D` `◑` `⌟`
76 78 79 `82` 83

This producer, in a punning reference to the village name, describes his wine as a 'vin de santé' – tonic wine – ideal for convalescents. The 1982 certainly has restorative properties with its solid, fruity, youthful taste. (1982) ✔ Santenay Premier Cru Clos Rousseau, Côte de Beaune-Villages, Bourgogne Blanc.
↬ Michel Delorme, Rue de la Charrière, Santenay-le-Haut 21590; tel. 80 20 63 41 ⟟ By appt.

DOMAINE FLEUROT LAROSE
Clos du Passetemps★

■   2ha   10500   `5` `D` `◑` `⌟`
71 76 78 79 80 *81 *`81` *82 83 84

The magnificent domaine cellars, hollowed out of the rock, have a capacity of some four thousand casks. This 1981 vintage is well developed and ready to drink. A light, subtle, wine with a good bouquet which would go well with game birds. (1981)
↬ René Fleurot, Ch. du Passe-Temps, 21590 Santenay; tel. 80 20 61 15 ⟟ By appt.

DOMAINE JEAN GIRARDIN
Clos Rousseau★★

■1er Cru   10ha   55000   `4` `D` `▮` `◑` `⌟`
79 80 81 ⑧② `82` 83

This 1982 stands out from this producer's other wines with its considerable finesse and bouquet. Beautiful, glistening colour and subtle flavour. Ready to drink. (1982) ✔ Santenay Comme, Santenay Maladière, Santenay Gravières, Côte de Beaune-Villages.
↬ Dom. Jean Girardin, Ch. de la Charrière, 21590 Santenay; tel. 80 20 61 95 ⟟ By appt. Closed during grape harvest.

DOMAINE DES HAUTES CORNIERES★★

■   13ha   60000   `4` `D` `◑` `⌟`
78 ⑦⑨ 81 `82`83

Pleasantly harmonious with all the fruit of a young wine. It lacks a bit of weight, though, and should be drunk young. (1982)
↬ Ph. Chapelle et Fils, Dom. des Hautes-Cornières, 21590 Santenay; tel. 80 20 60 09 ⟟ Mon.–Sat. 8.00–12.00/14.00–19.00. Closed Sun.

JESSIAUME PERE ET FILS
Gravières★★

■1er Cru   10ha   55000   `4` `D` `◑` `⌟`
*76 78 *79 *82 ⑧③ `83`

This is the fifth generation of wine growers to work this estate and they remain strongly attached to ancestral traditions. They make the wine without de-stalking the grapes to ensure plenty of tannic richness. This 1983 is nonetheless very well balanced with a deep colour and a fairly open bouquet. (1983) ✔ Santenay, Volnay Brouillards, Beaune Centvignes.
↬ MM. Jessiaume Père et Fils, 21590 Santenay; tel. 80 20 60 03 ⟟ By appt.

JOLY PERE ET FILS *Clos de Malte*★

■   7ha   38000   `4` `◑` `⌟`
78 ⑦⑨ 81 82 `83`

This vineyard is tucked away in the angle formed by two rocks which split in the Jurassic era. The land has a rich past and belonged to the Order of St John, then to the Knights of Malta. The entire pocket of land is classified vineyard and seven unbroken hectares of vines make up 'Le Clos'. It was destroyed by phylloxera a hundred years ago but has been patiently restored. This, the only wine made here, is always subtly flavoured and devoid of heaviness. The 1983 is more powerful than recent previous vintages but it preserves the characteristic fine, harmonious balance.
↬ MM. Joly Père et Fils, Clos de Malte, 21590 Santenay; tel. 80 20 60 07 ⟟ By appt.

DOMAINE LEQUIN-ROUSSOT
Commes★★

■1er Cru   2ha   10500   `5` `D` `◑` `⌟`
76 78 79 80 82 83

In 1734 two Lequin brothers brought two plots of vines totalling less than a tenth of a hectare. Their descendants have been working and expanding the property ever since. In 1872 the domaine's present buildings were put up. The latest generation jealously preserves the 'know-how' of its forefathers. This 1982 Premier Cru is just beginning to open out, and its fine, deep colour promises a wine for long-term keeping. (1982) ✔ Chassagne-Montrachet Rouge, Chassagne-Montrachet Blanc, Corton, Pommard.
↬ Dom. Lequin-Roussot, Rue de la Gare, 21590 Santenay; tel. 80 20 61 46 ⟟ By appt.

DOMAINE MESTRE PERE ET FILS
Le Passe-Temps★

■1er Cru   1.70ha   10800   `4` `D` `◑` `⌟`
78 79 80 82 ⑧③

A cherry robe hinting of orange with good fruit and extract and a tannic finish. This Santenay is still young and will age well. (1982)

➤ Dom. Mestre Père et Fils, 21590 Santenay; tel. 80 20 60 11 ☂ By appt.

MESTRE PERE ET FILS *Passe-Temps*★★

■1er Cru	1ha	5000	⑤ D ⅲ ↓
76 **78** 79 80 ⑧ **82** **83** **84**			

Yet another Burgundy vineyard name full of etymological conjecture. This one seems to refer to whiling away the time – a humorous reference perhaps to the difficulty of cultivating this vineyard and the time it took. This 1982 has a lovely colour and aromas of berries and oak. Good tannins ensure that it can be kept for a long time. (1982) ✔ Ladoix, Chassagne-Montrachet, Côte de Beaune-Villages, Aloxe-Corton.
➤ *MM*. Mestre Père et Fils, Place du Jet d'Eau, 21590 Santenay; tel. 80 20 60 11 ☂ By appt.

MOILLARD

■	48000	⑤ ⅲ ↓
7.9 ⑧ **82** **83**		

Ready to drink, this Santenay has a colour which has a bright, orangey tinge, but the aromas are still fresh and the flavours soft and delicate. (1982)
➤ SARL Moillard, 5 Rue F.-Mignotte, 21700 Nuits-St-Georges; tel. 80 61 03 34 ☂ No visitors.

LUCIEN MUZARD *Maladière*★★

■	4ha	25000	⑤ D ⅲ ↓
76 **78** 79 81 82 ⑧			

'Maladière' designates the original purpose of this spot – a leper hospital built in the 12th century. The ground was put to happier use when viticulture started up here several centuries later. This 1983 is very powerful but its aromas have not really developed yet, and it is still harsh on the palate. Needs at least ten years. (1983) ✔ Santenay les Champs Claude, Santenay les Gravières, Santenay Clos Faubard.
➤ Lucien Muzard, 21590 Santenay; tel. 80 20 61 85 ☂ By appt.

HERVE OLIVIER *Beaurepaire*★★

■1er Cru	2ha	10500	④ D ⅲ ↓
76 **78** 79 81 ⑧ **83**			

The Beaurepaire vineyard has been patiently replanted by two generations of wine growers anxious to preserve their heritage. This 1983 is marked by exceptionally fruity aromas and a solid, well-balanced flavour. It is already pleasant to drink, but will improve further with age. (1983) ✔ Santenay Premier Cru Beaurepaire, Savigny-lès-Beaune Premier Cru.
➤ Hervé Olivier, Rue Gaudin, 21590 Santenay-le-Haut; tel. 80 20 61 35 ☂ By appt.

DOMAINE PRIEUR-BRUNET
Maladière★

■1er Cru	5ha	28000	⑤ D ⅲ ↓
★76 **78** **79** 81 **82** ⑧ **84**			

The family-owned estate was established in 1804. The well-coloured 1982 has a good balance and could already be drunk. The 1983 is a great vintage which should be laid down. (1982) ✔ Chassagne-Montrachet Premier Cru Morgeot, Volnay Premier Cru Santenois, Beaune Premier Cru Clos-du-Roy, Platières Premier Cru Pom-

mard.
➤ Dom. Prieur-Brunet, 21590 Santenay; tel. 80 20 60 56 ☂ Daily 10.00–12.00/14.00–19.00.

DOMAINE SAINT-MICHEL★★

■	12ha	65000	④ D ⅲ ↓
79 80 **81** ★⑧ ★**82** **83**			

This 1982 has developed well and is quite full, although not without finesse, and has a fairly open-knit bouquet. The producer describes it as his best vintage for the last five years. (1982) ✔ Santenay Premier Cru Clos Rousseau, Santenay Premier Cru Comme, Bourgogne Rouge, Puligny-Montrachet.
➤ SCE Dom. St-Michel, Place de la Mairie, 21590 Santenay; tel. 80 20 60 67 ☂ Daily 9.00–12.00/14.00–20.00. Closed 10–25 Aug.

Côtes de Beaune-Villages

This secondary appellation is not to be confused with Côte de Nuits-Villages, which applies to only a very limited production area. The name Côte de Beaune-Villages, can be substituted for any red wine from the Côte de Beaune that has a commune appellation, except Beaune, Aloxe-Corton, Pommard and Volnay.

CHANSON PERE ET FILS★★

■	④ D ⅲ ↓
71 ⑦ **80****81** 82 **83**	

This wine has all the charms of its vintage; good colour, fruitiness, roundness, balance and lightness. These qualities are characteristic of this wine. (1982)
➤ *MM*. Chanson Père et Fils, 10–12 Rue Paul-Chanson, 21200 Beaune; tel. 80 22 33 00 ☂ No visitors.

THE COTE CHALONNAISE

Rully

The Côte Chalonnaise, acts as a transition between the Côte d'Or and Mâconnais vineyards. The Rully appellation area extends from its commune of origin into Chagny, where you will find one of the regions top restaurants. Equal amounts of white and red wine are produced – about 2500 hectolitres. They are pleasant wines that usually keep well. The best-known Premiers Crus are Les Cloux and La Renarde.

THOMAS BASSOT★

■	800	④ D
⑧ 83 84		

Deep garnet colour with classic red fruit Pinot bouquet. Fairly expressive, well-balanced flavour. (1983)
➤ Thomas Bassot, 5 Quai Dumorey, 21700 Nuits-St-Georges; tel. 80 62 31 05 ☂ By appt.

Côte Chalonnaise and The Mâconnais

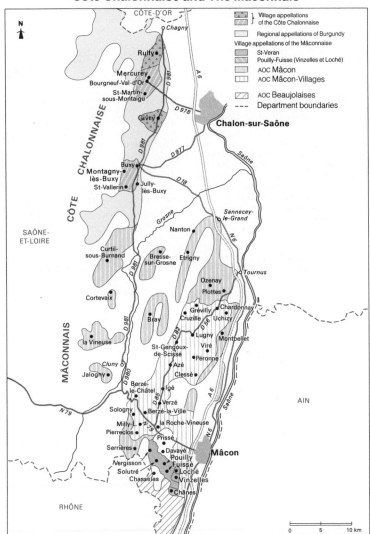

DOMAINE BELLEVILLE PERE ET FILS★

□		20 ha	45 000	🔲 D ▮ ⓦ ↓

78 79 ★82 **82** **83 84**

A straightforward wine with a promising bouquet, but slightly disappointing on the palate. Try it with snails. (1982) ✔ Mercurey, Crémant de Bourgogne, Bourgogne.
➼ *MM*. Belleville Père et Fils, Rue de la Loppe, Rully, 71150 Chagny; tel. 85 91 22 19 ☖ Daily 8.00–12.00/13.00–20.00.

EMILE CHANDESAIS★

□		6000	🔲 ⓦ ↓

79 80 **82**

This 1980 Rully offers some pleasant qualities such as the attractive nose and flavour of honey. Not as pleasing on the palate. (1980)
➼ Emile Chandesais, Ch. St-Nicolas, Fontaines, 71150 Chagny; tel. 85 91 41 77 ☖ By appt.

GUYOT-VERDIOT★

□		3 ha	9600	🔲 D ▮ ⓦ ↓

79 ★80 ★⑧₂ ★83

White Rully has a reputation for reliable quality. This 1982 is typical of its vintage, with a scented bouquet and clean, pleasant flavour. (1982)
✔ Bourgogne Aligoté, Crémant de Bourgogne, Rully Rouge, Bourgogne Mousseux.
➼ Hubert Guyot, Rue du Château Rully, 71150 Chagny; tel. 85 87 04 48 ☖ By appt.

ANDRE L'HERITIER★

□		4 ha	24 000	🔲 D ▮ ↓

78 ★79 ★82 **82** **83 84**

Excellent, very elegant white Rully with good fruit and a fat Chardonnay flavour. Will age well. (1982) ✔ Rully Rouge and Rosé, Bourgogne Alitoté Bouzeron, Bourgogne Rouge.
➼ André Lhéritier, 4 Bld de la Liberté, 71150 Chagny; tel. 85 87 00 09 ☖ By appt.

361

ANDRE L'HERITIER*

■   1ha   5000   4 D ▪ ↓

76 78 **78** 82

A firmly flavoured, deeply coloured, faultless Rully. Keep for two or three years. (1982)
ᐧ André Lhéritier, 4 Bld de la Liberté, 71150 Chagny; tel. 85 87 00 09 Ꙭ By appt.

DOMAINE DE L'HERMITAGE*

■   6ha   30000   4 D ⑪ ↓

77 **79** 80 **81 82** 83

This wine is very young and the bouquet is still undeveloped. However, in a few years it should provide a good accompaniment to meats in sauces. (1983) ✔ Aligoté Bouzeron, Bourgogne Clos de la Fortune Rouge, Rully Dom. de l'Hermitage, Mercurey Clos du Roy Premier Cru.
ᐧ *MM.* Chanzy Frères, Dom. de l'Hermitage, Bouzeron, 71150 Chagny; tel. 85 87 23 69 Ꙭ By appt.

H. ET P. JACQUESON *Les Clouds*

■1er Cru   1.5ha   6500   4 D ⑪

71 72 76 77 *78 80 81

This wine undergoes a very long vatting period during which the grapes are still trodden back down into the vat by human feet. The autumnal fragrances of woodland are dominant here, and persist on the palate. Try this wine with eggs in meurette sauce. (1981) ✔ Mercurey Naugues, Rully Premier Cru Grésigny, Rully les Chaponnières, Bourgogne Passe-Tout-Grain.
ᐧ H. et P. Jacqueson, Place Ste-Marie, Rully, 71150 Chagny; tel. 85 87 07 88 Ꙭ By appt. Closed Sat.

H. ET P. JACQUESON
Les Chaponnières

■   1.5ha   6500   4 D ⑪ ↓

71 72 73 76 ⑦⑧ 80 81 **82** 83

Dark ruby wine with a peppery and persistent flavour with well-judged tannin. Some of the best restaurants in France recommend this well-balanced Rully with meats or cheeses of character.
ᐧ H. et P. Jacqueson, Place Ste-Marie, Rully, 71150 Chagny; tel. 85 87 07 88 Ꙭ By appt. Closed Sat.

LEROY*

□   25000   5 ⑪ ↓

Light, brisk flavour very typical of a good white Rully. Pronounced Chardonnay varietal character on the nose with notes of vanilla and balm and a slightly animal note common to many white wines from Sâone-et-Loire. (1982)
ᐧ SA Leroy, Dom. de la Romanée-Conti, Vosne-Romanée, 21700 Nuits-St-Georges; tel. 80 61 04 57 Ꙭ No visitors.

YVES MARCEAU *Raboursay*

□1er Cru   3ha   13000   4 D ⑪ ↓

76 78 82 83

Light golden colour with a subtle and discreet aroma and slightly sweet finish. Suitable as an aperitif or as an accompaniment to river fish or poultry. ✔ Mercurey, Givry, Bourgogne.
ᐧ Yves Marceau, Grande-Rue, Mercurey, 71640 Givry; tel. 85 47 13 21 Ꙭ Mon.–Sat. 13.00–18.00.

ARMAND MONASSIER*

□   2ha   10000   4 D ▪ ⑪ ↓

74 79 81 **82 83**

Still rather reserved with considerable tannic firmness. Typical Rully character with aromas of ripe banana. Should age well. (1983)
ᐧ Armand Monassier, Dom. de Prieuré, Rully, 71150 Chagny; tel. 85 87 13 57 Ꙭ By appt.

ARMAND MONASSIER*

■   3ha   13000   4 D ⑪ ↓

76 78 79 80 81 82 **83**

Ripe cherry colour and aromas with an attractive rounded flavour. Good ageing potential. Should make a good accompaniment to roasts and dishes in red wine sauce. (1983)
ᐧ Armand Monassier, Dom. du Prieuré, Rully, 71150 Chagny; tel. 85 87 13 57 Ꙭ By appt.

DOMAINE NINOT RIGAUD*

■   2ha   6500   4 D ⑪ ↓

76 *82 ⑧③ 84

A typical red Rully, with its aromas of lilac, violet and wild raspberry. Still hard on the palate; should be left for a year or two. (1983) ✔ Rully Blanc, Rully Blanc Premier Cru, Mercurey Rouge, Crémant de Bourgogne.
ᐧ P.-M. Ninot, Dom. Ninot-Rigaud, Rully, 71150 Chagny; tel. 85 87 07 79 Ꙭ By appt.

DOMAINE DE LA RENARDE *Varot***

□   19ha   80000   4 D ▪ ↓

80 81 82 83 **83** 84

This inviting wine has a summer bouquet with aromas of hay, fresh straw and lime which persist on the palate. Will age harmoniously. (1983)
✔ Givry, Mercurey.
ᐧ Jean-François Delorme, Rue de la République, Rully, 71150 Chagny; tel. 85 87 10 12 Ꙭ By appt. Closed Aug.

CHATEAU DE RULLY *Molesme*

■1er Cru   1ha   3200   4 D ⑪ ↓

71 ⑦③ **74** 78 79 **80** 82 83

This full-bodied wine, crimson in colour with perfumes of raspberry and blackcurrant will develop fully in a few years. (1982) ✔ Rully Premier Cru la Bressande du Ch.
ᐧ C. d'Aviau-de-Ternay, Rully, 71150 Chagny; tel. 85 87 20 42 Ꙭ By appt.

CLOS SAINT-JACQUES***

□   9ha   36000   5 D ▪ ⑪ ↓

*78 *79 *80 *81 *82 **83** ⑧④

One of the very best white wines from the Côte Chalonnaise. Its outstandingly rich, complex flavours will allow it to age handsomely although it is already perfect today. The finesse of its bouquet and the excellent acid backbone give it great

versatility – drink as an aperitif, with shellfish in sauce or even with certain cheeses. (1983)
✔ Rully Clos de Bellecroix Rouge, Bourgogne Aligoté, Bourgogne Aligoté Bouzeron.
↦ E. Noël-Bouton Dom. de la Folie, 71150 Chagny; tel. 85 87 18 59 ☙ Mon.–Sat. 8.00–12.00/13.30–18.30. Closed winter.

CHARLES VIENOT★★

■	500	4 D
㉒ 83 84		

Bright red colour with aromas of game and musk and a crisply flavoured palate of red fruit, pepper and spice. Full, harmonious texture. (1982)
↦ Ets Charles Vienot, 5 Quai Dumorey, 21700 Nuits-St-Georges; tel. 80 62 31 05 ☙ By appt.

Mercurey

Mercurey lies about 12 km north-west of Chalon-sur-Saône, bordering the Chagny-Cluny road, and touching the southern tip of the Rully vineyard. This is the largest Chalonnais appellation by volume: 20 000 hectolitres are produced, less than 1000 of which is white. St-Martin-sous-Montaigu and Bourgneuf-Val-d'Or.

Several vineyards have recently been promoted to Premier Cru status; the wines often have a complex fruit flavour with considerable refinement, and keep well.

EMILE BERTRAND★

■	1 ha	5300	3 D ▮ ⑪ ↓
72 76 78 80 ㉒ 82			

Attractive aromas but still a bit harsh on the palate. Some richness and plenty of potential. Good value. (1982) ✔ Bourgogne Rouge et Blanc.
↦ Emile Bertrand, Barizey, 71640 Givry; tel. 85 44 38 68 ☙ No visitors.

DOMAINE BRINTET★

■	8 ha	50 000	4 D ⑪ ↓
63 76 78 79 82 83			

Raspberry aromas and woody flavour; needs to age. (1982) ✔ Mercurey, Bourgogne.
↦ L. Brintet et F. Charles, Grande Rue, Mercurey, 71640 Givry; tel. 85 47 14 50 ☙ By appt.
↦ GAEC La Charme Brintet-Charle.

DOMAINE DE CHAMEROSE
Clos des Baraults★★

■	7 ha	33 000	4 D ⑪ ↓
73 76 78 80 81 ㉒ 82 83			

This wine, with its magnificent colour, has a long tradition of success. It has good tannins and a fat persistent flavour. Recommended as an accompaniment to red meats and game. (1982) ✔ Mercurey Clos Laurent.
↦ Louis Modrin, Dom. de Chamerose, Mercurey, 71560 Givry; tel. 85 47 13 94 ☙ By appt.

DOMAINE DU CHATEAU DE CHAMILLY★★

■	3.5 ha	13 000	4 D ⑪ ↓
74 79 ㉒ 82 83 84			

Fine, deep colour and violet-scented aromas. Well balanced but needs to age. (1982) ✔ Bourgogne, Bourgogne Aligoté, Bourgogne Passetout-grain.
↦ Louis Desfontaine, Dom. du Ch. de Chamilly, Chamilly, 771510 St-Leger-sur-d'Heume; tel. 85 87 22 24 ☙ By appt.

CHATEAU DE CHAMIREY★

□	6 ha	25 000	5 ⑪ ↓
78 79 81 82 83			

This 1982 vintage has aromas of hazelnuts and toasted almonds. Fine golden colour and elegant, sappy flavour; well balanced on the palate; goes very well with foie gras, fish and shellfish. (1982)
↦ M. le Marquis de Jouennes, Ch. de Chamirey, 71640 Givry; tel. 85 45 22 22 ☙ By appt. Closed Aug.

CHATEAU DE CHAMIREY★★

■	22 ha	90 000	4 ⑪ ↓
㉗ 79 81 ★82 83			

Complex red-fruit flavour of redcurrants, raspberries and strawberries with good length on the palate. (1982) ✔ Mercurey Chamirey Blanc.
↦ Antonin Rodet, Mercurey, 71340 Givry; tel. 85 45 22 22 ☙ By appt. Closed Aug. ↦ M. le Marquis de Jouennes.

EMILE CHANDESAIS *Clos du Roy*★★

□	3000	4 ⑪ ↓
78 79 81 82 83		

Fine golden colour and fat, rich flavours. Distinguished aromas of almond and vanilla with a touch of new oak. Selected by the local Confrérie and bearing the 'Chanteflûte' label. (1982)
↦ Emile Chandesais, Ch. St-Nicolas, Fontaines, 71150 Chagny; tel. 85 91 41 77 ☙ By appt. Closed Mon. and Sun.

EMILE CHANDESAIS★

■ 12ha 120000 [4] ⅷ ⌁

★⑦⑧ ★81 82 [82] 83

Floral and red berry aromas. Soft and smooth. Despite fairly weak tannins, should continue to improve over the next two or three years. (1982) ☛ Emile Chandesais, Ch. St-Nicolas, Fontaines, 71150 Chagny; tel. 85 91 41 77 ⵝ By appt.

J. FAIVELAY *Clos du Roy*★★

■1er Cru 3ha 12000 [5] [D] ⅷ ⌁

71 76 78 [80] 82 83

An elegant wine with black cherry colour and roasted aromas. It is spicy (cinnamon and cloves) on the palate. Fairly firm body and long finish. (1980) ☛ Maison Faively, 8 Rue du Tribourg, 21700 Nuits-St-Georges; tel. 80 61 04 55 ⵝ By appt. Closed Aug.

J. FAIVELAY *Clos Rochette*★★★

☐ 3ha 10800 [5] [⑦] ⅷ ⌁

78 79 81 ★[82] 83

Light colour and fresh honeysuckle nose. Fat buttery flavour with perfectly weighted acidity. A fine bottle. (1982) ☛ Maison Faivelay, 8 Ru du Tribourg, 21700 Nuits-St-Georges; tel. 80 61 04 55 ⵝ By appt. Closed Aug.

CHANZY FRERES *Clos du Roy*★★

☐1er Cru 0.96ha 1500 [4] [D] ⅷ ⌁

★75 ★76 ★79 ★80 ★⑧⓪

Pale-gold colour, oak aromas on the nose and a hint of roasted almond on the palate. However, production of this medl-winning wine is limited. (1982) ☛ *MM*. Chanzy Frères, Dom. de l'Hermitage, Bouzeron, 71150 Chagny; tel. 85 87 23 69 ⵝ By appt.

MICHEL JUILLOT★

■ 16ha 70000 [5] [D] ⅷ ⌁

★78 79 80 82

Although this family have been producing wine since 1404, their oak casks are new, and contribute the elegant tannins in this wine. Ruby coloured, a lingering bouquet of wild red berries. Will develop well over the next few years. (1982) ☛ Aloxe-Corton Premier Cru, Corton, Bourgogne Rouge and Blanc. ☛ Michel Juillot, Mercurey, 71640 Givry; tel. 85 45 27 27 ⵝ By appt. Closed Jan. and Aug.

MARC LABORDE★

■ 1ha 4200 [4] [D] ⅷ ⌁

76 ★78 79 80 ★82 83

Glinting, ruby-tinged colour and very attractive aromas. Flattering on the palate, this is a deeply textured wine. (1982) ☛ Bourgogne Bourgogne Aligoté. ☛ Marc Laborde, St-Jean-de-Vaux, 71640 Givry; tel. 85 47 20 10 ⵝ By appt. Closed 20 Sept.–20 Oct.

ROBERT LANDRE *Le Clos Michaud*★

☐ 0.5ha 2000 [3] [D] [⑦] ⌁

76 78 [80] ⑧⓪

Bright, sharply coloured, rich and warm; not a typical Mercurey but worth trying nonetheless. (1980) ☛ Mercurey Chanteflûté, Mercurey, Bourgogne, Bourgogne Aligoté. ☛ Robert Landre, Mellecey, Mercurey, 71640 Givry; tel. 85 47 13 84 ⵝ By appt.

ROBERT LANDRE★

☐ 0.5ha 2000 [4] [D] ⅆ ⅷ ⌁

78 80 [80] ★83

Bright, rich and warm. Not characteristic of the appellation, which is not to say that it does not deserve to become well known. (1980) ☛ Robert Landre, Mellecey, Mercurey, 71640 Givry; tel. 85 47 13 84 ⵝ By appt.

LOUIS MORLAND★

☐ 0.4ha 2000 [4] [D] ⅷ ⌁

76 79 ★81 ⑧⓷

Very rich on the palate and has an excellent finish. Good with judru, the local Chagny version of the famous Lyonnais sausage. (1981) ☛ Mercurey Rouge, Bourgogne Rouge. ☛ Louis Morland, Le Bourg, St-Martin-sous-Montaigu, 71640 Givry; tel. 85 47 15 70 ⵝ By appt.

ANTONIN RODET★★

■ 120000 [4] [D] ⅷ ⌁

[80] [81] ⑧⓶ [82] [83]

Luminous crimson colour. Truffle and leaf aromas dominated by youthful raspberry note. Balance on the palate strongly marked by fairly hard tannins but the wine has plenty of future. Should be left to age for a few years. (1982) ☛ Antonin Rodet, Mercurey, 71640 Givry; tel. 85 45 22 22 ⵝ By appt. Closed Aug.

DOMAINE SAIER *Les Chenelots*★★

■ 18ha 100000 [D] ⅷ ⌁

76 78 79 82 ⑧⓷ ⑧⓹

Woody, very powerful. Rich in alcohol; should be drunk in three or four years' time. (1983) ☛ Bourgogne Rouge, Aloxe Corton Premier Cru Clos Maréchaudes, Corton Grand Cru Clos les Maréchaudes, Mercurey les Champs Martins. ☛ Ets Nicolas, 2 Rue Valmy, 94220 Charenton; tel. 01 37 59 20 ⵝ By appt. Closed Aug. ☛ Fabien et Louis Saier.

DOMAINE SAIER★

■ 18ha 100000 [4] [D] ⅷ ⌁

76 78 79 ⑧⓶ 83

Fairly light with the fruity aromas of a vin primeur. Round flavour with some finesse, although a little short on the palate. (1983) ☛ Bourgogne Rouge, Aloxe-Corton Premier Cru Clos Maréchaudes, Corton Clos des Maréchaudes, Mercurey les Champs Martins. ☛ Ets Nicolas, 2 Rue Valmy, 94220 Charenton; tel. 01 37 59 20 ⵝ By appt. Closed Aug. ☛ Fabien et Louis Saier.

YVES DE SUREMAIN *Clos Voyen*★

■1er Cru	6000	4 D ⊕ ↓

78 80 **82** 82 83

Round on the palate and has an exciting flavour that gives it a very pleasing character. Should be left for several years. (1982)
↜ Yves de Suremain, Mercurey, 71640 Givry; tel. 85 47 20 87 ✶ By appt.

YVES DE SUREMAIN *Les Crets*★★

■	1.5 ha	3600	4 D ⊕ ↓

78 80 **82** 82 ⑧

Well balanced with good length on the palate. Promises a good future. Should go remarkably well with game or a good meat in sauce. (1982)
↜ Yves de Suremain, Mercurey, 71640 Givry; tel. 85 47 20 87 ✶ By appt.

HUGUES DE SUREMAIN *Sazenay*★★

■	2 ha	10000	4 D ▮ ↓

64 66 **69** 71 76 78 ⑧ 82 83

Very successful, characterful Mercurey. Magnificent, deep robe and a flattering nose of blackcurrant. Kept for three years, it should be a perfect wine. (1982)
↜ Hugues de Suremain, Mercurey, 71640 Givry; tel. 85 47 11 10 ✶ By appt.

EMILE VOARICK★

■	15 ha	80000	4 D ⊕ ↓

71 78 79 **80** 81 82

The 1980 vintage was not an easy crop to vinify. This Mercurey is nevertheless a success, although it may be criticized for its short finish. (1980)
✔ Corton, Beaune, Givry, Bourgogne.
↜ SCV Emile Voarick, Le Bourg, St-Martin-sous-Montaigu, 71640 Givry; tel. 86 45 23 23 ✶ Mon.–Sat. 8.00–12.00/14.00–18.00.

Givry

Located 6 km south of Mercurey, this small town, typically Burgundian, has many historic monuments. Its chief wine is Givry Rouge (4000 hectolitres). All the Givry wines are very reasonably priced.

EMILE CHANDESAIS★

■	5000	4 ⊕ ↓

78 79 81 82 83

Selected by the Jurés Gourmets, this well-balanced ruby-coloured wine is beginning to soften as it ages. Over a background of animal aromas there is a touch of vanilla characteristic of its raising in oak casks. In a few years, it will provide a fine accompaniment to coq au vin. (1981)
↜ Emile Chandesais, Ch. St-Nicolas, Fontaines, 71150 Chagny; tel. 85 91 41 77 ✶ By appt. Closed Sun. and Mon. July and Aug.

LA CHAUME★

□	0.5 ha	2500	3 D ⊕ ↓

66 71 **76** 80 ⑧ 82 83

This pleasant hillside wine has a fine, bright colour. It is very fresh on the palate due to a slight presence of carbon dioxide. (1983)
✔ Givry, Bourgogne, Bourgogne Aligoté.
↜ Thierry Lespinasse, La Chaume, Rosey, 71390 Buxy; tel. 85 47 94 09 ✶ No visitors.

JEAN CHOFFLET★★

■	3 ha	15000	3 D ⊕ ↓

76 78 82

Light cherry colour and nose of blackcurrant that persists on the palate. The family have produced wine here since 1710; the present heir recommends opening this fine wine two hours before drinking. (1982)
✔ Givry Blanc, Bourgogne Passe-Tout-Grain, Bourgogne Aligoté.
↜ Jean Chofflet, Russilly, 71640 Givry; tel. 85 44 34 78 ✶ By appt. Closed Sun.

JEAN CLEAU *Clos Marceau*★★

■	4 ha	17500	3 D ⊕ ↓

81 82 82 83 84

Generous, rich, wine with good fruit. Good value for money. (1982)
↜ Jean Cléau, Rue des Berges, Poncey, 71640 Givry; tel. 85 44 31 35 ✶ By appt.

DESVIGNES *Clos du Vernoy*★

■	0.5 ha	4000	3 D ⊕ ↓

76 79 82 83 83

Typically tannic, vigorous example of this vintage. Although it should age well, it may be enjoyed from now on, as long as the bottle is opened well before drinking. (1983) ✔ Givry Clos du Vernoy, Givry.
↜ *MM.* Desvignes Aîné et Fils, Pontanevaux, 71570 La Chapelle-de-Guinchay; tel. 85 36 72 32 ✶ By appt.

DOMAINE JOBLOT
Clos du Cellier aux Moines★★

■1er Cru	2 ha	15000	3 D ⊕ ↓

76 78 81 81 82 82 83 83

Characteristic of the 1982 vintage. Good tannin enhances the ripe cherry aromas without impairing the balance of the flavour. Should age well. Very good with soft cheeses. (1982) ✔ Givry.
↜ Dom. Joblot, 71640 Givry; tel. 85 44 30 77 ✶ By appt. ↜ *M.* Joblot.

YVES MARCEAU *Pied-du-Clou*★

■	2 ha	5400	3 D ⊕ ↓

78 81 82

Wine growers for three generations and dedicated to traditional methods, this family produces a fruity wine with a dominant blackcurrant flavour. Pleasing on the palate, despite a slight touch of sugar. A good bottle at a reasonable price. (1982) ✔ Mercurey, Rully, Bourgogne.
↜ Yves Marceau, Grande-Rue, Mercurey, 71640 Givry; tel. 85 47 13 21 ✶ By appt.

JEAN MORIN★

■	5ha	22000	3 D ▤ ↓

80 *81 81 82

Colour and aroma evocative of redcurrant. This wine is very pleasing on the palate, although the finish is a little sharp. Fine to drink now, but should reach its peak in three or four years. (1981) ✔ Givry Blanc, Bourgogne Blanc.
↬ Jean Morin, Poncey, 71640 Givry; tel. 85 44 51 38 ⊺ By appt. Closed Sat. afternoons, second fornight in Aug.

GERARD MOUTON★

□	1.5ha	5000	3 D ◐ ↓

76 78 79 80 81 *82 83

A slight trace of carbon dioxide in this Givry adds a note of freshness to the pleasant, rounded flavour. (1980)
↬ Gérard Mouton, Poncey, 71640 Givry; tel. 85 44 37 99 ⊺ By appt.

DOMAINE RAGOT★★

■	4ha	24000	3 D ◐ ↓

76 78 79 81 *82 83

Having won the gold medal for his white wine, *M*. Ragot only just missed a double with his red which took second place. Attractive ruby red, with redcurrant aromas and compact, well-structured flavour. A wine of quality which should age well. (1982)
↬ *M*. Ragot, Poncey, 71640 Givry; tel. 85 44 38 84 ⊺ By appt. Closed Sun.

DOMAINE RAGOT★★

□	1.8ha	10800	3 D ◐ ↓

*76 *78 79 80 81 (82) 82

This very fine wine was a well-deserved gold-medal winner under the Concours Général de Paris. Full, balanced and round flavour with delightful floral aromas and a very long finish. Excellent value. (1982) ✔ Bourgogne Aligoté, Bourgogne Passe-Tout-Grain.
↬ *M*. Ragot, Poncey, 71640 Givry; tel. 85 44 38 84 ⊺ By appt. Closed Sun.

CLOS SALOMON★★★

■	6ha	30000	4 D ▤ ◐ ↓

*76 *78 *80 *82 *82

Clear purple colour. Aromas of blackcurrant, raspberry and bilberry. Full, spicy palate. Fermented in the old style, it will need several years to peak. (1982)
↬ *MM*. Dugardin et Dumas, Cidex 1044, 71640 Givry; tel. 85 44 32 24 ⊺ By appt.

LA SAULERAIE *Les Grandes Vignes*★

■	4ha	17000	3 D ◐ ↓

76 78 79 82 83

This wine, with its fine colour, won a silver medal in the Concours des Vins de France. It is delicate and refined, fruity and elegant. (1982) ✔ Bourgogne Clos de la Roche, Bourgogne Passe-Tout-Grain.
↬ Gérard Parize, 18 Rue des Faussillons, Poncey, 71640 Givry; tel. 85 44 38 60 ⊺ By appt.

LA SAULERAIE *Les Champs Pourrots*★

□	0.5ha	2000	3 D ▤

*80 *81 83

The light luminous colour reveals the youth of this wine, making the power of the aromas of woodland, hazelnut and meadow mushroom surprising. Enjoyable with many typical Burgundian first courses. (1983) ✔ Bourgogne Aligoté.
↬ Gérard Parize, 18 Rue des Faussillons, Poncey, 71640 Givry; tel. 85 44 38 60 ⊺ By appt.

BERNARD TARTRAUX★

■	3.5ha	20000	3 D ▤ ◐ ↓

*76 *78 *80 *82 82

Pleasant, good value drinking. Already at its peak. Drink with meat and game. (1982)
↬ Bernard Tartraux, 33 Rue de la Planchette, Poncey, 71640 Givry; tel. 85 49 82 57 ⊺ By appt.

Montagny

This is the southern-most village of the region, and the wines of Montagny, which are exclusively white, prepare us for the Mâconnais. The appellation area covers four communes; Montagny, Buxy, St-Vallerin and Jully-les-Buxy. Only wines from the commune of Montagny may mention the vineyard name on the label. The amount produced is approximately 3000 hectolitres.

COOPERATIVE DES VIGNERONS DE BUXY★

□1er Cru	80ha	80000	4 D ▤ ◐ ↓

73 76 78 81 82 83

This wine, with a pleasing nose and aromas of hazelnut and gunflint, is a little disappointing on the palate, although it remains crisp. (1982) ✔ Bourgogne Aligoté, Bourgogne, Mâcon.
↬ Coop. des Vignerons de Buxy, Les Vignes de la Croix, 71390 Buxy; tel. 85 92 03 03 ⊺ By appt.

DENIZOT PERE ET FILS

□	5ha	2000	3 D ▤ ◐ ↓

(82) 83

Aromas of walnut, yeast and mushrooms characterize this wine which still has a pronounced woody flavour and needs a year or two of bottle age to mature. (1982)
↬ GAEC Denizot Père et Fils, Les Moirots, Bissey-sous-Cruchaud, 71390 Buxy; tel. 85 42 16 93 ⊺ By appt.

CHATEAU DE LA SAULE**

☐   8ha   35000   ▨ D ▮ ◑ ⚓

76 79 *81 *82

This is a typical Chardonnay, with its fine golden-green colour, hazelnut bouquet and good balance. (1983) ✔ Bourgogne Aligoté, Bourgogne Passe-Tout-Grain.
☛ Alain Roy-Thevenin, Montagny-les-Buxy, 71390 Buxy; tel. 85 42 11 83 ⴹ By appt. Closed 15–30 Aug.

JEAN VACHET**

☐   3ha   19800   ▨ D ▮ ⚓

78 79 81 82 *⟨83⟩

A regular medal winner at the Concours Général de Paris. A clear, bright 1983 with an attractive aroma of dried fruits. A very fine bottle with considerable promise. (1983) ✔ Bourgogne, Bourgogne Aligoté, Bourgogne Passe-Tout-Grain.
☛ Jean Vachet, St-Vallerin, 71390 Buxy ⴹ By appt.

CHARLES VIENOT*

☐   400   ▨ D

⟨82⟩ 83 *84

Pale golden-green colour with typical aromas of hazelnut, almond and kirsch. Soft, round flavour. Ready to drink. (1982)
☛ Ets Charles Vienot, 5 Quai Dumorey, 21700 Nuits-St-Georges; tel. 80 62 31 05 ⴹ By appt.

THE MACONNAIS
Mâcon, Mâcon-Supérieur, and Mâcon-Villages

The white wines may also be called Pinot-Chardonnay-Mâcon. The appellations Mâcon, Mâcon-Superieur or Mâcon followed by the commune name are used for red, white and rosé wines. The production area is relatively large, and the diversity of vineyard sites, from the Tournus region to the Mâcon area, ensures a wide variety of wine styles.

The best-known area is that around Vire, Clesse, Lugny and Chardonnay, where the soil is perfect for producing pleasant, light white wines. Many wine-growers in this sector have organized themselves into cooperatives to produce and commercialize their wine together. The total production of white wine has increased to reach about 90 000 hectolitres. About 50 000 hectolitres of red are also produced; growers are now moving away from the Gamay grape, which originally earned the reputation of this appellation, in favour of the Pinot Noir.

Mâcon Supérieur

THOMAS BASSOT

▮   2500   ▨ D

83 84

Clear bright colour with light aromas and fresh, strong flavours which would suit charcuterie. (1983)
☛ Thomas Bassot, 5 Quai Dumorey, 21700 Nuits-St-Georges; tel. 80 62 31 05 ⴹ By appt.

BENAS FRERES*

▮   7.5ha   20000   ▨ D ▮ ⚓

73 76 ⟨76⟩ 77 *79 ⟨79⟩ *81 ⟨83⟩

Well-developed fruity aromas and a fresh lively flavour with a good finish. Very much in the 'house' style of this firm. (1983)
☛ Ets Bénas Frères, Serrières, 71960 Pierreclos; tel. 85 35 71 95 ⴹ By appt.

COOPERATIVE DE CHARNAY*

▮   20000   ▨ D ▮ ⚓

⟨83⟩ 84

Violet hints enrich the attractive, limpid red colour. The fruity nose is very open, with strong aromas of banana and fruit drops. Fresh, light smooth flavour; should be drunk young. (1984)
☛ Cave Coop. de Charnay, Charnay, 71000 Mâcon; tel. 85 85 34 54 2 ⴹ By appt.

COLLIN ET BOURISSET*

▮   25000   ▨ ▮ ⚓

*76 *78 79 81 *⟨83⟩

A clear raspberry colour and a nose of crushed soft fruit and vanilla. Well-balanced, round, rich flavour. (1983)
☛ MM. Collin et Bourisset, 71680 Crêche-sur-Saône; tel. 85 37 11 15 ⴹ No visitors.

RENE GAILLARD*

▨   1ha   2000   ▨ D ◑

81 82 ⟨83⟩ ▨

Very fine mature pink shade a clearly-flavoured aromatic wine that has reached its peak. Drink now. (1983)
☛ René Gaillard, La Roche-Vineuse, 71960 Pierreclos; tel. 85 37 72 49 ⴹ No visitors.

PRODUCTEURS DE LUGNY-ST-GENGOUX*

▮   140ha   150000   ▨ D ▮ ⚓

76 78 79 82 *⟨83⟩

This cooperative, one of the largest in the Mâconnais, is very good at making this type of fruity, thirst-quenching wine. The 1983 vintage is sufficiently firm to age well. (1983)
☛ Prod. de Lugny-St-Gengoux, Lugny-St-Gengoux, 71260 Lugny; tel. 85 33 22 85 ⴹ By appt.

LYCEE AGRICOLE DE MACON-DAVAYE*

▮   6ha   35000   ▨ D ▮ ◑ ⚓

⟨82⟩ 83

Produced by the students at the local college of agriculture. Deep ruby colour with high-toned, gamey aromas. Round, supple flavour. At its peak. (1982)

♦┑ Lycée Agricole Mâcon-Davayé, Davayé, 71960 Pierreclos; tel. 85 37 80 66 ⏃ By appt.

MAISON MACONNAISE DES VINS★★

■   14 000   🔳 D ■ ↓
76 78 79 82 ⑧ 🔳 84

When grown on granite soil, the Gamay generally produces excellent results. This red Mâcon vinified in the beaujolais style has a nose of fruit drops and grapes. Firm and well constructed, it should age well. (1983)
♦┑ Maison Mâconnais des Vins, 484 Ave de Lattre-de-Tassigny, 7100 Mâcon; tel. 85 38 36 70 ⏃ By appt. Closed 1 May, 25 Dec., 1st week in Jan.

PIERRE MAHUET★

■   3 ha   2000   🔳 D ⑪ ↓
81 82 ⑧ 🔳

Clear, purplish red. Nose gives off the scent of small red fruits (redcurrants and blackcurrants). Vivacity and freshness are noteable on the palate, making this a very pleasant bottle; to be drunk at once. (1984)
♦┑ Pierre Mahuet, La Roche-Vineuse, 71960 Pierreclos; tel. 85 37 70 82 ⏃ By appt.

CAVE DES VIGNERONS DE MANCEY★★

■   25 ha   80 000   🔳 D ■ ↓
★82 ★83 🔳 ★84

These growers have once again picked a winner. Crisp, fruity, densely flavoured wine with peppery aromas and good length on the palate. (1983) ✔ Bourgogne Pinot Noir, Crément de Bourgogne, Bourgogne Passe-Tout-Grain.
♦┑ Cave coop. de Mancey, Mancey, 71240 Sennecey-le-Grand; tel. 85 51 00 83 ⏃ By appt.

DOMAINE LES PROVENCHERES★

■   4.5 ha   15 000   🔳 D ■ ↓
75 76 81 82 ⑧ 🔳 84

This is an excellent mealtime wine, fruity, refreshing but somewhat tough. (1983)
♦┑ Maurice Gonon, Les Provenchères, Serrières, 71960 Pierreclos; tel. 85 35 71 96 ⏃ By appt.

DES VIEUX SAINT-SORCIN★★

■   3 ha   3000   🔳 D ⑪
⑧ 🔳

Bright, clear redcurrant colour. Interesting young, fresh slightly exotic bouquet. Round, fleshy flavour. Good value. (1983)
♦┑ René Gaillard, La Roche-Vineuse, 71960 Pierreclos; tel. 85 37 72 49 ⏃ By appt.

PIERRE SANTE★

■   1.5 ha   10 000   🔳 D ■ ⑪ ↓
76 79 81 82 ★83 🔳

Very lovely with beautiful ruby-red colour. Clear and light. Refreshing and fruity, and proves supple and round on the palate. (1983)
♦┑ Pierre Santé, La Roche-Vineuse, 71960 Pierreclos; tel. 85 37 80 57 ⏃ By appt.

JEAN SIGNORET★★

▨   0.65 ha   2000   🔳 D ■ ⑪ ↓
76 82 🔳 84

Light, pleasant wine, with a clear pink colour. Highly aromatic, refreshing flavour. Goes marvellously well with charcuterie. (1983)
♦┑ Jean Signoret, Hameau de Cray, Clessé, 71260 Lugny; tel. 85 36 93 74 ⏃ By appt.

JEAN-CLAUDE THEVENET
Mâcon Pierreclos★

■   12 ha   36 000   ② D ■ ↓
81 82 83 🔳 ★84

Fine, bright ruby colour and delicate fruity nose; very harmonious on the palate. (1983)
♦┑ Jean-Claude Thevenet, Le Bourg, 71960 Pierreclos; tel. 85 35 72 21 ⏃ Mon.–Sat. 7.30–12.00/ 13.30–19.00.

COOPERATIVE DE VERZE★★

■   86 ha   15 000   🔳 D ■ ↓
78 79 82 ★⑧

Attractive bright ruby colour, with a powerful well-developed bouquet with notes of game and vanilla. This wine has matured well, with good tannins and a rounded, fairly rich flavour. A pleasing bottle. (1983)
♦┑ Cave Coop. de Verze, Verze, 71960 Pierreclos; tel. 85 85 33 307 ⏃ By appt.

CHARLES VIENOT

■   2000   🔳 D
⑧ 84

Bright, deep red with a well-balanced bouquet. Slightly rustic, wild berry flavours on the palate. Drink with dried sausages.
♦┑ Ets Charles Vienot, 5 Quai Dumorey, 21700 Nuits-St-Georges; tel. 80 62 31 05 ⏃ By appt.

Mâcon-Villages

ADRIEN ARCELIN

☐   2 ha   🔳 D ■ ↓
★76 ★🔳 ★81 ★83

Attractive golden-yellow colour and smooth, round flavour with a fine note of verbena. (1983)
♦┑ Adrien Arcelin, La Roche-Vineuse, 71960 Pierreclos; tel. 85 36 61 38 ⏃ By appt.

THOMAS BASSOT★

☐   2500   🔳 D
⑧ 84

Limpid, golden-green colour and mild floral nose. Firmness on the palate, with a good overall balance. (1983)
♦┑ Thomas Bassot, 5 Quai Dumoray, 21700 Nuits-St-Georges; tel. 80 62 31 05 ⏃ By appt.

PAUL BEAUDET★

☐   15 ha   50 000   🔳 ■ ↓
82 ⑧ 🔳 84

With its complex nose of lemon and spices, this rich smooth wine would go very well with freshwater fish or goat's cheese. (1983) ✔ Pouilly Fuissé, St-Véran, Bourgogne Passe-Tout-Grain.

◆ Paul Beaudet, Pontanevaux, 71570 La Cha-pelle-de Guinchay; tel. 85 36 72 76 ⟁ Mon.–Fri. 8.00–12.00/14.00–17.00. Closed 15 July–15 Aug., 22 Dec.–2 Jan.

BENAS FRERES*

☐		3ha	5000	③ D ▮ ↓

73 76 **76** 77 ★79 ★**79** ★81 83

Attractive clear golden-yellow colour and oaky floral nose. Pleasant aroma of Chardonnay on the palate, with a hint of freshness. (1983)
◆ Ets Bénas Frères, 71960 Pierreclos; tel. 85 35 71 95 ⟁ By appt.

ETS BERTRAND *Vallières**

☐			10000	③ D ▮ ↓

76 78 79 81 ★⑧ ★**83**

A fine golden-yellow colour and a very well-developed nose. Smooth and light on the palate. (1983)
◆ Ets Bertrand, Sologny, 71960 Pierreclos; tel. 85 36 60 38 ⟁ By appt.

CHATEAU DES BOIS*

☐		3ha	22000	④ D ▮ ↓

78 79 ⑧ **82** 83 84

This Mâcon-Villages, with its elegant golden-green colour and slightly harsh young flavour will soften with age. Perfect with andouillette. (1982)
✔ Bourgogne Passe-Tout-Grain, Bourgogne Pinot Noir.
◆ Philibert Moreau, 4 Rue Georges Lecomte, 71003 Mâcon; tel. 85 38 42 87 ⟁ By appt. ◆ Héri-tiers Moreau.

DOMAINE DE LA BON GRAN**

☐		7ha	30000	④ D ▮ ◗ ↓

78 79 81 ⑧ 83

Famous for fine wines for three centuries, this vineyard produces only small quantities of this remarkably elegant golden wine. Very successful; aromatic and well balanced, with a very long finish. (1982)
◆ Jean-Claude Thevenet, Le Bourg, 71960 Pier-reclos; tel. 85 35 72 21 ⟁ By appt.

ANDRE BONHOMME *Mâcon-Viré**

☐		6ha	42000	④ D ▮ ◗ ↓

⑦⑤ 78 79 81 82 ★**83** ★84

Fine, bright yellow-gold; elegant, refined aromas and full, smooth flavour with good acidity and length. (1983)
◆ André Bonhomme, Cidex 2108, 71260 Viré; tel. 85 33 11 86 ⟁ By appt.

ROBERT BRIDON*

☐		4ha	1500	③ D ▮ ↓

⑦⑥ 78 79 81 82 ★**83** ★84

Fairly strong golden-yellow colour and refined Chardonnay aromas. On the palate, a touch of new oak, together with honey and gingerbread. Warmth, vigour and good length. (1983)
◆ Robert Bridon, Dom. de Thurissey, Montbel-let, 71260 Lugny; tel. 85 33 13 24 ⟁ By appt.

DOMAINE DES CARMES *Saint-Pierre**

☐		3ha	42000	④ D ▮

69 72 75 ⑧ 83 **84**

This wine is delicate in its pale golden colour, but has a reserved bouquet of laurel and thyme, and rather thin body. (1982) ✔ Mâcon Supérieur, Bourgogne Aligoté, Bourgogne Passe-Tout-Grain, Bourgogne Pinot Noir.
◆ Les Caves Rippe, le Prieuré, Bissy-la-Mâcon-naise, 71260 Lugny; tel. 85 33 23 22 ⟁ By appt.
◆ Ripe-Rattez.

COOPERATIVE VINICOLE DE CHAINTRE***

☐		15ha	20000	③ D ▮ ↓

71 73 78 79 82 ⑧ **83**

This white Mâcon-Villages is very fruity, crisp, round and well balanced. The bouquet is unusually persistent. (1983) ✔ Pouilly-Fuissé, St-Véran.
◆ Coop. Vinicole de Chaintré, Cedex 418, Chaintré, 71570 La-Chapelle-de-Guinchety; tel. 85 35 61 61 ⟁ By appt.

CHANSON PERE ET FILS**

☐				④ D ▮ ↓

68 78 79 **79** ⑧ 83

The marly soil and warm climate of southern Burgundy give Mâcon-Villages a very gulpable, round, rich flavour, here heightened by attractive aromas of banana and apple. A very good exam-ple of the appellation. (1982)
◆ *MM*. Chanson Père et Fils, 10–12 Rue Paul-Chanson, 21200 Beaune; tel. 80 22 33 00 ⟁ No visitors.

CAVE COOPERATIVE DE CHARDONNAY

☐		200ha	350000	③ D ▮ ↓

76 **76** 78 79 81 82 83 84

A light wine on the palate, with a pale golden colour and subtle slightly yeasty aromas. Should be kept for a year if it is to be enjoyed at its best. (1984)
◆ Cave Coop. de Chardonnay, Chardonnay, 71700 Tournus; tel. 85 51 06 49 ⟁ By appt.

CAVE COOPERATIVE DE CHARNAY *Elevage-sous-bois**

☐		30ha	15000	③ D ◗ ↓

★83 ★**83**

Bright colour and good varietal character with aromas of flowers, dried fruit and hazelnuts. Powerful oaky flavour with excellent acidity and a clean finish. (1983)
◆ Cave Coop. de Charnay, Charnay-les-Mâcon, 71000 Mâcon; tel. 85 34 54 24 ⟁ By appt.

CAVE COOPERATIVE DE CHARNAY**

☐		30ha	15000	③ D ▮ ↓

76 79 **79** ★81 ★82 ★83

A good example of the appellation with its fine golden-green colour and fresh bouquet; initially slightly reticent flavour which rounds out and finishes well. Excellent Chardonnay character. (1983)

369

➤ Cave Coop. de Charnay, Charnay-les-Mâcon, 71000 Mâcon; tel. 85 34 54 24 **Ⴘ** By appt.

DOMAINE DE CHAZELLES

☐ 4 ha 5000 **3** **D** **ⅰ** **⑪**

75 76 79 80 ⑧② *84

The wines of Viré, known as long ago as the 8th century, are generally crisp, with a pronounced earthy taste. This bottle has a dry, fruity flavour with good acidity and holds well on the palate. Its weight and length promise to make this a fine accompaniment to fish. (1982) ✔ Mâcon.
➤ Jean-Noel Chaland, En Chapotin, Cedex 2163, Viré, 71260 Lugny; tel. 85 33 11 18 **Ⴘ** By appt. Closed Sun. and public holidays.

COLLIN ET BOURISSET
*Les Giraudières**

☐ 12000 **4** **ⅰ** **↓**

*83 *■**83** *84

A fine colour, characteristic of this appellation, and an expressive floral nose. Rich, sustained flavour. (1983)
➤ *MM*. Collin et Bourisset, Rue de la Gare, 71680 Crêches-sur-Saône; tel. 85 37 11 15 **Ⴘ** No visitors.

COLLIN ET BOURISSET*

☐ 80000 **3** **ⅰ** **↓**

*83 *■**83** *84 *■**84**

Pale golden-green colour, mild but pleasant nose and soft, smooth flavour. (1983)
➤ *MM*. Collin et Bourisset, Rue de la Gare, 71680 Crêches-sur-Saône; tel. 85 37 11 15 **Ⴘ** No visitors.

DOMAINE DE LA CONDEMINE**

☐ 135 ha 9000 **4** **D** **ⅰ** **⑪**

82 83

The honeysuckle bouquet matches warm reflections that play in the golden-green colour. The rich, powerful, aromas hold up. (1982)
➤ Véronique et Pierre Janny, Péronne, 71260 Lugny; tel. 85 36 97 03 **Ⴘ** By appt.

RENE GAILLARD*

☐ 3.5 ha 3000 **3** **D** **⑪** **↓**

82 **■82**

Fine yellow-gold colour and aromatic nose, with touches of honeysuckle, mint and lemon; firm on the palate. (1982)
➤ René Gaillard, La Roche-Vineuse, 71960 Pierreclos; tel. 85 37 72 49 **Ⴘ** No visitors.

DOMAINE DES GRANGES*

☐ 6 ha 40000 **3** **D** **⑪** **↓**

82 ⑧③

This vineyard is ideally situated for the Chardonnay. Dry, fruity, fairly long, flavour. Will go well with the local charcuterie. (1983) ✔ Beaujolais Blanc, Pouilly Fuissé.
➤ Jean-François Cognard, Chaintré, 71570 La Chapelle-de-Guinchay; tel. 85 37 16 20 **Ⴘ** By appt.

CHATEAU DE LA GREFFIERE

☐ 4 ha 25000 **2** **D** **ⅰ** **↓**

69 76 78 82 *⑧③ **84**

This pale golden wine is fruity and floral, with a touch of lemony acidity typical of the 1983 vintage. Round and long on the palate. (1983)
✔ Mâcon la Roche-Vineuse, Bourgogne Passe-Tout-Grain, Marc de Bourgogne.
➤ Henri et Vincent Greuzard, La Roche-Vineuse, 71960 Pierreclos; tel. 85 37 79 11 **Ⴘ** By appt.

DOMAINE GUILLOT-BROUX
*Grévilly**

☐ 1 ha 13000 **3** **D** **ⅰ** **⑪** **↓**

79 81 **■81** **82 83**

The Chardonnay nose is enriched by a particularly pronounced oaky note. Warm, long flavour. (1983)
➤ Dom. Guillot-Broux, Cruzille, 71260 Lugny; tel. 85 33 21 89 **Ⴘ** By appt. Closed 1–15 Aug.

DOMAINE GUILLOT-BROUX
*Les Perrières**

☐ 1 ha 13000 **3** **D** **⑪** **↓**

79 81 **■81** **82 83**

Clear, pale yellow colour and well developed, refined aromas of flowers, honey and vanilla. A lively, well-rounded wine with a good finish. (1983)
➤ Dom. Guillot-Broux, Cruzille, 71260 Lugny; tel. 85 33 21 89 **Ⴘ** By appt. Closed 1–15 Aug.

CAVE COOPERATIVE D'IGE**

☐ 81 ha 120000 **3** **D** **ⅰ** **↓**

71 76 78 81 *■**82** *83 **84**

A warm powerful wine, typical of the 1983 vintage. Rich, bright golden colour and very developed aromas. (1983)
➤ Cave Coop. d'Igé, Igé, 71960 Pierreclos; tel. 85 33 33 65 **Ⴘ** By appt.

CAVE COOPERATIVE D'IGE
*Ch. London**

☐ 5 ha 25000 **3** **D** **ⅰ** **↓**

71 76 78 81 *82 *■**82** *83 **84**

Bright golden-yellow with remarkably full aromas of flowers and dried fruit. This wine has a firm, scented palate and good balance and length. (1983)
➤ Cave Coop. d'Igé, Igé, 71960 Pierreclos; tel. 85 33 33 56 **Ⴘ** By appt.

HENRI LAFARGE**

☐ 2.5 ha 10000 **3** **D** **ⅰ** **⑪** **↓**

73 78 79 81 82 ⑧③

A powerful wine, with a very fruity nose and long smooth flavour. Attractive finish. (1983)
➤ Henri Lafarge, Bray, 71250 Cluny; tel. 65 59 21 1 **Ⴘ** By appt.

LORON ET FILS*

☐ 30000 **3** **ⅰ** **↓**

82 **■82** **83 84**

Golden-yellow colour and well developed yeasty aromas. Clean, fresh flavour. (1983)
➤ Ets Loron et Fils, Pontanevaux, 71570 La

Chapelle-de-Guinchay; tel. 85 36 70 25 ☿ No visitors.

PRODUCTEURS DE LUGNY-ST-GENGOUX
Cuvée Henri Boulay★

□		150ha	150 000	**3** **D** **▮**
76 78 79 82 (83) 83 84				

This Mâcon-Villages, light golden in colour, is dry, fruity, round and well balanced, with persistent aromas of gunflint. (1983)
❧ Prod. Lugny-St-Gengoux, Lugny-St-Gengoux, 71260 Lugny; tel. 85 33 22 85 ☿ By appt.

PRODUCTEURS DE LUGNY-ST-GENGOUX *Charmes*★

□		88ha	600 000	**3** **D** **▮** **↓**
76 78 79 82 (83) 83				

From the home of the Chardonnay, this golden-green is dry, very aromatic, with a smooth full-bodied flavour. Should keep well. (1983)
❧ Prod. Lugny-St-Gengoux, Lugny-St-Gengoux, 71260 Lugny; tel. 85 33 22 85 ☿ By appt.

PRODUCTEURS DE LUGNY-ST-GENGOUX★★

☑		10ha	35 000	**3** **D** **▮** **↓**
76 78 79 82 ★(83) 83				

From the Gamay noir à jus blanc, this very fine rosé has all the finesse, lightness and smoothness of a white wine. This northern region of Mâconnais is famous for its rosés, which should be drunk chilled with pork dishes. (1983)
❧ Prod. Lugny-St-Gengoux, Lugny-St-Gengoux, 71260 Lugny; tel. 85 33 22 85 ☿ By appt.

MAISON MACONNAISE DES VINS★

□			10 000	**3** **D** **▮** **↓**
78 79 81 82 ★(83) 84				

This dry and well-balanced Mâcon-Villages exhales a summery bouquet of dog rose, honeysuckle and orange blossom. Smooth fat flavour with good acidity. (1983) ✔ Crément de Bourgogne, Pouilly Vinzelles, Mâcon Rosé, St-Amour.
❧ Maison Mâconnaise des Vins, 484, Ave de Lattre-de-Tassigny, 71000 Mâcon; tel. 85 38 36 70 ☿ Daily 8.00–21.00. Closed 1 May, 25 Dec., 1st week of Jan.

CLAUDE MANCIAT★

□		5ha	8400	**3** **D** **▯** **↓**
76 76 79 80 ★81 ★81 ★82 83 83				

Bright, clear colour and characteristic floral Chardonnay nose. Firm but round on the palate. Good balance and length. (1983)
❧ Claude Manciat, Lévigny-Charnay, 71000 Mâcon; tel. 85 34 18 77 ☿ By appt.

RENE MICHEL★★

□		2ha	24 000	**3** **D** **▮** **▯** **↓**
73 (78) ★80 ★81 ★82 ★83				

Lovely pale, white-gold colour and charming honeysuckle nose. On the palate, smooth, rich, round and agreeable. (1982)
❧ René Michel, Cray, Cléssé, 71260 Lugny; tel. 85 36 94 27 ☿ By appt.

CHATEAU DE MIRANDE★★

□		8ha	48 000	**3** **▮** **↓**
83 83 84				

This Mâcon-Villages is a fine golden colour and has a very typical expressive Chardonnay nose. A full but rather sharply flavoured wine. (1983)
❧ Ets Loron et Fils, Pontanevaux, 71570 La Chapelle-de-Guinchay; tel. 85 36 70 52 ☿ No visitors.

CHATEAU DE MIRANDE★★

□		15ha	90 000	**3** **D** **▮** **▯** **↓**
76 79 82 (83) 84				

The youthful aromas of peach and honeysuckle will develop notes of dry fruit, walnut and hazelnut when mature, making this a wine well suited to accompany freshwater fish. Dry, sappy flavour and good length. (1983)
❧ Patrice de l'Epine, La rivière, Montbellet, 71260 Lugny; tel. 85 33 13 45 ☿ By appt.

GILBERT MORNAND *Mâcon-Clessé*

□		6ha	36 000	**3** **D** **▮** **▯** **↓**
81 81 83 83				

A warm, powerful wine, with an attractive golden-yellow colour and a nose somewhat evocative of fresh yeast. (1983)
❧ Gilbert Mornand, Clessé, 71260 Lugny; tel. 85 36 94 90 ☿ By appt. Closed Aug.

NICOLAS★★★

□			74 000	**2** **▮**

An attractive wine with a light golden colour and a subtle nose of blackthorn flowers. Very long, fruity, floral flavour with a remarkable finish. (1983)
❧ Ets Nicolas, 2 Rue Valmy, 94220 Charenton; tel. 01 37 59 20 ☿ No visitors.

PRODUCTEURS DE PRISSE★★

□		55ha	200 000	**3** **D** **▮** **↓**
(76) 79 ★81 ★81 ★82 ★82 ★83 ★83				

Clear and bright with fine golden-yellow colour and floral and hazelnut aromas also found on the palate, which shows firm Chardonnay character. Round, harmonious, and very good length. (1983)
❧ Producteurs de Prissé, Prissé 71960 Pierreclos; tel. 85 37 82 53 ☿ By appt.

DOMAINE DE ROALLY
Mâcon Viré★★★

□		3ha	15 000	**4** **D** **▮** **▯**
75 76 77 78 79 (82) 83				

A very fine Viré, produced by a first-class estate. The wine is vinified in small quantities and fermentation is carried out at low temperatures to obtain the maximum bouquet. In all, one of the best Mâcons, full, round and smooth. (1983)
❧ Henri Goyard, Viré, '71260 Lugny; tel. 85 33 10 31 ☿ By appt. Closed 15–30 Aug.

371

PRODUCT OF FRANCE

GRAND VIN DE BOURGOGNE

MISE AU ~~DOMAINE~~ DOMAINE

MÂCON-VIRÉ
DOMAINE DE ROALLY
Appellation Mâcon-Viré Contrôlée   750 ml

HENRI GOYARD, Propriétaire-Récoltant à Viré - S.-&-L. - France

CLAUDIUS RONGIER★

□		6ha	15000	3 D ▪ ↓

74 75 76 79 81 ★⑧ 82 83

Attractive pale green-gold with a refined minty bouquet. Rich muscat-like flavour. (1982)
☛ Claudius Rongier, Clessé, 71260 Lugny; tel. 85 36 94 05 ϒ By appt.

PIERRE SANTÉ★★

□		15ha	12000	3 D ▪ ⑪ ↓

76 79 ★82 ★83 ★83

Pale golden colour and highly aromatic nose of honeysuckle; round and rich on the palate, with good finish. (1983)
☛ Pierre Santé, La Roche-Vineuse, 71960 Pierreclos; tel. 85 37 80 57 ϒ By appt.

PAUL ET PHILIBERT TALMARD
Cuvée Joseph Talmard

□		6ha	40000	3 D ▪ ↓

⑦⑤ 77 78 79 81 82 83

Fine golden colour with pleasant, clean aromas. Elegant, refreshing fairly lean flavour. A good 1984. (1984)
☛ Paul et Philibert Talmard, Uchizy, 71700 Tournus; tel. 85 51 10 37 ϒ By appt.

PAUL ET PHILIBERT TALMARD★

□		8ha	60000	3 D ▪ ↓

⑦⑤ 77 78 79 81 82 83

Very clear yellow with gold-green highlights. Attractive, young, fruity aromas. Dry, briskly acid flavour with a reasonable finish. (1984)
☛ Paul et Philibert Talmard, Uchizy, 71700 Tournus; tel. 85 51 10 37 ϒ By appt.

THORIN★★

□			100000	4 ▪ ↓

76 78 79 ★82 ★⑧

Delicate and elegant with a fine golden yellow colour and refined bouquet. Aromas evocative of dried fruits, with an overtone of almond. (1983)
☛ ETS Thorin, 71570 La Chapelle-de-Guyinchay; tel. 85 36 70 43 ϒ No visitors.

LES TOURNONS★★

□		5ha	40000	3 D ▪ ⑪ ↓

72 ⑦⑨ 79 82 83 84

Golden-yellow colour and grapey aromas with a note of honeysuckle. Smooth, round and pleasing on the palate. (1983)
☛ Ets Chevalier et Fils, Les Tournons, Charnay-les-Mâcon, 71000 Mâcon; tel. 85 34 26 74 ϒ By appt.

ANDRÉ TRENEL★

□			13000	3 ▪ ↓

⑦⑨ 81 82 83

Pale, clear colour and rich, subtle floral aromas; a dry, light, quaffing wine with good acidity. (1984)
☛ André Trenel, 71000 Mâcon; tel. 85 34 48 20 ϒ No visitors.

CHATEAU DE VERNEUIL
Clos des Tournons★★

□		4ha	22000	3 ▪ ↓

76 78 79 82 ⑧ 83 ★84

This fat, round and smooth 1983 wine has an aromatic bouquet of flowers and fruit and is characterized by crispness and elegance. The nose is floral and the palate fruity, with a pleasant persistence. Attractive golden-green colour; should age well. (1983) ✔ Mâconnais Rouge et Blanc, Beaujolais, Cotes-de-Beaune, Vins Mousseux.
☛ Ets Chevalier et Fils, Les Tournons, Charnay-les-Mâcon, 71000 Mâcon; tel. 85 34 26 74 ϒ By appt. Closed Aug.

CAVE COOPERATIVE DE VERZE★★

□		65ha	15000	3 D ▪ ↓

76 76 79 79 81 81 83 83

Bright, golden-yellow colour, with pronounced floral aromas. Good Chardonnay character on the palate with lingering scents of flowers, hazelnut and a trace of oak. Balance, length and well-judged acidity. (1983)
☛ Cave Coop. de Verzé, Verzé, 71960 Pierreclos; tel. 85 33 30 76 ϒ By appt. Closed during harvest.

CHARLES VIENOT★

□			3500	3 D ▪ ↓

⑧ 84

Attractive pale golden-green colour; discreet floral nose and good refreshing palate. (1983)
☛ Ets Charles Vienot, 21700 Nuits-St-Georges; tel. 80 62 31 05 ϒ By appt.

CAVE COOPERATIVE DE VIRE

□		275ha	2000000	3 D ▪ ⑪ ↓

★75 76 ★79 ★82 ★84

Clear, shining gold colour and powerful Chardonnay aromas. Well constructed and round, with a good long finish. (1983) ✔ Crémant de Bourgogne.
☛ Coop. de Viré, 71260 Lugny; tel. 85 33 12 64 ϒ Mon.–Thur.   8.30–12.00/14.00–18.30;   Fri. 8.30–12.00/14.00–17.00.

Pouilly-Fuissé
Above the village, the profiles of the Solutré and Vergisson Rocks rear upwards into the sky like the prow of a ship. At their feet lie the Pouilly-Fuissé vineyards – the most prestigious of the Mâconnais – located in the communes of Fuissé, Solutré, Pouilly, Vergisson and Chaintré.

About 32 000 hectolitres of wine are produced annually.

Vigorous, lively and fragrant, Pouilly wines have achieved world-wide fame, and their prices have always put them in keen competition with Chablis and even Meursault wines. When aged in oak casks, they acquire a distinctive aroma of roasted almonds or hazelnuts.

AUVIGNE-BURRIER-REVEL
La Frairie★★

□	2 ha	5000	5 ◫ ↓

76 78 79 ★80 81 **82** ⑧₃

Seductive, golden-green colour, floral bouquet and hazelnut flavour, round, fat and full. This wine promises a fine future. (1983) ✔ Maconnais Blanc.
➦ Ste Auvigne-Burrier-Revel, Charnay-les-Mâcon, 71000 Mâcon; tel. 85 34 17 36 ☎ Mon.–Thurs. 8.00–12.00/13.30–17.30. Fri. 8.00–12.00/13.30–16.30. Closed Aug.

DANIEL BALVAY★★

□	3.5 ha	2400	5 D ▮ ◫ ↓

★81 ★82 ★83

Pale golden-green colour and refined, expressive aromas. Light flavour marked by a note of gunflint. Should make a fine bottle. (1983)
➦ Daniel Balvay, Solutré, 71960 Pierreclos; tel. 85 37 82 36 ☎ No visitors.

ANDRE BESSON★★

□	6.5 ha	40000	4 D ▮ ↓

78 ★⑦₉ **80** ★82 83

Very attractive, with a subtle, shining hue the colour of old gold; interesting, spicy nose. Smooth, sharply etched flavour, good balance and excellent finish. (1983)
➦ André Besson, Solutré-Pouilly, 71960 Pierreclos; tel. 85 35 81 28 ☎ By appt.

COOPERATIVE VINICOLE DE CHAINTRE *Clos Ressier*★

□	95 ha	400000	4 D ▮ ↓

71 73 **78** 79 **82** ⑧₃

This fine white Burgundy is full of subtlety and distinction. It is for some the king of the Saône-et-Loire whites. An aromatic wine that will keep for a long time. (1983) ✔ St-Véran, Mâcon Chaintré.
➦ Coop. Vinicole de Chaintré, Cedex 418, Chaintré, 71570 La Chapelle-de-Guinchay; tel. 85 35 61 61 ☎ By appt. Closed Aug.

CHEVALIER ET FILS

□		30000	5 D ▮ ◫ ↓

79 ⁊⁹ **82 83** 84

An attractive, bright golden colour and a discreet, floral nose. Fairly rich on the palate with a mild, but elegant flavour. (1983)
➦ Ets Chevalier et Fils, Les Tournons, Charnay-les-Mâcon, 71000 Mâcon; tel. 85 34 26 74 ☎ No visitors.

COLLIN ET BOURISSET★

□		75000	6 ▮ ↓

78 79 **82 83** ★84

Attractive, old gold colour and well developed nose. Smooth and crisp on the palate, with a refined, scented flavour. A distinguished wine with good length. (1983)
➦ *MM*. Collin et Bourisset, Rue de la Gare, 71680 Crêches-sur-Saône; tel. 85 37 11 15 ☎ No visitors.

LOUIS CURVEUX★

□	3 ha	18000	4 D ◫ ↓

★75 ★76 ★78 **★79** ★83 84

Attractive, clear, green-gold colour and a typical, aromatic Chardonnay nose. Crisp on the palate; will develop even more character with ageing. (1983)
➦ Louis Curveux, Fuissé, 71960 Pierreclos; tel. 85 35 61 51 ☎ No visitors.

GEORGES DUBOEUF *Clos Reissier*★

□	4 ha	24000	5 D ▮ ↓

⁊⁸ 79 ⑧₁ 83

Light golden-green with a full, spicy nose; attractive flavour and finesse on the palate. (1983)
➦ Georges Duboeuf, 71720 Romanèche-Thorins; tel. 85 35 51 13 ☎ Mon.–Fri. 8.00–12.00/14.00–17.00. Closed Aug.

ROGER DUBOEUF *Les Plessis*★

□	5 ha	20000	4 D ◫ ↓

64 69 ★76 **★78** ★79 ★⑧₂ 83 84

This family estate, which dates back to the 15th century, produces a pale yellow-green Pouilly Fuissé. Should be a great white wine after a few years in bottle; one of the finest Mâconnais. (1983) ✔ Mâcon-Villages Blanc, Beaujolais Blanc.
➦ Roger Duboeuf et Fils, Savy, Chaintré, 71570 La Chapelle-de-Guinchay ☎ By appt.

MICHEL FOREST★

□	2.5 ha	10000	5 D ◫ ↓

⑦₁ 76 78 79 **81 83** ⁸³

Typical Pouilly-Fuissé, with its light colour, elegant, rich aromas and dense, lingering flavour. (1983)
➦ Michel Forest, Vergisson, 71960 Pierreclos; tel. 85 37 83 94 ☎ By appt.

CHATEAU FUISSE★★

□	20 ha	96000	5 D ▮ ◫ ↓

79 **81 82 83** 84

Light gold, with rich, clean aromas of fruit and vanilla. Firm, fat flavour with good acidity and length. Very attractive. (1983) ✔ St-Véran, Juliénas, Morgon Charmes.
➦ *MM*. M. Vincent et Fils, Ch. de Fuissé, Fuissé, 71960 Pierreclos; tel. 85 35 61 44 ☎ Closed Aug. and harvest time.

JEAN GOYON★★

| ☐ | | 4ha | 15000 | 5 D ▤ ↓ |

77 78 ★79 81 82 83

Bright golden-green with refined aromas of fruit and acidity. Clean, refreshing persistent flavour. A remarkable bottle and perfect example of the qualities of its appellation. (1983)
☛ Jean Goyon, Solutré, 71960 Pierreclos; tel. 85 35 81 15 ⟁ By appt.

ROGER LASSARAT *Clos de France*★

| ☐ | 0.36ha | 8000 | 5 D ▤ ◑ ↓ |

76 78 79 81 83 84

Fine golden-yellow colour; attractive verbena aromas. Light, crisp flavour and strong finish. (1983)
☛ Roger Lassarat, Vergisson, 71960 Pierreclos; tel. 85 37 82 37 ⟁ By appt.

ROGER LASSARAT *Vieilles Vignes*★

| ☐ | 2ha | 8000 | 5 D ▤ ◑ ↓ |

76 78 79 81 83 84

Attractive golden-yellow colour and rich nose strongly marked by oats. Deep, sharp flavour with good finish. (1983)
☛ Roger Lassarat, Vergisson, 71960 Pierreclos; tel. 85 37 82 37 ⟁ By appt.

LORON ET FILS *Les Vieux-Murs*★★

| ☐ | | 30000 | 5 ◑ ↓ |

⑦⑧ 80 82 83

Bright gold with a flowery nose and fruity, balanced flavour. It is fairly rich with a persistent aftertaste. (1983)
☛ Ets Loron et Fils, Pontanevaux, 71570 La Chapelle-de-Guinchay; tel. 85 36 70 52 ⟁ No visitors.

LORON ET FILS★

| ☐ | | 40000 | 5 ◑ ↓ |

⑦⑧ 80 82 83

Limpid, old gold colour, typical of a Pouilly-Fuissé which is begining to mature. Fairly rich harmonious flavour with crisp pleasing aromas. (1983)
☛ Ets Loron et Fils, Pontanevaux, 71570 La Chapelle-de-Guinchay; tel. 85 36 70 52 ⟁ No visitors.

LORON ET FILS *Rocquenvert*★★

| ☐ | | 30000 | 5 ◑ ↓ |

⑦⑧ 80 82 83

Clear, bright gold colour and warm aromas. Crisp, well-balanced persistent flavour. A very attractive bottle. (1983)
☛ Ets Loron et Fils, Pontanevaux, 71570 La Chapelle-de-Guinchay; tel. 85 36 70 52 ⟁ No visitors.

ROGER LUQUET

| ☐ | 5ha | 30000 | 4 D ▤ ↓ |

78 79 ★81 ⑧③ 84

Beautiful golden-green colour and a pronounced oaky nose. Very round with strong note of oak. (1983) ✔ St-Véran Les Grandes Bruyères, Macon Blanc Clos de Condemine.
☛ Roger Luquet, Le Bourg, Fuissé, 71960 Pierreclos; tel. 85 35 60 91 ⟁ Mon.–Sat. 8.00–12.00/ 13.30–19.00. Closed 15–31 Aug.

CLAUDE MANCIAT★

| ☐ | | 4ha | 6000 | 6 D ◑ ↓ |

76 78 ★80 ★81 82 83

Fine, bright, golden-green colour. Fruity and floral aromas with marked Chardonnay character. Smooth, fat flavour with a very long finish. (1983)
☛ Claude Manciat, Lévigny-Charnay, 71000 Mâcon; tel. 85 34 18 77 ⟁ By appt.

NICOLAS★★

| ☐ | | 5 ▤ ↓ |

An attractive wine with a promising future although it may be drunk now. Reserved for export to the U.S.A. Very light golden colour and an open, floral nose with warm tones, ranging from reseda to vanilla. A slightly surprising, sharp initial impression on the palate with a warm slightly alcoholic finish. (1984)
☛ Ets Nicolas, 2 Rue Valmy, 94220 Charenton; tel. 01 37 59 20 ⟁ No visitors.

CHATEAU POUILLY★

| ☐ | 3ha | 12000 | 6 D ◑ ↓ |

★76 77 ★78 79 80 ★82 83

Light gold colour with rich, warming aromas of caramel, vanilla and toasted almonds. Very clean, almost sharp fruit flavour with a long finish. (1983)
☛ Ets Mommessin, Charnay-les-Mâcon, 71000 Mâcon; tel. 85 34 47 74 ⟁ By appt.

Pouilly-Vinzelles

Two lesser-known small appellation areas are located in the communes of Loche and Vinzelles. They produce wines that are similar in character to a Pouilly-Fuissé but perhaps not quite as full-bodied. Only white wines are produced, totalling about 1000 hectolitres per year.

CHATEAU DE LAYE★

| ☐ | | 13 ha | 30000 | **4** **D** **▮** **⌄** |

★⑳ ★82 83 **84**

'Vinzelles' is an old Gallo-Roman word meaning 'small vine'. The winemaking tradition is indeed long-established here and this wine, with its delicate fruity bouquet and flavour, is a good example of the quality of the appellation. (1984) ✔ Mâcon-Villages Blanc, St-Véran, Beaujolais-Villages, Bourgogne Mousseux. ↬ Caves des Crus-Blancs, 71145 Vinzelles; tel. 85 61 38 ⏃ Mon.–Sat. 8.00–12.00/14.00–18.45.

CHARLES VIENOT★

| ☐ | | | 1000 | **4** **D** **▮** **⌄** |

82 ⑧

Bright yellow-gold with aromas of oak and fern. Full, well-balanced flavour. (1983) ↬ Ets Charles Vienot, 5 Quai Dumorey, 21700 Nuits-St-Georges; tel. 80 62 31 05 ⏃ No visitors.

Saint-Véran

This is the youngest Mâconnais appellation (1971) and is limited to the white wines produced in eight communes in Saône-et-Loire (15000 In the wine hierarchy, St-Véran would probably come between a Pouilly and a Mâcon-Villages. These are light, elegant and fruity wines that are ideal at the beginning of a meal.

Characterized by limestone soil, this appellation lies at the extreme south of the Mâconnais area; as one passes from the Mâconnais to Beaujolais, the soil changes from limestone to granite, and the grape variety from Chardonnay to Gamay.

DANIEL BARRAUD★

| ☐ | | 1 ha | 2000 | **3** **D** **▮** **⌄** |

⑧ **83**

Attractive, light colour with a slight oaky note on the palate. Smooth, full flavour with a good finish. (1983) ↬ Daniel Barraud, Vergisson, 71960 Pierreclos; tel. 85 37 60 17 ⏃

THOMAS BASSOT★

| ☐ | | | 500 | **3** **D** |

82 ⑧

Deep gold-yellow with delicate fern-scented aromas. Smooth, complete flavour. (1982) ↬ Thomas Bassot, 5 Quai Dumorey, 21700 Nuits-St-Georges; tel. 80 62 31 05 ⏃ By appt.

CAVE COOPERATIVE DE CHAINTRE★★

| ☐ | | 16 ha | 80000 | **3** **D** **▮** **⌄** |

71 73 78 79 82 ⑧ **83**

Established in 1928. Many good wines are made here, including this distinguished golden-green Saint-Véran. Its roundness and good length make it well suited to accompany fish, shellfish and seafood. (1983) ✔ Pouilly Fuissé, Mâcon Chaintré. ↬ Coop. Vinicole de Chaintré, Cedex 418, Chaintré, 71570 La Chapelle-de-Guinchay; tel. 85 35 61 61 ⏃ By appt. Closed Aug.

ROBERT DUPERRON

| ☐ | | 1.5 ha | 6000 | **3** **D** **▮** **◖◗** **⌄** |

★79 ★**82** ★83

Full golden-yellow colour, characteristic of the vintage. Fragrant and supple flavour. Drink at once. (1982) ↬ Robert Duperron, Leynes, 71570 La Chapelle-de-Guinchay; tel. 85 35 11 89 ⏃ No visitors.

MAURICE MARTIN★

| ☐ | | 5 ha | 20000 | **3** **D** **◖◗** **⌄** |

76 78 82 ⑧ **83**

Fine wine with vivid white-gold colour, and fruity aromas of apples and pears. Slightly sharp but thirst-quenching flavour. (1983) ↬ Maurice Martin, Aux Pegrins, Davaye, 71960 Pierreclos; tel. 85 37 84 14 ⏃ By appt.

PRODUCTEURS DE PRISSE★★

| ☐ | | 100 ha | 220000 | **3** **D** **▮** **⌄** |

Bright, clear colour. Nose is elegant and fruity, with smell of reinette apples and quince. On the palate, supple and round with a fairly long finish. (1983) ↬ Producteurs de Prissé, Prissé, 71960 Pierreclos; tel. 85 37 82 53 ⏃ By appt.

MARCEL ROBERT★★

| ☐ | | 7 ha | 20000 | **3** **D** **▮** **⌄** |

75 76 78 79 ★82 ★⑧ **83**

Excellent wine that expresses itself in subtle shades. Pale golden-green colour; fruity, aromatic nose and rich, full, soft flavour. (1983) ↬ GAEC Marcel Robert, Chasselas, 71570 La Chapelle-de-Guinchay; tel. 85 35 11 63 ⏃ By appt.

CHARLES VIENOT★

| ☐ | | | 300 | **3** **D** |

82 ⑧

Still rather young but with a firm, powerful flavour and attractive aromas of honeysuckle, fern and honey. (1982) ↬ Ets Charles Vienot, 5 Quai Dumorey, 21700 Nuits-St-Georges; tel. 80 62 31 05 ⏃ By appt.

CHAMPAGNE

CHAMPAGNE is the most northerly viticultural zone in France, situated some 140 km north-east of Paris. To the world, of course, it is the source of the universal wine of celebration which bears its name. Because of this, many people believe that the only wine made in Champagne is champagne. In fact, the Champagne region comprises three different appellations: Champagne, Coteaux Champenois and Rosé de Riceys.

The wine-growing region of Champagne is chiefly located in the departments of the Marne and the Aube, with minor areas extending into the Aisne, the Seine-et-Marne and the Haut-Marne. The whole area covers 34 000 hectares, of which 25 000 hectares are currently given over to vine-growing.

Geologically the region is formed of a chalky bedrock deposited by the ocean some 70 million years ago. Its porous quality and mineral richness give the wines of Champagne their finesse. A superficial layer of clay-limestone covers the bedrock almost 60 per cent of the land under vines. In the Aube – lying to the extreme south-west of the region – the composition of the soil is similar to the marl of its southern neighbour Burgundy. The Champagne growers increase the fertility of their land by generous dressings of organic compost.

At this northerly latitude frosts are common, making it difficult for wine-makers to achieve consistency of production. However, climatic extremes are moderated by the existence of huge tracts of forests: these help balance continental cold with Atlantic warmth, maintaining a relatively humid regional climate. The summers are rarely excessively hot, a fact which favours the quality of the wines. The grape varieties used are Pinot Noir, the noble black grape from which, paradoxically, much white champagne is made, and Chardonnay. Together they make up 52 per cent of the area under vines: the other 48 per cent is taken up by a third variety, Pinot Meunier. The Champagne wine trade employs 31 000 people, 14 000 of them proprietors who grow and make their own wine.

Dominating the trade, however, are the famous champagne houses of the twin capitals Reims and Epernay. These concerns make and sell two-thirds of all Champagne wines – amounting to 160 million bottles in 1983.

Wine has been made in the region since at least the time of the Roman invasion. It was originally white, then red, then 'gris' – that is, white, or almost white, wine produced from a pressing of black grapes only. Already it was known for its annoying habit of foaming up in the casks in which it was delivered. This was the result of a secondary fermentation, which began in the young wine after a period of suspended animation during the winter cold. The secondary fermentation released carbonic gases responsible for the bubbles.

Champagne was transported in casks until 1650. It was probably in England that the young wine was first bottled in any regular way. Early bottling was a crucial first step in transforming the simple Champagne wines of those days into the classic perfection of true champagne. In the bottle the wine continued to ferment, but the carbonic gases dissolved into the wine; when the bottle was opened the gases were released, giving the wine a lively, natural sparkle.

From then on the story was one of gradual development. It was found that by adding sugar and yeast, the quality of the wine – and its sparkle – could be radically improved. The first famous name in this process is that of Dom

Perignon, who was cellar-master of the abbey at Hautvillers at the end of the seventeenth century. A technician of genius, he refined the art of blending wines from different vineyards to achieve the best flavour. He experimented with stronger bottles, and invented the technique of tying on the corks with string, so that the bottled wine could ferment for longer, giving it greater strength and balance – and a longer-lived sparkle.

In 1728 the king's council authorized the distribution of wine in bottles; a year later the first wine-trading company of Champagne, Ruinart, was established. Others were to follow shortly (Möet began in 1743), but it was not until the nineteenth century that most of the large champagne houses were created, or given official recognition. Two further stages in the development of the champagne method took place. The widow Clicquot – who launched the first pink champagne in 1804 – found a way of removing the sediment which built up in the bottle during fermentation. She devised a wooden frame to hold the bottles upside down. Each day the cellarmen gently shook and twisted each bottle so that the sediment gradually accumulated on the cork. At the end of this process – known as the 'remuage' – the cork was swiftly removed and the small amount of wine containing the sediment was expelled (the 'dégorgement'). The bottle was then topped up with champagne of the same blend and vintage and re-corked.

In 1884 Raymond Abbelé added a refinement to this process, known as 'dégorgement à la glace'. The slug of wine containing the sediment was frozen solid by inserting the neck of the upturned bottle into a solution of very cold brine. Once frozen, it could be removed in one piece; the bottle was topped up and re-corked as before.

This is the 'méthode champenoise' as still practised by wine-makers in Reims, Epernay and Ay. Despite many advances in automation since 1945, the elements remain the same. Each house has its distinctive blend, which accounts for the particular flavour and balance of its product. The grapes are bought from the independent wine-growers of the region, the 'vendeurs au kilo'. A committee of growers and merchants fixes the price of grapes each year, and awards each wine-growing commune a 'cotation', or coefficient, reflecting the quality of its production. Those with a value of 100 per cent are permitted to use the title Grand Cru; the range 99–90 per cent is referred to as Premier Cru. The balance is drawn from the range 89–80 per cent. In setting the cotation, a higher value is given to the Pinot Noir and Chardonnay grapes than to Pinot Meunier. The maximum permitted yield per hectare is 13000kg, and no more than one hectolitre must be obtained from pressing 150kg of grapes.

Today the heart of the region is composed of three main areas: the Montagne de Reims in the north; below it, the Vallée de la Marne running from east to west, while, south of the river Marne, the Côte des Blancs extends down from Epernay for some 16km. This heartland is where the great champagne houses find the best grapes to blend. The Montagne, which includes north-facing slopes, is planted with the black Pinot Noir: the wine from here gives the blend structure and solidity. The Vallée de la Marne, with its south and south-east facing slopes, produces Pinot Noir and Pinot Meunier: the extra sun produces wine with a greater degree of roundness and fullness. The east-facing Côte des Blancs grows the white Chardonnay grape, which contributes a distinctive freshness and lightness to the blend.

Champagne is a white wine predominantly produced from black grapes. The clear juice must avoid contact with the outside skins to avoid discoloration. Because of this, extraordinary care is taken to press the grapes with as little delay as possible (so that the grapes should not be crushed under their own weight). Pressing takes place close to the vineyards, using specialized presses of traditional design in which the grapes are spread over a wide surface area so as not to be

Champagne

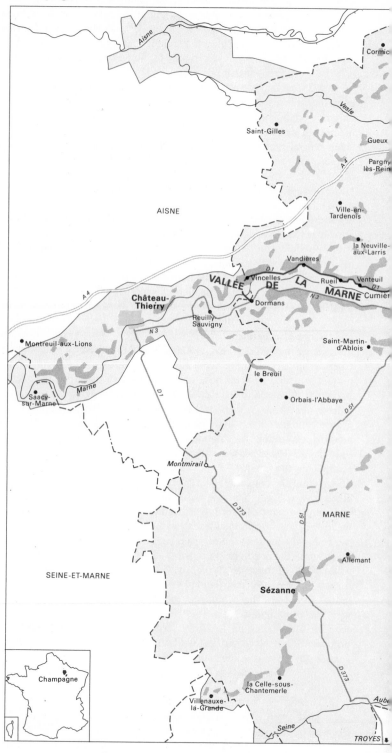

AISNE

SEINE-ET-MARNE

MARNE

Cormic

Vesle

Saint-Gilles

Gueux

Pargny
lès-Rein

Ville-en-
Tardenois

la Neuville-
aux-Larris

Vandières

Vincelles

Rueil   Venteuil

VALLÉE DE LA MARNE

Cumièr

Château-
Thierry

Dormans

Reuilly-
Sauvigny

Saint-Martin-
d'Ablois

Montreuil-aux-Lions

le Breuil

Marne

Orbais-l'Abbaye

Saacy-
sur-Marne

Montmirail

Allemant

Sézanne

la Celle-sous-
Chantemerle

Villenauxe-
la-Grande

Seine

Aube

TROYES

Champagne

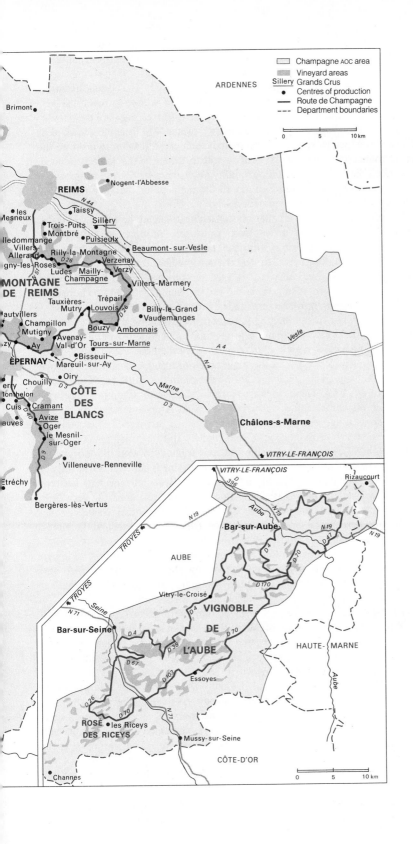

ARDENNES

Champagne AOC area
Vineyard areas
Sillery Grands Crus
• Centres of production
—— Route de Champagne
--- Department boundaries

0   5   10 km

Brimont•

REIMS
•Nogent-l'Abbesse
N 44
• les
Mesneux   •Taissy
•Trois-Puits   Sillery
•Montbré
Iledommange   •Puisieulx
Villers-   •Rilly-la-Montagne   •Beaumont- sur-Vesle
Allerand   D 26
gny-les-Roses •Verzenay
•Ludes Mailly- •Verzy
Champagne
MONTAGNE   •Villers-Marmery
DE REIMS
Tauxières-   Trépail
Mutry   •Louvois •Billy-le-Grand
autvillers   •Vaudemanges
•Champillon
Mutigny   Bouzy   Ambonnais
zy   •Ay   Avenay- •Tours-sur-Marne
Val-d'Or
ÉPERNAY •Bisseuil   Vesle
Mareuil-sur-Ay
•Oiry   A 4
erty   Chouilly D 3
lonchelon   N 4
Cuis   •Cramant   CÔTE
auves   Avize   DES   Marne
•Oger   BLANCS   D 3
le Mesnil-
sur-Oger   Châlons-s-Marne

•Villeneuve-Renneville
D 9
Étréchy
•Bergères-lès-Vertus   ♦ VITRY-LE-FRANÇOIS

♦ VITRY-LE-FRANÇOIS
D 396 Rizaucourt
D   Aube   N 19
N 19   N 19
TROYES   Bar-sur-Aube•   N 19   D 47
D 4   D 70
AUBE   N 19
D 4   D 170
TROYES   Vitry-le-Croisé   D 4   VIGNOBLE
N 71   Seine   DE
Bar-sur-Seine•   D 4   L'AUBE   D 70
D 38   HAUTE- MARNE
D 67
D 103   •Essoyes   Aube
D 26
N 71
ROSÉ •les Riceys
DES RICEYS
•Mussy-sur-Seine
CÔTE-D'OR
•Channes   0   5   10 km

over-crushed, and so that the juice can circulate more freely. The process is a very controlled one, designed to draw off the juice from each concentric zone of the grape, and to keep each pressing separate. Champagne grapes are never destemmed. The pressing procedure is strictly regulated. The 'pressoir' has to take 400 kg of grapes – no more, no less. The pressing is done in several stages. The first press, equivalent to ten barrels 'pièces' or 205 litres, is called the 'cuvée'. The pressing is then repeated, and another two pièces (410 litres) are produced. This is called the 'première taille'. The marc is then pressed again to produce the 'deuxième taille'. It is possible to press a fourth time but the juice produced, which is called the 'rebêche', is of low quality and cannot be used in champagne. The three musts are then taken by lorry to the main cellars and are fermented according to regular white-wine procedures.

At the end of the winter the cellar-master begins to blend the cuvée. He tastes all the available wines and mixes them in certain proportions to obtain a harmonious flavour in keeping with the taste of that particular brand of champagne. If he is making a non-vintage champagne he will use the reserve wines that have been made in previous years. It is even legally possible to add a little red wine to make a pink champagne; this is allowed in Champagne, but nowhere else. A few pink champagnes, however, are made by the saignée method.

The next stage begins the lengthy process of transforming still into sparkling wine. Sugar is added to the cuvée in the proportion of 24 grammes per litre; yeast, too, is added. The wine is then bottled (this stage is called the 'tirage'). The yeast converts the sugar into alcohol, at the same time producing carbonic gases which dissolve into the wine. This secondary fermentation in the bottle takes place at a low temperature (11°C). The bottles are stored in the famous Champagne cellars, many of which are carved out of subterranean chalk. After at least one year – or three years for vintage champagne – the bottles are disgorged. The sediment formed by secondary fermentation is removed by the dégorgement à la glace method already described. Finally, the bottle is topped up with the 'dosage', a wine that may or may not have sugar added. If pure wine is added, a 'Brut 100 per cent' is produced: examples are Piper Heidsieck's Brut Sauvage and Laurent Perrier's Ultra Brut, or any champagne that is called 'non dosé'. If very little sugar (1 per cent) is added, the champagne is Brut. The other classifications, related to the percentage of sugar, are Sec (dry, 2–5 per cent); Demi-sec (medium, 5–8 per cent) and Doux (sweet, 8–15 per cent).

After dosage the bottles are shaken to homogenize the contents, and left to rest while the yeasty taste disappears. Afterwards the bottles are labelled and despatched to customers. At that point the champagne is ready to be enjoyed at its best. Allowing it to age is generally considered unnecessary.

A successful champagne depends on a number of factors: the origin and quality of the grapes; the type of pressing; the blend of several reserve wines (in the case of non-vintage champagne); the talent of the master-blender, and the carefully judged dosage. During the maturation period all these elements are given the chance to blend harmoniously together.

The label on a bottle of champagne normally gives rather little information as to the history of the contents. Champagne producers have deliberately chosen a policy whereby the brand name is the consumer's guarantee of consistent character and quality. Accordingly, the label gives the name of the producer and the marque; the approximate dosage (Brut, Sec, etc.); the vintage (where applicable), or the words 'Non-Vintage'; the words 'Blanc de Blancs', if the champagne is made from white grapes only, and (rarely) the name of the commune where the grapes were grown. The words 'Grand Cru' indicate a champagne made from top-quality grapes grown in 12 designated communes, while 41 communes are permitted to classify their production as Premier Cru.

Finally, the status of the producer must be indicated (usually in very small type). Champagne producers are either NM (négociant-manipulant), RM (récoltant-manipulant), CM (coopérative-manipulant) or MA (marque auxiliaire). The RM is the exception to the standardized approach: he may only produce champagne from his own vines, which usually means from within a single commune. Such champagnes are called 'Mono-Cru'.

Although the single appellation Champagne covers the whole area, there are many and varied styles of champagne sufficient to fulfil any purpose and satisfy every taste. Champagne may be Blanc de Blancs (white wine from white grapes); Blanc de 80s (white wine from black grapes – Pinot Noir, Pinot Meunier, or both); or a mixture of these in every conceivable proportion. An individual champagne may come from one cru or several; if from a single cru, it could be a Premier Cru or a less prestigious one. It may be vintage or non-vintage, and, if non-vintage, may be made from young wine, or may include some older reserve wines in varying proportions – a non-vintage champagne may even be the result of blending vintage champagnes. It may be 'crémant' – less carbon dioxide and fewer bubbles –, or normally sparkling; it may be dosé to a greater or lesser extent, or not at all; it may be matured for a short or long time on its lees; it may have been disgorged a long time ago or recently; it may be white or rosé ... the permutations are infinite. Whatever the style, it is generally agreed that the best champagnes have spent a long time (five to ten years) on their lees and are consumed within a short period after disgorgement.

Taking into consideration all that has just been said, it may be easier to explain why the price of a bottle of champagne can vary so much, and how there come to be top-quality champagnes and special blends that are markedly superior to the standard product. It is unfortunately true that, at least among the big names, the cheapest champagnes are the least good. However, the large difference in price between the normal vintage champagnes and the most expensive does not always guarantee a corresponding jump in quality.

Champagne should be drunk at 7–9°C. Blanc de Blancs should be served cooler than vintage or more strongly flavoured champagnes. The bottle should be cooled in a champagne bucket containing ice and water. To open, remove the wire and the foil together. If the cork is being forced out by the pressure, let it come out with the foil and the wire 'muzzle' or cage. If the cork is resistant, hold it in one hand while turning the bottle with the other. Do not try to turn the cork – it may break. Pull the cork out slowly and gently, without a 'pop'.

Champagne should not be served in wide glasses but in long, thin ones, preferably made of crystal. The glass should be dry, not chilled, and totally free of any trace of detergent, which kills the sparkle and foam. Champagne can be drunk as an aperitif as well as with the meal, with an entrée or with non-oily fish. The fuller-flavoured wines, usually Blanc de Noirs or high-class vintage champagnes, are often served with meat or rich sauces. With pudding or sweet food, a Demi-Sec is preferable to a Brut, which would be too acid. Some recent vintages are: 1975: rich, full and well-balanced wines; 1976: often heavy, too expansive, lacking refinement and developing too quickly; 1979: a big vintage of good quality; 1980: clean, straightforward wines better than the reputation of the vintage.

ABELE *Grande Marque Impériale*★

| ○ | 150000 | ❸ Ⓓ |

Good colour, but the nose has been spoilt by oxidation. This is a shame as the wine has an agreeable palate despite a very noticeable dosage.
⌐ Abele, 52 Rue de Sillery, BP 18, 51051 Reims Cedex; tel. 26 85 23 86 ⟟ Closed Aug. ⌐ Cie Française des Grands Vins.

ABELE *Impérial Club Millésime*★

| ○ | 100000 | ❸ Ⓓ |

A characteristic example of the 1980 vintage: a pleasant brut, easy to drink, without harshness and with few defects, but little character. (1980)
⌐ Abele, 52 Rue de Sillery, BP 18, 51051 Reims Cedex; tel. 26 85 23 86 ⟟ Closed Aug. ⌐ Cie Française des Grands Vins.

ABELE *Le Sourire de Reims*★

| ○ | 400000 | ❸ Ⓓ |

This very old firm, established in 1757, perfected the remuage table – precursor of the famous rack (*pupitre*) – as well as the bench for disgorgement by ice, now universally used. The Sourire de Reims is a brut, perfect in appearance, slightly flowery and correctly dosed which remains lively on the palate.
⌐ Abele, 52 Rue de Sillery, BP 18, 51051 Reims Cedex; tel. 26 85 23 86 ⟟ Closed Aug. ⌐ Cie Française des Grands Vins.

GERARD AUTREAU★

| ○ 1er Cru | 40000 | ❷ Ⓓ |

A non-vintage brut, Blanc de Noirs, which is the result of a rare combination: 80 per cent Pinot Meunier and 20 per cent Pinot Noir. An easy-to-drink champagne, suited to the English palate, fruity and with a nose of mature Pinot. Ready to drink now. ✔ Blanc de Blancs, Rosé.
⌐ Gérard Autréau, 15 Rue René-Baudet, Champillon, 51160 Ay; tel. 26 51 54 13 ⟟ By appt.

GERARD AUTREAU
Cuvée de Réserve★★

| ○ | 30000 | ❷ Ⓓ |

A good example of a 1980 vintage brut. Bright and appealing colour, with a powerful nose of freshly cut hay. The combination is a success and the impression of balance is followed by a pleasing finish. (1980)
⌐ Gérard Autréau, 15 Rue René-Baudet, Champillon, 51160 Ay; tel. 26 51 54 13 ⟟ By appt.

AYALA★

| ◑ | 50000 | ❸ Ⓓ |

A healthy wine with good acidity, very similar to a Blanc de Blancs although it is made from 90 per cent black grapes, produced at the Château d'Ay. Because of its colour of dark rose petals, and its vigour, this wine makes a good aperitif. ✔ Ch. la Lagune (Haut-Médoc).
⌐ Ayala, 2 Bd du Nord, 51160 Ay; tel. 26 50 13 40 ⟟ By appt. Closed Aug. ⌐ J.-M. Ducellier.

AYALA *Extra Quality Brut*★

| ○ | 500000 | ❸ Ⓓ |

This champagne is not named after the Château d'Ay, where it is produced, but after a Columbian who has settled there. There are half a million of this non-vintage brut. Gold/straw-coloured, fruity and well balanced and, as intended, has no marked character.
⌐ Ayala, 2 Bd du Nord, 51160 Ay; tel. 26 50 13 40 ⟟ By appt. Closed Aug. ⌐ J.-M. Ducellier.

AYALA *Cuvée spéciale*★

| ○ | 50000 | ❸ Ⓓ |

Jean-Michel Ducellier, the owner of Ayala, claims that the character of his Blanc de Blancs evokes the music of the clarinet, flute and oboe. Green-gold in colour, with good fruit but with little body and acidity on the palate which does not diminish with age. Ideal as an aperitif and with shell-fish. (1979)
⌐ Ayala, 2 Bd du Nord, 51160 Ay; tel. 26 50 13 40 ⟟ By appt. Closed Aug. ⌐ J.-M. Ducellier.

BARA *Spécial Club*★

| ○Gd Cru | 10000 | ❸ Ⓓ |

A brut made from 75 per cent Pinot Noir and 25 per cent Chardonnay, full-bodied, high in alcohol, healthy and well balanced. Good to drink throughout a meal. Paul Bara is president of the Champagne region wine growers' club and all his wines are labelled 'grand cru 100%' – although all grand crus are rated 100 per cent. (1979) ✔ Other champagnes, Bouzy.
⌐ Paul Bara, 4 Rue Yvonnet, Bouzy, 51150 Tours-sur-Marne; tel. 26 57 00 50 ⟟ By appt. Closed Aug.

YVES BEAUTRAIT★

| ○Gd Cru | 50000 | ❸ Ⓓ |

Yves Beautrait owns several Grand Cru vineyards in the Montagne de Reims and has a modern 'cuvia', where the wine ferments. This brut consists of more than two-thirds Pinot Noir and under a third Chardonnay, giving it its principal characteristic of fruitiness. The juices from the black and white grapes are carefully blended, providing the backbone and elegance, respectively. ✔ Bouzy, Champagne Rosé.
⌐ Yves Beautrait, 4 Rue des Cavaliers, Louvois, 51160 Ay; tel. 26 57 03 38.

ALBERT BERGERE *Réserve*★

| ○ | 60000 | ❷ Ⓓ |

An interesting Blanc de Noirs, combining Pinot Meunier and Pinot Noir in equal proportions. Rounded and fruity, but heavy rather than light. Albert Bergère's best-selling wine. ✔ Other champagnes and Coteaux Champenois.
⌐ Albert Bergère, Fèrebrianges, 51270 Montmort; tel. 26 59 30 23 ⟟ By appt.

BESSERAT DE BELLEFON
Brut réserve★

| ○ | 600000 | ❸ Ⓓ |

New high-quality installations have allowed a tenfold increase in production on this estate in the last few years. A third of the bottles are labelled 'brut réserve'. The full colour suggests that this champagne is based on mature wines.

Specifically made for the English palate.

🐦 Besserat de Bellefon, Allée du Vignoble, BP 301, 51061 Reims Cedex; tel. 26 39 09 18 ℤ By appt. Closed Aug.

BESSERAT DE BELLEFON
Crémant des Moines★

| ○ | | ❸ Ⅾ |

This company makes both white and rosé crémants, both made from the same base. The very clear pale rosé colour is achieved by the addition of red wine from various sources, generally from the Marne département. A supple wine with a rather flowery nose, smooth on the palate and with a positive flavour.

🐦 Besserat de Bellefon, Allée du Vignoble, BP 301, 51061 Reims Cedex; tel. 26 39 09 18 ℤ By appt. Closed Aug.

BESSERAT DE BELLEFON
Cuvée spéciale★★

| ○ | | ❹ Ⅾ |

This prestige wine has no vintage, being a blend of wines from various years of vintage quality. A good colour, with small, quite persistent bubbles and a nose of freshly buttered brioches. On the palate it lives up to its vintage quality. A high-class wine, clear and light; made with precision and finesse.

🐦 Besserat de Bellefon, Allée du Vignoble, BP 301, 51061 Reims Cedex; tel. 26 36 09 18 ℤ By appt. Closed Aug.

BILLECART-SALMON★

| ◗ | 40 000 | ❸ Ⅾ |

A seductive rose-petal colour with hints of gold. A fine and lively nose; crisp, refreshing, light and lively on the palate which is very positive due to an above average acidity. The complete opposite of a heavy wine. An excellent summer aperitif.

🐦 Billecart-Salmon, 40 Rue Carnot, Mareuil-sur-Ay, 51160 Ay; tel. 26 50 60 22 ℤ By appt.

BILLECART-SALMON★★

| ○ | 70 000 | ❸ Ⅾ |

Deep colour, good size and consistency of bubbles and length of mousse. Yeast is still perceptible on the nose, although to drink it is extremely pleasant, perhaps even a little too easy. Excellent balance and a perfect dosage. (1979)

🐦 Billecart-Salmon, 40 Rue Carnot, Mareuil-sur-Ay, 51160 Ay; tel. 26 50 60 22 ℤ By appt.

BILLECART-SALMON★★★

| ○ | 300 000 | ❸ Ⅾ |

A remarkable champagne, yellow-gold in colour, with a continual renewal of tiny bubbles and a sustained mousse. Very pleasant on the nose; an elegant and lively wine.

🐦 Billecart-Salmon, 40 Rue Carnot, Mareuil-sur-Ay, 51160 Ay; tel. 26 50 60 22 ℤ By appt.

CHATEAU DE BLIGNY★

| ○ | 12 000 | ❷ Ⅾ |

From a region dedicated to the Pinot grape, this is a champagne made from Chardonnay. A good mousse; the grape is extremely, almost excessively, noticeable on the nose and a fresh apple aroma indicates that malolactic fermentation has not taken place. This is good, as the wine is round and full-bodied, while at the same time retaining a youthful acidity. Its firmness prevents it having the finesse of the great vintages of the Côte des Blancs. (1979) ✔ Blanc de Blancs.

🐦 Ch. de Bligny, 10200 Bligny; tel. 25 26 40 11 ℤ By appt. 🐦 MM. Lorin.

BOIZEL *Blanc de Blancs★*

| ○ | 10 000 | ❷ |

This small family firm from Epernay only labels a fiftieth of its produce as Blanc de Blancs: the Chardonnay harvested in the furthest communes of the Côte des Blancs, Chouilly and Vertus. This wine has a fine fragrant finesse and its roundness does not detract from its elegance. (1979)

🐦 Boizel, 16 Rue de Bernon, BP 149, 51205 Epernay Cedex; tel. 26 55 21 51 ℤ By appt. Closed Aug. 🐦 Mme Roques-Boizel.

BOIZEL *Grand Vintage★*

| ○ | 30 000 | ❷ |

This firm, which has no vineyards, produces half a million bottles each year. The Grand Vintage 1979 is good with meals: it has slight moderate acidity, is rather green and the nose opens up after a while. An attractive straw colour. (1979)

🐦 Boizel, 16 Rue de Bernon, BP 149, 51205 Epernay Cedex; tel. 26 55 21 51 ℤ By appt. Closed Aug. 🐦 Mme Roques-Boizel.

BOLLINGER *Spécial Cuvée★*

| ○ | 900 000 | ❸ Ⅾ |

The most prestigious champagne makers have their 'standard' blends, in this case called Special Cuvée. In fact, the house of Bollinger only produces special blends. Like others of this brand, it is well sparkled, and well balanced and suits the English taste. A very fine non-vintage (brut), intended to drink with meals.

🐦 J. Bollinger, 16 Rue Jules-Lobet, BP 4, 51160 Ay; tel. 26 50 12 34 ℤ By appt. Closed Aug.

BOLLINGER *R.D. 1975★★★*

| ○ | 200 000 | ❹ Ⅾ |

R.D. (recently disgorged) bottles have a back label showing the date of disgorgement – in this case 4.9.84, i.e. three months before the tasting session. It is important to check the date before buying a bottle of R.D., since this only has any meaning in the six months following disgorgement. A model champagne which has been left on its lees for nine years. It is both rich and lively, high in alcohol, full-bodied with a long finish. Drink it with a fine meal. (1975)

🐦 J. Bollinger, 16 Rue Jules-Lobet, BP 4, 51160 Ay; tel. 26 50 12 34 ℤ By appt. Closed Aug.

BOLLINGER *Grande année 1979*★★

| ○ | 250000 | ❹ Ⓓ |

An excellent vintage 1979 with a character typical of the round, powerful Pinot Noir wines. Deep gold, with a roasty nose (coffee) and a full, firm palate. Ideal to drink with meals. (1979)
☝ J. Bollinger, 16 Rue Jules-Lobet, BP 4, 51160 Ay; tel. 26 50 12 34 ☎ By appt. Closed Aug.

BOLLINGER
Vieilles Vignes Françaises★★★

| ○ Gd Cru | 2000 | ❺ Ⓓ |

This is the most expensive champagne in the world, a Blanc de Noirs produced from ungrafted vines (before phylloxera), cultivated 'en foule', as in the last century. Supreme finesse, complexity and richness. A fine long finish. A champagne to be drunk slowly and savoured. (1979)
☝ J. Bollinger, 16 Rue Jules-Lobet, BP 4, 51160 Ay; tel. 26 50 12 34 ☎ By appt. Closed Aug.

BONNAIRE *Blanc de Blancs*★

| ○ 1er Cru | 80000 | ❷ Ⓓ |

A straw-coloured brut with hints of green, full of fine bubbles. The nose has a fruity pear aroma while the taste is initially positive but in the end not quite convincing, doubtless because the dosage is too noticeable. ✍ Coteaux Champenois.
☝ A. Bonnaire, 105 Rue du Carrouge, Cramant, 51200 Epernay; tel. 26 57 50 85 ☎ By appt.

BONVILLE★

| ○ Gd Cru | 30000 | ❷ Ⓓ |

This wine grower and producer makes a Blanc de Blancs from Chardonnay harvested in the Avize commune and classed as a grand cru. There are 30 000 bottles from the 1978 vintage; full straw-yellow with an intense citrus fruit nose and well balanced to drink. (1978)
☝ Bonville, 9 Rue Pasteur, 51190 Avize; tel. 26 57 52 30 ☎ By appt.

CHATEAU DE BOURSAULT★

| ○ | 25000 | ❷ Ⓓ |

This château was built by the architect Arveuf in 1843–8 at the request of Madame Veuve Clicquot-Ponsardin. The park has been restored as a vineyard (Pinot Noir, Pinot Meunier and a little Chardonnay). After a supple beginning, the fruitiness of this wine, which is from a single vineyard, fills the mouth. Good with meals.
☝ Ch. de Boursault, Boursault, 51200 Epernay; tel. 26 58 42 21 ☎ By appt. ☝ N. Fringhian.

BRICOUT ET KOCH *Carte Noir*★

| ○ | 1000000 | ❸ Ⓓ |

There are two million signed bottles of this champagne in the cellars of the Château d'Avize. A good example of a non-vintage brut; its strong points are its deep, limpid colour, its mature fruitiness and its balance.
☝ Bricout et Koch, 7 Route de Cramant, 51190 Avize; tel. 26 57 53 93 ☎ By appt. Closed Aug.

BRICOUT ET KOCH *Vintage 79*★

| ○ Gd Cru | 40000 | ❸ Ⓓ |

A remarkable prestige wine and excellent value for money. The '79 has an amber-yellow colour and a fine steady mousse. Chardonnay provides its finesse, which is dominated by the fruity roundness of Pinot. To be drunk at mealtimes. (1979)
☝ Bricout et Koch, 7 Route de Cramant, 51190 Avize; tel. 26 57 53 93 ☎ By appt. Closed Aug.

BROCHET-HERVIEUX *Spécial Club*★

| ○ 1er Cru | 10000 | ❸ Ⓓ |

This 1980 was chosen by the Champagne region wine-growers' club. Consisting of Pinot Noir together with 20 per cent Chardonnay, with a fruity bouquet and a fine vinosity in the taste. Its backbone does not obscure its elegance. A good way to start a meal. (1980)
☝ Brochet-Hervieux, Eceuil, 51500 Rilly; tel. 26 49 74 10 ☎ By appt. Closed 24 Dec.–5 Jan. and 15 Aug.–5 Sept.

CANARD-DUCHENE★

| ○ | 2100000 | ❸ Ⓓ |

A non-vintage brut with a hint of gold within the deep colour and crowned by a fine mousse of small bubbles. Nose and taste suggest a contribution by black grapes. The dosage is correct.
☝ Canard-Duchêne, BP 1, Ludes, 51500 Rilly-la-Montagne; tel. 26 61 10 96 ☎ By appt. Closed Aug. and public holidays.

CANARD-DUCHENE★

| ○ | 110000 | ❸ Ⓓ |

A rather slight wine, lacking in depth, brilliant clear salmon-pink in colour; on the palate it has the fullness of a red wine, but with youthful freshness.
☝ Canard-Duchêne, BP 1, Ludes, 51500 Rilly-la-Montagne; tel. 26 61 10 96 ☎ By appt. Closed Aug. and public holidays.

CANARD-DUCHENE★★

| ○ | 70000 | ❸ Ⓓ |

There is a certain amount of risk involved in serving a 1976, given its rapid ageing. A full-bodied wine, with a very successful appearance, round and, above all, powerful; all the better for the judicious dosage. (1976)
☝ Canard-Duchêne, BP 1, Ludes, 51500 Rilly-la-Montagne; tel. 26 61 10 96 ☎ By appt. Closed Aug. and public holidays.

CANARD-DUCHENE *Charles VII*★

| ○ | 80000 | ❸ Ⓓ |

This special wine owes its name to the king consecrated in Reims in 1429 in the presence of Joan of Arc. Deep in colour with a light mousse and persistent bubbles; a hint of quince on the nose and a stony background on the palate.
☝ Canard-Duchêne, BP 1, Ludes, 51500 Rilly-la-Montagne; tel. 26 61 10 96 ☎ By appt. Closed Aug. and public holidays.

CASTELLANE *Croix de St-André★*

| ○ | 1 700 000 | ❸ Ⓓ |

A non-vintage brut, containing a significant pro-portion of reserve wine in the blending. Made from 25 per cent white and 75 per cent black grapes (of which 40 per cent is Pinot Meunier), deep yellow in colour, a spicy nose and an unremarkable, almost run-of-the-mill, round taste.
☙ Castellane, 57 Rue de Verdun, BP 136, 51204 Epernay Cedex; tel. 26 53 15 33 ⅄ By appt.☙ De Castellane-Mérand.

CASTELLANE★

| ○ | 32 000 | ❸ Ⓓ |

This company proudly maintains a battery of casks in its vast fermentation house at Epernay, although oxidized steel vats have also been intro-duced. Vintage and non-vintage Blanc de Blancs are produced. The green-gold colour proclaims a flowery nose, with a strong toasted bread aroma, and a hint of hazelnuts on the palate. The vintage wines age very well. ✔ Coteaux Champenois.
☙ Castellane, 57 Rue de Verdun, BP 136, 51204 Epernay Cedex; tel. 26 53 15 33 ⅄ By appt. ☙ De Castellane-Mérand.

CASTELLANE *Commodore★★*

| ○ | 42 000 | ❹ Ⓓ |

This prestige wine comes in a bottle that curves towards the bottom and carries a double label. Heavily influenced by the high proportion of Pinot Noir (75 per cent) with a full, fruity nose carried through on the palate which has a fine backbone, ensuring balance and length. (1975)
☙ Castellane, 57 Rue de Verdun, BP 136, 51204 Epernay Cedex; tel. 26 53 15 33 ⅄ By appt. ☙ De Castellane-Mérand.

CASTILLE *Brut réserve★*

| ○ | 200 000 | ❷ Ⓓ |

A non-vintage brut, consisting of 40 per cent Chardonnay and 60 per cent Pinot, including 15 per cent Pinot Meunier. The Pinot Meunier ensures the structure and fruitiness of the wine, while the white grapes provide a nose of freshly baked apple turnover.
☙ Castille, 11 Rue des Moissons, 51100 Reims; tel. 26 47 41 25 ⅄ By appt. Closed Aug.

CASTILLE *Couronne Blanche★*

| ○ | 50 000 | ❸ Ⓓ |

An interesting blend of the vigour of the '76 vintage and the finesse of Chardonnay. A musky nose, no doubt due to the great heat of that year, and an almost vanilla flavour on the palate. (1976)
☙ Castille, 14 Rue des Moissons, 51100 Reims; tel. 26 47 41 25 ⅄ By appt. Closed Aug.

CATTIER★

| ○ 1er Cru | 50 000 | ❷ Ⓓ |

This wine has escaped the rapid ageing associated with the '76 vintage but displays the characteris-tics of the vintage: a great deal of body, high alcohol content, a rich, full and fruity nose and the mature strength that overwhelms the finesse. A gold colour with tinges of pink. A typical mealtime champagne. (1976)

☙84 S. C. E. Cattier, 6–11 Rue Dom-Pérignon, Chigny-les-Roses, 51500 Rilly-la-Montagne; tel. 26 03 42 11 ⅄ By appt.

CATTIER★

| ◑1er Cru | 15 000 | ❷ Ⓓ |

Clear, rosé type with a fruity nose of peaches and soft fruit; an impression of crispness on the palate, but limited complexity. Good as an aperitif.
☙ S. C. E. Cattier, 6–11 Rue Dom-Pérignon, Chigny-les-Roses, 51500 Rilly-la-Montagne; tel. 26 03 42 11 ⅄ By appt.

CATTIER★★

| ○Gd Cru | 75 000 | ❷ Ⓓ |

The Cattier family have been wine growers at Chigny-les-Roses for several centuries and pro-duces a whole range of champagnes, all premier crus. This non-vintage brut is not too ambitious and achieves everything it sets out to do very well. A charming nose and a balanced taste, with good fruit.
☙ S. C. E. Cattier, 6–11 Rue Dom-Pérignon, Chigny-les-Roses, 51500 Rilly-la-Montagne; tel. 26 03 42 11 ⅄ By appt.

CATTIER *Clos du Moulin★★*

| ○1er Cru | 10 000 | ❸ Ⓓ |

This is one of the rare walled vineyards in Champagne. Non-vintage but a blend of years that have produced vintages – 1975, 1976 and 1978. Chardonnay and Pinot Noir are blended in equal proportions. Only the best part of the cuvée is retained, which is highly unusual, if not unique, and explains the delicate nose and the successful blend of fruitiness, finesse and com-plexity on the palate. Deep in colour, with a perfect mousse.
☙ S. C. E. Cattier, 6–11 Rue Dom-Pérignon, Chigny-les-Roses, 51500 Rilly-la-Montagne; tel. 26 03 42 11 ⅄ By appt.

CHARBAUT *Certificat★★*

| ○ | 10 000 | ❹ Ⓓ |

This company, established after the Second World War, produces two million bottles each year. This prestige wine is a Blanc de Blancs produced from Chardonnay harvested in the grand cru areas. Straw-gold in colour with light touches of green, a nose of baked bread and flavours of dried fruit on the palate. A precise and vigorous champagne. (1976)
☙ A. Charbaut, 35 Rue Maurice-Cervaux, BP 150, 51205 Epernay Cedex; tel. 26 54 37 55 ⅄ By appt. Closed Aug.

JACKIE CHARLIER *Carte Noire*★

| ○ | 50 000 | ❶ Ⓓ |

Jackie Charlier holds wine-tasting sessions in an enormous vat designed for this purpose – he is one of the last to make his wines 'in wood'. Perhaps this accounts for the amber colour and discreet, self-effacing nose. Low acidity due to the Pinot Meunier. ✔ Coteaux Champenois.
☛ Jackie Charlier, 4 Rue des Pervenches, Montigny-sous-Châtillon, 51700 Dormans; tel. 26 58 35 18 ⓣ By appt. Closed Sun. mornings.

J. CHARPENTIER *Cuvée impériale*★

| ○ | 15 000 | ❷ Ⓓ |

Based on 89 per cent Pinot Meunier, displaying all the characteristics of this grape: suppleness, fruitiness and low acidity. A limited number of small bubbles, full colour and a perceptible dosage.
☛ Jacky Charpentier, Villers-sous-Châtillon, 51700 Dormans; tel. 26 58 05 78 ⓣ By appt.

CHASSENEY D'ARCE

| ○ | 600 000 | ❶ Ⓓ |

The wine producers' association of the Coteaux de l'Arce produce, in their very modern installations, non-vintage, vintage, and rosé champagnes and even a vintage Blanc de Blancs, which is unusual in a region where the Chardonnay is rare because it characterizes wines too strongly. This is a Blanc de Noirs, well made, with a full and well-balanced roundness. A mealtime champagne.
☛ Chasseney d'Arce, Ville-sur-Arce, 10110 Bar-sur-Seine; tel. 25 38 74 07 ⓣ By appt ☛ Coop. Vinicole de Coteaux de l'Arce.

CHAUVET *Carte Blanche*★

| ○ | 25 000 | ❸ Ⓓ |

A small family firm for nearly 150 years, with an excellent vineyard in five communes, including three that have been classified as 'grand crus'. This is their most widely sold wine, consisting mainly of black grapes, well made and with a good balance between roundness and vigour.
☛ Chauvet, 11 Av. de Champagne, BP 4, 51150 Tours-sur-Marne; tel. 26 59 92 37 ⓣ By appt.

CHAUVET *Carte Verte*★

| ○ | 15 000 | ❷ Ⓓ |

A non-vintage green-gold wine from vineyards at Bisseuil and Vernezay. The bubbles are small and continuous. The fruity character is surprising for a Blanc de Blancs. ✔ Crémant.
☛ Chauvet, 11 Av. de Champagne, BP 4, 51150 Tours-sur-Marne; tel. 26 59 92 37 ⓣ By appt.

VEUVE CLIQUOT *Brut Carte d'Or*★★★

| ○ | 600 000 | ❹ |

The 1979 vintage has produced some great champagnes from those who were successful. Cliquot was one of these; perfect champagne colour, small, persistent bubbles and a persistent mousse. A fruity nose and the elegance and balance, discreetly lightened by the carbon dioxide, delight the palate. (1979)
☛ Veuve Clicquot-Ponsardin, 12 Rue du Temple, BP 102, 51054 Reims Cedex; tel. 26 40 25 42 ⓣ By appt. Closed Aug.

VEUVE CLICQUOT *Carte Jaune*★★★

| ○ | 4 500 000 | ❸ |

Widowed at the age of 27, Madame Clicquot-Ponsardin developed one of the greatest champagne-producing houses and created a vineyard that is outstanding in both quality and size. Nearly seven million bottles bear her signature each year. The non-vintage brut has perfect bubbles, sparkle and mousse, a delicate nose with vinosity and a taste without flabbiness.
☛ Veuve Clicquot-Ponsardin, 12 Rue du Temple, BP 102, 51054 Reims Cedex; tel. 26 40 25 42 ⓣ By appt. Closed Aug.

VEUVE CLICQUOT *La Grande Dame*★

| ○ | 100 000 | ❹ |

Madame Veuve Clicquot-Ponsardin was called 'La Grande Dame' and this name was given to the company's prestige wine to mark the company's bicentenary. The distinctively shaped bottles contain a bright brut champagne which sparkles perfectly. The nose highlights the elegance, while the taste reveals a perfect blend of the juice of black and white grapes.
☛ Veuve Clicquot-Ponsardin, 12 Rue du Temple, BP 102, 51054 Reims Cedex; tel. 26 40 25 42 ⓣ By appt. Closed Aug.

VEUVE CLICQUOT★★★

| ◐ | 150 000 | ❹ |

A rosé with a dark coral colour crowned by an extremely fine mousse, with a nose of strawberry and cherry on a floral base. The palate is well-constructed, with discreet acidity and a rich and well-blended fruit. Good with meals. (1978)
☛ Veuve Clicquot-Ponsardin, 12 Rue du Temple, BP 102, 51054 Reims Cedex; tel. 26 40 25 42 ⓣ By appt. Closed Aug.

CLOUET★

| ◐ Gd Cru | 8000 | ❷ |

A blend of 80 per cent Pinot Noir lightened by 20 per cent Chardonnay, coloured by a Bouzy red wine, produces this dark salmon-pink rosé. An abundant mousse, a raspberry nose, rich on the palate but spoilt by a rather tough background. This wine grower also produces an interesting champagne that is not blended. ✔ Coteaux Champenois.
☛ A. Clouet, 8 Rue Gambetta, 51150 Bouzy; tel. 26 57 00 82 ⓣ By appt.

RAOUL COLLET★

| ◕ | 40 000 | ❷ |

A coloured Blanc de Noirs, Pinot Noir forming the base with 20 per cent Pinot Meunier. Rosé colour with hints of gold and a fruity Pinot nose with a soft fruit aroma, also present in the delicate, positive taste. Good base crispness. The character is pleasant but lacks distinction.

☙ Raoul Collet, 34 Rue Jeanson, BP 8, 51160 Ay; tel. 26 55 15 88 ⵣ By appt. Closed Feb. (school holidays) and Aug. ☙ Coop. Générale des Vignerons.

RAOUL COLLET *Carte Rouge*

| ◯ | 460 000 | ❷ |

The 'carte rouge' label is given to the best non-vintage wines from the Ay cooperative consisting of a blend of 20 per cent Chardonnay, 10 per cent Pinot Meunier and 70 per cent Pinot Noir, from 15 communes. A well-made wine, but tending towards heaviness and a bit flashy.

☙ Raoul Collet, 34 Rue Jeanson, BP 8, 51160 Ay; tel. 26 55 15 88 ⵣ By appt. Closed Feb. (school holidays) and Aug. ☙ Coop. Générale des Vignerons.

RAOUL COLLET★

| ◯ | 100 000 | ❸ |

Raoul Collet was one of the founders of the first champagne cooperative, in 1921. Today, 400 growers supply their grapes to the COGEVI of Ay, which produces various wines including a vintage brut (the '76 and '79 are available). A fairly painstaking process is required to produce the balance of a blend which consists of 40 per cent Chardonnay and 60 per cent Pinot Noir selected from different growths. (1979)

☙ Raoul Collet, 34 Rue Jeanson, BP 8, 51160 Ay; tel. 26 55 15 88 ⵣ By appt. Closed Feb. (school holidays) and Aug. ☙ Coop. Générale des Vignerons.

DELAVENNE PERE ET FILS *Brut*★

| ◯ | 2000 | ❸ D |

A family concern established a century ago, with properties at Cramant and Bouzy. The 1979 vintage is full-bodied, well made, straightforward but too generously dosed. Its nose is open and high in alcohol; straw-yellow colour and a fine mousse. A champagne for mealtimes (1979).

✔ Coteaux Champenois.

☙ Delavenne Père et Fils, 6 Rue de Tours, Bouzy, 51150 Tours-sur-Marne; tel. 26 59 02 14 ⵣ By appt.

DELAVENNE PERE ET FILS★

| ◯ 1er Cru | 35 000 | ❷ D |

A good example of a wine with a dominant Bouzy character, Bouzy being a 'commune' (parish) classified as 'grand cru' and reputed to be the best situated commune in the Marne départe-ment. A powerful wine with a full-bodied palate preceded by a heavy alcoholic nose, with a background of fruit and honey. ✔ Coteaux Champenois.

☙ Delavenne Père et Fils, 6 Rue de Tours, Bouzy, 51150 Tours-sur-Marne; tel. 26 59 02 04 ⵣ By appt.

LAURENT DESMAZIERES★

| ◯ | 20 000 | ❷ D |

This small company produces a non-vintage brut, slightly acid with some roundness. A reserved nose with some weight due to the Pinot grape. ✔ Rosé, Coteaux Champenois.

☙ Laurent Desmazières, 11 Rue Dom-Pérignon, Chigny-les-Roses, 51500 Rilly-la-Montagne; tel. 26 03 44 46 ⵣ By appt ☙ J.-J. Cattier.

DESMOULINS *Cuvée Prestige*★

| ◯ | 150 000 | ❸ D |

Desmoulins is a small family firm three gener-ations old. White grapes are predominant in this blend; a deep colour with hints of green and streaked with regularly renewed, small bubbles. The nose, with aromas of brioche, apples and a hint of coffee, makes for a complex palate with a taste of quince, which gives the wine more body than lightness.

☙ Desmoulins, 44 Av. Hoche, BP 10, 51201 Eper-nay; tel. 26 54 24 24 ⵣ By appt. Closed Aug.

DETHUNE★

| ◯Gd Cru | 18 000 | ❷ D |

Paul Dethune produces only Grand Cru cham-pagnes. The blend of his non-vintage brut con-sists of two-thirds Pinot Noir and one-third Char-donnay harvested from south-facing vineyards, giving heady wines, high in alcohol, with strong bouquets. A champagne for mealtimes.

☙ Paul Dethune, Rue de l'Espérance, Ambon-nay, 51150 Tours-sur-Marne; tel. 26 57 01 88 ⵣ By appt. Closed 15 Aug.–5 Sept.

DETHUNE ★

| ◕ Gd Cru | 2000 | ❷ D |

Paul Dethune is a traditional wine grower-pro-ducer and one of the few who still use wood in making their wines. This rosé is coloured by adding a red Ambonnay wine to a blend of two-thirds Blanc de Noirs and one-third Blanc de Blancs. A fine pink colour, mature and full-bodied, almost fleshy; to be drunk during a meal. Remarkable value for money.

☙ Paul Dethune, Rue de l'Espérance, Ambon-nay, 51150 Tours-sur-Marne; tel. 26 57 01 88 ⵣ By appt. Closed 15 Aug.–5 Sept.

DEUTZ★★

| ◯ | 30 000 | ❹ D |

The Deutz company is 150 years old and one of the few to remain a family concern, with its own vineyards (also in the Côtes du Rhône, under the Delas brand name). The Blanc de Blancs is the result of a blend of Avize wine and Mesnil-sur-Oger. The Avize supplies suppleness, the Mesnil the body and enables the wine to be kept. A Blanc de Blancs that combines elegance and class. (1979)

☙ Deutz, 16 Rue Jeanson, 51160 Ay; tel. 26 55 15 11 ⵣ By appt. Closed Aug. ☙ Deutz and Geldermann.

DEUTZ★

| ◕ | 25 000 | ❹ D |

This firm is on the point of joining the four or five best large champagne-producing companies. This is a vintage rosé, a Blanc de Noirs, blended for

colour with a Bouzy wine. Pale salmon-pink with gold hints; a fruity87 alcoholic nose, while on the palate a good positive flavour supplants the richness of the fruit. (1979)
♠ Deutz, 16 Rue Jeanson, 51160 Ay; tel. 26 55 15 11 ☎ By appt. Closed Aug. ♠ Deutz and Gelderman S.A.

DEUTZ *Cuvée William Deutz*★★

| O | 30000 | ⑤ Ⓓ |

A special blend, in an old-style bottle, with 70 per cent Pinot (including a touch of Pinot Meunier) and 30 per cent Chardonnay classed as Grand Cru. Yellow-gold in colour; a balanced, well-made champagne with good body and length of finish. (1979)
♠ Deutz, 16 Rue Franson, 51160 Ay; tel. 26 55 15 11 ☎ By appt. Closed Aug. ♠ Deutz and Gellerman S.A.

DEUTZ *Cuvée Mathieu*★★

| O | 10000 | ④ Ⓓ |

The 1977 vintage brut is distinctively bottled, with a large white seal and brightly coloured label, and is very popular in the United States. Made from the '76 vintage, it has remained at its best and increased in complexity. Top of the range. (1979)
♠ Deutz, 16 Rue Jeanson, BP 9, 51160 Ay; tel. 26 55 15 11 ☎ By appt ♠ Deutz and Geldermann.

DOQUET JEANMAIRE *Carte d'Or*★★

| O 1er Cru | 80000 | ② Ⓓ |

A Blanc de Blancs produced from Chardonnay harvested in several communes of the Côte des Blancs. A subtle, complex nose and a well-defined, smooth taste. ✔ Champagne Rosé.
♠ Doquet Jeanmaire, Rue de Voipreux, 51130 Vertus; tel. 26 52 16 50 ☎ By appt. Closed 10–31 Aug. ♠ Michel Doquet.

DRAPPIER *Carte d'Or*

| O | 100000 | ② Ⓓ |

The vineyard has existed for more than eight centuries and has been worked by the Drappier family for more than a century. This is a Blanc de Noirs made from Pinot Noir and 10 per cent Pinot Meunier. It is slightly flashy; well made and full-bodied but too fruity.
♠ Drappier, Urville, 10200 Bar-sur-Aube; tel. 25 26 40 15 ☎ Mon.–Fri. 8.00–12.00/14.00–19.00.

DRAPPIER *Grande Sendrée*★

| O | 18000 | ③ Ⓓ |

A special vintage blend, combining Chardonnay (rare in this region) and Pinot Noir in equal parts. A plentiful and fine mousse, sunlight gold in colour, and a powerful palate with good length,

similar to that of a wine not made by the champagne method. (1979)
♠ Drappier, Urville, 10200 Bar-sur-Aube; tel. 25 26 40 15 ☎ Mon.–Fri. 8.00–12.00/14.00–19.00.

ROBERT DRIANT *Extra Brut Spécial*★★

| O 1er Cru | 30000 | ② Ⓓ |

A tiny business that produces only two champagnes. This one, undosed, has been made in the same way for a quarter of a century. Made predominantly from black grapes. This bottle uses a cork, held in place by a clip rather than by wiring. The wine is handled manually, in the old style. High in alcohol, well made, mature, with an excellent balance.
♠ Robert Driant, 12 Rue Marie-Coquebert, 51160 Ay; tel. 26 50 17 81.

DUVAL-LEROY *Fleur de Champagne*★

| O | 900000 | ② Ⓓ |

A dynamic company, still run by the family who established it. This non-vintage is healthy, well balanced, with a pleasant finish. The nose lacks body, but has a satisfying floral elegance. Gold colour with a hint of green. ✔ Champagne Rosé, Coteaux Champenois, Haut-Médoc (Bordeaux).
♠ Duval-Leroy, Rue de Mont-Chenil, BP 37, 51130 Vertus; tel. 26 57 00 70 ☎ By appt.

MICHEL EGLY★

| ◑ Gd Cru | 20000 | ① Ⓓ |

A Grand Cru rosé, the base wine coloured by red wines. The Pinot grape (at least 80 per cent) predominates as one would expect in the Aubonnay commune. Clear pink in colour, with a lot of fruit and alcohol. Easy to drink and excellent value for money.
♠ Michel Egly, Route de Trépail, BP 15, Ambonnay, 51150 Tours-sur-Marne; tel. 26 57 00 70 ☎ By appt.

MICHEL EGLY

| O | 5000 | ① Ⓓ |

This non-vintage brut is a blend of several wines, including, particularly, those from 1982, a huge harvest, part of which was converted into reserve wine, using the best grapes (80 per cent Pinot Noir and 20 per cent Chardonnay to provide the mousse). A round and fruity champagne whose suppleness is tempered by a moderate acidity. Excellent value for money. Good with meals.
♠ Michel Egly, Route de Trépail, BP 15, Ambonnay, 51150 Tours-sur-Marne; tel. 26 57 00 70 ☎ By appt.

ROLAND FLINIAUX *Carte Noire*★

| O Gd Cru | 12000 | |

Roland Fliniaux, one of a family of Champagne businessmen, has created his own wine-making company and has a vineyard of four hectares classified 'Grand Cru'. This is a Blanc de Noirs produced from a single vineyard, yellow-gold in colour with hints of pink; a powerful, alcoholic nose. On the palate the fruit masks the elegance. (1976)
♠ Roland Fliniaux, 1 Rue Léon-Bourgeois, BP 2, 51160 Ay; tel. 26 50 11 01 ☎ By appt.

GALLIMARD*

| ○ | 30000 | ❶ Ⓓ |

The commune of Riceys is famous for its still rosé (Rosé de Riceys). However, this grower makes white and rosé champagnes from a vineyard planted entirely with fine Pinot Noir. As a result, his brut is a fruity Blanc de Noirs, more round than vigorous, and goes well with meals.
⚲ Gallimard, 10340 Les Riceys; tel. 25 38 32 44 � By appt. Closed Sun.

GALLIMARD*

| ⚲ | 3000 | ❶ Ⓓ |

A rosé champagne obtained by a short fermentation in the vat using 100 per cent Pinot Noir. Fruity with a great deal of body; very good for drinking with a meal.
⚲ Gallimard, 10340 Les Riceys; tel. 25 38 32 44 � By appt. Closed Sun.

PIERRE GIMONNET ET FILS *Or*

| ○1er Cru | 125000 | ❷ Ⓓ |

This company owns vineyards in the communes of Cuis, Chouilly, and Cramant, to the north of the Côte des Blancs, and ferments only white grapes. Its vintage wine includes approximately 10 per cent reserve wine. Lively, light, lacking in complexity, and well balanced. ✔ Coteaux Champenois.
⚲ Pierre Gimonnet et Fils, 1 Rue de la République, Cuis, 51200 Epernay; tel. 26 55 12 54 � By appt.

PIERRE GIMONNET ET FILS
Spécial Club**

| ○1er Cru | 7000 | ❸ Ⓓ |

This Blanc de Blancs, vintage 1979, has been selected by the Champagne region Wine-Growers' Association and comes in the 'spécial club' bottle. It consists of two-thirds Premier Cru and one-third Grand Cru. A colour between gold and straw-yellow with a nose of buttered brioche; a light framework and an elegant balance. A refined aperitif. (1979)
⚲ Pierre Gimonnet et Fils, 1 Rue de la République, Cuis, 51200 Epernay; tel. 26 55 12 54 � By appt.

GOBILLARD *Carte Blanche*

| ○ | 100000 | ❷ Ⓓ |

This family has produced and sold champagne for over a century. The non-vintage brut is a blend of 75 per cent Pinot Meunier and 25 per cent Chardonnay, the white grapes providing the finesse and the Meunier contributing to the suppleness and fruitiness.
⚲ P. Gobillard, Ch. de Pierry, BP 1, Pierry, 51200 Epernay; tel. 26 54 05 11 � By appt. Closed Aug.

GOBILLARD *Grand Vin*

| ○ | 20000 | ❷ Ⓓ |

The '79, after five years in the bottle, is yellow-gold in colour with hints of green emphasized by the whiteness of the mousse. The nose introduces a round and (moderately) fruity taste. (1979) ✔ Jean-Paul Gobillard also produces a prestige wine (Régence), in special bottles.
⚲ P. Gobillard, Ch. de Pierry, BP 1, Pierry, 51200 Epernay; tel. 26 54 05 11 � By appt. Closed Aug.

MICHEL GONET*

| ○1er Cru | 300000 | ❷ Ⓓ |

The 1979 vintage is pale straw in colour, with a discreet aroma of fresh baking, a balanced vigour and is both delicate and very light. Perfect as an aperitif. (1979) ✔ Coteaux Champenois.
⚲ Michel Gonet, 21 Av. Jean-Jaurés, 51190 Avize; tel. 26 57 50 56 � By appt.

GOSSET *Cuvée Spéciale*

| ⚲ | 50000 | ❸ |

A pink-bronze colour; on the nose it appears mature, while on the palate it is full-bodied, interesting and rounded with a long finish. Well suited to the English palate. ✔ Vins de Chinon.
⚲ E. and L. Gosset, 69 Rue Jules-Blondeau, BP 7, 51160 Ay; tel. 26 50 12 51 � By appt. Closed Sept.

GOSSET *Grand Millésime*

| ○ | 25000 | ❺ |

This bottle, an exact copy of an old 18th-century bottle, contains one of the very few 1975 champagnes still available. The decade has not affected its colour – yellow-gold with tinges of pink. The nose is well developed and vinous, while the palate suggests that a touch of acidity has been compensated for by a perceptible dosage.
⚲ E. and L. Gosset, 69 Rue Jules-Blondeau, BP 7, 51160 Ay; tel. 26 20 12 51 � By appt. Closed Sept.

GOSSET *Quatrième Centenaire***

| ○ | 28750 | ❺ |

This special wine, celebrating the company's 400th anniversary, comes in a superb bottle. Good structure and balance are revealed on the palate. Bright, straw-yellow colour, streaked with small, rapid bubbles; a very delicate nose marked by the softness of mature Pinot.
⚲ E. and L. Gosset, 69 Rue Rules-Blondeau, BP 7, 51160 Ay; tel. 26 50 12 51 � By appt. Closed Sept.

GOSSET *Spécial Réserve***

| ○ | 65000 | ❸ |

Non-vintage, consisting of a blend of wines from two years – 1976 and 1977. A faultless appearance: pure gold, clear and bright, mousse and bubbles to match. A firm, discreet nose followed by a perfect taste, honest, with a hint of mead. A dry (minimum dosage) and honest wine.
⚲ E. and L. Gosset, 69 Rue Jules-Blondeau, BP 7, 51160 Ay; tel. 26 50 12 51 � By appt. Closed Sept.

ALFRED GRATIEN *Crémant*

| ○ | | ❸ Ⓓ |

This firm is well known for its large production of Loire 'crémant'. The 1976 champagne has the characteristics of its vintage: a powerful nose with a burnt aroma; full-bodied, round and powerful on the palate; an intense, pronounced, gold colour. The mousse and bubbles are what you would expect from a 'crémant'.
⚲ Alfred Gratien, 30 Rue Maurice-Cervaux, 51201, Epernay; tel. 26 54 38 20 � By appt.

ALFRED GRATIEN★★★

◔　　　　　　　　　　　❸ D

An excellent rosé, a fine amber-coral in colour with continually rising small bubbles. A characteristic nose with hints of balsam; youthful and fruity on the palate.
☛ Alfred Gratien, 30 Rue Maurice-Cerveaux, 51201 Epernay; tel. 26 54 38 20 ⚍ By appt.

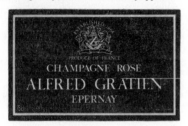

ALFRED GRATIEN★

○　　　　　　　　　　　❸ D

This firm, established in 1864, still uses traditional methods. This non-vintage brut has a marzipan aroma, while the palate reveals traces of cinnamon and an initial oxidation, appreciated by the English palate.
☛ Alfred Gratien, 30 Rue Maurice-Cerveaux, 51201 Epernay; tel. 26 54 38 20 ⚍ By appt.

GUIBORAT FILS★

○　　　　　　　　　　　❷ D

A yellow-gold colour, neither too clear nor too strong, indicating a delicate balance between the essential acids of the base and the round fruit; a light toasted bread aroma characteristic of Chardonnay.
☛ Guiborat Fils, 99 Rue de la Garenne, Cramant, BP 11, 51200 Epernay; tel. 26 57 54 08 ⚍ By appt.

HAMM ET FILS *Réserve Premier Cru★*

○ 1er Cru	60000	❷ D

A wine from a small firm – amber-yellow in colour, crisp and light. Good as an aperitif.
✔ Champagne Rosé, Coteaux Champenois.
☛ Emile Hamm et Fils, 16 Rue Nicolas-Philipponat, BP 27, 51160 Ay; tel. 26 50 12 87.

BERNARD HATTE *Cuvée Spécial Club★*

○ 1er Cru	1000	❷ D

A 1979 vintage, labelled by the Champagne region wine-growers' club. Dark gold in colour, with an excellent mousse formed by small, perfect bubbles. Particularly good with meals, with rather heavy winey scents, r89cting the fruity, round body. (1979)
☛ Bernard Hatté, 1 Rue Petite Fontaine, 51360 Vernenay; tel. 26 49 40 90 ⚍ By appt.

HEIDSIECK *Diamant Bleu★★*

○	80000	❹ D

This is a '50–50' blend, considered to be a good formula by many growers: 50 per cent Chardonnay and 50 per cent Pinot Noir from the best sources (Cramant, Ambonnay, Verzy, etc.) The finesse is appealing, and the house character, which is fruity, round, well made and distinctive, makes this a good bottle of champagne. (1979)
☛ Heidsieck et Cie Monopole, 83 Rue Coque-

bert, 51054 Reims Cedex; tel. 26 07 39 34 ⚍ By appt ☛ Seagram.

HEIDSIECK *Dry Monopole★*

◔	50000	❸ D

The 1979 vintage rosé consists of around one-third Chardonnay and two-thirds Pinot Noir and Pinot Meunier. The colour is obtained by adding a red Bouzy wine. Salmon-pink in colour, fruity, supple and round; given life by the carbon dioxide. (1979)
☛ Heidsieck et Cie Monopole, 83 Rue Coque-bert, 51054 Reims Cedex; tel. 26 07 39 34 ⚍ By appt ☛ Seagram.

HEIDSIECK *Dry Monopole★*

○	1 500 000	❸ D

This great firm, more than 100 years old, is controlled by Mumm, but has its own installations and cultivates its own vineyards. This wine is the firm's pride, consisting of 25 per cent Blanc de Blancs to 75 per cent wines from Pinot Noir and Pinot Meunier. It owes its success to its direct attack and the strong backbone supporting an honest fruit.
☛ Heidsieck et Cie Monopole, 83 Rue Coque-bert, 51054 Reims Cedex; tel. 26 07 39 34 ⚍ By appt ☛ Seagram.

CHARLES HEIDSIECK★★★

○	500000	❸ D

Very white in character. Includes large proportion of black grapes. Deep colour with small bubbles and an extraordinarily persistent mousse. Aromas of lightly toasted almond and buttered toast introduce a very well-balanced palate. The well-integrated acidic base heightens the almond flavours. (1979)
☛ Heidsieck-Henriot SA, 3 Place des Droits-de-l'Homme, BP 129, 51055 Reims Cedex; tel. 26 85 03 27 ⚍ By appt. Closed Aug.

CHARLES HEIDSIECK
Charlie Cuvée Spéciale★★

○　　　　　　　　　　　❺ D

This great wine contains 60 per cent Pinot Noir and 40 per cent Chardonnay. White-gold colour with small bubbles crowned by a snowy mousse. A nose of thinly buttered brioches, while on the palate the clear acidity of the base wine comes through. The dosage does not mask the finesse. (1979)
☛ Heidsieck-Henriot SA, 3 Place des Droits-de-l'Homme, BP 129, 51055 Reims Cedex; tel. 26 85 03 27 ⚍ By appt. Closed Aug.

HENRIOT *Crémant**

| ○ | 150000 | ❸ 35 |

One of the few firms making a crémant (semi-sparkling) Blanc de Blancs. The cheerful sparkle resembles that of champagne; an unpretentious wine with a smoky-charred nose.
➡ Heidsieck-Henriot SA, 3 Place des Droits-de-l'Homme, BP 129, 51055 Reims Cedex; tel. 26 85 03 27 ⏰ By appt. Closed Aug.

HENRIOT *Brut Souverain**

| ○ | 1 200 000 | ❸ Ⓓ |

A Brut based on 25 per cent Chardonnay and 75 per cent Pinot, including a touch of Meunier – a combination that is very black for Henriot. A typical example of a non-vintage Brut: skilfully dosed and with no striking character. The mousse and flow of bubbles are pleasing, the nose and palate faultless.
➡ Heidsieck-Henriot SA, 3 Place des Droits-de-l'Homme, BP 129, 51055 Reims Cedex; tel. 26 85 03 27 ⏰ By appt. Closed Aug.

HENRIOT *Cuvée Baccarat***

| ○ | | ❺ Ⓓ |

A 1976 vintage champagne which has avoided that vintage's pitfalls of excessive strength and heaviness. The use of 70 per cent Chardonnay from the best sources gives it elegance and finesse; the mousse is fine, the dosage successful. (1976)
➡ Charles Heidsieck-Henriot SA, 3 Place des Droits-de-l'Homme, BP 129, 51055 Reims Cedex; tel. 26 85 03 27 ⏰ By appt. Closed Aug.

BERNARD IVERNEL *Brut Réserve**

| ○ | 170000 | ❷ Ⓓ |

A non-vintage Brut with an exceptionally persistent mousse, delicate, herbaceous nose and balanced palate.
➡ Bernard Ivernel, 4 Rue Jules-Lobet, BP 15, 51160 Ay; tel. 26 50 11 00 ⏰ By appt. Closed Aug.

BERNARD IVERNEL*

| ◕ | 40000 | ❷ Ⓓ |

A perfect shade of pink crystal; the nose is of soft fruits and the taste has a good balance between acidity, fruit and alcohol.
➡ Bernard Ivernel, 4 Rue Jules-Lobet BP 15, 51160 Ay; tel. 26 50 11 00 ⏰ By appt. Closed Aug.

JACQUART*

| ○ | 300000 | ❹ |

Pleasant colour and mousse; a nose of toast and fruit (quince) confirmed on the palate. A noticeable dosage compensates for a slight acidity. (1978)
➡ Jacquart, 5 Rue Goset, BP 467, 51066 Reims Cedex; tel. 26 07 20 20 ⏰ Mon.–Fri. 8.00–11.00/ 14.00–16.00 ➡ Coopérative Régionale des Vins de Champagne.

JACQUART *Selection**

| ○ | 800000 | ❸ |

Thanks to a generous dosage the palate harbours a trace of honey at once bitter and sweet, while the yeasts can be detected.

➡ Jacquart, 5 Rue Gosset, BP 467, 51066 Reims Cedex; tel. 26 07 20 20 ⏰ Mon.–Fri. 8.00–11.00/ 14.00–16.00 ➡ Coopérative Régionale des Vins de Champagne.

JACQUESSON ET FILS***

| ○ Gd Cru | 70000 | ❷ |

Consists of many grapes from 1981, a little from 1980 and very few from 1979. A Brut with an extremely good balance between finesse, delicate acidity and a full palate. ✔ Rosé, Coteaux Champenois.
➡ Jacquesson et Fils, 68 Rue du Colonel Fabien, Dizy, 51200 Epernay; tel. 26 53 00 66 ⏰ By appt.

JACQUESSON ET FILS *Signature***

| ○ 1er Cru | 10000 | ❹ Ⓓ |

From 50 per cent black grapes (Ay, Dizy), 50 per cent white (Avize), fermented in wood. An intense colour, soft nose and full and round palate – this wine just avoids the pitfalls of the 1976 vintage. (1976)
➡ Jacquesson et Fils, 68 Rue Colonel-Fabien, Dizy, 51200 Epernay; tel. 26 53 00 66 ⏰ By appt.

KRUG *Clos du Mesnil****

| ○ | 15512 | ❺ |

A model Blanc de Blancs, with a smoky-charred nose with scents of quince, apple and a touch of yeast. A vigorous, deep and full palate with a finish of great length. (1979)
➡ Krug, 5 Rue Coquebert, BP 22, 51051 Reims Cedex; tel. 26 88 24 24 ⏰ By appt. Closed July–Aug. ➡ Krug, Vins Fins de Champagne SA.

KRUG *Cuvée Spéciale*

| ◕ | 10000 | ❺ |

A new wine for Krug, although still vinified from wines fermented in small oak casks. 'Blackest' of all the Krug wines, with 52 per cent Pinot Noir, and 24 per cent Pinot Meunier combined with 24 per cent Chardonnay. Pale salmon-pink gold in colour; the palate and the nose are well-balanced with a supple vigour. It has a rare fruitiness that is almost impossible to obtain.
➡ Krug, 5 Rue Coquebert, BP 22, 51051 Reims Cedex; tel. 26 88 24 24 ⏰ By appt. Closed July–Aug. ➡ Krug, Vins Fins de Champagne SA.

KRUG *Grande Cuvée***

| ○ | 400000 | ❺ |

This great blend of 35 per cent Chardonnay and 50 per cent Pinot Meunier from the best growths was conceived by the firm's founder. With elegant and delicately woody aromas and a deep palate dominated by a smooth balance.
➡ Krug, 5 Rue Coquebert, BP 22, 51051 Reims Cedex; tel. 26 88 24 24 ⏰ By appt. Closed July–Aug. ➡ Krug, Vins Fins de Champagne SA.

KRUG *Vintage 1976*★★★

| ○ | 100000 | ❺ |

Deep straw-yellow in colour; the nose is a skilful blend of fruit and vanilla, while the well-made, meaty and full-bodied palate has a long, complex and full finish. (1976)
❦ Kru91 Rue Coquebert, BP 22, 51051 Reims Cedex; tel. 26 88 24 24 ☎ By appt. Closed July–Aug. ❦ King, Vins Fins de Champagne SA.

LALLEMENT-DEVILLE *Dom Basle*★★★

| ○ | 6200 | ❷ Ⓓ |

There are few 1980 vintage champagnes, a year that saw a good, but limited harvest. This wine has a subtle nose of soft fruit, a vigorous balance and a bright straw-yellow colour. (1981)
❦ Lallement-Deville, 28 Rue Irénée-Gass, 51380 Verzy; tel. 26 97 95 90 ☎ By appt. Closed Aug.

LALLEMENT-DEVILLE★

| ○ 1er Cru | 1700 | ❷ Ⓓ |

This wine grower-producer will soon celebrate 100 years of family business. A pale straw-yellow Blanc de Blancs, with a subtle yet delicate bouquet, and a palate that is impulsively light. (1980)
❦ Lallement-Deville, 28 Rue Irénée-Gass, 51380 Verzy; tel. 26 97 95 90 ☎ By appt. Closed Aug.

LAMIABLE★

| ❷ | 7000 | ❷ Ⓓ |

A refreshing wine, tawny gold rather than rosé. It has a fairly simple taste and is very easy to drink, particularly as an apéritif. ✔ Coteaux Champenois Rouge.
❦ Lamiable Frères, 8 Rue de Condé, 51150 Tours-sur-Marne; tel. 26 59 92 69 ☎ By appt.

LAMIABLE★

| ○ Gd Cru | 45000 | ❷ Ⓓ |

Aged for four years in the cellar, a Blanc de Noirs produced from a single growth (Monocru) as well as Grand Cru. Supple, smooth and fruity, it is preceded by a full-bodied nose of blackcurrants and raspberries. Amber-gold in colour. Good with meals.
❦ Lamiable Frères, 8 Rue de Condé, 51150 Tours-sur-Marne; tel. 26 59 92 69 ☎ By appt.

LANG-BIEMONT *Cuvée Réservée*★

| ○ | 60000 | ❷ Ⓓ |

A delicate and light champagne, typical of the Côte des Blancs, which contains a large proportion of Chardonnay (80 per cent). Persistent bubbles form a light mousse above the green-gold wine. A fruity, smoky nose and similar palate. Moderate body; to drink with a light meal or as an aperitif. ✔ Rosé, Coteaux Champenois.
❦ Lang-Biémont, Les Ormissets, Oiry, 51200

Epernay; tel. 26 59 62 55 ☎ Mon.–Fri. 8.30–12.30/14.00–18.30.

LANSON *Black Label*★

| ○ | 5500000 | ❸ |

A pale straw-coloured champagne with impact. Lacking in complexity, but well-balanced. No aggressive acidity, but with a vigour well suited to its maturity.
❦ Lanson Père et Fils, 12 Bd Lundy, BP 163, 51056 Reims Cedex; tel. 26 40 36 26 ☎ By appt ❦ Groupe BSN.

LARMANDIER-BERNIER★

| ○ 1er Cru | 40000 | ❷ Ⓓ |

There is a slight shortage of bubbles and mousse in this non-vintage Brut. It is fairly ordinary on the nose and palate but is redeemed by the fine dominant elegance of the Chardonnay. ✔ Champagne Rosé, Crémant, Coteaux Champenois.
❦ Larmandier-Bernier, 43 Rue du 28 Août, 51130 Vertus; tel. 26 52 13 24 ☎ By appt.

LARMANDIER-BERNIER *Spécial Club*★★★

| ○ 1er Cru | 5000 | ❸ Ⓓ |

It is a shame the 1980 harvest was so small since the quality of the vintage is high. This special blend, selected by the Champagne region wine growers' club, is gold with hints of white-gold and green. A perfect sparkle and persistent mousse. A nose of great finesse introduces a wine that is mature, bright with crisp acidity, almost assertive, with a fine finish. (1980)
❦ Larmandier-Bernier, 43 Rue du 28-Aout, 51130 Vertus; tel. 26 52 13 24 ☎ By appt.

JULES LASSALLE *Cuvée Angeline*★★

| ○ 1er Cru | 5000 | ❷ Ⓓ |

A wine with the best qualities of a 1976 vintage: restrained colour, full bouquet and full-bodied palate. It avoids the high alcohol and lack of acidity of many '76s. (1976)
❦ Mme J. Lassalle et sa Fille, 21 Rue du Châtaignier, Chigny-les-Roses, 51500 Rilly-la-Montagne; tel. 26 03 42 19 ☎ By appt.

JULES LASSALLE★

| ○ 1er Cru | 10000 | ❷ Ⓓ |

A Blanc-de-Blancs which stands out (although discreetly) for its finesse and breeding; it lasts well on the palate for this type of wine. A pleasant finish. (1979)
❦ Mme J. Lassalle et sa Fille, 21 Rue du Châtaignier, Chigny-les-Roses, 51500 Rilly-la-Montagne; tel. 26 03 42 19 ☎ By appt.

JULES LASSALLE *Grandes Années*★

| ❷ 1er Cru | 10000 | ❷ Ⓓ |

A rosé suited to the English palate from a producer who exports very little wine. Pale salmon-pink in colour; a pronounced maturity on the nose and palate, which detracts from the crispness of the fruit.
❦ Mme J. Lassalle, 21 Rue du Châtaignier, Chigny-les-Roses, 51500 Rilly-la-Montagne; tel. 26 03 42 19 ☎ By appt.

LAUNOIS★

○ 1er Cru	20 000	❸ Ⓓ

Clear gold in colour, with a typical Blanc de Blancs nose, smoky and dry. Strong presence of carbon dioxide, together with acidity and a touch of bitterness on the palate, masked by a noticeable dosage. A good example of a non-vintage Brut.

↴ Launois Père et Fils, 3 Av. de la République, le Mesnil-sur-Oger, 51190 Avize; tel. 26 57 50 15 ⅄ By appt.

LAUNOIS★

○ 1er Cru	10 000	❷ Ⓓ

A mature vintage Brut, highly appreciated by the English, who import a large number of bottles. (1979)

↴ Launois Père et Fils, 3 Av. de la République, Le Mesnil-sur-Oger, 51190 Avize; tel. 26 57 50 15 ⅄ By appt.

LAUNOIS★

○ 1er Cru	15 000	❸ Ⓓ

A powerful well-made Premier Cru from the Côte des Blancs. Deep in colour, with a slightly smoky nose. On the palate the impact is immediate, strong acidity gives life to this good vintage Brut. (1980)

↴ Launois Père et Fils, 3 Av. de la République, Le Mesnil-sur-Oger, 51190 Avize; tel. 26 57 50 15 ⅄ By appt.

LAUNOIS *Cuvée Spécial*★★

○ 1er Cru	10 000	❷ Ⓓ

Selected by the Champagne region wine growers' club and therefore in a special bottle. Straw-yellow in colour with a perfect smoky-charred Chardonnay nose. On the palate it is well-structured, fine, full-bodied and lively. (1980)

↴ Launois Père et Fils, 3 Av. de la République Le Mesnil-sur-Oger, 51190 Avize; tel. 26 57 50 15 ⅄ By appt.

LAURENT-PERRIER *Brut LP*★

○	4 800 000	❸ Ⓓ

The main champagne from this dynamic firm, made for the English palate with its preference for mature wines: a strong colour and nose and a palate of black grapes. To be drunk without delay.

↴ Laurent-Perrier, Av. de Champagne, BP 13, 51150 Tours-sur-Marne; tel. 26 59 91 22 ⅄ By appt. Mon.–Fri. 8.00–12.00/13.30–17.00 ↴ B. de Nonancourt.

LAURENT-PERRIER *Ultra Brut*★

○	50 000	❹ Ⓓ

An undosed champagne, white-gold in colour with tawny hints. It has a full and mature nose and an appley fruitiness.

↴ Laurent-Perrier, Av. de Champagne, BP 3, 51150 Tours-sur-Marne; tel. 26 59 91 22 ⅄ By appt. Mon.–Fri. 8.00–12.00/13.30–17.00 ↴ B. de Nonancourt.

LAURENT-PERRIER *Cuvée Rosé Brut*★

◑	500 000	❹ Ⓓ

Produced by the process of running the wine off from the vat preceded by cold maceration. Pale cherry-red in colour, very much of the Pinot Type; the nose and palate have rich tones of blackcurrants and raspberries. Well-balanced, neither too full, nor too lively.

↴ Laurent-Perrier, Av. de Champagne, BP 3, 51150 Tours-sur-Marne; tel. 26 59 91 22 ⅄ By appt. Mon.–Fri. 8.00–12.00/13.30–17.00 ↴ B. de Nonancourt.

LAURENT-PERRIER
Cuvée Grand Siècle★★

○	600 000	❹ Ⓓ

A non-vintage prestige blend, in an old-fashioned bottle, which consists, however, of a blend of wines from vintage years. A fine, fruity nose indicates great art in the blending, with black grapes dominant. Well-made and full-bodied with a long and graceful finish. At a perfect stage of maturity.

↴ Laurent-Perrier, Av. de Champagne, BP 3, 51150 Tours-sur-Marne; tel. 26 59 91 22 ⅄ By appt. Mon.–Fri. 8.00–12.00/13.30–17.00 ↴ B. de Nonancourt.

LECHERE★

○ 1er Cru		❹

Pale in colour, reflecting the taste. It is round, but not very vigorous, justifying its classification as a non-vintage Brut.

↴ Lechère, 10 Rue de Constantinople, 75008 Paris; tel. 45 22 64 22

LECHERE★

◑		❹

A Blanc de Blancs with a typical Chardonnay nose, all finesse and subtlety. On tasting, the wine lacks acidity, doubtless because of the contribution made by the reserve wines. A very noticeable dosage.

↴ Lechère, 10 Rue de Constantinople, 75008 Paris; tel. 1 45 22 64 22.

LECHERE★

○		

A very successful, fresh colour – a blend of gold, peach and strawberry – which is better than the actual wine. Although it is delicate, its attack is flabby and the wine is too soft.

↴ Lechère, 10 Rue de Constantinople, 75008 Paris; tel. 45 22 64 22.

LECHERE *Blanc de Blancs Millésimé*★★

○		❹

Another 1980 vintage champagne, which suggests that this year deserves a better reputation. Very delicate, light, lively and vigorous. A crisp finish although a little short. Noticeable dosage (Brut). (1980)

↴ Lechère, 10 Rue de Constantinople, 75008 Paris; tel. 45 22 64 22.

LECHERE
Venise-Simplon Orient-Express

○   ❸

Selected for the Orient Express after a year of tasting. The nose of Chardonnay and a good balance of maturity and acidity make it equally good as an apéritif or with a meal. The pleasant finish does not completely hide the dosage.
♠ Lechére, 10 Rue de Constantinople, 75008 Paris, tel. 45 22 64 22.

LECLERC-BRIANT*

○   75 000   ❹ ⅅ

A rather full-bodied, self-assured wine, its finesse dominated by the robust body. However, the acidity is successfully balanced by a considerable alcohl content. Successful dosage (Brut). A meal-time champagne.
♠ Leclerc-Briant, 204 Rue G.-Poittevin, Cumières, 51200 Epernay; tel. 26 54 45 33 ⅄ By appt. Closed Aug. ♠ P. Leclerc.

LECLERC-BRIANT*

◑1er Cru   15 000   ❸ ⅅ

A dark-coloured rosé made by the run-off method after 48-hours fermentation of 100 per cent Pinot Noir. The nose is of Pinot with violets; on the palate it is well-structured, the roundness accompanied by a touch of bitterness in the finish. Recommended with meals.
♠ Leclerc-Briant, 204 Rue G.-Poittevin, Cumières, 51200 Epernay; tel. 26 54 45 33 ⅄ By appt. Closed Aug. ♠ P. Leclerc.

LECLERC-BRIANT *Spécial Club*

○1er Cru   20 000   ❹ ⅅ

A vintage Brut selected by the Champagne region wine growers' club, produced by an important wine grower-producer who owns land in six communes. Straw-yellow colour with a pleasing mousse and streaked with small bubbles. A burnt nose, balanced by good acidity. Delicate rather than full-bodied, perfect as an apéritif or with a first course. (1979)
♠ Leclerc-Briant, 204 Rue G.-Poittevin, Cumières, 51200 Epernay; tel. 26 54 45 33 ⅄ By appt. Closed Aug. ♠ P. Leclerc.

LEGRAS *Le Grand Vintage*

○   280 000   ❸ ⅅ

This is very pale in colour with hints of green, Blanc de Blancs with a smokey palate and a dense, vigorous texture.
♠ R. et L. Legras, 10 Rue des Patelaines, Chouilly, 51200 Epernay; tel. 26 54 50 79 ⅄ By appt.

LEGRAS *Cuvée Saint-Vincent**

○   25 000   ❹ ⅅ

A prestige wine, produced in a very modern fermentation house. It is a Chouilly single growth (Monocru) and almost a 'champagne de clos' (from grapes cultivated in a walled vineyard). Pure in colour and on the palate (brioche and hazelnuts), with a sustained, long finish. There is also a version made without dosage. (1979)
♠ R. et L. Legras, 10 Rue des Patelaines, Chouilly, 51200 Epernay; tel. 26 54 50 79 ⅄ By appt.

LEONZE-D'ALBE

○   400 000   ❶

This wine, produced by the Union des Coopératives Auboises, exists in two versions. The first is a blend which is essentially of an Aube-type character, while the second is a blend of wines from the Aube and Marne departments, although the Aube characteristic is dominant. A strong palate with an exuberant, fruity roundness. Good with meals, including cheeses.
♠ UCAVIC, Villeneuve, 10110 Bar-sur-Seine; tel. 25 29 85 57.

ABEL LEPITRE *Carte Blanche**

○   250 000   ❸ ⅅ

The best-selling wine from this firm which has recently been taken over by a Bordeaux owner (Château Dauzac). A typical example of a non-vintage Brut from a high-class producer; a blend of three champagne grapes without any being particularly dominant. A good overall balance with no attempt at complexity; noticeable dosage.
♠ Abel Lepitre, 4 Av. du Général-Gouraud, BP 124, 51055 Reims Cedex; tel. 26 85 05 77 ⅄ By appt. Closed Aug. ♠ Les Grands Champagnes de Reims.

ABEL LEPITRE

◑   50 000   ❸ ⅅ

Rosé champagnes range from very light yellow to red in colour, passing through all shades of apricot, peach, tawny yellow, copper red-gold, etc. This is almost a white wine with a touch of salmon-pink. Nose and taste are delicate but somewhat lacking in fruit and, despite its appearance, the wine seems excessively bitter.
♠ Abel Lepitre, 4 Av. du Général-Gourard, BP 124, 51055 Reims Cedex; tel. 26 85 05 77 ⅄ By appt. Closed Aug. ♠ Les Grands Champagnes de Reims.

ABEL LEPITRE *Crémant***

○   80 000   ❸ ⅅ

A special wine in an old-fashioned, long-necked bottle. Bright and light in colour with a moderate sparkle which allows the finesse of a Blanc de Blancs to be fully appreciated. The blending is noticeable, but well balanced; perfectly integrated bubbles and a long and pleasant finish. (1979)
♠ Abel Lepitre, 4 Av. du Général Gouraud, BP 124, 51055 Reims Cedex; tel. 26 85 05 77 ⅄ By appt. Closed Aug. ♠ Les Grands Champagnes de Reims.

ABEL LEPITRE
Prince A. de Bourbon-Parme★

○   70000   **D** **4**

A special wine produced in honour of the man after whom it is named. A blend of 60 per cent Chardonnay and 40 per cent Pinot Noir from eight different growths. The qualities of the 1976 vintage are noticeable in this harmonious and well-balanced wine. A finely balanced, rather imposing palate; must be drunk cool as it becomes soft and flabby if warm (typical of a '76). (1976)
✈ Abel Lepitre, 4 Av du Général Gouraud, BP 124, 51055 Reims Cedex; tel. 26 85 05 77 ✆ By appt. Closed Aug. ✈ Les Grands Champagnes de Reims.

MAILLY-CHAMPAGNE *Brut★★*

◑   50000   **3** **D**

This rosé bears the appellation of its comune, which is unusual in Champagne. Produced from Grand Cru Pinot Noir, obtained by running-off, a delicate and little-used technique. The very light colour indicates a short fermentation period. Similar to a very dry Blanc de Noirs in taste; direct, compact, with a very low dosage.
✈ Mailly-Champagne, 51500 Rilly-la-Montagne; tel. 26 49 41 10 ✆ Mon.–Fri. 8.00–11.00/14.00–17.30, Sat. and Sun. mornings during the summer.

MAILLY-CHAMPAGNE *Brut Réserve★*

○Gd Cru   35000   **2** **D**

This is a group of enterprising Mailly-Champagne producers who all have vineyards in the commune, classified as Grand Cru. The Brut Reserve is a single growth (Monocru) champagne in which Pinot Noir predominates, with good vinosity and more power than subtlety.
✈ Mailly-Champagne, 51500 Rilly-la-Mont94; tel. 26 49 41 10 ✆ Mon.–Fri. 8.00–11.00/14.00–17.30, Sat. and Sun. mornings during the summer.

MAILLY-CHAMPAGNE
Cuvée des Echansons★★

○Gd Cru   50000   **4** **D**

A Grand Cru special blend, in an 18th-century-style bottle, which has been fermented under cork. The carbon dioxide is well dissolved; aromas of dry flowers (lime?); a vigorous palate supported by a good acidic base. Clear, powerful and precise. To be drunk with fine meals.
✈ Mailly-Champagne, 51500 Rilly-la-Montagne; tel. 26 49 41 10 ✆ Mon.–Fri. 8.00–11.00/14.00–17.30, Sat. and Sun. mornings during the summer.

MARGAINE-BERNARD
Cuvée Traditionnelle★

○1er Cru   55000   **1** **D**

This wine grower-producer favours white grapes, which provide the hints of green and the burnt aromas in this deep coloured wine. Well-made with a supple finish. The dosage is, however, evident. ✓ Spécial Club, Champagne Rosé.
✈ Margaine-Bernard, 3 Av. de Champagne, Villiers-Marmery, 51150 Tours-sur-Marne; tel. 26 97 92 13 ✆ By appt. Closed Aug.

MARIE STUART★

○   450000   **2** **D**

Nearly half the bottles of Marie Stuart bear the 'Brut' label (non-vintage). The nose is close to toasted bread, but with a touch of toasted almond; the palate a little short and acid.
✈ Marie Stuart, 8 Place de la République, 51100 Reims; tel. 26 47 92 26 ✆ By appt. Closed Aug.
✈ Comptoir Vinicole de Champagne (C.V.C.).

MARIE STUART★★★

○   120000   **3** **D**

The nose is all finesse and elegance while the palate confirms the excellent appearance and nose. Everything a vintage wine should be. Chardonnay grapes (80 per cent) are largely responsible for this quality. (1979)
✈ Marie Stuart, 8 Place de la République, 51100 Reims; tel. 26 47 92 26 ✆ By appt. Closed Aug.
✈ C.V.C.

MARIE STUART *Cuvée de la Reine★*

○   100000   **3** **D**

This company, established at the beginning of the century, has changed hands frequently. After 30 years, René Griffant has given it a character of its own. This wine has a very distinctive nose while the taste reveals character and individuality. A very special blend.
✈ Marie Stuart, 8 Place de la République, 51100 Reims; tel. 26 47 92 26 ✆ By appt. Closed Aug.
✈ C.V.C.

MASSE★

○   500000   **2** **D**

A blend of non-vintage Bruts consisting of 40 per cent Chardonnay, 40 per cent Pinot Meunier and 20 per cent Pinot Noir – from second pressings of Grand Cru grapes and wines from outlying areas. It succeeds in its modest aim of providing a fruity champagne, without complexity, that is easy to drink. ✓ Vintage '76.
✈ Massé, 48 Rue de Courlancy, 51100 Reims; tel. 26 47 61 31 ✆ By appt ✈ Groupe B.S.N.

MERCIER★

○   4 000 000   **2** **D** **2**

A non-vintage Brut Blanc de Noirs containing as much Pinot Meunier as Pinot Noir from Aube. A fruity and fat champagne. ✓ Other champagnes.
✈ Mercier, 74 Av. de Champagne, BP 134, 51200 Épernay; tel. 26 54 71 11 ✆ Visits to the cellars by miniature electric train. Closed 25 Dec.–1 Jan.
✈ Moët-Hennessy.

MERCIER *Réserve de l'Empereur*★

○ ❺ D

Eugène Mercier was a great popularizer of champagne and also invented the prestige blend. This wine, originally made for Napoleon III, is a Blanc de Noirs, which is unusual for a special blend; full-bodied, vinous, with a finesse whose fruit is supported by a round base. (1978)
Mercier, 74 Av. de Champagne, BP 134, 51200 Épernay; tel. 26 54 71 11 Y Visits to the cellars by miniature electric train. Closed 25 Dec.–1 Jan. Moët-Hennessy.

JOSE MICHEL★

◑ 3000 ❶ D

7Pinot Meunier and Pinot Noir contribute equally to the light cherry colour and the nose of pear and Morello cherry. Fruity flavours, especially dried fruit, on the palate. A light, fairly elegant wine, good with white meat.
José Michel et Fils, 14 Rue Frelot, BP 16, Moussy, 51200 Épernay; tel. 26 51 04 69 Y By appt. Closed. Sun. morning.

JOSE MICHEL★

○ 100 000 ❷ D

Chardonnay and Pinot Meunier harvested in seven communes are blended in this 1979 vintage. Yellow-gold, streaked with small bubbles; the slightly musky nose follows through on the palate which is nicely balanced. (1979)
José Michel et Fils, 14 Rue Frelot, BP 16, Moussy, 51200 Épernay; tel. 26 51 04 69 Y By appt. Closed Sun. morning.

PIERRE MIGNON *Grande Réserve*★

○ 55 000 ❷ D

An original champagne: the blend is exclusively Blanc de Noirs from Pinot Meunier grown in outlying vineyards. A soft gold colour; floral scents and original, supple and round flavours, accompanied by a hint of *goût de terroir*.
Champagne Rosé.
Pierre Mignon, Rue des Grappes-d'Or, 51210 Montmirail; tel. 26 59 22 03 Y Daily 9.00–12.30/14.00–21.00. Closed 1–15 Jan.

MOET-ET-CHANDON *Dom Pérignon*★★★

○ ❺ D

Moët-et-Chandon launched its special Première Cuvée in 1936; it was imitated by all the producers, as was its presentation in an old-fashioned bottle. The blend contains more Chardonnay than Pinot Noir. The black grapes nevertheless ensure a solid framework in which the harmonious elegance of the Chardonnay stands out. (1975)
Moët-et-Chandon, 20 Av. de Champagne, BP 140, 51205 Epernay Cedex; tel. 26 54 71 11 Y By appt Moët-Hennessy.

MOET-ET-CHANDON *Brut Impérial*★

○ ❸ D

Established in 1743, this huge company produces more than a tenth of the Champagne wines. This is its best-selling wine, commemorating the visit of Napoleon to the residence of Jean-Rémy Moët, then Mayor of Épernay. It can be either vintage or non-vintage. The 1980 is a very pale, appealing colour. A floral fruity nose of apricot with hints of lemon and lime introduces a light taste with moderate acidity and no particular dominant character. (1980)
Moët-et-Chandon, 20 Av. de Champagne, BP 140, 51205 Epernay Cedex; tel. 26 54 71 11 Y By appt Moët-Hennessy.

MOET-ET-CHANDON *Brut Impérial*★★

◑ ❸ D

This is the 1980 rosé, salmon pink in colour with hints of gold; very fruity on the nose with cherry-blackcurrant scents and hints of pear, while a trace of bitterness in the taste is not masked by the suppleness. A wine that is easily appreciated and has a long finish. (1980)
Moët-et-Chandon, 20 Av. de Champagne, BP 140, 51205 Epernay Cedex; tel. 26 54 71 11 Y By appt Moët-Hennessy.

MONTEBELLO★

○ 200 000 ❸ D

A burnt nose with hints of apple. The palate is heavy rather than light. (1979)
Montebello, 2 Bd du Nord, 51160 Ay; tel. 26 55 03 22 Y By appt. Closed Aug. J.-M. Ducellier.

MOUTARD★

○ 80 000 ❶ D

A medium sized wine grower and producer, creating a Blanc de Blancs from one hectare of Chardonnay, a grape seldom grown in Aube, as this region accentuates its characteristics, giving the wine a 'taste of the soil'. The non-vintage Brut, sold at about three-years-old, is made from first and second pressings of Pinot Noir. A robust wine, round and fruity, to be drunk with meals.
Moutard Père et Fils, Buxeuil, 10110 Bar-sur-Seine; tel. 25 38 50 73 Y By appt.

MOUTARD★

○ 15 000 ❷ D

The Moutards have produced 1970, 1973 and 1975 vintages (no longer available) and this '76, reserving the 1979 and 1982 for the future. A thick, solid wine, the power of which emphasizes the full-bodied fruit, which develops to the detriment of the finesse. A mealtime champagne. (1976)
Moutard Père et Fils, Buxeuil, 10110 Bar-sur-Seine; tel. 25 38 50 73 Y By appt.

MOUTARDIER *Brut Sélection*★

○ 20 000 ❷ D

A prestige blend, in a specially shaped bottle, consisting of Pinot Noir and a third Chardonnay. Crisp, vigorous and with a light fruitiness; this is an inexpensive special blend. (1981)
Jean Moutardier, Le Brueil, 51210 Montmirail; tel. 26 59 21 09 Y By appt.

MOUTARDIER *Carte d'Or*★

○ 70 000 ❶ D

This wine grower-producer cultivates 15 hectares of vineyards situated in a fairly outlying area and his modern winery produces more than 100 000 bottles each year. His best seller is a wine from

Pinot Meunier, the blend ranging over three years on average. A fruity and supple wine, without great complexity.

⌐ Jean Moutardier, Le Breuil, 51210 Montmirail; tel. 26 59 21 09 ☎ By appt.

MOUTARDIER★

⌀	10000	❷ Ⓓ

A non-vintage rosé, but with no reserve wine. The base wine is 100 per cent Pinot Meunier, the colour coming from the addition of red wine from Pinot Meunier traditionally vinified, 70 per cent of the grapes being skinned. A light coloured rosé, fruity rather than lively.

⌐ Jean Moutardier, Le Breuil, 51210 Montmirail; tel. 26 59 21 09 ☎ By appt.

MUMM *Cordon Rouge*★★

○		❸ Ⓓ

Mumm has produced its Cordon Rouge since 1875. At several recent blind tastings, it was placed among the winners. An honest, round, very homogeneous wine, with a dominant characteristic of black grapes.

⌐ G.-H. Mumm, Rue du Champs-de-Mars BP 2712, 51053 Reims Cedex; tel. 26 40 22 73 ☎ By appt. Mon.–Fri. 9.00–12.00/14.00–18.00 ⌐ Seagram.

MUMM *Cordon Rouge*★

○	310000	❹ Ⓓ

Mumm owns a very large vineyard and makes a vast range of wines, from the well-known Crémant de Crémant to the René Lalou prestige blend. This is their main champagne; the 1979 is faultless, with its discreet straw-yellow colour, low-key bouquet and good alcohol-acidity balance. Well-made and will please all tastes. (1979)

⌐ G.-H. Mumm, 29 Rue du Champs-de-Mars, BP 2712, 51053 Reims Cedex; tel. 26 40 22 73 ☎ By appt. Mon.–Fri. 9.00–12.00/14.00–18.00 ⌐ Seagram.

MUMM *Cuvée René Lalou*★★★

○		❹ Ⓓ

A prestige blend in a luxuriously ribbed bottle which bears the name of a former chairman. It follows an old champagne recipe: half white, half black (Pinot Noir), making a wine with a great finesse and distinguished construction. It owes much to the quality of the Mumm vineyard, 220 hectares of the best growths. (1979)

⌐ G.-H. Mumm, 29 Rue du Champs-de-Mars, BP 2712, 51053 Reims Cedex; tel. 26 40 22 73 ☎ By appt. Mon.–Fri. 9.00–12.00/14.00–18.00 ⌐ Seagram.

NECTAR DES NOIRS★★

○	7000	❷

The cooperatives also produce prestige blends. This vintage wine is from the Union Champagne d'Avize and consists of a selection of the best black and white grapes, excluding second pressings: 70 per cent Noir to 30 per cent Chardonnay. A vinous champagne, without aggression, calm and self-assured. Full-bodied and round – good with meals. (1979)

⌐ Coop. Vin. d'Ambonnay, 2 Bd des Bermonts,

Ambonnay, 51150 Tours-sur-Marne; tel. 26 57 01 46 ☎ By appt.

NOMINE-RENARD *Cuvée Spéciale*★

○	140000	❷ Ⓓ

Despite the label, this is in fact the normal blend of Nominé-Renard champagne. Gold colour over a pink background, with a round rather than delicate nose, which does not detract from the elegance of the taste. ✓ Blanc de Blancs, Rosé, Reserve Blend, Vintage Blend.

⌐ Nominé-Renard, Villevenard, 51270 Montmortlucy; tel. 26 59 16 13 ☎ By appt.

CHARLES ORBAN *Special Club*★

○	7000	❸ Ⓓ

Selected by the Champagne region wine-growers' club. Unusual in being produced from a single grape variety, Pinot Meunier, giving it its fruity aromas, leafy background and fairly simple taste. It is, however, supple and high in alcohol. (1979)

⌐ Charles Orban, 44 Route de Paris, Troissy, 51700 Dormans; tel. 26 50 70 05.

OUDINOT★

○	360000	❷ Ⓓ

This house has recently been bought by a well-known Champenois. An amber-gold Brut with a moderate flow of small bubbles. The fruit is well-developed on the palate; a well-balanced wine.

⌐ Oudinot, 12 Rue Godard-Roger, 51200 Epernay; tel. 26 54 60 31 ☎ By appt ⌐ Michel Trouillard.

OUDINOT★

○	45000	❸ Ⓓ

Fermented in very modern installations, a Blanc de Blancs characterized by a very fine and remarkably persistent mousse, a delicate nose with a herbaceous background, and a vigorous taste – a good apéritif.

⌐ Oudinot, 12 Rue Godard-Roger, 51200 Epernay; tel. 26 54 60 31 ☎ By appt ⌐ Michel Trouillard.

OUDINOT★★★

⌀	20000	❸ Ⓓ

Produced by the difficult and little-used technique of running-off. Light salmon-pink colour, delicate nose of soft fruit which is confirmed on the palate. Elegance and a long finish. (1979)

⌐ Oudinot, 12 Rue Godard-Roger, 51200 Epernay; tel. 26 54 60 31 ☎ By appt ⌐ Michel Fouillard.

OUDINOT *Cuvée Particulière*★★

○	7500	❹ Ⓓ

A specially shaped bottle with a golden, numbered label, suggesting a prestige wine. This is a Blanc de Blancs, although an untypical one to taste, produced from prestige vineyars – Avize, Cramant (Grand Cru) and Chouilly (Premier Cru). All finesse on the nose and palate, with an assured vigour. A top-class wine. (1979)

⌐ Oudinot, 12 Rue Godard-Roger, 51200 Epernay; tel. 26 54 60 31 ☎ By appt ⌐ Michel Trouillard.

PALMER★★

| ○ | 15000 | ❷ 🄳 |

These owners of excellent vineyards have joined to ferment their grapes. A combination of 41 growths, half white, half black (of which only 10 per cent are Meunier) give a Brut champagne that is solid, round and clear, with immediate appeal and a good balance. A very pleasant dosage. (1979) ✔ Rosé, Blanc de Blancs.
↖ J.-C. Colson, 67 Rue Jacquart, 51100 Reims; tel. 26 07 35 07 ✹ Mon.–Fri. 8.00–12.00/14.00–18.00. Closed Aug. ↖ Coop. des Producteurs des Grands Terroirs de Champagne.

PANNIER *Cuvée Pure 81*★

| ◑ | 80000 | ❷ 🄳 |

Salmon pink in colour with hints of violet, harbouring surprising aromas of fruit drops. A sweet finish makes this a pleasant tea-time wine for those who prefer wine to tea! (1981)
↖ Pannier, 23 Rue Roger-Catillon, 02400 Ch.-Thierry; tel. 23 69 13 10 ✹ Mon.–Fri. 9.00–12.30/14.30–19.00. Closed 1 Jan.–15 Apr.
↖ COVAMA Champagne.

PANNIER★★

| ○ | 100000 | ❷ 🄳 |

A fine demonstration of the tenacity of the five-year-old Pinot Meunier, despite its reputation for delicacy. Small bubbles and a delicate burnt nose of roast hazelnuts. A well-balanced taste, supple rather than vigorous. At the time of tasting, this wine was presented in a magnum. (1979)
↖ Pannier, 23 Rue Roger-Catillon, 02400 Ch.-Thierry; tel. 23 69 13 10 ✹ Mon.–Fri. 9.00–12.30/14.30–19.00. Closed 1 Jan.–15 Apr.
↖ COVAMA Champagne.

PANNIER★

| ○ | 100000 | ❷ 🄳 |

A good champagne produced in conditions that are known to be difficult: the extreme north of the appellation, and using Pinot Meunier. Peach-coloured, with a dark mousse; a well balanced taste, without excessive complexity. (1980)
↖ Pannier, 23 Rue Roger-Catillon, 02400 Ch.-Thierry; tel. 23 69 13 10 ✹ Mon.–Fri. 9.00–12.30/14.30–19.00. Closed 1 Jan.–15 Apr.
↖ COVAMA Champagne.

PANNIER *Carte Blanche*★

| ○ | 95000 | ❷ 🄳 |

This is a Cuvée from a group of producers, based on Pinot Meunier. The winery and cellar are less than an hour from Paris. Pale gold enlivened by a touch of pink; crisp, light and pleasant, in the style of non-vintage Brut.
↖ Pannier, 23 Rue Roger-Catillon, 02400 Ch.-Thierry; tel. 23 69 13 10 ✹ Mon.–Fri. 9.00–12.30/14.30–19.00. Closed 1 Jan.–15 Apr.
↖ COVAMA Champagne.

JOSEPH PERRIER *Cuvée Royale Brut*★

| ○ | 500000 | ❸ 🄳 |

This firm was established at the end of the 18th century and the majority of its production bears this label. Made from equal amounts of grapes from three champagne vines, it has immediate appeal and a good balance between acidity and suppleness.

↖ Joseph Perrier Fils et Cie, 69 Av. de Paris, BP 31, 51005 Châlons-sur-Marne Cedex; tel. 26 68 29 51 ✹ By appt. Closed Aug.

PERRIER-JOUET *Brut Millésimé*★

| ○ | 160000 | ❸ 🄳 |

Light yellow with hints of amber; small, well-renewed bubbles; a fruity, vinous nose; the palate gives the impression of a strong construction. Full-bodied, with a noticeable dosage, (Brut). Good to drink throughout a meal.
↖ Perrier-Jouët, 28 Av. de Champagne, BP 31, 51201 Epernay Cedex; tel. 26 55 20 53 ✹ By appt.
↖ Seagram.

PERRIER-JOUET *Blason de France*★★★

| ○ | 35000 | ❸ 🄳 |

One of the few firms producing more than one special blend, in this case three, counting the rosé. The full body and high alcohol content makes it suitable for meals, although the dosage is noticeable. Good appearance and nose, the latter tending towards fruitiness.
↖ Perrier-Jouët, 28 Av. de Champagne, BP 31, 51201 Epernay Cedex; tel. 26 55 20 53 ✹ By appt.
↖ Seagram.

PERRIER-JOUET *Belle Epoque*★

| ○ | 325000 | ❺ 🄳 |

The model for this bottle was found in the firm's cellars and for many connoisseurs, it is the most successful champagne bottle. It contains a classy wine; a bright appealing colour, with a continuous flow of very small bubbles; a burnt nose of cut hay and a palate that is delicate rather than heavy; youthful and lively, perfectly dosed. Excellent as an apéritif or to start a meal. (1979)
↖ Perrier-Jouët, 28 Av. de Champagne, BP 31 51201 Epernay Cedex; tel. 26 55 20 53 ✹ By appt
↖ Seagram.

PERRIER-JOUET *Blason de France*★

| ◑ | 50000 | ❹ 🄳 |

A highly successful bright salmon-pink colour, streaked by a great many very small bubbles; with the characteristics of 70 per cent Pinot and the Bouzy wine added for colour. Full-bodied and well-made, graceful and appealing. A fine long finish.
↖ Perrier-Jouët, 28 Av. de Champagne, BP 31, 51201 Epernay Cedex; tel. 26 55 20 53 ✹ By appt.
↖ Seagram.

PERRIER-JOUET *Belle Epoque*★★

| ◑ | 70000 | ❺ 🄳 |

This superb, famous bottle reveals a salmon-pink colour tending towards apricot. The nose is discreet, almost dumb, but with extreme finesse in

keeping with the light and elegant taste. A very attractive, aristocratic wine. (1979)
➻ Perrier-Jouët, 28 Av. de Champagne, BP 31, 51201 Epernay Cedex; tel. 26 55 20 53 ♈ By appt.
➻ Seagram.

PERRIER-JOUET *Grand Brut*★

○	400 000	❹ Ⓓ

Established more than 150 years ago, this house owns a large and particularly successful vineyard in the Côte des Blancs. This is their best-selling champagne, made with a majority of black grapes; full-bodied and well-made with a pleasing finish, and fruity, heavy aromas.
➻ Perrier-Jouët, 28 Av. de Champagne, BP 31, 51201 Epernay Cedex; tel. 26 55 20 53 ♈ By appt
➻ Seagram.

DOMINIQUE PERTOIS★

○ 1er Cru		❹ Ⓓ

A large wine grower-producer from Mesnil-sur-Oger, a commune classified as premier cru but comparable to the grands crus (99 per cent). This yellow Blanc de Blancs develops a nose very characteristic of the Chardonnay. A burnt nose with scents of cut hay introduces a palate of immediate appeal which is perfectly dry. Noticeable dosage.
➻ D. Pertois 13 Av. de la République, Le Mesnil-sur-Oger, 51190 Avize; tel. 26 57 52 14 ♈ By appt. Closed Aug.

DOMINIQUE PERTOIS★

○ 1er Cru	9000	❷ Ⓓ

The commune of Mesnil-sur-Oger has the reputation of producing well-made wines that last well. This vintage Blanc de Blancs has a strong nose of burnt bread and a clear and honest taste. There is a good deal of carbon dioxide, not totally integrated into the wine. Good finish. Skilful dosage. (1978)
➻ D. Pertois, 13 Av. de la République, Le Mesnil-sur-Oger, 51190 Avize; tel. 26 57 52 14 ♈ By appt. Closed Aug.

PIERRE PETERS★

○ 1er Cru	140 000	❸ Ⓓ

A family business at Mesnil-sur-Oger, a commune rated 99 per cent in the grading of growths, but whose grapes are nevertheless sold at the same price as the 100 per cent Grands Crus. The 1980 Blanc de Blancs is a sparkling yellow – a cheerful appearance that is reflected in the taste, which is pure, direct, with a hint of hazelnuts. (1980)
➻ Pierre Peters, 26 Rue des Lombards, BP 10, Le Mesnil-sur-Oger, 51190 Avize; tel. 26 57 50 32 ♈ By appt. Closed Aug.

PETITJEAN *Carte d'Or Brut Tradition*★

○	5000	❸ Ⓓ

A small Epernay firm with a winery and cellars at Ambonnay. This wine is produced from Pinot Noir and Chardonnay in equal parts. A strong yellow-gold colour crowned by a fine mousse; a delicate, burnt nose followed by a palate that is full-bodied rather than delicate, with a noticeable dosage.
➻ Petitjean et Cie, Pl. Barancourt, Ambonnay,

51150 Tours-sur-Marne; tel. 26 54 44 52 ♈ By appt. Closed weekends.

PETITJEAN *Carte d'Or Brut Réserve*★

○	50 000	❷ Ⓓ

Made from two parts Chardonnay to two parts Pinot Noir. The gold colour reveals tinges of pink. Nose and palate give the impression of impeccable balance, which would be improved by greater complexity.
➻ Petitjean et Cie, Pl. Barancourt, Ambonnay, 51150 Tours-sur-Marne; tel. 26 54 44 52 ♈ By appt. Closed weekends.

PHILIPPONAT *Royale Réserve Brut*★

◑	30 000	❸ Ⓓ

A red-pink rosé based on Pinot, with 15 per cent Chardonnay added. The result is a supple wine that owes its vigour to the carbon dioxide. The fruit is highlighted by the dosage.
➻ Philipponat, 13 Rue du Pont, BP 2, Mareuil-sur-Ay, 51160 Ay; tel. 26 50 60 43 ♈ By appt. Closed Aug. ➻ SA Champagne Gosset.

PHILIPPONAT *Clos des Goisses*★★

○	25 000	❹ Ⓓ

One of the very few 'clos' champagnes, and without doubt the most prestigious. The special squat bottle suits its robust character. Rich and powerful – one could almost talk of a tannic base – with a long finish. A complete wine which goes well with meals. (1978)
➻ Philipponat, 13 Rue du Pont, BP 2, Mareuil-sur-Ay, 51160 Ay; tel. 26 50 60 43 ♈ By appt. Closed Aug. ➻ SA Champagne Gosset.

PHILIPPONAT *Royale Réserve Brut*

○	350 000	❸ Ⓓ

This firm, established in 1912, bears the name of a very old family from Ay. Both lively and supple, it is suitable for starting a meal.
➻ Philipponat, 13 Rue du Pont, BP 2, Mareuil-sur-Ay, 51160 Ay; tel. 26 50 60 43 ♈ By appt. Closed Aug. ➻ SA Champagne Gosset.

PHILIPPONAT *Cuvée Première*★★

○	130 000	❸ Ⓓ

Only Grand Cru Chardonnay grapes from the Côte des Blancs are used in to produce light mousse and buttery, almost vanilla, nose. Light, fruity and distinguished taste. Drink it as an apéritif or with fish dishes. (1980)
➻ Philipponat, 13 Rue du Pont, BP 2, Mareuil-sur-Ay, 51160 Ay; tel. 26 50 60 43 ♈ By appt. Closed Aug. ➻ S.A. Champagne Gosset.

PIPER-HEIDSIECK *Brut Extra*★

○	3 200 000	❸ Ⓓ

More than three million bottles are made every year. Pleasing nose of toasted bread and almond, and delicate, elegant palate with good acidity.
✔ Crémant de Loire.
➻ Piper-Heidsieck, 51 Bd Henri-Vasnier, BP 106, 51054 Reims Cedex; tel. 26 85 01 94 ♈ Daily 9.00–11.30/14.00–17.30.

PIPER-HEIDSIECK *Brut Sauvage*★

○	120000	

Full, round palate nose of mature Pinot, and straw colour with hints of amber-pink.
⚬┱ Piper-Heidsieck, 51 Bd Henri-Vasnier, BP 106, 51054 Reims Cedex; tel. 26 85 01 94 ⴲ Daily 9.00–11.30/14.00–17.30.

PIPER-HEIDSIECK *Brut Extra*★

○	400000	❹ Ⅾ

Straw-yellow in colour. Vigorous and well-bred, with a good, wholesome flavour rather than full-bodied; very subtly dosed. The nose is floral with a smoky-charred base. (1979)
⚬┱ Piper-Heidsieck, 51 Bd Henri-Vasnier, BP 106, 51054 Reims Cedex; tel. 26 85 01 94 ⴲ Daily. 9.00–11.30/14.00–17.30.

PIPER-HEIDSIECK *Brut Rosé*★★★

◑	240000	❹ Ⅾ

This vintage rosé owes its finesse to a high proportion of white grapes, while its pink colour, suffused with hints of copper, is due to the Pinot Noir, which also gives the full body. The blend is rich and balanced. Excellent as an apéritif or with meals. (1979)
⚬┱ Piper-Heidsieck, 51 Bd Henri Vasnier, BP 106, 51054 Reims Cedex; tel. 26 85 01 94 ⴲ Daily 9.00–11.30/14.00–17.30.

PIPER-HEIDSIECK *Rare*★★★

○	150000	❺ Ⅾ

A powerful, pale-coloured wine; very delicate and lively; supple and well made. (1976)
⚬┱ Piper-Heidsieck, 51 Bd Henri Vasnier, BP 106, 51054 Reims Cedex; tel. 26 85 01 94 ⴲ Daily 9.00–11.30/14.00–17.30.

POL ROGER★

○		❸ Ⅾ

An appealing bright colour. A dominant Chardonnay character on the nose and palate is surprising – it is unusual in non-vintage bruts. Finesse and elegance notably combined.
⚬┱ SA Pol Roger et Cie, 1 Rue Henri-Lelarge, BP 199, 51206 Epernay Cedex; tel. 26 55 41 95 ⴲ By appt. Closed Aug.

POL ROGER★

◑		❹ Ⅾ

This rosé bears a great vintage: 1975, renowned for its balance. Strong acidity and fruit, the Pinot ensuring a comfortable roundness highlighted by the dosage. (1975)
⚬┱ Pol Roger et Cie SA, 1 Rue Henri Lelarge, BP 199, 51206 Epernay Cedex; tel. 26 55 41 95 ⴲ By appt. Closed Aug.

POL ROGER *Blanc de Chardonnay*★★★

○		❹ Ⅾ

Seductive colour with tinges of gold, a charming nose of fresh butter, and an elegant, round, taste that delights the palate. An apéritif for very special occasions. (1975)
⚬┱ Pol Roger et Cie SA, 1 Rue Henri Lelarge, BP 199, 51206 Epernay Cedex; tel. 26 55 41 95 ⴲ By appt. Closed Aug.

POL ROGER★★★

○		❸ Ⅾ

A very fine and successful vintage 1979, consisting of 40 per cent Chardonnay and 60 per cent Pinot Noir. The golden colour is crowned by an attractive mousse. Aromas of frangipani in the bouquet give way to hints of toasted bread on the palate. A beautifully balanced wine. (1979)
⚬┱ Pol Roger et Cie SA, 1 Rue Henri-Lelarge, BP 199, 51206, Epernay Cedex; tel. 26 55 41 95 ⴲ By appt. Closed Aug.

POMMERY★★

◑	100000	❸ Ⅾ

The Chardonnay, slightly less than a third, gives character to this rosé with hints of coral colour. A generous nose, similar to a red wine; the palate is full-bodied and round. Should be drunk with a meal.

♠ Pommery et Greno, 5 Pl. du Général-Gouraud, BP 87, 51053 Reims Cedex; tel. 26 05 05 01 ⏺ Mon.–Fri. 9.00–11.00/14.00–17.00.

POMMERY*

| ○ | 200 000 | ❸ 🄳 |

A very fine 1979 in every detail: the colour, bubbles and mousse are all perfect. However, a slight taste of reduction spoils the nose (perhaps temporary). A very well-balanced palate. Ideal dosage. (1979)
♠ Pommery et Greno, 5 Place du Général Gouraud, BP 87, 51053 Reims Cedex; tel. 26 05 05 01 ⏺ Mon.–Fri. 9.00–11.00/14.00–17.00.

POMMERY *Brut Royale**

| ○ | 4 000 000 | ❸ 🄳 |

Noteworthy for its incredibly persistent, fine mousse and continuous flow of small bubbles. Gold colour, with tinges of pink. A full nose and a vinous, round and full-bodied palate.
♠ Pommery et Greno, 5 Place du Général Gouraud, BP 87, 51053 Reims Cedex; tel. 26 05 05 01 ⏺ Mon.–Fri. 9.00–11.00/14.00–17.00.

VIRGILE PORTIER *Brut Spécial**

| ○Gd Cru | 8000 | ❷ 🄳 |

Gold on a background of green. Fine mousse and a good flow of bubbles. A nose of toasted bread and green apples; the flavour of green apples is also on the palate (malic acid), giving the wine its vigour. ✓ Champagne Rosé, Coteaux Champenois.
♠ Virgile Portier, 21 Rte Nationale, Beaumont-sur-Vesle, 51400 Mourmelon-le-Grand; tel. 26 61 60 15 ⏺ By appt.

PREVOTEAU-PERRIER*

| ○ | 80 000 | ❶ 🄳 |

Gold in colour, with tawny hints. A very fruity palate but a little short, and without complexity.
♠ Prévoteau-Perrier, 13–15 Rue André-Maginot, Damery, 51200 Epernay; tel. 26 58 41 56 ⏺ By appt♠ Patrice Prévoteau.

PREVOTEAU-PERRIER*

| ◑ | 20 000 | ❷ 🄳 |

Very pale apricot-orange in colour; a fruity nose with a hint of roses. Very fruity to taste, and the round finish is marked by a touch of bitterness. Good overall balance.
♠ Prévoteau-Perrier, 13–15 Rue André-Maginot, Damery, 51200 Epernay; tel. 26 58 41 56 ⏺ By appt♠ Patrice Prévoteau.

PREVOTEAU-PERRIER
Grande Réserve*

| ○ | 20 000 | ❹ 🄳 |

A great many medium-sized bubbles, which are not completely integrated into a brut that is heavy rather than delicate. Short and predictable.
♠ Prévoteau-Perrier, 13–15 Rue André-Maginot, Damery, 51200 Epernay; tel. 26 58 41 56 ⏺ By appt♠ Patrice Prévoteau.

RENAUDIN *Brut Grande Réserve**

| ○ | 10 000 | ❹ 🄳 |

Avoids the weight and excessive strength associated with the 1976 vintage, which had a very high alcohol content. (1976)
♠ Renaudin, Domaine des Connardins, Moussy, 51200 Epernay; tel. 26 54 03 41 ⏺ By appt. Closed Aug. and weekends.

RENAUDIN *Brut Réserve**

| ○ | · 70 000 | ❷ 🄳 |

A fruity and supple wine; balanced, without unnecessary complexity.
♠ Renaudin, Dom. des Connardins, Moussy, 51200 Epernay; tel. 26 54 03 41 ⏺ By appt. Closed Aug. and weekends.

LOUIS ROEDERER*

| ○ | 1 200 000 | ❸ 🄳 |

A non-vintage brut suited to the English palate, as it has a touch of oxidation. Noticeable dosage.
♠ SA Louis Roederer, 21 Bd Lundy, BP 66, 51053 Reims Cedex; tel. 26 40 42 11 ⏺ By appt.

LOUIS ROEDERER *Cristal***

| ○ | | ❺ 🄳 |

Superb gold colour, streaked with abundant, small bubbles. Nose of brioche; clean on the palate; well-made, with immediate appeal. (1979)
♠ SA Louis Roederer, 21 Bd Lundy, BP 66 51053 Reims Cedex; tel. 26 40 42 11 ⏺ By appt.

ALFRED ROTHSCHILD *Millésime***

| ○ | 300 000 | ❸ 🄳 |

Liquid gold with tinges of green, streaked with small bubbles and crowned by a fine and continuous mousse. A subtle nose with aromas of brioche. The acidity of the base wine persist on the palate from start to finish; to round things off, a dosage to match. (1979)
♠ Marne-et-Champagne, 22 Rue Maurice Cerveaux, BP 138, 51205 Epernay; tel. 26 54 21 66 ♠ Gaston Burtin.

ALFRED ROTHSCHILD
Réserve Brut Rosé***

| ◑ | 400 000 | ❸ 🄳 |

A perfectly coloured vintage rosé with hints of coral and gold, and a mousse that seems to last for ever. The floral finesse of the nose is allied to the full-bodied fruitiness on the palate. (1979)
♠ Marne-et-Champagne, 22 Rue Maurice Cerveaux, BP 138, Epernay; tel. 26 54 21 66 ♠ Gaston Burtin.

ALFRED ROTHSCHILD
Spécial Réserve★

| ○ | 1 000 000 | ❸ Ⓓ |

Pleasing in appearance, but the light nose influences the palate, which is a little simple, although well-constructed and perfectly dosed.
🍷 Marne-et-Champagne, 22 Rue Maurice Cerveaux, BP 138, 51205 Epernay; tel. 26 54 21 66 🍷 Gaston Burtin.

ALFRED ROTHSCHILD
Grand Trianon★★

| ○ | 200 000 | ❻ Ⓓ |

Ideal, pale champagne colour, fine mousse, perfect stream of bubbles, delicate flowery nose and a distinguished and elegant palate. An incredible 1976! (1976)
🍷 Marne-et-Champagne, 22 Rue Maurice Cerveaux, BP 138, 51205 Epernay; tel. 26 54 21 66 🍷 Gaston Burtin.

RUINART *Dom Ruinart★★*

| ◔ | | ❺ Ⓓ |

Full, bright rosé colour with hints of red. Strong nose, with scents of soft fruits and blackcurrants on a floral background of violets. Marvellous accompaniment to a meal. (1976)
🍷 Ruinart, 4 Rue des Crayères, BP 85, 51053 Reims Cedex; tel. 26 85 40 29 ⏳ Mon.–Fri. 9.30–11.30/14.30–16.30 🍷 Moët-Hennessy.

RUINART *Dom Ruinart Cuvée Spécial★*

| ○ | | ❹ Ⓓ |

A vintage Blanc de Blancs, green-gold with an exuberant nose, and a rich palate derived from grapes exclusively harvested from Grand Cru vineyards. (1978)
🍷 Ruinart, 4 Rue Des Crayères, BP 85, 51053 Reims Cedex; tel. 26 85 40 29 ⏳ Mon.–Fri. 9.30–11.30/14.30–16.30 🍷 Moët-Hennessy.

RUINART *'R' de Ruinart★*

| ○ | | ❸ Ⓓ |

A widely sold bottle from the oldest champagne firm. The nose is both fruity and flowery, while the palate gives the impression of a mature wine. Very supple and soft.
🍷 Ruinart, 4 Rue des Crayères, BP 85, 51053 Reims Cedex; tel. 26 85 40 29 ⏳ Mon.–Fri. 9.30–11.30/14.30–16.30 🍷 Moët-Hennesy.

SAINT-NICAISE *Cuvée Prestige*

| ○ | 150 000 | ❸ Ⓓ |

A excessive vigour and relatively thin palate. The noticeable dosage compensates for an insistent acidity. Drink it with rich fish dishes. (1977)
✔ Champagne Rosé; Coteaux Champenois.
🍷 Bauchet-Frères, Rue de la Crayère, 51150 Bisseuil; tel. 26 59 92 12 ⏳ By appt.

SAINT-REOL★

| ○ | 35 000 | ❷ Ⓓ |

Consists of one-third Chardonnay to two-thirds Pinot Noir. Its positive taste is well suited to meals.
🍷 Cooperative Vinicole d'Ambonnay, 2 Bd des Bermonts, Ambonnay, 51150 Tours-sur-Marne; Tel. 26 57 01 46 ⏳ By appt.

SALON★★★

| ○ | 50 000 | ❺ Ⓓ |

Light straw-yellow, crowned with an immaculate, fine mousse. For a Blanc de Blancs the nose is surprisingly fruity, spicy and smoke-charred. The palate is also surprising, but seductive. It is crisp, vigorous and at the same time full-bodied. Good as an apéritif or with refined dishes. (1979)
🍷 SA Salon, Le Mesnil-sur-Oger, 51190 Avize; tel. 26 50 57 69 ⏳ By appt. Closed Aug.

SECONDE-PREVOTEAU
Fleuron de France★★

| ○ | 5000 | ❸ Ⓓ |

The deep colour conceals a hint of tawny gold. Small bubbles, but not very long-lasting. A strong nose reflected on the palate by a fruit that is round and full, with immediate appeal – perfect with meals. These are signs of a true Blanc de Noirs – a rarity. (1979)
🍷 A. Secondé-Prévoteau, 2 Rue du Cha. 51150 Ambonnay; tel. 26 57 01 59 ⏳ By appt. Closed Christmas and New Year.

SECONDE-PREVOTEAU
Brut Extra Princesses de France★

| ○ | 12 000 | ❸ Ⓓ |

Full colour and fine bubbles forming a small mousse. The nose and palate are normal. Moderate finesse, good overall balance and fruit. The base wine is a little light.
🍷 A. Secondé-Prévoteau, 2 Rue du Château, 51150 Ambonnay; tel. 26 57 01 59 ⏳ By appt. Closed Christmas and New Year.

SECONDE-PREVOTEAU
Princesses de France★★

| ◔ | 4500 | ❸ Ⓓ |

Salmon-pink colour, a full nose, and a palate that is balanced, full and harmonious with a long finish.
🍷 A. Secondé Prévoteau, 2 Rue du Cha., 51150 Ambonnay; tel. 26 57 01 59 ⏳ By appt. Closed Christmas and New Year.

SECONDE-PREVOTEAU
Brut Sélection Princesses de France★

| ○ | 5000 | ❸ Ⓓ |

Burnished gold colour streaked with slow bubbles. Rich aromas and direct, fruity flavour, with a smooth finish free of any bitterness.
🍷 A. Secondé-Prévoteau, 2 Rue du Cha., 51150 Ambonnay; tel. 26 57 01 59 ⏳ By appt. Closed Christmas and New Year.

JACQUES SELOSSE *Blanc de Blancs*★★★

○ Gd Cru	27000	❶ Ⓓ

Nose of toasted bread; rich and full-bodied, and supported by a mature base wine – all due to the Grand Cru.
☛ Jacques Selosse, Rue Ernest-Valle, 51190 Avize; tel. 26 57 53 56 ☏ By appt ☛ Anselme Selosse.

JACQUES SELOSSE *Spécial Club*★★★

○	6000	❸ Ⓓ

Full-bodied, with an elegant nose of fresh brioche; at once powerful and delicate. Very good balance. (1979)
☛ Jacques Selosse, Rue Ernest-Valle, 51190 Avize; tel. 26 57 53 56 ☏ By appt ☛ Anselme Selosse.

SUGOT-FENEUIL *Carte Rouge*★

○	❸ Ⓓ

Hints of pink in the colour; nose and palate are fruity with a touch of bitterness. A classic non-vintage brut.
☛ Sugot-Feneuil, 40 Impasse de la Mairie, Cramant, 51200 Épernay; tel. 26 57 53 54.

TAITTINGER *Brut Non Millésimé*★

○	3 600 000	❸ Ⓓ

The best-selling wine from this 250-year-old firm, fermented and made into champagne with the most modern equipment. The blend consists of a majority of black grapes, making it extremely full-bodied. ✔ Blanc de Blancs.
☛ Taittinger, 9 Place St-Nicaise, 51400 Reims; tel. 26 85 45 35 ☏ By appt.

TAITTINGER *Comtes de Champagne*★★★

○	400000	❺

A Blanc de Blancs of great finesse, which also has a fine full body – a rare balance favoured by a suitable dosage. (1976)
☛ Taittinger, 9 Place St-Nicaise, 51400 Reims; tel. 26 85 45 35 ☏ By appt.

TAITTINGER *Collection*★★

○	❺ Ⓓ

Solid and well-constructed wine. Drink before or during a meal. (1978)
☛ Taittinger, 9 Place St-Nicaise, 51400 Reims; tel. 26 85 45 35 ☏ By appt.

UNION-CHAMPAGNE *Orpale*★★★

○	20000	❸ Ⓓ

A Blanc de Blancs which remains 'sur point' (ready to drink) for three or four years. Very bright colour, with a subtle nose of baked bread and cut hay, together with a round and harmonious taste that has the elegance of the Chardonnay grape.
☛ Union-Champagne, 7 Rue Pasteur, 51190 Avize; tel. 26 57 94 22 ☏ By appt. Closed weekends.

DE VENOGE *Cordon Bleu*★

○	520000	❸ Ⓓ

This very old blend represents two-thirds of the sales of Venoge champagne. It combines the three champagne grapes in equal parts. A solid and fruity wine with a noticeable dosage.
☛ De Venoge, 30 Av. de Champagne, BP 103, 51204 Epernay Cedex; tel. 26 55 01 01 ☏ Mon.–Fri. office hours; weekends by appt ☛ Charles Heidsieck-Henriot.

DE VENOGE *Champagne des Princes*★★

○	100000	❺ Ⓓ

Very attractive. A lively Blanc de Blancs from Cramant, with a delicate nose and a round and mature palate. Noticeable dosage.
☛ De Venoge, 30 Av. de Champagne, BP 103, 51204 Epernay Cedex; tel. 26 55 01 01 ☏ Mon.–Fri. office hours; weekends by appt ☛ Charles Heidsieck-Henriot.

ALAIN VESSELLE★

○	70000	❸ Ⓓ

A non-vintage brut, pale in colour with tinges of pink, with a mousse of large bubbles. The nose is round, lively, almost heady, with a palate to match. A good non-vintage that achieves its aim.
★₮ Alain Vesselle, Bouzy, 51150 Tours-sur-Marne; tel. 26 57 00 88.

ALAIN VESSELLE *Saint-Eloi*★

○Gd Cru	20000	❹ Ⓓ

Light gold with hints of orange, crowned by a large mousse with a stream of persistent bubbles. The nose is burnt (smoky but not dry), the taste round, full and rich. Goes well with a meal.
★₮ Alain Vesselle, Bouzy, 51150 Tours-sur-Marne; tel. 26 57 00 88.

GEORGES VESSELLE
Bouzy Brut Zéro★★

○Gd Cru	18000	❸ Ⓓ

Clean and exact, yet full and high in alcohol. An excellent mealtime champagne. (1979) ✔ Coteaux Champenois.
★₮ Georges Vesselle, 16 Rue des Postes, Bouzy, 51150 Tours-sur-Marne; tel. 26 57 00 15 ⵏ By appt.

JEAN VESSELLE★★

○	50000	❸ Ⓓ

Deep gold-orange champagne, produced from 85 per cent Pinot Noir and 15 per cent Chardonnay. Tiny bubbles, perfectly renewed. Round and full, straightforward and clean on the palate. Very consistent. There is no dosage to affect the purity of the fruit or wine. For meals or as a vigorous apéritif.
★₮ Jean Vesselle, 2 Pl. J.-B.-Barnaut, BP 15, Bouzy, 51150 Tours-sur-Marne; tel. 26 57 01 55 ⵏ By appt.

JEAN VESSELLE *Œil-de-Perdrix*★

○	20000	❸ Ⓓ

A Blanc de Noirs, suitably tawny-gold. Very high in alcohol and full-bodied. To be drunk with substantial meals.
★₮ Jean Vesselle, 2 Pl. J.-B.-Barnaut, BP 15, Bouzy, 51150 Tours-sur-Marne; tel. 26 57 01 55 ⵏ By appt.

MARCEL VEZIEN★

○	50000	❶ Ⓓ

Made from Pinot Noir with just a touch of Pinot Meunier and Chardonnay. A pronounced character. Best drunk with a meal.
★₮ Marcel Vézien, Celles-sur-Ource, 10110 Bar-sur-Seine; tel. 25 38 50 22 ⵏ By appt.

MARCEL VEZIEN *Brut Prestige*★

○	20000	❷ Ⓓ

Yellow-gold in colour; well-renewed bubbles; a full, fruity and round palate.
★₮ Marcel Vézien, Celles-sur-Ource, 10110 Bar-sur-Seine; tel. 25 38 50 22 ⵏ By appt.

Coteaux Champenois

Formerly known as 'vins natures de Champagne', they gained their AOC in 1974 and took the name Coteaux Champenois. They are still wines which may be white, red or, very rarely, rosé. The whites should be drunk with indulgence, remembering that they are the survivors of a time long past, before champagne as we know it today was born. Like champagne, Coteaux Champenois may be Blanc de Noirs or Blanc de Blancs, or a combination of the two.

The most renowned Coteaux Champenois red wine, a Grand Cru wine from Pinot Noir grapes, is named after the famous commune of Bouzy. There, visitors may admire one of the two strangest vineyards in the world, the other being in Ay. A huge sign indicates 'vielles vignes françaises préphylloxerique' ('old French pre-phylloxera vines'). They would be indistinguishable from other vines were they not planted 'en foule', literally 'higgledy-piggledy', an ancient technique that has been abandoned elsewhere. All the work is done by hand with old-fashioned tools. Owned by the great champagne house of Bollinger, this vineyard produces the rarest and most expensive champagne in the world.

Coteaux Champenois wines should be drunk young, the whites at a temperature of 7–8°C with dishes that go well with very dry wines; and the reds at 9–10°C with fairly light dishes (white meat, or even oysters). Of the reds, a few exceptional years could even be laid down for a while. The great vintage reds bear some resemblance to Burgundy: the best years have been 1966, 1971 and 1976.

BONNAIRE★

☐1er Cru	5000	❶ Ⓓ

Made from the Chardonnay grape. Straw-gold colour with subtle silver highlights and a bouquet of fresh bread; firm and fresh acidity on the palate. André Bonnaire is one of the largest grower-distributors on the Côte des Blancs and owns an ultra-modern winery. (1983) ✔ Champagne.
★₮ Andre Bonnaire, 105 Rue de Carrouge, Cramont, 51200 Epernay; tel. 26 57 50 85 ⵏ By appt.

CLOUET**

■ Gd Cru | 5000 | ❷ Ⓓ

One of the very few Coteaux Champenois from 1977; the year suffered particularly by comparison with the excellent 1976 vintage. Dark pink colour with a complex bouquet of red fruit and a long, balanced finish. An interesting wine which has already reached its peak: 1977 is not a year to be kept. (1977) ✔ Champagne.
🕯 A. Clouet, 8 Rue Gambetta, 51150 Bouzy: tel. 26 57 00 82 ϒ By appt.

DELAVENNE Bozy Rouge

■ Gd Cru | 4000 | ❷ Ⓓ

This non-vintage wine is blended from 15 per cent 1979 and 85 per cent 1982 vinified from Pinot Noir grapes grown within the communal boundaries of Bouzy. Lovely red and purple colour and a bouquet reminiscent of stewed fruit. Fruity and rather light on the palate with a supple finish. ✔ Champagne.
🕯 MM. Delavenne Père et Fils, 6 Rue de Tours, Tours-sur-Marne, 51150 Bouzy; tel. 26 57 02 04 ϒ By appt.

LAURENT-PERRIER *Pinot Franc**

■ | 90 000 | ❷Ⓓ

This producer has established a good reputation for its Coteaux Champenois. Clear, shining appearance with a hint of rosy pink and discreetly fruity bouquet. Direct and wholesome on the palate, very supple and without any complexity. Owes its freshness to not having been matured in wood. ✔ Champagne.
🕯 Laurent-Perrier, Av. de Champagne, BP 3, 51150 Tours-sur-Marne; tel. 26 59 91 22 ϒ Mon.–Fri. 8.00–12.00/13.30–17.00 🕯 Bernard de Nonancourt.

LAURENT-PERRIER
*Blanc de Blancs de Chardonnay**

☐ | 300 000 | ❷ Ⓓ

Straw-coloured wine with a thin bouquet and relatively little acidity on the palate. Its softness is gained at the expense of freshness and firmness. ✔ Champagne.
🕯 Laurent-Perrier, Av. de Champagne, BP 3, 51150 Tours-sur-Marne; tel. 26 59 91 22 ϒ Mon.–Fri. 8.00–12.00/13.30–17.00 🕯 Bernard de Nonancourt.

ABEL LEPITRE*

■ | 30 000 | ❸ Ⓓ

A non-vintage Bouzy with a pale rosy tint and a bouquet of red fruit. Rather soft on the palate; supple, civilized and light overall. ✔ Champagne.
🕯 Abel Lepitre, 4 Av. du General-Giraud, BP 124, 50155 Reims Cedex; tel. 26 85 05 77 ϒ By appt. Closed Aug.

SECONDE-PREVOTEAU
*Ambonnay***

■ Gd Cru | 7500 | ❸ Ⓓ

Dark ruby red colour and generous nose of pulpy red fruit. Full, fleshy and sturdy on the palate but nonetheless complex and fine. Matured by the special solera method used in Jerez, Spain, and in Cahors. Can be kept. ✔ Champagne.
🕯 A. Secondé-Prevoteau, 2 Rue du Chateau, 51150 Ambonnay; tel. 26 59 01 59 ϒ By appt. Closed Christmas, New Year.

ALAIN VESSELLE *Bouzy**

■ Gd cru | 15 000 | ❷ Ⓓ

Red Bouzy with a light raspberry colour, made exclusively from grapes grown in the Bouzy commune. The bouquet is of small red fruit with overtones of banana. On the palate, rather light for a Bouzy but fine and perfumed with a supple finish. ✔ Champagne.
🕯 Alain Vesselle, Bouzy, 51150 Tours-sur-Marne; tel. 26 57 00 88.

JEAN VESSELLE *Bouzy Rouge**

■ Gd Cru | 5000 | ❸ Ⓓ

Made from the ripes grapes picked from the slopes with the best exposure to the sun. Jean Vesselle has done much to maintain the reputation of the red wines from the Montagne de Reims, as the 1959s from his own personal cellar bear witness. Shining ruby-garnet colour; raspberry, cherry and blackcurrant bouquet and lightness and balance on the palate. Not to be drunk with strongly flavoured food. (1982) ✔ Champagne.
🕯 Jean Vesselle, 2 Pl. J. B. Barnaut, BP 15, Bouzy, 51150 Tours-sur-Marne; tel.: 26 57 01 55 ϒ By appt.

GEORGES VESSELLE
*Cuvee Veronique Sylvie***

■ Gd cru | 5000 | ❸ Ⓓ

This special 'de luxe' Coteaux Champenois is named after Georges Vesselle's two daughters. Blended from a variety of years, but with a large proportion of 1976, and matured in Hungarian oak casks. Dark shining garnet colour with a rich Pinot Noir nose; harmonious and light on the palate, with good length. A very civilized bottle. ✔ Champagne.
🕯 G. Vesselle, 16 Rue des Postes, Bouzy, 51150 Tours-sur-Marne; tel. 26 57 00 15 ϒ By appt.

Rosé Des Riceys

The three Riceys villages (Riceys-Haut, Riceys-Haute-Rive and Riceys-Bas) are in the far south of the department of the Aube, not far from

Bar-sur-Seine. They are very old villages, parts of them dating back to the twelfth century. The commune of Riceys prides itself on having been judged worthy of three appellations: Champagne, Coteaux Champenois, and, of course, Rosé des Riceys. This is an extremely rare still wine (in a good year only 10000 bottles are produced) and is of very high quality – definitely one of the best rosés in France. It is a refined, distinguished wine with a long history, having been drunk at the Court of Louis XIV, supposedly because it was brought to Versailles by the men who came from Riceys to lay the foundations for the Palace.

This wine, which must have a natural potential alcohol content of at least 10 per cent, is made by a brief maceration of the Pinot Noir grapes with their skins. The juice is drawn off as soon as the 'goût de Riceys' (the flavour unique to the wine) becomes apparent – otherwise this flavour disappears. Only the rosé wines that have this special taste may be called Rosé de Riceys. The wine is aged either in large vats and drunk young, or in bottles, when it will mature for three to ten years. The young wine is most suitable as an aperitif, or at the start of a meal. It should be served at a temperature of 8–9°C. The mature wine should be served at 10–12°C at any stage of the meal. The most recent good vintages were in 1969, 1975, 1977, 1979 and 1982.

ALEXANDRE BONNET★

| | 20000 | ❷ Ⓓ |

The climate and sun of Aube give body to this orange-tinted rosé. Strong Pint aromas on the nose together with redcurrant, while on the palate the fruit is accentuated by a touch of hardness. A solid rosé, well suited as an accompaniment to a meal.
⤷ Alexandre Bonnet, 138 Rue Général-de-Gaulle, 10340 Les Riceys; tel. 25 38 30 93 ⵏ By appt.

ALEXANDRE BONNET★

| | 7000 | ❷ Ⓓ |

Alexandre Bonnet is the largest producer of rosé wines in Riceys. In his very modern winery he produces a light rosé similar in appearance to a Sancerre rosé, but with a typical Riceys nose. A light, smooth taste with aromas of bergamot. Drink young. (1980)
⤷ Alexandre Bonnet, 138 Rue Général-de-Gaulle, 10340 Les Riceys; tel. 25 29 30 93 ⵏ By appt.

PIERRE HORIOT★

| | 3000 | ❷ Ⓓ |

A relatively light rosé, with a bouquet of fruit and praline. The taste evokes cherry and blackcurrant. Drink within two years. (1983)
⤷ Pierre Horiot, 11 Rue de la Curé, 10340 Les Riceys; tel. 25 29 32 21 ⵏ By appt.

MOREL PERE ET FILS★★★

| | 2000 | ❷ Ⓓ |

The only grower to dedicate production entirely to Riceys rosé. Also the only one to age his wines for a long period in bulk storage (small casks). A dark rosé, almost a light red wine. Hints of bronze in the colour, typical Riceys nose together with a touch of vanilla. The flavour is very full for a rosé. Round and long on the palate. Reaches its peak after four or five years in bottle.
⤷ *MM.* Morel Père et Fils, Pressoir St-Vincent, 1 Grande-Rue-de-l'Ecole, 10340 Les Riceys; tel. 25 29 35 67 ⵏ By appt.

Jura, Savoie and Bugey

JURA

THE JURA region lies on the opposite side of the Saône valley to the Haut-Bourgogne vineyards. The appellation area covers the lower slopes which rise from the Saône plain to the Jura plateau, and runs in a band from Salins-les-Bains in the north to St-Amour in the south. The slopes are much more scattered and irregular than on the Côte d'Or, and have a highly varied exposure; only the sunniest slopes between the 250 m and 500 m contours are planted with vines. The AOC vineyards cover approximately 1400 hectares, from which an average of 42 000 hectolitres of wine is produced annually.

The climate is markedly continental in character, a factor emphasized by the mountainous terrain of the Jura, in particular the 'reculées' (steep-sided valleys) typical of the region. The winters are extremely harsh, and the summers unpredictable, although often very hot. The period of harvest may be quite extended: because the different grape varieties ripen at different rates, it is not unusual for it to continue into November. The soil, mostly of Triassic or Liassic origins, is rich in clay that, in the south, is often overlaid with limestone. The local grape varieties have adapted well to produce some wines of very high quality. The vines must, however, be kept off the ground, away from the dampness that would otherwise ruin the grapes. The local method of training the vines is called 'en courgées' after the thin, curved shoots from the vines. If one is to believe Pliny, vines have been cultivated in the region for almost two thousand years, and certainly Jura wines were already very popular by the Middle Ages.

The charming, peaceful and ancient city of Arbois is the centre of this wine region. The scientist Louis Pasteur (1822–95) spent his childhood here, returning frequently in later life. His studies on fermentation, conducted at his parents' house in Arbois, formed the basis of a true science of wine and led, among other things, to the development of the sterilization process which bears his name.

Jura wines come from local grape varieties such as the Poulsard (or Ploussard) and the Trousseau, along with the Burgundian Pinot Noir and Chardonnay. The Poulsard grows only in the Revermont, an area in the foothills of the Jura mountains which also includes the Bugey wine-growing region. The large, oval grapes, with their attractively pale, almost transparent skin, are very low in tannin and are perfectly suited to making rosé wines (vinified here in the same way as the reds). The Trousseau, by contrast, is rich in colour and tannin and gives the classic Jura reds, often blended with small amounts of Pinot Noir. It is also used to make Blanc de Noirs (white wine from black grapes) which, blended with Blanc de Blancs (white wine from white grapes), gives high-quality sparkling wines. Finally, the Chardonnay, which thrives on the clay soils of the Jura, provides Jura white wines with their unrivalled bouquet.

The most important grape of all, however, is the Savagnin, a local variety used to produce the famous Vin Jaune ('yellow wine'), sold in its own special bottle, the Jura 'clavelin'. To make the wine, white wine is first made in the usual way, then left in the barrel, where the level is allowed to drop as the wine evaporates. During this time a veil of yeast appears on the surface of the wine, which over the course of several years transforms the floral bouquet into a nutty, hazelnut and almond bouquet, similar to that of some types of Spanish sherry. The result of this long process is a great wine that at times can be in the same class as the very finest whites of Bordeaux or Burgundy. Its unusual ·bouquet allows it to complement even the most difficult of dishes, from duckling *à l'orange* or *à la sauce armoricaine*, to Roquefort, not forgetting Comté (another type of cheese) and, of course, any dishes, especially of white meat, made with the wine itself. It has the great practical advantage of keeping very well for several months once the bottle has been opened, even in the kitchen cupboard.

Vin de Paille ('straw wine') is another speciality of the Jura. This is a sweet wine made by storing the grapes (originally on straw mats) until Christmas to concentrate their sugar and reduce their acidity. The fermentation that follows is especially long, and the yield is very low; as a result, Vin de Paille is an expensive rarity.

Sparkling wines from the Jura vineyard are now of very high quality, the result of earlier picking, which preserves the acidity of the grape. Excellent sparkling wines are produced from a blend of Blanc de Noirs (Pinot) and Blanc de Blancs (Chardonnay).

In general the red and white wines of the Jura are rather old-fashioned in style, appearing very mature, almost oxidized in flavour. Fifty years ago there were still some hundred-year-old wines remaining, although nowadays the wines are not abnormally slow to develop.

The rosé wine made here is actually a low-tannin pale red wine, resembling other red wines more than other rosés. It can be kept for a short time, and is well-suited to light dishes; richer, more savoury food is best left to the true red wines. As usual, the whites go well with white meat and fish; an older bottle would be a good match for Comté cheese.

Arbois

This, the best-known of the Jura appellations, is applicable to all the wines – red, white, rosé – made in thirteen communes in the region of Arbois. About 25 000 hectolitres are produced annually from 700 hectares of AOC land. The soil quality is very distinctive here, and the rosés made from the Poulsard grape grown on this Triassic marl have a unique character.

FRUITIERE VINICOLE D'ARBOIS
Cuvée Vieilles Vignes★

■		20ha	10000	4 D ■ ↓

71 76 79 83

Beautiful colour and nose promises well, and the quality of this wine is indeed confirmed on the palate. The balance is a little angular and needs to be rounded by ageing, but this effect may also be achieved by serving the wine with the right sort of food – a liver pâté, for example. (1983)
•┑ Fruitière Vinicole d'Arbois, 2 Rue des Fossés, 39600 Arbois; tel. 84 66 11 67 ☎ By appt.

FRUITIERE VINICOLE D'ARBOIS
Grand Sélection★

□		80ha	200000	3 D ■ ↓

71 78 82 83

Brilliant colour and well-developed bouquet, with a hint of wood. On the palate, the flavour is very long and there is a hint of walnut to match the woodiness of the bouquet. An attractive bottle. (1982)
•┑ Fruitière Vinicole d'Arbois, 2 Rue des Fossés, 39600 Arbois; tel. 84 66 11 67 ☎ By appt.

Jura

Côtes du Jura
1 Arbois
2 Château-Châlon
3 l'Etoile

FRUITIERE VINICOLE D'ARBOIS
Vigne Saint-Jean*

| ◪ | | 70ha | 180000 | ③ D ⬛ ⬇ |

71 **73 76 79 83**

Marvellous colour and a bouquet full of promise, although still a little closed-up. Well balanced and very long on the palate. One to watch. (1983)
⬥ Fruitière Vinicole d'Arbois, 2 Rue des Fossés, 39600 Arbois; tel. 84 66 11 67 Ⓨ By appt.

FRUITIERE VINICOLE D'ARBOIS★★

| ○ | | 50ha | 250000 | ③ D ⬤ ⬇ |

Light golden colour and a fine, persistent mousse. Attractively fruity on the nose with a light, fresh, fashionably off-dry palate. A very agreeable sparkler.
⬥ Fruitière Vinicole d'Arbois, 2 Rue des Fossés, 39600 Arbois; tel. 84 66 11 67 Ⓨ By appt.

LUCIEN AVIET *Vin Jaune***

| □ | | | | ⑤ D ⬤ ⬇ |

The beautiful colour and complex bouquet are an excellent prelude to the quality on the palate. Unusually rich for a modern Vin Jaune, with flavours of roasted almonds, dried walnuts, hints of spice and a very long finish. A beautiful bottle which will go perfectly with a mature Comté cheese. (1976)
⬥ Lucien Aviet, Montigny-les-Arsures, 39600 Arbois; tel. 84 66 11 02 Ⓨ By appt.

LUCIEN AVIET
Caveau de Bacchus-Cuvée des Docteurs★★

| ■ | | 1ha | 9600 | ④ D ⬤ |

75 76 *79 **81** ⑧③

Another Arbois 'rosé' – really a light red – from the Poulsard grape. A well-balanced, refined and delicate wine which will improve with ageing. (1983)
⬥ Lucien Aviet, Montigny-les-Arsures, 39600 Arbois; tel. 84 66 11 02 Ⓨ By appt.

LUCIEN AVIET
Caveau de Bacchus-Cuvée des Géologues★★★

| ■ | | 1ha | 4800 | ④ D ⬤ ⬇ |

75 76 *79 **81** *⑧③

From the Trousseau grape. Dark red colour, with a reserved bouquet of good quality and a palate that is well balanced, full bodied, flavoury and outstandingly long. Soon to be a great bottle. (1983)
⬥ Lucien Aviet, Montigny-les-Arsures, 39600 Arbois; tel. 84 66 11 02 Ⓨ By appt.

PIERRE ET GEORGES BOUILLERET
Pupillin

| ◪ | | 2ha | 15000 | ③ D ⬛ ⬇ |

73 ⑦⑥ **79 82 83**

A pale red colour and discreet nose; fresh, light and supple on the palate. This is a wine which should be served chilled. (1982) ✔ Arbois Pupillin Cépage Pinot, Arbois Pupillin Savagnin, Arbois Pupillin Blanc, Arbois Pupillin Rosé, Arbois Pupillin Vin Jaune.
⬥ *MM.* Pierre et Georges Bouilleret, Pupillin, 39600 Arbois; tel. 84 66 20 05 Ⓨ By appt.

MAURICE CHASSOT
Vin Jaune*

| □ | | 0.5ha | 1000 | ⑥ D ⬤ |

67 71 73 76

Attractive pale-yellow colour, but still somewhat closed on the nose, suggesting that this wine needs to age a little longer. On tasting, this impression is confirmed: it is rich, full, and still quite lively. Wait a few years yet. (1976)
⬥ Maurice Chassot, 15 Route de Lyon, 39600 Arbois; tel. 84 66 15 36 Ⓨ By appt.

MAURICE CHASSOT★

| ◪ | | 2.25ha | 7000 | ③ D ⬤ ⬇ |

⑦⑥ 78 **79 81 82 83**

A brick-red wine with a well-developed bouquet, typical of the area. Light and feminine, almost 'lacy', the wine is ready to drink; in fact it should not be kept too long. (1981)
⬥ Maurice Chassot, 15 Route de Lyon, 39600 Arbois; tel. 84 66 15 36 Ⓨ By appt.

DOMAINE DE LA CROIX D'ARGIS★

| ■ | | 80ha | 360000 | ⑤ D ⬤ |

76 77 79 *80 *82 *83

Henri Maire has a passion for history, and the labels on his wines tell the history of his estates. This one, for example, is named after a medieval boundary stone that became a wayside altar. It produces a wine of an attractive, light colour, somewhere between red and rosé. Nose and palate, however, proclaim it unequivocally a red, a felicitous blend of the Poulsard, Pinot and Trousseau, present in equal quantities. (1983)
⬥ Henri Maire, Ch. Montfort, 39600 Arbois; tel. 84 66 12 34 Ⓨ By appt.

DANIEL DUGOIS★★

| □ | | 1ha | 4800 | ④ D ⬤ |

An attractive bouquet, elegant, delicate, and fruity. Distinctive wine that is warm and powerful, with a lot of potential. (1983)
⬥ Daniel Dugois, Les Arsures, 39600 Arbois; tel. 84 66 03 41 Ⓨ No visitors.

JACQUES FORET *Chardonnay★★*

| □ | | 4ha | 15000 | ④ D ⬛ ⬇ |

69 73 ⑦⑥ **79 82 83**

Brilliant colour, with a fine and expansive bouquet. On the palate the wine is powerful and very long. Already drinking very well and will make a beautiful bottle in a few years' time. (1982)
⬥ Jacques Forêt, 44 Rue de la Faïencerie, 39600 Arbois; tel. 84 66 11 37 Ⓨ By appt.

JACQUES FORET
Chardonnay Savagnin*

| □ | | 3ha | 12000 | ④ D ⬛ |

69 73 ⑦⑥ **79** *82 83

The nose is discreet at first, but more forthcoming once the wine has been allowed to breathe. Still very young on the palate, but showing roundness and finesse. (1982)
⬥ Jacques Forêt, 44 Rue de la Faïencerie, 39600 Arbois; tel. 84 66 11 37 Ⓨ By appt.

JACQUES FORET★★

■   6ha   23000 ·   4 D ⑪ ↓

69 73 ⑯ **79** 81 82 83

A complete, well-balanced wine, high in flavour and alcohol, with a good bouquet. Will age very well. (1981)
⊷ Jacques Forêt, 44 Rue de la Faïencerie, 39600 Arbois; tel. 84 66 11 37 ⌾ By appt.

JACQUES FORET★★

◪   6ha   23000   4 D ▮

73 76 79 82 **83**

A typical Arbois 'rosé', which is in fact a light red. This one contains a small proportion of the Trousseau grape, giving it good balance and flavour, and enabling it to mature successfully. On the palate, it shows finesse, class and length. A very attractive wine, to be served as a red. (1976)
⊷ Jacques Foret, 44 Rue de la Faïencerie, 39600 Arbois; tel. 84 66 11 37 ⌾ By appt.

JEAN-CLAUDE GALLOIS
Cuvée Spéciale★

□   0.6ha   2000   3 D ⑪ ↓

The vineyard is a relatively recent venture, and as yet only young wines are for sale. This example has a rather discreet nose but is promising to taste. Very pleasant to drink now, but also worth laying down for a while. (1983)
⊷ Jean-Claude Gallois, 39600 Arbois; tel. 66 12 87 ⌾ Mon.–Fri. 9.00–12.00/14.00–18.00.

JEAN-CLAUDE GALLOIS★

■   0.41ha   2000   3 D ⑪ ↓

Pale-red colour and delicate bouquet; supple and rich on the palate. Very satisfying drunk quite young with dishes that are not over-flavourful. (1983)
⊷ Jean-Claude Gallois, 39600 Arbois; tel. 84 66 12 87 ⌾ Mon.–Fri. 9.00–12.00/14.00–18.00.

DOMAINE DE LA GRANGE GRILLARD★★★

□   60ha   200000   5 D ⑪ ↓

76 77 79 *80 82 83

A gem of a bottle from a pedigree estate. (1977)
⊷ Henri Maire, Ch. Montfort, 39600 Arbois; tel. 84 66 12 34 ⌾ By appt.

ROGER LORNET★★

◪   1ha   6000   3 D ▮ ↓

79 82 83

A youthful pale red colour, and an undeveloped bouquet to match – but full of promise, none the less. Well balanced, round on the palate, and well worth waiting for. (1983)
⊷ Roger Lornet, Montigny-les-Arsures, 39600 Arbois; tel. 84 66 09 40 ⌾ By appt.

ROGER LORNET★★★

■   0.6ha   2000   3 D ⑪ ↓

⑭ **71 73 76 79** 81 82 83

Beautiful red colour and a powerful bouquet; well balanced, rich and vigorous on the palate. On the youthful side still, and so good with rich dishes, but probably better kept to develop into a

great bottle. (1983)
⊷ Roger Lornet, Montigny-les-Arsures, 39600 Arbois; tel. 84 66 09 40 ⌾ By appt.

ROGER LORNET★★

□   1.5ha   4000   3 D ⑪ ↓

76 79 *⑧③

A finely developed and beautifully presented wine with all the makings of a great and tempting bottle – provided one is prepared to wait. Five years, possibly? (1983)
⊷ Roger Lornet, Montigny-les-Arsures, 39600 Arbois; tel. 84 66 09 40 ⌾ By appt.

HENRI MAIRE *Vin Jaune*★★

□   30ha   60000   6 D ⑪ ↓

*74 *76 *78 79 82

A fine medieval winepress and a collection of 19th-century glasses are not the only treasures of the Château de Montfort. Its two floors of cellars contain the largest stock of Vin Jaune in the world. This example is a brilliant, golden-yellow colour, with a well-developed, complex bouquet in which the classic almonds-and-walnuts mingle with notes of game and even some warm, flowery hints of honey. All this is confirmed by the richness and finesse on the palate. (1974)
⊷ Henri Maire, Ch. Montfort, 39600 Arbois; tel. 84 66 12 34 ⌾ By appt.

DOMAINE DE MONTFORT★★

■   30ha   288000   5 D ⑪ ↓

76 ⑰ **79** *80 82 83

A wine of exceptionally deep colour, with a bouquet reminiscent of very ripe fruit. This Arbois is full, fat, supple and long on the palate. A bottle of sumptuous appeal for drinking with a fine game dish. (1982)
⊷ Henri Maire, Ch. Montfort, 39600 Arbois; tel. 84 66 12 34 ⌾ By appt.

JEAN-FRANCOIS NEVERS★

■   5ha   20000   4 D ▮ ↓

⑭ **73 75 79** 82 83

From one of the choicer Arbois hillsides, this is a wine with an attractive colour and a delightful bouquet. Crisp on the palate, but still a little harsh; a year or two's bottle age should do the trick. (1982) ✔ Other Arbois wines.
⊷ Jean-François Nevers, 4 Rue du Lycée, 39600 Arbois; tel. 84 66 01 73 ⌾ By appt.

OVERNOY-CRINQUAND *Pupillin*★★

□   0.7ha   2400   3 D ⑪ ↓

⑲ **76** *79 81 *82

Lovely straw-gold colour and an excellent nutty nose. Already good to drink but with a promising future too. (1982)
⊷ Overnoy-Daniel Crinquand, Pupillin, 36900 Arbois; tel. 84 66 01 45 ⌾ By appt.

OVERNOY-CRINQUAND *Pupillin*★★

◪   0.7ha   2400   3 D ⑪

⑲ **81 82 83**

With a lovely pale colour and fruity, Poulsard nose, this is a typical 'rosé d'Arbois'. Its structure and fullness on the palate suggest it be kept a while before drinking. (1983)

🐌 Overnoy-Crinquand, Pupillin, 39600 Arbois; tel. 84 66 01 45 ⍟ By appt.

DESIRE PETIT ET FILS *Pupillin*★★

◪		4 ha	19 200	**4** D 📷 ⪼
⑥⑨	71 73 **76 79 82 83**			

Attractive colour and promising bouquet for this rosé, which needs to develop before it displays all its qualities. Round and well balanced, this is certainly a wine with a good future. (1983) ✔ Côtes du Jura Rouge, Blanc et rosé.
🐌 Désiré Petit et Fils, Pupillin, 39600 Arbois; tel. 84 66 01 20 ⍟ By appt 🐌 Gérard et Marcel Petit.

DESIRE PETIT ET FILS *Pupillin*★★

■		2 ha	9600	**4** D 📷 ⪼ ⬇
⑥⑨	71 73 **76 79 82 83**			

Pupillin is the only village which may legally add its name to the Arbois appellation. This Pupillin shows attractive colour, with a fruity bouquet. Full bodied, powerful, warm, and remarkably long on the palate. A wine with a great future. (1983) ✔ Côtes du Jura Rouge, Blanc et Rosé.
🐌 Désiré Petit et Fils, Pupillin, 39600 Arbois; tel. 84 66 01 20 ⍟ By appt 🐌 Gérard et Marcel Petit.

DESIRE PETIT ET FILS *Pupillin*★★

■		5 ha	25 000	**4** D 📷 ⪼ ⬇
⑥⑨	71 73 **76 79 82 83**			

Beautiful red colour, the wine just beginning to reveal a delicate, distinctively Arbois bouquet and a palate of elegance, distinction, and excellent balance. Unlike the other Arbois-Pupillin wines, which need to be kept for a while, this one is ready for drinking now. (1983) ✔ Côtes du Jura Rouge, Blanc et Rosé.
🐌 Désiré Petit et Fils, 39600 Pupillin; tel. 84 66 01 20 ⍟ By appt 🐌 Gérard et Marcel Petit.

DESIRE PETIT ET FILS
Pupillin Vin Jaune★★★

☐		1.5 ha	3600	**5** D ⪼
59 ⑥④	69 73 76			

A fine Vin Jaune from Pupillin; golden-yellow in colour with a well-developed bouquet of pears and almonds; rich and long on the palate. A great wine. (1976) ✔ Côtes du Jura Rouge, Blanc et Rosé.
🐌 Désiré Petit et Fils, Pupillin, 39600 Arbois; tel. 84 66 01 20 ⍟ By appt 🐌 Gérard et Marcel Petit.

ROLET PERE ET FILS *Vin Jaune*★★★

☐		7 ha	7200	**6** D 📷
67 69 71 ★⑦⑥				

A great Vin Jaune, from the second largest estate in the Jura. Note the deep golden colour and powerful, expansive, and persistent bouquet with typical Vin Jaune nuttiness. On the palate it is rich, full, and well balanced. One of the jewels of the appellation. (1976)
🐌 *MM.* Rolet Père et Fils, Montigny, 39600 Arbois; tel. 84 66 00 05 ⍟ By appt.

VIN JAUNE D'ARBOIS
Appellation Arbois Contrôlée

1
9
7
6

Le Vin Jaune est exclusivement obtenu à partir du vin du cépage savagnin, mis vieillir six années durant en petits fûts de chêne sans ouillage, ni soutirages. C'est au cours de cette longue et lente élaboration que ce très grand vin acquiert son goût et caractéristique. Vin de très grande garde, il se sert légèrement chambré et débouché à l'avance. Mis en bouteille à la propriété. Médaille d'Or au Concours Général Agricole de Paris, le 3 Mars 1984.
ROLET Père et Fils, Vignerons à Montigny-les-Arsures · 39600 ARBOIS
63 cl

ROLET PERE ET FILS *Pinot*★★

■		5 ha	30 000	**3** D ⪼ ⬇
★79 ★82 83				

The Pinot grape marks this wine out from the other reds of the same appellation, usually made from the Trousseau grape. Attractively full bodied, with a delightful bouquet showing a hint of new oak. At present the wine can stand up to quite highly flavoured dishes, but in a few years it will be best suited to subtle flavours. (1982)
🐌 *MM.* Rolet Père et Fils, Montigny, 39600 Arbois; tel. 84 66 00 05 ⍟ By appt.

ROLET PERE ET FILS *Trousseau*★★

■		5 ha	15 000	**4** D ⪼ ⬇
★79 82 83				

Pale-red colour; well developed, expansive, fruity bouquet with a hint of redcurrant. Refined, rich and long on the palate. An attractive, typically Arbois wine that will improve with age. (1982)
🐌 *MM.* Rolet Père et Fils, Montigny, 39600 Arbois; tel. 84 66 00 05 ⍟ By appt.

ROLET PERE ET FILS *Poulsard*★

◪		15 ha	100 000	**3** D ⪼ ⬇
★79 80 81 ⑧② **82** 83				

An attractive, almost brick-red colour and a slightly woody bouquet that would improve if the wine were allowed to breathe. The wine is still quite firm and will improve with age. Decant immediately before serving. (1982)
🐌 *MM.* Rolet Père et Fils, Montigny, 39600 Arbois; tel. 84 66 00 05 ⍟ By appt.

ABBAYE DE SAINT-LAURENT★★

■		1 ha	4800	**3** D ⪼ ⬇
71 76 79 81 82 83				

Beautiful red colour, and a bouquet full of promise. Warm and powerful on the palate, this wine needs only a little more time to become an excellent bottle. (1983) ✔ Arbois, Rouge, Blanc et Rosé.
🐌 Jean-Marie Dole, Montigny-les-Arsures, 39600 Arbois; tel. 84 66 22 99 ⍟ By appt.

DOMAINE DU SORBIEF *Pupillin*★

◪		60 ha	240 000	**5** D ⪼ ⬇
76 77 79 ★80 ★82 ★83				

From a legendary champion of Arbois wines, a Pupillin of brilliant colour, with a discreet, but fine bouquet. Supple, fresh and light on the palate. A very pleasing bottle. (1979) ✔ Arbois

411

Dom. Du Sorbier 1982 Rosé, Arbois Dom. du Sorbier 1979 Blanc, Arbois Dom. du Sorbier 1979, Arbois Rouge.
☛ Henri Maire, Ch. Montfort, 39600 Arbois; tel. 84 66 12 34 ⌕ By appt.

ANDRÉ ET MIREILLE TISSOT★

☐	1 ha	10000	**3** D ◫
76 79 82 **83**			

Beautiful golden colour; nose discreet but typical. On the palate, the alcohol is rather dominant, masking the flavour, which is nevertheless long and of good quality. This wine should be served chilled with dishes in rich sauces. (1982)
☛ André et Mireille Tissot, Quartier Bernard, Montigny-les-Arsures, 39600 Arbois; tel. 84 66 08 27 ⌕ By appt.

ANDRÉ ET MIREILLE TISSOT★

☑	2 ha	20000	**3** D ☰
76 79 82 **83**			

Attractive, bright colour, with a slightly woody bouquet. Delicate, fresh and light on the palate; a very pleasant wine for immediate drinking. (1982)
☛ André et Mireille Tissot, Quartier Bernard, Montigny-les-Arsures, 39600 Arbois; tel. 84 66 08 27 ⌕ By appt.

ANDRÉ ET MIREILLE TISSOT★★

■	10 ha	55000	**3** D ☰ ◫ ⌄
76 79 83			

Fine colour and nose and a well-balanced, full-bodied palate. Should be very attractive after a little more time in bottle. (1983) ✔ Arbois, Blanc, Arbois Jaune.
☛ André et Mireille Tissot, Quartier Bernard, Montigny-les-Arsures, 39600 Arbois; tel. 84 66 08 27 ⌕ By appt.

Château-Châlon

Covering 30 hectares, this is the most prestigious Jura appellation, producing Vin Jaune only. The site itself is very striking, on an area of black Liassic marl overhung by cliffs, on the top of which perches the lovely old village. The amount of wine produced is quite small: 600 hectolitres on average. So concerned are the producers about maintaining the high standards of their wine that they actually refused to sell their wines under the AOC label in 1974 and 1980.

JEAN BOURDY

☐	0.5 ha	3600	**6** D ◫ ⌄
59 64 **67 69** 73 **76** ⑦⑧			

Fine bright yellow colour; fresh nose and palate, with a note of honey; a lively wine of elegance and finesse, and without a trace of heaviness. (1978)
☛ Jean Bourdy, Arlay, 39140 Bletterans; tel. 84 85 03 70 ⌕ By appt.

MARIUS PERRON *Vignes aux Dames*★

	2 ha	3000	**6** D ◫ ⌄
73 *76 *77 **78** **78**			

Attractively pale-yellow colour. At first, this wine appears to be closed-in but the bouquet becomes apparent after it has been allowed to breathe. In the mouth it is elegant and refined, and will probably improve with age. (1978)
☛ Marius Perron, 39210 Voiteur; tel. 84 85 20 83 ⌕ Mon.–Sat. 9.00–78.00.

Côtes du Jura

This catch-all appellation covers the complete vineyard area, around 14000 hectares, and includes red, white, and rosé wines.

CHATEAU D'ARLAY★

☐	3 ha	14400	**4** D ◫ ⌄
73 76 78 *79 *80 *82			

An attractive colour and a flowery, fruity, and slightly woody bouquet. This pleasant wine has good length on the palate, but still needs to mellow a little to lose that trace of bitterness. (1982)
☛ Renaud de Laguiche, Arlay, 39140 Bletterans; tel. 84 85 04 22 ⌕ By appt.

CHATEAU D'ARLAY★

☐	4 ha	9600	**6** D ◫ ⌄
73 75 76			

Brilliant golden-yellow colour and an expansive bouquet. Rich and harmonious on the palate, with flavours of almond, hazelnut, and coffee. (1976) ✔ Ch. d'Arlay Corail Rouge et Blanc.
☛ Renaud de Laguiche, Arlay, 31240 Bletterans; tel. 84 85 04 22 ⌕ By appt.

CHATEAU D'ARLAY★★

■	12 ha	42000	**4** D ◫ ⌄
76 ⑦⑧ *79 *80 **82**			

Light-red colour and distinctively Jura nose. On the palate, still pleasantly vigorous, a good match for its bouquet. An attractive wine with a long finish, to be drunk now or laid down. (1982)
☛ Renaud de Laguiche, Arlay, 39140 Bletterans; tel. 84 85 04 22 ⌕ By appt.

BERNARD BADOZ *Cru des Roussots*★★

☐	2 ha	9600	**4** D ◫
47 59 76 ⑧② **82** 83			

From a family concern using traditional methods, a wine of a brilliant colour and pronounced bouquet with notes of woodland and the farmyard. Smooth and generous on the palate, a wine of good quality, drinking well now but which will develop further yet. (1982) ✔ Côtes due Jura Cru des Roussots rosé, Rubis, Vin Jaune et Méthode Champenoise.
☛ Bernard Badoz, 15 Rue du Collège, 39800 Poligny; tel. 84 37 11 98 5 ⌕ By appt.

BAUD PERE ET FILS★

☑		3 ha	9600	③ D ▮ ↓

⑯ **79** 81 82 **83**

Fine light red colour and attractively distinctive bouquet. A wine with plenty of character but still youthful on the palate, needing time to mature, mellow and blossom. (1983)
↬ GAEC Baud Père et Fils, Le Vernois, 39210 Voiteur; tel. 84 25 31 41 ☖ By appt.

BAUD PERE ET FILS★

☐		10 ha	18000	③ D ▮ ⑪ ↓

⑯ **79** **79** 82 83

A lovely golden colour with shades of green, and a powerful bouquet, crisp, flowery and fruity. On the palate still quite young but with a long finish. A good wine overall. (1982) ✔ Côtes du Jura Rouge, Méthode Champenoise, Jaune et Macvin.
↬ GAEC Baud Père et Fils, Le Vernois, 39210 Voiteur; tel. 84 25 31 41 ☖ By appt.

ALAIN BLONDEAU★

☐		10 ha	36000	③ D ▮ ↓

72 ⑬ **79** 81 **82**

This golden-coloured wine has a pleasant bouquet with a hint of woodiness. These qualities are reflected on the palate, which is crisp, typical of its appellation and with good length. (1982) ✔ Côtes du Jura Rosé, Mousseux Blanc de Blancs Méthode Champenoise, Ch. Chalon.
↬ Alain Blondeau, Menetru-le-Vignoble, 39210 Voiteur; tel. 84 85 21 02 ☖ By appt.

JEAN BOURDY★★

▮		2 ha	9600	④ D ⑪ ↓

73 76 ★79 ★82 **82** 83

Colour shading to brick-red, with a bouquet suggesting that the wine will age in the true Jura fashion. This is a successful blend of Poulsard, Trousseau and Pinot grapes, well balanced, with an extremely attractive flavour and roundness. A delightful bottle that is very much in the tradition of this old estate. (1982)
↬ Jean Bourdy, Arlay, 39140 Bletterans; tel. 84 85 03 70 ☖ By appt.

EMILE BOURGUIGNON★

☐		2 ha	7000	③ D ↓

54 **59** 64 71 76 82

A fairly discreet bouquet, but the character of the Chardonnay grape is evident on the palate, together with both fruit and freshness. (1982)
↬ Emile Bourguignon, Vincelles, 39190 Beaufort; tel. 84 25 03 03 ☖ By appt.

EMILE BOURGUIGNON★

○		2 ha	8000	③ D ▮ ↓

79 ★80 ★82

Light golden colour with an abundant mousse and quite a fine bouquet. Fresh and fruity on the palate, making this a pleasant sparkling wine. (1980)
↬ Emile Bourguignon, Vincelles, 39190 Beaufort; tel. 84 25 03 03 ☖ By appt.

CHANTEMERLE *Poulsard*★

▪		0.8 ha	6000	③ D ▮ ↓

82 ⑧③ **83**

Pale-red Poulsard colour, with a typical Jura bouquet and a pleasant, smooth palate. Best drunk young. (1983)
↬ Joseph et Xavier Reverchon, 4 Rue du Clos, 39800 Poligny; tel. 84 37 16 78 ☖ By appt.

CHANTEMERLE *La Sauterette*★

○		1 ha	7000	③ D ▮ ↓

Pale golden colour and a fine sparkle; very 'ripe' nose with an earthy character from the soil, a note also present on the palate. This slightly unusual but very interesting wine should stand up to richer dishes – especially at a meal where a sparkling wine is to be served throughout.
↬ Joseph et Xavier Reverchon, 4 Rue du Clos, 39800 Poligny; tel. 84 37 16 78 ☖ By appt.

CHANTEMERLE *Les Boutasses*

☐		0.6 ha	4800	④ D ⑪ ↓

64 69 71 ⑯ 77 **79** 80 **81** 82

Bright colour, with a nose that still has a predominance of oak from the cask. On the palate, a tantalising hint of some very pleasant flavours that will emerge once the oakiness has mellowed. Needs keeping a while. (1982)
↬ Joseph et Xavier Reverchon, 4 Rue du Clos, 39800 Poligny; tel. 84 37 16 78 ☖ By appt.

CHARTREUX DE VAUCLUSE★★★

☐		8 ha	36000	④ D ⑪

⑯ **79** **82**

The 12th-century vaulted wine cellar, originally part of the monastery, is well worth a visit. A brilliant golden wine, with an attractive, refined and rather ethereal nose. Well balanced and pleasantly aromatic on the palate. A very handsome wine. (1982) ✔ Côtes du Jura Méthode Champenoise, Macvin, Eau-de-Vie de Marc, Vin de Paille.
↬ P. et F. Pignier, Montaigu, 39570 Lons-le-Saunier; tel. 84 24 24 30 ☖ By appt.

BERNARD CLERC★★

☐		1 ha	4800	④ D ⑪

82 ⑧③ **83**

Pale golden colour and an attractive, well developed Jura nose. The palate is refined and, while lighter overall, has some of the characteristics of a Vin Jaune. (1983) ✔ Côtes du Jura Rouge, Rosé and Mousseux.
↬ Bernard Clerc, Mantrey, 39230 Sellières, tel. 84 85 58 37 ☖ By appt. ↬ Gabriel Clerc.

GABRIEL CLERC *Pinot Brut*★★★

○		1 ha	9000	③ D ▮ ⑪ ↓

Very pale colour with a fine mousse, striking bouquet and a distinguished palate at once rich and light. A beautiful sparkling wine of high quality. It is only to be regretted that no batches were made from a combination of Blanc de Noirs and Blanc de Blancs, but this will soon be remedied by the producer.
↬ Gabriel Clerc, Mantry, 39230 Sellières, tel. 84 85 50 98 ☖ By appt.

GABRIEL CLERC★

◪		0.3 ha	2160	▣ 🄳 ⅲ ↓

79 79 (82) 82

A beautiful rosé with a light bouquet and a fresh palate. Still lively and youthful at 2½–3 years old. (1982)
🖐 Gabriel Clerc, Mantry, 39230 Sellières; tel. 84 85 50 98 🍷 By appt.

GABRIEL CLERC

■		0.4 ha	2880	▣ 🄳 ⅲ ↓

76 79 **79** 81 **82** (83)

Deep red colour; still discreet on the nose. Well structured, but firm on the palate and needing plenty of time to mellow and show its best. (1983)
🖐 Gabriel Clerc, Mantry, 39230 Sellières; tel. 84 85 50 98 🍷 By appt.

GABRIEL CLERC

□		0.94 ha	5400	▣ 🄳 ⬛

Fresh, floral, fruity on both nose and palate – plenty of youthful appeal. (1982)
🖐 Gabriel Clerc, Mantry, 39230 Sellières; tel. 84 85 50 98 🍷 By appt.

GRAND FRERES *Vin Jaune*★

		2 ha	6000	▣ 🄳 ⬛ ↓

(71) 75 76 79 82 **83**

A pale yellow colour and a nose rather unassertive for a Vin Jaune. In the mouth, however, the wine is delightful and refined, with good length. It would perhaps have benefited from being aged a little longer in cask, but will improve, albeit slowly, in bottle. (1976)
🖐 GAEC Grand Frères, Passenans, 39230 Sellières; tel. 84 85 28 88 🍷 Daily 9.00–12.00/13.30–19.00.

GRAND FRERES *Brut*★

○		5 ha	18000	▣ 🄳 ⬛ ↓

★**82** 82 83

Pale golden colour with a fine, persistent sparkle; delicately fruity, good length, distinguished overall. (1982) ✔ Côtes du Jura Rouge, Rosé and Blanc.
🖐 GAEC Grand Frères, Passenans, 39230 Sellières; tel. 84 85 28 88 🍷 Daily 9.00–12.00/13.30–19.00.

GRAND FRERES★★

□		4 ha	16000	▣ 🄳 ⬛ ↓

(71) 76 79 82 ★**83**

A lovely golden colour and a predominantly almond bouquet. Rich, sumptuous and fragrant in the mouth, with a long, attractive finish. Despite being relatively young it is a typical 'old Jura-style' wine. (1983)
🖐 GAEC Grand Frères, Passenans, 39230 Sellières; tel. 84 85 28 88 🍷 Daily 9.00–12.00/13.30–19.00.

GRAND FRERES★

■		5 ha	18000	▣ 🄳 ⬛ ⅲ ↓

76 79 82 ★**83**

With an attractive colour and rich bouquet, this is a delightfully smooth red wine that is ready to drink now. (1983)

🖐 GAEC Grand Frères, Passenans, 39230 Sellières; tel. 84 85 28 88 🍷 Daily 9.00–12.00/13.30–19.00.

CHATEAU GREA *Le Chanet*★★

□		3 ha	14400	▣ 🄳 ⅲ ↓

81 **81** 82 83

This lovely estate has been in the family since the 17th century. It has a few guest rooms as well as producing several different AOC Jura wines. This one has a beautiful straw-gold colour and a distinctive, fruity nose. On the palate it bears a family resemblance to a Vin Jaune. (1981) ✔ Côtes du Jura le Clos Blanc, Côtes du Jura sur la Roche Rosé, Côtes du Jura en Cury Vin Jaune, Côtes du Jura Ch. Gréa Brut.
🖐 Pierre de Boissie, Ch. Gréa, Rotalier, 39190 Beaufort; tel. 83 25 05 07 🍷 Mon.–Sat. 9.00–12.00/14.00–19.00.

CHATEAU GREA *Brut*★★

○		4 ha	18000	▣ 🄳 ⬛ ↓

A pale colour with hints of green, and fine, persistent sparkle. The bouquet is fruity if limited. Crisp and fruity on the palate, with an excellent finish. A very pleasant sparkling wine from an old estate with a traditional approach to wine-making. ✔ Côtes du Jura le Clos Blanc, Côtes du Jura le Chanet Blanc, Côtes du Jura sur la Roche Rosé, Côtes du Jura en Cury Vin Jaune.
🖐 Pierre de Boissieu, Ch. Gréa, Rotalier, 39190 Beaufort; tel. 84 25 05 07 🍷 Mon.–Sat. 9.00–12.00/14.00–19.00.

CAVEAU DES JACOBINS *Chardonnay*★

□			96000	▣ 🄳 ⅲ ↓

79 **79** 80 81 82 83

Lovely colour and fine Jura bouquet, very well developed. The nose is not fully confirmed on the palate, which suggests that the wine should be drunk fairly soon. But, for a six-year-old, this bottle is holding up very well. (1979)
🖐 Fruitière Vinicole de Poligny, 39800 Poligny; tel. 84 37 14 58 🍷 By appt.

CAVEAU DES JACOBINS *Poulsard*★★

■			9600	▣ 🄳 ⬛ ↓

81 **82** (83) **83**

Fine light colour typical of the pale Poulsard grape. Charming bouquet and remarkable balance on the palate, where there is considerable presence and finesse. A very nice bottle, already drinking well, but which can also be kept. (1983)
🖐 Fruitière Vinicole de Poligny, 39800 Poligny; tel. 84 37 14 58 🍷 By appt.

CAVEAU DES JACOBINS★★★

■			16200	▣ 🄳 ⅲ ↓

79 **79** 82 83

Very fine brilliant colour and well-developed bouquet with a great deal of finesse. Perfect balance on the palate with good body and aromas of great quality and persistence. A very good bottle. (1983)
🖐 Fruitière Vinicole de Poligny, 39800 Poligny; tel. 84 37 14 58 🍷 By appt.

CLAUDE JOLY★

□	3.5ha	18000	**3** **D** ◑

76 79 82 83

Brilliant colour and fine bouquet; strong Chardonnay aromas on the palate, as well as a marked freshness bordering on greenness. In time, other qualities will certainly develop to tone down the present light and aggressive character, but this itself could be a positive quality if matched with an acid dish (vinaigrette, for example). (1982)
➤ Claude Joly, Rotalier 39190 Beaufort; tel. 84 25 04 14 ♈ By appt.

PAUL PAVET★

□	2.5ha	12000	**3** **D** ◑ ⚓

78 ⑲ **82** **82** 83 84

From an old estate, recently completely replanted. Brilliant colour, fruity bouquet with a hint of green apples found again on the palate; however, its fresh, scented quality does not exclude a definite warmth. Still a little young and will improve with age. (1982)
➤ Paul Pavet, Domblans, 39210 Voiteur; tel. 84 44 61 92 ♈ By appt.

PAUL PAVET

■	5.5ha	3600	**3** **D** ◑ ⚓

78 ⑲ **82** **82** 83 84

Good nose and plenty of body; still seems to need a little more time to reach its best. (1982)
➤ Paul Pavet, Domblans, 39210 Voiteur; tel. 84 44 61 92 ♈ By appt.

MARIUS PERRON★

□	1.5ha	4800	**4** **D** ▮ ◑ ⚓

⑦⑥ 79 81 **82** 83

Star-bright colour and attractive bouquet of fresh-cut grass. Pleasing on the palate with a honeyed Chardonnay flavour. Altogether a very agreeable wine. (1982)
➤ Marius Perron, 39210 Voiteur; tel. 84 85 20 83 ♈ Mon.–Sat. 90.00–19.00.

PIERRE RICHARD *Brut*★★★

○	2ha	12000	**4** **D** ▮

From a small estate with very high standards, here is a pale-gold wine with a fine, long-lasting mousse. Distinguished and refined from first to last, this is among the best of sparkling wines.
✔ Côtes du Jura, Blanc, Rosé, Vin Jaune et Moussex Rosé.
➤ Pierre Richard. Le Vernois, 39210 Voiteur; tel. 84 25 33 27 ♈ By appt.

PIERRE RICHARD★

□	3ha	14400	**4** **D** ◑

⑲ ★81 ★82 **82**

Beautiful bright colour, with a faintly woody and very pleasing bouquet. Flowery and fruity on the palate, where a hint of the woodiness carries over. A delicate attractive wine. (1982) ✔ Côtes du Jura Blanc, Rosé, Vin Jaune et Mousseux Rosé.
➤ Pierre Richard, Le Vernois, 39210 Voiteur; tel. 84 25 33 27 ♈ By appt.

ROLET PERE ET FILS★★

□	7ha	30000	**4** **D** ◑ ⚓

78 81 ⑧② **82** 83

Brilliant golden colour. Classic ethereal quality on the nose, the mark of mature wines of the region. The 25 per cent proportion of Savagnin grapes gives both firmness and real quality. Very charming typical Jura that can only continue to improve over the next few years. (1982)
➤ *MM*. Rolet Père et Fils, Montigny, 39600 Arbois; tel. 84 66 00 05 ♈ By appt.

L'Etoile

The village takes its name from the star-shaped fossils that are found here. The area produces a little under 2000 hectolitres of white, yellow and sparkling wines.

CHATEAU L'ETOILE *Vin Jaune*★★★

□	3ha		**5** **D** ◑ ⚓

67 71 72 ★⑦⑥ **76** ★82 83

The best sort of Vin Jaune bouquet rises from this brilliant, golden yellow wine. Rich and mouth-filling palate, dominated by flavours of vanilla and hazelnut. Long aromatic finish. A great wine. (1976)
➤ J.-H. Vandelle et Fils, Ch. l'Etoile, 39570 Lons-le-Saunier; tel. 84 47 33 07 ♈ By appt.

CHATEAU L'ETOILE★★

□	12ha	45000	**3** **D** ◑ ⚓

⑤⑨ **76** **76** ★82 **83**

Bright yellow colour with green highlights. The bouquet is rich, warm and fruity. On the palate the wine is typically light and fresh, long, and elegant. A beautiful bottle. (1982)
➤ J.-H. Vandelle et Fils, Ch. l'Etoile, 39570 Lons-le-Saunier; tel. 84 47 33 07 ♈ By appt.

CLAUDE JOLY*

| ☐ | 1.5 ha | 8400 | 4 D ⦀ ⌇ |

76 *79 82 **83**

Brilliant straw-yellow colour and a flowery bouquet with a hint of honey. On the palate, this wine is well balanced with a flavour of dried fruit and a hint of oak wood. Decant before serving. (1982) ✔ Côtes du Jura, Blanc, Rouge et Mousseux.
•⌐ Claude Joly, 39190 Rotalier; tel. 84 25 04 14
Ⴌ By appt.

LYCEE AGRICOLE DU JURA

| ☐ | 4 ha | 18000 | 4 D ⦀ |

81 *82 *⑧③ 83

Produced by this agricultural college in its recently acquired fermenting room. On the palate this wine is well balanced and has a flavour similar to that of Vin Jaune, with hints of hazelnuts and roasted almonds. A specialized wine, but still with full Jura character. Production is still limited. (1982) ✔ Côtes du Jura Rouge et Rosé Etoile Blanc Méthode Champenoise.
•⌐ Lycée Agricole du Jura, Montmorot, 39570 Lons-le-Saunier; tel. 84 47 05 23 Ⴌ By appt.

DOMAINE DE MONTBOURGEAU
*Brut***

| ○ | | 6 ha | 18000 | 3 D ⬛ ⌇ |

⑧② 82 **83**

A beautiful, light golden green with a fine mousse. Attractive bouquet; fine and dry on the palate, with no trace of sweetness. Full marks! (1982) ✔ Macvin.
•⌐ Jean Gros, l'Etoile, 39570 Lons-le-Saunier; tel. 84 47 32 96 Ⴌ By appt.

DOMAINE DE MONTBOURGEAU**

| ☐ | | 6 ha | 25000 | 4 D ⬛ ⦀ ⌇ |

⑦⑨ 81 82 83

Bright yellow colour with green tints, and a fine nose of fruit and spice. Full, flavoury and well balanced on the palate with good length and an exceptional aromatic character. A fine wine which will age well and which probably owes its quality to its small Savagnin grape content. (1982)
•⌐ Jean Gros, l'Etoile, 39570 Lons-le-Saunier; tel. 84 47 32 96 Ⴌ By appt.

SAVOIE

THE Savoie vineyards stretch through the departments of Savoie and Haute-Savoie from Lake Geneva to the Isère valley, and are continually expanding. At present they occupy 1500 hectares on lowish Alpine slopes that have good growing conditions. The vineyards are scattered through the valleys, with large and small isolated areas of vines – a diverse topography which brings great variations in climate. Extremes may be heightened by the mountainous terrain or moderated by Lake Geneva and the Lac du Bourget nearby.

Two regional appellations, Vin de Savoie and Roussette de Savoie, cover all types of wine. For still wines, these may be followed by the name of the growth. All Rousette wines are white; wines from Crépy and Seyssel have their own appellation.

At first sight, there seems to be a wide variety of grape types in use, but in fact some of these, such as the Pinot and Chardonnay, are present only in very small quantities. There are two main red grape varieties and three white. The Gamay was imported from neighbouring Beaujolais after the phylloxera crisis, and produces crisp, light wines that should be drunk within a year of being made. The Mondeuse is a good-quality local variety which produces full-bodied red wines with marked regional character. This was the main pre-phylloxera variety used in Savoie, and it is once again growing in popularity. The Jacquère is the most common variety here, producing crisp, light wines that should be drunk young, while the Altesse is a very delicate grape, typical of Savoie, that produces the white wines sold as Roussette de Savoie. Finally, the Roussanne, known locally as Bergeron, gives high-quality white wines, especially the Chignin-Bergeron from Chignin.

Savoie and Bugey

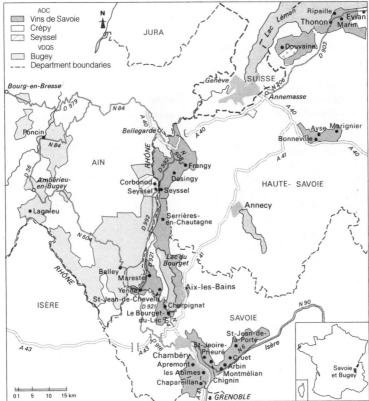

Crépy

Here, as elsewhere along the shores of Lake Geneva, the Chasselas grape is the predominant variety. The Crépy AOC area covers 800 hectares and produces 6000 hectolitres of light white wines which improve if laid down for a few years.

GOY FRERES★

	12ha 66000	

Very pleasant. Light-golden colour hints at the lightness of the whole wine. Very slightly sparkling, a characteristic that ensures its freshness and conserves its flowery aroma. Drink young. (1983)
MM. Goy Frères, Ballaison, 74140 Douvaine; tel. 50 94 10 82 By appt.

Vin de Savoie

The scattered areas that make up the Vin de Savoie AOC are situated mostly on old glacial moraines or scree-covered slopes. The diversity of the wines is recognized by the addition of the name of the local cru to the regional appellation. On both the French and Swiss shores of Lake Geneva, the Chasselas grape is used in Marin, Ripaille, and Marignan to produce the light, white Vins de Savoie that are often slightly sparkling and are usually drunk young. From north to south, the village appellations include Ayze, on the banks of the Arve, with its lightly sparkling wines; Chautagne, on the shores of the Lac du Bourget, south of the Seyssel appellation area, whose wines have a very distinctive character; and Charpignat, at the foot of the Mont du Chat. South of Chambéry, the Montgranier slopes, produce the crisp, white wines of Apremont and Les Abymes. Across from them lies Monterminot, a vineyard that has been invaded by urban development but which still manages to produce some remarkable wines. Next comes the St-Jean-Prieuré vineyard, on the other side of Challes-les-Eaux, and then Chignin, where the Bergeron has made a well-deserved name for itself. Travelling upstream along the east bank of the Isère, the south-east facing slopes are occupied

417

by the growths of Montmélian, Arbin, Cruet, and St-Jean-de-la-Porte. Finally, in the far south, halfway between Chambéry and Grenoble, lie the Ste-Marie-d'Alloix vineyard and its neighbour Gresivaudan, although the latter is now counted as part of Dauphiné rather than Savoie.

The amount of wine produced in this very picturesque area is really quite small – 100000 hectolitres – so that Savoie wines are mostly consumed locally; indeed, demand often exceeds supply. The white wines go very well with locally caught fish and shellfish. The easy-going Gamay reds can complement all manner of dishes. The Mondeuse reds, on the other hand, really need several years to mellow, when they can partner stronger-flavoured dishes (such as game) or regional cheeses such as the excellent Tomme Maigre de Savoie or the famous Reblochon.

COOPERATIVE DE CHAUTAGNE *Pinot**

■		8ha	60000	🖪 🗋 ⑪ ⬇
⑦⑥	83 84	84		

Clear, deep purple colour. Bouquet of fruit and mown hay and full aromatic Pinot character present on the palate. A light wine, with a touch of harshness which should disappear in time. Should not be drunk before it is a year old, when it will make a pleasant bottle. (1984) ✔ Vin de Savoie Chautagne Gamay, Vin de Savoie Chautagne Chautagnard, Vin de Savoie Chatagne blanc, Vin de Savoie Chautagne Mondeuse.
☛ Coop. de Chautagne, 73310 Ruffieux; tel. 79 54 27 12 ⏍ Mon.–Fri. 8.00–12.00/14.00–16.00, Sat. Sun. 14.00–18.00. Closed 30, 31 Aug.

CHIGNIN *Coteaux les Châteaux***

☐		6ha	48000	🖪 🗋 ■ ⬇
83	⑧⑤	84		

To judge the effects of malo-lactic fermentations, compare this wine with that of André Quénard. With malo-lactic fermentation, as here, the same grape produces a warmer, richer bouquet, suitable for shellfish. André Quénard's wine, without malo-lactic fermentation, is light and fresh – good to drink with oysters. (1984) ✔ Chignin Bergeron Blanc, Chignin Gamay Rouge, Chignin Mondeuse Rouge.
☛ Raymond Quénard, Le Villard 'Les Tours', Chignin, 73800 Montmélian; tel. 79 28 01 46 ⏍ Mon.–Sat. 8.00–12.00/14.00–20.00. Closed Oct. harvest.

CAVE COOPERATIVE DES VINS FINS CRUET *Arbin****

■		5ha	10000	🗲 🗋 ⑪ ⬇

Beautiful appearance, intense ruby to deep purple. Classic Mondeuse bouquet well in evidence. Full bodied, meaty and very long, leaving behind various fruity and somewhat spicy nuances. Gives overall impression of warmth. Beautiful bottle to keep. (1983)
☛ Cave Coop. des Vins Fins Cruet, 73800 Cruet; tel. 79 84 28 52 ⏍ Mon.–Sat. 8.00–12.00/14.00–16.00. Sat. closing 4.30. Closed 20 Aug.–10 Sept.

CAVE COOPERATIVE DES VINS FINS CRUET *Mondeuse**

■		60ha	240000	🗲 🗋 ⑪ ⬇
82 83				

Beautiful ruby colour. Nose little developed as yet. On the palate well balanced and promises solidity. Pleasant aroma. Classic Mondeuse but could use a little more spirit. (1983)
☛ Cave Coop. des Vins Fins Cruet, 73800 Cruet; tel. 79 84 28 52 ⏍ Mon.–Sat. 8.00–12.00/14.00–16.00. Sat. closing 16.30. Closed 20 Aug.–10 Sept.

CAVE COOPERATIVE DES VINS FINS CRUET *Chignin*

☐		18ha	156000	🗲 🗋 ⑪ ⬇

Light-golden colour. Developed bouquet with hints of herbalist's shop and underlying aroma of liquorice. Still pleasant on the palate, but regrettable it was not drunk younger. (1983)
☛ Cave Coop. des Vins Fins Cruet, 73800 Cruet; tel. 79 84 28 52 ⏍ Mon.–Sat. 8.00–12.00/14.00–18.00 Sat. closing 16.30. Closed 20 Aug.–15 Sept.

CLAUDE DELALEX *Marin***

☐		25ha	140000	🗲 🗋 ■ ⬇
⑦⑨	*83			

Claude Delalex keeps up high standards at his rather isolated lakeside vineyard. His efforts have just been rewarded by the official recognition of his Marin growth. This Chasselas wine – one of the last in Savoie still to be made with Crépy grapes – is crisp and fruity, with some finesse. The perfect bottle to drink outdoors with freshly caught lake perch. (1983)
☛ Claude Delalex, 74200 Marin; tel. 50 71 45 82 ⏍ By appt.

LA PLANTEE *Apremont****

☐		5ha	42000	🗲 🗋 ■ ⬇
⑧⑤	84			

One of the best bottles from Apremont, showing lightness, finesse and distinction. Its originality lies in a little touch of Sauvignon which goes well with the freshness. Beautifully long finish. (1984)
☛ Marcel Tardy et Fils, La Plantée, Apremont, 73190 Challes-les-Eaux; tel. 79 28 33 17 ⏍ By appt.

GAEC MIRIBEL-MASSON FRERES *Gamay*

■		15ha	144000	🗲 🗋 ■ ⬇

Tasted at 18 months and still had a beautiful colour, between ruby and purple. Must have been very pleasant in its first year, before being subdued by time. Interesting if consumed while very young. (1983) ✔ Vin de Savoie Blanc Sec, Rosé and Rouge.
☛ GAEC Masson Frères, 73170 Jongieux; tel. 79 36 83 68 ⏍

CHATEAU MONTERMINOD *Mondeuse Rosé***

◪ 3ha 10000 3 D ▮ ⫰

(75) **78 80 82** *83 *84

An attractive, bright pink colour and a generous, red-berry nose. In the mouth the wine has lots of fruit, substance, and a very long finish. A vigorous rosé, with a strong enough personality to stand up to most food combinations. (1983)
⊶ J. Girard, Ch. Monterminod, 73230 St-Alban-Lyesse; tel. 79 33 01 24 Ɏ By appt.

CHATEAU MONTERMINOD**

■ 2ha 15000 3 D ▮ ⫰

78 *(82) 83

A vivid ruby colour and an unusual, assertive wild fruit bouquet. On the palate there is a solid base of refined tannin and a general finesse particularly evident in the distinguished, fruity flavour. A top-quality wine, not to be drunk for a few years. (1983)
⊶ J. Girard, Ch. Monterminod, 73230 St-Alban-Lyesse; tel. 79 33 01 24 Ɏ By appt.

GAEC LES PERRIERES *Gamay**

■ 4ha 24000 2 D ▮ ⫰

Clear pale purple colour; very youthful nose with a hint of banana. Light, fruity, gulpable wine. (1984)
⊶ Edmond Jacquin, Les Perrières, 73170 Jongieux; tel. 79 36 82 35 Ɏ By appt. Closed Mon.

GAEC LES PERRIERES***

□ 3ha 24000 2 D ▮ ⫰

82 (84)

Pale greenish-gold colour. Extraordinary smoky nose, noble and fine, with an underlying fruitiness, fairly close to Sauvignon. The dominant aroma of blackcurrant leaves and rhubarb is reflected on the palate, which has a lively, long taste. This wine and certainly deserves its recent classification as 'Cru de Jongieux'. (1984) ✐ Vin de Savoie Rouge et Rosé.
⊶ Edmond Jacquin, Les Perrières, 73170 Jongieux; tel. 79 36 82 35 Ɏ By appt. Closed Mon.

DOMAINE DES ROCAILLES *Apremont*

□ 10ha 102000 3 D ▮ ⫰

82 83 84

Extremely light greenish-gold colour. Fruity, flowery nose. Well balanced on the palate. Classic Apremont. (1984)
⊶ Pierre Boniface, Dom. des Rocailles, St-André-les-Marches, 73800 Montmélian; tel. 79 28 14 50 Ɏ By appt.

DOMAINE DE TERMONT *Abymes**

□ 70000 2 ▮ ⫰

Very light colour and a nose that is subtle, delicate and evocative of flowers in undergrowth. Straightforward Jacquière style on the palate.
⊶ Ets Nicolas, 2 Rue de Valmy, 94220 Charenton; tel. 01 37 59 20 Ɏ No visitors ⊶ *M.* Allion.

COTEAU DE TORMERY *Chignin***

□ 4ha 36000 3 D ▮ ⫰

Light, golden colour. Broad, fruity bouquet with a dominant aroma of acid drops. Crisp and flowery on the palate; a very nice wine. (1984)
⊶ André Quénard et Fils, Torméry, 73800 Chignin; tel. 79 28 12 75 Ɏ By appt.

COTEAU DE TORMERY *Mondeuse***

■ 2ha 12000 3 D ⫰

Intense, brilliant purple-hued ruby colour. Refined, fruity bouquet with hints of pepper and cinnamon. Full bodied and solid, this remarkable wine should provide a great deal of pleasure for many years to come. (1983)
⊶ André Quénard et Fils, Torméry, 73800 Chignin; tel. 79 28 12 75 Ɏ By appt.

COTEAU DE TORMERY *Chignin-Bergeron***

□ 3ha 18000 3 D ▮ ⫰

Light, golden colour with harmonious and refined bouquet, dominated by warm tones of exotic fruits. Pleasing and rounded on the palate. Sweetish, full-bodied aroma starting to develop, which will tend towards pineapple in several months' time, as previous vintages have done. Long, with warm finish. Beautiful bottle. (1984)
✐ Vin de Savoie Chignin Cépage Jacquère Blanc, Vin de Savoie Chignin Cépage Mondeause Rouge, Vin de Savoie Chignin Cépate Gamay Rouge and Rosé.
⊶ André Quénard et Fils, Torméry, 73800 Chignin; tel. 79 28 12 75 Ɏ By appt.

COTEAU DE TORMERY *Gamay*

■ 2ha 12000 3 D ▮ ⫰

84 84

Youthful, deep purple colour. Fruity, floral bouquet of cherries and small red fruit; very attractive flavour. Smooth, supple and particularly fresh, this is one of the best Savoie wines made from the Gamay grape. (1984)
⊶ André Quénard et Fils, Torméry, 73800 Chignin; tel. 79 28 12 75 Ɏ By appt.

VARICHON-ET-CLERC *Pétillant de Savoie*

○ 120000 4 D ⫰

A pale colour and more sparkling on the palate than to the eye. A light, refreshing wine; ideal as an aperitif or thirst-quencher.
⊶ *MM.* Varichon et Clerc, 01420 Seyssel; tel. 50 59 23 15 Ɏ By appt.

DOMAINE DE LA VIOLETTE
Abymes★

□		4ha	36000	**3** **D** **▬** **↓**

83 ⑱ 84

Typically light, almost colourless apearance. An attractive bouquet, still dominated by banana but showing a lot of promise. Fresh and aromatic on the palate, and very slightly sparkling. A perfect young wine, excellent for drinking very soon. (1984) ✔ Vin de Savoie Apremont Blanc, Roussette de Savoie Blanc, Vin de Savoie Gamay Rouge, Vin de Savoie Gamay Rosé.
↱ Daniel Fustinoni, La Violette, Les Marches, 73800 Montmélian; tel. 79 28 13 30 ☖ Daily. 8.00–12.00/14.00–19.00.

Roussette de Savoie

The Roussette appellation wines come exclusively from the Altesse grape, although other wines may be made from a blend of Altesse, Chardonnay and Mondeuse Blanche. The Roussette is grown mainly in Frangy, along the banks of the Les Usses river, and in Monthou and Marestal, by the Lac du Bourget. It is customary to serve the Roussette crus quite young, which does them less than justice; once mature the wines can transform a simple fish or white-meat dish, as well as providing the perfect partner for the local Beaufort cheese.

CAVE COOPERATIVE DES VINS FINS CRUET

□		14ha	96000	**3** **D** **◑** **↓**

Light golden colour. Brilliant, with warm nose and very mature bouquet, which has hint of dried hay. Still pleasant on the palate, but has developed a little further than usual. Drink younger. (1983)
↱ Cave Coop. des Vins Fins Cruet, 73800 Cruet; tel. 79 84 28 52 ☖ Tues.–Sat. 8.00–12.00/14.00–18.00. Sat. closing 16.30. Closed 20 Aug.–15 Sept.

EDMOND JACQUIN★

□		3.5ha	10000	**2** **D** **▬** **↓**

79 81 82 ⑧ 84

A pale, greenish-gold colour and a very crisp nose with shades of lemon and nutmeg. On the palate, the wine is light and crisp, with just a hint of sweetness. A wine of some finesse. (1984)
↱ Edmond Jacquin, les Perrières,73170 Jonguieux; tel. 79 36 82 35 ☖ By appt. Closed Sun., Mon.

CHATEAU MONTERMINOD★★★

□		6ha	30000	**4** **D** **▬** **◑** **↓**

★70 ★75 ★⑦⑧ ★84

The low yield of 30 hectolitres per hectare is fundamental to the success of this wine, grown in a very unusual micro-climate that allows fig trees

to flourish. Pale golden colour, with a delicate, vanilla bouquet. Remarkable balance on the palate, a warm vanilla-and-caramel flavour and an underlying fruitiness. The finish is attractive and very long. A first-class Roussette. (1983)
↱ J. Girard, Ch. Monterminod, 73230 St-Alban-Lyesse; tel. 79 33 01 24 ☖ By appt.

ROYAL ALTESSE★

□		10ha	60000	**2** **D** **▬** **↓**

Light golden colour, with a fruity, flowery bouquet. On the palate, freshness and flavour are well balanced. A typical Roussette of a fairly high quality. (1984)
↱ GAEC Masson Frères, 73170 Jongieux; tel. 79 36 83 68

DOMAINE DE LA VIOLETTE
Apremont★

□		1ha	8400	**3** **D** **▬** **↓**

83 84 84

Pale golden colour; fine and faintly violet-like on the nose; off-dry, lightly sparkling and very fresh on the palate. Typical Apremont charm. (1984)
✔ Vin de Savoie Blanc, Roussette de Savoie Blanc, Vin de Savoie Gamay Rouge, Vin de Savoie Gamay Rosé.
↱ Daniel Fustinoni, La Violette, Les Marches, 73800 Montmélian; tel. 79 28 13 30 ☖ Daily 8.00–12.00/14.00–19.00.

Seyssel

The still Seyssel wines are produced from the Chasselas alone, but the variety is blended with Molette and Altesse to make sparkling wines which are marketed three years after the secondary fermentation. These local grape varieties give a very distinctive bouquet and finesse to the Seyssel wines, which have a markedly violet-like fragrance. The appellation covers approximately 75 hectares.

CLOS DE LA PECLETTE★★

□		6ha	30000	**3** **D** **▬** **↓**

Very pale greenish gold. An elegant bouquet with great finesse. Well balanced and warm on the palate with a long, aromatic finish. Good example of the Seyssel appellation. (1983)
✔ Seyssel la Tacconnière, Seyssel Mousseux.
↱ Maison Mollex, Corbonod, 01420 Seyssel; tel. 50 59 23 06 ☖ By appt. Closed last week Dec.

ROYAL-SEYSSEL
Cuvée Privée Brut 1980★

○		50ha	124000	**4** **D** **▬** **◑**

The pale yellow colour has an attractive sparkle, and there is a hint of honey among the floral aromas. A smooth and pleasantly lively wine, good as an aperitif or with biscuits. (1980)
↱ MM. Varichon et Clerc, 01420 Seyssel; tel. 50 59 23 15 ☖ By appt. Closed Aug.

VARICHON-ET-CLERC
Roussette Cépage Altesse*

☐ 10ha 45500 **4** **D** ▮ ⦿ ⬇

This lively and slightly smoky wine has a pale colour and subtle nose. It would be perfect with fish, hors d'oeuvres, and, of course, *raclette* or *Savoie fondue*. It would also be fun to try as an aperitif. (1983)
⬥ *MM*. Varichon et Clerc, 01420 Seyssel; tel. 50 59 23 15 ⵣ By appt. Closed Aug.

Bugey VDQS

The Bugey vineyards in the Ain department occupy two areas on the lower slopes of the Jura mountains; from Bourg-en-Bresse to Ambérieu, in the extreme south of the Revermont, and from Seyssel to Lagnieu on the east bank of the Rhône. The area cultivated was once quite large, but is now much smaller and more scattered. The vines are planted mostly on fairly steep slopes of limestone scree. The region is a natural geographical crossroads, and the grape varieties planted here reflect this, juxtaposing the Jura Poulsard, Savoie Mondeuse and Burgundian Pinot and Gamay to make red wines. Similarly, the Jacquère, Altesse, Chardonnay, Aligoté, Mondeuse Blanche and Molette – this last the only local varietal – are all used to make whites. The designation Vin de Bugey applies to wines made from the distinctive Altesse grape, to which some Chardonnay may be added.

CELLIER DE BEL-AIR *Chardonnay***

☐ 6ha 60000 **3** **D** ▮ ⬇
83 ⑧④ **84**

Very light green-gold colour; light, fresh floral nose. On the palate the very slight prickle of this 'perle' wine reinvigorates the aroma. A little miracle of balance and harmony between perle, freshness and perfume. Serve very cool and

young; an unexpectedly sophisticated wine.
✔ Vin de Bugey Pinot Rouge, Vin de Bugey Gamay Rouge.
⬥ Dom. du Cellier Bel-Air, 01350 Coluz; tel. 79 87 04 20.

CAVEAU BUGISTE *Chardonnay*

☐ 9ha 60000 **2** **D** ▮ ⬇
82 **83** 84

A light colour and a subtle nose that begins with dry hay, but which, as the wine is allowed to breathe, becomes more flowery. On the palate the wine is a little dried out, but leaves a pleasant impression nonetheless. Should have been drunk sooner. (1983)
⬥ Caveau Bugiste, Vongnes, 01350 Culoz; tel. 79 87 92 37 ⵣ By appt.

CAVEAU BUGISTE *Pinot**

■ 3.5ha 20000 **2** **D** ▮ ⬇
83 84 **84**

An attractive ruby colour, and a mature, slightly spicy Pinot bouquet. Smooth and round in the mouth, with a pleasing flavour, and a definite warmth that inspires one to drink it young, and chilled. (1983)
⬥ Caveau Bugiste, Vongnes, 01350 Culoz; tel. 79 87 92 37 ⵣ By appt.

EUGENE MONIN *Mondeuse**

■ 10ha 3000 **2** **D** ▮ ⬇
79 **83** 84

A lovely purple colour and a generous fruity nose augur well for the future of this wine, even though it could do with a little more fullness. Time will tell. Lovely Mondeuse flavour with distinctive liquorice and cinnamon qualities. All in all, a combination which should prove excellent after a due amount of bottle age. (1984)
⬥ Eugène Monin et Fils, Vongnes, 01350 Culoz; tel. 79 87 92 33 ⵣ By appt.

EUGENE MONIN*

☐ 8ha 60000 **2** **D** ▮ ⬇

Pale golden green in colour with an attractive and long-lasting 'mousse'. The nose is particularly delicate. In the mouth it is crisp and charming, with a hint of sweetness on the long finish.
⬥ Eugène Monin et Fils, Vongnes, 01350 Culoz; tel. 79 87 92 33 ⵣ By appt.

LANGUEDOC AND ROUSSILLON

LANGUEDOC

BETWEEN the southern fringe of the Massif Central and the eastern Pyrénées lies a mosaic of vineyards producing a wide range of wines that originate from four neighbouring departments: Gard, Hérault, Aude, and Pyrénées-Orientales. The hills form a vast amphitheatre, their steep slopes running down towards the sea in four stages. The highest of these is made up of mountainous terrain originating from the Massif Central. The second, a region of foothills and scrubland, is the oldest part of the vineyards. The third is the fairly well-sheltered alluvial plain, with a few low (200m) hills; and the fourth is the coastal zone made up of flat beaches and saltwater lakes, which have recently been developed to make this a very popular resort area now served by the A9 autoroute, 'La Languedocienne'.

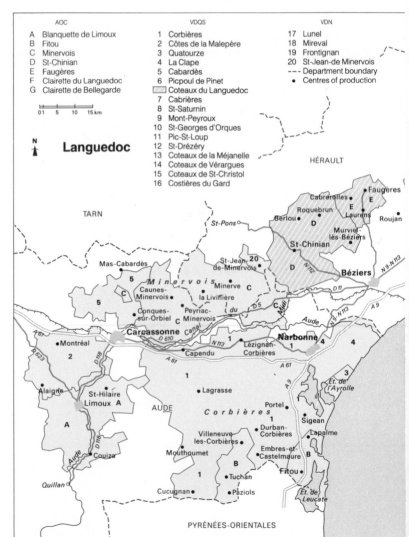

AOC		VDQS		VDN	
A	Blanquette de Limoux	1	Corbières	17	Lunel
B	Fitou	2	Côtes de la Malepère	18	Mireval
C	Minervois	3	Quatourze	19	Frontignan
D	St-Chinian	4	La Clape	20	St-Jean-de Minervois
E	Faugères	5	Cabardès		--- Department boundary
F	Clairette du Languedoc	6	Picpoul de Pinet		• Centres of production
G	Clairette de Bellegarde		Coteaux du Languedoc		
		7	Cabrières		
		8	St-Saturnin		
		9	Mont-Peyroux		
		10	St-Georges d'Orques		
		11	Pic-St-Loup		
		12	St-Drézéry		
		13	Coteaux de la Méjanelle		
		14	Coteaux de Vérargues		
		15	Coteaux de St-Christol		
		16	Costières du Gard		

The vines in this area are thought to have been established by the Greeks, probably some time during the eighth century BC. The Languedoc vineyards expanded rapidly in Roman times, and in fact became such a serious rival to Roman viticulture back home that in AD 92 the Emperor Domitian ordered half of the Languedoc vineyards to be grubbed up! For two hundred years, vine cultivation was restricted to the Narbonnais region. Probus lifted the ban in AD 270, and the Languedoc-Roussillon vineyards were given a new lease of life. They thrived under the Visigoths, but perished with the arrival of the Saracens. The next viticultural initiative took place early in the ninth century, with extensive planting carried out by the monasteries and abbeys. Vines were planted on good hillside locations and the flat plains were given over to agriculture.

In the fourteenth and fifteenth centuries the wine trade expanded considerably, new technologies were introduced, and many more people became employed in viticulture. The commercial distillation of eaux-de-vie was also developed during the sixteenth and seventeenth centuries.

During the seventeenth and eighteenth centuries, the region experienced an economic boom with the opening of the port of Sète and the digging of the Canal des Deux Mers. The old Roman Road was repaired and the wool-weaving and silk-making trades were developed. With the increase in trade and prosperity

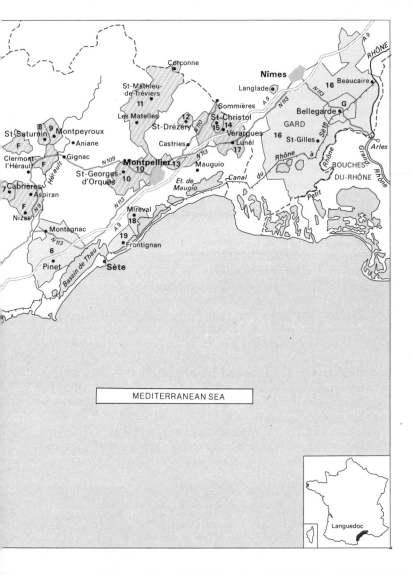

came an increase in viticultural activity and the exportation of wines and eaux-de-vie was made easier by more efficient transportation methods.

Vineyard expansion meant that once again the coastal plains were planted with vines, but we find for the first time the explicit link between vineyard site and quality of wine. Much of the wine made in those days was sweet, often crudely obtained by simply adding honey to a dry wine. The development of the railway between dramatically reduced distances and opened new markets for wine – markets which turned increasingly to the huge volume of cheap wine produced by these vineyards once the phylloxera crisis was over.

Next door to the celebrated Languedoc vineyards lie those of Roussillon, planted with traditional grape varieties on the hillsides of Gard, Hérault, Minervois, and Corbières. They began to expand and develop around 1950 when some of the wines acquired VDQS and AOC status, and wine-makers began to concentrate on improving the quality of their wines.

Today the production areas of Languedoc-Roussillon vary greatly with regard to altitude, proximity to the sea, vineyard site and type of soil. The common factor throughout the region is its Mediterranean climate, making it the hottest part of France. There is not much rainfall, and what little there is tends to be unevenly distributed – each summer from 15 May to 15 August there is a serious lack of water. In many parts of Languedoc-Roussillon only vines and olives may be grown. The strong inland winds (the Mistral, Cers and Tramontane) make the climate even drier, although sea breezes help to moderate the heat and bring some welcome humidity.

There is a particularly dense network of watercourses here; twenty or so rivers that can be torrential after a storm and completely dry during the droughts. These rivers have helped to shape the relief from the Rhône valley to the Têt in the Pyrénées-Orientales.

The soils and subsoils are extremely varied. These include schist from primary massifs, such as that found in Banyuls, Maury, Corbières, Minervois, and St-Chinian; Triassic or Liassic sandstone interspersed with areas of marl, as in Corbières and St-Jean-de-la-Blaquière; terraces of round pebbles from the Quaternary Era, excellent for vines, in Rivesaltes, Val-d'Orbieu, Caunes-Minervois, Mejanelle, and Costières du Gard; stony limestone soils on slopes or plateaus as in Roussillon, Corbières, Minervois, or Coteaux du Languedoc, as well as some areas of young alluvial soils.

The soil types and climate of Languedoc-Roussillon are ideally suited to viticulture; 40 per cent of France's wine is produced here. This is 1.5 million hectolitres of AOC wine (10 per cent of national AOC production) and 1.5 million hectolitres of VDQS wines (65 per cent of national VDQS production).

AOC production is made up of 700000 hectolitres of 'vins doux naturels', mostly from Pyrénées-Orientales but also from Hérault; 80000 hectolitres of sparkling wines from Aude; and 25000 hectolitres of white wines. Ninety-five per cent of the VDQS wines that are made in the four departments is red.

Since 1950, there have been significant changes in the type of grape varieties planted. The Aramon, a coarse varietal planted during the nineteenth century to produce a light table wine, is now much less common, having been replaced by the traditional Languedoc-Roussillon varieties – Carignan, Cinsault, Grenache, Syrah, and Mourvèdre – and also by more aromatic newcomers such as Cabernet-Sauvignon, Cabernet-Franc, and Merlot. The grape varieties most commonly used for red wines are:

Carignan The principal variety, accounting for between 50 and 90 per cent; this hardy varietal gives the wine body, colour, and structure.

Cinsault Usually grown on poor soil to produce a smooth, pleasantly fruity wine.

Grenache A rather fragile varietal prone to 'coulure'. It gives richness and bouquet to the wine, although it tends to oxidize as it ages.

Mourvèdre Ages well and gives full-bodied, well-coloured, tannic wines.

Syrah A high-quality varietal which contributes tannin and its distinctive aroma, which evolves as the wine ages.

For white wines, the varieties used are Carignan, Grenache Blanc, Picpoul, Bourboulenc, and Macabeu. Clairette, which gives the wine a certain warmth, is also used, but maderizes (turns brown) quite rapidly. For sparkling wines, there are Mauzac, Chardonnay, and Chenin.

Blanquette de Limoux

This is the only sparkling wine cru in Languedoc-Roussillon. Various grape varieties are used to make the wine; Mauzac (80 per cent of the area planted), called Blanquette in the Limoux dialect, and Chenin and Chardonnay, both of them introduced to replace the Clairette and to give the wines acidity and aromatic delicacy.

Three types of wine may use the appellation – a still wine called Limoux, and two sparkling wines, Blanquette de Limoux and Vin de Blanquette (a sparkling white wine made by traditional methods).

Blanquette de Limoux is now made by the Méthode Champenoise, and can be either brut, medium dry, or sweet. Present production may exceed eight million bottles a year.

ALDERIC BRUT AIMERY★

○	400000	3 D ↓

A very delicate sparkle and a light greeny-gold colour make this a good-looking wine. It has a fresh nose and its pleasantness is confirmed on the palate. A classic, well-produced Blanquette. (1982)
↜ Coop. Aimery Avenue du Mauzac, 11300 Limoux; tel. 68 31 14 59 ⓣ By appt.

MAISON GUINOT
Flascon Maistres Blanquetiers★

○	11ha	62000	4 D ▮ ↓

*75 78 78 *80 81

Light gold colour, with a delicate, abundant and persistent sparkle and a fresh, fragrant bouquet. Elegance, freshness, lightness and distinction on the palate, with a good finish. A very well-balanced and delightful dry white. (1978)
↜ Maison Ginot 11300 Limoux; tel. 68 31 01 33 ⓣ Mon.–Sat. 9.00–12.00/14.00–18.00.

SIEUR D'ARQUES★

○	100000	4 D ↓

78 78 79

Light greeny-golden colour, with a delicate, abundant and persistent sparkle. The bouquet has a burnt, somewhat coffee-like aroma with a hint of greenery. Clean and fresh on the palate with a very agreeable taste. Fresh and fragrant finish. A good-quality sparkling aperitif wine. (1979)
↜ Coop. Aimery Avenue du Mouzac, 11300 Limoux; tel. 68 31 14 39 ⓣ By appt.

DOMAINE DE TREILHES
Flascon Roussel Maistres Blanquetiers★

○	25ha	120000	4 D ▮ ↓

78 79 *80 81 82

Golden-coloured wine with a slight green tinge, fine, long-lasting bubbles. The nose is forthcoming, flowery and fruity. The perfume on the finish is pleasant; in all a good-quality, fresh wine. A pleasure to drink. (1982)
↜ Gérard Roussel, Dom. de Treilhes, Gardie, 11250 St-Hilaire; tel. 68 69 40 82 ⓣ By appt.

Clairette de Bellegarde

These wines are grown on red pebbly soils in the south-eastern part of Costières du Gard in two small areas, between Beaucaire and St-Gilles, and Arles and Nîmes. The area acquired AOC status in 1949, and at present 6000 hectolitres of this distinctively scented wine are produced a year.

DOMAINE DE L'AMARINE★★

□	32500	2 D ▮ ↓

82 *83 *83 *(84) *84

Nicolas (everyone calls him by his first name) is a leading figure in the renaissance of the light red wines of Bellegarde. Modern wine-making techniques have allowed him to produce a wine which, despite being grown in the South, yields nothing to its northern counterparts, whether in bouquet, freshness or longevity. This is a lovely bottle of wine to be drunk young. (1984)
↜ Nicolas Godebski, Dom. de l'Amarine, 30127 Bellegarde; tel. 66 01 11 19 ⓣ Mon.–Sat. 9.00–12.00/15.00–19.00. Closed Feb.

LA CLAIRETTE★★

☐	200ha	500000	② Ⓓ ▮ ↓

A very light and beautiful golden-green wine with a youthful, crisp bouquet. Good balance on the palate (light-bodied with positive crisp acidity) and a pleasantly lingering fragrance make this an attractive wine. (1984)
✦ Cave Coop. 'La Clairette', 30127 Bellegarde; tel. 66 01 10 39 ☖ By appt.

DOMAINE SAINT-LOUIS-LA-PERDRIX★★

☐	50ha	130000	② Ⓓ ▮ ↓

82 ★⑧③ ★83 84

Light colour and youthful nose with the typical fruity bouquet of a light red wine confirmed on the palate. A sensation of alcohol on the palate which leads to a pleasant finish scented with a fine perfume. A nice feminine wine. (1984)
✦ Philippe Lamour, Dom. St-Louis-la-Perdrix, 30127 Bellegarde; tel. 66 01 11 27 ☖ Mon.–Sat. 9.00–12.00/14.30–18.30.

Clairette du Languedoc

The vines are grown in eight communes in the central Hérault valley, and produce 10 000 hectolitres of wine a year. Vinification takes place at a low temperature so as to prevent oxidation, and the result is a rich white wine with a clear yellow colour. It may be dry, medium dry, or medium sweet. As it ages it acquires a characteristic 'rancio' flavour, which has its admirers.

CHATEAU DE LA CONDAMINE BERTRAND★★

☐	10ha	20000	② Ⓓ ▮ ↓

⑧⓪ 83 ★84

From one of the oldest wine-growing areas, a brilliant pale-yellow wine with a fine fruity nose of peach and apricot. An attractive wine grown below a beautiful château. (1984)
✦ M. Jany, 34230 Paulhan; tel. 67 24 46 01.

CHATEAU SAINT-ANDRE

☐	3ha	6000	② Ⓓ ▮ ↓

83 ★⑧④

Brilliant pale-yellow wine with a nose reminiscent of apples. Its acidity is a little excessive which makes it severe in the mouth. (1984)
✦ Coteaux du Languedoc Rouge.
✦ Jean-Louis Randon, Ch. St-André, 34120 Pézenas; tel. 67 98 12 58 ☖ By appt.

Faugères

Like those of neighbouring St-Chinian, these wines have been classified AOC since 1982. The production area includes seven communes north of Beziers and south of Bedarieux, and 40 000 to 50 000 hectolitres of wine are produced each year. The vines are planted on steeply sloping hillsides at a height of 250 m, in the poor schistous soils of the first Cévennes foothills. Faugères wine has a deep colour with purplish tints and a firm, rather heavy, fruity flavour.

GILBERT ALQUIER★

■	25ha	108000	③ Ⓓ ▮ ⑪ ↓

★79 ★80 ★82 ★83 ★83

Although slightly dry, this wine has good tannin and a lovely deep colour. Its nose is scented with vanilla-flavoured prunes and a full, mature quality is to be found on the palate. Should age well, to be drunk in two to six years' time. (1983)
✦ Gilbert Alquier et Fils, Faugères, 34600 Bédarieux; tel. 67 23 07 89 ☖ By appt.

DOMAINE DES ESTANILLES

■	20ha	120000	③ Ⓓ ▮ ↓

79 ★81 ★82 ★83 ★83

When he entered the wine-growing industry in 1976 this young producer replanted his scrubland estate with top-quality grape varieties. Limpid colour, with a fruity nose and taste of cherries. It is pleasant in the mouth and should be drunk young. (1983) ✔ Faugères Blanc de Blancs Cuvée Guillen.
✦ Michel Louison, Lenthérie-Cabrerolles, 34480 Magalas; tel. 67 90 29 25 ☖ By appt.

CAVE COOPERATIVE DE FAUGERES *Sélection*★

■		1 500000	② Ⓓ ▮ ↓

The village is at a height of 250 m, on hilly ground ideal for producing wines of quality. The cooperative produces a clean wine of spicy elegance. It is very characteristic of the schistous soil on which the vines are grown and is silky with a smooth, flowing quality. (1983)
✦ Cave Coop. de Faugères, Faugères, 34600 Bédarieux; tel. 67 95 08 80 ☖ By appt.

DOMAINE DU FRAISSE★★

■	17ha	80000	② Ⓓ ▮ ↓

79 ★81 ★82 ★83 ★83

A deep purple colour, intense and slightly spicy nose with a full palate all indicate an excellent balance between the grape varieties and good production techniques. A nicely made wine. (1983) ✔ Vin de Table.
✦ Jacques Pons, Rue du Chemin-de-Ronde, Autignac, 34480 Magalas; tel. 67 90 23 40 ☖ By appt.

CHATEAU HAUT-FABREGES★★★

■	10ha	50000	③ Ⓓ ⑪ ↓

This very pretty château is an ancient fortified stronghold. The wine tasted here has a slightly rich, meaty nose with notes of spices and liquorice. Well made and full bodied, this deep red wine should be opened an hour before drinking. (1983)
✦ M. Saur, Cabrerolles, 34480 Magalas; tel. 67 90 28 67 ☖ By appt.

CAVE COOPERATIVE DE LAURENS
Cuvée Valentin-Duc

■ 958ha 1200000 [3] [D] ▮ ⌄
★82 ★82 83

The vineyard where this wine grows is near the marble quarries at Laurens. Its colour is clear and the nose has a meaty note, slight but rich. Recommended for both trout and *magret de Canard*. (1983) ✔ Faugères, VDQS Coteaux du Languedoc Rouge, Vin de Pays les Coteaux de Laurens Rouge.
↦ Cave Coop. de Laurens, Laurens, 34480 Magalas; tel. 67902823 � Mon.–Sat. 8.00–12.00/14.00–18.00.

NICOLAS★

■ 93000 [2] ▮
Unexceptional colour, nose earthy and lightly fruity. Assertive on the palate, with high acidity and tannin fading a little too quickly. (1984)
↦ Ets Nicolas, 2 Rue de Valmy, 94220 Charenton; tel. 01375920 � No visitors.

DOMAINE C. ET B. VIDAL

■ 20ha 50000 [2] [D] ▮ ⌄
Only average colour, but remarkably elegant nose with complex vegetal, floral and fruity aromas. These carry through to the palate, and there is a long finish. A good, lingering wine. (1984)
↦ M. et *Mme* Vidal, La Liquière, Cabrerolles, 34480 Malagas; tel. 67902920 � By appt. Closed Feb.

Fitou
The oldest (1948) red AOC appellation in Languedoc-Roussillon, Fitou is situated in the Mediterranean zone of Corbières. It covers nine communes, which also have the right to make Rivesaltes Vins Doux Naturels. About 60000 hectolitres of Fitou wines are produced each year. They must have an alcoholic content of at least 12 per cent; aged in oak casks for nine months or more, they have a lovely deep ruby colour.

PAUL COLOMER★

■ 7ha 25000 [2] [D] ▮ ⑾ ⌄
★83 ★83

Both colour and nose are good, the latter being clean, powerful and vigorous and giving way to an impression of youthful delicacy on the palate. Recommended for spicy dishes which are not too highly seasoned; under those conditions this is a very pleasant bottle of wine. (1983) ✔ Muscat de Rivesaltes Blanc, Rivesaltes Rouge.
↦ Paul Colomer, 11350 Tuchan; tel. 68454634 � Daily 8.00–12.00/14.00–22.00.

CAVE DES PRODUCTEURS DE FITOU *Terre Natale*★★

■ 180ha 200000 [3] [D] ▮ ⌄
76 80 82

This wine's colour is lovely and its bouquet pleasant, powerful and slightly spicy with a range of scents of heathland flowers. On the palate it is warm, full bodied and fairly refined, quite characteristic of the appellation. Perfect with wild boar stew, the most important game speciality of the region. (1982) ✔ VDQS Corbières Rouge, VDQS Corbières Rosé, VDQS Corbières Blanc, Rivesaltes VDN.
↦ Cave des Prod. de Fitou, RN9, Les Cabanes, 11510 Fitou; tel. 68457141 � Daily 8.00–12.00/14.00–19.00.

CAVES DU MONT-TAUCH★

■ 408ha 1680000 [3] [D] ▮ ⌄
Lovely colour; discreet and elegant bouquet with hints of wildflowers and truffles. Loose-knit and soft on the palate, it should be drunk while it is young. (1984) ✔ Vin de Pays Rouge, VDN Rivesaltes Rancio, Muscat de Rivesaltes.
↦ Caves de Mont-Tauch, 11350 Tuchan; tel. 68454013 � By appt.

CAVE COOPERATIVE DE PAZIOLS
Côtes de Tauch★

■ 300ha 150000 [3] [D] ▮ ⌄
79 ★81 ★81

A lovely, strong, deep ruby colour; the bouquet does not open out until the wine has been allowed to breathe for some time; indeed the bottle should be opened at least an hour before drinking. On the palate, it shows character, richness and subtlety. (1981) ✔ Rivesaltes Rouge, Rivesaltes Maccabeo Blanc de Blancs, Muscat de Rivesaltes, Corbières VDQS.
↦ Cave Coop. de Paziols, Paziols, 11350 Tuchan; tel. 68454056 � Mon.–Sat. 8.00–12.00/14.00–18.00.

COOPERATIVE PILOTE DE VILLENEUVE★

■ 168ha 900000 [4] [D] ⑾ ⌄
★⑦⑧

The lovely cherry colour and pleasant nose give way to good balance on the palate with a decent length of finish. Still young and needs time to become more refined and reveal its fragrance properly. (1978) ✔ Corbières Rosé, Rivesaltes Blanc, Muscat de Rivesaltes Rouge.
↦ Cave Villeneuve-les-Corbières, Villeneuve-les-Corbières, 11360 Durban-Corbières; tel. 68459159 � No visitors.

Minervois
AOC Minervois wine is produced in 61 communes, 45 of which are in Aude and 16 in Hérault. It is a region of gentle south-facing limestone hills sheltered from cold winds by the Montagne Noire. The appellation produces one white wine and two types of red. The first is vinified rapidly, sometimes by carbonic maceration; the second is

427

a wine for keeping longer and under-goes a longer vatting time.

The Minervois vineyards are criss-crossed by many scenic routes, one of which is a designated vineyard trail signposted 'La Route du Vin', with several tasting cellars along the way. The ancient city of Minerve – a famous Cathar site – has many small Romanesque chapels, and the churches of Rieux and Caunes are major local tourist attractions. The local confrérie, 'Les Compagnons du Minervois', is based in Olonzac.

DOMAINE BARROUBIO★★

| ■ | | 10ha | 25000 | 2 D ◫ ↓ |

80 *81 *82 *83 83

The estate, which dates from the 15th century, is set among hundred-year-old oak woods. This wine shows a lively red colour and a delicate, restrained, subtle bouquet. Perhaps a little short on the palate, but pleasantly delicate and well balanced. (1983) ✔ Minervois Rosé, Saint-Jean de Minervois Muscat Rouge.
•↑ Jean Miquel, Dom. de Barroubio, Saint-Jean-de-Minervois, 34360 Saint-Chinian; tel. 67 38 20 42 ⵘ Daily 9.00–12.00.

DOMAINE CABEZAC

| □ | | 2ha | 12000 | 2 D ▤ ↓ |

Pale yellow colour with green highlights. Nose with scent of plants and scrubland honey. Slightly blunt, but pleasantly well balanced on the palate. (1983)
•↑ Serge Azais, Dom. de Cabezac, Bize-Miner-vois, 11120 Ginestas; tel. 68 27 02 57 ⵘ By appt.

DOMAINE CABEZAC★

| ■ | | 3ha | 20000 | 2 D ◫ ↓ |

Beautifully deep colour and discreet, closed-in nose. Despite passing coarseness shows good balance on the palate. Fairly short finish with taste of liquorice. (1983) ✔ VDQS Minervois Dom. de Cabezac Rosé, VDQS Minervois Dom. de Cabezac Blanc.
•↑ Serge Azais, Dom. de Cabezac, Bize-Miner-vois, 11120 Ginestas; tel. 68 27 02 57 ⵘ By appt.

LE CALVEZ★

| ■ | | 10ha | 96000 | 2 D ▤ ↓ |

75 (79) 80 81 83 84

High proportion of Grenache Noir grapes and traditional production methods produce this fragrant wine. Garnet-red with amber highlights. Distinctive, rather delicate bouquet. Well balanced on the palate; pleasantly authentic. (1981)
•↑ Jacqueline Le Calvez, La Caunette, 34210 Olonzac; tel. 68 91 23 12 ⵘ By appt.

COOPERATIVE CAUNES-MINERVOIS
Réserve du Palais Abbatial★★

| ■ | | 50ha | 40000 | 2 D ◫ ↓ |

*78 *81 *81 *83

Well-developed garnet-red colour and a delicate nose with a hint of oak. Pleasant, elegant and well-balanced on the palate. (1981) ✔ Minervois Amboise Le Veneur Rouge.
•↑ Coop. de Caunes-Minervois, 11160 Caunes-Minervois; tel. 68 78 00 98 ⵘ By appt.

CHATEAU DU DONJON

| ■ | | 15ha | 40000 | 2 D ▤ ↓ |

74 77 79 81 83 *(84)

Well-developed colour and delicate, slightly toasty nose. Powerful, despite slight lack of maturity. (1981) ✔ Corbières Dom. du Parc.
•↑ Guy Panis, Bagnoles, 11600 Conques-sur-Orbiel; tel. 68 77 18 33 ⵘ By appt. Closed 15 July–15 Aug.

CHATEAU DE FABAS★

| ■ | | 39ha | 36000 | 2 D ▤ ↓ |

80 (81) 81 82

The estate was a fortified farm in earlier days, and its origins go back to well before the 16th century. The wine is garnet-red in colour, while the bouquet is well developed with a hint of oakiness; it is well balanced with tannin on the palate. (1981) ✔ Minervois Rouge, Minervois Rosé.
•↑ J.-P. Ormières, Fabas, 11800 Laure-Minervois; tel. 68 78 17 82 ⵘ By appt.

CHATEAU DE GOURGAZAUD★

| ■ | | 35ha | 250000 | 2 D ▤ ◫ ↓ |

79 83 84

Light, pleasant wine with pronounced youth and fruit. Intense colour and light and delicate nose. Reasonable amount of body without being too full. (1983)
•↑ SCA du Ch. de Gourgazaud, La Livinière, 34210 Olonzac; tel. 68 78 10 02 ⵘ By appt. Closed Sat. and Sun.

DOMAINE DE GRANIES★

| ■ | | 15ha | 10000 | 2 D ▤ ↓ |

*79 *82 *82 *83 *84

The name means 'granary', and there were certainly cornfields on this estate, which used to be the falconry of the Counts of Minerve, but the stony ground was always planted with vines. This wine is thus the result of centuries of experience. It has a beautiful deep colour, slightly over-developed, and a powerful, aromatic bouquet, with a slight 'goût de terroir' from the soil. Fairly full bodied and heavy in the mouth, if a little unsophisticated. (1982) ✔ Minervois Dom. de Graniès Rosé, Minervois Dom. de Graniès Blanc.
•↑ Roseline Bourdiol, Dom. de Graniès, Aigne, 34210 Olonzac; tel. 68 91 22 54 ⵘ By appt.

COOPERATIVE DU HAUT-MINERVOIS
Les Trois Blasons★★

■   12ha   30000   **2** **D** ◀◀ ↓

76 78 80 *82 **82** 83

This wine is made in stout cellars built in 1889. It has an attractive colour, verging on tile-red, and a very delicate bouquet with a hint of truffles. It is full-bodied in the mouth and will become better balanced as it ages. (1981) ✔ Minervois Les Trois Blasons Rosé.
↜ Coop. du Haut-Minervois, Azillanet, 34210 Olonzac; tel. 68 91 22 61. ☈ Mon.–Fri. Closed Sat., Sun. and public holidays.

COOPERATIVE COTEAUX DU HAUT-MINERVOIS
Cuvée Jacques de la Jugie★★

■   120ha   1 000 000   **3** **D** ◀◀ ↓

*78 *⑧① *⑧① *83

Beautifully deep garnet-red colour, and unassuming but very delicate and complex nose, with hints of oak. Its palate is full and high in alcohol. (1981) ✔ Minervois Cuvée Jacques de la Jugie, Minervois, Minervois Rosé, Minervois Rouge. 1980.
↜ Coop. Coteaux du Ht-Minervois, 34210 La Livinière, 34210 Olonzac; tel. 68 91 42 67. ☈ By appt.

DOMAINE DES HOMS★★

■   4ha   20000   **2** **D** ◼ ◀◀ ↓

80 81 ⑧② **83**

Particularly marked by the Syrah grape. Full-coloured with a nose whose dominant scent is of ripe cherries. The palate is high in alcohol with fine tannin. Ample and full bodied. Drink within two years. (1983)
↜ Bernard de Crozals, Dom. des Homs, Rieux-Minervois, 11160 Caunes-Minervois; tel. 68 78 10 51 ☈ By appt. Closed Sun. afternoon.

COOPERATIVE DE LAURE-MINERVOUS
Jordanne de Lauran★

■   20ha   60000   **2** **D** ◀◀ ↓

80 81 ⑧② 83 84

An unusual blend of the Grenache Noir and Syrah grapes. Bright colour with a slightly heavy bouquet displaying hints of roast almonds. Rather fat and meaty on the palate. (1980) ✔ Minervois Ch. de Villarlong Rouge, Minervois Ch. de Villarlong Blanc, Minervois Dom. de Fontanilles Rosé, Minervois Dom. de Fontanilles Rouge.
↜ Coop. de Laure-Minervois, 11800 Trèbes; tel. 68 78 12 12 ☈ Daily 8.00–12.00/14.00–17.30.

DOMAINE DE LA LECUGNE★★

■   8ha   20000   **2** **D** ◼ ↓

79 80 81 82 *83 ***83** 84

Madame Bonnet thoroughly deserves her role as ambassadress for the Minervois wine district. Her garnet-coloured wine has a bouquet of ripe fruit; it is round and pleasant on the palate, with a spicy hint of soft fruit. A powerful and ample wine, with a good finish. (1983) ✔ Lécugne Rouge, Rosé, Blanc.
↜ Christian Bonnet, Dom. de la Lécugne, Bize-

Minervois, 11120 Genestas; tel. 68 91 22 59 ☈ Daily 8.00–12.00.

DOMAINE DE MAYRANNE★

◪   1ha   6000   **3** **D** ◼ ↓

79 81 82 ⑧③ **83** 84

Fresh, light colour. Delicate nose with scent of plants. Very slight sparkle and is pleasant and well balanced on the palate. (1983) ✔ Minervois Dom. de Mayranne Rouge.
↜ René Maynadier, Dom. de Mayranne, Minerve, 34210 Olonzac; tel. 68 91 22 93 ☈ Daily 10.00–12.00/14.30–19.30. Closed 15 Sept.–15 Jun.

DOMAINE DE MAYRANNE★

■   4ha   96000   **2** **D** ◼ ↓

⑧② **82** 83

The main grape here is the Carignan, which produces a wine with good keeping qualities. Deep colour verging on tile-red; the nose is light, with a hint of oak and pepper. Lively and youthful on the palate. This is a substantial wine which needs two to three years to mature. (1982) ✔ Minervois Dom. de Mayranne.
↜ René Maynadier, Dom. de Mayranne, Minerve, 34210 Olonzac; tel. 68 91 22 93 ☈ By appt.

DOMAINE DE MAYRANNE★★

■   10ha   60000   **2** **D** ◀◀ ↓

*73 77 79 81 83 **83**

Beautiful, deep ruby colour. Powerful, very elegant, flowery bouquet with hint of mushroom. Powerful, aromatic, well balanced and long, with hints of liquorice and blackcurrant in the finish. (1983) ✔ Minervois Dom. Tailhades Mayranne Blanc.
↜ André Tailhades, Dom. de Mayranne, Minerve, 34210 Olonzac; tel. 68 91 22 93 ☈ Daily 10.00–12.00/14.30–19.30. Closed 15 Sept.–15 Jun.

DOMAINE MEYZONNIER★

■   7ha   42000   **2** **D** ◼ ↓

*78 *80 *81 *83 **83**

Deep colour with garnet highlights. Powerful, rich bouquet. To be kept; not yet completely balanced and will mature fully in two years. (1983)
↜ Jacques Meyzonnier, Dom. Meyzonnier, Pouzols-Minervois, 11120 Ginestas; tel. 68 46 13 88 ☈ By appt.

MAISON DU MINERVOIS

◪   100ha   5000   **1** ◼ ↓

This rosé has beautiful garnet colour and an unassuming flowery bouquet. Delicate, pleasant and fresh on the palate.
↜ UCARO Maison du Minervois, 34210 Olonzac; tel. 68 91 35 74. ☈ By appt. Closed Sat. and Sun.

DOMAINE DU PECH D'ANDRE★

■   15.7ha   35000   **2** **D** ◀◀ ↓

75 76 78 79 80 81 82 *⑧③ **83**

Somewhat feminine. Deep colour verging on violet, and delicate, flowery nose. Well balanced and light on the palate. (1983)
↜ Marc Rémaury, Dom. du Pech d'André, Azil-

429

lanet, 34210 Olonzac; tel. 68912266 ℐ Daily
8.00–18.00.

SICA VINICOLE DE PEYRIAC
*Cuvee Jean d'Alibert**

■   500ha 200000   2 D ⑪ ↓

㊄ 78 79 81 ⑧⑪ 82

Deep garnet colour. The bouquet, with its hint of
cocoa, is not yet fully developed, but the wine is
well balanced on the palate, with hints of liquorice and oak. Good finish. (1981) ✔ Minervois
Phalippou.
✦ SICA Vinicole de Peyrac, Rieux-Minervois,
11160 Caunes-Minervois; tel. 68782214 ℐ Daily
8.00–12.00/14.00–18.00.

CAVE COOPERATIVE PEYRIAC-
MINERVOIS *Tour Saint-Martin**

☐   2ha 7000   2 D ▄ ↓

75 76 78 82 ㊷

Brightly coloured, with distinctive bouquet of
honey, pine resin and wildflowers. Mature on the
palate, with fairly long finish. (1983)
✦ Cave Coop. Peyriac-Minervois, Peyriac-Minervois, 11160 Caunes-Minervois; tel. 68781120
ℐ Mon.–Fri. 8.00–1200/14.00–18.00.

CAVE COOPERATIVE PEYRIAC-
MINERVOIS *Tour Saint-Martin*

▨   2ha 10000   2 D ▄ ↓

75 76 78 82 ㊷

Little rosé with fairly delicate nose; very well-
balanced on the palate. (1983)
✦ Cave Coop. Peyriac-Minervois, Peyriac-Minervois, 11160 Caunes-Minervois; tel. 68781120
ℐ Mon.–Fri. 8.00–12.00/14.00–18.00.

CAVE COOPERATIVE PEYRIAC-
MINERVOIS *Tour Saint-Martin**

■   26ha 36000   2 D ⑪ ↓

75 ⑯ 78 ㊴ 82 83

Deep, slightly mature colour. Hint of vanilla in
its fruity bouquet. Long and elegant on the
palate; powerful. (1976)
✦ Cave Coop. Peyriac-Minervois, Peyriac-Minervois, 11160 Caunes-Minervois; tel. 68781120
ℐ Mon.–Fri. 8.00–12.00/14.00–18.00.

CUVÉE DENIS PHALIPPOU*

■   1000000   2 ▄ ↓

81 ㊂ ⑫ 83

Full but not very deep colour. Fairly powerful,
complex nose of cocoa and tobacco. Full-bodied
and pleasant in the mouth, but the finish is a bit
short. (1982) ✔ Minervois Alibert.
✦ SICA Vinicole de Peyrac, Rieux-Minervois,
11160 Caunes-Minervois; tel. 68782214 ℐ Daily
8.00–12.00/14.00–18.00.

COTEAUX DE POUZOLS-
MINERVOIS**

■   5ha 50000   3 D ▄ ↓

73 75 78 ㊲ ⑫ 83

Beautiful ruby colour with elegant bouquet and
hint of cocoa. Well-balanced palate, with hints of
fruit and vanilla. Good finish. (1982)
✦ Coteaux de Pouzols-Minervois, Pouzols-Minervois, 11120 Ginestas; tel. 68461376 ℐ Mon.–

Sat. 8.00–12.00/14.00–18.00. Closed 1 Oct.–30
Jun.

DOMAINE DE SAINTE-EULALIE**

▦   15ha 100000   2 D ▄ ↓

78 79 80 81 82 *㊳ ⑧⑬ 84

Deep colour tinted with garnet. Powerful and
flowery nose, with hint of violets. Very good
qualities on the palate, rich, round, powerful and
full-bodied, lingering taste and excellent finish.
Drink now or keep for a few years. (1983)
✦ Gérard Blanc, Dom. de St-Eulalie, La Livinière, 34210 Olonzac; tel. 68914272.

COOPERATIVE DE TRAUSSE-
MINERVOIS *Cuvée Gaston Dhomps***

■   20ha 110000   2 D ⑪ ↓

75 76 81 ㊱ ⑫ 83

The power and character of the Mourvèdre (or
Mataro) grape are reflected in the wines from the
Cave de Trausse. This one has a good cherry-red
colour and a powerful, oaky nose with a hint of
coffee. Full, soft and well balanced on the palate,
although the finish is a little short. (1982)
✦ SCAV Costos Roussos, Trausse-Minervois,
11160 Caunes-Minervois, tel. 68783115
ℐ Mon.–Fri. 8.00–12.00/14.00–18.00.

CHATEAU VILLEGLY MOUREAU**

■   5ha 25000   2 D ▄ ↓

*80 ⑧⑯ *81 *82 *83

Pretty, slightly fullish colour. Flowery, slightly
fruity nose, with some acidity. Long, and full on
the palate, with well-balanced tannins and distinctive aromas. The finish is long and pleasantly
perfumed. (1980)
✦ Marceau Moureau et Fils, Ch. de Villerambert,
11160 Caunes-Minervois; tel. 68780026 ℐ Daily
8.00–19.00.

CHATEAU VILLERAMBERT
MOUREAU

■   32ha 32000   2 D ▄

*80 ⑧⑯ *81 *82 *83

Slightly over-developed cherry-red. Delicate
bouquet with hint of oak. Good tannin. An
every-day wine but well balanced. (1980)
✦ Marceau Moureau et Fils, Ch. de Villerambert,
11160 Caunes-Minervois; tel. 68780026 ℐ Daily
8.00–19.00.

St-Chinian VDQS

A VDQS since 1945, St-Chinian acquired
AOC status in 1982. The appellation
area, in Hérault, north of Narbonne,

covers 20 communes and produces 83000 hectolitres of red and rosé wines. The vines grow at an altitude of 100–200 m on hillsides that face towards the sea. The vineyard soils are schistous, especially in the northern section, with limestone pebbles in the south. St-Chinian wines have a very long-standing reputation going back as far as the fourteenth century. A 'Maison des Vins' has been set up in St-Chinian itself.

DOMAINE DES CALMETTE★★

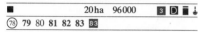

| | | 20 ha | 96 000 | 3 D ▮ ↓ |

⑦ 79 80 **81 82 83** 83

Deep ruby colour. First impression in the mouth is surprisingly soft and rich, developing tannin and a long finish of blackcurrant. Powerful nose. (1983)
🍷 G. Calmette, Cazedarnes, 33460 Cessenon; tel. 67 38 02 37 ☎ By appt. Closed during harvest.

CHATEAU COUJAN★★★

| | | 20 ha | 26 000 | 3 D ◑ ↓ |

⑦ 79 80 **81 82 83** 83

Handsome deep red colour. Extremely inviting nose of oak. Elegant fruit supported by pleasant tannin that needs to age well. The brightest jewel of the only great appellation in this region. (130
🍷 *MM*. Guy et Peyre, Ch. de Coujan, 34490 Murviel-les-Béziers; tel. 67 36 01 12 ☎ Mon.–Sat. 10.00–13.00/16.00–20.00.

DOMAINE DES JOUGLA★★

| | | 25 ha | 129 600 | 2 D ◑ ↓ |

★82 83 83

Brilliant colour. Distinguished by intense, refined nose smelling of figs, blackcurrants and prunes. Well balanced, mature and long finish. (1983)
🍷 Alain Jougla, Prades-sur-Vernazobre, 34360 St-Chinian; tel. 67 38 06 02 ☎ By appt.

LIBES-CAVAILLE

| | | 7 ha | 60 000 | 3 D ▮ ◑ ↓ |

Light nose with slight hint of tobacco. Pleasant on the palate. ✔ Coteaux du Languedoc Rouge, Coteaux de urviel Blanc Liquoreux.
🍷 André Libes-Cavaillé, St-Nazaire-de-Ladarez, 34490 Murviel-les-Béziers; tel. 67 89 64 69 ☎ By appt.

NICOLAS
Cave des Vignerons de Roquebrun★★

| | | | 100 000 | 2 ▮ ↓ |

Deep purple colour and pleasant fruity bouquet. Balanced and full-bodied on the palate, with a spicy finish that lingers.
🍷 Ets Nicolas, 2 Rue de Valmy, 94220 Charenton; tel. 01 37 59 20 ☎ No visitors.

NICOLAS★

| | | | 420 000 | 2 ▮ |

Lovely colour. Distinguished, fruity nose; at first light in the mouth, but then the distinctive body emerges. Pleasantly fragrant.
🍷 Ets Nicolas, 2 Rue de Valmy, 94220 Charenton; tel. 01 37 59 20 ☎ No visitors.

LES COTEAUX DE RIEU-BERLOU
Berlou Prestige★

| | | 12 ha | 20 000 | 3 D ▮ ↓ |

81 ★⑧ **83** 83 84

Clean wine of quality with complex nose. Tannin content will enable it to age another three years. (1983)
🍷 Cave Coteaux de Rieu-Berlou, Ave des Vignerons, Berlou, 34360 St-Chinian; tel. 67 38 03 19 ☎ By appt. Closed Sun. and public holidays.

Cabardès VDQS

These wines come from the Côtes de Cabardes et de l'Orbiel, a region north of Carcassonne and west of Minervois. The vineyards extend over 2200 hectares and 14 communes, and produce 10 000 hectolitres of red wine, up to 30 per cent of which may be from Carignan grapes. Produced in the western-most part of the Languedoc-Roussillon region, where the maritime influence is stronger, these wines have a marked local character. The appellation is quite recent, but has great potential.

431

LES CAPITELLES

■	80 ha	12 000	2 D ◑ ↓

*80 *81 *82 ⑧

31eRich ruby colour. Aged in oak and made from traditional grape varieties. (1983) ✔ Minervois Rouge.
↜ UC du Cabardès et du Fresque, Villalbe, 11000 Carcassonne; tel. 68 47 18 50 ☥ By appt. Closed Sun.

CHATEAU DE PENNAUTIER*

■	22 ha	7000	2 D ◑ ↓

Deep cherry colour. Already very fragrant and well balanced. Room for further ageing; should peak in 1986. (1983)
↜ Francoise de Lorgeril, Ch. de Pennautier, 11000 Carcassonne; tel. 68 25 02 11 ☥ By appt.

DOMAINE DE RAYSSAC**

■	20 ha	120 000	2 ▦ ◑ ↓

75 77 80 ⑧ *83 84

Deep ruby colour. Lingers on the palate. Very pleasant. (1983)
↜ Jean de Cibeins, Dom. de Rayssac, 11600 Conques-sur-Orbiel; tel. 68 77 16 12 ☥ By appt. Closed Aug.

CHATEAU RIVALS**

☑	20 ha	10 000	2 D ▦ ↓

*⑧ *83 *84

Pleasant salmon-pink summer wine. Very fruity nose. Well balanced palate. (1984)
↜ Charlotte Capdevila, Ch. Rivals, Villemoustaussou, 11600 Conques-sur-Orbiel; tel. 68 25 80 96 ☥ By appt. Closed Sun.

Cabrières VDQS

Cabrières is a VDQS appellation within the Coteaux du Languedoc area. The vines grow on steep slopes in a schistous valley between the two production areas of Faugères and Clairette de Languedoc. This commune produces an annual total of 7000 hectolitres of red and rosé wines, the most famous being Estabel, known as 'vin vermeil' after its vermilion colour.

DOMAINE DU TEMPLE
Cuvée Jacques de Molay

■	6 ha	30 000	3 D ◑ ↓

Hints of nutmeg and flavours of violet. Very warm and heady suggesting good alcohol content. (1982)
↜ Maurice Muller, Cabrières, 34800 Clermontl'Hérault; tel. 67 96 07 98 ☥ By appt.

Corbières VDQS

The largest VDQS production area in France, Corbières is now in the process of acquiring AOC status. The appellation covers 92 communes, producing 600 000 hectolitres of wine, 10 per cent of which is white and 90 per cent red. The wines are powerful, with an alcoholic content of between 11 and 13 per cent. The appellation Corbières Supérieurs is reserved for wines produced in 39 of the communes with a maximum yield of 40 hectolitres per hectare, and an alcohol content of at least 12 per cent.

This is a typical viticultural region; in fact it is hardly possible to grow anything else. With its Mediterranean and maritime climate, its pockets of vineyards isolated by the sharp relief of the terrain and its highly varied soils, mostly planted with Carignan, the area is difficult to classify. A local confrérie, 'L'Illustre Cour des Seigneurs du Corbières', is based in Lezignan-Corbières.

CAVE DES COTES D'ALARIC
Montagne Alaric

□	22 ha	48 000	2 D ▦ ↓

Pleasant, green ('*vert*') Corbières wine. To appreciate this freshness, drink youngest vintage available. (1983) ✔ Montagne Alaric Rouge 1982, Peyres Nobles 1980, Carignan Primeur Rouge.
↜ Cave des Côtes d'Alaric, Camplong, 11200 Lézignan-Corbières; tel. 68 43 60 86 ☥ Mon.–Fri. 8.00–12.00/14.00–18.00. Closed winter weekends.

CHATEAU DE LA BARONNE
*Montagne d'Alaric***

■	25 ha	40 000	2 D ◑ ↓

81 82 *83 ⑧ *84

Lovely colour with well-developed nose, powerful, with good balance on the palate and good finish. (1983) ✔ Vin de Pays Dom. des Lanes Rouge, Rosé and Primeur Rouge.
↜ Suzette Liguères, Ch. de la Baronne, Fontcouverte, 11700 Capendu; tel. 68 43 90 64 ☥ Daily 8.00–12.00/14.00–19.00.

CHATEAU DE CARAGUILHES

□	7 ha	48 000	2 D ▦ ↓

79 80 81 82 83

Classic white. Well balanced, fresh and pleasant on the palate. Drink while young. (1983) ✔ Corbières Ch. de Caraguilhes Rouge, Corbières Ch. de Caraguilhes Rosé, Côteaux de Cabrerisse Rouge.
↜ Lionel Faivre, St-Laurent-de-la-Cabrerisse, 11220 Lagrasse; tel. 68 43 62 05 ☥ By appt.

COOPERATIVE DE CASTELMAURE
Cuvée de Pompadour

■	8 ha	36 000	3 D ▦ ◑ ↓

78 80 *81 82 83

Lovely burnt-ruby colour. Nose displays all the developed, refined qualities of maturity; on the palate richness and warmth, full bodied with tannin. Marked fruity character. (1981) ✔ Castelmaure Rosé and Blanc.

✦ Sté Vinicole Agricole Castelmaure, Embres-et-Castelmaure, 11360 Durban-Corbières; tel. 68 45 91 83 ☎ Mon.–Fri. 8.00–12.00/14.00–18.00.

CHATEAU L'ETANG DES COLOMBES★★

■   66 ha   6000   ② D ⃞ ⬤ ⬇

78 *79 *80 *81 ⑧ ⑧

Pleasing in all its qualities. Combines refinement with balance, fullness and length. Well-developed nose and full bodied. (1982)
✦ Henri Gualco, Ch. l'Etang des Colombes, Cruscades, 11200 Lézignan-Corbières; tel. 68 27 00 03 ☎ Daily 8.00–12.30/14.00–20.00

COOPERATIVE DES CORBIERES MARITIMES
Rocbère Rouge Maceration

■   400 ha   127 000   ② D ⬤ ⬇

75 76 ⑧ ⑧ 83 84

Carbonic maceration is the basic influence behind the roundness, softness and fruity spiciness. Pleasant. Drink as young as possible. (1982)
✦ Coop. des Corbières Maritimes, 11490 Portel-des-Corbières; tel. 68 48 28 05 ☎ By appt.

CAVE COOPERATIVE DE FABREZAN *Cuvée Charles Cros**

■   237 ha   70 000   ② D ⃞ ⬇

*⑧ 83

Lovely colour, well-developed bouquet and roundness on the palate, where the characteristic baked flavour is experienced to the full. (1982)
✦ Cave Coop. de Fabrézan, Fabrézan, 11200 Lézignan-Corbières; tel. 68 43 61 18 ☎ By appt.

CHATEAU DU GRAND CAUMONT

■   75 ha   45 000   ② D ⬤ ⬇

82 ⑧ 84

Amber-ruby tinges. As yet undeveloped nose, nevertheless well-balanced and has a pleasant tannic finish. Needs time to become softer and to mature. (1983) ✔ Pays Dom. de Gaumont St-Paul.
✦ Louis Rigal, Ch. du Grand Caumont, 11200 Lézignan-Corbières; tel. 68 27 10 82 ☎ Daily 9.00–12.00/13.30–18.30.

CHATEAU HELENE

□   2 ha   10 800   ② D ⬤ ⬇

This little white wine is made by a lady wine-grower. Although the blend, predominantly white Grenache grapes, is not very inspired, it is nevertheless a well made wine, a pleasant aperitif. (1984) ✔ Corbières Ch. Hélène Rouge and Rosé, Vin de Pays Côteaux Miramont Rouge and Rosé.
✦ Marie-Hélène Gau, Ch. Hélène, Barbaira, 11800 Trèbes; tel. 68 79 02 38 ☎ By appt.

CHATEAU HELENE★

■   3 ha   16 200   ② D ⃞ ⬤ ⬇
⑧

Light colour. Fruity bouquet with marked scent of banana that quickly fades. Fresh and aromatic on the palate. (1984) ✔ Ch. Hélène Rouge and Blanc, Vin Pays Côteaux Miramont Rouge and Rosé.

✦ Marie-Hélène Gau, Ch. Hélène, 11800 Barbaira; tel. 68 79 02 38 ☎ By appt.

LHATEAU DE LASTOURS
*Cuvée Simone Descamps**

■   93 ha   420 000   ② D ⃞ ⬇

77 79 82 84

Light, tile-red colour and balanced taste. With ageing the bouquet should take on a distinctive southern French quality. (1982) ✔ Chatellenie de Lastours Rouge, Ch. de Lastours Tradition Rouge, Muscat, Rosé.
✦ Centre d'Aide par le Travail, Ch. de Lastours, 11490 Portel-des-Corbières, tel. 68 48 29 17 ☎ By appt.

CHATEAU DE LASTOURS★★

□   10 ha   42 000   ② D ⃞ ⬇

77 82 83 84

Bright and pretty. Pleasant nose if a little light, but fresh and fruity on the palate and should be drunk young. (1984)
✦ Centre d'Aide par le Travail, Ch. de Lastours, 11490 Portel-des-Corbières, tel. 68 48 29 17 ☎ By appt.

DOMAINE DE MANDOURELLE★★

■   65 ha   300 000   ② D ⃞ ⬤ ⬇

*80 ⑧ *83

Beautifully coloured with hint of tile-red. Powerful nose and full-bodied and aromatic on the palate. Long, pleasant finish. (1982) ✔ Corbières Cuvée Henri de Monfreid Rouge, Corbières Rosé.
✦ Eric Latham, Dom. de Mandourelle, Villesque-des-Corbières, 11360 Durban-Corbières; tel. 67 28 38 17 ☎ By appt.

CAVES DU MONT-TAUCH
*Fleur de Bruyère**

■   165 ha   960 000   ② D ⃞ ⬇

81 ⑧ 82 83

Lovely burnt-ruby-tinge. Well-developed nose. Full bodied and long-lived on the palate. Has retained its rugged and powerful character. (1981) ✔ Vin de Pays, Fitou, Rivesaltes Rancio, Muscat de Rivesaltes.
✦ Caves du Mont-Tauch, 11350 Tuchan; tel. 68 45 40 13 ☎ By appt.

LES VIGNERONS D'OCTAVIANA★

■   100 ha   300 000   ② D ⃞ ⬇

*78 *80 ⑧ 81 82

Lovely deep-purple colour. Pleasant bouquet. Full bodied yet harmonious. On the palate, fleshy, solid character. Pleasantly aromatic. Drink now. ✔ Corbières Rouge, Vin de Pays Hauteurine Rouge.
✦ Les Vignerons d'Octaviana, Ornaisons, 11200 Lézignan-Corbières, tel. 68 27 09 76 ☎ Mon.–Sat. 8.00–12.00/14.00–18.30. Closed Sun.

CHATEAU D'OLIVERY

■   40 ha   20 000   ② D ⃞ ⬇

*81 *82 *⑧

Pleasant, prettily coloured and light on the nose and palate. (1983) ✔ Vin de Pays Côteaux Lézignannais.

➤ Pierre Salles, Ch. d'Olivery, Cruscades, 11200 Lézignan-Corbières; tel. 68 27 08 66 ⊤ No visitors.

CHATEAU LES OLLIEUX

☑	35 ha	35 000	🟥3 🇩 ⬇

77 *78 *79 *81 *82 Ⓑ

Bright, slightly salmon-pink colour. Bouquet of honey and acid drops. Light and fresh on the palate, with plenty of distinction and good finish. Drink young. (1983)
➤ Françoise Surbezy-Cartier, Ch. les Ollieux, Montseret, 11200 Lézignan-Corbières; tel. 68 43 32 61 ⊤ By appt.

CHATEAU LES OLLIEUX★★

■	35 ha	35 000	🟥2 🇩 ⬛ ⬇

77 *78 *79 *81 Ⓑ 🟥

Powerful in all aspects: colour, bouquet, balance and harmony; all well blended. Temper its warm character by serving slightly chilled.(1983)
➤ Françoise Surbezy-Cartier, Ch. les Ollieux, Montseret, 11200 Lézignan-Corbières; tel. 68 43 32 61 ⊤ By appt.

CHATEAU LES PALAIS★★

■	105 ha	804 000	🟥2 🇩 ⬛ ⬇

73 Ⓐ 78 80 🟥 82 84

Strong-coloured. Fruity, rich and expressive nose. Very attractive mature, fat, fleshy character on the palate, with a long, lingering finish. (1981)
➤ M. de Volontat, Ch. les Palais, St-Laurent-de-la-Cabrerisse, 11220 Lagrasse; tel. 68 44 01 63 ⊤ Daily 8.00–12.00/14.00–18.00

CAVE COOPERATIVE DE PAZIOLS★★

■	50 ha	35 000	🟥3 🇩 ⬛ ⬇

77 79 *83 84

Pleasing and aromatic on the palate, introduced by a fragrant nose of wild herbs. Ready for drinking now. (1980)
➤ Cave Coop. de Paziols, Paziols, 11350 Tuchan; tel. 68 45 40 56 ⊤ Mon.–Sat. 8.00–12.00/14.00–18.00.

CHATEAU DE PECH-LATT
Blanc de Macabeu★★

☐	4 ha	30 000	🟥2 🇩 ⬥ ⬇

Fine and spicy with a good, fresh quality. Drink while young. (1983) ✔ Rosé de Grenache VDQS, VDQS Macération Carbonique Rouge, Pétillant Brut or Demi-sec, VDQS Grenache Rancio Blanc.
➤ SC Ch. de Pech-Latt, Ribauté, 11220 Lagrasse; tel. 68 25 22 88 ⊤ Mon.–Sat. 9.00–12.00/14.00–18.00.

DOMAINE PRIEURE DE SAINT-AMANS★

■	11 ha	66 000	🟥2 🇩 ⬛ ⬥ ⬇

80 81 🟥

Attractive ruby colour. Rather light nose. Good body and alcohol make it promising; worth waiting for. (1983)
➤ GFA *Mme* Paule Roger, Bizanet, 11200 Lézignan-Corbières; tel. 68 45 11 94 ⊤ By appt.

CHATEAU DE QUERIBUS★★

■	65 ha	180 000	🟥2 🇩 ⬛ ⬇

78 80 82 🟥 84

Pleasant, spicy bouquet. Well balanced and powerful on the palate, and very fragrant. (1983)
✔ Vin de Pays de Cucugnan Blanc and Rouge, Corbières Rosé.
➤ Coop. de Cucugnan, Ch. de Quéribus, Cucugnan, 11350 Tuchan; tel. 68 45 41 61 ⊤ By appt.

CAVE COOPERATIVE DE RIBAUTE★

☑	11 ha	30 000	🟥2 🇩 ⬛ ⬇

Youthful, with a bright, pretty, cherry-pink hue, fruity bouquet of redcurrants and fresh, fragrant taste. Drink young. (1984)
➤ Cave Coop. de Ribauté, Ribauté, 11220 Lagrasse; tel. 68 43 11 09 ⊤ Mon.–Sat. 8.00–12.00/14.00–18.00 Closed weekends in winter.

CAVE COOPERATIVE DE RIBAUTE★★

■	12 ha	50 000	🟥2 🇩 ⬥ ⬇

73 *79 *81

Deep colour tending to violet; as yet undeveloped. Fruity, cherry-scented nose that is quite flowery. Lingering finish, balance and fruitness give considerable charm on the palate, and the tannin content is just right to sustain these features. (1981)
➤ Cave Coop. de Ribauté, Ribauté, 11220 Lagrasse; tel. 68 43 11 09 ⊤ Mon.–Sat. 8.00–12.00/14.00–18.00. Closed weekends in winter.

SAINT-LAURENT DE LA CABRERISSE *Cuvée des Vignerons*★

■	9 ha	20 000	🟥3 🇩 ⬛ ⬇

Good, dark colour. Powerful, well balanced bouquet and full-bodied palate. (1982) ✔ Corbières 3 Ans d'Age Rouge, Corbières Blanc de Blancs, Corbières Rosé.
➤ Coop. St-Laurent-de-la-Cabrerisse, St-Laurent-de-la-Cabrerisse, 11220 Lagrasse; tel. 68 44 02 73 ⊤ Mon.–Fri. 8.00–12.00/14.00–19.00.

DOMAINE DE VILLEMAJOU★

■	50 ha	250 000	🟥3 🇩 ⬥ ⬇

78 79 82 83

Mature. Nose reminiscent of undergrowth and hay. Charm and suppleness on the palate, and pleasant finish. (1981)
➤ Georges Bertrand, St-André-de-Roquelongue, 11200 Lézignan-Corbières; tel. 68 45 10 43 ⊤ By appt.

COOPERATIVE PILOTE DE VILLENEUVE

◨   6ha   10000   **2** **D** ▮ ⌂

80 81 82 83

Clear, full pink. Fruity nose and fairly youthful on the palate. Drink young. (1983)
⬩ Cave Villeneuve-les-Corbières, Villeneuve-les-Corbières,   11360   Durban-Corbières;   tel. 68 45 91 59   ⵙ Daily   8.30–13.00/14.00–19.00. Closed in winter.

DOMAINE DE LA VOULTE-GASPARETS★★

■   50ha   240000   **3** **D** ⑪ ⌂

76 78 80 ⑧ 82 *83

Lovely bright colour, rich and strong nose, and full, distinguished palate. Altogether, a bottle worth considering. (1982)
⬩ M. Berges-Reverdy, Dom. de la Voulte Gasparets, Boutenac, 11200 Lézignan-Corbières; tel. 68 27 07 86 ⵙ Daily 9.00–18.00.

Costières du Gard VDQS

These straightforward red, white and rosé wines are produced from vineyards planted on sunny, pebbly slopes in the Rhône delta. They lie within a rectangle bounded by Meynes, Vauvert, Saint-Gilles, and Beaucaire, south-west of Nîmes between the Rhône and the Vidourle, north of the Camargue. Twenty-six communes produce 100000 hectolitres of wine annually, 75 per cent of which is red, 20 per cent rosé, and the remainder white. L'Ordre de la Boisson de la Stricte Observance des Costières du Gard – a local wine brotherhood – perpetuates a tradition established in 1703. A vineyard trail runs through this region, beginning at Nîmes.

DOMAINE DE L'AMARINE
Cuvée des Bernis★

■   13ha   169000   **2** **D** ▮ ⑪ ⌂

⑧ 81 82 83 84 84

Light ruby colour, light nose with warm, fruity tones. On the palate there is low acidity. Although made to age in bottle, the lack of acidity counsels caution, could be drunk from now onwards. (1983) ✔ Costières du Gard, Clairette de Bellegard Blanc.
⬩ Nicolas Godebski, Dom. de l'Amarine, 30127 Bellegarde; tel. 66 01 11 19 ⵙ Mon.–Sat. 9.00–12.00/15.00–19.00. Closed Feb.

DOMAINE DE L'AMARINE★★

☐   4ha   32500   **2** **D** ▮ ⌂

Interesting fragrance and finesse, having a warm aspect coming from a quite high alcohol and extract, which in turn brings a touch of sweetness. Serve cool. (1984) ✔ Costières du Gard.
⬩ Nicolas Godebski, Dom. de l'Amarine, 30127 Bellegarde; tel. 66 01 11 19 ⵙ Mon.–Sat. 9.00–1200/15.00–19.00. Closed Feb.

MAS AUPELLIERE

■   22ha   130000   **2** **D** ⑪ ⌂

⑧ 81 82 *83 84 84

Warm, full-bodied, southern wine. Rustic character. (1982)
⬩ M. Grootmaat, Mas Aupellière, Gallician, 30600 Vauvert; tel. 66 73 30 75 ⵙ By appt.

MAS AUPELLIERE

◨   22ha   14000   **2** **D** ▮ ⌂

82 ⑧ 84 80

Extremely pale with fresh nose. The palate is very light in character and lacks body, but easy to drink. (1984)
⬩ M. Grootmaat, Mas Aupellière, Gallician, 30600 Vauvert; tel. 66 73 30 75 ⵙ By appt.

CHATEAU BELLE-COSTE
Cuvée Saint-Marc★★

◨   10ha   68000   **2** **D** ▮ ⌂

82 83 84 84

From a distinctive soil that gives the Grenache grapes – the only variety used – an unusual character and distinctive, spicy bouquet. (1984)
⬩ Bertrand du Tremblay, Ch. de Belle-Coste, 30230 Caissargues; tel. 66 20 26 48 ⵙ By appt.

CHATEAU BELLE-COSTE
Cuvée Saint-Marc★★

☐   50ha   50000   **2** **D** ⑪ ⌂

⑧ 81 82 83 84

Light in colour, nose, and balance on the palate. Above all, a remarkable finish. Very pleasant. (1984)
⬩ Bertrand du Tremblay, Ch. de Belle-Coste, 30132 Caissargues; tel. 66 20 26 48 ⵙ By appt.

CHATEAU BELLE-COSTE
Cuvée Saint-Marc★★

■   40ha   520000   **2** **D** ⑪ ⌂

⑧ 81 82 *83 84 84

Beautiful, bright ruby-tinted wine. Very distinctive, pleasant and distinguished nose of fresh herbs. On the palate it is well made; plenty of elegance can be discerned. (1983)
⬩ Bertrand du Tremblay, Ch. de Belle-Coste, 30132 Caissargues; tel. 66 20 26 48 ⵙ By appt.

CHATEAU DE CAMPUGET★★

■   40000   **2** **D** ▮ ⌂

⑧ 83 84

Very light colour and original, meaty nose. Full bodied on the palate without being heavy, and has a light but pleasant base with elegant aromas. Full of distinction. (1983)
⬩ M. Dalle, Ch. de Campuget, 30129 Manduel; tel. 66 20 34 92 ⵙ By appt.

CHATEAU DE CAMPUGET

◨   6000   **2** **D** ▮ ⌂

⑧ 83 84

Attractive appearance and on the palate. Fruity bouquet and balance that is best when served very cool. (1984)
⬩ M. Dalle Ch. du Campuget, 30129 Manduel; tel. 66 20 34 92 ⵙ By appt.

CAVE LES COSTIERES
Cuvée Spéciale★★

■   70ha   400000   2 D ▮ ↓
81 82 83 *(84) *84

Very light colour. Nose is extremely soft, a quality rediscovered in the mouth. Well balanced fruit and velvety, perfumed finish.
🕊 Cave les Costières, 30510 Générac; tel. 66013131 ⊻ By appt.

CAVE LES COSTIERES★

▨   900ha   150000   2 D ▮ ↓
82 83 (84) 84

Traditional light colour, elegant style and warm, fruity quality. Serve young and cool unless you prefer well-developed rosés. (1984)
🕊 Cave les Costières, 30510 Générac; tel. 66013131 ⊻ By appt.

DOMAINE DE MOURIER★

▨   55ha   39000   2 D ◫ ↓

Pretty rosé with hidden depths and distinctive character that is revealed in burnt, leathery tones on the nose, and reaffirms itself in the fullness and softness on the palate. (1984) ✔ Costières du Gard.
🕊 Simone Camfrancq, Dom. de Mourier, 30000 Nîmes; tel. 66380527 ⊻ Daily 8.00–12.00.

NICOLAS

▨   156000   2 ▮ ↓

Light-coloured wine whose light nose evolves into a flowery, fruity taste on the palate. Serve cool.
🕊 Ets Nicolas, 2 Rue de Valmy, 94220 Charenton; tel. 01375920 ⊻ No visitors.

NICOLAS★★

■   164000   2 ▮

Beautifully deep colour and positive nose of soft fruits. On the palate well-balanced and full-bodied with strong perfume, good, sustained length and plenty of charm.
🕊 Ets Nicolas, 2 Rue de Valmy, 94220 Charenton; tel. 01375920 ⊻ No visitors.

DOMAINE SAINT-LOUIS-LA-PERDRIX★★

■   55ha   325000   2 D ▮ ↓
80 81 82 82 *(83) 84

Lovely bright purple. Nose is still not developed, and will not be at its best until end 1985. Initially on the palate it seems slight, but its essential nature is charming; fullness and length of its fruity fragrance guarantees it will attain good quality soon. (1983) ✔ Costières du Gard Rosé, Clairette de Bellegard Blanc.
🕊 *Mme* Philippe Lamour, Dom. St-Louis-la-Perdrix, 30127 Bellegard; tel. 66011127 ⊻ Mon.–Sat. 9.00–12.00/14.30–18.30.

DOMAINE SAINT-LOUIS-LA-PERDRIX★

▨   80ha   96000   2 D ▮ ↓

Nicely presented, with light but pleasant nose. Light, easily drunk. Beginning to lose body – drink now. (1983)
🕊 *Mme* Philippe Lamour, Dom. St-Louis-la-Per-

drix, 30127 Bellegard; tel. 66011127 ⊻ Mon.–Sat. 9.00–12.00/14.30–18.30.

CHATEAU DE LA TUILERIE★★

▨   3ha   40000   2 D ▮ ↓

Very bright and light. Forthcoming and fruity nose. Freshness is emphasized on the palate, where a trace of carbon dioxide sparkles pleasantly on the tongue. (1984)
🕊 SCIAM de la Tuilerie, Route de St-Gilles, 30000 Nîmes; tel. 66701055 ⊻ By appt 🕊 *Mme* Guy Serres.

CHATEAU DE LA TUILERIE★

□   6ha   40000   2 D ▮ ↓

Extremely light colour with a light nose characteristic of fermentation at low temperature. Fresh palate with hint of softness. Technological success. (1984)
🕊 SCIAM de la Tuilerie, Route de St-Gilles 30000 Nîmes; tel. 66701055 ⊻ By appt 🕊 *Mme.* Guy Serres.

CHATEAU DE LA TUILERIE★

■   35ha   28000   2 D ▮ ↓
81 82 83 (84) 84

Light coloured. Nose has scents of warm fruit, vanilla and trace of caramel. Well-developed and elegant. Easy to drink, very soft, fine and fruity. Ready to drink.
🕊 SCIAM de la Tuilerie, Route de St-Gilles 30000 Nîmes; tel. 66701055 ⊻ By appt 🕊 *Mme.* Guy Serres.

Coteaux du Languedoc VDQS

Ninety-one communes, five of them in Aude, two in Gard, and the rest in Hérault make up this scattered Languedoc vineyard area, in the zone of hills and scrubland that extends from Narbonne to Nîmes. The basic classification of these distinctive red and rosé wines is VDQS Coteaux du Languedoc, but within this eleven areas are considered to be of special merit and worth an individual VDQS label. Clape and Quatourze in Aude, Cabrières, Montpeyroux, St-Saturnin, Pic-St-Loup, St-Georges-d'Orques, Coteaux de Mejanelle, St-Drézery, St-Christol, and Coteaux de Verargues in Hérault. There are also two separate AOC wines, St-Chinian and Faugères. Finally, there are twenty communes which are only allowed to use the regional appellation Coteaux du Languedoc.

All eleven VDQS areas will be promoted to AOC in 1986. A wine brotherhood, L'Ordre des Ambassadeurs des Coteaux du Languedoc, has been established in Montpellier, at the

Hotel Montpelliériain des Vins du Languedoc.

COOPERATIVE LA CARIGNANO

■   8ha   60000   2 D 🍷 ⬇

*80 *81 **82** ⑧③

Ruby colour with light brown edges. Nose of soft fruit. Tannin, although present, does not destroy the softness and harmony. (1983)
🍴 Cave Coop. la Carignano, Route de Pouzolles, Gabian 34320, Roujan; tel. 67 24 65 64 ⏋ By appt.

CHATEAU CARRION-NIZAS

■   9ha   65400   2 D 🍷 ⬤

Clean and bright. Well balanced with tannin. As yet its oak-scented bouquet has not fully opened out. ✔ Vin de Pays de Caux Dom. de Salleles Rouge, Rosé, and Blanc Sec.
🍴 SCA du Ch. Carrion-Nizas, 34320 Roujan; tel. 67 25 15 44 ⏋ By appt.

DOMAINE DE LA COSTE

■   22ha   54000   2 D 🍷 ⬇

82 84 **84**

Clear and limpid. Fruity and slightly rich, meaty nose. Spicy ripe fruit apparent in the mouth. (1982)
🍴 Luc Moynier, Mas de la Coste, St-Christol, 34400 Lunel; tel. 67 71 28 63 1 ⏋ By appt.

DOMAINE DE LANGLADE★★

■   8ha   48000   2 D 🍷 ⬇

An industrialist with a love of wine has taken on the task of restoring the estate to its former rank. Drop in to see him, and perhaps he will sell you a few bottles of his 1983, a very charm36wine.
✔ Vin de Pays de la Vaunage Rouge, Vin de Pays de la Vaunage Rosé, Vin de Pays de la Vaunage Blanc.
🍴 Henri Arnal, 30980 Langlade; tel. 66 81 31 37 ⏋ Daily 8.00–12.00/14.00–19.00.

CHATEAU SAINT-FERREOL★

■   60ha   360000   2 D ⬤ ⬇

A famous family and one of the oldest estates in Languedoc produces Vins de Pays d'Oc and this AOC. Tones of liquorice, spices and oak combined with great softness. (1983)
🍴 Vignobles d'Ormesson, Ch. Lézignan, 'Lézignan-la-Cèbe, Pézenas 34120; tel. 67 98 23 80 ⏋ No visitors🍴 *Comte* Jérôme d'Ormesson.

PRIEURE SAINT-JEAN DE BEBIAN★★★

■   25ha   150000   3 D 🍷 ⬇

⑧① *82 *83 84

Brilliant, deep red. Develops well. Powerful nose of red fruit reminiscent of cherry and plum stones, with a hint of cherries in eau-de-vie. Full bodied, well made. Will still be good five years hence. (1984)
🍴 Alain Roux, Dom. de St-Jean de Bebian, 34120 Pézenas; tel. 67 98 13 60 ⏋ By appt.

Coteaux de St-Christol VDQS

The commune of St-Christol lies between St-Drézery and Verargues, to the north of la Grande-Motte. Its red wines (7000 hectolitres per year) are enjoyed from Montpellier to Central France. In 1778 Le Chevalier de Suffren, Lord of St-Christol and Admiral of France, devised a special hallmark with which to brand the barrels and guarantee the wine's authenticity.

GABRIEL MARTIN★★

■   8ha   45000   2 D 🍷 ⬇

⑦⑨ *80 *81 **82** 83 84

Soft and smooth on the palate, and full of flavour. Nose is spicy and reminiscent of nutmeg. Lingers on the palate. Best drunk between 16–17°C. (1984)
🍴 Gabriel Martin, St-Christol, 34400 Lunel; tel. 67 86 01 15 ⏋ By appt.

Côtes de la Malepère VDQS

Some 13000 hectolitres of these VDQS wines are produced by 31 communes in Aude. The vineyard areas are protected from the Mediterranean influence by the Hauts-de-Corbières to the south-east. Full-bodied and fruity red and rosé wines are made from the Grenache and Syrah, with Bordeaux varieties such as the Cabernet-Sauvignon, Cabernet-Franc and Merlot.

DOMAINE DE FOURNERY

■   250ha   1500000   1 D 🍷 ⬇

Lovely colour. Nose has nuances of young vegetation. On the palate the 'Bordeaux' character noticed on the nose is confirmed. Depth, harmony and good, long finish. Interesting wine that needs time to develop. (1983)
🍴 Cave du Razès Routier, 11240 Belvèze-du-Razès; tel. 68 69 02 71 ⏋ No visitors.

CHATEAU DE LAMOTHE

■   8ha   50000   2 🍷 ⬇

82 *83 **83**

Deep colour with dark hues. On the nose, flavours of Bordeaux and Mediterranean grape varieties blend together. Although pleasant on

the palate, the slightly dominant tannin content advises ageing for a bit longer. (1983)
⚲ Jacques de Fonde Montmaur, Ch. de Lamothe, Routier, 11240 Belvèze; tel. 68 69 026 ☖ By appt.

CAVE COOPERATIVE DE LA MALEPERE *Dom. de Foucauld*

■ 6ha 35000 **2** **D** 🖍 ↓

82 *83

Light and bright. Spicy bouquet in which Bordeaux and Mediterranean grape flavours blend together. In the mouth, soft and quite well balanced. (1982)
⚲ Cave Coop. de la Malpère, Arzens, 11290 Montréal; tel. 68 76 21 31 ☖ By appt.

CHATEAU DE MALVIES-GUILHEM★★

☑ 5ha 20000 **2** **D** 🖍 ⑪ ↓

83 ⑧④ 84

The Cabernet Franc has just replaced the Cinsault as the grape for this strongly coloured wine. Very flowery nose. Drink cool. (1983)
⚲ GFA du Ch. de Malvies, Malvies,11300 Limoux; tel. 68 31 14 41 ☖ By appt ⚲ Brigitte Gourdou-Guilhem.

CHATEAU DE MALVIES-GUILHEM

■ 20ha 100000 **2** **D** 🖍 ⑪ ↓

⑧⓪ *82 *83 84

Strong colour, elegant yet unobtrusive bouquet. First impression on the palate is of youth and suppleness followed by an almost dried-out sensation. Full bodied; likely to improve if left to mature for a few months. (1983)
⚲ M. Gourdou Ch. de Malviès, Malviès, 11240 Belvèze-du-Rozès; tel. 68 31 14 41 ☖ By appt.

CHATEAU DE MALVIES-GUILHEM★★

■ 20ha 100000 **2** **D** 🖍 ⑪ ↓

*⑧③ ⑧③ 84

Pretty, clear, ruby colour. Delightfully clean and fruity. (1983)
⚲ GFA du Ch. de Malvies, Malvies; 11300; tel. 68 31 14 41 ☖ By appt ⚲ Brigitte Gourou-Guilhem.

CHATEAU DE ROUTIER

■ 46ha 30000 **2** **D** 🖍 ↓

*⑧② 84

Bright and lively colour. Rather soft and only slightly developed nose. Impact on the palate is good, with an oaky note, but could be more lasting. Ready to drink. (1984)
⚲ Mme Lezerat, Routier, 11240 Belvèze-du-Razès; tel. 68 69 06 13 ☖ By appt.

La Clape vDQs

The vines of La Clape are grown on a wooded limestone massif at an altitude of 200m, on the coast to the north of Narbonne. The area is made up of many separate vineyards, distributed among woods and scrubland. Annual production is 28 000 hectolitres, 26 000

hectolitres of which are red and rosé wines with a full-bodied, rich, fruity character and good keeping properties. The remaining 2000 hectolitres are crisp, smooth, white wines.

CHATEAU PECH-REDON

☑ 15ha 40000 **2** 🖍 ↓

⑧⓪ **81 82** 83 84

Light cherry colour. Powerful nose of liquorice and caramel, with hint of banana. Fruity on the palate, with good finish. (1984)
⚲ Jean Demolombe, Ets, Saignes, 11100 Narbonne; tel. 68 41 04 04 ☖ By appt.

DOMAINE DE RIVIERE-LE-HAUT

☐ 10ha 100000 **2** **D** 🖍 ↓

80 ⑧① *82 83

Straw yellow colour. Full, mainly floral nose, indicating it is already well developed. Has slight acidity and is full bodied on the palate. Perfect with fish in sauce. (1983)
⚲ Jean Ségura, Dom. de Rivière-le-Haut, 11560 Fleury-d'Aude; tel. 68 33 61 33 ☖ Daily 7.00–12.00/14.00–20.00.

DOMAINE VIRES★

■ 50ha 150000 **2** **D** ⑪ ↓

⑧⓪ *81 **82** 83

Purple-coloured, with a nose of soft fruit. On the palate, slightly tannic and meaty. Would go well with game. (1981)
⚲ Yves Lignères, 29 Bd de Gaulle, 1110 Narbonne; tel. 68 32 04 11.

Montpeyroux vDQs

The Montpeyroux vineyards adjoin those of St-Saturnin to the east, on predominantly schistous land. Some 15000 hectolitres of robust red wine are produced, most of which is vinified by the local cooperative.

CAVE COOPERATIVE DE MONTPEYROUX★

■ 250ha 300000 **2** **D** 🖍 ↓

Strong ruby colour and complex bouquet, with aromas of overripe red fruits and dried fruit. Full-bodied, round and warm on the palate, with good persistent flavour. (1980)
⚲ Cave Coop. de Montpeyroux, 34150 Gignac; tel. 67 96 61 08 ☖ By appt.

Picpoul de Pinet vDQs

This is the only vDQs white wine made in Hérault. It comes from a vineyard on limestone soil on the banks of Lake Thau, south of Pézenas. The greeny-yellow wine is fruity and should be drunk young. In 1713, an edict was issued allowing each barrel of wine produced in Pinet to be branded to guarantee its authenticity of origin.

DOMAINE DE LA ROQUETTE
Cuvée Ludovic Gaujau★★

| □ | 7ha | 25000 | [2] [D] [■] [↓] |

The Picpoul gives this wine its brilliant pale-yellow colour and fine nose of dried fruits and hazelnuts. Soft, lingering and warm in the mouth. (1984)
↪ Claude Gaujal, Dom. de la Roquette, 34850 Pinet; tel. 67 38 70 02 12 ☿ By appt.

Pic-St-Loup VDQS
The vineyards are spread over 14 communes, dominated by the 658m-high 'pic' (peak) from which the wine takes its name; 35000 hectolitres of smooth, fruity red and rosé wines are produced, along with 300 hectolitres of white wine. There are several tasting cellars in this area, which is also noted for its wild game.

COOPERATIVE DE VALFLAUNES

| ■ | | 15000 | [2] [D] [■] [↓] |

Light-coloured wine with a notes of soft fruit, liquorice and coffee. Very smooth, flowing combination that should be drunk without delay. (1984)
↪ Coop. de Valflaues, 34270 Valflauvnes; tel. 67 55 22 05 ☿ By appt.

Quatourze VDQS
The vineyards here, only a few metres above sea-level, are close to Narbonne and the coastal Lake Bages. They produce 10000 hectolitres per year of robustly flavoured red wines which keep well.

CHATEAU NOTRE-DAME-DU-QUATOURZE

| ◪ | 3ha | 10000 | [2] [D] [■] [↓] |
| ★⑧③ 84 | | | |

Pleasant summer wine, well-balanced and crisp. (1983)
↪ Yvon et Georges Ortola, Ch. Notre-Dame-du-Quatourze, 11100 Narbonne; tel. 68 41 58 92 ☿ Mon.–Sat. 8.00–12.00/14.00–18.00.

CHATEAU NOTRE-DAME-DU-QUATOURZE

| ■ | 35ha | 10000 | [2] [D] [■] [↓] |
| ★80 ★⑧① ★82 83 | | | |

Characteristic Syrah and Mourvèdre style, tending to lightly spicy aroma and roundness on the palate. Drink at room temperature with red meat dishes. (1982)
↪ Yvon et Georges Ortola, Ch. Notre-Dame-du-Quatourze, 11100 Narbonne; tel. 68 41 58 92 ☿ Mon.–Sat. 8.00–12.00/14.00–18.00.

St-Georges d'Orques VDQS
Six communes, including part of Montpellier, produce red and rosé wines which have had VDQS status

since 1957, and became part of Coteaux du Languedoc in 1972. Annual production of these wines, which are very popular locally, is now 14000 hectolitres. In fact they have been well known since the eighteenth century; in 1730 the authorities devised a barrel stamp (depicting St George and the dragon) to guarantee the wine's authenticity.

CHATEAU DE L'ENGARRAN

| ■ | | 2ha | 7000 | [2] [D] [◑] [↓] |

Pale with nose of dried flowers. Ready to drink. (1982)
↪ *Mme* Grill, GFA du Ch. de l'Engarran, 34880 Laverune; tel. 67 27 60 89 ☿ By appt.

COOPERATIVE SAINT-GEORGES-D'ORQUES
Cuvée du Millénaire de Montpellier★

| ■ | 200ha | 80000 | [3] [D] [■] [↓] |

Clear bright colour, with a nose of soft red fruit. This is a vin nouveau, fruity and pleasant to drink, with a typical banana note.
↪ Coop. St-Georges-d'Orques, 34680 St-Georges-d'Orques; tel. 67 75 11 16 ☿ No visitors.

St-Saturnin VDQS
The name of this vineyard area commemorates St Saturnin, the first bishop of Toulouse. He was born in Patras, in Greece, but was a disciple in Languedoc and was subsequently martyred in Toulouse. The vineyards run between Montpellier and Lodève, north of Clermont-l'Hérault, and below the Rocher des Deux Vierges and Mont Baudile, under the Causse du Larzac. The commune of Larzac, like its three neighbours, has predominantly schistous soils, and together they produce 19000 hectolitres of red and rosé wines. These have acquired some prominence mostly because of the 'vin d'une nuit', a red wine that is macerated only very briefly, and the 'Vin Cardinal', a fine, deeply coloured wine that is excellent with roast leg of lamb.

COOPERATIVE DES VINS DE SAINT-SATURNIN *Le Lucian*★

| ■ | 52ha | 24000 | [3] [D] [■] [↓] |

Deep and attractive colour. Nose smells of fruit drops, but round enough on the palate. (1981)
↪ Cave Coop. de St-Saturnin, Avenue de la Cave, St-Saturnin 34150 Gignac; tel. 67 96 61 52 ☿ Mon.–Fri. 8.00–12.00/14.00–18.00, Sat. 8.00–12.00/14.00–17.00

ROUSSILLON

Vines were originally planted in Roussillon in the seventh century BC, by Greek seafarers who, were attracted to the Catalan coast by its abundance of minerals. The vineyards expanded during the Middle Ages and the sweet wines of the area enjoyed a considerable reputation, being known at that time as 'Vin d'Espagne' (Spanish wine). After the phylloxera catastrophe, vines were replanted extensively on the hillsides of these, the southern-most vineyards of France.

The Roussillon vineyards stretch over a semicircle of hills facing the Mediterranean Sea. They are bounded by three mountain ranges; Les Corbières to the north, Le Canigou to the west and Les Albères, forming the Spanish border, to the south. In past eras, the rivers Têt, Tech and Agy have shaped the landscape into terraces of washed and gravelly soil which now produce high-quality wines, notably 'vins doux naturels', the famous fortified sweet wines of the region. Other soil formations include schist, expanses of granite and hills of detritus from the Pliocene era.

The vineyards enjoy a particularly sunny climate with mild winters and hot summers. Rainfall is rather unevenly distributed, much of it falling as thunderstorms. There is, however, a long dry period in the summer which encourages the grapes to ripen, often accentuated by 'La Tramontane', the warm southern wind.

Vines here are pruned and trained in the 'gobelet' fashion, and planted at a density of 4000 stocks per hectare. Wine-making is still carried out in the traditional way, often with very little machinery. Cellar equipment is being modernized as more grape varieties and different wine-making techniques are introduced. Only after rigorous tests as to the ripeness of the crop are the grapes

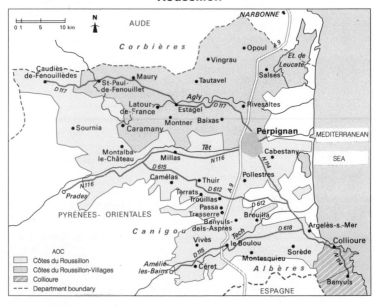

Roussillon

picked; they are then transported in 'comportes' or small baskets to prevent their being crushed and therefore spoiled by oxidation before they reach the cuverie. A proportion of the crop may be vinified by the carbonic maceration process (the bunches are tipped whole into a vat which has been filled with carbon dioxide, and are pressed later after a certain amount of fermentation has taken place). Tradition and technology work side by side, with a growing reliance on technology to regulate temperature during vinification and so maintain the freshness of the wine's aromas.

Côtes du Roussillon, Côtes du Roussillon-Villages

The wines of these appellations come from the best vineyards in the region. The area concerned is about 6000 hectares and produces up to 300 000 hectolitres of wine a year. The Côtes du Roussillon-Villages come from the northern part of the Pyrénées-Orientales department, and two communes – Caramany and Latour-de-France – are allowed to add their own names to the appellation. Gravel-based terraces, granite and schistous soils provide a richness and diversity in quality that the wine-makers have exploited to advantage.

The grape varieties used for white wines are the Macabéo and the Malvoisie de Roussillon; the grapes are pressed and fermentation begins immediately. The wines have a greenish tinge and a light, refreshing style, with a pronounced flowery aroma. They are perfect with the local fish and seafood.

The red and rosé wines are made from several grape varieties. Carignan Noir (a maximum of 70 per cent), Grenache Noir, Ladoner Pelut and Cinsault predominate, but the Syrah, Mourvèdre and Macabéo (maximum of 10 per cent in red wines) are used as complementary grape types. All wine must include one principal and one complementary varietal. All the grape varieties except the Syrah are pruned very short. Often a proportion of the crop is vinified by carbonic maceration, especially the Carignan, which gives excellent results when processed in this way. The rosé wines must be made by the 'saignée' method, in which black grapes are macerated on their skins until the correct colour is obtained.

The rosés are fruity, full bodied and refreshing; the red wines are fruity and spicy, with an alcoholic content of around 12 per cent. The Côtes du Roussillon-Villages wines are full bodied and warmly flavoured. Some can be drunk young, while others keep longer and develop an intense and complex bouquet. Their very distinctive and varied qualities of bouquet and flavour can partner a wide range of dishes.

Côtes du Roussillon

LES VIGNERONS DE BAIXAS**

■ 300 000 3 D ▪ ⫰

78 80 82 83

Cherry-ruby colour and intense bouquet that blends fragrances of redcurrant and cherry. On the palate there are shades of spice and liquorice. Smooth, full-bodied, with a certain meatiness. (1982)

🗝 Les Vignerons de Baixas, 66390 Baixas; tel. 68 64 22 37 Y By appt.

PRODUCTEURS DE LA BARNEDE
*Blanc de Blanc**

□ 17ha 60 000 2 D ▪ ⫰

(66) 78 79 81 83

Bright golden colour. Subtle flowery fragrance. Balanced and youthful with a hint of freshness in the finish. (1983) ✔ Côtes du Roussillon Rouge, Côtes du Roussillon Rosé, Vins de Pays Primeur, Rivesaltes.

🗝 Les Producteurs de la Barnede, 66670 Bages; tel. 68 21 60 30 Y Mon.–Sat. 8.15–12.00/14.00–19.00. Closed Sun. and public holidays.

MOULIN DE BREUIL*

□ 6ha 24 000 2 D ▪ ⫰

*(82) *82 *84 *84

Pale gold shot with spring-like green highlights. A nose at once flowery, fine and clean, leading to freshness coupled with a youthful quality on the palate. (1983) ✔ Rivesaltes Vieux 76 Ambré.

🗝 Albert de Massia, Moulin de Breuil, Montesquieu, 66740 St-Genis-des-Fontaines; tel. 68 89 61 01 Y Daily by appt. 9.00–19.00.

CALVET-MARTY**

■ 10ha 15 000 2 D ▪ ⫰

77 79 80 81 *82 *(83) *84

Deep, garnet-red colour. Very spicy quality on the nose that is also present on the palate. Good body and tannin. (1983)

🗝 *M.* Calvet-Marty, 36 Av. du Maréchal-Joffre, 66300 Thuir; tel. 68 53 42 62 Y By appt.

DOMAINE DE CANTERRANE★★

■ *102ha 400000 **3** D ▊.↓

74 76 78 **78** 79 80 81 82

Ruby colour with tile-red highlights. Nose of cooked fruits and plums. Liquorice flavour on the palate, which is pleasant, well balanced and soft. (1978) ✔ Muscat de Rivesaltes, Rivesaltes Rouge AOC 10 ans d'age, Côtes du Roussillon AOC Blanc, Côtes due Roussillon AOC Rosé.

⌘ Maurice Conte, Dom. de Canterrane, Trouillas, 66300 Thuir; tel. 68 53 47 24 Ⅰ Mon.–Fri. 9.00–12.00/14.00–18.00. Sat. 9.00–12.00.

CHATEAU CAP DE FOUSTE★

■ 5.50ha 84000 **3** D ⑴ ↓

*79 *80 *81 *81

Good colour, with orange highlights. Complex nose. Well-structured, fleshy and lingering on the palate, with slight vanilla flavour. (1981) ✔ Côtes du Roussillon Blanc, Muscat de Rivesaltes.

⌘ Vignerons Catalans, Route de Thuir, 66011 Perpignan; tel. 68 85 04 51 Ⅰ By appt.

CARBASSE★

■ 5ha 15000 **2** D ⑴ ↓

Bright colour. Sound, fruity, slightly peppery bouquet, and enough tannin to create good body. (1982)

⌘ M. Carbasse, Fourques, 66300 Thuir; tel. 68 38 80 39 Ⅰ By appt.

VITICULTEURS CATALANS
Taïchat★★

□ 50ha 120000 **3** D ▊ ↓

81 83 **83** 84

White to pale green colour and fruity vine flower nose. Fresh, harmonious taste. (1983) ✔ Côtes du Roussillon Taïchat Rosé.

⌘ Viticulteurs Catalans, Route de Thuir, 66011 Perpignan; tel. 68 85 04 51 Ⅰ By appt.

CAZES★★

□ 3ha 16200 **2** D ▊ ↓

75 76 77 78 **83** *84

Fine nose with an aroma of vine flowers that leads on to a pleasant freshness in the mouth. (1983) ✔ Muscat de Rivesaltes, Rivesaltes, Cotes du Rousillon Villages.

⌘ MM.Cazes Frères, 4 Rue Francisco Ferrer, 66600 Rivesaltes; tel. 68 64 08 26 Ⅰ Mon.–Sat. 8.00–12.00/14.00–18.00.

CAZES★★

◪ 5ha 27000 **3** D ▊ ↓

75 76 77 78 **83** *84

Peony and 'onion-skin' colour. Fruity and spicy nose with slightly toasted flavour. Fresh and creamy on the palate. (1983) ✔ Muscat de Rivesaltes, Rivesaltes, Côtes du Rousillon Villages.

⌘ MM. Cazes Frères, 4 Rue Francisco-Ferrer, 66600 Rivesaltes; tel. 68 64 08 26 Ⅰ Mon.–Sat. 8.00–12.00/14.00–18.00.

CAZES★★

■ 20ha 96000 **2** D ▊ ↓

At once tannic and supple. The numerous flavours are well balanced. Dominant fruity aroma tinged by scents of liquorice and leather, and a noteworthy, original 'roasted' scent on the nose. (1981) ✔ Muscat de Rivesaltes, Rivesaltes, Côtes de Rousillon Villages.

⌘ MM. Cazes Frères, 4 Rue Francisco-Ferrer, 66600 Rivesaltes; tel. 68 64 08 26 Ⅰ Mon.–Sat. 8.00–12.00/14.00–18.00.

CHATEAU L'ESPARROU★★

■ 17ha 96000 **2** D ⑴ ↓

*⑧ *81

Cherry-red with a developing fragrance; fruity at first, then spicy. Quite full on the palate, with good, lingering finish. (1981) ✔ Rivesaltes Ambré, Muscat de Rivesaltes.

⌘ Ch. L'Esparrou, BP 15, 66140 Canet-en-Roussillon; tel. 68 80 30 93 Ⅰ Mon.–Sat. 9.00–12.00/ 14.00–17.30. Closed fortnight over Christmas.

ILLIBERIS★★

■ 101ha 300000 **2** ▊ ⑴ ↓

*⑧⓪ *80

Slight tile-red tinges. Intense nose, subtly blending scents of fruits, leather and spices, all confirmed on the palate. The body has oakiness and is well-balanced. Good finish. (1980)

⌘ Les Viticulteurs Réunis, Route de Thuir, 66002 Perpignan; tel. 68 85 06 07 Ⅰ By appt.

JAUBERT-NOURY★★

◪ 3ha 18000 **2** D ▊ ↓

*⑧③ *83 84

Onion-skin colour with slightly developed nose reminiscent of dead leaves. Fairly firm and long-lasting on the palate, with slight taste of beeswax. (1981)

⌘ Jaubert-Noury, Rue des Artisans, St-Jean-Lasseille, 66300 Thuir; tel. 68 21 71 43 Ⅰ Daily 10.00–12.00/16.00–20.00. Closed Oct.–June.

JAUBERT-NOURY★★

□ 5ha 30000 **2** D ▊ ↓

*⑧③ *83 84

Whitish-green. Distinctive fine, flowery fragrance. Youthful balance and freshness on the palate. (1983)

⌘ M. Jaubert-Noury, Rue des Artisans, St-Jean-de-Lasseille, 66300 Thuir; tel. 68 21 71 43 Ⅰ Daily 10.00–12.00/16.00–20.00. Closed Oct.–June.

CHATEAU DE JAU★

■ 26ha 5400 D ▊ ↓

78 80 *81 *82 83

Deep purple, with a nose of sweet spices and blackcurrant. On the palate, full-bodied with fine tannin content, and complex, lingering aromas, which give it a superb finish. (1982) ✔ Muscat de Rivesaltes, Rivesaltes, Banyuls.

⌘ Robert Doutres, Ch. de Jau, Cases-de-Pène, 66600 Rivesaltes; tel. 68 64 11 38 Ⅰ Daily 9.00–19.00. Closed, Sat., Sun. off season ⌘ GFA De Château de Jau.

Château de Jau

COTES DU ROUSSILLON
APPELLATION COTES DU ROUSSILLON CONTROLEE

1982

MIS EN BOUTEILLES AU CHATEAU

DIFFUSION DES DOMAINES DE JAU
CHATEAU DE JAU   750ml
66600 CASES DE PENE FRANCE

LUC DE JONCLARE*

■ 200ha 720000 **1** D ▤ ↓
*⑧ *83 *84 *84

Ruby colour tending slightly to garnet-red. Fragrance of crushed red fruit and hint of spiciness on the nose, which leads to a faintly peppery palate. Well-structured wine. (1983)
🍷 Vignerons Catalans, Route de Thuir, 66011 Perpignan; tel. 68 85 04 51 ⏳ Mon.–Sat. 8.00–12.00/14.00–18.00.

CAVE COOPERATIVE LESQUERDE**

■ 110ha 65000 **1** D ▤ ↓
75 78 80 82

Ruby colour with brick-red shades. Light, fragrance of venision and spice. Smooth and round. (1982)
🍷 Cave Coop. Lesquerde, St-Vincent, Lesquerde 66220 St-Paul-de-Fenouillet; tel. 68 59 02 62 ⏳ Mon.–Sat. 8.00–12.00/14.00–18.00.

LIMOUZY**

■ 35000 **3** D ▤ ❶ ↓
*81 *⑧ *82

Ruby-red, tending to tile-red. Note aromas of cooked fruit and spices. Good body, with a hint of liquorice. (1982)
🍷 Henri Limouzy, Celliers du Tate-Vin, 66000 Perpignan; tel. 68 34 01 27 ⏳ By appt.

CAVE COOPERATIVE DE MONTALBA**

■ 200ha 13000 **6** D ▤ ↓
76 82 83

Intense nose of ripe fruit and sweet, spicy aromas. Well-balanced and meaty on the palate, with a long-lasting fragrance. (1983)
🍷 Cave Coop. de Montalba, 66130 Ille-sur-Têt; tel. 68 84 76 53 ⏳ Mon.–Thurs. 8.00–12.00/14.00–18.00. Fri. 8.00–12.00/14.00–17.00.

NICOLAS *Redan***

■ 0ha 195000 **2** ▤

Excellent wine with exceptional quality-price ratio. (1983)
🍷 Ets Nicolas, 2 Rue de Valmy; 94220 Charenton; tel. 01 37 59 20 ⏳ No visitors.

COOPERATIVE DE PEZILLA-LA-RIVIERE**

■ 47ha 305880 **2** D ▤ ↓
73 81 *82 *83 84

Light colour contrasts with a slightly spicy aroma, overlaying a full, ripe, fruity taste. Well balanced, round and pleasant on the palate (1982) ✔ Rivesaltes, Rivesaltes Grenache Noir, Muscat de Rivesaltes.
🍷 Coop. de Pézilla-la-Rivière, 66370 Pézilla-la-Rivière; tel. 68 92 00 09 ⏳ Mon.–Sat. 9.00–13.00/15.00–19.00.

MAS RANCOURE*

■ 12ha 72000 **2** D ▤ ❶ ↓
*80 *⑧ 83

Characteristic, and fine ruby-red hue. Pleasantly fruity fragrance, suppleness and maturity. Spicy aromas give it individuality. (1983) ✔ Rivesaltes.
🍷 Dr Pardineille, Mas Rancoure, 66740 St-Genis-des-Fontaines; tel. 68 89 03 69 ⏳ Daily 15.00–19.00.

DOMAINE SAINT-LUC**

■ 15ha 60000 **3** D ▤ ↓
⑦ 75 78 79 81 82 83

Beautiful, deep red colour; well-made and fairly high in tannin. (1982) ✔ Rivesaltes, Muscat de Rivesaltes.
🍷 Luc-Jérôme Talut, Passa-Llauro-Turderes 66300 Thuir; tel. 68 38 80 38 ⏳ Daily 8.00–12.00/18.00–20.00.

COOPERATIVE DE SAINT-PAUL DE FENOUILLET**

◩ 55ha 231000 **2** D ▤ ↓
78 80 *83

Orange highlights in deep, peony-coloured wine. Intense fruity and flowery fragrances on the nose, and a hint of spiciness. Fat and full-bodied on the palate. (1983)
🍷 Coop. de St-Paul de Fenouillet, 17 Ave Jean-Moulin, 66220 St-Paul-de-Fenouillet; tel. 68 59 02 39 ⏳ By appt. Mon.–Fri. 8.00–12.00/14.00–18.00. Sat. 8.00–12.00.

DOMAINE SARDA-MALET**

■ 40ha 120000 **2** D ▤ ❶ ↓
*82 *82 83

Bright, very promising ruby colour. Confirmed in the mouth by supple, well-balanced character and aromas of well-ripened fruits, such as blackcurrants or Morello cherries. (1982) ✔ Rivesaltes.
🍷 M. Sarda-Malet, 134 Av. Victor Dalbiez, 66000 Perpignan; tel. 68 54 59 95 ⏳ Daily by appt.

BLANC DE SARRAT*

□ 34ha 142800 **2** D ▤ ↓
80 82 83 84 84

Bright gold tinged with green. Fine and lightly flowery bouquet. Fresh, well balanced, youthful and pleasant. (1983)
🍷 Coop. de St Paul-de-Fenouillet, 17 Ave Jean-Moulin, 66220 St-Paul-de-Fenouillet; tel. 68 59 02 39 ⏳ By appt. Mon.–Fri. 8.00–12.00/14.00–18.00. Sat. 8.00–12.00.

TAICHAC★★

☐   16ha   60000   **2** D 🍾 ↓

⑧⁴ **84**

Subtle and typical vine-flower nose. Young and fresh on the palate. (1983) ✔ Muscat de Rivesaltes.

↤ *MM.* Salvat Père et Fils, 66610 Villeneuve-la-Riviere; tel. 68 92 17 96. ⚥ By appt. Mon.–Sat.

TERRASSOUS★★

■   200ha   1600000   **2** D 🍾 ↓

77 79 ⑧⁰ **80** 82 **82**

Earthy qualities confirmed by *goût de terroir* with ripe-fruit and liquorice scents. On the palate, the spicy aroma complements good tannins and a nicely balanced finish. (1980) ✔ Muscat de Rivesaltes, Rivesaltes.

↤ Les Vignerons de Terrats, BP 32, Terrats, 66300 Thuir; tel. 68 53 02 50 ⚥ Mon.–Fri. 8.00–12.00/14.00–18.00. Sat.–Sun. 8.00–12.00.

CHATEAU DE VESPEILLE★

■   15ha   60000   **2** D 🍾 ⑾ ↓

75 ★82 ★**82** ★⑧³ **84**

Marked fruitiness on the nose confirmed on tasting. Well constituted, clean and sound. Fairly easy tannin. (1983)

↤ Les Vignerons de Rivesaltes, 2 Rue de la Roussillonnaise, 66600 Rivesaltes; tel. 68 64 06 63 ⚥ Mon.–Sat. 9.00–12.00/14.00–18.00

Côtes du Roussillon-Villages

CAVE COOPERATIVE D'AGLYA★★

■   200ha   600000   **3** D 🍾 ↓

★77 ★80 ★82 ★**82**

Bright ruby red. Scents of well-ripened, soft fruit on the nose. On the palate, a mature, full-bodied quality with good fruit. (1982) ✔ Rivesaltes AOC, Muscat de Rivesaltes AOC, Côtes du Roussillon AOC Rosé, Vin de Pays Côtes Catalanes Rouge, Vin de Pays Côtes Catalanes Rouge.

↤ Cave Coop. d'Aglya, 66310 Estagel; tel. 68 29 82 45 ⚥ Mon.–Sat. 8.00–12.00/14.00–19.00.

COOPERATIVE VINICOLE DE L'AGLY★★

■   28ha   167000   **3** D 🍾 ⑾ ↓

82 ★⑧³ ★**83**

Elegant purple colour tending to tile-red. Spicy nose with hint of leather. Good body and oakiness in the mouth. (1982) ✔ Côtes du Roussillon Rouge, Côtes du Roussillon Blanc, Côtes du Roussillon Villages, Muscat de Rivesaltes.

↤ Coop. Vinicole de l'Agly, L'Agly, Cases-de-Pène, 66600 Rivesaltes; tel. 68 64 11 91 ⚥ Mon.–Sat. 8.00–12.00/14.00–18.00. Closed Sun. and public holidays.

LES VIGNERONS DE BAIXAS
Domiane Brial★★

■   200ha   120000   **3** D ⑾ ↓

71 75 80 **80**

Elegant, spicy, liquorice bouquet. On the palate, nice tannin content and oak and vanilla flavours. Good finish. (1980) ✔ Muscat de Rivesaltes

Dom. Brial, Rivesaltes Dom. Brial, Côtes du Roussillon, Rivesaltes Vieille Réserve.

↤ Les Vignerons de Baïxas, 66390 Baïxas; tel. 68 64 22 37 ⚥ Mon.–Sat. 8.00–12.00/14.00–18.00.

BOUDAU ET FILS★★

■   50ha   24000   **2** 🍾 ↓

Spicy and positive on the nose. Reveals fruity aromas and a well-rounded, full-bodied tannin content on the palate. (1982)

↤ Sté Vve Boudau et Fils, 7 Av. Gambetta, 66600 Rivesaltes; tel. 68 64 07 40 ⚥ By appt.

CUVEE RENE-JEAN CAMO★★

■   15ha   15000   **2** D ⑾ ↓

80 ★⑧² ★**82**

Unusual touches of mahogany in the colour. The nose has scents of old leather and roasting coffee, with hints of meaty richness. In the mouth it is well made, with lingering fragrances of coffee and vanilla. (1980)

↤ Vignerons Catalans, Route de Thuir, 66011 Perpignan; tel. 68 85 04 51.

CASSAGNES★★★

■   110ha   12000   **2** D 🍾

82 **82** ★⑧³

Fairly consistent ruby colour. Effect of maceration carbonique detectable through the nose of fruits and spices. On the palate, well put together with a dominant peppery note. (1982)

↤ Vignerons Catalans, Route de Thuirs, 66011 Perpignan; tel. 68 85 04 51.

VITICULTEURS CATALANS
Cave de Vingrau★

■   52ha   240000   **3** D 🍾 ↓

79 80 ⑧¹ **81**

Ruby with hints of tile-red. Well-developed bouquet in which rich aromas of plums and spices intermingle. Full bodied and well made, but not yet quite ready. (1981)

↤ GIAR Viticulteurs Catalans, Banguls-dels-Aspres, 66300 Thuir; tel. 68 85 04 51 ⚥ Mon.–Sat. 8.00–12.00/14.00–18.00.

VITICULTEURS CATALANS★

■   150ha   36000   **2** D 🍾 ↓

★⑧³ ★84 ★**84**

Deep garnet colour. Characterized by a nose of ripe fruit and full-bodied quality in the mouth. (1983)

↤ GIAR Viticulteurs Catalans, Banyuls-dels-Aspres, 66300 Thuir; tel. 68 85 04 51 ⚥ Mon.–Sat. 8.00–12.00/14.00–18.00.

CAVEAU-DU-PRESBYTERE★★

■   188ha   840000   **3** D 🍾 ↓

78 80 82 **83** 84

Lovely deep red to bright garnet colour. Nose reminiscent of well-ripened, refined and elegant red soft fruit and spices. On the palate, cinnamon predominates; sweetish, full-bodied and soft character and nice tannin content. (1983)

↤ Vignerons Catalans, Route de Thuir, 66011 Perpignan; tel. 68 85 04 51 ⚥ By appt.

CAZES★★

■   15ha 72000 **2** **D** ■ ◑ ♨

77 78 79 ★80

Well-developed nose reminiscent of toasted bread and hint of vanilla. Oak is more marked on the palate. Fine, well-balanced tannin content and spicy finish are features to note. (1979)
◑ᴛ *MM.* Cazes Frères, 4 Rue Frnacisco-Ferrer, 66600 Rivesaltes; tel. 68 64 08 26 ☎ Mon.–Sat. 8.00–12.00/14.00–18.00.

CELLIER DE LA DONA★

■   30ha 96000 **3** **D** ◑ ♨

76 78 80 ⑧⑴ **81** 82   ♦

Striking nose of sweet spices gives way to a well-made, smooth wine with a lingering aroma. (1981) ✔ Côtes du Rousillon, Vin de Pays Blanc, Rivesaltes.
◑ᴛ Cellier de la Dona, 66000 Perpignan; tel. 68 54 67 78 ☎ By appt.

COOPERATIVE ESPIRA-DE-L'AGLY★★

■   90ha 420000 **2** ◑ ♨

★⑺⑼ ★**79** ★**80**

Light purple with slight tile-red highlights. Intense and spicy bouquet and slight flavour of cooked fruit. In the mouth, full-bodied balance and high tannin content. (1980) ✔ Côtes du Rousillon, Rivesaltes, Muscat de Rivesaltes.
◑ᴛ Coop. Espira-de-l'Agly, 39 Rue Thiers, Espira-de-l'Agly, 66600 Rivesaltes; tel. 68 64 17 54 ☎ Mon.–Sat. 8.00–12.00/14.00–19.00.

LATOUR-DE-FRANCE★★

■   237ha 180000 **3** **D** ■ ♨

70 74 76 78 ★80 ★82 ★⑻⑷

Ruby colour with shades of brick-red. Spicy, somewhat toasty nose, and well balanced and robust on the palate. (1980)
◑ᴛ Cave Coop. de Latour-de-France, 2 Av. du Général-de-Gaulle, 66720 Latour-de-France; tel. 68 29 11 12 ☎ By appt.

CAVE COOPERATIVE LESQUERDE
Cuvée Georges Pons★★★

■   13ha 20000 **2** **D** ■ ♨

82

Deep, bright ruby-red colour. Striking, powerful, ripe-fruit fragrance on the nose. Very full-bodied and meaty on the palate, and has refined and elegant tannins, as well as good length. (1982)
◑ᴛ Cave Coop. Lesquerde, Lesquerde St Vincent, 66220 St-Paul-de-Fenouillet; tel. 68 59 02 62 ☎ Mon.–Sat. 8.00–12.00/14.00–18.00.

LES VIGNERONS DE MAURY★

■   255ha 50000 **2** ◑ ♨

81 ⑧⑵ **82** 83

The nose is reminiscent of ripe fruit, but in the mouth it becomes more spicy. Full-bodied and fleshy. (1982) ✔ AOC Maury, AOC Muscat de Rivesaltes, AOC Côtes du Roussillon.
◑ᴛ SCV Les Vignerons de Maury, 66460 Maury; tel. 68 59 00 95 ☎ By appt.

COOPERATIVE DE MONTNER★★

■   105ha 25000 **3** **D** ■ ◑ ♨

Garnet colour shot with tile-red highlights. Well-developed nose and powerful and meaty smell of leather and dried fruits. Soft, full-bodied palate. (1981)
◑ᴛ Coop. de Montner, 66720 Montner; tel. 68 29 11 91 ☎ By appt.

COOPERATIVE DE PLANEZES★★

■   20ha 10000 **3** **D** ■ ♨

76 78

Ruby colour with glints of bronze. Pleasant, quite developed, and meaty nose. In the mouth, a certain smoothness that blends well with liquorice-like aromas. (1982)
◑ᴛ Cave Coop. de Planèzes, Planèzes, 66720 Latour-de-France; tel. 68 29 11 52 ☎ By appt.

CUVEE DE PRESIDENT SALY★★

■   112ha 7500 **3** **D** ■ ♨

Ruby-red tending towards cherry-red. The intense nose is spicy and reminiscent of overripe redcurrants. On the palate, well balanced, full bodied with light tannin. (1982)
◑ᴛ Union des Vignerons de Belesta, Belesta, 66720 Latour-de-France; tel. 68 84 75 14 ☎ By appt.

RASIGUERES-TREMOINE
Tours de Tremoine★

☑   200ha 150000 **3** **D** ■ ♨

Pink-and-peony colour. Spicy nose with subtle hints of flowers and fruits. On the palate there is a good, positive quality and softness.
◑ᴛ Vignerons Catalans, Route de Thuir, 66011 Perpignan; tel. 68 85 04 51 ☎ Mon.–Fri. 9.00–12.00/14.00–18.00. Sat. 9.00–12.00.

CUVEE DES SAINTES★★★

■   4ha 6000 **3** **D** ■ ♨

This deep purple wine needs to be inhaled deeply to appreciate its intense and complex nose, with fragrances of spice and blackcurrant. On the palate, it has a generous, full bodied finish with quite persistent notes of pepper and liquorice. (1981)
◑ᴛ Francis Bomzoms, 1 Rue Voltaire, Tautavel, 66720 Latour-de-France; tel. 68 29 04 39 ☎ By appt. Closed June–Sept.

COOPERATIVE DE SAINT-PAUL DE FENOUILLET *Cuvée des Champions★★*

■   40ha 168000 **3** **D** ■ ♨

78 80 ⑧⑴ **81** ★**82**

Lovely, deep, garnet colour. Intense nose reminiscent of ripe or cooked fruit, with marked spiciness. Full bodied and well balanced on the palate, with peppery bouquet. (1981)
◑ᴛ Coop. de St-Paul de Fenouillet, 17 Av. Jean-Moulin, 66220 St-Paul-de-Fenouillet; tel. 68 59 02 39 ☎ By appt.

VIGNERONS DE SAINT-VINCENT★★

■   130ha   780000   ③ Ⓓ 🍷 ↓

80 82 83 83

Deep garnet colour. Elegant, full nose, with a hint of violets against a background of ripe soft fruit. Finishes well on the palate and will keep well. (1983) ✔ Rivesaltes Tradition, Muscat de Rivesaltes St-Vincent, Rivesaltes Sève de Macabeo, Rivesaltes Grenache d'Or.
↥ Vignerons de St-Vincent, BP. 22, 66310 Estagel; tel. 68 29 00 94 ☎ By appt.

COOPERATIVE DE VINS FINS DE SALSES★★

■   60ha   110000   ④ Ⓓ ⑾ ↓

78 80

Deep ruby colour and nose reminiscent of ripe soft fruit. Excellent balance on the palate, with a liquorice fragrance. (1978)
↥ Coop. de Vins Fins de Salses, Salses, 66600 Rivesaltes; tel. 68 38 62 07 ☎ Mon.–Sat. 8.00–12.00/14.00–18.00.

CELLIERS DU TATE-VIN★★

■   10ha   30000   ④ Ⓓ 🍷 ⑾ ↓
Ruby colour with hints of tile-red. Scents of smoke and leather on the nose. Spicy aromas, and a powerful structure in the mouth. (1982)
↥ ETS. Limouzy, Celliers du Tâte-Vin, 66000 Perpignan; tel. 68 34 01 27 ☎ Mon.–Sat. 8.00–12.00/14.00–18.00.

MAITRES VIGNERONS DE TAUTAVEL★★

■   150ha   720000   ④ Ⓓ ⑾ ↓

★⑦⑨ ★79 80 81 82

Rich, meaty nose with oak and spices. Powerful and full bodied on the palate, with a remarkably long finish. (1979) ✔ Côtes du Roussillon Rouge, Côtes du Rousillon Blanc, Rivesaltes Rouge, Rivesaltes Blanc.

↥ Maitres Vignerons de Tautavel, 24 Route de Vingrau, Tautavel, 66720 Latour-de-France; tel. 68 29 12 03 ☎ By appt.

COOPERATIVE DE VINGRAU★

■   0.63ha   240000   ④ Ⓓ 🍷 ↓

⑦⑧ 80 81

Ruby to tile-red wine; nose at first spicy, then rich. Balanced and quite full bodied on the palate, with some tannin. (1978) ✔ Rivesaltes Rouge, Rivesaltes Blanc, Muscat de Rivesaltes.
↥ Coop. de Vingrau, 3 Rue Maréchal-Joffre 66600 Vingrau; tel. 68 29 40 41 ☎ Mon.–Fri. Closed Oct.

Collioure

This appellation area is very small, presently comprising about 50 hectares that produce 2000 hectolitres of wine per year, and sharing the same boundaries as the Banyuls appellation. Only four communes are involved: Collioure, Port-Vendres, Banyuls-sur-Mer and Cerbère.

The principal grape varieties are the Grenache Noir, Carignan and Mourvèdre, with Syrah and Cinsault as the junior partners. The wine is exclusively red and is made near the beginning of the harvest, before the grapes destined for Banyuls have been harvested. The low yield of these vines, planted on narrow terraces, explains the beautiful dark-red colour of these warm, full-bodied reds, with their ripe, concentrated flavour.

DOMAINE DU MAS BLANC
Cuvée les Piloums★★

■   5ha   15600   ④ Ⓓ 🍷 ↓

76 78 ★82 ★83

Bouquet of ripe soft fruit and full-bodied palate. Good tannin content, ensuring longevity and a nice, lingering spicy finish. (1983) ✔ Banyuls.
↥ MM. Parcé et Fils, Dom. du Mas Blanc, 66650 Banyuls-sur-Mer; tel. 68 88 32 12 ☎ By appt. Closed Aug.

CELLIERS DES TEMPLIERS★★

■   40ha   180000   ③ Ⓓ ⑾ ↓

78 79 ★80 ★81 ★82 ★82 83

Purple with orange highlights. Well-developed bouquet with hint of venison and dominant smell of leather. In the mouth, soft tannin and lingering aroma of ripe fruit. (1980)
↥ Celliers des Templiers, Route du Mas-Reig, 66650 Banyuls-sur-Mer; tel. 68 88 31 59 ☎ Mon.–Sat. 9.00–12.00/14.00–18.00.

PROVENCE AND CORSICA

PROVENCE

For most people, Provence is holiday France, where the sun 'always shines', and life moves to the slower rhythms of the south. For the wine-makers, too, it is a land of blue skies, where the sun shines for 3000 hours every year, but also a land of infrequent but violent rains, wild winds and tortuous hills. The Phocaeans, who arrived in Marseilles about 600 BC, found the same varieties of vine as in their native Asia Minor, and set to increasing their potential, just as the Romans did six centuries later. The medieval abbeys and monasteries, and after them the feudal nobles (one of whom was the wine-maker king René d'Anjou, who was Count of Provence), continued the process of consolidation.

Provence wines were once famous, favoured by Eléonore de Provence, wife of the French king Henry III, in preference to the Gascony wines introduced by the king's mother-in-law, Eleanor of Aquitaine. Subsequently, the Provence wine trade went into decline except for those fortunate producers who happened to be on important trade routes. But, after centuries of eclipse, the rise in tourism has created a new demand for these wines, in particular for the rosés. For millions of visitors over the last few decades, Provence wines have become the very symbols of happy summer holidays, recalling many an al fresco Provençal meal eaten in the shade amid the scents of pine and frangipani.

Today, the annual wine production of Provence reaches almost four million hectolitres, of which approximately 800000 are from the five AOC areas (Cassis, Bandol, Palette, Côtes de Provence and Bellet). In the department of the Var alone, wine accounts for 45 per cent of overall agricultural production, and vines occupy 51 per cent of the surface area under cultivation.

As is common in all the vineyards of southern France, many different grape types are planted; thirteen are permitted in the Côtes de Provence appellation, even though the Muscat wines which were the pride of many parts of Provence have disappeared following the phylloxera crisis. At present, the vines are mostly pruned and trained on the 'gobelet' system, although a method of training the vines along supporting wires is becoming more common. The rosé and white wines (the latter less common but often surprisingly good) are usually drunk young. This custom should perhaps be rethought, now that wines are bottled young, and not exposed to such extremes of climate. The same is true of the lighter red wines. In any case, the fuller-bodied red wines of all these appellations age very well indeed, and Bandol in particular may last two or more decades. And finally, since Provençal is still spoken on a few estates, it is worth knowing that an 'avis' is a branch of vine, a 'tine' is a vat and a 'crotte' is a cellar! And there are local names, too, for the grape varieties themselves, based on the way that the bunches of grapes hang; for example 'pecoui-touar' (twisted tail) or 'ginou d'agasso' (magpie's knee).

Côtes de Provence

This extremely large appellation (almost 700 000 hectolitres per year) covers over one-third of the department of the Var, extending into the Bouches-du-Rhône, up to the outskirts of Marseilles, and also into a small part of the Alpes-Maritimes. Three different types of soil characterize the area: the clayey clumps of les Maures in the south-east, bordered to the north by a band of red sandstone that stretches from Toulon to Saint-Raphaël; and beyond that the large mass of limestone hills and plateaux which form foothills of the Alps. The wines produced in this region come from different grape types, blended in varying proportions, grown on vineyards of highly varied soil and exposure. The result is a range of different wines showing only a family resemblance due to the southern sun.

The smooth, aromatic but dry white wines from the coastal region are absolutely perfect with fresh fish, whereas those from the north are a little sharper, standing up better to écrevisses à l'américaine or strong cheeses. The rosés, which may appear as full bodied or refreshing, depending on personal taste, make a splendid accompaniment to the strong flavours of Provençal cuisine – soupe au pistou, anchoïade, aïoli, bouillabaisse, red mullet or sea urchins.

Finally, the red wines, which are rounded and smooth, go well with a leg of mutton or a roast, but also with pot-au-feu, especially cold pot-au-feu served as a salad. Some of the fuller-bodied red wines, powerful and generous as they are, would go well with jugged hare, daube and woodcock.

Provence

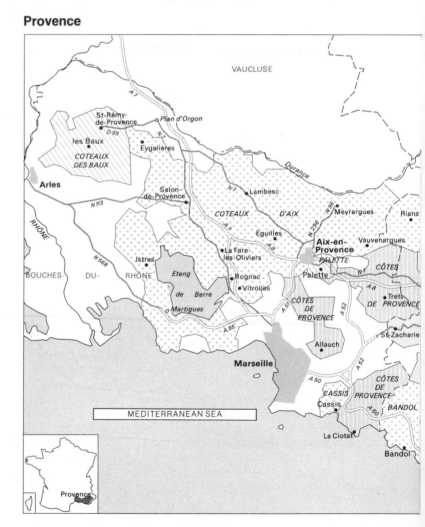

448

DOMAINE DU VAL D'ANRIEU*

■   25 ha   45 000   2 D ⬛ ⬛

*79 *81 ㉘

The 1983 red bears the stamp of the Mouvèdre grape. Drink at room temperature, as its nose has the delicacy of youth. (1983) ✔ Côtes de Provence le Val d'Anrieu Rosé, Côtes de Provence le Val d'Anrieu Blanc.
🍷 Jean Poussel, Dom. le Val d'Anrieu, 83590 Gonfaron; tel. 94 78 30 93 ⵌ By appt.

CAVE COOPERATIVE L'ARCOISE**

◩   250 ha 400 000   2 D ⬛ ⬛

83 84 .

A very fine rosé smelling of small fruits. Soft, full bodied, pleasant with good acidity. ✔ Côtes de Provence Rouge, and Blanc.
🍷 Cave Coop. l'Arcoise, Quartier le Lauron, 83460 Les Arcs-sur-Argens; tel. 94 73 30 29 ⵌ By appt.

DOMAINE DES ASPRAS***

☐   7 ha   4800   2 D ⬛ ⬛

81 82 *83 *84

The right grape varieties and a combination of soil and technique have resulted in this fine, elegant wine. Out-of-the-ordinary quality at an ordinary price. (1983) ✔ Côtes de Provence Rouge, Côtes de Provence Rosé, Vin de Pays du Var Blanc Sec, Vin de Pays du Var Rouge.
🍷 Lisa Latz, Dom. des Aspras, Correns, 83123 Carces; tel. 94 59 59 70 ⵌ By appt.

CHATEAU BARBEYROLLES***

■   10 ha   25 000   3 D ⬛ ⬛ ⬤ ⬛

83 84

Soft and warm, red. Made from a blend of six grape varieties. (1983)
🍷 *Mlle* Régine Sumeire, Ch. Barbeyrolles, Gassin, 83990 St-Tropez; tel. 94 56 33 58 ⵌ By appt.

CHATEAU BARBEYROLLES***

◩   10 ha   25 000   3 D ⬛ ⬛

83 84

Fine rosé, typical of Côtes de Provence. Pale colour, delicate aroma of aniseed on the nose. (1983)
🍷 *Mlle* Régine Sumeire, Ch. Barbeyrolles, Gassin, 83990 St-Tropez; tel. 94 56 33 58 ⵌ By appt.

CHATEAU BARON-GEORGES★★

■ | 35ha | 50000 | 2 D ◑ ⬩

82 *83 *84

Well-chosen blend of grape varieties gives a nose of flowers and plants. The fragrances of liquorice, beeswax, vanilla and cinnamon are still developing, but it is good and youthful on the palate; has distinction and lingers well. (1983)
☙ Anthony Gassier, Ch. Baron-Georges, 13114 Puyloubier; tel. 94 59 48 68 ☍ No visitors.

DOMAINE DU GRAND BATAILLER★★

■ | 10ha | 4000 | 2 D ▬ ⬩

A very well-balanced, clean, healthy, vinous and soft wine. A recent production, but worth following up. (1983)
☙ *M.* Courty, Dom. du Grand Batailler, 83230 Bormes-les-Mimosas; tel. 94 64 89 37 ☍ Daily 10.00–12.00/17.00–19.00. Closed 20 Sept.–1 Nov.

DOMAINE DE LA BERNARDE
Cuvée Saint-Germain★★★

■ | 3ha | 7000 | 4 D ▬ ⬩

78 80 ⑧ 82 83 84

Brightly coloured from selected grapes. Surprising nose with dominant rich, meaty character giving way to fruity, flowery aromas characteristic of carbonic maceration. On the palate, considerable body and great fragrance. (1981)
✔ Côtes de Provence Dom. de la Bernarde Rouge.
☙ Jacqueline Meulnart. Dom. de la Bernarde, 83340 Le Luc; tel. 94 60 71 31 ☍ By appt.

DOMAINE DE LA BERNARDE
Cuvée Saint-Germain★★★

□ | 4ha | 15000 | 4 D ▬ ⬩

80 81 82 83 84

Made only from Ugni Blanc grapes. Intense, distinctive flowery nose. Well balanced. Smooth and pleasantly crisp on the palate. (1983)
☙ Jacquline Meulnart, Dom. de la Bernarde, 83340 Le Luc; tel. 94 60 71 31 ☍ By appt.

DOMAINE DE LA BERNARDE★★

▨ | 15ha | 45000 | 3 D ▬ ⬩

82 84

Elegant and fruity. Particularly firm, soft texture and lingers on the palate. (1982)
☙ Jacqueline Meulnart, Dom. de la Bernarde, 83340 Le Luc; tel. 94 60 71 31 ☍ By appt.

DOMAINE DE BERTAUD

□ | 4ha | 8000 | 3 D ▬ ⬩

*⑧ *84

Flowery and young. A little too vinous on the palate. (1983)
☙ Yves Lemaître, Dom. de Bertaud, 83990 Gassin; tel. 94 56 16 83 ☍ By appt.

DOMAINE DE BERTAUD★

■ | 10ha | 40000 | 3 D ◑ ⬩

73 78 81 83 *84

Aged by the Bordeaux method. Very good colour. Still a little closed, but its body promises good longevity. (1983)
☙ Yves Lemaître, Dom. de Bertaud, 83990 Gassin; tel. 94 50 16 13 ☍ By appt.

MAS DE CADENET★★

▨ | 50ha | 100000 | 3 D ▬ ⬩

74 78 80 82 83

Very attractive rosé. Lovely fragrance of broom and seringa flowers; pleasantly crisp and delicate palate. (1983) ✔ Côtes de Provence Rouge, Côtes de Provence Blanc.
☙ M. Negrel, Mas de Cadenet, 13530 Trets-en-Provence; tel. 42 29 21 59 ☍ By appt.

DOMAINE DE CAMPDUNY★★

□ | 15ha | 90000 | 2 D ▬ ⬩

82 83 84

Lovely colour and distinctive fragrance. (1983)
☙ M. Gavoty, Dom. de Campduny, Flassans-sur-Issole, 83340 Le Luc; tel. 94 69 72 16 ☍ By appt.

DOMAINE DE CAMPDUNY★★

■ | 30ha | 180000 | 2 D ◑ ⬩

78 82 83

One of the first estates to ferment grapes whole, giving the flowery fragrances of faded roses and honeysuckle. (1983)
☙ M. Gavoty, Dom. de Campduny, Flassans-sur-Issole, 83340 Le Luc; tel. 94 69 72 16 ☍ By appt.

DOMAINE DE CAMPDUNY★★

▨ | 60ha | 360000 | 2 D ▬ ⬩

82 83 84

Full colour and characteristic fragrances of well-vinified rosés. Pleasantly crisp. Attractive. (1983)
☙ M. Gavoty, Dom. de Campduny, Flassans-sur-Issole, 83340 Le Luc; tel. 94 69 72 16 ☍ By appt.

DOMAINE DES CANEBIERES★★

■ | 14ha | 13000 | 2 D ▬ ◑ ⬩

81 82 *83 83

Lovely, flowery red. Very soft, easy and well balanced. (1983)
☙ Louis et Luce Maille, Dom. St-Jean, 83570 Carcès; tel. 94 04 50 97 ☍ By appt.

DOMAINE DE LA CARONNE★

▨ | 20ha | 4800 | 6 D ▬ ⬩

81 82 *83 84

Good representative of Côtes-de-Provence. Luminous, with a crisp, full scent; soft without being flabby. Leaves a lingering silkiness on the palate. (1983) ✔ Côtes de Provence Rouge, Côtes de Provence Blanc Sec.
☙ Denis Baccino, Dom. de la Caronne, 83340 Le Luc; tel. 94 60 71 28 ☍ Mon.–Sat. 8.30–12.00/14.00–19.00.

CASTEL ROUBINE★★

◪ 18ha 120000 **4** **D** ▮ ↓

81 *83 **83**

Clear, very warm and silky. Low-temperature fermentation has given it a distinctive nose. (1983)
☙ DPMVR SA, Castel Roubine, 83510 Lorgues; tel. 94 73 71 55 ⟂ Daily 9.00–12.00/14.00–18.00
☙ *M.* Hallgren PDG.

CASTEL ROUBINE★

☐ 6ha 42000 **3** **D** ▮ ↓

81 *83

The knowledgeable taster will detect an echo of the Gironde. Bears the stamp of the Sémillon grape and has aromas of linden blossom. Pleasantly crisp and well balanced. (1983)
☙ DPMVR SA, Castel Roubine, 83510 Lorgues; tel. 94 73 71 55 ⟂ Daily 9.00–12.00/14.00–18.00.
☙ *M.* Hallgren PDG.

CASTEL ROUBINE★

■ 50ha 300000 **4** **D** ⑪ ↓

*81 *82 *83 84

The 1981 red, with its uniform colour, is mature and supple, with hints of Bordeaux. (1981)
✔ Méthode Champenoise Brut Blanc de Blancs.
☙ DPMVR SA, Castel Roubine, 83510 Lorgues; tel. 94 73 71 55 ⟂ Mon.–Sat. 9.00–12.00/14.00–18.00.

DOMAINE DE CLASTRON★

☐ 2ha 10000 **2** **D** ▮ ↓

82 **83**

Pale yellow with delicate perfume of tropical fruit. Good acidity to complement seafood and fatty cheeses. (1983)
☙ GFA du Dom. de Clastron, 83920 La Motte; tel. 94 70 24 57 ⟂ Mon.–Sat. 8.00–12.00/13.00–18.00

DOMAINE DE CLASTRON★

■ 5ha 30000 **2** **D** ▮ ⑪ ↓

81 82 **83**

Aromas bear the imprint of a high proportion of Cabernet-Sauvignon vines and storage in wood. Fine wine with excellent structure and balance. (1983) ✔ Côtes de Provence wines.
☙ GFA du Dom. de Clastron, 82390 La Motte; tel. 94 70 24 57 ⟂ Mon.–Sat. 8.00–12.00/13.00–1800.

DOMAINE DE CLASTRON★

◪ 10ha 70000 **2** **D** ▮ ↓

82 **83** 84

Syrah grape gives this rosé its 'peony' tint and floral scent. Its softness and good acidity is partly due to the vintage and partly to expertise in its making. (1983)
☙ GFA du Dom. de Clastron, 83920 La Motte; tel. 94 70 24 57 ⟂ Mon.–Sat. 8.00–12.00/13.00–18.00.

CAVE COOPERATIVE DE COLLOBRIERES★

◪ 18ha 100000 **2** **D** ▮ ↓

83 84

Low-temperature fermentation of the decanted must has given Collobrières a well-deserved reputation for its rosés. Light hint of the Syrah and highly perfumed.
☙ Cave Coop. de Collobrières, 83610 Collobrières; tel. 94 04 50 97 ⟂ By appt.

DOMAINE DE LA CROIX★★

■ 100ha 200000 **2** **D** ⑪ ↓

70 77 78 80 **81** 82

The nose has good varietal character and the firm, slightly rough body is a guarantee that the wine will age well. (1981) ✔ Côtes de Provence wines.
☙ Dom. de la Croix SA, 83420 La Croix-Valmer; tel. 94 79 60 02 ⟂ By appt.

DOMAINE DE CUREBEASSE★

■ 15ha 96000 **2** **D** ▮ ↓

77 82 *83

Strong Provençal accent, and blackberry and blackcurrant scents. (1983)
☙ Jean Paquette, Dom. de Curebéasse, 83600 Fréjus; tel. 94 52 10 17 ⟂ Mon.–Sat. 8.00–12.00/14.00–18.00. Closed 20 Dec.–5 Jan.

DOMAINE DU DEFFENDS★★

☐ 3ha 15000 **2** **D** ▮ ↓

83 **84**

The Ugni Blanc is surprisingly full of perfume and flavour. Who says good white wines cannot be made in Provence? (1984) ✔ Côtes de Provence Rouge and Rosé.
☙ Michel Donon, Le Deffends, 83660 Carnoules; tel. 94 28 33 12 ⟂ Daily 8.00–12.00/14.00–19.00.

DOMAINE DU DEFFENDS★

■ 6ha 80000 **2** **D** ▮ ↓

81 82 **83**

Classic selection of Cinsaut, Grenache, a little Carignan and hint of Mourvèdre. Lovely fragrance of wild herbs, vanilla and soft, full body. (1983) ✔ Côtes de Provence Rosé and Blanc Sec .
☙ *Mme* Michel Donon, Le Deffends, 83660 Carnoules; tel. 94 28 33 12 ⟂ Daily 8.00–12.00/14.00–19.00.

DOMAINE DU DEFFENDS★

◪ 8ha 90000 **2** **D** ▮ ↓

83 **84**

Pale and fresh as the sweetbriar and a highly suitable partner for local culinary delights, such as *poulpe à la provençal* (octopus). (1984)
☙ *Mme* Michel Donon, Le Deffends, 83660 Carnoules; tel. 94 28 33 12 ⟂ Daily 8.00–12.00/14.00–19.00.

DOMAINE DU DRAGON★★

☐ 10ha 12000 **2** **D** ▮ ↓

82 ⑧③ 84

A white wine made exclusively from Ugni Blanc grapes. Highly scented, delicate and elegant. (1983)

Paul Garro, Dom. du Dragon, 83300 Draguignan; tel. 94 68 00 34 ☿ Mon.–Sat. 8.00–12.00/ 14.00–18.00. Closed Sun. and public holidays.

L'ESTANDON★★

■   1200 000   2   D   🍶   🍷   ⚱

74 ⑲ 81

The high standards of this vineyard have been maintained in this fleshy yet supple red wine, which will keep well. (1983)

J. Bagnis et Fils, Quartier des Aubregades, 83390 Cuers; tel. 94 48 55 20 ☿ By appt.

L'ESTANDON★★

◪   1400 000   2   D   🍶   🍷   ⚱

⑲ 83 84

A supple rosé, light in colour with a slightly fruity character, which should go well with spicy foods. (1983)

J. Bagnis et Fils, Quartier des Aubregades, 83390 Cuers; tel. 94 48 55 20 ☿ By appt.

L'ESTANDON★★

☐   450 000   2   D   🍶   🍷   ⚱

⑦ 74 79

The white wines here are as respected as the red, and noted for being supple and fruity. This delicate wine has all these qualities and is a good example. (1983)

J. Bagnis et Fils, Quartier des Aubregades, 83390 Cuers; tel. 94 48 55 20 ☿ By appt.

DOMAINE DES FERAUD★

■   12 ha   60 000   3   D   🍶   ⚱

78 *81 *82 *⑧ 84

Bordeaux aromas are dominant, but the Provençale scents of vanilla, blackcurrant and raspberry can be detected. (1983) ✔ Côtes de Provence Dom. Feraud Blanc, Côtes de Provence Dom. Feraud Rosé.

SCA Les Feraud, Dom. des Feraud, 83550 Vidauban; tel. 94 73 03 12 ☿ By appt.

DOMAINE DES FOUQUES★★

■   3 ha   20 000   2   D   🍶   ⚱

81 82 ⑧

Pleasant, sumptuous red, with a deeply flowery palate. Very pleasant drinking. (1983)

GFA des Borrels, Dom. des Fouques, 83400 Hyères. tel. 94 57 21 84 ☿ Mon.–Sat. 8.00–12.00/ 14.00–18.00.

DOMAINE DES FOUQUES★

◪   12 ha   60 000   2   D   🍶   ⚱

83 ⑧

Attractive, clear rosé with an honest nose. Easy to drink and full of flavour. (1984)

GFA des Borrels, Dom. des Fouques, 83400 Hyères; tel. 94 57 21 84 ☿ Mon.–Sat. 8.00–12.00/ 14.00–18.00.

CHATEAU DE GAIROIRD★★

◪   25 ha   1800   2   D   🍶   ⚱

81 82 *⑧ ⑧ *84

The scents of berried fruit are typical of wines from the soil of this dry, stony plain. (1983) ✔ Côtes de Provence Rouge, Côtes de Provence

Blanc.

Deydier de Pierrefeu, Ch. de Gairoird, 83390 Cuers; tel. 94 48 50 60 ☿ No visitors.

DOMAINE DU GALOUPET★★
Cru Classé

☐   4 ha   13 500   2   D   🍶   ⚱

83 ⑧

Excellent white from the Sémillon and Rolle (Mourvèdre). Gleams of golden-green, and flowery perfume of lilac and citrus fruit skins. Will surprise some lovers of more northerly whites. (1984) ✔ Côtes de Provence wines.

Dom. du Galoupet, 83250 La Londes-les-Maures; tel. 94 66 40 07 ☿ Daily 8.00–12.00/ 13.00–18.00.

DOMAINE DU GALOUPET★★

■   5 ha   30 000   2   D   🍶   🍷   ⚱

81 82 ⑧

Made mainly from Syrah grapes (aromas of strawberry and violet) and still a little immature. Should be laid down to develop fully. (1983) ✔ Côtes de Provence Rosé and Blanc Sec, Vin de Pays du Var Rosé and Rouge.

Dom. du Galoupet, 83250 La Londes-les-Maures; tel. 94 66 40 07 ☿ Daily 8.00–12.00/ 13.00–18.00.

DOMAINE DU GALOUPET★

◪   12 ha   80 000   2   D   🍶   ⚱

81 82 ⑧ 84

Pale rosé reminiscent of light music. Elegant and fine – a reminder of sunlit holidays. (1983) ✔ Côtes de Provence Blanc Sec and Rouge, Vin de Pays du Var Rosé and Rouge.

Dom. du Galoupet, 83250 La Londes-les-Maures; tel. 94 66 40 07 ☿ Daily 8.00–12.00/ 13.00– 18.00.

VIGNOBLES GASPERINI★★

■   15 ha   35 000   3   D   ⚱

80 ⑧

Full bodied and forthcoming; not very well developed as yet. (1982)

Guy et Alain Gaspérini, 83260 La Crau; tel, 94 66 70 01 ☿ Mon.–Fri. 8.00–12.00/14.00–18.30.

VIGNOBLES GASPERINI★★

◪   15 ha   50 000   3   D   🍷   ⚱

82 83

Attactive rosé. Full and delicate; for drinking with grilled fish. (1982) ✔ Gastillant Mousseau Rosé.

Guy et Alain Gaspérini, 83260 La Crau; tel. 94 66 70 01 ☿ Mon.–Fri. 8.00–12.00/14.00–18.30.

LA GORDONNE★★

■   50 ha   260 000   2   D   🍶   ⚱

⑧

Just beginning to open out and already pleasing; aromas of green pepper, undergrowth and venison can be detected. Firm and smooth on the palate. (1981)

Dom. de la Gordonne, 83450 Pierrefeu; tel. 94 66 81 46 ☿ By appt Salins du Midi.

CHATEAU GRAND BOISE★★

◩ 43ha 216000 ③ Ⓓ ■ ↓

81 82 *83 83 ***84**

Crisp, with high acidity, flowery, scented and delicate. Interesting. (1983) ✔ Côtes de Provence Rouge, Côtes de Provence Blanc Sec, Vin de Pays des Bouches-du-Rhône Rouge, Vin de Pays des Bouches-du-Rhône Rosé.
↰ M. Gruey, Ch. de Grand Boise, 13530 Trets-en-Provence; tel. 42 29 22 95 ☎ By appt.

DOMAINE DE GRAND'BOISE★★

■ 43ha 234000 ③ Ⓓ ■ ↓

71 74 *78 *79 80 81 *82 ⑧③

Deeply coloured, well made and full-bodied. Rich, meaty nose with hint of damp plants. Well balanced on the palate. Lingering aromas; well above average for this appellation. (1983) ✔ Côtes de Provence Rouges et Blancs, Vin de Pays des Bouches-du-Rhône Rouge et Rosé.
↰ M. Gruey, Ch. Grand'Boise, 13530 Trets-en-Provence; tel. 42 29 22 95 ☎ By appt.

DOMAINE DE LA GRANDE BASTIDE★

☐ 2ha 2500 ② Ⓓ ■ ↓

82 83

Lovely yellow colour with green glints, and a pleasant yet discreet nose. On the palate it is warm and supple, fat and persistent. (1983)
↰ Laure Hairs, Dom. de la Grande Bastide, 83400 Hyères; tel. 94 28 20 79 ☎ By appt. Closed Sun.

DOMAINE DE LA GRANDE BASTIDE★

■ 10ha 25000 ② Ⓓ ■ ⑪ ↓

77 81 82 **83**

Lovely, well-made red. Very pleasant, with slightly cooked nose. (1983)
↰ Laure Hairs, Dom. de la Grande Bastide, 83400 Hyères; tel.94 28 20 79 ☎ By appt. Closed Sun.

DOMAINE DE GRAND-PRE★

☐ 1ha 5000 ③ Ⓓ ■ ↓

83 84

Attractive, well made, and rather unobtrusive but very youthful! ✔ Côtes de Provence Rosé et Rouge. (1984)
↰ Emmanuel Plauchut, Dom. de Grand-Pré, 83750 Puget-Ville; tel. 94 48 32 16 ☎ Daily 9.00–19.00

DOMAINE DE GRAND-PRE★★

■ 2ha 12000 ③ Ⓓ ■ ↓

81 82 83

A rich, meaty nose and liquorice arise from a full body, which needs only the maturity it will gain with age. (1983)
↰ Emmanuel Plauchut, Dom. de Grand-Pré, 83750 Puget-Ville; tel. 94 48 32 16 ☎ Daily 9.00–1900.

DOMAINE DE GRAND-PRE★★

◩ 5ha 40000 ③ Ⓓ ■ ↓

83 84

Elegantly tinted salmon-pink. Flavour of wood strawberries. Delicate but not too mellow. High class. (1984) ✔ Côtes de Provence Rouge and Blanc Sec.
↰ Emmanuel Plauchut, Dom. de Grand-Pré, 83750 Puget-Ville; tel. 94 48 32 16 ☎ Daily 9.00–19.00.

DOMAINE DE L'ILE DE PORQUEROLLES★★

■ 8ha 42000 ② Ⓓ ⑪ ↓

82 ***83**

Attractive, light, delicate mature and crisp; ideal for a Mediterranean holiday. (1982)
↰ Mme Le Ber, Porquerolles, 83400 Hyères; tel. 94 58 30 21 ☎ By appt.

DOMAINE DE L'ILE DE PORQUEROLLES★★★

◩ 12ha 36000 ② Ⓓ ■ ↓

82 ⑧③ 83 ***84**

Lively rosé with a powerful, exotic nose of banana and lychee, confirmed on the palate. Very round and well balanced. The perfect rosé? (1983)
↰ Mme Le Ber, Porquerolles, 83400 Hèyres; tel. 94 58 30 21 ☎ By appt.

DOMAINE JAS D'ESCLANS★★

■ 50ha 240000 ③ Ⓓ ■ ⑪ ↓

74 *77 *80 80 **82 83**

Very successful. Brilliant, clear ruby-red. Powerful nose of vanilla. Flows well and has great quality and charm. Lingers on the palate. (1980)
↰ M. et Mme. Lorgues-Lapouge, Route de Callas, 83920 La Motte; tel. 91 70 27 86 ☎ By appt.

DOMAINE DE LA JEANETTE★★

☐ 2ha 13000 ② Ⓓ ■ ↓

Soft, tender and full of the charm and good qualities of this appellation.
↰ MM. Mouette Frères, La Jeanette, 83400 Hyères; tel. 94 65 68 30 ☎ By appt.

DOMAINE DE LA JEANETTE★★

■ 5ha 30000 ② Ⓓ ⑪ ↓

81 83 84

Light and easy to drink. Pleasing and uncomplicated. A good bottle, typical of its appellation. (1984)

🗝 *MM.* Mouette Frères, La Jeanette, 83400 Hyères; tel. 94 65 68 30 🍷 By appt.

DOMAINE DE LA JEANETTE**

◪ 12ha 91000 2 D ▮ ↓

84

The three brothers who run this vineyard deserve their good reputation. This rosé is not only of a high quality but excellent value for money.
🗝 *MM.* Mouette Frères, La Jeanette, 83400 Hyères; tel. 94 65 68 30 🍷 By appt.

CHATEAU DE LEOUBES**

◪ 70ha 250000 3 D ▮ ↓

Full reds and warm white are produced at this château, but, above all, their rosés are deep in colour and well structured. A good example of a traditional Provençal wine. (1983) ✔ Other Côtes de Provence.
🗝 *MM.* Engelson et Lebel, Ch. des Leoubes, 83230 Bormes-les-Mimosas; tel. 94 64 80 03 🍷 By appt.

CAVE COOPERATIVE LA LONDE-LES-MAURES**

■ 150ha 100000 2 D ▮ ↓

78 79 82 84

The Londe reds and rosés have a distinctive 'goût de terroir' from vineyard soils which contain traces of iodine. (1984)
🗝 Cave Coop. La Londe-les-Maures, Le Pansard, 83250 La Londe-les-Maures; tel. 94 66 80 23 🍷 By appt.

DOMAINE DE LA MALHERBE***

□ 8ha 15000 4 D ▮ ↓

Very pale, golden-green colour. Rolle grapes, very careful vinification, soil, and the unique microclimate all give extra flavour and bouquet. Particularly well presented. (1984)
🗝 Serge Ferrari, La Malherbe, 83230 Borues-les-Mimosas; tel. 94 64 80 40. 🍷 Daily 9.00–12.00/14.00–18.00. Closed Sat. and Sun. out of season.

DOMAINE DE LA MALHERBE***

◪ 13ha 35000 4 D ▮ ↓

A rosé with an extraordinarily, even surprisingly, intense nose. Do not underestimate. (1984)
🗝 Serge Ferrari, La Malherbe, 83230 Bormes-les-Mimosas; tel. 94 64 80 40 🍷 Daily 9.00–12.00/14.00–18.00. Sat. and Sun. Closed out of season.

CHATEAU MINUTY**

■ 30ha 62000 4 D ⊕ ↓

Grenache gives alcohol, Cinsaut elegance and Syrah and Mourvèdre spices and a raspberry nose. Ageing in wood has given a flavour of vanilla, and whole grape fermentation makes it reminiscent of a faded rose. Rich and enchanting; lacking for nothing. (1983)
🗝 Jean Farnet, Ch. Minuty, Gassin, 83990 St-Tropez; tel. 94 56 12 09 🍷 Mon.–Sat. 9.00–12.00/14.00–19.00.

CLOS MIREILLE***

□ 40ha 160000 5 D ⊕ ↓

The land and climate here are said to be the least favourable for white wine: schistous rock close to the sea. Despite this the Ott family have produced a firm, well-made, flavoursome white. Curiously shaped bottle. (1983)
🗝 Dom. Ott, 22 Bld d'Aiguillon, 06600 Antibes; tel. 93 34 38 91 🍷 Daily 8.00–12.00/14.00–18.00.

DOMAINE DE LA NAVARRE**

■ 10ha 5400 4 D ▮ ⊕ ↓

(80) 80 *81 *82 *83 84

This 1980 red *'Darrie li Faïs'* is full-bodied, with good alcohol, and promises to age well. (1980) ✔ Côtes de Provence Rouge, Côtes de Provence Rosé, Côtes de Provence Blanc Sec.
🗝 *M.* Viguier, Fondation Dom. la Navarre, 83260 La Crau; tel. 94 66 73 10 🍷 By appt.

NICOLAS
*Caves des Vignerons de Collobrières**

◪ 304000 2 ▮ ↓

Attractive pink colour and fresh, floral, fruity bouquet. Smooth and fresh on the palate, this is a pleasing wine which should be well cooled before serving.
🗝 Ets Nicolas, 2 Rue de Valmy, 94220 Charenton; tel. 01 37 59 20.

DOMAINE DE PEISSONNEL*

◪ 15ha 15000 3 D ▮ ↓

75 78 80 *82 *83 *84

Amber-coloured rosé with flowery and, oddly, slightly tannic nose. On the palate the tannin takes over. (1983) ✔ Côtes de Provence Rouge.
🗝 Pierre Lemaître, Dom. de Peissonnel, 83550 Vidauban; tel. 94 73 02 96 🍷 Daily 9.00–12.00/14.00–20.00.

LA PELLEGRINE

◪ 25ha 15000 3 D ▮ ↓

79 81 83

Classic rosé. Keeps its youthful nose for a long time. Drink cool, but not chilled. (1983) ✔ Côtes de Provence le Val d'Anrieu Rouge and Blanc.
🗝 Jean Poussel, Dom. le Val d'Anrieu, 83590 Gonfaron; tel. 94 78 30 93 🍷 By appt.

COMMANDERIE DE PEYRASSOL
*Marie-Estèlle***

■ 1ha 5000 4 D ⊕ ↓

81 81 82 *83

Fine red colour, with intense perfume of ripe fruit and apricot. Elegant and pleasant on the palate, with good balance and long finish. A very fine bottle, without doubt the best from this property. (1981) ✔ Vin de Pays du Var.
🗝 Yves Rigord, Dom. de Peyrassol, Flassans-sur-Issole, 83340 Le Luc; tel. 94 69 71 02 🍷 By appt.

COMMANDERIE DE PEYRASSOL
Cavalier Rose★★

| 🗺 | | 25ha | 125000 | 🔳3 D 🍾 ⬇ |

81 83 **83** 84 **84**

Bright, lively rosé revealing scents of exotic fruit. Flavour and delicacy without any lack of crisp acidity, and enriched by a hint of spice. (1983) ✔ Vin de Pays du Var. ◄► Yves Rigord, Dom. de Peyrassol, Flassans-sur-Issole, 83340 Le Luc; tel. 94 69 71 02 ⵣ By appt.

COMMANDERIE DE PEYRASSOL
Cuvée Eperon d'Or★

| ☐ | | 4ha | 25000 | 🔳3 D 🍾 ⬇ |

78 80 83 **83** 84 **84**

Extremely pale, attractive colour. Delicate, light, flowery nose. Elegance is confirmed on the palate, with a distinguished, bitter finish. (1983) ✔ Vin de Pays du Var. ◄► Yves Rigord, Dom. de Peyrassol, Flassans-sur-Issole, 83340 Le Luc; tel. 94 69 71 02 ⵣ By appt.

COMMANDERIE DE PEYRASSOL
Cuvée Eperon d'Or★

| ◼ | | 30ha | 125000 | 🔳3 D 🔵 ⬇ |

78 80 *81 *82 **82** *83 **83**

Deep, garnet-red colour and a nose with perfumes of vanilla and spices, in which stock is the strongest. Warm, pleasing and soft. Pleasing wine that may be drunk from now on. (1982) ◄► Yves Rigord, Dom. de Peyrassol, Flassans-sur-Issole, 83340 Le Luc; tel. 94 69 71 02 ⵣ By appt.

DOMAINE DES PLANES★★

| ◼ | | 5ha | 5400 | 🔳2 D 🔵 ⬇ |

78 81 82 *83 84

Firm and sound on the palate and should keep well. Spicy and fruity nose should develop further. (1983) ✔ Côtes de Provence Tibouren Rosé, Côtes de Provence Blanc de Blancs, and Vin de Var Muscat Fruité Sec. ◄► Christophe et Ilsé Rieder, Dom. des Planes, 83520 Roquebrune-sur-Argens; tel. 94 45 70 49 ⵣ Mon.–Sat. 8.30–12.00/14.00–19.00. Closed Sun. and public holidays.

ETS PRADEL★

| 🗺 | | 100ha | 240000 | 🔳3 D 🍾 ⬇ |

Relatively full-bodied and has passed lengthy testing with flying colours. Good alcohol, youth and fruit. (1982) ◄► Ets Pradel, Le Logis de Bonneau, 06270 Villeneuve-Loubet; tel. 93 20 81 71 ⵣ No visitors.

COOPERATIVE LA PUGETOISE
Coste Brulade★★

| 🗺 | | 200ha | 300000 | 🔳2 D 🍾 ⬇ |

64 72 ⑦ 83 84

Successful blend in both red and rosé wines. Well balanced, warm, and gives off the perfume of raspberries and spices. The colour of the rosés holds up, and they are relatively full-bodied. (1983) ◄► Coop. la Pugetoise, 83750 Puget-Ville; tel. 94 48 31 05 ⵣ By appt.

DOMAINE CHRISTIANE RABIEGA★★

| ◼ | | 3ha | 11000 | 🔳4 D 🍾 🔵 ⬇ |

*78 *80 **80** *82 **82** *83 **83**

Lovely dark ruby colour. Powerful but fleeting meaty scents accompanied by spices. Still young and a little harsh on the palate, but a powerful, slightly alcoholic body confirms it will age without difficulty. (1983) ◄► *M.* et *Mme* Lengagne-Rabiega, Clos Dière-Méridional, 83300 Draguignan; tel. 94 68 44 22 ⵣ Daily 9.00–12.00/14.00–19.00. ◄► *M.* Lengagne.

DOMAINE CHRISTIANE RABIEGA★★

| 🗺 | | 8ha | 46000 | 🔳3 D 🍾 ⬇ |

78 80 **82** 83

Very pale rosé. Light, elegant nose and surprising palate of body and substance, with spicy flavours developing. Unique and extremely pleasant. (1982) ✔ Côtes de Provence Rouge, Côtes de Provence Blanc. ◄► *M.* et *Mme* Lengagne-Ragiega, Clos Dière-Méridional, 83300 Draguignan; tel. 94 68 44 22 ⵣ Daily 9.00–12.00/14.00–19.00. ◄► *M.* Lengagne.

COOPERATIVE DE RAMATUELLE
Cuvée Tibouren★★

| 🗺 | | 178ha | 850000 | 🔳2 D 🍾 ⬇ |

80 82 83 ⑧④

Pleasant, refreshing rosé. Unique aromas of the Tibouren grape on the nose. Unusual but appealing. (1984) ◄► Coop. de Ramatuelle, les Boutinelles, 83350 Ramatuelle; tel. 94 79 23 60 ⵣ By appt.

DOMAINE DE RIMAURESQ★★★

| ◼ | | 22ha | 50000 | 🔳3 D 🔵 ⬇ |

78 *79 80 82 **82** 83 84

Exceptionally good colour, warmth, fruit and body. Rare white made from the Rolle, which has a good reputation of its own. (1982) ◄► SCI du Dom. de Rimauresq, 83790 Pignans; tel. 94 48 80 45 ⵣ Daily 8.00–12.00/14.00–18.00.

domaine de
Rimauresq
1982 *cru classé* e 75cl
Côtes de Provence
Appellation Côtes de Provence contrôlée

Mis en bouteille au Domaine FRANCE
Société Civile du Domaine de Rimauresq
Propriétaire à Pignans (Var)

CHATEAU DU ROUET★★

| ◼ | | 25ha | 130000 | 🔳2 D 🍾 🔵 ⬇ |

78 79 80 82 **83** 84

Fine garnet-coloured red. Spicy nose and full-bodied power. Has potential to age well. (1983) ✔ Côtes de Provence Ch. du Rouet Rosé, Côtes de Provence Ch. du Rouet Blanc, Mousseux Methode champenoise le Rouet Brut.

Bernard Savatier, Ch. du Rouet, 83490 Le Muy; tel. 94 45 16 00. ⵣ Daily 8.00–12.00/14.00–18.00.

CHATEAU DE ROUX★★★

◼		30 ha	50 000	3 D 🍷 ↓

78 80 82 83 ★84

Deep, velvety wine full of red fruit. Balanced and pleasant; warm and delicate. (1983) ✔ Côtes de Provence Rosé, Côtes de Provence Blanc.
Elisabeth Giraud, Ch. de Roux, Cannet-des-Maures, 83340 Le Luc; tel. 94 60 73 10 ⵣ By appt.

DOMAINE DE SAINT-ANDRE DE FIGUIERE★★

☐		2 ha	14 500	3 D 🍷 ↓

80 81 ★82 ★83 84

Beautiful pale colour. Flowery apricot nose and great length make it almost perfect. (1983) ✔ Côtes de Provence Cuveé de Marquis 82/83 Rouge, Côtes de Provence Cuveé Spéciale 82/83 Rouge, Côtes de Provence 83 Rosé, Côtes de Provence Grand Roy 83 Rouge.
André Connesson, Dom. de St-André de Figuière, 83250 La Londe-les-Maures; tel. 94 66 92 10 ⵣ By appt. Closed Jan.

DOMAINE DE SAINT-ANDRE DE FIGUIERE *Cuveé Spéciale*★★★

◼		4 ha	26 000	3 D 🍷 ↓

★82 82 ★83

Well made and soft, with rich, meaty overtones. The 1982 will probably open out more. (1982)
André Connesson, Dom. de St-André de Figuière, 83250 La Londe-les-Maures; tel. 94 66 92 10 ⵣ By appt. Closed Jan.

DOMAINE DE SAINT-ANDRE DE FIGUIERE *Cuvée du Marquis*★★

◼		3 ha	20 000	3 D 🍷 ↓

79 80 82 82 ★83

Splendid. At the peak of its powers. Powerful, pleasant meaty nose of Havanas, and a rich, flowing, lingering palate. (1982)
André Connesson, Dom. de St-André de Figuière, 83250 La Londe-les-Maures; tel. 94 66 92 10 ⵣ By appt. Closed Jan.

DOMAINE DE SAINT-BAILLON *Cuvée Roudaï*★★

◼		9 ha	3000	3 D 🍶 ↓

★82 ★83

Soft fruit, vanilla and pepper note with oak. Soft, alcoholic and lingering. Attractive. (1982)
Hervé Goudard, Dom. de St-Baillon, Flassans, 83340 Le Luc; tel. 94 69 74 60 ⵣ Daily 8.00–20.00.

DOMAINE DE SAINT-BAILLON★★

◼		9 ha	48 000	3 D 🍷 ↓

78 81 82 83

Strong nose of soft fruit. On the palate, full bodied, soft and lingering. (1982) ✔ Côtes de Provence Dom. de St-Baillon.
Hervé Goudard, Dom. de St-Baillon, Flassans 83340 Le Luc; tel. 94 69 74 60 ⵣ Daily 8.00–18.00.

DOMAINE DE SAINT-BAILLON★★

☑		9 ha	50 000	3 D 🍷 ↓

78 ★82 ★83

Traditional full body and very modern, exotic nose, indicating vinification at controlled temperatures. (1983)
Hervé Goudard, Dom. de St-Baillon, Flassans 83340 Le Luc; tel. 94 69 74 60 ⵣ Daily 8.00–20.00.

DOMAINE SAINT-JEAN★

◼		17 ha	10 000	2 🍷 ↓

81 ★82 ★83 83

Still rather youthful on the palate, but has alcohol and fullness. The Syrah is revealed on the nose. (1983)
Louis et Luce Maille, 42 Ave Ferrandin, 83570 Carcès; tel. 94 04 50 97 ⵣ By appt.

SAINT-PIERRE-DES-BAUX★★★

☐		6 ha	25 000	3 D 🍷 ↓

77 80 81 82 83 ★84

Light straw colour, the nose of the Sémillon with just the right amount of youthful acidity. (1983)
M. Kennel, Dom. des Baux, 83450 Pierrefeu; tel. 94 28 20 39 ⵣ By appt.

SAINT-PIERRE-DES-BAUX★★★

◼		10 ha	65 000	3 D 🍶 ↓

77 80 81 82 ★83 ★84

Partial ageing in casks has given a characteristic harmony, blending fruity flavours with rich meaty flavour and vanilla. (1983)
M. Kennel, Dom. des Baux, Pierrefeu-du-Var, 83390 Cuers; tel. 94 28 20 39 ⵣ By appt.

SAINT-PIERRE-DES-BAUX★★

☑		15 ha	100 000	3 D 🍷 ↓

76 77 80 82 83 ★84

Delicately coloured rosé with crisp nose that develops well on the palate. (1983)
M. Kennel, Dom. des Baux, Pierrefeu-du-Var, 83390 Cuers; tel. 94 28 20 39 ⵣ By appt.

CHATEAU SAINT-PIERRE★★★

☐ 1 ha 6000 [2] [D] [▮] [↓]

82 ⑧ 🄳 84

Very fine white. Intense perfume of lemon verbena, mandarin skin, acacia and honey. Full bodied and persistent. (1983)
➦ J. Victor, Ch. St-Pierre, 83460 Les Arcs-sur-Argens; tel. 94 47 41 47 ♈ By appt.

CHATEAU SAINT-PIERRE★★★

[▪] 6 ha 25 000 [2] [D] [▮] [↓]

79 81 82 83 🄳 ★84

Exhibits the raspberry and violet perfume of the Syrah and the spiciness of the Mourvèdre. Youthful and pleasant on the palate. A high-quality wine. (1983)
➦ J. Victor, Ch. St-Pierre, 83460 Les Arcs-sur-Argens; tel. 94 47 41 47 ♈ By appt.

CHATEAU SAINT-PIERRE★★★

[◪] 18 ha 100 000 [2] [D] [▮] [↓]

⑧ 83 🄳 84

One of the most famous rosés of this appellation. Smooth-drinking, with aromas of candied fruits. Richly endowed with all the qualities of a very good Côtes de Provence. (1984)
➦ J. Victor, Ch. St-Pierre, 83460 Les Arcs-sur-Argens; tel. 94 47 41 47 ♈ By appt.

DOMAINE LA SOURCE SAINTE-MARGUERITE★★

[▪] 6 ha 20 000 [2] [D] [▮] [↓]

⑧ 84 🄳

A bright, lively rosé, with a very clear colour; fresh and unaggressive. (1984)
➦ J.-R. Fayard, Dom. la Source Ste-Marguerite, 83250 La Londe-des-Maures; tel. 94 66 81 46 ♈ By appt. Closed in Feb.

CHATEAU SAINTE-ROSELINE★★★

[▪] 53 ha 250 000 [4] [D] [◑] [↓]

65 67 69 71 74 ★78 ★79 80 81

Very fine deep red, smelling of truffles and richly meaty. Lingering flavour. (1981)
➦ *Baron* Louis de Rasque de Laval, Ch. Ste-Roseline, 83460 Les Arcs-sur-Argens; tel. 94 73 32 57 ♈ By appt.

CHATEAU SAINTE-ROSELINE★★

☐ 10 ha 25 000 [4] [D] [▮] [↓]

80 81 82 83 84

Pale colour. Fragrances of pear, a little raspberry and almond shell. Crisp; good length. Very attractive. (1982)
➦ *Baron* Louis de Rasque de Laval, Ch. Ste-Roseline, 83460 Les Arcs-sur-Argens; tel. 94 73 32 57 ♈ By appt.

COOPERATIVE DE MONT-SAINTE-VICTOIRE★★

[◪] 100 ha 70 000 [1] [D] [▮] [↓]

82 83 84

Soft, rich and appealing. A perfect rosé. (1984)
➦ Coop. de Mont-Ste-Victoire, 13114 Puyloubier; tel. 42 29 24 07 ♈ By appt.

COOPERATIVE DE MONT-SAINTE-VICTOIRE★★

[▪] 200 ha 100 000 [1] [D] [▮] [↓]

74 75 76 77 ★82 ⑧

Lovely quality. Perfect product from the foot of Cézanne's beloved Ste-Victoire. (1983)
➦ Coop. de Mont-Ste-Victoire, 13114 Puyloubier; tel. 42 29 24 07 ♈ By appt.

CHATEAU DE SELLE

[◪] 30 ha 120 000 [5] [D] [◑] [↓]

Well-balanced rosé with distinctive aromas and a long finish. Low in acidity. (1983) ✔ Côtes de Provence Chateau de Selle Blanc Sec and Rouge, Bandol Coeur-de-Grain, Bandol Rosé, Bandol Rouge.
➦ Dom. Ott, 22 Bld d'Aiguillon, 06600 Antibes; tel. 93 34 38 91 ♈ Daily 9.00–12.00/14.00–18.00.

COOPERATIVE VINICOLE DE VIDAUBAN★★

[◪] 12 ha 56 000 [2] [D] [▮] [↓]

★⑧ ★84

Excellent, clear colour. Full of flavour on the palate, soft and lingering, with hint of toasted almond. (1983)
➦ Cave Coop. de Vidauban, 83550 Vidauban; tel. 94 73 00 12 ♈ By appt.

VIGNERONS PRESQU'ILE SAINT-TROPEZ *Carte Noire*★

[◪] 50 ha 300 000 [3] [D] [▮] [↓]

80 ★83 ★84

Particularly elegant bottle. Fruity rosé; fragrant and elegant. (1983)
➦ Vign. Presqu'Ile St-Tropez, Gassin, 83580 St-Tropez; tel. 94 56 32 04 ♈ Mon.–Thur. 8.00–12.00/14.00–18.00; Fri. 8.00–12.00/14.00–17.00. Closed 13 Oct.–4 Nov.

VIGNERONS PRESQU'ILE SAINT-TROPEZ *Carte Noire*★

[▪] 15 ha 100 000 [3] [D] [▮] [↓]

80 ★83 ★84

Substantial wine from balanced blend in which Syrah and Mourvèdre varieties can be noticed, with notes of raspberry and iodine. (1983)
➦ Vign Presqu'Ile St-Tropez, Gassin, 83990 St-Tropez; tel. 94 56 32 04 ♈ Mon.–Thur. 8.00–12.00/14.00–18.00; Fri. 8.00–12.00/14.00–17.00. Closed 13 Oct.–4 Nov.

Cassis

The small port of Cassis lies in an inaccessible rocky bay at the foot of imposing hill country west of Marseilles. Famous for its picturesque coves, its anchovies and a restorative natural spring, Cassis is also the principal town of a vineyard celebration in medieval times. In the eleventh century, the Pope was on hand to arbitrate in a dispute over ownership among powerful Church foundations. Today, Cassis produces red and rosé wines, but chiefly whites, described as smelling like rosemary, heather and myrtle. The wines are unpretentious (although not inexpensive) and go well with bouillabaisse, grilled fish, or shellfish cooked in a wine from the same appellation.

CLOS BOUDARD**

| □ | | | 4 D |

A good vintage despite the dreadful weather in this region. Pale greenish-gold with exotic aromas reminiscent of summer tones of almond and linden. (1984)
🌢 Pierre Marchand, Route de La Ciotat, 13160 Cassis; tel. 42 01 72 66 🍷 No visitors.

CHATEAU DE FONTBLANCHE**

| □ | 20ha | 140000 | 4 D ▣ ⌄ |
| 71 77 78 82 83 |

This estate is one of the pioneers in re-establishing one of the oldest of French wines. Its white is a brilliant yellow, soft but not feeble, developing slightly spicy aromas of linden. (1983)
🌢 J.J. bontoux-Bodin, Ch. de Fontblanche, La Tant, 13160 Cassis; tel. 42 01 00 11 🍷 By appt. Closed one week from 15 Aug.

CLOS SAINTE-MAGDELEINE*

| □ | 10ha | 40000 | 4 D ▣ ⌄ |
| 82 83 |

This wine has a straw-gold colour and is already mature. Aromas give an elegant hint of toasted almonds. Rich in alcohol (and should therefore be drunk thoroughly chilled). Honey flavoured with a slight touch of acidity. (1983)
🌢 GFA Sack-Zafiropulo, Clos Ste-Magdeleine, 13260 Cassis; tel. 42 01 70 28 🍷 Mon.–Sat. 10.00–18.00.

Bellet

Few people know this minute appellation in the hills behind Nice, and the wine is rarely found outside the area of production. Bellet's aromatic white wines come from two varieties: Rolle, a very distinctive grape, and Chardonnay, which can still produce fair-quality wine at this latitude if it has a northern exposure and a relatively high altitude. Bellet rosés are fresh and silky, and the reds are sumptuous, owing their original and distinctive character to the two local grape types, Fuella and Braquet. They should be served with the spicy and inventive Niçois cuisine.

CHATEAU DE CREMAT***

| ■ | 5ha | 19000 | 5 D ⦀ ⌄ |
| ★70 ★72 ★74 ★⑦⑧ 82 |

The classic Folle Noire and the Braquet produce red wines with a high alcohol content and exceptional lightness. Unforgettable nose. (1974)

458

🌢 *MM*. Bagnis et Fils, 42 Chemin de Crémat, 06200 Nice; tel. 93 86 14 71 🍷 By appt.

CHATEAU DE CREMAT**

| □ | 5ha | 19000 | 4 D ▣ ⌄ |

Lovely white wine bearing all the characteristics of the Rolle: toasted almonds with orange blossom and mandarin skins. (1983)
🌢 *MM*. Bagnis et Fils, 42 Chemin de Crémat, 06200 Nice; tel. 93 86 14 71 🍷 By appt.

Bandol

These noble wines are not actually produced in Bandol but on the sunburnt terraces of the surrounding villages. They may be white or rosé, but it is the reds, full-bodied and high in tannin from the Mourvèdre grape, which make up more than half of the appellation. Their generous flavour goes well with venison or red meat which enhance the subtle aromas of pepper, cinnamon, vanilla and black cherries. Bandol red wines can be kept for many years: 1983 should last for more than ten years, as did the 1965 and 1975 vintages.

CHATEAU DES BAUMELLES*

| ◪ | 6.5ha | 15000 | 4 D ⦀ ⌄ |

Still young and a little closed-in. A good buy if you have patience.
🌢 Thierry Grand, Ch. des Baumelles, 83270 St-Cyr-sur-Mer; tel. 94 26 46 59 🍷 By appt.

DOMAINE DU CAGUELOUP***

| ■ | 18ha | 120000 | 3 D ▣ ⌄ |
| ⑦⑥ ★78 80 82 |

Sumptuous and velvety, with aromas of vanilla, cinnamon, banana, coffee and toast. A surprising and attractive bottle. (1983)
🌢 Gaston Prébost, Dom. de Cagueloup, 83270 St-Cyr-sur-Mer; tel. 94 26 15 70 🍷 By appt.

MOULIN DES COSTES***

| ■ | 30ha | 120000 | 4 D ⦀ ⌄ |
| 74 75 76 77 78 79 80 81 82 83 |

The Moulin des Costes is an example of the success of enthusiastic young vine-growers who came from Algeria to resettle in the South of France. This red is already superb – mature and full bodied, with fragrances of vanilla, raspberry and cinnamon. (1981) 🖋 Bandol Rosé and Blanc.
🌢 Paul Bunan, Moulin des Costes, 83740 La Cadière-d'Azur; tel. 94 98 72 76 🍷 Mon.–Sat. 8.00–12.00/14.00–18.00.

DOMAINE DE FREGATE**

| ■ | 20ha | 25000 | 4 D ⦀ ⌄ |
| 71 ⑦⑤ ★78 ★79 80 81 ★82 84 |

The estate is situated on a pretty seaside cove, and has a splendid wine-cellar cut into hard rock. This fine 1981 is a deep ruby colour with fruity scents mingling with pepper and cinnamon. It still has a little too much tannin but will open up and

gain maturity. (1981) ✔ Bandol Rosé and Blanc.
➤ Dom. N.-Dame du Port d'Alon. Dom. de Fregate, 83270 St-Cyr-sur-Mer; tel. 94 26 17 02 ⚓ Mon.–Fri. 9.00–12.00/14.00–18.00.

DOMAINE LE GALANTIN★★

■   12ha   28 000   ▣ Ⓓ ⑪ ⌄
78 **80** 82 83

Beautiful colour, and powerful fragrant scents of cinnamon and spices. A very alcoholic wine at the peak of perfection. (1980) ✔ Bandol, Blanc and Rosé.
➤ Pascal Achille, Dom. le Galantin, Le Plan-du-Castellet, 83330 Bandol; tel. 94 98 75 94 ⚓ By appt.

DOMAINE DE L'HERMITAGE★★★

■   36ha   105 000   ▣ Ⓓ ⑪ ⌄
⑦⑤ 81 **82**

Le Rouve is a part of Le Beausset which overlooks most of the Bandol area. M. Duffort has totally restored this estate incuding the vines and the cellars. His 1982 red is a splendid affair, full, flowing and lingering, with a warm, spicy nose. (1982) ✔ Bandol Blanc de Blancs, Bandol Rosé.
➤ G. Duffort, Dom. de l'Hermitage, 83330 Le Beausset;˙ tel. 94 98 71 31 ⚓ Mon.–Fri. 8.00–18.00. Sat. 8.00–12.00.

DOMAINE LAFRAN-VEYROLLES★★★

■   8ha   25 000   ▣ Ⓓ ⑪ ⌄
80 **81** 82

This wine, raised at a Cadière-d'Azur, has the powerful and complex nose one would expect. Good balance. Lingering on the palate. (1981)
➤ *Mme* Jouve-Férec, Dom. Lafran-Veyrolles, 83740 La Cadière-d'Azur; tel. 94 29 33 37 ⚓ By appt. Closed Sun.

DOMAINE LAFRAN-VEYROLLES★

▨   1500   ▣ Ⓓ ⑪ ⌄
81 82 83

Pale pink, elegant and fine. Possibly a little unobtrusive. Its true value can only be appreciated by those who take time to savour it. (1981)
➤ *Mme* Jouve-Férec, Dom. Lafran-Veyrolles, 83740 La Cadière-d'Azur; tel. 94 29 33 37 ⚓ By appt. Closed Sun.

DOMAINE DE LA LAIDIERE
Carte Noire★★★

■   8ha   400 000   ▣ Ⓓ ⑪ ⌄
75 78 **79** 80 81 **82**

A superb, brilliant deep red. Strong nose of cinnamon, banana, vanilla and raspberry, coupled with body which is both powerful and soft. A sumptuous wine with a long life ahead of it. (1982) ✔ Bandol Blanc Liquoreux, Rosé La Laidière.
➤ GAEC Estienne, Dom. de la Laidière, Evenos, 83330 Le Beausset; tel. 94 90 37 07 ⚓ Mon.–Fri. 8.00–12.00/14.00–18.00; Sat. 8.00–12.00.

DOMAINE DE LA NOBLESSE★★

■   10ha   25 000   ▣ Ⓓ ⫞ ⑪ ⌄ .
78 79 **80** 82 83

A powerful and well-made wine, characteristic of its output. The colour is good and the nose becomes gradually firmer, taking five to ten years to develop. (1983)
➤ Jean-Pierre Gaussen, Dom. de la Noblesse, 83740 La Cadière-d'Azur; tel. 94 98 75 54 ⚓ By appt.

DOMAINE DE PIBARNON★

□   3ha   10 000   ▣ Ⓓ ⫞ ⑪ ⌄
83 84

This vintage has a pale, straw-gold colour and a flowery, hawthorn-like fragrance. In the mouth it is smooth, well-balanced, with a long finish. (1983)
➤ Comte de St-Victor, Dom. de Pibarnon, 83740 La Cadière-d'Azur; tel. 94 29 32 73 ⚓ Daily 9.00–12.00/14.00–19.00.

DOMAINE DE PIBARNON★

▨   24ha   30 000   ▣ Ⓓ ⑪ ⌄
83 84

A well-balanced wine with a rather light but very delicate nose. Warm and smooth, this is a true Provence wine. (1983)
➤ Comte de St-Victor, Dom. de Pibarnon, 83740 La Cadière-d'Azur; tel. 94 29 32 73 ⚓ Daily 9.00–12.00/14.00–19.00.

CHATEAU PRADEAUX★★★

■   24ha   40 000   ▣ Ⓓ ⑪ ⌄
64 66 69 72 74 **75** ⑦⑧ 78 79

A very big wine, as yet a little hard but also noble and powerful. Aromas of West Indian hardwood, fine leather, havana, liquorice and prune on the nose. (1975)
➤ *Mlle* de Portalis, Ch. Pradeaux, 83270 St-Cyr-sur-Mer; tel. 94 26 10 74 ⚓ By appt.

CHATEAU ROMASSON★★

■   10ha   40 000   ▣ Ⓓ ⑪ ⌄

These wines, in their distinctive bottles, live up to the reputation of the Ott properties. Fragrant reds, bright in colour and lighter than is customary of Provence reds. (1981)
➤ Dom. Ott, Bld d'Aiguillon, 06600 Antibes; tel. 93 34 38 91 ⚓ Daily 9.00–12.00/14.00–18.00.

459

LE MOULIN DE LA ROQUE★

■	100ha	160000	**3** D ▮ ↓

76 78 80 **81** 82

A carefully made wine with a nose of violet and liquorice, long on the palate. An excellent buy. (1982) ✔ Bandol Rosé and Blanc, Bandol Rouge Tradition.
•┓ Coop. des Vins de Bandol, Caves du Moulin de la Roque, 83740 La Cadière-d'Azur; tel. 94293039 ⊤ Mon.–Fri. 8.00–12.00/13.30–17.30; Sat. 8.00–12.00. Closed Sun. and public holidays.

CHATEAU SAINTE-ANNE★★

■	6ha	25000	**4** D ⚌ ↓

79 81 **82** 83 84

This excellent vineyard straddles the Aires de Bandol and the Côtes de Provence. Its very fine wines include an 1982 Bandol with a deep full colour, and a very characteristic full nose. The wine has tannin and is suitable for laying down. (1982)
•┓ M. Dutheil de la Rochère, Ch. Ste-Anne, Evenos, 83330 le Beausset; tel. 94903540 ⊤ Mon.–Sat. 8.00–12.00/14.00–18.00.

CHATEAU SAINTE-ANNE★

◪	6ha	25000	**3** D ▮ ↓

82 ⑧② 83 84

A very pale rosé with a fine nose and an elegant body, so light that it almost vanishes. (1983) ✔ Bandol Ch. Ste-Anne Rouge and Blanc Côtes de Provence Ch. Ste-Anne Rosé.
•┓ M. Dutheil de la Rochère, Ch. Ste-Anne, Evenos, 83330 Le Beausset; tel. 94903540 ⊤ Mon.–Sat. 8.00–12.00/14.00–18.00.

DOMAINE DES SALETTES★★

■	17ha	35000	**4** D ⚌ ↓

70 ⑦⓪ 75 78 79 **80** 81 82

Wines from the stony slopes of the Mal Passé. The reds are full-bodied and complex, the rosés delicate and the whites lively. (1982)
•┓ M. Boyer, Dom. des Salettes, 83740 La Cadière-d'Azur; tel. 94293086 ⊤ By appt.

DOMAINE TEMPIER★★

■	20ha	50000	**4** D ⚌ ↓

70 71 78 81 82 83

Richly coloured; flowery palate; full bodied, with good tannin. Generous and lingers on the palate. Allowed to age before drinking a little below room temperature.
•┓ GAEC Peyraud, Dom. Tempier, 83330 Le Plan-du-Castelet; tel. 94987021 ⊤ By appt.

DOMAINE TEMPIER

■	25ha	90000	**5** D ⚌ ↓

M. Peyraud is justly regarded as the mainspring of the revival of the Bandol area. He promotes the Mourvèdre grape and cask-matured wines and his estate is known for its powerful tannic reds which age so well. (1982)
•┓ GAEC Peyraud, Dom. Tempier, 83330 Le Plan-du-Castelet; tel. 94987021 ⊤ By appt. Closed Sun., and public holidays.

CHATEAU VANNIERES★★

■	27ha	108000	**4** D ⚌ ↓

75 ⑦⑤ 78 79 81 **82** 84

This 1982 vintage has the true Bandolais colour, bouquet and structure. Spices and fine tannin on the palate, together with lingering aromas. It should be at its peak in three to four years' time. (1982) ✔ Côtes de Provence Rouge, and Rosé, Bandol Rosé.
•┓ M. Boisseaux, Ch. Vannières, 83740 La Cadière-d'Azur; tel. 94293119 ⊤ Daily 8.00–12.00/14.00–18.00. Closed Jan.

Coteaux d'Aix-en-Provence

The Coteaux d'Aix vineyards are dotted amongst the woods and scrubland east of Aix-en-Provence and north-west of Marseilles. They fall mostly within the Bouches-du-Rhône department, although they also extend westwards into the Var. About 3000 hectares of vines are planted on hillsides that are sheltered from the Mistral wind. Despite a past history of underinvestment and indifferent viticulture in the region, today's wine-makers have made great strides to improve the quality of their wine, efforts that have recently been rewarded by the promotion of the wines from VDQS to AOC. The vineyards are gradually being replanted with better grape varieties. Among the red wines, for example, the Syrah, Mourvèdre, or Cabernet now contribute quality to the previously dominant Grenache, and the Cinsault is steadily replacing the Carignan as the grape type to give the wine tannic structure. Temperature control is also an important technological development.

The red wines, grown mostly on clay-limestone soils, have good structure. The bouquet varies according to the type of grape used; if Mourvèdre is the predominant variety, the wine has a delicate, slightly gamey bouquet; if it is Syrah, the wine is flowery and fruity, while Cabernet wines have a fragrance of balsam. They all age quite rapidly and so are best drunk after two or three years. The younger they are, the more versatile they prove at partnering food.

The rosé wines often come, at least in part, from quite tannic grape varieties. They are vigorous enough to match dishes that may be difficult for a white or red wine, such as aïoli, bourride, brandade de morue (a cod dish), or poutargue. A few refreshing white wines are also made; they are best drunk young.

CHATEAU BARBERELLE *Cuvée Jas d'Amour**

■   28ha 177000 **2 D ▮ ⅰ ⅰ**

Beautiful, rather youthful colour. The bouquet has a high pitch with notes of violet, cherry and plum, confirmed on the palate, which has warm richness, perhaps too warm for some tastes. An attractive wine of its type. (1982)
🍷 Brice Herbeau, Ch. Barberelle, 13840 Rognes; tel. 42 50 22 12 ⌘ Daily 8.30–18.30.

COMMANDERIE DE LA BARGEMONE**

■   60ha 360000 **D ▮ ⅰ ⅰ**

Light ruby in colour, with a rich, pleasant fruity nose. On the palate it is full and well balanced, with a flowery, fruity fragrance dominated by muscari and freesia. Very seductive, with excellent staying power. (1983) ✔ Coteaux d'Aix Cuvée Tournebride 80 Rouge.
🍷 Jean-Pierre Rozan, RN 7, 13760 St-Cannat; tel. 42 28 22 44 ⌘ By appt. Closed Sun. afternoon.

CHATEAU BAS*

■   60ha 360000 **2 D ⅰ ⅰ**

Very pleasant wine with a pronounced purple-ruby colour. Fruity on the nose and palate, with length, roundness and a good finish. (1983) ✔ Vin de Pays Dom. de St-Césaire Rouge, and Rosé.
🍷 Georges de Blanquet, Dom. de Ch. Bas, 13116 Vernègues; tel. 90 59 13 16 ⌘ Mon.–Sat. 8.00–12.00/13.30–18.00.

DOMAINE LES BASTIDES *Cuvée Saint-Pierre*

■   5ha 30000 **3 D ⅰ ⅰ**

A nose of stone fruit and berries, with hint of greenery. Very warm character on the palate. Finish is a little dry. Those who like a very warm wine will appreciate this one, which should be drunk young. (1982) ✔ Other Coteaux d'Aix wines.
🍷 Jean Salen, Dom. les Bastides, St-Canadet, 13610 Le-Puy-Ste-Réparade; tel. 42 28 62 66 ⌘ Daily 8.00–13.00/14.00–19.00.

CHATEAU DE BEAULIEU*

☐   20ha 168000 **2 D ▮ ⅰ**

Characteristically southern; pleasant and rather warm. Drink young. (1983)
🍷 Robert Touzet, Ch. de Beaulieu, 13840 Rognes; tel. 42 50 24 07 ⌘ By appt.

CHATEAU DE BEAULIEU**

■   75ha 360000 **2 D ▮ ⅰ**

Lively colour with lovely range of fruity and flowery notes. Mature nose. Full bodied and lingering on the palate. Well balanced with plenty of flavour and longevity.
🍷 Robert Touzet, Ch. de Beaulieu, 13840 Rognes; tel. 42 50 24 07 ⌘ By appt.

CHATEAU DE BEAULIEU*

◪   180ha 720000 **2 D ▮ ⅰ**

Its fruity nose is rather light, but there is a touch of liveliness on the palate. A light wine that is best drunk very young. (1983)
🍷 Robert Touzet Ch. de Beaulieu 13840 Rognes; tel. 42 50 24 07 ⌘ By appt.

CHATEAU DE CALISSANNE***

■   15ha **3 D ⅰ ⅰ**

Beautiful deep red with very full nose of stone fruit. On the palate full and substantial with flavour of very ripe 'cooked' fruit with hints of vanilla and caramel. High-quality. May be left for some time to develop but is already drinking well. (1983) ✔ Coteaux d'Aix-en-Provence Rosé and Blanc, Vin de Pays des Bouches-du-Rhône Rouge, Rosé and Blanc.
🍷 Les toques Gourmardes, 29 bis Route de Versailles, 78560 Port-Marly; tel. 01 91 61 17 ⌘ By appt.

CHATEAU LA COSTE**

◪   20ha 240000 **2 D ▮ ⅰ**

A 'vigorous' rosé. Powerful flavour from grape varieties with good tannin. Justifies the existence of the rosé type that cannot be replaced by a white or red. Very noteworthy. ✔ Other Coteaux d'Aix wines.
🍷 SICA Bordonado, Ch. la Coste, 13610 Le Puy-Ste-Réparade; tel. 42 61 89 98 ⌘ Mon., Wed. and Sat. 8.00 –12.00/14.00–18.00.

CHATEAU LA COSTE**

☐   10ha 60000 **2 D ▮ ⅰ**

Full nose; very fruity; enlivened with a touch of saucisson. Well made and full on the palate, with excellent balance and plenty of flavour and elegance. (1984) ✔ Other Coteaux d'Aix wines
🍷 SICA Bordonado, Ch. la Coste, 13610 Puy-Ste-Réparade; tel. 42 61 89 98 ⌘ Mon., Wed. and Sat. 8.00–12.00/14.00–18.00.

CHATEAU LA COSTE***

■   110ha 1200000 **2 D ▮ ⅰ**
82

Pleasing, bright, intense ruby colour. Range of aromas which are woody and of very ripe fruit lie over a background of green forests. Full and perfectly balanced on the palate. Round, with solid structure, yet not harsh. Fine length and an excellent aromatic, warm finish. A bottle full of quality and charm. ✔ Coteau-d'Aix Rosé and Blanc Sec.
🍷 SICA Bordonado, Ch. La Coste, 13610 Le Puy-Sainte-Réparade; tel. 42 61 89 98 ⌘ By appt.

CHATEAU DE FONSCOLOMBE★★

☐   160ha 126000 ▣ D ◧ ↓

Attractive, soft pale colour. Intensely fruity nose with scent of lychees. Very pleasant on the palate with good acidity not often found in the southern region. Drink young. (1983) ✔ Other Vin de Pays des Bouches-du-Rhône wines.
✦ SCA Ch. de Fonscolombe, 13610 Le Puy-Ste-Réparade; tel. 42 61 89 62 ▾ By appt. Closed 6–20 Aug. ✦ M. le Marquis de Saporta.

MAS DE GOURGONNIER *Coteaux des Baux-de-Provence*

▨   5ha 30000 ▣ D ▤ ↓

Pink colour beginning to take on a yellowish tinge. Light fruity nose, and very warm on the palate. Could have more positive acidity. Drink young (1983)
✦ Nicolas Cartier, Mas de Gourgonnier, Le Destet, 13890 Mouriès; tel. 90 47 50 45 ▾ Mon.–Sat. 8.00–12.00/13.30–19.00. Sun. 9.00–12.00/15.00–18.00.

MAS DE GOURGONNIER *Coteaux des Baux-de-Provence*★★

■   5ha 25000 ▣ D ▤ ↓

Softly fruited nose. Full and generous on the palate, with the rather dominant warmth of the 1982s. Very good. (1982)
✦ Nicolas Cartier, Mas de Gourgonnier, Le Destet, 13890 Mouriès; tel. 90 47 50 45 ▾ Mon.–Sat. 8.00–12.00/13.30–19.00. Sun. 9.00–12.00/15.00–18.00.

DOMAINE DE LA GRANDE SEOUVE★★

■   35ha 200000 ▣ D ▤ ↓

Remarkably crisp and fruity. Drink young. (1983) ✔ Chateau la Coste.
✦ GFA de la Grande Séouve, Dom. de la Boulangère, 13490 Jouques; tel. 42 28 60 28 ▾ By appt.

CHATEAU GRAND-SEUIL★

▨   45ha 240000 ▣ D ▤ ◧ ↓

The youthful nose is obtained by growing varieties of grape that have been very carefully chosen; the results are very happy. (1984) ✔ Other Coteaux d'Aix wines.
✦ M. et *Mme* Carreau-Gaschereau, Ch. du Seuil, 13540 Puyricard; tel. 42 92 15 99 ▾ Daily 8.00–12.00/14.00–18.30.

CHATEAU MAS DE L'HOPITAL★★

☐   4ha 25000 ▣ D ▤ ↓

Good-looking wine with fruity nose and light hint of Sauvignon. Flowery and well balanced palate. Drink young. (1983)
✦ Charles Sardou, Ch. Vignerolles, Gignac-la-Nerthe, 13700 Marignane; tel. 42 88 55 15 ▾ By appt.

CHATEAU MAS DE L'HOPITAL★★

▨   14ha 90000 ▣ D ▤ ↓

Good fruity nose followed by fine fragrant qualities on the palate, together with a light refreshing acidity. Easy to drink. A very attractive rosé. (1984)
✦ Charles Sardou, Ch. Vignerolles, Gignac-la-Nerthe, 13700 Marigrane; tel. 42 88 55 15 ▾ By appt ✦ Sté Civ. du Mas de l'Hôpital.

CHATEAU MAS DE L'HOPITAL★

■   52ha 300000 ▣ D ▤ ↓

Lovely yellow colour. Very attractive, open nose. Full and fat on the palate, with a slight coarseness characteristic of this region. Already very fruity and full of promise. (1984)
✦ Charles Sardou, Ch. Vignerolles, Gignac-la-Nerthe, 13700 Marignane; tel. 42 88 55 15 ▾ By appt.

DOMAINE DES LAUZIERES
Coteaux des Baux-de-Provence★

■   30ha 18000 ▣ D ▤ ↓

Pleasant, classic wine. Nose of stone fruits. Well balanced on the palate, with a severity that should disappear with age. (1982)
✦ Les Filles de Joseph Boyer, Dom. des Lauzières, 13890 Mouriès; tel. 42 04 70 39 ▾ Mon.–Sat. 8.00–12.00/13.30–18.30. Closed Sun. and public holidays.

MAS DE LA DAME
Coteaux des Baux-de-Provence★★

■   50ha 300000 ▣ D ▤ ◧ ↓

Beautiful burnt-ruby colour. Fully mature nose, complex and long-lived. Well-balanced, rich, full-bodied palate, with a touch of new-mown hay in its fruit. Lovely and warm; fills the mouth with the scent of tropical fruits. (1982) ✔ Coteaux des Baux Rosé, Coteaux des Baux Cuvée Gourmande Rouge.
✦ Sté Fermière du Mas de la Dame, Dom. de Vilmorin, 13520 Les Baux-de-Provence; tel. 90 97 32 24 ▾ By appt.

MAS DE LA DAME
Coteaux de Baux-de-Provence★★

▨   12ha 60000 ▣ D ▤ ↓

Beautiful light-pink colour. Rich-fruit nose. Well-balanced in the mouth, with positive acidity predominant in its elegant style. An interesting rosé with a lingering aftertaste. (1984)
✦ Ste. Fermière du Mas de la Dame, Dom. de Vilmorin, 13520 Les-Baux-de-Provence; tel. 90 97 32 24 ▾ By appt. Closed Sun. and public holidays.

MAS SAINTE-BERTHE *Coteaux des Baux-de-Provence*

◪ 35ha 192000 2 D ▮ ◖◗ ⫰

Pleasant, light colour and bouquet of banana and berries. A little unripe on the palate. Would suit dishes requiring a lively wine. (1984)
Mme Hélène David, Mas Ste-Berthe, 13520 Les Baux-en-Provence; tel. 90 97 34 01 Y By appt.

CHATEAU DU SEUIL *Chateau du Grand Seuil***

■ 25ha 120000 3 D ▮ ◖◗ ⫰

Elegant, deep ruby colour. Slightly spicy, very unique nose. On the palate this spiciness is confirmed, with an added touch reminiscent of lichen – rare in a red wine. Well made and of good quality. (1983) ✔ Coteaux d'Aix-en-Provence Chateau du Seuil Rosé, Le Grand Seuil
M. et *Mme* Carreau-Gaschereau, Ch. du Seuil, 13540 Puyricard; tel. 42 92 15 99 Y Daily 8.00–12.00/14.00–18.30.

TERRES BLANCHES *Coteaux des Baux-de-Provence*

■ 5ha 150000 3 D ◖◗ ⫰

Lovely colour. Fruity nose contains a hint of greenery. This classic example of the appellation will be enjoyed by those who like their wines austere. (1982)
Noel Michelin, Terres Blanches, 13210 St. Rémy-de-Provence; tel. 90 95 91 66 Y Mon.–Sat. 8.00–12.00/14.00–18.00.

DOMAINE DE LA VALLONGUE *Coteaux des Baux-de-Provence***

■ 34ha 228000 3 D ◖◗ ⫰

The nose hovers between youthful tones, including an exotic fruity aroma, and a maturity revealed in hints of leather, tobacco and game. Its unique quality is confirmed on the palate, mature and full bodied with a distinctive fragrance. A very fine bottle. (1983) ✔ Vin de Pays des Bouches-du-Rhône '3 Mas'
Philippe-Paul Cavallier, Dom. de la Vallongue, 13810 Eygalières; tel. 90 95 91 70 Y By appt.

DOMAINE DE LA VALLONGUE *Coteaux des Baux-de-Provence***

◪ 11ha 75000 2 D ◖◗ ⫰

Pretty 'old rose' colour. Lovely fruity nose. Very crisp, with fruited, flowery aromas, light on the palate and well balanced. Has kept well, but would have been even better when younger. Serve chilled. (1983) ✔ Vin de Pays des Bouches-du-Rhône '3 mas'.
Philippe-Paul Cavallier, Dom. de la Vallongue, 13810 Eygalières; tel. 90 95 91 70 Y By appt.

COOPERATIVE VINICOLE DE VELAUX-COUDOUX*

■ 75ha 400000 2 D ▮ ⫰

Classic red colour. The nose is already mature, still fruity but developing towards new-mown hay; confirmed on the palate where the wine is very pleasant and round.
Coop. de Velaux-Coudoux, 13880 Velaux-Coudoux; tel. 42 87 92 09 Y By appt.

CHATEAU VIGNELAURE***

■ 55ha 5000 4 D ◖◗ ⫰

(82)

Perhaps more typical of Aquitaine than Provence. Undoubtedly has class. Richly varied bouquet, remarkable fullness on the palate, and a character which makes it good to drink with game fowl. (1979)
Georges Brunet, Ch. Vignelaure, 83560 Rians; tel. 94 80 31 93 Y Mon.–Sat. 8.00–12.30/14.00–18.30. Sun. 10.30–12.30/14.30–18.30.

Coteaux Varois VDQS

Recently created VDQS, Coteaux Varois wines are produced around Brignoles, in the centre of the department of Var. The wines (red and rosé) should be drunk young and are cheerful, fruity and lively, in keeping with the image of this pretty little Provençal village, once the summer retreat of the medieval counts of Provence.

DOMAINE DU DEFFENDS *Rosé d'Une Nuit*

◪ 1ha 5000 2 D ▮ ⫰

*83 83

Attractive, light rosé. Honey nose. On the palate, finishes with a touch of raspberry and a slight bitterness. (1983)
J.S. de Lanversin, 83470 St-Maximin; tel. 94 78 03 91 Y By appt.

DOMAINE DE FONTAINBLEAU

◪ 4ha 26000 2 D ▮ ⫰

Attractive, clear colour with tinges of orange, and aromas of cherry brandy. Warm on the palate, it leaves a flavour which is beautifully long. (Limited production only.)
Hector Serra, Dom. de Fontainebleau, 83143 Le Val; tel. 94 59 59 09 Y Daily 8.00–12.00/14.00–18.00.

DOMAINE DE FONTAINBLEAU

■ 9ha 60000 2 D ▮ ◖◗ ⫰

This attractive red wine, with its bright colour and light, chestnut nose has a slightly thin palate, which will improve with age. (1983)
Hector Serra, Dom. de Fontainebleau, 83143 Le Val; tel. 94 59 59 09 Y Daily 8.00–12.00/14.00–18.00.

LA GAREOULTAISE *Carte Noire**

■ 60ha 30000 2 ▮ ⫰

Fine colour with mature aromas of venison and dishes cooked in wine. Ready to drink from now on. (1983) ✔ Coteaux du Varois Rosé.
Coop. Roguebrusanne la Garéoultaise, Garéoult 83136; tel. 94 04 92 09 Y By appt.

LA GAREOULTAISE *Carte Or**

◪ 70ha 40000 2 ▮ ⫰

Slightly brick-red colour and aromas of toasted hazelnut. Fresh and harmonious. (1983)
Coop. la Garéoultaise, Garéoult 83136 Roguebrusanne; tel. 94 04 92 09 Y By appt.

DOMAINE DE LA LIEUE★★

☑ 10ha 50000 **2 D ▮ ↓**
⑧ **84**

Deep nasturtium colour. Nose reminiscent of liquorice. Supple, flowing, harmonious and lingering on the palate. (1983) ✔ Coteaux Varois Rouge, Vin de Pays du Var Blanc.
↝ Jean-Louis Vial, Dom. de la Lieue, 83170 Brignoles; tel. 94 69 00 12 ⍭ Daily 9.00–18.00.

DOMAINE DE LA LIEUE★

■ 10ha 50000 **2 D ▮ ↓**

Light red wine with a fine but easily perceptible perfume of red fruit. Very pleasant drinking. (1983)
↝ Jean-Louis Vial, Dom. de la Lieue, 83170 Brignoles; tel. 94 69 00 12 ⍭ Daily 9.00–18.00.

DOMAINE DU LOOU★★

■ 3ha 12500 **2 D ⑪**

Good, clear colour. Rich aromas of vanilla and blackcurrant. Firm body that is powerful yet elegant. Will develop further if left to age for a few more years. (1983)
↝ M. Dominique di Placido, 83136 La Roque-brussanne; tel. 94 86 94 97 ⍭ By appt.

DOMAINE DU LOOU★★

☑ 5ha 25000 **2 D ▮ ↓**

Classic 'Rosé de Saignée' colour. Rich aromas of peach and plum give an attractive, full flavour, which is both refreshing and lively. (1983)
↝ M. Dominique di Placido, 83136 La Roque-brussan; tel. 94 86 94 97 ⍭ By appt.

CAVE SAINT-ANDRE★★

■ 6ha 20000 **2 D ⑪ ↓**

Fine, honest red colour with aromas of raspberry, blackcurrant and blackberry. Very rich, but the tannins are still a little aggressive. Will improve with age. (1984)
↝ Cave St-André, Seillons-Source-d'Argens, 83470 St-Maximin-la-Ste-Baume; tel. 94 78 02 9 ⍭ Mon.–Sat. 8.00–12.00/14.00–18.00. Closed public holidays.

CAVE SAINT-ANDRE★

☑ 11ha 20000 **2 D ▮ ↓**

Young and floral. Aromas of raspberry. Fresh and lively. Should retain its characteristics for at least a year. (1984)
↝ Cave St-André, Seillons-Source-d'Argens, 83470 St-Maximin-la-Ste-Baume; tel. 94 78 02 91 ⍭ Mon.–Sat. 8.00–12.00/14.00–18.00. Closed public holidays.

CHATEAU SAINT-ESTEVE★★

■ 30ha 200000 **2 D ⑪ ↓**

A pleasing wine, with an attractive, slightly brick-red colour and a floral aroma mixed with vanilla. Although the tannin is still strong, there is good balance on the palate. (1982)
↝ M. Anthony Gassier, Ch. St-Estève, 83119 Brue-Auriac; tel. 94 59 48 68 ⍭ Daily 8.00–12.00/13.30–18.00.

DOMAINE DE SAINT-JEAN
Cuvée Spéciale★★

■ 8ha 50000 **3 D ⑪ ↓**

Pleasing and serious. Bright-red colour, rich aromas and, on the palate, good balance. (1982)
↝ GFA du Dom. St-Jean, Villecroze, 83690 Salernes; tel. 94 70 63 07 ⍭ By appt.

DOMAINE DE SAINT-JEAN★

☑ 5ha 40000 **3 D ▮ ↓**

Very pale, attractively clear, corn-coloured wine. The aromas of ripe fruit open out slowly on the palate; cheerful, elegant and feminine. (1983)
↝ GFA du Dom. St-Jean, Villecroze, 83690 Salernes; tel. 94 70 63 07 ⍭ By appt.

CLOS DE LA TRUFFIERE★★

■ 6ha 40000 **3 D ⑪ ↓**
⑧

Attractive dark red. Interesting aromas of green peppers and vanilla. On the palate, good structure and body, with suppleness that holds well. (1982)
↝ J.S. de Lanversin, 83470 St-Maximin; tel. 94 78 03 91 ⍭ By appt.

CORSICA

THE traditional description of Corsica is 'a mountain in the sea'. The topography of the whole island is very tortuous, and even the so-called eastern plain would almost certainly be called hilly on the mainland. These hundreds of small hills and slopes are mostly exposed to sun, but also remain fairly humid thanks to the maritime influence, the rainfall, and the vegetation. This allows vines to be grown almost everywhere, the only restriction being altitude. Of the 28 000 hectares, 4000 are AOC. The main soil type is granite, which covers most of the south and the west of the island. Schistous soils are found to the north-east, and between these two zones is a small area of limestone.

Corsican wines are mostly classified as Vins de Pays and Vins de Table. As well as the traditional grape varieties imported from the mainland, Corsica has its own, highly original varieties. The Niellucio in particular is a very tannic grape which excels on limestone soil. Another local variety, the Sciarello, gives a quite full-bodied and very fruity wine which is usually drunk young. Among the white varieties, the Malvasia (also known as Vermentino or Malvoisie) seems particularly well suited to the Mediterranean climate.

As a rule the Corsican whites and, particularly, the rosés should be drunk quite young. They are very good with all types of seafood, and with the excellent local goat's cheese and broccio. Depending on their age and tannic strength, the red wines go well with a wide range of meat dishes and with various types of Corsican sheep's cheese.

Vin de Corse

The appellation covers wine produced anywhere on the island except within the limits of the two other appellation areas described below. However, the wines have many different nuances of quality depending on the region, the estate, the grape varieties used, and the soil type. Because of these factors, local wines are allowed to add the name of the specific area where they were made to the Vin de Corse appellation. Most of the 30 000 hectolitres of wine produced each year come from the east coast, where there are several cooperatives.

NICOLAS

| ■ | 77 000 | 2 ▮ ↓ |

A fine ruby-purple colour, with a discreet, light fruity nose. Firm but not aggressive on the palate, which has pleasing aromas and a good finish.

➧ Ets Nicolas, 2 Rue de Valmy, 94220 Charenton; tel. 01 37 59 20.

NICOLAS

| ◪ | 93 000 | 2 ▮ ↓ |

Mature pink colour and very discreet nose and palate. Fresh, with a light, slightly rubbery aroma. Serve well chilled.

➧ Ets Nicolas, 2 Rue de Valmy, 94220 Charenton; tel. 01 37 59 20.

Corsica

AOC	Corsican wines
▢ Ajaccio	1 Coteaux du Cap Corse
	2 Calvi
▨ Patrimonio	3 Sartène
	4 Figari
▢ Corsican wines	5 Porto Vecchio

CLOS NICROSI *Coteaux du Cap Corse*★★

☐   7ha   25000   ▣ Ⓓ ▪ ↓

82 83

A typical wine from the Malvoisie grape, known locally as the Rolle. Very elegant, understated mandarin-skin pink colour and good acidity. (1983)
➻ A. Luigi, Clos Nicrosi, 20247 Rogliano; tel. 95 35 42 02 ⚔ No visitors.

DOMAINE DE TORRACCIA
Porto Vecchio Oriu★★

▪   8ha   30000   ▣ Ⓓ ▪ ↓

80 ★ 83 ★84

Made from selected grapes. Slightly veiled ruby-red colour. Smells of spices and Havanas. An original combination. Soft and well made.
➻ Christian Imbert, Dom. de Torraccia, Lecci, 20137 Porto-Vecchio; tel. 95 71 43 50 ⚔ Mon.–Sat. 8.00–12.00/14.00–18.00. Closed Sun., public holidays.

DOMAINE DE TORRACCIA
Porto-Vecchio★

☐   4ha   21600   ▣ Ⓓ ▪ ↓

83 84

Very brilliant clear yellow colour, and Malvoisie grape fragrance. Warm, soft and full on the palate. (1984)
➻ M. Christian Imbert, Dom. de Torraccia, Lecci, 20137 Porto-Vecchio; tel. 95 71 43 50 ⚔ Mon.–Sat. 8.00–12.00/14.00–18.00. Closed Sun. and public holidays.

DOMAINE DE TORRACCIA
Porto-Vecchio

☑   12ha   50000   ▣ Ⓓ ▪ ↓

83 84

Brilliant 'oeil-de-perdrix' colour; a sinewy, vigorous rosé with a reserved nose and rather firm finish. Good with difficult Mediterranean dishes such as *bourride* (a pungent fish stew with garlic). (1984)
➻ M. Christian Imbert, Dom. de Torraccia, Lecci, 20137 Porto-Vecchio; tel. 95 71 43 50 ⚔ Mon.–Sat. 8.00–12.00/14.00–18.00. Closed Sun. and public holidays.

CLOS VALLE-VECCHIA
Porto Vecchio★★★

☑   35ha   30000   ▣ ▪ ↓

Fine, bright pink colour. Very original, meaty bouquet, and excellent fruit. Lively and vigorous on the palate, with a very pleasing aroma. Will go very well with the highly flavoured dishes from the Mediterranean coast. Exclusive to Nicolas.
➻ Ets Nicolas, 2 Rue de Valmy, 94220 Charenton; tel. 01 37 59 20 ⚔ No visitors.

Ajaccio

The city of Ajaccio is the capital of southern Corsica, and its appellation area covers a broad sweep of the hills surrounding the famous gulf. The soil is mostly granite and the main grape variety the Sciarello. Annual production averages 700 hectolitres, the majority of which is red wine that will age quite well.

CLOS CAPITORO★★

▪   10ha   40000   ▣ Ⓓ ▪ ↓

71 75 ★78 ★79 80

Garnet colour and bouquet of dried flowers, tobacco and vanilla. A delicate though full-bodied wine, well balanced on the palate with a good finish. (1980) ✔ Ajaccio Clos Capitoro Rose, Ajaccio Clos Capitoro Blanc.
➻ MM. Bianchetti Frères et Fils, Route de Sartène, Pisciatella, 20166 Porticcio; tel. 95 20 02 63 ⚔ Mon.–Sat. 9.00–12.00/14.00–17.30. Closed Christmas Day and New Year's Day.

COMTE PERALDI★★

▪   27ha   100000   ▣ Ⓓ ▪ ⑾ ↓

68 79 82 83

The Sciaccarello is the traditional Corsican varietal. This wine, from selected grapes, has spent some time in the cask, making it soft, alcoholic, warm and full-bodied, rich with the scents of red fruit, tobacco and caramel. (1983) ✔ Ajaccio 1983, Ajaccio Cuvée Spéciale, Vin de Corse Clos de Tollisa.
➻ M. de Poix, Dom. Peraldi, 20167 Ajaccio; tel. 95 22 37 30 ⚔ By appt.

THE WINES OF THE SOUTH-WEST

THIS is a somewhat artificial category that lumps together such dissimilar wines as Irouléguy and Marcillac. In fact, there are two distinct traditions here: wines of the Pyrenean foothills around Béarn and Jurançon, and those of the region stretching east and south from the Gironde. The wine-growing areas in the South-West, scattered between Bergerac and Fronton, Cahors and Jurançon, have always had to struggle against the strong image of Bordeaux wines. Until the arrival of the railway, Bordeaux more or less laid down the law for these 'subservient' vineyards. It was able to do this because of its geographical location and its strong ties with England and, subsequently, with the French court. The Pyrenean wines were in a different position; at the price of negotiating the river Adour they could reach the port of Bayonne and be freely exported. However, the Cahors, Gaillac, Buzet, Duras and other Fronton wines had no choice but to wait patiently for the Gironde harvest to be sold to consumers on the other side of the Channel or to the trade in Holland – or else be sold as 'vins médicins', to beef up the lighter and weaker cuvées of 'claret' for the English market. In these circumstances it is understandable that their reputation rarely spread beyond their immediate vicinity.

Yet these vineyards are among the oldest in France, a monument to so many once-famous grape types. Nowhere else can such a wide variety be found – no surprise to those who know the Gascon individualism and fierce local pride.

The grape varieties used here – Manseng, Tannat, Negrette, Auxerrois, Duras, Len-de-l'El, Mauzac, Fer Servadou, Folle Noire, Arrufiat and Barroque –

The South-West

467

originated in the dark ages of wine-making history, and give these wines their distinctive authenticity. 'Peasant' wines in the noblest sense of the word, they are true 'vins du terroir' taking their place in a pattern of mixed farming as one of a huge range of agricultural products. The local cuisine has a special kinship with the wines of the region that gives south-west France a particularly enviable gastronomic tradition.

All these vineyards are presently being given a new lease of life through the efforts of the cooperatives and some keen and committed individual producers. Enormous efforts are being made to improve the quality of the wines through the most advanced methods of viticultural science, and these efforts are paying off, making the wines of the South-West some of the best value in France.

Cahors

The Cahors vineyards are amongst the oldest in France, dating from the late Roman occupation. Pope Jean XXII, installed at Avignon, had vignerons come from this region to tend the vines of Châteauneuf-du-Pape, while François I planted Cahors vines in Fontainebleau. The Greek Orthodox Church adopted Cahors as its communion wine, and the court of the Russian Tsars served it to distinguished visitors. And yet, despite this illustrious history, Cahors underwent a long period of neglect and has had to work hard to reestablish its prominence. Totally destroyed by the frosts of 1956, the area under vine fell to only one per cent of its previous extent. Replanted along the windy valley of the River Lot with traditional varieties, such as Auxerrois, Tannat and Merlot, the Cahors vineyards

have regained their rightful place in the ranks of high-quality wines. There are even some brave efforts at present to replant the 'causses', areas of very sparse vegetation where vineyards flourished long ago.

Cahors wines are generally powerful and robust with a very deep colour; indeed the English nicknamed them 'black' wines. There is no doubt that they are better laid down for a few years. Some people drink them very young, however, and, in that case, these meaty, aromatic, fruity wines should be served slightly chilled, with grills or with Roquefort cheese. After two or three years of bottle age they become hard and austere, but after a further two or three years they recover and display a round, full flavour that makes them the ideal accompaniment to such local specialities as truffes sous la cendre (ash-covered truffles), mush-

Cahors

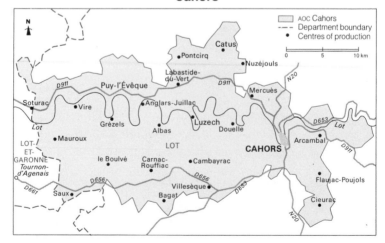

rooms, and game. The ability of these wines to age depends on many factors, including the vineyard location, the grape varieties used in the blend and the method of vinification. Not all Cahors age well, however, and the current trend is towards producing lighter wines for short-term drinking.

DOMAINE DE LA BERGERIE★

| ■ | | 6ha | 30000 | 2 | D | 🍾 | 🍷 |

67 70 71 75 *77 *79 *81 *82 83

Nice, dark ruby colour. Undeveloped but promising nose. Assertive and quite rich and stylish on the palate, with a good finish. (1983)
🔑 Les Côtes d'Olt, Parnac, 46140 Luzech; tel. 65 30 71 86 ⟁ By appt 🔑 R. Baudel.

DOMAINE DE LA CAMINADE★★

| ■ | | 15ha | 96000 | 2 | D | 🍾 | ◑ | 🍷 |

75 78 80 82

Rich and full-bodied with a touch of austerity. Now close to its peak. An excellent bottle. (1982)
🔑 L. Resses, Dom. de la Caminade, Parnac, 46140 Luzech; tel. 65 30 73 05 ⟁ Mon.–Sat. 8.00–12.00/14.00–19.00.

DOMAINE DE CAUNEZIL★

| ■ | | 6ha | 30000 | 2 | D | 🍾 | 🍷 |

59 67 70 71 ⑦⑤ *77 *79 *81 *82 83

Another lightweight 'commercial' Cahors with an agreeable bouquet and good balance; could last for a while. (1982)
🔑 Les Côtes d'Olt, Parnac, 46140 Luzech; tel. 65 30 71 86 ⟁ By appt 🔑 M. Lafage.

CHATEAU DU CAYROU★

| ■ | | 30ha | 21600 | 3 | D | 🍾 | 🍷 |

⑦⑤ 79 80 81 82 82 83

Magnificent colour; full and firm on the palate. Stainless steel and oak cellars make it a touch austere, but will open up with age. (1982)
🔑 Jean Jouffreau, Clos de Gamot, 46220 Prayssac; tel. 65 22 40 26 ⟁ Daily 9.00–13.00/14.00–20.00.

CHATEAU DE CHAMBERT★★★

| ■ | | 50ha | 25000 | 3 | D | ◑ | 🍷 |

*81 *82 *83 *83

Shows signs of quality; powerful, full-bodied, well balanced and refined. An encouraging successor to generations of winemakers. (1983)
✔ Cahors Pech-de-Sirech, Cahors Hauts-de-Chambert.
🔑 SCA Ch. Chambert, Floressas, 46700 Puyl'Evêque; tel. 65 87 24 58 ⟁ By appt.

LES COTES D'OLT *Imperial*

| ■ | | | 30000 | 3 | D | 🍾 | ◑ | 🍷 |

67 70 71 75 *77 *79 *81 *82 83

Good colour but closed-up on the nose. Rather tannic on the palate. Needs time to develop. (1982)
🔑 Les Côtes d'Olt, Parnac, 46140 Luzech; tel. 65 30 71 86 ⟁ By appt.

LES COTES D'OLT
Comte André de Monpezat★

| ■ | | | 30000 | 2 | D | 🍾 | 🍷 |

59 67 71 75 *77 *79 *81 *82 83

A classic Cahors that is at present closed-up, but which shows signs of potential development. (1982)
🔑 Les Côtes d'Olt, Parnac, 46140 Luzech; tel. 65 30 71 86 ⟁ By appt.

CLOS LA COUTALE★★

| ■ | | 35ha | 180000 | 3 | D | 🍾 | 🍷 |

75 78 79 *⑧① 82 83 83

Small proportions of Tannat and Merlot blended with the predominating Auxerrois give the Cahors wines their famed characteristics. The 1982 is true to type, with a lovely colour, expansive bouquet and roundness and richness on the palate. Good ageing potential. (1982)
🔑 V. Bernède et Fils, Vire, 46700 Puy-l'Evêque; tel. 65 36 51 47 ⟁ By appt.

DOMAINE DE DAULIAC★★

| ■ | | 9ha | 48000 | 2 | D | 🍾 | 🍷 |

59 67 70 71 ⑦⑤ *77 *79 *81 *82 83

Good, deep ruby colour with a full, rich nose. Full bodied but with finesse and distinction. Will age well. (1983)
🔑 Les Côtes d'Olt, Parnac, 46140 Luzech; tel. 65 30 71 86 ⟁ By appt 🔑 A. Resseguier.

DOMAINE EUGENIE *Cuvée Reservée★*

| ■ | | 19ha | 114000 | 4 | D | ◑ | 🍷 |

81 82 83 83

Descended from vine stock much prized by the Tsars, this 1982 vintage has a powerful bouquet with a slight scent of truffles. Substantial, weighty and well balanced on the palate. (1982)
🔑 Jean et Claude Couture, Rivière-Haute, 46140 Albas; tel. 65 30 73 51 ⟁ By appt.

JEAN GALBERT★★

| ■ | | 7ha | 5300 | 3 | D | 🍾 |

*80 *81 *83 *83

At its best now; should be drunk young. (1982)
🔑 Jean Galbert, 46700 Puy-l'Evêque; tel. 65 21 32 64 ⟁ By appt.

CLOS DE GAMOT★★★

| ■ | | 10ha | 57600 | 3 | 🍾 | 🍷 |

55 75 76 78 *⑧② *82 *83

Magnificent deep colour, promising nose, fullness and long finish. For those patient enough to wait a few years before drinking. (1983)
🔑 Jean Jouffreau, Clos de Gamot, 46220 Prayssac; tel. 65 22 40 26 ⟁ Daily 9.00–20.00.

DOMAINE DE GAUDOU★★

| ■ | | 20ha | 96000 | 3 | D | 🍾 | ◑ | 🍷 |

77 78 78 79 80 81 82

Lovely bright colour; powerful, fruity nose and full-bodied on the palate. Harmonious and well balanced. Shows its class and will keep well. (1982)

◆┐ Durou et Fils, Domaine de Gaudou, Vire-sur-Lot, 46700 Puy-l'Evêque; tel. 65 36 52 93 ⟐ By appt.

DOMAINE DE GRAUZILS★★

■ 17ha 107 000 **2** **D** ▮ ◑ ↓

*75 *76 *78 *79 81 **82** 83

A rich wine, whose current astringency denotes good ageing potential. (1983)
◆┐ Pontie et Fils, Gamot, 46220 Prayssac; tel. 65 30 65 44 ⟐ By appt.

CHATEAU DE HAUTE-SERRE★★

■ 40ha 228 000 **3** **D** ◑ ↓

78 81 ✶⟨82⟩ *82 83

Light in colour, has substantial body and is full of flavour; ready for drinking. (1982)
◆┐ Georges Vigouroux, Cieurac, 46230 Lalben-que; tel. 65 38 70 30 ⟐ Daily 10.00–12.00/15.00–18.00.

DOMAINE LABARRADE★

■ 14ha 72 000 **2** **D** ▮ ↓

59 67 70 71 ⟨75⟩ *77 *79 *81 *82 83

Pleasant, light, modern-style Cahors, with good fruit. For immediate consumption. (1982)
◆┐ Les Côtes d'Olt, Parnac, 46140 Luzech; tel. 65 30 71 86 ⟐ By appt◆┐ *M*. Viallatte.

CHATEAU LACAPELLE-CABANAC★★

■ 8ha 7000 **2** **D** ▮ ↓

82 83 **83**

Rich and complex nose and, although rather loose-knit, not without finesse. An interesting wine for the connoisseur. (1983)
◆┐ Alex Denjean, Lacapelle-Cabanac, 46700 Puy-l'Evêque; tel. 65 36 51 92 ⟐ By appt.

DOMAINE DES LANDES★

■ 28ha 14 800 **2** **D** ▮ ↓

67 70 71 75 *77 *79 *81 *82 83

Good colour. An initially backward bouquet that develops in the glass. A certain finesse. Nice balance on the palate, with a good finish. (1982)
◆┐ Les Côtes d'Olt, Parnac, 46140 Luzech; tel. 65 30 71 86 ⟐ By appt◆┐ GAEC Cap-des-Orts.

DOMAINE LOU-CAMP-DEL-SALTRE★★

■ 13ha **2** **D** ▮ ◑ ↓

80 81 ✶⟨82⟩ *82 83 **83**

Unusual, slightly gamey bouquet. Light on the palate and a pleasing appearance. The 1983 vintage of this type will be a great wine. (1982)
◆┐ Roland Delbru et Fils, Route du Collège, 46220 Prayssac; tel. 65 22 42 40 ⟐ By appt.

DOMAINE DE MASSABIE★

■ 13ha 36 000 **2** **D** ▮ ↓

67 70 71 75 *77 *79 *81 *82 83

Recently bottled. Was suffering from bottle sick-ness when tasted, but showed some potential on the palate. (1983)
◆┐ Les Côtes d'Olt, Parnac, 46140 Luzech; tel. 65 30 71 86 ⟐ By appt◆┐ J. Delcros.

DOMAINE DE PAILLAS★★★

■ 27ha 202 000 **3** **D** ▮ ↓

78 ⟨82⟩ **82** 83

Drink now to take advantage of its current overt fruitiness and full-bodied character. (1982)
◆┐ SCEA de St-Robert, 46700 Puy-l'Evêque; tel. 65 21 34 42 ⟐ By appt.

CHATEAU PARNAC★★

■ 3ha 18 000 **2** **D** ▮ ↓

59 67 70 71 ⟨75⟩ *77 *79 *81 *82 83

Good, deep colour and more body than average among those tasted; some potential for ageing. (1982)
◆┐ Les Côtes d'Olt, Parnac, 46140 Luzech; tel. 65 30 71 86 ⟐ By appt◆┐ J.-P. Brunet.

DOMAINE DU PECH-DE-CLARY★

■ 4ha 30 000 **2** **D** ◑ ↓

*82 *82 83

Light in colour with an aroma of ripe fruit. Ready to drink. (1982)
◆┐ Antonia Valette-Clary, Lamagdelaine, 46090 Cahors; tel. 65 35 37 08 ⟐ Daily 9.00–20.00
◆┐ Frederic Valette-Clary.

DOMAINE DU PIC★

■ 6ha 25 000 **2** **D** ▮ ↓

80 81 82 *83 *83

Classic example of the 1983 vintage, whose fruity bouquet is still green and needs to age. (1983)
◆┐ Jose Roucanières, Douelle, 46140 Luzech; tel. 65 20 04 28 ⟐ By appt.

DOMAINE DE LA PINERAIE★★★

■ 20ha 126 000 **3** **D** ◑ ↓

*80 *81 *82 *82 83

At the time of tasting, this 1982 had the best nose of all the 1982s we tasted. Supple and rounded, with a touch of refinement from the ten per cent Merlot added to the Auxerrois. (1982)
◆┐ Burc et Fils, Peygues, 46700 Puy-l'Evêque; tel. 65 30 82 07 ⟐ Mon.–Sat. 7.00–12.00/14.00–20.00. Closed Sun. and public holidays.

DOMAINE DU PRADEL★

■ 12ha 63 000 **2** **D** ◑ ↓

80 81 82 **82** *83

Nicely coloured. Its warm bouquet has an unusual burnt aroma; soundly tannic on the palate with good body and some delicacy. Ready to drink. (1983)
◆┐ Gérard Maerten, Les Roques, St-Vincent-

Rive-d'Olt, 46140 Luzech; tel. 65 30 71 55 ☎ No visitors.

METRAIRIE GRANDE DU THERON★★

■ 2.5 ha 88 000 [2] [D] ▮ ↓
75 78 80 82 *[83]

Has the typical fine colour of young Cahors. Warm and fruity, vegetal, but with a hint of redcurrants; fine and lingering aromas make it a pretty, distinguished wine. (1983) ♈ Liliane Sigaud, 46220 Prayssac; tel. 65 22 41 80 ☎ By appt.

CLOS TRIGUEDINA★★

■ 35 ha 210 000 [3] [D] ▮ ⬥ ↓
71 75 78 79 [80]*(81) *(82) *(83)

A 1982 noteworthy for its finesse and harmony. Considerable promise for the future. (1982) ✐ AOC Cahors Prince-Probus. ♈ Mm. Baldès et Fils, Clos Triguedina, 46700 Puy-l'Evêque; tel. 65 21 30 81 ☎ By appt.

DOMAINE DE VERDOU★

■ 5 ha 38 000 [2] [D] ▮ ↓
82 [82] 83

Nicely presented, with a classic colour and attractive and forthcoming bouquet. Weighty and a good, lingering finish on the palate. Should lose its broad rustic character with ageing. (1983) ♈ Emile Arnaudet, Douelle, 46140 Luzech; tel. 65 30 91 34 ☎ By appt.

DOMAINE DE VIGNALS★★

■ 8 ha 42 000 [2] [D] ↓
67 70 71 75 *77 *79 *81 *82 83

Deep-coloured but reticent on the nose, with a pleasant vinous quality. Nicely balanced, with an attractive, soft tannin – a pretty wine. (1982) ♈ Les Côtes d'Olt, Parnac, 46140 Luzech; tel. 65 30 71 86 ☎ By appt ♈ A. Labrande.

Gaillac

The origins of the Gaillac vineyards go back to the first century AD. In the thirteenth century Raymond VII, Count of Toulouse, established what amounted to a local appellation contrôlée, while Auger Gaillard, the Occitan poet, praised Gaillac sparkling wine well before champagne was invented. The vineyards are traditionally divided into the Premières-Côtes, Hauts-Coteaux (east bank of the Tarn), the plain, and the Cunac and Cordais regions.

The limestone slopes are particularly suited to the cultivation of traditional white grape types such as the Mauzac, Len-de-l'El (local dialect for 'loin de l'oeil' meaning 'far from view'), Odenc, Sauvignon, and Muscadelle. The gravel areas support red grape varieties – Duras, Braucol, Syrah, Gamay, Negrette, Cabernet-Franc, Cabernet-Sauvignon, Juran-

Gaillac

471

çon, Merlot, and Portugais Bleu. The long list of varieties explains why the Gaillac vineyards are capable of producing almost every style of wine.

Among the whites there are the fresh, slightly sparkling, aromatic dry wines, and the full, rich, sweet wines of the Premières Côtes. These wines, strongly marked by Mauzac varietal character, have made Gaillac famous. Gaillac Mousseux, a sparkling wine, can be made either by a natural secondary fermentation or by the Méthode Champenoise: the former type is fruity and has more character. The rosés, produced by the saignée method, are light and refreshing. The red wines age well and have a distinctive style and bouquet. Gaillac cuisine is a natural complement to the diversity of these wines, with such dishes as freshwater fish, crayfish, daube or pigeon pie.

MAS D'AUREL**

| ■ | 10 ha | 24 000 | 2 D ▪ |

76 82 83 83

First-class wine that shows the Duras grape characteristics to good effect. Bright ruby colour and complex fruit aromas. Full-bodied with some tannin; will keep well. (1983) ✔ Gaillac Mas d'Aurel Rosé, Gaillac Mas ☙ Albert Ribot, Mas d'Aurel, Donnazac, 81170 Cordes; tel. 63 56 06 39 ⌇ Daily 9.00–12.00/14.00–17.00.

MAS D'AUREL*

| □ | 3.5 ha | 11 400 | 2 D ▪ |

79 80 82 84

Successful white from Len-de-l'el, Sauvignon and Mauzac, which takes much of its character from a diverse mixture of soils. Delicate colour, good fruit on the nose, crisp and fresh on the palate with good length. (1984) ✔ Gaillac Rouge, Gaillac Rosé, Gaillac Mousseux.
☙ Albert Ribot, Mas d'Aurel, Donnazac, 81170 Cordes; tel. 63 56 06 39 ⌇ Daily 9.00–12.00/14.00–17.00.

DOMAINE DES BOUSCAILLONS**

| ■ | 3 ha | 18 000 | 2 D ▪ |

80 81 *82 *82 83

Distinctively Gaillac wine made from Duras and Braucol with Syrah and Cabernet adding a deeper tone to the colour. Rich, aromatic, spicy and burnt nose. Needs keeping for a while to lose its tannin. (1982)
☙ Yvon Maurel, Dom. des Bouscaillons, Montels, 81140 Castelnau-Montmirail; tel. 63 57 10 16 ⌇ By appt.

DOMAINE DES BOUSCAILLONS**

| ■ | .60 ha | 3240 | 2 D ▪ |

83 84 84

Interesting wine with greenish tinge from Sauvignon and Len-de-l'el grapes. Fresh, aromatic nose and necessary acidity on the palate. Good, all-purpose white. (1984) ✔ Gaillac Dom. des Bouscaillons Rouge, Gaillac Dom. des Bouscaillons Rosé, Gaillac Dom. des Bouscaillons Blanc Moelleux, Gaillac Dom. des Bouscaillons Pétillant.
☙ Yvon Maurel, Dom. des Bouscaillons, Montels, 81140 Castelnau-Montmirail; tel. 63 57 10 16 ⌇ By appt.

CHATEAU CLARES
Blanc 'Moustillant'**

| ○ | 6 ha | 3600 | 2 D ▪ |

Soft and sparkling. For any convivial occasion, either as an aperitif or as a dessert wine. (1984)
☙ Pierre Clarès, Ch. Clarès, Florentin, 81150 Marssac-sur-Tarn; tel. 63 55 40 12 ⌇ By appt.

DOMAINE JEAN CROS*

| ■ | 4 ha | 24 000 | 3 D ▪ |

71 72 76 78 81 82

Most unusual and original. Fine ruby colour and spicy, soft-fruit aroma. Full-flavoured and well balanced, with a long finish. Elegant and distinguished. (1982) ✔ Gaillac Dom. Jean Cros Perlé Blanc Sec, Gaillac Dom. Jean Cros Rouge Primeur.
☙ Jean Cros Père et Fils, Mas des Vignes, 81140 Cahuzac-sur-Vère; tel. 63 33 92 62 ⌇ Mon.–Sat. 11.00–19.00; Sun. 16.30–18.00.

DOMAINE JEAN CROS**

| ○ | 6 ha | 36 000 | 3 D ▪ |

78 82 83 83

Excellent example of Perlé, the Gaillac speciality. Distinctive colour and particularly fruity aroma. Light and fresh. (1983) ✔ Gaillac Ch. Larroze Blanc Sec, Gaillac Ch. Larroze Rouge, Gaillac Dom. Jean Cros Méthode Rurale Blanc.
☙ Jean Cros Père et Fils, Mas des Vignes, 81140 Cahuzac-sur-Vère; tel. 63 33 92 62 ⌇ Mon.–Sat. 11.00–19.00; Sun. 16.30–18.00.

DOMAINE DE GRADDE
Moustillant Doux*

| ○ | 4 ha | 24 000 | 3 D ▪ |

76 78 81 82 *83 *84

For those who like sweet things, the attraction of *méthode gaillacoise* lies in the fact that it is more fruit than wine. A pleasant colour that is not too strong, a characterstic aroma of fruit and flowers and a good mousse. (1984) ✔ Gaillac Rouge, Gaillac Rosé, Gaillac Blanc Sec.
☙ Etienne Coursières, 81140 Campagnac; tel. 63 33 12 61 ⌇ By appt.

DOMAINE DE GRADDE

| ■ | 5 ha | 30 000 | 2 D ▪ |

76 78 81 *82 *82

Soft ruby-red tinged with purple. Solid, velvety and elegant, with overtones of vegetation on the palate. Wine-lovers will appreciate its discreet charm. Ready to drink. (1982)

♠ Etienne Coursières, Dom. de Graddé, Campagnac, 81140 Castelnau-de-Montmiral; tel. 63 33 12 61 ☒ By appt.

DOMAINE DE GRADDE★★

| ○ | 8ha | 48000 | 2 | D | ■ |

75 76 78 81 ◀82 ▸83 84

Vinification as a *perlé* gives a touch of humour to this serious wine, which many will appreciate. (1983) ✔ Gaillac Rouge, Gaillac Rosé, Gaillac Blanc Sec.
♠ Etienne Coursières, Dom. de Gradde, 81140 Campagnac; tel. 63 33 12 61 ☒ By appt.

DOMAINE DE LABARTHE★★★

| ○ | 2ha | 12000 | 3 | D | ■ |

79 80 81 ▸82 ⑧③ 83

Here at its best, the Mauzac has beautiful colour without patina and a rounded, flowery, spicy and slightly exotic bouquet. Elegant and well made. Suitable as an aperitif. (1983) ✔ Gaillac Rouge, Gaillac Rosé, Gaillac Blanc Sec.
♠ Jean Albert, Dom. de Labarthe, Castanet, 81150 Marssac-sur-Tarn; tel. 63 56 80 14 ☒ By appt.

DOMAINE DE LABARTHE★★

| □ | 5ha | 30000 | 2 | D | ■ |

79 80 81 ▸82 ▸84

Greenish-white in colour. Initially reticent on the nose, it develops a distinguished bouquet. Refined, well balanced and aromatic on the palate. (1984)
♠ Jean Albert, Dom. de Labarthe, Castanet, 81150 Marssac-sur-Tarn; tel. 63 56 80 14 ☒ By appt.

COOPERATIVE DE LABASTIDE-DE-LEVIS *Demi-sec*★

| ○ | 40ha | 840000 | 3 | D | ■ ↓ |

78 79 80 81 82 ⑧③ 83

A medium-sweet wine from equal proportions of Mauzac and Len-de-l'el. Distinctive, sweet, Mauzac rosé, suggesting flowery and fruity aromas of acacia, almonds, hawthorn broom, with apples, bananas and walnuts. Fine and long-lasting mousse. (1983)
♠ Coop. de Labastide-de-Lévis, Labastide-de-Lévis, 81150 Marssac-sur-Tarn; tel. 63 55 41 83 ☒ By appt.

COOPERATIVE DE LABASTIDE-DE-LEVIS★★

| ☑ | 15ha | 93480 | 2 | D | ■ ↓ |

79 82 83 84 84

Highly coloured rosé from mainly Syrah and Gamay. Good fruit on the nose and agreeably long on the palate. (1984)
♠ Coop. de Labastide-de-Lévis, Labastide-de-Lévis, 81150 Marssac-sur-Tarn; tel. 63 55 41 83 ☒ By appt.

COOPERATIVE DE LABASTIDE-DE-LEVIS★

| ○ | 18ha | 108000 | 3 | D | ■ ↓ |

78 79 80 81 82 ⑧③ 83

The brut 1983, from 60 per cent Mauzac and 40 per cent Len-de-l'el, compares well with many single estate wines, and shows consistency over the years. (1983)
♠ Coop. de Labastide-de-Lévis, Labastide-de-Lévis, 81150 Marssac-sur-Tarn; tel. 63 55 41 83 ☒ By appt.

COOPERATIVE DE LABASTIDE-DE-LEVIS

| ■ | 120ha | 840000 | 2 | D | ■ ↓ |

73 75 76 78 79 ⑧③

Delightfully drinkable wine, mainly from Syrah and Gamay, with the local Duras and Braucol very much to the background. (1983)
♠ Coop. de Labastide-de-Lévis, Labastide-de-Lévis, 81150 Marssac-sur-Tarn; tel. 63 55 41 83 ☒ By appt.

DOMAINE DE LACROUX★

| □ | 6ha | 24000 | 2 | D | ■ |

79 ⑧① ▸82 ▸83

A classic Gaillac. Straightforward colour; some finesse on the nose. Round and full on the palate, with a teasing edginess, making a satisfyingly harmonious wine. (1983) ✔ Gaillac Dom. de Lacroux Rouge, Gaillac Dom. de Lacroux Blanc Liquoreux, Gaillac Dom. de Lacroux Mousseux.
♠ GAEC Derrieux Pierre et Fils, Dom. de Lacroux, Cestayrols, 81150 Marssac-sur-Tarn; tel. 63 56 81 67 ☒ Daily 8.00–12.00/14.00–18.00.

CHATEAU LARROZE★

| ■ | 5ha | 30000 | 3 | D | ■ |

82 82 83

Duras, Merlot and Cabernet grapes are particularly apparent on the nose. Most attractive, with very little tannin. At its best now. (1982) ✔ Gaillac Dom. Jean Cros Perlé Blanc Sec, Gaillac Dom. Jean Cros Rouge.
♠ Jean Cros Père et Fils, Mas des Vignes, 81140 Cahuzac-sur-Vère; tel. 63 33 92 62 ☒ Mon.–Sat. 11.00–19.00; Sun. 16.30–18.00.

CHATEAU LASTOURS *Brut*★★

| ○ | .60ha | 3600 | 3 | D | ■ |

83 84

You will like this sparkling wine, with its beautiful colour tinged with gold. A distinctly dry brut with a subtle aroma of flint, vanilla, walnuts and toast. (1983) ✔ Gaillac Ch. Lastours Rouge, Gaillac Graviers Blancs Ch. Lastours Rosé, Gaillac Graviers Blancs Ch. Lastours Blanc Sec.

➤ J.H.F. de Faramond (GAEC), Ch. de Lastours, 81310 Lisle-sur-Tarn; tel. 63 57 07 09 ℐ By appt.

CHATEAU LASTOURS*

◪		1 ha	6000	2 D ▬

⑦⑧ 80 82 84 84

Fruity, supple and of great elegance, accentuated by a slight patina. Most attractive on the palate. (1984) ✔ Gaillac Ch. Lastours Rouge, Gaillac Graviers Blancs Ch. Lastours Blanc Sec, Gaillac Ch. Lastours Méthode Champenoise Mousseux.
➤ J.H.F. de Faramond (GAEC), Ch. de Lastours, 81310 Lisle-sur-Tarn; tel. 63 57 07 09 ℐ By appt.

CHATEAU LASTOURS*

□		4 ha	24 000	2 D ▬

75 78 *⑧② *82 83

Agreeably full and rounded, with a touch of fresh Sauvignon acidity, and finished with the fragrance and colour of the Muscadelle. Made to please. (1982)
➤ J.H.F. de Faramond (GAEC), Ch. de Lastours, 81310 Lisle-sur-Tarn; tel. 63 57 07 09 ℐ By appt.

CHATEAU LASTOURS*

■		15 ha	90 000	2 D ▬

75 78 *⑧② *82 *83

Syrah and Cabernet compensate for its defects, adding a touch of sweetness on the nose. Loose-knit and on the lighter side. (1982)
➤ J.H.F. de Faramond (GAEC), Ch. de Lastours, 81310 Lisle-sur-Tarn; tel. 63 57 07 09 ℐ By appt.

DOMAINE DE MAZOU**

◪		.26 ha	1560	2 D ▬

*⑧④ *84

A satisfying blend of Syrah, Cabernet and Merlot complement the distinctive character of the Duras. Appealing pinkish colour, harmonious and distinctive nose, and well balanced, with a hint of earthiness on the palate. (1984)
➤ Boyals Père et Fils, 10 Rue St-Louis, 81310 Lisle-sur-Tarn; tel. 63 33 37 80 ℐ Daily 9.00–12.00/14.00–19.00.

DOMAINE DE MAZOU*

□		.80 ha	5040	2 D ▬

*⑧④ *84

Purists will find a characteristic nose with a discreet touch of lactic acid. The mist of sparkle that guarantees authenticity will be reticent only if one is in a hurry and does not wait for the temperatures to balance out. (1984)
➤ Boyals Père et Fils, 10 Rue St-Louis, 81310 Lisle-sur-Tarn; tel. 63 33 37 80 ℐ Daily 9.00–12.00/14.00–19.00.

DOMAINE DE MAZOU*

■		8.6 ha	52 000	2 D ▬

75 78 79 80 81 ⑧③ 83

Attractive ruby colour. Syrah and Cabernet on the nose and Duras on the palate, with a hint of tannin and an almost imperceptible trace of Merlot. Ready to drink. (1983) ✔ Gaillac Dom.

de Mazou Rosé, Gaillac Dom. de Mazou Blanc Sec.
➤ Boyals Père et Fils, 10 Rue St-Louis, 81310 Lisle-sur-Tarn; tel. 63 33 37 80 ℐ Daily 9.00–12.00/14.00–19.00.

DOMAINE DE MOUSSENS*

■		1 ha	5400	3 D ▬

82 82 83

Despite its light colour, a fruity wine with a hint of cherry on the nose, characteristic of Syrah grown on the clayey-chalk soil at Moussens. Well balanced, rounded and ready to drink. (1982) ✔ Other Gaillac Primeur wines, sparkling grape juice.
➤ Alain Monestié, Dom. de Moussens, Cestayrols, 81150 Marssac-sur-Tarn; tel. 63 56 81 66 ℐ Mon.–Sat. 8.00–1200/14.00–18.00.

DOMAINE DE MOUSSENS**

■		.40 ha	1200	2 D ▬

Rich and highly aromatic, with a fine glossy colour. From pure Syrah grown on a clayey-chalk soil. (1984)
➤ Alain Monestié, Dom. de Moussens, Cestayrols, 81150 Marssac-sur-Tarn; tel. 63 56 81 66 ℐ Mon.–Sat. 8.00–12.00/14.00–18.00.

DOMAINE DE PIALENTOU**

■		5.16 ha	30 960	2 D ▬

78 79 79 81 *82

Enough tannin to keep, but fully developed on the nose. Well made wine from Syrah, Cabernet and Duras given long fermentation. For those who prefer younger wines, the rich 1982 is recommended. (1979) ✔ Gaillac Pétillant.
➤ Jean-Louis Ailloud, Dom. de Pialentou, Brens, 81600 Gaillac; tel. 63 57 17 99 ℐ By appt.

MAS PIGNOU*

■		4.8 ha	25 000	3 D ◐

79 80 81 *⑧② *82 83

Distinctive and characterful. Bright red colour with a ripe-fruit aroma, which contrasts with the soft, round flavour and promises early maturity. (1982) ✔ Gaillac Blanc Sec.
➤ Jacques Auque, Mas Pignou, 81600 Gaillac; tel. 63 57 10 04 ℐ By appt.

CHATEAU DE RHODES**

■		2.5 ha	14 000	3 D ▬

81 ⑧② 83 83

A seductive wine made from traditional grape varieties. Inviting, bright, clear ruby colour. Subtle and complex fruit, full and round on the palate with good length. Ready to drink despite a little tannin. (1983) ✔ Gaillac Mousseux Doux, Gaillac Brut Demi-sec, Gaillac Perlé, Gaillac Blanc de Blancs, Gaillac Primeur Rouge.
➤ GAEC Boissel Rhodes, Boissel, 81600 Gaillac; tel. 63 57 06 02 ℐ Mon.–Sat. 8.00–12.30/14.00–20.00. Closed during major holidays ➤ René Assie.

RENE RIEUX *Doux*★★

○	1.20ha	7200	3 D i ↓

80 82 **83** 83

To make sparkling wine by the *méthode rurale*, in this case the *méthode gaillacoise*, requires more than just technical expertise. The vigneron must belong to an old tradition of wine makers, of which this Cuvée Rieux is a fine expression. (1983)

✦┱ René Rieux, GAEC de Boissel et Rhodes, Rhodes Boissel, 81600 Gaillac; tel. 63 57 06 07 ⲧ Daily 8.00–13.00/13.30–20.00.

RENE RIEUX *Brut*★

○	3ha	18000	3 D i

★80 ★82 ★**83** ★83

A first-class sparkling wine. Fine mousse and golden colour; fresh, light, fruity and well balanced. (1983) ✔ Gaillac Doux René Rieux Mousseux, Gaillac Ch. de Rhodes Rouge, Gaillac Sec et Perlé Blanc Sec, Gaillac Rosé.

✦┱ René Rieux, GAEC de Boissel et Rhodes, Rhodes Boissel, 81600 Gaillac; tel. 63 57 06 07 ⲧ Daily 8.00–13.00/13.30–20.00.

DOMAINE DE ROUCOU CANTEMERLE *Sauvignon*★★★

□	1ha	60000	2 D i

⑧① 82 **83** 84 **84**

Recommended to those who like discovering something new. Traditionally made and successful Sauvignon; very characteristic of the grape variety. (1984)

✦┱ Robert Plageoles, Dom. de Roucou Cantemerle, 81140 Castelnau-de-Montmiral; tel. 63 57 10 18 ⲧ By appt.

DOMAINE DE ROUCOU CANTEMERLE *Mauzac*★★

□	1ha	4800	2 D i

⑧② 83 **84**

Clear, bright, pale colour with hints of green. Refined, full and well-developed nose and a good, long finish, which gives it a refined charm and places it amongst the best. (1984) ✔ Gaillac Moelleux Blanc, Gaillac Duras Rouge, Gaillac Gamay Rouge, Gaillac 'Vin de Voile' Blanc Sec.

✦┱ Robert Plageoles, Dom. de Roucou Cantemerle, 81140 Castelnau-de-Montmiral; tel. 63 57 10 18 ⲧ By appt.

LA CROIX SAINT-SALVY★★★

■	3ha	18600	2 D i ↓

78 ⑧① **81** 82

Fine ruby colour with an orange tinge. Elegant nose, with a hint of blackcurrant, strawberry and vanilla. Good depth and length on the palate – at its best now. (1981)

✦┱ Group. des Vign. Rabastens, 33 Route d'Albi, 81800 Rabastens; tel. 63 33 73 80 ⲧ By appt.

CAVE COOPERATIVE DE TECOU *Primeur*★★

■	4ha	24000	2 D i ↓

★81 ★⑧④ ★**84**

A classic *primeur*. Strong primary fruit aromas of black- and redcurrants and violets, accentuated by the flinty nature of the soil. (1984)

✦┱ Coop. Agri. de Técou, 81600 Gaillac; tel. 63 33 00 80 ⲧ Mon.–Sat. 8.00–12.00/14.00–18.00.

CAVE COOPERATIVE DE TECOU

■	6ha	36000	3 D i ↓

79 82 83 ★84

Fine, youthful purple colour and original and elegant aroma. Full bodied and well made. To drink now. (1983) ✔ Gaillac Tradition Rouge, Gaillac St-Vincent Rouge, Gaillac Perlé Blanc Liquoreux, Gaillac Moelleux Blanc Moelleux.

✦┱ Coop. Agri. de Técou, 81600 Gaillac; tel. 63 33 00 80 ⲧ Mon.–Sat. 8.00–12.00/14.00–18.00.

CAVE COOPERATIVE DE TECOU★★★

○	10ha	60000	2 D i ↓

81 82 ⑧ **83** ★84

Lively and characterful 1983 *perlé* with a hint of Sauvignon. Typical, pale-coloured and well balanced; satisfyingly petillant. (1983)

✦┱ Coop. Agri. de Técou, 81600 Gaillac; tel. 63 33 00 80 ⲧ Mon.–Sat. 8.00–12.00/14.00–18.00.

DOMAINE CLEMENT TERMES

○	7ha	42000	3 D i ↓

77 78 79 81 82

A sparkling wine made from equal quantities of Mauzac and Len-de-l'el grapes. Light golden colour and discreet bouquet; excellent structure and balance on the palate. Very good as an aperitif. (1983) ✔ Gaillac Dom. Clement Termes Blanc Sec, Gaillac Rosé, Gaillac Mousseux.

✦┱ MM. David Père et Fils, Les Fortis, 81310 Lisle-sur-Tarn; tel. 63 57 23 19 ⲧ By appt.

DOMAINE CLEMENT TERMES★★

■	10ha	60000	2 D i

77 78 79 81 ★⑧② ★**82**

Syrah, Merlot and Cabernet give this excellent wine a touch of class. Fine, deep-purple colour with a hint of spicy blackcurrant from the Cabernet coming through on the rather caramel nose. With very little tannin, it is ready to drink, but the 1983 needs time to mature. (1982) ✔ Gaillac Dom. Clément Termes Blanc Sec, Gaillac Dom. Clément Termes Mousseux, Gaillac Dom. Clément Termes Rosé.

✦┱ David Père et Fils, Dom. Clément Termes, 81310 Lisle-sur-Tarn; tel. 63 57 23 19 ⲧ By appt.

DOMAINE DES TERRISSES *Brut*★

○	.80ha	4800	3 D ⑪

83 **83**

A dry sparkling wine, made by the *méthode gaillacoise*, that retains much of the grape aromas of the Mauzac and Len-de-l'el with a touch of Sauvignon. Agreeably light, fruity and well balanced, but with a gentle mousse. (1983) ✔ Gaillac Rouge, Gaillac Banc Sec, Gaillac Blanc Moelleux, Gaillac Rosé.

✦┱ Gazottes et Fils, Dom. des Terrisses, St-Laurent, 81600 Gaillac; tel. 63 57 16 80 ⲧ By appt.

DOMAINE DES TERRISSES *Demi-sec*★

○ .80 ha 4800 ③ Ⓓ ⑪
83 83

From the same grape varieties, in the same proportions, as the brut. Clear, bright colour with a good firm mousse, and a complex, refined, if reticent, aroma. (1983)
☞ Gazottes et Fils, Dom. des Terrisses, St-Laurent, 81600 Gaillac; tel. 63 57 16 80 ℤ By appt.

DOMAINE DES TERRISSES *Doux*★

○ .80 ha 4800 ③ Ⓓ ⑪
82 83 83

Reminiscent of the brut, but with the addition of sugar, giving a ripe-apple and caramelized grape aroma. Very typical, sweet Gaillac; full, rounded and good sparkle. (1983)
☞ Gazottes et Fils, Dom. des Terrisses, St-Laurent, 81600 Gaillac; tel. 63 57 16 80 ℤ By appt.

LE TONNEAU DE GAILLAC
Demi-sec★

○ 12 000 ③ Ⓓ ▮
83

A medium-sweet sparkling wine with class. Youthful, clear, bright colour; good, tight and long-lasting mousse, and an assertive flowery and fruity aroma. (1983)
☞ Georges Rolland, 36 Rue de la Marne, 81600 Gaillac; tel. 63 57 01 37 ℤ By appt. Closed 16 Sept.–14 June.

LE TONNEAU DE GAILLAC *Brut*★

○ 8000 ③ Ⓓ ▮ ⑪
83

This *Méthode Champenoise* brut is agreeable and typical, with a Mauzac and Len-de-l'el character. Interesting wine for those looking for something out of the ordinary. (1983)
☞ Georges Rolland, 36 Rue de la Marne, 81600 Gaillac; tel. 63 57 01 37 ℤ By appt. Closed 16 Sept.–14 June.

DOMAINE DE TRES CANTOUS
Le Gamay de R. Plageoles★★

■ 1 ha 5400 ② Ⓓ ▮
⑧② 82 83

Lovely, intense, deep-purple colour. Can be ranked with the best. Concentrated and powerful nose with a full, ripe-fruit aroma. On the palate, a well-balanced flavour and weight, rich and nicely rounded, makes it easy to drink. (1983)
☞ Robert Plageoles, Dom. de Tres Cantous, 81600 Gaillac; tel. 63 33 90 40 ℤ By appt.

DOMAINE DE TRES CANTOUS *Les*
Côtes 'Le Vin de Voile'★★★

□ 1 ha 4800 ④ Ⓓ ⑪
66 ⑦① 71 73 75 79

Old and very dry white. Amber-coloured, with hints of vermouth and sherry from being aged in cask since 1971. Unusual aroma, with hints of crushed walnut leaves, quince, dried figs and walnuts. (1971) ✔ Gaillac Moelleux Dom. de Tres Cantous, Gaillac Sauvignon Dom. Roucou Cantemerle Blanc Sec, Gaillac Duras Dom. de Tres Cantous Rouge, Gaillac Gamay Dom. de

Tres Cantous Rouge, Gaillac Mauzac Dom. Roucou Cantemerle Blanc.
☞ Robert Plageoles, Dom. de Tres Cantous, 81140 Gaillac; tel. 63 33 90 40 ℤ By appt.

DOMAINE DE TRES CANTOUS★★

□ 1 ha 6000 ② Ⓓ ▮
82 ★83 ★⑧④ ★84

A mature, deeply coloured wine, not due to oxidation. Well balanced, with a concentrated sweet fruitiness. (1984)
☞ Robert Plageoles, Dom. de Tres Cantous, 81600 Gaillac; tel. 63 33 90 40 ℤ By appt.

DOMAINE DE TRES CANTOUS★★★

■ 1 ha 6000 ② Ⓓ ▮
★81 ★⑧② ★82 ★83

Splendid, deep, intense colour with typical, ripe soft-fruit aroma. Refined and with good length; leaving aside its fine tannin it is good for at least four more years. Extremely well balanced. (1982)
☞ Robert Plageoles, Dom. de Tres Cantous, 81600 Gaillac; tel. 63 33 90 40 ℤ By appt.

Côtes de Buzet

Considered an integral part of the Bordeaux vineyard area since the Middle Ages, the Buzet vines used to stretch from Agen to Marmande. They were cultivated first of all around the abbeys of Fonclaire, Buzet and St-Vincent; further planting was carried out by the inhabitants of Agen. After the phylloxera crisis and the virtual disappearance of the vine, the vineyards were replanted thanks to the efforts of the Coopérative des Producteurs Réunis. Today the vines occupy the terraces and hills of the left bank of the Garonne river. The grape types planted are typically Bordelais – Cabernet-Franc, Cabernet-Sauvignon, Merlot and Malbec for red and rosé wines, Sémillon and Muscadelle for the whites. But what gives Buzet wines their quality and originality is the way they are 'raised'. The Coopérative des Producteurs Réunis, for example, unlike any other Buzet producer, raises all its wine in wood. It has more than 3000 barrels, the old ones being replaced regularly by its own coopers. The same traditional wine-making methods that are used in the big châteaux of the Gironde are used here to produce wines that are classically smooth, yet meaty, tannic and long-lived. The cooperative vinifies the harvest from other estates, such as the châteaux of Gueyze and Bouchet, separately, and a few independent owners are marketing their own wines with success. The red Buzet wines go marvellously with local dishes such as duck, goose and rabbit.

CHATEAU DE GUEYZE★★

■ 80ha 200000 **3** **D** ⑪ ↓
★75 79 80 ⑧ **81** 82 **82**

Deep garnet colour; complex ripe-fruit nose with hints of venison and leather. Full flavour and fine tannin suggest that with age this will make a fine bottle. A well-bred, elegant wine. (1981)
↦ Vign. Réunis des Côtes-de-Buzet, Buzet-sur-Baïse, 47160 Damazan; tel. 53 79 44 30 ▾ By appt.

NICOLAS★

■ 695000 **2** ▪
Light colour; intense vanilla bouquet, with good fruit and balance on the palate. A good example of the appellation. (1983)
↦ Ets Nicolas, 2 Rue Valmy, 94220 Charenton; tel. 01 37 59 20 ▾ No visitors.

CHATEAU PIERRON★

■ 14ha 70000 **2** **D** ⑪ ↓
★71 ★75 ★⑦ 81 ★⑧ ★**82** 83

This lovely estate still has some old vines, which account for the quality of its wines. The 1982 has fine bright ruby colour, with concentrated ripe-fruit aroma. Supple and rounded on the palate, showing genuine quality. Needs ageing for a few years. (1982)
↦ René Van den Bosch, Route de Mézin, 47600 Nérac; tel. 53 65 05 52 ▾ By appt. Mon.–Fri. 9.00–12.00/14.00–19.00.

VIGNERONS REUNIS DES COTES-DE-BUZET *Cuvée Napoleon*★★★

■ 200000 **3** **D** ⑪ ↓
79 ★80 81 **81** 82

From carefully selected grapes grown in the best areas, this wine spends 18 months in new oak casks. Deep garnet colour and on the nose a harmonious blend of blackberry, blackcurrant and vanilla. Firm, well structured and full of tannin on the palate; a fine wine which requires ageing. (1981)
↦ Vign. Réunis des Côtes-de-Buzet, Buzet-sur-Baïse, 47160 Damazan; tel. 53 79 44 30 ▾ By appt.

VIGNERONS REUNIS DES COTES-DE-BUZET★★

■ 100000 **3** **D** ⑪ ↓
★79 80 **80** 81 **81** 82

This cooperative maintains its own stock of more than 3000 oak barrels for ageing its wine Bordeaux-style. 1981 has a vivid red colour with soft fruit aromas. The predominant Merlot gives a noticeable suppleness. A well-balanced wine to be drunk from now onwards. (1981) ✔ Côtes de Buzet Ch. du Bouchet, Côtes de Buzet Ch. de Sevèze.
↦ Vign. Réunis des Côtes-de-Buzet, Buzet-sur-Baïses, 47160 Damazan; tel. 53 79 44 30 ▾ By appt.

DOMAINE DE VERSAILLES★

■ 8ha 48000 **3** **D** ▪ ↓
★78 ★⑦ ★80 ★82 ★83 84

From an old estate well known for its quality wines made and aged the traditional way. Beautiful garnet-tinged colour, gamey, leathery nose, and fairly long, supple finish. Ready to drink from now onwards. (1979)
↦ J. Ryckman; Dom. de Versailles, Montagnac sur-Auvignon, 47600 Nérac; tel. 53 97 10 53 ▾ Daily 9.00–12.00/14.00–19.00.

Côtes du Frontonnais

Fronton, the well-known wine of Toulouse, along with its twin, Villaudric, come from very old vineyards which once belonged to the Knights of St John. During the siege of Montauban, Louis XIII and Richelieu are said to have whiled away the time in comparative tastings. The vineyards were revived after the phylloxera catastrophe thanks to the creation of the Fronton and Villaudric cooperatives, and a little-known grape variety, the Negrette – otherwise found only in Gaillac – was reinstated. The other varieties blended with it are the Cot, Cabernet-Franc, Cabernet-Sauvignon, Fer, Syrah, Gamay, Cinsaut and Mauzac.

The red wines with a high proportion of Cabernet, Gamay or Syrah are light, fruity and aromatic. Those with more Negrette are more powerful and tannic with a distinctive bouquet from the soil. Côtes du Frontonnais should be drunk with cassoulet or Toulouse sausage. The area also produces some fresh, pleasantly fruity rosés.

DOMAINE DE BAUDARE★★

■ 4ha 25000 **2** **D** ▪ ↓
77 78 ⑧ **82** 83

Attractive colour and fine, discreet aromas. Well balanced on the palate and very fruity. (1982)
✔ Vin de Pays de Comté Tolosan.
↦ Claude Vigouroux, Dom. de Baudare, 82370 La Bastide-St-Pierre; tel. 63 30 51 33 ▾ By appt.

DOMAINE DE BAUDARE★★

◪ 4ha 5500 **2** **D** ▪ ↓
84 ⑧

Dry and aromatic, well balanced, and has a pleasant fruitiness. (1984)
↦ Claude Vigouroux, Dom. de Baudare, 82370 La Bastide-St-Pierre; tel. 63 30 51 33 ▾ By appt.

CHATEAU BELLEVUE LA FORET★★

■ 96ha 76000 ❸ Ⓓ ▮ ⬇

77 78 79 82 ★🔳

A pacesetter in the appellation. Astonishingly rounded, very fruity and flowery. Drink young and slightly chilled. (1983)
🌶 SCEA Ch. Bellevue la Forêt, 31620 Fronton; tel. 61 82 43 21 ⵋ Mon.–Fri. 8.00–12.00/14.00–18.00 🌶 P. Germain and H. de Galard.

CHATEAU BELLEVUE LA FORET★★

◪ 96ha 48000 ❸ Ⓓ ▮ ⬇

82 83 🔳

A refined rosé characterized by its outstanding fruitiness. The 1983 has turned out particularly well. (1983)
🌶 SCEA Ch. Bellevue la Forêt, 31620 Fronton; tel. 61 82 43 21 ⵋ Mon.–Fri. 8.00–12.00/14.00–18.00 🌶 P. Germain and H. de Galard.

DOMAINE CAZE *Villaudric*★

◪ 4ha 24000 ❷ Ⓓ ▮

80 ★81 82 ★83 🔳 .

Attractive rosé with beautiful colour and clean, fruity aroma. Lively and delicate on the palate. (1984) ✔ Côtes de Frontonnais Villaudric Dom. Caze Rouge.
🌶 Maurice Rougevin-Baville, Dom. Caze, Villaudric, 31620 Fronton; tel. 61 82 90 30 ⵋ By appt.

DOMAINE DE LA COLOMBIERE
Villaudric Réserve★★

■ 8ha 48000 ❷ Ⓓ ▮

Similar aromatic and fruity characteristics to the Cuvée Chabanon. Light, fruity and ready for drinking. ✔ Côtes de Frontonnais Vin Gris Villaudric.
🌶 Baron F. de Driesen, Dom. de la Colombière, Villaudric, 31620 Fronton; tel. 61 82 44 05 ⵋ Mon.–Sat. 8.00–12.00/14.00–18.00. Closed on public holidays.

DOMAINE DE LA COLOMBIERE
Cuvée Chabanon★★★

■ 7ha 22000 ❸ Ⓓ ▮

78 79 80 ★81 ★Ⓑ ★🔳 ★83

The 1982 is typical, with an intense aroma of blackcurrants and violets. On the palate, very concentrated and full of fruit; a successful wine for the appellation. (1982)
🌶 Baron F. de Driesen, Dom. de la Colombière, Villaudric, 31620 Fronton; tel. 61 82 44 05 ⵋ Mon.–Sat. 8.00–12.00/14.00–18.00. Closed on public holidays.

CHATEAU CRANSAC★★★

■ 10ha 60000 ❸ Ⓓ ⬙

Ⓑ 🔳

Deep colour and a subtle and elegant aroma, characteristic of the Negrette grape. Well balanced on the palate with an elegant finish. Ready to drink now. (1982)
🌶 Cave Coop. de Fronton, Route de Montauban, 31620 Fronton; tel. 61 82 41 27 ⵋ By appt 🌶 Mme de Beaumont.

DOMAINE DE FAOUQUET★

■ 4.63ha 16000 ❷ Ⓓ ▮ ⬙ ⬇

82 Ⓐ 🔳 84

The 1983 has great concentration. Beautiful, intense colour, jammy aroma and flavour result in a powerful but rounded wine. (1983)
🌶 Robert Beringuier, Dom. de Faouquet, Bouloc, 31620 Fronton; tel. 61 82 06 66 ⵋ By appt.

CHATEAU DE LAUROU★

■ 30ha 660000 ❷ Ⓓ ⬙

80 81 Ⓑ 🔳 Ⓑ

Characterized by its flowery aroma, fruitiness and lightness on the palate. (1982)
🌶 Campillo-Perry, Dom. de Laurou, 31620 Fronton; tel. 61 82 40 88 ⵋ No visitors.

CHATEAU MONTAURIOL★★★

■ 30ha 96000 ❷ Ⓓ ▮ ⬇

82 83 🔳

Deep red colour and a heady, elegant bouquet. Full-bodied on the palate. Typical Villaudric that can be kept for several years before drinking. (1983) ✔ Côtes de Frontonnais Vin de Pays.
🌶 Cave Coop. de Villaudric, Villaudric, 31620 Fronton; tel. 61 82 44 14 ⵋ By appt. Closed Sun.

CHATEAU LA PALME★

■ 17ha 77000 ❷ ▮ ⬇

Ⓐ 🔳 83 84

Light and fruity. Easy to drink. Ready now. (1982)
🌶 Martine Ethuin, Ch. la Palme, 31340 Villemur-sur-Tarn; tel. 61 09 02 82 ⵋ By appt.

PIERRE DE SEGUIER★

■ 176ha 220000 ❷ Ⓓ ▮ ⬇

81 Ⓐ 🔳 83

Attractive, well-developed colour, and fine, fruity aroma. Beautifully rounded on the palate; ready for drinking in two or three years' time. (1982)
🌶 Cave Coop. de Villaudric, Villaudric, 31620 Fronton; tel. 61 82 44 14 ⵋ By appt. Closed Sun.

Lavilledieu VDQS

To the north of the Fronton region, on the Tarn and Garonne terraces, the small vineyard of Lavilledieu produces red and rosé wines. The production, which is classified VDQS, is still very limited.

HUGUES DE VERDALLE**

■   16ha   96 000   2 D ■
*⑦⑤ *81 *82 *83

A harmonious blend of Gamay, Syrah, Cabernet, Tannat and a small quantity of Négrette gives this wine, despite its youth, maturity and individuality together with the roundness and smoothness characteristic of the appellation. (1983)
↱ Coop. La Ville-Dieu-du-Temple, 82290 La Ville-Dieu-du-Temple; tel. 63 31 60 05 ☎ By appt.

Côtes du Brulhois VDQS

COOPERATIVE DES COTES-DU-BRULHOIS*

■   150ha   500 000   2 D ■ ↓
*80 *81 *⑧② *82

The cooperative has recently been promoted to VDQS status. Its 1982 is particularly successful, with fine, fruity aromas; warmth and body on the palate, and a long finish. Good drinking with the regional cuisine. (1982)
↱ Cave Coop. des Côtes-du-Brulhois, Donzac, 82340 Auvillar; tel. 63 39 91 92.

Côtes du Marmandais VDQS

Surrounded by the gravel soils of Entre-Deux-Mers, Duras and Buzet, Côtes du Marmandais wines are produced by the cooperatives of Beaupuy and Cocumont. The whites are made from Sémillon, Sauvignon, Muscadelle and Ugni Blanc grapes, and are dry, lively and fruity. The reds, made from Bordeaux grape varieties as well as Abouriou, Bovillet and Grappu grapes, have a fruity bouquet and are relatively soft.

CAVE COOPERATIVE DE BEAUPUY*

■   200ha   100 000   2 D ■ ↓
*80 *81 *⑧② *82

Lovely brick-red colour with a youthful ripe-fruit nose; fleshy and robust on the palate, although beginning to show a certain maturity. A well-balanced wine worth giving two or three years more in bottle. (1982) ✔ Côtes-de-Marmandais, Rouge, Côtes-de-Marmandais Blanc Sec.
↱ Cave Coop. de Beaupuy, 47200 Marmande; tel. 53 64 32 04 ☎ By appt.

CAVE COOPERATIVE DE COCUMONT*

□   3ha   25 000   2 D ■ ↓
80 *81 *⑧② *82

A dry white made from classic Aquitaine grapes, vigorous and aromatic. The 1982 is distinguished by its fullness and length. (1982)
↱ Cave Coop. de Cocumont, 47250 Cocumont; tel. 53 94 50 21 ☎ By appt.

DOMAINE DES GEAIS*

■   2ha   15 000   2 D ■ ↓

Lovely ruby-red colour and powerful blend of red fruit and flowers on the nose. Round and pleasant on the palate with good balance. (1982)
↱ MM. Boissoneau Pere et Fils, Ch. de la Vieille-Tour, St-Michel-Lapujade, 33190 La Réole; tel. 56 61 72 14 ☎ By appt.

Entraygues, Estaing, Marcillac

Flanked by the causses of Aubrac, the Cantal mountains and the Lévezou plateau, the Aveyron region is properly part of the Massif Central. The small appellations of Marcillac, Estaing, Entraygues and Fel were founded by the monks of Conques during the ninth century.

Marcillac produces rustic red wines from the Fer Servadon or Mansoi varieties. The very distinctive aromas, a mixture of fruity and vegetal notes, make these wines instantly recognizable. The wines from Estaing are divided between fresh, perfumed reds, based on the Fer and Gamay varieties, and very individual whites, made from a blend of Chenin, Mauzac and Rousselon grapes. These lively wines have a marked perfume from the local soil. The white wines of Entraygues are produced from equal amounts of Chenin and Mauzac grapes, grown on narrow schistous terraces cut into steep hillsides. These fresh, fruity wines are perfect with river trout and Cantal Doux cheese. The red wines of Fel are solid and earthy and should be drunk with mountain lamb and the charcuterie of the Auvergne.

Vins d'Entraygues VDQS

HENRI AVALLON**

□   1ha   6000   2 D ■
*83

Pale-yellow with a flinty, vegetal nose, good acidity and balance. (1983) ✔ Vin d'Entraygues et du Fel Rouge, Vin d'Entraygues et du Fel Rosé.
↱ Henri Avallon, St-Georges, 12140 Entraygues; tel. 65 44 53 38 ☎ By appt.

Vins D'Estaing VDQS

LE VIALA**

□   1ha   6000   2 D ⅲ ↓
*83

From a combination of Chenin Blanc and the more southerly Mauzac, which tones down the

479

acidity. A unique wine with a more vegetal than flowery nose. (1983) ✔ Vin d'Estaing le Viala Rouge, Vin d'Estaing le Viala Rosé.
♠ Pierre Rieu, Le Viala, 12190 Estaing; tel. 65 48 20 96 ☎ By appt.

Vins de Marcillac VDQS

LE CROS DE CASSAGNES-COMTAUX★★

■		4 ha	12 000	② Ⓓ ◐ ⌂
83				

An intense, deep and dark-coloured wine of a rustic nature. Individual on the nose and palate, with a surprising range of unusual flavours. Balanced, light, with scarcely any tannin. (1983)
♠ Laurens-Teulier, Goutrens, 12390 Rignac; tel. 65 72 71 77 ☎ By appt.

PIERRE LACOMBE★★

■		3 ha	3000	② Ⓓ ◐
83				

Very special bouquet. Light, harmonious and fairly tannic. Although lacking depth, an unbeatable thirst-quencher. (1983)
♠ Pierre Lacombe, Avenue de Rodez, 12330 Marcillac; tel. 65 71 80 05 ☎ By appt.

CAVE VIGNERONS DU VALLON VALADY★★

■		80 ha	300 000	② Ⓓ ▤
83				

Typically highly coloured, with a soft-fruit aroma. Should be drunk quickly, despite a hint of tannin. (1983) ✔ Marcillac Cuvée Réservée Rouge, Marcillac Tradition Rosé.
♠ Cave Vign. Vallon-Vallady, Valady, 12330 Marcillac; tel. 65 72 70 21 ☎ Mon.–Sat. 9.00–12.00/14.00–18.00.

Béarn

Côtes de Béarn wines may be produced in three different areas. The first two are identical to the appellation areas of Jurançon and Madiran; the third covers the communes around Orthez and Salies-de-Béarn.

Following the phylloxera crisis, vineyards were replanted on the foothills of the Pyrenees and the gravelly soils of the Gave valley. The red wines are made from Tannat, Cabernet-Sauvignon, and Cabernet-Franc (Bouchy) grapes, and also from the older varieties of Manseng Noir, Courbu Rouge and Fer Servadou. They are rich and full bodied, and go well with garbure – a local goose dish – or grilled pigeon. The best Béarn appellation wines are

the rosés; they are lively, delicate and well-balanced, with the subtle aromas of a Cabernet wine.

FEBUS ABAN★

□		3.20 ha	12 000	② Ⓓ ▤ ⌂
★83				

Made from the local Raffiat grape, this is a good example of wine from the foothills of the Pyrenees. Very aromatic with scents of wild flowers; a lively, dry wine with the characteristic gun-flint taste. Good with salmon. (1983) ✔ Béarn Cuvée Henri de Navarre Rouge, Béarn Cuvée des Vignerons Rouge, Béarn Bellocq Rosé.
♠ Coop. Vinicole de Bellocq, 64270 Salies-de-Béarn; tel. 59 38 00 30 ☎ By appt.

Irouléguy

The Irouléguy vines (called Chacoli on the Spanish side of the border) are the last remains of the huge Basque vineyard complex that dates back to the eleventh century, and show how determined the local wine-makers have been in perpetuating an ancient tradition. The vines are planted on the foothills of the Pyrenees, and spread over the communes of St-Etienne de Baïgorry, Irouléguy and Anhaux.

The older grape varieties are gradually being displaced by Cabernet-Sauvignon, Cabernet-Franc and Tannat for red wines, and Courbu, Gros Manseng and Petit Manseng for whites. All the grapes are vinified at the cooperative in Irouléguy. The cherry-coloured rosés are light, lively and fragrant, very good with piperade – a type of pizza – or charcuterie. The Irouléguy reds are strongly scented, sometimes quite tannic wines that go well with the local confits and regional cheeses.

CAVE COOPERATIVE D'IROULEGUY★★

■		18 ha	150 000	② Ⓓ ▤
81 ★⑧② ★⑧② 83				

Attractive dark-red colour. Highly aromatic, with a raspberry aroma. Lively and virile on the palate. May be kept for two or three years. (1982)
♠ Cave Coop. d'Irouléguy, 64430 St-Etienne-de-Baïgorry; tel. 59 37 41 33 ☎ By appt.

Jurançon

Jurançon wines have an ancient pedigree. They were drunk at the christening of Henri of Navarre (later Henri IV) and for centuries were the staple of French family celebrations. In Jurançon we find the earliest example of quality control and market intervention: the wines were legally protected from foreign competition, while the Parliament of Navarre instituted the classification of vineyard land according to the standard of the wine produced on each parcel. Exported via Bayonne, the wines were highly prized by the Dutch and the English. In fact, Jurançon reached a pitch of celebrity which faded only because of phylloxera. Through the efforts of the 'Cave de Gan' and a few dedicated growers, the vineyards were replanted with the old grape varieties and the traditional methods of wine making revived.

In this appellation the vintage is of primary importance; sweet Jurançon wines need a slow, late ripening and have to be picked in stages, as they reach the correct degree of overripeness. The traditional grape varieties are all white; Gros Manseng, Petit Manseng and Courbu. Because it is not unusual for the harvest to last until the first snows, the vines are grown on trellisses to avoid frost damage.

Jurançon Sec is a very aromatic dry Blanc de Blancs wine (a white wine from white grapes) that has a beautiful light colour with greenish tints, and a hint of honey on the nose. It goes very well with trout and salmon from the river Gave. The sweet wines from Jurançon have a fine golden colour, and a complex nose that suggests tropical fruit and spices, with a hint of nutmeg and cinnamon. Their balance of acidity and sweetness make them obvious partners for foie gras. The wines can age for many years, and may be drunk at any stage throughout the meal, going particularly well with fish in cream sauce and sheep's cheese from the Ossau valley. The best vintages are 1970, 1971, 1975, 1981, 1982 and 1983.

CLOS CANCAILLAU *Crème de Tête*★★★

□	16ha	77000	🟥3 🟦D 🔲
81 ⓐ2 🟦82			

Highly aromatic, with typical scents of guava and pineapple. Very rounded but with good acidity – very elegant and delicate. (1982)
🍷 Alfred Barrère, Lahourcade, 61450 Mourenx; tel. 59 60 08 15 ⵏ By appt.

DOMAINE CAUHAPE★★★

□	7.5ha	30000	🟥3 🟦D 🔲 🔲 ⬇
82 🟦82 83			

A superbly balanced sweet wine, full, rich and well-structured. Its lovely aromas of tropical fruit make it an excellent example of its appellation. Drink this with fresh foie gras. (1982) ✓ Jurançon Sec Blanc.
🍷 Henri Ramonteu, Dom. Cauhape, 64360 Monein; tel. 59 21 33 02 ⵏ By appt.

COOPERATIVE DE GAN-JURANCON *Prestige Moelleux*★★

□	18ha	45000	🟥3 🟦D 🔲 ⬇
60 70 71 **73 75** 80 ★⑧ ★🟦81 82 🟦82 ★83			

The slopes around Jurançon produce a soft, rich, very highly perfumed wine from grapes that have dried on the vine without being affected by *pourriture noble* (noble rot). Characterized by a fresh and delicate aroma, good body and balance between sweetness and acidity. (1981) ✓ Other Jurançon.
🍷 Cave Coop. de Gan-Jurançon, 64290 Gan; tel. 59 21 57 03 ⵏ Mon.–Sat. 9.00–12.00/14.00–19.00.

CRU LAMOUROUX★★★

□	4ha	18000	🟦4 🟦D 🔲
79 81 82 🟦82 **83** 🟦83			

Exceptionally rich and luscious wine made in mid-November from late-picked grapes. Complex pineapple, honey and wild-flower aromas and perfect balance between richness and acidity. (1983)
🍷 J. Chigé et R. Ziemek, La Chappelle-de-Rousse, 64110 Jurançon; tel. 59 21 74 41 ⵏ Daily.

CLOS-UROULAT★★★

□	2ha	50000	🟥3 🟦D 🔲 🔲
★82 83 🟦83			

Classic sweet Jurançon with a marvellous balance between acidity and sugar. An ideal aperitif, with lingering aromas of peach, pineapple and cinnamon. Try it with ewe's milk cheese. (1982)
🍷 Charles Hours, Quartier Trouilh, 64360 Monein; tel. 59 21 43 19 ⵏ Daily 8.00–12.00/14.00–18.00. Closed Sun.

Jurançon Sec

COOPERATIVE DE GAN-JURANCON *Grain Sauvage*★★

□	25ha	15000	2 D ▪ ⬥

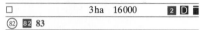

Flowery aroma and full-bodied character. Chewy on the palate. (1983) ✔ Juançon Sec Brut Réserve, Jurançon Sec Peyre Or 1981, Jurançon Apéritif Henri IV Jurançon Cuvée du Quadricentenaire, Jurançon Prestige 1981.
➤ Cave Coop. de Gan-Jurançon, Gan, 64290 Jurançon; tel. 59 21 57 03 � Mon.–Sat. 9.00–12.00/14.00–19.00.

CLOS MIRABEL★★

□	3ha	16000	2 D ▪

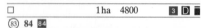

A dry Jurançon, very lively and aromatic. The 1982 has the fruity aromas typical of the appellation. Crisp and fresh. (1982)
➤ Raymond Dubois, Clos Mirabel, 64110 Jurançon; tel. 59 06 24 14 ☵ No visitors.

NICOLAS★

□		2 ▪

Dry and rather flat to start with, followed by a hint of bitterness. (1983)
➤ Ets Nicolas, 2 Rue Valmy, 94220 Charenton; tel. 01 37 59 20 ☵ No visitors.

CLOS-UROULAT★★★

□	1ha	4800	3 D ▪
⑧₃	84	84	

The present owner of this vineyard uses a mixture of modern and traditional methods to produce this aromatic, lively, vigorous yet elegant wine, which should be drunk now. (1983)
➤ Charles Hours, Quartier Trouilh, 64360 Monein; tel. 59 21 43 19 ☵ Daily 8.00–12.00/14.00–18.00. Closed Sun.

Madiran

Originating in Gallo-Roman times, the wine from Madiran was already being served to ninth-century pilgrims passing to or from the shrine of Saint-Jacques de Compostelle (Santiago de Compostela) in Spain. The main grape is the Tannat, producing a dark-red wine that, when young, is quite tough but with an immediate raspberry scent; it definitely needs bottle age to reach its full potential. The other grapes that may be blended with it are Cabernet-Sauvignon, Cabernet-Franc, and Fer Servadou (or 'Pinenc').

Madiran is a good example of a 'virile' wine. However, it may be made in a lighter style with a higher proportion of Cabernet and should then be drunk young to make the most of its round fruitiness. Madiran goes very well with confit d'oie or magrets de canard, always underdone. The traditional-style Madiran wines, with a higher proportion of Tannat, need to age for a few years. A well-aged Madiran has a faintly burnt aroma and is rich, full-bodied and meaty, a good accompaniment to game, or the sheep's cheeses that come from the high valleys.

CHATEAU D'AYDIE★★

■	22ha	550000	3 D ▪ ⬥ ⬥
79 81 ⑧₂ 82 83			

From a leading producer of Madiran in the modern style. Rich aromas of concentrated fruit and toast. Rounded, firm and powerful on the palate; a few years' ageing will make a great bottle. (1983)
➤ GAEC Vignobles Laplace, Ch. d'Aydie, 64330 Garlin; tel. 59 04 01 17 ☵ Mon.–Sat. 8.00–13.00/14.00–20.00.

DOMAINE BARREJAT★★

■	13ha	60000	2 D ▪ ⬥
⑧₃			

Dark colour, slightly woody aroma and full-bodied tannic character. A typical Madiran, to be kept for at least seven years. (1983)
➤ Maurice Capmartin, Dom. Barréjat, 32400 Maumusson; tel. 62 69 74 92 ☵ Mon.–Sat. 8.00–12.00/14.00–20.00.

DOMAINE DU CRAMPILH★

■	20ha	132000	2 D ▪
74 79 ★81 ⑧₂ 82			

A short maceration method is used here to produce this supple and easy-to-drink wine. Ready now. (1982)
➤ Lucien Oulié, Aurion-Idernes, 64350 Lembeye; tel. 59 04 01 61 ☵ By appt.

CHATEAU DE GAYON★★

■	6ha	33000	3 D ▪ ⬥
⑧₁			

Lovely dark colour; a spicy, vanilla-and-toast nose, and still-perceptible tannin which it should lose after a few years. Round, full bodied with a long finish; keep for a few years in order to enjoy it at its best. (1981)
➤ Vign. Réunis du Vic-Bilh Madiran, Crouseilles, 64350 Lembeye; tel. 59 68 10 93 ☵ Mon.–Sat. 8.30–12.30/14.00–16.30.

DOMAINE DE MAOURIES★★

■	4ha	18000	2 D ▪ ⬥
78 79 81 ★82 83			

Intense, powerful nose full of Tannat fruit. Very typically Madiran, both in aroma and flavour. Very attractive. Will keep for a long time but can be drunk now. (1981)
➤ André Dufau Père et Fils, Labarthète, 32400 Riscle; tel. 62 69 80 36 ☵ By appt.

CHATEAU MONTUS★★★

■ 19ha 48000 ☐2 D ⦿ ⚲
㉒ 82

With a striking intensity of colour and a vanilla and oaky aroma, an impressively full-bodied and tannic wine that will keep for a long time. (1982)
⮑ Alain Brumont, Maumusson, 32400 Riscle; tel. 69 74 67 ⟐ By appt.

CHATEAU DU PERRON★★

■ 8ha 60000 ☐2 D ▮
80 81 ㉒ 82

Typically tannic and long-lasting. Very ripe soft-fruit aromas and very well structured. Keep for several years. (1982)
⮑ J.-P. Crouzet, Ch. du Perron, Madiran, 65700 Maubourguet; tel. 62 31 97 49 ⟐ No visitors.

DOMAINE PICHARD★★

■ 12.5ha 55000 ☐2 D ⦿
78 79 80 ★㉒ ★82

Pleasantly supple. Fine vanilla nose. Vigorous and very full on the palate, with tannins that will soften in several years' time. Will be a fine bottle. (1982)
⮑ Auguste Vigneau, Soublecause, 65700 Maubourguet; tel. 62 96 35 73 ⟐ By appt.

PRODUCTEURS DE PLAIMONT
Collection Plaimont★★

■ 100ha 250000 ☐4 D ⦿ ⚲
79 ★80 81 82 82

Fine ruby colour and powerful but still closed-up nose with a hint of vanilla and new oak. On the palate a touch of caramel and vanilla, with excellent balance and a long, warm finish. A bottle for keeping and drinking with strongly flavoured dishes. (1982) ✔ VDQS Côtes de St-Mont Blanc, Rouge Tradition, Rouge Collection; Vin de Pays Côtes de Gascogne Rouge, Vin de Pays Côtes de Gascogne Blanc.
⮑ Producteurs de Plaimont, 32400 St-Mont; tel. 62 69 78 87 ⟐ By appt.

DOMAINE DE TESTON★★

■ 18ha 65000 ☐3 D ▮ ⚲
80 81 ㉒ 82 83

The Lafitte family has made wine for several generations, producing particularly high-quality supple Madirans with 50 per cent Tannat. The 1982 has a lovely concentrated ripe-fruit aroma but is robust and full bodied on the palate. Well balanced and easy to drink, it will be at its peak in three to four years. (1982)

⮑ Lafitte Père et Fils, 32400 Maumusson; tel. 62 69 74 54 ⟐ Daily 8.00–12.00/14.00–19.00.

VIGNERONS REUNIS DU VIC-BILH
Rot du Roy★★

■ 20ha 95000 ☐3 D ▮ ⚲
81 81 ㉒ 83

From the cooperative which revived the Madiran appellations. A fruity-scented wine, full bodied and well structured, with soft tannin, good balance and lingering finish. (1981)
⮑ Vign. Réunis du Vic-Bilh Madiran, Crouseilles, 64350 Lembeye; tel. 59 68 10 93 ⟐ Mon.–Sat. 8.30–12.30/14.00–16.30.

VIGNERONS REUNIS DU VIC-BILH★

■ 150ha 330000 ☐2 D ▮ ⚲
㉓

This Madiran is given a short fermentation to be ready sooner. Suppleness and soft tannins distinguish it from the traditional style. Note, too, its youthful soft-fruit aromas. Drink now. (1983)
⮑ Vign. Réunis du Vic-Bilh Madiran, Crouseilles, 64350 Lembeye; tel. 59 68 10 93 ⟐ Mon.–Sat. 8.30–12.30/14.00–16.30.

Pacherenc du Vic-Bilh

This white wine comes from the same area as Madiran. Local grape varieties – Arrufiat, Manseng and Courbu – are used in combination with the Bordeaux Sauvignon and Sémillon, a fact which explains the extraordinary range of aromas in the wines. Depending on the weather pattern of the vintage, the wines may be dry and fragrant, or sweet with good acidity. The latter version is an astounding wine, rich and full bodied with well-married aromas of almond, hazelnut and tropical fruits – perfect with pâté de foie gras. The drier wines make an excellent aperitif.

DOMAINE BOUSCASSE★★

☐ 400000 ☐3 D ⦿
82 82 83

Rich and complex aromas hinting of wild flowers and exotic fruits. Lively on the palate, with good body, and ready to drink now. Recommended as an aperitif, or to accompany freshwater fish. (1983)
⮑ Alain Brumont, Dom. de Bouscassé, Maumusson, 32400 Riscle; tel. 62 69 74 67 ⟐ By appt.

LAPLACE★★★

☐ 2ha 9000 ☐3 D ▮ ⚲
㉒ 82 83

Pacherenc wine is a rarity which you absolutely must discover. This 1983 has a very rich range of aromas with hints of pineapple and wild flowers. Particularly well-vinified, vigorous and full-bodied, this is a great white wine to accompany fish in sauce or poultry, and also makes an ideal

apéritif. (1983)
↞ GAEC Vignoble Laplace, Ch. d'Aydie, 64330, Garlin; tel. 59 04 01 17 **Ⓨ** By appt.

DOMAINE DE TESTON★★

□		6000	**2** **D** **▪** **↓**
㉓			

Pale-green colour, with characteristic flowery aromas. A dry, vigorous wine, with a taste of gunflint. (1983)
↞ *M.* Lafitte Père et Fils, Dom. de Teston, Maumusson-Laguian, 32400 Riscle; tel. 62 69 74 58 **Ⓨ** By appt.

VIGNERONS REUNIS DU VIC-BILH★★

□	20ha	40000	**2** **D** **↓**

A lovely soft Pacherenc with rich aromas; both lively and sweet on the palate, this very original wine may be drunk as an aperitif or with the local foie gras.
↞ Vignerons Réunis du Vic-Bilh, Crouselles, 64350 Lembeye; tel. 59 68 10 93 **Ⓨ** By appt.

Tursan VDQS

Once owned by Eleanor of Aquitaine, the Tursan vineyards produce red, white and rosé wines. Best of all are the whites, made from the very distinctive Barroque grape variety. With its refreshing flavour and characteristic bouquet, a white Tursan goes well with freshwater fish, especially eels and shad.

LES VIGNERONS DE TURSAN
Etiquette Noire★

■	250ha	350000	**2** **D** **⑾** **↓**

Attractive, deep-red colour and pleasant nose. The hint of pine is a reminder of the Landes countryside. Interestingly light on the palate, with a slight sparkle.
↞ Lea Vignerons de Tursan, 40320 Géaune; tel. 58 44 51 55 **Ⓨ** By appt.

LES VIGNERONS DE TURSAN★★

□	40ha	260000	**1** **D** **▪** **↓**
★71 72 81 ㉘ ㉚ ㉚ 84			

The ancient Barroque grape variety, of unknown origin, is only to be found in the Tursan district. Dry and vigorous white wine with its own unsophisticated aromas unique to the *terroir* – very flowery, fresh and scented. (1983)
↞ Les Vign. de Tursan, 40320 Geaune; tel. 58 44 51 25 **Ⓨ** Mon.–Sat. 8.00–12.00/14.00–17.30. Closed Sun.

LES VIGNERONS DE TURSAN★★

■	250ha	350000	**2** **D** **⑾** **↓**
81 ㉒ 83 84			

With a darker, denser colour than that of the 'etiquette noire' (black label) wine from the same vineyard, this seems an altogether richer and more complex wine. This is confirmed on the nose, fruitier and less 'primeur', evidence of ageing in oak. Good fruitiness on the palate, with a gamey nose.

↞ Les Vignerons de Tursan, 40320 Géaune; tel. 58 44 51 25 **Ⓨ** By appt.

Côtes de St-Mont VDQS

This, the most recently created Pyrenean appellation, is an extension of the Madiran vineyard. Here, too, the main red grape is the Tannat, whereas for white wines the Clairette, Arrufiat, Courbu, Gros Manseng and Petit Manseng are used. Most of the wine is produced by the dynamic Union de Caves Coopératives in Plaimont. The richly coloured red wines are full bodied, quickly becoming rounded and very pleasing. They should be drunk with grilled meat or the famous Gascony garbures. The delicate rosé wines are worth seeking out for their fruity aromas. The dry and refreshing white wines have the typical bouquet of the region.

PRODUCTEURS DE PLAIMONT
Tradition★★

■	660ha	2 700000	**3** **D** **▪** **↓**
80 81 ★82 ★㉚			

Distinctly traditional wine dominated by the local Tannat, although blended with other varieties that moderate its more astringent properties. Good at any age. (1983) ✔ Madiran, VDQS Côtes de St-Mont Collection, VDQS Côtes de St-Mont Blanc, Vin de Pays Côtes de Gascogne.
↞ Producteurs de Plaimont, 32400 St-Mont; tel. 62 69 78 87 **Ⓨ** By appt.

PRODUCTEURS DE PLAIMONT
Collection★★★

■	100ha	250000	**3** **D** **▪** **↓**
81 ㉛ 82			

Original wine made from high proportion of Tannat, which accounts for its still youthful colour, intense and austere bouquet, full of fruit with earthy overtones, and its firm tannic structure. An outstanding bottle. (1981) ✔ Madiran VDQS Côtes de St-Mont Blanc, VDQS Côtes de St-Mont Tradition, Vin de Pays Côtes de Gascogne.
↞ Producteurs de Plaimont, 32400 St-Mont; tel. 62 69 78 87 **Ⓨ** By appt.

The Dordogne

Coming from land adjacent to the Libourne vineyards, the wines of the Dordogne are separated from those of Bordeaux only by an administrative boundary. The Bordelais refer to them as Vins du Haut-Pays. The regional appellation, Bergerac, comprises red, white and rosé wines. The Côtes du Bergerac produce only red and white wines; the whites are sweet and have a delicate bouquet, the reds are full bodied and round, ideal with poultry or meat cooked in sauce. The Saussignac appellation produces some excellent sweet wines that have a perfect balance of sharpness and sweetness. They are aperitif wines halfway between a white Bergerac and a Monbazillac. The Montravel vineyards, near Castillac, have a strong historical association with the sixteenth-century French writer Montaigne. Production is divided between dry white Montravel, with firm Sauvignon character, and Côtes de Montravel and Haut-Montravel, both elegant, sweet pudding wines. Pécharmant is a red wine harvested on the hills around Bergerac, where the iron-rich soils give it a very distinctive flavour. These wines keep well and, with their delicate bouquet, are the ideal accompaniment to traditional Périgord cuisine.

Monbazillac is one of the most famous dessert wines in France. Established since the fourteenth century, the vineyards face north, on a clay-and-limestone soil. The local micro-climate particularly favours the development of noble rot. As in Sauternes and Barsac, the grapes are harvested in successive batches, picking each individual grape bunch at its optimum ripeness. The wines have a beautiful golden colour, an aroma of honey and wild flowers, and a long finish. They may be drunk as an aperitif, with foie gras, with Roquefort or with most puddings except those based on chocolate. Rich and quite high in alcohol, these fine sweet wines acquire a roasted flavour with age.

Bergerac

DOMAINE DES COMBERIES*

■ 15ha 100000 ② Ⅾ ▤ ⤓

*81 *⑧③

Nose still undeveloped, but a well-structured wine with a long finish. Ready to drink now. (1983)
⚲ Jean-Paul Lhomme, Singleyrac, 24500 Eymet; tel. 53 58 80 19 ⵏ Daily 8.00–12.00/14.00–18.00.

CLOS LA CROIX-BLANCHE**

■ 1.30ha 10000 ② Ⅾ ▤ ⤓

*79 *81 *82 83

This wine has good potential, but is also supple and easy to drink now. (1983) ✔ Côtes de Bergerac Clos la Croix-Blanche.
⚲ Michel Brouilleau, Clos la Croix-Blanche Moelleux, Monestier, 24240 Sigoulès; tel. 53 58 45 82 ⵏ Daily 9.00–12.00/14.00–19.00.

DOMAINE DU DENOIX**

■ 10ha 50000 ② Ⅾ ▤ ⤓

*81 *⑧② *83

Attractive aroma of violets; well balanced and full-bodied; a nice wine which will age well. (1982)
⚲ Claude Ledemé, Le Denoix, Montcaret, 24230 Velines; tel. 53 58 61 08 ⵏ No visitors.

Bergerac

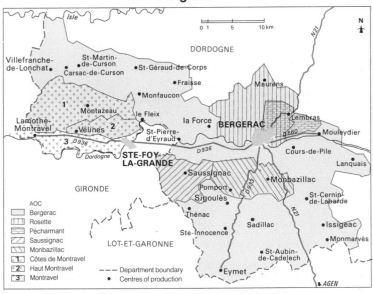

DOMAINE DE FRAYSSE*

■　18ha　120000　２　Ｄ　🍷　⌁

78 79 81 ⑧

This wine, from an exceptional year, has a beautifully delicate scent; it can be drunk from now onwards. (1979) ✔ Bergerac Sec Sauvignon, Bergerac Rosé, Côtes de Bergerac Moelleux, Bergerac Méthode Champenoise.
🍷 Marcel Murer, Dom. de Fraysse, 24500 Eymet; tel. 53 23 81 38 ⊤ Daily 14.00–18.00. Closed Jan. and second week Sept.

DOMAINE DU GOUYAT**

■　7ha　33600　２　Ｄ　🍷　⌁

79 *82 *⑧ ⑧

A wine which needs to be drunk fairly young; good colour and pleasantly rounded on the palate. (1982) ✔ Bergerac Sec. Dom. du Gouyat, Bergerac Rosé Dom.-du-Gouyat, Méthode Champenoise.
🍷 GAEC du Gouyat, Dom. du Gouyat, St-Meard-de-Gurçon, 24610 Villefranche-de-Lonchat; tel. 53 82 45 26 ⊤ Daily 8.00–12.00/14.00–18.00 🍷 *MM.* Dubard Frères

CHATEAU LA JAUBERTIE**

■　20ha　110000　３　Ｄ　🍷　⌁

*75 *76 *81 *⑧ 83

The château – once the property of Henri IV – is rich in historical associations. The estate produces this very good wine, exceptionally rounded and full-bodied. (1982) ✔ Bergerac Ch. la Jaubertie Rosé, Bergerac Sec Ch. la Jaubertie.
🍷 Henry Ryman SA, Ch. la Jaubertie, Colombier 24560 Issigeac; tel. 53 58 32 11 ⊤ By appt.

CHATEAU DE MONTAIGNE*

■　15ha　50000　３　Ｄ　🍷　⌁

*82 ⑧ *83

A typical Bergerac, full-bodied and round, with rather more ageing potential than usual for this appellation. (1982)
🍷 Malher-Besse, Ch. de Montaigne, St-Michel-de-Montaigne, 24230 Velines; tel. 53 58 60 56 ⊤ By appt.

MOULINS-DE-BOISSE**

■　7ha　55000　２　Ｄ　🍷　⌁

*73 75 *76 77 ⑧ ⑧ *83 84

Aromatic, balanced and well-structured wine which will age well. (1983)
🍷 Jean-Louis Molle, Moulins-de-Boisse, 24560 Boisse; tel. 53 58 71 18 ⊤ Daily 8.00–20.00.

CHATEAU DE PANISSEAU*

■　25ha　140000　２　Ｄ　🍷　⌁

*73 78 81 *⑧ *⑧ *83

The château here dates from the 13th century. A nicely presented wine, supple and light, best drunk young. The estate also produces outstandingly subtle dry white wines. (1982) ✔ Bergerac Rosé Panisseau.
🍷 *M.* Becker, Ch. Panisseau, Thenac, 24240 Sigoulès; tel. 53 58 40 03 ⊤ Mon.–Sat. 9.00–12.00/14.00–18.00.

CHATEAU PUY-SERVAIN***

■　7ha　55000　２　Ｄ　🍷

75 76 79 82 ⑧ ⑧

Attractive colour, with an assertive nose, excellent structure and a fine tannin; an excellent keeping wine. Put it to the back of the cellar and forget about it for a while. (1982) ✔ Bergerac Sec Ch. Puy-Servain, Côtes de Bergerac Moelleux Ch. Puy-Servain.
🍷 Paul Hecquet, Cantalouette, Port-St-Foy, 33220 Ponchapt; tel. 57 46 11 46 ⊤ By appt.

CHATEAU LA RAYE***

■　11ha　80000　２　Ｄ　🍷　⌁

76 79 80 81 ⑧ ⑧ 83 84

Although it already has good colour and balance, this wine is worth giving a long ageing period. The château also produces soft, rich wines of great distinction. (1982) ✔ Côtes de Montravel.
🍷 Itey de Peironin, La Raye, 24230 Velines; tel. 53 27 50 14 ⊤ No visitors.

DOMAINE DE LA VAURE*

■　14ha　100000　３　Ｄ　🍷　⌁

*⑧ *83 84

An easy-to-drink wine with a nice colour, to be consumed from now onwards. The estate produces rich, round wines that are usually much better than this 1983 vintage; 1982 especially produced excellent wines in magnum. (1983)
✔ Bergerac Dom. de la Vaure.
🍷 Cave Coop. Le Fleix, Le Fleix, 24130 La Force; tel. 57 46 20 15 ⊤ By appt.

Bergerac Sec

DOMAINE DE COMBRILLAC***

☐　7ha　44000　２　Ｄ　⌁

⑧

'Concombre' (cucumber) was the old name for this château, but one of the former owners found this had little commercial appeal. The wine is slightly sparkling and fresh, fruity and remarkably delicate. (1983) ✔ Côtes de Bergerac Ch. Combrillac Rouge, Côtes de Begerac Ch. Combrillac Moelleux.
🍷 Jean Priou, Dom. de Combrillac, Prigonrieux, 24130 Le Force; tel. 53 58 91 67 ⊤ By appt. Closed 8–20 Aug.

CAVE COOPERATIVE DU FLEIX
*Sauvignon***

☐　10ha　60000　２　Ｄ　🍷

⑧ *84

Extremely aromatic and powerful wine from 100 per cent Sauvignon grapes, with a lovely round character. Good quality and excellent value for money. (1983)
🍷 Cave Coop. du Fleix, Le Fleix, 24130 La Force; tel. 53 46 20 15 ⊤ By appt.

CHATEAU DE MASBUREL★★

☐   3ha   25000   **2** **D** ⬛ ↓
Ⓧ

Lively, slightly petillant Sauvignon, with a delicate nose lent a fullness on the palate by the soil
on which it is grown. (1983) ✔ Côtes de Bergerac,
Bergerac, Haut-Montravel.
↾ Roland Barthoux, Ch. de Masburel, Fouguey-
rolles, 33220 Ste-Foy-La-Grande; tel. 57 46 15 78
Ⓨ By appt.

DOMAINE LA VAURE★★

☐   6ha   40000   **2** **D** ⬛ ↓
Ⓧ

Fresh and fruity and agreeably long on the
palate; perfect example of a dry white Bergerac,
produced by blending traditional grape varieties.
(1983)
↾ Cave Coop. Le Fleix, Le Fleix, 24130 La Force;
tel. 57 46 20 15 Ⓨ By appt.

Côtes de Bergerac

DOMAINE DE L'ANCIENNE CURE★★

■   8ha   43000   **2** **D** ⬛ ↓
78 79 80 81 Ⓧ

This wine has pronounced Cabernet characteristics and a well-developed bouquet. The tasting
room, on the road to Agen, is very popular with
visitors; also try the Monbazillac. (1982) ✔ Monbazillac Dom. de l'Ancienne Cure Blanc Liquoreux, Bergerac Sauvignon Sec, Bergerac Moelleux, Bergerac Rosé.
↾ Pierre Roche, Colombier, 24560 Issigeac; tel.
53 58 32 28 Ⓨ By appt.

CHATEAU COURTS-LES-MUTS★★★

■   10ha   50000   **3** **D** ⬛ ⑪ ↓
79 80 81 82 Ⓧ

Flowery nose with a slight scent of wood. A
good, well-balanced wine aged in wood and
ready to drink. Visitors are warmly welcomed by
the young wine-growers running this vineyard.
(1983) ✔ Bergerac Ch. Court-les-Muts Sec, Saussignac Ch. Court-les-Muts Blanc Moelleux, Vin
de Fête Ch. Court-les-Muts Mousseux.
↾ Pierre Sadoux, Razac-de-Saussignac, 24240
Sigoulès; tel. 53 27 92 17 Ⓨ Mon.–Sat. 9.00–
11.30/14.00–17.30.

**Château
Court-Les-Muts**

APPELLATION CÔTES DE BERGERAC CONTROLÉE
P. SADOUX
PROPRIÉTAIRE-VIGNERON À RAZAC DE SAUSSIGNAC (DORDOGNE)
MIS EN BOUTEILLE AU CHÂTEAU

DOMAINE DE GOLSE★★★

■   7ha   40000   **3** **D** ⬛ ↓
75 79 81 ★Ⓧ

A wine to keep. Full-bodied and with delicate
aromas; in a few years this will be a very great

wine. (1982) ✔ Côtes Montravel Ch. la Cabanelle
Blanc Moelleux.
↾ Jean Bertrand, Golse, Pontchapt, 33220 Ste-
Foy-La-Grande; tel. 57 46 22 53 Ⓨ By appt.

DOMAINE DU GRAND-BOISSE★★

■   7ha   30000   **3** **D** ⑪ ↓
80 82

Produced by the Bergerac cooperative, this is a
generous, well-rounded wine with a fine nose.
(1982)
↾ Cave Coop. de Bergerac, Bd de l'Entrepôt,
24100 Bergerac; tel. 53 57 16 27 Ⓨ By appt.

LA TOUR DE GRANGEMONT★★

■   12ha   45000   **2** **D** ⬛ ↓
76 77 78 79 80 81 ★Ⓧ ★**82**

Forward and well balanced. Will keep. Typical of
the 1982 vintage. (1982) ✔ Côtes de Bergerac
Rouge, Côtes de Bergerac Moelleux, Bergerac
Sec, Bergerac Rosé.
↾ Marie-Louise Lavergne, La Tour de Grange-
mont, 24560 St-Aubin-de-Lanquais; tel.
53 58 27 54 Ⓨ Mon.–Sat. 9.00–12.00/14.00–18.00.

CHATEAU LE MAYNE★★

■   22ha   164000   **2** **D** ⬛ ↓
★64 ★66 ★70 ★Ⓧ ★83

Has the fullness and elegance to develop into a
great wine in a few years. (1982) ✔ Côtes de
Bergerac Moelleux 1980, Bergerac Sec Ch. le
Mayne, Bergerac Rosé Ch. le Mayne, Méthode
Champenoise.
↾ J.-P. Martrenchard, Les Vignobles du Mayne,
24240 Sigoulès; tel. 53 58 40 01 Ⓨ Daily 8.00–
12.00/14.00–19.00. Closed 18 Dec.–3 Jan. and
Sun. in winter.

CHATEAU LE PARADIS★

■   20ha   140000   **2** **D** ⬛ ⑪ ↓
76 78 81 Ⓧ

Good colour and a refined nose, firm vinous
quality and a long lingering finish. The property
produces red wines only. (1982)
↾ Roger Chambaud, Ch. le Paradis, Perdoux,
24560 Issigeac; tel. 53 58 36 69 Ⓨ By appt.

CHATEAU LA PLANTE★★

■   5ha   30000   **3** **D** ⬛ ⑪ ↓
79 80 81 Ⓧ 83

This property makes long-lived wines for keeping, using traditional methods and oak ageing. A
generous wine but lacking suppleness and needing a few years in bottle. (1982) ✔ Ch. la Plante
Rosé Sec and Moelleux, Méthode Champenoise.
↾ Jacques Mournaud, Minzac, 24610 Villefranche-de-Lonchat; tel. 53 80 77 43 Ⓨ By appt.

CHATEAU LES PLAQUETTES★★★

■   10ha   72000   **2** **D** ⬛ ↓
★Ⓧ ★**82** 83

A vinous wine which is full, supple and already
very pleasant. Red wines from this property are
often medal-winners in competitions. (1982)
✔ Côtes de Bergerac Moelleux Ch. les Plaquettes, Bergerac Blanc Sec Ch. les Plaquettes,
Bergerac Rosé Ch. les Plaquettes.
↾ Jean Gazziola, Ch. les Plaquettes, Saussignac,
24240 Sigoulès; tel. 53 27 93 17 Ⓨ By appt.

CHATEAU LE PONTET★

■   16ha 35000   2 D ▪ ↓
*74 75 *76 78 **82**

An elegant, slightly tannic wine which can nonetheless be drunk now. The Bergerac Sauvignon is also worth looking at. (1982) ✔ Bergerac Sauvignon Sec.
↤ Alain Garcia, Ch. le Pontet, 24230 Velines; tel. 53 27 51 53 ⱺ Daily 8.00–12.00.

DOMAINE DE SAINT-AULAYE-DE-BREUIL★

■   15ha 95000   2 D ▪
75 *79 *81 (82)

A light, aromatic wine best drunk young. Consistent quality from this vineyard, situated halfway between St-Emilion and Monbazillac. (1982)
↤ Marius Marceteau, St-Antoine-de-Breuil, 24230 Velines; tel. 57 46 23 67 ⱺ By appt.

ABBAYE DE SAINT-MAYNE★★★

□   12ha 63000   2 D ▪ ↓
83

With its elegance and youthful delicacy, this will be a pleasant surprise to those people who do not usually like mellow wines. Visitors receive a warm welcome. (1983) ✔ Monbazillac Ch. de BélingardBlanc Liquoreux, Côtes de Bergerac Ch. Chayne Rouge, Bergerac Sec Ch. Chayne.
↤ De Bosredon, Ch. de Bélingard, Pomport, 24240 Sigoulès; tel. 53 57 05 01 ⱺ By appt.

CHATEAU DE VALLADOUX★

■   10ha 50000   2 D ▪
(75) *(82) *82

Lovely colour but has a closed-up nose and is still rather assertively tannic. (1982) ✔ Montravel Dom. du Haut-Montbrun Blanc Sec, Côtes de Bergerac Ch. de Valladoux Moelleux, Bergerac Dom. du Haut-Montbrun Rouge.
↤ Philippe Poivey, Montravel, Montcaret, 24230 Velines; tel. 53 58 66 93 ⱺ By appt. Closed during harvest.

Côtes de Bergerac Moelleux

DOMAINE DE LA GRANGE-NEUVE★★

□   10ha 60000   2 D ▪ ↓
75 76 79 *82 83

This easy-to-drink wine is recommended, as are the red and dry wines from the same estate. Made from fully-ripened grapes, it has a good alcohol-sugar balance. (1982) ✔ Monbazillac Dom. de Grange-Neuve, other Bergerac wines.
↤ R. et R. Castaing, GAEC de Grange Neuve, Pomport, 24240 Sigoulès; tel. 53 58 42 23 ⱺ By appt.

LES HAUTS PERROTS★★

□   7ha 40000   2 D ▪
76 79 (81) 81 **82 83**

A rich and full wine from overripe grapes. Typical of the appellation. (1981) ✔ Côtes de Bergerac Les Hauts-Perrots.
↤ Jean Moulinier, Les Hauts Perrots, St-Nexans, 24520 Mouleydier; tel. 53 58 34 37 ⱺ By appt.

Monbazillac

CHATEAU LA BORDERIE★★

□   5ha 18000   2 D ▪ ⅰ ↓
*64 *75 *79 80 *(81) *81 **82**

Attractive colour, toasted, overripe-grape aroma and excellent length. Also an excellent red, and dry white Sauvignon, and beautiful *chai*. (1981) ✔ Bergerac Rosé.
↤ Dominique Vidal, Ch. la Borderie, Monbazillac, 24240 Sigoulès; tel. 53 57 00 36 ⱺ By appt. Closed Sun.

CHATEAU GRAND-CHEMIN-BELINGARD★★

□   9ha 6000   2 D ▪
69 69 *70 *71 *75 *78 *79 *80 *81 *82 *83

A lively yellow colour lends brilliance to this wine which has the characteristic aroma of overripe grapes and a vigorous sappy quality on the palate. (1981)
↤ Albert Monbouche, Ch. Grand-Chemin-Belingard, Pomport, 2424 Sigoulès; tel. 53 58 30 57 ⱺ By appt.

CHATEAU LE FAGE★★

□   30ha 70000   4 D ▪ ↓
67 *(70) 75 78

Only the great years are bottled, among them this 1975 which has reached its peak and shows a good toasted warmth on the palate. (1975)
✔ Côtes de Bergerac Ch. le Fagé Rouge.
↤ Maurice Gerardin, Le Fagé, Pomport, 24240 Sigoulès; tel. 53 58 32 55 ⱺ Daily 8.00–20.00.

CHATEAU HAUTE-FONROUSSE★

□   16ha 70000   3 D ▪ ↓
78 **80** (82)

This yellow-gold wine, somewhat lacking in bouquet, is characteristic of the vintage; not very full bodied, but pleasantly light and fresh. (1978)
↤ Serge Geraud, GAEC des Ganfards, Haute-Fonrousse, 24240 Sigoulès; tel. 53 58 30 28 ⱺ By appt.

DOMAINE DU HAUT-MONTLONG★

□   15ha 57000   3 D ▪ ⅰ ↓
*75 *76 *77 *(80) *82 *83

Pleasant-looking pale-yellow wine, with a distinctive but delicate nose, easy on the palate; despite adverse weather conditions, surprisingly successful. (1980)
↤ R. Sergenton, Dom. du Haut-Montlong, Pomport, 24240 Sigoulès; tel. 53 58 44 88 ⱺ Daily 9.00–20.00

REPAIRE DU HAUT-THEULET★★★

□   5ha 15000   4 D ⅰ ↓
75 76 **78** (82)

The amber-coloured wine from this vineyard is traditionally aged in barrels. Rich, complex nose with a hint of honey; weighty and characterful on the palate. Visitors are warmly welcomed and the tasting building has a fine view. (1982)
↤ *Mme* Bardin, Repaire du Haut-Theulet, Monbazillac, 24240 Sigoulès; tel. 53 58 30 30 ⱺ By appt.

CHATEAU LADESVIGNES*

□	4ha	21600	**3** D ▪

*62 *64 *70 *75 ⊛78 *82

This nicely presented wine has all the characteristics of the 1978 vintage; slightly lacking in body, but pleasantly light. (1978) ✔ St-Emilion Grand Cru Classé, Grand-Barrail-Anarzelle Rouge, Bourgeois Haut-Médoc Cambon-la-Pelouse Rouge.
☞ Edmond Carrère et Fils, Ch. Ladesvignes, Pomport, 24240 Sigoulès; tel. 53 58 30 67 ☎ By appt.

CHATEAU MONBAZILLAC**

□	22ha	50000	**4** D ▪ ↓

⊛76 **80 81**

This château has a medieval appearance, although it was built at the height of the Renaissance. The wine has a lovely golden colour, fine bouquet and a raisiny fruit on the palate, but has not yet reached its peak. Of the other vintages the 1976 is worth keeping. (1980) ✔ Monbazillac Ch. Septy Blanc Liquoreux, Monbazillac Ch. la Brie Blanc Liquoreux, Bergerac Sec, Bergerac Rouge, Pécharmant Rouge.
☞ Cave Coop. de Monbazillac, BP2 Monbazillac 24240 Sigoulès; tel. 53 57 06 38 ☎ By appt.

CHATEAU LES OLIVOUX*

□	10ha	50000	**3** D ▪ ↓

⊛67 **79** *82 **83**

With its bright yellow colour, fresh nose, suppleness on the palate and good balance, this is typical of the 'modern', easy-to-drink Monbazillac. (1982) ✔ Bergerac Ch. les Olivoux Rouge, Bergerac Rosé.
☞ Jean Dailliat, Les Olivoux, Pomport, 24240 Sigoulès; tel. 53 58 41 94 ☎ By appt.

CHATEAU DE SANXET*

□	8ha	30000	**2** D ▪ ↓

*82 *82 *83 *83 84

This bright, pale-yellow wine is served at the Norwegian royal court and is light and supple. The 15th-century château is the family home. (1982) ✔ Bergerac Sec. Ch. de Sanxet.
☞ B. de Passemar, Ch. de Sanxet, Pomport, 24240 Sigoulès; tel. 53 58 37 46 ☎ By appt.

CHATEAU TREUIL-DE-NAILHAC***

□	10ha	44000	**3** D ▪ ⊕ ↓

*64 69 ⊛75 77 **79** 80 81 82

Pretty golden colour, and a refined, ripe and grapey bouquet make an excellent keeping wine, well balanced and rounded; recommended for those who like sweet wines. (1979) ✔ Bergerac Sec Ch. Treuil-de-Nailhac, Bergerac Rouge Ch. Treuil-de-Nailhac.
☞ Vidal-Hurmic, Monbazillac, 24240 Sigoulès; tel. 53 57 00 36 ☎ Daily 8.00–20.00.

Haut-Montravel

DOMAINE DE LIBARDE***

□	4ha	20000	**2** ▪ ⊕ ↓

69 75 77 79 *82 **82** 83

Attractive, fruity aromas proclaim a well-balanced and harmonious wine with good length. One of the rare examples of this appellation. (1982) ✔ Montravel Dom. de Libarde, Bergerac Rouge.
☞ Jean-Claude Banizette, Nastringues, 24230 Vélines; tel. 57 46 11 25 ☎ No visitors.

Pécharmant

CAVE COOPERATIVE DE BERGERAC*

■	80ha	300000	**3** D ▪ ⊕ ↓

*69 *75 *81 82

This Pécharmant is the main wine from the Bergerac cooperative, which makes several different estate wines. Plenty of fruit, but needs time to develop further. (1981)
☞ Cave Coop. de Bergerac, Bd de l'Entrepôt, 24100 Bergerac; tel. 53 57 16 27 ☎ Mon.–Sat. 8.30–12.00/14.00–18.00.

CHATEAU CHAMPAREL***

■	6ha	25000	**3** D ▪ ⊕ ↓

*75 *76 *78 *82 83

An intense red colour, this wine, although young, shows a noteworthy balance and delicacy with refined tannin. When fully developed in a few years, it will make an excellent bottle. (1982)
☞ *Mme* Bouche, Ch. Champarel, Pécharmant, 24100 Bergerac; tel. 53 57 34 76 ☎ No visitors.

CHATEAU CORBIAC**

■	11ha	60000	**4** D ▪ ↓

*82 83

The same family has owned this château (which was restored under Napoleon III) since the Middle Ages. The 1982 has a lovely, deep red colour, with a complex and scented nose, and is full bodied and rounded on the palate. Worth ageing but already drinking well. (1982)
☞ Bruno Durand de Corbiac, Ch. de Corbiac, 24100 Bergerac; tel. 53 57 20 70 ☎ By appt.

489

GRAND-JAURE★

■   1 ha   5000   ② Ⓓ ▮
★73 ★75 78 79 81 ⑧② 82

Tile-red, with a weighty and powerful nose, this wine undoubtedly takes its traditional rustic character from being vinified, without de-stalking, in oak barrels. (1981)
⊷ Georges Baudry, Jaure, 24100 Bergerac; tel. 53 57 35 65 ⏸ Daily 9.00–12.00/14.00–18.00.

DOMAINE DU HAUT-PECHARMANT★

■   18 ha   124 000   ③ Ⓓ ▮
80 81 ⑧②

Needs several years ageing; like most of the wines from this estate it does not show well when tasted young. (1981)
⊷ *Mme* Reine Roches, Dom. du Haut-Pécharmant, Pécharmant, 24100 Bergerac; tel. 53 57 29 50 ⏸ Daily 8.00–12.00/14.00–19.00.

CLOS PEYRELEVADE★★

■   10 ha   43 000   ③ Ⓓ ▮
⑧② 83

Rich in body and extract, full-bodied and well knit, this wine has all the qualities of a keeping wine; after a few years, it will go well with game. (1982)
⊷ Edith Girardet, Clos Peyrelevade, 24100 Bergerac; tel. 53 57 43 30 ⏸ By appt.

CHATEAU LA RENAUDIE★★

■   22 ha   100 000   ③ Ⓓ ▮ ⬇
★⑧②

With an attractive ripe-fruit aroma, and powerful but supple on the palate, this is an excellent keeping wine from the Monbazillac cooperative. (1982) ✔ Monbazillac.
⊷ Cave Coop. de Monbazillac, BP2, Monbazillac, 24240 Sigoulès; tel. 53 57 06 38 ⏸ By appt.

CHATEAU DE TIREGAND★

■   30 ha   150 000   ③ Ⓓ ⑩ ⬇
70 75 78 79 81 ⑧② 83

A fine family business producing wines of consistent quality, Tiregand is also famous for its magnificent 17th-century château with its histori(1982) ✔ Ch. de Tiregand Blanc Sec.
⊷ SEA du Ch. de Tiregand, Creysse, 24100 Bergerac; tel. 53 23 21 08 ⏸ Mon.–Sat. 8.00–12.00/14.00–18.00.

DOMAINE DU VIEUX SAPIN★

■   5 ha   20 000   ④ Ⓓ ⑩ ⬇
⑧②

Already rich and full although not yet fully developed, with a fine colour and still closed-up nose. (1982)
⊷ Cave Coop. de Bergerac, Bd de l'Entrepôt, 24100 Bergerac; tel. 53 57 16 27 ⏸ Mon.–Sat. 8.30–12.00/14.00–18.00.

Rosette

CHATEAU PUYPEZAT★★

☐   20 ha   60 000   ② Ⓓ ▮ ⬇
⑧② 83

Well-rounded, although still closed up on the nose, this wine is worth ageing. One of the last of the Rosette appellation, which are often more refined and lively than their Bergerac counterparts produced on the south bank of the river Dordogne. (1982) ✔ Bergerac Rouge, Rosé, Blanc Sec.
⊷ Bernad Frères, Ch. Puypezat, Rosette, 24100 Bergerac; tel. 53 57 27 69 ⏸ Daily 8.00–21.00.

Saussignac

CHATEAU COURT-LES-MUTS★★★

☐   1.2 ha   10 000   ③ Ⓓ ▮ ⬇
73 74 75 76 77 78 79 **80 81** 83

An excellent wine from Sémillon grapes, the variety used for the best white Bordeaux. This bottle can be kept for some time yet, to be served as an aperitif or as a partner for foie gras. (1980)
✔ Bergerac Ch. Court-les-Mûts Rouge, Bergerac Ch. Court-les-Mûts Blanc Sec.
⊷ Pierre Sadoux, Ch. Court-les-Mûts, Razac-de-Saussignac, 24240 Sigoules; tel. 53 27 92 17 ⏸ Mon.–Sat. 9.00–11.30/14.00–17.30; Sat. by appt only.

Côtes de Duras

The Duras region is the natural extension of the Bordeaux Entre-Deux-Mers plateau. Duras wine was a favourite at the court of François I. It is said that, following the revocation of the Edict of Nantes, the exiled Huguenots of Gascony had wine sent from Duras to their refuge in Holland, and that they marked with a tulip each row of vines that was reserved for them.

Situated on slopes of clay-and-limestone soil carved out by the river Dourdèze and its tributaries, the Côtes de Duras provide good conditions for the Bordeaux grape varieties. Sémillon, Sauvignon and Muscadelle are grown for whites, and the Cabernet-Franc, Cabernet-Sauvignon, Merlot and Malbec for reds; small amounts of Chenin, Ondenc and Ugni Blanc are also found. The reputation of Duras rests on its white wines; the sweet whites are very pleasant, but the most successful wines are the dry whites made from the Sauvignon. Refined and refreshing, they have a very special bouquet and are a marvellous accompaniment to fish and shellfish from the Atlantic. The red wines are round and meaty with a good colour. The different grape varieties are often vinified separately. A few Vins Primeurs are made by the carbonic maceration method.

DOMAINE AMBLARD *Sauvignon**

☐ 2ha 15000 ⬛ Ⓓ ■ ↓

82 ⑧⑬

Particularly successful, with its fresh, clean aroma. Fine and elegant on the palate. (1983) ✔ Côtes de Duras Dom. Amblard Rouge and Blanc Moelleux.
♠ Guy Pauvert, Dom. Amblard, St-Germain-de-Duras, 47120 Duras; tel. 53 94 77 92 ♈ Daily 8.00–12.30/13.30–20.00.

BERTICOT *Merlot**

■ 25ha 150000 ⬛ Ⓓ ■ ↓

81 ⑧ 83 ⑬

The Merlot, made by *macération carbonique*, is particularly fruity and easy to drink. Supple and light, and can be drunk now. (1983)
♠ Cave Coop. de Duras, Berticot, 47120 Duras; tel. 53 83 71 12 ♈ By appt.

BERTICOT *Sauvignon***

☐ 58ha 400000 ⬛ Ⓓ ■ ↓

83 ⑬

Beautiful, greenish colour and very flowery grape aroma. A slight prickle on the tongue gives it a crisp, dry finish. (1983)
♠ Cave Coop. de Duras, Berticot, 47120 Duras; tel. 53 83 71 12 ♈ By appt.

DOMAINE DES COURS *Sauvignon***

☐ 6ha 35000 ⬛ Ⓓ ■ ↓

81 ⑧ 83 ⑬

Pale-coloured, with a typical, fruity, firm aroma. Dry, lively and well balanced, with character and flavour. A successful vintage. (1983)
♠ Régis Lusoli, St-Colombe, 47120 Duras; tel. 53 83 74 35 ♈ By appt.

DOMAINE DE DURAND***

☐ 3ha 12000 ⬛ Ⓓ ■ ↓

82 ⑧ ⑬

Superb dry white made completely from Sauvignon grapes. Beautiful yellow colour with green tints; very fine fruity and musky aroma; lively and fresh on the palate. All finesse and lace. A success. (1983) ✔ Côtes de Duras Dom. de Durand Rouge, Rosé, Blanc Moelleux, Mousseux.
♠ Jean Fonvielhe, Dom. de Durand, St-Jean-de-Duras, 47120 Duras; tel. 53 84 02 04 ♈ By appt.

DOMAINE DE DURAND*

■ 9ha 44000 ⬛ Ⓓ ■ ↓

80 81 ⑧⓵ ⑧

Fairly assertive and round. The 1982 has a jammy ripe-fruit aroma and is round and full on the palate. With a few years in bottle this will become a lovely wine. (1982) ✔ Côtes de Duras Dom. de Durand Blanc Mousseux and Rosé.
♠ Jean Fonvielhe, Dom. de Durand, St-Jean-de-Duras, 47120 Duras; tel. 53 83 02 04 ♈ By appt.

DOMAINE DE FERRANT *Sauvignon**

☐ 3ha 25000 ⬛ Ⓓ ■ ↓

⑧ 83

Beautiful pale-yellow with green reflections. Aroma of wild flowers. Very lively on the palate, fresh and light. (1983)
♠ Lucien Salesse, Esclottes, 47120 Duras; tel. 53 83 73 46 ♈ By appt.

DOMAINE DE FERRANT**

■ 4ha 25000 ⬛ Ⓓ ■ ↓

⑧ 83

A very Cabernet Sauvignon-style wine with fresh fruity aroma. The 1982 is fairly full bodied and well balanced, needing several years to lose its tannin and round out. One to wait for. (1982) ✔ Côtes de Duras Ferrant Blanc Sec, Blanc Moelleux, Rosé.
♠ Lucien Salesse, Esclottes, 47120 Duras; tel. 53 83 73 46 ♈ By appt.

DOMAINE LAS-BRUGUES MAU-MICHAU**

■ 3ha 85000 ⬛ Ⓓ ■ ↓

80 81 ⑧ ⑧⓶

Well known for its strength and character. The 1982 is particularly full bodied and well balanced, but needs time to lose its considerable tannin. Promises well for the future. (1982) ✔ Côtes de Duras Sauvignon and Sémillon.
♠ Michel Prévot, Monteton, 47120 Duras; tel. 53 20 24 51 ♈ By appt.

491

THE LOIRE VALLEY AND CENTRAL FRANCE

THE VARIED countryside of the Loire valley is bathed in a single light, which comes from a gentle blending of the sky and the majestic river that rises here in the 'Garden of France'. The produce of this garden, of course, includes the vine, and from the Massif Central right up to the Loire estuary, vineyards are scattered along the River Loire and its major and minor tributaries. This huge wine-producing region is called the Vallée de la Loire et Centre even though it extends beyond the actual Loire valley and its central section. There are many pleasures for the tourist here, be they cultural, gastronomic, or oenological, along the scenic routes that follow the course of the river and the less obvious by-ways that wind through the vineyards and forests.

From Roanne to Nantes and St-Pourçain to St-Nazaire, through changing soils, climate and viticultural practices, the hillsides that run along the river banks are occupied by vines. Along 1000 kilometres, more than 80000 hectares of vines are planted, producing 2.5–3.5 million hectolitres of wine a year, with considerable annual variation. A factor common to all the wines produced in this huge region is their lively acidity, which may be explained by the northerly location of most of the wine-growing areas.

However, it would be wrong to lump all of these wines together, bearing in mind the huge diversity of climate and vineyard locations. St-Pourçain is on the same latitude as Mâcon and Roanne on the same latitude as Villefranche-sur-Saône. Local variations in the terrain, and the shelter they provide from the Atlantic airstream, create marked differences in micro-climate along the length of the Loire valley.

The vineyards that really do form a unity are those of the Pays Nantais,

The Loire Valley and Central France

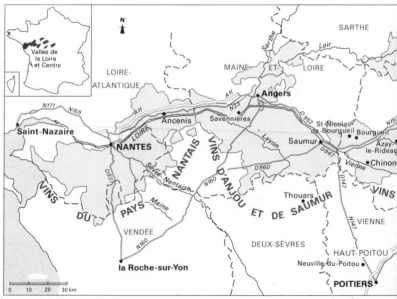

Anjou-Saumur and the Coteaux de Touraine, although others lacking a firm regional identity – those in Berry, the Côtes d'Auvergne, and the Côtes Roannaises – have now also been added. If these vineyards were larger they would have been able to form a separate region by themselves. As it is, the region as a whole may be divided into four general areas; the first three already mentioned, and those of central France.

In the Loire valley proper, the Pays Nantais and part of Anjou lie on the Armoricain massif, which is made up of schist, sandstone, granite, and other sedimentary or eruptive rocks from the Primary Era. The soil that has evolved here is perfect for vine-growing, and the wines are of excellent quality. The Pays Nantais, at the far west of the Loire valley, has a relatively gentle relief, although the hard rocks of the Armoricain massif are quite sharply grooved by the small rivers of the region. Viticulture being impossible in these steep valleys, the vines occupy hilltops on the plateau. The climate is reasonably consistent throughout the year, since the maritime influence acts to moderate the effects of the seasons. The winters may nevertheless be quite harsh and the summers hot and often wet; the region receives a great deal of sunshine, but spring frosts can cause problems.

The Sèvre-et-Maine region to the west of the city of Nantes produces 80 per cent of the Pays Nantais wines, chiefly Muscadet and Gros-Plant. Anjou-Saumur, upstream from the Pays Nantais, lies almost entirely to the south of the Loire, in the department of Maine-et-Loire. The western-most sub-region of Anjou, the Coteaux de la Loire, is a continuation of the Pays Nantais vineyard and is situated on gentle, north-facing slopes, where the vines occupy the edge of the Armoricain plateau. Coteaux du Layon, in the central sub-region, is an area of steeply sloping schist along the valley of the Layon; to the north lies the Coteaux de l'Aubance and, further east, the transitional zone between Anjou and the Coteaux de Touraine, where much rosé is produced.

The Saumurois, on the eastern limit of the Anjou region, marks the beginning of Touraine proper, and the vines grow on distinctive tufa chalk. The soft soils make cellar construction very easy, and there are numerous underground cellars and tunnels carved out of the chalk in which the racks of bottles compete for space with the 'champignons de Paris' (button mushrooms) which account for thirty per

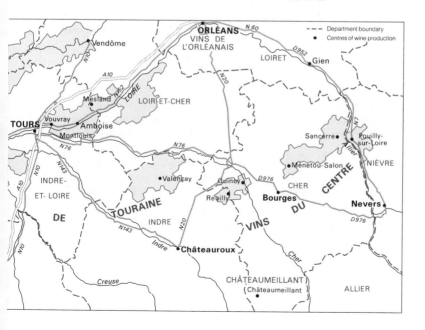

cent of the national production. The hills – slightly higher here – hold back the westerly winds and help to create a climate that is half maritime, half continental.

On the east bank, opposite the Saumurois, are the vineyards of St-Nicolas-de-Borgeuil, which fall within the Touraine regional boundary. Still in western Touraine, but on the west bank of the Loire, the Vienne valley is the home of Chinon, most famous of Touraine wines. Thirty kilometres upstream, on the other side of Tours, lie Vouvray and its smaller neighbour Montlouis. Less well known, but worthy of interest, are Azay-le-Rideau, Amboise, Mesland and the Coteaux de Cher. Finally, the small satellite vineyards of Coteaux du Loir, Cheverny, Valencay, and even the Orléanais and Coteaux de Giennois, may also be considered part of the Touraine area.

Far to the south-west of Touraine, the Berry (or central) vineyards make up an independent fourth region that differs from the others in two ways; its soil is Jurassic and its climate semi-continental, with hot summers and cold winters. For ease of presentation we include St-Pourçain, Côtes Roannaises and Forez in this region, despite their different soil (primary Massif Central) and climate (semi-continental to continental).

From west to east, Loire wines begin with Muscadet, which is both the local name for the Melon de Bourgogne and of the dry white wine it produces. The Folle Blanche is also planted here, producing a dry white of modest quality, the Gros-Plant du Pays Nantais. The Ancénis region has been colonized by the Gamay Noir.

In Anjou, the Chenin, or Pineau de la Loire, is the main grape variety used for white wines, although the Chardonnay and Sauvignon have recently been introduced. Chenin grapes are used to produce great sweet white wines of intense depth, as well as the now more popular dry and sparkling style. For red wines, the oldest grape variety is the Grolleau Noir, traditionally used to make medium-dry rosés and good red vins ordinaires. The Cabernet-Franc and Cabernet-Sauvignon have been introduced more recently and help produce refined yet full-bodied red wines that age well. The diversity of Anjou production can at times be somewhat disconcerting.

In Touraine, the principal grape varieties used are as follows: to the west the Chenin in Vouvray, Montlouis and the Coteaux du Loir; the Cabernet-Franc in Chinon, Bourgueil and Champigny; and the Grolleau in Azay-le-Rideau. To the east, the Gamay Noir (for reds) and Sauvignon (for whites) produce pleasant, light and fruity wines. Finally, we should include the slightly peppery Pinot d'Aunis used in Coteaux du Loir, and the Gris Meunier from the Orleans region.

In the vineyards of central France, the Sauvignon holds pride of place in the white wines of Reuilly, Quincy, Menetou-Salon, Sancerre and Pouilly, where the varietal is also called Blanc-Fumé. In addition to the Sauvignon, Pouilly has a few remaining Chasselas vineyards that produce dry, lively white wines. The red wines underline the proximity of Burgundy in the Pinot Noirs of Sancerre and Menetou-Salon.

Mention should also be made of the Haut-Poitou vineyards, which have built a deserved reputation for their refreshing, fruity Sauvignon white wines, fuller-bodied Chardonnays and light but firm reds from the Gamay Noir, Pinot Noir, and Cabernet. With its semi-continental climate, Haut-Poitou is a stepping stone between Val de Loire and Bordeaux.

Finally there are the Fiefs Vendéens vineyards planted along the Atlantic coast (the wines used to be called Vins des Fiefs du Cardinal) which have recently acquired vDQS status. The most famous wines are the rosés de Mareuil, made from Gamay Noir and Pinot Noir grapes, and the regional curiosity, very difficult to find, called 'Ragoûtant' or 'Dégoûtant', made from the Negrette grape.

For Loire wines, as in all northern areas, the year on the label is crucial, since the richness and aromatic strength of the wines depend to a great extent on the climatic conditions of the vintage. The size and quality of the harvest are more than usually affected by spring frosts, cold Junes (when the vine flowers) and variations in the late summer and early autumn. Vintages, then, are by no means uniform, and it is impossible to generalize, for example, about when the wines should be drunk.

Rosé de Loire

These are dry rosé wines, classified AOC since 1974, produced within the regions of Anjou, Saumur, and Touraine. They may be made from the following grape varieties: Cabernet-Franc, Cabernet-Sauvignon, Gamay Noir à jus blanc, Pinot d'Aunis, and Grolleau.

CLOS DE L'ABBAYE*

☑		2ha	12000	2 D ■ ↓

★84 ★84

Good, attractive rosé colour, with the aromatic nose of the Cabernet-Sauvignon grape. A well-made wine to be served at 10–12°C (45–50°F) with entrées and crudités, or in summer with pizzas. (1983)
↬ Henri Aupy, Clos de l'Abbaye Puy Notre-Dame, 49260 tel. 41 52 26 71 � By appt. Mon.–Thurs.

DOMAINE DE BEILLANT*

☑		7ha	30000	2 D ■ ↓

79 81 82 ⑧ 83

Well-developed colour. Attractive aromas and spicy scents contributed by the varieties of grape used. Ideal for serving with crudités and charcuterie, but because of its structure it can also accompany an entire evening meal. (1983)
✔ Anjou Blanc, Anjou Rouge, Cabernet d'Anjou Rouge, Coteaux du Layon Blanc.
↬ Jacques Peltier, Passavent-sur-Layon, 49560 Neuil-sur-Layon; tel. 41 59 51 32 � By appt.

PIERRE ET PHILIPPE CADY*

■		2ha	2000	2 D ■ ◖ ↓

Tile-red with hint of pink, the normal colour for this type and age of wine. Slightly woody nose. To taste, pleasant, slightly tough but well bred. (1983)
↬ P. et P. Cady, Valette, St-Aubin-de-Luigné, 49190 Rochefort-sur-Loire; tel. 41 78 33 69 � By appt.

DOMAINE DE LA CROIX DE MISSION*

☑		60ha	57600	2 D ■ ↓

The colour has become sightly tile-red, as the Anjou Grolleau and Cabernet varieties tend to do as they get older. The nose is light, and the wine is far from being aggressive – indeed, it is quite easy to drink, charming and well balanced. Drink it slightly cool. (1983) ✔ Bonnezeaux Blanc Moelleux, Anjou Blanc Sec, Anjou, Anjou Gamay Rosé.

↬ René Renou, Place du Champ-de-Foire, 49380 Thouarcé; tel. 41 54 04 05 � By appt.

VIGNOBLES GAUDARD*

☑		15ha	6000	2 D ■ ↓

81 ⑧4

Gleaming, tempting colour. Pleasant fruity and floral aromas. Although light on the palate, makes a refreshing bottle for drinking with a light meal in summer. (1984)
↬ M. Aguilas-Gaudard, La Brosse, Chaudefonds-sur-Layon, 49290 Chalonnes-sur-Loire; tel. 41 78 10 68 � By appt.

LOGIS DU PRIEURE*

■		6ha	36000	3 D ■ ↓

Colour already well developed with an initial scent that is elegant, if slightly peppery and sulphured. Light structure on the palate. Drink chilled in summer. (1983)
↬ Jousset et fils, Coucourson-sur-Layon, 49700 Doué-la-Fontaine; tel. 41 59 11 66 � By appt.

DOMAINE DES VARINELLES**

☑		2ha		2 D ■ ◖ ↓

A light colour and a very attractive floral, fruity and spicy nose. Great elegance from the Cabernet grape. A wine to drink with light charcuterie, or throughout a summer meal. (1983) ✔ Saumur-Champigny, Saumur Tranquille, Sauvignon Blanc Sec, Saumur Brut Méthode Champenoise.
↬ Claude Daheuiller, 28 Rue de Ruau, 49400 Saumur, Varrains; tel. 41 52 90 94 � By appt. Closed public holidays, Sat. afternoons and Sun.

Crémant de Loire

The area covered by this sparkling wine appellation includes Anjou, Saumur, and Touraine. The Méthode Champenoise gives excellent results here, and the production of these 'vins de fête', or celebration wines, keeps on increasing (at present it is more than 30000 hectolitres). Many different grape varieties are used, principally the Chenin or Pineau Blanc de Loire, Cabernet-Sauvignon, and Cabernet-Franc, Pinot Noir and Chardonnay. The appellation mainly produces white wines, but there are also a few rosés and even some reds.

CLOS DE L'ABBAYE*

○   2ha   10000   🔳 D ▪ ↓

Attractive aroma is due to the combination of grapes used, with the Chenin being the foremost. Elegant and true to form of the area. (1982)
🍴 Henri Aupy, Clos de l'Abbaye, 49260 Puy-Notre-Dame; tel. 41 52 26 71 ⊥ By appt.

ALAIN ARNAULT**

○   1ha   3124   🔳 D ▪

78 81 ⑧

Magnificently presented. Slightly pink tinge indicating the presence of Blanc de Noirs. Very delicate, long-lasting mousse. Refined fruity scent gives a very favourable impression, and the palate is well balanced, with finesse, lightness and character. (1981)
🍴 Alain Arnault, Les Landes, Bouillé-Loretz, 79220 Argenton-l'Eglise; tel. 49 67 04 85 ⊥ By appt.

CHATEAU DU GAILLARDIN**

□   1ha   3600   🔳 D ▪ ↓

A slight tinge in the colour suggests that this a Blanc de Noirs. Good, delicate, long-lasting bubbles, and a very good fruity nose. Well balanced, easy and elegant. A success.
🍴 Noel Pinot, Dampière-sur-Loire, 49460 Saumur; tel. 41 51 14 35 ⊥ By appt.

GRATIEN-MEYER*

□   250000   🔳 D ↓

The colour is good and the mousse delicate and intense. Strong varietal aroma. A good wine of its type; pleasant and with a good finish.
🍴 *MM*. Gratien-Meyer et Fils, Route de Montsoreau, 49100 Saumur; tel. 41 51 01 54 ⊥ Daily 9.00–12.00/14.00–17.00.

PRINCE DE LA HALLE*

□   1ha   6000   🔳 D ▪ ↓

A blanc de noirs with a charming rosé colour. The aromas are still closed up and are not showing well. To taste, however, it shows its vigour and depth.
🍴 Henri Rochais et Fils, Ch. de Plaisance, Chaume 49190 Rochefort-sur-Loire; tel. 41 78 33 01 ⊥ By appt. Closed Sun. afternoon.

CHATEAU DE MIDOUIN**

□   18ha   205000   🔳 D ▪ ↓

*81 *82 ⑧ 83

Fine biscuity note that is not disappointing and foretaste of softness yet to develop fully. Pleasant and successful. (1982)
🍴 Maurice Rémy, Ch. de Midouin, St-hilaire-St-Florent, 49400 Saumur; tel. 41 50 22 42 ⊥ No visitors.

PERRY DE MALEYRAND
*Brut Tradition***

○   12ha   100000   🔳 D ▪ ↓

Pretty yellow wine with a delicate and long-lasting mousse and very distinctive nose. Well balanced on the palate with remarkable aromas. Renowned for its lightness. (1980)
🍴 Michel Lateyron, 1 Bis Quai des Violettes, 37400 Amboise; tel. 47 57 33 48 ⊥ By appt.

CHATEAU DE SAINT-FLORENT*

○   4ha   40000   🔳 D ▪ ↓

⑧ ⑧ ⑧

Lively, a little bit aggressive, with a delicate, long-lasting mousse. A very characteristic wine which will fine-down as it ages. Drink as an aperitif. (1982) ✔ Saumur, Saumur.
🍴 SA Langlois-Château BP6. St-Hilaire-St-Florent, 49416 Saumur Cedex; tel. 41 50 28 14 ⊥ Daily 9.30–11.30/15.30–17.00.

LE SALVARD*

○   1.5ha   3000   🔳 D ↓

Young and floral. Dense, well made and lively, with an aroma of bergamot fruit.
🍴 *M*. G.-M. Gilbert Deiaille, Dom. le Salvard, 41120 Fougères-sur-Bièvre, 41120 Les Montils; tel. 54 20 28 21 ⊥ By appt.

CAVE DES VIGNERONS DE SAUMUR**

○   40ha   300000   🔳 D ▪ ↓

76 ⑦ *⑧

A pretty wine with very delicate mousse; elegant, subtle and well-made. Ageing in cellars and a constant temperature of 10–12°C (50–54°F) have allowed the qualities of vine and soil to develop in the wine. (1982) ✔ Saumur Blanc Sec, Saumur Rouge, Saumur Mousseux, Cabernet de Saumur.
🍴 Coop. des Vignerons de Saumur, St-Cyr-en-Bourg, 49260 Montreuil-Bellay; tel. 41 51 61 09 ⊥ By appt. Closed 1 Oct.–30 Apr.

PAYS NANTAIS

Two thousand years ago the Roman legions brought the vine to the Nantes region, the crossroads of Brittany, Vendée, the Loire and the Atlantic Ocean. The terrible winter of 1709 – when the sea along the coast froze – totally destroyed the vineyards. They were replanted mainly with the Melon de Bourgogne, which later became known as Muscadet.

Today the Pays Nantais wines production area covers 12 900 hectares, and extends into the department of Loire-Atlantique, south of Nantes, the regional capital. The vines are grown on sunny hillsides that come under the influence of the maritime climate. The soil is mostly light and stony, composed of ancient sub-soils mixed with volcanic rock. The Pays Nantais vineyard produces three appellations: the AOC Muscadet and the VDQS wines Gros-Plant du pays Nantais and Coteaux d'Ancenis.

Pays Nantais

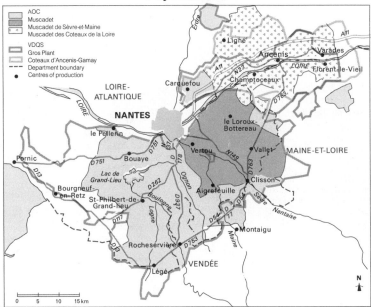

	AOC
	Muscadet
	Muscadet de Sèvre-et-Maine
	Muscadet des Coteaux de la Loire
	VDQS
	Gros Plant
	Coteaux d'Ancenis-Gamay
- - -	Department boundary
●	Centres of production

Muscadet

Muscadet is a dry white wine that has had an AOC classification since 1936. It comes exclusively from the grape variety known as Melon de Bourgogne or Muscadet. The total production area for this wine is 9800 hectares, and an average 450 000 hectolitres is made each year. There are three separate areas of AOC wines: Muscadet de Sèvre-et-Maine, which accounts for 85 per cent of production; Muscadet des Coteaux de la Loire (5 per cent) and Muscadet (10 per cent).

A traditional Pays Nantais technique is to bottle the wine directly off its 'lees' – the light sediment deposited during fermentation. This sur lie method is now subject to certain controls. To be able to use the description 'sur lie' on the label, the wine must spend only one winter in the vat or the barrel and still be on its lees left from the wine-making process at the time that it is bottled. The method accentuates the freshness, delicacy and bouquet of the Muscadet wines.

By nature Muscadet is a dry white wine without too pronounced greenness and having a well-developed bouquet. Its style makes it the ideal accompaniment to fish, and shellfish, but it also makes an excellent aperitif.

It should be served chilled, (8–9°C) but not iced.

DOMAINE DE LA GARANDERIE★★

○	5ha 27000	2 D 🍷 👃

Well balanced and can stand comparison with the famous Muscadets de Saône-et-Loire. Clouds of tiny bubbles appear through its lovely colour. Lively nose; most attractive. (1983) ✔ Gros Plant sur Lie.
↠ M. de la Garanderie, Le Poirier, La Limouzinière 44310; St-Philbert-de-Grand-Lieu; tel. 40 69 03 28 ☎ By appt.

DOMAINE DE LA HAUTE MAISON★

☐	8ha 85000	3 D 🍷 👄 👃

Typical iodized character gives a certain charm; best drunk chilled between 10°–12°C. (1983) ✔ Gros Plant du Pays Nantais, Gamay Vin de Pays Rouge, Gamay Vin de Pays Rosé, Cabernet Vin de Pays Rouge.
↠ J.-N. Schaeffer-Bronckhorst, Dom. de la Haute Pont-St-Martia Maison, St-Aignan-de-Grand-Lieu 44860; tel. 40 26 84 92 ☎ Mon.–Sat. 9.00–12.00/14.00–19.00.

DOMAINE DES HERBAUGES★★

☐		2 D 🍷 👃

Supple, slightly sparkling and characterized by very good nose and length on the palate. (1983) ✔ Gros Plant du Pays Nantais.
↠ Pierre et Luc Choblet, Dom. des Herbauges, 44340 Bouaye; tel. 40 65 44 92 ☎ Mon.–Sat. 9.30–12.00/14.00–19.00.

CHATEAU DE LA ROULIERE★★

| □ | 9ha | 15000 | **2** **D** ▬ ↓ |

82 **83** 84

Crystal-clear. Light, very fragrant nose, which is reminiscent of banana and fruit drops on the palate. (1983)
✦ René Erraud, Ch. de la Roulière, St-Colomban, 44310 St-Philibert-de-Grand-Lieu; tel. 40 05 80 24. ☎ By appt.

Coteaux de la Loire

CHATEAU LA BERRIERE
Clos Saint-Roch★

| □ | 6ha | 36000 | **2** **D** ▬ ⅲ ↓ |

Elegant, with pronounced earthy taste, deep colour and distinctive, musky fragrance. (1983)
✦ Armelle de Boscher, Ch. la Berrière, 44450 St-Julian-de-Concelles; tel. 40 54 01 22. ☎ By appt. Closed Aug.

DOMAINE DE LA CASSARDERIE★★

| □ | 4ha | 3000 | **2** **D** ▬ ↓ |

81 82 83 *84

Slightly tawny colour. Somewhat tired, with a faintly flinty taste. (1983)
✦ Fernand Alix, La Cassarderie, St-Méen, 44820 Ligné; tel. 40 25 40 48 ☎ By appt.

DOMAINE DES GENAUDIERES
Sur Lie★

| □ | 20ha | 144000 | **2** **D** ⅲ ↓ |

Woody vanilla nose typical of the region. Pleasant to drink; ready now. (1983)
✦ Augustin Athimon, Les Genaudières, Le Cellier, 44850 Ligné; tel. 40 25 40 27 ☎ By appt.

DOMAINE DES GENAUDIERES★

| □ | 20ha | 42000 | **2** **D** ⅲ ↓ |

Pleasant and well made, with a yellow colour and lively nose. (1983)
✦ Augustin Athimon, les Genaudières, Le Cellier, 44850 Ligne; tel. 40 25 40 27 ☎ By appt.

Muscadet de Sèvre-et-Maine

BARRE *Les Mesnils*★

| □ | | | **2** **D** ▬ ⅲ ↓ |

Despite the unassertive nose, this pale-yellow wine turns out to be a well-balanced and satisfying bottle. (1983)
✦ Ets Barré Frères, Beau Soleil, Gorges, 44190 Clisson; tel. 40 06 90 70 ☎ No visitors.

CHATEAU LA BERRIERE★

| □ | 10ha | 72000 | **2** **D** ▬ ⅲ ↓ |

Distinctive wine dominated by the country flavours that influence the fruitiness and balance.
✔ Muscadet de Sèvre-et-Maine les Audelières, Muscadet Sèvre-et-Maine St-Clément, Muscadet des Côteaux de la Loire St-Roch.
✦ Armelle de Boscher, Ch. la Berrière, 44450 St-Julian-de-Concelles; tel. 40 54 01 22 ☎ By appt. Closed Aug.

DOMAINE DE LA BIGOTIERE★★

| □ | 12ha | 72000 | **2** **D** ▬ ↓ |

An elegant wine, round, supple and balanced. (1983)
✦ André Batard, La Bigotière, Maisdon-sur-Sevre, 44690 La Haie-Fouassiedre; tel. 40 06 62 61 ☎ By appt.

DOMAINE DE LA BLANCHETIERE★

| □ | 18ha | 50000 | **2** **D** ▬ ⅲ ↓ |

76 **79** 82 83 84

Finesse and delicacy throughout. Very typical of the region – light, fruity and easy to drink. (1983)
✦ Serge Luneau, La Blanchetière, 44430 Le Loroux-Bottereau; tel. 40 33 82 14.

DOMAINE DU BOIS BRULEY★★

| □ | 9ha | 54000 | **3** **D** ▬ ⅲ ↓ |

Pale yellow in colour with a rather undeveloped nose but firm, vigorous and attractive palate. (1983)
✦ Ets Chéreau-Carre, Dom. de Chasseloir, BP 49 St-Fiacre-sur-Maine, 44690 La Haie-Fouassière; tel. 40 54 81 15 ☎ Mon.–Sat. 8.00–18.30 ✦ Bernard Chéreau et Fils.

DOMAINE DU BOIS-JOLY *Sur Lie*★

| □ | 10ha | 60000 | **2** **D** ▬ ↓ |

Beautifully strong colour, a nose which is perhaps a little bit too backward, and a supple and charming flavour. (1983) ✔ Gros Plant du Pays Nantais.
✦ Henri Bouchard, Le Bois-Joli, Le Pallet 44330 Vallet; t'el. 40 26 40 83 ☎ By appt. Closed 15 to 31 Aug.

DOMAINE DE LA BOTINIERE★★

| □ | 30ha | 180000 | **2** ▬ ↓ |

Excellent colour and fresh, youthful nose. A well-balanced and very full-bodied wine from this long-established (16th-century) estate. (1983)
✦ Jean Beauquin, Dom. de la Botinière, 44330 Vallet; tel. 40 06 73 83 ☎ By appt.

DOMAINE DE BOURGUIGNON
Sur Lie★★

| □ | 14ha | 44000 | **2** **D** ▬ ↓ |

82 83

Good pale colour and a fresh, clean and light nose; full of vitality. (1983)
✦ *Mme* Henri Piou, Dom. De Bourguignon, 44330 Vallet; tel. 40 33 93 43 ☎ By appt.

ANDRE-MICHEL BREGEON★★★

| □ | 6ha | 33000 | **2** **D** ▬ ⅲ ↓ |

Pale colour and elegant nose give way to good balance and lingering qualities in the mouth. Harmonious *coup de coeur* wine, ideal with seafood and as an aperitif. (1982) ✔ Gros Plant du Pays Nantais, Vin de Pays des Marches de Bretagne.
✦ André-Michel Bregeon, Les Guisseaux, Gorges 44190 Clisson; tel. 40 06 93 19 ☎ By appt.

CHATEAU DE LA BRETESCHE★★

☐   20ha   120000   2 D ☷ ◑ ⌀

Very good-quality wine that perfectly blends a bright, pale-gold colour, delicate and elegant nose, and light finish. (1983)
◑┑ Barre Frères, Plessis Brezot, Gorges 44190 Clisson, tel. 40 06 90 70 ⊥ No visitors.

FIEF DE LA BRIE★★

☐   15ha   90000   2 D ☷ ◑ ⌀

A pleasant wine of good colour, well presented in a Nantaise bottle. Very stable and long on the palate. (1983)
◑┑ Auguste Bonhomme, Dom. de Baucheveau, Gorges, 44190 Clisson; tel. 40 06 91 61 ⊥ By appt. Closed 10–30 Aug.

CHATEAU DE LA CANTRIE★★

☐   11ha   60000   2 D ☷ ◑

Very delicate and fruity nose, reminiscent of acid drops. The same fruitiness is there in the mouth, with plenty of length. (1983)
◑┑ Laurent Bossis, Le Bourg, 44690 St-Fiacre-sur-Maine; tel. 40 36 94 64 ⊥ Mon.–Sat. 14.00–19.00.

CHATEAU DE LA CASSEMICHERE★

☐   17ha   100000   2 D ☷ ⌀

A lovely pale golden wine, young and dashing. Nose lightly developed; supple on the palate. (1983)
◑┑ Ch. de la Cassemichère, La Chapelle-Heullin, 44330 Vallet; tel. 40 06 70 05 ⊥ By appt.

DOMAINE DE LA CHAMBAUDIERE★★

☐   6ha   36000   2 D ☷ ⌀

Plenty of elegance and a good attack. A slightly bitter finish typical of the Muscadet. (1983)
⌀ Gros Plant du Pays Nantais Blanc Sec.
◑┑ Bruno Cormerais, La Chambaudière, St-Lumine-de-Clisson, 44190 Clisson; tel. 40 03 85 84 ⊥ By appt.

LES MOULINS DE LA CHAROUILLERE★★

☐   11ha   20000   2 D ☷ ⌀

83 83

Well made with floral nose and flavour. All the indications are that it will keep well. (1983)
◑┑ Jean Bouyer, La Charouillère, 44330 Vallet; tel. 40 36 23 77 ⊥ By appt.

DOMAINE CHARPENTIER★

☐   12ha   72000   2 D ☷

Beautiful colour and well-balanced on the palate; supple and charming with a long finish. A very good accompaniment to fish and shellfish, but equally enjoyable between meals. (1983)
◑┑ Guy Charpentier, Les Noues, 44430 Le Loroux-Bottereau; tel. 40 06 43 76

CHATEAU DE CHASSELOIR★★★

☐   20ha   150000   4 D ☷ ◑ ⌀

⑦⑥ 82 83

Pretty yellow colour and a very developed nose, with hints of vanilla and bay. Powerful, long and fruity on the palate. The 1983 is well balanced with a lively and delicate nose with hints of hawthorn. (1976) ⌀ Ch. de Chasseloir Gde Réser, Comte Lelou.
◑┑ Ets Chéreau-Carre, Dom. de Chasseloir, BP 49, Saint-Fiacre-sur-Maine, 44960 La Haie-Fouassière; tel. 40 54 81 15 ⊥ Daily 8.00–18.30
◑┑ Edmond Chéreau.

DOMAINE DES CHAUSSELIERES★★

☐   7ha   42000   2 D ☷ ◑

Full of character, with a subtly perfumed nose. Easy to drink and very typical of the Muscadet. (1982) ⌀ Gros Plant du Pays Nantais Blanc, Vin de Pays des Marches-de-Bretagne Rouge.
◑┑ Joseph Bosseau, La Bouillère, 44330 Le Pallet; tel. 40 26 40 12 ⊥ By appt.

CHATEAU DU CLERAY★★

☐   30ha   150000   3 D ◑ ⌀

Attractive light-yellow colour, and delicate mineral nose. Fairly round on the palate, with a touch of aggression. Always a pleasure to drink. (1983) ⌀ Gros Plant.
◑┑ MM. Sauvion et Fils, Ch. du Cléray, 44330 Vallet; tel. 40 36 22 55 ⊥ Mon.–Fri. 8.00–12.00/14.00–17.30. Closed Oct.–Easter.

CHATEAU DU COING★

☐   23ha   200000   4 D ☷ ◑ ⌀

76 79 82 83

Typical 1983, characterized by strength, fully developed flavours and richness on the palate. (1983)
◑┑ Véronique Chéreau, Ch. du Coing, St-Fiacre-sur-Maine, 44690 La Haie-Fouassière; tel. 40 54 81 15 ⊥ Mon.–Sat. 8.00–12.00/14.00–18.30
◑┑ Véronique Gunther-Chéreau.

GRAND FIEF DE LA CORMERAIE★★

☐   4.26ha   26400   4 D ☷ ◑ ⌀

A very charming wine with a rather sharp nose, not greatly developed but very pleasing. (1983)

⋆┑ Ets Chéreau-Carre, Dom. de Chasseloir, BP 49 St-Fiacre-sur-Maine 44690 La Haie-Fouassière; tel. 40 54 81 15 ϒ Mon.–Sat. 8.00–18.00. ┑ Véronique Gunther-Chéreau.

DOMAINE DES CROIX⋆

| □ | 12ha | 57500 | 2 D ▮ |

Bottling a wine on the lees keeps the wine fresh for longer, giving us extra time in which to appreciate the light yellow colour, attractive nose and elegant balance of this wine. (1983) ✔ Gros Plant du Pays Nantais, Vin de Pays du Jardin de la France.
┑ Bernard Pichon, Dom. des Croix, 44330 Vallet; tel. 40 36 23 18 ϒ By appt.

DOMAINE DE LA DEBAUDIERE
Sur Lie⋆⋆

| □ | 10ha | 60000 | 2 D ▮ |
| 69 76 76 78 83 84 |

Beautiful pale colour with fruity, elegant nose. High-spirited finesse and lightness on the palate. (1983)
┑ Albert Frères, La Varenne, 49270 St-Laurent-des-Autels; tel. 40 83 50 02 ϒ No visitors.

DOMAINE DE L'ECU *Sur Lie*⋆

| □ | 12ha | 75000 | 2 D ▮ ⊕ ⌄ |
| 83 84 |

Delicate nose and light on the palate; a thoroughly elegant wine (1983).
┑ Guy Bossard, La Brettonière, Le Landréau, 44430 Le Louroux-Bottereau; tel. 40 06 40 91 ϒ By appt.

DOMAINE DE LA FEVRIE *Sur Lie*⋆⋆⋆

| □ | 13ha | 40000 | 2 D ▮ ⌄ |

Very good colour, and a delicate, attractive nose. Rewarding length and softness on the palate. A very great pleasure to drink. (1983)
┑ Claude Branger, La Févrie, Maisdon-sur-Sèvre, 44690 La Haie Fouassiéré; tel. 40 36 94 08 ϒ By appt.

LA FOLLIETTE⋆⋆

| □ | 12ha | 15000 | 2 ▮ ⌄ |
| ⑧③ 83 |

Good, well-balanced example of the 1983 vintage. The elegant white colour and powerful nose make this a delicate wine of fine quality. (1983)
┑ Louis Brosseau, La Folliette, 44690 La Haye-Fouassière; tel. 40 54 83 16.

DOMAINE DE LA FRUITIERE⋆⋆

| □ | 20ha | 96000 | 2 D ▮ ⌄ |

The vineyard soil gives elegance and finesse to this pale-yellow wine. Light and fruity, with a long finish. (1983) ✔ Gros Plant du Pays Nantais, Vin de Pays des Marches de Bretagne, Cabernet.
┑ Jean Douillard, La Fruitière, 44690 Châteauthébaud; tel. 40 06 53 05 ϒ By appt.

GABARE DE SEVRE⋆

| □ | 69ha | 310000 | 3 D ▮ ⊕ |

Pale-yellow colour leading to a powerful, earthy nose characteristic of the area, and a pronounced iodine flavour. (1983)
┑ GIE Gabare de Sèvre, Le Pé-de-Sèvre, 44330 Le Pallet; tel. 40 26 97 30 ϒ By appt.

DOMAINE DE LA GAUTRONNIERE⋆⋆

| □ | 9ha | 40000 | 2 D ▮ ⌄ |
| 82 ⋆83 |

Tasting this wine is a real pleasure. Beautifully pale in colour and delicate, subtle, long and powerful on the palate. (1983)
┑ Jean Forget, La Gautronnière, 44330 La Chapelle-Heulin; tel. 40 06 74 13 ϒ By appt.

DOMAINE DES GENAUDIERES⋆

| □ | 4ha | 25000 | 2 D ⊕ ⌄ |

Well-developed nose, good body and easy to drink. (1983)
┑ Augustin Athinon, Les Genaudières, Le Cellier 44850; tel. 40 25 40 27 ϒ By appt.

CHATEAU DES GILLIERES⋆

| □ | 40ha | 240000 | 2 D ▮ ⌄ |

Clean white colour, slightly developed nose and strength and tautness in the mouth. (1983)
✔ Gros Plant sur lie, Vin de Pays Cabernet.
┑ Louis Nogue, Ch. des Gillières, 44690 La Haye-Fouassière; tel. 40 54 80 05. ϒ By appt.

MARQUIS DE GOULAINE
Château Les Montys⋆⋆

| □ | | 70000 | 2 D ▮ ⊕ ⌄ |

Beautiful white wine with lovely colour and restrained nose, good balance and finesse on the palate. (1983)
┑ Marquis de Goulaine, Ch. de Goulaine, 44115 Haute Goulaine; tel. 40 54 91 42 ϒ By appt.

MARQUIS DE GOULAINE⋆⋆

| □ | 12ha | 64800 | 2 D ▮ ⊕ ⌄ |

Lovely yellow colour. Delicate and elegant nose confirmed by fullness on the palate. Great quality (1983) ✔ Muscadet Sèvre-et-Maine, Gros Plant du Pays Nantais.
┑ Le Marquis de Goulaine, Ch. de Goulaine, 44115 Haute-Goulaine; tel. 40 54 91 42 ϒ By appt.

DOMAINE DU GRAND-MOUTON
Sur Lie⋆⋆

| □ | 22ha | 150000 | 4 D ▮ ⌄ |

A very light and lively wine whose colour hints at a slightly acid nose reminiscent of pear drops. Very firm and vigorous on the palate.
┑ GIE Louis Métaireau, La Févrie, Maisdon-sur-

Sèvre, 44690 La Haie-Fouassière; tel. 40 54 81 92 ⵊ By appt.

GRAND-MOUTON HUISSIER*

☐ 23 ha 140 000 **4** **D** ⵊ ⵊ

81 82 83

Bright yellow colour and lively, fairly fruity nose with aromas of fresh apples. On the palate short finish with hints of coffee and aniseed. (1983) ✔ Métaireau Grand-Mouton Cuvée No. 2. ⵊ GIE Louis Métaireau, La Févrié, 44690 Maisdon-sur-Sèvre; tel. 40 54 81 92 ⵊ By appt. Closed Aug.

DOMAINE DE LA GRANGE**

☐ 12 ha 72 000 **3** **D** ⵊ ⵊ ⵊ

Deep-yellow colour. Nose still lively and defined. Well made and unusual to taste, due to its age. (1980) ✔ Gros Plant du Pays Nantais sur Lie. ⵊ Pierre et Rémy Luneau, Dom. de La Grange, 44430 Le Loroux-Bottereau; tel. 40 06 43 90 ⵊ By appt.

MOULIN DE LA GRAVELLE**

☐ 8.5 ha 51 000 **4** **D** ⵊ ⵊ ⵊ

Splendid colour and full (but not overpowering) nose. A well-made wine with reasonable length on the palate. (1983) ⵊ Ets Chéreau-Carre, Dom. de Chasseloir, BP 49 St-Fiacre-sur-Maine, 44690 La Haie-Fouassière; tel. 40 54 81 15 ⵊ Mon.–Sat. 8.00–18.00.

LA GRENADIERE *Tiré Sur Lie**

☐ 15 ha 72 000 **2** **D** ⵊ ⵊ

Pale-gold in colour, with quite a fresh young nose, and satisfyingly well balanced on the palate. A little flighty, but will go well with crudités or with goat's cheese after dinner. (1983) ⵊ *MM.* Brochard Frères, La Grenadière, 44690 Maisdon-sur-Sèvre; tel. 40 03 80 00 ⵊ By appt.

JOSEPH HALLEREAU
*Clos le Patis de la Noé**

☐ 20 ha 6000 **2** **D** ⵊ ⵊ

A well-made wine with a lightly developed colour. (1983) ⵊ Joseph Hallereau, Les Chaboissières, 44330 Vallet; tel. 40 78 21 62 ⵊ By appt.

DOMAINE DE LA HAUTE-POEZE**

☐ 8 ha 48 000 **2** **D** ⵊ

Beautiful, slightly sparkling appearance, fresh young nose; balance and charm on the palate. (1983) ⵊ Pierre Mabit, Haute-Poeze, 44330 Le Landreau; tel. 40 06 43 88 ⵊ Daily by appt.

DOMAINE DES HAUTES-PERRIERES*

☐ 20 ha 120 000 **2** **D** ⵊ

This wine is in its prime. Lightly developed nose and a lovely white colour. A pleasure to drink. (1983) ⵊ Alexandre Gauthier, Les Hautes-Perrières, 44115 Haute-Goulaine; tel. 40 06 10 08 ⵊ By appt.

DOMAINE DE LA HAUTIERE**

☐ 15 ha 72 000 **3** **D** ⵊ ⵊ

Good colour and body, well-made and full-bodied. To keep. (1982) ✔ Gros Plant du Pays Nantais. ⵊ Gabriel Thebaud, La Hautière, 44690 St-Fiacre-sur-Maine; tel. 40 54 81 13 ⵊ Mon.–Fri. 10.00–12.00/15.00–18.00. Closed 10 Aug.–5 Sept.

DOMAINE DES HAUTS PEMIONS**

☐ 12 ha 60 000 **2** **D** ⵊ

Clear white colour and woody nose. On the palate, well balanced, well made and has long finish. Good value for money. (1983) ⵊ Joseph Drouard, La Hollopière, 44620 Monnières; tel. 40 26 43 48 ⵊ By appt.

DOMAINE DE L'HYVERNIERE*

☐ 30 ha 180 000 **2** ⵊ ⵊ

Slight bitterness typical of the Muscadet, nonetheless very pleasant to taste. (1983) ✔ Gros Plant du Pays Nantais Blanc. ⵊ *Mme* Veuve Marcel Sautejeau, Dom. de l'Hyvernière, 44330 Le Pallet; tel. 40 06 73 83 ⵊ By appt.

DOMAINE DU LANDREAU-VILLAGE**

☐ 9 ha 55 000 **2** ⵊ ⵊ ⵊ

Good colour, fresh young nose and, although slightly bitter on the palate, pleasant to drink. Suitable for laying down. A wine of great character. (1983) ⵊ *MM.* Drouet Frères, 6 Rue Emile Gabory, 44330 Vallet; tel. 40 78 15 94 ⵊ By appt. Closed 15–22 Aug. ⵊ Héritiers Sautejeau.

DOMAINE DE LA MARTINIERE**

☐ 21 ha 160 000 **2** **D** ⵊ ⵊ

76 79 81 *82 *83

Pale yellow in colour, with light, floral nose; a delicate, clean and pleasant thirst-quencher. (1983) ⵊ GAEC Baron Brevet, La Martinière, 44330 La Chapelle-Heulin; tel. 40 06 70 34 ⵊ By appt.

CHATEAU DE LA MERCREDIERE**

☐ 30 ha 180 000 **3** **D** ⵊ ⵊ

This 14th-century château produces a wine with a beautiful colour, elegant nose and supple roundness on the palate. (1982) ⵊ *Mm.* Futuel Frères, Ch. de la Mercredière, Le Pallet, 44690 La Haie-Fouassière; tel. 40 54 80 10 ⵊ Mon.–Sat. 9.00–12.30/14.00–18.00.

LOUIS METAIREAU *Cuvée One**

☐ 75 ha 40 000 **4** **D** ⵊ ⵊ

81 82 83 **83**

Pale yellow. Delicate and elegant; slightly sparkling. Powerful, aromatic nose, with a hint of herbs. Well made. Quite easy to drink, with a definite aftertaste of coffee. (1983) ⵊ GIE Louis Métaireau, La Févrie, 44690 Maisdon-sur-Sèvre; tel. 40 54 81 92. ⵊ By appt. Closed Aug. ⵊ Groupement des Viticulteurs.

LOUIS METAIREAU
Cuvée Louis Metaireau★★

☐   75ha   60000   **4** **D** ▋ ⬇

Pale yellow. Apple and pear flavours predominate. Very slightly sparkling, with a supple, rounded taste. (1983)
➍ GIELouisMétaireau,LaFévrie,44690Maisdon-sur-Sèvre; tel. 40 54 81 92 ☗ By appt. Closed Aug.

LOUIS METAIREAU★

☐   75ha   110000   **3** **D** ▋ ⬇
81 82 ⑧⑬ **83**

Bright transparent-yellow colour and nose dominated by aromas of apples. On the palate, supple and attractive, with hint of coffee and aniseed. (1983)
➍ GIE Louis Métaireau, La Févrié, 44690 Maisdon-sur-Sèvre; tel. 40 54 81 92 ☗ By appt. Closed Aug.

DOMAINE DE LA MINIERE★★

☐   30ha   50000   **2** **D** ▋ ⬇
83

Delicate and perfumed white with a yellow tinge. Woody nose. Well balanced and very well made. (1983)
➍ André Ménard-Gaborit, La minière, 44620 Monnières; 40 26 43 21 ☗ By appt.

DOMAINE DES MORTIERS-GOBIN★★

☐   8ha   48000   **3** **D** ▋ ⬇

This wine is a lovely colour with a slight sparkle from being bottled 'sur lie'. Elegant nose, revealing good structure, balance and body on the palate. Ready for drinking, but will age well. (1983)
➍ Robert Brosseau, Dom. des Mortiers-Gobin, 44690 La Haie-Fouassière; tel. 40 54 80 66 ☗ By appt. Closed 10–30 Aug.

DOMAINE DU MOULIN★

☐   10ha   60000   **2** **D** ▋ ⬗ ⬇
⑧⑬

Good bright colour and light palate, with a pleasant finish. (1983) ✔ Gros Plant du Pays Nantais Dom. l'Épau Blanc.
➍ Bernard Derame, La Bourchinière, 44690 St-Fiacre-sur-Maine; tel. 40 54 83 80 ☗ By appt. Closed 15–30 Aug.

DOMAINE DE LA MOUTONNIERE★

☐   4ha   25000   **2** **D** ▋ ⬗ ⬇

The very distinctive nose of this wine shows the advantage of bottling on the lees. Lovely pale colour; soft and pleasant to drink. (1983)
➍ Marcel Guilbaud et Frères, Les Lilas, Mouzillon 44330 Vallet; tel. 40 36 30 55 ☗ Mon.–Fri. 8.00–12.30/14.00–18.00.

RESERVE DES NOE-GUERETS★★

☐   12ha   50000   **2** **D** ▋ ⬇
83 **83**

Subtle, elegant bouquet and delicate flavour. (1983)
➍ M. et J.-C. Lebas, 38 Rue de Bazoges, 44330 Vallet; tel. 40 78 20 61 ☗ By appt. Closed Aug.

DOMAINE DES NOELLES-DE-SEVRE★

☐   12ha   65000   **2** **D** ▋ ⬗

A strong yellow colour and developed nose. The prickling sensation on the tongue is characteristic of wines bottled 'sur lie'. (1983)
➍ Théophile Chéreau, Rue de la Poste, 44690 Monnières; tel. 40 26 43 27 ☗ By appt.

VIGNERONS DE LA NOELLE★★

☐   200ha   500000   **2** **D** ▋ ⬇
81 82 83 **83**

Good example of the appellation characterized by aromas of apples and pears, with a slight touch of iodine. Well-balanced structure. (1983)
➍ Coop. Vignerons de la Noelle, Groupe Cana, St-Géréons, 44150 Ancenis; tel. 40 83 02 40 ☗ By appt.

CHATEAU DE LA NOE★★

☐   30ha   120000   **2** **D** ▋
83 84

Beautiful yellow colour; balsam with a hint of vanilla on the nose, developing into a slightly woody taste on the palate. A pleasure to drink. (1983)
➍ M. le Comte de Malestrait, Ch. de la Noé, 44330 Vallet; tel. 40 78 20 59 ☗ By appt.

CHATEAU L'OISELINIERE DE LA RAMEE★★

☐   8.55ha   25000   **4** **D** ▋ ⬗ ⬇

To taste this elegant wine is alive and vital. It has a lovely colour, pale, with a young gutsy nose. (1983)
➍ Ets Chéreau-Carre, Dom. de Chasseloir, BP 49 St-Fiacre-sur-Maine, 44690 La Haie-Fouassière; tel. 40 54 81 15 ☗ Mon.–Sat. 8.00–18.00.

CHATEAU DE L'OISELINIERE★★

☐   32ha   190000   **2** **D** ▋ ⬗ ⬇

Beautiful pale wine with a delicate, elegant nose; very well balanced and harmonious on the palate. (1983) ✔ Gros Plant du Pays Nantais Blanc.
➍ Jean Aulanier, Ch. de l'Oiselinière, Gorges, 44190 Clisson; tel 40 06 91 59 ☗ By appt.

CLOS DES ORFEUILLES★

☐   30ha   80000   **2** ⬗ ⬇

Full-bodied, pale-yellow wine. If kept properly will last two to five years, which is unusual for a Muscadet. (1983)
➍ Mme Veuve Marcel Sautejeau, Dom. de l'Hyvernière, 44330 Le Pallet; tel. 40 06 73 83 ☗ By appt.

DOMAINE DU PIED DE GARDE★

☐   15ha   72000   **2** **D** ▋ ⬇

Clean, supple and lightly fruity. Lovely colour. (1983)
✔ Gros Plant du Pays Nantais Blanc, Vin de Pays du Marche-de-Bretagne Rouge
➍ Jean-Louis Hervouet, 2 Rue de la Margerie, Gorges, 44190 Clisson; tel. 40 06 92 29 ☗ By appt.

CHATEAU PLESSIS BREZOT★★

☐ 11ha 66000 **2 D ▬ ◐ ↓**

Intense, elegant colour. The fine, wood-scented nose is matched by its length and fullness in the mouth. Perfect (1983)
🍷 Barre Frères, Pleasis Brezot, 44190 Gorges; tel. 40 06 90 70 ☎ No visitors 🍷 Sté. Civ. Plessis-Brezot.

DOMAINE DES QUATRE ROUTES★

☐ 20ha 120000 **2 D ▬ ◐ ↓**

Pale yellow with an unripe nose and an attractive, easy-to-drink quality in the mouth. (1983)
🍷 Henri Poiron, Dom. des Quatre Routes, 44690 Maisdon-sur-Sèvre; tel. 40 26 42 07. ☎ Mon.–Sat. 8.00–12.00/14.00–18.00.

DOMAINE DE LA QUILLA★★

☐ 16ha 86500 **2 D ▬ ↓**

A wine with a lovely colour and slight sparkle. Young elegant, nose and good balance and charm on the palate; very characteristic of the region. (1983)
🍷 Gérard Vinet, La Croix-Moriceau, 44690 La Haie-Fouassière; tel. 40 54 83 28 ☎ By appt.

CHATEAU DE LA RAGOTIERE★★

☐ 28ha 120000 **2 D ▬ ↓**

Nose reminiscent of gunflint and characteristic of the flinty soil; plenty of body. (1983) ✔ Gros Plant du Pays Nantais VDQS 1982.
🍷 GAEC la Ragotière, Ch. de la Ragotière, 44330 La Regrippière; tel. 40 36 35 11 ☎ By appt.

DOMAINE DE LA REBOURGERE★★

☐ 8ha 35000 **2 D ▬ ↓**
83 84

Straw-coloured Muscadet. Delicate and fruity, with aromas of apples and pears. (1983)
🍷 Joseph Launais, La Rebourgère, Maisdon-sur-Sèvre, 44690 La Haye-Fouassière; tel. 40 26 43 58 ☎ By appt.

DOMAINE DE LA ROCHERIE★

☐ 5.6ha 28500 **2 D ▬**

A delicate wine with a classic colour. Slightly aggressive nose, but nonetheless pleasant, (1983) ✔ Gros Plant du Pays Nantais, Vin de Pays Gamay grape, Vin de Pays Cabernet grape.
🍷 Daniel Gratas, La Rocherie, 44430 Le Landreau; tel. 40 06 41 55 ☎ By appt.

CLOS DES ROSIERS★★

☐ 10ha 60000 **2 D ▬ ◐ ↓**

Beautiful light colour, with a very floral and powerful nose; long on the palate and easy to drink. (1983)
🍷 Philippe Laure, Le Clos-des-Rosiers, 44330 Vallet; tel. 40 78 17 52 ☎ By appt.

LE SOLEIL NANTAIS★★

☐ 8ha 100000 **2 D ▬ ◐ ↓**

A refeshing wine with a beautiful white colour, lively and not overpowering on the nose and well balanced on the palate. (1983) ✔ Chinon AC, St-Nicolas de Bourgueil AC, Saumur-Champigny.
🍷 Ets Guilbaud et Frères, Les Lilas, Mouzillon,

44330 Vallet; tel. 40 36 30 55 ☎ Mon.–Sat. 8.00–12.30/14.00–18.00.

DOMAINE DE LA TOURMALINE★

☐ 22ha 120000 **2 D ▬ ◐**

The light colour of this wine is a good sign. Pale gold with a very fresh young nose and an earthy background; very easy to drink. (1983)
🍷 *MM*. Gadais Frères, Le Coteau, 44690 St-Fiacre-sur-Maine; tel. 40 54 81 23 ☎ Mon.–Sat. 8.00–18.00.

CHATEAU DE LA TURMELIERE★★

☐ 7ha 42000 **2 D ▬ ↓**

This wine has a good colour and lively nose; the flavour is well balanced and pronounced. To be drunk young. (1983)
🍷 Sté Donatien Bahuaud, BP 1, 44330 La Chapelle-Heulin; tel. 40 06 70 05 ☎ By appt.

LE VERGER★★

☐ 8ha 35000 **3 D ▬ ↓**
82 83 83

Pale colour with very floral nose. On the palate, full bodied and very earthy influence. (1983)
🍷 Léon Dollet, Le Verger, 44620 La Haye-Fouassière; tel. 40 36 90 19 ☎ By appt.

DOMAINE FRANCIS VIAUD LA FEVRIE★★

☐ 12ha 72000 **3 D ▬ ↓**

Attractive and elegant nose, balanced and firm structure confirms the harmony of its rich bouquet. (1983) ✔ Gros Plant du Pays Nantais.
🍷 Francis Viaud, La Févrie, 44690 Maisdon-sur-Sèvre; tel. 40 54 81 17 ☎ By appt. Closed second fortnight Aug.

Gros-Plant VDQS

Gros-Plant du Pays Nantais is a dry white wine which has had VDQS status since 1954. It is made from a single grape variety, the Folle Blanche of Charentes, which is here called the Gros-Plant. The area of the vineyard is around 2800 hectares (6900 acres) and average annual production is 160000 hectolitres. Like the Muscadet, Gros-Plant wine may be bottled 'sur lie'. Its refreshing dryness suits it to seafood in general and shellfish in particular. It should be served chilled but not iced (8–9°C).

DOMAINE DU BOIS-BRULEY★★

☐ 3ha 18000 **3 D ▬ ◐ ↓**

Beautiful colour, lingering taste, excellent balance. (1983)
🍷 ETS Chéreau-Carré, Dom. de Chasseloir, BP 49 St-Fiacre-sur-Maine 44690; La Haie-Fouassière; tel. 40 54 81 15 ☎ Daily. Closed Sun. 20–20.30 🍷 Bernard Chéreau.

DOMAINE DU BOIS-JOLY★

☐ 3ha 18000 **2** D 🍷 ⬇

Extremely easy to drink; pale-yellow colour, well-developed bouquet of scented wood, and quite round to taste. (1983)
🍷 Henri Bouchard, Le Bois-Joly, 44330 Le Pallet; tel. 40 26 40 83. ⏳ By appt. Closed 15–31 Aug.

ANDRE-MICHEL BREGEON★★

☐ 0.75ha 4000 **2** D 🍷 ⬤ ⬇

Has a good strong colour and delicate nose. A slight touch of acidity on the palate, but nonetheless a very pleasant example of this particular wine. (1983)
🍷 André-Michel Bregeon, Les Guisseaux, Gorges, 44190 Clisson; tel. 40 06 93 19. ⏳ By appt.

DOMAINE GUY CHARPENTIER★★

☐ 4ha 24000 **2** D 🍷 ⬇

Good pale colour, with an elegant nose; charming and very attractive to taste. (1983)
🍷 Guy Charpentier, Les Noues, 44430 Le Loroux-Bottereau; tel. 40 06 43 76 ⏳ Closed early Sep.

CHATEAU DE CLERAY
Domain de la Seigneurie du Cléray★★

☐ 3ha 25000 **3** D ⬤ ⬇

Beautiful colour and delicate, fruity nose. Elegant and classy. Lingers on the palate. Clear, bright and jaunty. (1983)
🍷 Sauvignon et Fils, Ch. de Cléray, 44330 Vallet; tel. 40 36 22 55 ⏳ Mon.–Fri. 8.00–12.00/14.00–17.30. Closed Oct.–Easter.

DOMAINE DES CROIX★

☐ 3ha 18000 **1** D 🍷

Light-yellow colour and mature nose; from the very heart of the region. (1983) ✔ Muscadet de Sevre-et-Maine, Vin de Pays des Jardins de la France.
🍷 Bernard Pichon, Dom. des Croix, 4430 Valley; tel. 40 36 23 18 ⏳ By appt.

GABARE DE SEVRE★★

☐ 28ha 168000 **2** D 🍷 ⬤ ⬇

Pale yellow colour and delicately developed nose. Well balanced to taste. Slightly flinty finish that is rather pleasant. (1983)
🍷 GIE Cabare de Sèvre, St-Pé-de-Sèvre, La Vallet, 44330, Pallet; tel. 40 26 98 30 ⏳ By appt.

CHATEAU DES GILLIERES★★

☐ 40ha 240000 **2** D 🍷 ⬇

·A pretty wine with a very good white colour, whose charm increases as you sniff the flowery nose; excellent balance on the palate. (1983)
🍷 Louis Nogue, Ch. des Gillières, 44690 La Haie-Fouassière; tel. 40 54 02 80 ⏳ By appt.

CHATEAU DE LA GRANGE★

☐ 50000 **2** D 🍷 ⬤ ⬇

Clear coloured, with a strong farmyard nose and fairly well-developed palate. (1983)
🍷 *M. le Marquis* de Goulaine, Ch. de Goulaine, 44115 Haute-Goulaine; tel. 40 54 91 42 ⏳ By appt. Closed 2 Nov.–Easter.

DOMAINE DE LA HAUTE POEZE★★

☐ 4ha 24000 **2** D 🍷 ⬇

Straightforward, lively nose; well made and harmonious on the palate, with a certain suppleness. Demonstrates brilliantly that the Gros Plant is not the poor relation of the Nantes region. (1983)
🍷 Pierre Mabit, Dom. de la Haute-Poeze, Le Landreau 44430; le Loroux-Bottereau; tel. 40 06 43 88 ⏳ By appt.

DOMAINE DE LA HAUTE-MAISON★

☐ 7ha 40000 **2** D 🍷 ⬇

Yellow-tinged colour. Full bodied, with well-developed, woody nose. (1983)
🍷 J.-N. Schaeffer-Bronckhorst, Dom. de la Haute-Maison, St-Aignan-de-Grand-Lieu 44860; Pont-St-Martia; tel. 40 26 84 42 ⏳ Mon.–Sat. 9.00–12.00/14.00–19.00.

DOMAINE DES HERBAUGES★★

☐ 7.5ha 50000 **2** D 🍷 ⬇

An attractive wine with a plain, honest nose presenting the palate with *une dominante de vivacité*, but will improve if left to mature for a while. (1983)
🍷 Pierre et Luc Choflot, Dom. des Herbauges, 44340 Bouaye; tel. 40 65 44 92 ⏳ Mon.–Sat. 9.30–12.00/14.00–19.00.

DOMAINE DU LANDREAU-VILLAGE★

☐ 4ha 24000 **2** D 🍷 ⬤ ⬇

Despite a lively acidity, an attractive wine with a pale colour and a spicy nose. Very easy to drink. (1983)
🍷 Drouet Frères, 6 Rue Emile Gabory, 44330 Vallet; tel. 40 78 15 94 ⏳ By appt. Closed the week of the 15 Aug. 🍷 Héritiers Sautejean.

DOMAINE DES NOELLES-DE-SEVRE★

☐ 1.5ha 5000 **2** D 🍷 ⬤ ⬇

Lovely yellow colour. Impulsive and cheeky. Well-developed and woody nose, and light acidity. (1983)
🍷 Théophile Chéreau, Rue de la Poste, Monnières 44690; tel. 40 26 43 27 ⏳ By appt 🍷 M. Th. Chéreau-Merrière.

CHATEAU DE L'OISELINIERE★★

☐ 32ha 192000 **2** D 🍷 ⬤ ⬇

A wine with the full spirit and flavour of its type, having a bright colour and a delicate, fruity nose. Good attack, well balanced and long in the mouth. (1983)
🍷 Jean Aulanier, Ch. de l'Oiselinière, Gorges 44190, Clisson; tel. 40 06 91 59 ⏳ By appt 🍷 SC Aulanier.

CHATEAU DE LA RAGOTIERE★★

☐ 2ha 12000 **2** D 🍷 ⬇

Well-balanced. A nose that literally jumps out of the glass and lingers on the palate. (1983)
🍷 Couillaud Frères, Ch. de la Ragotière, 44330 Vallet; tel. 40 36 35 11 ⏳ By appt.

DOMAINE DE LA ROCHERIE★

☐ 2ha 14400 **2 D ▪ ↓**

A pretty, yellow-coloured wine with a lightly, developed nose; very charming and will appeal to delicate palates. (1983)
➥ Daniel Gratas, La Rocherie, 44430 Le Landreau, Le Loroux-Bottereux; tel. 40 06 41 55
☖ By appt.

CLOS DES ROSIERS★★★

☐ 3ha 24000 **2 D ▪ ⑴ ↓**

A magnificent wine with an excellent and extremely delicate nose, and with very good fruit on the palate. Elegant and well-bred, its brilliance is like that of a fine, white rose. (1983) ✔ Muscadet Sèvre-et-Maine 'sur lie', Gros-plant Méthode Champenoise.
➥ Philippe Laure, Le Clos-des-Rosiers, 44330 Vallet; tel. 40 78 17 52 ☖ By appt.

GABRIEL THEBAUD★

☐ 5ha 40000 **2 D ▪ ↓**

Beautiful, pale-yellow colour and delicately developed nose, with no sharp edges. Very well balanced. (1982)
➥ Gabriel Thébaud, La Hautière, 44690 St-Fiacre-sur-Maine; tel. 40 54 81 13 ☖ Mon.–Fri. 10.00–12.00/15.00–18.00. Closed 10 Aug.–5 Sept.

DOMAINE FRANCIS VIAUD-LA-FEVRIE★★

☐ 1ha 7000 **2 D ▪ ↓**

Good white colour, a fresh, young and lively bouquet, and all the good characteristics of gros-plant sur lie. (1983)
➥ Francis Viaud, La Févrié, Maisdon-sur-Sèvre, 44690 La Haie-Foussière; tel. 40 54 81 17 ☖ By appt. Closed 2nd fortnight Aug.

Fiefs Vendéens VDQS

Formerly in the hands of the church, these vineyards have a very long history. In the seventeenth century, the local wines were firm favourites of Cardinal Richelieu. The region was granted VDQS status in 1984, a recognition of the growers' sustained efforts to maintain and improve quality.

Five communes make up the 380 hectares of the appellation. The Mareuil region produces fragrant, light and fruity red wines from the Gamay, Cabernet, and Pinot Noir. The

amount of white wine produced is still very limited. The vineyards, at Brem near the coast, produce some dry white wines from the Chenin and Grolleau Gris, and also some red and rosé wine. Around Fontenay-le-Comte, dry white wines from the Chenin, Colombard, Melon and Sauvignon grapes are produced in the regions of Pissotte and Vix together with reds and rosés from the Gamay and Cabernet. The wines should be drunk young.

DOMAINE DE LA CHAIGNEE
Blanc de Blanc Sauvignon★★

☐ 5ha 30000 **2 D ▪ ↓**

82 ⑧ ★84 84

Brilliant golden-green colour, and the elegant, well-developed floral nose characteristic of the Sauvignon. Crisp on the palate, with strongly persistent aromas, this attractive and pleasing wine is perfect for hot summer days. Serve well-chilled (below 12°C). (1984) ✔ Fiefs Vendéens Rouge, Fiefs Vendéens Rosé.
➥ MM. Mercier Frères, Dom. de la Chaignée, 85770 Vix; tel. 51 00 65 14 ☖ By appt.

DOMAINE DE LA CHAIGNEE★★

◪ 5ha 15000 **2 D ▪ ↓**

83 ⑧ 84

Lovely, mature rose colour, well-developed fruity nose, crisp and light on the palate with a delicate aroma. A full, vigorous wine which could be drunk well-chilled with salads. (1984) ✔ Fiefs Vendéens Rouge, Fiefs Vendéens Rosé.
➥ MM. Mercier Frères, Dom. de la Chaignée, 85770 Vix; tel. 51 00 65 14 ☖ By appt.

DOMAINE DE LA CHAIGNEE★★

■ 10ha **2 D ▪ ↓**

76 79 ⑧ 83 ★84

Light in colour and flavour, with the full character of the Cabernet grape. Round and flowing on the palate, and a perfect partner for roast or grilled white meat. Serve extremely cool. ✔ Fiefs Vendéens Rouge, Fiefs Vendéens Rosé.
➥ MM. Mercier Frères, Dom. de la Chaignée, 85770 Vix; tel. 51 00 65 14 ☖ By appt.

PHILIPPE ET XAVIER COIRIER
Pissotte★★

☐ 13ha 6000 **2 D ⑴ ↓**

Fine colour, with an excellent, well-developed, fruity nose, typical of the Chenin grape. Very attractive, crisp and persistent on the palate. A great pleasure to drink, particularly in summer. Serve well-chilled, with seafood.
➥ Philippe et Xavier Coirier, Rue des Gélinières, Pissotte, 85200 Fontenay-le-Comte; tel. 51 69 34 19 ☖ No visitors.

DANIEL GENTREAU *Mareuil*

| ■ | 3 ha | 2150 | 2 D ▮ ↓ |

A strawberry-coloured wine with a pleasant nose. For a wine that was only four months old when tasted, it showed great promise on the palate and should develop well.
↱ Daniel Gentreau, Follet, 85320 Rosnay; tel. 51 30 55 39 ⵏ By appt.

MICHEL LUCAS *Blanc de Brem*★

| □ | 3 ha | 36000 | 1 D ▮ ⑪ ↓ |

Lovely colour and very crisp nose; smooth and round on the palate; a very charming wine. Its freshness would make it a good accompaniment to all types of fish. (1983) ✔ Fiefs Vendéens Rosé de Brem, Fiefs Vendéens Rouge de Brem.
↱ Michel Lucas, 14 Rue du Petit-Marais, Brem-sur-Mer, 85470 Bretignolles-sur-Mer; tel. 51 90 50 24 ⵏ No visitors.

DANIEL PAJOT *Blanc de Brem*★

| □ | 6 ha | 29000 | 2 D ▮ ⑪ |

Attractive colour and, despite a rather discreet bouquet, a classic wine typical of the region; very well balanced on the palate. A very pleasing bottle. (1983)
↱ Daniel Pajot, La Corde, Brem-sur-Mer, 85470 Bretignolles-sur-Mer; tel. 51 90 50 56 ⵏ Daily 10.00–18.00.

MICHEL PAUPION *Blanc de Brem*★

| □ | 2.5 ha | 9000 | 2 D ▮ ↓ |

This wine has the brilliant colour and characteristic bouquet of the Sauvignon, with a dominant aroma of broom. This is confirmed on the palate and lasts well. A good accompaniment for all types of fish.
↱ Michel Paupion, 85470 Bretignolles-sur-Mer; tel. 51 90 03 81 ⵏ By appt.

MICHEL PAUPION *Rouge de Brem*★

| ■ | 2.5 ha | 12000 | 2 D ⑪ ↓ |

A lovely, strong colour and attractive blackcurrant nose. With body, bite and fullness on the palate, the aroma and structure of this wine are very characteristic of the Cabernet grape.
↱ Michel Paupion, 85470 Bretignolles-sur-Mer; tel. 51 90 03 81 ⵏ By appt.

ARSENE RAMBAUD *Mareuil*★★

| ◪ | 4 ha | 19000 | 2 D ⑪ ↓ |

A strong, salmony-pink colour and very aromatic bouquet. Smooth, supple and delicate on the palate – the dominant Pinot blended with Gamay – this wine cannot fail to please. (1984)
↱ Arsène Rambaud, 'Follet', Rosnay, 85320 Mareuil-sur-Lay-Dissais; tel. 51 30 54 08 ⵏ By appt.

PIERRE RICHARD *Rosé de Brem*★

| ◪ | 2 ha | 6000 | 2 D ▮ ↓ |

A beautiful salmon-pink colour with a very fruity nose reminiscent of well-ripened cherries. This Gamay rosé is crisp and pleasant on the palate and should be drunk young. (1983)
↱ Pierre Richard, Brem-sur-Mer, 85470 Bretignolles-sur-Mer; tel. 51 90 56 84 ⵏ By appt.

DOMAINE DES ROCHETTES *Mareuil*★★

| ■ | 8 ha | 42000 | 2 ▮ ↓ |

Beautiful, intense colour; crisp and full bouquet over a fruity background, which is confirmed on the palate. The Gamay grape is dominant but the combination with the Pinot and Cabernet is perfectly balanced. Serve this wine well chilled. (1984) ✔ Fiefs Vendéens Rouge, Fiefs Vendéens Rosé.
↱ *MM.* Laurent Frères, Dom. des Rochettes, 85310 Chaillé-sous-les-Ormeaux; tel. 51 98 92 53 ⵏ By appt.

Coteaux d'Ancenis VDQS

Coteaux d'Ancenis has been classed as a VDQS wine since 1954. There are four types of wine, each made from a single grape variety: Gamay (80 per cent), Cabernet, Chenin and Malvoisie. The area of the vineyard is 300 hectares and average annual production is 10000 hectolitres. The Gamay used in the Coteaux d'Ancenis is the Gamay Noir à jus blanc, a red grape with clear juice, giving light, dry and fruity wine that may be either red or rosé, depending on how it is vinified – a good partner for hors d'oeuvre, charcuterie or meat. It may be drunk slightly chilled or at room temperature.

DOMAINE DES GENAUDIERES *Gamay*★★

| ■ | 4 ha | 25000 | 2 D ⑪ ↓ |

Good quality but still young. Remarkable for its ruby colour, blackcurrant nose, and slight tannic flavour in the mouth. (1983)
↱ Augustin Athinon, Les Genaudières, 44850 Le Cellier; tel. 40 25 40 27 ⵏ By appt.

DOMAINE DES GENAUDIERES *Cabernet*★

| ■ | 4 ha | 25000 | 2 D ⑪ ↓ |

The strength of the 1983 vintage is apparent in this deep ruby wine, which has a well-developed nose and is easy to drink, despite the continuing presence of tannin. (1983)
↱ Augustin Athimon, Les Genaudières, 44850 Le Cellier; tel. 40 25 40 27 ⵏ By appt.

DOMAINE DES GENAUDIERES *Pinot*★

| □ | 2 ha | 12000 | 2 D ⑪ ↓ |

A good-value wine which is characterized by its strong yellow colour, reserved nose and supple, slightly sweet finish. (1983)
↱ Augustin Athimin, Les Genaudières, 44850 Le Cellier; tel. 40 25 40 27 ⵏ By appt.

Anjou-Saumur

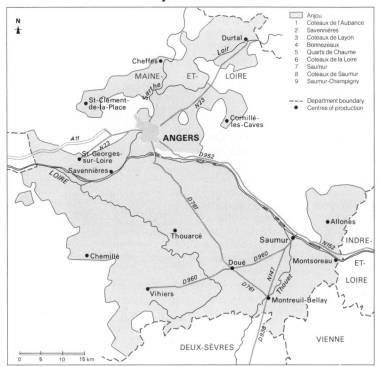

	Anjou
1	Coteaux de l'Aubance
2	Savennières
3	Coteaux de Layon
4	Bonnezeaux
5	Quarts de Chaume
6	Coteaux de la Loire
7	Saumur
8	Coteaux de Saumur
9	Saumur-Champigny

– – – Department boundary
● Centres of production

ANJOU-SAUMUR

The vineyards of Anjou and Saumur lie mostly in the department of Maine-et-Loire, but spill over into the north of Vienne and also into Deux-Sèvres. These vines, in one of the northern-most viticultural areas of France, grow in an Atlantic climate on gentle slopes amid a countryside of rivers and streams.

Vines have long been cultivated on the hillsides of the Loire, the Layon, the Aubance, the Loir and the Thouet. These rivers have always played an important part in the local wine trade: even today, traces of tiny embarkation ports can be found along the Layon. The area under vines reached its greatest extent at the end of the nineteenth century – 31 000 hectares in Maine-et-Loire alone. Here, as elsewhere, the vineyard was destroyed by phylloxera. Replanting began at the beginning of the twentieth century, increased during the 1950s and 1960s, but later fell off again.

The character of the wines of this region is determined not only by the climate, of course, but also the soil.

There is a clear distinction between the wines grown on 'l'Anjou bleu' – schist and other primary rocks of the Armoricain massif – and those grown on 'l'Anjou blanc', the chalky tufa which also extends to the Saumurois. The vines, which used to be mostly trained on the gobelet system, are now being replaced according to the guyot system, and are planted at a density of 4500–5000 stocks per hectare.

Anjou's reputation is built on its sweet white and rosé wines, the most famous area being the Coteaux du Layon. These days, however, there is a trend towards producing dry or medium-dry wines and also red wines. The red wines of Saumur have a high reputation, along with the sparkling wines which have increased considerably in the past few years, especially the AOCS Saumur-Mousseux and Crémant de Loire.

Anjou

Nearly 200 communes are included in this appellation producing white (60 000 hectolitres), red and rosé wines (90 000 hectolitres). For many people the name of Anjou is synonymous with the sweet or semi-sweet white wines made from the Chenin, also known as Pineau de la Loire. However, with the current trend towards drier wines, producers here have now begun to use Chardonnay or Sauvignon grapes to a maximum of 20 per cent. Red wine production, using Cabernet-Franc and Cabernet-Sauvignon, is now changing the image of the area. Producers in this region have made great efforts to ensure a high standard of quality, and these efforts should soon be rewarded by the advent of an Anjou-Villages appellation. The best wines come from the vineyards that border the Aubance and Layon rivers. These wines are characterized by a wonderful ruby colour and fruity aroma, together with a tannin content that allows them to age well. With age, their bouquet becomes more intense and slightly gamey; in fact they will go very well with game, as well as red meat.

ALAIN ARNAULT★

☐ 2ha 2500 ▨ **D** ▤ ⤓

★⑦⑧ 81 **82** 83 **84**

A well-presented wine with a little carbon dioxide, which accentuates the fairly strong Sauvignon aromas. A pleasant sugariness is perceptible on the palate, which makes it better drunk on its own. (1984)
➼ Alain Arnault, Les Landes, Bouillé-Loretz 79290, Argenton-l'Eglise; tel. 49 67 04 85 ▾ By appt.

ALAIN ARNAULT★

■ 5.5ha 7000 ▨ **D** ▤ ⤓

78 ⑧② **83**

Fairly light, developed colour and attractive scents that are at once peppery, floral and reminiscent of soft red fruits; its attack, however, is quite light. To taste, its astringency is not strong and it is quite well put together. Should be drunk young, preferably with grilled meat. (1983)
➼ Alain Arnault, Les Landes, Bouillé-Loretz, Argenton-l'Eglise; tel. 49 67 04 85 ▾ By appt.

DOMAINE DE BABLUT★

■ 26ha 100000 ▨ **D** ▤ ⤓

⑧② **82**

A well-developed colour, almost tile-red, and attractive taste, with the spicy flavours of perfectly ripe Cabernet-Sauvignon blended with the tobacco flavour of the Cabernet Franc. Its fruitiness lacks a little backbone to last long, and it should therefore be drunk young with grilled meat. (1982) ✔ Côteaux de l'Aubance Blanc Moelleux, Rosé de Loire Sec, Cabernet d'Anjou Rosé,Crémant de Loire.

➼ MM. Daviau Frères, Dom. de Bablut, 49320 Brissac-Quince; tel. 41 91 22 59 ▾ By appt.

DOMAINE BANCHEREAU
Le Tirchaud★

■ 2ha 10000 ▨ **D** ▤ ⤓

73 76 79 ⑧② **82** **83**

Typical Cabernet-Sauvignon nose and a well-developed colour. This unusual wine needs to be opened well in advance to be fully appreciated. Should go well with game or strong cheese. (1982) ✔ Rosé d'Anjou.
➼ P. Banchereau et Fils, Le Bourg, St-Aubin-de-Luigné, 49190 Rochefort-sur-Loire; tel. 41 78 33 24 ▾ By appt. Closed 1 Aug.–15 Sept.

JACQUES BEAUJEAU★

☐ 10ha 60000 ▨ **D** ▤ ⑴ ⤓

A rather light wine with attractive nose and taste. It has been aged in oak casks and would be good with charcuterie at the beginning of the meal. (1983)
➼ Jacques Beaujeau, 8 Rue de l'Eglise, 49380 Thouarcé; tel. 41 91 41 17 ▾ By appt. Closed Aug.

JACQUES BEAUJEAU★

■ 15ha 90000 ▨ **D** ▤ ⤓

A pleasant light coloured wine, rich in tannin and slightly acid which will allow it to age. Should be drunk with red meat. (1983)
➼ Jacques Beaujeau, 8 Rue de l'Eglise, 49380 Thouarcé; tel. 41 91 41 17 ▾ By appt. Closed Aug.

DOMAINE DE BEILLANT★★

☐ 3ha 18000 ▨ **D** ▤ ⤓

A very delicate floral wine with excellent balance and very good finish. Altogether a great success and an excellent accompaniment to freshwater fish or charcuterie. (1983) ✔ Rosé de Loire, Anjou Rouge, Cabernet d'Anjou Demi-Sec Rosé, Côteaux-du-Layon Blanc Liquoreux.
➼ Jacques Peltier, Passavant-sur-Layon, 49560 Nueil-sur-Layon; tel. 41 59 51 32 ▾ By appt.

BORE FRERES★

■ 3ha 18000 ▨ **D** ⑴ ⤓

64 69 76 78 79 **80** **81** ⑧② 83

This wine combines the finesse of the Cabernet Franc (which makes up a quarter of the blend) with the strength of the Cabernet-Sauvignon. Although it has good balance and generous tannin, the rather strong acidity means it should be kept before drinking, but buy now to take advantage of the price. (1982)
➼ GAEC Boré Frères, Le Freshe, 49620 La Pommeraye; tel. 41 77 74 63 ▾ By appt.

CLAUDE BRANCHEREAU★

■ 6ha 24000 ▨ **D** ▤ ⑴

This wine is remarkably light and elegant, already beginning to develop scents and aromas of soft red fruit combined with liquorice. It may be served with red meat and robust cheeses. (1982) ✔ Coteaux de Layon-Villages, Anjou Rouge, Anjou Gamay Rouge, Cabernet d'Anjou Rosé.
➼ Claude Branchereau, Les Barres, St-Aubin-de-

Luigné, 49190 Rochefort-sur-Loire; tel. 41 78 33 56 ℐ By appt. Closed last fortnight.

DOMAINE CADY *Brut**

○		1 ha	6000	**3** **D** 📷 ↓

㉃ 83

A wine for parties, with good, long-lasting mousse. Fruity nose, due to the Chenin grapes, with a yeasty background, giving it an attractive aroma of brioches. It would go well with boudoir biscuits as an aperitif. A vigorous wine. (1983)
☙ Pierre et Philippe Cady, Valette, St-Aubin-de-Luigné, 49190 Rochefort-sur-Loire; tel. 41 78 33 69 ℐ Daily 9.00–20.00.

DOMAINE CADY*

□		3 ha	1500	**2** **D** 📷 ↓

㉃ 83 84

Well developed in colour, this wine clearly shows the character of the Chenin grape, combined with the soil of the region. The addition of a little Chardonnay has given the wine some fullness, making it attractive and ready to drink. Its hard finish, due to natural acidity, makes it an obvious choice to accompany seafood and shellfish. (1983)
☙ Pierre et Philippe Cady, Valette, St-Aubin-de-Luigné, 49190 Rochefort-sur-Loire; tel. 41 78 33 69 ℐ Daily 9.00–20.00.

DOMAINE CADY*

■		4 ha	4000	**2** **D** 📷 ↓

79 81 82 82 83 **84**

An attractive, well-made ruby-coloured wine with a fruity bouquet and good balance. Not very alcoholic, it is ready for drinking now and over the next five years with white meat and entrées. (1983)
☙ Pierre et Philippe Cady, Valette, St-Aubin-de-Luigné, 49190 Rochefort-sur-Loire; tel. 41 78 33 69 ℐ Daily 9.00–20.00.

DOMAINE DES CHARBOTTIERES**

■		3 ha	15000	**2** **D** 📷 ↓

78 78 **81** 81 **82** ㉃ 83

Clear, intense colour, a shade between purple and deep ruby. Fruity and tobacco fragrances on the nose, characteristic of the great red wines from this region. Fleshy, well-balanced and tannic palate, with a lingering aromatic finish that augurs well for the future. A very good wine. (1983) ✔ Anjou Blanc, Cabernet d'Anjou Rouge, Côteaux-de-l'Aubance Blanc Liquoreux, Rosé de Loire.

☙ *MM*. Fillion Frères, Les Charbottières, Vauchrétien, 49320 Brissac-Quincé; tel. 41 91 22 87 ℐ By appt. Closed Sun.

DOMAINE LE CHAUMIER*

■		3 ha	18000	**2** **D** 📷 ↓

㉒ 82 83

This young wine is technically very good. Classic deep ruby colour, although a little unsophisticated. Definitely a wine to keep. (1983) ✔ Anjou Gamay Rouge, Rosé de Loire, Cabernet d'Anjou Rosé, Anjou Blanc.
☙ Gilles Musset, Le Chaumier, 49620 La Pommeraye; tel. 41 77 75 72 ℐ By appt ☙ Jean Musset.

CLOS DE COULAINE**

■		5 ha	25000	**3** **D** ◖◗ ↓

75 76 78 82 83

Good colour and fascinatingly rich fragrances of well-ripened soft red fruits. Good potential despite its high alcohol content. (1983)
☙ François Roussier, Coulaine, 49170 St-Georges- sur Loire; tel. 41 72 21 06 ℐ Mon.–Fri. 10.00–12.00/14.00–18.00, Sat. 10.00–12.00.

DOMAINE DE LA CROIX DES LOGES**

■		15 ha	80000	**2** **D** 📷 ↓

69 70 74 *75 *76 76 ㉒ 83 84

A very well-made wine from a good quality harvest. It has an attractive colour and nose reminiscent of redcurrants and raspberries. Well balanced with a long and intensely aromatic finish. It can be kept but need not be opened long before drinking. (1983) ✔ Bonnezeau Blanc Liquoreux, Cabernet d'Anjou Rosé, Rosé de Loire, Saumur mousseux.
☙ Christian Bonnin, Dom. de la Croix des Loges, 49540 Martigné-Briand; tel. 41 59 43 66 ℐ Mon.–Sat. 9.00–12.00/15.00–19.00. Closed Oct.

DHOMME FRERES**

■		4 ha	20000	**2** **D** 📷 ◖◗ ↓

76 78 81 *82 82 ***83** 83

Lovely intense colour but disappointing on the nose because it has not opened out yet. A little heavy to taste, with a lot of alcohol which deadens the aromas. Nevertheless worth keeping for four or five years to allow it to develop. (1982)
☙ *MM*. Dhomme Frères, Le Petit Fort Girault, 49290 Chalonnes-sur-Loire; tel. 41 78 24 27 ℐ By appt.

CHATEAU DE FESLES*

■		5 ha	25000	**2** **D** 📷 ↓

75 78 81 ㉒ 82 83

A good strong ruby-coloured wine; the fruity scents and fragrance of Cabernet Sauvignon give an impression of fullness. The tannin is powerful and a little green on the palate. Should be left to age for a few years. Drink with meat or poultry in sauce. (1983)
☙ Jacques Boivin, Ch. de Fesles, 49380 Thouarcé; tel. 41 91 40 40 ℐ By appt.

DOMAINE DE HAUTE PERCHE★

■ 9ha 50000 ③ D ▮ ↓
76 80 ⑧ 82 ▨ 83

At present austere and closed-up, but a well-made wine which will develop well with age. (1983) ✔ Anjou Gamay Rouge, Rosé de Loire, Cabernet d'Anjou Rosé.
↬ Christian Papin, Haute Perche, St-Mélaine-sur-Aubance, 49320 Brissac-Quincé; tel. 41 91 15 20 ⵉ By appt. Closed first week Aug.

DOMAINE DES HAUTS-PERRAYS★★

□ 2ha 9000 ② D ▮ ↓
⑧ 83 ▨

Very fine colour and agreeable, flowery bouquet, predominantly young and fresh; good structure and perfect balance on the palate, without the usual aggressiveness of this type of wine. Drink with hors d'oeuvre or fish, either grilled or in sauce. (1984)
↬ GAEC Fardeau-Robin, Les Hauts-Perrays, Chaudefonds-sur-Layon 49290, Chalmnes-sur-Loire; tel. 41 78 04 38 ⵉ By appt. Closed May.

DOMAINE DES HAUTS-PERRAYS★

■ 8ha 13000 ② D ▮ ↓
⑦ 78 82 *83

Lovely, vivid ruby colour. The fragrance of well-ripened, soft red fruit has a complex, aromatic side that is already well developed. Satisfactory body, strong structure, a slightly dried feeling in the mouth and a woody, vegetal finish. A little high in alcohol. (1983)
↬ GAEC Fardeau-Robin, Les Hauts-Perrays, Chaudefonds-sur-Layon 49290, Chalonnes-sur-Loire; tel. 41 78 04 38 ⵉ By appt.

ROBERT LECOMTE-GIRAULT★

■ 2.5ha 25000 ② D ▮ ↓
78 79 ⑧ ▨▨ 84

Attractive, light ruby colour, with slight hints of soft red fruit on the nose. Well made, with a slightly bitter finish; with less alcohol on the nose it would be perfect. Serve fairly cool and young with grilled meat. (1984)
↬ Robert Lecomte-Girault, Le Sablon, Faye-d'Anjou, 49380 Thouarcé; tel. 41 91 41 34 ⵉ By appt. Closed 15 Aug.–15 Sept.

DOMAINE LEDUC-FROUIN
La Seigneurie★

■ 5ha 12000 ② D ▮ ↓
⑥ 76 78 81 82 83 ▨▨

A good, clear-coloured wine with a very attractive nose blending soft fruits with aromas of peach and tobacco. Good balance, and the delicate and reserved tannin content gives it good body. May be drunk now or left to age, which it will do elegantly. A nice bottle. (1983)
↬ Georges Leduc, Soussigné, 49540 Martigné-Briand; tel. 41 59 42 83 ⵉ By appt.

JOEL LHUMEAU★

□ 1ha 5000 ② D ▮ ↓
59 ⑦ *80 *81 84

A good balance of alcohol, acid and sugar. Well-presented, but with a faint sulphur smell and not much body. Its scope is not great, but an interesting wine for the vintage. (1984)
↬ Joel Lhumeau, Linières, Brigné-sur-Layon, 49700 Doué-la-Fontaine; tel. 41 59 30 51 ⵉ By appt.

JOEL LHUMEAU★

■ 15ha 15000 ② D ▮ ↓
⑦ 82 83 *84 ▨▨

An attractive, light colour tending towards ruby, with a slightly limited bouquet dominated by the distinctive aromas of Cabernet-Sauvignon (plants and tobacco). Good structure and an attractive finish. Decant before drinking with grilled red meats. (1984)
↬ Joel Lhumeau, Linières, Brigné-sur-Layon, 49700 Doué-la-Fontaine; tel. 41 59 30 51 ⵉ By appt.

LES CAVES DE LA LOIRE★

■ ha 4 000 000 ② D ▮ ↓
⑧ 83

An attractive, warm, quite deep-ruby coloured wine which, because of its youth, is still closed in. The bouquet is reminiscent of soft red fruits. Well-made, with quite a strong structure; very easy to drink. A straightforward wine which should be served with grilled meat and should not be kept too long. (1984)
↬ Les Caves de la Loire, 49320 Brissac-Quincé; tel. 41 91 22 71 ⵉ By appt.

GAEC LONGEPE★

■ ② D ▮ ↓

Pleasant, light ruby-cherry colour. On the nose an equally pleasant aroma of red, spicy fruit. Rather woody on the palate, with good tannin. Drink immediately. (1983)
↬ GAEC Longepe, Les Brosses, 49380 Champ-sur-Layon; tel. 41 54 02 99 ⵉ By appt.

DOMAINE DES MAURIERES★

■ 2ha 10000 ③ D ▮ ↓
79 80 81 82 ▨ ⑧ ▨▨ ▨▨

Bright ruby-coloured wine with a nice fruity fragrance, light, fresh, lingering nose and good, well-constituted vinous character. Full in the mouth, its acidity not too strong and balanced well with the tannin. It should be allowed to age four or five years. (1983)
↬ Fernand Moron, 8 Rue de Périnelle, St-Lambert-du-Lattay, 49190 Rochefort-sur-Loire; tel. 41 78 30 21 ⵉ By appt.

CHATEAU MONTBENAULT★

■ 3ha 12000 ② D ◗ ↓

Light colour and rather closed-up nose; a little thin and tannic to taste, but its strong and lingering aromatic finish points to a good origin. (1983) ✔ Anjou Blanc, Anjou Gamay Rouge, Cabernet d'Anjou Rosé, Côteaux-du-Layon Faye-d'Anjou Blanc Liquoreux.
↬ Yves Leduc, Ch. Montbenault, Faye-d'Anjou,

49380 Thouarcé; tel. 41 78 31 14 ♈ Mon.–Sat. 9.00–12.00/14.00–20.00.

CHATEAU MONTBENAULT★

○   9ha   2000   🄷 D ↓

Fine light bubbles and classic green nose so typical of the area and the Chenin grape, also known as Pinot de la Loire. Well balanced in the mouth, slightly closed to balance the natural acidity. This estate specializes in sweet white wines.
�r Yves Leduc, Ch. Montbenault, Faye-d'Anjou, 49380 Thouarcé; tel. 41 78 31 14 ♈ Mon.–Sat. 9.00–12.00/14.00–18.00.

DOMAINE DE LA MOTTE★

◼   4ha   25000   2 D ◗ ↓
71 75 76 78 81 ★⑧ ⑧ ⑧

Lovely strong ruby colour and typical spicy fragrance of the Cabernet-Sauvignon grape variety. The producer has tried to compensate for the high acidity with a fairly strong alcohol content which means the wine can be served with strong meats and will age well. (1983)
�r André Sorin, 31 Avenue d'Angers, 49190, Rochefort-sur-Loire; tel. 41 78 71 13 ♈ Mon.– Sat. 9.00–12.00/13.30–19.00.

CHRISTIAN PAPIN★

☐   2ha   10000   2 D ◼ ↓
76 78 81 82 ★⑧ ⑧

Delicate, reserved and complex nose; well balanced on the palate, with good structure. Must be drunk young to appreciate its qualities fully. (1983) ✔ Anjou Gamay Rouge, Rosé de Loire, Cabernet d'Anjou Rosé.
�r Christian Papin, Haute Perche, St-Mélaine-sur-Aubance, 49320 Brissac-Quincé; tel. 41 91 15 20 ♈ By appt. Closed first week Aug.

DOMAINE DES PARAGERES★

☐   3ha   13000   2 D ◼ ↓
82 ⑧ ⑧

A well-presented wine which needs to be opened a little in advance of tasting, due to having been bottled recently. The character of the Chenin grown on good soil can then be appreciated. On the palate it is quite full bodied, well-made and with good balance; ideal for fish in strongly flavoured sauces. (1984)
�r M. Aguilas-Gaudard, La Brosse, Chaude-fonds-sur-Layon, Chaltonnes-sur-Loire; tel. 41 78 10 68 ♈ By appt.

GAEC DU PETIT CLOCHER★

◼   10ha   50000   2 D ◼ ↓
80 81 82 ★83 ⑧ ⑧

Although bright in colour and attractive, this wine is still a little rough and severe. After a while it will be good with red meat casseroles. (1983) ✔ Cabernet d'Anjou Rosé, Rosé de Loire, Côteaux de Layon Blanc Moelleux, Crémant de Loire.
�r P. et F. Denis, GAEC du Petit Clocher, Cléré-sur-Layon, 49560 Nueil-sur-Layon; tel. 41 59 54 51 ♈ Mon.–Sat. 8.00–12.30/14.00–19.30.

DOMAINE DU PETIT VAL.★

◼   4.5ha   19200   2 D ◼ ↓

Intensely deep colour and fruity nose, not fully mature. All the basic characteristics of Cabernet-Sauvignon, but also a slightly unpleasant acidity which should, however, fade with age. Wait a while before drinking. (1983) ✔ Bonnezeaux Blanc Liquoreux, Côteaux du Layon Blanc Moelleux, Anjou Blanc, Cabernet d'Anjou Rosé.
�r Vincent Goizil, Le Petit Val, Chavagnes-les-Eaux, 49380 Thouarcé; tel. 41 91 43 09 ♈ By appt.

DOMAINE DE LA PIERRE BLANCHE★

◼   7ha   40000   🄷 D ◼ ↓
69 70 71 ⑧ ⑧ ★⑧

A light-coloured wine, quite well developed despite a closed-in nose. Good balance between its different fruits, but needs to be opened well before drinking to allow it to breathe; it could even be decanted. Well made and sturdy and should be kept to age. (1983)
�r GAEC Ogereau Fils, Rue de la Belle-Angevine, St-Lambert-du-Lattay, 49190 Rochefort-sur-loire; tel. 41 78 30 53 ♈ By appt.

DOMAINE DE PIERRE BISE

◼   3ha   20000   🄷 D ◼ ◗ ↓

Beautiful, intense but rather dense garnet colour. Nose rather closed-up and insignificant, not immediately apparent but showing fruit when in the glass. To taste, it is rather rough and crude, being naturally tannic and slightly too high in alcohol. An interesting wine which will age well. (1983) ✔ Coteaux du Layon Chaume et Beaulieu, Anjou Blanc, Anjou Gamay Rouge, Cabernet d'Anjou Rouge.
�r Claude Papin, Dom. de Pierre Bise, Beaulieu-sur-Layon, 49190 Rochefort-sur-Loire; tel. 41 78 31 44 ♈ By appt.

CHATEAU DE PLAISANCE★

◼   6ha   36000   🄷 D ◼ ↓

Pale colour and correspondingly light nose and palate, compensated for by a certain elegance. (1983)
�r Henri Rochais et Fils, Ch. de Plaisance, Chaume, 49190 Rochefort-sur-Loire; tel. 41 78 33 01 ♈ By appt.

LOGIS DU PRIEURE★

◼   10ha   60000   🄷 D ◼ ↓
★76 78 80 81 82 83

A lovely light ruby colour, and attractive fruity nose of red fruit. The aromas develop well in the mouth, but is light and lacking in substance overall. Best drunk young with grilled meat rather than risk disappointment by keeping it too long. (1983)
�r Jousset et Fils, Coucourson-sur-Layon, 49700 Doué-la-Fontaine; tel. 41 59 11 66 ♈ By appt.

DOMAINE DES QUINZE DENIERS★

◼   14ha   25000   2 D ◼ ↓
81 82 ⑧ ⑧ ⑧

A well-presented wine quite high in tannin but with rather too high an alcohol content. It will age well. (1983) ✔ Anjou Gamay Rouge,

Côteaux de l'Aubance Blanc Moelleux, Cabernet d'Anjou Rosé, Rosé d'Anjou.
↬ Maugin Père et Fils, GAEC du Haut Coudray, Charcé-St-Ellier/Aubance, 49320 Brissac-Quincé; tel. 41 54 20 01 **Ⲧ** Mon.–Sat. 8.00–17.00.

DOMAINE DES QUINZE DENIERS★

☐ 1 ha 4800 **2 D ■ ↓**

A vigorous, straightforward wine to accompany shellfish. (1983) **✔** Anjou Gamay Rouge, Anjou Rouge, Blanc Côteaux, Cabernet d'Anjou Rosé.
↬ MM. Maugin Père et Fils, Charcé-St-Ellier, 49320 Brissac-Quincé; tel. 41 54 20 01 **Ⲧ** By appt
↬ GAEC du Haut-Coudray.

REVEILLERE-GIRAUD★

○ 2 ha 12000 **3 D ■ ↓**

An attractive clear wine with a good delicate long-lasting mousse and a distinct aroma of the Chenin grape. A great success. (1982) **✔** Anjou Rouge, Anjou Gamay Rouge, Cabernet d'Anjou Rosé, Anjou Blanc.
↬ GAEC Reveillère-Giraud, La Gonorderie, 49320 Brissac-Quincé; tel. 41 91 22 80 **Ⲧ** By appt.

REVEILLERE-GIRAUD★

■ 10 ha 60000 **2 D ■ ↓**
76 81 82 **82** 83

A well-made wine with a good nose; full bodied, but a little neutral in character. It should be laid down. (1983) **✔** Anjou Gamay Rouge, Cabernet d'Anjou Rosé.
↬ GAEC Reveillère-Giraud, La Gonorderie, 49320 Brissac-Quincé; tel. 41 91 22 80 **Ⲧ** By appt.

RICHOU PERE ET FILS★★★

☐ 5 ha 35000 **2 D ■ ↓**
76 78 81 83 **⟨84⟩ 84**

A very attractive nose of fruit and flowers with a hint of newly mown hay can be found in this perfect blend of the Chardonnay and Chenin grapes. Best served at the beginning of a meal but could accompany plain fish. (1983) **✔** Anjou Gamay Rouge, Cabernet Anjou Rosé, Côteaux de l'Aubance Blanc Moelleux, Crémant de Loire.
↬ Henri et Didier Richou, Chauvigné, Mozé-sur-Louet, 49190 Rochefort-sur-Loire; tel. 41 78 72 13 **Ⲧ** Mon.–Sat. 8.00–19.00.

DOMAINE RICHOU★

■ 6 ha 35000 **3 D ■ ⅏ ↓**
78 81 **⁺82 82** 83 **83**

The vanilla nose indicates that the tannin is already well developed. A well-made wine which will benefit from ageing. Good with red meat. (1983)
↬ Henri et Didier Richou, Chauvigné, Mozé-sur-Louet, 49190 Rochefort-sur-Loire; tel. 41 78 72 13 **Ⲧ** Mon.–Sat. 8.00–19.00.

DOMAINE DES ROCHELLES★

■ 5 ha 15000 **3 D ■ ↓**
78 79 81 **⟨82⟩ 82** 83

With a good colour and of subtle, delicate aromas, this well-balanced wine has the slight touch of acidity which promises an easy ageing process. (1983) **✔** Côteaux de l'Aubance Blanc Moelleux.
↬ MM. Lebreton et Fils, Les Rochelles, St-Jean-des-Mauvrets, 49320 Brissac-Quincé; tel. 41 91 92 07 **Ⲧ** By appt.

DOMAINE DES ROCHELLES★

▣ 15 ha 50000 **2 D ■ ↓**
78 79 81 **⟨82⟩ 82 ⁺83**

A lovely well-developed ruby colour, intense nose and rich fruitiness can all be found in this wine, which should definitely be laid down. A specialized cellar, being one of the first to produce the new Anjou red wines. (1983) **✔** Côteaux de l'Aubance Blanc Moelleux.
↬ Mm. Lebreton et Fils, Les Rochelles, St-Jean-des-Mauvrets, 49320 Brissac-Quincé; tel. 41 91 92 07 **Ⲧ** By appt.

DOMAINE DE SAINTE-ANNE★★

■ **3 D ■ ↓**
76 78 **⟨81⟩ 81 82 83** 84

The colour still appears purple and young for the vintage, but the nose of red soft fruits is attractive and the balance is good. A good wine from a good estate. (1981) **✔** Côteaux de l'Aubance Blanc Moelleux.
↬ Henri Brault, Ste-Anne, St-Saturnin-sur-Loire, 49320 Brissac-Quincé; tel. 41 91 24 58 **Ⲧ** Mon.–Sat. 8.30–12.00/14.00–19.00.

DOMAINE DE SAINTE-ANNE
Cabernet-franc★★

■ 14 ha 70000 **2 D ■ ↓**
76 **80** **⟨81⟩ 81 82 82 83 83**

This wine has a pretty, dark colour and blackcurrant nose. Its slight toughness in the mouth is due to marked acidity and strong tannin. Ageing is essential for a few years to make it drinkable. (1983) **✔** Côteaux de l'Aubance Blanc Moelleux.
↬ Henri Brault, Ste-Anne, St-Saturnin-sur-Loire; 49320 Brissac-Quincé; tel. 41 91 24 58 **Ⲧ** Mon.–Sat. 8.30–12.00/14.00–19.00.

DOMAINE SAINT-PIERRE★

☐   24ha   240000   **2** **D** **⊟** **⊪** ↓

Full of life, well made and original with a sappy quality typical of the Chaudefonds soil. This prettily coloured wine should be opened for some time before drinking as it is stifled by too much sulphur dioxide. Good with all kinds of fish. (1983)

↪ Antoine Renouard, Chaudefonds-sur-Layon, 49290 Chalonnes-sur-Loire; tel. 41 78 04 21 ☿ By appt.

DOMAINE DES SAULAIES★

■   4ha   30000   **3** **D** **⊟** ↓

⑦ **77** 78 **79** **81** 83 84 **84**

It is an achievement to be able to offer a wine of this vintage, since 1977 was a poor year, when the grapes did not ripen properly. Although this is not a great wine, it has been vinified very well and has developed elegance with age. Not very full bodied, but it should be good with grilled meat or game. (1977) ✔ Cabernet d'Anjou Rosé, Rosé d'Anjou, Rosé de Loire, Coteaux du Layon Faye Blanc Moelleux.

↪ Philippe Leblanc, Les Saulaies, Faye-d'Anjou, 49380 Thouarcé; tel. 41 91 41 13 ☿ By appt. Closed end Aug.–early Sept.

BERNARD SECHET-CARRET★

☐   1ha   2000   **2** **D** **⊟** ↓

82 ⑧③ 84

A well-presented wine; still closed in and needs to be opened a long time in advance. Behind its present condition a certain delicacy can be detected. Substantial body, but there is a lack of balance between the alcohol content and its other constituents. A slightly bitter finish – would go well chilled with charcuterie. Wait a few months before drinking. (1984)

↪ Bernard Sechet-Carret, Maligné, 49540 Martigné-Briand; tel. 41 59 43 40 ☿ By appt.

DOMAINE DE LA TOUCHE★

■   10ha   50000   **2** **D** **⊟** ↓

78 81 ⑧② **83** **84**

A wine of very intense colour, spicy fragrance and robust character but not yet fully developed. Its alcoholic richness means it would be perfect with red meat, possibly even game and cheese. (1983) ✔ Crémant de Loire, Rosé de Loire, Cabernet d'Anjou Rosé.

↪ Didier et Robert Hauret, Rue Chanoine Panaget, 49540 Martigné-Briand; tel. 41 59 42 06 ☿ By appt.

DOMAINE DE LA VIAUDIERE
Rouge★

■   10ha   35000   **2** **D** **⊟** ↓

81 ⑧② **82** 83

This wine has a pleasant and stylish quality. Fairly generous alcohol content, but a little thin, so best with grilled meat or not-too-spicy first courses. (1982) ✔ Côteaux du Layon Blanc Moelleux, Anjou Blanc, Rosé de Loire, Cabernet d'Anjou Rouge.

↪ Olivier Gelineau, Dom. de la Viaudière, Le-Champ-sur-Layon   49380   Thouarcé;   tel. 41 91 41 64 ☿ By appt. Closed Aug.

Anjou Gamay

This is a red wine made from Gamay Noir grapes. When grown on the main schist areas, they can produce an excellent everyday wine. About 10000 hectolitres are produced each year.

JACQUES BEAUJEAU★

■   4ha   24000   **3** **D** **⊟** ↓

The colour and the well-developed nose show that this wine is quite light and will not last more than a year. A name to remember provided you drink these wines while they are still young. (1983)

↪ Jacques Beaujeau, 8 Rue de l'Eglise, 49350 Thouarcé; tel. 41 91 41 17 ☿ By appt.

DOMAINE CADY★

■   0.5ha   1200   **2** **D** **⊟** ↓

84 **84**

Good cherry colour with the typical rustic fragrance that Gamay wines produce at the end of 18 months. Gamay wines should be light and easy to drink, and this one is typically uncomplicated and correct. Drink when it is one year old, with entrées, charcuterie and goat's cheese. In 1985 look for the 1984 vintage. (1983)

↪ Pierre et Philippe Cady, Valette, St-Aubin-de Luigné,   49190   Rochefort-sur-Loire;   tel. 41 78 33 69 ☿ Daily 9.00–20.00.

DOMAINE DE SAINTE-ANNE★

■   5ha   30000   **2** **D** **⊟** ↓

76 81 82 83 ⭐⑧④ **84**

A pleasant Anjou-Gamay wine made by carbonic maceration; should be drunk young with grilled meats. (1983) ✔ Anjou Blanc Sec, Côteaux de l'Aubance, Anjou Mousseux Méthode Champenoise.

↪ Henri Brault, Ste-Anne, St-Saturnin-sur-Loire, 49320 Brissac-Quincé; tel. 41 91 24 58 ☿ Mon.– Sat. 8.30–12.00/14.00–19.00. Closed Sun. and public holidays.

Rosé d'Anjou

With production varying from year to year between 150000 and 250000 hectolitres, this is the largest of the Anjou appellations in terms of quantity. It used to be exported with great success, but sells less well nowadays. The main grape variety is the Grolleau or Gros Lot. The light rosés that were formerly produced were called 'rougets', but it is now more common to make a light red wine, a Vin de Table or Vin de Pays.

CHATEAU DE BEAULIEU Brut★

○   70000   **3** **D** ↓

This wine is a lovely pink colour with delicate bubbles which, however, do not last long; a pleasant, well-balanced party wine.

↪ *MM.* Gratien et Meyer, Route de Montsoreau,

49100 Saumur; tel. 41 51 01 54 🍷 Daily 9.00–12.00/14.00–17.00.

ROBERT LECOMTE-GIRAULT*

◪ 6ha 50000 ❷ Ⓓ ▮ ↓

(82) **83 84**

A quite successful wine for the appellation. Attractive but rather too amber colour. Limited bouquet due to early stopping of the fermentation process, but the aromas of the grape variety show through nonetheless. (1984)
⊶ Robert Lecomte-Girault, Le Sablon, Faye-d'Anjou, 49380 Thouarcé; tel. 41 91 41 34 🍷 By appt. Closed 15 Aug.–15 Sept.

DOMAINE DES QUINZE DENIERS*

◪ 5.5ha 2500 ❷ Ⓓ ▮ ↓

Orange tinge gained from Grolleau and Cabernet vines. Good example of its appellation. (1983)
✓ Anjou Gamay Rouge, Anjou Blanc Sec, Cabernet d'Anjou Rosé, Rosé de Loire.
⊶ Maugin Père et Fils, GAEC du Haut Coudray Charcé-St-Ellier/Aubance, 49320 Brissac-Quincé; tel. 41 54 29 01 🍷 By appt.

Cabernet d'Anjou

This appellation includes some excellent, fragrant medium-dry rosé wines made from Cabernet-Franc and Cabernet-Sauvignon grapes. Served chilled, they go very well with melon as an hors d'oeuvre, or with certain puddings, as long as they are not too sweet. The volume produced is in the order of 100000 – 150000 hectolitres. The most famous wines come from the Tigné region, rather than from the Layon.

AGUILAS-GAUDARD**

◪ 3ha 13000 ❷ Ⓓ ▮ ↓

(73) **78** 83 [84]

Pale salmon-pink in colour with discreet, characteristically fruity and pleasant aromas. Full bodied, with good structure and balance and a certain delicacy. A benchmark for the appellation. Should be served quite cool during the afternoon, or with iced melon. (1984)
🍷 *M.* Aguilas-Gaudard, La Brosse, Chaudefonds-sur-Layon, Chalonnes-sur-Loire; tel. 41 78 10 68 🍷 By appt.

DOMAINE DE BABLUT*

◪ 50ha 25000 ❷ Ⓓ ▮ ↓

Beautiful colour of faded tiles, with a hint of orange. Nose fruity, mature and well made. To taste, this medium-dry wine is very well balanced, but this is not a wine to drink with a meal, except with chilled melon, or on a hot summer's day. It is worth mentioning that this vineyard has a good stock of old vintages. (1983)
✓ Anjou Rouge, Coteaux de l'Aubance Blanc Moelleux, Rosé de Loire, Anjou Gamay Rouge.
⊶ *MM.* Daviau Frères, Dom. de Bablut, 49320 Brissac-Quincé; tel. 41 91 22 59 🍷 By appt.

CHATEAU DU BREUIL*

■ 15ha 12000 ❸ Ⓓ ▮ ↓

76 81 82 *83 *84

Beautifully clear with scent of honey and gingerbread. Good balance between residual sugar and acidity. Good example of Cabernet grapes. Drink chilled. (1983)
⊶ Marc Morgat, Ch. du Breuil, Beaulieu-sur-Layon, 49190 Rochefort-sur-Loire; tel. 41 78 32 54 🍷 By appt.

DOMAINE CADY*

◪ 1ha 2500 ❷ Ⓓ ▮ ↓

83 [83]

This Cabernet is an admirable tile-red in colour, and should be decanted to let it breathe fully and remove any traces of sulphur. The finish is a little hard and the wine should be kept to improve with age. (1983)
⊶ Pierre et Philippe Cady, Valette, St-Aubin-de Luigné, 49190 Rochefort-sur-Loire; tel. 41 78 33 69 🍷 Daily 9.00–20.00.

DOMAINE DE LA CROIX-DES-LOGES*

◪ 5ha 18000 ❷ Ⓓ ↓

69 70 74 76 (83) [83] [84]

A light pink colour with a tile-red background. Should be opened a little in advance to allow the lactic acid smell to disappear. It is light and well balanced and should be served chilled between meals. (1983) ✓ Bonnezeau Blanc Liquoreux, Rosé de Loire, Anjou Blanc, Saumur Mousseux.
⊶ Christian Bonnin, Dom. de la Croix-des-Loges, 49540 Martigné-Briand; tel. 41 59 43 66 🍷 Mon.–Sat. 9.00–12.00/15.00–19.00. Closed Oct.

ROBERT LECOMTE-GIRAULT*

◪ 2ha 15000 ❷ Ⓓ ▮ ↓

(82) **83 *84** *[84]

Agreeable both in colour and on the nose, with a wealth of flowery aromas due to the grape variety. Technically it is well made and displays good balance between sugar content and other components. A successful wine which makes the cellar a specialist in Angevin wines. (1984)
⊶ Robert Lecomte-Girault, Le Sablon, Faye-d'Anjou, 49380 Thouarcé; tel. 41 91 41 34 🍷 By appt. Closed 15 Aug.–15 Sept.

GAEC LONGEPE*

◪ ❷ Ⓓ ▮

Characteristic orange-yellow colour. Rather undeveloped fragrance, but good balance. (1984)
⊶ GAEC Longepe, Les Brosses, 49380 Champ-sur-Layon; tel. 41 54 02 99 🍷 By appt.

DOMAINE DES MAURIERES★★

| ☑ | 5ha | 2200 | 3 D ▮ ↓ |

69 70 71 ★⑧⑧ 83 ★84

Deep, pure, slightly tile-red colour with typical Cabernet nose. On the palate, the balance is pleasantly influenced by the taste of residual sugar, A very good example of an old-style wine and should age well. To be served in the evening, by itself or with dessert. (1983)
↬ Fernand Moron, 8 Rue de Périnelle, St-Lambert-du-Lattay, 49190 Rochefort-sur-Loire; tel. 41 78 30 21 ☎ By appt.

GAEC DU PETIT CLOCHER
Moelleux

| ▪ | 10ha | 7000 | 2 D ▮ ↓ |

Not yet showing its true quality. Slight smell of acid drops and still reserved. Allow to breathe before serving. (1983)
↬ Denis Père et Fils, GAEC du Petit Clocher, Cléré-sur-Layon 49560; tel. 41 59 54 51 ☎ By appt. Closed Sun.

DOMAINE LES CAVES DU ROCHER★

| ☐ | 4ha | 18000 | 2 D ▮ ↓ |

Attractive deep tile-red colour, the mark of a well-developed Cabernet. Good balance tending towards sweetness with a floral bouquet reminiscent of geranium. Ideal served cool outdoors on summer afternoons. (1983) ✔ Coteaux du Layon Chaume Blanc Moelleux, Coteaux du Layon Saint-Aubin-de Luigné Blanc Moelleux, Anjou Rouge, Anjou Gamay Rouge, Vin de Pays Rouge.
↬ MM. Baffet Père et Fils, St-Aubin-de-Luigné, 49190 Rochefort-sur-Loire; tel. 41 78 33 36 ☎ By appt. Closed first fortnight Aug.

DOMAINE DE SAINTE-ANNE
Moelleux

| ☑ | 3.6ha | 20000 | 2 D ▮ ↓ |

76 ★81 81 82 83

A tile-red colour typical of the Cabernet after a little ageing; good sugar-alcohol balance and distinctly woody nose. A good wine with which to relax at the card table. (1983) ✔ Anjou Blanc, Côteaux de l'Aubance Blanc, Anjou Mousseux.
↬ Henri Brault, Ste-Anne, St-Saturnin-sur-Loire, 49320 Brissac-Quincé; tel. 41 91 24 58 ☎ Mon.–Sat. 8.30–12.00/14.00–19.00. Closed Sun. and public holidays.

BERNARD SECHET-CARRET★

| ☑ | 1ha | 2500 | D ▮ |

A classic amber-coloured wine with the characteristic, clean, leafy aromas of the Cabernet variety, and a satisfactory balance with slight traces of reduction, indicating that it should be opened a fairly long time before drinking. (1984)
↬ Bernard Sechet-Carret, Maligné, 49540 Martigné-Briand; tel. 41 59 43 40 ☎ By appt.

Coteaux de L'Aubance

Very old Chenin vines grow on the schistous hillsides that border the small Aubance river. From these vines, a sweet white wine is made that improves with age. Much is changing in this area of ten villages or so: Cabernet is gradually replacing the Chenin vines, resulting in some good red wines. Quality has been further improved through the annual competition in Brissac-Quince. Production is about 1000 hectolitres.

DOMAINE DE HAUTE-PERCHE★

| ○ | 2ha | 7000 | 2 D ▮ ↓ |

76 78 81 82 ⑧ 83

A good example of a Chenin wine: fat, and fruity with good ageing potential. In ten years' time it will make an excellent aperitif. (1983) ✔ Anjou Gamay, Rosé de Loire, Cabernet d'Anjou Rosé.
↬ Christian Papin, Dom. Haute-Perche, St-Mélaine-sur-Aubance, 49320 Brissac-Quincé; tel. 41 91 15 20 ☎ By appt. Closed 1–15 Aug.

RICHOU PERE ET FILS★

| ○ | 3ha | 10000 | 3 D ▮ ↓ |

59 64 69 76 79 80 ⑧

From a vineyard which usually produces red Gamay and dry white Chenin and Chardonnay wines comes this aristocratic speciality which although difficult to taste now shows great promise and deserves to be successful. (1983)
↬ Henri et Didier Richou, Chauvigné, Mozé-sur-Louet, 49190 Rochefort-sur-Loire; tel. 41 78 72 13 ☎ Mon.–Sat. 8.00–19.00.

Anjou-Coteaux de la Loire

This appellation is restricted to white wines made from Chenin (Pineau de la Loire) grapes. Very little is produced (1500 hectolitres) considering the area involved (about twelve communes). All the vineyards are located on the schist and limestone of Montjean. The grapes are left to become overripe and then picked in stages; the wines made in this way differ in colour from those of Coteaux du Layon, having a more greenish tinge. They are usually medium dry or slightly sweet. Here, too, the vineyard is gradually being given over to red wine production.

BORE FRERES *Cuvée Vieille Sève*★

☐		2ha	6000	**3** **D** ⑪ ↓

59 76 78 ⑲ **79 80 82** 83

A prettily coloured wine with a generous nose of almost-ripe apricots and lime flowers, slightly hidden by an excess of sulphur dioxide, which will pass. This, however, will enable the wine to last for a good thirty years. A very well balanced wine which should only be opened for friends as an aperitif in five to ten years. (1982) ✔ Anjou Coteaux de la Loire Blanc Sec, Anjou Gamay Rouge, Anjou Rouge Cabernet, Anjou Méthode Champenoise.

♠ GAEC Boré Frères, Le Fresche, 49620 La Pommeraye; tel. 41 77 74 63 � By appt. Closed Sun.

Savennières

These are dry white wines made from Chenin grapes, and mostly come from the commune of Savennières. The schist and purplish clay of the area give the wines a distinctive style. For many years they have been identified with Coteaux de la Loire, but in fact they deserve to have a place of their own. The Savennières appellation is the more consistent, and should really establish and develop itself. The wine is vigorous, sometimes slightly acidic and goes wonderfully well with fish dishes.

CHATEAU DE CHAMBOUREAU *Clos du Papillon*★

☐		2ha	3000	**3** **D** ⬛ ↓

64 69 71 78 83 84

This vineyard produces a medium-sweet wine purely for commercial demand. This is a pity, for the sugar that has to be added masks good raw materials. (1983)

♠ SCEA Pierre et Yves Soulez, Ch. Chamboureau, Savennières, 49170 St-Georges-sur-Loire; tel. 41 77 20 04 � By appt. Closed Sun.

CHATEAU DE CHAMBOUREAU★

☐		7ha	20000	**4** **D** ⬛ ↓

64 69 71 78 84

This is a classic Savennières wine, characteristic of the 1983 vintage with its slightly aggressive nose and quite strong floral aromas. It will keep well, and makes a good accompaniment to dried fish and chabichou (goat's milk cheese). (1983) ✔ Savennières Roche-aux-Moines, Savennières Dom. de la Bizolière, Anjou Ch. de Chamboureau, Sauvignon Vin de Pays.

♠ SCEA Pierre et Yves Soulez, Ch. Chamboureau, Savennières, 49170 St-Georges-sur-Loire; tel. 41 77 20 04 � By appt. Closed Sun.

DOMAINE DU CLOSEL★

☐		12ha	35000	**4** **D** ⬛ ⑪ ↓

56 78 81 82 ★⑧③ 83

Immediately establishes itself as a well-made wine, well bred and showing good balance, along with the characteristic iodine flavour typical of

late-harvested Chenin grapes. A rather woody flavour in the finish, but the slightly sharp edge shows it will age well and be ideal with fish. (1983) ✔ Anjou Rouge Cépage Cabernet.

♠ Bazin-de-Jessey, Les Vault Savennières, 49170 St-Georges-sur-Loire; tel. 41 72 21 31 � By appt.

CLOS DE COULAINE★

☐		3ha	10000	**4** **D** ⑪ ↓

47 75 76 82 ⑧④ 84

This wine's colour is excellent, pale and clear, with a floral nose typical of the grape variety when grown here at Savennières. A little aggressive at present, it is well made and worth buying now to drink in a few years when it will show its true qualities. (1983) ✔ Anjou Clos de Coulaine.

♠ François Roussier, Coulaine, 49170 St-George-sur-Loire; tel. 41 72 21 06 � By appt.

Savennières Roche-aux-Moines, Savennières Coulée de Serrant

Although these two crus have separate names, they are so similar in quality and character that it is difficult to distinguish between them. Coulée de Serrant, the smaller of the two, is situated on both sides of the Petit Serrant valley, most of it having a south-westerly exposure. The appellation is owned exclusively by the Joly family and has made a reputation for itself equal to that of the French Grands Crus, not only for high quality, but for the high prices it fetches. It needs to be laid down for five to ten years to allow its qualities to mature and blossom. La Roche-aux-Moines is owned by several growers and covers 33 hectares, not all of it planted. It is mostly situated on the southern slopes of the Loire; while not as consistent as its twin it does offer some cuvées which are almost as fine.

CHATEAU DE CHAMBOUREAU★

☐		3ha	12000	**4** **D** ⬛ ↓

80 81 ★**82** 82 ★83

Distinctively presented wine, very typical of the appellation. Unfortunately, the 1982 yield was very high and the wines, although pleasant, were a little watery. This one may be drunk now, and will also age well. (1982) ✔ Savennières Ch. de Chamboureau, Savennières Dom. de la Bizoliere, Savennières Clos du Papillon Demi-Sec.

♠ SCEA Pierre et Yves Soulez, Ch. de Chamboureau, Savennières, 49170 St-Georges-sur-Loire; tel. 41 77 20 04 � By appt.

COULEE DE SERANT
*Clos de la Coulée de Serrant***

☐		7ha	24000	5 D ⦀ ⌣

76 83 84

A remarkable wine with a very fine golden yellow colour and subtle aromas of nuts and dried figs on the nose. Full, glowing and very long on the palate. Best drunk in about ten years' time. (1976)

↬ *M. et Mme* Nicolas Joly, Ch. de la Roche-aux-Moines, Savennières, 49170 St-Georges-sur-Loire; tel. 41 72 22 32 ⵏ By appt.

Coteaux du Layon

These medium-dry, sweet or dessert wines come from the hills of the twenty-five communes that border the river Layon from Neuil to Chalonnes. Chenin is the only grape type used for this appellation, which is becoming better known again after many years of neglect. Ranging from the greeny-golden colour of the Concourson wines, to the more yellowy and powerful wines that come from nearer the mouth of the river, all the Layon wines are delicate, with aromas of honey and acacia from the overripe grapes. They age astoundingly well. Some 40000 hectolitres are produced from the 1300 hectares under cultivation.

CLOS DE L'AIGLERIE*

☐		3ha	8000	3 D ⵏ ⦀ ⌣

67 69 71 79 **79** ⑧ 83 **83**

An old-style wine whose high sulphur dioxide content conceals aromas that will reveal themselves to those who look. A rich, sappy wine, well worth buying and laying down for at least 10 years. (1982) ✔ Rosé de Loire, Cabernet d'Anjou Rosé, Anjou Blanc.

↬ *MM.* Gousset et Fils, Clos de l'Aiglerie, St-Aubin-de-Luigne, 49190 Rochefort-sur-Loire; tel. 41 78 33 05 ⵏ By appt. Closed Sept.

JACQUES BEAUJEAU**

☐		12ha	43200	3 D ⵏ ⦀ ⌣

64 75 76 78 79 ⑧ 83

As with all sweet white wines at this stage of development, it is difficult to assess, as the wine is meant for laying down. This seems to be developing well, is warm and rich in aromas, will be good as an aperitif in one to two years' time, and will very soon be a perfect accompaniment to foie gras. (1983)

↬ Jacques Beaujeau, 8 Rue de l'Eglise, 49380 Thouarcé; tel. 41 91 41 17 ⵏ By appt.

CLAUDE BRANCHEREAU*

☐		8ha	15000	3 D ⵏ ⦀ ⌣

55 *59 *69 71 *76 ⑧ 82

This wine is already a beautiful golden colour, indicative of a harvest where the grapes were able to ripen fully. It is not yet showing well, as the added sulphur dioxide masks characteristics which may not show through fully for some 10–15 years. A fine bottle, to be put away and, eventually, served as an aperitif. (1982) ✔ Anjou Gamay Rouge, Cabernet d'Anjou Rosé, Méthode Champenoise.

↬ Claude Branchereau, Les Barres, St-Aubin-de-Luigné, 49190 Rochefort-sur-Loire; tel. 41 78 33 56 ⵏ By appt.

CHATEAU DU BREUIL*

☐		48ha	30000	4 D ⵏ ⌣

*59 64 66 69 71 73 75 76 78 82

This wine is not yet revealing its true qualities, and despite the difficult year in which it was grown is still a success. Should develop more rapidly than other vintages. (1979) ✔ Anjou Rouge, Cabernet d'Anjou Rosé, Vin de Pays Chardonnay Blanc Sec, Vin de Pays Sauvignon Blanc Sec.

↬ Marc Morgat, Ch. du Breuil, Beaulieu-sur-Layon, 49190 Rochefort-sur-Loire; tel. 41 78 32 54 ⵏ Tue.–Sat. 10.00–12.00/15.00–19.00. Closed Oct.–Nov. ↬ *MM.* Dubreuil et De La Roche.

DOMAINE CADY*

☐		10ha	10300	2 D ⵏ ⌣

59 69 71 73 74 75 76 78 ⑧ 84

Despite the influence of the sulphur used during the making of this wine, it has an attractive, fruity and floral nose. To taste, the acidity, allied with the sulphur, makes it hard. It may be bought now for drinking in about 10 years' time, but, because it is not very full bodied, it should be tasted periodically in order to drink it at its best. (1983)

↬ Pierre et Philippe Cady, Valette, St-Aubin-de-Luigné, 49190 Rochefort-sur-Loire; tel. 41 78 33 69 ⵏ Daily 9.00–20.00.

DHOMME FRERES*

☐		3ha	10000	3 D ⵏ ⦀ ⌣

76 78 **78** *⑧ 82 *83

Greeny-gold colour and iodine nose. Slightly maderized wine, very powerful, unusual and characteristic of the wines from the Côteaux de la Loire or the Côteaux du Layon. The taste backs up these qualities and shows good balance. A difficult wine to serve but at its best with blue cheeses. For the connoisseur. (1978) ✔ Anjou Rouge, Anjou Gamay Rouge, Anjou Blanc Sec, Rosé de Loire.

↬ Dhomme Frères, Le Petit Fort Girault, 49290 Chalonnes-sur-Loire; tel. 41 78 24 27 ⵏ By appt.

VIGNOBLE DIOT-ANTIER**

☐		3ha	9000	3 D ⵏ ⌣

⑦⑥ 78 82 82 83

A very floral wine with a well-developed colour and attactive, soft nose. To taste it is also attractive, fat and full-bodied, well blended with delicate, discreet structure and vigour. A pretty wine to be laid down and kept until it reaches its peak of perfection. (1982)

↬ GAEC Fardeau-Robin, Les Hauts-Perrays, Chaudefonds-sur-Layon 49290, Chalonnes-sur-Loire; tel. 41 78 04 38 ⵏ By appt. Closed May.

CHATEAU DE FESLE★★

☐ 12ha 50000 **2** ▪ ⑪

The light golden colour of this eleven-year-old wine is still youthful. Characteristic Blanc Moelleux nose, generous and fruity, and a perfect balance between sweetness, acidity and bitterness on the palate. (1974)
⊷ Ets Nicolas, 2 Rue de Valmy, 94220 Charenton tel. 01 37 59 20 ⊺ No visitors.

ROBERT LECOMTE-GIRAULT★

☐ 2ha 10000 **2** D ▪ ⑪

69 71 ⑦⑥ **7̶6̶** ★79 **82**

A typical Val de Loire wine: pale-coloured, bright and clear, with the iodine nose characteristic of the Chenin variety. Quite complex aromas, which develop well on opening. Its balance is on the sweet side, which gives it very little body. Although well made, it is essentially a technically made wine that could do with a little more character. To be drunk cool. (1984)
⊷ Robert Lecomte-Girault, Le Sablon, Faye-d'Anjou, 49380 Thouarcé; tel. 41 91 41 34 ⊺ By appt. Closed 15 Aug.–15 Sept.

DOMAINE LEDUC-FROUIN★

☐ 4ha 20000 **4** D ⑪ ⬇

④⑦ **64 69** 6̶9̶ **70 71 74 76 78**

A good, well-developed yellow-gold colour, and pleasant scents of quince, dried figs and honey – the typical maturing aromas of sweet wines. On the palate it has a quality of fullness with a slightly raw taste, due to the initial acidity which must be quite high, making this a good wine to drink with foie gras. Can also be served as an aperitif. (1969)
⊷ *Mme* Georges Leduc, Soussigné, 49540 Martigné-Briand; tel. 41 59 42 83 ⊺ By appt.

LOGIS DU PRIEURE★★

☐ 12ha 15000 **3** D ▪ ⬇

⑤⑨ **78** 8̶3̶

The Coteaux du Layon wines produced in this region often have a slight greenness blending with the gold of the over-ripe Chenin, and this is no exception. It has a very pleasant scent of quince on the nose. Good balance and a delicate complexity, typical of the producer, make this a very good wine which combines lightness with class. (1983) ✔ Anjou Rouge, Anjou Blanc Sec, Rosé de Loire, Cabernet d'Anjou Rosé.
⊷ *MM.* Jousset et Fils, Concourson-sur-Layon, 49700 Doué-la-Fontaine; tel. 41 59 11 66 ⊺ By appt.

DOMAINE DU PETIT VAL★

☐ 4.5ha 13000 **3** D ▪ ⬇

64 69 76 78 ★8̶0̶ ★8̶2̶ 8̶3̶ ⑧④ 8̶4̶

Attractive nose typical of the Chenin. To taste has good balance between acidity and sugar content; an aristocratic wine. In five to six years it will go well with foie gras and if kept longer will develop into a good aperitif. (1983) ✔ Anjou Rouge Cépage Cabernet, Anjou Rouge Cépage Gamay, Anjou Blanc Sec, Cabernet d'Anjou Rosé.
⊷ Vincent Goizil, Le Petit Val, Chavagnes-les-Eaux, 49380 Thouarcé; tel. 41 91 43 09 ⊺ By appt.

CHATEAU DES ROCHETTES★★

☐ 4ha 10000 **3** D ⑪ ⬇

69 ⑦⑥ **77 78 82** 8̶2̶ **83**

This wine is a lovely golden colour, but has a very unpleasant nose due to a high degree of sulphur. However we decided to list it because of its class which can be attributed to its background of old vines, careful grape selection and meticulous production. We advise you to open and decant it a good 24 hours in advance of drinking. (1982)
✔ Anjou Rouge Cépage Cabernet, Saumur Méthode Champenoise, Cabernet d'Anjou Rouge, Rosé de Loire.
⊷ Jean Douet, Les Rochettes, Concourson sur-Layon, 49700 Doué-La-Fontaine; tel. 41 59 11 51 ⊺ By appt.

BERNARD SECHET-CARRET★

☐ 1ha 2000 **2** D ▪

79 80 ⑧① **82 83** 8̶4̶

A well-presented wine with a delicate, fruity, starchy nose and good structure and balance in the mouth. Well-bred and certainly made from good grapes, it is a successful wine from a difficult year and has a good finish. It could be kept for several years. (1984)
⊷ Bernard Sechet-Carret, Maligné, 49540 Martigné-Briand; tel. 41 59 43 40 ⊺ By appt.

Coteaux du Layon-Villages

The most famous of these villages is Chaume, in Rochefort-sur-Loire, with 1500 hectolitres of wine produced on 70 hectares of land. Six others may have this name added to the appellation: Rochefort-sur-Loire; St-Aubin-de-Luigne; St-Lambert-du-Lattay; Beaulieu-sur-Layon; Rablay-sur-Layon and Faye-d'Anjou. The producers of these excellent wines have joined ranks in a 'Club des Villages', cultivating 120 hectares to produce 2500–3000 hectolitres annually.

DOMAINE D'AMBINOS *Beaulieu*★

☐ 11ha 19000 **3** D ▪ ⬇

78 79 82 ⑧③ 8̶3̶

The well-developed straw colour is characteristic of the vintage which, for those growers who waited long enough, ripened to perfection. Well-developed nose, with its exotic character confirmed; a successful balance on the palate, which has a distinct fruitiness. This wine is still young; needs opening in advance and requires patience. It will be ready to drink in ten years' time. (1983)
⊷ Jean-Pierre Chené, Impasse des Jardins, Beaulieu-sur-Layo 49190, Rochefort-sur-Loiren; tel. 41 78 48 09 ⊺ By appt.

DOMAINE BANCHEREAU
Saint-Aubin★

☐ 10ha 15000 **3** D ▪ ⬇

59 76 ★78 ★⑧① **82** 8̶3̶ 8̶4̶

Colour already quite well developed, nose full with a pleasant beeswax scent; this wine could easily be drunk as an aperitif now. Its rich softness will ensure it ages well, reaching its peak in a few years' time. (1981) ✔ Rosé d'Anjou, Anjou Rouge, Côteaux du Layon Chaumé, Anjou Gamay.

⌐ Paul Banchereau et Fils, Le Bourg, St-Aubin-de-Luigné, 49190 Rochefort-sur-Loire; tel. 41 78 33 24 ⊤ By appt. Closed 1 Aug.–15 Sept.

DOMAINE DE PIERRE BISE
Beaulieu

☐	5 ha	10000	3 D ▐ ◫ ↓

69 70 76 77 **78** ⑧² **83**

This wine looks absolutely correct but is very difficult to taste. It has a rather closed nose with a hint of hay, is hard in the mouth and leaves an impression which is difficult to define. It should be good and is now obviously undergoing a period of bottle-sickness and should be left for a few years. It will be good with foie gras, for example, or a blue cheese. (1983) ✔ Anjou Blanc, Anjou Rouge, Anjou Gamay Rouge, Cabernet d'Anjou Rosé.

⌐ Claude Papin, Dom. de Pierre Bise, Beaulieu-sur-Layon, 49190 Rochefort-sur-Loire; tel. 41 78 31 44 ⊤ By appt. Closed end Aug.–early Sept.

CADY PERE ET FILS *Saint-Aubin*

☐	4 ha	10000	2 D ◫ ↓

75 78 ★**79** ⑧¹ ⑧² ⑧³ ⑧⁴

This wine is still too young, so the complex nose which hints at something good is slightly closed-in. The aggressive taste is correct and behind the acidity it is clean and distinct, suggesting the qualities it will have after ageing. A little too much sulphur at present. (1983) ✔ Anjou Sec Sauvignon ou Chardonnay, Anjou Rouge Cépage Cabernet, Cabernet d'Anjou, Anjou Méthode Champenoise.

⌐ Pierre et Philippe Cady, Valette, St-Aubin-de-Luigné, 49190 Rochefort-sur-Loire; tel. 41 78 33 69 ⊤ Daily 9.00–20.00.

JEAN-PIERRE CHENE *Beaulieu**

☐	11 ha	12000	4 D ◫ ↓

⑥⁹ ⑥⁹ **70 71** 73 **76** ⑦⁶ 79 80 81 ★82 ★83 ★84

Sparkling golden colour; well-developed and complex aromas of wood, leather, tobacco and honey. To taste, it is the body with its fruity nuances that is most noteworthy. This wine is still developing and, despite its age, is only just beginning to be drinkable; it is still a little closed up. Will age well. A good example of the speciality of this producer. (1969)

⌐ Jean-Pierre Chené, Impasse des Jardins, Beaulieu-sur-Layon 49190, Rochefort-sur-Loire; tel. 41 78 48 09 ⊤ By appt.

GROSSET *Rochefort*

○	14 ha	10000	3 D ◫ ↓

61 62 69 70 71 73 75 76 **78** ⑦⁸ **80 81 82**

Although easy on the eye this wine has only just started to age, but the honey scent characteristic of great vintages can be detected. Allow to breathe and scents of truffles and iodine mix with the honey, creating an intriguing blend. To taste the balance is excellent. (1978) ✔ Côteaux du Layon, Anjou Blanc, Cabernet d'Anjou, Anjou Rouge.

⌐ R. Grosset, Rue René-Gasnier, 49190 Rochefort-sur-Loire; tel. 41 78 70 80 ⊤ By appt.

CHATEAU DE LA GUIMONIERE
*Chaume**

☐	16 ha	50000	3 D ◫ ↓

⑷³ ⑷⁵ ⑸⁹ ⑹⁶ 70 **71** 73 **79** 80 **81** ⑧² 83

Beautiful, well-developed colour, attractive and interesting nose exactly right for this stage in the ageing process. The acidity in this wine is rather high and aggressive. It has developed fairly rapidly but still possesses the qualities to age further. (1970) ✔ Côteaux du Layon Blanc, Anjou Blanc Sec, Cabernet d'Anjou.

⌐ Michel Doucet, Ch. de la Guimoniere, 49190 Rochefort-sur-Loire; tel. 41 78 31 56 ⊤ By appt. Closed 1 Oct.–15 Nov.

LES CAVES DE LA LOIRE *Beaulieu**

☐	80 ha	250000	2 D ▐ ↓

⑥⁹ ⑺⁸ ⑻¹ ⑻²

A wine for the enlightened wine-lover, with a brilliant, luminous colour that is already maturing. Lightly starchy taste, symptomatic of wines vinified at low temperature; balance satisfactory and the structure properly formed. An unpretentious yet pleasant wine which is worth acquiring at the right moment. (1984)

⌐ Les Caves de la Loire, 49320 Brissac-Quincé; tel. 41 91 22 71 ⊤ By appt.

DOMAINE DES MAURIERES
*Saint-Lambert**

☐	3 ha	10000	4 D ▐ ↓

⑺⁵ ⑺⁸ 79 **80 81** 82 83

The closed-in nose and general appearance is that of a young wine. Still aggressive: the 1978 wines are all slow developers and this one will need a good ten years to show its full potential. (1978) ✔ Anjou Blanc, Cabernet d'Anjou, Rosé d'Anjou, Anjou Rouge.

⌐ Fernand Moron, 8 Rue de Périnelle, St-Lambert-du-Lattay, 49190 Rochefort-sur-Loire; tel. 41 78 30 21 ⊤ By appt. Closed beginning Aug. 1–15 Sept.

CHATEAU MONTBENAULT
*Faye-d'Anjou**

☐	9 ha	18000	3 D ◫ ↓

73 74 75 **76** ⑺⁸ 80 **81** ⑻³

The scents and aromas of the Chenin are already evident in a very pleasant initial bouquet. Good balance, but a little too aggressive, as is to be expected at this youthful stage. Very good potential quality which suggests that 1983 will maintain the reputation of Château Montbenault as specialists in this type of wine. (1983) ✔ Anjou Blanc, Anjou Méthode Champenoise, Anjou Gamay Rouge, Cabernet d'Anjou Rosé.

⌐ Yves Leduc, Ch. Montbenault, Faye d'Anjou, 49380 Thouarcé; tel. 41 78 31 14 ⊤ Mon.–Sat. 9.00–12.00/14.00–19.00.

DOMAINE DE LA MOTTE *Rochefort**

☐	5 ha	18000	4 D ▐ ↓

69 70 73 ⑺⁴ 75 ⑺⁶ **78** ⑺⁸ ⑺⁹ ⑻² 83

A lovely colour which indicates a good vintage for late harvested wine. The scents and bouquet are rich, delicate and subtle. The good first

519

impression is confirmed in the taste of dried-out, over-ripe grapes. A very good bottle which will age well. (1976) ✓ Anjou Rouge, Anjou Gamay, Cabernet d'Anjou, Rosé d'Anjou.

↪ André Sorin, Ave d'Angers, 49190 Rochefort-sur-Loire; tel. 41 78 71 13 ⍙ By appt. Closed beginning Jul.

DOMAINE DE LA PIERRE BLANCHE *Saint Lambert*★

☐		5 ha	15 000	**4** **D** ⑪ ↓

69 70 ★71 **71**

Lovely, well-developed old gold colour, full and mature nose though still far from its peak. A top-class wine to taste but obviously needs longer to express its qualities to the full. Nonetheless, if opened well in advance of drinking, will make a spendid aperitif or accompaniment to blue cheese. (1971)

↪ GAEC Ogereau et Fils, Rue de la Belle-Angevine, St-Lambert-du-Lattay, 49190 Rochefort-sur-Loire; tel. 41 78 30 53 ⍙ By appt.

CHATEAU DE PLAISANCE *Chaume*★★★

☐		14 ha	35 000	**5** **D** ▮ ⑪ ↓

67 **68** **69** 70 **70** 75 76 79 80 81 ★**83**

Perfect colour. The aromas and scents of old wax mixed with candied fruits are gradually released as the wine breathes. Very good and very elegant on the palate. This wine may be drunk now but should be decanted to allow it to breathe. (1970) ✓ Anjou Blanc, Cabernet d'Anjou.

↪ Henri Rochais et Fils, Ch. de Plaisance, Chaume, 49190 Rochefort-sur-Loire; tel. 41 78 33 01 ⍙ By appt. Closed Sun. afternoon.

CHATEAU DE LA ROULERIE *Chaume les Aunis*★

☐		6 ha	15 000	**3** **D** ⑪ ↓

68 **69** 70 71 75 76 **81** ⑧⑴ **82** **83**

M. Jaudeau is one of the great specialists in this type of wine and this well-balanced example already has the attractive scents and aromas characteristic of this area. The high standards of his vineyards, coupled with his exacting vinification technique are reflected in this fine wine. (1983) ✓ Anjou Rouge, Anjou Blanc.

↪ Dominique Jaudeau, Ch. de la Roulerie, St-Aubin-de-Luigné, 49190 Rochefort-sur-Loire; tel. 41 78 33 02 ⍙ By appt. Closed Oct.

DOMAINE DES SAULAIES *Faye-d'Anjou*★

☐		2.5 ha	10 000	**3** **D** ▮ ↓

69 71 ★76 77 84 **84**

Not very well forward for the year, but the quality is there. The high proportion of sulphur dioxide must be allowed to evaporate by opening the wine well in advance of drinking. Nevertheless the wine works well and is ideal for ageing, to make a fine aperitif. (1976) ✓ Anjou Rouge Cabernet, Cabernet d'Anjou, Rosé d'Anjou, Anjou Gamay.

↪ Philippe Leblanc, Les Saulaies, Faye d'Anjou, 49380 Thouarcé; tel. 41 91 41 13 ⍙ By appt. Closed end Aug.–early Sept.

Bonnezeaux

This has long been recognized as an unrivalled pudding wine. In earlier days good dessert wines were usually served only at the appropriate point in the meal. Today this Grand Cru is enjoyed more as an aperitif. Full of vigour and extremely fragrant, Bonnezeaux wine owes its various characteristics to the special quality of the terroir on which the vines are planted. They face full south on three precipitous schist slopes – La Montagne, Beauregard and Fesles – above the village of Thouarcé.

The annual production varies between 700 to 1200 hectolitres from 50 hectares. The production area as a whole covers 130 hectares. This very reliable wine represents excellent value for money.

DOMAINE DE LA CROIX-DE-MISSION★★

☐		6 ha	15 000	**4** **D** ⑪ ↓

64 71 75 76 79 ⑧③ **83**

Mature colour indicating noble rot on the grapes. Bouquet still closed up, and rather coarse palate. Nevertheless, signs of good breeding make this wine definitely worth waiting for, especially in view of the general superiority of Bonnezeuax ✓ Anjou Blanc Sec, Anjou Rouge, Anjou Gamay, Cabernet Anjou.

↪ René Renou, Place du Champ-de-Foire, 49380 Thouarcé; tel. 41 54 04 05 ⍙ By appt.

DOMAINE DE LA CROIX-DES-LOGES★★

☐		2 ha	6000	**4** **D** ↓

70 71 74 75 76 ⑦⑧ 79 **82** **83**

Although young the colour is a well-developed straw yellow due to the over-ripeness of the grapes and late picking. Attractive and powerful on the nose; rather too high an alcohol content on the palate, and time is needed to allow the honey and acacia fragrances to develop. Keep this wine to go with foie gras. (1983) ✓ Anjou Rouge, Anjou Blanc, Cabernet d'Anjou, Rosé de Loire.

↪ Christian Bonnin, Dom. de la Croix-des-Loges,

49540 Martignée-Briand; tel. 41 59 43 66 ☎ By appt. Mon.–Sat. 9.00–12.00/15.00–19.00. Closed Oct.

CHATEAU DE FESLES★★★

□	12 ha	25000	4 D ⅲ ↓

75 76 78 82 *83 83

Certainly the greatest wine produced from the 1983 Anjou harvest. Every grape with 'noble rot' was hand picked resulting in a lovely straw coloured wine that has all the right qualities, classic scents of lime flowers, acacia, honey and crystallized fruit. A truly excellent bottle, to be drunk with foie gras or later in its life as an aperitif. (1983) ✔ Anjou Rouge Cépage Cabernet, Rosé de Loire, Anjou Blanc Sec.
🍷 Jacques Boivin, Ch. de Fesles, 49380 Thouarcé; tel. 41 91 40 40 ☎ By appt.

DOMAINE DU PETIT VAL★

□	1.8 ha	5000	4 D ▪ ↓

72 73 76 78 *79 79 *81 82 83 83 84

The taste of this wine is masked by a rather high sulphur dioxide content, which will, however, ensure good aging. Once this has faded the powerful scents will come through. This cellar usually produces successful wines of this type. (1982)
🍷 Vincent Goizil, Le Petit Val, Chavagnes-les-Eaux, 49380 Thouarcé; tel. 41 91 43 09 ☎ By appt.

Quarts de Chaume

In feudal days, the local aristocratic family of Chaume used to reserve a quarter of the annual wine production for itself. Naturally, the wine was from the best section of the vineyard. Today, the area produces 600–800 hectolitres of wine in the 40 hectares of the appellation. It is located right on the tip of a hill, facing south, near the village of Chaume in Rochefort-sur-Loire.

Most of the vines are old ones, and this factor, combined with the southerly exposure and the characteristics of the Chenin grape, leads to a small yield of very high quality. Harvesting takes place in several stages, so that each grape is picked as and when it is ripe. These are sweet wines that are rich in flavour and fruit, but with good acidity. They age well.

CHATEAU DE L'ECHARDERIE★

□	20 ha	40000	4 D ⅲ ↓

59 69 ⑦⑤ 76 78 79 80 81

Good well-developed colour with attractive highlights. Rather closed-up for the vintage, but if opened for a while has quite a high aromatic potential and a richness confirmed on the palate with good balance. In all, a fleshy wine with a firm finish, which will age well. To be served with blue cheese or foie gras or as an aperitif. (1978)
✔ Coteaux du Layon Chaume, Anjou Rouge Cépage Cabernet, Anjou Gamay, Cabernet d'Anjou.
🍷 Simone Laffourcade, Ch. de l'Echarderie 49190 Rochefort-sur-Loire; tel. 41 78 42 14 ☎ By appt.

Saumur

This appellation covers 36 communes, producing 20000 hectolitres of dry, refreshingly tart white wine and also 15000 hectolitres of red. The same grape varieties are used as in the Anjou AOC wines. They age very well.

The vineyards are spread over the hillsides above the Loire and the Thouet. The appellation was once famous for white wines from Turquant and Brezé but some of the red wines have now earned a good reputation, including those from Puy-Notre-Dame, Montreuil-Bellay and Tourtenay. However, the appellation is much better known for its sparkling wines, of which ten to twelve million bottles are produced every year, and whose high quality has been maintained by the efforts of the producers. All the production takes place in Saumur; the cellars there, dug out of the surrounding tufa rock, are well worth a visit.

CLOS DE L'ABBAYE
Cuvée des Chanoines★

▪	4.5 ha	4500	2 D ▪ ↓

74 78 80 82 83 83

A ruby-coloured wine with the nose of soft red fruits, typical of Cabernet-Franc and Cabernet-Sauvignon grapes. Fairly full bodied. (1983)
🍷 Henri Aupy, Clos de l'Abbaye, 49260, Le Puy-Notre-Dame; tel. 41 52 26 71 ☎ By appt.

CLOS DE L'ABBAYE★

□	5 ha	7000	2 D ▪ ↓

83 *84 84

Chardonnay grapes give this wine its pretty gold colour, attractive nose and good balance. (1983)
🍷 Henri Aupy, Clos de l'Abbaye, 49260 Puy-Notre-Dame; tel. 41 52 26 71 ☎ By appt.

CLOS DE L'ABBAYE★★

■ 4.5ha 4500 **2** **D** **ī** ↓

(64) **74 75** 76 77 **78** 79 80 ★**81** ★**82** **82** ★83

Pretty, deep, well-developed colour, and rich organic bouquet characteristic of the good '82 vintage. This wine is good to drink now and would, possibly, be even better if kept. (1982)
↦ Henri Aupuy, Clos de l'Abbaye, 49260 Puy-Notre-Dame; tel. 41 52 26 71 ⊥ By appt.

BADET-LHERIAU★

■ 20ha 55000 **2** **D** **ꝗ** ↓

64 70 (76) 78 79 80 **81** 82 83

Sustained dark colour, indicating a tannin-rich wine, confirmed on the palate. Some attractive characteristics that will appear in a few years. (1983)
↦ Badet-Lhériau, 49260 Montreuil-Bellay; tel. 41 52 31 36 ⊥ By appt.

CHATEAU DE BEAULIEU★

○ 1560000 **4** **D** ↓

Lovely and bright, with delicate bubbles, but is rather too closed. Wait a while before drinking. ✔ Crémant de Loire Brut, Anjou Rosé Brut.
↦ MM. Gratien et Meyer, Route de Montsoreau, 49100 Saumur; tel. 41 51 01 54 ⊥ Daily 9.00–12.00/14.00–17.00.

BOUVET-LADUBAY *Brut*★

○ 1400000 **3** **D** **ī** ↓

A fine and persistent mousse, with predominantly fruity fragrances on the nose. Full, rich and vigorous, and very representative of the region. Good served as an aperitif or at a soirée.
↦ Bouvet-Ladubay, St-Hilaire-St-Florent, 49400 Saumur; tel. 41 50 11 12 ⊥ By appt.

BOUVET-LADUBAY *Blanc de Blanc*★

○ 150000 **4** **D** **ī** ↓

The attractive yellow shade indicates good development, although the mousse is rather soft. An elegant, fruity bouquet is confirmed on the palate, with mature, refined aromas and a good finish. A fine aperitif wine.
↦ Bouvet-Ladubay, St-Hilaire-St-Florent, 49400 Saumur; tel. 41 50 11 12 ⊥ By appt.

CHATEAU DE BREZE★

□ 12ha 65000 **2** **D** **ꝗ** ↓

72 ★**78** (82) ★**82** ★**83**

Patience is needed with this wine as it is tough at present, and the sulphur dioxide makes it even more so. But over the course of ten years or so will become a desirable bottle. (1982) ✔ Côteau de Saumur, Saumur Rouge, Saumur Brézé 'Brut'.
↦ Bernard de Colbert, Ch. de Brézé, Brézé 49260 Montreuil-Bellay; tel. 41 51 62 06 ⊥ By appt.

JEAN DOUET *Nemrod*★

□ 5ha 60000 **3** **D** **ꝗ** ↓

76 78 80 81 (82) **82**

This beautiful wine with its fine mousse would be ideal for any celebration. (1982) ✔ Coteaux de Layon, Anjou Rouge, Rosé de Loire, Cabernet d'Anjou.
↦ Jean Douet, Les Rochettes, Concourson-sur-Layon, 49700 Doué-la-Fontaine; tel. 41 59 11 51 ⊥ By appt.

LYCEE D'ENSEIGNEMENT PROF. AGRICOLE★★

■ 5.5ha 30000 **2** **D** **ī** ↓

79 80 ★**81** ★**82** ★**83** ★84

Crystal-clear, with deep cherry-red colour and scent richly reminiscent of soft fruits. Full but slightly tough and tannic to taste. Will age well but needs to be opened well in advance. (1983).
↦ Lycée d'Enseign. Prof. Agricole, 49260 Montreuil-Bellay; tel. 41 52 31 96 ⊥ By appt.
↦ M. Louvet.

CHATEAU DE MONTREUIL-BELLAY★

■ 9ha 50000 **2** **D** **ī** ↓

75 76 79 ★**80** ★**81** ★(82) **82**

Dark and smelling of chalk; undeveloped, very tannic, rather aggressive and dry. Would be best to wait a while before drinking. (1982) ✔ Saumur Blanc.
↦ Mme. De Thuy, Ch. de Montreuil, 49260 Montreuil-Bellay; tel. 41 52 33 06 ⊥ By appt.

DOMAINE DES NERLEUX★

○ 10ha 60000 **4** **D** **ī** **ꝗ** ↓

A good-looking wine with an attractive colour. The bubbles could be finer, but they last well and look good, indicating recently added *liqueur d'expedition*. Easy on the nose and to taste, the dosage is rather high which will make this wine easy to drink on its own. ⊥ Saumur-Champigny, Saumur Blanc, Crémant de Loire, Sauvignon d'Origine Mousseux.
↦ Robert et Régis Néau, Dom. des Nerleux, St-Cyr-en-Bourg, 49260 Montreuil-Bellay; tel. 41 51 61 04 ⊥ By appt.

DOMAINE DES NERLEUX★★

□ 10ha 60000 **2** **D** **ī** **ꝗ** ↓

64 76 ★**83** **83** 84

A well-developed wine, with good colour and rich aromas, and, above all, good balance. The acidity which is often rather high in a Saumur wine is not present here, due to the richness of its other features. A joy to drink, preferably at the beginning of a meal or with fish, although it could also accompany a morning snack. (1983) ✔ Saumur-Champigny, Saumur Brut Méthode Champenoise, Crémant de Loire, Sauvignon Vin de Pays Blanc Sec.
↦ Robert et Régis Néau, Dom. des Nerleux, St-Cyr-en-Bourg, 49260 Montreuil-Bellay; tel. 41 51 61 04 ⊥ By appt.

NOEL PINOT *Brut*★

○　　　　　　1ha　3500　　🔲 Ⓓ ▮ ⬥
78 82 **82** 83

Slightly yellow tone to this lively, grapey wine which has a strong aroma of the Chenin grape. A very straightforward wine. (1983)
⬥ Noël Pinot, Dampierre-sur-Loire, 49460 Saumur; tel. 41 51 14 35 Ⓣ By appt.

NOEL PINOT★

▢　　　　　　5ha　12000　　🔲 Ⓓ ◐ ⬥
78 **78** 82 **82** 83 **83** 84

Quite good colour, slightly evocative of forest undergrowth. This wine has been dosed with rather a lot of sulphur dioxide which makes it hard, so that it must be allowed to breathe before serving. Will age well. (1983)
⬥ Noël Pinot, Dampierre-sur-Loire, 49460 Saumur; tel. 41 51 14 35 Ⓣ By appt.

CHATEAU DE SAINT-FLORENT★

■　　　　　　3ha　18000　　🔲 Ⓓ ◐ ⬥
76 78 81 ★**82** ★83 **83** **84**

A dark-coloured wine with a rich, fruity, untamed nose which develops well on opening. Fairly light to drink. (1983) ✔ Saumur Blanc Ch. de St-Florent, Crémant Loire Langlois Ch.
⬥ SA Langlois-Ch., BP 6, St-Hilaire-St-Florent, 49416 Saumur; tel. 41 50 28 14 Ⓣ By appt ⬥ Baron Jean de Bodman.

CHATEAU DE SAINT-FLORENT★★

▢　　　　　　6ha　35000　　🔲 Ⓓ ▮ ⬥
★82 **82** ★83 **83**

A lovely, well-developed colour matches this floral, subtly scented, typical Saumur wine. Slightly acidic sharpness and lingering aromatic finish on the palate. (1983) ✔ Saumur, Crémant de Loire Langlois-Ch.
⬥ SA Langlois-Ch., St-Hilaire-St-Florent, 49416 Saumur; tel. 41 50 28 14 Ⓣ By appt ⬥ Baron Jean de Bodman.

CAVE DES VIGNERONS DE SAUMUR *Brut*★

○　　　　　　200ha　1200000　　🔲 Ⓓ ▮ ⬥
★81 **81**

Delicate, plentiful bubbles in this light, elegant, aristocratic wine. Once it has settled down it will make an excellent aperitif. (1981) ✔ Saumur Blanc, Cabernet de Saumur, Saumur Rouge, Saumur-Champigny.
⬥ Coop. des Vignerons de Saumur, St-Cyr-en-Bourg, 49260 Montreuil-Bellay; tel. 41 51 61 09 Ⓣ By appt. Closed 1 Oct.–30 Apr.

CAVES DES VIGNERONS DE SAUMUR★

▢　　　　　125ha　700000　　🔲 Ⓓ ▮ ⬥
76 ★82 **82**

The powerful, high-toned aromas typical of the Chenin are particularly obvious in the nose of this wine. A slight toughness blended with its delicacy will enable it to be drunk with fish – especially fish cooked in white butter sauce. (1983) ✔ Saumur-Champigny, Saumur Rouge, Cabernet de Saumur, Saumur Mousseux.
⬥ Coop. des Vignerons de Saumur, 49260 Montreuil-Bellay; tel. 41 51 61 09 Ⓣ By appt. Closed 1 Oct.–30 Apr.

CAVES DES VIGNERONS DE SAUMUR★★★

■　　　　　185ha　1000000　　🔲 Ⓓ ▮ ⬥
76 ★82 **82**

A very pretty wine with a light, clear ruby colour. Grapey nose with subtle fragrances; excellent balance in the mouth, where delicacy and finesse blend well together, leaving a lingering, aromatic finish. Easy to drink. (1982) ✔ Saumur Blanc, Cabernet de Saumur.
⬥ Coop. des Vignerons de Saumur, St-Cyr-en Bourg, 49260 Montreuil-Bellay; tel. 41 51 61 09 Ⓣ By appt. Closed 1 Oct.–30 Apr.

MICHEL SUIRE★

▢　　　　　　6ha　40000　　🔲 Ⓓ ▮ ◐ ⬥
★83 **83** ★84

The soft, porous sub-soil of this small winegrowing area suits the Chenin variety well and gives good balance. Can easily be left to age a while. (1983) ✔ Saumur Rouge, Saumur Méthode Champenoise.
⬥ Michel Suire, Pouan-Berrie, 86120 Trois-Moutiers; tel. 49 22 92 61 Ⓣ By appt. Closed 15 Sept.–15 Nov.

CHATEAU DE TARGE★★

■　　　　　15ha　75000　　🔲 ▮ ◐ ⬥
78 81 82 ★83 **83**

A lovely deep purple wine which is very well made. It shows good ageing potential and does credit to the hard work of this talented young wine producer. (1983)
⬥ Edouard Pisani-Ferry, Ch. de Targé, Parnay, 49730 Montsoreau; tel. 41 38 11 50 Ⓣ By appt.

DOMAINE DES VARINELLES★

☐   4ha   20000   2 D ▮ ↓

69 70 72 76 81 32 ⑧ 84

A good example of its type, which should be allowed to age a little before drinking, when it will show to better advantage. (1983) ✔ Saumur-Champigny, Saumur Blanc, Rosé de Loire, Sauvignon Blanc.
↳ Claude Daheuiller, 28 Rue du Ruau, Varrains, 49400 Saumur; tel. 41 52 90 94 ☎ By appt. Closed public holidays, Sat. afternoon.

CHATEAU DE VILLENEUVE★★★

☐   8ha   60000   2 D ▮ ↓

76 81 82 ★83

Full, aromatic richness produced by a happy combination of Chenin grapes and Saumur soil. Aristocratic, complete and elegant. Perfect with perch or pike in a white butter sauce. (1983)
↳ Robert Chevallier, Villeneuve, Souzay-Champigny, 49400 Saumur; tel. 49 51 14 04 ☎ By appt. Closed Sun.

Cabernet de Saumur

This wine (3000 hectolitres), made near the town of Saumur, is somewhere between a Rosé de Loire and a Cabernet d'Anjou. Essentially, it is a rosé made from Cabernet grapes. It is neither dry nor sweet, though usually on the drier side, and can be attractive and fruity if it is well made.

CAVES DES VIGNERONS DE SAUMUR★

◪   100ha   600000   2 ▮ ↓

76 ⑧ ★83

A fairly deep and floral wine, slightly sweet to taste. A very good example of its type. (1983) ✔ Saumur-Champigny, Saumur Rouge, Saumur Blanc, Saumur Mousseux Brut.
↳ C. Coop. des Vignerons de Saumur, St-Cyr-en Bourg, 49260 Montreuil-Bellay; tel. 41 51 61 09 ☎ By appt. Closed 1 Oct.–30 Apr.

Saumur-Champigny

Although the vineyard has been widely developed only recently, the red wines of Champigny have been known for many centuries. They are made in nine communes from Cabernet-Franc or Breton grapes, and are light, fruity and easy to drink.

Between 30000 and 35000 hectolitres are produced. The Cave des Vignerons in St-Cyr-en-Boix has played an important part in developing the vineyard. For a glimpse of the history of the region, it is worth visiting some of the many ancient wine cellars to be found in the villages around Saumur.

DOMAINE DU BOURGNEUF★

▮   6.5ha   30000   3 D ▮ ⑪ ↓

47 49 76 82 ★⑧ 83

A prettily coloured wine with a distinctive nose of soft red fruits and blackcurrant. Will open out in several years' time. (1983)
↳ Christian Joseph, 31 Rue de Bourgneuf, Varrains, 49400 Saumur; tel. 41 52 92 10 ☎ By appt. Closed public holidays.

CHATEAU DE CHAINTRES★

▮   20ha   120000   3 D ▮ ⑪ ↓

75 76 79 81 ★⑧ 32 83 84

Following an exceptional 1982, this vintage seems still closed in. However, a sound investment. (1983) ✔ Saumur Blanc, Rosé Cabernet de Loire.
↳ Gael de Tigny, Ch. de Chaintres, Dampierre-sur-Loire, 49400 Saumur; tel. 41 52 90 54 ☎ By appt. Closed July, Aug.

PAUL FILLIATREAU★★

▮   30ha   300000   3 D ▮ ⑪ ↓

75 76 78 79 ⑧ 83 ★84

Well-developed colour; nose a little small due to the method used to produce this wine. Good balance, but decanting before drinking will help. Should age well. (1983) ✔ Lena Filliatreau Rouge, Dom. Filliatreau Jeunes Vignes, Dom., Filliatreau Vieilles Vignes Rouge.
↳ Paul Filliatreau, Chaintres, Dampierre-sur-Loire, 49400 Saumur; tel. 41 52 90 84 ☎ By appt.

DOMAINE DES NERLEUX★

▮   15ha   80000   3 D ▮ ⑪ ↓

76 82 ★⑧ 83

Clean, bright colour. Cabernet bouquet that is spicy and interesting. Little hard in the mouth, but pleasant. Will age well. (1983) ✔ Saumur Blanc, Crémant de Loire.
↳ Robert et Régis Neau, Dom. des Nerleux, St-Cyr-en-Bourg, 49260 Montreuil-Bellay; tel. 41 51 61 04 ☎ By appt. Closed Sun.

CHATEAU DE PARNAY★

▮   12ha   70000   3 D ⑪ ↓

70 76 82 ★⑧ 83 ★84

A well-presented, pleasant, light wine which is ready to drink now. (1983) ✔ Saumur Blanc.
↳ Gilles Collé, Ch. de Parnay, 49730 Montsoreau; tel. 41 38 10 85 ☎ Mon.–Sat. 9.00–12.00/14.00–18.00. Closed Sun.

DOMAINE DES ROCHES NEUVES★★★

■   10ha   50000   🔳 🅳 🍶 ⅏ ⌁

74 76 78 ⑧ 🔳 83 🔳

Well made, full bodied and aristocratic. Typical of the vintage. With age will develop into a truly great wine. (1983)
♠ Denis Duveau, 27 Rue de la Mairie, Varrains, 49400 Saumur; tel. 41 52 90 14 ⅄ By appt.

DOMAINE DU VAL BRUN★

■   10ha   50000   🔳 🅳 ⅏ ⌁

76 78 🔳 ★83 🔳 ★🔳

Well-developed colour and a certain lightness confirmed on the palate indicate that this wine is ready for drinking. (1983) ✔ Saumur Méthode Champenoise, Saumur Blanc, Côteau de Saumur.
♠ Jean-Pierre Charrvau, Rue Valbrun, Parnay, 49730 Montsoreau; tel. 41 38 11 85 ⅄ By appt.

DOMAINE DES VARINELLES★

■   13ha   60000   🔳 🅳 ⅏ ⌁

81 ★⑧ ★🔳 🔳

The colour is attractive, the aromatic richness very expressive. Its lightness suggests it should be drunk young with grilled meat. (1983) ✔ Saumur, Saumur d'Origine, Rosé de Loire, Cabernet d'Anjou.
♠ Claude Daheuiller, 28 Rue du Ruau, Varrains, 49400 Saumur; tel. 41 52 90 94 ⅄ By appt.

CHATEAU DE VILLENEUVE★

■   12ha   70000   🔳 🅳 🍶 ⌁

76 78 81 82 ★⑧ 🔳

Attractive, but undeveloped bouquet and slightly hard, green character mean it would be better to keep it for a little before drinking. (1983) Saumur Blanc.
♠ Robert Chevallier, Villeneuve, Souzay-Champigny, 49400 Saumur; tel. 41 51 14 04 ⅄ By appt. Closed Sun.

TOURAINE

The wine museum at Tours bears witness to the long history of the vine in this area. Legendary tales of the life of St Martin, Bishop of Tours about AD 380, contain many allusions to wine and viticulture. Bourgueil abbey with its famous walled vineyard was home to the Breton or Cabernet-Franc grape around the year AD 1000 and, later, the sixteenth-century French author Rabelais celebrated the good life in a famous history of the region. These rich associations can be relived from Mesland to Borgueil on the east bank (passing through Reugny, Tours, Lugnes, and Langeais), and from Chaumont to Chinon on the west bank (passing through Amboise, Chenonceaux, the Cher valley, Saclié, Azayle-Rideau, and the Forest of Chinon).

The Touraine vineyards were at their largest in the late nineteenth century. Today, they cover some 10000 hectares, an area smaller than that before the phylloxera crisis. They are principally situated in the departments of Indre-et-Loire and Loir-et-Cher, spreading into Sarthe to the north. Tasting some of the very old wines (1921, 1893, 1874, or even 1858), one finds that, despite modern advances in growing and wine-making techniques, the style of Touraine wine has remained essentially unchanged. This may be partly due to the fact that each of the appellations is made from a single grape variety. Climate, too, plays an important part; the Loir slopes form a screen against the northerly winds, and the interplay of maritime and continental influences is evident in the wines. From north to south stretch a succession of valleys running east-west; the Loir, Loire, Cher, Indre, Vienne and Creuse valleys provide a profusion of tufa hillsides that are perfect for vines. The valley soils are a mixture of clay–limestone and sand, with flinty outcrops. There are also some gravelly soils along the Loire and the Vienne.

The various characteristics of the 'Garden of France' are reflected in the wines. Each valley has its own appellation, and the character of each wine is strongly marked by the climatic conditions of the vintage. The year 1976 was hot and dry, and the wines from that vintage are full bodied and rich, with exceptional ageing potential. In 1977 the vines blossomed late and the weather was more humid, so that the white wines are drier, the red wines lighter, and only today are they really ready to drink. If one were to rank the wines of the last few decades according to their richness, the order would be as follows: 1959, 1976, 1964, 1982, 1961, 1970, 1969, 1981 and 1983.

Touraine

There is however a tendency to fluctuate between the tannic reds of Chinon or Bourgueil (the smoother wines come from the valleys, the more robust wines from the hills), and the lighter (Gamay) reds of the Touraine appellation. In a good year, average production exceeds 380000 hectolitres, and this is divided more or less equally between owner-growers, cooperatives, and négociants.

Touraine

The Touraine appellation covers the whole region, although the growing area is mostly located between the valleys of the Loire and the Indre, with the Cher in the centre. The soil is basically sand and clay, with some limestone, and is mainly planted with Gamay Noir, along with more tannic varietals, such as the Cabernet and Côt, depending on the area. Each year about 150000 hectolitres of light and fruity wines are produced, especially

the Vins Primeurs made from the Gamay Noir. The reds, made from a blend of two or three grape varieties, can age in bottle, while the still, dry, white wines (between 100000 and 180000 hectolitres, depending on the year) are made from the Sauvignon, Chenin, Pineau Blanc de la Loire or the Pineau Blanc d'Arbois. A large proportion of the white wine is, however, made into sparkling wine. Finally, a few thousand hectolitres of dry or medium-dry light, fruity, rosé wine are made from red grapes.

The cellars carved out of the tufa rock provide perfect conditions for ageing wine, with a constant temperature of around 12°C. White wine vinification takes place at a low temperature. Fermentation may last for several weeks, or even months in the case of the sweeter wines. On the other hand, the light-bodied Touraine red Vins Primeurs spend only a short time in the vat, although Bourgueil and Chinon wines customarily have a longer fermentation of two to four weeks. The reds undergo malo-lactic fermentation; the whites and rosés do not, since they depend on the presence of malic acid for their crispness.

On the outskirts of Tours lies a very old vineyard now being re-cultivated to produce dry rosé wines under the Touraine appellation. The wines used to be called 'noble joué', a name that has begun to be used again. The grape varieties planted are the three Pinots; Pinot Gris, Pinot Meunier and Pinot Noir.

LE CLOS NEUF DES ARCHAMBAULTS *Cabernet*★★★

■	1.25ha	6000	3 D ◖ ↓

76 81 ⑧ 83

Deep carmine red, with complex farmyard aromas and scents of cherries and truffles. Develops well in the mouth, the taste slightly coffee-flavoured and the finish fairly long. It is still a little young to be at its best. (1976)
➟ Jean-François Dehelly, Les Archambults, 37800 Ste-Maure-de-Tourraine; tel. 47 65 48 70
Ⴤ By appt.

LE CLOS NEUF DES ARCHAMBAULTS
Cabernet Vielles Vignes★★★

■	1.25ha	6000	5 D ◖ ↓

75 76 78 ⑧ **82** 83

The vivid ruby colour, with hues of raspberries, truffles and peaches, heralds a full, harmonious, tannic and easy-to-drink wine, which shows good length and a slight vanilla flavour. (1982)
➟ Jean-François Dehelly, Les Archambhaults, 37800 Ste-Maure-de-Tourraine; tel. 47 65 48 70
Ⴤ By appt.

CLOS BAUDOIN
Méthode Champenoise★★★

◔	2ha	9000	3 D ◖ ↓

A lovely copper-pink coloured wine with delicate, consistent bubbles and a nose of sloes, almonds and soft red fruits. A nice dryness on the palate, with a good balance between firmness and suppleness. An original wine with a long finish. (1980)
➟ Philippe Poniatowski, Le 'Close Baudoin', 37210 Vouvray; tel. 47 52 71 02 Ⴤ By appt.

J.-M. BEAUFRETON★

◪	1.6ha	3600	2 D ▮ ↓

Beautiful coppery colour. Rather fruity nose with a hint of green pepper. Balanced and supple on the palate. (1983)
➟ J.-M. Beaufreton, Rue de Grand-Verger, 37230 Luynes; tel. 47 55 67 13 Ⴤ By appt.

ANDRE BLANCHARD
Cabernet Sauvignon

■	0.68ha		D ▮ ◖

★⑧ **84** 84

Dark red colour, with a hint of ruby. Slightly milky nose mingling with coffee grounds and spiced bread. The taste is balanced with a slight bitterness, and the aroma of the nose re-appears on the palate. Interesting. (1984)
➟ André Blancard, Ch. du Penon, Lemère, 37120 Richelieu 957168 Ⴤ By appt.

JEAN-CLAUDE BODIN *Cabernet*

■	2ha	10000	2 D ▮ ◖ ↓

The tannic, supple and rustic nature of this wine could be gauged from its ruby-garnet colour, which is backed up by the scent of blackberries and capsicum. (1983)
➟ Jean-Claude Bodin, La Bergeonnière, St-Romain, 41140 Noyers-sur-Cher; tel. 54 71 70 43

JEAN-CLAUDE BODIN *Gamay*★

■	4ha	15000	2 D ▮ ◖

A light redcurrant colour with a quite leafy nose. Scents of plums and liquorice. (1983)
➟ Jean-Claude Bodin, La Bergeonnière, St-Romain, 41140 Noyers-sur-Cher; tel. 54 71 70 43.

JEAN-CLAUDE BODIN★★

□	4ha	7000	2 D ▮ ◖ ↓

⑧ 83 **83**

A dry, firm and lively wine with fresh almond aromas and a bright straw-yellow colour. (1983)
✔ Touraine Sauvignon, Touraine Côt, Pineau d'Aunis Rose, Méthode Champenoise Rosé.
➟ Jean-Claude Bodin, La Bergeonnière, St-Romain, 41440 Noyers-sur-Cher; tel. 54 71 70 43. Daily 8.00–12.00/14.00–18.00.

JEAN BOUTON *Cabernet*★

■	2ha	10000	2 D ▮ ↓

Intense ruby-red colour. Complex nose that has yet to mature. Rich and delicate on the palate. Should age well. (1982) ✔ Touraine Gamay Rouge.
➟ Jean Bouton, Parcay, St-Georges-sur-Cher, 41400 Montrichard; tel. 54 32 31 28 Ⴤ By appt.

JOSE CHOLLET★★

◪	2ha	15000	2 D ▮ ↓

⑥ 69 ★81 ★82 83

Beautiful pink with a touch of amber. Complex scent of almonds and caramel on the nose. Balanced and characteristic on the palate. (1983)
➟ Jose Chollet, 23 Chemin de Rabelais, 41150 Onzain, tel. 65 42 07 95 Ⴤ By appt.

DOMAINE DES CORBILLIERES
Cabernet★

■	2ha	15000	3 D ▮ ↓

83

Long-lasting, rich in tannin and very typical of the region. Noteworthy for its rustic character, its leafy, animal nose redolent of vanilla and liquorice, and, finally, for its brilliant, ruby colour. (1982)
➟ Maurice Barbou, Les Corbillières, Oisly, 41700

Contres; tel. 54 79 52 75 ⊺ Mon.–Sat. 8.00–12.00/14.00–18.00.

DOMAINES DES CORBILLIERES
Sauvignon★

☐	0.9 ha	40 000	⓷ Ⓓ ⬛ ↓
⑧⑴ 83			

Bright straw colour. A full-bodied wine, powerful, well made, lively and finishes well. (1983)
☛ Maurice Barbou, Les Corbillières, Oisly, 41700 Contres; tel. 54 79 52 75 ⊺ Mon.–Sat. 8.00–12.00/14.00–18.00.

LA CROIX DE MOSNY★★★

☐	3 ha	10 000	② Ⓓ ⬛ ↓

Golden-green colour. On the nose, full freshness of spring flowers with a touch of aniseed. Elegant palate and delicious, aromatic persistence. A delightful and original wine. (1983)
☛ Michel Lateyron, 1 Bis Quai des Violettes, 37400 Amboise; tel. 47 57 33 48 ⊺ By appt. Closed Easter, 1 Nov.

DOMAINE JOEL DELAUNAY
Sauvignon★★

☐	2.5 ha	20 000	② Ⓓ ⬛ ↓

Platinum-yellow colour. Aromas of gingerbread, new-mown hay and light tobacco. Charming and well made; lingers on the palate. (1983) ✔ Touraine Gamay, Touraine Cabernet, Touraine Cabotières Rosé, Touraine Méthode Champenoise.
☛ Joel Delaunay, La Tesnière, Pouillé, 41110 St-Aignan; tel. 54 71 45 69 ⊺ By appt. Closed Oct.

DOMAINE JOEL DELAUNAY
Cabernet★★

⬛	1.28 ha	10 000	② Ⓓ ⬛ ↓

Rich, garnet-red colour. Red, soft fruits scent also present in a vegetal, coffee-like aroma. Full, harmonious and perfectly combined on the palate. Good length. (1983) ✔ Touraine Sauvignon et Cabernet, Touraine Cabotières, Méthode Champenoise.
☛ Joel Delaunay, La Tesnière, Pouillé 41110 St-Aignan; tel. 54 71 45 69 ⊺ By appt. Closed Oct.

GUY DELETANG ET FILS
Sauvignon★★

☐	1 ha	8000	② Ⓓ ⬛ ⑪ ↓
82 83 ⑻⑶			

Golden-yellow colour and a nose that at first seems immature, but then reveals new-mown hay and medlar scents. Full, dry, lively and light on

the palate, and very typical, with its fresh, long-lasting taste. (1983) ✔ Montlouis.
☛ Guy Deletang, St-Martin-le-Beau, 37270 Montlouis; tel. 47 50 67 25. ⊺ Daily 10.00–12.00/14.00–18.00.

JEAN-MARIE DUVOUX *Cabernet★★*

⬛	3.5 ha	26 000	② Ⓓ ⬛ ↓
⑧② ⑻⑶			

A remarkable wine whose distinguishing features are its aromas of soft red fruits and slight farmyardy nose, together with a tannic, attractive taste – a good example of its type. (1983)
☛ Jean-Marie Duvoux, Le Pernas, Angé 41400 Montrichard; tel. 54 32 05 63 ⊺ By appt.

JEAN-MARIE DUVOUX *Gamay★*

⬛	2.5 ha	20 000	② Ⓓ ⬛ ↓
⑧② ⑻⑶			

Bright ruby colour and well-developed bouquet, with scents of warm, soft fruits and new-mown hay. To taste it is well balanced, chewy and easy to drink, with a spicy flavour. The finish is of average length, and fairly rough. (1983)
☛ Jean-Marie Duvoux, Le Pernas, Angé 41400 Montrichard; tel. 54 32 05 63 ⊺ By appt.

JEAN-MARIE DUVOUX
Cabernet Rosé★

☑	1 ha	5000	② Ⓓ ⬛ ↓
⑧② 83			

The copper-pink colour and scent of fresh almonds introduce a dry, young and lively wine, a perfect example of its type.
☛ Jean-Marie Duvoux, Le Pernas, Angé 41400 Montrichard; tel. 54 32 05 63 ⊺ By appt. Closed Oct.

DOMAINE DES ECHARDIERES
Cabernet★★

⬛	3 ha	4800	② Ⓓ ⬛ ⑪ ↓
76 79 81 ⑻② ⑻⑶			

A good, ruby-coloured wine with scents of capsicum and soft red fruits. The taste reveals very good quality, characterized by a lot of tannin. Still a little young. (1982)
☛ Lucien Launay, Angé, 41400 Montrichard; tel. 54 32 05 73 ⊺ By appt.

DOMAINE DES ECHARDIERES
Gamay★★

⬛	3 ha	48 000	② Ⓓ ⬛ ⑪ ↓
76 79 81 82 ⑻⑶			

Light ruby colour with a scent of crystallized soft red fruits. A well-balanced wine, typical of its kind; easy to drink. (1983)
☛ Lucien Launay, Angé, 41400 Montrichard; tel. 54 32 05 73 ⊺ By appt.

GERARD GABILLET *Gamay★★*

⬛	3 ha	7000	② Ⓓ ⬛ ⑪ ↓
82 ⑻⑶			

Brick-red colour. Developing scents of vegetal and animal character. Pleasant, light and spicy. (1981)
☛ Gérard Gabillet, 31 Rue des Charmoises, Thésée, 41140 Noyers-sur-Cher; tel. 54 71 45 02

Y Mon.–Sat. 8.00–12.00/14.00–20.00. Sun. 8.00–12.00.

GERARD GABILLET *Cabernet**

■ 1 ha 4000 [2] [D] ▮ ⦀ ⫰

The aromatic blend of capsicum, cherry, almonds and apple makes an interesting, tannic and fairly firm wine, although a little short in the mouth. Ruby colour, tending to garnet-red. (1981)

⚷ Gérard Gabillet, 31 Rue des Charmoises, Thésée, 41140 Noyers-sur-Cher; tel. 54 71 45 02 Y Mon.–Sat. 8.00–12.00/14.00–20.00, Sun. 8.00–12.00.

GERARD GABILLET *Sauvignon***

□ 2 ha 10000 [2] [D] ▮ ⦀ ⫰

82 83 [83]

Slightly straw-beige colour with well-developed and characteristic scents. Still young and lively to taste, with the lingering aromas so typical of this variety; very promising. A successful, very typical wine. (1983)

⚷ Gérard Gabillet, 31 Rue des Charmoises, Thésée, 41140 Noyers-sur-Cher; tel. 54 71 45 02 Y Mon.–Sat. 8.00–12.00/14.00–20.00, Sun. 8.00–12.00.

GAEC GALLAIS *Gamay***

■ 2 ha 5000 [2] [D] ▮ ⦀ ⫰

[78] *(82) *83 *84

Bold red colour, and nose of spring violets mixed with a touch of liquorice. Balanced and well made despite a light astringency. Will become more supple with time. (1984)

⚷ GAEC Gallais, Valleres, 37190 Azay-le-Rideau; tel. 47 43 35 32 Y By appt.

DOMAINE DE LA GARRELIERE*

◪ 2 ha 15000 [2] [D] ▮ ⫰

This pale pink wine, with its aroma of peaches, is dry, vigorous, firm and flowing on the palate. A typical rosé from the Richelieu area of the Touraine. (1982)

⚷ Pierre Plouzeau, 37120 Razinnes; tel. 47 93 16 34 Y By appt.

DOMAINE DE LA GARRELIERE*

□ 5 ha 30000 [2] [D] ▮ ⫰

The vineyard was once the property of the Richelieu family and now produces this lively straw-coloured wine, very typical of the appellation. Firm and full on the nose, with a palate to match and a lingering flavour. (1984)

⚷ Pierre Plouzeau, 37120 Razinnes; tel. 47 93 16 34 Y By appt.

CHATEAU DE LAUNAY**

□ 4 ha 25000 [3] [D] ▮ ⫰

*(83) *84

Nice, light golden colour with tinges of green. Good floral nose, still very youthful. Fresh and light on the palate with a fruity, slightly acid finish which is very pleasant. (1983)

⚷ Vignobles Michel Lateyron, 1 bis Quay des Violettes, 37400 Amboise; tel. 47 57 33 48 Y By appt.

CHATEAU DE LAUNAY**

◪ 15 ha 100000 [3] [D] ▮ ⫰

(82) 83

A pretty 'vieux rosé' colour, with a blend of flowers and fruit on the nose. Very fresh; has the vigour to accompany difficult dishes, particularly fish. (1983)

⚷ Vignobles Michel Lateyron, 1 Bis Quai des Violettes, 37400 Amboise; tel. 47 57 33 48 Y By appt. Closed Easter, 1 Nov.

LECLAIR PERE ET FILS *Cabernet***

■ 2 ha 6000 [2] [D] ▮ ⫰

An interesting wine with a light, carmine colour and a nose which is still closed in but has a hint of almonds. Good, long finish. (1983)

⚷ GAEC Leclair Père et Fils, La Foltière, Angé, 41400 Montrichard; tel. 54 32 09 72 Y Daily 8.00–20.00.

LECLAIR PERE ET FILS *Gamay**

■ 5 ha 9000 [2] [D] ▮ ⫰

(76) 79 81 82 83

The carmine colour is reinforced by the developing but still closed-in nose, and the light, fruity and vigorous finish, making an easy-to-drink wine. (1983)

⚷ GAEC Leclair Père et Fils, La Foltière, Angé, 41400 Montrichard; tel. 54 32 09 72 Y Daily 8.00–20.00.

MAURICE LELARGE *Cabernet Sauvignon**

■ 1 ha 4200 [2] [D] ▮

81 *(82)

Garnet colour. Powerful, spicy nose with a nuance of game. Rich. (1982)

⚷ Maurice Lelarge, Les Feuilleteries Nouy, 37270 St-Martin-le-Beau; tel. 47 50 61 31 Y No visitors.

CAVE CLAUDE LEVASSEUR

◪ 2000 [2] [D] ⦀ ⫰

Simple pink colour, and a blend of plums and peppers on the nose. Rather full, long-lasting, waxy taste. (1982)

⚷ Claude Levasseur, 38 Rue des Bouvineries, Husseau, 37270 Montlouis-sur-Loire; tel. 47 50 84 53 Y By appt. Closed 20 Aug.–10 Sept.

JEAN LOUET***

■ 2.5 ha 19000 [2] [D] ▮ ⫰

(82) [82] [83]

Rich ruby-red with scents of coffee and tobacco together with slight animal scent. Long on the palate, and the tannins blend well with the faintly spicy aromas of the nose. (1982) ✔ Touraine Blanc, Touraine Rosé, Touraine Sauvignon, Touraine Pineau de la Loire.

⚷ Jean Louet, 3 Rue de la Paix, Monthou-sur-Bièvre, 41120 Les Montgils; tel 54 44 04 54 Y By appt. Closed Sun. PM.

JACKY MARTEAU *Gamay***

■ 7 ha 50000 [2] [D] ▮ ⫰

82 (83)

A well-balanced wine combining a ruby colour, soft-fruit scents with a hint of flowers, and a powerful, long-lasting finish. ✔ Touraine Caber-

net Touraine Sauvignon.
🍷 Jean & Jacky Marteau, La Tesnière, Pouillé,
41110 St-Aignan; tel. 54 71 50 00 ⏳ By appt.

JACKY MARTEAU *Sauvignon*★★

☐	2ha	8000	② Ⓓ ▮ ↓

82 ⑧⑧

A typical, liquorice bouquet and straw-beige
colour introduces a dry, powerful and vigorous
wine which finishes long.
🍷 Jean & Jacky Marteau, La Tesniére, Pouillé,
41110 St-Aignan; tel. 54 71 50 00 ⏳ By appt.

JACKY MARTEAU *Cabernet*★★

▮	2ha	16000	② Ⓓ ▮ ↓

82 ⑧⑧

This wine has a good balance between its clear
ruby, carmine-tinted colour, its complex soft,
fruit aromas and its full, strong body.
🍷 Jean et Jacky Marteau, La Tesnière, Pouillé,
41110 St.-Aignan; tel. 54 71 50 00 ⏳ By appt.

JACKIE MASNIERE *Sauvignon*★★

☐	4ha	15000	② Ⓓ ▮ ↓

★76 ★82 ⑧⑧ ★83 ★84 ⑧⑧

Greenish-yellow colour. Subtle, flowery nose.
Balanced and very delicate on the palate. (1984)
✔ Touraine Rouge.
🍷 Jackie Masnière, Le Coteau, 41120 Monthou-
sur-Bievre; tel. 54 44 02 25 ⏳ By appt.

DOMAINE CHRISTIAN MAUDUIT

▱	2ha	15000	② Ⓓ ▮ ↓

Light, coppery-pink colour characteristic of the
grape variety. Dry and fruity, easy to drink;
vigorous and powerful, with developing aromas
of fading rose petals. (1983)
🍷 Christian Mauduit, La Meschinière, Mareuil-
sur-Cher, 41110 St-Aignan; tel. 54 75 15 80
⏳ Mon.–Sat. 8.00–12.00/14.00–20.00, Sun. 8.00/
12.00.

DOMAINE CHRISTIAN MAUDUIT★

▮	5ha	30000	② Ⓓ ▮ ↓

⑧⑧ ⑧⑧

Light carmine in colour with a well-developed
fruity, flowery nose. Tannic, full, easy to drink
and finishes well. (1983) ✔ Touraine Gamay,
Touraine Cabernet, Touraine Sauvignon, Touraine Pineau d'Aunis, Touraine Méthode Champenoise.
🍷 Christian Mauduit, La Meschinière, Mareuil-
sur-Cher, 41110 St-Aignan; tel. 54 75 15 80
⏳ Mon.–Sat. 8.00–12.00/14.00–20.00, Sun.
8.00–12.00.

DOMAINE CHRISTIAN MAUDUIT

▮	0.7ha	4000	② Ⓓ ▮ ↓

82 ⑧⑧ 83

The soft, red fruit scents already suggested by the
deep ruby hue make a powerful and tannic wine
which is still a bit young. (1982)
🍷 Christian Mauduit, La Meschinière, Mareuil-
sur-Cher, 41110 St-Aignan; tel. 54 75 15 80
⏳ Mon.–Sat. 8.00–12.00/14.00–20.00, Sun.
8.00–12.00.

ROBERT MESLIAND

○	2ha	6000	③ Ⓓ ↓

A straw-coloured wine with delicate and abundant mousse, characterized by a firm, supple and
lively attack, and by its young aromas ✔ Touraine
Sauvignon.
🍷 Robert Mesliand, Limeray 37400, Amboise;
tel. 47 30 11 15 ⏳ By appt.

ROBERT MESLIAND

▮	1.5ha	5000	② Ⓓ ▮ ⑪ ↓

The light ruby colour, leafy nose and palate, and
liquorice-flavoured fruitiness, all go to make up a
well-balanced, tannic and fairly easy to drink
wine, which is, however, still thin and very
young. (1982)
🍷 Robert Mesliand, Limeray 37400, Amboise;
tel. 47 30 11 15 ⏳ By appt.

CHATEAU MONTRESOR★★

▱	2.2ha	7500	② Ⓓ ▮ ↓

⑧⑧

Very light-pink colour. Seasoned nose that is
almost spicy and very delicate. The refinement
and originality of the aroma is confirmed on the
palate, which is still very young. Very distinguished rosé. (1983)
🍷 Michel Lateyron, 1 Bis Quai des Viollette,
37400 Amboise; tel. 47 57 33 48 ⏳ By appt.
Closed Easter, 1 Nov.

CONFEDERATION VIGNERON DE OISLY ET THESEE *Cabernet*★

▮	40ha	200000	② Ⓓ ▮ ↓

A perfectly balanced, easy to drink, quality wine
which is tannic and lingering to taste. Bright ruby
hue and animal nose of tobacco and capsicum.
(1983) Touraine Baronnie d'Aignan Rouge,
Touraine Baronnie d'Aignan Blanc Sec. Crémant
de Loire Baronnie d'Aignan.
🍷 Conf. Vig. de Oisly et Thésée, Cidex 112,
Oisly, 41700 Contres; tel. 54 79 52 88 ⏳ Daily
9.00–12.00/14.00–17.00.

CONFEDERATION VIGNERON DE OISLY ET THESEE *Sauvignon*★★

☐	100ha	700000	② Ⓓ ▮ ↓

⑧⑧ 83 ⑧⑧

A typically delicate dry wine, quite charming,
firm and fresh; distinguished by its straw-yellow
colour and good finish. (1983)
🍷 Conf. Vig. de Oisly et Thésée, Cidex 112,
Oisly, 41700 Contres; tel. 54 79 52 88 ⏳ Daily
9.00–12.00/14.00–17.00.

CONFEDERATION VIGNERON DE OISLY ET THESEE *Pineau de Loire*★★

☐	15ha	100000	③ Ⓓ ▮ ↓

⑧⑧ 82 83

An excellently well-balanced dry wine, remarkable for its finish and dominant quince flavour.
(1982)
🍷 Conf. Vig. de Oisly et Thésée, Cidex 112,
Oisly, 41700 Contres; tel. 54 79 52 88 ⏳ Daily
9.00–12.00/14.00–17.00.

CONFEDERATION VIGNERON DE OISLY ET THESEE *Gamay*★★

■ 50ha 350000 **2** **D** ▌ ⬗

81 82 83 🅱

Quite clear, ruby colour with a scent of warm, soft red fruits and a hint of rhubarb. Light to taste, well balanced, tannic and spicy, with a long finish. (1983)
↝ Conf. Vig. de Oisly et Thésee, Cidex 112, Oisly, 41700 Contres; tel. 54 79 52 88 ⏺ Daily 9.00–12.00/14.00–17.00.

PERCEVAL PERE ET FILS *Sauvignon*★

□ 5ha 25000 **2** **D** ▌ ⬗ ⬗

82 🅗

A wine with a fairly strong straw colour and typical Sauvignon fragrance. Full and powerful, but with a quite short finish. (1983)
↝ Perceval Père et Fils, GAEC du Clouzeau, Sassay, 41400 Contas; tel. 54 79 57 52 ⏺ Daily 9.00–12.00/14.00–17.00

COMTE DU PETIT THOUARS★

■ 12ha 20000 **2** **D** ⬗ ⬗

76 82 ★🅱 **84**

Full, young, intensely ruby coloured wine. Lingering aromas of capsicum and lightly spiced peony. (1983)
↝ Yves du Petit-Thouars, Ch. du Petit Thouars, 37000 St-Germain-sur-Vienne; tel. 47 95 96 40 ⏺ By appt.

RENE PINON *Cabernet*★★

■ 3.5ha 8000 **2** **D** ▌ ⬗ ⬗

🅖 🅱

Remarkable for its excellent ruby-red colour and smoky nose of soft red fruits, with a hint of peppers and spice. Lingers nicely on the palate. (1983)
↝ René Pinon, L'Ormeau, St-Julien-de-Chédon, 41400 Montrichard; tel. 54 32 03 69 ⏺ By appt.

FRANÇOIS PIRONNEAU★★

○ 1.5ha 10000 **3** **D** ▌ ⬗

Charming, straw-coloured, with tiny bubbles and faint mousse. Well-developed peach and lime aromas harmonize with good structure, which is true to type.
↝ François Pironneau, Le Bourg, Monteaux, 41150 Onzain; tel. 54 70 23 75. ⏺ By appt.

DOMAINE DU PRE SARON *Sauvignon*★

□ 4ha 30000 **2** **D** ▌ ⬗

🅗 **83**

The straw-yellow colour indicates a typical Sauvignon wine which is dry and quite vigorous. (1983) ✒ Touraine Gamay, Touraine Cabernet, Crémant de Loire.
↝ Guy Mardon, Oisly, 41700 Contres; tel. 54 79 52 87 ⏺ Daily 8.00–12.00/14.00–17.00.

DOMAINE DU PRE SARON *Cabernet*★

■ 2.5ha 12000 **2** **D** ▌ ⬗

🅖 🅱

Good, strong colour with a touch of ruby. Prune and red fruit scents blend with the tannins to produce a well-structured taste. (1983).
↝ Guy Mardon, Oisly, 41700 Contres; tel. 54 79 52 87 ⏺ Daily 8.00–12.00/14.00–19.00.

DOMAINE DE LA PRESLE *Gamay*★★

■ 24ha 80000 **2** **D** ▌ ⬗

Ruby-red colour. Nose of cooked peppers manifested in the rather vigorous palate, which nevertheless has good balance and length. (1983)
↝ Jean-Marie Penet, Dom. de la Presle, Oisly, 41700 Contres; tel. 54 79 52 65 ⏺ By appt.

JACQUES PREYS *Gamay*★

■ 25ha 90000 **2** **D** ▌ ⬗

82 ★83 ★84

Ruby red colour and developed nose. Balanced on the palate, with a spicy aroma suggesting a hint of coffee. Slightly astringent and quite smooth. (1984)
↝ Jacques Preys, Bois-Pontois, 41130 Meusnes, Selles-sur-Cher; tel. 54 71 00 34 ⏺ By appt.

JACQUES PREYS
Sauvignon 'Produit sur Pierre à Fusil'★★

□ 8ha 60000 **2** **D** ▌ ⬗

83 🅘

Pale-yellow colour with a flowery, quite developed nose. Good balance. (1984)
↝ Jacques Preys, Bois-Pontois, 41130 Meusnes, Selles-sur-Cher; tel. 54 71 00 34 ⏺ By appt.

DOMAINE DU PRIEURE★★

■ 2ha 10800 **2** **D** ⬗ ⬗

🅖 🅱

Good, strong ruby colour. Complex nose of peppers and blackcurrants. On the palate, full, quite tannic, and blends well with the nose. (1983) ✒ Touraine Sauvignon, Touraine Gamay, Touraine Cabernet, Touraine Chenin..
↝ Jean-Marc Gallou, Dom. du Prieuré, Valaire 41120 Les Montils; tel. 54 44 11 62 ⏺ By appt.

DOMAINE DU RHIN-DU-BOIS *Gamay*★

■ 5ha 30000 **3** **D** ▌ ⬗

80 81 82 🅚

The ruby colour and scent of soft red fruits introduce a well-balanced wine with a tannic, spicy body. (1983)
↝ Jean-Marie Jusselin, Dom. Rhin-du-Bois, 41230 Soings-en-Sologne; tel. 54 98 71 87 ⏺ Daily 9.00–12.00/14.00–17.00.

DOMAINE DU RHIN-DU-BOIS *Sauvignon*★

□ 3ha 18000 **3** **D** ▌ ⬗

80 81 82 🅚 **83 84**

Greeny-straw colour. The nose develops characteristic scents but has been cut off a bit short. Easy to drink, well-made and finishes powerfully. (1983)
↝ Jean-Marie Jousselin, Dom. du Rhin-du-Bois,

41230 Mur-de-Sobogne Soings-en-Sologne; tel. 54 98 71 87 ☎ Daily 9.00–12.00/14.00–17.00.

DOMAINE DES SABLONS
Pineau d'Aunis*

◩		1 ha	6500	**2** **D** ▦ ♨

⑦⑥ **78** **80** **81** *82 **82** *83

Average intensity of colour. Nose of bread and onions. Lightly acidic; thirst-quenching. Ideal on a sunny day. (1983)
☙ Jacques Delaunay, Dom. des Sablons, Pouille, 41110 St-Aignan; tel. 54 71 44 25 ☎ By appt.

JEAN-JACQUES SARD *Noble Joué****

◩		1 ha	60000	**2** **D** ⑪ ♨

80 ⑧② **83** **83**

A good-value wine; pink in colour, the nose dominated by peach, chestnut and aniseed. Finesse, elegance and freshness are well blended on the palate. (1983)
☙ Jean-Jacques Sard, La Chambrière, 37320 Esvres-sur-Indre; tel. 47 26 42 89 ☎ By appt.

ETIENNE SAULQUIN

☐		5 ha	10000	**2** **D** ⑪ ♨

Finesse in the gentle sparkle of this straw-coloured wine. Very little nose, but peach, lime and mineral scents do develop. Tangy, well made, full bodied.
☙ Etienne Saulquin, Athée-sur-Cher, 37270 Montlouis; tel 47 50 68 04 ☎ By appt.

ETIENNE SAULQUIN**

◼		5 ha	12000	**2** **D** ⑪ ♨

⑧② **82** **83**

Ruby colour. Bouquet of pepper, blackcurrants and coffee; complex aromas confirmed on the palate. Rich in tannin and rather supple. Lasts well in the mouth and should age well. (1982)
☙ Etienne Saulquin, Athée-sur-Cher, 37270 Montlouis; tel. 47 50 68 04 ☎ By appt.

GAEC SAUVETE *Sauvignon***

☐		1.8 ha	4000	**2** **D** ▦ ⑪ ♨

83 **83**

Very pronounced straw colour. Undeveloped nose suggesting crystallized fruits and light tobacco. Dry, tangy, well made; light and full of characteristic aromas. (1983)
☙ GAEC Sauvète, La Bocagerie, 41400 Monthou-sur-Cher; tel. 54 71 43 62 ☎ Mon.–Sat. 8.00–12.00/14.00–18.00.

GAEC SAUVETE *Mousseux**

○		1.5 ha	5000	**3** **D** ▦ ⑪ ♨

Delicate, gentle sparkle and straw colour. Full-bodied, lively and true to type on the palate. Apples, lemons and dried flowers predominate.
☙ GAEC Sauvète, La Bocagerie, 41400 Monthou-sur-Cher; tel. 54 71 43 62 ☎ Mon.–Sat. 8.00–12.00/14.00–18.00.

GAEC SAUVETE *Cabernet***

◼		1 ha	2000	**2** **D** ▦ ⑪ ♨

Beautiful, rich garnet-red colour. Complex nose with a leafy, fruity character. Well balanced, slightly spicy. Tannins have been developed to perfection. Good length in the mouth. (1983)
☙ GAEC Sauvète, La Bocagerie, 41400 Monthou-sur-Cher; tel. 54 71 43 62 ☎ Mon.–Sat. 8.00–2.00/14.00–18.00.

HUBERT SINSON**

◼		14 ha	20000	**2** **D** ▦

A well-balanced wine of a strong red hue, with a fresh, flowery nose. To taste, balanced and fruity, as well as velvety, with a firm background; a good finish. (1982) ✔ Valencay Dom. de la Maison Blanche.
☙ Hubert Sinson, Le Muza, Meusnes, 41130 Selles-sur-Cher; tel. 54 71 00 26 ☎ By appt.

J.-P. TROUVE**

◼		1 ha	2000	**2** **D** ▦ ⑪ ♨

78 **79** *82 *⑧③

Ruby-red colour, and rich, fruity aromas on the nose. Particularly successful for its appellation and vintage. (1983)
☙ J.-P. Trouve, St-Martin-le-Beau, 37270 Montlouis; tel. 47 60 63 62 ☎ By appt.

CLOSERIE DU VAU-DE-LA-LEU
Gamay**

◼		15 ha	90000	**2** **D** ▦ ♨

***64** *⑦⑥ ***78** *84

Brilliant ruby colour. Well-developed nose. Very fruity Gamay character on the palate and classic red-fruit aroma. Pleasant, refreshing and easy to drink. (1984)
☙ SCA du Vau-de-la-Leu, Chouzy-sur-Cisse, 4 41150 Onzain; tel. 54 20 72 99 ☎ No visitors.

CLOSERIE DU VAU-DE-LA-LEU
Pineau d'Aunis**

◩		4 ha	24000	**2** **D** ▦ ♨

***83** *⑧④ **84**

The Pineau d'Aunis, which always produces rosé, gives a distinctive type of wine with a peppery aroma. This Chouzy is a good example. Elegant floral nose, and somewhat pale, translucent colour, absolutely right for this Vin Gris style. Nicely proportioned on the palate with spicy aromas: a spring and summer wine to be served cool in the open air. (1984)
☙ SCA du Vau-de-la-Leu, Chouzy-our-Cisse, 41150 Onzain; tel. 54 20 72 99 ☎ Closed.

LE VIEUX CHAI *Gamay*

■ 3.5 ha 20000 **2 D ▪ ⌄**
⑧ 82

A powerful wine with a light carmine colour, and strength, fruitiness and spiciness on the palate. (1983)
➦ Jean-Claude Barbeillon, Oisly, 41700 Contres; tel. 54 79 54 75 ☎ Mon.–Sat. 8.00–20.00, Sun. by appt. Closed 15 Sept.–30 Oct.

LE VIEUX CHAI *Sauvignon***

□ 3 ha 20000 **2 D ▪ ⌄**
82 ⑧ 83

A straw-yellow coloured wine with a very pronounced scent of blackcurrant leaves. It has fullness, power and vigour, and a good long finish. (1983) ✔ Touraine Gamay, Touraine Côt, Pineau d'Aunis, Méthode Champenoise Rosé.
➦ Jean-Claude Barbeillon, Oisly, 41700 Contres; tel. 54 79 54 57 ☎ Mon.–Sat. 8.00–20.00, Sun. by appt. Closed 15 Sept.–30 Oct.

LE VIEUX CHAI

◪ 1 ha 4500 **2 D ▪ ⌄**
83

Pale, copper-pink colour, coupled with a fruity, fragrant nose. Dry, full wine with a slight firmness. (1983)
➦ Jean-Claude Barbeillon, Oisly, 41700 Contres; tel. 54 79 54 57 ☎ Mon.–Sat. 8.00–20.00, Sun. by appt. Closed 15 Sept.–30 Oct.

Touraine-Amboise

The Touraine-Amboise appellation vineyards (150 hectares) are situated on both banks of the Loire. The château, built in the fifteenth and sixteenth centuries, keeps vigil over the river near Clos-Lucé, where Leonardo da Vinci spent his final years. About 8000 hectolitres of wine are produced, mainly reds from Gamay blended with Côt and Cabernet. They are full, round, not overly tannic wines and, if predominantly from Côt and Cabernet, will age well. The white wines (3000 hectolitres), too, may keep well, depending on the year.

JACQUES BONNIGAL ET FILS
*Cuvée François 1er***

■ **2 D ⦀ ⌄**
81 81 *82

A ruby-coloured wine; well-developed nose scented with soft red fruits and new-mown hay. The same aromas are found on the palate, which is balanced, full bodied and quite powerful. Still a young wine, but has a very promising future. (1982)
➦ Jacques Bonnigal, 6 Rue D'enfer, Limeray 37400, Amboise; tel. 47 30 11 02 ☎ Daily 8.00–13.00/14.00–20.00.

JACQUES BONNIGAL ET FILS**

□ 3 ha 12000 **2 D ⦀ ⌄**
76 81 82 82 83

A straw-coloured wine with complex aroma, of peaches, honey and wax. Still very young but already powerful. Full and dry on the palate, and looks as if it will develop well. (1982)
➦ Jacques Bonnigal, 6 Rue d'Enfer, Limeray 37400, Amboise; tel. 47 30 11 02 ☎ Daily 8.00–13.00/14.00–20.00.

DUTERTRE *Cuvée François Ler***

■ 6 ha 32000 **2 D ⦀ ⌄**
74 78 *82 *83 *84

Good ruby colour. Fairly spicy nose with touch of the farmyard and hint of tobacco. Fairly powerful, tannic structure makes for a balanced wine. (1982) ✔ Touraine Amboise, Touraine Amoboise, Touraine Sauvignon, Touraine Crémant.
➦ MM. Dutertre et Fils, 20 Rue d'Enfer, 37530 Limeray; tel. 47 30 10 69 ☎ By appt.

DUTERTRE

■ 6 ha 32000 **2 D ⦀ ⌄**
74 78 *82 *83 *84

Young, clear, light, with a nose of plant aromas. Well-balanced on the palate, but a very tannic structure. (1982)
➦ MM. Dutertre et Fils, 20 Rue d'Enfer, 37530 Limeray; tel. 47 30 10 69 ☎ By appt.

DUTERTRE*

■ 6 ha 32000 **2 D ⦀ ⌄**
76 *80 *81 *⑧ *83 *84

Beautiful straw colour with nose of dried fruits and flowers. On the palate, fresh and firm, with aromas of apple and rose petals. (1981)
➦ MM. Dutertre et Fils, 20 Rue d'Enfer, 37560 Limeray; tel. 47 30 10 69 ☎ By appt.

DUTERTRE*

◪ 6 ha 32000 **2 D ⦀ ⌄**
⑧ *83 *84

Copper-pink colour, with a complex nose of plants and fruit. Charming and fresh on the palate, aromas of peaches and a hint of cocoa. (1983)
➦ MM. Dutertre et Fils, 20 Rue d'Enfer, 37530 Limeray; tel. 47 30 10 69 ☎ By appt.

DOMAINE DE LA GABILLERE**

■ 5 ha 36000 **2 D ▪ ⦀ ⌄**
*81 *82 *83 *83

Characteristic of Touraine: light in colour, with a floral nose and hint of new-mown hay. Light, well made, with a slightly spicy taste. (1983) ✔ Touraine Sauvignon, Touraine Primeur Gamay, Touraine Méthode Champenoise Blanc and Rosé, Crémant de Loire.
➦ LEP Viti. Dom. de la Gabillère, 13 Route de Bléré, 37400 Amboise; tel. 47 30 48 58 ☎ By appt.

YVES MOREAU *Réserve***

■ 6 ha 26000 **2 D ▪ ⌄**

Strong ruby-garnet colour; complex, high-toned bouquet. A very good wine, well-balanced and long-lasting, with tannins that blend perfectly

into the total composition. (1982) ✔ Touraine Sauvignon et Mousseux, Touraine Amboise Gamay et Assemblage Rouge, Touraine Mesland Gamay.
➤ Yves Moreau, 20 Route de Mesland, Cangey, 37400 Ambroise; tel. 47 30 09 93 ☎ By appt. Closed 20 Aug.–5 Sept.

YVES MOREAU★★

■	1 ha	4000	2 D 🍸 ⑪ �

An attractive light ruby colour; well-developed nose with scents of soft red fruit a hint of spices. To taste, this spiciness is accentuated. A fruity wine, well-balanced and well-structured. (1983)
☎ Yves Moreau, 20 Route de Mesland, Cangey, 37400 Amboise; tel. 47 30 09 03 ☎ By appt. Closed 20 Aug.–5 Sept.

YVES MOREAU★★

☑	0.6 ha	2600	2 D 🍸 ⑪ �
⑧② 83 🔳			

Pleasing to the eye, with a light fruity nose hinting of almond and ripe fruits. Dry, balanced, full and long on the palate. (1983) ✔ Touraine Sauvignon et Mousseux, Touraine Mesland Gamay, Touraine Amboise Gamay et Assemblage Rouge, Touraine Mesland Gamay.
➤ Yves Moreau, 20 Route de Mesland, Fleuray, 37400 Amboise; tel.47 30 09 93 ☎ By appt. Closed 20 Aug.–5 Sept.

MARCEL PERCEREAU *Gamay*★★

■	2.5 ha	3000	2 D 🍸 ⑪ �
81 ★82 ★🔳			

A typical wine with a lovely light ruby colour; blended scents, both animal and vegetable, on the nose, which is still a little closed-in. However, good body and tannin content make this a well-balanced, long-lasting wine. (1983) ✔ Touraine Amboise Rosé, Blanc Sec, Demi-Sec, Touraine Sauvignon, Touraine Méthode Champenoise Bl.Brut, Touraine Méthode Champenoise Rosé Sec.
➤ Marcel Percereau, 85 Rue de Blois, Limeray, 37400 Amboise; tel. 47 30 11 40 ☎ By appt.

MARCEL PERCEREAU *Cabernet*★★

■	0.5 ha	1500	2 D 🍸 ⑪ �

Light-coloured wine from the Cabernet grape. Well-balanced, with good length, it will improve still further if left to mature. (1983) ✔ Touraine Amboise Rosé, Blanc Sec, Demi-Sec, Touraine Sauvignon, Touraine Méthode Champenoise Blanc Brut, Touraine Méthode Champenoise Rosé Sec.
➤ Marcel Percereau, 85 Rue de Blois, Limeray, 37400 Amboise; tel. 47 30 11 40 ☎ By appt.

MARCEL PERCEREAU★★

☐	1.5 ha	1500	2 D 🍸 ⑪ �
81 ★82 ★⑧③			

Light straw-yellow colour with a complex nose of soft fruits and flowers, and an unexpected trace of menthol. A typical, dry, well-balanced and quite lively wine, which it will be a pleasure to drink for a long time. (1981) ✔ Touraine Amboise Rouge, Touraine Amboise Blanc Sec, Touraine Sauvignon, Touraine Méthode Champenoise.
➤ Marcel Percereau, 85 Rue de Blois, Limeray, 37400 Amboise; tel. 47 30 11 40 ☎ By appt.

ROLAND PLOU *Cabernet*★★

■	3 ha	14500	2 D 🍸 ⑪ �

Beautiful, shimmering ruby colour typical of the Cabernet grape. A nose hinting of raspberries, still backward but well balanced and full of flavour on the palate. The aroma is a complex combination of hot coffee and cherries, with a long finish of medlar fruit. (1983)
➤ Roland Plou, Chargé, 37400 Amboise; tel. 47 57 05 47 ☎ By appt.

ROLAND PLOU★★

☐	5 ha	25000	2 D 🍸 �

Straw-coloured wine, with well developed floral nose dominated by lilac and, strangely, rhubarb. Attractive, delicate, firm and lively on the palate with a good finish. (1983)
➤ Roland Plou, Chargé, 37400 Amboise; tel. 47 57 05 47 ☎ By appt.

ROLAND PLOU★

☑		15000	2 D 🍸 �

Beautiful pink colour. Nose of soft red fruits with hints of almonds and aniseed. Dry and firm, fresh and long in the mouth. Just right for quenching one's thirst. (1983)
➤ Roland Plou, Chargé, 37400 Amboise; tel. 47 57 05 47 ☎ By appt.

Touraine Azay-le-Rideau

The elegant Château Azay-le-Rideau gives its name to this appellation, covering 50 hectares on both banks of the Indre river. Production is predominantly white (1500 hectolitres) and the wines, made from the Chenin or Pineau Blanc de la Loire, are delicate yet quite long-lived. In addition, 1000 hectolitres of dry, refreshing red wine are made from the Grolleau.

ROBERT DENIS★★★

☑	1.5 ha	9000	D ⑪ �

Fine, pure rosé colour. Quite developed bouquet with a hint of strawberries. Balanced and rather full on the palate, complementing the aromas on the nose. (1983)
➤ Robert Denis, La Chapelle-St-Blaise, 37190 Cheille; tel. 47 43 36 57 ☎ By appt.

GASTON PIBALEAU★★

☑ 2ha 3000 ② D ⑪ ↓

㉘ 🏷 83 84

Beautiful pale pink colour, and quite reserved, delicate nose. On the palate, dry, well made and fresh, with a good finish. (1982)
➤ Gaston Pibaleau, Luré, 37190 Azay-le-Rideau; tel. 47 43 31 41 ☎ Daily 8.00–20.00.

GASTON PIBALEAU★★★

☐ 2ha 9600 ② D ⑪

🏷 ㉘ 84

Lovely straw colour. Pronounced and typical nose revealing a floral fragrance with hints of medlars, new-mown hay, lime and almond. Young and dry, nicely made and easy to drink; lasts well on the palate. (1982) ✔ Touraine Azay-le-Rideau Rosé, Touraine Gamay and Cabernet, Touraine Méthode Champenoise Blanc and Rosé.
➤ Gaston Pibaleau, Luré, 37190 Azay-le-Rideau; tel. 47 43 31 41 ☎ Daily 8.00–20.00.

Touraine-Mesland

The AOC area lies north of Chaumont on the east bank of the Loire, in the eastern part of Touraine. Its 200 hectares produce 10 000 hectolitres of red wine, mostly from the Gamay. The wines are not too tannic and have good structure and balance. The appellation also produces rosés (1000 hectolitres) and whites (13 000 hectolitres), both types being dry.

DOMAINE D'ARTOIS
Vieilles Vignes★★★

■ 4ha 192 000 ③ D ▮

★81 ★82 ★🏷 83

Delightful, strong deep-red, almost garnet, colour. Beefy and well made, with characteristic soft red-fruit aroma of the Touraine-Mesland grape. Lasts well on the palate. (1982) ✔ Touraine Mesland Blanc and Rouge, Touraine Sauvignon, Gris de Touraine Meslands, Touraine Crémant Extra Brut de la Morandière.
➤ M. Girault-Artois, 7 Quai des Violettes, 37400 Amboise; tel. 47 57 07 71 ☎ By appt.

CHATEAU GAILLARD★★

■ 6ha 60 000 ② D ▮ ↓

78 81 ㉘ 🏷 83 🏷

True to its type, with a light, bright colour and a leafy nose. Well-balanced, smooth, light and fruity. (1983) ✔ Touraine Primeur, Touraine Sauvignon, Gris de Touraine Mesland.
➤ Vincent Girault, Ch. Gaillard, Mesland, 41150 Onzain; tel. 54 70 27 14 ☎ Mon.–Fri. 9.00–12.00/ 14.00–19.00; Sat. 9.00–12.30. Closed second Sat. in Aug.–end Aug.

HOGU PERE ET FILS★

☑ 6ha 2000 ② ▮

★78 ★83

Unusual copper tinge to the colour. The nose is complex, at first lactic, then evolving into green almonds and new-mown hay. Although a little lively, it is well balanced, with good consistency and quite good finish. (1983)
➤ Hogu Père et Fils, Villesavoir-Choissy-sur-Cisse, 41150 Onzain; tel. 54 20 47 77 ☎ By appt.

DOMAINE DE LUSQUENEAU★★

■ 30ha 180 000 ② D ▮ ↓

73 76 80 ㉘ 🏷 ★83

Ruby-coloured and lovely to look at. Complex, well-developed nose blending leafy and farmyard scents. Full and well-balanced, with long-lasting taste. (1982) ✔ Touraine Mesland Gamay and Chenin, Touraine Méthode Champenoise Rosé and Blanc.
➤ Philippe Brossillon, Dom. de Lusqueneau, Mesland, 41150 Onzain; tel. 54 70 28 23 ☎ Daily 8.00–20.00.

CHATEAU DE MONTEAUX
Cuvée de l'Ambassadeur★★

■ 2.5ha 2000 ② D ⑪ ↓

㉘ 84 🏷

Bright colour with a fruity, spicy aroma. Slight harsh on the palate, but this is balanced by an overall lightness. A very fresh wine. (1984) ✔ Touraine Mesland, Touraine Mesland, Touraine Mesland, Touraine Mesland Sauvignon.
➤ E. de Grouy-Chanel, Ch. de Monteaux, 41150 Onzain; tel. 54 70 23 06 ☎ By appt. Closed Aug.

CHATEAU DE MONTEAUX★

☐ 12ha 10 000 ② D ⑪ ↓

㉘ 84

Fairly strong colour and well-developed nose reminiscent of beeswax. A fresh, dry wine with an aroma of roast almonds on the palate.
➤ E. de Crouy-Chanel, Ch. de Monteaux, 41150 Onzain; tel. 54 70 23 06 ☎ By appt. Closed Aug.

YVES MOREAU *Gamay★★*

■ 10ha 26 000 ② D ▮ ⑪ ↓

Honest ruby-red colour and typical nose suggesting leaves and farmyards. Well balanced and well made, with a pleasing freshness. Long-lasting unusual taste reminiscent of soft, red fruits. ✔ Touraine Sauvignon, Touraine Amboise Gamay, Touraine Amboise Rouge, Touraine Mousseux.
➤ Yves Moreau, 20 Route de Mesland, Cangey, 37400 Amboise; tel. 47 30 09 93 ☎ By appt. Closed 20 Aug.–5 Sept.

FRANCOIS PRIONNEAU★

■ 14ha 25 000 ② D ▮ ⑪ ↓

76 78 79 80 🏷 81 🏷 83

Good colour, typical of a 1982. Fairly powerful, balanced and easy to drink, with good body and aromas of soft red fruits. (1982)
➤ François Prionneau, Le Bourg, Monteaux, 41150 Onzain; tel. 54 70 23 75 ☎ By appt. Closed for harvest.

Bourgueil and St-Nicolas de Bourgueil

Still on the east bank of the Loire, Bourgueil is in the west of Touraine, next to Anjou. The Cabernet-Franc (or Breton) is the main variety of the 800 hectares of the appellation area. Its red wines have a certain refinement, with a well-balanced tannic structure which is more or less pronounced depending on the site – limestone-and-clay slope or gravel terrace. They can age very well indeed, and wines which have undergone a long fermentation may, in the best vintages (1947 or 1964, for example), keep for several decades. A few hundred hectolitres of dry rosé wine are also made. The wine-makers who belong to the cooperative in Bourgeuil usually raise their wines in their own cellars.

St-Nicolas-de-Bourgueil red wines are lighter, but otherwise similar to those of Bourgueil with respect to the grape varieties used and the techniques of vinification and maturing. About 30000 hectolitres of wine are produced from 400 hectares of AOC vineyard. The wines may be marketed under the Bourgueil appellation, although the reverse does not apply.

CLOS DE L'ABBAYE★★

■ 7ha 34000 ③ Ⓓ 🖩 🕪 ↓
78 81 ⑧ 82 83 84

Strong ruby colour and aromas of peppers, biscuits and spices. The tannin, while not too obvious, suggests that the wine will keep well. (1982) ✔ Bourgueil.
↦ GAEC de la Dime, Ave. Jean Causeret, 37140 Bourgueil; tel. 47 97 76 30 ☎ By appt ↦ Congrég. des Soeurs St-Martin.

MARCEL AUDEBERT★★

■ 10ha 42000 ④ Ⓓ 🖩 🕪 ↓
70 73 75 *76 *78 80 81 82 82

Lovely ruby-red colour with aromas of biscuit and liquorice. This wine is full bodied, with well-balanced tannin and will age well. (1982)
↦ Marcel Audebert, 37410 Mestigue; tel. 47 97 31 31 ☎ By appt.

DOMAINE HUBERT CALLOT-CALBRUN★★

■ 12ha 25000 ③ Ⓓ 🖩 ↓
73 74 75 *76 78 81 *82 *83

A pretty wine that has kept its youthful colour. Floral on the palate, with perfect balance and mature taste of tannin. (1981)
↦ GAEC Callot-Calbrun, La Hurolaie, Benais, 37140 Bourgueil; tel. 47 97 30 59 ☎ By appt.

DOMAINE DE LA CHANTELEUSERIE★★

■ 8.75ha 42000 ③ Ⓓ 🖩 🕪 ↓
64 76 78 81 *82 83 84

Good ruby colour; aromas of cherries and liquorice, with farmyard background, add to the finesse and balance of this wine. Quite concentrated tannin, which means that this wine will age well. (1982)
↦ Moïse Boucard, La Chanteleuserie, Benais, 37140 Bourgueil; tel. 47 97 30 20 ☎ By appt.

MARC DELAUNAY★★

■ 8ha 38000 ② Ⓓ 🕪 ↓
64 *81 *82 82 *83 83

Bright red colour and complex 'animal' nose with scents of cherry and peach. Well balanced and very dense on the palate, with youthful tannin. A perfect representative of its type. (1983) ✔ Chinon Rouge.
↦ Marc Delaunay, La Lande, 37140 Bourgueil; tel. 47 97 80 73 ☎ By appt.

CAVE DES ESVOIS★

■ 10ha 35000 ③ Ⓓ 🖩 🕪 ↓
76 *78 81 82 83

This Bourgueil is a lovely deep-red colour with a nose of biscuits, liquorice and rose petals. On the palate it is full and powerful, with well-balanced tannins and lingering, delicate aromas of sloe and coffee. (1982)
↦ Marc Mureau, Lossay, Restigné, 37140 Bourgueil; tel. 47 97 32 60 ☎ By appt.

DOMAINE DES GALLUCHES★★

■ 10ha 53000 ③ Ⓓ 🕪 ↓
⑦⑤ 76 77 78 79 80 82 83 84

Limpid, ruby colour. Quite developed nose reminiscent of coffee. Bold and characteristic of this vintage. Still young, but very promising. (1984)
↦ STEA Dom. des Regunières, Le Machet, Benais, 37140 Bourgueil; tel. 47 97 30 76 ☎ By appt.

DOMAINE DU GRAND CLOS★★

■ 9ha 48000 ③ Ⓓ 🕪 ↓
76 79 81 *82 83 84

Brilliant ruby colour and complex nose of peppers and biscuits with a farmyard background. A beautifully balanced, long wine with soft tannin. Should age well. (1982) ✔ Saint-Nicolas-de-Bourgueil, Bourgueil.
↦ MM. Audebert Père et Fils, Ave. Jean Causeret, 37140 Bourgueil; tel. 47 97 70 06 ☎ By appt.

DOMAINE HUBERT★★

■   11 ha   53 000   2 D ◖ ↓
76 78 80 ⑧⑴ 82 83 84

A first-rate example of its appellation. Deep red colour and well-developed nose combining animal and flowery aromas, with a hint of tobacco. On the palate, balanced, very full and long. Will keep well. (1982)
↝ Robert Caslot, La Hurolaie, Benais, 37140 Bourgueil; tel. 47 97 30 59 ☎ By appt ↝ Robert Caslot-Galbrun

JEAN MOREAU-DUGIE★

■   4 ha   12 000   3 D ◖ ↓
★80 ★81 ★82 82 ★83

Fairly strong colour but subtle nose. On the palate, balanced and softly tannic, with characteristic Bourgueil aroma and persistence. (1982)
↝ Jean Moreau Dugie, Rue Basse, Restigne, 37140 Bourgueil; tel. 47 97 33 17 ☎ By appt.

REGIS MUREAU★

■   5 ha   30 000   4 D ◖ ↓
83 ★84

Ruby-coloured wine, clearly showing its time in cask. A hint of cherry on the nose, and power, balanced and great persistence on the palate, all typical of its appellation. (1983)
↝ Régis Mureau, La Gaucherie, Ingrandes-de-Touraine, 37140 Bourgueil; tel. 47 96 97 60 ☎ By appt.

DOMAINE DES OUCHES★★

■   7 ha   34 000   3 D ◖ ↓
69 75 76 78 81 ★⑧② 82 ★83

A balanced and powerful wine, distinguished by its ruby colour, scent of mown hay and its good body. Aged in oak; certainly worth laying down. (1982)
↝ Paul Gambier, Fontenay, Ingrandes-de-Touraine, 37140 Bourgueil; tel. 47 96 98 77 ☎ By appt.

PAUL POUPINEAU★★

■   8 ha   31 000   3 D ▮ ◖ ↓
75 76 81 82 83

Ruby colour and delicate nose combining aromas of peppers, cherries and fresh flowers. Beautifully balanced, full and long. (1983)
↝ Paul Poupineau, Le Bourg, Benais, 37140 Bourgueil; tel. 47 97 30 30 ☎ By appt.

DOMAINE DES RAGUENIERES★★

■   12.5 ha   65 000   3 D ◖ ↓
⑥④ 76 78 80 81 82 83

Medium-intense cherry colour; a good wine, with a complex nose of marc, raspberry and pepper. Well balanced and very characteristic of the appellation, it promises a harmonious maturity. (1983)
↝ SCEA Dom. des Raguenières, Le Machet, Benais, 37140 Bourgueil; tel. 47 97 30 76 ☎ By appt.

Chinon

The AOC Chinon vineyards (800 hectares) are located within the triangle formed by the confluence of the Vienne and the Loire rivers. They lie on south-facing slopes around the medieval town. The Cabernet-Franc produces an average of 55 000 hectolitres of fine, long-lived red wines. A very small amount of white Chinon is produced (250 hectolitres); it is an unusual wine, normally dry, but may in some years be faintly sweet.

GUY CAILLE★★★

◲   12 ha   2500   2 D ▮ ◖ ↓
⑧③ 84

Beautiful copper colour; well-developed nose, fine and elegant with a hint of sloes. Smooth, delicate and youthfully persistent on the palate. More wines like this one, please! (1984)
↝ Guy Caillé, 37500 Panzoult; tel. 47 58 53 16 ☎ By appt.

DOMAINE RENE COULY
Clos de l'Echo★★

■   13 ha   65 000   4 D ▮ ◖ ↓
78 79 ★81 81 ★82 ⑧③ 83 84

Beautiful, bright ruby colour, with flavours of prune and pimento over a spicy aroma. A full wine with delicate tannic structure, only just beginning to open up; with further age will develop into a perfect example of its type. A potentially great bottle. (1981)
↝ Couly Dutheil, 12 Rue Diderot, 37502 Chinon; tel. 47 93 05 84 ☎ By appt.

DOMAINE RENE COULY
Madeleine Baronnie★★

■   4 D ↓
★78 ★⑦⑨ 79 ★82

A blend of the best vintages, which shows in the brilliant ruby colour and the well-developed aromas of soot, peony, pimentoes and violet, which are balanced by a fullness on the palate. The tannin is still young, allowing for even further improvement. (1982)
↝ Couly Dutheil, 12 Rue Diderot, 37502 Chinon; tel. 47 93 05 84 ☎ By appt.

DOMAINE RENE COULY★★

■   15 ha   80 000   3 D ▮ ◖ ↓
78 79 81 ★82 82 83 84

Lively ruby colour and biscuity nose combining scents of cherries and pimentoes. Elegant and well-balanced on the palate, with firm and flow-

ing qualities characteristic of the light, fine type of Chinon wine. (1983)
🛒 Couly Dutheil, 12 Rue Diderot, 37502 Chinon; tel. 47 93 05 84 ⊺ By appt.

CLOS DE LA DIOTERIE
Cuvée des Varennes★★

■   3.5 ha   12000   3 D ⦀ ↓
⑦⑥ ★78 ★81 ★82 83 84

An elegant harmony has been achieved between the ruby colour, the bouquet of flowers and soot, and the soft firmness of its flowing and lively structure. A youthful wine which is a perfect example of those grown on the left bank of the Vienne. (1984)
🛒 Charles Joguet, Clos de la Dioterie, Sazilly, 37220 L'Ile-Bouchard; tel. 47 58 55 53 ⊺ No visitors.

CLOS DE LA DIOTERIE
Vieilles Vignes★★

■   2.5 ha   9000   3 D ⦀ ↓
⑦⑥ ★78 ★82 84

This young, bright-red wine is already showing its paces. Lively fullness on the palate, excellent astringency and authentic Chinon character. (1984) ✔ Chinon Clos de la Cure Jeunes Vignes, Chinon Clos du Chêne Vert, Chinon Varenne du Grand Clos.
🛒 Charles Joguet, Clos de la Dioterie, Sazilly, 37220 L'Ile Bouchard; tel. 47 58 55 53 ⊺ No visitors.

NICOLAS★★

■   90 000   3 ■

Light in colour for this vintage. Fruity, youthful nose, but the palate shows that the wine has yet to achieve real balance. (1984)
🛒 Ets Nicolas, 2 Rue Valmy, 94220 Charenton; tel. 01 37 59 20 ⊺ No visitors.

DOMAINE DE LA NOBLAIE★★

■   8 ha   25 000   2 D ⦀ ↓
⑦⑥ 82 ★83 84

Brilliant ruby-red colour, with aromas of peony and liquorice. A fine, elegant wine, still very young, which will age well in the bottle. (1983)
🛒 Pierre Manzagol, Dom. la Noblaie, Ligré, 37500 Chinon; tel. 47 93 10 96 ⊺ By appt.

DOMAINE DE LA NOBLAIE★★

☐   8 ha   4000   2 D ⦀ ↓
⑦⑥ 82 ★83 84

An original wine with a well-developed nose. On the palate it is floral with hints of liquorice. Dry and full with a long finish. (1983)
🛒 Pierre Manzagol, Dom. la Noblaie, Ligré, 37500 Chinon; tel. 47 93 10 96 ⊺ By appt.

DOMAINE DE LA NOBLAIE★★

◪   8 ha   5000   2 D ⦀ ↓
⑦⑥ 83 84

Brilliant pale, pink colour, almost 'oeil de perdrix'. Aromas of bees wax, peony and liquorice on the nose, all confirmed on the palate with an additional hint of sloes. Dry, fruity and lively with good length. (1983)

🛒 Pierre Manzagol, Dom. la Noblaie, Ligré, 37500 Chinon; tel. 47 93 10 96 ⊺ By appt.

PLOUZEAU★

■   3 ha   10 000   3 D ■ ↓
★82 82 ★83

An extremely harmonious, ruby-coloured wine with a bouquet of red fruit followed by a good balance of astringency and body on the palate. A perfect example of the Chinon appellation. (1982)
🛒 Pierre Plouzeau, 37120 Razinnes; tel. 47 93 16 34 ⊺ By appt.

DOMAINE OLGA RAFFAUT★★

■   15 ha   70 000   3 D ■ ⦀

Beautiful crimson colour. Complex aroma of leather, prunes and peppers. Elegant tannin and silky structure of natural distinction. Fairly persistent taste. Should mature well. (1981)
🛒 Olga Raffaut, Roguinet, 37420 Savigny-en Evron; tel. 47 58 42 16 ⊺ No visitors.

DOMAINE DU RAIFAULT★★

■   17 ha   96 000   3 D ⦀ ↓
★80 ★81 ★⑧②

Biscuit-flavoured wine with a strong red colour. On the palate it shows power and promise, while the tannin suggests that it will keep well. (1982)
✔ Touraine Cépage Gamay grape.
🛒 Raymond Raffault, Le Raifault, Savigny-en-Véron, 37420 Avoine; tel. 47 58 44 01 ⊺ By appt. Closed Sun.

DOMAINE DU RONCEE★★

■   10 ha   52 000   3 D ■ ↓
76 82 82 ★83 84

A bright ruby colour typical of the appellation with a very firm nose reminiscent of pimento. Suitable for laying down. (1982)
🛒 *Mme* Anne-Marie Donabella, Dom. du Roncée, 37270 Panzoult; tel. 47 58 53 01 ⊺ No visitors.

CLOS DU SAUT-AU-LOUP★

■   18 ha   87 000   3 D ■ ↓
76 78 79 81 81 ⑧② ★83 84

A fine combination of beautiful, shimmering, deep ruby-red colour and nose of peaches and apricots. Well balanced on the palate, quite delicate and easy to drink. (1983)
🛒 Jean-Marie Dozon, Clos du Saut-du-Loup, Ligré, 37500 Chinon; tel. 47 93 26 38 ⊺ By appt.

SPELTY★

■   10 ha   22 000   3 D ⦀ ↓
★71 ★76 ★79 ★82 83 84

Very clear, pale ruby colour, with scents of pepper and peonies on the nose. Well-balanced on the palate, combining a lively, astringent structure with an easy-to-drink quality. A good regional wine. (1983)
🛒 Gérard Spelty, Le Bourg, Cravant-les-Coteaux, 37500 Chinon; tel. 47 93 08 38.

St-Nicolas-de-Bourgeuil

DOMAINE DU BOURG★★

■   12ha   60000   3 D ⦀ ⌀

61 62 64 67 70 71 74 75 76 77 78 80 81

Brilliant ruby colour and floral nose of peach and roses. Perfectly balanced on the palate, with lovely tannins and aromas of tobacco, coffee and peach. This lively wine is still young and will age well.
✚ Jean-Paul Mabileau, Le Bourg, 37140 St-Nicolas-de-Bourgueil; tel. 47 97 82 02 ⲧ By appt.

DOMAINE DE LA CAILLARDIERE★★

■   12ha   60000   3 D ⦀ ⌀

★⑧⑴ **81 82 83**

Still young and full of promise. On the nose, flowery with touch of prune. On the palate, gentle tannin perfectly complements the balance. (1981)
✚ James Morrisseau, La Caillardière, St-Nicolas-de-Bourgueil, 37140 Bourgueil; tel. 47 97 75 40 ⲧ By appt.

LA CHEVALLERIE★★

■   5ha   30000   3 D ⦀ ⌀

76 79 81 ★⑧⑵ **83 83** 84

Very brilliant crimson colour, with a nose of soft red fruits with a farmyard background. Delicate and well balanced on the palate, and an aroma reminiscent of rose petals. (1983)
✚ MM. Audebert Père et Fils, Ave. Jean Causeret, 37140 Bourgueil; tel. 47 97 70 06 ⲧ By appt.

DOMAINE DE CHEVRETTE
Jeunes Vignes★★

■   12ha   60000   3 D ▊ ⌀

76 78 81 ★**83 83** 84

Ruby colour, with a nose of flowers and soft fruits. Fresh, yet warm on the palate, showing a good balance of tannins. Full of life. (1983)
✚ Joel Taluau, Dom. de Chevrette, 37140 St-Nicolas-de-Bourgueil; tel. 47 97 78 79 ⲧ By appt.

DOMAINE DE CHEVRETTE
Vieilles Vignes★★

■   3ha   12000   3 D ⌀ ▊

75 76 78 **79 80 82 83 83**

Lovely ruby colour and biscuity nose with scents of pears and sloes. Full and powerful on the palate, with firm tannic structure and beautifully persistent aromas of prunes and cherries in brandy. This wine will keep well and is definitely worth waiting for. (1983)
✚ Joel Taluau, Dom. de Chevrette, 37140 St-Nicolas-de-Bourgueil; tel. 47 97 78 79 ⲧ By appt.

MAX COGNARD★★

■   0.5ha   34000   3 D ⦀ ⌀

75 76 79 81 ⑧⑵ **82 83 83**

Scintillating ruby colour, with scents of peony heightened by blackcurrant and a musky note. Balanced on the palate, with well-structured tannins and the same aromas as the nose with the addition of sloe. A persistent wine for its age, and well worth laying down.
✚ Max Cognard, Dom. de Chevrette, 37140 St-Nicolas-de-Bourgueil; tel. 47 97 76 78 ⲧ By appt.

MAX COGNARD★★

☑   6.5ha   2000   2 D ⦀ ⌀

79 82 83 **83**

A beautiful old rose colour with a fairly well-developed aroma of peaches. Dry, lively and balanced on the palate, with a long finish: a good example of its appellation. (1983)
✚ Max Cognard, Dom. de Chevrette, 37140 St-Nicolas-de-Bourgueil; tel. 47 97 76 78 ⲧ By appt.

LA COTELLERAIE★★

■   13ha   60000   3 D ▊ ⦀ ⌀

★**82** ★**83 83**

Lively colour and fresh nose; characteristic aromas on the palate, which is rich in elegant tannins. (1983)
✚ Claude Vallée, La Cotelleraie, St-Nicolas-de-Bourgueil; tel. 47 97 75 53 ⲧ 8.00–13.00/14.00–19.30; closed Sun.

DOMAINE DU FONDIS★★

■   17ha   85000   2 D ▊ ⦀ ⌀

56 59 74 **76** 78 82 ⑧⑵ **83**

Light cherry-red colour; scents of peony, with a fine tannic structure on the palate. Flowing, powerful and elegant, with a lingering finish and good ageing potential. (1983)
✚ Pierre Jamet, Gaec du Fondis, 37140 St-Nicolas-de-Bourgueil; tel. 47 97 75 02 ⲧ By appt.

VIGNOBLE DE LA JARNOTERIE★

■   8ha   20000   3 D ▊ ⦀

★74 ★75 ⑺⑹ ★78 **84**

A pleasant and floral wine with a pale but bright colour. On the palate it is full, with good tannins and a distinctive style. (1984)
✚ Jean-Claude Mabileau, La Jarnotie, 37140 St-Nicolas-de-Bourgueil; tel. 47 97 75 49 ⲧ By appt.

NICOLAS★

■   100000   3 ⦀

Typically light-coloured 1984 with red-fruit nose; very closed-up on the palate; needs time to round out. (1984)
✚ Ets Nicolas, 2 Rue Valmy, 94220 Charenton; tel. 01 37 59 20 ⲧ No visitors.

CLOS DES QUARTERONS★

■   20ha   96000   2 D ⦀ ⌀

★**82 82** ★**83 83**

Lively colour; aroma of acacia on the nose and floral and mineral fragrances on the palate. Well balanced, with gentle tannin and good persistence. (1982)
✚ MM. Amirault, Close des Quarterous, St-Nicolas-de-Bourgueil, 37140 Bourgueil; tel. 47 97 75 25 ⲧ Mon.–Sat. 8.00–20.00.

CLOS DU VIGNEAU★★

■   18ha   95000   3 D ⦀ ⌀

55 59 64 69 ★71 ★74 ★75 ★76 82 ⑧⑶ **83**

Typical terroir character for this clear, bright-red wine. Very well-developed nose of peony and roses, with hints of pepper and candied fruits. Elegant tannic palate, with aromas of tobacco and cherry. This wine is a perfect example of its

appellation, and will age well. (1983)
⊶ Anselme et Marc Jamet, Clos du Vigneau, 37140 St-Nicolas-de-Bourgueil; tel. 47 97 75 10.

Montlouis

The area of this appellation (300 hectares) is bounded by the Loire to the north, the Forest of Amboise to the east, and the outskirts of Tours to the west. A few vines are planted south of the river Cher, in the region of St-Martin-le-Beau. The clay-limestone soils, planted with Chenin or Pineau Blanc de la Loire, produce 1000 hectolitres of white wine with plenty of finesse, which may be dry or sweet, still or sparkling. Like the wines of Vouvray, they improve with some bottle age.

CLAUDE BOUREAU**

□ 2ha 4800 ❷ Ⓓ ⦀ 🌡
(69) **70 76 81 82** ■83

Limpid, straw-coloured, lightly pétillant. Quite intense nose, characteristic of the appellation. Balanced, full bodied and fleshy, and still youthful; very successful for its vintage. (1983)
⊶ Claude Boureau, St-Martin-le-Beau, 37270 Montlouis; tel. 50 61 39 𝐈 By appt.

JEAN CHAUVEAU*

□ 3ha 18000 ❷ Ⓓ ⦀ 🌡
76 78 ■78 (82) **83**

Green-yellow colour. Fairly weak nose, but quite balanced on the palate and should become smoother with age. (1983)
⊶ Jean Chauveau, 19 Route de Tours, St-Martin-le-Beau, 37270 Montlouis; tel. 47 50 66 97 𝐈 By appt.

JEAN CHAUVEAU**

○ 4ha 22000 ❸ Ⓓ ⦀ 🌡

Straw-yellow wine with a flowery nose and a slight sparkle.
⊶ Jean Chauveau, 19 Route de Tours, St-Martin-le-Beau, 37270 Montlouis; tel. 47 50 66 97 𝐈 By appt.

J. ET M. COURTEMANCHE**

□ 2ha 96000 ❷ Ⓓ ⦀ 🌡
(59) ***70 71 *76 *78 *82** ■82

Pale-yellow colour with a developed nose of grilled almonds and herbal tea. Will age well. (1982)
⊶ J.etM.Courtemanche,15Rued'Amboise,37270 Montlouis, St-Martin-le-Beau; tel. 47 50 61 68 𝐈 By appt.

GUY DELETANG ET FILS***

□ 16ha 7000 ❷ Ⓓ ▮ 🌡
82 83 ■83

Lovely golden straw-colour with delicate floral fragrance containing traces of jasmine. Well made, full bodied and charming, with a good balance between stability and liveliness. Should mature very nicely. (1983)
⊶ Guy Deletang et Fils, St-Martin-le-Beau, 37270 Montlouis; tel. 47 50 67 25 𝐈 Mon.–Sat. 10.00–12.00/14.00–17.00.

GUY DELETANG ET FILS***

○ 16ha ❸ Ⓓ ▮ 🌡

Light pétillance with a lovely yellow-green colour. Distinct appley nose with a hint of flowers. On the palate, well balanced and well made, young and soft, with an extra hint of bergamot. Extremely good finish.
⊶ Guy Deletang et Fils, St-Martin-le-Beau, 37270 Montlouis; tel. 47 50 67 25 𝐈 Mon.–Sat. 10.00–12.00/14.00–17.00.

JEAN GUESTAULT*

□ 2ha 6000 ❷ Ⓓ ▮ 🌡
76 79 (81) ■81 **84**

Green-yellow colour and lightly acidic nose. Flowery aroma and hint of bitter almonds. Still young. (1984)
⊶ Jean Guestault, St-Martin-le-Beau, 37270 Montlouis; tel. 47 50 25 52 𝐈 By appt.

JEAN GUESTAULT**

□ 3ha 12000 ❷ Ⓓ ▮ 🌡
76 79 81 82 83 (84) ■84

Straw-yellow colour. Vegetable aroma with a prevalent nuance of crusty bread. Balanced and gentle. One of the year's successes. (1984)
⊶ Jean Guestault, St-Martin-le-Beau, 37270 Montlouis; tel. 47 50 25 52 𝐈 By appt.

ALAIN JOULIN★★

○		4200	**2** **D** ⑴ ↓

64 76 ⑧₂ **84**

Slightly pétillant. Jolly wine with nice straw-yellow colour and flowery nose, which combines the aromas of acacia, honey and mint. Balanced and lively palate, slightly bitter, but this is typical. Should smooth out with age. (1984)
↖ Alain Joulin, 2 Rue Traversiere, St-Martin-le-Beau, 37270 Montlouis, tel. 47 50 28 49 Ⴈ By appt.

MAURICE LELARGE★★

☐	5 ha	4900	**2** **D** ▪ ↓

81 ⑧₂ **8₂**

Limpid, light colour with green reflections. Average nose with a hint of burnt toast. Balanced, gentle and full taste, with slight sparkle. Aroma could still develop further. Quite mature and characteristic of its vintage. (1982)
↖ Maurice Lelarge, Les Feuilleteries Nouy, Montlouis 37270 St-Martin-le-Beau; tel. 47 50 61 31 Ⴈ Mon.–Fri. 9.00–19.00.

CAVE CLAÛDE LEVASSEUR
Méthode Champenoise★★

○	2 ha	10000	**3** **D** ⑴ ↓

76 81 82 8₂ 83

Golden straw colour and cheerful sparkle. Balanced, powerful, firm and long in the mouth. A charming wine. (1982) ✔ Montlouis Nature 1981/1982/1983, Montlouis Nature Blanc Sec, Demi-Sec Touraine.
↖ Claude Levasseur, 38 Rue des Bouvineries, Husseau, 37270 Montlouis-sur-Loire; tel. 47 50 84 53 Ⴈ By appt. Closed 20 Aug.–10 Sept.

CAVE CLAUDE LEVASSEUR★★

☐	4 ha	16000	**2** **D** ⑴ ↓

76 81 82 8₂ 83

A pretty wine of great finesse. Fresh hay and stocks on the nose; well-balanced on the palate, with a good finish. (1982)
↖ Claude Levasseur, 38 Rue des Bouvineries, Husseau, 37270 Montlouis-sur-Loire; tel. 47 50 84 53 Ⴈ By appt. Closed 20 Aug.–10 Sept.

DANIEL MOSNY★★

☐	12 ha	10000	**3** ⑴ ↓

81 82 ⑧₃

Balanced and harmonious wine with a light-yellow colour. Fairly developed nose dominated by a hint of grape juice. Leaves a pleasant impression, full of freshness. ✔ Montlouis Methode Champenoise, Touraine Rouge, Rosé et Sauvignon.
↖ Daniel Mosny, 37270 Montlouis, St-Martin-le-Beau; tel. 47 50 61 84 Ⴈ By appt.

Vouvray

Lengthy ageing – in cellar and in bottle – is required to bring out all the qualities of Vouvray wines. These distinguished wines come from a growing area (2000 hectares) north of the Loire that is divided by the River Brenne

and cut off to the north by the A10 autoroute. The white Touraine grape variety, Chenin (Pineau de la Loire), is used to make 50000 hectolitres of fine, still white wine which varies from dry to medium-sweet depending on the year; the same variety is also used to produce 40000 hectolitres of very rich sparkling wines. Both styles keep very well, although the sparkling wines can be drunk quite young. The still wines go well with fish and cheese, especially goat's cheese; light, delicate dishes or puddings are the most satisfactory partners for the sparkling wines.

BERTIER PICHOT

☐	12 ha		**3** **D** ⑴

⑤₉ **64** ⑦₀ **76** 78 79 ★**81** ★82 ★83

Pale-yellow colour; young nose; immature on the palate. To lay down. (1983)
↖ Bertier Pichot, Coteau de la Biche, 37210 Vouvray; tel. 47 52 16 64 Ⴈ By appt.

CHATEAU DES BIDAUDIERES★

○			**4** **D** ▪ ↓

★**81** ★⑧₂ **8₂**

Persistent mousse and fruity, but rather undeveloped, nose. Fairly long and balanced on the palate. (1982)
↖ Bernard Avignon, Dom. des Bidaudieres, 37210 Vouvray; tel. 47 52 78 29 Ⴈ By appt.

BERNARD BONGARS★★

○	6 ha	30000	**2** **D** ⑴ ↓

⑦₆ ★78 ★**7₀** ★**8₃**

Limpid, straw-yellow colour. Fruity, developed aroma strongly reminiscent of figs. Fairly long and fragrant in the mouth. Now at its peak. (1982)
↖ Bernard Bongars, Noizay, 37210 Vouvray; tel. 47 52 11 64 Ⴈ By appt.

CLOS DU BOURG★★★

☐	6 ha	25000	**3** **D** ⑴

70 ⑦₆ **81** ★82 **8₃**

Noteworthy for its straw colour, full bouquet redolent of dried fruits, and its well-balanced, supple and fresh taste, which lasts well on the palate. (1983)
↖ Gaston Huet, Dom. du Haut-Lieu, 37210 Vouvray; tel. 47 52 78 87 Ⴈ By appt. Closed Sun. and public holidays.

MICHEL BRUNET

○	7 ha	3000	**3** **D** ▪ ⑴ ↓

Pale yellow. Still young, with persistent bubbles and immature nose. Slightly fruity on the palate; balanced and honest overall.
↖ Alain Ferrand, Angibault, Vernou-sur-Brenne. 37210 Vouvray; tel. 47 52 14 78 Ⴈ By appt.

CHEVREAU-VIGNEAU★★

○ 14ha 28000 **3** **D** ▪ ⊕ ⬇
64 **69 71 76 81** ★83

Fine bubbles go well with the straw colour. Peach, apricot and lime fragrances precede a full, mellow taste. (1983) ✔ Vouvray Méthode Champenoise.
➛ *MM.* Chevreau-Vigneau, 4 Rue du Clos-Baglin, Chançay, 37210 Vouvray; tel. 47 52 93 22 ⊥ By appt.

CHEVREAU-VIGNEAU★★

○ 15ha 60000 **3** **D** ▪ ⊕ ⬇
64 **69 71 76 81** ★83

Fine mousse and straw colour, with the scents of peach, apricot and lime, make a fresh and young wine with good body. (1983)
➛ *MM.* Chevreau-Vigneau, 4 Rue du Clos-Baglin, Chançay, 37210 Vouvray; tel. 47 52 93 22 ⊥ By appt.

BERNARD COURSON
Blanc Demi-sec★

□ 1ha 5000 **3** **D** ⊕ ⬇
⑦⑥ ★78 ★80 ★**80** ★81 ★82 ★83

Strong straw colour with scents of new-mown hay and flowers; charming and well balanced on the palate, with the delicate flavour of new honey. Allow to mature. (1982)
➛ Bernard Courson, Les Patys, 37410 Vouvray; tel. 47 52 73 74 ⊥ By appt.

BERNARD COURSON★★

○ 2ha 18000 **3** **D** ▪ ⬇
⑦⑥ ★78★ **80** ★81 **82** ★⑧⑧

Well balanced, with a golden straw colour, tiny persistent bubbles and a floral and fruity nose, predominantly quince. Well made and easy to drink; true to its type, with a good finish. (1982)
➛ Bernard Courson, Les Patys, 37210 Vouvray; tel. 47 52 73 74 ⊥ By appt.

BERNARD COURSON★★

□ 6ha 30000 **3** **D** ⊕
★⑦⑥ ★**76** 78 **80** 81 82 83

Lovely golden colour and complex nose of fruits and nuts. Powerful and well balanced; perfectly made, with a good finish. (1976)
➛ Bernard Courson, Les Patys, 37210 Vouvray; tel. 47 52 73 74 ⊥ By appt.

ALAIN FERRAND
Méthode Champenoise★★

○ 10ha 12000 **3** **D** ▪ ⬇
⑧⓪ **82**

Straw coloured with delicate, light mousse and scent of red fruits, with a farmyard quality on the palate. Powerful but well made and full bodied. Lingers beautifully on the palate, a marvellous example of its type.
➛ Alain Ferrand, Angibault, Vernou-sur-Brenne, 37210 Vouvray; tel. 47 52 14 78 ⊥ By appt.

ALAIN FERRAND★★

□ 10ha 60000 **2** **D** ▪ ⊕ ⬇
★78 ★79 ★⑧⓪ ★82 ★83 ★**83**

Straw coloured, good to drink being well balanced and fairly lively. Does not give much away at present on the nose. (1983) ✔ Vouvray Pétillant and Demi-sec, Vouvray Méthode Champenoise Brut and Demi-sec.
➛ Alain Ferrand, Angibault, Vernou-sur-Brenne, 37210 Vouvray; tel. 47 52 14 78 ⊥ By appt.

ALAIN FERRAND★★

○ 8000 **3** **D** ⊕ ⬇

Pale straw coloured with a steady pétillance backed by a rather reticent mineral and floral nose. Well-structured, with a mild, soft taste.
➛ Alain Ferrand, Angibault, Vernou-sur-Brenne, 37210 Vouvray; tel. 47 52 14 78 ⊥ By appt.

ANDRE FOUQUET★★

□ 18ha 25000 **3** **D** ▪ ⊕ ⬇
⑤⑤ **59** 64 70 75 76 80 ★81 ★82 ★**83**

Handsome, fleshy and more gentle than dry. Pretty golden colour. Complex aroma of acacia, honey and buttered bread. Has aged well. (1983)
➛ Andre Fouquet, 47 Rue Bambetta, 37210 Vouvray; tel. 47 52 70 23 ⊥ By appt.

BERNARD FOUQUET★

○ 18ha 25000 **3** **D** ▪ ⊕ ⬇

Pretty, straw-coloured sparkling wine, with a delicate and plentiful mousse which brings out a strong aroma of nuts on the nose. This in turn evolves on the palate as apples and redcurrants. Balanced and interesting, but could be livelier. (1982)
➛ Bernard Fouquet, 17 Rue Gambetta, 37210 Vouvray; tel. 47 52 61 55 ⊥ By appt.

JEAN-PIERRE FRESLIER
Blanc Demi-sec★★

□ 8ha 5400 **2** **D** ⊕ ⬇
80 **80** ⑧① 82 83

Colour of slightly faded straw, and a nose reminiscent of truffles and quinces. Charming, vigorous and very fruity. Finishes well. (1980)
➛ *M.* J.-P. and *Mme* C. Freslier, La Caillerie, 37210 Vouvray; tel. 47 52 76 61 ⊥ Mon.–Sat. 8.30–20.00; Sun. 8.30–12.00.

JEAN-PIERRE FRESLIER★★

□ 8ha 5400 **3** **D** ⊕ ⬇
80 **81** 82 83

Straw coloured and reminiscent of white truffles. Full, well-balanced and lively on the palate, typical of the appellation. (1981) ✔ Other Vouvray wines.
➛ *M.* J.-P. and *Mme* C. Freslier, La Caillerie, 37210 Vouvray; tel. 47 52 76 61 ⊥ Mon.–Sat. 8.30–20.00; Sun. 8.30–12.00.

JEAN-PIERRE FRESLIER★⁂

○ 8ha 7200 **3** **D** ⊕ ⬇

Straw-gold with tiny bubbles, and scents of quinces and lime. True to type; a good example of a well-balanced and well-made wine.
➛ *M.* J.-P. and *Mme* C. Freslier, La Caillerie,

37210 Vouvray; tel. 47 52 76 61 ☎ Mon.–Sat. 8.30–20.00; Sun. 8.30–12.00.

SYLVAIN GAUDRON★★

○ 6.5ha 10000 **2** **D** 🍷 ⦿ 🥄
79 81 ⑧ **83** 🟦

Attractive, bright colour and light, fruity nose. On the palate soft, rich and well balanced, its liveliness making a pleasant surprise. (1983)
☙ Sylvain Gaudron, 59 Rue Neuve, Vernou-sur-Brenne, 37210 Vouvray; tel. 47 52 12 27 ☎ By appt. Closed 15 Aug.–10 Sept.

SYLVAIN GAUDRON★

□ 6.5ha 30000 **2** **D** 🍷 ⦿ 🥄
76 78 79 80 ⑧ *83

Transparent, yellow-green colour and aromas of banana make a complex, balanced, lively, full wine that is quite firm and very clean. (1983)
☙ Sylvain Gaudron, 59 Rue Neuve, Vernou-sur-Brenne, 37210 Vouvray; tel. 47 52 12 27 ☎ By appt. Closed 15 Aug.–15 Sept.

SYLVAIN GAUDRON★★★

○ 6.5ha 49000 **3** **D** 🍷 ⦿ 🥄
⑧ **83**

Straw colour and steady mousse. A very vinous wine, with a complex nose of peaches, apricots and lime blossom. Fairly dense, balanced and long in the mouth.
☙ Sylvain Gaudron, 59 Rue Neuve, Vernou-sur-Brenne, 37210 Vouvray; tel. 47 52 12 27 ☎ By appt. Closed 15 Aug.–10 Sept.

LIONEL GAUTHIER-L'HOMME★★

□ 1ha 3600 **3** **D** ⦿
78 80 ⑧ 82 83

Pale colour and an aroma of potato on the nose. A handsome wine, harmonious and expressive. (1983)
☙ Lionel Gauthier-l'Homme, Meolotin, 37280 Reugny; tel. 47 52 96 41 ☎ By appt.

GERMAIN GAUTIER-PELTIER★★

■ 10ha 24000 **3** **D** 🍷 ⦿ 🥄
76 ⑦ 🟦 81 82 🟦

A straw-coloured wine with scents of flowers and liquorice but slightly shut-in at present. On the palate, delicate, lively and firm, with persistent aromas of warm plums, lime blossom and mown hay. Already powerful, despite its youth. (1983)
☙ Germain Gautier-Peltier, La Rocauderie, Parçay-Meslay, 37210 Vouvray; tel. 47 51 30 47 ☎ Daily 8.00–12.00.

GERMAIN GAUTIER-PELTIER★★

○ 10ha 5000 **3** **D** 🍷 ⦿ 🥄
⑦ 🟦 81 82

Straw-coloured Vouvray with delicate bubbles, rich in aromas of beeswax, camomile and liquorice. Lively, young and full, with complex aromas which linger on the palate. ✔ Vouvray Blanc Sec et Blanc Moelleux, Touraine Méthode Champenoise, Vin de Table Rosé.
☙ Germain Gautier-Peltier, La Rocauderie, Parçay-Meslay, 37210 Vouvray; tel. 47 51 30 47 ☎ Daily 8.00–21.00

JEAN-PIERRE GILET
Blanc Demi-sec★★

○ 3ha 18000 **2** **D** ⦿
76 81 ★⑧ ★🟦

Lovely golden colour and strongly developed nose with fragrances of wax, new-mown hay and flowers. Well balanced but still young on the palate. (1982) ✔ Vouvray Méthode Champenoise Brut and Sec, Vouvray Pétillant.
☙ Jean-Pierre Gilet, 5 Rue de Parcay, Parçay-Meslay, 37210 Vouvray; tel. 47 51 22 99 ☎ No visitors.

JEAN-PIERRE GILET★★

○ 3ha 30000 **3** **D** ⦿

Sustained golden colour and light but short-lived mousse. Well-balanced and robust on the palate. A nose reminiscent of apples and pears. Better with a meal than as an aperitif.
☙ Jean-Pierre Gilet, 5 Rue de Parcay, Parçay-Meslay, 37210 Vouvray; tel. 47 51 22 99 ☎ No visitors.

LE HAUT-LIEU★★★

□ 6ha 28000 **3** **D** 🍷 🥄
⑦ 80 81 82 🟦

Straw-coloured wine with well-developed scents of hay, honey, lime blossom and acacia, with a mineral touch. On the palate it is full, firm, lively and long. A dry, young wine of strong regional character. (1983)
☙ Gaston Huet, Dom. du Haut-Lieu, 37210 Vouvray; tel. 47 52 78 87 ☎ By appt. Closed Sun. and holidays.

DANIEL JARRY
Méthode Champenoise★

○ 8ha 43000 **3** **D** 🥄
69 76 ★80 ★81 ★82 ★**83**

Straw-coloured with a good, persistent mousse and nose of quinces, medlars, camomile and lime. True to type: rather heavy, lively yet solid. Good finish.
☙ Daniel Jarry, La Vallée Coquette, 37210 Vouvray; tel. 47 52 78 75 ☎ By appt.

JEAN-PIERRE LAISEMENT★★

○ 3ha 12000 **3** **D** ⦿
59 64 76 ★78 ★79 ★80 ★**81** ★82 ★83

Golden straw colour, with background of tiny bubbles, blending well with the complex and subtle scents of honey and lilac. On the palate, well balanced and supple, with a long finish. Typical of the region. (1983)
☙ Jean-Pierre Laisement, La Vallée Coquette, 37210 Vouvray; tel. 47 52 74 47 ☎ By appt.

MME HENRI LAISEMENT*

☐ 10ha 54000   2 D ◑

59 64 76 *78 *79 *80 *81 *81 82 *83

Nose with aromas of chestnuts and white truffles; powerful and full on the palate. ✦ Vouvray Méthode Champenoise, Vouvray Pétillant.
✦ *Mme* Henri Laisement, La Vallée Coquette, 37210 Vouvray; tel. 47 52 74 47 ℐ By appt.

PIERRE LOTHION *Blanc Demi-sec***

☐ 4ha 60000   3 D ◑

75 ⑦ 77 78 79 82 83

Many points for this straw-coloured wine with its subtle nose of beeswax, white lilac and ginger-bread. Well balanced, easy to drink and lively on the palate, leaving a delicate and lingering taste. (1983)
✦ Pierre Lothion, 37 Rue Gambetta, 37210 Vouvray; tel. 47 52 71 24 ℐ By appt. Closed 15–31 Aug.

PIERRE LOTHION**

☐ 4ha 18000   3 D ◑

75 ⑦ 77 78 79 82 83

Light straw in colour, with a nose of beeswax, flowers and minerals with a hint of truffles. Well balanced and well made with hints of liquorice and lime on the palate. Finishes well but is still too young. (1982)
✦ Pierre Lothion, 37 Rue Gambetta, 37210 Vouvray; tel. 47 52 71 24 ℐ By appt. Closed 15–31 Aug. ✦

CLAUDE METIVIER**

○ 7ha 45000   3 D ▮ ◑

*82 *83

Good, deep straw colour, with a delicate, steady mousse. Fruity and floral nose with hint of dried apricots. On the palate, well made, full bodied, lively and grapey. The nose is borne out on the palate, with an additional hint of apples. Good example of its type. (1983)
✦ Claude Métivier, 51 Rue Neuve, Vernou-sur-Brenne, 37210 Vouvray; tel. 47 52 01 95 ℐ By appt.

MAISON MIRAULT**

○ 30000   3 D ▮ ◑

Refreshing, pale-yellow wine with immature vegetable nose. Well balanced. With luck, it will become more refined in time.
✦ Maison Mirault, 15 Ave Brule, 37210 Vouvray; tel. 47 52 16 27 ℐ By appt.

LE MONT***

☐ 6ha 24000   4 D ◑

70 ⑦ 76 80 ⑧ 82 83

A wine of great quality, noteworthy for its golden straw colour and pronounced nose of warm plums and meadow flowers, with a trace of white truffles and peaches. Well balanced, charming, easy to drink and fresh; finishes very well. (1982)
✦ Vouvray le Haut-Lieu, Vouvray le Clos du Bourg, Vouvray Pétillant, Vouvray Mousseux.
✦ Gaston Huet, Dom. du Haut-Lieu, 37210 Vouvray; tel. 47 52 78 87 ℐ By appt. Closed Sun. and public holidays.

NICOLAS*

◪ 70000   3 ◑

Slightly soft Vouvray with characteristic Chenin nose. Good acidity-sugar balance and support on the palate. (1983)
✦ Ets Nicolas, 2 Rue Valmy, 94220 Charenton; tel. 01 37 59 20 ℐ No visitors.

JEAN-CLAUDE PICHOT*

☐ 12ha 7500   3 D ◑

64 ⑦⓪ 76 78 79 *81 *82 *83 85

Limpid, straw-yellow colour and light, flowery nose. Rather sweet on the palate, but its smooth-ness will be appreciated. To lay down. (1983)
✦ Jean-Claude Pichot, Le Peu de La Moriette, 37210 Vouvray; tel. 47 52 72 45 ℐ By appt.

PRINCE PONIATOWSKI *Aigle Blanc***

☐ 18ha 150000   3 D ◑ ⏚

70 ⑦ 80 81 *82 83

Golden beige colour, a well-balanced scent of chestnuts, angelica and citrus fruits. Full-flavoured, with good body and aromas, and a rather rustic feel. (1983)
✦ Philippe Poniatowski, Le Clos Baudouin, 37210 Vouvray; tel. 47 52 71 02 ℐ By appt.

PRINCE PONIATOWSKI
*Clos Baudouin***

☐ 5ha 13000   3 D ▮ ◑ ⏚

⑦ 79 80 81 82 83

Golden colour, a fresh nose reminiscent of wal-nuts, hazelnuts, country flowers and hay, add up to a well-balanced wine, full bodied and fla-voured on the palate, with aromas of liquorice and flowers. It is distinctive and finishes well. (1982) ✔ Vouvray Aigle Blanc et Blanc Sec, Vouvray Méthode Champenoise Brut Blanc, Touraine Rosé Méthode Champenoise.
✦ Philippe Poniatowski, Le Clos Baudouin, 37210 Vouvray; tel. 47 52 71 02 ℐ By appt.

PRINCE PONIATOWSKI
*Clos Baudouin***

○ 18ha 75000   3 D ▮ ⏚

⑦ 79 80 81 82 83

A clear straw colour, with plenty of small bub-bles. The reserved nose hinting of flowers charac-terizes this well-structured, young, full and lively sparkling wine. On the palate it is long, with fruity and flowery aromas. (1982)
✦ Philippe Poniatowski, Le Clos Baudouin, 37210 Vouvray; tel. 47 52 71 02 ℐ By appt.

VITICULTEURS DE VOUVRAY**

○ 150ha 1000000   4 D ▮

Lovely yellow colour and fine, regular mousse. A strongly characteristic Vouvray, complete with a light scent of brioche on the nose and delicate aromas on the palate.
✦ Les Viticulteurs de Vouvray, 37210 Vouvray; tel. 47 52 60 20 ℐ By appt; closed in winter.

Cheverny VDQS

These vineyards, which acquired VDQS status in 1973, are situated on 200 hectares on the west bank of the river between Loire and Sologne, extending to the fringe of the Orléans area. A number of different grape types are planted, with local varieties complementing the classic stalwarts. In general, the wines are produced to be drunk young. The reds (8000 hectolitres), from Gamay, Cabernet and Pinot Noir, are light and fruity; the rosés (1000 hectolitres), from Gamay, Pinot d'Aunis and Pinot Gris, are dry. The whites (8000 hectolitres), from Sauvignon, Chenin and Chardonnay, are dry and light.

MICHEL CADOUX *Romorantin*★★

□	1 ha	6000	2 D ▪ ⬇

⑲ **82 83**

Pale-yellow colour with a hint of green. Flowery nose with a powerful aroma of jennet. Gentle, fragrant and savoury; smooth on the palate. (1983)
↬ *M. et Mme* Michel Cadoux, Le Portail, Cheverny, 41700 Contres; tel. 54 79 91 25 ⊥ By appt.

MICHEL CADOUX *Gamay*★

■	2 ha	13000	2 D ▪ ⬇

76 79 ⑧

Representative of its appellation and year. Pale cherry colour and aromas of vegetation and spice. (1984) ✔ Other Cheverny
↬ *M. et Mme* Michel Cadoux, Le Portail, Cheverny, 41700 Contres; tel. 54 79 91 25 ⊥ By appt.

BERNARD CAZIN★★

■	1.5 ha	50000	2 D ⬩ ⬇

80 81 ★⑧ **83 84**

Pretty, light cherry-coloured wine. Robust, spicy nose, and a typically supple, balanced and savoury palate. (1983)
↬ Bernard Cazin, Cheverny, 41700 Contres; tel. 54 79 93 75 ⊥ By appt.

GILBERT CHESNEAU *Gamay*★★

■	1.5 ha	10000	2 D ▪ ⬇

75 ★⑧ ★**83**

Cherry colour and spicy, lightly acidic nose. On the palate it is well-balanced, with a noticeable hint of liquorice. An elegant wine. (1983)
↬ Gilbert Chesneau, Le Bourg, Sambin, 41120 Les Montils; tel. 54 20 28 04 ⊥ By appt.

JEAN-MICHEL COURTIOUX★

■	11.5 ha	50000	2 D ▪ ⬇

Cherry-red colour typical of the appellation. Light and fragrant wine with aromas of strawberry and herbs on the nose. Well-balanced palate characterized by a pronounced flavour of herbs. (1983)
↬ Jean-Michel Courtioux, L'Hermitage, Cellettes, 41120 Les Montils; tel. 54 70 41 50 ⊥ By appt.

ANDRE COUTOUX *Gamay*★★

■	2 ha	60000	2 D ▪ ⬩ ⬇

80 81 ⑧ **83 84**

Fairly dark ruby colour, very pleasing to the eye, and a fruity nose with aromas of orange intermingled with undergrowth. On the palate, well balanced, with a hint of pepper.
↬ André Coutoux, Closerie-des-Mûrs, Seur, 41120 Les Montils; tel. 54 44 04 58 ⊥ By appt.

DOMAINE DE LA DESOUCHERIE
Romorantin★

□	8 ha	35000	2 D ▪ ⬇

⑲ **82**

Pale colour. Flowery nose, with a hint of vegetable, and nuances of yeast and burnt toast. Rustic, balanced, lively and slightly astringent. Would go well with the local charcuterie. (1983) ✔ Other Cheverny wines.
↬ Christian Tessier, Dom. de la Desoucherie, Cour-Cheverny, 41700 Contres; tel. 54 79 90,08 ⊥ By appt. Closed Sun. afternoon.

FRANCOIS GAZIN *Romorantin*★★

□	1 ha	3000	2 D ▪ ⬇

★⑧ **83** ★**84**

Very pretty and flowery straw-coloured wine with green reflections. Delicate nose of honey and acacia. Lightly acidic, balanced and dry. (1983)
↬ Francois Gazin, Le Petit Chambord, 41700 Cheverny; tel. 54 79 93 75 ⊥ By appt.

GENDRIER *Romorantin*★★

□	5 ha	36000	2 D ▪ ⬇

⑦ 80 81 ⑧ **83 84**

Balanced wine whose green-yellow colour is characteristic of the Romorantin grape. Delicate, flowery nose with a hint of beeswax. (1983)
↬ *M.* Gendrier, Les Muards, Cour-Cheverny, 41700 Contres; tel. 54 79 97 90 ⊥ By appt.

PATRICE HAHUSSEAU *Gamay*★

■	5 ha	10000	2 D ▪ ⬇

⑦ **82**

Pale red colour. Fairly intense nose, and a lightly astringent palate with hints of strawberry and liquorice. (1983) ✔ Cheverny Méthode Champenoise.
↬ Patrice Hahusseau, 12 Rue des Chaumettes, Muides-sur-Mer, 41500 Mer; tel. 54 87 50 28 ⊥ Mon.–Sat. 9.00–12.30/14.00–19.00.

EDGARD HUGUET *Romorantin**

☐ 3ha 5000 [2] [D] [i] [↓]

Good, typical, pale-yellow wine. Well balanced and quite delicate, with an elegant aroma. Open a little while before drinking. (1983)
☛ Edgard Huguet, 7 Rue Bon-Leyrault, St-Claude-de-Dinay, 41350 Vineuil; tel. 54 20 65 01 ⏰ By appt.

PIERRE PARENT *Romorantin*

☐ 1.3ha 7000 [2] [D] [i] [↓]
⑧⑫ [82] 83

Pale-yellow colour with a hint of green. A balanced wine with a rather intense nose combining aromas of wax and orange peel. (1982)
✔ Other Cheverny wines.
☛ Pierre Parent, Mont-pres-Chambord, 51250 Bracieux; tel. 54 70 73 57 ⏰ Daily 9.00–20.00.

DOMAINE DE LA PLANTE D'OR
*Pineau d'Aunis**

◪ 1.25ha 4000 [2] [D] [i] [↓]

Pale-pink colour and an agreeable nose with a hint of redcurrant. Typical wine, balanced, delicate and very warming. (1982)
☛ Claude Locquineau, 25 Rue de la République, Cormeray, 441120 Les Montils; tel. 51 44 23 09 ⏰ By appt.

MICHEL REPINCAY *Gamay**

■ 5ha 48000 [2] [D] [i] [↓]
⑦⑥ 78 79 81 82

Cherry colour. Vegetal nose with notes of lichen and mint; the same aromas are found on the palate and give this pleasant wine its originality.
☛ Michel Repinçay, l'Atelier, Cour-Cheverny, 41700 Cheverny; tel. 54 70 48 40 ⏰ By appt.

LE SALVARD *Gamay**

■ 15ha 25000 [2] [D] [i] [⑪] [↓]

Famous since the Middle Ages, the Cheverny vineyard produces a light wine the colour of redcurrants, with lightly spicy aromas. (1983)
☛ G.-M. Delaille, Dom. le Salvard, Fougères-sur-Bièvre, 41120 Les Montils; tel. 54 20 28 21 ⏰ By appt.

LE SALVARD *Sauvignon**

☐ 15ha 25000 [2] [D] [i] [⑪] [↓]
82 83

A pale yellowy green wine which is easy to drink, well developed, dry and lively, with aromas of peaches and bananas. (1983)
☛ G.-M. Delaille, Dom. le Salvard, Fougères-sur-Bièvre, 41120 Les Montils; tel. 54 20 28 21 ⏰ By appt.

LE SALVARD*

○ 15ha 15000 [3] [D] [i] [⑪] [↓]

A straw-coloured wine with plenty of bubbles, developing a scent of dried hay and aromas of strawberries.
☛ G.-M. Delaille, Dom. le Salvard, Fougères-sur-Bièvre, 41120 Les Montils; tel. 54 20 28 21 ⏰ By appt.

CLOS DE TUEBOEUF*

■ 7ha 15000 [2] [D] [i]
⑦⑥ *82 [82] *83 [83] 84

Cherry-coloured wine with a green-pepper nose. Supple but powerful on the palate; should mature further. (1982)
☛ Jean Puzelat, 6 Route de Seur, 41120 Les Montils; tel. 54 44 05 16 ⏰ By appt.

Coteaux du Vendômois VDQS

The normal range of Touraine grape varieties is found here on each side of the Loir valley, upstream of the Coteaux du Loir and Jasnières vineyards. Some 60 hectares produce light and dry red, white, and (from the Pineau d'Aunis) rosé wines.

MINIER *Pineau d'Aunis***

◪ 3ha 4000 [2] [D] [i] [↓]
*83

Fine pink colour. Lightly acidic nose reminiscent of apples, pears and bananas. Finely balanced, and as supple on the palate as it is smooth and tasty. (1983)
☛ M. Minier, Les Monts, Lunay 41360, Savigny-sur-Braye; tel. 54 72 02 36 ⏰ By appt.

Valençay VDQS

About 60 km south-east of Tours, these vineyards are in the department of Indre, quite close to the vineyards of Central France. Twenty hectares or so are planted with Gamay, Cabernet, Pinot Noir and Côt vines, producing light, fruity red wines and drier rosés. The dry, fairly full-bodied whites come from the Arbois, Sauvignon, and Chardonnay varieties. All these wines should be drunk young.

JACKY AUGIS *Gamay***

■ 5ha 18000 [1] [D] [i] [↓]
⑦⑥ 80 83 84

Ruby-coloured wine with fruity aromas of raspberry and orange on the nose. Fine, rich and well balanced. Serve it with mixed grill. (1983)
☛ Jacky Augis, Le Muza, Meusnes, 41130 Selles-sur-Cher; tel. 54 71 01 89 ⏰ By appt.

HUBERT SINSON *Côt***

■ 17ha 26000 [2] [D] [i] [⑪] [↓]
76 *82 [82] *83 [83]

A ruby-coloured wine with aromas of raspberry and peach and a hint of milkiness. Balanced, full and tannic, with an additional powerful hint of violet on the palate. Could mature further.
☛ Hubert Sinson, Le Muza, Meusnes, 41130, Selles-sur-Cher; tel. 54 71 00 26 ⏰ By appt. Closed Aug.

POITOU

Haut-Poitou VDQS

In 1865, the eminent Dr Guyot reported that the Vienne vineyard covered 33560 hectares. Nowadays the only areas of viticultural interest, apart from the vineyards included in the Saumur region, are around the cantons of Neuville and Mirebeau, home of the VDQS wines of Haut-Poitou. The commune of Marigny-Brizay has the largest number of independent wine-growers for its size. Most growers are part of the Cave de Neuville-Poitou, which began Haut-Poitou production, and which still makes 90 per cent of the 30000 hectolitres produced each year.

The Neuvillois plateau is a mixture of hard limestone, marl, and the chalk of Marigny. This soil provides excellent growing conditions for the grape varieties that go to make up the appellation, the best known being the Sauvignon Blanc. Benefiting from first-class promotion, these light and fragrant Haut-Poitou wines are known throughout the entire restaurant trade in France, and are now well established abroad.

FOURNIER FRERES★

■		10ha	48000	2 D ▮ ⅲ ⅃
76 79 82 ★84				

Well balanced. Well-developed colour. Good example of the Cabernet grape. Could be drunk now with cheese or roast meat, but if allowed to age will go well with game. (1983) ✔ Haut-Poitou Gamay, Haut-Poitou Sauvignon, Haut-Poitou Chardonnay, Haut-Poitou Pinot Noir Rouge.
↬ *MM*. Fournier Frères, Marigny-Brizay, 86380 Vendeuvre-du-Poitou; tel. 49 52 09 46 ☍ By appt.

FOURNIER FRERES★

□		0.5ha	2400	2 D ▮ ⅲ ⅃
76 79 80 81 ★82 82 ★83 83				

Lovely floral nose but still a little hard on the palate. Made from the Chenin, this wine is worth laying down. (1983)
↬ *MM*. Fournier Frères, Marigny-Brizay, 86380 Vendeuvre-du-Poitou; tel. 49 52 09 46 ☍ By appt.

COOPERATIVE DU HAUT-POITOU
Chardonnay★★

□		100ha	400000	2 D ⅲ ⅃
80 80 ★82 82 83 83				

A pretty, bright, golden-coloured wine with a delicate and well-balanced nose. Full bodied,

attractive and long in the mouth. Shows good breeding. (1983)
↬ Cave coop. du Haut-Poitou, 86170 Neuville-de-Poitou; tel. 49 51 21 65 ☍ By appt. Closed Sun.

COOPERATIVE DU HAUT-POITOU
Cabernet★★★

☑		48ha	100000	2 D ▮ ⅃
80 81 82 83 ★(84) 84				

A lively and very attractive colour and a nose of soft red fruits. Plenty of character; worth going out of your way for. (1983)
↬ Cave Coop. du Haut-Poitou, 86170 Neuville-du-Poitou; tel. 49 51 21 65 ☍ By appt. Closed Sun.

COOPERATIVE DU HAUT-POITOU
Sauvignon★★★

□		195ha	1 000000	2 D ▮ ⅃

Fine green-gold colour. The Sauvignon nose, overpowering at first, develops pleasantly. Should be wonderful with *chabis du Poitou* or mussels cooked in the same wine. A model of harmony and elegance. (1983) ✔ Haut-Poitou Chardonnay, Haut-Poitou Cabernet, Haut-Poitou Gamay.
↬ Cave Coop. du Haut-Poitou, 86170 Neuville-de-Poitou; tel. 49 51 21 65 ☍ Mon.–Fri. 8.30–12.00/13.30–18.00.

COOPERATIVE DU HAUT-POITOU
Gamay★★

■		310ha	1 500000	2 D ▮ ⅃

A beautiful light colour, clear, with a very attractive nose highly typical of new Gamay. This wine is a little more sophisticated than the 1983 and will be pleasant to drink during the year. A successful wine in a difficult vintage. (1984)
↬ Cave Coop. du Haut-Poitou, 86170 Neuville-de-Poitou; tel. 49 51 21 65 ☍ Mon.–Fri. 8.30–12.00/13.30–18.00.

MANOIR DE LAVAUGUYOT★

□		3ha	6000	2 D ▮ ⅃
(62) 74 76 79 ★82 82 ★84				

A lightly woody nose and rather hard taste. Could still age well. (1982) ✔ Haut-Poitou

547

Cabernet, Haut-Poitou Gamay Rouge, Haut-Poitou Chardonnay Blanc Sec.
↖ Robert Champalou, Marigny-Brizay, 86380 Vendeuvre-du-Poitou; tel. 49 52 09 73 ℐ By appt.

CAVE DE LA ROTISSERIE
Chardonnay*

☐	11 ha	20000	2 Ⓓ ▮ ↓

82 **83** ***84** 84

Takes some time to develop a nose but then has nice Chardonnay aromas. Suppleness in the mouth means it will age well. (1983)
↖ Gérard Descoux, Marigny-Brizay, 86380 Vendeuvre-de-Poitou; tel. 49 52 09 02 ℐ By appt. Closed Sun.

CAVE DE LA ROTISSERIE
Cabernet***

◼	2.5 ha	12000	2 ▮ ↓

Very beautiful, dark ruby-violet colour. Lively and tannic on the palate. A very original wine which will age well. (1982)
↖ Gerard Descoux, Marigny-Brizay, 86380 Vendeuvre-du-Poitou; tel. 49 52 09 02 ℐ No visitors.

CAVE DE LA ROTISSERIE *Sauvignon**

☐	11 ha	20000	2 ▮ ↓

Limpid, discreet and fine Sauvignon. Pleasant, even lively, on the palate. (1983)
↖ Gerard Descoux, Marigny-Brizay, 86830 Vendeuvre-du-Poitou; tel. 49 52 09 06 ℐ No visitors.

CENTRAL FRANCE

The principal wine-growing areas of central France are scattered along a 300 km stretch between the Côtes du Forez and Orléans. This is a quiet, green countryside of wide horizons and changing scenery. The vines occupy prime sites on the hills and plateaus shaped over the course of geological time by the river Loire and its tributaries, the Allier and the Cher. Even the vineyards that are planted on the northern and eastern slopes of the Massif Central – such as those on the Côtes d'Auvergne, in Châteaumeillant, or in parts of St-Pourçain – still face the Loire basin.

The soils exploited for vine-growing here are either sand or limestone and are always in a good location with a favourable exposure. In either case, only a limited number of grape varieties are planted, mainly Gamay for red and rosé wines and Sauvignon for white wines. Occasionally other varietals are used for local speciality wines; examples are the Tresallier in St-Pourçain, the Chasselas in Pouilly-sur-Loire (both for white wines), and the Pinot Noir in Sancerre and Menetou-Salon for reds and rosés (and also the delicate Pinot Gris in the latter). Finally there is the Meunier grape, which provides the interesting 'gris meunier' near Orléans.

All the regional wines made from these grape varieties have the common characteristics of lightness, freshness, and fruitiness. These combine to make them particularly pleasant, attractive and very drinkable – qualities which make them the perfect accompaniment to the regional cuisine. The wine-makers themselves, whether from around Auvergne, Bourges, Nevers, Berry or Orléans, promote their wines with energy and enthusiasm – and admittedly the wines deserve it, coming as they do from family, artisan-style vineyards which genuinely reflect the character and traditions of the region.

Central France

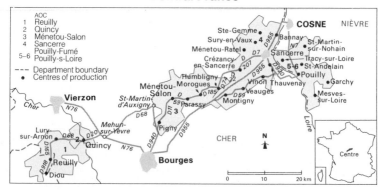

Chateaumeillant VDQS

The Gamay thrives on this area's soils and its long association with them can be traced in the local museum. Châteaumeillant's reputation is based on its famous 'vin gris', a pale rosé made from the immediate pressing of Gamay grapes which possesses a remarkable grapiness, freshness and fruitiness. The reds, grown on volcanic soils have a similar if slightly firmer character, and should be drunk young and chilled; they are clean and light, with a good bouquet. The average annual production of the 100 hectares is 4500 hectolitres, most of which is produced by the cooperative in Châteaumeillant.

DOMAINE DU FEUILLAT *Pinot**

☑	1 ha	7200	② Ⅾ ■ ↓

There is a definite amber tinge in the clear colour of this wine. It has a fresh and lightly woody nose which is confirmed on the palate. (1983)
➤ Maurice Lanoix, Beaumerle, 18370 Châteaumeillant; tel. 98 61 33 89 ☧ By appt.

DOMAINE DU FEUILLAT *Gamay**

☑	3 ha	78000	② Ⅾ ■ ↓

Visually this wine is clear and a charming slightly straw-pink. The distinctive nose is dominated by the scent of ripe pears and this rustic background is also present in the mouth, with a bouquet mainly composed of pear and cherry. (1983)
➤ Maurice Lanoix, Beaumerle, 18370 Châteaumeillant; tel. 98 61 33 89 ☧ By appt.

DOMAINE DU FEUILLAT*

■	3 ha	18000	② Ⅾ ■ ↓

A clear wine with a strong ruby colour. At present the nose is closed up but should open with age, but the artemisia scent of the Gamay is recognizable. On the palate the wine is firm, slightly tannic, peppery and quite herbal, still young, with a touch of caramel. Wait a little longer for this one. (1983)
➤ Maurice Lanoix, Beaumerle, 18370 Châteaumeillant; tel. 98 61 33 89 ☧ By appt.

HENRI RAFFINAT**

☑	1 ha	5000	② Ⅾ ■ ↓
⑧ 83			

Clear, lively salmon-pink colour. Pronounced scents of ripe prunes and almonds on the nose, while ripe cherries are dominant on the palate. A fresh wine, lively and full. (1983)
➤ Henri Raffinat, Rue des Tanneries, 18370 Châteaumeillant; tel. 48 61 35 16 ☧ Daily 8.30–12.30/ 14.00–20.00.

HENRI RAFFINAT*

■		5 ha	20000	② Ⅾ ■ ↓
82 ⑧ 83				

Clear ruby colour with hints of amber; lively and fresh on the palate, with a taste of slightly acid red fruits and an aroma of leather. (1983)
➤ Henri Raffinat, Rue des Tanneries, 18370 Châteaumeillant; tel. 48 61 35 16 ☧ Daily 8.30–12.30/ 14.00–20.00.

Côtes d'Auvergne VDQS

Whether they come from the Les Puys vineyards in Limagne or from the hillside vineyards on the eastern side of the Massif Central, all good Auvergne wines are made from the Gamay, a variety that has long been grown here. This area (500 hectares) was granted a VDQS appellation in 1977, and produces 21000 hectolitres of wine annually. The refreshing rosé wines – sometimes called 'blancs' – and the fuller reds are particularly good with the famous charcuterie of Auvergne or with the well-known regional dishes.

CAVES DES COTEAUX *Corent***

☑	20 ha	80000	② Ⅾ ■ ↓
⑧ 83 84			

A fine rosé of grey-pink, slightly salmon colour. Well-defined, lively and spring-like aromas, and a finish evocative of fresh hazelnuts. Lightly acidic on the palate with the savour of ripe cherries. (1983)
➤ Cave des Coteaux, 63960 Veyre-Monton; tel. 73 69 60 11. ☧ By appt.

PIERRE LAPOUGE ET FILS *Châteaugay***

■		200000	② Ⅾ ■ ⑪ ↓
⑧ 83 84			

Bright redcurrant colour, with a slight crimson hue. Full and harmonious aromas that are distinctly plant-like. Very rounded on the palate; lightly acidic, easy to drink, with a peppery taste at the back of the mouth. (1983)
➤ Pierre Lapouge et Fils, 63100 Châteaugay; tel. 76 87 24 31. ☧ By appt.

PIERRE LAPOUGE ET FILS

■	10 ha	35000	② Ⅾ

Lovely deep ruby colour, fresh herbal nose, and good balance between tannin and fruit on the palate. A well-blended wine with an initial flavour of dark tobacco and an overall earthy quality. ✔ Other Côtes d'Auvergne.
➤ Pierre Lapouge et Fils, 8 Rue du Port, 63100 ChâteauGay; tel. 73 87 24 31 ☧ By appt.

Côtes du Forez VDQS

The continued existence of these beautiful vineyards is a tribute to the determination of the local growers.

The small (150 hectares) growing area includes some twenty communes around Boën-sur-Lignon (Loire). The excellent red and rosé wines are dry and lively, made solely from Gamay grapes, and are usually drunk young. They are practically all produced by the local cooperative. This concern has recently expanded with the aim of improving the quality of the wine.

CAVE COOPERATIVE DES COTES DU FOREZ★★★

■   50ha   60000   **2 D** ■ ↓

★82 83 83

Lovely ruby-coloured wine with clean, crisp, leafy nose and easy roundness on the palate; its complex evocation of spring flowers and herbs is irresistible. Yet this wine will open out even more splendidly after another few years, if you can bear to wait. (1983) ✔ Côtes du Forez Rosé and Demi-sec, Moussette.

➤ Les Vignerons Foréziens, Trélins, 42130 Boens; tel. 77 24 00 12 ☎ Mon.–Sat. 8.00–12.00/ 14.00–18.00.

CAVE COOPERATIVE DES COTES DU FOREZ *Rosé Sec*★★

◩   8ha   30000   **2 D** ■ ↓

⑧⑬ 83 84

This attractive rosé has a lively, honest colour, crisp leafy nose and salty, peppery aromas which give way to a flavour of full, fat, green nuts. (1983) ✔ Côtes du Forez Rosé and Demi-sec Moussette.

➤ Les Vignerons Foréziens, Trélins, 42130 Boens; tel. 77 24 00 12 ☎ Mon.–Sat. 8.00–12.00/ 14.00–18.00.

CAVE COOPERATIVE DES COTES DU FOREZ *Rosé Demi-sec*★

◩   5ha   10000   **2 D** ■ ↓

⑧⑬ 83

This pretty rosé is a pleasure to drink. Its colour is pinkish straw and it has an honest nose with a touch of artemisia, which is confirmed on the palate, where it can be detected against a soft, perhaps even slightly flat background. (1983) ✔ Côtes du Forez Rosé and Demi-sec, Moussette.

➤ Les Vignerons Foréziens, Trélins, 42130 Boens; tel. 77 24 00 12 ☎ Mon.–Sat. 8.00–12.00/ 14.00–18.00.

Coteaux du Giennois VDQS

These well-known slopes extend into the Nièvre and the Loiret departments. Three traditional grape types, Gamay, Pinot and Sauvignon, produce almost 4000 hectolitres of light, fruity wines with the distinctive character of the local sandy and limestone soils. They are tannic enough to keep for a few years and go well with all types of meat dishes.

DOMAINE BALLAND-CHAPUIS★★

■   2ha   10000   **2 D** ■ ↓

⑦⑥ 78 79 82 83 83

Bright, deep ruby colour, with a delicate, balanced quality on the nose. Clean and full on the palate, with not too much body, recalling dog-roses and incense. (1983)

➤ Joseph Balland-Chapuis, BP 24, Bué, 18300 Sancerre; tel. 48 54 06 67 ☎ By appt.

DOMAINE BALLAND-CHAPUIS★

◩   2ha   3000   **2 D** ■ ↓

76 78 79 82 83

A clear, grenadine-pink wine with a gentle scent of passionflower. Marked fruitiness on the palate, with a touch of acidity and a light taste of mild Maryland tobacco and honey. (1983)

➤ Joseph Balland-Chapuis, BP 24, Bué, 18300 Sancerre; tel. 48 54 06 67 ☎ By appt.

PAUL PAULAT ET FILS★★

■   4ha   25000   **2 D** ◐ ↓

81 81 ★⑧② 82 83

Beautiful, clear, dark ruby red, if a little lacking in brilliance, and the very positive nose combines various leafy scents, but is dominated by the typical Gamay grape scent of artemisia. It is easy to drink and combines different cooked and smoky flavours. (1982) ✔ Coteaux du Giennois Pinot Rouge, Coteaux du Giennois Gamay Biologique Rouge, Coteaux du Giennois Sauvignon Blanc Sec, Coteaux du Giennois Gamay and Pinot Rosé.

➤ Paul Paulat et Fils, Villemoison-St-Père, 58200 Cosne-sur-Loire; tel. 86 28 22 39 ☎ Daily 8.00– 21.00.

STATION VITICOLE INRA★★

■   3ha   12000   **2 D** ◐ ↓

★⑧② 82 83 83

Clear bright ruby-coloured wine with a nose strongly influenced by a hint of banana. Crisp, lively and very pleasant on the palate. (1983) ✔ Coteaux du Giennois Cosne-sur-Loire Blanc and Rosé, Sancerre Pleurs de St-Etienne Blanc Sec, Sancerre Pleurs de St-Etienne Blanc Sec and Rouge.

➤ Station Viticole INRA, Cours, 58200 Cosne-sur-Loire; tel. 86 82 17 30 ☎ By appt.

TROCADERO★★

■   4ha   25000   **2 D** ■ ◐ ↓

81 81 ★⑧② 82 83

Beautiful, bright ruby colour; nose is a combination of ripe plums and artemisia typical of the Gamay grape. Very supple and round. (1982) ✔ Coteaux du Giennois Ousson Blanc Sec and Rouge, Coteaux du Giennois Gien Blanc Sec and Rosé.

➤ *MM.* Poupat et Fils, 47 Rue Clémenceau, 45500 Gien; tel. 38 67 03 54 ☎ By appt.

St-Pourçain VDQS

The peaceful and fertile Bourges region, possesses fine vineyards that extend over nineteen communes to the south-west of Moulins. With a growing area of 500 hectares, this local region produces 23 000 hectolitres of wine annually. The vineyards themselves are planted on hills and plateaux along the River Sioule. On these limestone and gravel soils the Gamay grape is the major variety, producing red and rosé wines that are notably fruity and thirst-quenching. The equally refreshing white wines also have a very distinctive character, strongly marked by the Tresallier grape.

GUY ET SERGE NEBOUT*

□	2ha	11 000	2 D ▮ ↓

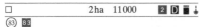

The Nebout family estate is one of only a handful of independent Saint-Pourçain producers, all of whom have to compete with a powerful local cooperative. This wine is a clear amber colour with a marked combination of scents, among which one can identify vanilla, honey and a hint of broom. The taste is supple and round, and sets the seal on a wine which is well developed in all other respects. (1983)
↪ GAEC Guy et Serge Nebout, Route de Montluçon, 03500 St-Pourçain-sur-Sioule; tel. 70 45 31 70 ☎ By appt.

GUY ET SERGE NEBOUT*

■	66ha	35 000	2 D ▮ ↓

Clear, deep ruby colour, with good leafy scents, combining artemisia and vanilla. Firm and tannic on the palate, with crisp, herby fruit and a hint of caramel. (1983)
↪ GAEC Guy et Serge Nebout, Route de Montluçon, 03500 St-Pourçain-sur-Sioule; tel. 70 45 31 70 ☎ By appt.

GUY ET SERGE NEBOUT*

◪		8000	2 D ▮ ↓

A clear sustained salmon-pink colour combines with a positive nose dominated by caramel. A big, lively wine, but a little short in the finish, even though it has a complex vegetal taste. (1983)
↪ GAEC Guy et Serge Nebout, Route de Montluçon, 03500 St-Pourçain-sur-Sioule; tel. 70 45 31 70 ☎ By appt.

JEAN ET FRANÇOIS RAY**

□	2ha	8000	2 D ▮ ↓

Clear pale-gold colour, with a lively nose of vanilla and almond. The supple, crisp taste confirms the impression of fresh almonds. The Ray family's estate is in a good position in St-Pourçain and they make various different cuvées of each wine. (1983) ✔ St-Pourçain, Mousseux Méthode Champenoise.
↪ MM. Ray Père et Fils, Saulcet, 03500 St-Pourçain; tel. 70 45 35 46 ☎ By appt.

JEAN ET FRANÇOIS RAY**

■	6ha	25 000	2 D ▮ ↓

First impressions are of clarity and a bright ruby-red colour, backed up by a nose which is crisp and floral but slightly smoky. The taste is full, slightly tannic and reminiscent of dried apricots. (1983) ✔ St-Pourçain Rosé Mousseux Méthode Champenoise.
↪ MM. Ray Père et Fils, Saulcet, 03500 St-Pourçain; tel. 70 45 35 46 ☎ By appt.

Côtes Roannaises VDQS

This is an area of volcanic soils on west-, south- and south-west-facing slopes – a perfect environment for the Gamay grape. Twenty-four communes and 80 hectares on both sides of the river produce some excellent red, and, more rarely, crisp rosé wines. Some good local wine-making has attracted many of the region's best chefs to these comparatively humble wines. The local history of the area may be studied at the Musée Forézien in Ambierle. Annual wine production is 4000 hectolitres.

ALAIN DEMON *La Perrière**

■	2ha	18 000	3 D ▮ ↓

*82 ⑧₃

Limpid, sustained ruby colour. Intense nose reminiscent of grape juice and black tobacco. Lively, slightly acidic taste of boiled sweets and green pepper. (1982)
↪ Alain Demon, La Perrière, 42820 Ambierle; tel. 77 65 65 49 ☎ By appt.

PIERRE GAUME *Les Millets***

■	1.5ha	8000	2 D

82 *⑧₃ *84

A wine that has remained remarkably youthful. Bright ruby colour with crimson reflections. Well-rounded palate, lively, smooth and strong. Just the right salty, herbal touch of a good Gamay. (1983)
↪ Pierre Gaume, 'Les Millets', 42155 Lentigny; tel. 77 63 14 29. ☎ By appt.

DOMAINE DU PAVILLON**

■	3ha	15 000	2 D ⑾

⑺₈ *84

Beautiful colour shading to ruby. Lively, fresh nose, vinous and full of the grape. On the palate, lightly acidic, balanced and meaty, with vanilla and pepper undertones. (1984)
↪ Maurice Lutz, Dom du Pavillon, 42820 Ambierle; tel. 77 65 64 35 ☎ No visitors.

Vins de l'Orléanais VDQS

Cultivating 100 hectares of plateau land on both sides of the River Loire, today's wine-makers ensure that vines still have their traditional place amongst the famous gardens, orchards and pastures of the Orléanais. The Gris Meunier grape provides the area's speciality, a fresh rosé wine with a gooseberry-and-blackcurrant bouquet, to be drunk with roast partridge or pheasant, game pâtés from nearby Sologne, or goat's cheese rolled in ash from the Gatin region. Total wine production is about 4000 hectolitres with far more red than white being produced.

CAVE COOPERATIVE COVIFRUIT
Pinot Noir★

| ☑ | | 7ha | 35000 | **1** **D** ▤ |

83 **84**

Good colour, with clear trace of amber. Dumb but straightforward aroma of dried figs. Complex taste, in which the flavour of Parma violets is predominant, with very good finish. Drink now. (1983) ✔ Orléanais Cabernet Rouge, Orléanais Gris Meunier Rouge, Orléanais Auvernat Blanc Sec, Prince d'Auvernat Chardonnay Mousseux, Prince d'Auvernat Pinot Rosé Mousseux.
⊶ Cave Coop. Covifruit, 45160 Olivet; tel. 38 63 40 20 ☎ By appt.

A. JAVOY ET FILS *Cabernet Franc*★★

| ▪ | | 9ha | 5000 | **2** **D** ▤ ◑ ↓ |

*82 ★**82** **83**

Pale, ruby-red. Subtle fragrance mingling the scents of blackcurrants and ripe strawberries. Somewhat sparkling and slightly tangy, preventing these flavours being carried through on tasting. (1983) ✔ Vins d'Orléanais Cabernet Sec, Vins d'Orléanais Gris Meunier Rouge, Orléanais Pinot Rouge, Orléanais Auvernat Blanc.
⊶ A. Javoy et Fils, 196 Rue du Buisson, 45370 Mézières-lès-Cléry; tel. 38 45 61 91 ☎ By appt. Closed Sun.

JACKY LEGROUX *Auvernat Blanc*★

| ☐ | | 0.60ha | 3000 | **2** **D** ▤ |

An Auvernat Blanc that is among the specialities of the Orléanais region. Greenish-gold, with full, rich fragrance of acacia root and honeysuckle about to flower. To taste, very fresh, slightly tangy and reminiscent of green apples. (1984) ✔ Orléanais Gris Meunier Rouge, Orléanais Pinot Rouge, Orléanais Cabernet Rosé.
⊶ Jacky Legroux, 315 Rue des Muids, Mareau-aux-Prés, 45370 Cléry-St-André; tel. 38 45 60 31 ☎ No visitors.

CAVE COOPERATIVE DE MAREAU-AUX-PRES★★

| ☑ | | 40ha | 10000 | **2** **D** ▤ ↓ |

Pale but definite and sustained cherry-red tint. Pronounced nose, with scent of ripe raspberries and liquorice. Full, well-rounded, warm taste, suggesting liquorice and rather tart damsons. (1983)
⊶ Cave Coop. de Mareau aux-Prés, 550 Rue des Muids, Mareau-aux-Prés, 45370 Cléry-St-André; tel. 38 45 61 08 ☎ By appt.

CAVE COOPERATIVE DE MAREAU-AUX-PRES★★★

| ▪ | | 40ha | 200000 | **2** **D** ▤ ↓ |

★⑧ ★**8.3**

Rather veiled deep garnet-red colour. Subtle nose reminiscent more of blackcurrants than of damson scent. Well-blended, fleshy taste, with subtle hint of cinnamon. Despite some tannin, well balanced. Astonishingly good for the region, and should mature very well. (1983)
⊶ Cave Coop. de Mareau-aux-Prés, 550 Rue des Muids, Mareau-aux-Prés, 45370 Cléry-St-André; tel. 38 45 61 08 ☎ By appt.

CLOS DE SAINT-FIACRE *Cabernet*★★

| ▪ | | 1ha | 2000 | **2** **D** ▤ ↓ |

Beautiful ruby-red to garnet colour. Powerful nose, with character reminiscent of sloes. On the palate, quite supple and light. Flavour should be left to develop. (1983)
⊶ Roger Montigny et Fils GAEC, Clos St-Fiacre, Mareau-aux-prés, 45370 Cléry-St-André; tel. 38 45 61 55 ☎ By appt.

CLOS DE SAINT-FIACRE
Gris Meunier★

| ☑ | | 1ha | 2000 | **2** **D** ▤ ↓ |

A local speciality. Pale, salmon-pink tinge and subtle, delicate fragrance. Its damsony taste is still rather bittersweet. (1984)
⊶ Roger Montigny et Fils, GAEC Clos de St-Fiacre, Mareau-aux-Prés, 45370 Cléry-St-André; tel. 38 45 61 55 ☎ By appt.

CLOS DE SAINT-FIACRE
Gris Meunier★

| ▪ | | 1.10ha | 2000 | **2** **D** ▤ ↓ |

Brilliant, strong ruby-red with orange tinge. Nose of Morello cherries and violets, with slight suggestion of iodine. On the palate, slightly tangy and a little green, with overtones of peppers and walnuts. Will mature well in the bottle. (1984)
⊶ Roger Montigny et Fils, GAEC Clos de St-Fiacre, Mareau-aux-Prés, 45370 Cléry-St-André; tel. 38 45 61 55 ☎ By appt.

CLOS DE SAINT-FIACRE
Auvernat Pinot Rouge★

| ▪ | | 1.10ha | 2000 | **2** **D** ▤ ↓ |

Made from the Auvernat Noir (Pinot Noir) grape, a brilliant, bright ruby-red. The nose is vaguely reminiscent of ripe plums. Rather thin, faintly mineral taste. Will develop in the bottle. (1984)
⊶ Roger Montigny et Fils, GAEC Clos de St-Fiacre, Mareau-aux-Prés, 45370 Cléry-St-André; tel. 38 45 61 55 ☎ By appt.

Ménetou-Salon
This appellation owes its viticultural origins to nearby Bourges, a powerful centre in medieval times. Unlike many once-famous vineyards, this one has remained under vines and indeed has retained its high reputation. It covers about 500 hectares.

Ménetou-Salon shares its favourable exposure and fine soils with its prestigious neighbour, Sancerre. The Sancerrois grape varieties Sauvignon Blanc and Pinot Noir are grown here to produce fresh and herby white wines, delicate and fruity rosés, and well-balanced and aromatic reds that should be drunk young. All these wines go very well with the famous Berrichon cuisine; the whites with aperitifs or hot entrées, and the reds served chilled with fish, rabbit or charcuterie.

GAEC DES BRANGERS★★

□	5 ha	30000	3 D ▐ ↓

82 ★⑧ 83 84

This light gold coloured wine has a leafy nose, light and fresh with a hint of liquorice. To taste it is reminiscent of fresh fruit salad with a touch of liquorice. It can be purchased in large bottles (up to the 'salmanazar' which holds 9 litres) – with a label bearing the customer's name. (1983) ✔ Ménetou-Salon Rouge et Rosé. ✚ GAEC des Brangers, 18510 Menetou-Salon; tel. 48 64 80 87 ☎ Daily 7.00–21.00. ✚ Georges Chavet et Fils.

GAEC DES BRANGERS★★

■	25 ha	30000	3 D ▐ ↓

72 76 78 82 ★83

Sustained redcurrant colour. The nose is quite fresh, with a dominant note of blackcurrant confirmed in the lively young taste together with a hint of citronella. (1983) ✚ GAEC des Brangers, 18510 Ménetou-Salon; tel. 48 64 80 87 ☎ Daily 7.00–21.00. ✚ Georges Chavet et Fils.

GAEC DES BRANGERS★★

◩	2.5 ha	30000	3 D ▐ ↓

76 78 82 ★83

This wine is a lively salmon colour with a clean, caramel nose. Full and firm on the palate with a dominant raspberry taste. (1983) ✚ GAEC des Brangers, 18510 Ménetou-Salon; tel. 48 64 80 87 ☎ Daily 7.00–21.00. ✚ Georges Chavet et Fils.

DOMAINE DE CHATENOY★★

◩	1 ha	4000	3 D ▐ ↓

76 78 80 81 82 83

Attractive rosé made from the Pinot Noir grape. Salmon-pink in colour, lively and clear, with a fresh taste reminiscent of ripe plums. (1983) ✚ Bernard Clément, Chatenoy, 18510 Menetou-Salon; tel. 48 64 80 25 ☎ Mon.–Sat. 8.00–19.00, Sun. 8.00–12.00.

DOMAINE DE CHATENOY★

■	2 ha	20000	3 D ⑾ ↓

76 78 80 81 82 83

Good strong ruby colour. Oaky nose with a hint of graphite. Still young, tannic and rather closed-up. (1983) ✚ Bernard Clément, Chatenoy, 18510 Menetou-

Salon; tel. 48 64 80 25 ☎ Mon.–Sat. 8.00–19.00, Sun. 8.00–12.00.

DOMAINE DE CHATENOY★★

□	12 ha	45000	3 D ▐ ↓

76 78 80 81 82 83

A good wine from the ultra-modern winery of this old-established (1773) family estate. Pure gold colour, distinctive boxwood nose and a clear hint of liquorice on the palate. Round, charming and easy to to drink. (1983) ✔ Menetou-Salon Rouge et Rosé.
✚ Bernard Clément, Chatenoy, 18510 Ménetou-Salon; tel. 48 64 80 25 ☎ Mon.–Sat. 8.00–19.00, Sun. 8.00–12.00.

CAVES JACQUES COEUR★

■	35 ha	30000	2 D ▐ ↓

⑧² ★83 84

Brilliant ruby 'red-tile' colour. The combined aromas of strawberry and raspberry evoke the garden in summer. Wait for it to become fuller and more rounded. (1983)
✚ Caves Jacques Coeur, Menetou-Salon, 18510, St-Martin-d'Auxigny; tel. 48 64 09 96 ☎ Mon.–Fri. 8.00–12.00/14.00–17.30. Closed 23 Dec., 3 Jan.

DOMAINE HENRI PELLE
Menetou-Salon-Morogues★★★

□	13 ha	40000	3 D ▐ ↓

70 76 81 82 ⑧ 83 84

Clear golden colour with a nose combining the scents of *pain d'épice* and blackcurrant. Round and full bodied in the mouth, opening out to a very floral aroma. (1983) ✔ Menetou-Salon Rouge et Rosé.
✚ Henri Pellé et Fils, Morogues, 18220 Les Aix-d'Augillon; tel. 48 64 42 48 ☎ By appt.

Pouilly-sur-Loire, Pouilly Blanc Fumé

The dry white wine vineyards of Pouilly-sur-Loire were originally established by Benedictine monks. The river turns north-west at this point, its course blocked by a limestone promontory which is the site of 470 hectares of fine vineyards with an excellent southerly and south-easterly exposure. Traditionally, Pouilly has always made delicate, light and drinkable white wines from the Chasselas grape. Today, although there are still some Chasselas vines, they will soon have been totally replaced by the other grape variety found here, the Sauvignon Blanc-Fumé. However, the Sauvignon Blanc-Fumé has many qualities, drawing its character from the limestone soils. It combines freshness and vigour with a blend of aromas, specific to the grape variety, that have been mellowed by the growing medium and fermentation conditions.

Current annual production from the Sauvignon is 18000 hectolitres, as against 4000 hectolitres from the Chasselas.

The magnificent Loire scenery, the rolling vineyards and the charm of such spots as Les Cornets, Les Loges and Le Calvaire de St-Andelain, give visitors to Pouilly a perfect visual counterpoint to the character of the wines themselves. Particularly suited to dry cheeses and seafood, they are also delightful served well chilled as an aperitif.

DOMAINE DU BUISSON-MENARD
Clos du Chailloux***

☐	4.8ha	36000	4 D 🍷 ↓

75 76 80 81 82 82 * ⑧ 83

This family have been producing excellent wines here for eight generations, a fact confirmed in this bottle. Clear golden colour, full clean nose evocative of linden blossom. Full, soft and harmonious on the palate with a dominant note of liquorice. (1983)
♠ Didier Dagueneau, Les Berthiers, St-Andelain, 58150 Pouilly-sur-Loire; tel. 86 39 15 62

DOMAINE DES COQUES**

☐	5ha	25000	3 D 🍷 ↓

69 75 82 83

This hillside vineyard produces a brilliant gold-green wine with a lively bouquet of yellow peaches, and a full, distinguished taste is crowned by a hint of tobacco. (1983) ✔ Pouilly-sur-Loire.
♠ Patrick Coulbois, Les Berthiers, St-Andelain, 58150 Pouilly-sur-Loire; tel. 86 39 15 69 ☎ By appt. Closed last week Aug.

GITTON PERE ET FILS
Clos Joanne d'Orion**

☐	3ha	20000	4 D 🍷 ⅲ ↓

76 78 80 * 82 * 83

Limpid, straightforward gold colour with very musky scent. On the palate, full of flavour and well balanced. Typical of the vintage. (1982)
♠ Gitton Père et Fils, Ménétréol, 18300 Sancerre; tel. 48 54 38 84 ☎ By appt.

DOMAINE MASSON-BLONDELET
Les Bacoins***

☐	3ha	20000	4 D 🍷 ↓

69 76 80 81 82 *83 83

Pure golden colour, strong scent of acacia blossom and fat, round taste, very long and reminiscent of flowers and honey. (1983) ✔ Pouilly-Fumé, Pouilly-Fumé les Criots, Pouilly-sur-Loire, Sancerre Blanc.
♠ Jean-Michel Masson, 58150 Pouilly-sur-Loire; tel. 86 39 00 34 ☎ By appt.

LA LOGE AUX MOINES**

☐	8ha	40000	3 D 🍷 ↓

78 *81 *82 *83 **84**

This vineyard used to belong to the Benedictines of La Charité-sur-Loire, who created the Pouilly style in wine. The wine is a dark golden colour and has a nose with a fragrance of honey and musk. Full and firm on the palate, combining aromas of vanilla and pepper. (1983)
♠ Patrice Moreux, Les Loges, 58150 Pouilly-Loire; tel. 86 39 00 52 ☎ By appt.

LES MOULINS A VENT*

☐	12ha	150000	3 D 🍷 ↓

80 81 82 82 *83 83

The Caves de Pouilly vinify, grow and bottle the best wines from well-known vineyards covered by the appellation 'Blanc Fumé de Pouilly-sur-Loire'. This particular wine is a clear gold colour with a clean nose of pepper and new-mown hay. Its full fat mature taste combines honey and tobacco. (1983) ✔ Pouilly-sur-Loire les Moulins à Vent.
♠ Coop. de Pouilly-sur-Loire, 58150 Pouilly-sur-Loire; tel. 86 39 10 99 ☎ By appt.

GAEC ROGER PABIOT ET FILS
Coteau de Girarmes*

☐	9ha	50000	3 D 🍷 ↓

76 79 81 *83 83

This wine is a pure gold colour with a clean fruity nose of honey and plums. Its balanced Sauvignon taste is full, round, fat and aromatic. This family-run vineyard produces wines of individuality and quality. (1983)
♠ GAEC Roger Pabiot Père et Fils, Tracy-sur-Loire, 58150 Pouilly-sur-Loire; tel. 86 39 12 41 ☎ By appt.

LA RENARDIERE★

| ☐ | 5 ha | 30000 | 3 D 🍷 ↓ |
| 76 81 83 | | | |

The grandfather of the present grower planted the first non-grafted Blanc-Fumé vine. The wine is pale gold in colour with a discreet nose of vanilla and honey. On the palate it is charming and lively, dominated by the taste of dried almond. (1983) ✔ Pouilly-sur-Loire.
↜ Pascal Bouchié, La Renardière, St-Andelain, 58150 Pouilly-sur-Loire; tel. 86 39 14 01 ☥ By appt. Closed Aug.

DOMAINE SAGET *Les Roches*★★

| ☐ | 15 ha | 70000 | 4 D 🍷 ↓ |
| ⑧⑵ ⑧⑵ 83 83 | | | |

This 1982 'Les Roches' has been regularly served at State banquets. Classic pure gold colour and lively bouquet, fully confirmed on the palate. (1982) ✔ Pouilly-sur-Loire les Moulins à Vent.
↜ Guy Saget, Caves St-Vincent, 58150 Pouilly-sur-Loire; tel. 86 39 16 37 ☥ Daily 8.00–12.00/ 14.00–18.00.

CHATEAU DE TRACY★

| ☐ | 22 ha | 100000 | 4 D 🍷 ↓ |
| 77 78 **79** 81 82 83 | | | |

This famous family, dating back to the 15th century, produce wine that is amber-gold in colour, with a well-developed nose reminiscent of dried walnuts. It is easy to drink leaving an impression of honey and wax. (1983)
↜ Alain Destutt d'Assay, Ch. de Tracy-sur-Loire, 58150 Pouilly-sur-Loire; tel. 86 39 10 55 ☥ By appt.

Quincy

On the banks of the river Cher, not far from Bourges or from Mehun-sur-Yèvre, the vineyards of Quincy and Brinay extend over 100 hectares of sand- and gravel-covered plateaus.

Quincy is made solely from the Sauvignon Blanc (about 3500 hecto-litres) and is characterized by a simple, light, fruity flavour and crisp acidity. If, as Dr Guyot wrote last century, the grape variety dominates the cru, Quincy wines show, however, that the same grape variety planted in the same region produces different results depending on the nature of the soil. All the better for the wine-lover, who will find very elegant Loire wines here to go with fish, seafood, or goat's cheese.

GERARD MEUNIER-LAPHA★

| ☐ | 6 ha | 35000 | 3 D 🍷 ◑ ↓ |
| ★79 ★80 ★81 ⑧⑵ 83 83 ★84 | | | |

A pale golden wine with a light but distinctive nose of new leather dominated by fennel. The flavour is round and warm leaving a pleasant aftertaste of caramel. (1983) ✔ Vin de Pays du

Cher Blanc Sec, Rosé et Rouge, Méthode Champenoise Meunier.
↜ Gérard Meunier, Quincy, 18120 Lury-sur-Arnon; tel. 48 51 31 16 ☥ By appt.

RAYMOND PIPET★

| ☐ | 12 ha | 75000 | 3 D 🍷 ↓ |
| **74 79** 82 ★83 83 84 | | | |

Fine, deep golden colour, with an attractive fragrance of fresh herbs, and a flavour recalling young wood and green apples. A good, round and supple wine produced by an old-established family estate. (1983) ✔ Vin de Pays du Cher-Arnon Rosé and Rouge.
↜ Raymond Pipet, Quincy, 18120 Lury-sur-Arnon; tel. 48 51 31 17 ☥ Daily 9.00–12.00/ 14.00–18.00.

Reuilly

Reuilly, in Berry, is one of the best vineyards of the whole region, albeit modest in size (only 30 hectares) and in the amount of wine it produces (1200 hectolitres). With its steep, sunny hillsides and its excellent soils, Reuilly is perfectly suited to vine cultivation and produces some first-rate wines.

The appellation covers seven communes in the Indre and Cher department – a delightful region traversed by the green valleys of the Rivers Cher, Arnon and Théols. The Sauvignon Blanc is the main grape variety for Reuilly's dry, yet full and fruity white wines. The Pinot Gris is used here to produce a soft, delicate and distinguished rosé, but it is in imminent danger of being replaced by Pinot Noir vines. These also produce excellent rosés, clean and fresh, that have more colour than the Pinot Gris wines. More importantly, however, this variety gives full and well-rounded red wines that are always light, complex and distinctively fruity, with seductive aromas of violets and raspberries.

DOMAINE HENRI BEURDIN
Sauvignon★

| ☐ | 5 ha | 25000 | 2 D 🍷 ↓ |
| 81 ★82 ★83 ★83 ★84 | | | |

Deep golden colour, with well-developed nose of dried lime flowers. Well-rounded, smooth, slightly woody taste. (1983)
↜ Henri Beurdin, Preuilly, 18120 Lury-sur-Arnon; tel. 48 51 30 78 ☥ By appt. Closed 26 Dec.–3 Jan.

DOMAINE HENRI BEURDIN
Pinot Noir★★

■   2ha   9000   2 D ⦀ ↓

★82 ★83 ★83 ★84

Beautiful, deep ruby-red colour, with distinctive nose of tanned leather. The firm, well-rounded taste contains complex, fruity flavours, particularly banana. (1983)
� Henri Beurdin, Preuilly, 18120 Lury-sur-Arnon; tel. 48 51 30 78 ⵝ By appt. Closed 26 Dec.–3 Jan.

CLAUDE LAFOND *Pinot Noir*★

■   1ha   6000   3 D ▮ ↓

81 82 83 83 84

Beautiful, rich cherry-red colour with a strong, complex nose, full of leafy scents. Taste is full and subtle, with a pleasant background of fresh apples. (1983)
� Claude Lafond, Bois St-Denis, 36260 Reuilly; tel. 54 49 22 17 ⵝ Daily 9.00–19.00.

CLAUDE LAFOND *Pinot Gris*★

◩   1ha   6000   3 D ▮ ↓

76 ⑦⑧ 81 82 83 83 84

Strong salmon-pink colour, with a light nose. Delicate, distinctive taste that is very well balanced.(1983)
� Claude Lafond, Bois St-Denis, 36260 Reuilly; tel. 54 49 22 17 ⵝ Daily 9.00–19.00.

CLAUDE LAFOND★

□   4ha   25000   3 D ▮ ↓

76 81 82 83 83 84

Very clear white with slightly golden tinge. Strong scent of gingerbread on the nose. On the palate, light and fresh, with a scent of acacia flowers. (1983) ✔ Reuilly Pinot Gris, Reuilly Pinot Noir.
� Claude Lafond, Bois St-Denis, 36260 Reuilly; tel. 54 49 22 17 ⵝ Daily 9.00–19.00.

GUY MALBETE *Pinot Gris*★★

◩   1.5ha   8000   2 D ▮ ⦀ ↓

79 80 81 82 ⑧⑨ 83 84

Fine rosé, faintly salmon-pink in colour. Straightforward nose with subtle touch of raisins. Full-flavoured, with fruitiness in which complex scents combine with a touch of camphor. (1983)
� Guy Malbète, Bois St-Denis, 36260 Reuilly; tel. 54 49 25 09 ⵝ By appt. Closed Sun. afternoon.

GUY MALBETE *Sauvignon*

□   3ha   12000   3 D ▮ ⦀ ↓

79 80 81 82 83 84

Distinct, clear gold colour and well-developed nose combining musk and liquorice. Well-rounded taste, full of flavour, with slight touch of resin. (1983)
� Guy Malbète, Bois St-Denis, 36260 Reuilly; tel. 54 49 25 09 ⵝ By appt. Closed Sun. afternoon.

GUY MALBETE★

■   1ha   5400   2 D ▮ ⦀ ↓

82 83 83 84

Cherry-red with a touch of orange. Fresh scent of wild strawberries. On the palate seems quite tannic, with a raspberry fruitiness. (1983)
� Guy Malbète, Bois St-Denis, 36260 Reuilly; tel. 54 49 25 09 ⵝ By appt. Closed Sun. afternoon.

DIDIER MARTIN★★★

◩   1ha   3000   3 D ⦀

64 71 76 81 82 ★83

Fine example from the Pinot Gris, an increasingly uncommon speciality of Reuilly, but which is well worth continuing with if the wines are as good as this one. Beautiful, clear amber colour and straightforward scent of heather honey. Mild and delicate on the palate, and honeyed in taste. (1983)
� Didier Martin, Route d'Issoudun, 36260 Reuilly; tel. 54 49 20 77 ⵝ By appt. Closed Aug.

DIDIER MARTIN

□   2ha   8000   3 D ⦀

64 71 76 81 82 ★83

Good, clear wine with distinct gold colour, backed by lively nose of honey and wax. Mature, dry taste with a certain woodiness. (1983)
� Didier Martin, Route d'Issoudun, 36260 Reuilly; tel. 54 49 20 77 ⵝ By appt. Closed Aug.

GILBERT ROUSIE *Pinot*★

◩   1ha   2000   3 D ⦀ ↓

76 82 83 84

Pale salmon-pink colour with a faint scent of fruit drops. Mild taste, with a hint of light tobacco. (1983)
� Gilbert Rousié, 17 Rue du Dr-Apard, 36260 Reuilly; tel. 54 49 20 15 ⵝ By appt.

GILBERT ROUSIE *Sauvignon*★

□   1ha   4000   3 D ⦀ ↓

76 82 83 83 84

Beautiful, clear, golden colour and distinct fragrance of acacia honey. Good, firm flavour, but rather short-lived on the palate, though with a pleasantly resinous finish. (1983)
� Gilbert Rousié, 17 Rue du Dr-Apard, 36260 Reuilly; tel. 54 49 20 15 ⵝ By appt.

SORBE ET FILS★

☑	1.5ha	4800	**2** **D** **ɪ** **◉** **↓**

76 78 81 82 ★83 84

Distinct salmon-pink colour with slightly woody fragrance. Warm, supple taste with hint of caramel. (1983) ✔ Vin de Pays du Cher.
➜ *MM*. Sorbe et Fils, La Quervée, Preuilly, 18120 Lury-sur-Arnon; tel. 48 51 03 07 ☓ By appt.

Sancerre

Sancerre is an especially privileged wine-growing location, proudly dominating some of the most beautiful scenery of the Loire valley. The vineyards extend over eleven communes and a magnificent network of hills which could have been designed specifically for the cultivation of the vine. The hills provide sheltered locations, with a sunny exposure and limestone or sandy soils well suited to making high-quality wine. Around 1400 hectares are planted, the predominant varieties being the Sauvignon Blanc and Pinot Noir. Both are highly distinguished grape types which do very well here, translating the particular qualities of the terroir into a uniquely local style of wine. The largest part of the production (about 45000 hectolitres per year) is given over to white wines which are fresh, fruity and usually drunk young. The rosé wines (3500 hectolitres) are subtle and delicate, while the reds (about 6500 hectolitres) are light, fragrant, and well rounded.

Sancerre is an area with a very strong local identity: a community of growers taking pride in their land, their work and their wines. It is not an easy task producing this fine wine on land that is close to the northern-most limits of French wine-growing, and at an altitude of 200–300 metres – especially when the main grape variety, Sauvignon (not an early variety), is grown on slopes which are among the steepest in France, and the delicately balanced fermentation process takes place at the end of this late growing season!

White Sancerre goes particularly well with a dry goat's cheese such as the famous 'crottin' from Chavignol (a village which also produces wine), with fish, or a hot, mildly spicy entrée. The red wines are good with poultry or local meat dishes.

JACQUES AUCHERES *Clos du Désert*★

☐	2ha	12000	**3** **D** **ɪ**

⑧³ **83** **84**

Clear, pale gold with a nose of honey and wax. To taste, well made but vigorous, with a background of boxwood. Ready to drink. (1984) ✔ Sancerre Rouge and Rosé.
➜ Jacques Auchères, Bué, 18300 Sancerre; tel. 48 54 06 61 ☓ By appt.

BAILLY-REVERDY *Chêne Marchand*★★

☐	8ha	40000	**3** **D** **ɪ** **↓**

73 81 82 ★83 84

Clear, golden wine with fruity fragrance of apples and quinces. To drink, vigorous and faintly sparkling, full-flavoured with pleasant hint of liquorice. (1982)
➜ GAEC Bailly-Reverdy et Fils, Bué, 18300 Sancerre; tel. 48 54 18 38 ☓ By appt.

DOMAINE BALLAND-CHAPUIS
Clos Vallon★

☐	3ha	15000	**4** **D** **ɪ** **↓**

⑦⁶ **78 79 82 83**

Bright, slightly greeny-gold colour, with a musky scent. On the palate, it is round, a little flat and has a touch of greenness. (1983) ✔ Sancerre Clos du-Chêne Marchand Blanc Sec, Sancerre Rouge and Rosé, Côteaux du Giennois Blanc Sec and Rouge.
➜ Joseph Balland-Chapuis, BP 24, Bué, 18300 Sancerre; tel. 48 54 06 67 ☓ By appt.

DOMAINE BALLAND-CHAPUIS★

■	3ha	3000	**4** **D** **ɪ** **↓**

⑦⁶ **78 79 82 83 84**

Definite ruby colour, and a reserved nose with a hint of vanilla. On the palate, a slight astringency from the wood tannins hides the fruit in the structure which is still undeveloped. (1983)
➜ Joseph Balland-Chapuis, BP 24, Bué, 18300 Sancerre; tel. 48 54 06 67 ☓ By appt.

CELLIER CROIX-SAINT-URSIN
Chêne Marchand★★

☐	3.6ha	15000	**3** **D** **ɪ** **↓**

74 76 79 82 ★83 ★84

Good, clear gold colour. Full nose with hint of liquorice. Straightforward taste typical of the Sauvignon grape, quite complex, well balanced and fully mature. (1983) ✔ Sancerre Rouge and Rosé.
➜ Sylvain Bailly, Bué, 18300 Sancerre; tel. 48 54 06 32 ☓ Mon.–Sat. 8.00–12.00/13.30–19.00.

DOMAINE DAULNY ET FILS★★

☐	7ha	45000	**3** **D** **◉**

71 73 75 78 ★83 ★⑧⁴ ★84

Beautiful, limpid, greenish-gold colour. Pronounced floral fragrances, especially rose. On the palate, full, fat, well built and vigorous, with fruitiness suggesting blackcurrants and passion-fruit. (1983) ✔ Sancerre Rouge and Rosé.
➜ René Daulny et Fils, Chaudenay-Verdigny, 18300 Sancerre; tel. 48 54 22 93 ☓ Daily 8.00–12.00/14.00–19.00.

GITTON PERE ET FILS *Les Romains**

■   1 ha   7000   🔲 Ⓓ 🖩 ⑪ ⌊

62 73 76 ⋆82 ⋆⑧③

Good, strong ruby-red colour, with slight touch of amber. Straightforward, obvious nose which has a pleasant hint of oak. Full, firm taste reminiscent of sparkling spring water, with trace of iodine. Still a bit dumb, particularly on the nose, but full of promise. (1983)
❧ Gitton Père et Fils, Ménétréol, 18300 Sancerre; tel. 48 54 38 84 ⏺ By appt.

GITTON PERE ET FILS
*Les Belles Dames****

☐   7 ha   50000   🔲 Ⓓ 🖩 ⑪ ⌊

55 62 73 76 ⋆⑧③ ⋆83

Limpid, pale gold, with full, subtle fragrance reminiscent of gingerbread and mint. Well-rounded, well-made taste, typical of flinty soils, and curiously reminiscent of dry casks. Fine example of wines grown on this type of soil. (1983)
❧ Gitton Père et Fils, Ménétréol, 18300 Sancerre; tel. 48 54 38 84 ⏺ By appt.

GITTON PERE ET FILS
*Vigne du Larrey***

☐   1.5 ha   7000   🔲 Ⓓ 🖩 ⑪ ⌊

55 62 73 76 80 ⑧② ⋆83

Particularly interesting to the connoisseur, and may well surprise the wine-lover familiar with the usual Sancerres. Limpid, pale gold, but its scent recalls bay, juniper and broom-flowers. Full, rich, heavy taste confirms the complex nose. (1982)
❧ Gitton Père et Fils, Ménétréol, 18300 Sancerre; tel. 48 54 38 84 ⏺ By appt.

DOMAINE DE LA MERCY-DIEU**

◪   4 ha   10000   🔳 Ⓓ 🖩 ⌊

81 82 83 ⋆84

Rosé with attractive, greyish, salmon-pink colour and delicate, subtle fragrance, very floral in character. On the palate, lively and vigorous, with fresh hazelnut taste. (1983)
❧ GAEC Bailly-Reverdy et Fils, Bué, 18300 Sancerre; tel. 48 54 18 38 ⏺ By appt.

DOMAINE DE LA MERCY-DIEU***

■   4 ha   8000   🔳 Ⓓ 🖩 ⌊

73 76 78 ⋆⑧② ⋆82

Beautiful, strong, ruby or garnet colour. Nose is full and strongly redolent of Russian leather. To

taste, well made and rather high in tannin, with fruity flavour of cherries in brandy. Has a good future. (1982)
❧ GAEC Bailly-Reverdy et Fils, Bué, 18300 Sancerre; tel. 48 54 18 38 ⏺ By appt.

DOMAINE DE LA MERCY-DIEU*

☐   8 ha   40000   🔳 Ⓓ 🖩 ⌊

73 81 82 ⋆83 84

Clear, greenish-gold colour. Very aromatic nose, with pleasant hint of bracken. On the palate, a well-made, warm, rounded taste, with leafy fruitiness. (1983) ✔ Sancerre Pinot Rouge and Rosé, Sancerre Clos du Chêne Marchand Blanc Sec.
❧ GAEC Bailly-Reverdy et Fils, Bué, 18300 Sancerre; tel. 48 54 18 38 ⏺ By appt.

DOMAINE DE LA MOUSSIERE

☐   35 ha   130000   🔲 Ⓓ 🖩 ⑪ ⌊

⑧③ 84

Clear, slightly effervescent. Pale, greenish-white colour with nose of pears and green apples, and light, gentle taste. ✔ Sancerre la Moussière '83, Sancerre Rouge and Rosé.
❧ Alphonse Mellot, 3 Rue Porte-César, 18300 Sancerre; tel. 48 54 07 41 ⏺ By appt. Closed Sat. and Sun.

CAVE DES PIERRIS**

☐   9 ha   30000   🔳 Ⓓ 🖩 ⑪ ⌊

76 79 82 83 84

Good, clear wine with distinct gold colour and straightforward, well-balanced fragrance with a delicate scent of bergamot. Full, fresh taste, with complex, spicy flavours, which develops slowly but surely. (1983)
❧ Roger Champault, Crézancy, 18399 Sancerre; tel. 48 79 00 03 ⏺ By appt.

DOMAINE PAUL PRIEUR ET FILS***

■   4 ha   10000   🔳 Ⓓ 🖩 ⑪ ⌊

78 79 ⋆82 ⋆82 ⋆83 84

Lovely ruby colour; fine distinctive nose with a hint of truffles. Very round, full and well-balanced on the palate, where it develops yet more aromas. A strikingly individual wine which will keep well. (1982) ✔ Sancerre Blanc Sec and Rosé.
❧ Paul Prieur et Fils, Verdigny, 18300 Sancerre; tel. 48 54 20 28 ⏺ By appt.

DOMAINE PAUL PRIEUR ET FILS**

☐   4 ha   25000   🔳 Ⓓ 🖩 ⑪ ⌊

78 79 80 ⑧② 82 ⋆83 84

Clear and brilliant, with pale greenish-gold colour. Strong and fresh fragrance, with blend of fresh fruits and peppermint that is soft and well made. Full-flavoured, with traces of toasted almonds and liquorice. (1983)
❧ Paul Prieur et Fils, Verdigny, 18300 Sancerre; tel. 48 54 20 28 ⏺ By appt.

BERNARD REVERDY ET FILS*

☐   5 ha   33000   🔲 Ⓓ 🖩 ⌊

70 75 76 82 83 ⋆84

Clear greenish-gold with slightly pepperminty fragrance. Full, warm taste on the palate, with pronounced fruitiness. (1983) ✔ Sancerre Rouge and Rosé.

🕯 Bernard Reverdy et Fils, Chandoux-Verdigny, 18300 Sancerre; tel. 48 54 26 13 ⅄ By appt.

BERNARD REVERDY ET FILS★★★

| ☑ | 2ha | 12000 | 4 D ▮ ⅏ ⅃ |

74 75 78 82 ★83 ★⑧④ ★84

Clear, gently sparkling wine with distinct salmon-pink tinge. Delicate nose, with most attractive, complex, spring-like fragrance, and background of fennel. Taste is full and vigorous for a rosé, with an aftertaste of Morello cherries. To keep for a few years. (1983) ✔ Sancerre Blanc Sec and Rouge.

🕯 Bernard Reverdy et Fils, Chandoux-Verdigny, 18300 Sancerre; tel. 48 54 26 13 ⅄ By appt.

DOMAINE DE SAINT-PIERRE★★

| ■ | 2ha | 8000 | 4 D ▮ ⅏ |

78 79 82 ★83 ★84

Clear, light ruby-red colour. Strong, young fragrance, with attractive scent of tar and leaves mixed with violets. On the palate, the taste is quite closed up and youthful but with a good blend of oak, currants and cherries. (1983)

🕯 Pierre Prieur et Fils, Verdigny, 18300 Sancerre; tel. 48 54 08 45 ⅄ By appt. Closed end Aug.

DOMAINE DE SAINT-PIERRE★★★

| ☐ | 8ha | 25000 | 4 D ▮ ⅏ |

78 79 80 82 ★83 ★84

Limpid and faintly sparkling, with greenish-gold colour. Very floral nose, with the strong spring-like smell of May-blossom. To taste, fresh, vigorous and full of lovely aromas, strongly reminiscent of the agave, characteristic of the Sauvignon grape. (1983)

🕯 Pierre Prieur et Fils, Verdigny, 18300 Sancerre; tel. 48 54 08 45 ⅄ By appt. Closed end Aug.

DOMAINE DE SAINT-PIERRE★★

| ☑ | 8ha | 5000 | 4 D ▮ ⅏ |

78 79 82 83 84

A clear, vivid salmon-pink wine whose fresh nose of ripe cherries develops in the mouth into a full, fat, warm wine, evoking the taste of crystallized cherries. (1983)

🕯 Pierre Prieur et Fils, Verdigny, 18300 Sancerre; tel. 48 54 08 45 ⅄ By appt. Closed end Aug.

CHRISTIAN SALMON
Chêne Marchand★

| ☐ | 10ha | 35000 | 4 D ▮ ⅏ ⅃ |

79 81 ★83 ★84

Good, clear wine. Pale gold, with full aroma of ripe fruits and hint of fennel. To taste, full bodied, well made, quite round, with faint flavour of banana. Very promising, if left to age. (1983)

🕯 Christian Salmon, Bué, 18300 Sancerre; tel. 48 54 20 54 ⅄ By appt. Closed Aug.

CHRISTIAN SALMON *Petit Chemarin*★★

| ☐ | 10ha | 35000 | 4 D ▮ ⅏ ⅃ |

79 81 ★83 ★84

Coming from one of the best areas of Bué, a clear, pale-gold wine, with a strongly aromatic, spicy scent of agave. Well-knit, smooth and fruity taste, with the agave still predominant. (1983)

🕯 Christian Salmon, Bué, 18300 Sancerre; tel. 48 54 20 54 ⅄ By appt. Closed Aug.

CHRISTIAN SALMON★

| ■ | 2ha | 10000 | 4 D ▮ ⅏ ⅃ |

76 81 ★83 ★84

Strong, brilliant cherry-red colour combined with slightly woody nose reminiscent of raspberries; very oaky tannin taste, with traces of blackcurrant, and an attractive resinous flavour. (1983)

🕯 Christian Salmon, Bué, 18300 Sancerre; tel. 48 54 20 54 ⅄ By appt. Closed Aug.

CHATEAU DE THAUVENAY

| ☐ | 12ha | 70000 | 3 D ▮ ⅏ ⅃ |

66 76 77 ⑧② ⑧③ 84

Clear, amber colour with faintly woody, pronounced waxy scent. Full flavoured, well made and mature on the palate, with hint of Russian leather. (1983)

🕯 Georges de Choulot, Ch. de Thauvenay, 18300 Sancerre; tel. 48 54 07 22 ⅄ By appt.

DOMAINE DES TROIS-NOYERS★

| ☐ | 5ha | 35000 | 3 D ▮ ⅃ |

76 78 82 ⑧③ 84

Beautiful, limpid greenish-gold with spicy fragrance of stocks. Attractive, full and well made, with aftertaste of vanilla. (1983) ✔ Sancerre Rouge and Rosé.

🕯 Roger Reverdy-Cadet, Chandoux-Verdigny, 18300 Sancerre; tel. 48 54 18 92 ⅄ By appt. Closed late Aug.–early Sept.

DOMAINE DES VILLOTS★★★

| ☐ | 7ha | 25000 | 4 D ▮ ⅃ |

76 79 82 ⑧③ 84

Beautifully clear, pale-gold colour, with a delicate fragrance that is nevertheless strongly vanilla in character. Full-flavoured and fruity, with an attractive taste of cooked pears. (1983) ✔ Sancerre.

🕯 Jean Reverdy et Fils, Verdigny, 18300 Sancerre; tel. 48 54 07 62 ⅄ No visitors.

THE RHONE VALLEY

THE POWERFUL River Rhône sweeps through France towards the Midi – and the southern sun. Far from dividing the areas of countryside that it flows through, the Rhône appears to unite them, and along each bank stretch some of France's most ancient vineyards.

After Bordeaux, the Rhône valley is the largest wine-producing region in France. It can compete in quality, too, and some of its growths arouse as much interest among connoisseurs as the top-echelon wines of Bordeaux or Burgundy. For many years, however, Côtes du Rhône wine was underestimated. It was seen as a nice enough wine to be drunk by the glass at the counter, but a little vulgar nevertheless; only very rarely would it appear on an elegant dinner table. The average Rhône was a 'one-night wine', so-called because it spent less than twenty-four hours in vat and so would be light, fruity, and not very tannic; typically, it could be found alongside Beaujolais in the 'bouchons', or local wine bars, of Lyons.

Nevertheless, true wine lovers still appreciated the better wines of the Rhône, tasting a Hermitage with the respect appropriate to a great bottle. Today, thanks to a continual improvement in the quality of the wine, the image of Côtes du Rhône has changed dramatically. Although the jug wines happily continue to appear on the metal counters of the bouchons, the fine wines of the Rhône are now fully established at the best dinner tables.

Very few vineyards can pride themselves on a past as glorious as those of the Côte du Rhône. From Vienne to Avignon, the names of its towns and villages recall some of the most exciting pages of French history. And the story goes back even further – more than two thousand years. On the outskirts of Vienne is one of the oldest vineyards in France. Established by Phoenician colonists from Marseilles, it was later developed by the Romans. Vineyards are mentioned during the fourth century BC in the areas which are today called Hermitage and Côte-Rôtie, while vines appeared in the Die region about the beginning of the first century. Twelfth-century Templar Knights planted the first Chateauneuf-du-Pape vines, and this work was continued by Pope Jean XXII two centuries later. As for the Côtes du Rhône wines from the Gard, they first enjoyed major popularity during the seventeenth and eighteenth centuries.

This extraordinary tradition is continued by the promotional efforts of the Rhône growers, shippers and local organizations. A sustained international campaign has educated consumers to recognize the quality and diversity of Rhône wines, while at the same time new opportunities have been created within the region itself for visitors who want to know more about the wines. In the southern half of the region, for example, the medieval château of Suze-la-Rousse houses L'Université du Vin, which organizes courses for amateurs and professionals, as well as holding regular exhibitions. In addition, the Interprofessional Committee has created a wine trail, or Route des Vins. Nine different routes, each with special signposts painted by artist Georges Mathieu, give tourists the chance to explore the region, enjoy its scenery, learn something of its incredible history – and taste its wines!

Along most of the length of the Rhône valley, vines are grown on both banks of the river. Some people make the distinction between right-(west-) bank wines, which are full-bodied and heady, and the lighter wines of the left bank. It is more usual, however, to make the distinction between two very different areas: the northern Côtes du Rhône, to the north of Valence, and the southern Côtes du Rhône, to the south of Montélimar. There is a stretch of 50 kilometres between these two sectors where no vines are grown.

We must not forget the lesser-known appellations bordering southern Côtes du Rhône, which produce some distinctive, high-quality wines. To the north lie the Coteaux de Tricastin; to the east, the Côtes de Ventoux and VDQS Côtes de Luberon; and to the north-west, VDQS Côtes du Vivarais. There are three further appellations which are situated farther away from the valley proper. Clairette de Die and Clairette de Chatillon-en-Diois, made near the Vercors in the Drôme valley; and VDQS Coteaux de Pierrevert, produced in the department of Alpes-de-

The Northern Rhône

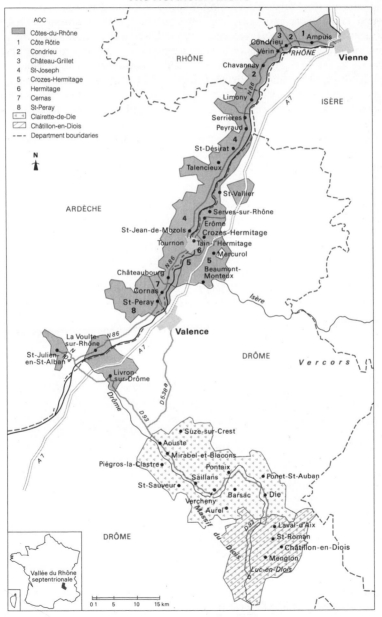

Hautes-Provence. Finally, the two Vaucluse sweet wine appellations should be mentioned; these are Muscat de Beaumes de Venise and Rasteau (see Vins Doux Naturels section, pp. 609–610).

It is possible to divide the vast area of the Rhône valley in yet another way; into three subdivisions according to climate and soil type. North of Valence there is a temperate climate with a continental influence; here the soil is mostly granite and the terrain one of steep hillsides. The red wines of the region are made solely from the Syrah grape; white wines come from the Marsanne and Roussanne, with a small production of the Viognier grape, used to make Château Grillet and Condrieu. In the Diois region the climate is influenced by the mountainous terrain, and the limestone soils of the vineyards are made up of scree fallen from the lower mountain slopes. Clairette and Muscat vines have adapted well to the local growing conditions. Finally, to the south of Montelimar the Mediterranean climate takes over, and some very diverse soils cover a limestone bedrock (terraces of round pebbles, red clay and sand, and sandstone). Here, the main grape variety is Grenache, but climatic extremes force the growers to use several different grape varieties in order to obtain a perfectly balanced wine; these include Syrah, Mourvèdre, Cinsault, Carignan, Clairette, and Bourboulenc.

Following a sharp decline during the nineteenth century, the Rhône valley vineyard area has expanded once more, and is still increasing in size. It now covers a total of 63 975 hectares, includes more than 160 communes, and in an average year produces 3 million hectolitres of wine. In the southern sector almost 50 per cent of the production is marketed by négociants, and in the northern sector almost 70 per cent by cooperatives.

Côtes du Rhône

The regional appellation Côtes du Rhône was created in 1937 and covers six departments; the Gard, Ardèche, Drôme, Vaucluse, Loire and Rhône. The 40800 hectares of vines are almost all in the southern half of the region and annual production averages 2.1 million hectolitres.

With dozens of micro-climates and a rich diversity of soils and grape types, these vineyards are capable of producing a wine to please every palate. The warmest regions – on the alpine diluvium soils of Domazan, Esterzargues, Courthezon or Orange – produce full, tannic and generous red wines that need a certain amount of bottle age before they can be served with red meat dishes. The lighter soils of Puymeras, Nyons, Sabran or Bourg-St-Andéol produce lighter, fresher wines. Following the success of Beaujolais Nouveau, there are now Côtes du Rhône Vins Primeurs which are enjoying an ever-increasing popularity; clean and fruity, they are ready to drink by 15 November of the same year and go well with white meat dishes or charcuterie.

The summer heat and dryness tend to give the white and rosé wines a high alcohol content and low acidity. Technological advances have enabled the wine-makers to produce increasingly fresh, aromatic and delicate wines, for which demand is growing apace. The whites should be served with saltwater fish and the rosés with a salad or charcuterie.

AMPHORE DE DIONYSOS★

☑	485 ha	3 D ▮ ↓

78 82 83

With its fairly dark-pink, almost light-red colour, this wine has a faint scent of redcurrant and is notable above all for its structure. (1983) *MM.* Ch. de Seresin et Fils, Dom. de Bruthel, Colombier, Sabran, 30200 Bagnols-sur-Cèze; tel. 66 79 96 24 ☎ Mon.–Sat. 9.00–12.00/14.00–19.00. Sun. 14.00–18.00. ⚓ UCVF Bagnols-sur-Cèze, 12 Rue St-Victor, 30201 Bagnols-sur-Cèze; tel. 66 89 56 04 ☎ By appt.

AMPHORE DE DIONYSOS★

☐	485 ha	3 D ▮ ↓

78 82 83

A gleaming light-yellow in colour, this is a fresh wine, firm on the palate, which should be drunk well cooled. (1983) ⚓ UCVF de Bagnols-sur-Cèze, 12 Rue St-Victor, 30200 Bagnols-sur-Cèze; tel. 66 89 56 04 ☎ By appt.

DOMAINE LES ROCHES D'ARNAUD

■ 18ha 100000 🔲 🔲 🔲 ⬤

79 80 *82* *83* ⓐ 🔲

This wine is a little short, but nevertheless holds well on the palate. (1982)
➻ Jean-Paul Arnaud, Dom. des Roches d'Arnaud, Donazan, 30390 Aramon; tel. 66 57 05 39 ⏺ Mon.–Fri. 14.00–17.00; weekends 9.00–12.00/14.00–17.00.

UCVF BAGNOLS-SUR-CEZE

■ 400ha 🔲 🔲 🔲 ⬤

78 82 🔲 **83**

Brick-red in colour, with a well-developed but quite supple bouquet of blackcurrant and ripe fruit. To be drunk young. (1983)
➻ UCVF de Bagnols-sur-Cèze, 12 Rue St-Victor, 30201 Bagnols-sur-Cèze; tel. 66 89 56 04 ⏺ By appt.

DOMAINE DE BANVIN*

☐ 2ha 4800 🔲 🔲 ⬤

Very floral aromas of white hawthorn and elder. Neither too sweet nor too crisp; a very pleasant, rich wine.
➻ Cave Zanti-Cumino, Dom. du Banvin, 84290 Cairanne; tel. 90 30 82 38 ⏺ Mon.–Sat. 8.00–12.00/14.00–20.00. Sun. 8.00–12.00. Closed Christmas, New Year's Day, Easter.

THOMAS BASSOT*

■ 15000 🔲 🔲

84

Beautiful colour. Fruity and well-balanced structure. Classic Côtes du Rhône. (1984)
➻ Thomas Bassot, 5 Quai Dumorey, 21700 Nuits-St-Georges: tel. 80 62 31 05 ⏺ By appt.

LE BENJAMIN*

☐ 200000 🔲 ⬤ ⬤

Straw-yellow colour. Already mature aroma. Roundness on the palate, with a touch of dryness in the finish. Drink immediately.
➻ Paul Etienne et Fils, 07130 St-Péray; tel. 75 40 30 18 ⏺ No visitors.

LE BENJAMIN*

■ 300000 🔲 ⬤ ⬤

A fine bottle with a beautiful red colour. Well balanced.
➻ Paul Etienne et Fils, 07130 St-Péray; tel. 75 40 30 18 ⏺ No visitors.

LE BENJAMIN*

◪ 300000 🔲 ⬤ ⬤

Very structured rosé that tends towards the balance found in a red wine; it is here that its originality lies.
➻ Paul Etienne et Fils, 07130 St-Péray; tel. 75 40 30 18 ⏺ No visitors.

CAVE J.-P. BENOIT**

■ 8ha 48000 🔲 🔲 🔲 ⬤ ⬤

79 80 *82*

A wine full of character, with powerful aromas which will please connoisseurs of original wines. Matte red-brown colour, and very individual nose, woody and spicy, with a touch of leather and civet. Good structure on the palate, with good tannin balance. (1982)
➻ Jean-Paul Benoit, Quartier la Chapelle, 84470 Châteauneuf-de-Gardagne; tel. 90 22 29 76 ⏺ Wed. and Sat. 9.00–12.30/14.00–20.00; Mon., Tues., Thurs. and Fri. 17.40–20.00.

DOMAINE DE LA BERTHETE**

☐ 5ha 6000 🔲 🔲 🔲 ⬤

🔲 ⓐ 🔲

A clear bright yellow colour with a floral nose and a vigorous palate. Closed and still very young; this is a very pleasant wine. (1983)
➻ *MM.* Cohendy-Gonnet et Fils, Route de Jonquiere, Camaret-sur-Aigues, 84150 Jonquières; tel. 90 37 22 41 ⏺ Daily 10.00–12.00/15.00–19.00.

DOMAINE DE LA BERTHETE**

◪ 12000 🔲 🔲 🔲 ⬤

83 84

This wine is an attractive candy-pink colour, with a delicate, pleasing nose. It is well balanced and a pleasure to drink. (1983)
➻ *MM.* Cohendy-Gomet et Fils, Route de Jonquières, Camaret, 84150 Jonquières; tel. 90 37 22 41 ⏺ Daily 10.00–12.00/15.00–19.00.

DOMAINE DE LA BERTHETE*

■ 30ha 140000 🔲 🔲 🔲 ⬤

80 81 82 84

A good-looking wine, with a plant-like, slightly herby bouquet and a tannic finish. (1982)
➻ Cohendy-Gomet et Fils, Route de Jonquières, Camaret, 84150 Jonquières; tel. 90 37 22 41 ⏺ Daily 10.00–12.00/15.00–19.00.

DOMAINE BERTHET-RAYNE**

■ 1ha 5040 🔲 🔲 ⬤ ⬤

64 78 79 81 82 83

After picking, the grapes are fermented for a long time. This produces well-constructed wines with a light red colour and pleasant aromas of fruit and spices. (1982) ✔ Châteauneuf-du-Pape.
➻ Christian Berthet, Route de Rauquemaure, 84350 Courthezon; tel. 90 70 74 14 ⏺ Daily 8.00–12.00/ 14.00–20.00 ➻ Christian Berthet-Rayne.

DOMAINE BLAYRAC*

■ 2ha 9600 🔲 🔲 ⬤ ⬤

78 79 80 81 ⓐ 🔲 **83**

Not a particularly attractive bouquet, but nevertheless a very full-bodied wine, with a good, dark-red colour. (1982)
➻ Pierre Blayrac, 40 bis, Rue de la République, 30400 Villeneuve-lès-Avignon; tel. 90 25 66 68 ⏺ Daily 9.00–13.00/17.00–20.00.

The Southern Rhône

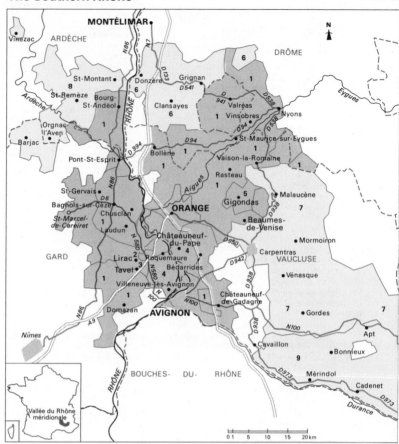

CHARTREUSE DE BONPAS★

☐   1 ha   6000   **2 D ▮ ↓**

This wine has a bright, pale yellow colour and traces of carbon dioxide which give it a touch of crispness. Round on the palate with a pleasantly warm finish. (1984)
↣ Jean Olphe-Gailliard, Chartreuse de Bonpas, 84510 Caumont-sur-Durance; tel. 90 22 54 03
Ⲧ By appt.

CHARTREUSE DE BONPAS★

▮   15 ha   60000   **2 D ▮ ↓**

The Bonpas ('good journey') monastery was founded in 1320 on the border between Comtat and Provence. The original site was a post-house at the crossing point over the Durance river. Fine terraces have replaced the ruined buildings and those that survive house the installations which produce this light red wine. The aromas are fruity and pleasing and the wine is generous, warm and slightly tannic. (1983) ✔ Côtes du Rhône Blanc 1984.
↣ Jean Olphe-Gailliard, Chartreuse de Bonpas, 84510 Caumont-sur-Durance; tel. 90 22 54 03
Ⲧ By appt.

CHATEAU DE BOUCARUT

▮   15 ha   88000   **2 D ▮ ↓**

★⑧② 8̄²̄ ★83 **84**

These vines produce unfailingly well-bred wine – usually more successful than this 1982, which tends to dry a little on the palate and, therefore, would be best for immediate drinking. (1982)
✔ Lirac.
↣ Robert Fuget, Ch. de Boucarut, 30150 Roquemaure; tel. 66 50 16 91 Ⲧ Mon.–Sat. 8.30–12.00/14.00–18.30; Sun. 10.00–12.00/14.00–17.00.

CHATEAU BOURDINES★

▮   27 ha   5000   **2 D ▮ ↓**

★⑧③ 8̄³̄

This red wine should be allowed to breathe for a good while before drinking, to give the pleasing bouquet plenty of time to present itself.
↣ Gérard Baroux, Ch. Bourdines, 84700 Sorgues; tel. 90 39 36 77 Ⲧ Mon.–Sat. 16.00–19.00.

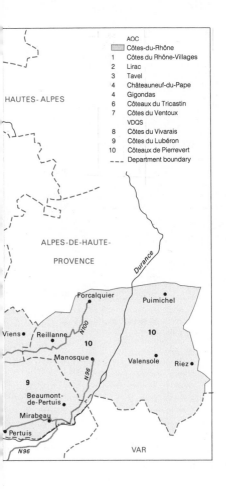

		AOC
	▨	Côtes-du-Rhône
	1	Côtes du Rhône-Villages
	2	Lirac
	3	Tavel
	4	Châteauneuf-du-Pape
	4	Gigondas
	6	Côteaux du Tricastin
	7	Côtes du Ventoux
		VDQS
	8	Côtes du Vivarais
	9	Côtes du Lubéron
	10	Côteaux de Pierrevert
	- - -	Department boundary

BROTTIERS★

■ 100000 ③ Ⓓ ▤ ↓

79 80 81 82 ★⑧③ 🔳

A special attraction at this property is a museum of wine-grower's tools, with more than 500 exhibits. This 1983 is a fine Côtes du Rhône, with an extremely good balance and a bouquet of ripe fruit. It is ready for drinking now, but would be equally suitable for laying down. (1983) ✹ Lirac Rouge, Lirac Rosé.
☛ Jean-Pierre Brotte, Châteauneuf-du-Pape, 84230 Châteauneuf-du-Pape; tel. 90 83 70 07 ☥ Daily 8.00–12.00/14.00–18.00.

DOMAINE DE LA BRUISSIERE★★

■ 26ha 180000 ② Ⓓ ▤ ⅏ ↓

80 81 82 83

Attractive red colour with shades of brown, and a gamey nose. Strong indications of ageing on the palate: a wine to be drunk without delay. (1980)
☛ Jean Gorecki, Le Mas des Collines, Gigondas, 84190 Beaumes-de-Venises; tel. 90 65 86 40 ☥ By appt ☛ Régis de Taxis du Poet.

DOMAINE BRUN-HUPAYS★

▨ 2ha 10000 ② Ⓓ ▤ ↓

82 83 84

Pink, slightly salmon colour. A well-structured wine, but a little more freshness would not come amiss. Best for summer meals.
☛ Paul Brun de Prémorel, Le Grès, 84430 Mondragon; tel. 90 30 15 42 ☥ By appt.

DOMAINE BRUN-HUPAYS★★

☐ 0.5ha 3000 ② Ⓓ ▤ ↓

Distinctive wine with a fine, pale yellow colour. Delicate floral aromas of acacia and honeysuckle are followed by smoothness and a good acid base, most noticeable in the finish.
☛ Paul Brun de Prémorel, Le Grès, 84430 Mondragon; tel. 90 30 15 42 ☥ By appt.

DOMAINE BRUN-HUPAYS★★

■ 10ha 60000 ② Ⓓ ▤ ↓

79 82 ★83 84

Rich colour: deep red, with garnet-coloured tinges and a slight nuance of yellow. The aromas are beginning to develop towards ripe red fruit and cooked fruit. Good balance on the palate, with delicate tannins which are also present in the finish. (1983)
☛ Paul Brun de Prémorel, Le Grès, 84430 Mondragon; tel. 90 30 15 42 ☥ By appt.

DOMAINE DE BRUTHEL★★

☐ 3ha 9600 ③ Ⓓ ⅏ ↓

78 79 81 ⑧③ 🔳

Yellow with sparkling green tint. Fine floral aromas on the nose and palate, and light refreshing taste. A pleasant bottle which may be drunk from now on. (1983) ✹ Côtes du Rhône Rosé, Côtes du Rhône Blanc.
☛ *MM.* Ch. de Seresin et Fils, Dom. de Bruthel, Colombier, Sabran, 30200 Bagnols-sur-Cèze; tel. 66 79 96 24 ☥ By appt.

DOMAINE DE BRUTHEL★

■ 12ha 60000 ③ Ⓓ ▤ ↓

78 79 80 81 82 83

Good cherry red colour and aromas with nuances of sugar almonds and vanilla. Fleshy and round with a good structure, it leaves a pleasant fruity aftertaste. (1983)
☛ *MM.* Ch. de Seresin et Fils, Dom. de Bruthel, Colombier, Sabran, 30200 Bagnols-sur-Cèze; tel. 66 79 96 24 ☥ Mon.–Sat. 9.00–12.00/14.00–18.00.

DOMAINE DU CABANON★★

■ 9ha 44000 ② Ⓓ ⅏ ↓

82 ★⑧③ 🔳 84

A combination of vinification methods (conventional and carbonic maceration) helps to give this wine a lovely bouquet of red fruit and spices. Fairly powerful, with a good finish. Best drunk young. (1982)
☛ Achille Payan, Dom. du Cabanon, Saze, 30650 Rochefort-du-Gard; tel. 90 31 70 74 ☥ Sun. 10.00–12.00/14.30–19.00.

DOMAINE DE CABASSE★

■   14ha   60000   🔳 D ▥ ⅲ ↓

78 79 80 ★82 83

Fine and elegant. Extremely supple and easy to drink. (1982)
☙ Nadine Latour, Dom. de Cabasse, 84000 Séguret; tel. 90 36 91 12 ⊤ By appt.

DOMAINE DE COURON

■   15ha   12500   🔳 D ▥ ↓

Peony-red colour of average intensity. Complex aromas of wood, leather and tobacco. Very pronounced alcoholic richness on the palate. (1983)
☙ M. Quelin, Quartier Labégude, St-Marcel-d'Ardèche, 07700 Bourg-St-Andéol; tel. 75 04 66 10 ⊤ By appt.

FERME DU CUBERT★

■   29ha   150000   🔳 D ▥ ↓

81 82 ⑧ 83

A dark red wine characterized by a nose with overtones of game. It is at its peak and should be drunk now. (1982)
☙ Véronique Marres-Monnier, Ferme de Cubert, 84820 Visan; tel. 75 98 31 95 ⊤ By appt.

CHATEAU DE DOMAZAN★★★

■   30ha   150000   🔳 D ▥ ⅲ ↓

★78 79 80 81 ★82

Dark, luminous red that announces a fine structure, finishing on a note of confidence. (1982)
☙ MM. Chauderac et Fils, Ch. de Domazan, 30390 Domazan; tel. 66 57 03 18 ⊤ By appt.

CELLIER D L'ENCLAVE DES PAPES★

■   80000   🔳 D ▥ ↓

72 73 74 ★⑧⓪ 82 ⑧③ ⑧③ 84 ⑧④

Good balance and bouquet of gooseberries and perhaps wild mulberries. (1983)
☙ Cellier de l'Enclave des Papes, 11 Av. du Général-de-Gaulle, 84600 Valréas; tel. 90 41 91 42 ⊤ By appt.

DOMAINE DE L'ESPIGOUETTE★★

◩   2ha   4800   🔳 D ⅲ ↓

81 82 83 84

This rosé has an outstanding character and finely aged nose in which crystallized fruit combines with coffee beans. A wine of great distinction and excellent structure, this bottle is highly recommended. (1982) ✔ Côtes du Rhône Rouge.
☙ Edmond Latour, Dom. de L'Espigouette, Violes, 84150 Joncquières; tel. 90 70 90 81 ⊤ By appt.

DOMAINE DE L'ESPIGOUETTE★★

■   7ha   26400   🔳 D ▥ ⅲ ↓

81 ⑧① ⑧② ⑧② 83 ⑧③

Edmond Latours 1982 Côtes-du-Rhône is one of his best: fruity, woody, well balanced and with a long finish. (1982)
☙ Edmond Latour, Dom. de l'Espigouette, Violes, 84150 Jonquières; tel. 90 70 90 81 ⊤ By appt.

DOMAINE DE L'ESPIGOUETTE★

■   10ha   50000   🔳 D ⅲ ↓

★81 ★82

This is a wine typical of the Grenache grape. The dominant fruity character is accompanied by a touch of vanilla. This bottle has aged well for a 1982. (1982) ✔ Côtes du Rhône Rouge, Côtes du Rhône Blanc.
☙ Edmond Latour, Dom. de L'Espigouette, Violes, 84150 Joncquières; tel. 90 70 90 81 ⊤ By appt.

DOMAINE ESTOURNEL★★
Cuvée Réservée

☐   0.75ha   5000   🔳 D ▥ ↓

This round and very supple wine is bright yellow-gold in colour. Slightly oxidized, it has aromas of apple and rum. It should be well cooled before drinking.
☙ Rémy Estournel, Dom. Estournel, 30790 St-Victor-de-la-Coste; tel. 66 50 01 73 ⊤ By appt.

DOMAINE ESTOURNEL★
Cuvée du Festival de Cannes

■   00ha   70000   🔳 D ▥ ↓

⑦⑨ ⑧① 83

A cuvée spéciale used to promote these Côtes du Rhone; while this wine has a pleasant appearance and is lively on the palate, the weak aromas are somewhat disappointing.
☙ Rémy Estournel, Dom. Estournel, 30790 St-Victor-de-la-Coste; tel. 66 50 01 73 ⊤ By appt.

CHATEAU DE FAREL

■   16ha   95000   🔳 D ▥ ↓

78 79 80 81 ★⑧② ⑧② ★83

The proprietor is a fervent believer in traditional methods. His red wine, bright and lively, is bottled only after a long period in cask. A well-rounded wine, with a bouquet of dried fruit. (1982)
☙ Pierre Sylvestre, Ch. de Farel, Comps, 30300 Beaucaire; tel. 66 74 50 83 ⊤ Mon.–Fri. 10.00–12.00/14.00–16.00; Sat. 8.00–12.00/14.00–19.00.

DOMAINE DE LA FOURMONE★★

■   16ha   63000   🔳 D ▥ ⅲ ↓

★⑧① 82 ⑧② 83 ⑧③

Bouquet of spices and woodland plants, a velvety feel, full in the mouth and strong in tannin. The 1981 is particularly successful. (1981)
☙ GAEC Roger Combe et Fils, Dom. de la Fourmone, Vacqueyras, 84190 Beaumes-de-Venise; tel. 90 65 86 05 ⊤ Daily.

VIEUX MANOIR DU FRIGOULAS
Cuvée Bel Air★★

◩   5ha   31000   🔳 D ▥ ↓

⑧③ ⑧③ ⑧④

Lively, honest and muscular, has an attractive freshness and goes extremely well with charcuterie. Good value for money. (1983)
☙ Alain Robert et Fils, Vieux Manoir du Frigoulas, St-Alexandre, 30130 Pont-St-Esprit; tel. 66 39 18 71 ⊤ Mon.–Sat. 8.00–12.00/14.00–19.00; Sun. 14.00–18.00.

VIEUX MANOIR DU FRIGOULAS
Clos du Sauzet★★

| □ | 5 ha | 30 000 | 2 D ▮ ↓ |

79 80 81 82 ★⑧ 83

The Grenache, Ugni Blanc, Clairette, Picpoul and Bourboulenc grape varieties combine to produce this simple, light and perfumed white wine. With a good level of acidity, firm and well balanced, it should be drunk young and cool. (1983) ↩ Alain Robert et Fils, Vieux Manoir du Frigoulas, St-Alexandre, 30130 Pont-St-Esprit; tel. 66 39 18 71 ⵟ Mon.–Sat. 8.00–12.00/14.00–19.00; Sun. 14.00–18.00.

DOMAINE LE GARRIGON★★

| □ | 3 ha | 17 000 | 2 D ▮ ↓ |

83 ★84

Attractive white wine, with shades of light yellow. Slightly maderized nose, but supple on the palate; it should be drunk soon. (1983) ↩ Daniel et Jean Couston, Dom. le Garrigon, Tulette, 26970 Suze-la-Rousse; tel. 75 98 31 95 ⵟ By appt.

DOMAINE LE GARRIGON★

| ◪ | 10 ha | 60 000 | 2 D ▮ ↓ |

81 82 83 ★84

Attractive, slightly brick-red colour. The nose, now mature, indicates advanced ageing. Although still perfectly satisfactory, it would have been better to have drunk it a year or two ago. An interesting wine. (1980) ↩ Daniel et Jean Couston, Dom. le Garrigon, Tulette, 29690 Suze-la-Rousse; tel. 75 98 31 95 ⵟ By appt.

DOMAINE LE GARRIGON★★

| ■ | 30 ha | 180 000 | 2 D ▮ ↓ |

80 81 82 ★83

Dark red wine with a powerful nose; fleshy on the palate and still has good tannin. It has aged well and is ready to drink. (1981) ↩ Daniel et Jean Couston, Dom. le Garrigon, Tulette, 26970 Suze-la-Rousse; tel. 75 98 31 95 ⵟ By appt.

LA GLOIRE DE SAINT-ANDRE★★

| □ | 4 ha | 22 000 | 2 D ▮ ↓ |

78 79 80 ★81 ★82

This wine has a bright, light yellow colour with hints of green. The nose is light and floral, with aromas of peach blossom. Crisp on the palate, it has a good overall balance. (1982) ✔ Côtes du Rhône le Trésor de St-Chétin Rouge, Dom. des Hauts de St-Pier Rouge. ↩ scp André Gras et Fils, Dom. de St-Chétin, 84600 Valréas; tel. 90 35 06 68 ⵟ By appt.

DOMAINE DU GRAND CYPRES★★

| ■ | 7 ha | 41 000 | 2 ▮ ↓ |

★⑧ 81 ★82 ★83 84

A deep-red wine with a rich, powerful nose both peppery and spicy. Still tannic on the palate, it needs to age before reaching its peak. A good Côtes du Rhône. (1981) ↩ Gérard Lindeperg, 470 Av. Mal-Foch, 84100 Orange; tel. 90 34 05 24 ⵟ By appt. Closed Jan.

CHATEAU DU GRAND MOULAS★

| ■ | 29 ha | 96 000 | 2 D ▮ ↓ |

⑦ 80 81 ★83 83 84

From its clifftop position, the château looks down on the vineyard, established when the uncultivated land was cleared fourteen years ago. A light but very brightly coloured wine, with aromas of red fruit and quince, and smooth, balanced flavour. Extremely elegant and ready to drink. (1983) ↩ M. Ryckwaert, Ch. du Grand Moulas, Mornas, 84420 Piolenc; tel. 90 37 02 90 ⵟ Mon.–Sat. 8.00–12.00/14.00–18.00.

DOMAINE DU GRAND-RELAIS★★★

| ◪ | 1 ha | 6 000 | 2 D ▮ ⑾ ↓ |

⑧ 84

Very attractive, bright raspberry-pink colour, with a youthfully fruity nose of strawberry and redcurrant. A touch of carbon dioxide on the palate gives great finesse to this wine which is both firm and fresh. A very good rosé which should be drunk young. (1984) ↩ Daniel Pelissier, Dom. du Grand-Relais, Mirabel-aux-Baronnies, 26110 Nyons; tel. 75 27 14 80 ⵟ Mon.–Fri. 15.00–18.30; Sat. 9.30–12.00/15.00–18.30.

DOMAINE DU GRAND-RELAIS★★

| □ | 1 ha | 6 000 | 2 D ▮ ⑾ ↓ |

★⑧ ★84

This is a pale yellow wine, crisp and firm on the palate, which should be drunk while young. It has very distinct floral aromas (eglantine and a touch of jasmine). (1984) ↩ Daniel Pelissier, Dom. du Grand-Relais, Mirabel-aux-Baronnies, 26110 Nyons; tel. 75 27 14 80 ⵟ Mon.–Fri. 15.00–18.30; Sat. 9.30–12.00/15.00–18.30.

DOMAINE DU GRAND-RELAIS★

| ■ | 18 ha | 60 000 | 2 D ▮ ⑾ ↓ |

The estate takes its name from the old post House where the wines are produced. The 1983 has a cherry-red colour and distinctive nose characterized by perfumes of leather and incense, with slight vegetal aromas. On the palate, the tannin makes for an attractively slender wine with 'bite'. (1983) ✔ Côtes du Rhône Blanc and Rosé. ↩ Daniel Pelissier, Dom. du Grand-Relais Mirabel-aux-Baronnies, 26110 Nyons; tel. 75 27 14 80 ⵟ Mon.–Fri. 15.00–18.30; Sat. 9.30–12.00/15.00–18.30.

DOMAINE DE LA GRAND'RIBE★

| ■ | 5.5 ha | 200 000 | 3 D ▮ ↓ |

79 79 81 83

Traditional growing methods are strictly adhered to – hand-hoeing, organic manure, no herbicides, the grapes graded and the wine stored underground in amphorae, at a constant temperature. The wines are fruity, well made and have a long finish. They are typified by this very good 1979, which is ready to drink yet still capable of further improvement with age. (1979) ↩ Abel Sahuc, Dom. de la Grand'Ribe, 84290 Ste-Cécile-les-Vignes; tel. 90 30 83 75 ⵟ Daily 10.00–12.00/14.00–19.00.

DOMAINE DE LA JANASSE*

■   12ha   20000   3 D ■ ◉

(79) *80 *81 83 83

On one of the region's oldest vineyards, the Sabon family uses three grape varieties – Grenache, Syrah and Mourvèdre – to grow powerfully scented red wines. The family believes in the advantages of maturing the wines in cask – as exemplified by this 1983, with its clearly tannic finish. (1983) ✔ Châteauneuf-du-Pape. ⊶ Aimé Sabon, Dom. de la Janasse, 84350 Courthezon; tel. 90 70 86 29 ⵣ Mon.–Sat. 8.00–12.00/14.00–20.00.

CAVES C. N. JAUME*

■   30ha   80000   2 D ↓

80 80 *81 81 82

This is a pleasant, very floral wine at a very reasonable price. It may be drunk from now on. (1980) ✔ Côtes du Rhône de Vinsobres. ⊶ GAEC. Caves C. N. Jaume, Rue Reynarde, Vinsobres, 26110 Nyons; tel. 75 27 61 01 ⵣ Mon.–Sat. 8.00–12.00/14.00–19.00.

LAMBERT-FLORIMOND

☐   8.5ha   42000   2 D ■ ↓

(67) 74 76 79 80 82

Lambert Florimond is the sixth generation of his family to work this estate. His white côtes du rhône 1982 is already well developed, as borne out by the hints of amber in the yellow colour and the wine's subtle bouquet, redolent of ripe fruit. (1982) ⊶ Lambert-Florimond, Roaix, 84100 Vaison-la-Romaine; tel. 90 46 11 33 ⵣ By appt. Closed Tues. morning and during harvesting.

LES LAMBERTINS**

■   8ha   30000   2 D ◉ ↓

(78) 79 80 81 82 83

An extremely floral, aromatic wine, with a lot of character. It is also round, which gives it a good overall balance. (1983) ✔ Côtes du Rhône Blanc, Côtes du Rhône Rosé. ⊶ MM. Lambert Frères, GAEC des Lambertins, 84000 Vacqueyras; tel. 90 65 85 54 ⵣ By appt. Closed Sun. afternoon.

CAVE DES VIGNERONS DE LAUDUN*

☑   6ha   37000   2 D ■ ↓

80 81 82 *83

A dark rosé; warm on the palate. (1983) ✔ Côtes du Rhône Laudun, Côtes du Rhone-Villages Rouge. ⊶ Cave des Vignerons de Laudun, 2 Route de l'Ardoise, 30290 Laudun; tel. 66 79 49 97 ⵣ By appt.

JEAN-MARIE LOMBARD Brezeme***

■   2ha   12000   3 D ◉ ↓

81 (82) 83

This wine is a very fine dark red, with a fruity nose developing strongly towards ripe fruit and pear and strawberry jam. The tannins blend well with the smoothness on the palate; lingering aromas and a finish of spices and vanilla. (1982)

⊶ Jean-Marie Lombard, Quartier Piquet, 26250 Livron; tel. 75 61 64 90 ⵣ By appt.

DOMAINE DE MALAIGUE**

■   75ha   60000   3 D ◉ ↓

81 82 *83

A limpid, brick-red wine, fragrant and generous with a certain crispness. This vintage is now reaching its best. (1982) ⊶ Jean-Claude Reboul, Dom. de Malaïgue, Sagriès, 30700 Uzès; tel. 66 22 25 43 ⵣ Mon.–Sat. Closed Sun.

DOMAINE MARTIN DE GRANGENEUVE**

■   33ha   50000   3 D ◉ ↓

76 78 *(80) *82

Bright, cherry colour. Aroma of undergrowth on the nose, and pepper and liquorice on the palate. Delicate and well balanced. Could be left to age. A nice bottle. (1980) ✔ Côtes du Rhône Rosé et Blanc, Vin de Pays de la Principauté d'Orange. ⊶ Hélène et François Martin, Dom. de Grangeneuve, 84150 Jonquières; tel. 90 70 62 62 ⵣ Mon.–Sat. 8.00–12.00/13.30–20.00. Sun. by appt.

DOMAINE DU MAS D'EOLE**

■   21ha   130000   2 D ■ ◉ ↓

78 79 82 83

An attractive, shimmering colour, with aromas of ripe fruit which are immediately apparent to the nose and then even stronger on the palate, where they seem to acquire an additional touch of cold coffee and cocoa. Pleasing finish. (1982) ⊶ Serge Galon, Dom. du Mas d'Eole, 30390 Domazan; tel. 66 37 10 98 ⵣ Daily 9.00–12.00/14.00–18.00. Closed Christmas, New Year's Day.

LES VINS MATHELIN
*Cuvée Costebelle**

■   30000   2 D

Bold, fruity and very characteristic red. Pleasant, with a fine structure evident on the palate. Drink without delay. (1984) ⊶ Vins Mathelin, BP 3, Châtillon-d'Azerques, 69380 Lozanne; tel. 74 84 39 24 ⵣ Mon.–Sat. 8.30–12.00/14.00–19.00.

CHATEAU DE MONTPLAISIR*

■   5ha   30000   2 D ■ ◉ ↓

(78) 79 80 *82 *83

Deep red and aromatic, a pleasing fruity wine with a touch of raspberry and good balance between tannin and smoothness on the palate. (1983) ⊶ Henri Davin, 84600 Valréas; tel. 90 35 05 87 ⵣ By appt.

DOMAINE DU MOULIN**

■   20ha   40000   2 D ◉ ↓

81 82 83 83

From a scent of Morello cherries in its youth, the bouquet gradually becomes more reminiscent of kirsch. Although the tannin seems a little mouth-puckering at first, the finish leaves one with a marvellous impression of this wine. Stored with care, a good wine to keep. (1982)

🕿 Jean Vinson, 26490 Vinsobres; tel 75 27 60 47
🍷 By appt Mon.–Sat.

NICOLAS★★

■   940000   2 🍴

A fine ruby colour and a warm bouquet for a wine with a very full and aromatic palate. The charming finesse of the perfume lingers for a long time. (1984)
🕿 Ets Nicolas, 2 Rue de Valmy, 94220 Charenton; tel. 01 37 59 20 🍷 No visitors.

NOTRE-DAME DES VIGNETS★

■   40ha   192000   3 D 🍴 ⬤ ↓
76 78 **78** ★79 **79** ★80

It is generally accepted that 1978 was an outstanding year for Côtes du Rhône wines. This wine is generous and tannic, with a bouquet of blackcurrant and raspberry, and is capable of further improvement in bottle, even now. (1978)
🕿 Cave Coop. les Coteaux, Notre-Dame des Vignets, 84820 Visan; tel. 90 41 91 12 🍷 Daily 8.30–12.00/14.00–18.30.

CAVE COOPERATIVE DU NYONSAIS★

■   730ha   27000   2 D 🍴 ↓
78 81 **83**

Still has signs of youth. The nose is still immature, but on tasting fills the mouth well. Leave to age further. (1983)
🕿 Cave Coop. Agricole du Nyonsais, BP 9, 26110 Nyons; tel. 75 26 03 44 🍷 Daily 8.00–12.00/14.00–18.00. Closed to groups.

DOMAINE DE L'OLIVET★

■   9ha   20000   3 D 🍴 ⬤ ↓
⑦⑧ 79 81 ★82

A redcurrant-like colour, and a fruity nose. Rich, with a fine balance on the palate; delicate and elegant. Drink now. (1982)
🕿 Rodolphe Gassens, 0770 Bourg-St-Andéol; tel. 75 54 52 74 🍷 By appt.

DOMAINE PALESTOR LA FAGOTIERE★★★

■   3ha   15000   2 D 🍴 ⬤ ↓
78 79 80 **80** 81 ★82 ★83

This is a bright, light red, wine. It is well constructed and delicate on the palate, with aromas of vanilla. A good finish; will age well. (1980)
🕿 André Chastan-Pierry, Dom. Palestor la Fagotière, 84100 Orange; tel. 90 34 51 81 🍷 Mon.–Sat. 8.00–12.00/14.00–19.00. Closed Sun. and public holidays.

DOMAINE DE LA PRESIDENTE★

☑   50000   2 D 🍴 ↓

A generous wine that will warm any meal of game. Aroma of mature fruit. Ready to drink.
🕿 Max Aubert, Ch. de Gallifet, 84290 Ste-Cécile-les-Vignes; tel. 90 30 80 34 🍷 By appt.

DOMAINE DE LA PRESIDENTE★

■   107ha   200000   2 D 🍴 ↓
71 76 78 ⑧② **83**

Although this wine is produced largely for export, great care is taken that the quality does not suffer. The aromas and the structure of this wine give it undeniable originality. (1982)
🕿 Max Aubert, Ch. De Gallifet, 84290 Sainte-Cécile-les-Vignes; tel. 90 30 80 34 🍷 Mon.–Sat.

DOMAINE DE LA PREVOSSE★

■   10ha   53000   2 D 🍴 ⬤ ↓
78 ⑦⑨ 80 82 83

Dark red colour with yellow tinges, and mature nose with strong aromas – spicy and evocative of ripe fruit – symptomatic of ageing. Well constructed and powerful on the palate. This wine has matured well: a bottle to drink now. (1979)
🕿 Henri Davin, 84600 Valréas; tel. 90 35 05 87 🍷 By appt.

DOMAINE DE LA PREVOSSE

☑   10ha   7200   2 D 🍴 ⬤ ↓
82 ⑧③

This rosé shows tinges of yellow in the robe and good structure on the palate. It has already aged well and should be drunk now. (1982)
🕿 Henri Davin, 84600 Valréas; tel. 90 35 05 87 🍷 By appt.

DOMAINE DE LA PREVOSSE★

☐   1.5ha   6000   2 D 🍴 ⬤ ↓
82 ⑧③

Straw-yellow colour and a pleasing, fruity nose. Warm and thick on the palate—no need to be allowed to breathe. Ready to drink. (1982)
🕿 Henri Davin, 84600 Valréas; tel. 90 35 05 87 🍷 By appt.

DOMAINE RABASSE-CHAVARIN★★★

☐   2ha   8400   2 D 🍴 ↓
83

A pretty, pale wine which is vigorous and solid. On the nose the aromas of flowers and fruits promise a fine character which is confirmed on the palate. (1983)
🕿 Corine Couturier, Les Coteaux-St-Martin, Cairanne, 84290 Ste-Cécile-les-Vignes; tel. 90 30 82 27 🍷 Daily 8.00–12.00/13.00–20.00.

DOMAINE DE LA REMEJEANNE**

■ 10ha 17000 2 D ■ ↓

79 80 81 *⟨82⟩ 82 83

A careful balance between old and young Syrah vines goes to make this 'big in the mouth' wine, blood-red in colour, with a very pleasant, smooth touch of tannin and a bouquet offering hints of coffee and quince. Soft and appealing, it is very reasonably priced for a wine of this quality. (1982) ↪ François Klein, Dom. de la Réméjeanne, Cadignac, 30200 Bagnols-sur-Cèze; tel. 66 89 69 95 ☏ Daily 8.00–12.00/14.00–19.00.

DOMAINE DE LA REMEJEANNE**

□ 20ha 108000 2 D ■ ↓

*83 83 *84 84

In contrast to the Syrah for its reds, the domaine relies on the Bourboulenc and Ugni Blanc grape varieties to give its white wines their light, flower-scented character. This 1983 is a virile wine, to be drunk well cooled – and, once again, with a considerably higher quality than one would normally expect for the price. (1983) ↪ François Klein, Dom. de la Réméjeanne, Cadignac, 30200 Bagnols-sur-Cèze; tel. 66 89 69 95 ☏ Daily 8.00–12.00/14.00–19.00.

DOMAINE DE LA RENJARDE**

■ 51ha 300000 2 D ■ ↓

81 82 ⟨83⟩ 83 84

Rich bouquet not only of red fruit but also pine, spices and, above all, pepper. A splendid introduction to such a very pleasing wine. (1983) ↪ Dom. de la Renjarde, Sérignan-du-Comtat, 84830 Orange; tel. 90 70 00 15 ☏ By appt. Mon.–Sat.

DOMAINE DE LA RENJARDIERE**

■ 100ha 2 ■ ⦿ ↓

75 79 81 *82 83 ⟨84⟩

Summery, peony colour and aroma of red fruit. Has the liveliness of youth and good persistence on the palate. May be left to age. (1984) ↪ Pierre Dupond, 339 Rue de Thizy, 69653 Villefranche-en-Beaujolais; tel. 74 65 24 32 ☏ By appt.

LA REUISCOULADO *Cuvée Louis***

■ 1ha 40000 3 D ■ ↓

71 78 79 *83 83

The Trintignant family have succeeded in making a fine example of a typical good côtes du rhône with this wine – its colour an attractive dark red, its bouquet offering the characteristic scents of ripe fruit, notably redcurrants and cherries. Full-bodied and smooth, it is a wine with a particularly good, long finish. (1983) ✔ Châteauneuf-du-Pape Blanc, Châteauneuf-du-Pape Rouge, Côtes du Rhône Rosé, Côtes du Rhône Blanc. ↪ Je83Trintignant, 84230 Châteauneuf-du-Pape; tel. 90 83 73 23 ☏ By appt. Closed Jan., Feb.

LA REUISCOULADO *Cuvée Louis***

□ 1ha 7000 4 D ■ ↓

78 79 82

Also produced by the Trintignants is this crisp, firm white wine, with a light yellow colour and rich bouquet of flowers. A very fine bottle. (1982)

↪ Jean Trintignant, 84230 Châteauneuf-du-Pape; tel. 90 83 73 23 ☏ By appt. Closed Jan., Feb.

ROBERT ET FILS**
Grande Cuvée

■ 8ha 75000 2 D ■ ↓

⟨77⟩ 78 82 82 83 84

For thirteen generations the Robert family have cultivated their vines in the traditional way. This is a cherry-red wine with aromas of ripe fruit dominated by quince. Round and with a pleasant finish; a fine bottle worth adding to your cellar. (1982) ↪ Alain Robert et Fils, Vieux Manoir du Frigoulas, St Alexandre 30130; tel. 66 39 18 71 ☏ Mon.–Sat. 8.00–12.00/14.00–17.00.

LES VIGNERONS DE ROCHEGUDE
*Cuvée du Docteur Barbe**

■ 15000 2 D ■ ↓

83 84

Cherry red colour, not too intense, with fruity aromas of cherry, redcurrant and blackcurrant. Pleasing, supple and well balanced on the palate; ready for drinking. (1983) ↪ Coop. des Vign. de Rochegude, Rochegude, 26130 St-Paul-Trois-Châteaux; tel. 75 04 81 84 ☏ By appt.

LES VIGNERONS DE ROCHEGUDE**

□ 12000 2 D ■ ↓

82 83 84

Bright, light yellow colour. Elderflower and beeswax aromas of good finesse on the nose. Fine balance on the palate between acidity, body and smoothness. A very pleasing wine, ready for drinking now. (1984) ↪ Coop. des Vign. de Rochegude, Rochegude, 26130 St-Paul-Trois-Châteaux; tel. 75 04 81 84 ☏ By appt.

LES VIGNERONS DE ROCHEGUDE*

◩ 15000 2 D ■ ↓

83 84

Although the colour is a little intense, the extremely delicate aromas are pleasing (fruit drops, banana, acetone and a very slight herbaceous undertone, this last being characteristic of low-temperature vinification). Attractively supple and fresh on the palate, and should not be kept long before drinking. (1984) ↪ Coop. des Vign. de Rochegude, Rochegude, 26130 St-Paul-Trois-Châteaux; tel. 75 04 81 84 ☏ By appt.

LES VIGNERONS DE ROCHEGUDE

■ 60000 2 D ■ ↓

81 82 83 84

Very light colour with strong yellow tints. Highly vegetal, even grassy, aroma. Supple, with great warmth in its balance. (1982) ↪ Coop. des Vignerons de Rochegude, Rochegude, 26130 St-Paul-Trois-Châteaux; tel. 785 04 81 84 ☏ By appt.

DOMAINE DU ROURE★★★

■   12ha   12000   **2** **D** ▮ ♨
⑦⑧ 81 82 83

A very good red colour with slight hints of very brilliant brown. Rich and complex aromas denoting a good intense and delicate ageing. On the palate it is quite remarkable, perfectly balanced and powerful. It is a very good bottle which can be drunk now but which will also keep for two or three years. (1981)
↬ *M.* J. Terrasse, St-Marcel-d'Ardèche, 07700 Bourg-St-Andéol; tel. 75 04 67 67 ⋎ Daily 9.00–12.00/14.00–18.00.

DOMAINE DE SAINT-CHETIN★

■   16ha   110800   **2** **D** ◑ ♨
78 81 82 **82** 83

This wine has the colour of dark-red cherries, and fruity aromas. The structure is very tannic. (1982)
✔ Le Trésor de St-Chétin, La Gloire de St-André.
↬ scp André Gras et Fils, Dom. de St-Chétin, 84600 Valréas; tel. 90 35 06 68 ⋎ By appt ↬ GFA Mathilde et André Gras.

DOMAINE SAINT-CLAUDE★

☐   1.5ha   7000   **2** **D** ▮ ♨
81 82 83 ★⑧④ **84**

This is a light yellow wine with floral aromas which is very lively on the palate, due to its acidity. (1984)
↬ Claude Charasse, Dom. St-Claude, 84110 Vaison-la-Romaine; tel. 90 36 23 68 ⋎ By appt.

DOMAINE SAINT-CLAUDE★★

■   28.5ha   130000   **2** **D** ▮ ♨
⑧① 82 ★83 ★84

Peony red colour, with a nose which is floral and fruity over a background of musk. Elegant and fairly delicate on the palate. (1984)
↬ Claude Charasse, Dom. St-Claude, 84110 Vaison-la-Romaine; tel. 90 36 23 68 ⋎ By appt.

BARON SAINT-ELZEAR★★

☐   **3** **D** ▮ ♨
81 82 83

With hints of autumn in its yellow colour, this wine is fresh to the taste but already well developed in character. One very much for keeping, particularly if you love old wines.
↬ UCVF de Bagnols-sur-Cèze, 12 Rue St-Victor, 30201 Bagnols-sur-Cèze; tel. 66 89 56 04 ⋎ By appt.

CHATEAU SAINT-ESTEVE★★

☑   4ha   25000   **3** **D** ▮ ♨
81 82 ★⑧③ **84**

Good colour. Very fruity, with a nuance of fennel and green pepper. Very elegant on the palate. An attractive bottle. (1983)
↬ Gérard Français et Fils, Dom. de St-Estève, Uchaux, 84100 Orange; tel. 90 34 34 04 ⋎ By appt.

CHATEAU SAINT-ESTEVE★★★

☐   5ha   31000   **3** **D** ▮ ♨
81 82 ★⑧③ **83** 84

Although this proprietor has only been established here since 1981, he already produces wines of high class and deserves to be more widely known. This remarkable white wine, with its aromas of fruit, honey and spring flowers, is the result of an unusual blend of grape varieties: Clairette, Roussanne, Grenache and Viognier. (1983)
↬ Gérard Français et Fils, Ch. St-Estève, Uchaux, 84100 Orange; tel. 90 34 34 04 ⋎ By appt.

CHATEAU SAINT-ESTEVE★★★

■   15ha   76000   **3** **D** ▮ ♨
⑧⓪ **80** ★82 83 84

A chapel dedicated to St-Estève (the Provencal for Etienne, or St Stephen) once stood on this spot. This is an extremely pleasant wine – a deep, bright cherry in colour, with a rich and complex bouquet made up of blackcurrant, liquorice and faint vegetable smells. One of the best wines of this appellation. (1980)
↬ Gérard Français et Fils, Dom. de St-Estève, Uchaux, 84100 Orange; tel. 90 34 34 04 ⋎ By appt.

DOMAINE SAINT-GEORGES★★

■   15ha   93000   **3** **D** ▮ ♨
76 81 **81** ⑧② **82** 83 **83** 84

The vineyard lies on terraces of smooth pebbles shaped by the river over thousands of years: its wines are fruity, powerful, and with a constant colour. This 1982 is vinified by carbonic maceration and has a bouquet redolent of ripe fruit. It is strong in tannin – so, while already an outstanding Côtes du Rhône, could improve even more with age. (1982)
↬ André Vignal, Dom. St-Georges, Vénéjan, 30200 Bagnols-sur-Cèze; tel. 66 89 73 14 ⋎ By appt daily.

DOMAINE DE SAINT-GEORGES**

□ 5ha 30000 **3 D 📓 🐧 ⬇**
82 83 84

This is a wine to drink while young. Hints of green in the colour, reveal a floral nose with a scent of hawthorn. Crisp and light on the palate. (1983) ✔ Côtes du Rhône Rouge, Côtes du Rhône Villages.
📬 André Vignal, Dom. St-Georges, Vénéjan, 30200 Bagnols-sur-Cèze; tel. 66 89 73 14 ☎ By appt.

COOPERATIVE SAINT HILAIRE-D'OZILHAN *La Clastre**

■ 150ha 87500 **2 D 📓 ⬇**

Handsome, light ruby colour. Very warm nose of ripe fruit, tending towards aromas of game; expansive and rich in its nuances. Quite fruity on the palate, with much charm in the finish.
✔ Other Côtes du Rhone wines.
📬 Coop. St Hilaire-d'Ozilhan, St-Hilaire-d'Ozilhan, 30210 Remoulins; tel. 66 37 16 47 ☎ By appt.

COOPERATIVE SAINT HILAIRE-D'OZILHAN*

■ 150ha 87500 **2 D 📓 ⬇**
⑧① ⑧②

Ruby-crimson colour. Initially the nose is of overripe fruit and becomes fresher. Full and round on the palate, with good balance and discreet, fruity aromas. Appears to have had everything going for it, but cannot retain these qualities for a great length of time; a good reason to choose its brother of a more recent vintage. (1982) ✔ Other Côtes du Rhône and Côtes du Rhone-Villages wines.
📬 Coop. St Hilaire d'Ozilhan, St-Hilaire-d'Ozilhan, 30210 Remoulins; tel. 66 37 16 47 ☎ By appt.

COOPERATIVE DE SAINT-MAURICE-SUR-EYGUES*

◪ 8500 **2 D 📓 ⬇**
80 81 ⑧② 84

A delicate light rosé colour with a hint of yellow. The youthful aromas have already developed towards ripe fruit, with a touch of resin. This delicate wine has a supple, smooth, structure and should be drunk now. (1982)
📬 Coop. de St-Maurice-sur-Eygues, 26110 St-Maurice-sur-Eygues; tel. 75 27 63 44 ☎ By appt.

DOMAINE SAINTE-ANNE***

□ 5ha 30000 **2 D 📓 ⬇**
79 81 82 *83 ⑧③ 84

A light yellow wine, with a bright, clear appearance. The floral nose hints of strawberries. Crisp and firm on the palate, it holds well. This is a delicate, and truly exceptional white Côtes du Rhone. (1983) ✔ Côtes du Rhône, Côtes du Rhône- Villages.
📬 GAEC Dom. Ste-Anne, Mas Célettes, St-Gervais, 30200 Bagnols-sur-Cèze; tel. 66 89 67 41 ☎ Mon.–Sat. 9.00–11.00/14.00–19.00 📬 MM. Steinmaier et Fils.

DOMAINE DU SARRAZIN**

■ 20ha 120000 **2 D 📓 🐧 ⬇**
78 79 80 81 *82 83

A pleasant wine that has kept much of its freshness. A solid finish indicates it should keep well. (1981)
📬 Daniel Charre, Place de la Porte, 30390 Domazin; tel. 66 57 47 03 ☎ Daily 9.00–12.00/14.00–18.30.

DOMAINE DE SIGNAC*

■ 37ha 80000 **3 D 📓 ⬇**
80 *⑧① 82 83 84

This vineyard, re-established in 1960, lies at the foot of the Dent de Signac and has the advantage of a very good exposure. The 1981 has a complex bouquet, combining the scents of ripe fruit and woodsmoke. Light and with a fairly short finish, it should be drunk without delay. (1981)
📬 Dom. de Signac, Route d'Orsan, BP 34, 30200 Bagnols-sur-Cèze Cedex; tel. 66 89 58 47 ☎ Mon.–Sat. 8.30–12.00/14.00–18.30; Sun. 10.00–12.00/14.00–17.00.

LA SUZIENNE *Grande Réserve**

■ 999ha 40000 **2 D 📓 ⬇**
80 ⑧② ⑧② *83 84

Garnet-coloured wine which, although the nose is very discreet, has a very good balance on the palate. Full, velvety, tannic and well-structured. (1982)
📬 Cave Coop. la Suzienne, 26130 Suze-la-Rousse; tel. 75 04 80 04 ☎ By appt.

LA SUZIENNE*

■ 6ha 35000 **2 D 📓 ⬇**
81 ⑧① *⑧② ⑧② *83

Made predominantly from Syrah grapes. The bouquet of cooked red fruit proclaims a well-balanced and very pleasant wine. Allow to breathe before drinking. (1982)
📬 Cave Coop. la Suzienne, 26130 Suze-la-Rousse; tel. 75 04 80 04 ☎ By appt. Closed 1 Jan., 1 May and 25 Dec.

LE CELLIER DES TEMPLIERS*

■ 450ha 2400000 **2 D 📓 ⬇**
73 78 79 *81 *83

This firm, light and crisp wine has a very good finish. Aromas of blackcurrant, cherry and a little spice all add to the pleasure of this bottle, which is one of the most reasonably priced. (1981)
✔ Coteaux du Tricastin.

┡ Coop. Le Cellier des Templiers, 84600 Richer-
enches; tel. 90 35 05 09 ☎ Mon.–Sat. 8.00–12.00/
14.00–18.00.

DOMAINE DE LA TOUR-COUVERTE

■   7 ha   36 000   2 D ▄ ♨
⑧⓪ 81 *82 83

A bright lively red colour for a slightly thin wine
which is nevertheless pleasing.
┡ R. Couston et G. Monnier, Dom. de la Tour-
Couverte, Tulette, 26790 Suze-la-Rousse; tel.
75 98 31 95 ☎ By appt.

TRESOR DE SAINT-CHETIN★★

■   25 ha   110 800   3 D ◑ ♨
★⑦⑧ *79 **80** 81 *82 83

A lively red in colour, this wine has aromas that
are plant-like and spicy in character. Round,
powerful and full-bodied on the palate, it promises to be a fine bottle if kept for some time.
(1983)
┡ scp André Gras et Fils, Dom. de St-Chétin,
84600 Valréas; tel. 90 35 06 68 ☎ By appt.

VAL DES ROIS★

■   2 ha   12 000   3 D ▄ ♨
71 74 81 82 *83

The Bouchard family has been selling fine wines
for eight generations. This is a lively wine, with a
pleasant, bright cherry red. To be drunk now.
(1983) ✔ Côtes du Rhône Valréas AOC Rouge,
Côtes du Rhône 'Petit Roi' Rouge, Cuvée de la
Huitième Génération.
┡ Romain Bouchard, Dom. du Val des Rois,
84600 Valréas; tel. 90 35 04 35 ☎ By appt.

CHARTREUSE DE VALBONNE★★

■   4 ha   20 000   3 D ▄ ♨
83 ⑧④ 84

Guillaume de Vénégan, Bishop of Uzès, founded
this Carthusian monastery in 1203. Today, the
building – noteworthy for its size and fine roof –
houses a medical centre. The neighbouring
vineyard, abandoned after the monks left, is now
in process of restoration and some excellent
wines are on offer. One such is this red wine,
highly typical of the Syrah grape (the Shiraz, in
other parts of the world), with a nice balance and
a good level of tannin. To be drunk young. (1983)
┡ ASVHT, Dom. Chautreuse de Valbonne, St-
Paulet-de-Caisson, 30130 Pont St-Esprit; tel.
66 89 68 32 ☎ By appt.

CHATEAU DE VALPINSON★

■   15 ha   60 000   2 D ▄ ♨
⑦⑧ 79 82 83

A delightful name for this monastery, which was
declared a 'national asset' during the Revolution
and was subsequently sold to a Jewish musician/
magician who died at the age of 103. Today it is a
peaceful family home where very good wines are
carefully produced. This 1982 is light, supple and
should be drunk immediately. (1982) ✔ Côtes du
Rhône Ch. de Valpinson Rosé, Côtes du Rhone
Réserve du Rossignol Rouge.
┡ Gérard Allauzen, Ch. de Valpinson, St-Alexandre, 30130 Pont-St-Esprit; tel. 66 39 23 67
☎ Mon.–Fri. 10.00–12.00/13.00–20.00.

DOMAINE DE LA VERQUIERE★★

■   45 ha   200 000   3 D ◑ ♨
★⑦⑧ *79 *81 *82 82 **83**

Beautiful garnet-red colour. Still a little immature on the nose. Solid and powerful; will need
ageing to realize its potential. (1982) ✔ Côtes du
Rhône Rouge, Rosé et Blanc.
┡ Louis Chamfort et Frères, Dom. de la Verquière, Sablet, 84110 Vaison-la-Romaine; tel.
90 36 90 11 ☎ Daily 8.00–12.00/14.00–18.00.

DOMAINE DE LA VERQUIERE★

◩   5000   3 D ▄ ♨
⑦⑧ **80** 81 82 *83 84

Ruby-pink with a vegetal and floral perfume.
Good constitution. Drink now. (1983) ✔ Côtes
du Rhône-Villages Rouge, Côtes du Rhone
Rouge.
┡ Louis Chamfort et Freres, Dom. de la Verquière, Sablet, 84110 Vaison-la-Romaine; tel.
90 36 90 11 ☎ Daily 8.00–12.00/14.00–18.00.

FERME LA VERRIERE★

◩   2 ha   4000   2 D ▄ ◑ ♨
82 83 84

Bright, clear rosé characterized by vegetal aromas of ivy leaves and small fruit. A pleasingly
fresh and balanced wine. Ready to drink. (1982)
┡ Pierre Rosati, Route du Pègre, 84600 Valréas;
tel. 90 35 13 63 ☎ Daily 8.00–12.00/13.00–19.30.

FERME LA VERRIERE★★

■   18 ha   85 000   2 D ▄ ◑ ♨
81 82 83 84

While the colour is a good, bright cherry red, the
aromas of small red fruit, although delicate, are a
little reserved. Overall, however, this is an extremely supple, round wine, rich and very fleshy. A
particularly pleasing Côtes du Rhône, ready to
drink now. (1982)
┡ Pierre Rosati, Route du Pègre, 84600 Valréas;
tel. 90 35 13 63 ☎ Daily 8.00–12.00/13.00–19.30.

FERME LA VERRIERE★

☐   2.1 ha   4000   2 D ▄ ◑ ♨
82 83

Light yellow colour with very bright green highlights and floral aromas of narcissus on the nose.
A pleasing wine, delicate and with good length.
There is a little excess acidity which gives a great
deal of freshness. Ready to drink.
┡ Pierre Rosati, Route du Pègre, 84600 Valréas;
tel. 90 35 13 63 ☎ Daily 8.00–12.00/13.00–19.30.

DOMAINE DE LA VIEILLE-JULIENNE★

■   10 ha   20 000   3 D ▄ ◑ ♨
⑦⑧ 79 81 82 83

A yellowish tint to this wine's medium-red col-
our. Aromas of cooked fruit, dry fig and prune.
Generous and warm. (1982) ✔ Côtes du Rhône
Rosé et Blanc.
┡ MM. Arnaud-Daumen, Dom. de la Vieille-
Julienne, Le Grès, 84100 Orange; tel. 90 34 20 10
☎ Mon.–Sat. 8.30–12.00/13.30–20.00. By appt.
on public holidays.

DOMAINE DE LA VIEILLE-JULIENNE★★

☐   10ha   3000   **3** **D** ▮ ⑾ ↓
82 83

Beautiful, straw-like colour. The aroma is pleasant and flowery, although rather brief, with a hint of honey. Roundness without acidity. Pleasant finish.
➡ *MM.* Arnaud-Daumen, Dom. de la Vieille-Julienne, Le Grès, 84100 Orange; tel. 90 34 20 10
☓ Mon.–Sat. 8.30–12.00/13.30–20.00. By appt on public holidays.

DOMAINE DE LA VIEILLE-JULIENNE★

◩   10ha   3000   **3** **D** ▮ ⑾ ↓
83 84

Delicately aged tint. Will please those who like strong, already matured rosés. ✓ Other Côtes du Rhônes wines.
➡ *MM.* Arnaud-Daumier, Dom. de la Vieille-Julienne, Le Grès, 84100 Orange; tel. 90 34 20 10
☓ Mon.–Sat. 8.30–12.00/13.30–20.00. By appt on public holidays.

CHARLES VIENOT★

■   10000   **3** **D**

Light, shining red colour; lively on the palate with good structure. (1984)
➡ Ets Charles Vienot, 5 Quai Dumorey, 21700 Nuits-St-Georges; tel. 80 62 31 05 ☓ By appt.

DOMAINE DU VIEUX CHENE★★

■   22ha   120000   **2** **D** ▮ ↓

The carbonic maceration of Grenache and Syrah grapes, carried out to perfection, results in a pleasing, fruity bouquet which, in conjunction with the good general balance, makes this a remarkably successful wine. (1983)
➡ J.-C. et D. Bouche, Route d'Avignon, 84150 Camaret; tel. 90 37 21 58 ☓ By appt. daily.

Côtes du Rhône-Villages

Within the Côtes du Rhône area, there are seventeen communes with particularly good vineyard land which produce wines of special quality and local character. Together these form the Côtes du Rhône-Villages appellation. The wines may be marketed under the general appellation or, as in Beaujolais and Mâcon, may appear with the designation Côtes du Rhône followed by the name of an individual village. All the wines in this appellation are subject to stricter standards concerning vineyard area, maximum permitted yield-per-hectare, minimum potential alcohol content and specific grape varieties to be used. The communes involved are as follows: Rochegude, Rousset-les-Vignes, St-

Pantaléon-les Vignes, St-Maurice-sur-Aygues, Vinsobres, Chusclan, audun, St-Gervais, Cairanne, Beaumes-de-Venise, Rasteau, Roaix, Sablet, Séguret, Vaquéyras, Visan, Valréas. The total vineyard area is some 2800 hectares and produces an average of 145 000 hectolitres of wine per year.

Most of the production is devoted to red wines, rich in aromas and with enough tannin to age well – excellent with poultry and meat dishes, especially meat in sauce.

UCVF DE BAGNOLS-SUR-CEZE
Laudun★

■   80ha   380000   **2** **D** ▮ ⑾ ↓
78 ⑧

Bright colour and very animal nose. Warm and pleasant. Already mature. Drink immediately. (1981)
➡ UCVF de Bagnols-sur-Cèze, 12 Rue St-Victor, 30201 Bagnols-sur-Cèze; tel. 66 89 56 04 ☓ By appt.

UCVF BAGNOLS-SUR-CEZE
Chusclan★

◩   50ha   200000   **3** **D** ▮ ↓
78 82 83

This orangey-pink wine is well rounded and has a warm finish. (1983)
➡ UCVF Bagnols-sur-Cèze, 30201 Bagnols-sur-Cèze; tel. 66 89 56 04 ☓ By appt.

DOMAINE DU BANVIN *Cairanne*★★

■   15ha   30000   **3** **D** ▮ ↓
78 ★⑲ ★80 ★81 **82** 83

Drink immediately, if you want to enjoy its best qualities before the onset of oxidation. (1982)
➡ Cave Zanti-Cumino, Dom. du Banvin, 84290 Cairanne; tel. 90 30 82 38 ☓ By appt. Closed Christmas, 1 Jan., Easter and Sun. afternoons.

JEAN-PIERRE BROTTE *Séguret*★★

■   40000   **3** **D** ⑾ ↓
79 81 ⑧ **82** 83 84

Cherry-red colour with the atmosphere of a beautiful late summer's day: aromas of wood, very ripe fruit, peaches, apricots, and a hint of vanilla in the finish. A slight predominance of alcohol does not spoil its delicate and elegant nature. (1982) ✓ Lirac Rosé, Côtes du Rhône Vacqueyras Rouge, Lirac Rouge, Côtes du Rhône Brottiers.
➡ Ets Jean-Pierre Brotte, 84230 Châteauneuf-du-Pape; tel. 90 83 70 07 ☓ Daily 9.00–12.00/14.00–18.00.

DOMAINE DE CABASSE★★★

■   10ha   36000   **3** **D** ▮ ⑾ ↓
⑱ 79 80 ★82 83 **83**

A deep red colour and a bouquet with highly concentrated aromas which should develop quite a bit more. Those immediately presenting them-

selves are of fruit, but there are also complex overtones of spices, vanilla and cinnamon, with a good attack, good balance, good length and pleasing finish. It all adds up to a wine of very fine quality. (1983)
↪ Nadine Latour, Dom. de Cabasse, 84000 Séguret; tel. 90 36 91 12 ⟗ By appt.

GRAND VIN DU CAMP ROMAIN
Laudun★★

| ■ | 230ha | 696 000 | 3 D ▪ ◑ ⬥ |

80 81

Full-bodied, dark red wine which, in the mouth, gives off generous scents of blackcurrant and cooked fruit. (1981) ✔ Côtes du Rhône Laudun Blanc, Côtes du Rhône Laudun Rosé.
↪ Cave des Vignerons de Laudun, Route de l'Ardoise, 30290 Laudun; tel. 66 79 49 97 ⟗ By appt Mon.–Sat.

DOMAINE DU CLOS DU CAVEAU
Vacqueyras★

| ■ | 9ha | 25 000 | 3 D ▪ ⬥ |

79 80 ★81 81

A very dark, brick-coloured wine of complex flavour with a tannic finish. A robust bottle that goes well with highly seasoned dishes. (1979) ✔ Côtes du Rhône Rouge.
↪ SCA Dom. du Clos du Caveau, Vacqueyras, 84190 Beaumes-de-Venise; tel. 90 65 85 33 ⟗ Mon.–Sat. 8.00–12.00/14.00–18.00.

DOMAINE CLOS DES CAZEAUX
Cuvée Saint-Roch★★

| ■ | 8ha | 38 000 | 3 D ▪ ⬥ |

76 78 79 ★81 82 (83)

If drunk this year, you will discover great refinement and harmony in this rich, cherry-red wine. If kept, it will retain all its qualities. (1981) ✔ Côtes du Rhône Vacqueyras Cuvée Templier, Gigondas Cuvée de la Tour Sarrasine.
↪ Archimbaud et Vache, Dom. Clos des Cazeaux, Vacqueyras 84190 Beaumes-de-Venise; tel. 90 65 85 83 ⟗ Mon.–Sat. 9.00–12.00/14.00–19.00. Closed public holidays.

DOMAINE CLOS DES CAZEAUX
Cuvée des Templiers★★★

| ■ | 10ha | 44 000 | 3 D ▪ ⬥ |

76 78 79 ★81 82 (83) 83

As the name of the wine indicates, this walled property dates from the time of the Knights Templar. The 1983, cherry-red in colour, is very much a wine to keep, holding out exceptional promise thanks to the good balance between its tannins, alcohol and general mellowness. Its attractive bouquet seems likely to develop a marvellous finesse. (1983) ✔ Côtes du Rhône Vacqueyras Cuvée St-Roch, AC Gigondas Cuvée de La Tour Sarrazinne.
↪ MM. Archimbaud et Vache, Dom. Clos des Cazeaux, Vacqueyras, 84190 Beaumes-de-Venise; tel. 90 65 85 83 ⟗ Mon.–Sat. 9.00–12.00/14.00–19.00.

DOMAINE LE CLOS DES CAZAUX
VACQUEYRAS
CÔTES DU RHÔNE
APPELLATION CÔTES DU RHÔNE CONTRÔLÉE
MIS EN BOUTEILLE AU DOMAINE
75 cl
ARCHIMBAUD L. ET VACHE M.
PROPRIÉTAIRES-RÉCOLTANTS A VACQUEYRAS (VAUCLUSE) FRANCE

CELLIER DE L'ENCLAVE DES PAPES

| ■ | | 240 000 | 2 D ▪ ⬥ |

(78) 79 80 81 82 83 83

On this land, which was purchased in 1317 by John XXII, the Cellier de l'Enclave des Papes produces a dark-red wine with a heady nose that hints at cooked fruit and resin. A good bottle, to be drunk now. (1981) ✔ Coteaux du Tricastin, Côtes du Rhône.
↪ Cellier de l'Enclave des Papes, 11 Av. du Général-de-Gaulle, 84600 Valréas; tel. 90 30 91 42 ⟗ Mon.–Sat. 8.00–12.00/15.00–19.00. Sun. 9.00–12.00/15.00–18.00.

DOMAINE ESTOURNEL *Laudun*★

| ▨ | 1ha | 4800 | 3 D ▪ |

(79) 81 81

A highly original wine, bright salmon-pink in colour, with a complex nose revealing aromas of beeswax, honey and quince. Fascinating. (1983)
↪ Rémy Estournel, Dom. Estournel, 30790 St-Victor-la-Coste; tel. 66 50 01 73 ⟗ By appt.

DOMAINE ESTOURNEL *Laudun*★★

| ■ | 600ha | 500 000 | 2 D ▪ |

(81) 81 83

From a blend of five grape varieties. Dark red-brown wine with a good structure on the palate. Rather undeveloped nose. (1979).
↪ Rémy Estournel, Dom. Estournel, 30790 St-Victor-la-Coste; tel. 66 50 01 73 ⟗ By appt.

CHATEAU DE LA GARDINE★★

| ■ | 48ha | 200 000 | 3 D ◑ ⬥ |

78 79 80 ★81 82 83

This wine has a fine, strong, red colour, though with a slight hint of chestnut, and a very delicate and elegant bouquet. It is equally pleasing on the palate, full and quite fleshy. (1980)
↪ SCP Ch. de la Gardine, 84230 Châteauneuf-du-Pape; tel. 90 83 73 20 ⟗ By appt.

DOMAINE DE LA GARRIGUE★★

| ■ | 7ha | | 3 D ▪ ⬥ |

78 79 80 (82) 82 83 83

This rugged wine is made without clarifying or filtration, by a traditional vinification method used for a century or more. Connoisseurs will be delighted by its musky animal flavours. However, it is still a touch hard on the palate and should be kept a little longer. (1982) ✔ Côtes du Rhône, Gigondas.
↪ A. et L. Bernard, Dom. de la Garrigue, Vac-

queyras, 84190 Beaumes-de-Venise; tel. 90 65 84 60 ☎ Mon.–Sat. 8.00–20.00; public holidays by appt. Closed Sun.

LAMBERTINS *Vacqueyras**

■   12ha   70000   2 **D** ⅏ ⅃
78 ⑦⑨ **80 81 82** 83

A straightforward, pleasing wine with fine colour and good structure on the palate. (1983)
↜ *MM*. Lambert Frères, GAEC des Lambertins, Vacqueyras, 84000; tel. 90 65 85 54 ☎ By appt. Closed Sun. pm.

CAVE DES VIGNERONS DE LAUDUN
*Grand Vin du Camps Romain**

■   230ha   696000   3 **D** ▪ ⅃
73 ⑦⑧ 79 80 80 81 83

Seductively fine, bright colour. Fruity nose, fresh and delicate with a touch of strawberry. Good structure and balance on the palate. A pleasing bottle which may be drunk at any time. (1980)
✔ Côtes du Rhône Laudun Blanc, Côtes du Rhône Laudun Rouge, Côtes du Rhône Laudun Rosé.
↜ Cave des Vignerons de Laudun, Route de l'Ardoise, 30290 Laudun; tel. 66 79 49 97 ☎ By appt.

CAVE DES VIGNERONS DE LAUDUN
*Laudun Grand Blanc du Haut-Claud**

□   50ha   114000   3 **D** ▪ ⅃
⑦⓪ **82** 83 84

Renowned for producing wines of consistent quality, the Cave des Vignerons de Laudun has not failed here. A very pleasing bottle for an all occasions. (1983)
↜ Cave des Vignerons de Laudun, Route de l'Ardoise, 30290 Laudun; tel. 66 79 49 97 ☎ By appt.

CAVE COOPERATIVE DU NYONSAIS**

■   60ha   18000   2 **D** ▪ ⅃
78 81 *83

Beautiful, sombre red. Pleasant nose. Good on the palate, with good tannin. Drink immediately. (1982)
↜ Cave Coop. du Nyonsais, BP 9, 26110 Nyons; tel. 75 26 03 44 ☎ By appt.

DOMAINE RABASSE-CHARAVIN
*Cairanne***

■   7ha   40000   3 **D** ▪ ⅃
72 74 77 81 ⑧⑨ 82 83

Charming dark peony colour and woodland aromas of moss, pine and resin – a bouquet which strengthens with age. A very full-bodied wine, but this in no way detracts from its balance. (1983)
↜ *Mme* Corine Couturier, Les Coteaux-St-Martin, 84290 Cairanne; tel. 90 30 82 27 ☎ Daily 8.00–12.00/13.00–20.00.

CAVE DES VIGNERONS DE RASTEAU *Rasteau**

■   70ha   506000   3 **D** ⅏ ⅃
78 79 81 ⑧② 82 83

Rich Grenache, Cinsault; subtle Syrah and Mourvèdre combine to produce this beautiful, brilliant red wine with a very delicate nose. Warm and full bodied, its structure indicates interesting results with ageing. To be laid down; offered at an attractive price. (1982) ✔ Rasteaux Vin Doux Naturel Rouge et Rosé, Côtes du Rhône Rouge et Rosé.
↜ Cave des Vignerons de Rasteau, Rasteau 84110 Vaison-la-Romaine; tel. 90 46 10 43 ☎ Daily 8.00–12.00/14.00–18.00.

LES VIGNERONS DE ROCHEGUDE
*Cuvée du Président**

■   25000   2 **D** ▪ ⅃

Moderately intense but clear colour. Discreet aromas of small red fruit (redcurrant, blackberry and blackcurrant). Fairly well balanced, but very vigorous, showing a combination of suppleness and aggression. Drink now. (1984)
↜ Coop. des Vign. de Rochegude, Rochegude, 26130 St-Paul-Trois-Châteaux; tel. 75 04 81 84 ☎ By appt.

LES VIGNERONS DE ROCHEGUDE
*Cuvée de la Cassuise**

■   12000   2 **D** ▪ ⅃
82 83 84

The peony-red colour is not particularly intense, while the aromas of small red fruit are still young. A supple wine, but short and weak on the palate, where the alcohol dominates. (1982)
↜ Coop. des Vign. de Rochegude, Rochegude, 26130 St-Paul-Trois-Châteaux; tel. 75 04 81 84 ☎ By appt.

CHATEAU SAINT-ESTEVE**

■   24ha   152000   3 **D** ▪ ⅃
78 80 81 *82 *⑧③

This is a very pleasing wine, with spicy aromas of thyme and seasoning. Good grip on the palate and excellent tannins. Drink immediately. (1983)
↜ G. Français et Fils. Dom. de St-Estève, Uchaux, 84100 Orange; tel. 90 34 34 04 ☎ Mon.–Sat. 8.00–12.00/14.00–18.00.

VIGNERONS DE SAINT-GERVAIS**

■   35ha   130000   3 **D** ▪ ⅃
78 79 80 *82 *83

With its fine dark-red colour, this is a rich, generous, fleshy but well-balanced wine which may be drunk now or kept for a fair while. (1982)
↜ Vignerons de St-Gervais, 30200 St-Gervais; tel. 66 89 67 05 ☎ By appt.

COOPERATIVE SAINT-HILAIRE-D'OZILHAN**

■   30ha   144000   2 **D** ▪ ⅃

Intense ruby purple wine, with a powerful nose of fruit over woody and forest perfumes, as well as undertones of fresh leather and venison. A great deal of character on the palate with a fine base and good structure. Well made with very pleasing aromas which persist well. All adds up to a fine

bottle; full and powerful. (1983) ✔ Other Côtes du Rhône wines, Côtes du Rhône Villages.
✚ Coop. St-Hilaire-d'Ozilhan, St-Hilaire d'Ozilhan, 30210 Remoulins; tel. 66 37 16 47 ⅄ By appt.

FERME SAINT-MARTIN
Beaumes-de-Venise

■		5 ha	22 000	🅱 🅳 ▮ ◐ ⬇
81 **82** 83 84				

Produced within the walls of a 12th-century convent, this is an attractively coloured, peppery, tannic wine which should be drunk now; does not need to breathe. (1982) ✔ Côtes du Rhone.
✚ Guy Jullien, Coteaux de la Ferme St-Martin, Suzette, 84190 Beaumes-de-Venise; tel. 90 62 96 40 ⅄ Mon–Sat. 10.00–19.00.

COOPERATIVE DE SAINT-MAURICE-SUR-EYGUES
*Saint-Maurice**

■		6 ha	96 000	🄲 🅳 ▮ ⬇
66 68 70 82 **82** ⑧⑬				

A straightforward, honest and pleasant enough wine, the colour of redcurrant, that should develop well with time. (1983)
✚ Coop. de St-Maurice-sur-Eygues, 26110 St-Maurice-sur-Eygues; tel. 75 27 63 44 ⅄ By appt.

COOPERATIVE SAINT-PANTALEON-LES-VIGNES
*Rousset-les-Vignes**

■		58 ha	288 000	🄲 🅳 ▮ ◐ ⬇
70 78 79 ★81 ★82 ★83				

A pleasant wine, with a red-tile colour, notable for two principal characteristics: suppleness and lightness. (1981)
✚ Coop. St-Pantaléon-les-Vignes, Route de Nyons, 26770 St-Pantaléon-les-Vignes; tel. 75 26 26 43 ⅄ By appt.

COOPERATIVE SAINT-PANTALEON-LES-VIGNES*

■		53 ha	300 000	🄲 ▮ ◐ ⬇
70 78 79 80 81 82 **82** 83 84				

Supple and round on the palate. Light nose. Drink immediately. (1982) ✔ Rousset-les-Vignes Rouge, St-Pantaléon-les-Vignes Rosé, Côtes du Rhône Rouge, Coteau du Tricastin Rouge.
✚ Coop. St-Pantaléon-les-Vignes, Route de Nyons, 26770 St-Pantaléon-les-Vignes; tel. 75 26 26 43 ⅄ By appt.

COOPERATIVE SAINT-PANTALEON-LES-VIGNES
*Saint-Pantaléon***

■		70 ha	360 000	🅱 🅳 ▮ ◐ ⬇
70 78 79 81 82 ★83				

This wine, a beautiful dark-red in colour, has acquired a powerful, aromatic nose from its ageing in oak casks – characteristics fully borne out in the taste. (1982) ✔ St-Pantaléon les Vignes Rouge, Côtes du Rhône Rouge, Coteaux du Tricastin Rouge.
✚ Coop. St-Pantaléon-les-Vignes, Route de Nyons, 26770 St-Pantaléon-les-Vignes; tel. 75 26 26 43 ⅄ By appt.

DOMAINE SAINTE-ANNE
*Cuvée Notre-Dame des Cellettes***

■		18 ha	80 000	🅱 🅳 ▮ ⬇
79 81 82 ⑧⑬ **83**				

Beautiful ruby colour and flowery nose, with a hint of apricot, are immediately reminiscent of high summer. On the palate, it offers the pleasures of good balance, elegance and harmony, while a light but not unduly assertive touch of tannin indicates that this is a wine still worth keeping. (1979) ✔ Côtes du Rhône Blanc, Côtes du Rhône-Villages Blanc, Côtes du Rhône Rouge.
✚ GAEC Dom. Ste-Anne, Mas de Cellettes, St-Gervais, 30200 Bagnols-sur-Cèze; tel. 66 89 67 41 ⅄ Mon.–Sat. ✚ *MM*. Steinmaier et Fils.

LE SANG DES CAILLOUX
*Vacqueyreas***

■		16 ha	74 400	🄲 🅳 ▮ ◐

This exceptional wine should be allowed to breathe for a good while before drinking, to bring out all its lovely moorland aromas with overtones of carob and bay-leaf; the bouquet is matched by a well-rounded taste and a long finish. (1983)
✚ SCEA Le Sang des Cailloux, Route de Vacqueyras, 84260 Sarrians; tel. 90 65 85 67 ⅄ By appt Mon–Sat.

DOMAINE DE LA SOUMADE
*Rasteau***

■		4 ha	12 000	🅱 🅳 ▮ ⬇
★82 **82** ⑧⑬				

Rasteau has already established a reputation for producing 'vin doux natural' (naturally sweet wine). But there are also some excellent reds, such as this example. Warm and very tannic, with a rather burnt nose, this is a good bottle to keep. (1982) ✔ Côtes du Rhône Rouge, Côtes du Rhône Villages Rouge, Vin Doux Naturel Rasteau Doré.
✚ André Romero, Dom. de la Soumade, Rasteau, 84110 Vaison la Romaine; tel. 90 46 11 26 ⅄ Mon.–Sun. 8.00–12.00/14.00–22.00.

LA SUZIENNE**

■		200 ha	760 000	🄲 🅳 ▮ ⬇
66 70 72 78 ⑧② **82**				

Classic fruit-and-vegetable bouquet of a good Côtes du Rhône-Villages – a wine which would go well, as soon as you wish, with a fine *gigot*, the succulent leg of lamb that is one of the specialities of the Drôme region. (1982)
✚ Cave Coop. la Suzienne, 26130 Suze-la-Rousse; tel. 75 04 80 04 ⅄ By appt. Closed 1 Jan., 1 May, 25 Dec.

DOMAINE DES COTEAUX DES TRAVERS *Rasteau*★★

| ■ | 10ha 50000 | 3 D ▮ ⬤ |

76 78 79 80 ★⑧⑴ ★82 ★83 84

Cherry-red colour and an aroma of blackcurrants, myrtle berries and quinces. Well balanced, warm and rich; not too tannic. (1983)
↬ GAEC Robert Charavin et Fils, Rasteau, 84110 Vaison-la-Romaine; tel. 90 46 10 48 ⟂ By appt.

DOMAINE DU VAL DES ROIS
Valréas★★

| ■ | 5ha 22000 | 3 D ▮ ⬤ |

⑥④ **78** ⑧② **83**

The Val des Rois once belonged to the popes. In keeping with this venerable past, Romain Bouchard guarantees the wines he now produces there for ten years (provided they are stored properly in cellar) and undertakes to reimburse anyone who is not satisfied. His 1982, with its bouquet of red fruit, is still a little closed-in but is sure to develop well as the tannin softens. (1982)
✔ Côtes du Rhône 'Petit Roi' Rouge, Côtes du Rhône 'Petit Roi' Rosé, Côtes du Rhône Cuvée de la Huitième Génération Rouge.
↬ Romain Bouchard, Dom. du Val des Rois, 84600 Valréas; tel. 90 35 04 35 ⟂ By appt.

DOMAINE DE LA VERQUIERE★★

| ■ | 10ha 38000 | 3 D ⬤ ⬤ |

★78 ★79 ★81 ★82

As handsome as it is good. Magnificent colour; delicate and elegant aroma based on fruit, leather, truffles, vanilla and spices. Powerful structure, with a fine balance between the alcohol and tannin. Already full, the extent of its fullness will not be reached for another two or three years. (1979) ✔ Côtes du Rhône 1982/1983 Rouge et Blanc, Vin doux Naturel Rasteau.
↬ Louis Chamfort et Frères, Dom. de la Verquière, Sablet, 84110 Vaison-la-Romaine; tel. 90 36 90 11 ⟂ Daily 8.00–12.00/14.00–18.00.

COOPERATIVE LES COTEAUX DE VISAN★

| □ | 200ha 180000 | 2 D ▮ ⬤ |

78 79 ⑧⑴ **82 83**

One of the first 'brotherhoods of wine' was founded at Visan in 1475. This light-yellow wine, from the Visan cooperative, is rather weak on the nose, but vigorous and a little sweet on the palate. (1982) ✔ Visan Rosé 1982, Visan Blanc 1983, Grande Réserve 1979 Rouge, Notre-Dame-des-Vignes 1979 Rouge.
↬ Coop. Les Coteaux de Visan, 84820 Visan; tel. 90 41 91 12 ⟂ Daily 8.30–12.00/14.00–18.30. Closed 25 Dec., 1 Jan.

COOPERATIVE LES COTEAUX DE VISAN★★

| ◪ | 200000 | 3 D ▮ ⬤ |

79 80 81 ⑧⑴ **82** ★83

A gleaming light colour, with a touch of yellow, and a well-developed bouquet in which you can detect a hint of Morello cherries. It has lasted well, for a 1981, and has a good finish. To be drunk now. (1981) ✔ Other Côtes du Rhônes.
↬ Coop. les Coteaux de Visan, 84820 Visan; tel.

90 41 91 12 ⟂ Daily 8.30–12.00/14.00–18.30. Closed 25 Dec., 1 Jan.

DOMAINE DE WILFRIED★★★

| ■ | 25ha 120000 | 3 ⬤ D ⬤ |

78 80 ★82 ★83

Aromatic nose, combining strawberry jam, ripe fruit and a touch of leather. Powerful tannins in harmony with the smoothness and fullness of the palate. A highly successful example of the vintage. (1982)
↬ Emile Charavin, Quartier Blorac, Rasteau, 84110 Vaison-la-Romaine; tel. 90 46 10 66 ⟂ By appt.

Château Grillet

This white-wine appellation is unique among all French wines. Made on a single estate of 2.5 hectares, it is France's smallest AOC, producing only 90 hectolitres per year. The vineyard is planted on sunny granite terraces, well-sheltered from the wind, in an isolated amphitheatre overlooking the Rhône valley. The wine, made from Viognier grapes, is high in alcohol, fat, crisply acidic, very fragrant and astoundingly refined. Although it may be drunk young, bottle age gives it a bouquet and an elegance that can make it a wine of exceptional quality, ideal for serving chilled (under 10°C) with fish.

CHATEAU GRILLET★★★

| □ | 3ha 1100 | 6 D ⬤ ⬤ |

66 68 ⑦② ⑦⑤ ⑦⑧ **78** ⑦⑧ **79 81 82 83**

Very bright pale yellow wine with a smoky bouquet followed by floral, fruity aromas. Concentrated and full on the palate, its strongest flavours being peach and apricot. Remarkable wine of character, possessing harmony, subtlety, elegance and complex aromas. (1981)
↬ M. Neyret-Gachet, Ch. Grillet, Vérin, 42410 Pelussin; tel. 74 59 51 56 ⟂ By appt.

Clairette de Die

The Clairette de Die vineyards are situated on slopes of the central Drôme valley between Luc-en-Diois and Aouste-sur-Sye; the sparkling white wine made here is one of the oldest known. It is produced from Clairette and Muscat grapes in two different ways. The traditional method is to allow the wine to ferment naturally in bottle; this is an unusual method ideal for preserving the aromas of the Muscat grape, which has to make up at least 50 per cent of the blend. The second method is the Méthode Champenoise, in which secondary fermentation in the bottle is caused by the addition of a sweetened wine mixture to the dry wine. In wine made by this method, Clairette has to be the predominant grape variety – at least 75 per cent. Total production is in the order of 55000 hectolitres from 1000 hectares.

UNION DES PRODUCTEURS DU DIOIS *Brut Voconces**

| ○ | 50ha | 100000 | 4 D ▮ ↓ |

This sparkling wine, made by the champagne method, is a very good example of the Clairette de Die appellation. Served at between 6° and 8°C it goes well with dessert and also makes an enjoyable aperitif. (1981) ✔ Cuvée Impériale Brut, Tradition Cuvée Impériale.
➤ Coop. de la Clairette de Die, Av. de la Clairette, 26150 Die; tel. 75 22 02 22 ☎ Daily 8.00–12.00/13.30–18.30.

UNION DES PRODUCTEURS DU DIOIS *Tradition Cuvée Impériale***

| ○ | 750ha | 300000 | 4 D ▮ ↓ |

Instead of the Clairette grape variety, the fine bouquet of this attractive wine shows it to stem from Muscat grapes. Again, though, equally pleasant either as an aperitif or with dessert. ✔ Cuvée Impériale Brut.
➤ Coop. de la Clairette, Av. de la Clairette, 26150 Die; tel. 75 22 02 22 ☎ Daily 8.00–12.00/13.30–18.30.

DOMAINE DE MAGORD *Brut***

| ○ | 3ha | 11000 | 3 D ▮ ↓ |

Fine colour, enhanced by a light mousse. Pleasing to look at. The aromas are floral over a vegetal background, and show good finesse. A pleasing sparkling wine, balanced and satisfyingly fresh. (1983)
➤ Jean-Claude Vincent, Dom. de Magord, Barsac, 26150 Die; tel. 75 21 71 43 ☎ By appt.

DOMAINE DE MAGORD *Méthode Traditionelle 1/2 Sec**

| ○ | 3ha | 25000 | 3 D ▮ ↓ |

This attractive, very pale yellow wine, with its light mousse, has a very marked aroma of the Muscat grape. Predominantly sweet; a good bottle to follow the pudding.
➤ Jean-Claude Vincent, Dom. de Magord, Barsac, 26150 Die; tel. 75 21 71 43 ☎ By appt.

DOMAINE DE MAGORD****

| ○ | 3ha | 3000 | 2 D ▮ ↓ |

Attractive pale-yellow colour with tinges of green. Aromas of vine flowers and a slight scent of musk over a vegetal background of ivy leaves. This well-balanced wine is supple, smooth, and delicate on the palate. Drink now. (1983)
➤ Jean-Claude Vincent, Dom. de Magord, Barsac, 26150 Die; tel. 75 21 71 43 ☎ By appt.

GEORGES RASPAIL *Méthode dioise traditionnelle***

| ○ | 3ha | 20000 | 3 D ▮ ↓ |
| 83 |

Excellent presentation confirmed in the delicacy and refinement of its aromas. Keeps its body well. Lingering finsh. Very good bottle, produced according to traditional methods. (1983)
➤ Georges Raspail, Aurel, 26340 Saillans; tel. 75 21 71 89 ☎ By appt.

GEORGES RASPAIL****

| ○ | 3ha | 24000 | 3 D ▮ ↓ |

Typical Clairette aromas, and releases a stream of delicate bubbles. A wine of good quality.
➤ Georges Raspail, Aurel, 26340 Saillans; tel. 75 21 71 89 ☎ By appt.

CAVES SALABELLE *Brut**

| ○ | 2ha | 8000 | 3 D ▮ ↓ |

A well-made wine, light yellow in colour. The finish is pleasing, with a slight hint of bitterness at the end.
➤ Pierre Salabelle, Barsac, 26150 Die; tel. 75 32 72 21 ☎ By appt.

CAVES SALABELLE *Méthode Dioise***

| ○ | 3ha | 22000 | 3 D ▮ ↓ |

A very attractive wine, with delicate aromas of the Muscat grape. Good balance, and strong, persistent bubbles. Lingering aromas on the finish. Above all, a great deal of finesse.
➤ Pierre Salabelle, Barsac, 26150 Die; tel. 75 32 72 21 ☎ By appt.

Chatillon-en-Diois

The Chatillon-en-Diois vineyards cover 50 hectares of the slopes of the high Drôme valley between Luc-en-Diois (550m) and Pont-de-Quart (465m). Both red and white wines are produced under this appellation; the reds, made from Gamay grapes, are light, fruity, and ready to drink when young; the whites are made from Aligoté and Chardonnay and are lively and very pleasant. Total production is 2500 hectolitres.

UPVF DE DIOIS *Cuvée du Reviron**

| ■ | 40ha | 300000 | 2 D ▮ ↓ |
| (83) |

Very pretty colour. Supple and light on the palate. Drink without delay. (1983)
➤ Coop. de la Clairette de Die, Ave de la Clairette, 26150 Die; tel. 75 22 02 22 ☎ Daily 8.00–13.00/13.30–18.30.

UPVF DE DIOIS *Chardonnay***

| □ | 15ha | 90000 | 2 D ▮ ↓ |
| (84) |

Straw-coloured. Rich, with complex and powerful aromas of flowers and fruit. Vegetables and green fruit on the palate. Both smooth and fresh at the same time, with a good finish. Elegant.

Drink young. (1982)
♠ Coop. de la Clairette de Die, Ave de la Clairette, 26150 Die; tel. 75 22 02 22 ⊤ Daily 8.00–13.00/13.30–18.30.

UPVF DE DIOIS *Aligoté**

| □ | 15 ha | 90 000 | ② Ⓓ 🍾 ↓ |

⑭

Straw-yellow. Bright and transparent. Flowery, with a hawthorn aroma. Well balanced. Drink young. (1983)
♠ Coop. de la Clairette de Die, Ave de la Clairette, 26150 Die; tel. 75 22 02 22 ⊤ Daily 8.00–13.00/13.30–18.30.

Condrieu

The Condrieu vineyards lie on the east bank of the Rhône about 11 kilometres to the south of Vienne. Only white wines made entirely from Viognier grapes are allowed to use the appellation. The AOC area is divided between seven communes, but totals less than 16 hectares, and only about 400 hectolitres of wine are produced annually. These factors combine to make Condrieu very rare. High in alcohol, smooth, fat and very fragrant, it nevertheless has a certain freshness, and a flowery aroma, predominantly of apricot and violets. It is a unique, exceptional and unforgettable wine that may either be drunk young, served chilled with any freshwater fish dish, or kept to develop in the bottle.

PIERRE ET ANDRE PERRET
Coteau de Chéry***

| □ | 2 ha | 7200 | ⑤ Ⓓ 🍾 ⑪ ↓ |

81 82 83 83

Bright, light yellow colour with tinges of green; rich and complex nose, with slightly smoky aromas of tobacco, spices and exotic fruit. A very original wine, thick yet dry and full on the palate. (1983) ✔ Côtes du Rhône Rouge.
♠ Pierre et André Perret, Verlieu, 42410 Chavanay; tel. 74 87 24 74 ⊤ By appt.

Cornas

This appellation, to the south of Hermitage, lies entirely within the single commune of Cornas. The AOC area covers 53 hectares and produces 2300 hectolitres annually. The vineyard slopes are very steep, and the soil – sandy granite – has to be retained by careful cultivation. Cornas is a virile

and robust wine that needs at least three years in bottle – and may sometimes be kept quite a bit longer – in order to develop its fruity and spicy aromas. It goes well with red meat and game.

PAUL ETIENNE PERE ET FILS*

| ■ | | 6000 | ⑤ ⑪ ↓ |

⑤⑨ 62 70 81

A wine with a deep, slightly hazy colur and rich nose with woody overtones and a touch of liquorice. A very tannic bottle, typical of its appellation. (1981)
♠ Paul Etienne et Fils, 07130 St-Péray; tel. 75 40 30 18 ⊤ No visitors.

PAUL JABOULET AINE***

| ■ | 42 ha | 30 000 | ④ Ⓓ 🍾 ⑪ ↓ |

70 71 73 76 *⑦⑧ *79 *80 *82 83

Lovely ruby colour and a delicate and seductive bouquet of overripe fruit. Full on the palate, with finesse and elegance. The aroma is remarkably long-lasting. Quite austere at the finish, but after a year or two it will make a very smart and enticing bottle. (1983)
♠ SA Paul Jaboulet Ainé, RN 7, BP 46, La Roche-de-Glun, 26600 Tain-l'Hermitage; tel. 75 84 68 93 ⊤ No visitors.

MARCEL JUGE***

| ■ | 3 ha | 13 000 | ④ Ⓓ ⑪ ↓ |

78 79 80 *82 82 ⑧③

Strongly characterized by its fine, dark red colour, this wine's wild-fruit aromas are still slightly restrained by its tannin. However, the excellent value for money and the promise of ageing well make it worthwhile buying this wine now. (1983) ✔ Cornas St-Péray Blanc.
♠ Marcel Juge, Place de la Salle-des-Fêtes, Cornas, 07130 St-Péray; tel. 75 40 36 68 ⊤ No visitors.

MICHEL ROBERT**

| ■ | 4 ha | 13 000 | ④ Ⓓ 🍾 ⑪ ↓ |

78 79 81 ⑧② 83 83

Matured in oak casks, which gives the wine its full-bodied quality and the reason why the bouquet of cooked fruit and truffles can take four or five years to reach its best. (1982) ✔ Cornas Pied-de-Coteau Rouge.
♠ Michel Robert, Grande-Rue, Cornas, 07130 St-Péray; tel. 75 40 38 70 ⊤ Mon.–Sat.

UPVF DE TAIN-L'HERMITAGE*

| ■ | 10 ha | 38 000 | ④ Ⓓ ⑪ ↓ |

78 79 80 *⑧② 82 *83

The Cave Coopérative des Vins Fins has just celebrated its fiftieth anniversary. Its honest Cornas will be ready for drinking – any moment now. (1982) ✔ Hermitage Rouge, Crozes-Hermitage Rouge, St-Joseph Rouge.
♠ UPVF de Tain-L'Hermitage, 22 Route de Larnage, BP 3, 26600 Tain-l'Hermitage; tel. 75 08 20 87 ⊤ Mon.–Sat. Closed public holidays.

NOEL VERSET★★★

■ 2.5ha 9600 **4** **D** ◗ ↓

82 83

Fine deep colour with tinges of brown, a powerful, wild fruit bouquet, still slightly closed-in; confirmed on the palate by good balance despite very strong tannins. If left for two or three years it will mature into a great wine, which will last for several more years. (1983)
♦⌐ Noel Verset, Rue de la Coulèse, Cornas, 07130 St-Péray; tel. 75 40 36 66 ☒ By appt.

Côte Rôtie

This vineyard, at Vienne, on the east bank of the Rhône, is the oldest of the entire Côtes du Rhône. The 106 hectares of AOC production are divided between the communes of Ampuis, St-Cyr-sur-Rhône and Tupins-Sémons; the vines grow on very steep, almost vertiginous slopes. Traditionally, but not legally, a distinction is made between the Côte Blonde and the Côte Brune; the tradition supposedly stems from a local landowner called Maugiron who in his will divided his land between his two daughters, one blonde, the other brunette.

There is more schist here than elsewhere in the region, and only red wines are produced; these are made mostly from Syrah grapes, but the Viognier is also used, up to a maximum of 20 per cent. The Côte Brune wines are fuller-bodied, the Côte Blonde wines more delicate.

Côte Rôtie wine (4500 hectolitres) is deep red in colour and has a subtle and delicate bouquet of spice and raspberry, with a touch of violets. It has good structure and a very long finish, and must be classed among the top Côte du Rhône wines – a perfect complement for any dish with which one would expect to serve a great red wine.

DOMAINE DE BOISSEYT
Côte-Blonde★★★

■ 0.6ha 2000 **5** **D** ◗ ↓

78 79 81 82 **82**

Woody, vegetal nose, with a touch of flowers. The flavour is still closed in around an assertive tannin, although this is softened by a hint of vanilla. With ageing, a wine that holds out great promise. (1981)
♦⌐ Jean Chol et Fils, Route Nationale 86, Ampuis, 42410 Chavanay; tel. 74 87 23 45 ☒ Tues.–Sun. 9 00–12.00/14.00–19.00.

A. ET L. DREVON★★

■ 5ha 25000 **4** **D** ◗ ↓

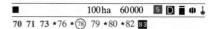
★76 ★78 ★80 ★82 83

Purple-red colour and a very backward, pungent bouquet. A very powerful, amply flavoured wine which is tannic and acid on the palate. This will be a good bottle in six to eight years' time. (1983)
♦⌐ A. et L. Drevon, La Roche, 69420 Ampuis; tel. 74 56 11 38 ☒ By appt.

PAUL JABOULET AINE
Les Jumelles★★★

■ 100ha 60000 **5** **D** ⌷ ◗ ↓

70 71 73 ★76 ★⑦⑧ 79 ★80 ★82 **83**

Terrific, bright, ruby colour. Attractive, powerful and expansive Syrah nose combining cherry and violet fragrances. Robust but very full bodied on the palate, with a lingering aroma. Extremely rich finish which leaves strong fragrances in the mouth. Remarkably attractive. (1983)
♦⌐ SA Paul Jaboulet Aîné, RN 7, BP 46, La Roche-du-Glun, 26600 Tain-l'Hermitage; tel. 75 84 68 93 ☒ No visitors.

DOMAINE DE VALLOUIT★★

■ 20ha 72000 **D** ◗ ↓

76 78 80 ★81 ★82 ★⑧③

Dark-red colour with a spicy, vegetal nose. The good tannin-alcohol balance suggests it will mature well. (1982) ✔ Hermitage, Crozes-Hermitage.
♦⌐ L. de Vallouit, 26240 St-Vallier; tel. 75 23 10 11 ☒ By appt.

LA VIAILLERE★

■ 3ha 15000 **5** **D** ◗ ↓

★76 ★77 ⑦⑧ ★79 ★80 ★81 82 **83**

Although a little light, the colour is bright and attractive. Aromas, which include vanilla, have great finesse but lack fullness and intensity. A very light style of Côte Rôtie, which is to be drunk now. (1982)
♦⌐ Albert Dervieux-Thaize, Vérenay-Ampuis, 69920 Condrieu; tel. 74 53 37 75 ☒ By appt. Closed 20 Aug.–5 Sept.

Crozes-Hermitage

The vineyard land of this appellation is more easily cultivated than in Hermitage, and extends into eleven communes surrounding Tain-l'Hermitage. About 43000 hectolitres of wine are produced on 822 hectares, making Crozes-Hermitage the largest-yielding appellation of the northern Côtes du Rhône. The rich soil produces fruity wines, less powerful than in Hermitage, that are best drunk young. The reds are smooth and aromatic, the whites dry and fresh, with a pale colour and flowery aromas; like white Hermitage, they make a perfect accompaniment to freshwater fish.

PERE ANSELME★

■ 120000 ③ D ▪ ↓

80 81 81 82

The red colour has some brown tinges and its aromas are correspondingly old, hinting of leather and liquorice and rather too strong a smell of wood. It has only average balance and softness, all of which make it a classic example of a wine which, while not disappointing, is pretty nondescript. ✓ Chateauneuf-du-Pape Rouge, Tavel Rosé, Gigondas Rouge, Côtes du Rhone-Villages Rouge.

☛ Père Anselme, 84230 Châteauneuf-du-Pape; tel. 90 83 70 07 ☍ Daily 9.00–12.00/14.00–18.00.

THOMAS BASSOT★★

■ 3000 ③ D ▪ ↓

83

A wine characterized by its complex aromas which combine red fruit with that of cooked fruit; good character. (1983)

☛ Thomas Bassot, 5 Quai Dumorey, 21700 Nuits-St-Georges; tel. 80 62 31 05 ☍ By appt.

CAVE DES CLAIRMONTS★★

☐ 67ha 430000 ③ D ▪ ↓

⑦⑨ 81 ★82 83

Pale yellow colour, with tinges of green. Nose initially closed-in, but develops aromas typical of the Roussane and Marsanne grapes. Floral, slightly spicy and very firm to taste, this is a wine to drink with a meal rather than as an aperitif and will easily keep for two or three years. ✓ Crozes-Hermitage Blanc.

☛ SCA des Caves de Clairmonts, Beaumont-Monteux, 26600 Tain-l'Hermitage; tel. 75 84 61 91 ☍ Mon.–Sat. 8.00–12.00/14.00–18.00. Closed public holidays.

CAVE DES CLAIRMONTS★★

■ 70ha 420000 ③ D ▪ ↓

78 79 81 ★83

A very attractive, deep red colour accompanies good balance on the palate. The wine has aromas of spiced fruit with a touch of vanilla. To be drunk now. (1983).

☛ SCA des Caves de Clairmonts, Beaumont-Monteux, 26600 Tain-l'Hermitage; tel. 75 84 61 91 ☍ Mon.–Sat. 8.00–12.00/14.00–18.00. Closed public holidays.

DOMAINE DES ENTREFAUX★★★

■ 11ha 50000 ③ D ⑪ ↓

★78 79 80 ★82 ★⑧③ 83

A perfect example of its appellation; its deep, young red colour has purplish tinges, and a very peppery nose with aromas of blackberry and blackcurrant. The wine has great finesse and length, together with a slightly rustic, earthy tang. This is an exemplary wine which may be enjoyed until 1988 without any problem. (1983)

☛ C. Tardy et B. Ange, GAEC de la Syrah, Chanos-Curson, 26600 Tain-l'Hermitage; tel. 75 07 33 38 ☍ By appt.

JULES FAYOLLE ET FILS★★

☐ 1ha 800 ④ D ⑪ ↓

74 75 76 **76** ★78 **78** ★80 ⑧① 82

Slightly golden colour with good brightness and already well-developed aromas. Round and crisp, with a pleasing finish. This wine may be aged for several years and is similar to the wines produced in the Hermitage appellation. (1982)

☛ Jules Fayolle et Fils, Gervans, 26600 Tain-l'Hermitage; tel. 75 08 33 74 ☍ By appt. Closed three weeks Aug.

PAUL JABOULET AINE
Domaine de Thalabert★★★

■ 30ha 108000 ④ D ▪ ⑪ ↓

70 71 73 76 ★⑦⑧ ★79 ★80 ★82 **83**

Sumptuously purplish-red colour. Generous nose rich and persistent fruitiness. Plenty of fullness and good, firm balance on the palate, with a slight predominance of tannin at the finish. A good bottle which still needs two or three years to soften and open up, but already with the right food. (1983) ✓ Hermitage Rouge, Crozes-Hermitage la Mule Blanche Blanc, Hermitage Chevalier de Sterimberg.

☛ SA Paul Jaboulet Ainé, RN 7, BP 46, La Roche-de-Glun, 26600 Tain-l'Hermitage; tel. 75 84 68 93 ☍ No visitors.

DOMAINE LA NEGOCIALE★

☐ 2ha 7000 ③ D ▪ ↓

83 ★84

Light golden colour containing a great deal of carbon dioxide, released in very small bubbles on opening. The original bouquet is fairly generous, with aromas of fruit and fresh grass. Quite smooth on the palate, with a soft beginning but a fresher, more lively finish. This wine seemed to be at a difficult age when tasted, but should become more rounded and refined after its first year. (1984)

☛ Cave Collonge, Dom. la Négociale, Mercurol, 26600 Tain-l'Hermitage; tel. 75 08 11 47 ☍ By appt.

DOMAINE LA NEGOCIALE★

■ 25ha 120000 ③ D ▪ ↓

80 ⑧② **82** 83 84

A very striking and attractive purple colour, with an open, intense and fruity bouquet of very ripe plum-type fruit. Surprisingly soft on the palate, with very evolved and lingering flavours. This is a charming wine which, because of its low acidity, should be drunk fairly soon. (1983)

☛ Cave Collonge, Dom. la Négociale, Mercurol, 26600 Tain-l'Hermitage; tel. 75 08 11 47 ☍ By appt.

CLOS LES PONTAIX★★

■ 8ha 43000 ③ D ▪ ⑪ ↓

⑧① 82 83 **83**

Dark red colour with tinges of purple, the aromas are damp and herbaceous. Aged in cask and has character. May be drunk now but will also keep well. (1982)

☛ Jules Fayolle et Fils, Gervans, 26600 Tain l'Hermitage; tel. 75 08 33 74 ☍ By appt. Closed three weeks in Aug.

UPVF DE TAIN-L'HERMITAGE★★

■ 650ha 500000 ▣ Ⓓ ◐ ⌣
★80 ▣ ★81 ▣ ★82 ▣

An attractive bright red colour and a delicious bouquet of small red fruit and (above all) blackcurrant, with a touch of vanilla, are rounded off by the good balance of this wine. It is ready for drinking now, but will reach its peak in one or two years' time. (1982) ✔ Hermitage Rouge, Crozes-Hermitage Blanc, St-Joseph Blanc, St-Péray Méthode Champenoise.
♦ UPVF de Tain-l'Hermitage, 22 Route de Larnage, BP 3, Tain-l'Hermitage; tel. 75 08 20 87 Ⅱ Mon.–Sat. Closed public holidays.

DOMAINE DES VOUSSIERES★★★

■ 0.25ha ▣ Ⓓ ▤ ⌣
▣ 76 78 79 ★⑧ 81 82 83

Ten years is a fine age for a Crozes-Hermitage. The rich, complex aromas dominated by truffle and musk. This 1975 is now fully mature. It would be a pity not to make the most of it. (1975)
♦ Jules Fayolle et Fils, 26600 Gervans, 26600 Tain-l'Hermitage; tel. 75 08 33 74 Ⅱ By appt. Closed three weeks in Aug.

Hermitage

The Hermitage hillside is situated to the north-east of Tain-l'Hermitage and has a fine southern exposure. Vines have been cultivated here since the fourth century BC but the appellation name is attributed to the knight Gaspard de Sterimberg who, on returning from the crusade against the Albigensians in 1224, decided to go into retreat from the world. He built a hermitage for himself, cleared the surrounding land and planted vines.

The appellation covers 125 hectares and produces 4700 hectolitres of wine. The western side of the Tain massif is made of sandy granite, a terroir ideal for producing red wines such as Les Bessards, Le Méal, or Les Greffieux. The eastern and south-eastern vineyards (such as Les Rocoules or Les Murets) are made up of pebbly soils and fine loam and are best suited to white wines.

Hermitage Rouge is a big, tannic, very aromatic wine, and may require up to twenty years in bottle for it to develop its bouquet of rare depth and quality. It is, therefore, definitely a wine for laying down and should be served at 16–18°C with game or solidly flavoured red meat dishes.

Hermitage Blanc is made from Roussane and, above all, Marsanne grapes and is a very delicate wine: smooth, fat, not too acidic, and very fragrant. It can easily be enjoyed the year after the harvest but may not develop fully for five years or more. Wine from a good vintage can be kept for much longer, as long as forty years.

PERE ANSELME★★

■ 30000 ▣ ▤ ⌣
77 78 79 80 ⑧ ▣

Beautiful garnet colour with biscuity glints. One can already appreciate the elegance of its flowery, fruity, slightly spicy bouquet, as well as the lightly acidic balance on the palate. Much will be gained by leaving it to age for a few years. (1981)
♦ Père Anselme, 84230 Châteauneuf-du-Pape; tel. 90 83 70 07 Ⅱ Daily 8.00–12.00/14.00–18.00.

MAX CHAPOUTIER
Chante Alouette★★★

☐ 13ha 63000 ▣ Ⓓ ▤ ⌣

The Chapoutier firm has a fine reputation. This wine, evocative of honey and orange, is remarkably round and smooth, which guarantees it a good future. Good with fish in sauce, shellfish, foie gras and curried dishes. (1981) ✔ Hermitage Rouge Monier-de-la-Sizeranne, Châteauneuf-du-Pape la Bernardine Rouge, Côte-Rôtie Rouge.
♦ Max Chapoutier, 18 Av. de la République, 26600 Tain-l'Hermitage; tel. 75 08 28 65 Ⅱ By appt.

PAUL ETIENNE PERE ET FILS★

■ 35000 ▣ ◐ ⌣
57 59 64 66 ★▣

Distributed by a St-Péray shipper, this wine has kept well and may be drunk from now on. (1973)
♦ Paul Etienne et Fils, 07130 St-Péray; tel. 57 40 30 18 Ⅱ No visitors.

JULES FAYOLLE ET FILS
Les Dionnières★★

■ 0.3ha ▣ Ⓓ ▤
78 79 80 **81** 82

This dark red wine initially has a gassy smell which quickly disappears when decanted. Good structure supported by slightly hard tannins, it should be left for some time to mature fully. (1983)
♦ Jules Fayolle et Fils, Gervans, 26600 Tain-l'Hermitage; tel. 75 08 33 74 Ⅱ By appt. Closed for three weeks in Aug.

JEAN-LOUIS GRIPPAT★★★

☐   1.2ha   6000   5 D ▮ ◑ ⚲

64 76 ★78 ★⑧② 82 83

Bright yellow colour and rich, complex aromas of honey with a hint of smokiness. Very well balanced on the palate and has a long finish. This classy bottle has still not fully aged and requires patience. (1982) ✔ St-Joseph Rouge and Blanc, Hermitage Rouge.
✦ Jean-Louis Grippat, La Sauva, 7300 Tournon-sur-Rhône; tel. 75081551 ☎ By appt. Closed Sun.

JEAN-LOUIS GRIPPAT★★★

■   1ha   1900   5 D ◑ ⚲

72 78 79 ⑧③ 83

Jean-Louis Grippat has been known for some years for his exceptional St-Joseph wines. He is currently pursuing a similar standard for his Hermitages. The 1983 vintage has great class, and should age remarkably well. A rich, spicy nose that ranges from red fruit to green pepper, with elegant balance on the palate. A marvellous wine. (1983)
✦ Jean-Louis Grippat, La Sauva, 07300 Tournon-sur-Rhône; tel. 79081551 ☎ By appt. Closed Sun.

PAUL JABOULET AINE
Le Chevalier de Sterimberg★★

☐   5ha   21000   5 D ▮ ⚲

70 71 73 76 ★78 ★79 ★80 ★82 ⑧③ 83

Shining gold. Warm, rich, and very flowery bouquet, with shades of vanilla and roasted almonds. Opulent, meaty and very long in the mouth. Remarkably harmonious and round. (1983)
✦ SA Paul Jaboulet Ainé, RN 7, BP 46, La Roche-de-Glun, 26600 Tain-l'Hermitage; tel. 75846893 ☎ No visitors.

PAUL JABOULET AINE
La Chapelle★★★

■   20ha   84000   6 D ▮ ◑ ⚲

70 71 73 76 ★78 ★79 ★80 ★82 ⑧③ 83

Very deep ruby colour. Bouquet is still a little closed-up but sustained and full of promise. Magnificent in the mouth: very full, still dominated by a very tannic base, but also nicely meaty, guaranteeing perfect roundness in a few years' time. Has potential greatness. (1983)
✔ Crozes-Hermitage Mule Blanche Blanc, Crozes-Hermitage Dom. de Thalabert Blanc, Hermitage Chevalier de Sterimberg Rouge.
✦ SA Paul Jaboulet Ainé, RN 7, BP 46, La Roche-de-Glun, 26600 Tain-l'Hermitage; tel. 75846893 ☎ No visitors.

MARC SORREL *Vieilles Vignes*★★

■   3ha   4000   5 D ◑ ⚲

69 70 71 72 73 74 76 77 ⑦⑧ 79 80 82

This wine has a very concentrated, peppery nose, with aromas of red fruit, blackcurrant, raspberry and a slight gamey scent. It has a fine purple-red colour and looks very young, as, indeed, it is. Although very tannic, it has quality and should be allowed to age for at least 10 years. (1983)
✦ Marc Sorrel, 128 bis, Av. Jean-Jaurès, 26600 Tain-l'Hermitage; tel. 75084716 ☎ By appt.

MARC SORREL *Les Rocoules*★★★

☐   0.5ha   2000   5 D ◑ ⚲

78 79 81 82 ★⑧③

Very clear, bright yellow wine; youthful aromas, are still closed-up. Full and smooth on the palate, it is well balanced and has a long finish. This is a fine bottle which should be left to age. (1983)
✦ Marc Sorrel, 128 bis. Av. Jean-Jaurès, 26600 Tain l'Hermitage; tel. 75082945 ☎ By appt.

St-Joseph

On the easten bank of the Rhône, in the department of the Ardèche, the St-Joseph appellation area spans 23 communes, covering 298 hectares in all. The hillsides, of steeply sloping granite, command excellent views of the Alps, Mont Pilat and the Doux gorge.

St-Joseph red wines are elegant, refined, soft and relatively light-bodied, with subtle aromas of raspberry, pepper and blackcurrant that show especially well when served with grilled poultry or certain cheeses. The white wines are reminiscent of the Hermitage whites – fat, with a delicate, flowery-fruity and honey fragrance. These wines are best drunk young.

VIGNERONS ARDECHOIS★★

■   200ha   360000   3 D ◑ ⚲

81 82 ★⑧③

Fine red colour with light-yellow tinges, normal in a 1981. Delicate aromas of blackcurrant liqueur, violet and liquorice, and a touch of truffle. Supple, elegant and well-balanced, this is a wine with all the character of its appellation; very satisfying if drunk immediately. (1981)

➤ UCO Vignerons Ardéchois, BP 8, 07120 Ruoms; tel. 75 93 50 55 ⟁ By appt. Closed 25 Dec.–1 Jan.

DOMAINE DE BOISSEYT★

■		2 ha	8800	4 D ◖◗ ⌁

⑥ 74 76 81 **81 82 83**

The influence of its length in cask is still noticeable, but it has a proud allure that is already attracting local attention. (1982)
➤ Jean Chol et Fils, 86 Route Nationale, Ampuis, 42410 Chavanay; tel. 74 87 23 45 ⟁ By appt.

PIERRE COURSODON★★★

□		1 ha	5400	4 D ◼ ⌁

79 82 ★83

Bright yellow colour has additional yellowish tinges. The floral, fruity nose is rich and complex, with a mixture of floral, smoked and resinous tones. This wine is full-bodied on the palate and has good, lively depth with a flavour of hawthorn blossom which lasts well. It needs to be kept to enable it to develop further. (1983)
➤ Pierre Coursodon, Place du Marché, Mauves, 07300 Tournon-sur-Rhône; tel. 75 08 29 27 ⟁ By appt.

PIERRE COURSODON★

■		7 ha	30000	4 D ◖◗ ⌁

61 63 *67* 70 *78* 79 80 ★⑧ **82** 83

A dull red colour with tinges of brown and nose which releases aromas of cherry, ripe pear, slightly underripe blackcurrant, leather and truffle. The taste is initially a little bitter, but is followed by a very good finish with strong tannin. To be drunk now. (1982)
➤ Pierre Coursodon, Place du Marché, Mauves, 07300 Tournon-sur-Rhône; tel. 75 08 29 27 ⟁ By appt.

PAUL ETIENNE ET FILS★

■			40000	4 ◖◗ ⌁

★⑥ 71 **78** **81**

Very characteristic of its appellation; should be drunk without delay if it is to be enjoyed at its peak. (1981)
➤ Paul Etienne et Fils, 07130 St-Péray; tel. 75 40 30 18 ⟁ No visitors.

EMILE FLORENTIN
Clos de l'Arbalestrier★★

□		1 ha	3500	4 D ◖◗ ⌁

79 80 81 82 ⑧ **83**

Bright gold colour, attractively crisp, despite an early mellowness. A smoky, vanilla flavour accompanies the floral and fruity bouquet, which make this wine a suitable accompaniment to shellfish. (1982) ✔ St-Joseph 'Clos de l'Arbalestrier' Rouge.
➤ Emile Florentin, Clos de l'Arbalestrier, Mauves, 07300 Tournon-sur-Rhône; tel. 75 08 12 11 ⟁ By appt.

EMILE FLORENTIN
Clos de l'Arbalestrier

■		3.5 ha	12000	4 D ◖◗ ⌁

64 66 67 69 76 77 78 79 80 ★**81** 83 ⑧

Light red with tinges of brown, this wine has a typical bouquet. Tannic, vigorous and generous, with a dry finish. To be drunk now. (1982) ✔ St-Joseph Blanc.
➤ Emile Florentin Clos de l'Arbalestrier, Mauves, 07300 Tournon-sur-Rhône; tel. 75 08 12 11 ⟁ By appt.

PIERRE GONON

■		2 ha	9500	4 D ◼ ⌁

76 78 79 ⑧ **82** 83 **83**

The nose has surprisingly little character. The touch of lactic acid on the palate is also surprising . . . could this be due to a slight accident during the vinification process? (1982) ✔ St-Joseph Blanc.
➤ Pierre Gonon, Rue des Launays, Mauves, 07300 Tournon-sur-Rhône; tel. 75 08 07 95 ⟁ By appt.

BERNARD GRIPA★★

■		3 ha	15000	4 D ◖◗ ⌁

76 **78** 81 ⑧ **82** 83 **83**

The Syrah here displays flavours characteristic of blackcurrant, with a touch of liquorice. A very good, powerful wine that requires four to five years' ageing and should be well aired before drinking. (1982) ✔ St-Joseph Blanc, St-Péray Blanc.
➤ Bernard Gripa, Mauves, 07300 Tournon-sur-Rhône; tel. 75 08 14 96 ⟁ By appt Mon.–Sat. Closed end Aug.

JEAN-LOUIS GRIPPAT★★★

□		1 ha	3500	4 D ◼ ◖◗ ⌁

74 75 76 **78** 79 ★**82** **82**

A very delicate wine with floral aromas of hawthorn and acacia, with a touch of lemon peel. Elegant and well balanced, a good example of this appellation that may be left to age. (1982)
➤ Jean-Louis Grippat, La Sauva, 07300 Tournon-sur-Rhône; tel. 75 08 15 51 ⟁ By appt. Closed Sun.

JEAN-LOUIS GRIPPAT★★★

■		2 ha	12000	4 D ◼ ◖◗ ⌁

64 72 73 **78** 81 ★⑧ **82** 83

A richly aromatic wine in which blackcurrant, strawberry and violet are dominant. The flavours hold well on the palate with a pleasing finish. It is ready to drink, but it would do no harm to keep it for two to three years. (1982) ✔ Hermitage Blanc and Rouge, St-Joseph Blanc.
➤ Jean-Louis Grippat, La Sauva, 07300 Tournon-sur-Rhône; tel. 75 08 15 51 ⟁ By appt. Closed Sun.

DOMAINE GUILLERMAIN

■		3 ha	10000	3 D ◖◗ ⌁

81 82 83 84

Very deep purple with woody aromas over a background of cocoa. This wine is very well-constructed but still hard; so should be kept before drinking. (1983)

⚫ Pierre Guillermain, La Tuillière, Lemps, 07610 Vion; tel. 75 08 11 50 ⟁ By appt.

PAUL JABOULET AINE
Le Grand Pompée★★

■	38 ha	150 000	4 D ▮ ⦿ ↓

70 71 73 76 ★⑦⑧ ★79 ★80 ★82 83

Attractive ruby colour, and a lovely, intensely fruity, young Syrah nose. Full and meaty in the mouth, remarkably robust but also well rounded. Fruity enough to drink now, but will certainly improve over the next few years. (1983)
⚫ SA Paul Jaboulet Ainé, RN 7, BP 46, La Roche-de-Glun, 26600 Tain-l'Hermitage; tel. 75 84 68 93 ⟁ No visitors.

UPVF DE TAIN-L'HERMITAGE★

■	35 ha	114 000	3 D ⦿ ↓

78 79 ⑧⓪ ★82 82 83

A rather aggressive tannin which is very typical of the Syrah, but should soften within a few months. (1982) ✓ Hermitage Rouge, Crozes-Hermitage Blanc, St-Joseph Blanc, St-Péray Méthode Champenoise.
⚫ UPVF de Tain-l'Hermitage, 22 Route de Larnage, BP 3, 26600 Tain-l'Hermitage; tel. 75 08 20 87 ⟁ By appt Mon.–Sat. Closed public holidays.

St-Péray
Situated opposite Valence, the vineyard of St-Péray is overlooked by the ruins of the Château de Crussols. It covers 35 hectares and produces 2000 hectolitres of wine. A somewhat cooler micro climate and richer soils combine to produce dry, acidic wines with a low alcohol content that are made into one of the best Méthode Champenoise sparkling wines in France. Much more of the St-Péray AOC Mousseux is produced than the AOC still wine.

DARONA PERE ET FILS *Les Faures*

○	8 ha	45 000	3 ⦿ ↓

Honest, fresh, dry, fruity and aromatic, with a slight sparkle which makes it an ideal accompaniment for desserts. ✓ St-Péray Tranquilla Rouge.
⚫ MM. Darona Père et Fils, Route de Toulaud, 07130 St-Péray; tel. 75 40 34 11 ⟁ By appt.

DARONA PERE ET FILS★

▢	8 ha	50 000	3 D ▮ ↓

This very likeable sweet still wine evokes the lovely smell of a cellar full or ripe apples. Just one good reason why the St-Peray vineyard, under serious threat from urbanization, ought to be declared a protected zone! (1982)
⚫ MM. Darona Père et Fils, Route de Toulaud, 07130 St-Péray; tel. 75 40 34 01 ⟁ By appt.

DARONA PERE ET FILS *Les Faures*★

▢	8 ha	50 000	3 D ▮ ↓

An attractive clear yellow colour, with tinges of green, this dry, vigorous wine has a flowery bouquet and needs to be given a chance to breathe a little before serving. Ready for drinking now. (1982) ✓ St-Péray Méthode Champenoise.
⚫ MM. Darona Père et Fils, Route de Toulaud, 07130 St-Péray; tel. 75 40 34 11 ⟁ By appt.

PAUL ETIENNE PERE ET FILS★★

▢		5000	4 ⦿ ↓

Shows well-defined and slightly acidic qualities typical of its appellation. Very fresh and pleasant to drink. (1980)
⚫ Paul Etienne et Fils, 07130 St-Péray; tel. 75 40 30 18 ⟁ No visitors.

Châteauneuf-du-Pape
In 1931 this appellation area became the first Côtes du Rhône to define its conditions of production. As well as covering practically the whole of the commune which bears its name, it also extends into parts of several neighbouring communes where the soil type is the same: Orange, Courthezon, Bedarrides and Sorgues. This vineyard area of 3050 hectares lies on the west bank of the Rhône about 15 km north of Avignon. The landscape is distinctive; vast terraces of varying height covered with a mixture of red clay and pebbles. Many different grape varieties are planted, predominantly Syrah, Mourvèdre, Muscadin and Cinsault.

Châteauneuf-du-Pape wines always have a deep colour. The age at which they should be drunk varies according to the vintage, but they always need at least some bottle age. Well-rounded, full-bodied and robust, these wines have a powerful and complex bouquet and go well with red meats, game and strong cheeses. White wines are also produced, but only in small quantities. Nevertheless, they conceal considerable strength behind their flavour and aromas. Total production is in the region of 104 000 hectolitres.

THOMAS BASSOT★★

■		1500	4 D ⦿

★83

Beautiful dark-red colour for this generous and full-bodied wine. Powerful and heady bouquet typical of its appellation. (1983)
⚫ Thomas Bassot, 5 Quai Dumorey, 21700 Nuits-St-Georges; tel. 80 62 31 05 ⟁ By appt.

CHATEAU DE BEAUCASTEL★★★

■ 70ha 228000 **4** **D** ❶ ⚭

★⑧⓪ ⑧⓪ **81** ⑧① **82** **82**

The Perrin family, have perfected a technique which avoids the need for sulphur dioxide, used in conventional vinfication. Their 1980, a very intense red wine, with purplish-blue tinges, is redolent of both game and plants. With a long finish; generous, elegant as well as powerful, it is a remarkable wine which will keep its great qualities for many years to come. ✔ Côtes du Rhône Cru de Coudelet Rouge. (1980)
❧ Ste Ferm. des Vignobles Perrin, Ch. de Beaucastel, 84350 Courthezon; tel. 90 70 70 60 ☎ By appt. Closed weekends.

MAURICE BOIRON
Bosquet des Papes★

■ 22ha 22500 **4** **D** ▮ ❶ ⚭

79 ★⑧① **81** **82** **83** **83**

With a slight touch of tile pink in its red colour, it has a strong scent of faintly burnt cooked fruit. Strong evidence of tannin, contributing unquestionably to its ruggedness. A classic wine, already fully matured and ripe for immediate drinking. (1982)
❧ Maurice Boiron, Route d'Orange, 84230 Châteauneuf-du-Pape; tel. 90 83 72 33 ☎ By appt. Closed during harvest.

MAURICE BOIRON
Bosquet-des-Papes★

☐ 22ha 39600 **4** **D** ▮ ❶ ⚭

61 67 69 70 ★79 ★81 82 ★⑧③ **83**

A wine that gives the impression of having been well vinified and well stored. With its gleaming light yellow colour and its bouquet (slightly on the weak side) of flowers, with a touch of rum, it is a very honest wine – smooth and vigorous to the taste. (1983)
❧ Maurice Boiron, Route d'Orange, 84230 Châteauneuf-du-Pape; tel. 90 83 72 33 ☎ By appt. Closed during harvest.

JEAN PIERRE BROTTE★★

■ **5** **D** ▮ ⚭

⑦⑧ **78** 79 81 82 83

Another lovely Châteauneuf from one of the best vintages on record. Its dominant scents are of pepper and leather, with touches of liquorice and truffle. Generous and very powerful, it is remarkable in every way. There is a museum of wine grower's tools, with nearly five hundred exhibits, on the property. (1978) ✔ All Rhône valley wines.
❧ Ets Brotte Jean-Pierre, 84230 Châteauneuf-du-

Pape; tel. 90 83 70 07 ☎ Daily 8.00–12.00/14.00– 18.00.

DOMAINE DU PERE CABOCHE★

☐ 5ha 14400 **4** **D** ▮ ⚭

79 **83** ⑧④

This estate derives its name from the marriage in 1777 between the then proprietor's daughter, Elizabeth Chambellan, and a blacksmith, Jean-Louis Boisson: 'caboche' is the Provencal word for a horseshoe nail. The couple's descendants produce a white Châteauneuf with a shining colour and a bouquet in which a scent of flowers is topped off by a touch of honey. An elegant wine, to be drunk young. (1983) ✔ Châteauneuf-du-Pape rouge, Côtes du Rhône Rouge, Vin du Pays de Vaucluse Rouge.
❧ Jean-Pierre Boisson, Dom. du Père Caboche, 84230 Châteauneuf-du-Pape; tel. 90 83 71 44 ☎ By appt.

DOMAINE DU PERE CABOCHE★★

■ 30ha 110000 **4** **D** ❶ ⚭

78 81 **82** 83 ⑧④

A deep red wine, with distinctive aromas of small red fruit and a touch of spices. Good balance; can be drunk immediately. (1982)
❧ Jean-Pierre Boisson, Dom. du Père Caboche, 84230 Châteauneuf-du-Pape; tel. 90 83 71 44 ☎ By appt.

DOMAINE DE CABRIERES LES SILEX★★★

■ 56ha 170000 **4** **D** ❶ ⚭

61 67 73 ★⑦⑦ **77** ★80 **80** 81 **81** **82** 83

The soil here is covered by a layer of flint pebbles that prevent precious moisture from evaporating and also store up the heat of the sun by day, reflecting it back on the vines at night. An excellent terrain, producing superb wines. The 1981 has a delicate but powerful bouquet, evocative of aniseed, thyme and plants over a veritable explosion of spices. An exceptional wine, with a magnificent balance, which should retain its qualities at their best for several years yet. (1982)
✔ Côtes de Rhône Rouge.
❧ Louis Arnaud et Fils, 84230 Châteauneuf-du-Pape; tel. 90 83 73 58 ☎ By appt.

DOMAINE CHANTE-CIGALE★★

■ 40ha 140000 **D** ❶ ⚭

78 ★⑦⑨ 80 ★81 ★82 83

A nice, dark, red wine with a nose reminiscent of the smell of leather, supple palate. Ready for drinking. (1982) ✔ Côtes du Rhône.

587

•┐ *MM.* Sabon-Favier, Dom. Chante-Cigale, 84230 Châteauneuf-du-Pape; tel. 90 83 70 57 ϒ Mon.–Sat. 8.00–12.00/14.00–18.00.

DOMAINE CHANTE PERDRIX★★

■ 18 ha 44 000 [4] [D] ▮ ↓

★⑲ ★80 [8C] ★81 82

Elegant colour and a rich nose that is already developing aromas of ageing. Generous on the palate, where truffles and musk combine along with the solidity of a good tannin. All the hallmarks of an excellent Châteauneuf, just as it should be. (1982)
•┐ GAEC Nicolas Fréres, 84230 Châteauneuf-du-Pape; tel. 90 83 71 86 ϒ Daily 8.00–12.00/14.00–18.00.

DIFFONTY ET FILS
Cuvée du Vatican★★★

■ 17 ha 60 000 [4] [D] ▮ ⑾ ↓

79 80 ⑧ [81] 82 [82]

This vineyard has several tenants and its grapes are harvested from strips of land facing in different directions. They combine to produce a wine with a very complex bouquet of flowers and fruit, rich and of great finesse. Warm, generous, elegant and supple, the 1982 is a wine that may be kept. (1982) ✔ Vin de Pays Blanc, Vin de Pays Rouge.
•┐ Félicien Diffonty et Fils, 84230 Châteauneuf-du-Pape; tel. 90 83 70 51 ϒ By appt.

CHATEAU DE LA FONT DU LOUP★

■ 15 ha 50 000 [4] [D] ▮ ⑾ ↓

⑲ 80 81 82 [82] 83

This 1979 is still marked by a very aggressive tannin, though it is partially masked by the wine's velvety feel and the dominant ripe blackcurrant of its bouquet. (The 1980, in contrast, tends much more towards a 'gamey' nose and the tannin is less obvious.) (1979) ✔ Châteauneuf-du-Pape.
•┐ Charles Mélia, 84350 Courthezon; tel. 90 33 06 34 ϒ Closed Feb.

CHATEAU FORTIA★★★

■ 27 ha 84 000 [4] [D] ⑾ ↓

61 64 67 77 ★⑦⑧ [78] 80 81

A beautiful deep red colour and a bouquet of red fruit and game that is just right for a well matured wine but only just beginning to open out. Full bodied and vigorous, it is a wine that may be recommended to people looking for well made wines that are sure to age well. (1978)
•┐ SARL Ch. Fortia, 84230 Châteauneuf-du-Pape; tel. 90 83 70 06 ϒ Daily 9.00–11.00/14.00–17.00.

CHATEAU FORTIA★★

□ 2.50 ha 10 800 [4] [D] ▮ ↓

83 [83] 84

A golden yellow-white wine, with its very delicate flowery bouquet, topped off by slight touches of apricot and lemon. Extremely well balanced, elegant and fresh, it is ready for drinking now. (1983) ✔ Châteauneuf-du-Pape.
•┐ SARL Ch. Fortia, 84230 Châteauneuf-du-Pape; tel. 90 83 70 06 ϒ Daily 9.30–11.30/14.00–17.30.

DOMAINE LOU FREJAU★

■ 3 ha 12 000 [4] [D] ▮ ↓

The first wine to be made by this young new wine grower. Appropriately, it stands out for its 'youthful' bouquet, characterized by red fruit and spices. A pleasing wine that should be kept for three or four years. (1983) ✔ Côtes du Rhône Rouge.
•┐ Serge Chastan, Chemin de la Gironde, 84100 Orange; tel. 90 39 01 07 ϒ Daily 10.00–19.00.

CHATEAU DE LA GARDINE★★★

■ 54 ha 216 000 [5] [D] ⑾ ↓

78 79 ⑧ [80] 81 82 83

Nobody knows the origin of the name of this château, high on its pebble-strewn plateau, but it is suspected that there might once have been a guardpost on the site, overlooking the valley. The present-day owner, current president of the Cuvée des Hospices de Châteauneuf-du-Pape, the local wine order, recommends this distinctive, harmonious 1980, with its bouquet of blackcurrant and spices and very long finish. A wine to keep. (1980) ✔ La Cuvée des Générations Gaston-Philippe.
•┐ Gaston Brunel, Ch. de la Gardine, 84230 Châteauneuf-du-Pape; tel. 90 83 73 20 ϒ By appt. Closed for New Year.

PIERRE JACUMIN
Cuvée de Boisdauphin★★

■ 11 ha 33 000 [4] [D] ⑾ ↓

78 79 80 81 [82] 83

The nose reveals an aroma of undergrowth that develops quickly and offers smells of spice (cinammon, vanilla) and leather. The palate confirms the good balance of a persistent bouquet. Will keep all of its qualities for some years yet. (1980)
•┐ Pierre Jacumin, 84230 Châteauneuf-du Pape; tel. 90 83 73 71 ϒ By appt. Closed Aug.

DOMAINE LE LA JANASSE★★

■ 8 ha 30 000 [4] [D] ▮ ⑾ ↓

⑦⑧ 81 [81] ★82

A well developed bouquet redolent of spices: origano and vanilla, with a touch of woodland. Very deep red in colour, generous and powerful, it is a fine example of wines of this appellation. Ready for drinking. (1982) ✔ Côtes du Rhône Rouge, Côtes du Rhône Blanc, Châteauneuf-du-Pape Blanc.
•┐ Aimé Sabon, Dom. de la Janesse, 84350 Courthezon; tel. 90 70 86 29 ϒ Mon.–Sat. 8.00–12.00/14.00–20.00.

DOMAINE MATHIEU★★

■ 12 ha 42 000 [4] [D] ⑾

80 ★⑧ ★82 ★83

Deep red wine with very deep, vegetal nose. Good alcohol structure on the palate with aromas of red fruit and pepper. A round wine with good tannins. (1981)
•┐ Charles Mathieu, Route de Courthézon 84230 Châteauneuf-du-Pape; tel. 90 83 72 09 ϒ By appt. Closed 17–21 Jun. and 30 Nov.–5 Dec.

DOMAINE DE MONTPERTUIS★★

□   3 ha   4000   4 D 🍶 💧

80 81 82 ★⑧③ 8̲3̲ 84

A typical southern white, with clear yellow colour and apple-like bouquet, proclaiming a rapid development. Very pleasing on the palate. Good balance between body and mellowness and pleasant acidity. To be drunk without delay. (1983) ✔ Châteauneuf-du-Pape Rouge, Côte du Rhône Rouge.
🍷 Paul Jeune, 7 Av. St Joseph, Châteauneuf-du-Pape; tel. 90 83 73 87 ⵏ By appt.

DOMAINE DE MONTPERTUIS★★

■   23 ha   63 000   4 D 💧 💧

78 80 8̲0̲ 81 82 8̲2̲

The fine, honest red colour, the first-class vigour and the still slightly under-developed nose have led this wine to be selected – with great success – for receptions at the Hôtel Matignon (the French prime minister's official residence), the Elysée (the presidential palace) and several ministries . . . Fine balance and an aroma of cooked vanilla-flavoured fruit. (1981) ✔ Côtes du Rhône Rouge, Vin de Pays de Vaucluse, Châteauneuf-du-Pape Blanc.
🍷 Paul Jeune, 7 av. St-Joseph, 84230 Châteauneuf-du-Pape; tel. 90 83 73 87 ⵏ By appt.

DOMAINE DU MONT-REDON★

□   95 ha   54 000   4 D 🍶 💧

This vineyard is able to trace its owners back over more than six centuries, among them the provençal poet Anselme Mathieu. This is a much beflowered, remarkably elegant white wine. (1983) ✔ Châteauneuf-du-Pape Rouge, Côtes du Rhône Rouge.
🍷 SCEA du Dom. de Mont-Redon, 84230 Châteauneuf-du-Pape; tel. 90 83 72 75 ⵏ By appt
🍷 MM. Abeille et Fabre.

DOMAINE DE MONT-REDON★

■   95 ha   380 000   4 D 💧 💧

★80 8̲0̲ 8̲1̲ 82 8̲2̲ 83 8̲3̲

This estate belonged to the provençal poet Anselme Mathieu. It is one of the best spots for Châteauneuf, renowned for the consistent quality of its wines. The 1981 is characterized by a bouquet in which you can discern woodland plants, blackcurrant and raspberry. Although a little light-bodied, it is harmonious and elegant. Ready for drinking now, but could still be kept another three or four years. (1981) ✔ Côtes du Rhône.
🍷 SCEA du Dom. de Mont-Redon, 84230 Châteauneuf-du-Pape; tel. 90 83 72 75 ⵏ By appt
🍷 MM. Abeille et Fabre.

NICOLAS *Chateau des Fines Roches*★★

■   🍶 💧

A full, deep, generously fruity wine. Extremely supple, so recommended to accompany rich food. (1983)
🍷 Ets Nicolas, 2 Rue de Valmy, 94220 Charenton; tel. 01 37 59 200 ⵏ No visitors.

DOMAINE PALESTOR LA FAGOTIERE★★

■   20 ha   66 000   4 D 🍶 💧 💧

⑦⑧ 7̲8̲ ★79 ★81

This 1978 (an excellent year) has a shining purple colour and bouquet of red fruit and woodland plants. Well-made, powerful, strong in alcohol, it would be a pity not to drink it straight away. (1978) ✔ Côtes du Rhône Rouge.
🍷 André Chastan-Pierry, Dom. Palestor la Fagotière, 84100 Orange; tel. 90 34 51 81 ⵏ Mon.–Sat. 8.00–12.00/14.00–18.00. Closed Sun. and public holidays.

DOMAINE DE PALESTOR★★

■   4 ha   15 000   4 D 💧 💧

⑦⑧ 7̲8̲ 7̲9̲ 8̲0̲ 81 82

A long maturation in cask has resulted in a fine plant-like bouquet, with a touch of spices. Rich and fleshy, this well-balanced wine will need several more years to reach its peak. Well worth buying to lay down. (1979) ✔ Côtes du Rhône Rouge.
🍷 André Chastan, Dom. Palestor le Grès, 84100 Orange; tel. 90 34 50 96 ⵏ Daily 10.00–19.00.

DOMAINE DU CLOS DES PAPES★★

□   3 ha   12 000   4 D 💧 💧

★78 ★79 ★80 ★81 ★8̲3̲ ⑧④

A gleaming light yellow wine dedicated to those 14th-century Popes who did so much for the vine in this part of the world. It has a bouquet of flowers – a bit faint, but clearly in evidence – and a very good balance. A typical white Châteauneuf-du-Pape, which should reach its peak this year. ✔ Châteauneuf-du-Pape Rouge.
🍷 Paul Avril, 84230 Châteauneuf-du-Pape; tel. 90 83 70 13 ⵏ By appt.

DOMAINE DU CLOS DES PAPES★★★

■   30 ha   114 000   4 D 🍶 💧

78 ★⑧① 8̲1̲ 82 83

A magnificent wine to keep. It has just reached the turning point where the attractive aromas of its youth are beginning to give way to the more sophisticated perfumes of a fine maturity. Its power in no way detracts from its remarkable elegance. (1981)
🍷 Paul Avril, 84230 Châteauneuf-du-Pape; tel. 90 83 70 13 ⵏ By appt.

DOMAINE DE LA PINEDE★★

■   10ha   36000   4 D 🍷 ⊕ 🍴
★82 ★83 ★84

Green oaks as well as century-old pine trees shade the vineyard on which this bright red wine is produced. The nose evokes kitchens of times gone by, where mulberry jam simmered beneath a shelf of spices. A full-bodied wine, powerful and well balanced. (1981) ✔ Côtes du Rhône Rouge.
⬥ Georges-Pierre Coulon, 84230 Châteauneuf-du-Pape; tel. 90 83 71 50 ⏳ By appt.

DOMAINE DES RELAGNES★

■   14ha   42000   4 D 🍷 ⊕ 🍴
81 ★82 ★⑧②

The aromas evoke red fruit and spices. A quality wine with a clear cherry-red colour and a full, round, long palate with good balance. (1983)
⬥ Henri Boiron, Route des Bédarrides, 84230 Châteauneuf-du-Pape; tel. 90 83 73 37 ⏳ By appt.

DOMAINE DE LA ROQUETTE★★★

■   30ha   114000   4 D 🍷 ⊕ 🍴
77 80 ⑧⓪ 81 ★82 ★83

The fine, strong red colour proclaims all the power that one expects from a Châteauneuf. Complex bouquet, predominantly of plants but with a trace of musk and even a hint of wood-smoke – goes extremely well with rich game dishes. The good level of tannin provides the foundation for a superb balance. (1981)
⬥ René Laugier, Dom. de la Roquette, 84230 Châteauneuf-du-Pape; tel. 90 83 71 25 ⏳ Daily 7.30–12.00/13.30–18.00.

DOMAINE TRINTIGNANT
La Réviscoulado★★★

■   25ha   125000   4 D 🍷 ⊕ 🍴
80 ⑧⓪ 81 ⑧① 82 ⑧② ⑧③

Those with the patience to keep this already very good wine in cellar will be well rewarded, because it should develop into a really marvellous wine. Scents of thyme, resin and spices, well rounded and with good length, the wine success-fully unites tannin with smoothness and richness in a most harmonious balance. (1983) ✔ Côtes du Rhône Rouge, Côtes du Rhône Blanc.
⬥ Jean Trintignant, 84230 Châteauneuf-du-Pape; tel. 90 83 73 23 ⏳ By appt.

CHATEAU DE VAUDIEU★

■   70ha   270000   4 D ⊕ 🍴
74 **78** 79 80 ★⑧① ⑧① ★82

A Florentine nobleman built this castle in the 'Valley of God' from which the estate takes its name. The wine is vinified at low temperature and has great elegance, with a bouquet of spices and truffles. Although a little lacking in body and power at preent, it could still improve with age. (1981)
⬥ SCA du Ch. de Vaudieu, Gigondas, 84190 Beaumes-de-Venise; tel. 90 65 86 09 ⏳ By appt.

DOMAINE DE LA VIEILLE-JULIENNE★★

■   7ha   25000   4 🍷 ⊕ 🍴
76 77 ⑦⑧ 79 80 81 **82 83**

Attractive, dark-red colour. Distinctly woody aroma strongly reminiscent of spices and toast. Structure characteristic of a traditional Châteauneuf-du-Pape: rich in alcohol, and with a strong, tannic body. (1982) ✔ Côtes du Rhône Rouge et Blanc.
⬥ *MM*. Arnaud-Daumen, Dom. de la Vielle-Julienne, Le Grès, 84100 Orange; tel. 90 34 20 10 ⏳ By appt.

CHARLES VIENOT★★

■   2000   4 D ⊕
★83

Bright red, with a fresh nose not yet matured. Noticeable for its youth and slightly acidic qua-lity. Keep to mature. (1983)
⬥ Ets Charles Vienot, 5 Quai Dumorey, 21700 Nuits-St-Georges; tel. 80 62 31 05 ⏳ By appt.

Coteaux du Tricastin

This appellation covers 2000 hectares on the west bank of the Rhône. It stretches from Beaume-de-Transit in the south, through St-Paul-les-Trois-Châteaux, to Granges-Gontardes in the north. The soils, made up of very old alluvium, are extremely stony, and the sandy hillsides (here at the limits of the Mediterranean climate) pro-duce some elegant, delicate but lively red wines as well as a few rosés. Total production is about 100 000 hecto-litres.

DOMAINE DU BOIS NOIR★

■   2.5ha   12000   2 D 🍷 🍴

The bouquet – evocative of soft red fruit, above all redcurrant – is still fairly restrained, but has great finesse. It is still a very young wine but has a good balance, though a trifle lacking in acidity. (1984) ✔ Côtes du Rhône Rouge, Côtes du Rhône Rosé, Coteaux du Tricastin Rouge, Coteaux du Tricastin Rosé.
⬥ Jean-Pierre Esteve, Dom. du Bois Noir, 26130 La Baume-de-Transit; tel. 75 98 11 02 ⏳ By appt.

DOMAINE DU BOIS NOIR★

☑   10ha   12000   ② Ⓓ ▮ ⌄

83 84 84

The fine, delicate pink colour is enticing. An immediate smell of fruit drops, but the bouquet is spoilt by the vegetal aroma that follows it. A pretty vigorous and very pleasing wine to taste. (1984)
➻ Jean-Pierre Esteve, Dom. du Bois Noir, 26130 La Baume-de-Transit; tel. 75 98 11 02 ⵊ By appt.

DOMAINE BOUR *Cuvée Spéciale*★

▮   65ha   3000   ③ Ⓓ ▮ ⌄

74 78 81 83

Beautiful purplish-red colour. Nose evoking red fruit and spices (peppers). Pleasant tannins give it good structure and balance. (1980)
➻ O. et H. Bour, Dom. de Grangeneuve, Roussas, 26230 Grignan; tel. 75 98 51 80 ⵊ By appt.

DOMAINE BOUR *Cépage Syrah*★

▮   30ha   140000   ③ Ⓓ ▮ ⌄

74 78 81 83

Dark-red wine with ageing aromas and nose of violets and red fruit. Drink with red meats. (1980)
➻ O. et H. Bour, Dom. de Grangeneuve, Roussas, 26230 Grignan; tel. 75 98 51 80 ⵊ By appt.

CELLIER DE L'ENCLAVE DES PAPES★

▮   200ha 1000000   ② Ⓓ ▮ ⌄

⑧③ 83 84 84

A light wine, with a pleasant, bright red colour and bouquet with overtones of spicy plants. To be drunk young. (1983)
➻ Cellier de l'Enclave des Papes, 11 Av du Général de Gaulle, 84600 Valréas; tel. 90 30 91 42 ⵊ Daily.

CHATEAU DES ESTUBIERS★★

☑   19ha   100000   ② Ⓓ ▮ ⌄

82 83

Lively colour tending towards cherry. Fine nose with pleasant mixture of smell red fruits. Long on the palate for a rosé. Drink without delay. (1982)
➻ H. Roth et L. Morel, Les Estubiers, Les Granges-Gontardes, 26290 Donzère; tel. 75 98 53 86 ⵊ By appt.

CHATEAU DES ESTUBIERS★★

▮   73ha   430000   ② Ⓓ ▮ ⌄

80 ⑧① ★ 82 83

Crimson red with a hint of chestnut. Full and pleasant; aromas of ageing fruit. Drink now. (1981)
➻ H. Roth et L. Morel, Les Estuviers, Les Granges-Gontardes, 26290 Donzière; tel. 75 98 53 86 ⵊ By appt.

DOMAINE DE GRANGENEUVE★★

☑   8ha   36000   ② Ⓓ ▮ ⌄

81 ★ 82 ★ 83

Very beautiful colour – tender but bright pink – and delicate, flowery nose. On the palate it has great character. Very nice bottle, whose price reflects the quality. (1983)

➻ O. et H. Bour, Dom. de Grangeneuve, Roussas, 26230 Grignan; tel. 75 98 51 80 ⵊ By appt.

DOMAINE DE GRANGENEUVE★★

▮   65ha   130000   ② Ⓓ ▮ ⌄

74 78 81 ⑧③

Mingles aromas of ripe fruit and leather beneath its carmine colour. Good balance. Ready to drink. (1983)
➻ O. et H. Bour, Dom. de Grangeneuve, Roussas, 26230 Grignan; tel. 75 98 51 80 ⵊ By appt.

COOPERATIVE SAINT-PANTALEON- LES-VIGNES★★

▮   39ha   250000   ② Ⓓ ▮ ⑪ ⌄

70 78 79 ★ 81 82 ★83

With its very bright cherry-red colour and a delicate, pleasing bouquet redolent of woodland plants, this is a well balanced, harmonious wine, rich and supple. Ready for immediate drinking. (1983) ✔ Côtes du Rhône-Villages St-Pantaléon Rouge, Côtes du Rhône Rouge.
➻ Coop. St-Pantaléon-les-Vignes, Route de Nyons, 26770 St-Pantaléon-les-Vignes; tel. 75 26 26 43 ⵊ By appt.

DOMAINE DU SERRE ROUGE★

☐   2ha   12000   ② Ⓓ ▮ ⌄

80 ⑧② 82 83 84

The wines of Tricastin, once included with those of the Côtes du Rhône, have regained their own identity. This wine has a distinctive bouquet of great finesse. A little lacking in smoothness and power, but a most pleasing wine overall, ready for immediate drinking. (1983)
➻ Jean Brachet et Fils, Dom. du Serre Rouge, 26230 Valaurie; tel. 75 98 50 11 ⵊ By appt.

DOMAINE DU SERRE ROUGE★

▮   21ha   13000   ② Ⓓ ▮ ⌄

80 ⑧② 82 83 84

This is a young vineyard, entirely replanted in 1975 with grape varieties better suited to the soil (mainly Syrah and Grenache). That is all it took to produce an elegant light red wine from this historic terrain – an area praised in the letters of the Marquise de Sévigné. The wine is not quite as full as it might be, but this does not obtrude. (1983) ✔ Coteaux du Tricastin Blanc, Coteaux du Tricastin Rosé.
➻ Jean Brachet et Fils, Dom. du Serre Rouge, 26230 Valaurie; tel. 75 98 50 11 ⵊ By appt.

LA SUZIENNE★★

▮   999ha 40000   ② Ⓓ ▮ ⌄

82 83 ⑧④ 84

Cherry-red colour with purplish tinges. Aromas of banana and fruit drops make for a very youthful-seeming nose. This good, very fruity Tricastin has character on the palate and should be drunk young. (1984)
➻ Cave Coop. la Suzienne, 26130 Suze-la-Rousse; tel. 75 04 80 04 ⵊ By appt. Closed 1 Jan. and 1 May.

DOMAINE DU VIEUX MICOCOULIER★★

■ 124ha 480000 ② D ■ ↓
⑦⑨ 82 ★83 ⑧⑧ 84

A very fine red wine produced from a very stony site. Characterized by its bouquet of leather, truffles and spices, it is a powerful, generous and well balanced wine, which only just falls short of being really outstanding. All that is missing, perhaps, is a touch more finesse. (1983)
➴ SCGEA les Granges-Gontardes, Cave Vergobbi, 26290 Les Granges-Gontardes; tel. 75 04 02 72 ⅄ By appt.

Côtes du Ventoux

At the base of the limestone Ventoux massif lies the 'Giant of Vaucluse' (1909m). On these soils of tertiary sediment grow 6400 hectares of vines, stretching from Vaison-la-Romaine in the north to Apt in the south.

The AOC area produces mainly red and rosé wines, and the climate, cooler than in the Côtes du Rhône, means that the grapes ripen later. The reds are lower in alcohol but are fresh and elegant when young, and fuller-bodied if produced in the westernmost communes of Caromb, Bédoin and Mormoiron. The very pleasant rosés are best drunk young. Total annual production can reach 240000 hectolitres.

LES VINS DE SYLLA★

■ 1500000 ② D ■ ⑪ ↓
⑦⑧ 79 80 ⑧②

This Cave gets its name from a Roman general who waged fierce battles in this region. It produces very attractive wines – well made and with a long finish. (1982) ✔ Côtes du Lubéron Rouge, Blanc and Rosé. Côtes du Venteoux Blanc.
➴ Cave les Vins de Sylla, 84400 Apt; tel. 90 74 05 39 ⅄ By appt.

Gigondas

At the foot of the spectacular Dentelles de Montmirail, the Gigondas vineyards extend over a series of rolling hills. Gigondas itself has a very long wine-making tradition, although the main expansion (the Colombier and Bosquets areas) did not take place until the nineteenth century under the auspices of Eugène Raspail. The Gigondas area received AOC status in 1971. Today, it covers 1080 hectares and produces 35000 hectolitres per year. Soil and climate combine to produce powerful, robust and well-balanced reds that are very high in alcohol yet subtly aromatic, combin-

ing scents of liquorice, spices, plums and peaches. A good accompaniment to game, they develop slowly and can be kept for many years. Finally, Gigondas also produces a few powerful and heady rosé wines.

PERE ANSELME★★

■ 60000 ④ D ■ ↓
80 81 82 83 ⑧⑧

Purple red, with browny glints, this wine has an already well developed bouquet of cooked fruit and spices (particularly green pepper). Well made. To be drunk now. (1982) ✔ Hermitage, Côte Rôtie, Cornas, Crozes Hermitage.
➴ Père Anselme, 84230 Chateauneuf-du-Pape; tel. 90 83 70 07 ⅄ By appt.

LA BASTIDE SAINT-VINCENT★★

■ 7ha 6000 ③ D ■ ↓
★⑦⑧ ★79 80 81 ★83

An attractive-looking wine, red with purplish-blue glints; a bouquet based on spices and red fruit, with touches of vanilla and cocoa butter. The taste achieves a happy compromise between the level of acidity and tannins, making this a balanced and elegant wine. One to be kept. (1983)
➴ Guy Daniel, la Bastide St-Vincent, 84150 Violes; tel. 90 70 94 13 ⅄ Daily 9.00–12.00/ 14.00–18.00.

DOMAINE DU CAYRON★★

■ 13ha 21000 ③ D ⑪ ↓
77 78 79 80 ★⑧① ⑧① 82

A lively but deep red in colour, this wine has all the characteristics afforded by a classic vinification culminating in a long maturation in cask. Powerful, generous and well-balanced, though not particularly elegant, it has a bouquet of spices and woodland plants, against a background of cold coffee. A wine to be kept. Will go well with game. (1981)
➴ Georges Faraud, Dom. du Cayron, Gigondas, 84190 Beaumes-de-Venise; tel. 90 65 86 71 ⅄ By appt.

DOMAINE DU CLOS DES CAZEAUX
Cuvée de la Tour Sarrazine★★★

■ 12ha 54000 ④ D ■ ↓
76 78 79 ★⑧① ⑧① 82

Harmony, elegance, power and generosity: a great wine, with a purple colour and a bouquet of woodland plants, topped-off by truffles, vanilla and spices. It will reach its peak in two or three years' time and thereafter will keep its qualities for a good long while. (1981)
➴ MM. Archimbaud et Vache, Dom. Clos des Cazeaux, Vacqueyras, 84190 Beaumes-de-Venise; tel. 90 65 85 83 ⅄ Mon.–Sat. 9.00–12.00/ 14.00–19.00. Closed Sun. and public holidays.

LE MAS DES COLLINES★

■ 14ha 42000 **4** **D** ■ **◑** ↓
82 83

A very fine, deep colour. Powerful and supple wine with a light aroma of pond water, spices and green pepper. Ready for drinking. (1982) ✔ Côtes du Rhône.
◑ Jean Gorecki, Le Mas des Collines, Gigondas, 84190 Beaumes-de-Venise; tel. 90 65 86 40 ⊤ By appt ◑ *M.*Régis de Taxis du Poet.

DOMAINE DE LA FOURMONE
L'Oustau Fauquet★★

■ 9ha 38000 **4** **D** ■
78 79 80 **80** (81) **81** 82

A gleaming red colour, the perfumes of flowers combined with musk and spices – and much finesse and elegance. May seem feminine in character, but comes out undeniably virile. A good wine for keeping. (1981)
◑ GAEC Roger Combe et Fils, Dom. de la Fourmone, Vacqueyras, 84190 Beaumes-de-Venise; tel. 90 65 86 05 ⊤ No visitors.

COOPERATIVE VIGNERONS DE GIGONDAS *Cuvée du Président*★

■ 230ha 1 020000 **4** **D** **◑** ↓
78 79 80 (81) **81** ★82 83

Attractive ruby red colour; a very delicate nose of red fruit, vanilla, liquorice and then resin, against a background of spices. Besides the finesse of its aromas this balanced and harmonious wine is notable for its richness in alcohol. It will keep its best qualities for at least another two years. (1981) ✔ Côtes du Rhône.
◑ Coop. Vignerons de Gigondas, Gigondas, 84190 Beaumes-de-Venise; tel. 90 65 86 27 ⊤ Daily 8.00–12.00/14.00–18.00.

CLOS DE JONCUAS★

■ 10ha 30000 **4** **D** **◑** ↓
(78) 79

Lovely deep red colour with hints of brown. Tannic and powerful; destinctly woody. Alcoholic strength suggests too much Grenache. (1979) ✔ Côtes du Rhone Séguret Dom. la Garancière Rouge and Blanc, Côtes du Rhone Vacqueyras la Font-de-Papier Rouge, Clos du Joncuas Rouge.
◑ Fernand Chastan, Clos de Joncuas, Gigondas, 84190 Beaumes-de-Venise; tel. 90 65 86 86 ⊤ Mon.–Sat. 8.00–12.00.

DOMAINE DU PESQUIER★★★

■ 15ha 63000 **4** **D** ■ **◑** ↓
72 76 78 80 ★(81) **81**

Lovely colour and a nose with an impression first of spices then vanilla and a touch of rosemary. On the palate, it is elegant and has quite a long finish. A wine for keeping. (1981) ✔ Côtes du Rhône-Villages.
◑ Raymond Boutière et Fils, Dom. du Pesquier, Gigondas, 84190 Beaumes-de-Venise; tel. 90 65 86 16 ⊤ Mon.–Sat. 8.00–19.00. Closed Sun. afternoon.

DOMAINE RASPAIL-AY★★★

■ 18ha 35000 **3** **D** ■ ↓
78 80 81 ★(82) **82** 83

A very intense colour; aromas of cold coffee, dark tobacco and a hint of kirsch, above a fundamentally woodland bouquet; an explosion of spices on the palate. A virile, powerful and generous wine. One to be laid down for a very long time. (1982)
◑ François Ay, Dom. Raspail-Ay, Gigondas, 84190 Beaumes-de-Venise; tel. 90 65 83 01 ⊤ By appt.

CHATEAU RASPAIL★

■ 18ha 63000 **3** **◑** ↓
79 **81** 82 83

This wine, with its fine ruby red colour, has a very 'gamey' character, marked by a bouquet which has been described as smelling of hare's fur over a vinous base. On the palate, it seems quite harmonious and has a good balance. A very sellable wine. To be drunk now. (1981)
◑ Gabriel Meffre, Gigondas, 84190 Beaumes-de-Venise; tel. 90 65 86 09 ⊤ By appt Tues.–Wed.

DOMAINE ROMANE-MACHOTTE★

■ 120ha 342000 **1** **D** ■ ↓
74 76 78 79 (80) ★**82**

This wine grower matures his wines in large casks, kept in a disused tunnel. His 1982 offers a nose with a very pleasant savour of wood – of plant-like aromas dominated by spices. Very strong in tannin; to be drunk with highly-seasoned meats or game. (1982)
◑ SCA Pierre Amadieu, Dom. Romane-Machotte, Gigondas, 84190 Beaumes-de-Venise; tel. 90 65 84 08 ⊤ Daily 8.00–12.00/14.00–18.00.

Lirac

Lirac has been producing high-quality wines since the sixteenth century. In those days, the wines' authenticity was guaranteed by the magistrates of Roquemaure who branded the barrels with the letters 'C d R'. To the north of Tavel, and with similar climate and soils, the vineyard is divided between the communes of Lirac, St-Laurent-des-Arbres, St-Génies-de-Comolas and Roquemaure. It is the only southern cru to produce three types of wine. The whites and rosés are charming and fragrant and make a perfect match for seafood from the nearby Mediterranean. They are best drunk young and chilled. The powerful and generous red wines have a pronounced earthy flavour and are an excellent accompaniment for red meats.

CHATEAU D'AQUERIA★

■   3ha   12000   3 D ◧ ⌂

⑦ **81** ★82 ★83

This vineyard produces a fine Tavel rosé and also some excellent Liracs. This 1982, yielding a bouquet of ripe fruit with a touch of newly-toasted bread, is a good example. (1982) ✔ Tavel Ch. d'Aqueria Rouge.

↞ Jean Olivier, Ch. d'Aqueria, 30126 Tavel; tel. 66 50 04 56 ⊺ Mon.–Fri. 8.30–12.00/14.00–17.30.

J.-C. ASSEMAT *Les Garrigues*★

■   20ha   190000   4 D ⌂ ⌂

82 83 83 **84** 84

The Syrah accounts for 60 per cent of the grape varieties used here. Result: a well-made wine, with a good balance between tannin and acidity, and a predominantly plant-like bouquet. (1983) ✔ Lirac Blanc, Lirac Rosé, Lirac Rouge d'Été, Lirac Rouge Classique.

↞ J.-C. Assemat, Dom. des Causses et St-Eymes, St Laurent-des-Arbres, 30150 Roquemaure; tel. 66 50 29 76 ⊺ Mon.–Sat. 8.00–18.00.

CHATEAU DE BOUCARUT★

■   20ha   50000   3 D ⌂ ◧ ⌂

★76 ★78 ★82 82 ★83

Notable all for its bouquet of ripe fruit, blackcurrant and cherry. Although it has a good balance overall, its main drawback is a relative lack of elegance. (1982) ✔ Côtes du Rhône AOC, Rouge and Rosé.

↞ Robert Fuget, Ch. de Boucarut, 30150 Roquemaure; tel. 66 50 16 91 ⊺ No visitors.

CHATEAU DE BOUCARUT★

◰   30000   3 D ⌂ ◧ ⌂

82 83

The youthful colour of this wine – tile-pink with orange tints – should not mislead you. The development of its bouquet confirms that it should be drunk without delay. (1982) ✔ Côtes du Rhône Rouge, Côtes du Rhône Rosé.

↞ Robert Fuget, Ch. Boucarut, 30150 Roquemaure; tel. 66 50 16 91 ⊺ By appt.

CHATEAU DE BOUCHASSY★

☐   1ha   2000   3 D ⌂ ⌂

80 ⑧ 84

Beautiful, clear colour, slightly golden. At the peak of its maturity. Full and smooth but also delicate enough to drink now. (1982)

↞ Robert. Degoul, Ch. de Bouchassy, 30150 Roquemaure; tel. 66 50 12 49 ⊺ Daily 8.00–12.00/14.00–19.00.

CHATEAU DE BOUCHASSY★★

■   5ha   24000   3 D ⌂ ⌂

★⑦ 78 79 81

Degoul of Roquemaure – a name and place to remember, so good is the wine. Full, powerful, well balanced and of great consistency, after a further three to five years in bottle, it will be absolutely excellent. Distinguished exceptional finesse of its bouquet (redolent of woodland plants and spices). Equally noteworthy is the remarkable 1978, which is still capable of improving with age. (1981) ✔ Lirac Blanc, Lirac Rosé, Côtes du Rhône Rouge.

↞ Robert Degoul, Ch. de Bouchassy, 30150 Roquemaure; tel. 66 50 12 49 ⊺ Mon.–Sat. 8.00–12.00/14.00–19.00.

CHATEAU DE BOUCHASSY★

◰   30ha   5000   3 D ⌂ ⌂

82 84

Attractive, with a good lively red colour and a nose smelling predominantly of peardrops. Can be drunk now. (1984)

↞ Robert Degoul, Ch. de Bouchassy, 30150 Roquemaure; tel. 66 50 12 49 ⊺ Daily 8.00–12.00/14.00–19.00.

DOMAINE CASTEL-OUALOU★

■   50ha   222000   3 D ⌂ ⌂

79 80 81 ★82 ★83 83

A North African name for this winery, the proprietors of which were formerly wine-growers in Algeria. Their cherry-red Lirac has a youthful, flowery bouquet, predominantly of violets but shading towards ripe raspberries. Although the aromas do not hold as long as they might, the wine is pleasantly full on the palate. (1982) ✔ AOC Lirac Rouge, AOC Lirac Rosé, AOC Lirac Blanc.

↞ Mme Marie Pons-Mure, Dom. Castel-Oualou, 30150 Roquemaure; tel. 66 50 12 64 ⊺ By appt.

DOMAINE DES CAUSSES ET SAINT-EYMES★

◰   10ha   55000   4 D ⌂ ⌂

83 84

A deep, attractive, bright pink colour with a nose which, although weak, still has the aroma of ripe strawberries. Pleasing and well balanced on the palate; ready to drink.

↞ J. C. Assemat, Dom. des Causses et St-Eymes, St-Laurent-des-Arbres, 30150 Roquemaure; tel. 66 50 29 76 ⊺ By appt.

DOMAINE DES CAUSSES ET SAINT-EYMES

■   15ha   72000   4 D ⌂ ⌂

81 82 83 84

Dark-red colour; a well-balanced Lirac with aromas of fruit and fruit jelly. Uncomplicated and easy to drink. (1983)

↞ J. C. Assemat, Dom. des Causses et St-Eymes, St-Laurent-des-Arbres, 30150 Roquemaure; tel. 66 50 29 76 ⊺ By appt.

DOMAINE DES CAUSSES ET SAINT-EYMES

☐   5 ha   25 000   🔳 D ▮ ⬇

83 84

Golden-yellow colour, with aromas of ripe fruit and rum on the nose. Round and very supple on the palate, with a certain extra crispness. Ready to drink. (1982)
↞ J.-C. Assemat, Dom. des Causses et St-Eymes, St-Laurent-des-Arbres, 30150 Roquemaure; tel. 66 50 29 76 ☎ By appt.

CHATEAU DE CLARY*

◼   7500   🔳 D ⪧ ⬇

Deep and dark. Aroma of gentle spices that evoke the Rhône valley. Balanced on the palate. (1982)
↞ Manuel Seguin, Rue Paul Maldaut, 21420 Savigny-lès-Beaune; tel. 80 21 50 42 ☎ By appt.

DOMAINE DU DEVOY*

◪   15 ha   19 000   🔳 D ▮ ⬇

78 80 81 83

This rosé is renowned for the finesse of its tannins. Despite a high alcholic content, it is never aggressive on the palate and the aromas, enhanced by a touch of carbon dioxide, are remarkable. An attractive, balanced wine. (1983)
↞ GAEC Lombardo Frères, Dom. du Devoy, St-Laurent-des-Arbres, 30125 Tavel; tel. 66 50 01 23 ☎ By appt.

DOMAINE LES GARRIGUES**

◪   20 ha   84 000   🔳 D ▮ ⬇

⑦⑥ 80 🔳 *84

If you are fond of sardines grilled over a wood fire, then you will enjoy this well-balanced rosé. It goes perfectly with such dishes – although, as a wine of class, it can equally well be drunk with many other kinds of food or even on its own. (1983) ✔ Lirac Blanc, Lirac Type Syrah Rouge.
↞ Jean-Claude Assemat, Dom. des Causses et St-Eymes, St-Laureat-des-Arbres, 30150 Roquemaure; tel. 66 50 29 76 ☎ By appt.

DOMAINE DE LA GENESTIERE*

◼   11 ha   50 000   🔳 D ⪧ ⬇

74 78 *🔳 *82 🔳

A powerful red colour. Its strong tannins make it a wine that goes well with highly seasoned dishes. (1981)
↞ Mme Andrée Bernard, Dom. de la Genestière, 30126 Tavel; tel. 66 50 07 03 ☎ Mon.–Sat. 8.00–12.00/13.30–17.30.

DOMAINE MABY *La Fermade***

◼   23 ha   60 000   🔳 D ▮ ⪧ ⬇

77 79 *80 🔳 81 🔳

Still very fresh for a 1980, this wine has developed extremely well. It has an attractive dark red colour and a bouquet of small berries. (1980) ✔ Lirac Blanc.
↞ GAEC Dom. A. Maby, 30126 Tavel; tel. 66 50 03 40 ☎ Daily 8.00–12.00/14.00–18.00. Closed 1–15 Aug.

DOMAINE DU SEIGNEUR*

☐   0.5 ha   2200   🔳 D ▮ ⬇

*83 🔳 *84 🔳

Yellow colour flecked with gold; a mainly plant-like, slightly herby bouquet; well rounded overall. A wine that goes particularly well with oysters. (1983)
↞ Jean Duseigneur, Route de St-Victor, St Laurent-des-Arbres, 30150 Roquemaure; tel. 66 50 02 57 ☎ Mon.–Fri. 9.00–12.00/15.00–18.00. Closed 1–18 Aug.

DOMAINE DU SEIGNEUR*

◪   13 ha   25 000   🔳 D ▮ ⬇

79 83 *84 🔳

This wine starts with a deep pink colour, leading on to a bouquet with aromas which are powerful if not very diverse, and then finally to a slight astringency in the finish. (1983)
↞ Jean Duseigneur, Route de St-Victor, St Laurent-des-Arbres, 30150 Roquemaure; tel. 66 50 02 57 ☎ Mon.–Fri. 9.00–12.00/15.00–18.00. Closed 1–18 Aug.

DOMAINE DU SEIGNEUR*

◼   13 ha   69 000   🔳 D ▮ ⪧ ⬇

79 *81 🔳 *82 🔳 *83 🔳

Bouquet has the scent of roses just before they begin to fade, plus a slight touch of spiced quince. A rich and supple wine, to be drunk immediately. (1981) ✔ Lirac Rosé, Lirac Blanc, Côtes du Rhône-Villages Rouge, Côtes du Rhône Rouge.
↞ Jean Duseigneur, Route de St-Victor, St Laurent-des-Arbres, 30150 Roquemaure; tel. 66 50 02 57 ☎ Mon.–Fri. 9.00–12.00/15.00–18.00. Closed 1–18 Aug.

DOMAINE DE LA TOUR**

◪   31 ha   6000   🔳 D ▮ ⬇

*82 *83

The Andréo family sell barely a quarter of their production in France, exporting most of their wine to England, West Germany and Canada; which sometimes makes it difficult to buy direct from them. If you do succeed, however, you will not be disappointed. This Lirac Rosé, for example, is aromatic, fruity, fresh and balanced. (1982)
↞ François Andréo, St-Laurent-des-Arbres, 30126 Tavel; tel. 66 50 01 19 ☎ No visitors ↞ Mme Raymonde Andréo.

Tavel

Considered by many to be the best rosé produced in France, this wine comes from a variety of sandy, clay-alluvial and pebbly soils on the east bank of the Rhône. It is the only Rhône appellation that makes nothing but rosé wine; the area covers Tavel and one or two pieces of land in the commune of Roquemaure. Tavel is an expansive wine, strong and dry, with a fruity, flowery bouquet; it goes well with fish in sauce, charcuterie and white meats. The total AOC area is 836 hectares, producing some 3600 hecto-litres annually.

CHATEAU D'AQUERIA**

| ☑ | 50ha | 228000 | ③ Ⓓ ▮ ↓ |

74 77 80 82 ⋆ ⑧③ ⑧③ ⋆ ⑧④

Cherry-coloured rosé. Very fruity, with a plea-sant, flowery hint. Fine finish on the palate. (1983)
↱ Jean. Olivier, Ch. d'Aqueria, 30126, Tavel; tel. 66 50 04 56 ☎ Mon.–Fri. 8.00–12.00/14.00–18.00. Closed 1–15 Oct.

DOMAINE DE LA FORCADIERE***

| ☑ | 46ha | 216000 | ③ Ⓓ ▮ ↓ |

78 80 ⋆ ⑧④ ⑧④

The very pink colour and the fruity nose are pleasing, and the beautiful combination of aro-mas is still clearly evident on the palate. To be drunk young. (1984)
↱ GAEC Dom. A. Maby, 30126 Tavel; tel. 66 50 03 40 ☎ Daily 8.00–12.00/14.00–18.00. Closed 1–15 Aug.

DOMAINE DE LA GENESTIERE**

| ☑ | 26ha | 125000 | ③ Ⓓ ▮ ↓ |

71 74 77 ⋆84 ⑧④

A very honest rosé, fairly dark. While the deli-cate nose does not have much personality, the firmness and good balance evident on the palate make it a very pleasing wine. (1983) ✔ Lirac Rouge.
↱ *Mme* Andrée Bernard, Dom. de la Genestière, 30126 Tavel; tel. 66 50 07 03 ☎ Mon.–Sat. 8.00–12.00/13.30–17.30.

LEVEQUE *Seigneurs de Vaucrose*

| ☑ | 30ha | 96000 | ④ Ⓓ ▮ |

78 79 80 ⋆81 ⋆ ⑧②

The proprietors family specialize in Tavel rosé, which is aged in cask, giving their wines a very distinctive character. This salmon pink 1981, for instance, has a very developed bouquet, in which you can detect bayleaf, mint, resin and newly toasted bread. (1981)
↱ SCA Levêque, Seigneurs de Vaucrose, 30126 Tavel; tel. 66 50 12 66 ☎ Mon.–Fri. 14.00–18.00.

PRIEURE DE MONTEZARGUES***

| ☑ | 30ha | 125000 | ③ Ⓓ ▮ ↓ |

78 79 80 81 ⋆ ⑧③ ⑧③

Visitors are given a warm welcome in this ancient priory, dating from the 13th century, where they are sure to appreciate the elegance of its salmon-pink Tavel rosé. Full, rounded and well-balanced, with a subtle and delicate bouquet, it is a wine fit to accompany the most refined dishes. (1983)
↱ GAFF Allauzen, Prieuré de Montezargues, 30126 Tavel; tel. 66 50 04 48 ☎ By appt.

DOMAINE DE ROC EPINE***

| ☑ | 30ha | 126000 | ③ Ⓓ ▮ ↓ |

73 74 75 ⋆82 ⋆ ⑧③ ⋆84

Excellent barbecue wine. Attractive purple col-our with a touch of yellow; bouquet of flowers and fruit, and elegant balance on the palate. An ideal match for the fragrances of a garden in summer. Like most Tavels, it is liable to mader-ize after about five years. (1983) ✔ Lirac Rouge, Côtes du Rhône Rouge.
↱ J.-P. et P. Lafond, Dom. de Roc Epine, 30126 Tavel; tel. 66 50 24 59 ☎ By appt.

DOMAINE DE TOURTOUIL*

| ☑ | 10ha | 35000 | ③ Ⓓ ▮ ↓ |

65 79 81 82 ⑧③ 84

This is a good-looking pale rosé, well made, with a strong alcohol content. (1981)
↱ Edouard Lefèvre, Dom. de Tourtouil, 30126 Tavel; tel. 66 50 05 68 ☎ By appt.

CHATEAU DE TRINQUEVEDEL**

| ☑ | 25ha | 100000 | ③ Ⓓ ▮ ↓ |

82 ⋆ ⑧③ ⑧③ ⋆84 ⑧④

Moorland scents characterize this clear, bright rosé, glimmering with golden tints. A well-balanced and quite powerful wine. (1983)
↱ F. Demoulin, Ch. de Trinquevedel, 30126 Tavel; tel. 66 50 04 04 ☎ No visitors.

Les Coteaux de Pierrevert

Most of the 400 hectares of vines in the department of Alpes-de-Haute-Provence are on the eastern bank of the River Durance (e.g. Corbières, Sainte-Tulle, Pierrevert or Manos-que). The rather severe weather con-ditions restrict vine-growing to only a quarter of the 42 communes that lie within the authorized appellation area. The red, white and rosé wines have a fairly low alcohol content and refreshing acidity, and are much appreciated by visitors to the area.

DOMAINE DE LA BLAQUE*

| ☐ | 5ha | 10000 | ② Ⓓ ▮ ↓ |

78 81 82 ⑧② 83 ⋆84

This 1982 wine, its yellow colour flecked with gold, has kept its original freshness. A likeable, fairly delicate wine, it has a slightly bitter after-

taste. To be drunk now. (1982)
☙ Charles Pons-Mure, St-Laurent-des-Arbres; 31026 Tavel; tel. 66 50 09 90 ☈ By appt.

DOMAINE DE LA BLAQUE★

☑	12000	2 D 🍾 ⬇

78 81 82 83 ★84

This rosé has the distinctive 'onion skin' colour and a bouquet of fading roses. A relatively neutral wine, easy to drink. (1982)
☙ Charles Pons-Mure, St-Laurent-des-Arbres, 30126 Tavel; tel. 66 50 09 90 ☈ By appt.

DOMAINE DE LA BLAQUE★★

■	52ha 360000	2 D 🍾 ⬇

78 81 82 82 ★84

A bouquet of cooked fruit and always well balanced and pleasant to drink. (1982)
✔ Coteaux de Pierrevert Rosé, Coteaux de Pierrevert Blanc.
☙ Charles Pons-Mure, St-Laurent-des-Arbres, 30126 Tavel; tel. 66 50 09 90 ☈ By appt.

Côtes du Luberon VDQS

Thirty-five communes make up this appellation of 2850 hectares stretching over the northerly and southerly slopes of the limestone Luberon massif. The vineyard soils produce light and fruity reds of good quality, quite similar in style to the wines of Ventoux. However, the appellation is best known for its white and rosé wines, which gain a certain elegance and freshness from the cooler climate and later harvest of the region. Annual production of all Côtes de Luberon wines averages 120000 hectolitres.

CHATEAU LA CANORGUE★★

■	12ha 48000	3 D 🍾 ⬛ ⬇

79 ★81 ★82 82 84

A fine cherry-red colour and a nose of red fruit, above all blackcurrant, with cocoa butter in the background. Very drinkable, harmonious and well balanced; a wine to enjoy now – but which will keep its qualities for several years yet. (1982)
✔ Côtes du Lubéron Ch. la Canorgue Rosé, Côtes du Lubéron Ch. la Canorgue Blanc.
☙ Jean-Pierre Margan, Ch. la Canorgue 84480 Bonnieux; tel. 90 75 81 01 ☈ Daily 8.00–12.30/ 13.30–20.00.

CHATEAU LA CANORGUE★★

☑	12ha 8000	3 D 🍾 ⬛ ⬇

79 82 ⟨83⟩ 83 84

This glimmering light rosé has a most effective and elegant bronzed colour and a flowery bouquet of great finesse. Equally elegant and pleasing on the palate, it is an attractive wine, ready for immediate drinking. (1983)
☙ Jean-Pierre Margan, Ch. la Canorgue, 84480 Bonnieux; tel. 90 75 81 01 ☈ Daily 8.00–12.30/ 13.30–20.00.

DOMAINE DE FONTENILLE★

■	13ha 9000	3 D 🍾 ⬇

⟨78⟩ 80 82 ★84

A purply-red wine with a light nose and a pleasing palate. For immediate drinking. (1982)
☙ Michel Levêque, Dom. de Fontenille, 84360 Lauris; tel. 90 68 10 37 ☈ By appt.

CHATEAU DE L'ISOLETTE★★★

■	5ha 24000	5 D ⬛ ⬇

⟨76⟩ 76 80 ★82 ★83 83 84

Although this wine is by no means cheap, the price is well justified by its exceptional quality. A delicate, complex bouquet, with aromas of roses, vanilla, kirsch and even newly cured leather; a taste which holds to perfection. In short, a first-rate product which is an outstanding ambassador for wines of this appellation. (1979)
☙ Luc Pinatel, Ch. de l'Isolette, 84000 Apt; tel. 90 74 16 70 ☈ Mon.–Sat. 8.00–11.30/14.00–17.30.

CHATEAU DE L'ISOLETTE★★

☐	6ha 30000	4 D 🍾 ⬇

82 ★83 84

The Clairette and Roussanne grape varieties, when grown in the type of soil predominating here, can sometimes produce surprisingly good results. The only criticism that could be made of this 1983 is that it may seem a little pricey; but it is a well-made wine and has an interesting nose, with a very characteristic touch of apple (Cox's pippins, say). Ready for immediate drinking. (1983)
☙ Luc Pinatel, Ch. de l'Isolette, 84000 Apt; tel. 90 74 16 70 ☈ Mon.–Sat. 8.00–11.30/14.00–17.30.

CHATEAU DE L'ISOLETTE★★

☑	18ha 84000	3 D 🍾 ⬇

76 80 82 ⟨83⟩ 84

A particularly well-made wine, this rosé has an elegant bouquet and good long finish. It goes exceptionally well with fine foods (foie gras, etc.) and charcuterie. (1983)

↱ Luc Pinatel, Ch. de l'Isolette, 84000 Apt; tel. 79741670 ⊥ Mon.–Sat. 8.00–11.30/14.00–17.30.

CELLIER DE MARRENON★★

◩   300000   2 D 🞖 ⑪ ⬇
78 80 82 83 83

Fresh, delicate and well balanced rosé, which goes very well with hors d'oeuvres and charcuterie. (1983)
↱ Cellier de Marrenon, 84240 La Tour-d'Aigues; tel. 90744065 ⊥ Daily 8.00–18.00. Closed Sun. afternoon, Christmas and Aug.

CELLIER DE MARRENON★

☐   300000   2 D 🞖 ⑪ ⬇
78 80 82 83

A dry, limpid wine, well bred and distinctive. Its strongly floral bouquet is still relatively discreet. Very typical of wines of this appellation, it goes extremely well with fish, seafood and pastries. (1983)
↱ Cellier de Marrenon, 84240 La Tour-d'Aigues; tel. 90774065 ⊥ Daily 8.00–18.00. Closed Sun. afternoon, Christmas and Aug.

CELLIER DE MARRENON★★

■   500000   2 D 🞖 ⑪ ⬇
78 80 82 83 83

Although the public at large has started to become aware of them only in quite recent years, the Côtes du Lubéron are pleasant, fruity wines which may be drunk young. The 1983 from the Cellier de Marrenon is a very typical example. (1983)
↱ Cellier de Marrenon, 84240 La Tour-d'Aigues; tel. 90774065 ⊥ Daily 8.00–18.00. Closed Sun. afternoon, Christmas and Aug.

CHATEAU TURCAN★★

■   14ha   60000   3 D 🞖 ⬇

Louis Turcan planted one of the first vineyards to be established in the Ansouis region. The present-day proprietors produce wines by entirely natural methods and refuse to use any inorganic fertilizers on the vineyard's soil. Harvesting is carried out solely by hand, which allows the grapes to be carefully graded. This 1982 is a deep red wine with a pervasive bouquet; despite strong tannins, it is well made and has a good finish. (1982)
↱ MM. Laugier et Fils, Ch. Turcan, 84690 Ansouis; tel. 90792214 ⊥ Daily 8.00–20.00.

CHATEAU VAL-JOANIS★★

■   70ha   456000   3 D 🞖 ⬇
82 83

Beautiful, bold red colour. The aroma is also bold, fruity and has a touch of kirsch. Well made with good balance between alcohol, acid and tannin. (1983)
↱ Famille Chancel, Ch. Val-Joanis, 84120. Pertuis; tel. 90792077 ⊥ By appt.

Côtes du Vivarais VDQS

The growing area of this VDQS wine is at the extreme north-west of the southern Côtes du Rhône on the bor-

ders of the two departments of the Ardèche and Gard. Three communes are allowed to add their names to the appellation; Orgnac (famous for its natural well), St-Remèze and St-Montant.

Grown on limestone soil, these wines, principally reds and rosés, have a characteristic freshness and should be drunk young. Total annual production averages 36000 hectolitres from 739 hectares.

VIGNERONS ARDECHOIS★

☐   50ha   360000   2 D 🞖 ⬇
83 84

Fairly strong yellow colour. Discreet vegetal nose slightly reminiscent of green undergrowth. Despite fairly faint aromas, it has a good, subtle balance, although the finish is slightly acid. Ready to drink.
↱ UCO Vignerons Ardéchois, BP 8, 07120 Ruoms; tel. 75935055 ⊥ By appt. Closed 25 Dec.–1 Jan.

VIGNERONS ARDECHOIS★

◩   100ha   360000   2 D 🞖 ⬇
83 ★84

Very pale, clear rosé which is characterized by its floral aromas. Pleasing to drink; harmonious and round, almost smooth, with a very fresh finish. Ready to drink.
↱ UCO Vignerons Ardéchois, BP 8, 07120 Ruoms; tel. 75935055 ⊥ By appt. Closed 25 Dec.–1 Jan.

DOMAINE GALLETY★★

☐   1ha   5000   2 D 🞖
★83 83 ★84

Fine bright colour for a wine with a taste of honey; smooth and long on the palate while retaining all its crispness. (1983)
↱ Caroline Gallety, La Montagne, St-Montan, 07220 Viviens; tel. 75526318 ⊥ 8.00–12.00/ 14.00–18.00.

DOMAINE GALLETY★

■   7ha   42000   2 D 🞖 ⑪ ⬇
81 ★82 ★83 ★84

Rather light-red colour and aromas of small red fruit. Pleasing on the palate. Should go well with pork. Should be drunk quite soon. (1983)
↱ Caroline Gallety, La Montagne, St-Montan, 07220 Viviens; tel. 75526318 ⊥ Daily 8.00–12.00/14.00–18.00.

COOPERATIVE VIGNERONS DE SAINT-MONTANT *Cépage Syrah*★★★

■   31250   3 D 🞖 ⬇

Dark red colour with deep purple glints. Highly perfumed, with characteristic nose: fruity nature over an animal, liquorice base that has a peppered and spicy hint. Nicely full bodied on the palate. An original bottle; pleasant and easy to drink. Could age further. (1983)

☞ Coop. Vignerons de St-Montan, St-Montan, 07220 Viviers; tel. 75 52 61 75 ☎ By appt.

PRODUIT REUNIS DE SAINT-REMEZE-GRAS★★

■　　　40ha　10000　　2 D ■ ↓

83 84

Dark-red colour, and a fruity nose with a vegetal undertone. Good structure on the palate, and an attractive tannin. Ready for drinking. (1983)
☞ Prod. Réunis de St-Remèze-Gras, 07700 St-Remeze; tel. 75 04 08 56 ☎ By appt. Closed Sun. and public holidays.

DOMAINE DE VIGUIER★★

■　　　35ha　480000　　2 D ■ ↓

81 84

Good cherry red colour. Very fresh and young with a primal, vegetal nose of laurel leaves and ivy, and a fruitiness mainly of gooseberries and blackcurrants. Good, long finish makes tasting pleasant. Quite acidic on the palate, which may not suit all tastes. Good for the year. (1984)
☞ Francis Dupré, Dom. du Viguier, Lagorce, 07150 Vallon-Pont-d'Arc; tel. 75 88 01 18 ☎ By appt.

VINS DOUX NATURELS

THE EXCELLENT fortified sweet wines of Roussillon, the Vins Doux Naturels, have been produced for a very long time. They are made by adding grape spirit (eau-de-vie) to red or white wine while the fermentation is still in full swing. The additional alcohol kills the fermenting yeasts and fermentation comes to a halt, leaving a certain amount of unfermented grape sugar in the must. The discovery of this process, called 'mutage', is credited to a certain Arnau de Vilanova in the thirteenth century.

Today, Vins Doux Naturels AOC areas are found in several departments of southern France, but never far from the Mediterranean; Pyrénées-Orientales, Aude, Hérault and Vaucluse. The grape varieties used are the Grenache Blanc, Grenache Gris, Grenache Noir, Macabéo, Roussillon Malvoisie (called Tourbat here), Muscat à Petits Grains and Muscat d'Alexandrie. In all cases the vines have to be short pruned.

The yield per hectare is low, and at the time of harvest the grapes need to have a sugar content of at least 252 grams per litre of must. Appellations are not awarded until the wines have been aged for a fixed period, which varies between appellations. The wines are only granted the appellation after being tested and analysed; they must have an actual alcohol content of 15–18 per cent; a sugar content of at least 45 g/l, (up to 100 g/l for the Muscat wines); and a total alcohol level (actual alcohol content plus potential alcohol content) of at least 21.5 per

Vins Doux Naturels

cent. They are not marketed until they are three years old; some are aged in the traditional way, in wooden casks which are topped up with younger wines. These wines, called 'rancio', are closely related to Spanish sherry.

Banyuls and Banyuls Grand Cru

The land covered by this appellation is unusual, almost unique. The vineyards are located in the far eastern section of the Pyrénées where precipitous cliffs drop down to the Mediterranean. Only four communes may use this appellation; Collioure, Port-Vendres, Banyuls-sur-Mer and Cerbère. The vineyards cover about 2000 hectares and cling onto schistous terraces where the bedrock shows through a thin layer of soil. In the poor and often acid, soil conditions, only very hardy grape varieties such as the Grenache can be grown. The yield is extremely low, often less than 20 hectolitres per hectare. Annual production varies between 30000 and 40000 hectolitres. Cultivation of the vine is, needless to say, particularly arduous; the slightest storm can blow away the precious topsoil, and the vignerons work the steep terraces by hand, thus protecting the soil from the elements. However, on the credit side, the terraces maximize the amount of sunshine that the vines receive, and the nearby Mediterranean provides the area with a favourable micro-climate – two factors which undoubtedly contribute to the exceptional quality of these grapes, so rich in sugar and aromatic elements. Grenache is the main variety with a high proportion of old vines. The wine is made by macerating the whole bunches of grapes. Sometimes eau-de-vie is added at this stage, allowing an extended maceration time of more than twelve days.

The next stage of vinification is of vital importance. In general, the ageing process involves indirect contact with the air, either in wooden casks or in demi-johns exposed to the sun. Thus aged, the various cuvées are then blended with the greatest of care by the cellarmaster in order to create many different types of Vins Doux Naturels. In certain instances, however, the wine is kept from all contact with air so as to conserve all its original fruitiness. The result of this process is a highly individual wine with its own unique taste and bouquet; these wines are called 'rimages'.

Wines with the appellation Grand Cru must have been aged in wood for at least 30 months. These ruby-coloured wines have a bouquet of raisins, cooked fruit, roasted almonds, coffee, and plum liqueur. The rimages wines, on the other hand, preserve their young aromas of kirsch, cherry and red berries. Banyuls wines should be drunk at a temperature of 12–17°C depending on their age. They are drunk as an aperitif, with dessert (some Banyuls are the only wine that can be drunk with chocolate), or with coffee and a cigar; but equally they may be served with foie gras, duck with cherries or figs or with certain types of cheese.

Banyuls

ROBERT DOUTRES★★

| ■ | 6ha | 2700 | 4 D ◗ D |

A Banyuls of great distinction, produced by Robert Doutres who owns vines at the heart of the Banyuls land. He demonstrates a genuine passion in the way he makes this lovely, fine wine which is fat and beautifully tannic. (1980)
✔ Côtes-de-Roussillon Rouge, Muscat-de-Rivesaltes, Rivesaltes.
↬ Diff. des Dom. de Jau, Ch. de Jau, Casses-de-Pène, 66600 Rivesaltes; tel. 68 54 51 67 ⊺ Daily 9.00–19.00. Closed Sat., Sun. out of season.

L'ETOILE *Extra Vieux*★

| ■ | 140ha | 24000 | 5 D ◗ ♦ |

Brick-red and amber colour. Scent reminiscent of dried fruit, especially almond, and a balance in the mouth that is medium-sweet, combined with an aroma of nut. (1970)
↬ Cave Coop. l'Etoile, 26 Av. du Puig-del-Mas, 66650 Banyuls-sur-Mer; tel. 68 88 00 10 ⊺ Mon.–Fri. 8.00–12.00/14.00–18.00.

L'ETOILE *Grand Rèserve*★

| ■ | 140ha | 12000 | 4 D ◗ ♦ |

Brick-red colour. Roasting and coffee on the nose, rounded off by a hint of old wood. On the palate, fleshy and persistent aroma of dried fruit. Sufficient qualities to make it a good Banyuls. (1962)
↬ Cave Coop. l'Etoile, 26 Av. du Puig-del-Mas, 66650 Banyuls-sur-Mer; tel. 68 88 00 10 ⊺ Mon.–Fri. 8.00–12.00/14.00–18.00.

L'ETOILE *Macere*★★

■ 120ha 36000 ④ Ⅾ ⑪ ↓

Colour wavers between brick-red and mahogany. Dash of nutmeg strengthens the nose, which is primarily of cooked fruit. Thick and powerful, and in the mouth discloses a tannic structure and persistent aroma. (1975)
➻ Cave Coop. l'Etoile, 26 Av. du Puig-del-Mas, 66650 Banyuls-sur-Mer; tel. 68 88 00 10 ⵂ Daily 8.00–12.00/14.00–18.00.

DOMAINE DU MAS BLANC *Rimage*★★

■ 6ha 28800 ④ Ⅾ ⬛ ↓

Intense scent of fruit and plum brandy. Preserves its solid structure and fleshiness for the mouth, and links them with a bouquet of red berries and a trace of blackberries. Has considerable length in the mouth. (1982)
➻ MM. Parcé et Fils, Dom. du Mas Blanc, 66650 Banyuls-sur-Mer; tel. 68 88 32 12 ⵂ By appt. Closed Aug.

DOMAINE DU MAS BLANC
Vieilles Vignes★★

■ 6ha 32400 ⑤ Ⅾ ⑪ ↓

Mahogany colour and an intense bouquet of dried fruit and coffee liqueur. Good structure in the mouth, combined with strong tannin verging on a plum taste. (1967)
➻ MM. Parcé et Fils, Dom. du Mas Blanc, 66650 Banyuls-sur-Mer; tel. 68 88 32 12. ⵂ By appt. Closed Aug.

SICA DES VINS DU ROUSSILLON
Templiers Vieux★

■ 200ha 360000 ④ ⬛

Bright ruby colour. Scent of fairly well-baked red fruits. Vigorous sensation on the palate. Fairly thick, with slightly spicy aroma. All the characteristics seem almost a little too marked. (1982)
➻ SICA des Vins du Roussillon, Route des Crêtes, 66650 Banyuls-sur-Mer; tel. 68 88 31 59 ⵂ Daily 9.00–1200/14.00–18.00.

CELLIER DES TEMPLIERS
Vieille Réserve

■ 100ha 240000 ④ Ⅾ ⑪ ↓

Nose of red fruits and spices. Becomes lively in the mouth, with an aroma of dried fruit. (1982)
➻ Cellier des Templiers, Route de Mas-Reig, 66650 Banyuls-sur-Mer; tel. 68 88 31 59 ⵂ Daily 9.00–12.00/14.00–18.00.

Banyuls Grand Cru

HOSPICES DE BANYULS
Castell dels Templiers★★

■ 10ha 24000 ⑥ Ⅾ ⑪

Shaded by ruby reflections. Less complex than the bouquet that conjures up ripe fruit, peach and, to a lesser degree, musk. In the mouth, a touch of woodiness reminiscent of pine. (1970)
➻ Cellier des Templiers, Route du Mas-Reig, 66650 Banyuls-sur-Mer; tel. 68 88 31 59 ⵂ Daily 9.00–12.00/14.00–18.00.

L'ETOILE *Select-Vieux*★★★

■ 5ha 1500 ⑤ Ⅾ ⑪ ↓

A great vintage that has aged beautifully. Bouquet is just *ranciote* (under the influence of dried fruit and honey). On the palate, beneath a very long aroma, an elegant touch of rancio reappears at the finish, but is sufficiently discreet to be pleasing. (1966)
➻ Cave Coop. l'Etoile, 26 Av. du Puig-del-Mas, 66650 Banyuls-sur-Mer; tel. 68 88 00 10 ⵂ Mon.–Fri. 8.00–12.00/14.00–18.00.

CELLIERS DES TEMPLIERS
Cuvée Viviane Le Roy Sec★★

■ 10ha 24000 ⑥ Ⅾ ⑪ ↓

Bright-red mahogany concealing scents of old wood, resin and cocoa beans. Trace of rancio on the palate. (1974)
➻ Cellier des Templiers, Route du Mas-Reig, 66650 Banyuls-sur-Mer; tel; 68 88 31 59 ⵂ Daily 9.00–12.00/14.00–18.00.

CELLIER DES TEMPLIERS
Cuvée du Président Vidal★★

■ 10ha 24000 ⑥ Ⅾ ⑪ ↓

This splendid wine cellar, has been superbly restored and opened to the public. It is now the shop window of the GICB, the producer of this great Banyuls vintage. It has been allowed to age in small *tuns* and, has a nose of old wood, thickness and good tannin content. (1970)
➻ Celliers des Templiers, Route du Mas-Reig, 66650 Banyuls-sur-Mer; tel. 68 88 31 59 ⵂ Daily 9.00–12.00/14.00–18.00

Rivesaltes

This is the biggest of the Vin Doux Naturel appellations: its 20000 hectares produce 400000 hectolitres of wine. The vineyards – mostly in Roussillon, but with a small area in Corbières – show the typical combination of poor soil and hot, dry climate, excellent for ripening the grapes. Four grape varieties are permitted here; Grenache, Macabéo, Malvoisie and the Muscat family. In general the wines are made according to white-wine vinifying procedures, except for the Grenache Noir which is left on the skins for a while to give it maximum colour and tannin.

The way that Rivesaltes wines are

aged is fundamental to quality. The bouquet that the wine develops will vary tremendously according to whether it is stored in stainless steel vats or wooden barrels. There is a possible declassification, into the appellation Grand Roussillon.

The colour of the wines varies from amber to almost brick-red. The bouquet is reminiscent of roasted coffee, dried fruit or, when most developed, rancio wine. When young, a Rivesaltes wine has aromas of cherry, blackcurrant or blackberry. It should be drunk as an aperitif or with pudding, at 11–15°C; the younger the wine, the cooler it should be.

AGLYA PRESTIGE★★

■　　194ha　132000　　3 D ■ ⅃

Garnet-red colour with dash of brick-red. Nose evocative of cooked fruits and cocoa, which the palate confirms with hint of chocolate. Fleshy and very persistent, with good tannin level. (1982) ✔ Rivesaltes Doré, Muscat de Rivesaltes, Côtes du Roussillon-Villages Rouge, Vin de Pays Côtes Catalanes.
✦┐ Cave Coop. d'Aglya, 66310 Estagel; tel. 68 29 00 45　Ⅰ Mon.–Sat.　8.00–12.00/14.00–19.00.

CAVE D'ARGELES *Vieille Réserve*★★

■　　10ha　96000　　3 D ⅉ ⅃

Supple, thick and tannic. Evocative of cooked fruits with a hint of cherry brandy. (1979) ✔ Côtes de Roussillon Rouge. Muscat de Rivesaltes.
✦┐ Cave Coop. d'Argelès, Route de Sorède, 66700 Argèles-sur-Mer; tel. 68 81 01 04　Ⅰ Daily 9.00–12.00/14.00–18.00.

LES PRODUCTEURS DE LA BARNEDE *Rancio*★★

■　　124ha　2400　　4 D ⅉ ⅃

Intense and complex bouquet with hints of cherry brandy and old wood. On the palate it is very thick and strongly constructed, with a long rancio finish. (1965)
✦┐ Producteurs de la Barnède, 66670 Bages; tel. 68 21 60 30　Ⅰ Mon.–Sat.　8.15–12.00/14.00–19.00. Closed Sun. and public holidays.

BARTISSOL BIANCO★★

□　　　　　　　　4 ⅉ ⅃

A golden colour and on the nose delicate aromas of honey and bay. The palate is well balanced, thick and harmonious.
✦┐ Ets Bartissol, 8 Bd Violet, 66000 Perpignan; tel. 01 30 75 70　Ⅰ No visitors.

BARTISSOL ROUGE★★

■　　　　　　　　3 ■ ⅃

Beneath its cherry red colour, this wine is round, supple and thick with aromas of small red fruits mingled with those of dried fruits.

✦┐ Ets Bartissol, 8 Bd Violet, 66000 Perpignan; tel. 01 30 75 70　Ⅰ No visitors.

BOUDAU ET FILS★★★

■　　24ha　12000　　4 ■ ⅃

A mahogany colour and an intense nose evoking cooked fruits. On the palate it is well structured with a powerful and long-lasting aroma of cocoa.
✦┐ Sté Vve Boudau et Fils, 7 Ave Gambetta, 66600 Rivesaltes; tel. 68 64 07 40　Ⅰ By appt.

DOMAINE BRIAL★★

■　　10ha　120000　　4 D ⅉ ⅃

Subtle wine with a brick-red, crimson colour. Intense, characteristic nose, evoking blackcurrant and cherry, and tannin, which is mild but nonetheless in evidence. (1978) ✔ Muscat de Rivesaltes Dom. Brial, Côtes du Roussillon-Villages Dom. Brial, Rivesaltes Vieille Réserve, Côtes du Roussillon Rouge.
✦┐ SCV les Vignerons de Baixas, 66390 Baixas; tel. 68 64 22 37　Ⅰ Mon.–Sat.　8.00–12.00/14.00–18.00.

CHATEAU DE CALADROY
Al Vi Réal★★

■　　20ha　10000　　3 D ■ ⅃

Nose gives off roasting and old wood aromas with a dash of kirsch. On the palate there is an overriding impression of thickness and mellowness combined with persistent aromas.
✦┐ Ch. de Caladroy, Balesta, 66720 Latour-de-France; tel. 68 57 10 25　Ⅰ By appt ✦┐ *M.* Arnold.

LES VIGNERONS DE CASCASTEL
Rancio★

■　　　　24000　　4 D ⅉ ⅃

Cherry-red colour that shines out of the glass and gives off a bouquet of overripe fruits, with a slight hint of cocoa. Syrupy and heavy, with a pleasant dash of gooseberry on the palate. ✔ Fitou, AOC, VDN AOC Rivesaltes, Corbières.
✦┐ Les Vign. de Cascastel, 11360 Cascastel-des-Corbières; tel. 68 45 91 74　Ⅰ Mon.–Sat.　8.00–12.00/14.00–18.00. Sun. 8.00–12.00.

VITICULTEURS CATALANS
Hors d'Age★★

■　　920ha　70000　　5 D ⅉ ⅃

Amber shade, a sign of quality, and nose of old barrels, mingling honey with candied fig. On the palate, mellow, thick and persistent, with a dash of rancio. (1963)
✦┐ GIAR Viticulteurs Catalans, Rue des Vendanges, BP 1, 66300 Banyuls; tel. 68 21 72 18　Ⅰ Mon.–Sat. 8.00–12.00/14.00–18.00.

VITICULTEURS CATALANS
Santa-Clara★★

■　　200ha　48000　　3 D ⅉ ⅃

Brick-red, mahogany colour. Very persistent in the mouth. Supple and thick, with a nose of vanilla and prune. (1979)
✦┐ GIAR Viticulteurs Catalans, Rue des Vendanges, BP 1, 66300 Banyuls; tel. 68 21 72 18　Ⅰ Mon.–Sat. 8.00–12.00/14.00–18.00.

CAZES CUVEE AIME CAZES
Très Vieux Cazes★★★

☐ 20ha 48000 6 D ▪ ↓

Pleasant amber colour. Attractive, has aged well and acquired a complex bouquet of honey and candied fig. Smooth in the mouth, and develops a good syrupy balance and beautiful, strong aroma reminiscent of nuts, raisins and candied orange. (1963) ✔ Rivesaltes Ambré, Muscat de Rivesaltes, Côtes du Roussillon Rouge, Rosé and Blanc, Côtes du Roussillon Villages Rouge.
➤ MM. Cazes Frères, 4 Rue Francisco Ferrer, 66600 Rivesaltes; tel. 68 64 08 26 ☎ Mon.–Sat. 8.00–12.00/14.00–18.00.

CHATEAU DE CORNEILLA★

▪ 7ha 20000 4 D ▪ ↓

Balanced structure and fruity aroma. Like the château, combines medieval power with southern warmth. (1977) ✔ Côtes du Roussillon Ch. de Corneilla, Vins de Pays Catalan Chapelle du Paradis.
➤ GFA Jonqueres d'Oriola, Ch. de Corneilla, Corneilla del Vercol, 66200 Elné; tel. 68 22 12 56 ☎ Mon.–Sat. 16.00–19.30. Closed winter except Mon. morning.

JOSEPH COUDINE★★

▪ 3 ▪ ↓

A brick-red mahogany colour and on the nose aromas of dried fruit and roasting which change to those of coffee and cooked prunes on the palate. Thick and smooth, it has a good finish.
➤ Joseph Coudine, Rue Valmagne, 66160 Le Boulou; tel. 68 83 34 56 ☎ No visitors.

ANDRE CREMADEILS★

☐ 15ha 36000 3 D ▪ ◑ ↓

Amber colour. Characterized by nose of dried fruit with hint of honey, and fairly thick syrupy taste.
➤ André Cremadeils, 17 Av. Jean-Jaurès, 66670 Bages; tel. 68 21 72 72 ☎ By appt.

CHATEAU L'ESPARROU *Tuilé*★

▪ 10ha 24000 3 D ◑ ↓

Ruby-red colour with brick-red glints. Scent of ripe fruit, grape mark and prunes. On the palate, thick and well constructed; the prune smell re-emerges in the aroma. ✔ Rivesaltes Ambré. Muscat de Rivesaltes, Côtes du Roussillon Rouge and Rosé.
➤ M. Rendu, Ch. l'Esparrou, BP 15, 66140 Canet-en-Roussillon; tel. 68 80 30 93 ☎ By appt. Closed Christmas fortnight.

DOMAINE DE GARRIA★★★

☐ 30ha 6000 5 D ▪ ↓

Very fine, with lustrous bronze, amber colour. Exhales powerful scent of roasted hazelnuts and candied fig mingled and followed by walnut bark and honey. Particularly thick and smooth, with superb length on the palate.
➤ René Mitjaville, Dom. de Garria, Pollestres, 66300 Thuir; tel. 68 54 50 93 ☎ By appt.

MAS DE LA GARRIGUE★★

▪ 36ha 100000 4 ▪ ↓

Mahogany shade with a touch of old-brick. Nose has scents of cooked cherry and dried prune. On the palate, very long, fat and discreetly tannic, with distinct aromas of animal hide and roasting. (1959) ✔ Muscat de Rivesaltes.
➤ Marcel Vila, 17 Av. du Général-de-Gaulle, 66240 St-Estève; tel. 68 92 06 56 ☎ No visitors.

CHATEAU DE JAU *Jean Dauré*★★

▪ 9ha 4900 4 D

Light mahogany colour and nose of cooked fruits. On the palate, very *fondu*, and decidedly smooth. ✔ Côtes du Roussillon Rouge, Muscat de Rivesaltes, Banyuls.
➤ Diff. des Dom. de Jau, Ch. de Jau, Cases-de-Pène, 66600 Rivesaltes; tel. 68 54 51 67 ☎ Daily 9.00–19.00. Closed Sat., Sun. out of season
➤ GFA du Ch. de Jau.

CHATEAU DE JAU★★

▪ 9ha 3600 4 D

Colour somewhere between topaz and amber. Thick and fat, with aromas evoking cooked fruits–cherry and prune in particular. ✔ Côtes du Roussillon Rouge, Muscat de Rivesaltes, Banyuls Rouge.
➤ Diffusion des Dom. de Jau, Ch. de Jau, Cases de Pène, 66600 Rivesaltes; tel. 68 54 51 67 ☎ Daily 9.00–19.00. Closed Sat., Sun. out of season.

LACROIX *Cuvée Valérie*★★

☐ 4ha 18480 4 D ▪ ↓

Golden amber colour. Bouquet of garrigue honey, dried fruit and nuts. Very persistent in the mouth. (1975) ✔ Côtes du Roussillon, Rouge and Rosé, Muscat de Rivesaltes.
➤ Pierre Lacroix, 17 Av. de la Méditerranée, 66670 Bages; tel. 68 21 72 46 ☎ No visitors.

COOPERATIVE DE MONTNER★

▪ 16ha 15000 3 D ▪ ↓

Mahogany, tile-red colour. Nose of cooked fruits and old wood. Syrupy taste and cocoa aroma dominant on the palate. (1977) ✔ Muscat de Rivesaltes, Rivesaltes Doré, Côtes du Roussillon-Villages Rouge.
➤ Coop. de Montner, Montner, 66720 Latour-de-France; tel. 68 29 11 91 ☎ By appt.

NOETINGER *Mas Palegry*★★

▪ 4 D ▪ ↓

Deep mahogany colour and intense bouquet of cooked prunes and cocoa, which is rather *raci*. Thick and long on the palate, giving off candied cherry and chocolate aromas. (1977) ✔ Côtes de Roussillon Mas Palegry Rouge and Rosé, Muscat de Rivesaltes, Rivesaltes Mas Palegry.
➤ Charles Noetinger, Mas Palegry, Route d'Elné, 66000 Perpignan; tel. 68 54 08 79 ☎ By appt.

CHATEAU DE NOUVELLES *Rancio*★

▪ 13ha 24000 4 D ◑ ↓

Syrupy, thick, fat and long, with nose of roasting and chocolate, and aroma of plum brandy. (1978)
➤ Robert Daurat-Fort, Ch. de Nouvelles, 11350 Tuchan; tel. 68 45 40 03 ☎ By appt.

CAVE COOPERATIVE DE LA PALME★★

☐ 240ha 60000 ③ Ⅾ ⓘ ↓

Golden amber colour. Thick and syrupy. Aroma of dried fruit before taking shape on the palate, where dried fig is predominant. (1981) ✔ Muscat de Rivesaltes, Fitou Rouge, Corbières Rouge.
✚ Cave Coop. de la Palme, 11480 La Palme; tel. 68 48 15 17 ☎ By appt.

CAVE COOPERATIVE DE PAZIOLS
Grenache★★

■ 70ha 50000 ③ Ⅾ ⓘ ↓

Both round and well constructed, with a nose of red fruits (cherry) and an aroma on the palate with a hint of vanilla.
✚ Cave Coop. de Paziols, Paziols, 11350 Tuchan; tel. 68 45 40 56 ☎ By appt.

CAVE COOPERATIVE DE PAZIOLS★★

☐ 75ha 50000 ③ Ⅾ ⓘ ↓

Gilded colour and scent reminiscent of honey and beeswax. On the palate, pleasant, round, thick and long.
✚ Cave Coop. de Paziols, Paziols, 11350 Tuchan: tel. 68 45 40 56 ☎ By appt.

GRENACHE NOIR PEZILLA★★

■ 70ha 50000 ② Ⅾ ⓘ ↓

Ruby coloured with tile-red hints. Highly developed bouquet dominated first by red fruit smells, then by coffee. On the palate, cocoa aromas emerge along with the impression of slipperiness and considerable persistence.
✚ Cave Coop. de Pézilla, 66370 Pézilla-la-Rivière; tel. 68 92 00 09 ☎ By appt.

CAVE COOPERATIVE DE POLLESTRES *Vieux Rivesaltes*★★★

☐ ④ Ⅾ ◑ ↓

Amber colour bordering on rust. Scent of honey and candied bitter orange. Long and thick on the palate, with hints of resin. Not without nobility. (1975) ✔ Muscat de Rivesaltes.
✚ SCV. de Pollestres, 66300 Pollestres; tel. 68 54 22 86 ☎ Mon.–Fri. 8.00–12.00/14.00–18.00.

MAS RANCOURE★

■ 5ha 5000 ③ Ⅾ ⓘ ◑ ↓

Light tile-red. Strawberry distinctly predominent in the cooked-fruit aroma. On the palate, syrupy with good persistence. (1980)
✚ M. Pardineille, Mas Rancoure, 66740 St-Génis-des-Fontaines; tel. 68 89 03 69 ☎ By appt.

CHATEAU DE REY★★

■ 25ha 75000 ③ Ⅾ ◑ ↓

Brick-red, mahogany colour. Complex and intense bouquet that conjures up baked cherry and cocoa. Very long on the palate, with mild tannin and hints of a prune aroma. (1975) ✔ Côtes de Roussillon Rouge, Muscat de Rivesaltes, Vin de Pays Cabernet Sauvignon Rouge.
✚ Mme Georges Sisqueille, BP 2, 66140 Canet-en-Roussillon; tel. 68 80 20 44 ☎ Mon.–Sat. 8.00–12.00/14.00–18.00.

SICA DES VINS DU ROUSSILLON
Byzans★

150ha 360000 ④ Ⅾ ↓

Attractive amber-gold colour. Pleasantly mellow and balanced. Its dried-fruit aroma is not, however, as intense as that of the Muscat by the same producer.
✚ SICA des Vins du Roussillon, Route des Crètes, 66650 Banyuls-sur-Mer; tel. 68 88 31 59 ☎ No visitors ✚ SIVIR.

CAVE COOPERATIVE DE SAINT-ANDRE *Vieux Foudre*★

■ 211ha 18000 ⑤ Ⅾ ⓘ ↓

Soft amber colour and an open scent suggestive of almonds and dried fruits. Sweet and honeyed on the palate. (1968) ✔ Vin de Pays Rouge, Côtes du Roussillon Rouge and Blanc Sec, Muscat de Rivesaltes.
✚ Cave Coop. de St-André, Rue du Stade, 66690 St-André; tel. 68 89 03 03 ☎ By appt.

DOMAINE SAINT-LUC★★

■ 12ha 5000 ③ Ⅾ ⓘ ↓

Maghogany colour. Fairly thick, smooth and harmonious. Nose of small, cooked fruits (strawberry and cherry in particular), and palate with aroma of cocoa.
✚ Luc Talut, Dom. St-Luc, Passa-Llauro-Tordères, 66300 Thuir; tel. 68 38 80 38 ☎ Daily 7.00–12.00/14.00–18.00.

SAINT-VINCENT-TRADITION★★★

■ 15ha 36000 ④ Ⅾ ⓘ ↓

Crimson colour with touches of brick-red. Intense and elegant aroma evoking overripe, cooked fruits. Finish reveals thick tannin, giving a strong structure, while the bouquet (of alcohol, fruit and cocoa) is very long. (1980)
✚ Vignerons de St-Vincent, BP 22, 66310 Estagel; tel. 68 29 00 94 ☎ By appt.

DOMAINE SAINTE HELENE★

■ 8ha 5000 ③ Ⅾ ◑ ↓

Brick-red, mahogany colour. Nose suggestive of cooked fruits, with hint of cocoa. Fairly thick on the palate and leaves a persistent aroma. ✔ Muscat de Rivesaltes, Côtes du Roussillon Rouge.
✚ André Cavaillé, 10 Rue du Moulin, Cassarya, 66690 Sorède; tel. 68 89 20 15 ☎ Mon.–Sat. 9.00–19.00.

COOPERATIVE DES VINS FINS DE SALSES★★

■ 200ha 720000 ④ Ⅾ ◑ ↓

Beneath the tile-red colour, a scent combining dried fruit and roasting. Well balanced and syrupy on the palate. (1977) ✔ Côtes du Roussillon Rouge and Blanc Sec, Vin de Pays Catalan Rouge and Rosé.
✚ Cave Coop. des Vins Fins de Salses, Salses, 66600 Rivesaltes; tel. 68 38 62 08 ☎ Mon.–Sat. 8.00–12.00/14.00–18.00.

DOMAINE SARDA-MALET
20 Ans d'Age★★

☐ 39ha 240000 [5] [D] [≣] [⌄]

Amber coloured with lovely green reflections. Has a great deal of personality. Intense bouquet reminiscent of nuts and dried fruits. Becomes thick and mellow on the palate, with a slight rancio aroma, which will either delight or surprise. ✔ Côtes du Roussillon Rouge and Blanc Sec, Vin de Pays des Côtes Catalanes Blanc. ↬ *MM*. Sarda-Malet, 134 Av. Victor Dalbiez, 66000 Perpignan; tel. 68 54 59 95 ☎ By appt.

CELLIERS DU TATE-VIN★

■ 9000 [5] [D] [⊕] [⌄]

Fine and elegant with a bouquet of red-fruit jam. Thick on the palate, and has hints of cherries in brandy. (1972) ↬ Ets Limouzy Celliers Tate-Vin, Ancienne Route d'Espagne 66000 Perpignan; tel. 68 85 13 04 ☎ Daily 8.00–12.00/14.00–18.00.

TERRASSOUS *Vieux Rivesaltes*★★

☐ [4] [D] [⊕] [⌄]

Golden amber colour. Nose of dried fruit and roasting precede the aroma of honey and old barrels. (1974) ↬ SCV Les Vignerons de Terrats, BP 32, 66300 Terrats; tel. 68 53 02 50 ☎ Mon.–Sat. 8.00–12.00/14.00–18.00.

TORRE DEL FAR★★

■ 125ha 330000 [4] [D] [⊕] [⌄]

Distinguished by an intense bouquet that moves from red berries to cherry and blackcurrant, and finishes well with an aroma of strawberries. (1982) ✔ Côtes du Roussillon Rouge and Rosé, Côtes du Roussillon-Villages Rouge, Muscat de Rivesaltes. ↬ Maitres Vign. de Tautavel, 24 Route de Vingrau, 66720 Tautavel; tel. 68 29 12 03 ☎ By appt.

COOPERATIVE DE TROUILLAS
Rancio★★

■ 80ha 96000 [3] [D] [⊕] [⌄]

It was probably in Trouillas that the writer and doctor Arnau de Vilanova 'invented' the natural sweet wine. This wine can therefore lay claim to a long heritage. (1978) ✔ Muscat de Rivesaltes, Rivesaltes Doré, Côtes Rouge and Blanc Sec. du Roussillon. ↬ Coop. de Trouilles, 1 Ave du Mas Deus, 66300 Thuir; tel. 68 53 47 08 ☎ Mon.–Sat. 8.00–12.00/14.00–18.00.

CHATEAU VALMYA *Vieux Sélection*★★

■ 20ha 65000 [3] [D] [≣] [⌄]

Tannic, fat and balanced. (1980) ✔ Muscat de Rivesaltes Cachet d'Or, Côtes du Roussillon Valmya Rouge, Rosé and Blanc. ↬ Vit. Réunis de Thuir, BP 208, 66002 Perpignan Cedex; tel. 68 85 06 07 ☎ By appt ↬ *M*. Peix.

CHATEAU DE VESPEILLE
Rivesaltes Rosé★★

☑ 10ha 8400 [3] [D] [≣] [⌄]

Distinguished more by its label than by its peony-red colour. Thick, mellow and well balanced, offering a succession of persistent gooseberry, grenadine and strawberry aromas. (1983) ↬ Les Vignerons de Rivesaltes, 2 Rue de la Roussillonaise, 66600 Rivesaltes; tel. 68 64 06 63 ☎ Mon.–Sat. 9.00–12.00/14.00–18.00.

COOPERATIVE PILOTE DE VILLENEUVE *Vieux Grenache Rancio*★★

■ 20ha 36000 [4] [D] [⊕] [⌄]

Highly characteristic of a typical *rancio*. Nose evokes roasting and grilled almonds. Well balanced with an aroma of smoked vanilla in the mouth. (1977) ↬ Cave Villeneuve-les-Corbières, Villeneuve-les-Corbières, 11360 Durban-Corbières; tel. 68 45 91 59 ☎ Daily 8.15–12.00/14.00–18.00.

COOPERATIVE DE VINGRAU★★

■ 97ha 240000 [3] [D] [≣] [⊕] [⌄]

Strong ruby, tile-red colour. Nose evokes smell of cooked, small red fruits. On the palate, fat, full bodied and highly persistent, with hints of blackcurrant and prune. (1977) ↬ Coop. de Vingrau, 3 Rue Maréchal-Joffre, Vingrau, 66600 Rivesaltes; tel. 68 29 40 41 ☎ By appt. Closed Oct.

Maury

This appellation area (2000 hectares) covers the commune of Maury to the north of the river Agly, and parts of the neighbouring communes. The landscape is one of steep hills covered with crumbling schistous rock; only 40000 hectolitres of wine are produced, all from the Grenache Noir. Vinification often involves a long maceration, and the ageing process improves the wine to produce some remarkable blends.

Maury is a pale pomegranate colour when young, but with age the wine acquires a mahogany tint; its bouquet, which starts off very aromatic, with a scent of red berries develops notes of cocoa, cooked fruit or coffee. These wines may be enjoyed as an aperitif or with dessert, and make a good accompaniment to any sweet and spicy dish.

MAS AMIEL★★

■   128.09 ha   110000   **5** **D** ☙ ⬇

Lustrous mahogany-bronze. Intense nose of cocoa and spices. Fat, full and very long on the palate, with dashes of prune and rancio. (1979)
☙ Charles Dupuis, Dom. du Mas Amiel, 66460 Maury; tel. 68 59 15 99 ☥ By appt.

JEAN-LOUIS LAFAGE *Prestige*★★

■   30 ha   800   **3** **D** ▮ ☙ ⬇

Mahogany colour clothing fragrances of woody rancio. Supple and thick on the palate, with dash of caramel. (1973)
☙ Jean-Louis Lafage. Av. Jean-Jaurès, 66460 Maury; tel. 68 59 12 66 ☥ By appt.

VIGNERONS DE MAURY *Rancio*★

■   200000   **4** **D** ▮ ⬇

Mahogany shaded with tile-red. Nose is met with aromas of roasting and prunes. Generous and full on the palate, with a predominant aroma of cocoa.
☙ SCV les Vignerons de Maury, 66640 Maury; tel. 67 59 00 95 ☥ Mon.–Fri. 8.00–12.00/14.00–18.00.

VIGNERONS DE MAURY
Vieille Réserve★★

■   20 ha   50000   **4** **D** ▮ ⬇

Powerful, pure-bred bouquet and scent of coffee. Long, warm and balanced on the palate. Rich in aromas containing old leather, coffee and prune. (1977) ✔ Maury Ans d'Age, Maury Rancio 3 Ans, Maury Doré.
☙ SCV les Vignerons de Maury, 66460 Maury; tel. 68 59 00 95 ☥ Mon.–Fri. 8.00–12.00/14.00–18.00.

VIGNERONS DE MAURY
6 Ans d'Age★★

■   500000   **3** **D** ▮ ⬇

Tile-red, ruby colour. Nose conjures up cherry, blackcurrant and cocoa. Fat and elegant on the palate, creating an impression of youth and development.
☙ SCV les Vignerons de Maury, 66460 Maury; tel. 68 59 00 95 ☥ Mon.–Fri. 8.00–12.00/14.00–18.00.

Muscat de Rivesaltes

The appellation covers wine from 100 per cent Muscat vines grown in Rivesaltes, Maury or Banyuls. The AOC area is about 5000 hectares and produces 100000 hectolitres of wine per year. Two types of Muscat are allowed: the Muscat à Petits Grains and Muscat d'Alexandrie. The former, also known as Muscat Blanc or Muscat de Rivesaltes, is an early-ripening variety and likes a cool climate and preferably lime-rich soil. The latter, also called Muscat Romain, is a later variety which is highly resistant to drought.

The grapes are made into wine either by a direct pressing or by maceration. The wine has then to be kept in an oxygen-free atmosphere to conserve the primary aromas, which would otherwise spoil due to oxidation.

These are sweet wines, with a minimum sugar content of 100 g/l. They are best drunk young at a temperature of 9–10°C and make an excellent pudding wine. Particularly good with lemon, apple or strawberry tart, sorbet, ice cream, fruit or tourrons a Spanish nougat-and-marzipan dessert.

ETIENNE AMOUREUX★★

□   5 ha   12000   **3** **D** ▮ ⬇

Pale golden colour succeeded by a fine, open, floral nose with a tiny hint of lemon. Sweet freshness and good balance are revealed in the mouth. (1982) ✔ Côtes du Roussillon Rouge, Rivesaltes.
☙ Etienne Amoureux, 15 Av. de Passa, Tresserre 66300 Thuir; tel. 68 38 80 35 ☥ Mon.–Sat. 9.00–12.00/14.00–19.00.

APHRODIS★★

□   150 ha   320000   **4** ▮ ⬇

Golden colour. Intense to the nose and thick on the palate. (1983)
☙ SICA des Vins du Roussillon, Route des Crêtes, 66650 Banyuls-sur-Mer; tel. 68 88 31 59 ☥ Daily 9.00–12.00/14.00–18.00.

LES VIGNERONS DE BAIXAS
Dom Brial★★

□   25 ha   150000   **4** **D** ▮ ⬇

The nose gives off strong scents of flowers and fresh grapes. On the palate, an aroma of currants coupled with good, smooth balance, leading up to a pleasant finish. (1983) ✔ Rivesaltes Dom. Brial, Côtes du Roussillon-Villages Dom. Brial, Rivesaltes Vieille Réserve, Côtes du Roussillon Rouge.
☙ SCV les Vign. de Baïxas, 66390 Baïxas; tel. 68 64 22 37 ☥ Mon.–Sat. 8.00–12.00/14.00–18.00.

DOMAINE DE BELLEVISTE★

□   2 ha   7200   **4** **D** ▮ ⬇

Thick and syrupy with a fruity aroma. (1983) ✔ Côtes du Roussillon Rougé, Rosé and Blanc, Rivesaltes.

➥ P. Baillon et Fils, Dom. de Belleviste, Came-las, 66300 Thuir; tel. 68 53 50 55 ⟑ Daily.

CHATEAU DE CAP DE FOUSTE★★

| ☐ | 6.6ha | 20000 | 🔳 🅳 🔳 ↓ |

Intense and characteristic bouquet presenting succession of flower and raisin scents. Balanced smoothly and well on the palate, but has strong aroma of grapes' mark. (1983) ✔ Côtes du Roussillon Rouge.

➥ Caisses de Mutual. Agr. 30 Rue Bretonneau, Villeneuve-de-la-Raho, 66020 Perpignan; tel. 68 50 45 28 ⟑ Mon.–Fri.

CAZES★★★

| ☐ | 20ha | 54000 | 🔳 🅳 🔳 ↓ |

Pale golden colour. Intense bouquet of flowers and green lemon, which on the palate gives way to aroma of raisins. Thick, syrupy savour emerges as lovely, harmonious finish. Very great wine. (1983) ✔ Côtes du Roussillon-Villages Rouge, Côtes du Roussillon Rouge, Rosé and Blanc, Rivesaltes.

➥ MM. Cazes Frères, 4 Rue Francisco- Ferrer, 66600 Rivesaltes; tel. 68 64 08 26 ⟑ Mon.–Sat. 08.00–12.00/14.00–18.00.

COLL-ESCLUSE★★

| ☐ | 32ha | 60000 | 🔳 🅳 ⑪ ↓ |

Beautiful old-gold colour gives this wine persona-lity, as does its powerful, highly characteristic nose, which has hints of lemon liqueur. On the palate it shows length and good, smooth balance, with an aroma of grapes roasted by the sun. (1983) ✔ Rivesaltes Tradition 1979, Rivesaltes Prestige 1969, Rivesaltes Ambré 1978, Muscat Moelleux 1983.

➥ M. Coll-Escluse, 1Rue Cuvier, 66000 Perpig-nan; tel. 68 54 58 69 ⟑ Daily 9.00–12.00/14.00–19.00.

CORDON DE LA VIGUERIE★★★

| ☐ | 13ha | 18000 | 🔳 🅳 🔳 ↓ |

Band-style label, linking discretion with ele-gance. Very beautiful wine. Powerful flower and lemon aromas, combined with sumptuously smooth balance in the mouth. (1983) ✔ Côtes du Roussillon Rouge, Rivesaltes Tuilé, Rivesaltes Blanc.

➥ Bernard Marie, 21 Rue Alexis-Alquier, 66000 Perpignan; tel. 68 56 90 66 ⟑ No visitors.

CHATEAU ESPARROU★

| ☐ | 7ha | 24000 | 🔳 🅳 🔳 ↓ |

Fairly syrupy and golden in colour, with a floral nose. (1983) ✔ Rivesaltes Ambré, Côtes du Roussillon Rouge.

➥ Ch. Esparrou, BP 15, 66140 Canet-en-Roussil-lon; tel. 68 80 30 93 ⟑ Mon.–Fri. Closed Christ-mas fortnight.

FOURQUES★★

| ☐ | 7ha | | 🔳 🅳 🔳 ↓ |

This wine has a golden colour and a delicate nose with flowery hints. On the palate it is well balanced and thick with a long-lasting aroma.

➥ Augustin Coronat, 20 Chemin Lamartine, 66430 Bompas; tel. 68 63 26 09 ⟑ By appt.

GALERA★★

| ☐ | 40ha | 96000 | 🔳 🅳 🔳 ↓ |

Golden colour. Intense perfumes of flowers and fresh grapes on the nose. On the palate, pleasant sensation of a well-balanced liqueur. (1983) ✔ Rivesaltes Rouge Rancio, Rivesaltes Blanc, Corbières Blanc and Corbières Rouge.

➥ Cave Coop. de Tuchan, 11350 Tuchan; tel. 68 45 40 13 ⟑ Mon.–Fri. 08.00–12.00/14.00–18.00.

CHATEAU DE JAU★★

| ☐ | 8ha | 3400 | 🔳 🅳 🔳 ↓ |

Magnificent shining gold. Quite intense nose mingling scents of flowers and freshly pressed grapes. Sumptuous, syrupy and pleasantly per-sistent on the palate with powerful aromas. (1983) ✔ Côtes du Roussillon Rouge, Rivesaltes, Banyuls.

➥ Diff. des Dom. de Jau, Ch. de Jau Cases-de-Pène, 66600 Rivesaltes; tel. 68 54 51 67 ⟑ Daily 9.00–19.00. Closed Sat., Sun. out of season.

SAN JOUAN★

| ☐ | 27ha | 60000 | 🔳 🅳 🔳 ↓ |

Sun coloured. Very floral nose. Well balanced, smooth and persistent in the mouth. (1983) ✔ Côtes du Roussillon, Rouge Rivesaltes.

➥ Cave St Jean Lasseille, St-Jean-Lasseille, 66300 Thuir; tel. 68 21 72 06 ⟑ Mon.–Sat. 8.00–12.00/14.00–18.00.

LES VIGNERONS DE MAURY★★

| ☐ | 45ha | 20000 | 🔳 🅳 ↓ |

Straw-yellow, honey and old-gold colour, con-ceals a subtle, floral nose reminiscent of candied lemon. The wine seems to melt on the palate, and becomes syrupy, pleasant and very persistent. (1983) ✔ Maury, Muscat de Rivesaltes, Côtes du Roussillon-Villages Rouge, Côtes duRoussillon Rouge.

➥ SCV les Vign. de Maury, 66460 Maury; tel. 68 59 00 95 ⟑ Mon.–Fri. 8.00–12.00/14.00–18.00.

COOPERATIVE DE MONTNER★★

| ☐ | 21ha | 15000 | 🔳 🅳 🔳 ↓ |

Classic golden colour. Initially gives off subtle floral fragrances before developing fruitier aro-mas on the palate, where it proves fairly thick and mellow. (1983) ✔ Rivesaltes Rouge and Blanc, Côtes du Roussillon-Villages Rouge.

➥ Coop. de Montner, Montner, 66720 Latour de France; tel. 68 29 11 91 ⟑ By appt.

ANDRE PARCE★★

| ☐ | 2ha | 12000 | 🔳 🅳 🔳 ↓ |

Clear golden colour and floral nose with traces of peach create a spring-time air. Thick, well balanced and long in the mouth, with an aroma of raisins. (1983) ✔ Côtes du Roussillon Rouge and Blanc Sec, Rivesaltes.

➥ André Parcé, 6 Rue Jean-Jaurès, 66670 Bages; tel. 68 21 80 45 ⟑ Daily 10.00–12.00/16.00–20.30.

DOMAINE DE LA ROUREDE★★

| ☐ | 4ha | 38400 | 🔳 🅳 🔳 ↓ |

Beneath the old gold colour a wine with a powerful nose, which evokes the mark of the grapes. Balanced and very thick on the palate,

with a highly individual aroma of raisins. (1983)
✔ Rivesaltes.
⌂ Jean-Luc Pujol, Dom. de la Rourède, Four-
ques, 66300 Thuir; tel. 68 38 84 44 ⌶ By appt.

LA ROUSSILLONNAISE★★

☐		160ha	420000	**4** **D** **⊟** **↓**

Intense; floral, highly Muscatel nose and dashes
of rose and lemon flower. Syrupy and powerful
on the palate, with predominant aroma of raisins.
(1983)
⌂ Les Vign. de Rivesaltes, 2 Rue de la Roussillonnaise, 66600 Rivesaltes; tel. 68 64 06 63
⌶ Mon.–Sat. 9.00–12.00/14.00–18.00.

DOMAINE SAINTE-HELENE★★

☐		8ha	2400	**3** **D** **⊟** **↓**

Elegant yet intense nose. Persistent aromas that
conjure up the taste of fresh grapes and roses in
the mouth. (1983) ✔ Côtes du Roussillon Rouge,
Rivesaltes.
⌂ André Cavaillé, 10 Rue du Moulin, Cassanya,
66690 Sorède; tel. 68 89 20 15 ⌶ Daily 9.00–
12.00/14.00–19.00.

COOPERATIVE DES VINS FINS DE SALSES★★

☐		170ha	360000	**4** **D** **⊟** **↓**

Light golden colour shot through with green
reflections. Subtle floral nose. Becomes harmonious, long and very aromatic on the palate, with
a dash of lemon. (1984) ✔ Rivesaltes Vieillis en
Fûts de Chêne, Côtes du Roussillon-Villages
Rouge.
⌂ Coop. des Vins Fins de Salses, Salses, 66600
Rivesaltes; tel. 68 38 62 08 ⌶ Mon.–Sat. 8.00–
12.00/14.00–18.00.

MAITRES VIGNERONS DE TAUTAVEL★★

☐		50ha	132000	**4** **D** **⊟** **↓**

Balanced, woody, very fine, syrupy and persistent. Flower and lemon aromas enhanced with a
touch of peppermint. (1983) ✔ Côtes du Roussillon Rouge, Rivesaltes, Côtes du Roussillon-Villages Rouge.
⌂ Maitres Vign. de Tautavel, 24 Route de
Vingrau, 66720 Tautavel; tel. 68 29 12 03 ⌶ Daily
9.00–12.00/14.00–18.00.

TERRASOUS★

☐		40ha	132000	**3** **D** **⊟** **↓**

Golden, with slight sheen and powerful nose of
flowers and fruit. Syrupy in the mouth, with a
dash of honey and raisins. (1983)
⌂ SCV les Vignerons de Terrats, BP 32, 66300
Terrats; tel. 68 53 02 50 ⌶ Mon.–Fri. 8.00–12.00/
14.00–18.00.

COOPERATIVE DE VINGRAU★★

☐		58ha	120000	**4** **D** **⊟** **↓**

Hints of fig evident in a rather surprising wine,
but far fewer than in the vineyard where it is
produced. ✔ Rivesaltes Rouge and Blanc, Côtes
du Roussillon-Villages.
⌂ Coop. de Vingrau, 3 Rue Maréchal-Joffre,
Vingrau, 66600 Rivesaltes; tel. 68 29 40 41 ⌶ By
appt.

Muscat de Frontignan, Muscat de Mireval

Sweet, fruity, round wines from a
region stretching from Sète towards
Montpellier, along the shore of the
coastal lake Vic. The soil is of Jurassic
origins, predominantly limestone with
ancient alluvium and pebbles. The
only grape variety planted is Muscat à
Petit Grains.

The 'mutage' takes place early on
in the vinification because the wine
must have a minimum of 125 grams of
sugar per litre. Under the Frontignan
appellation, wines may also be made
by adding eau-de-vie to the must
before fermentation, producing wine
with an even higher sugar content
(185 g/l). In some cases, Muscat wine
is aged in very old casks which permit
a slight oxidation of the wine, giving it
a pronounced flavour of raisins.

COOPERATIVE DE FRONTIGNAN★

☐		670ha	1700000	**4** **⊟** **◑** **↓**

Old-gold colour followed by vanilla aromas with
hints of dried fruits. On the palate it is syrupy
with an aromatic finish evoking lemon liqueur.
(1983) ✔ Muscat de Frontignan Vin de Liqueur.
⌂ Coop. de Frontignan, 14 Av. du Muscat, 34110
Frontignan; tel. 67 48 12 26 ⌶ Mon.–Fri. 8.00–
12.00/13.30–17.30.

CHATEAU LA PEYRADE★

☐		25ha	60000	**4** **D** **⊟** **↓**

Lovely golden colour. Subtle nose with hints of
flowers and candied orange. On the palate the
aromas change to *passerillé* grapes creating a
vigorous, syrupy impression.
⌂ Yves Pastourel et Fils, Ch. de la Peyrade, 34110
Frontignan; tel. 67 48 61 10 ⌶ No visitors.

CAVE RABELAIS★

☐		150ha	25000	**4** **D** **⊟** **↓**

Light golden colour. Retains some subtle fragrances with hints of lemon and fresh grape for
the nose. On the palate these give way to aromas,
which are reminiscent of overripe grapes.
⌂ Cave Coop. Rabelais, 112 Route Nationale,
34840 Mireval; tel. 67 78 15 79 ⌶ Mon.–Fri. 8.00–
12.00/14.00–18.00. Closed May.

Muscat de Beaumes-de-Venise

To the north of Carpentras, beneath
the imposing Dentelles de Montmirail, the countryside takes on the
appearance of greyish limestone and
red marl. In some places the soil is
composed of sand, marl, and sandstone; elsewhere the soils are the result of violent geological shifts during
the Triassic and Jurassic Ages. The
single grape variety planted is the

Muscat à Petits Grains, but in some areas one can see mutant red or pink grapes. The wines, which have a minimum sugar of 110g/l, are aromatic, fruity and refined, and are perfect as an aperitif or with certain types of cheese.

CAVE COOPERATIVE BEAUMES-DE-VENISE**

☐	240ha 800000	**3** **D** ■ ↓	

Classic golden colour. Fine and subtle nose as the scent of freshly pressed grapes is aroused. On the palate, well balanced with persistent lemon aromas.
↜ Cave Coop. Beaumes-de-Venise, 84190 Beaumes-de-Venise; tel. 90 62 94 45 ⵟ By appt.

DOMAINE DE DURBAN**

☐	10.5ha 30000	**4** **D**

The colour is quite light for this type of wine. Subtle bouquet. Very pleasant to the nose and on the palate, where it gives evidence of good balance, thickness and very fruity, persistent aromas.
↜ *MM.* Leydier et Fils, Dom. de Durban, 84190 Beaumes-de-Venise; tel. 90 62 94 26 ⵟ By appt.

Muscat de Lunel

The countryside around Lunel is the classic Mediterranean landscape of red clay soils covered with pebbles, where vines are planted at the top of the hills. Only the Muscat à Petits Grains is used for this sweet wine, which must have a sugar content of at least 125g/l.

COOPERATIVE DE LUNEL*

☐	211ha 840000	**4** **D** ■ ↓

Delicate old-gold colour and intensely expressive nose of very floral scents, including rose and geranium. Becomes quite vigorous in the mouth.
↜ Coop. de Lunel, Vérargues, 34400 Lunel; tel. 71 86 00 09 ⵟ Mon.–Fri. 8.00–12.00/14.00–18.00.

Muscat de St-Jean-de-Minervois

The vineyards perch some 200 metres above sea level, the vines interwoven with a classic scrubland landscape. The harvest here is about three weeks later than the other Muscat appellations. There are a few vines on primary schistous soils, but most are planted on limestone, where the redness of the clay sometimes shows through. Once again, the only permitted grape variety is the Muscat à Petits Grains, and the minimum sugar content of the wine is set at 125g/l. The wines are very aromatic with plenty of finesse and a distinctive floral note.

DOMAINE DE BARROUBIO**

☐	8ha 18000	**4** **D** ■

Discreet, pale-gold colour precedes an intense and subtle nose suggestive of lemon liqueur and rose with a dash of mint. Slightly exotic impression created on the palate by passion-fruit aromas. Worth noting the good balance and rather sumptuous, syrupy quality. (1983) ✔ Minervois, Rouge and Rosé.
↜ Jean Miquel, Dom. de Barroubio, St-Jean-de-Minervois, 34360 St-Chinian; tel. 67 38 20 42 ⵟ By appt.

LE PARDEILLAN**

☐	80ha 180000	**4** **D** ■ ↓

Golden colour followed by an intense, complex nose that conjures up fresh grapes, lemon and rose. These are replaced by tropical fruit aromas on the palate, and the whole has good balance and persistence. ✔ Minervois Coop. St-Jean Rouge.
↜ Coop. St-Jean-de-Minervois, St-Jean-de-Minervois, 34360 St-Chinian; tel. 67 38 03 24 ⵟ By appt.

Rasteau

The vineyards cover two very different areas in the far north of the Vaucluse department: to the north, soils of sand, marl, and stones, and to the south, terraces of very old (Quaternary) Rhône alluvium with round pebbles. Throughout, only the Grenache (Noir, Blanc, or Gris) is planted.

DOMAINE LA SOUMADE

■	4ha 9000	**4** **D** ■ ↓

Quite dark mahogany, tile-red colour. Intense and highly developed nose evoking dried fruits combined with old alcohol and dead leaves. Good balance emerges on the palate, in which cooked fruits predominate.
↜ André Roméro, Dom. de la Soumade, Rasteau, 84110 Maison-la-Romaine; tel. 90 46 11 26 ⵟ Daily 8.00–12.00/14.00–20.00.

VINS DE LIQUEUR

THIS APPELLATION applies only to the fortified Pineau de Charentes wine produced in the Cognac region, famous for its liqueur brandy. The appellation area lies to the north of Aquitaine and takes the form of a vast undulating slope that, from an altitude of 180 m, gradually descends westwards towards the Atlantic. The gentle relief becomes progressively less pronounced as it approaches the coast. The maritime climate, with its remarkable amount of sunshine and a fairly constant temperature, allows for a slow but sure ripening of the grapes.

Pineau des Charentes

The vines cover some 80000 hectares planted on predominantly limestone slopes on both sides of the Charente river. Most of the wine produced here is destined to be made into cognac. The rest is fortified by blending with cognac to make a versatile sweet wine.

According to legend, it was chance that led a sixteenth-century winemaker to pour some grape must into a cask which still contained cognac. Seeing that the wine in the barrel was not fermenting, he put it to the back of the store and forgot all about it. A few years later when he came to empty the cask, he discovered a clear, delicate liquid that had a sweet and fruity flavour – and Pineau des Charentes was born. This 'blend' subsequently spread to other estates and is still made in the same traditional way, after each harvest. For a long time the wine remained a local speciality, but it has now become more widely known throughout France and has even acquired a small export market.

White Pineau des Charentes is made primarily from the Ugni Blanc, Colombard, Montils and Sémillon grape types; the rosé uses such red varieties as Cabernet-Franc, Cabernet-Sauvignon and Merlot. The vines have to be short pruned, grown without nitrate fertilizers, and limited to a yield of 50 hectolitres per hectare. Under these conditions the grapes achieve a good degree of ripeness. The must should have a potential alcohol content of 10 per cent.

The 'mutage' – the addition of cognac to the must – is done with 'rancio' cognac previously aged in oak casks. The blend which results has an overall alcoholic strength of 16–22 per cent, and is then aged in oak casks for at least a year, when it is tasted and approved for general sale. In accordance with the Pineau de Charentes AOC regulations, the wine must be bottled in the region of production, and each bottle must carry the stamp or seal of the producers' Syndicat.

As with cognac, the vintage of Pineau des Charentes is not indicated on the label. However, there may be a more general mention of the age. The term 'Vieux Pineau' means that the wine is over five years old, has been aged in small casks, and that its quality is endorsed by the tasting committee. In its final form, Pineau des Charentes usually has an alcoholic strength, stated on the label, of 17–18 per cent, and contains between 125–150 grams per litre of residual sugar. The rosés are in general sweeter and fruitier, the whites drier and more firmly flavoured. Average annual production during the last ten years has exceeded 7500 hectolitres, two-thirds being white. 1982 had the highest yields, with 120000 hectolitres.

With its enchanting bouquet and wonderful sweetness, deceptively concealing the high alcohol level, Pineau des Charentes may be drunk as young as two years after the harvest. At this time its fruity aromas are fully developed – even more so with the rosé than the white. However, with age it acquires the very distinctive 'rancio', sherry-like nose which makes it into a connoisseur's bottle. It is traditionally drunk as an aperitif or with pudding, although several gourmets have discovered that its roundness lends itself remarkably well to foie gras or to Roquefort, and that its sweetness enhances the taste of certain fruits, in particular (Charentes) melon and strawberries. It can also be used in cooking, for example in mousclades and other regional dishes, and it gives a delicious flavour to white meat in sauce.

DOMAINE DE BEAUGRENY★★

| □ | 16ha 15000 | 4 D ⦿ |

Honeyed scent; very fat and rich and displays exquisite delicacy on the palate.
↱ Jean Hillaireau, La Pinelle, Haimps, 17160 Matha; tel. 46 26 64 82 ℐ By appt.

CHATEAU DE BEAULON★★

| ◩ | 40ha 96000 | 5 D ⦿ |

Well-developed, highly coloured rosé Pineau des Charentes.
↱ Christian Thomas, Ch. de Beaulon, St-Dizant-du-Gua, 17240 St-Genis-de-Saintonge; tel. 46 49 96 13 ℐ By appt.

BERNARD BEGUET★★

| □ | 20ha 20000 | 4 D ⦿ |

Pleasant fragrance and creamy taste make a lovely wine. ✔ Pineau des Charentes Rosé, Vieux Pineau des Charentes Blanc.
↱ Bernard Beguet, Chenac-sur-Gironde, 17120 Cozes; tel. 46 90 64 84 ℐ By appt. Closed Sun.

DOMAINE DE CAILLERES★★★

| □ | 20ha 30000 | 4 D ⦿ |

Fifteen-year-old Pineau made from blend of white and rosé wines. Lovely amber colour, sumptuous, delicate perfume and magnificent taste, with perfect harmony and fullness.
✔ Pineau des Charentes Jeunes Blanc et Rouge, Cognac, Armagnac.
↱ SARL Briat-Savarin, Dom. des Chiots, 16130 St-Preuil-Ségonzac; tel. 45 81 95 87. ℐ By appt.

LE LOGIS DU COUDRET★★

| □ | 30ha 30000 | 4 D ⦿ |

Smooth and delicate. Still displaying scents of grapes which, along with the distinction of the cognac, makes an excellent blend, with its own particular delicate taste. ✔ Pineau des Charentes 2 à 3 Ans Rosé.
↱ Michel Baron, 16370 Cherves-de-Cognac; tel. 45 83 24 72 ℐ By appt.

FRANCOIS Ier★★★

| □ | 15ha 4000 | 5 D ⦿ |

Aged about 20 years. Magnificent bouquet and smooth taste, which are wrapped in beautiful harmony. ✔ Cognac, Pineau des Charentes Grande Tradition 3 à 5 Ans.
↱ Philippe Rivière, Les Gatinauds, Angeac, 16120 Châteauneuf; tel. 45 97 02 66 ℐ By appt.

ILLREA★

| ◩ | 500000 | 4 D ⦿ ↓ |

Typical Pineau from the Ile de Ré district. Good product that can be enjoyed while visiting the castle at Vauban. ✔ Pineau des Charentes Blanc.
↱ Coop. de l'Ile de Ré, 17580 Le Bois-Plage-en-Ré; tel. 46 09 23 09 ℐ By appt.

LE MAINE GIRAUD★★

| ◩ | 20ha 15000 | 4 D ⦿ |

Highly fragranced, with dominant scent of Cabernet; taste is full, fat and flowing. Very harmonious. ✔ Cognac.
↱ Jacques Durand, Le Maine Giraud, Champagne-Vigny, 16250 Blanzac; tel. 45 64 04 49 ℐ By appt.

MENARD★★

| ◩ | 40ha 18000 | 4 D ⦿ |

Characteristic fruity aroma. Bouquet from red Merlot grapes, mixed with scents of roses and reseda. ✔ Cognac Grande Champagne, Pineau des Charentes 3 Ans Rosé, Pineau des Charentes Très Vieux 10 Ans.
↱ MM. Ménard Frères, 16720 St-Même-des-Carrières; tel. 45 81 92 02 ℐ By appt. Closed Sat., Sun.

GERARD PAUTIER★★

| ◩ | 30ha 15000 | 4 D ⦿ |

Lovely rosé Pineau des Charentes whose colour is like ripe cherries. Bouquet has the scent of Merlot grapes and hint of Cabernet, giving it weight; deliciously fat and rich.
↱ Gérard Pautier, Veillard, Bourg-Charente, 16200 Jarnac; tel. 45 81 30 15 ℐ By appt.

UNICOGNAC★★

| □ | 17000 | 4 D ⦿ |

Beautifully coloured, lovely old Pineau, with smell and taste of honey mixed with woodsmoke, making good harmony.
↱ Coop. de Jonzac, Unicognac, 17500 Jonzac; tel. 46 48 10 99 ℐ Daily 8.00–12.00/14.00–18.00.

VIEUX LOGIS★★

| ◩ | 100000 | 4 D ⦿ |

Of moderate, but pretty, colour and fine fruit aromas. Fruity taste is well blended. Exquisitely soft. ✔ Pineau des Charentes.
↱ Ets Héraud, St-André-de-Lidon, 17260 Gemozac; tel. 46 94 28 01 ℐ Daily 9.00–12.00/14.00–18.00. Closed Sept.–June. ↱ Jacques Héraud.

VINS DE PAYS

VINS DE PAYS simply means wines of the region. This is underlined by the fact that all Vins de Pays are followed by the name of the region or commune. Thus, Vin de Pays du Gard will come from the Gard department and Vin de Pays des Côteaux du Pont du Gard from the Pont du Gard region within the same department. Today, more and more wine drinkers are recognizing the variety, enjoyment and value for money offered by these regional, or 'country', wines, which combine authentic local character with high standards of quality.

Vins de Pays form the base of the pyramid of French wine, supporting the more prestigious Vins Delimités de Qualité Supérieur (VDQS) and Appellations d'Origine Controlées (AOC). Even in this lowly position they are subject to the same rules and regulations, although to a less strict degree. Yet in a country where the majority of AOC wines have a style and character that has evolved over several generations, and which began to be classified fifty years ago, the Vins de Pays classification is relatively new. It first came into being officially in 1968 when a decree was passed by the Ministry of Agriculture authorizing certain Vins de Table to indicate the region of origin of the wine. This was designed to inform the consumer and to give him a guarantee of quality. It was also the first step in what was to become a very successful campaign to move French wine production away from Vin Ordinaire ('le gros rouge' or the common red), sold purely on its degree of alcohol, towards wines where character and taste played a part. In 1973, a further decree did away with the Vins d'Appellation d'Origine Simple (AOS), an earlier set of regulations designed to improve the anonymous Vins de Table, and fixed precisely the conditions to which a Vin de Pays must adhere in order to have the right to its own appellation. These rules are the same as for the AOC and VDQS wines, covering geographical identity, grape varieties, permitted yield per hectare, degree of alcohol and even level of sulphur dioxide and of volatile acidity. Finally, in 1979 these rules were refined in a further drive to increase quality. The aim throughout has been the same as for the commercially more important AOC and VDQS categories, namely that the consumer must be offered a bottle with a level of guarantees that will assure him as to the quality of the wine in the glass. The Vins de Pays regulations are supervised by the Office National Interprofessionel des Vins (ONIVIN).

In all, there are three basic types of Vins de Pays, corresponding to different geographical interpretations.

1 *Vins de Pays Régionaux* These may come from several departments, providing they correspond to an accepted style of wine, for example Vin de Pays d'Oc for the whole of the Languedoc-Roussillon; Vin de Pays du Jardin de la France for the wines from the Loire valley.

2 *Vins de Pays Départementaux* These must carry the name of the department where they are produced, for example Vin de Pays du Gard, Vin de Pays de l'Ardèche.

3 *Vins de Pays de Zone* These wines may state the name of the individual commune where they are produced, for example Vin de Pays du Val d'Orbieu (Aude), Vin de Pays des Côteaux de Peyriac (Hérault).

Vins de Pays

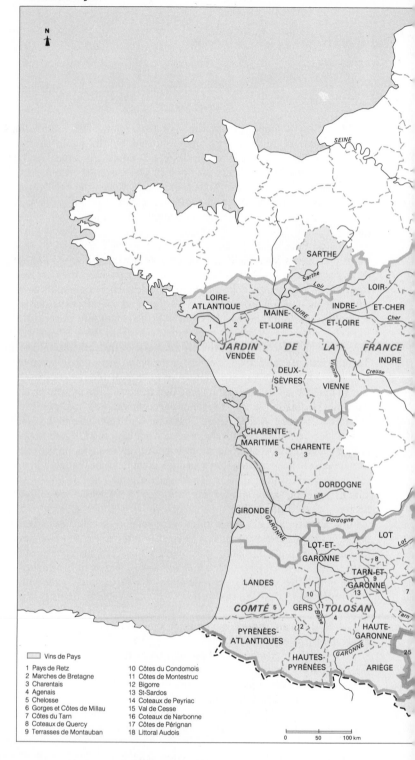

N

SEINE

SARTHE

Sarthe

Loir

LOIR-

LOIRE-
ATLANTIQUE

MAINE-

INDRE-

ET-CHER

Cher

ET-LOIRE

LOIRE

ET-LOIRE

1

2

JARDIN   *DE*   *LA*   *FRANCE*

VENDÉE

INDRE

DEUX-
SÈVRES

Vienne

Creuse

VIENNE

CHARENTE-
MARITIME

CHARENTE

3

3

DORDOGNE

Isle

GIRONDE

GARONNE

Dordogne

LOT

Lot

LOT-ET-
GARONNE

8

TARN-ET-
GARONNE

9

LANDES

13

7

COMTÉ 5

GERS

11

TOLOSAN

Brise

4

Tarn

10

12

HAUTE-
GARONNE

PYRÉNÉES-
ATLANTIQUES

GARONNE

25

Vins de Pays

HAUTES-
PYRÉNÉES

ARIÈGE

1 Pays de Retz	10 Côtes du Condomois
2 Marches de Bretagne	11 Côtes de Montestruc
3 Charentais	12 Bigorre
4 Agenais	13 St-Sardos
5 Chelosse	14 Coteaux de Peyriac
6 Gorges et Côtes de Millau	15 Val de Cesse
7 Côtes du Tarn	16 Coteaux de Narbonne
8 Coteaux de Quercy	17 Côtes de Pérignan
9 Terrasses de Montauban	18 Littoral Audois

0   50   100 km

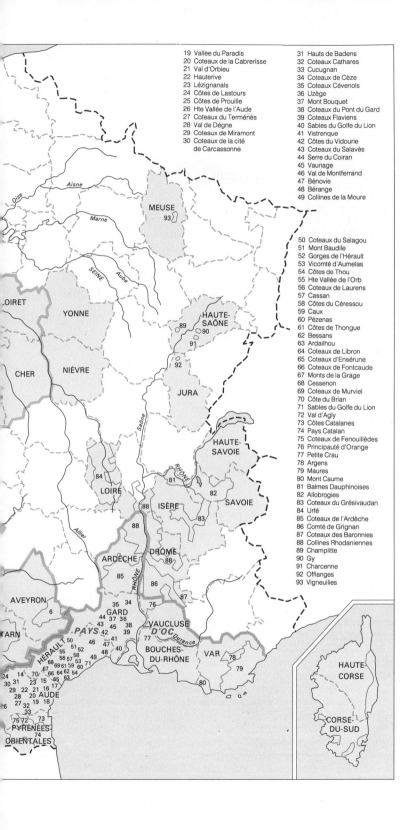

19 Vallée du Paradis
20 Coteaux de la Cabrerisse
21 Val d'Orbieu
22 Hauterive
23 Lézignanals
24 Côtes de Lastours
25 Côtes de Prouille
26 Hte Vallée de l'Aude
27 Coteaux du Terménès
28 Val de Dègne
29 Coteaux de Miramont
30 Coteaux de la cité
   de Carcassonne

31 Hauts de Badens
32 Coteaux Cathares
33 Cucugnan
34 Coteaux de Cèze
35 Coteaux Cévenols
36 Uzège
37 Mont Bouquet
38 Coteaux du Pont du Gard
39 Coteaux Flaviens
40 Sables du Golfe du Lion
41 Vistrenque
42 Côtes du Vidourie
43 Coteaux du Salavès
44 Serre du Coiran
45 Vaunage
46 Val de Montferrand
47 Bénovie
48 Bérange
49 Collines de la Moure

50 Coteaux du Salagou
51 Mont Baudile
52 Gorges de l'Hérault
53 Vicomté d'Aumelas
54 Côtes de Thou
55 Hte Vallée de l'Orb
56 Coteaux de Laurens
57 Cassan
58 Côtes du Céressou
59 Caux
60 Pézenas
61 Côtes de Thongue
62 Bessans
63 Ardailhou
64 Coteaux de Libron
65 Coteaux d'Ensérune
66 Coteaux de Fontcaude
67 Monts de la Grage
68 Cessenon
69 Coteaux de Murviel
70 Côte du Brian
71 Sables du Golfe du Lion
72 Val d'Agly
73 Côtes Catalanes
74 Pays Catalan
75 Coteaux de Fenouillèdes
76 Principauté d'Orange
77 Petite Crau
78 Argens
79 Maures
80 Mont Caume
81 Balmes Dauphinoises
82 Allobrogies
83 Coteaux du Grésivaudan
84 Urfé
85 Coteaux de l'Ardèche
86 Comté de Grignan
87 Coteaux des Baronnies
88 Collines Rhodaniennes
89 Champlitte
90 Gy
91 Charcenne
92 Offlanges
93 Vigneulies

All Vins de Pays fit into one or another of these categories; since category 3 is the most closely defined, it is plain that these wines may be sold under the category 2 and 1, and category 2 may be sold under the category 1 label if desired.

The volume of Vins de Pays produced is immense, averaging 5.5 million hectolitres a year (630 million bottles), about 14 per cent of total French wine production. Vins de Pays are produced in 45 departments, but are concentrated in the Languedoc-Roussillon region, which represents 75 per cent of the total, with the department of the Pyrénées-Orientales alone accounting for 20 per cent. Provence-Côte d'Azur accounts for a further 12 per cent and the Loire valley for 6 per cent. There are 92 separate Vins de Pays de Zone, to which must be added the 45 Vins de Pays Départementaux and the three Vins de Pays Régionaux, making a total of 140 possible types of Vin de Pays. It should also be remembered that over 10 per cent of the wines presented for classification are rejected by local Tasting Commissions, where the wines are judged blind.

It is not surprising that a large part of this volume is produced by local growers' cooperatives. On a national level, the 1200 Caves-Coopératives in France produce a fraction over half the total of all table wine. For the Vins de Pays, this rises to 64 per cent and many of the Vins de Pays de Zone are produced almost entirely by one cooperative. Furthermore, with the vast quantity of wine involved, some cooperatives are now marketing their wine as well as producing it.

For the everyday drinker, Vins de Pays offer an almost unlimited range of genuine 'country' wines. The majority are produced from local grape varieties, for the most part the 'cépages méridionaux', but the last few years have seen the successful introduction of 'cépages nobles' from Burgundy and Bordeaux, proving that the grapes that make France's most famous wines can also produce wines of quality outside their region of origin. Thus, from Touraine to Corsica, we are seeing Cabernet-Sauvignon, Merlot, Chardonnay and Sauvignon appearing on the labels of Vins de Pays. The result of the commitment of the Ministry of Agriculture to controlling quality wine production in France, combined with the positive reaction of the vignerons and cooperatives, has resulted in an increasing amount of fine table wine available for home and foreign consumption at extremely reasonable prices.

The Loire Valley

As far as the Vins de Pays legislation is concerned, this region comprises the twelve departments of Loire-Atlantique, Vendée Maine-et-Loire, Deux-Sèvres, Vienne, Indre-et-Loire, Indre, Cher, Loir-et-Cher, and Loiret, as well as Sarthe and Nièvre. The first ten of these form the regional category Jardin de France which accounts for 60 per cent of Vins de Pays production in the Loire Valley. Each of the twelve is also entitled to the departmental category of Vins de Pays (25 per cent of production). Finally, the remaining 15 per cent of Vins de Pays production comes under the sub-regional category, with Vin de Pays des Coteaux du Cher and Vin de Pays des Coteaux de l'Amour (both to the south of Vierzon, near Quincy and Reuilly); Vin de Pays des Marches de Bretagne (part of the Sèvre-et-Maine vineyards) and Vin du Pays de Retz, to the south of the Loire estuary. The Vin de Pays des Fiefs Vendéens acquired VDQS status in 1984.

The amount of wine produced in these different areas varies tremendously – from 300 hectolitres to 400000 hectolitres. Half of this is in the form of fruity, red wines that are mostly drunk young. The whites are in general dry and fruity, and have some finesse if they come from the Chardonnay or Pinot Gris. A slight pepperiness from the Pinot d'Aunis grape enlivens the Loir and Cher valley rosé wines. Most rosés are produced from a single traditional grape variety, whose name will appear on the label.

Vin de Pays du Jardin de la France

CAVES DU PERE AUGUSTE*

■   8ha   10000   1️⃣ Ⅾ 📷 ⚲

This south-facing vineyard, between Chenonceau and Givray, produces a light wine from the three local grape varieties. Traditional vinification techniques are used. (1984) ✓ Touraine Rouge, Touraine Rosé, Touraine Blanc Sec, Touraine Mousseux.
☛ Caves du Pierre Auguste, 14 Rue des Caves, Civray-de-Touraine 37150 Bléré; tel. 47 23 93 04 ⚲ Daily   8.00–12.00/14.00–19.00   ☛ Robert Godeau.

BESNARD ET FILS*

☐   3ha   2500   2️⃣ Ⅾ 📷 ⚲

Dry, light and fruity Vin de Pays, well structured with a nutty flavour. The cellars here date from the 16th century. (1984) ✓ Vin de Pays Gamay Rouge.
☛ *MM.* Besnard et Fils, Rue Colin, Cheverny, 41700 Contres; tel. 54 44 27 87 ⚲ By appt.

BUISSE *Caves de la Boule Blanche*

■   100000   1️⃣ Ⅾ 📷 ⚲

To be drunk young and fresh within two years; goes perfectly with cold cooked meat. Should be served at 12°C. (1984) ✓ Touraine Rouge, Chinon Rouge, Bourgueil Rouge.
☛ Ets Buisse, 69 Route de Vierzon, 41400 Montrichard; tel. 54 32 00 01 ⚲ By appt.

BUISSE *Caves de la Boule Blanche*

☐   200000   1️⃣ Ⅾ 📷 ⚲

A dry wine from this modern winery. Distinctive nose blends floral and untamed aromas with a touch of flint. (1984) ✓ Touraine Blanc Sec.
☛ Ets Buisse, 69 Route de Vierzon, 41400 Montrichard; tel. 54 32 00 01 ⚲ By appt.

PIERRE CHAINER *Gamay***

■   130ha 1 200000   1️⃣ 📷 ⚲

Light in colour, with a discreet aroma and a gentle acidity. Its very low price makes it extremely popular. Drink chilled. (1984) ✓ Touraine Rouge, Bourgueil Rouge, Chinon Rouge.
☛ Ets Pierre Chainier, La Boitardière, 37400 Amboise; tel. 47 57 15 96 ⚲ By appt.

PIERRE CHAINIER *Gris de Gamay**

◨   10ha 98 000   1️⃣ 📷 ⚲

A rare vin gris with a delicate, fruity and lively nose. Would go well with charcuterie. (1984)
☛ Ets Pierre Chainier, La Boitardière, 37400 Amboise; tel. 47 57 15 96 ⚲ By appt.

CLOS DES CINQ ROUTES*

◨   2ha 10000   1️⃣ Ⅾ 📷 ⚲

Very light rosé with a subtle, delicate nose; it has the same pleasant freshness as the red from this producer. (1984) ✓ Muscadet et Gros Plant, Rosé de Grolleau, Gris de Grolleau.
☛ Louis Gilet, Cinq Routes, Paulx 44270 Machecoul; tel. 40 26 00 45 ⚲ By appt.

CLOS DES CINQ ROUTES*

■   3ha 10000   2️⃣ Ⅾ 📷 ⚲

From a blend of Cabernet-Franc and Cabernet-Sauvignon grapes. Light, very fruity wine of great character, without acidity but nicely fresh. (1984) ✓ Rouge Gamay.
☛ Louis Gilet, Cinq Routes, Paulx 44270 Machecoul; tel. 40 26 00 45 ⚲ By appt.

JEAN-MICHEL DESROCHES**

■   3ha 2000   1️⃣ Ⅾ 📷 ⚲

The youngest of four generations of winegrowers, M. Desroches took over in 1980 and, like his forebears uses the traditional methods of vinification; he is trying to develop direct selling. This red is fruity, light and smooth, very typical of the grape variety. (1984) ✓ Touraine Rouge, Touraine Rosé, Touraine Blanc Sec.
☛ Jean-Michel Desroches, Les Raimbaudières, St-Georges-sur-Cher, 41400 Montrichard; tel. 54 32 33 13 ⚲ By appt.

DOMAINE DES HAUTS-DE-SANZIERS*

☐   3ha 10000   2️⃣ Ⅾ 📷 ⚲

This wine, from the Chardonnay grape, is dry, perfumed, well balanced and long on the palate. It should be served chilled. The Tessier family have been wine-growers and producers for two centuries and welcome visitors in their cellars, which are hollowed out of the rock. (1984) ✓ Saumur Blanc Liquoreux, Saumur Rouge, Saumur Mousseux.
☛ SCEA Tessier et Fils, 'Sanziers' Le Puy-Notre-Dame, 49260 Montreuil-Bellay; tel. 41 52 26 75 ⚲ By appt.

JOEL LHUMEAU**

☐   2ha 5000   1️⃣ Ⅾ 📷 ⚲

Very light dry white wine that is nevertheless velvety and seductive, with great finesse. (1984) ✓ Rosé d'Anjou, Cabernet d'Anjou Rosé, Cremant de Loire.
☛ Joel Lhumeau, Linières, Brigne-sur-Layon, 49700 Doué-la-Fontaine; tel. 41 59 30 51 ⚲ By appt.

JOEL LHUMEAU**

■   5ha 12000   1️⃣ Ⅾ 📷 ⚲

The vineyard has grown from three hectares in 1962 to its present 30; the winery is equipped with centrally heated chais and inert gas installations for keeping the wine. The wine is nice and fruity, light and smooth. (1984) ✓ Anjou Rouge.
☛ Joel Lhumeau, Linières, Brigne-sur-Layon, 49700 Doué-la-Fontaine; tel. 41 59 30 51 ⚲ By appt.

CAVES DE LA LOIRE-BRISSAC
*Sauvignon**

☐   20000   2️⃣ Ⅾ 📷 ⚲

Dry, aromatic and supple wine with good length on the palate. (1984) ✓ Anjou Rosé, Cabernet d'Anjou Rosé, Anjou Blanc Sec, Anjou Rouge.
☛ Caves de la Loire-Brissac, 49320 Brissac-Quincé; tel. 41 91 22 71 ⚲ Mon.–Fri. 8.00–12.30/14.00–17.30.

CAVES DE LA LOIRE-BRISSAC★

■   50000   1 D ▮ ⌟

Fruity, supple and aromatic light red wine from a large-scale producer with very modern equipment. (1984) ✔ Anjou Rouge.
☍ Caves de la Loire-Brissac, 49320 Brissac-Quincé; tel. 41912271 ▼ Mon.–Fri. 8.00–12.30/14.00–17.30.

NICOLAS *Chenin*★★

☐   163000   1 ▮ ⌟

Very aromatic nose shows modern vinification methods. On the palate a dominant acidity gives it a pronounced liveliness. To be drunk chilled.
☍ Ets Nicolas, 2 Rue Valmy, 94220 Charenton; tel. 43759200.

LES NOUES *Gamay*★

■   1 ha   10000   2 D ▮ ⌟

Pale colour, but nicely fruity nose. Refreshing and with good acidity on the palate, this wine would be better drunk younger so that its Gamay qualities could be fully appreciated. (1982)
☍ Guy Charpentier, Les Noues, 44430 Le Loroux-Bottereau; tel. 40064376 ▼ By appt.

CHATEAU DU PERRON

■   5 ha   20000   2 D ▮ ⌟

Tannic, fruity red from a vineyard established about 1900 by M. Blanchard's grandfather. (1983) ✔ Touraine Rouge.
☍ André Blanchard, Ch. du Perron, Lémeré, 37120 Richelieu; tel. 57957104 ▼ Mon.–Sat. 8.30–12.30/13.30–18.00.

CHATEAU DU PERRON★

☐   5 ha   20000   2 D ▮ ⌟

Very dry and well-balanced white with a floral nose; to be drunk with rillettes, the regional coarse pork paté, or with pike in butter sauce. (1984) ✔ Touraine Blanc Sec, Touraine Rosé.
☍ André Blanchard, Ch. du Perron, Lémeré, 37120 Richelieu; tel. 57957104 ▼ Mon.–Sat. 8.30–12.30/13.30–18.00.

RABIER ET FILS *Gamay*★★

■   300000   1 ▮ ⌟

A fine fruity red, well-balanced with a pleasant persistence, from an old-established family concern. (1984)
☍ Ets Rabier et Fils, Menars, 41500 Mer; tel. 54468103.

PATRICK ROBERT

■   2 ha   1000   1 D ▮ ⌟

In 1982 Patrick Robert set out to produce high-quality wines and, within a few years, will have completely replanted his vineyard. This light, smooth, fruity red should be served chilled. (1983) ✔ Vins de Pays Sauvignon.
☍ Patrick Robert, Vitray, 41130 Billy; tel. 54974743 ▼ By appt.

ANTOINE SIMONEAU *Gamay*★

■   7 ha   2000   2 D ▮ ⌟

Another young wine-producer renovating his vineyard offers this very fruity, light and smooth

red which should be drunk young. (1984) ✔ Touraine Rouge.
☍ Antoine Simoneau, La Poterie, St-Georges-sur-Cher, 41400 Montrichard; tel. 54323158 ▼ By appt.

CELLIERS DE ST-GEORGES *Chenin*★

☐   143000   1 ▮ ⌟

Gold colour characteristic of the Chenin grape and a harmonious vigour on the palate. Its sinewy quality makes this wine the perfect accompaniment for whitebait. (1984) ✔ Vin de Pays Sauvignon, Touraine Blanc Sec, Touraine Mousseux.
☍ Ets Pierre Chainier, La Boitardière, 37400 Amboise; tel. 47571596 ▼ By appt.

CAVE DES VIGNERONS DE SAUMUR *Sauvignon*★

☐   80000   2 D ▮ ⌟

A dry, perfumed and well-structured white with good length on the palate. It should be served chilled but not frappé (10–12°C). (1984) ✔ Saumur Blanc Sec, Saumur Rouge, Saumur Champigny Rouge, Saumur Mousseux.
☍ Coop. des Vignerons de Saumur, St-Cyr-en-Bourg, 49260 Montreuil-Bellay; tel. 41516109 ▼ By appt. Closed 1 Oct. to 30 Apr.

Vin de Pays des Marches de Bretagne

LES NOUES *Cabernet*★

■   0.6 ha   5400   2 D ▮ ⌟

Good dark colour and a nose that is pure concentrated blackcurrants. This wine is astonishingly young for the vintage, and has kept a little of its tannin. Now at its peak. (1979)
☍ Guy Charpentier, Les Noues, 44430 Le Loroux-Bottereau; tel. 40064376 ▼ By appt.

DOMAINE DE LA ROCHERIE *Cabernet*★★

■   1 ha   1500   2 D ◑ ⌟

Attractive red colour and young, flowery nose that evokes blackcurrants and their leaves. Well balanced, fruity yet solid and has good length. Basically well made; would adapt itself to any part of a meal. (1982)
☍ Daniel Gratas, La Rocherie, Le Landreau, 44430 Le Loroux-Bottereau; tel. 40400641 55 ▼ By appt.

DOMAINE DE LA ROCHERIE *Cépage Gamay*★★★

■   1 ha   8500   2 D ◑

Attractive pale red, slightly purple colour typical of a Gamay in this area. Fruity, flowery and very pleasant nose. Persistent and satisfying. Well made; probably the best of the appellation. (1983)
☍ Daniel Gratas, La Rocherie, Le Landreau, 44430 Le Loraux-Bottereau; tel. 40400641 5 ▼ By appt.

Vin de Pays de Retz

DOMAINE DES HERBAUGES★

| | 2.5ha | 12000 | 2 D ▪ ⬚ |

Made from the Grolleau grape alone, and bottled off its lees. Pale coloured, pleasant and light, with little bouquet and slight acidity. Delightfully refreshing in summer; good as an aperitif or with food. (1983)
↬ Luc et Pierre Choblet, Dom. des Herbauges, 44830 Bouaye; tel. 40 65 47 05 ☎ By appt.

DOMAINE DES TREIZE VENTS
Gris de Grolleau★

| | 3ha | 15000 | 2 D ▪ ⬚ |

Whether easterly or westerly, the winds of this vineyard's name seem to do nothing but good, judging by this attractive, fragrant, and well-balanced white wine. (1984) ✔ Gros Plant.
↬ Freuchet Père et Fils, Dom. des Treize Vents, 44310 La Chevrolière; tel. 40 31 30 42 ☎ Mon.–Sat. 8.00–12.30/14.00–17.00.

DOMAINE DES TREIZE VENTS
Grolleau Rosé★★

| | 6ha | 70000 | 2 D ▪ ⬚ |

Fruity, spicy, smooth and balanced rosé wine. (1984) ✔ Vin de Pays Gamay Rose.
↬ Freuchet Père et Fils, Dom. des Treize Vents, 44310 La Chevrolière; tel. 40 31 30 42 ☎ Mon.–Sat. 8.00–12.30/14.00–17.00.

Vin de Pays du Maine-et-Loire

CHATEAU D'AVRILLE *Pinot Blanc*★

| | 7ha | 35000 | 2 D ▪ ⬚ |

Smooth, fruity and nicely full white. (1984) ✔ Anjou Blanc Sec, Vin de Pays Gamay Rouge, Vin de Pays Cabernet Rouge, Rosé d'Anjou.
↬ GAEC Bottieau Frères, Dom. d'Avrillé, 49230 St-Jean-des-Mauvrets, 49230 Brissac-Quincié; tel. 41 91 22 46 ☎ By appt.

Aquitaine and Charentes

This is a vast area engulfing the whole Bordeaux region, made up of the departments of Charente, Charente-Maritime, Gironde, Landes, Dordogne and Lot-et-Garonne. Production reaches 60000 hectolitres, mostly smooth and fragrant red wines from Aquitaine, made from Bordeaux grape varieties complemented by a few hardier local types, such as Tannat, Abourian, Bouchales, and Fer. Charentes and Dordogne produce mostly white Vins de Pays that may be light and delicate (the Ugni Blanc or Colombard), round (the Sémillon, blended with other varieties), or powerful (the Baroque). The two sub-regional classifications are Charentais and Agenais (Côtes de Brulhois is now VDQS). Dordogne, Gironde and Landes are the departmental classifications.

Vin de Pays Charentais

COOPERATIVE DE COZES-SAUJON★

| | 250ha | 150000 | 2 D ▪ ⬚ |

The Charentais have recently made great progress in producing wines that are for direct consumption rather than for use in cognac. This dry, lively wine would be perfect with snails. (1984)
↬ Coop. de Cozes-Saujon, BP6, Saujon, 17120 Cozes; tel. 46 90 70 44 ☎ By appt.

COOPERATIVE DE L'ILE DE RE★

| ■ | 400ha | 150000 | 2 D ▪ ⬚ |

A wine that is not very common in France. Has good colour and fine qualities. You could try it with seafood, but if you prefer a traditional choice this cooperative also has rosé and white wines. (1984)
↬ Coop. de l'Ile de Ré, 17580 Le Bois-Plage-en-Ré; tel. 46 09 23 09 ☎ By appt.

COTEAUX DE MONTAGAN★

| | 120ha | 100000 | 2 D ▪ ⬚ |

A little white wine where 'little' is very complimentary, meaning a wine that is refreshing and slips down well. Drink within the year. (1984)
↬ Union des Coteaux de Montagan, Le Bout des Ponts, Gondeville, 16200 Jarnac; tel. 45 81 39 44 ☎ By appt.

CAVE COOPERATIVE DE ST-SORNIN★

| ■ | 200ha | 100000 | 2 D ▪ ⬚ |

Charentais also produces some red wine which perhaps owes its particular style to the more usual white. It has a fine, intense colour, with the same lightness as a white and much charm. (1984)
↬ Cave Coop. de St-Sornin, St-Sornin, 16220 Montbron; tel. 45 70 61 29 ☎ By appt.

Vin de Pays de l'Agenais

CAVE COOPERATIVE DE COCUMONT★

| ■ | 350ha | 150000 | 2 D ▪ ⬚ |

The Cocumont cooperative has developed this well-structured Vin de Pays by selecting vines and wine-producing estates from the Marmandais region. (1984)
↬ Cave Coop. de Cocumont, BP1, Cocumont, 47250 Bouglon; tel. 53 94 50 21 ☎ By appt.

COOPERATIVE DE GOULENS EN BRULHOIS★

| ■ | 250ha | 100000 | 2 D ▪ ⬚ |

A well-structured and balanced red wine which is very reasonable in price and extremely satisfying. (1984)
↬ Coop. de Goulens en Brulhois, 47390 Layrac; tel. 53 87 01 65 ☎ By appt.

COOPERATIVE DES COTES DU MARMANDAIS★

■   250ha   150000   2 D 🖬 ↓

Produced in a region famed for its tomatoes and strawberries, this very pleasant Vin de Pays is inexpensive, with plenty of body and a good red colour. (1984)
◆┐ Coop. des Côtes du Marmandais, Beaupuy, 47200 Marmande; tel. 53 64 32 04 ⏰ By appt.

COOPERATIVE DES SEPT MONTS★

■   200ha   100000   2 D 🖬 ↓

Excellent colour and good structure.
◆┐ Coop. des Sept Monts, Au Lidon, 47150 Monflanquin; tel. 53 36 43 69 ⏰ By appt.

Vin de Pays de Dordogne

DOMAINE DE JARRAUTY★★

■   9ha   10000   2 D 🖬 ↓

A well-made wine with very good colour and fine structure. It stands up well to competition from the equally interesting white and rosé wines produced by the estate. (1984)
◆┐ Jean Leconte, Jarrauty, 24700 Montpon-Ménestérol; tel. 53 80 31 74 ⏰ By appt.

Vin de Pays des Landes

COOPERATIVE DE HAUTE-CHALOSSE★

■   120ha   200000   2 D 🖬 ↓

Deep coloured and fairly tannic. The cooperative produces dry whites and rosés under the same name. (1984)
◆┐ Coop. de Haute-Chalosse, 40250 Mugron; tel. 58 97 70 75 ⏰ By appt.

Pays de la Garonne

This region, centred on Toulouse, groups together eleven departments under the name Pays du Comté Tolosan. The departments concerned are Ariège, Aveyron, Haute-Garonne, Gers, Landes, Lot, Lot-et-Garonne, Pyrénées-Atlantiques, Hautes-Pyrénées, Tarn and Tarn-et-Garonne. The sub-regional or local denominations include Côtes-du-Tarn, Gorges et Côtes de Millau (red Vins Primeurs), Coteaux de Glanes (in Haut-Quercy, to the north of Lot – producing red wines that will age well); Coteaux de Quercy (south of Cahors – full-bodied reds); St-Sardos (west bank of the Garonne); Coteaux et Terrasses de Montauban (light, quaffing reds); Côtes de Gascogne (includes Côtes de Eaudonnois and Côtes de Montestruc)

and Gers (the area where Armagnac is produced – mostly white wines). The three departmental denominations are Haute-Garonne, Tarn-et-Garonne, and Pyrénées-Atlantiques.

The styles of wine of the whole region are extremely varied, and production amounts to around 200000 hectolitres of red and rosé wines, with a few whites from Gers, Tarn, and Béarn. Because of the wide diversity of soil types, climate and grape varieties, the growers blend their wines in an effort to achieve a product with a consistent style. The regional category Vin de Pays du Comté Tolosan was set up in 1982 with precisely this aim but the amount produced is still very limited; 22000 hectolitres out of a total of 200000 hectolitres.

Vin de Pays du Comté Tolosan

DOMAINE DE CANDIE★

■   15ha   60000   2 D 🖬 ↓

This historic château is renowned for its annual wine competition and excellent wines. A pretty Vin de Pays produced by the city of Toulouse.
◆┐ Régie Agricole de Toulouse, Dom. de Candie, 31000 Toulouse; tel. 61 07 51 65 ⏰ No visitors.

Vin de Pays des Côtes du Tarn

COOPERATIVE DE LABASTIDE-DE-LEVIS★

□   500ha   4000000   1 D 🖬 ↓

A classic little white wine, pleasant if drunk very young.
◆┐ Coop. de Labastide-de-Lévis, Labastide-de-Lévis, 81150 Marssac-sur-Tarn; tel. 63 55 41 83 ⏰ No visitors.

DOMAINE DE LABERTHE★

■   5ha   20000   2 D 🖬 ↓

Has all the qualities to be expected of this estate, which produces a wide range of different types.
◆┐ Jean Albert, Dom. de Laberthe, Castanet, 81150 Marssac-sur-Tarn; tel. 63 56 80 14 ⏰ By appt.

COOPERATIVE DE RABASTENS★

■   500ha   4000000   1 D 🖬 ↓

A smart young red Vin de Pays developed by carbonic maceration. It should be drunk during the winter following the harvest.
◆┐ Coop. de Rabastens, 33 Route d'Albi, 81800 Rabastens; tel. 63 33 73 80 ⏰ No visitors.

Vin de Pays des Coteaux du Quercy

XAVIER DIEUZAIDE★★★

| ■ | 6ha | 15000 | 2 D 🍷 ⚓ |

It is apparently a local tradition to produce wines that have body and plenty of colour; in any case this wine is a success.
🍷 Xavier Dieuzaide, La Combarade, 46170 Castelnau Montratier; tel. 65 21 95 95 ☎ No visitors.

GAEC DE MAEZUC★★

| ■ | 5ha | 6000 | 1 D 🍷 ⚓ |

Lengthy fermentation has given this wine great character and an excellent structure, together with a fine aroma.
🍷 Fernand Carlet, Puylaroque, 82240 Septfonds; tel. 63 31 90 91 ☎ No visitors.

Vin de Pays de St-Sardos

CAVE COOPERATIVE DE ST-SARDOS★

| ■ | 50ha | 150000 | 2 D 🍷 ⚓ |

The vines cultivated on the stony limestone terraces of the Garonne provide this cooperative with red wines of appreciable quality.
🍷 Cave Coop. de St-Sardos, 82600 Verdun-sur-Garonne; tel. 63 02 52 44 ☎ No visitors.

Vin de Pays des Coteaux et Terrasses de Montauban

DOMAINE DE MONTELS★★

| ■ | 16ha | 15000 | 1 D 🍷 ⚓ |

A high-quality wine from the Aveyron; extremely rich nose and good mature character. Goes well with all types of food. (1983)
🍷 Aline Romain, 82350 Albias; tel. 63 31 02 82 ☎ By appt.

Vin de Pays des Côtes de Gascogne

OLIVIER GALABERT★★

| ■ | 2ha | 10000 | 2 D 🍷 ⚓ |

Good colour and solid structure. The Tannat and Cabernet assure its good quality.
🍷 Olivier Galabert, Mathalin, Beaucaire-sur-Baise, 32410 Castera-Verduzan; tel. 62 68 15 45 ☎ By appt.

GRASSA-DUBUC★★★

| □ | 35ha | 300000 | 1 D 🍷 ⚓ |

Ugni Blanc grapes provide freshness, and Colombard adds finesse to produce a high-quality Vin de Pays.
🍷 *Mme* Dubuc and *M.* Grassa, Le Tarriquet, 32800 Eauze; tel. 62 09 87 82 ☎ By appt.

UNION DE PRODUCTEURS PLAIMONT *Colombard*★★★

| □ | 150ha | 800000 | 1 D ⑪ ⚓ |

A fresh white wine with a delicate aroma; well balanced and well developed. One of the best of the Vins de Pays.

🍷 Producteurs de Plaimont, St-Mont, 82400 Riscle; tel. 62 69 78 87 ☎ Mon.–Sat. 8.00–12.00/ 14.00–18.30.

Vin de Pays de Bigorre

DOMAINE DU BOUSCASSE★★

| ■ | 15ha | 100000 | 1 D 🍷 ⚓ |

A red wine with the tonal qualities and above all the beautiful structure of the Tannat and Cabernet vines. Perfect with duck and pâté.
🍷 Alain Brumont, Dom. du Bouscasse, Maumusson, 32400 Riscle; tel. 62 62 74 67 ☎ By appt.

Vin de Pays de la Haute-Garonne

DOMAINE DE RIBONNET★★★

| ■ | 15ha | 100000 | 2 D 🍷 ⑪ ⚓ |

The Merlot, which is typical of this estate, is perhaps one of the best-loved of the excellent range of Vins de Pays produced here.
🍷 SARL Dom. de Ribonnet, Beaumont-sur-Léze, 31190 Auterive; tel. 61 08 71 02 ☎ By appt.

Vins de Pays du Tarn-et-Garonne

DOMAINE DE CALLORY★

| ■ | 12ha | 20000 | 2 D 🍷 |

A wine with body, tenacity and a certain amount of charm. (1982)
🍷 *MM.* Perez and Montels, Dom. de Callory, 82370 Labastide-St-Pierre; tel. 63 30 50 30 ☎ No visitors.

Vin de Pays des Pyrénées-Atlantiques

CAVE COOPERATIVE GAN-JURANÇON★★

| □ | 20ha | 100000 | 1 D 🍷 ⚓ |

A light, dry white wine with an intense nose. Very inexpensive and popular with tourists.
🍷 Cave Coop. de Gan-Jurançon, 64290 Gan; tel. 59 21 57 03 ☎ By appt.

CAVE COOPERATIVE DU VIC-BILH-MADIRAN★★

■   500ha   45000   1️⃣ 🄳 📷 ♨

A fruity and fresh wine in full youth, sold under the name of Vin de Fleur.
➤ Cave Coop. du Vic-Bilh-Madiran, Cruseilles, 64350 Lembeye; tel. 59 68 10 93 ☎ No visitors.

Languedoc and Roussillon

This is the major table-wine producing area in France, supplying 70 per cent (4 million hectolitres) of all Vins de Pays. Most comes from the departments Aude, Gard, Hérault, Pyrénées-Orientales (these are the four departmental classifications), and also from Ardèche, Vaucluse, Bouches-du-Rhône and Var, which constitute the regional classification of 'Vins de Pays d'Oc'. Production is 80 000 to 100 000 hectolitres per year, 75 per cent being red and the rest rosé. The Vins de Pays de Languedoc and Roussillon are made from selected grapes and vinified separately. Various grape varieties are used; mostly Carignan for reds and rosés, along with some Grenache and Cinsault, although increasingly Merlot, Cabernet-Sauvignon, and Syrah are being used to give the wines more body. For white wines, Clairette, Grenache Blanc, Macabeu, Ugni Blanc and Carignan Blanc are the main varieties. There are quite a few wines made from a single grape variety, and this is mentioned in the name. Many Vins Primeurs are made here, too. The Vins de Pays d'Oc have to undergo a second approved tasting before they can use the classification.

In this huge area, which extends from Bigorre to Catalan and Cévennes on the Spanish border, there is a large number of sub-regional or local Vins de Pays (see map on p.614–15). Co-operatives play a major rôle throughout the region.

Vin de Pays d'Oc

ETS SKALI *Fortant de France*★
■   200ha   200000   2️⃣ 🄳 📷 ♨

Powerful aroma on the nose, with complex grassy and flowery overtones. Very harmonious on the palate, as these aromas develop further. Rich, smooth and long-lasting finish. (1984) ✔ Vin de Pays d'Oc Cépage Cinsaut, Vin de Pays d'Oc Cépage Merlot Rouge.
➤ Ets Skali, BP 376, 34204 Sète; tel. 67 48 61 10 ☎ No visitors.

Vin de Pays de la Haute-Vallée de l'Aude

DOMAINE DES ASTRUC★★
■   8ha   20000   2️⃣ 🄳 📷 ♨

Displays all the characteristics of Merlot, Cabernet-Franc, Cabernet-Sauvignon and Malbec. Bouquet of overripe fruit, full on the palate, and long, intense finish. (1981) ✔ Vin de Pays Haute-Vallée de l'Aude Rouge, Vin de Pays Haute-Vallée de l'Aude Rosé, Vin de Pays Haute-Vallée de l'Aude Blanc, Blanquette de Limoux Moelleux.
➤ Pierre et Jacques Astruc, Malras, 11300 Limoux; tel. 68 31 13 26 ☎ Daily 7.30–12.30/13.30–20.00.

Vin de Pays des Côtes de Prouille

JACQUES GUILHEM★
☑   10ha   20000   2️⃣ 🄳 📷

A very flowery and somewhat mellow wine with a strong colour. Should be drunk young and chilled. (1984)
➤ Brigitte Gourdou-Guilhelm, Ch. de Malviés, 11300 Limoux; tel. 68 31 14 41 ☎ By appt.

Vin de Pays des Côtes de Lastours

COTES DE LASTOURS *Les Capitelles*★★
■   55ha   160000   1️⃣ 🄳 📷 ♨

Lovely ruby colour. Powerful, long-lasting, wild-berry aroma. Clean beginning and long, flowing finish. (1983)
➤ Cabardes et Fresquel, Villalbe, 11000 Carcassonne; tel. 68 47 18 50 ☎ Mon.–Sat. 9.00–12.00/14.00–18.00.

Vin de Pays de Cucugnan

COOPERATIVE DE CUCUGNAN★★
■   90ha   20000   1️⃣ 🄳 📷 ♨

Red wine that has a distinctive taste of the soil ('goût de terroir') from the grape varieties used – Carignan, Cinsault, and Grenache. Nicely aromatic, with body and structure. (1984) ✔ Corbières.
➤ Coop. de Cucugnan, Ch. de Quéribus, Cucugnan, 11350 Tuchan; tel. 68 68 45 41 6 ☎ By appt.

COOPERATIVE DE CUCUGNAN★★
☐   36ha   6000   1️⃣ 🄳 📷 ♨

Quite high in alcohol for a Vin de Pays. Called green because it comes from Grenache Blanc and Maccabeu varieties. Fruity and very crisp. (1984)
➤ Coop. de Cucugnan, Ch. de Quéribus, Cucugnan, 11350 Tuchan; tel. 68 68 45 41 6 ☎ By appt.

Vin de Pays des Coteaux du Littoral Audois

COOPERATIVE DES CORBIERES MARITIMES *Berval*★

| ■ | | 800ha | 38000 | 2 D ▋ ↓ |

Intense colour that goes from bright red to garnet. Fragrant, very smooth, yet full bodied. (1984) ✔ Corbières Rouge, Corbières Rosé.
�﬌ Coop. des Corbières Maritimes, 11490 Portel-des-Corbières; tel. 68 48 28 05 ☎ By appt.

Vin de Pays de l'Aude

JEAN-FRANCOIS BOURZEIX
Vin Coeur★★

| ■ | | | 40000 | 2 D ▋ ↓ |

Why *vin coeur*, or 'heart wine'? A medicinal wine that may well conquer (*vainquer*) all one's problems. At present closed-in, but just as good as the other wines in its category. (1984)
�﬌ Jean-François Bourzeix, Route de Marcorignan, 11100 Narbonne; tel. 88 42 29 34 ☎ By appt.

NICOLAS *Cépage Merlot*★

| ■ | | | | 1 ▋ |

Attractive, purplish, ruby colour and expansive bouquet characteristic of the grape variety. Full and aromatic with good length. A delight.
�﬌ Ets Nicolas, 2 Rue de Valmy, 94220 Charenton; tel. 01 37 59 20 ☎ No visitors.

NICOLAS

| ■ | | | 330000 | 1 ▋ ↓ |

Has class, depth of colour, body, and a marked Cabernet style, which will improve by ageing and rounding out.
�﬌ Ets Nicolas, 2 Rue de Valmy, 94220 Charenton; tel. 01 37 59 20 ☎ No visitors.

Vin de Pays des Coteaux du Salavès

VIGNERONS DE CARNAS★

| ■ | | 4ha | 21000 | 1 D ▋ ↓ |

Still young and has predominant fruitiness of the Syrah grape. (1984)
�﬌ Coop. des Vignerons de Carnas, 30260 Quissac; tel. 66 77 30 76 ☎ By appt. Mon.–Sat. 8.00–12.00/14.00–18.00.

COOPERATIVE ST-HIPPOLYTE-DU-FORT★

| ◪ | | 4ha | 25000 | 1 D ▋ ↓ |

Intense, bright colour and delicate nose; a full wine with a long finish. (1984) ✔ Vins de Pays des Coteaux du Salavés Rosé, Vins de Pays des Coteaux du Salavés Blanc.
�﬌ Coop. St-Hippolyte-du-Fort, 30170 St-Hippolyte-du-Fort; tel. 66 77 21 30 ☎ Mon.–Sat. 8.00–12.00/14.00–18.00.

COOPERATIVE VIC-LE-FESQ★

| ■ | | 4ha | 24000 | 1 D ▋ ↓ |

Intense, bright colour, well-developed secondary aromas, full and smooth, with a slightly tannic note on the palate. (1983) ✔ Vins de Pays des

Coteaux du Salavés Rosé, Vins de Pays des Coteaux du Salavés Blanc.
�﬌ Coop. de Vic-le-Fesq, 30260 Quinsac; tel. 66 80 82 11 ☎ By appt.

Vin de Pays de Coteaux Cévenols

DOMAINE DE LA BEGUDE

| ■ | | 20ha | 10000 | 3 D ▋ ↓ |

Bright ruby-red with pleasant nose. (1979)
�﬌ Christian Silhol, Ch. de St-Victor-de-Malcap, 30500 St-Ambroix; tel. 66 24 10 83 ☎ By appt.

Vin de Pays des Coteaux de Cèze

COOPERATIVE DE LA CEZARENQUE

| ■ | | 200ha | 26000 | 1 D ▋ ↓ |

Light, lively colour. Clear traces of the Syrah grape variety in the bouquet, while aromas of the Grenache grape come through on the palate. (1983) ✔ Côtes du Rhône Rouge, Rosé and Blanc.
↮ Coop. de la Cézarenque, Roquebrune-Saint-Alexandre, 30130 Pont-St-Esprit; tel. 66 39 02 00 ☎ By appt.

Vin de Pays de l'Uzège

DOMAINE DE GOURNIER★★

| □ | | 15ha | 15000 | 2 D ▋ ↓ |

Blanc de Blancs with a straw-gold, almost crystalline colour. Very slightly sparkling. Aromatic, delicate and flowery nose; warm, flowing, expansive, and full of Sauvignon-Blanc aromas on the palate. Very long finish. (1983)
↮ Maurice Barnouin, Ste-Anastasie, 30910 St-Chaptes; tel. 66 81 20 28 ☎ By appt.

DOMAINE DE GOURNIER★★

| ■ | | 15ha | 15000 | 2 D ▋ ↓ |

Extremely rich. Light, clear, purplish colour. Intense aromatic richness and persistence, but very pleasant. Smooth, solid and tannic. Will become elegant, distinguished and well resolved after a few months of bottle age. (1983)
↮ Maurice Barnouin, Ste-Anastasie, 30190 St-Chaptes; tel. 66 81 20 28 ☎ By appt.

DOMAINE DE MALAIGUE★

| ◪ | | 8ha | 30000 | 2 D ▋ ↓ |

Crystal-clear colour that glistens and shimmers; aromatic, very fragrant, crisp and classy. (1983) ✔ Côtes du Rhône.
↮ Jean-Claude Reboul, Dom. de Malaigue, Sagriès, 30700 Uzès; tel. 66 22 25 43 ☎ Closed Sun. and public holidays.

DOMAINE DE MALAIGUE★

| ■ | | 20ha | 50000 | 2 D ◑ ↓ |

Star-bright ruby colour. Generous and clean; really flows over the palate. (1982) ✔ Côtes du Rhône.
↮ Jean-Claude Reboul, Dom. de Malaigue, Sagriès, 30700 Uzés; tel. 66 22 25 43. ☎ Closed Sun. and public holidays.

CAVES DE L'UZEGE *Bermonde***

◼ 212ha 120000 [1] [D] [画] [↓]

The proportion of Syrah adds deep colour and a flowery note to the typically aromatic Grenache grape.
◆ Union des Caves de l'Uzège, St-Quentin-la-Poterie, 30700 Uzès; tel. 66 22 56 55 ⊺ By appt.

CAVES DE L'UZEGE *La Fenestrelle***

[◪] 125ha 50000 [1] [D] [画] [↓]

Has the warmth of the dominant Grenache and the bouquet of the Syrah.
◆ Union des Caves de l'Uzege, St-Quentin-la-Poterie, 30700 Uzès; tel. 66 22 56 55 ⊺ By appt.

Vin de Pays des Coteaux du Pont du Gard

COOPERATIVE DU PONT-DU-GARD**

[◪] 65ha 50000 [2] [画] [↓]

A pretty, lively colour with a very fruity nose; pleasant on the palate. Should be drunk young and well chilled.
◆ Union des Coteaux Pont-du-Gard, Vers-Pont-du-Gard, 30210 Remoulins; tel. 66 22 80 35 ⊺ Daily 8.00–12.00/14.00–18.00.

COOPERATIVE DU PONT-DU-GARD**

◼ 540ha 2000000 [2] [画] [↓]

The character of the Syrah vine is very apparent in this very supple wine.
◆ Union des Coteaux Pont-du-Gard, Vers-Pont-du-Gard, 30210 Remoulins; tel. 66 22 80 35 ⊺ Daily 8.00–12.00/14.00–18.00.

LES VIGNERONS DE REMOULINS*

◼ 23ha 200000 [2] [D] [画] [↓]

A fruity, supple and well-balanced wine with a good colour; very pleasant to drink. (1984)
◆ Cave Coop. des Vign. Remoulins, Route d'Avignon, 30210 Remoulins; tel. 66 37 14 51 ⊺ By appt. Closed Sat. afternoon, Sun. and public holidays.

CAVES DE L'UZEGE*

[☐] 20ha 40000 [1] [D] [画] [↓]

This little white wine has all the character of the wines from this ancient region.
◆ Union des Caves de l'Uzege, St-Quentin-la-Poterie, 30700 Uzès; tel. 66 22 56 55 ⊺ By appt.

Vin de Pays des Sables du Golfe du Lion

U.V. LA BAIE D'AIGUES-MORTES
*Gris de Gris***

[◪] 90ha 3000000 [2] [D] [画] [↓]

A Gris-de-Gris of distinctive colour. Floral nose; supple and harmonious on the palate. A nice summer-holiday wine. (1984)

◆ U.V. La Baie d'Aigues-Mortes, Bld Diderot, BP 31, 30220 Aigues-Mortes; tel. 66 53 75 20 ⊺ By appt.

DOMAINE DU BOSQUET *Listel***

◼ 600ha 4000000 [2] [D] [画] [↓]

The Cabernet-Sauvignon and Cabernet-Franc grape varieties thrive here, as shown by this full-bodied red with developed aromas. (1982)
◆ Dom. Viticole Salins-du-Midi, 68 Cours Gambetta, 34063 Montpellier Cedex; tel. 66 58 23 77 ⊺ By appt ◆ S.A. Cie des Salins-du-Midi.

DOMAINE DE JARRAS *Listel gris***

[◪] 404ha 3000000 [2] [D] [画] [Ⅲ] [↓]

Fine, fruity and delicate wine with a characteristic light smoky flavour.
◆ Dom. Viticole Salins-du-Midi, 68 Cours Gambetta, 34063 Montpellier Cedex; tel. 66 58 23 77 ⊺ By appt ◆ S.A. Cie des Salins-du-Midi.

DOMAINE DE VILLEROY *Listel**

[☐] 287ha 2000000 [2] [D] [画] [Ⅲ] [↓]

An aromatic and sinewy Blanc de Blancs, bottled on its lees; gains a pleasant finesse from the favourable local micro-climate. (1983)
◆ Dom. Viticole Salins-du-Midi, 68 Cours Gambetta, 34063 Montpellier Cedex; tel. 66 58 23 77 ⊺ By appt ◆ S.A. Compagnie des Salins-du-Midi.

Vin de Pays du Gard

DOMAINE DE LA BARBEN**

[☐] 5ha 10000 [2] [D] [画] [↓]

Greenish-gold highlights, caused by chalk in the soil, in an otherwise crystal-clear wine. Full bodied, lively and pleasantly fruity. (1984)
◆ MM. Brunel Frères, Dom. de la Barben, 30000 Nîmes; tel. 66 81 10 52 ⊺ No visitors.

DOMAINE DE LA BARBEN**

[◪] 10ha 15000 [2] [D] [画] [↓]

Pleasing, crystal-clear, shimmering rosé colour. Rich in fruity aromas and delicate fragrances. Crisp, classy and flows agreeably over the palate. (1984)
◆ MM. Brunel Frères, Dom. de la Barben, 30000 Nîmes; tel. 66 81 10 52 ⊺ No visitors.

DOMAINE DE LA BARBEN*

◼ 20ha 50000 [2] [D] [画] [↓]

From an estate formerly owned by the Counts of Toulouse. Purplish, bright and clear. Full bodied, meaty and distinguished.
◆ MM. Brunel Frères, Dom. de la Barben, 30000 Nîmes; tel. 66 81 10 52 ⊺ No visitors.

VIGNERONS DE CARNAS
Lou Requines★★

◪ 6ha 53000 **1** **D** 🖷 ⌄

Attractive, unoxidized colour. Seductive nose. Dry with hint of richness on the palate. (1984) ✔ Vin du Pays du Gard Lou Requines Rouge et Blanc Sec, Vin du Pays du Gard Cabernet Rouge. ☙ Coop. des Vignerons de Carnas, 30260 Quissac; tel. 66773076 ⏳ Mon.–Sat. 8.00–12.00/ 14.00–18.00.

DOMAINE DE CHIRAC★

□ 2ha 5000 **2** **D** 🖷 ⌄

Pale, slightly golden-yellow colour and fruity, southern-style nose, although on the palate it is dry and well balanced. The vintage is not stated, but a more recent blend would probably display a little more crispness. ☙ MM. Reinaud Frères, Dom. de Chirac, 30140 Bagard, 30140 Anduze; tel. 66521822 ⏳ By appt.

DOMAINE DE CHIRAC★★

◪ 12ha 30000 **2** **D** 🖷 ⌄

Light, bright rosé, with faint, attractive shades of violet. Nose is somewhat reserved; peony aromas on the palate. Unusual and pleasant. Made from a blend of classic southern French grape varieties and the Italian Barbera varietal. ☙ MM. Reinaud Frères, Dom. de Chirac, 30140 Bagard, 30140 Anduze; tel. 66521822 ⏳ By appt.

VIGNERONS DES GARRIGUES★

▣ 100000 **2** **D** ⌄

This blended wine is constantly sought after for its flowery character and intense colour. Persistent on the palate. Heady, well blended, aromatic. (1984) ☙ Vignerons des Garrigues, Marché Gare, 30000 St-Césaire, 30000 Nîmes; tel. 66380478 ⏳ No visitors.

DOMAINE LE PIAN

▣ 45ha 500000 **2** **D** 🖷 ◑ ⌄

Purplish, light and clear. Meaty, full bodied, well resolved, clean and easy to drink. The estate has been in the family since 1635. (1983) ☙ F. Durand et Fils. Dom. le Pian, 30350 Moulézan; tel. 66808125 ⏳ Mon.–Sat. 9.00–12.00/ 14.00–19.30.

DOMAINE LE PIAN★

◪ 8ha 10000 **2** **D** 🖷 ⌄

Deep, crystal clear colour. Full of predominantly fruity aromas. Crisp and well bred; very easy to drink. (1983) ☙ F. Durand et Fils, Dom. le Pian, 30350 Moulézan; tel. 66808125 ⏳ Mon.–Sat. 9.00–12.00/ 14.00–19.30.

DOMAINE DE PUECHREDON★★★

▣ 40ha 600000 **2** **D** ◑ ⌄

Very full and round with an attractive dark-red colour. Marvellous, slightly spicy, pomegranate nose. Long and elegant on the palate. Remarkable quality for a Vin de Pays. (1983) ✔ Vin du Pays du Gard Rosé.

☙ Michel Cuche, Dom. de Puechredon, 30640 Suave; tel. 66773125.

COOPERATIVE ST-HIPPOLYTE-DU-FORT *Le Cigalois*★

▣ 6ha 45000 **1** **D** 🖷 ⌄

Produced close by the famous Demoiselle grotto; a golden wine with primary aromas of the Syrah grape on the nose. Fat and long on the palate. (1984) ☙ Coop. St-Hippolyte-du-fort; tel. 66772130 ⏳ Mon.–Sat. 8.00–12.00/14.00–18.00.

COOPERATIVE DE VIC-LE-FESQ *Le Fesco*★

▣ 4ha 26000 **1** **D** 🖷 ⌄

Intense colour and characteristic Cabernet aromas go well together. Smooth; long finish. ✔ Vin de Pays du Gard le Fesco Rosé et Blanc Sec, Vin de Pays du Gard Cabernet Rouge, Vin du Pays du Gard Syrah Rouge. ☙ Coop. de Vic-le-fesq, 30260 Quissac; tel. 66808211 ⏳ By appt.

Vin de Pays des Coteaux d'Ensérune

LES VIGNERONS DE NISSAN★★

▣ 4ha 34500 **2** **D** 🖷 ⌄

Deep, ruby coloured with shades of violet. Made from Merlot grapes; delicate and light, clean and easy to drink, and well-structured on the palate. (1984) ☙ Cave Coop. de Nissan, Av de la Gare, 34440 Nissan-lez-Enserune; tel. 67370031 ⏳ Mon.–Fri. 8.00–12.00/14.00–18.00. Closed during harvest.

Vin de Pays des Coteaux de Fontcaude

DOMAINE DE MALLEMORT★★

▣ 50ha 120000 **3** **D** ◑ ⌄

Deep, young violet colour. Intense fruit nose of blackberry and bilberry, also apparent on the palate. At first smooth but a little harsh at the finish, due to the time spent in oak. A good wine. (1982) ☙ Jean Peitavy, Dom. de Mallemort, 34620 Puisserguier; tel. 67937420 ⏳ By appt.

Vin de Pays des Coteaux de Murviel

CHATEAU DE COUJAN★

□ 1ha 7000 **3** **D** 🖷 ⌄

Most attractive, very pale and very clean yellow colour. Richly fruity and very aromatic with good, dry finish. Lots of character. Drink young to enjoy its fruitiness and crispness. (1983) ☙ Guy et S. Payre, Ch. de Coujan, 34490 Murviel-les-Beziers; tel. 67360112 ⏳ Mon.–Sat. 10.00–13.00/16.00–20.00.

CHATEAU DE COUJAN★★★

■ 10ha 50000 ③ D ⦿ ↓

Deep mahogany with brick-red shades. Rich, complex and mature Pomerol-style nose of truffles and undergrowth. Round and smooth on the palate. Distinctive and high-class; could almost be mistaken for one of the great appellation wines, probably due to the high proportion of Merlot grapes (75 per cent), and careful ageing (2 years in wooden vats). (1979)
☞ Guy et S. Peyre, Ch. de Coujan, 34490 Murviel-les-Beziers; tel. 67 36 01 12 ℤ Mon.–Sat. 10.00–13.00/16.00–20.00.

CAVE COOPERATIVE DE PUIMISSON★★★

■ 5ha 25000 ② D ↓

Attractive Cabernet-Sauvignon with deep garnet colour and powerful passion fruit nose. Harmonious, aromatic and especially full bodied. (1984)
☞ Cave Coop. de Puimisson, Puimisson 33480 Magalas; tel. 67 36 09 74 ℤ By appt.

Vin de Pays du Mont Baudile

SICA DE MONROC★★

■ 500ha 250000 ① D ■ ↓

Smooth and round. Pleasant on the palate. Discreet nose but very elegant finish; secondary aromas still very much in evidence. (1984)
☞ SICA Monroc, St-Saturnin, 34150 Gignac; tel. 67 96 61 52 ℤ By appt.

Vin de Pays des Gorges de l'Hérault

DOMAINE DU BOSC *Syrah*★

■ 9ha 75000 ③ D ■ ↓

Very young, violet-red colour. Concentrated fruit nose; has preserved all its fruitiness and natural Syrah tannin. Although made by carefully controlled vinification along *maceration carbonique* lines, must be laid down for at least three years. (1982)
☞ Pierre Bésinet, Dom. du Bosc, 34450 Vias; tel. 67 94 00 39 ℤ By appt.

DOMAINE DU BOSC *Cinsaut-Syrah*★

■ 15ha 120000 ③ D ■ ↓

Lovely garnet-red, lighter than Merlot-Cabernet-Sauvignon, and fruity nose characteristic of the *maceration carbonique* process. On the palate

fruitiness is sustained by Cinsaut, and Syrah grapes (the former predominant, adding firmness to this particular cuvée). May be drunk throughout a meal. (1983)
☞ Pierre Bésinet, Dom. du Bosc, 34450 Vias; tel. 67 94 00 39 ℤ By appt.

DOMAINE DU BOSC
Cépage Grenache★★★

□ 20ha 175000 ③ D ■ ↓

Lovely, very pale-yellow colour and pleasantly subtle, boiled-sweet nose. Lively and fruity on the palate; very well made. Could be drunk as an aperitif or with a meal. Sets itself apart by its elegance and exceptional aromatic crispness. (1983)
☞ Pierre Bésinet, Dom. du Bosc, 34450 Vias; tel. 67 94 00 39 ℤ By appt.

DOMAINE DU BOSC
Merlot-Cabernet-Sauvignon★

■ 10ha 85000 ③ D ■ ↓

Very deep colour still immature for the year; extremely fruity nose (blackcurrant and blackberry) with all the richness of an Hérault wine. Distinct structure on the palate, which is still somewhat tannic; should either age a little longer, or be served with meat in sauce. (1982)
☞ Pierre Bésinet, Dom. du Bosc, 34450 Vias; tel. 67 94 00 39 ℤ By appt.

CAVE COOPERATIVE
LA CARIGNANO★

■ 120ha 50000 ② D ■ ↓

Bright ruby-coloured wine with an animal nose. Solid, smooth, light to drink and fleshy on the palate.
☞ Cave Coop. la Carignano, Route de Pouzolles, Gabian, 34320 Roujan; tel. 67 24 65 64 ℤ Daily 8.00–12.00/13.30–17.30.

CAVE COOPERATIVE COTEAUX
DE NEFFIES *La Mazade*★★

■ 80ha 15000 ② D ■ ↓

A very deep red wine. Its floral nose has aromas of red fruits and cocoa, and it is lively and well structured on the palate. (1984)
☞ SCAV Coteaux de Neffiès, Neffiès, 34320 Roujan; tel. 67 24 61 98 ℤ Mon.–Fri. 8.00–12.00/ 14.00–18.00.

FONTAMOUR★★

■ 25ha 200000 ② D ⦿ ↓

A harmonious blend of Bordeaux vines (Merlot, Cabernet, Sauvignon) with traditional Languedoc varieties (Carignan, Cinsaut). A fruity and balanced wine which is good with Roquefort cheese or Cévennes ham.
☞ UCOVI Clermont-l'Hérault, 34800 Clermont-l'Hérault; tel. 67 96 83 97 ℤ Mon.–Fri. 8.00–12.00/ 14.00–18.00.

DOMAINE GRANGE ROUGE

□ 9ha 96000 ② D ■ ↓

Pale golden colour. Nose typical of a white wine from a sunny country; plenty of aroma but not much finesse. Drink young to enjoy fully its fruitiness; good accompaniment to any Mediterranean fish. (1984)

♠ *MM*. Pourthié Frères, Dom. Grange Rouge, 34300 Agde; tel. 67 94 21 76 ✆ By appt. Closed 1 Sept.–15 Oct.

DOMAINE GRANGE ROUGE★

■   8ha   66 000   `2` `D` `▮` `⬇`

Planted only 4 km from the sea, the estate's vines ripen slowly, preserving grape aromas. Violet-red wine with slightly grassy nose. On the palate, fruity with typical Carignan solidity. A hearty bottle – perfect with game. (1983)
♠ *MM*. Pourthié Frères, Dom. Grange Rouge, 34300 Agde; tel. 67 94 21 76 ✆ By appt. Closed 1 Sept.–15 Oct.

DOMAINE GRANGE ROUGE
Rosé de Saignée★★

☑   15ha   12 000   `2` `D` `▮` `⬇`

Attractive pale rosé with mauvish tints. Lively, boiled-sweet aromas. On the palate, clean, fruity and pleasant. Made from Grenache and Cinsaut grapes; a good example of successful, modern winemaking methods. (1984)
♠ *MM*. Pourthié Frères, Dom. Grange Rouge, 34300 Agde; tel. 67 94 21 76 ✆ By appt. Closed 1 Sept.–15 Oct.

DOMAINE DE GRANGE ROUGE
Cabernet Sauvignon★

■   8ha   60 000   `2` `D` `▮` `⬇`

Deep, dark red, giving rich appearance. Mature and complex nose, with blackberry and eucalyptus fragrances. On the palate, rich and tannic; would need a robust meal to balance its strength.
♠ *MM*. Pourthié Frères, Dom. Grange Rouge, 34300 Agde; tel. 67 94 21 76 ✆ By appt. Closed 1 Sept.–15 Oct.

CAVE COOPERATIVE DE LESPIGNAN★★

■   8ha   67 000   `2` `D` `⬥` `⬇`

A dark-red wine with hints of brown and a warm, rather complex nose with aromas of Russian leather and cocoa. Would go well with mixed grills.
♠ Cave Coop. de Lespignan, Route de Fleury, 34710 Lespignan; tel. 67 37 02 05 ✆ Mon.–Fri. 8.00–12.00/14.00–17.30. Closed during harvest.

DOMAINE DE MAIRAN★

☑   20ha   25 000   `3` `D` `▮` `⬇`

Pale rosé enriched by shades of orange. Fragrances of crushed fruit. Quite full bodied, pleasant and round.
♠ Jean Peitavy, Dom. de Mallemort, 34620 Puisserguier; tel. 67 93 74 20 ✆ By appt.

DOMAINE DE MAIRAN★

☐   28ha   50 000   `3` `D` `▮` `⬇`

Attractive pale yellow. Aromatic, fruity and very lively. Well made and presented in its 'Véronique' bottle. (1983)
♠ Jean Peitavy, Dom. de Mallemort, 34620 Puisserguier; tel. 67 93 74 20 ✆ By appt.

DOMAINE DE PREIGNES-LES-VIEUX★

■   1ha   10 000   `2` `D` `⬥` `⬇`

A well-structured and supple wine, fruity and round – very pleasant on the nose and the palate. (1983)
♠ Robert Vic, 38 Rue Diderot, 34500 Béziers; tel. 67 76 38 89 ✆ By appt.

DOMAINE DE LA SERRE★★★

☑   10 000   `2` `D` `▮` `⬇`

Lovely pale rosé with orange shades. Nose is at first quite reserved but then displays some character. A complexity rarely found in a rosé, the result of a judicious, well-balanced blend of local grape varieties: Carignan, Cinsaut and Grenache, with a hint of Syrah.
♠ P. Tobena, Dom. de la Serre, 34630 St-Thibery; tel. 67 98 55 66 ✆ By appt.

DOMAINE ST-MARTIN DE LA GARRIGUE *Cuvée Réserve*★★★

■   4ha   19 000   `3` `D` `⬥` `⬇`

Parts of this estate date from the 9th century. Attractive, deep ruby wine; still immature. Interesting concentration of fruits and spices on the nose. Elegant composition, and harmonious and rich blend of fruit and tannin, suggesting excellent development. Very fine wine way above its appellation; even the elegance of its presentation shows as much care as the wine itself.
♠ Henry Père et Fils, Dom. St-Martin de la Garrigue, 34530 Montagnac; tel. 67 98 30 20 ✆ By appt.

DOMAINE ST-MARTIN DE LA GARRIGUE *Cuvée Tradition*★★

☑   2ha   16 000   `2` `D` `▮` `⬇`

Very attractive violet-rosé colour precedes a fragrant nose with striking aromas. Lively for a southern rosé, and one of the few that will keep for more than a year in the bottle. (1983)
♠ Henry Père et Fils, Dom. St-Martin de Garrigue, 34530 Montagnac; tel. 67 98 30 20 ✆ By appt.

CAVE COOPERATIVE THEZAN-LES-BEZIERS★

■   10ha   60 000   `2` `D` `▮` `⬇`

Deep cherry colour and a fine, powerful nose. Fruity and rather tannic; not yet matured but quite pleasant.
♠ Coop. de Thézan-lès-Béziers, Les Clos de Thézan, Thézan-lès-Béziers, 34490 Murviel-lès-Béziers; tel. 67 36 00 35 ✆ By appt.

DOMAINE DES TOURELLES★

■   25ha   8 000   `2` `D` `▮` `⬇`

Deep purple-black colour and an animal nose. Not yet mature, very mellow and full. Should be drunk slightly chambré.
♠ André Cabanes et Fils, Rue de la Source, Sauvian, 34410 Sérignan; tel. 67 32 18 27 ✆ Mon.–Sat. 9.00–12.00/15.00–19.00.

Vin de Pays de la Bénovie

COOPERATIVE DE LA BENOVIE★★

■   540ha   100000   ② Ⓓ 🖩 ⬇

Thanks to the Grenache and Cinsaut grapes and adequate fermentation, this wine is supple, round and pleasant. (1983)
➤ Coop. de la Benovie, Beaulieu, 34160 Castries; tel. 67 86 58 44 ⵊ Mon.–Fri. 8.00–12.00/14.00–18.00.

Vin de Pays du Bérange

CAVES DU BERANGE★

☐   20000   ① Ⓓ 🖩 ⬇

Good fermentation emphasizes the attributes of the local vines and produces a white wine with a pleasant, flowery aroma. (1985)
➤ Group. des Caves du Bérange, Cave Coop. de Castries, 34160 Castries; tel. 67 70 06 85 ⵊ By appt. Closed 1 Sept.–31 Oct.

CAVES DU BERANGE★

■   40000   ① Ⓓ 🖩 ⬇

This is a 'little', quality wine at an unbeatable price. It displays all the aromas of its vines, is harmonious and has good length. (1984)
➤ Group. des Caves du Bérange, Cave Coop. de Castries, 34160 Castries; tel. 67 70 06 85 ⵊ By appt. Closed 1 Sept.–31 Oct.

CAVES DU BERANGE★

☑   260ha   20000   ① Ⓓ 🖩 ⬇

Supple and fruity for a rosé, it has the charms and attributes of its red brother. On the palate it is very supple, with persistent aromas. (1984)
➤ Group. des Caves du Bérange, Cave Coop. de Castries, 34160 Castries; tel. 67 70 06 85 ⵊ By appt. Closed 1 Sept.–31 Oct.

Vin de Pays des Collines de la Moure

FABREGOU★★

☐   125ha   750000   ① Ⓓ 🖩 ⬇

Well balanced, with a freshness just right for the shellfish produced locally. (1984)
➤ UC de la region de la Moure, Chai de Bouzigues, Bouzigues, 34140 Mèze; tel. 67 78 30 40 ⵊ By appt.

FABREGOU★★

☑   150ha   750000   ② Ⓓ ⑪ ⬇

A fresh and fruity rosé which, in the absence of a white, would go well with oysters or mussels. (1984)
➤ UC de la Région de la Moure, Chai de Bouzigues, Bouzigues, 34140 Mèze; tel. 67 78 30 40 ⵊ By appt.

FABREGOU★★

■   300ha   1250000   ① Ⓓ ⑪ ⬇

An elegant red, supple and fleshy with a fine, discreet bouquet. (1984)

➤ UC de la Région de la Moure, Chai de Bouzigues, 34140 Mèze; tel. 67 78 30 40 ⵊ By appt.

COOPERATIVE DE GRABELS★

☑   10ha   3000   ① Ⓓ 🖩 ⬇

Very fresh, fruity rosé from this small village in the hills near Montpellier. (1984)
➤ Coop. de Grabels, 37790 Grabels; tel. 67 75 10 45 ⵊ Closed Sep.–Oct.

COOPERATIVE DE GRABELS★

■   15ha   10000   ① Ⓓ 🖩 ⬇

Fruity, supple and lively wine from vineyards set amid aromatic scrubland.
➤ Coop. de Grabels, 34790 Grabels; tel. 67 75 10 45 ⵊ Closed Sep.–Oct.

CAVE COOPERATIVE DE PIGNAN★

☐   12ha   175000   ① Ⓓ 🖩 ⬇

A rather supple white wine; quite round and refreshing. Ideal for sunny days. (1984)
➤ Cave Coop. de Pignan, 34570 Pignan; tel. 67 47 70 15 ⵊ No visitors.

CAVE COOPERATIVE DE PIGNAN★

☑   15ha   244000   ① Ⓓ 🖩 ⬇

A fruity, fresh and spirited wine which will quench the thirst of visitors to the very picturesque 'old village' of Pignan.
➤ Cave Coop. de Pignan, 34570 Pignan; tel. 67 47 70 15 ⵊ By appt.

CAVE COOPERATIVE DE PIGNAN★

■   47ha   444000   ① Ⓓ 🖩 ⬇

A supple wine with harmonious aromas; pleasant and straightforward. (1984)
➤ Cave Coop. de Pignan, 34570 Pignan; tel. 67 47 70 15 ⵊ By appt.

DOMAINE DE L'ABBAYE DE VALMAGNE *Cuvée Cardinale*★

■   30ha   500000   ② Ⓓ ⑪ ⬇

Extremely rich colour and rich fruity nose with mature and intense aromas strongly reminiscent of blackberry. These carry onto the palate, where the finish is without acidity or tannin. (1981)
✔ Cuvée Tradition Rouge, Cuvée de Turenne Rouge.
➤ Gaudard d'Allaines, Dom. de l'Abbaye de Valmagne, 34140 Ville veyrac; tel. 67 78 06 09 ⵊ By appt.

Vin de Pays de la Vicomté d'Aumelas

UCOVIA★★

■   500ha   2000000   ② Ⓓ 🖩 ⬇

Aromatic and ruby-coloured. Full-bodied, has a long finish and is very pleasant to drink. (1983)
✔ Vin du Pays de la Vicomté d'Aumelas Cabernet.
➤ UCOVIA, Plaissan 34230 Pauchan; tel. 67 96 32 87 ⵊ Mon.–Fri. 8.00–12.00/14.00–18.00.

Vin de Pays des Côtes de Ceressou

VIGNERONS DU CERESSOU★★

☑   145ha   220000   2 D ☷ ↓

Vines clinging to the hillsides grow well in the strong Languedoc sunshine, producing this lovely, crisp, fruity rosé.
☞ Les Vignerons du Ceressou, Aspiran, 34800 Clermont-l'Hérault; tel. 67 96 50 16 ☎ By appt.

VIGNERONS DU CERESSOU★★

■   350ha   300000   2 D ☷ ↓

Technology plays servant to tradition, giving us this fragrant, drinkable red wine.
☞ Les Vignerons du Ceressou, Aspiran, 34800 Cleremont-l'Hérault; tel. 67 96 50 16 ☎ By appt.

Vin de Pays de Pézenas

DOMAINE DE LAVAL★★

☐   15ha   68000   2 D ☷ ◑ ↓

The first glimpse of its pale golden colour suggests a rich wine. Very aromatic (peaches and pears); smooth, fruity, and obviously southern, due to the grape varieties and amount of sunshine they have received. Dry and well-made but should be drunk young. Well presented with particularly attractive label. Deserves recognition. (1983)
☞ Jean Chazottes, Dom. de Laval, Tourbes, 34120 Pézenas; tel. 67 98 15 11 ☎ By appt.

Vin de Pays des Côtes de Thongue

DOMAINE DU PRIEURE
D'AMILHAC *Cuvée Jean de Bonsi*★★

■   100ha   400000   2 D ◑

Exclusively from the Cabernet-Sauvignon grape, using modern methods of vinification. Before going on sale the wine has been matured for two years in cask and one in bottle, and the result is a very generous and powerful wine. (1980)
☞ Régis and Max Cazottes, Prieuré d'Amilhac, BP 11, 34290 Servian; tel. 67 39 10 51

DOMAINE DU PRIEURE
D'AMILHAC★

☐   100ha   100000   2 D ☷ ↓

A tasting cellar and wine museum have been established in a 17th-century hall on the estate. This wine has a rich, fruity nose from the grape varieties Sauvignon Blanc and Chardonnay – an unusual combination in the south of France. (1983)
☞ Régis and Max Cazottes, Prieuré d'Amilhac, BP 11, 34290 Servian; tel. 67 39 10 51 ☎ Mon.–Sat. 8.00–12.00/14.00–19.00.

DOMAINE LA CONDAMINE-
L'EVEQUE★★★

■   40ha   30000   2 D ◑ ↓

Deep colour, moderately powerful fine and floral nose with hints of sage. Round, fat and well structured, it leaves a light taste of liquorice on the palate. A lovely Vin de Pays. (1984)

☞ *M.* and *Mme* Bascou, Dom. de la Condamine, Nézignan-l'Evêque,   34120   Pézenas;   tel. 67 98 27 61 ☎ By appt.

DOMAINE DESHENRYS★★

☑   1ha   8000   2 D ☷ ↓

Attractive pale, orange-pink colour. Pleasant, fruity, subtle, and harmonious bouquet. Lively and easy to drink.
☞ Henri-Ferdinand Bouchard, Dom. Deshenrys, 34920 Alignan-du-Vent; tel. 67 24 91 67 ☎ Tues.–Fri. 8.00–12.00.

DOMAINE DESHENRYS★★

■   34ha   26000   2 D ☷ ↓

Attractive, young and seductive deep-red colour. Nose is still quite discreet but has good fruit. Well-balanced, delicate, very drinkable; very good for a Vin de Pays. (1983)
☞ Henri-Ferdinand Bouchard, Dom. Deshenrys, Alignan-du-Vent 34290 Servien; tel. 67 24 91 67 ☎ Tues.–Fri. 8.00–12.00.

DOMAINE DE LAVAL★★

■   38ha   300000   2 D ☷ ◑ ↓

Young-coloured, deep-purplish wine that will keep well. Peony and citrus fruit bouquet; lively, peppery. Robustness due to high proportion of Cabernet-Sauvignon and Syrah gapes from vines averaging thirty years old. (1983)
☞ Jean Chazottes, Dom. de Laval, Tourbes, 34120 Pézenas; tel. 67 98 15 11 ☎ By appt.

COOPERATIVE VIGNERONS DE MONTBLANC

■   30ha   30000   2 D ☷ ↓

Deep garnet colour. A full, fat, supple and round wine which goes well with grills and roasts. (1984)
☞ Cave Coop. de Montblanc, Montblanc, 34290 Servian; tel. 67 98 50 26 ☎ Daily 7.30–12.00.

VIGNERONS DE POUZOLLES-
MARGON *Cuvée des sept Pechs*★

■   30ha   30000   2 D ☷ ◑ ↓

Deep garnet colour and young fruity nose. Round and well-structured on the palate. (1984)
☞ Vignerons de Pouzolles-Margon, Pouzolles, 34480 Magalas; tel. 66 24 61 62 ☎ By appt.

DOMAINE DE LA SERRE
Cuvée Spéciale★★

■   4ha   25000   2 D ☷ ↓

Attractive colour that is neither too dark nor too developed. Pleasant nose. Elegant and very harmonious; plenty of finesse. The result of careful, traditional winemaking. (1982)

629

⚑ P. Tobena, Dom. de la Serre, 34630 St-Thibery; tel. 67 28 38 00 ☎ By appt. Closed Oct.–May.

DOMAINE DE LA SERRE

■ 20ha 120000 ☐ ☐ ☐ ⬇

Colour is very full; beginning to lose its youth. Four grape varieties – Carignan, Cinsaut, Grenache and Syrah – produce mature and spicy aromas. A somewhat harsh finish is in keeping with its style. (1980)
⚑ P. Tobena, Dom. de la Serre, 34630 St-Thibery; tel. 67 28 38 00 ☎ By appt. Closed Oct.–May.

CAVE COOPERATIVE DE SERVIAN

■ 370ha 150000 ☐ ☐ ☐ ⬇

The blend of Syrah and selected Carignan grapes gives this wine its deep garnet colour. Powerful floral nose, predominantly violet; balanced, fresh and aromatic on the palate. (1984)
⚑ Cave Coop. de Servian, 34290 Servian; tel. 67 39 11 17 ☎ Mon.–Fri. 8.00–12.00/2.00–6.00.

P. & L.-M. TEISSERENC
Cuvée de l'Arjolle★★

■ 18ha 20000 ☐ ☐ ☐ ⬇
83 84

Ruby-red colour with violet glints and a fine spicy nose of green peppers; should be uncorked two hours before drinking to allow the bouquet to reach its best. (1983)
⚑ P. and L.-M. Teisserenc, Pouzolles, 34480 Magalas; tel. 67 24 69 72 ☎ By appt.

CAVE COOPERATIVE DE VALROS★

■ 20ha 15000 ☐ ☐ ☐ ⬇

After a visit to the ruined Roman bastion, Garda de Valrano, at the very top of the village, one can taste this pleasant wine. Bright red colour and a very powerful nose of exotic fruits; a fresh, smooth Vin de Pays. (1984) ✔ Other Côtes de Thongue.
⚑ Cave Coop. de Varos, La Tour, Valros, 34290 Servian; tel. 67 98 52 65 ☎ By appt.

Vin de Pays des Coteaux du Libron

LA TREILLE BITERROISE★

■ 20ha 40000 ☐ ☐ ☐ ⬇

Brownish red with purplish tints. Animal-like aromas on the nose, and the bouquet becomes more intense on the palate, where it is well-composed, rich and round. (1983)
⚑ Cave Coop. Treille Biterroise, Route de Pézenas, 34500 Béziers; tel. 67 31 27 23 ☎ By appt.

Vin de Pays de l'Ardailhou

COOPERATIVE LA CERSOISE★★

■ 50ha 12000 ☐ ☐ ☐ ⬇

Rich, bright coloured. Powerful and fruity nose reminiscent of blackcurrants. On the whole perhaps a little closed-in; nevertheless, fresh and well balanced on the palate. (1984)

⚑ Sté Coop. la Cersoise, Cers 34420 Villeneuve-les-Béziers; tel. 67 39 31 79 ☎ By appt.

Vin de Pays Catalan

DOMAINE DE JAU★★

■ 7ha 25000 ☐ ☐ ☐ ⬇

Attractively coloured, aromatic and well-balanced; full and lively.
⚑ Diff. des Dom. de Jau, Ch. de Jau, Cases-de-Pène, 66600 Rivesaltes; tel. 68 54 51 67 ☎ Daily 9.00–19.00. Closed out of season.

Vin de Pays des Côtes Catalanes

LES VIGNERONS DE BAIXAS★★

■ 65ha 150000 ☐ ☐ ☐ ⬇

Light, smooth and fruity, with delicate and varied aromas. (1983) ✔ Côtes du Roussillon-Villages Rouge, Côtes du Roussillon Rouge, Muscat de Rivesaltes Blanc, Rivesaltes Rouge.
⚑ SCV les Vignerons de Baixas, 14 Av. du Mal-Joffre, 66390 Baixas; tel. 68 64 22 37 ☎ Mon.–Sat. 8.00–12.00/14.00–18.00.

VITICULTEURS CATALANS
Dom. Castel de Blé★★

■ 12ha 12000 ☐ ☐ ☐ ⬇

Light red colour with hints of violet. Delicate and fruity aromas and attractive flavour. Light, but also round, easy to drink, and well-balanced. (1984)
⚑ GIAR Les Viticulteurs Catalans, Rue des Vendanges, BP1, Banyuls-dels-Aspres, 66300 Thuir; tel. 68 21 72 18 ☎ By appt.

Vin de Pays des Pyrénées-Orientales

PRODUCTEURS DE LA BARNEDE★★

■ 230ha 100000 ☐ ☐ ☐ ⬇

Attractive and pleasant on the palate. Would go well with 'Les Boules de Picoulat', a regional dish. (1984) ✔ Côtes du Roussillon, Rivesaltes, Muscat de Rivesaltes.
⚑ SCV des Prod. de la Barnède, Av. du 8 Mai-1945, 66670 Bages; tel. 68 21 60 30 ☎ By appt. Closed public holidays.

DOMAINE JAMMES★★

☐ 10ha 5000 ☐ ☐ ☐ ⬇

Crisp and fruity. Good with cassis as an aperitif, or served as is with shellfish. (1984) ✔ Côtes du Roussillon, Muscat de Rivesaltes, Rivesaltes.
⚑ Dom. Jean Jammes, St-Jean-Lasseille, 66300 Thuir; tel. 68 21 64 94 ☎ By appt.

COOPERATIVE DE TROUILLAS★★

■ 250ha 200000 ☐ ☐ ☐ ⬇

Solid and very pleasantly round.
⚑ Sté Coop. Vini. de Trouillas, 1 Av. du Mas Deus, Trouillas, 66300 Thuir; tel. 68 53 47 08 ☎ Daily 8.00–12.00/14.00–18.00.

Provence and the Southern Rhône Valley

Here, too, most of the wine produced is red, accounting for 70 per cent of the 700000 hectolitres that come from the departments within the administrative zone, Provence-Alpes-Côte d'Azur. Of the rosés, 25 per cent of the total come mostly from the Var; the whites from the Vaucluse and the northern Bouches-du-Rhône. The many and varied grape varieties of the south are found here, normally blended in varying proportions according to climatic conditions and local custom. However, it is becoming increasingly common to blend the standard varieties with more unusual types – some traditional but neglected, others 'imported' from other regions. Examples of the former would be the Cournoise and Roussanne in the Var, and of the latter, the Cabernet-Sauvignon and Merlot, which are Bordeaux varieties, or the Syrah and Mourvèdre from the Rhône valley. Departmental classifications apply to Vins de Pays from Vaucluse, Bouches-du-Rhône, Var, Alpes-de-Haute-Provence, and Alpes-Maritimes; and there are five sub-regional or local denominations: Principauté d'Orange, Petite Crau (south-east of Avignon), Mont Caune (west of Toulon), Argens (between Brignoles and Draguignan, in Var), and Maures.

Vin de Pays de l'Ile de Beauté

CASANIS *Cirnéa*★★

■		650000	2 ■ ↓

Intense ruby colour and an expansive bouquet of very ripe fruit. Fullness, charm and a very persistent warm and aromatic character on the palate. An excellent Vin de Pays with nothing to apologize for. (1982)
✦ Sté Casanis, 75 Ave. Sainte-Marthe, 13014 Marseilles; tel. 91 63 63 63

DOMAINE DU LISTINCONE★

□	14ha	60000	2 D ■ ↓

Pale yellow with shades of gold. Very definite Muscat aromas. Surprisingly pleasant; sweetish yet has dry finish. Unusual and well made. Best served chilled as an aperitif.
✦ F. Vieles Tristani, Dom. de Listincone, 20270 Aghione; tel. 95 56 13 89 ⵝ By appt.

Vin de Pays de Petite Crau

CAVE COOP. DE NOVES
Cuvée des Amours★★

■		300ha	300000	1 D ■ ↓

A *vin de pays de la petite Crau* that is warm, smooth and generous. Reflects the area sung of by Mistral and painted by Van Gogh. Full of sunshine. (1983)
✦ Cave Coop. Vinicole de Noves, 13550 Noves; tel. 90 94 01 30 ⵝ By appt.

Vin de Pays du Mont Caume

SAN-CERI★★

■		130ha	150000	2 D ■ ↓

Makes a favourable first impression with its beautiful colour and rather fine nose. On the palate this is confirmed by great warmth of character. (1984)
✦ Coop. la St-Cyrienne, 29 Blvd J.-Jaurès, 83270 St-Cyr-sur-Mer; tel. 94 26 10 56 ⵝ By appt.

Vin de Pays d'Argens

CASTEL ROUBINE★★

☑		4ha	40000	2 D ■ ↓

Attractive rosé from a noble estate. Lovely pale colour, well-developed aromatic strength, and very delicate on the palate. ✔ Côtes-de-Provence.
✦ DPMVR Castel Roubine, Castel-Roubine, 83510 Lorgues; tel. 94 73 71 55 ⵝ Mon.–Fri. 8.00–12.00/14.00–18.00. Closed Nov. and holidays ✦ Ojvind Hallgren.

CASTEL ROUBINE★★★

■		4ha	40000	2 D ■ ↓

The estate is mostly known for its Côtes-de-Provence AOC wines. The red Vin de Pays is an attractive ruby colour, and very round and full. Tannic, with a clean finish. (1984)
✦ DPMVR Castel Roubine, Castel-Roubine, 83510 Lorgues; tel. 94 73 71 55 ⵝ Mon.–Fri. 8.00–12.00/14.00–18.00. Closed Nov. and holidays ✦ Ojvind Hallgren.

631

Vin de Pays des Maures

CAVE COOPERATIVE L'ARCOISE★★
☑   70ha   600 000   🔢 🄳 📷 ↓

The cooperative's Vin de Pays is in the same family as its Côte-de-Provence. Bright colour and quite delicate nose. Perfect Provence rosé, to be drunk young and served chilled. (1984) ✔ Côtes de Provence Rouge, Côtes de Provence Rosé, Côtes de Provence Blanc Sec.
↜ Cave Coop. l'Arçoise, Quartier le Lauron, 83460 Les Arcs-sur-Argens; tel. 94 73 30 29 ⓧ Mon.–Sat. 8.00–12.00/14.00–18.00.

COMMANDERIE DE PEYRASSOL
Vin nouveau Syrah pure★
■   12ha   72 000   🔢 🄳 📷 ↓

Attractive purplish colour, crushed fruit nose and lovely fruity flavour. Of quite high standard for a vin nouveau. Made exclusively from Syrah grapes. (1983)
↜ Yves Rigord, Dom. de Peyrassol, Flassans-sur-Issole, 83340 Le Luc; tel. 94 69 71 02 ⓧ By appt.

COOPERATIVE DE RAMATUELLE
Lou Siblaïre★★★
☐   17ha   15 000   🔢 🄳 📷 ↓

The type of fermentation and extraction set this dry wine apart. Made from Ugni Blanc, a traditional grape variety. Lively but very fragrant. Drink chilled. (1984) ✔ Côtes de Provence Rouge, Côtes de Provence Rosé, Côtes de Provence Blanc Sec.
↜ Coop. de Ramatuelle, Les Boutinelles, 83350 Ramatuelle; tel. 94 79 23 60 ⓧ Mon.–Sat. 8.30–12.00/14.00–17.45 (summer, 18.30). Closed two weeks in Feb.

DOMAINE FR. RAVEL★★
■   30ha   250 000   🔢 🄳 📷 ↓

A Cabernet-Sauvignon made to be full-bodied. Tannic acid evident on the palate is typical of this type, which is allowed to infuse for ten days. Will quickly smooth out and reveal the style of its origins – the Maures Massif. (1984) ✔ Côtes de Provence Rosé, Vin de Pays des Maures Tibouren.
↜ SCE Vignobles Ravel, Ch. Montaud, Pierrefeu-du-Var, 83390 Cuers; tel. 94 28 20 30 ⓧ Mon.–Thurs. 8.00–12.00/13.30–17.30. Closed public holidays ↜ François Ravel.

CAVE COOPERATIVE LA VIDAUBANAISE★★
■   260ha   80 000   🔢 🄳 📷 ↓

Deep-red and smooth, typical of the wines pro-
duced from the region's red marl soil. (1984) ✔ Côtes de Provence Roubertas Rouge, Côtes de Provence Provencal Rouge, Côtes de Provence Provençal Rosé, Côtes de Provence Provençal Blanc.
↜ Cave Coop. la Vidaubanaise, Av. Mouries, 83550 Vidauban; tel. 94 73 00 12 ⓧ By appt. Closed Sun.

Vin de Pays du Vaucluse

JEAN-LOUIS CHANCEL★★★
☑   40ha   100 000   🔢 ◑ ↓

Lovely 18th-century residence in the centre of a 'restored' vineyard, already famous for its antiquity in the Middle Ages. Pale red wine, with good fruit and long finish. (1984) ✔ Côtes du Luberon Val-Joanis.
↜ Jean-Louis Chancel, Ste. Civ. Ch. des Vaux, 84120 Pertuis; tel. 90 79 20 77 ⓧ By appt.

CAVE DES COTEAUX DU RHONE
Principauté d'Orange
■   150ha   30 000   🔢 📷 ↓

Pale red and clean tasting. (1984) ✔ Côtes du Rhône.
↜ Cave Coop. Coteaux du Rhône, Sérignan-du-Comtat, 84100 Orange; tel. 90 70 04 22 ⓧ By appt.

LA GAREOULTAISE★★
☑   275ha   100 000   🔢 🄳 📷

Pale, clean rosé colour; delicate and complex aroma. Lively wine that successfully marries traditional Midi grape varieties and local soil character. (1984).
↜ Coop. la Garéoultaise, Garéoult, 83136 Roquebrussanne; tel. 94 04 92 09 ⓧ By appt.

COOPERATIVE VINICOLE DE GRAMBOIS★★
■   28ha   288 000   🔢 🄳 ◑ ↓

Fruity and quite full-bodied; plenty of finesse. Pleasantly lively on the palate. Drink young. (1983) ✔ Côtes du Luberon.
↜ Coop. Vinicole de Grambois, Grambois, 84240 La Tour-d'Aigues; tel. 90 77 92 04 ⓧ Mon.–Fri. 8.00–12.00/14.00–18.00; Sat. 8.00–12.00.

DOMAINE DE GRANGE-BLANCHE★★★
■   5ha   50 000   🔢 🄳 📷 ↓

Deep ruby colour; richly fruity nose; full-bodied and surprisingly fruity on the palate. Complex, due to the time spent in wood. Very good Vin de Pays. (1983) ✔ Côtes du Rhône Dom. Font-du-Rouge, Châteauneuf-du-Pape Dom. de Tout-Vent.
↜ Jacques Mousset, Les Fines-Roches, 84230 Châteauneuf-du-Pape; tel. 90 83 70 30. ⓧ Mon.–Sun. 8.00–12.00/14.00–19.00. Closed Jan.

CELLIER DE MARRENON★★
■   600 000   🔢 🄳 📷 ↓

Ruby-coloured, fragrant and fruity. Delicate nose and average persistence on the palate. Drink young. (1984) ✔ Côtes du Luberon.
↜ Cellier de Marrenon, Quartier Notre Dame,

84240 La Tour-d'Aigues; tel. 90 77 40 65.
☎ Mon.–Sat. 8.00–12.00/14.00–18.00. Sun. 8.00–12.00.

DOMAINE DU VIEUX-CHENE★★★

■ 12ha 50000 ② Ⅾ 🍷 ⬇

Made by carbonic maceration. Combines smoothness with fruitiness. A headiness usually associated with Côtes du Rhône wines and their predominance of Grenache grapes. Handsome wine. (1984) ✔ Côtes du Rhône.
🍇 J.-C. et D. Bouche, Route de'Avignon, Camaret-sur-Aigues, 84150 Jonquières; tel. 90 37 21 58 ☎ By appt.

Vin de Pays des Bouches-du-Rhône

UCV DES BOUCHES-DU-RHONE
Sommelière★

■ 220ha 2 500 000 ② 🍷 ⬇

Made from traditional Midi grape varieties: Grenache, Cinsaut and Carignan. Crisp, smooth and fruity. Drink young. (1984) ✔ Côtes de Provence, Coteaux d'Aix-en-Provence.
🍇 UCV des Bouches-du-Rhône, Maison des Agriculteurs, 13626 Aix-en-Provence; tel. 42 23 06 11 ☎ Mon.–Sat. 8.00–12.00/14.00–17.45. Closed Sun. and public holidays.

DOMAINE DE BOULLERY★★★

■ 50ha 1 000 000 ② Ⅾ 🍷 ⬇

When near Aix-en-Provence, stop and admire the gardens and superb buildings of the Château de Fonscolombe, where this soft, supple, cherry-coloured wine is made. Drink young to appreciate the fruit. (1984) ✔ Coteaux d'Aix-en-Provence.
🍇 SCA Ch. de Fonscolombe, 13610 Le Puy-Ste-Reparade; tel. 42 61 89 62 ☎ By appt.

DOMAINE DE LA DURANCOLE

■ 20ha 72000 Ⅾ 🍷 ⬇

Fruity and smooth for a Vin de Pays. Good match for southern cuisine. (1983) ✔ Coteaux d'Aix-en-Provence; Vin de Pays des Bouches-du-Rhône, Rosé, Blanc Sec.
🍇 SCA la Durancole, Dom. de Calissanne, 78560 Lancon-de-Provence; tel. 01 91 61 17 ☎ By appt.

COOPERATIVE DE LA FARE-LES-OLIVIERS★

■ 25ha 240 000 ② Ⅾ 🍷 ⬇

From the home of vines and olives. Deep-coloured, robust, well-balanced red wine. Drink

young. (1984) ✔ Coteaux d'Aix-en-Provence.
🍇 Coop. de la Fare-les-Oliviers, Av. de Roquefavour, 13580 La Fare-les-Oliviers; tel. 90 42 61 47 ☎ By appt.

CHATEAU GRAND' BOISE★

◪ 1ha 6000 ① Ⅾ 🍷 ⬇

Subdued rose colour and concentrated fruit aromas. Good deal of character and fruit on the palate, no doubt the result of Cabernet and Syrah grapes.
🍇 Famille Gruey, Ch. Grand' Boise, 13530 Trêts-en-Provence; tel. 42 29 22 95. ☎ By appt.

CHATEAU GRAND' BOISE★★★

■ 1ha 6000 ① Ⅾ 🍷 ⬇

Fine, deep colour. Lively and interesting bouquet of red and blackcurrants. Persistence of fruit on the palate and touch of tannin due to the Cabernet Sauvignon grape. Elegant and well-balanced; exceptional for a Vin de Pays; from a fine vineyard. ✔ Côtes de Provence
🍇 Famille Gruey, Ch. Grand' Boise, 13530 Trêts-en-Provence; tel. 42 29 22 95 ☎ By appt.

DOMAINE DE LUNARD★★

■ 22ha 50000 ② Ⅾ 🍷 ⑪ ⬇

Ruby colour, with honest, clean aroma brought out by maceration. Underlying fruitiness, characteristic of this early ripening area. (1983)
🍇 François Michel, Dom. de Lunard, 13140 Miramas; tel. 90 50 93 44 ☎ Tues.–Sat. 9.00–12.00/15.00–19.00.

MAS DE REY★★★

■ 5ha 150000 ② Ⅾ 🍷 ⑪ ⬇

Characteristic old Camargue-style *mas*. Strikingly lovely red colour. Bouquet dominated by Cabernet aromas; fairly solid structure. Still young, but full of promise. (1984)
🍇 SCA du Mas de Rey, Route de St-Gilles, 13200 Arles; tel. 90 96 11 84 ☎ By appt.

MAS DE REY★★★

◪ 4ha 150000 ② Ⅾ 🍷 ⬇

Star-bright, pale-pink wine with overriding Cabernet aroma and pleasant roundness on the palate. (1984)
🍇 SCA du Mas de Rey, Rte de St-Gilles, 13200 Arles; tel. 90 96 11 84 ☎ By appt.

COOPERATIVE DE ROQUEFORT-LA-BEDOULE★★

☐ 75ha 150000 ② Ⓓ 🍶 ↓

Brilliant green-tinted colour. Distinctive, aromatic and delicate nose coming from Rolle or Vermentino grapes included in the blend. Successful and well made; very pleasant to drink. (1983) ✔ Côtes de Provence Cuvée Spéciale.
↳ Coop. de Roquefort-la-Bédoule, 13830 Roquefort-la-Bédoule; tel. 42 70 32 80 ⊥ By appt.

Vin de Pays du Var

DOMAINE DE CAMPDUMY

■ 25ha 180000 ② Ⓓ 🍶 ↓

Ruby colour and fine, complex nose. Generous and long on the palate. (1983)
↳ M. P. Gavoty, Cabasse, 83340 Le Luc; tel. 94 69 72 39 ⊥ By appt.

DOMAINE DE CAMPDUMY★★★

☐ 7ha 50000 ② Ⓓ 🍶 ↓

White Vin de Pays from the Gavoty estate, better known for its Côtes-de-Provence. Bright, pale straw-colour. Lively and refreshing. Light, flowery bouquet. (1984) ✔ Côtes de Provence. Rouge, Côtes de Provence Rosé, Côtes de Provence Blanc Sec.
↳ P. Gavoty, Cabasse, 83340 Le Luc; tel. 94 69 72 39 ⊥ By appt ↳ P. et B. Gavoty.

DOMAINE DE LA LIEUE★★

■ 11ha 50000 ② Ⓓ 🍶 ↓

Full coloured and tannic, with good persistence of flavour. The Mourvèdre grape will allow it to age well. Full of promise; to be laid down. (1984) ✔ Coteaux Varois.
↳ Jean-Louis Vial, Route de Cabasse, Dom. de la Lieue, 83170 Brignoles; tel. 94 69 00 12 ⊥ Daily 9.00–12.00/14.00–19.00.

DOMAINE DU LOOU★★★

■ 4ha 25000 ② Ⓓ 🍶 ⑪ ↓

Full-bodied wine of lovely ruby colour and persistent flavour marked by Syrah grapes. Vin de Pays that lives up to the year. (1981) ✔ Coteaux-Varois 1982 Rouge, Coteaux-Varois 1983 Rosé, Coteaux Varois Rouge et Rosé, Cuvée Speciale Rouge, Vin de Pays du Varois Cabernet-Sauvignon Rouge.
↳ Dominique di Placido, Dom. du Loou, 83136 La Roquebrussanne; tel. 94 86 94 97 ⊥ By appt.

DOMAINE ST-JEAN-DE-VILLECROZE
Cabernet Sauvignon★★

■ 31ha ③ Ⓓ ⑪ ↓

Extremely striking, rich and very deep colour, and a developed and concentrated nose with aromas of red fruits and high game. A wine of great class, lingering and elegant on the palate, without any alcoholic heaviness. A perfect dinner wine. (1981)
↳ GFA du Dom. de St-Jean, Villecroze, 83690 Salernes; tel. 94 70 63 07 ⊥ Daily 8.00–12.00/14.00–18.00. ↳ M. et Mme A. and D. Hirsh.

Vin de Pays de Layres

DOMAINE FRANCOIS RAVEL★

■ 45ha 300000 ③ Ⓓ 🍶 ↓

A pretty, dark-red wine with a beautiful nose of crushed fruits. The Cabernet-Sauvignon grape (100 per cent) gives it concentration and finesse. Still hard on the palate, it needs to mature, or to be drunk with meat casseroles or game. (1983)
↳ SCE Vignobles François Ravel, Ch. Montaud, Pierrefeu-du-Var, 83390 Cuers; tel. 94 28 20 30 ⊥ By appt.

Alpes and Pays Rhodaniens (Rhône)

This region runs along both sides of the Rhône valley from Auvergne to the Alps, grouping together the departments of Puy-de-Dôme, Loire, Rhône, Ain, Isere, Haute-Savoie, Savoie, Drôme, Haute-Loire, and Ardèche. The range of wines is enormous, as one would expect of wines made from different grape varieties grown in all manner of natural conditions. The area includes Burgundy varietals (Pinot, Gamay, and Chardonnay), those of the Midi (Grenache, Cinsault, Clairette, etc), as well as some from the Côtes du Rhone and Bordeaux. The local red grape variety is of course the Syrah, but in Savoie there is the Mondeuse, which has an unusual bouquet, and the Etraire de la Dui, a curiosity from the Isère valley. For white wines, Marsanne is sometimes blended with Roussanne, while the Molette is grown in the Ain department, the Jacquère in Savoie, and the Chasselas, or Fendant, in Haute-Savoie. Some 200000 hectolitres of wine are produced each year; the majority is red, and much of that comes from Ardèche and Drôme. On the whole, the regional tendency is to make wines from a single grape variety.

Ain, Drôme, Ardèche, and Puy-de-Dôme form the four departmental classifications, and there are eight subregional or local denominations in the region. These are: Vin de Pays d'Allobrogie (Savoie and Ain; 5000 hectolitres – most of which is white); Coteaux du Grésivaudan (from the Isère valley, 4500 hectolitres); Balmes Dauphinoises (Isère, 1500 hectolitres); Coteaux de Baronnies (in the south-east of Drôme; 20000 hectolitres of red wine); Comté de Grignan;

(20000 hectolitres of red wine); Collines Rhodaniennes (15000 hectolitres, mostly red); Coteaux de l'Ardèche (140000 hectolitres, mostly red) and Pays d'Urfi (Forez and Roannais, 1500 hectolitres of Gamay reds).

Vin de Pays d'Allobrogie

PIERRE DEMEURE★★

| ☐ | 3ha | 35000 | 2 D ⑪ ↓ |

Fresh, lively wine, pale-yellow with greenish tints. Hint of almonds and faint gun-flint flavour typical of the Jacquère grape. Drink young. (1983) ✔ Vin de Pays d'Allobrogie Gamay, Vin de Pays d'Allobrogie Chardonnay.
↪ Pierre Demeure, Joudin, 73240 St-Genix-sur-Guiers; tel. 76 31 61 74 ☎ By appt.

DOMAINE DE VILLY★★

| ☐ | 9ha | 60000 | 2 D ⑪ |

The Dumonts have resuscitated a centuries-old wine-making tradition. A wine that stands up for itself: light, fruity, with a faint sparkle. Drink cold with the local cuisine. (1984)
↪ Claude Dumont et Fils, Dom. de Villy, Contamine-sur-Arve, 74130 Bonneville; tel. 50 09 62 00 ☎ By appt.

Vin de Pays des Coteaux du Grésivaudan

CAVE COOPERATIVE DU HAUT-GRESIVAUDAN★

| ■ | 26ha | 20000 | 2 ■ ↓ |

Firm, fruity and straightforward. Based on the Etraire de la Dui grape, grown only in Gresivaudan. (1984)
↪ Cave Coop. du Haut-Gresivaudan, Barraux, 38530 Pontcharra; tel. 76 97 60 66 ☎ By appt.

Vin de Pays des Balmes Dauphinoises

MARC BONNAIRE★★

| ☐ | 5ha | 30000 | 2 D ■ ↓ |

Agreeable Vin de Pays. Bouquet of Chardonnay grapes and freshness of Jacquère. Pleasingly elegant combination. (1984) ✔ Vin de Pays des Balmes-Dauphinoises Rouge et Rosé
↪ Marc Bonnaire, La Remonde, St-Savin, 38300 Bourgoin-Jallieu; tel. 74 93 65 47 ☎ By appt.

Vin de Pays des Coteaux Baronnies

CAVE COOPERATIVE DU NYONSAIS★

| ■ | 200ha | 15000 | 2 D ■ ↓ |

Light and uncomplicated. Agreeable bouquet. Drink within a year of vintage. (1983) ✔ Côtes du Rhône-Villages Rouge, Côtes du Rhône Rouge, Côtes du Rhône Rosé, Côtes du Rhône Blanc Liquoreux.
↪ Cave Coop. du Nyonsais, Les Pilles, 26110 Nyons; tel. 75 26 03 44 ☎ Mon–Sat 9.00–12.00/14.00–18.00. Closed Sunday.

DOMAINE LA ROSIERE★★

| ■ | 2ha | 13000 | 2 D ■ ↓ |

From the Syrah grape. Solid colour. and rich, fruity-flowery aroma of violets, raspberries and strawberries. Rounds out on the palate with pleasantly long flavour. Drink 1–5 years after vintage. (1984)
↪ Serge Liotaud Dom. Rosière, Ste-Jalle, 26110 Nyons; tel. 75 27 30 36 ☎ By appt. Closed Oct.

Vin de Pays du Comté de Grignan

COOPERATIVE LA VINSOBRAISE
Cuvée de la Marquise de Sévigné★★

| ■ | 124ha | 950000 | 1 D ■ ↓ |

From the same mix of grape varieties as the cooperative, AOC Côtes-du-Rhône production. Fine, soft red colour. Supple and fruity. Drink young to appreciate the finesse. (1983) ✔ Côtes du Rhône, Côtes du Rhône-Villages, Vin de Pays de la Drôme.
↪ Coop. la Vinsobraise, Tulette, 26110 Vinsobres; tel. 75 27 64 22 ☎ By appt.

Vin de Pays des Collines Rhodaniennes

COOPERATIVE DE ST-DESIRAT-CHAMPAGNE★★★

| ■ | 30ha | 350000 | 2 D ■ ↓ |

Lovely deep-red colour. Bouquet reminiscent of violets, blackcurrants and truffles. Rounded and full-bodied. At its best after 2–3 years. (1983) ✔ Vin de Pays de l'Ardèche, Vin de Pays des Collines Rhodaniennes.
↪ Coop. de St-Désirat-Champagne, 07340 Serrières; tel. 75 34 22 05 ☎ By appt.

635

UPVF DE TAIN L'HERMITAGE
Syrah★★

| ■ | 60 ha | 280 000 | 2 ■ 🛦 |

From the Syrah grape; like the more prestigious AOC wines. Fine, deep-red colour. Delicate aroma of berried fruit. Outstanding suppleness. Perfect for early drinking. (1984) ✔ Hermitage Rouge, Hermitage Blanc; Crozes-Hermitage Rouge, Crozes-Blanc.
🛦 Coop. de Tain l'Hermitage.

UPVF DE TAIN-L'HERMITAGE

| ■ | 60 ha | 290 000 | 2 ■ 🛦 |

Very dark colour. Bouquet still shut in. Rich and full-bodied rather than delicate. Drink with fairly spicy food. ✔ Hermitage Rouge, Hermitage Blanc; St-Péray Méthode Champenoise, Crozes-Hermitage Rouge, Crozes-Hermitage Blanc, St-Joseph Rouge, St-Joseph Blanc.
🛦 Coop. de Tain-l'Hermitage, 26600 Tain-l'Hermitage; tel. 75 08 20 87 ☎ By appt. Closed 1 Jan., Easter, 1 Nov., Christmas.

Vin de Pays des Coteaux de l'Ardèche

VIGNERONS ARDECHOIS
Cabernet Sauvignon★★

| ■ | 120 ha | 700 000 | 2 🄳 ■ 🛦 |

This dynamic group of wine producers, situated close by the Ardèche gorge, sells a large range of wines. Among these, the Cabernet-Sauvignon is one of the most remarkable: fruity, characteristic, elegant and well balanced on the palate. It can be kept for several years and is one of the region's best value-for-money wines. (1983) ✔ Côtes du Rhône Rouge, Côtes du Rhône-Villages Rouge, Côtes du Vivarais Rouge, Côtes du Vivarais Rosé.
🛦 Vignerons Ardéchois, BP 8, 07120 Ruoms; tel. 75 93 50 55 ☎ By appt 🛦 *M. G.* Champetier.

DOMAINE DU BELVEZET *Syrah*★★

| ■ | 4 ha | 10 000 | 2 🄳 🕪 🛦 |

Dark-red in colour, powerful and generous, its solid structure should allow its aromas to develop fully in a few years. (1984) ✔ Côtes du Vivarais St-Remèze.
🛦 GAEC Belvezet, Dom. du Belvezet, St-Remèze, 07700 Bourg-St-Andéol; tel. 75 04 24 50 ☎ By appt 🛦 *MM.* Brunel and Deschamps.

DOMAINE DE BOURNET *Merlot*★★★

| ■ | 3 ha | 20 000 | 2 🄳 🕪 🛦 |

Full-bodied wine, with powerful aromas and a remarkable balance on the palate. (1984) ✔ Vin de Pays Coteaux de l'Ardèche Syrah.
🛦 Gérard Sauzon, Dom. de Bournet, Grospierres, 07120 Ruoms; tel. 75 39 68 20 ☎ By appt.

CAVES DE LA CEVENNE ARDECHOISE★★

| ■ | 8 ha | 60 000 | 2 🄳 ■ 🛦 |

Excellent wine: lively, cheerful, fruity, aromatic, full of charm. Soft finesse–drink within the year. (1984) ✔ Côtes du Vivarais VDQS.
🛦 Caves de la Cévenne Ardèchoise, Route Natio-

nale, St-Didier-sous-Aubenas, 07200 Aubenas; tel. 75 93 67 94 ☎ Mon–Sat 8.00–12.00/14.00–18.00.

DOMAINE DU COLOMBIER★★

| ■ | 25 ha | | 🄳 |

A blend of Carignan for strength of body, Grenache for warmth and fruitiness, and Syrah for distinction and bouquet. Fermented in the most natural way it has a light, lively and brilliant colour, a good constitution and a pleasant bouquet. When served at its best temperature, not too chambré, it has finesse and slips down well. (1984)
🛦 Philippe and Alain Walbaum, Dom. du Colombier, 07150 Vallon-Pont-d'Arc; tel. 75 88 01 70 ☎ By appt. Closed Oct.–May.

CAVE COOPERATIVE DE LABLACHERE *Gamay*★

| ■ | 15 ha | 70 000 | 2 🄳 ■ 🛦 |

Light, fruity and agreeably aromatic wine from vineyards near the magnificent dolmens (Celtic standing stones). Drink as young as possible. (1984) ✔ Vin de Pays Coteaux de l'Ardèche Syrah.
🛦 Cave Coop. de Lablachère, 07230 Lablachère; tel. 75 36 65 37 ☎ Mon–Fri. 8.00–12.00/14.00–18.00. Closed holidays.

Vin de Pays d'Urfé

COOPERATIVE 'LES VIGNERONS FORENZIENS' *Gamay*★★

| ■ | 8 ha | 20 000 | 2 🄳 ■ 🛦 |

An excellent Vin de Pays from the Gamay vine: supple, round and light to drink, with a beautiful ruby colour and a taste of raspberry. (1984)
🛦 Les Vignerons Foréziens, Trelins, 42130 Boens; tel. 77 24 00 12 ☎ By appt.

Vin de Pays de la Drôme

CAVE DES CLAIRMONTS
Bouquet de Syrah★

| ■ | 12 ha | 120 000 | 2 🄳 ■ 🛦 |

A good example of Syrah, this spicy and complete wine is violet-red in colour, young, and has a lightly rustic nose. (1983) ✔ Crozes-Hermitage.
🛦 SCA des Caves de Clairmonts, Beaumont-Monteux, 26600 Tain-l'Hermitage; tel. 75 84 61 91 ☎ By appt.

The Eastern Section

Some interesting, if modest, wines are grown here in the last remains of a vineyard area that had its hour of glory, thanks to its prestigious neighbours Burgundy and Champagne, but was then completely destroyed by phylloxera. Local grape varieties are used along with others from Alsace and Jura. Single-variety wines predominate and show good varietal character – whether of Chardonnay, Pinot Noir, Gamay, or Pinot Gris (this last being used for rosé wines). Auxerrois is sometimes added if the wine is being blended.

The Vins de Pays from Franche-Comté, Meuse, and the Yonne are light, crisp and aromatic. The amount of wine produced, especially white wine, is on the increase, but as yet amounts only to 30 000 hectolitres per year.

Vin de Pays de Franche-Comté

GROUPT. VITICOLE CHANITOIS
Coteaux de Champlitte★★★

| ☐ | 4ha | 25 000 | 2 D 🍷 ↓ |

A slightly amber wine, very supple and full, with exceptional balance. The finesse and lightness of the aromas are remarkable and special to the region. (1983) ✔ Vin de Pays de Franche-Comté Chardonnay, Vin de Pays de Franche-Comté Pinot Noir.
🖘 Groupt. Viticole Chanitois, 70600 Champlitte; tel. 84 31 65 09 ☎ By appt.

GUILLAUME PERE ET FILS★★★

| ■ | 2ha | 10 000 | 2 D 🍷 ↓ |

From the Bourgogne Pinot Noir, the Guillaume family produce red wines which are good examples of their type, with complex and rich aromas. These are class wines which would improve if left to mature for some years; show full varietal character.

🖘 Guillaume Père et Fils, Charcenne, 70700 Gy; tel. 84 32 80 55 ☎ By appt.

GAEC DE LA SERRE★

| ☐ | 2ha | 10 000 | 2 D 🍷 ◑ ↓ |

A light wine with discreet aromas and all the finesse which characterizes Chardonnay. The characteristics of each vintage are complemented by the Méthode Champenoise. (1983)
🖘 GAEC de la Serre, Offlanges, 39290 Moissey; tel. 84 70 24 36 ☎ By appt.

Vin de Pays de la Meuse

PHILIPPE ANTOINE★★

| ☐ | 1ha | 6000 | 2 D 🍷 ↓ |

On its home ground, the Auxerrois reveals all its finesse and special qualities. This dry white is a good example of the characteristics of this region. (1983) ✔ Vin de Pays de la Meuse.
🖘 M. et Mme Philippe Antoine, 2 Rue de l'Eglise, St-Maurice-sous-les-Côtes, 55210 Vigneulles-lès-Hattonchâtel; tel. 29 89 38 31 ☎ By appt.

GAEC DES COTES DE MEUSE★★

| ☐ | 2ha | 12 000 | 2 D 🍷 ↓ |

A fine example of the subtle aromas of the Auxerrois; an agreeable vivacity gives it a plea-Very original owing to the richness and complexity of its nose. (1983) ✔ Vin de Pays de la Meuse Pinot Noir.
🖘 GAEC des Côtes de Meuse, Billy-sous-les-Côtes, 55210 Vigneulles-lès-Hattonchâtel; tel. 29 89 37 43 ☎ By appt.

TABLE OF MAPS

GLOSSARY

AC Appellation Contrôlée. see **AOC**, Appellation d'Origine Contrôlée.

Acidity A vital component of a wine's **balance** giving freshness and vigour. If there is not enough acidity a wine tends to be flabby. Too much is also a fault, though apparently high acidity in young wines will often even out with age.

After-taste The lingering impression of a wine's characteristics which remains on the senses after every drop of the wine itself has left the mouth.

Age Often thought to be desirable in all wines – but this is not so. While a good number of wines do improve with age (notably clarets and red Burgundies) there are many more which should be drunk, at the latest, within three to five years of the harvest. Among these are virtually all rosés, generic Beaujolais and most dry Loire wines.

Alcohol After water, ethyl alcohol is the main component of wine. All clarified wines in France must respect a minimum and maximum alcoholic content, in accordance with local regulations. Too much alcohol in a wine gives a sharp, burning sensation in the throat and stomach.

Aligoté White grape variety used mainly in Burgundy.

Altesse White grape variety, lending great finesse to the Roussette de Savoie wines.

Amber Describes the hue sometimes taken on by white wines which have aged for a long time in bottle, or which have oxidized prematurely (*See* **oxidation**).

Ampelography The scientific study of grape varieties.

Ample Said of a harmonious wine which gives the impression of filling the mouth.

AOC Appellation d'Origine Contrôlée (also Appellation Contrôlée, **AC**): the highest classification category of French wines, legally defined by governmental decree. Although not a guarantee of high quality, as such, it does confirm that the wine comes from its stated origin and that its production has met certain specified requirements. All French wines granted an appellation are likely to be above average quality.

Aramon Black grape variety from the Midi, much in favour after the phylloxera crisis in the latter part of the nineteenth century, but now rarely planted.

Arbois Everyday white grape variety grown in Touraine. It has no connection with the Jura wine of the same name.

Aroma In wine-tasting terms, refers to the olfactory sensations experienced when the wine is in the mouth or, more generally, to the complete smell or bouquet of a wine.

Arrufiac White grape variety, used in the production of certain Béarn wines.

Assemblage French term for **blending**.

Astringency The somewhat mouth-puckering tartness often present in young red wines which are rich in tannin but not yet well-rounded. Disappears as the wine ages.

Auxerrois Grape variety grown in Lorraine, yielding Alsace Pinot or Alsace Klevner. Also the name used locally in the Cahors region for the Malbec grape variety.

Balance Denotes that the acidity and sweetness of a white wine, or the acidity, sweetness and tannin of a red wine, are harmoniously balanced on the palate.

Balsamic A broad category describing a number of different but related scents given off by wine – including (among others) vanilla, incense, resin and balsam.

Balthazar Outsize champagne bottle, equivalent to 16 ordinary bottles. (*See also* **magnum**, **Jeroboam**, **Rehoboam**, **Methusaleh**, **Salmanazar** and **Nebuchadenezzar**.)

Ban des vendanges Official proclamation, in each wine region, of the date when grape-picking for the latest vintage should begin.

Baroque White grape variety used in Béarn, producing a wine suitable for laying down.

Barrique French word for wooden cask in which wines are matured after fermentation. In Bordeaux, a *barrique* holds the equivalent of 225 litres. As another commonly used measurement of the volume of productions, four *barriques* equal one *tonneau* (though huge wooden tuns of this size are, in practice, hardly ever used nowadays).

Baumé A scale of measurement used in France to describe the amount of sugar in grape must. 10.7° Baumé indicates a potential alcoholic content of 10 per cent.

Blanc de Blancs May describe any white wine made solely from white grapes, though usually the term is applied only to champagne.

Blanc Fumé The local name for the white grape variety of the upper Loire region – in fact, the **Sauvignon** grape. Hence the wine Pouilly Fumé (*not* to be confused with the Pouilly Fuissé of Burgundy).

Blending (cf **assemblage**.) The practice of 'marrying' or mixing wines, usually of similar origin but of slightly different characteristics or ages. Strictly controlled by EEC wine-making laws, its main objectives are either to produce a wine of consistent quality and style, year in year out, or to create one which, in the aggregate, is better than any of the individual wines which form its ingredients. Most (though not all) champagnes are blends.

Body Designates the 'weight' of flavour of a wine. A full body is an essential characteristic of most fine red wines and also of such great sweet white wines as Sauternes. For many other white wines, though, it is the last property one would want. The finesse and elegance of champagne, for example, would be spoilt by too much body.

Bottle age The length of time a wine has spent in bottle. By implication, this is of significance only when the wine is capable of improvement during this period. Some quite inexpensive wines can improve very greatly if allowed to rest in bottle for 3–4 years or so. In contrast, others would develop no further, however long they were kept.

Botrytis cinerea The mould or fungus responsible for **pourriture noble**, or 'noble rot'. It forms on the skins of ripening grapes in certain wine districts, notably Sauternes, and is 'noble' because it results in wines of supremely high quality. The mould's spores suck water from the grape juice until the grapes become shrivelled and brown; in consequence, the almost glycerine-like juice retains a higher proportion of sugar to water than is usual, giving wines of extra sweetness and luscious flavour.

Bouquet The pleasing smell(s) a wine gives off, a short while after the bottle is opened. Also known as the 'nose'. It may be reminiscent of fruit, flowers, plants, fresh earth, even animal odours such as musk, venison or leather. In general, wines made in difficult conditions tend to have the most pronounced bouquets, while those grown in easy conditions and hot temperatures usually (though not always) have much less distinctive bouquets. 'Bouquet' is often taken to refer narrowly to the developed smell of wine after some bottle age, in contrast to 'aroma' the smell of an undeveloped wine.

Bourboulenc Good quality white grape variety, used in the Mediterranean region (Provence and parts of the Rhône valley).

Breton Local name in the Loire valley for the **Cabernet-Franc** grape variety.

Brut The driest normal grade of champagne and other sparkling wines. In practice, a small, carefully controlled amount of sweetening (the **dosage**) is added to all such wines; but the word *brut* indicates that very little has been used – just enough to moderate the wine's acidity. Champagne described as *brut zéro*, fashionable in some quarters, has had no *dosage* whatever added; but it is only in rare years that wines of this type are entirely satisfactory.

Cabernet-Franc Black grape variety, used in the Bordeaux region with the **Cabernet-Sauvignon** and **Merlot** to produce long-keeping wines of great finesse. Also makes the best red wines of the Loire region.

Cabernet-Sauvignon The greatest of Bordeaux's black grapes, predominant in the Médoc and Graves – but also found in other regions throughout France and elsewhere. Almost invariably produces wines which are firm, assertive and initially strong in tannin and which need to be laid down for several years before reaching their peak.

Carbonic maceration Method of vinification now being used increasingly to produce fruity wines for immediate drinking. Many local wines, once pretty rough and unknown outside their own community, have been improved by the process to the point where, today, they are reaching a much wider audience.

Carignan The most widely planted black grape variety in France, particularly in the south. Tends to produce robust, full-bodied wines – of no great subtlety or distinction, but pleasant enough (and especially so when used in blends with other grapes).

Cépage French word encountered incessantly in the wine field. Simply the general term for 'grape variety'.

César Very tannic grape variety, a small proportion of which is used at Irancy, giving a special character to Pinot Noir wines. Also known as the Romain.

Chai Ground-floor cellar used for storing wines in those regions where it would be unwise or impracticable to dig underground cellars (e.g. Bordeaux, with its high water table).

Chaptalization Practice of adding sugar to grape musts, officially permitted (under strict controls) to help fermentation in some districts with difficult climatic conditions. Named after the chemist and statesman Jean Chaptal, Comte de Chanteloup, who was Napoleon Bonaparte's minister of agriculture.

Chardonnay Best of the white Burgundy grapes; also used extensively in Champagne and Franche-Comté (and in many other parts of the world). Yields fine, subtle dry wines, often capable of considerable age.

Chasselas White grape variety (also widely cultivated as a table grape), which is used for growing eveyday wines in a number of French regions, such as Pouilly-sur-Loire, Savoie and Alsace.

Château (Literally, 'castle'.) Word often used to designate a vineyard estate or winery – even if the site does not incorporate an actual château.

Chenin Blanc White grape variety used for making the best white wines of Anjou and Touraine.

Cinsault (or Cinsaut) Black grape, grown especially in the Rhône valley and producing very fruity wines.

Clairet Can be either a light, fruity red wine *or* a rosé produced in Bordeaux and Burgundy.

Clairette White Mediterranean grape, producing fairly fine wines.

Claret Word invented by the British (probably a corruption of clairet, above) to describe all red wines from Bordeaux. The word has no legal status in France itself.

Clavelin Specially shaped bottle, holding 60cl, used for Jura wines.

Climat Literally 'climate' – but, in Burgundy, has a special meaning, designating a particular vineyard site.

Clone A group of vine shoots propagated from a single master shoot, either by cuttings or grafting.

Clos Commonly used in some regions to describe a vineyard enclosed by walls (e.g. Clos de Vougeot); but has also acquired a much wider meaning, sometimes being used to denote an entire winery or wine estate.

Closed in (French, *fermé.*) Describes a good quality wine which is still too young to have developed a pronounced bouquet. Until it begins to open up to reveal its best qualities, it will not be ready for tasting.

Colombard White grape variety used in the south-west of France, yielding fairly ordinary wines.

Commune A synonym of village; equivalent to an English parish.

Côt Name used for the Malbec grape variety in some regions (particularly the Loire).

Coteaux, Côtes Geographical terms, habitually followed by the name of a district, village or river, showing that the wines come from vineyards situated (respectively) on hillsides or slopes. Côtes probably designates a steeper terrain than coteaux – but both, by implication, are more favoured situations than vineyards on the plains.

Coulure A pollination failure of the young vine. This problem often arises from cold weather conditions during the period when the vines are flowering.

Courbu White grape variety grown in Béarn and the Basque country.

Crémant Describes a champagne or other effervescent wine fermented so as to produce a gentler sparkle than ordinary champagne (though still considerably more sparkling than **pétillant** wines). Does not apply to the excellent Crémants d'Alsace, which *are* fully sparkling.

Cru Literally, 'growth'. For example, the Grands Crus or Crus Classés (the great growths or classed growths). However, while always conveying the sense of a wine's identity with the specific place where it is grown, the precise meaning of the term varies slightly from region to region.

Crus Classés The classed growths (*see above*) are usually taken to refer to Bordeaux's historic 1855 classification, when the 62 best clarets of the day were listed in five Grand Cru – since followed by Crus Bourgeois, Crus Artisans and other gradings somewhat lower down the scale. However, in more recent years, the wines of nearly all the other main French vineyard regions have now been classified as well.

Cuverie; Cuvaison; cuve; cuvée Respectively: a vat-room; the process of fermenting in vats; the vat or tank itself; and a vatful or tunful. More particularly, the *cuvaison* is the period during which, after the harvesting of black grapes, the skins and other solids remain in contact with the grape juice (which is more or less colourless) as it begins fermenting in the *cuve*. The length of this period will determine the eventual depth of colour and tannic strength of the wine. On the basis that juice from the first grape pressing produces better wine than subsequent pressings, the phrase *tête de cuvée* on a label denotes that the contents come from a vat (or vats) regarded as holding the best of that particular batch of wine.

Cuve close A method of producing sparkling wines whereby the secondary fermentation is carried out in a sealed tank instead of in bottle. Quicker than the **Méthode Champenoise**, but the wines have less finesse.

Débourbage The clarification of unfermented grape juice.

Decanting Process of transferring wine from its bottle into a decanter or carafe, often required for fine old wines which show a sediment in bottle (and needing great care if the sediment is not to be disturbed). Rarely necessary for younger wines.

Déclassement Withdrawal of a wine's right to an appellation, after which it is marketed as an ordinary Vin de Table.

Dégorgement Under the **Méthode Champenoise**, the process for removing the deposit formed during the secondary fermentation. Withdrawal of this deposit, gradually brought down to the neck of the bottle by the **remuage**, also permits the insertion of the bottle's second, final cork.

Degree A wine's richness in alcohol used to be expressed in degrees, corresponding to the percentage of the volume of alcohol in the wine. The great majority of table wines rate between 10 and 12 degrees or so. Today, EEC law requires that the alcohol content be expressed as a percentage of the whole.

Demi-sec The literal translation of 'half-dry' is misleading. Demi-sec wines (notably champagne and other sparkling wines) are quite sweet.

Deposit Unless left at the bottom of the bottle, solids thrown by a wine as it matures, particularly a wine of some age, could often spoil the colour and be unpleasant in the mouth. Hence the advisability of **decanting** the wine (*see above*).

Depth A wine is said to have depth when it offers more and more subtleties of bouquet and flavour, etc., the more you taste it.

Destemming Separation of the grapes from the stems. For some wines, this takes place before the pressing. For others, the stems are kept in contact with the juice for a while, enhancing the level of tannin.

Dosage The additional sweetening added to champagne and other sparkling wines, by means of a *liqueur de tirage*, after the **dégorgement** and before insertion of the final cork (*see above*).

Doux Descriptive term for sweet wines.

Duras Black grape variety, grown above all in the Gaillac region.

Durif Black grape of the Dauphiné.

Elevage Literally, 'bringing up' or 'raising' the wine. Term used to describe all the various operations entailed in wine-making after the alcoholic fermentation and up to the time of bottling, and most specifically, the maturation period in barrel or vat.

Eye (*Oeil.*) Synonym for a vine bud.

Fer Black grape variety, producing wines capable of age

Fermentation Turbulent process through which the 'must' or grape juice is converted into wine – brought about by the action of yeasts, which change the natural sugar in the grapes into alcohol. *Malo-lactic fermentation* often called 'secondary' fermentation is the transformation of malic acid into lactic acid and carbonic gas – the effect being to render the wine less acid.

Fillette A half-bottle size (35cl), used in the Loire valley.

Fining Process for clarifying a wine by removing particles which have remained in suspension in the liquid. Agents permitted for this purpose may include egg whites or isinglass. (An alternative or complementary method of clarification is *filtration*.)

Finish The impression a wine leaves on the nose and palate as you swallow it. When this impression is long-lasting, the wine is said to have a 'long finish'. (Not to be confused with **after-taste**, which is the following stage.)

Flûte Tall, narrow glass, generally regarded as the best type for drinking champagne or other sparkling wine.

Folle Blanche White grape variety, producing very tangy wines. Known as the Gros Plant in Brittany and the Picpoul in the Midi.

Foudre Very large wooden tun holding up to 300 hectolitres.

Foulage Process by which the skins of red grapes are punctured in a coarse mill before alcoholic fermentation to liberate the grape juice and promote a rapid start to the fermentation. May alternatively designate the traditional practice in some wine growing areas of trampling the grapes by foot in the vat.

Foxy Describes the high-toned animal smell given off by wines made from certain hybrid grape varieties. (Inherited from description originally applied to the taste of wine produced from the American native wild vine.)

Full Describes a wine which gives a sensation of filling the mouth.

Gamay Noir à jus blanc Black grape best known for producing the light, fruity wines of Beaujolais (where it is the only variety grown). But it is now being used successfully in several other regions as well, notably Touraine.

Generic Often used to denote a regional appellation wine, as distinct from a more specific local appellation.

Gewürztraminer Highly scented Alsace grape variety, markedly spicy in both bouquet and taste.

Glycerol A tri-alcohol, produced by fermentation, with a sweetish taste. Glycerine gives the wine its unctuosity.

Grafting Since the phylloxera crisis of the 1870s, which threatened to destroy France's vineyards, this has been the only way to keep the deadly phylloxera louse at bay. American vinestocks which are resistant to phylloxera provide the roots of the vine plant and the desired varietal shoot is grafted onto the American rootstock.

Graves Soil containing a large proportion of rounded pebbles and gravel, very favourable for the production of high quality wines. In the Bordeaux region, is found especially in the Médoc and, of course, the Graves district.

Grenache Black grape, grown above all in parts of the Midi and the Rhône valley (e.g. Banyuls and Châteauneuf-du-Pape). Yields a perfumed, strong wine. Also used for making good rosés, such as Tavel.

Grip The firmness of flavour, normally contributed by acidity, of a wine in the mouth.

Grolleau Black grape variety grown in the Loire valley.

Gros Plant (*See* **Folle Blanche**.) Grape used for making the second main wine of the Muscadet region (after **Muscadet** itself).

Hard Describes a red wine with an uncomfortably high level of tannin or acidity (though this may ease with age).

Hectare 10,000 square metres ('ha', for short). As a rough rule of thumb, equals 2½ acres. (Actually, 2.471.)

Hectolitre 100 litres ('hl'). As a rough guide, equals 22 UK gallons or 26½ US gallons. (Actually, 21.997 or 26.417, respectively.)

INAO Institut National des Appellations d'Origine. The French Government Agency with responsibility for determining and controlling the production conditions of AOC wines.

ITV Institut Technique de la Vigne et du Vin. Professional body responsible for experimentation and research into vines and wines.

Jacquère White grape, grown in Savoie and the Dauphiné, producing a good wine that is best drunk fairly young.

Jeroboam Large-size bottle, holding the equivalent of four ordinary bottles. (See also **magnum**, **Rehoboam**, **Methusaleh**, **Salmanazar**, **Balthazar** and **Nebuchadnezzar**.)

Jurançon If white, a grape variety still used in Charentes but not much elsewhere. If black, either a subsidiary grape variety in south-west France or a fairly everyday wine.

Keeping *See* **Vin de garde**.

Lactic acid *See* **Fermentation**, **Malic acid**.

Larmes Literally, 'tears' although the English use the term 'legs'. Describes the traces left on the side of a glass by the wine. Often taken to denote a wine of high alcoholic content.

Lees The natural deposit left behind in a cask or vat when a wine is racked (i.e. clarified by being transferred to another container). A few wines – above all, Muscadet *sur lie* – are kept in the same cask on the original lees throughout the maturation process until they are bottled, thereby seeming to acquire extra richness of flavour.

Liquoreux Describes white wines that are richly sweet, thanks to 'noble rot' (*see* **Botrytis cinerea**).

Long Said of a wine when its aromas and flavour linger pleasantly in the mouth for quite a while after tasting. Hence 'a good length'.

Maceration Contact between the **must** and solids from the grape (e.g. skins, pips, perhaps even stalks) during the fermentation.

Maderized Describes a white wine which has begun to turn brownish with age – often also acquiring a taste somewhat reminiscent of Madeira (hence the term). Such wines may still, on occasion, be perfectly drinkable.

Magnum Double-size bottle (i.e. holds the equivalent of two standard bottles – about 1½ litres).

Malbec *See* **Côt**. Besides its cultivation in the Loire and Bordeaux regions, also helps to make the dark red wines of Cahors.

Malic acid One of the main types of acid found naturally in many wines. During the malo-lactic **fermentation** process, is turned into lactic acid and carbon dioxide.

Manseng Gros Manseng and Petit Manseng are the two basic white grape varieties of the Jurançon region.

Marc Solids remaining after the grape pressing. Also a strong, distilled liquor made from them.

Marsanne White grape variety, grown above all in the Hermitage region.

Mauzac White grape, grown above all in the Languedoc and Toulouse regions, yielding a wine that is quite elegant but not long-lasting.

Melon White grape, once found in the Côte d'Or area of Burgundy, but now better known as the Muscadet of Brittany.

Merlot Black grape variety grown throughout much of the Bordeaux region – used in smaller proportions with Cabernet grapes in the Médoc, but of predominant importance in St-Emilion and Pomerol.

Méthode Champenoise Used for all the best sparkling wines, as well as for champagne. The long, painstaking process whereby the precious bubbles are produced through a secondary fermentation in bottle.

Methusaleh (Or Imperial.) Large-size bottle, holding equivalent of eight ordinary bottles.

Meunier (Literally, 'miller'.) Member of the Pinot grape family, so named because the underside of its vine leaves has a floury white appearance, like a miller's coat.

Mildew Vine disease caused by a fungus attacking the plant.

Millésime The year a wine was harvested (cf **vintage**).

Mis en bouteille Literally, 'put into bottle'. When the label confirms that this was done at the château or estate where the wine was grown, it can nearly always be taken as a mark of added quality.

Mistelle Fresh grape must, rich in sugar, whose fermentation has been halted by the addition of alcohol.

Mondeuse Black grape grown in Savoie and the Dauphiné, producing a long-keeping wine of excellent quality.

Mourvèdre Black grape variety used mainly in Provence, yielding long-lived wines of some elegance.

Mousseux General term denoting sparkling wines.

Muscadelle White grape of the Bordeaux region, mostly used in conjunction with Sémillon and Sauvignon grapes.

Muscadet Fresh dry white wine from western end of the Loire region (near Nantes, Brittany). Also the grape variety from which it takes it name. (*See* **Melon.**)

Muscat Widespread family of very scented grapes. Also the name of wines made from such grapes.

Must The sugar-rich juice extracted from grapes.

Mutage Process for arresting the alcoholic fermentation of the must.

Nebuchadnezzar Largest of the outsize bottles, equal to 20 ordinary bottles. (N.B. These large-size bottles, from Rehoboam upwards, are virtually always used only for champagne.)

Négoce In a wine context, denotes commerce in wine and the various professions involved therein.

Négociant-eleveur In particular the professional engaged in buying wine from individual growers and 'raising', bottling and selling it.

Négociant-manipulant Term used in the Champagne region for a *négociant* who also buys in grape crops to make his own champagne.

Négrette Black grape variety of south-west France, giving a deep-coloured, rich wine of low acidity.

Niellucio Black grape grown in Corsica, yielding long-keeping wines of high quality (particularly at Patrimonio).

Noble rot *See* **Pourriture noble.**

Nose Frequently used synonym for a wine's smell or **bouquet.**

Nouveau Literally, 'new'. Describes wine from the latest harvest. Best known, of course, is Beaujolais Nouveau – but there are a good few others well worth trying.

Oaky Describes the flavour sometimes clearly discernible in wine which has been matured in wooden casks.

Oenology The scientific study of wine.

Oidium Wine disease caused by a small fungus and manifesting itself by the vine leaves turning powdery grey and the grapes becoming dehydrated. The disease, akin to mildew, can be treated with sulphur.

OIV Office International de la Vigne et du Vin. Inter-governmental body studying technical, scientific and economic questions posed by viniculture and wine production.

ONI VINS Office National Interprofessional des Vins. An official organisation, representing all main sections of the wine business, responsible for directing and controlling the wine market.

Organoleptic Vogue word to denote the qualities or properties of wine perceived by the senses, such as colour, smell or flavour.

Oxidation What happens when oxygen in the air gets at wine. A brief exposure may be beneficial (e.g. opening a bottle an hour before serving). But too much can adversely affect both the colour and bouquet of a wine.

Passerillage Process of drying grapes in the open air, enhancing their sweetness.

Pasteurization The technique of sterilizing wine (or other beverages) by heat, to kill off unwanted bacteria, as developed by the French scientist Louis Pasteur in the latter half of the nineteenth century.

Perfume *See* **Bouquet.** Perfume has an additional shade of meaning in that, implicitly, the word is always complimentary when applied to wine.

Perlant Very slightly sparkling (less so than **crémant** and **pétillant.**)

Pétillant Describes wines which have an evident tingle, though the sparkle is much less than that in *vins mousseux* and also, in nearly all cases, lower than the 'foaming' quality of **crémant** (q.v.).

Petit Verdot One of the minor grape varieties sometimes used in conjunction with Cabernet and Merlot grapes in the Bordeaux region.

Phylloxera Aphis (full name, *phylloxera vastatrix*) which drills into vine roots, usually killing off the plant within three years. Arrived from the USA in the early 1860s and, over not quite 20 years, threatened the virtual extinction of the entire French wine industry. Once in the soil, the aphis cannot be eradicated. It fails to survive only if vineyards lie on sand (which few do) or if they are flooded – when, of course, the vines could not be cultivated. The solution eventually discovered was **grafting**.

Pièce In full, *pièce de vin* – a Burgundian cask holding 216 or 228 litres.

Pineau Pineau des Charentes or Pineau Charentais: a sweet aperitif from the general Cognac area, made by adding brandy to the fermenting juice of fresh grapes.

Pineau d'Aunis Black grape grown in some parts of the Loire valley, yielding an extremely light-coloured wine.

Pineau de la Loire Local name for the **Chenin Blanc**.

Pinot Among the most prolific of grape families. Pinot Noir is *the* black grape of Burgundy, producing the greatest red wines of the Côte d'Or. Is also used in Champagne and sometimes in other regions for making white wine.

Pinot Blanc A member of the Pinot family but a white grape. Grown mainly in Alsace and also in Champagne.

Pinot Gris Grape variety otherwise known as the Tokay d'Alsace, producing a full-bodied Alsace white wine with a spicy character. (*See also* **Meunier.**)

Piqûre A disease caused by bacteria which results in sour acetic wine. Thus, as a tasting expression, a wine described as *piqué* is one suffering from sourness of taste and probably a vinegar-like smell as well.

Poulsard Black grape grown above all in the Jura; yields very elegant though only lightly coloured wines.

Pourriture noble 'Noble rot', a beneficent mould or fungus that forms on certain white grapes and makes possible the great sweet wines of Sauternes, in particular. (*See* **Botrytis cinerea.**) Although the phenomenon is also found in Germany, Hungary and other parts of the world, it is only in the Sauternes district (including Bordeaux) that it appears with such consistency, year after year.

Pressing Process of crushing the grapes to produce the juice which will be fermented to become wine. A *vin de presse* is a red wine made by pressing the grape solids which have been left behind after the grape juice proper, the must, has been extracted.

Primeur *Vin de primeur:* wine made to be drunk very young (e.g. Beaujolais primeur, released on the market only about eight weeks after the harvest). *Achat en primeur:* method of buying wine soon after the harvest (usually at an advantageous price), long before the wine itself will be anywhere near ready to drink.

Racking Process of clarifying a maturing wine by moving it from one cask or vat to another, leaving behind any deposit or **lees**. This operation may be performed 2–3 times or more throughout the maturation period before bottling depending on the kind of wine.

Rancio Describes character acquired by certain natural sweet wines (*vins doux naturels*) as they mature in cask. Gives them the taste and colour of old wines – broadly equivalent to 'tawny', as applied to port.

Ratafia Liqueur made in Champagne and Burgundy by mixing marc with grape juice; can be flavoured with almonds or the kernels of peach, apricot or cherry.

Récoltant-manipulant In Champagne region, describes vine-grower who also makes his own champagne. (cf **Négociant-manipulant**.)

Rehoboam Large-size champagne bottle, holding equivalent of six ordinary bottles.

Remuage Intrinsic part of the **Méthode Champenoise**, whereby deposits thrown off during the secondary fermentation are gradually, over a period of time, eased down to the neck of the bottle (pointing downwards), so that they can be removed at the moment of **dégorgement** (q.v.) The operation is still often performed manually.

Richness In wine-tasting terms, implies more than just sweetness. A rich wine is one with a powerful yet well-balanced flavour.

Riesling The greatest white grape of Alsace, producing dry wines of real distinction.

Rolle White grape variety used in Provence and the Nice area, yielding wines of some elegance.

Romorantin Fairly ordinary white grape, cultivated in a few parts of the Loire valley.

Rounded Describes the impression left in the mouth by a wine that is supple, rich (*see above*) and agreeably full and fleshy.

Roussanne White grape variety grown in the Drôme department, yielding very fine long-living wines. Best known for the white wines of Hermitage (and also of St-Péray, on the opposite bank of the Rhône).

Sacy White grape cultivated in the Yonne and Allier departments, producing a very fresh dry wine.

Saignée The process of drawing off excess liquid from the fermenting vat to achieve a better balance of solids to liquids during fermentation. Rosé de Saignée: a rosé wine drawn from a vat of black grapes after a short period of **maceration**.

St-Pierre White grape giving a somewhat acid wine found in the Allier department.

Salmanazar Large-size champagne bottle, holding equivalent of 12 ordinary bottles.

Sauvignon A very versatile white grape variety, used notably in Sauternes, the upper Loire (for Sancerre and Pouilly) and numerous other French regions. Produces an elegant wine, likely to keep well, with a distinctive sharp, sometimes 'smoky' bouquet (hence Pouilly Fumé).

Savagnin Grape variety used for making the *vins jaunes* ('yellow wines') of the Jura.

Sciacarello Black grape variety cultivated in Corsica, yielding a fleshy, fruity red wine.

Sec Literally, 'dry' – but in sparkling and other effervescent wines, particularly, is still likely to have some sweetness.

Sémillon One of the great white grape varieties, cultivated above all in the Bordeaux region, where it contributes lusciousness to Sauternes (being one of the type of grape most likely to attract **noble rot**). Also used for making soft dry white wines.

Short Said of a wine which leaves little trace of its qualities in the mouth after tasting. (Direct opposite to **long**).

Sulphur Sulphur dioxide, used judiciously, has been an important tool for wine growers over many centuries. The benefits it offers include helping to preserve wine, killing off harmful bacteria, sterilizing equipment and preventing or inhibiting oxidation. *Sulfatage* is a vine treatment, formerly carried out with copper sulphate, to prevent cryptogamic infections. *Sulfitage* is the process of adding a sulphur solution to must or wine, as protection against bacterial disease and other mishaps and to encourage a clean and healthy fermentation.

Sylvaner White grape variety, widely cultivated in Alsace. Makes fresh light wines, a little less dry than Alsace Riesling.

Syrah Best black grape of the Rhône valley, making powerful, deep-coloured wines capable of great distinction (e.g. Hermitage). Also grown in the Languedoc-Roussillon region.

Taille Pruning of the vines, to control growth and prevent excessive production.

Tannat Black grape found in the Pyrénées-Atlantiques department, yielding very full-bodied but elegant wines, capable of long life.

Tannic Having a discernible taste of **tannin**.

Tannin Astringent, naturally occurring substance that gives wine its ability to live for a long time – as much as a century or so for a few really great red wines – as well as providing certain elements in the wine's taste. Young wines may be unduly tannic, because their strong tannin tends to have a mouth-puckering effect, but this usually softens with age. Most of the tannin in wine comes from the pips and stalks of the grapes.

Tastevinage Mark of honour conferred by the Chevaliers du Tastevin wine order on selected Burgundies (chosen at 'blind' tastings, where members of the panel judge wines without knowing their complete identity).

Terroir Used in a wine context to denote a vineyard area with particular physical characteristics which are decisive in determining the nature and taste of the wine produced there.

Thermorégulation Technique enabling the temperature of the vats to be kept under control during the fermentation process.

Tokay d'Alsace *See* **Pinot Gris**. (N.B. This wine has *no* connection with the Tokay of Hungary.)

Tranquille (vin) Still wine.

Tressallier Alternative name for the white **Sacy** grape variety.

Ugni Blanc White grape variety, grown above all in the south of France and making a number of light white wines which, though quite pleasant, have a fairly high level of acidity and need to be drunk young. Also known as the St-Emilion in the Cognac region, but has no connection whatever with the Bordeaux district of that name.

Ullage Refers to the gap, occupied by air, between the top of the wine and the bottom of the cork, in a wine bottle. However, as an extension of the same thought, people in the wine trade also use the term to describe the practice of regularly topping up wine in a barrel, to keep the container full and prevent air from getting at the wine.

VDL *Vin de liqueur* – a sweet wine produced either by mixing wine and alcohol (as with Pineau des Charentes, q.v.), or by other processes not conforming to those for **VDN**.

VDN *Vins doux naturels:* naturally sweet wines, slightly above normal table wine strength. Usually made from Muscat Grenache or Malvoisie grapes, they are produced in accordance with strict regulations governing their method of fermentation, level of richness, and so on.

VDQS Vins Délimités de Qualité Supérieure. Like **AOC** is an officially backed guarantee that the wines concerned come from a specified area, are made only with the approved grape varieties and meet the regulations regarding maximum permitted yield per acre, traditional local production methods, and so on. Although **VDQS** is one below **AOC** in status, it is still a difficult distinction to obtain. Wines qualifying for the classification have to be tasted and approved first by a committee of impartial experts.

VQPRD Vin de Qualité Produit dans une Région Délimitée. The official EEC term to designate wines above table wine status. In France the term encompasses **AOC** and **VDQS** wines.

Vermentins White grape variety, also known as Rolle in Provence and the Nice area and as Malvoisie in Corsica.

Villages Used in some regions to designate wines from approved individual communes which are slightly better in quality (and probably also a trifle stronger) than those of the general appellation, e.g. Beaujolais-Villages, Côtes du Rhône-Villages.

Vin de garde Wine worth keeping or laying down, because it is almost certain to improve with age.

Vin Gris Wine made by vinifying black grapes as if they were white grapes.

Vinification The whole process of turning grape juice into wine.

Vintage Denotes the annual grape harvest and the wine made from it. (*See* **Millésime**.)

Viognier White grape variety of the Rhône valley, used in particular to make the superbly soft and fragrant white wines of Condrieu.

LIST OF SELECTED UK WINE MERCHANTS

B RITAIN IS fortunate in having a tradition of specialist wine merchants offering their own selection of French wines. Wine merchants, or their agents, make frequent trips to France to visit growers and buy their stock direct. The historical relationship of the English wine trade with Bordeaux and Burgundy is well known. But in recent years especially, an increasing number of independent wine merchants have established reputations in previously lesser-known regions. This section contains a representative list of wine merchants, from small concerns to countrywide chains, including supermarkets, which offer French wines of quality. The list is arranged geographically to cover the British Isles, and suppliers and merchants have been coded as follows:

M   = MULTIPLE
S   = SPECIALIST
W   = WHOLESALER (minimum order 1 case)

Where a merchant has a particular speciality, this is marked as below. It does not mean that he stocks nothing else. On the other hand, some merchants have extremely comprehensive ranges, covering all regions, but do not have a particular speciality – here, no symbol is used.

A   = ALSACE
B   = BEAUJOLAIS
Bo   = BORDEAUX
Bu   = BURGUNDY
C   = CHAMPAGNE
La   = LANGUEDOC
Lo   = LOIRE
P   = PROVENCE
R   = RHONE
Sw   = SOUTH-WEST
VdP = VIN DE PAYS

LONDON

S   *Les Amis Du Vin*
      Bo, Bu, La, Lo, P, Sw, VdP

SW   7 Ariel Way, Wood Lane,
      Shepherds Bush, London W12
      7SN; tel: (01) 743 2066/
      740 0053.

S   51 Chiltern Street, London
      W1M 1HQ; tel: (01) 847 3419.

S   30 James Street, London WC2;
      tel: (01) 836 4666.

S   *Balls Brothers* 313 Cambridge
      Heath Road, London E2 9LA;
      tel: (01) 739 6466.
      Bo, C

S   *Berkmann Wine Cellars*
      12 Brewery Road, London
      N7 9NH; tel: (01) 609 4711.
      Be, Bu

S   *Berry Bros & Rudd* 3 St James's
      Street, London SW1A 1EG;
      tel: (01) 930 1888.
      Bo, Bu

S   *Bibendum* 113 Regents Park
      Road, London NW1 8UR;
      tel: (01) 586 9761.
      Bo, Bu, Lo, R, Sw, VdP

S   *Bow Wine Vaults* 10 Bow
      Churchyard, London EC4M
      9DQ; tel: (01) 248 1121.
      Bo, Bu, La, R

S   *Camden Wine & Cheese* 214
      Camden High Street, London
      NW1; tel: (01) 482 2553.
      C

S *Caves de la Madeleine* 301
Fulham Road, London SW10
9AH; tel: (01) 351 5863.
Be, Bo, Bu, Lo, R, Sw, VdP

SW *The Champagne House* 15
Dawson Place, London W2;
tel: (01) 221 5538.
C

S *Christopher & Co.* 4 Ormond
Yard, London SW1; tel:
(01) 930 5557.
Bu, VdP

S *Corney & Barrow*
Bo, Bu

12 Helmet Row, London EC1V
3QJ; tel: (01) 251 4051.

118 Moorgate, London EC2;
tel: (01) 628 2894.

M *J. T. Davies & Sons Ltd
(Davisons)* Head Office, 7
Aberdeen Road, Croydon,
Surrey CR10 1EQ; tel:
(01) 681 3222.
Bo

S *Dolamore* 15 Craven Road,
London W2; tel: (01) 723 8894.
Bo

SW *Domaine Direct* 29 Wilmington
Square, London WC1; tel:
(01) 837 3521.
Bu

M *Peter Dominic* Head Office,
Vintner House, River Way,
Harlow, Essex; tel: (0279)
26801.

S *Ehrmanns Ltd* 26 Old Church
Street, London SW3; tel:
(01) 352 4114.

29 Heath Street, London NW3;
tel: (01) 435 6845.

56 Lambs Conduit Street,
London WC1; tel:
(01) 405 3106.

SW *Ellis Son & Vidler Ltd* 57
Cambridge Street, London
SW1V 4PJ; tel: (01) 834 4101.
Bo, Lo, VdP

S *Alexander Findlater* 77 Abbey
Road, London NW8; tel:
(01) 624 7311.
Bo, Bu, VdP

S *Findlater, Mackie, Todd*
Findlater House, 92 Wigmore
Street, London. W1H 0BB;
tel: 935 9264.
Bo, Bu, C, R

S *Greens Ltd* 34 Royal Exchange,
London EC3;
tel: (01) 626 8801.
Bo, Bu, R, VdP

S *John Harvey & Sons* 27 Pall
Mall, London SW1; tel:
(01) 839 4695.
Bo

S *Haynes Hanson & Clark*
Be, Bo, Bu, Lo, R

36 Kensington Church Street,
London W8 4BX; tel:
(01) 937 4650.

W 17 Lettice Street, London SW6
4EH; tel: (01) 736 7878.

S *Hedges & Butler* 153 Regent
Street, London W1R 4HQ;
tel: (01) 734 4444.
A, Bo

S *Justerini & Brooks* 61 St James's
Street, London SW1 A 1LZ;
tel: (01) 493 8721.
Bo

S *Laytons* 20 Midland Road,
London NW1; tel:
(01) 388 5081.
Bo, Bu

S   *O. W. Loeb & Co.* 15 Jermyn Street, London SW1Y 6LT; tel: (01) 734 5878. **A, Bu, R**

S   *Mackie & Co.* 4 Apothecary Street, London EC4V 6EU; tel: (01) 236 7080. **Bo, L**

M   *Majestic Wine Warehouses* Head Office, Colina Mews, Park Road, London N15; tel: (01) 889 9380.

Albion Wharf, Hester Road, London SW11; tel: (01) 223 2983.

Arch 84, Goding Street, London SE11; tel: (01) 587 1830.

West Ealing Station, Hastings Road, London W13; tel: (01) 567 9251.

229–233 The Broadway, London SW19; Tel: (01) 543 8125.

SW   *Malmaison Wine Club* 28 Midland Road, London NW1 2AD; tel: (01) 388 5086. **Bo, Bu, Lo, R, VdP**

S   *The Market* 700–702 Fulham Road, London SW6; tel: (01) 736 4295.

M   *Marks & Spencers PLC* Head Office, Michael House, 47–67 Baker Street, London W1; tel: (01) 935 4422.

S   *Milroys* 3 Greek Street, London W1V 5LA; tel: (01) 437 0893. **Be, Bu, C**

M   *Oddbins UK Ltd* Head Office, 80 Wapping High Street, London E1; tel: (01) 488 0109. **Bo, C, La, R, VdP**

M   *Arthur Rackham's Wine Shops* Head Office, Winefare House, Byfleet, Surrey; tel: (09323) 51585.

S   *La Reserve* **Bo, Bu**

56 Walton Street, London SW3; tel: (01) 589 2020.

47 Kendal Street, London W2; tel: (01) 402 6920.

S   *Russell & McIver* The Rectory, St Mary at Hill, London EC3; tel: (01) 283 3575. **Bo, Bu, R, VdP**

M   *J. Sainsbury* Stamford House, Stamford Street, London SE1; tel: (01) 921 6000.

SW   *Sookias & Bertaut* The Cottage, Cambal Road, Putney Hill, London SW15 6EW; tel: (01) 788 4193. **Sw**

M   *Tesco Stores Ltd* Head Office, Tesco House, Delamare Road, Cheshunt, Hertfordshire; tel: (0992) 32222.

M   *Thresher & Co. Ltd* Head Office, Sefton House, 42 Church Road, Welwyn Garden City, Hertfordshire; tel: (07073) 28244.

M   *Victoria Wine Company* Head Office, Brook House, Chertsey Road, Woking, Surrey; tel: (04862) 5066.

S   *La Vigneronne* 105 Old Brompton Road, London SW7; tel: (01) 589 6113. **Bo, L, R**

657

M   *Waitrose Supermarkets* Head
Office, Doncastle Road,
Southern Industrial Area,
Bracknell, Berkshire; tel:
(0344) 24680.

S   *Wine Growers Association* 230
Great Portland Street, London
W1N 5HG; tel: (01) 451 0981.

SOUTH EAST AND HOME COUNTIES

SW *Bordeaux Direct*
Bo, VdP

87 Caversham Road, Reading,
Berkshire; tel: (0743) 589990.

Shop 2 Dorna House, West
End, Woking, Surrey; tel:
(04862) 6133.

4 Alston Road, Barnet,
Hertfordshire; tel:
(01) 441 1255.

121 Arthur Road, Windsor,
Berkshire; tel: (07535) 66192.

3 Holtspur Parade,
Beaconsfield,
Buckinghamshire;
tel: (04946) 77564.

19 Denmark Street,
Wokingham, Berkshire;
tel: (0734) 785113.

24 Market Place, Henley-on-
Thames, Oxfordshire; tel:
(0491) 577355.

144 High Street, Bushey,
Hertfordshire; tel:
(01) 950 0747.

S   *Chaplin & Son* 35 Rowland
Way, Worthing, Sussex BN11
3JJ; tel: (0903) 35888.

M   *Peter Dominic* Head Office,
Vintner House, River Way,
Harlow, Essex; tel:
(0279) 26801.

SW *Andrew Gordon Wines*
Glebelands Centre, Vincent
Lane, Dorking, Surrey RH4
3YX; tel: (0306) 885711.
Bo

S   *Gerard Harris* 2 Green End
Street, Aston Clinton,
Aylesbury, Buckinghamshire
HP22 5HP; tel: (0296) 631041.
Bo

SW *High Breck Vintners* Spats
Lane, Headley, Hampshire
GU35 8SX; tel: (0428) 713689.

M   *Majestic Wine Warehouses*
79 Sumner Road, Croydon,
Surrey; tel: (01) 681 8130.

S   *Hungerford Wine Co.* 128 High
Street, Hungerford, Berkshire
RG17 0DL; tel: (0488) 83238.
Bo, R

M   *Marks & Spencer PLC* Head
Office, Michael House, 47–67
Baker Street, London W1;
tel: (01) 935 4422.

M   *Oddbins UK Ltd* Head Office,
80 Wapping High Street,
London E1; tel: (01) 488 0109.
Bo, C, La, R, VdP

M   *Arthur Rackham's Wine Shops*
Head Office, Winefare House,
Byfleet, Surrey; tel:
(09323) 51585.

M   *J. Sainsbury PLC* Stamford
House, Stamford Street,
London SE1; tel: (01) 921 6000.

SW *Seymour Ramsey* Watcombe
Manor Farm Office, Ingham
Lane, Watlington, Oxfordshire;
tel: (049161) 3266.

SW   *Stapylton Fletcher Wines* North
View, Oast Forge Lane, East
Farleigh, Maidstone, Kent;
tel: (0622) 20200.
Lo, R, Sw, VdP

M   *Tesco Stores Ltd* Head Office,
Tesco House, Delamare Road,
Cheshunt, Hertfordshire; tel:
(0992) 32222.

M   *Thresher & Co. Ltd* Head
Office, Sefton House, 42
Church Road, Welwyn Garden
City, Hertfordshre; tel:
(07073) 28244.

SW   *Henry Townsend & Co.* York
House, Oxford Road,
Beaconsfield,
Buckinghamshire; tel:
(04946) 78291.
Bo, Bu, C, R

M   *Victoria Wine Company* Head
Office, Brook House, Chertsey
Road, Woking, Surrey; tel:
(04862) 5066.

M   *Waitrose Supermarkets* Head
Office, Doncastle Road,
Southern Industrial Area,
Bracknell, Berkshire; tel:
(0344) 24680.

S   *Wine Growers Association* 135
Western Road, Brighton, East
Sussex; tel: (0273) 28408.

SOUTH-WEST

S   *Avery's* 11 Park Street, Bristol;
tel: (0272) 214141.
Bu

M   *Peter Dominic* Head Office,
Vintner House, River Way,
Harlow, Essex; tel:
(0279) 26801.

M   *Eldridge Pope* Head Office,
Weymouth Avenue,
Dorchester, Dorset; tel:
(0305) 64801.
Be, Bu, Bo

S   *John Harvey & Sons* 12
Denmark Street, Bristol BS99
7JE; tel: (0272) 836161.
Bo

SW   *Richard Harvey Wines* The
Auction House, East Street,
Wimborne Minster, Dorset
BH21 1DX; tel: (0202) 881111.

SW   *Hicks & Don* 4 The Market
Place, Westbury, Wiltshire
BA13 3EA; tel: (0373) 864723.

M   *Majestic Wine Warehouses*
St Bartholomew's Almshouses,
Westgate Street, Gloucester;
tel: (0452) 33949.

M   *Marks & Spencer PLC* Head
Office, Michael House, 47–67
Baker Street, London W1; tel:
(01) 935 4422.

M   *Oddbins UK Ltd* Head Office,
80 Wapping High Street,
London E1; tel: (01) 488 0109.
Bo, C, La, R, VdP

M   *J. Sainsbury PLC* Stamford
House, Stamford Street,
London SE1; tel: (01) 921 6000.

M   *Victoria Wine Company* Head
Office, Brook House, Chertsey
Road, Woking, Surrey; tel:
(04862) 5066.

SW   *Yapp Brothers* The Old
Brewery, Mere, Wiltshire;
tel: (0747) 860423.
Lo, P, R

EAST ANGLIA

S   *Adnams*
     Bo, Bu, Lo, R, VdP

     Sole Bay Brewery Southwold,
     Suffolk; tel: (0502) 722424.

     Adnams Wine Shop South
     Green, Southwold, Suffolk;
     tel: (0502) 722138.

     Market Place, Halesworth,
     Suffolk; tel: (09687) 2563.

     Olde Wine Shop Aldeburgh,
     Suffolk; tel: (072885) 2298.

SW   *Chesterford Vintners* The Old
     Greyhound, Great Chesterford,
     Saffron Walden, Essex; tel:
     (0799) 30088.
     Bo, Bu

S   *Dolamore* Joshua Taylor,
     Market Passage, Cambridge
     CB2 3JN; tel: (0223) 316455.
     Bo, Bu

M   *Peter Dominic* Head Office,
     Vintner House, River Way,
     Harlow, Essex; tel:
     (0279) 26801.

SW   *Roger Harris Wines* Loke Farm,
     Weston Longville, Norfolk NR9
     5LG; tel: (0603) 880171.
     Be

SW   *Hicks & Don* Park House,
     Elmham, Dereham, Norfolk
     NR20 5AB; tel: (036281) 571.
     Bo, R

S   *Lay & Wheeler* 6 Culver Street
     West, Colchester, Essex CO1
     1JA; tel: (0206) 67261.
     Bo, Bu, R, VdP

M   *Majestic Wine Warehouses*
     7/9 Coldhams Lane,
     Cambridge; tel: (0223) 313133.

M   *Marks & Spencer PLC* Head
     Office, Michael House, 47–67
     Baker Street, London W1; tel:
     (01) 935 4422.

M   *Oddbins UK Ltd* Head Office,
     80 Wapping High Street,
     London E1; tel: (01) 488 0109.
     Bo, C, La, R, VdP

M   *Peatling & Cawdron* Head
     Office, Westgate House, Bury
     St Edmunds, Suffolk IP33 1QS;
     tel: (0284) 5949.

M   *J. Sainsbury PLC* Stamford
     House, Stamford Street,
     London SE1; tel: (01) 921 6000.

M   *Tesco Stores Ltd* Head Office,
     Tesco House, Delamare Road,
     Cheshunt, Hertfordshire; tel:
     (0992) 32222.

M   *Thresher & Co. Ltd* Head
     Office, Sefton House, 42
     Church Road, Welwyn Garden
     City, Hertfordshire; tel:
     (07073) 28244.

M   *Victoria Wine Company* Head
     Office, Brook House, Chertsey
     Road, Woking, Surrey; tel:
     (04862) 5066.

M   *Waitrose Supermarkets* Head
     Office, Doncastle Road,
     Southern Industrial Area,
     Bracknell, Berkshire; tel:
     (0344) 24680.

S   *Wine Growers Association*
     5 Castle Meadow, Norwich;
     tel: (0603) 27112.

MIDLANDS

SW   *Bordeaux Direct* Market
     Square, Newbury; tel:
     (0635) 36052.
     Bo, VdP

S   *Dolamore* 106 Walton Street,
     Oxford OX2 6AJ; tel:
     (0865) 57734.

M   *Peter Dominic* Head office, Vintner House, River Way, Harlow, Essex; tel: (0279) 26801.

S   *S. H. Jones & Co. Ltd* 27 The High Street, Banbury,   -   Oxfordshire; tel: (0295) 51177.

M   *Majestic Wine Warehouses* 381 Cowley Road, Oxford; tel: (0865) 716959.

M   *Marks & Spencer PLC* Michael House, 47–67 Baker Street, London W1; tel: (01) 935 4422.

M   *Oddbins UK Ltd* Head Office, 80 Wapping High Street, London E1; tel: (01) 488 0109. **Bo, C, La, R, VdP**

M   *J. Sainsbury PLC* Stamford House, Stamford Street, London SE1; tel: (01) 921 6000.

S   *Edward Sheldon Ltd.* New Street, Shipston-on-Stour, Warwickshire; tel: (0608) 61409. **Bo**

S   *Tanners of Shrewsbury* Head Office, 26 Wyle Cop, Shrewsbury, Shropshire; tel: (0743) 53421.

M   *Tesco Stores Ltd* Head Office, Tesco House, Delamare Road, Cheshunt, Hertfordshire; tel: (0992) 32222.

M   *Victoria Wine Company* Head Office, Brook House, Chertsey Road, Woking, Surrey; tel: (04862) 5066.

M   *Waitrose Supermarkets* Head Office, Doncastle Road, Southern Industrial Area, Bracknell, Berkshire; tel: (0344) 24680.

NORTH

M   *T. F. Ashe & Nephew Ltd* Head Office, Ellis Ashton Street, Huyton Industrial Estate, Liverpool L36 6JB; tel: (051) 4805678.

S   *D. Byrne & Co.* 12 King Street, Clitheroe, Lancashire BB7 2EP; tel: (0200) 23152. **Bo**

M   *Peter Dominic* Head Office, Vintner House, River Way, Harlow, Essex; tel: (0279) 26801.

S   *Eaton Elliot Winebrokers* 12 London Road, Alderley Edge, Cheshire; tel: (0625) 582354.

M   *Marks & Spencer* Head Office, Michael House, 47–67 Baker Street, London W1; tel: (01) 935 4422.

M   *Oddbins UK Ltd* Head Office, 80 Wapping High Street, London E1; tel: (01) 488 0109. **Bo, C, La, R, VdP**

S   *Quellyn Roberts* The Old Crypt, 11–23 Watergate Street, Chester CH1 2JX; tel: (0244) 20515. **Bo**

M   *J. Sainsbury PLC* Stamford House, Stamford Street, London SE1; tel: (01) 921 6000.

M   *Tesco Stores Ltd* Head Office, Tesco House, Delamare Road, Cheshunt, Hertfordshire; tel: (0992) 32222.

M   *Victoria Wine Company* Head Office, Brook House, Chertsey Road, Woking, Surrey; tel: (04862) 5066.

M   *Waitrose Supermarkets* Head
Office, Doncastle Road,
Southern Industrial Area,
Bracknell, Berkshire; tel:
(0344) 24680.

S   *Willoughby's* 53 Goss Street,
Manchester M2 4JB; tel:
(061) 834 6850.
Bo, C

SW   *Yorkshire Fine Wines* Nun
Monkton, York YO5 8ES;
tel: (0901) 30131.

SCOTLAND

M   *Peter Dominic* Head Office,
Vintner House, River Way,
Harlow, Essex; tel:
(0279) 26801.

S   *Peter Green* 37 Warrender Park
Road, Edinburgh EH9 1HJ;
tel: (031) 229 5925.

S   *J. E. Hogg* 61 Cumberland
Street, Edinburgh EH3 6RR;
tel: (031) 556 4025.
Bo, Bu

S   *Justerini & Brooks* 39 George
Street, Edinburgh EH2 2HN;
tel: (031) 226 4202.
Bo

M   *Marks & Spencer PLC* Head
Office, Michael House, 47–67
Baker Street, London W1;
tel: (01) 935 4422.

M   *Oddbins UK Ltd* Head Office,
80 Wapping High Street,
London E1; tel: (01) 488 0109.
Bo, C, La, R, VdP

M   *Tesco Stores Ltd* Head Office,
Tesco House, Delamare Road,
Cheshunt, Hertfordshire; tel:
(0992) 32222.

WALES

M   *Peter Dominic* Head Office,
Vintner House, River Way,
Harlow, Essex; tel:
(0279) 51177.

S   *Luc Lacerre Et Fils Ltd* 78–80
City Road, Cardiff; tel:
(0222) 482302.
Bo, Bu, Lo, R, VdP

M   *Marks & Spencer PLC* Head
Office, Michael House, 47–67
Baker Street, London W1;
tel: (01) 935 4422.

M   *Oddbins UK Ltd* Head Office,
80 Wapping High Street,
London E1; tel: (01) 488 0109.
Bo, C, La, R, VdP

M   *J. Sainsbury PLC* Stamford
House, Stamford Street,
London SE1; tel: (01) 921 6000.

S   *Tanners of Shrewsbury* Head
Office, 26 Wyle Cop,
Shrewsbury, Shropshire;
tel: (0743) 53421.

M   *Tesco Stores Ltd* Head Office,
Tesco House, Delamare Road,
Cheshunt, Hertfordshire; tel:
(0992) 32222.

M   *Victoria Wine Company* Head
Office, Brook House, Chertsey
Road, Woking, Surrey; tel:
(04862) 5066.

NORTHERN IRELAND

S   *Duncairn Wines Ltd* Downtown
Shopping Centre, Downpatrick;
tel: (0396) 3392.

555 Antrim Road, Belfast;
tel: (0232) 771694.

IRISH REPUBLIC

S   *Findlater (Wine Merchants) Ltd*
149 Upper Rathmines Road,
Dublin 6; tel: Dublin 976130.

USEFUL ADDRESSES
IN FRANCE

WHILE history, sociology and ethnology all have their own views on the subject, nothing evokes the business of wine and its social role better than the museums devoted to it. The geographical side, too, is important: study it in its most seductive form – tourism – along the Routes du Vin, which are more often than not extremely well sign-posted by the Unions or Comités Interprofessionnels (listed below) or by the Comités de Tourisme in each department. (The most important routes are shown on the regional maps in this guide.) Besides this, organized trips with all aspects of wine as their theme have become increasingly common in France over the last few years (further details can be obtained from travel agents and the regional or departmental Comités de Tourisme). Finally, there is a newly formed chain of hotels consisting of thirty-seven top establishments in the wine-producing regions of France, called the Hostelleries du Vignoble Français (Auberge de Tavel, 30126 Tavel; tel. 66 50 03 41.) The places where business and folklore meet, such as fairs, fêtes and markets, or the ceremonial meetings of wine societies are excellent places to start your exploration of the world of wine.

Learning About Wine

Wine-tasting is not something that depends on innate skills, and you have to train your senses before you will be able to analyse different tastes and smells. Learning to drink wine is like learning to read – practice makes perfect. Introductory courses on the study of wine and wine-tasting are widely available nowadays, but it is certainly best to take your very first steps in your 'apprenticeship' under the guidance of a wine merchant, wine-buyers' club, or a knowledgeable cellarman. Wine bars ('bistros à vin') and top restaurants with good cellars are also splendid places to extend your knowledge, and will complement your visits to the producers' tasting cellars or 'caveaux de dégustation', and farms in the wine-producing areas.

TRADE BODIES

These are responsible both for maintaining the quality of wines and for the promotion of wine in their region, but they are also excellent sources of information for the general public (inquiries should be made by letter where possible.)

L'Alsace

Comité Interprofessionnel des Vins d'Alsace, 12 Av. de la Foire-aux-Vins, 68003 Colmar Cédex; tel. 89 42 06 21.

Beaujolais

Union Interprofessionnelle des Vins du Beaujolais, 210 Bld Vermorel, 69400 Villefranche-sur-Saóne; tel. 74 65 45 55.

Bordeaux

Conseil Interprofessionnel du Vin de Bordeaux, 1 Cours du XXX Juillet, 33000 Bordeaux; tel. 56 52 82 82.

Burgundy

Comité Interprofessionnel de la Côte-d'Or et de l'Yonne pour les Vins AOC *de Bourgogne,* Rue Henri-Dunant, 21200 Beaune; tel. 80 22 21 35.
Comité Interprofessionnel des Vins de Bourgogne et Mâcon, Av. du Maréchal-de-Lattre-de-Tassigny, 71000 Mâcon; tel. 85 38 20 15.

Champagne

Comité Interprofessionnel du Vin de Champagne, BP 135, 51204 Epernay Cédex; tel. 26 54 47 20.

Languedoc and Roussillon

Comité Inerprofessionnel des Vins de Fitou, Corbières et Minervois, et des Coteaux Occitans, RN 113, 11200 Lézignan-Corbières; tel. 68 27 03 64.

Provence and Corsica

Comité Interprofessionnel des Vins des Côtes-de-Provence, 3 Av. Jean-Jaurès, 83460 les Arcs-sur-Argens; tel. 94 73 33 38.
Groupement Interprofessionnel des Vins de l'Ile de Corse, 6 Rue Gabriel-Péri, 20000 Bastia; tel. 95 31 37 36.

The South-West

Comité Interprofessionnel des Vins de Gaillac, 8 Rue du Père-Gibrat, 81600 Gaillac; tel. 63 57 15 40.
Comité Interprofessionnel des Vins de la Région de Bergerac, 2 Place du Docteur-Cayla, 24100 Bergerac; tel. 53 57 12 57.

Loire Valley and Central France

Comité Interprofessionnel des Vins d'Origine du Pays Nantais, 17 Rue des Etats, 44000 Nantes; tel. 40 47 15 58.
Comité Interprofessionnel des Vins de Touraine, 19 Square Prosper-Mérimée, 37000 Tours; tel. 47 05 40 01.
Conseil Interprofessionnel des Vins d'Anjou et de Saumur, 21 Bld Foch, 49000 Angers; tel. 41 87 62 57.

Rhône Valley

Comité Interprofessionnel des Vins des Côtes du Rhône, Maison du Tourisme et du Vin, 41 Cours Jean-Jaurès, 84000 Avignon; tel. 90 86 47 09.

Vins Doux Naturels

Comité Interprofessionnel des Vins Doux Naturels, 19 Av. de Grande-Bretagne, 66000 Perpignan; tel. 68 34 42 32.

Vins de Liqueur

Comité National du Pineau des Charentes, 45 Av. Victor-Hugo, 16100 Cognac; tel. 45 32 09 27.

WINE MUSEUMS

Wine has played a part in French history for more than 2000 years, and many museums throughout the country bring to life an activity that is fundamental to French civilization. Whether set up in old vine-growers' houses, abbey precincts, Gothic cellars, as in Tours, or in superb hotels, as in Beaune, these museums contain a comprehensive collection of traditional implements and works of art ranging from Gallo-Roman *amphorae* to Jean Lurcat tapestries, from medieval wine presses to collections of bottles and glasses. Sometimes the exhibits are no more than a few tools lovingly collected by a vine-grower; elsewhere they may fill two rooms in an unassuming provincial museum. The main museums are listed below.

Alsace and the East

Musée de Kientzheim In the Château, headquarters of the Confrérie St-Etienne (Kientzheim, 68240 Kayserberg; tel. 89 78 21 36).
Musée Unterlinden This superb museum has more visitors than any other provincial museum in France. Large section devoted to wine containing, amongst other things, the famous Isenheim Altarpiece (1 Place Unterlinden, 68000 Colmar; tel. 89 41 89 23).
Musée Départemental d'Arts et Traditions Populaires Albert-Demard In the château at Champlitte; exceptional (70600 Champlitte; tel. 84 41 64 94).

Bordeaux

Musée des Outils de la Vigne et du Vin Château Loudenne (St-Yzans-de-Médoc, 33340 Lesparre-Médoc; tel. 56 41 15 03).
Musée du Vin et la Vigne dans l'Art Château Mouton-Rothschild; superb collections dating back over thirteen centuries (33250 Pauillac; tel. 56 59 22 22).

Burgundy

Musée du Vin de Bourgogne In the Hôtel des Ducs; a beautiful building constructed in the fourteenth and fifteenth centuries; a panoramic view of the history of wine in Burgundy (Rue d'Enfer, 21200 Beaune; tel. 80 22 08 19).

Champagne

Musée Municipal d'Epernay History and techniques of champagne production (13 Av. de Champagne, 51200 Epernay; tel. 26 51 49 91).
Musée d'Hautvillers In the abbey of Dom Pérignon (51160 Ay; tel. 26 59 40 01). (Most of the big champagne houses that admit visitors frequently have collections on display.)

Jura and Savoie

Musée de la Vigne et du Vin At the Hôtel de Ville in Arbois, where you can also visit Pasteur's house (Hôtel de Ville, 39600 Arbois; tel. 84 66 07 45).
Musée de la Vigne et du Vin Beside the River Loue, and not far from the Gorges de la Loue (Route d'Athoze, 25930 Lods; tel. 81 62 24 98).

Languedoc and Roussillon

Musée du Bitterois Collection devoted to the vine (7 Rue Massol, 34500 Béziers; tel. 67 76 90 10).
Musée de la Vigne et du Vin A rich collection devoted to art and popular traditions (Caves Savey-Serres, 3 Rue Turgot, 11200 Lézignan-Corbières; tel. 68 27 07 57).
Musée des Corbières In the *mairie* at Sigean (11130 Sigean; tel. 68 48 20 04).

Maison Vigneronne At Narbonne (Rue de l'Ancienne Porte-Neuve, 11100 Narbonne; tel. 67 32 64 82).
Musée de la Vigne et des Outils du Vin At the Teissier Domaine (Gallician, 30600 Vauvert; tel. 66 73 30 85).

Provence and Corsica

Musée International des Vins At the Paul Ricard Domaine; an impressive collection of bottles (Ile de Bendor, 83150 Bandol; tel. 94 29 44 34).

The South-West

Musée du Vin Mainly tools (24100 Bergerac; tel. 53 57 80 92).

The Loire Valley and Central France

Musée des Vins de Touraine Situated in cellars dating from the thirteenth century (Celliers St-Julien, 16 Rue Nationale, 37000 Tours; tel. 47 61 07 93).
Musée Animé du Vin et de la Tonnellerie (12 Rue Voltaire, 37500 Chinon; tel. 49 93 25 63).
Musée du Vin An annexe of the Musée Lurcat (4 Bld Arago, 49000 Angers; tel. 41 87 41 06).
Musée de la Vigne et du Vin In the cellars of La Coudraye (Place des Vignerons, 49190 St-Lambert-de-Lattay; tel. 41 78 30 69).
Musée Pierre-Abélard Devoted to the history of vine cultivation around Nantes (Chapelle St-Michel, Le Pallet, 44330 Vallet; tel. 40 26 40 24).
Musée de la Vigne et du Vin (Cour des Bénédictines, 03500 St-Pourçain-sur-Sioule; tel. 70 45 32 73).
Musée Municipal d'Histoire et des Traditions Locales In the cloisters of the old abbey of Selles (Place Charles-de-Gaulle, 41130 Selles-sur-Cher; tel. 54 97 40 19).

The Rhône Valley

Musée du Vigneron In the Beauregard Domaine, recently opened by a vine grower from Châteauneuf-du-Pape (84110 Rasteau; tel. 90 46 11 75).
Musée des Outils de Vignerons (84230 Châteauneuf-du-Pape; tel. 90 63 70 07).

Other Museums

There are several museums in the Cognac region, which also have displays devoted to Pineau Charentes. (Bld Denfert-Rochereau, 16000 Cognac; tel. 45 32 07 25; Le Bourg, Salles-D'Angles, 16130 Ségonzac; tel. 45 83 71 13).

In the Paris Area

Musée du Vin Situated in the cellars of an old convent (3 Rue des Eaux, 75016 Paris; tel. 45 25 63 26).
Musée Municipal René-Sordes Has an important collection of artefacts connected with the history of viticulture in the area (92150 Suresnes; tel. 47 72 38 04).

WINE FAIRS AND MARKETS

The first French wine fair was held in 1214; since that time, fairs – whether local, regional, national or even international – have been taking place regularly all over the country. They constitute a real shop window for the French wine industry, as well as places to buy and sell wine, meet other enthusiasts and to exchange ideas with vine growers and wine merchants. They are also places where you may discover exceptional wines – even excellent ones. Many of these fairs include competitions, the most prestigious being the Foire de Mâcon and the Foire du

666

Salon de l'Agriculture de Paris. Many excellent wines, however, are never entered in these competitions, and there are special competition wines, and even sometimes wines produced specifically to please the judges of a particular competition. But these are the exception, and a trip to a wine fair is usually an occasion for gleaning plenty of useful information about good-quality wines.

Large Wine Fairs

Foire Nationale des Vins de France de Mâcon During the 1985 open event of this highly respected competition, 7200 samples were tasted! (Parc des Expositions, annually, second half of May).

Salon International de l'Agriculture de Paris The competition is broadly similar to the one in Mâcon (Parc des Expositions de la Porte-de-Versailles, annually in March).

Foire de Paris Numerous wine producers, merchants and caves coopératives are represented at the Salon des Vins (annually in Paris, end of April and beginning of May).

Salon National des Caves Particuliéres This 'salon', which is stimulating and of a high standard, every year brings together several hundred independent wine producers from all over France. Sometimes remarkable discoveries are made (Paris, beginning Dec.) (Confédération Nationale des Caves Particulières, BP 227, 84108 Orange Cédex; tel. 90 34 36 04).

Large Regional Fairs

Alsace *Foire du Vin de Colmar* (first half Aug.).

Beaujolais and Lyonnais *Concours-Exposition de Ville-Franche-sur-Saône* (first Sun. in Dec.).

Bordeaux *The Foire de Bordeaux* attracts several wine producers' stands, but the biennial *Salon International Vinexpo-Vinotech* is exclusively for professionals.

Burgundy *Foire Gastronomique et des Vins de Dijon* (end of Oct.–beginning Nov.); *Fêtes Internationales de la Vigne et du Vin* (Dijon, Sept.); *Vente des Hospices de Beaune* (see *Festivals* below); Champagne *Foires-Expositions de Reims et de Troyes* (June).

The Rhône Valley *Foire aux Vins d'Orange* (end Jan.).

Provence *Foire de Brignoles;* with a competition for wines from the Midi.

The Loire Valley *Foire aux Vins de Tours* (middle Feb.)

Foire aux Vins du Mans (Jan.–Feb.).

FESTIVALS AND CELEBRATIONS

Countryside life has always included festivals. Initially these festivals, linked to a Christian tradition that is in turn rooted in much older, pagan rituals, were meant to protect or improve the harvest. Throughout the centuries they have given rhythm to peasant life, and still have a great significance in the world of wine. They are also an expression of joy and conviviality, without which wine would be meaningless. On 22 January every year, for example, many villages celebrate the feast of St Vincent with a procession and a banquet. The 'ban des vendanges', officially marking the beginning of the harvest, is itself an occasion for celebration. Since the Middle Ages these festivities have often been accompanied by trade shows, the most prestigious of which is still the *Vente des Hospices de Beaune.*

Alsace

There are many village festivals in July and August, as well as in October at harvest time; *Journée des Grands Crus d'Alsace* (mid-May).

Beaujolais and Lyon

Fête Raclet at Romanèche-Thorins (Nov.) is the first tasting of the year's wines in Beaujolais and Mâconnais.
Vente des Hospices de Beaujeu (second Sun. in Dec.) Many towns and villages also exhibit the year's best Beaujolais Crus every Sunday in November.

Bordeaux

The majority of confréries celebrate the harvest, and the feast of St Vincent is kept in all villages (22 Jan.).

Burgundy

Les Trois Glorieuses The first, held in mid-November, is the *Chapitre de la Confrérie du Tastevin*, which takes place at the Château du Clos-Vougeot. It is a large gathering, and a great many speeches and toasts are made. The second, held the next day, is the famous *Vente des Hospices de Beaune* during which the administration of the town's hospices auctions the wine from its domaines in accordance with an ancient tradition; buyers come from all over the world and the prices they pay fix those of the best Grands Crus. The third takes place on the third day at Meursault. It is known as *La Paulée*, and is a banquet to which everyone brings his own wines. A literary prize is also awarded. The *St-Vincent 'Tournante'* is held in a different place each year. Volnay has been chosen as the venue for 1986, and Santenay for 1987. Worth mentioning also are the *Fête des Vins de Chablis*, one week after the *Trois Glorieuses*; the *Exposition des Vins de Chablis* (end of Dec.); the *Fête du Roi Chambertin* at Gevrey-Chambertin; the *Carrefour de Dionysos* at Morey-St-Denis; and the *Vente des Hospices de Nuits* (spring).

Champagne

In the Aube, just like everywhere else, St Vincent is celebrated, but in addition the feast of St Paul is also kept (25 Jan.).
Journées de la Choucroute et du Champagne at Brienne-le-Château (Aube) (third Sat. and Sun. in Sept.).
Festival du Champagne, with concerts, songs and tastings, is held from time to time on an irregular basis.

Jura and Savoie

The *Fête du Biou d'Arbois* has very ancient origins, and has retained its religious character to this day. The finest grapes are fixed to a wooden mould filled with straw and then covered with wire netting. The effect is that of a huge bunch of grapes, which is then carried from Pasteur's house to the church.
Fête des Vins d'Arbois (second half July); plus numerous local festivities in Savoie.

Languedoc and Roussillon

Fête du Vin Nouveau at Perpignan, with a mass and blessing in the cathedral and a procession through the town (Oct.); *Fête de la Jacquetout* at Carcassonne and Narbonne (last weekend in Aug.); *Ste-Catherine* at Carcassonne (autumn); the *Foire aux Vins de Rivesaltes* (July); *Fêtes des Vins* at Nîmes (Nov.); and the *Fête du Vin d'Uzès* (first weekend in Aug.). *Les Paillasses de Courmontéral* Hérault. On the day of the carnival mattress fights take place in a flood of wine dregs. Faces, clothes and bodies are soaked, much to the delight of all!

Provence and Corsica

The *Fête des Vins de Bandol* (first and second Sun. in Dec.); the *Fête du Vin* in Cassis (first Sun. in Sept.); *Fête des Vignerons* at Antibes (19 May). The *Procession des Bouteilles* at Boulbon (Bouches-du-Rhône) (1 June) in honour of St Marcellin. Singing Provençal hymns, everyone moves in a procession to a Romanesque chapel where, after a sermon in Provençal, a blessing is given. All then brandish a bottle of wine and take a single swig. The remaining wine is kept for the sick.

The South-West

The *Cocagne des Vins de Gaillac* (first weekend in Aug.); the *Fête des Vins* in Lisle-sur-Tarn (mid-July). Also in the Tarn the *Fête du Cayla* is celebrated (Aug.), and the *Fête du Grand Fauconnier* at Cordes-sur-Ciel (mid July).

The Rhône Valley

There are a great number of festivals in villages, for example the *Fête des Côtes du Rhône Villages à Vacqueyras* (14 July, 'en tour' in Aug.); the *Baptême des Côtes-du-Rhône* is held in Avignon (14 Nov.), and the *Foire aux Vins Primeurs* takes place at Vaison-la-Romaine (end of the year).

WINE CONFRERIES

Although the tradition of the confréries can be traced back to the Middle Ages and beyond, almost all the confréries of today were founded relatively recently. The most famous, the Confrérie des Chavaliers du Tastevin, has been so successful in promoting the trade in Burgundy that its example has been widely followed; and in certain regions, such as Bordeaux, Anjou and Touraine, confréries flourish in ever-increasing numbers. While the ceremonial costume, the insignia, the solemn initiation ceremonies and the happy, flushed faces all make for a picturesque, even folksy, scene, the confréries are by no means frivolous. The members, who are for the most part elected to membership, whether they be vine growers or simply enthusiasts, will usually have had to prove their knowledge of wines. The confréries play a significant role in preserving the quality of wine, and to this end many of them award a seal of approval to the best wines in comparative tastings. (*Chevaliers du Tastevin, Compagnons de St-Vincent et Disciples de la Chanteflûte, Confrérie Alsacienne St-Etienne, Jurade de St-Emilion*, etc.).

Alsace

Hospitaliers d'Andlau; the *Confrérie St-Etienne* at the château at Kientzheim.

Beaujolais

Compagnons de Beaujolais (Villefranche-sur-Saône); *Confrérie du* GOSIERSEC *de Clochemerle* (Vaux-en-Beaujolais.)

Bordeaux

Commanderie du Bontemps du Médoc et des Graves, Pauillac; *de Sauternes-Barsac*, Langon; *De St-Croix-du-Mont. Jurade de St-Emilion; Compagnons de Bordeaux* (Génissac); *Hospitaliers de Pomerol; Gentilshommes du Duché de Fronsac; Compagnons de Loupiac; Vignerons de Montagne-St-Emilion.*

Burgundy

Chevaliers du Tastevin (Nuits-St-Georges, Ch. du Clos de Vougeot); *Cousinerie de Bourgogne; Confrérie St-Vincent* and *Disciples de la Chanteflûte de Mercurey; Confrérie des Vignerons de St-Vincent* (Mâconnais); *Piliers chablisiens; Trois Ceps de St-Bris* (Yonne).

Champagne

Ordre des Coteaux de Champagne; Commanderie du Saute-Bouchon de Champagne; Echevinage de Bouzy.

Languedoc and Roussillon

Confrérie des Coteaux du Languedoc; Maîtres Tasteurs du Roussillon and *Commande Majeure du Roussillon à Perpignan; Confrérie du Fitou; Illustre Cour des Seigneurs de Corbières* (Lézignan); *'Capitol dals Tastevins e Cargamelos de Limos'* (Limoux).

Provence

Confrérie de l'Ordre Illustre des Chevaliers de la Méduse (les Arcs-sur-Argens); *Confrérie des Comtés de Nice et de Provence.*

The South-West

Commanderie des Chevaliers de Tursan.

The Loire Valley and Central France

Commanderie des Grands Vins d'Amboise; Confrérie des Compagnons de Grandgousier; Confrérie des Maîtres de Chais; Confrérie des Tire-Douzils de la Grande-Brosse; Confrérie des Chevaliers de la Chantepleure (Vouvray); *Commanderie de la Dive Bouteille des Vins de Bourgueil et St-Nicolas-de-Bourgueil; Entonneurs Rabelaisiens* (Chinon); *Commanderie du Taste-Saumur; Chevaliers du Sacavin* (Angers); *Confrérie des Vins Gouziers d'Anjou; Chevaliers de la Canette; Confrérie des Hume-Pinot du Loudunais; Chevaliers de Sancerre.*

The Rhône Valley

Confrérie de la Syrah-Roussette (Valence); *Echansonnerie des Papes*, Château-neuf; *Commanderie des Costes-du-Rhône* (Ste-Cécile-des-Vignes); *Compagnons de la Côte du Rhône Gardoise* (Bagnols-sur-Cèze); *Commanderie de Tavel; Confrérie St-Vincent de Visan; Confrérie des Vignerons de la Cave de Beaumes-de-Venise; Grand Ordre de St-Romain; Confrérie des Chevaliers de Gouste-Seguret; Confrérie des Maîtres Vignerons de Vacqeyras; Confrérie de Crozes-Hermitage.*

Vins Doux Naturels

'As Templars de la Serra', Banyuls.

Finally, there are the *Compagnons de la Capucine*, Toul, and three groups in Paris: the *Commanderie des Vins de France*, the *Conseil des Échansons de France* (at the Flusée du Vin); and the *Association des Courtiers-Jurés-Piqeurs de Vins.*

WINE-TASTING COURSES

DRINKING a glass of wine is one thing; wine-tasting is quite another. You must use your eyes, studying the wine's radiance and colour, then your nose, which will tell you what the wine has to offer; then, and only then, does it pass your lips, at which point the wine is savoured and particular qualities that make it memorable are noted. It is of course possible to learn these techniques from books, but there comes a point when only practical experience will do. And of course, doing it is much more pleasant than reading about it! A growing number of schools, clubs, confréries and academies now offer courses in the study of wine. These range in length from a few hours to an academic year, and the wide selection available means you certainly should be able to find a course that fits your timetable. The initial outlay for such courses is usually high, but once your tutors have introduced you to the fascinating world of wine, with visits to vineyards and maybe even their own cellars, you will feel it is money well spent. A list of a few organizations that offer courses is given below.

The Paris Area

La Maison de la Vigne et du Vin Although not a formally established body, it offers a two-hour mini-course that ends with a wine-tasting. (21 Rue François 1er, 75008 Paris; tel. (1) 47 20 20 76).

L'Institut Technique du Vin Offers highly technical courses of one to four days (viticulture, setting up production facilities for vine growing and wine-making, study of wines, techniques of wine-tasting). (21 Rue François 1er, 75008 Paris; tel. (1) 47 23 42 00).

L'Académie du Vin The English in Paris, with all the wisdom they bring to the study of wine. A classic, twinned with the Caves de la Madeleine. (Cité Berryer, 25 Rue Royale, 75008 Paris; tel. (1) 42 65 09 82).

La Boutique du Vin Courses consisting of two or three sessions, in the form of social evenings with dinner. (33 Rue de l'Arcade, 75008 Paris; tel. (1) 42 65 27 27).

La Carte des Vins Perhaps the only remaining lunatics in Paris: courses were still being given free last year! Simply call round and sign-up. (10 Rue Papillon, 75009 Paris; tel. (1) 42 46 37 62 and 8 Bis Bld Richard-Lenoir, 75011 Paris; tel. (1) 43 38 74 99).

Le Caveau des Echansons Courses of four two-hour sessions over a period of two weeks, by qualified wine experts. (5 Square Charles-Dickens, 75016 Paris, tel. (1) 45 25 63 26).

Le Centre d'Information de Documentation et de Dégustation des Vins Wide range of courses (tasting, serving wines, study of wines, the vineyards of France). Monthly sessions on the wines of different regions, with guest producers from that region. (45 Rue Liancourt, 75014 Paris; tel. (1) 43 27 67 21).

Le Club Amical du Vin Theoretical and practical course. (10 Rue Cerisaie, 75004 Paris; tel. (1) 42 72 33 05).

Les Bons Mardis de Loïc de Rocquefeuil Two principal three-hour courses: 'Le Bordélais et ses appellations' and 'Les grands fleuves du vin français'. (48 Rue Ste-Anne, 75002 Paris; tel. (1) 42 61 99 88).

L'Invitation à Découvrir Five courses for amateurs, professionals and restaurateurs. (Caveau Valréas, 13 Rue Linné, 75005 Paris; tel. (1) 47 07 22 91).

671

Vinum Courses are held in the evening behind the shop, which, incidentally, stocks some splendid wines. Maximum of six for each course, with the accent on the 'nose' of the wines. (3 Rue de la Condamine, 75017 Paris; tel. (1) 42 93 61 61).

Hobby Vins Introductory courses to wine and wine-tasting; meetings specializing in regional themes. (La Défense, 92400 Courbevoie; tel. (1) 47 75 03 99).

L'Association des Gastronomes-Oenophiles A club for amateurs in the Chantilly area; a certain amount of drinking for pleasure, but it does help you to get to know your wines. (3 Place Gambetta, Noisy-sur-Oise, 95270 Luzarches; tel. (1) 40 34 11 47).

Alsace

Ecole Hôtelier de Strasbourg Given by the twice-crowned King of French Sommeliers, the courses consist of fourteen sessions, from September to February. (75 Route du Rhin, 67400 Illkirch-Graffinstaden; tel. 88 66 23 00).

Beaujolais and Lyons

Le Pavillon Daniele Carre-Cartal, one-time Best Sommelier of France, gives twelve lessons in the restaurant (the physiology of taste, wine-making, varieties of vines, the regions of France, and so on), complete with tastings. A similar course has been established in a restaurant in Lyon. (4 Av. de la Gare, 42700 Firminy; tel. 77 56 00 45).

Le Cavon de Lyon Bernard Tremblay, formerly of the Tour d'Argent and Lenôtre, has established himself in Lyon, close to the Place Bellecour. The course offered consists of fifteen sessions, each on a different theme. (6 Rue de la Charité, 69002 Lyon; tel. 78 42 86 87).

Bordeaux

Institut d'Oenologie de L'Université de Bordeaux The 'Oxbridge' of wine-tasting and the study of wine. Really for students, but welcomes amateurs, knowledge-able or not. Many courses, from one week to one year. (351 Cours de la Libération, 33405 Talence Cédex; tel. 56 90 91 28).

L'Hôtel de Vins de Bordeaux Courses on request, for groups of ten. (106 Rue de l'Abbé-de-l'Epée, 33000 Bordeaux; tel. 56 48 01 29).

Burgundy

Comité Interprofessionnel des Vins de Bourgogne (Rue Henri-Dunant, BP 166, 21202 Beaune Cédex; tel. 80 22 21 35).

L'Ambassade du Vin Tastings to suit everyone. (23 Rue des Tonneliers, 21200 Beaune; tel. 80 22 80 43).

Fondation Wine School Three courses: the geography of wines, the principles of wine-tasting and matching wines and food, and wine production. (22 Rue Paradis, 21200 Beaune; tel. 80 24 70 87).

La Cour aux Vins Introduction to the techniques of wine-tasting and 'soirées villages', for getting to know the wines of a particular area. (3 Rue Jeannin, 21200 Dijon; tel. 80 67 85 14).

La Maison des Vins de la Côte Chalonnaise Two sessions annually, and by request for larger groups. (Promenade Ste-Marie, 71100 Châlon-sur-Saône; tel. 85 41 64 00).

Lycée Agricole de Davayé Fairly technical. (389 Av. de-Lattre-de-Tassigny, 71960 Pierreclos; tel. 85 38 20 15).

Jura

André Jeunet Courses given on request by this jovial and enthusiastic restaurateur, who was voted best sommelier in France in 1966. (10 Rue du Vieux-Château, 39600 Arbois; tel. 84 66 07 50).

Languedoc and Roussillon

ANFOPAR, Domaine de la Bastide. (Route de Générec, 33000 Nîmes; tel. 66 38 09 56).
Comité Interprofessionnel des Coteaux Occitans Introduction to wine-tasting, dealing with all the wines of France, as well as Corbières. (RN 113, 11200 Lézignan-Corbières; tel. 68 27 03 64).
Université des Vins de Roussillon In the midst of the vineyards, discover the calm wisdom of the university. (Station Viti-Vinicole de Tresserre, 66300 Thuir; tel. 68 38 83 79).

Provence

Lycée Agricole de Hyères One of the best places for an introduction to wine. Open to all. A longer residential course can be arranged through INRA. (Quartier 'Les Grès', 83400 Hyères).
Le Club des Amis du Vin (Les Escassades, 13710 Fuveau; tel. 42 58 52 84).
Les Sommeliers de Provence, Lycée Hôtelier de Nice Courses right through the academic year, for amateurs as well as professionals. (144 Rue de France, 06000 Nice; tel. 93 86 92 11).

The South-West

Club 'Connaissance du Vin' (13 Rue Boulbonne, 31000 Toulouse; tel. 61 52 36 13).

The Loire Valley and Central France

Jacques Puisais au Château d'Artigny Four week-long residential courses every year, given by one of the great wine experts in a lovely hotel in a château. (Montbazon, 37250 Veigne; tel. 47 26 24 24).

The Rhône Valley

Université du Vin de Suze la-Rousse Forty short (3 or 4 days) residential courses, three long residential courses, plus 'wine-lovers' weekend'. This magnificent château also houses an excellent information centre. Video-cassettes on tasting, champagne and Côtes du Rhône are available. (Château de Suze-la-Rousse, 26130 St-Paul-Trois-Châteaux; tel. 75 04 86 09).

The North

Maison de l'Oenologie Courses in the study of wine, right in the middle of beer country. (14 Rue du Gard, 59000 Lille; tel. 20 51 06 77).

SUPPLIERS
Nothing beats buying direct from the grower or shipper, and tasting wines in a cellar owned by a group of wine-growers or a syndicate is the best way of finding out about country wines. This is almost certainly why there are so few cellarmen to be found in the provinces. But in town – and when you do not have the time to

build up a cellar yourself – the best thing is to enlist the help of a real cellarman. He will be a wine-lover, and often will travel thousands of miles every year in search of the best crus. You should not feel ashamed of asking his advice: in doing so you will be paying homage to his knowledge, learning more about it for yourself, and quite often assuring the success of a meal in the future. Certain 'bistros à vin' (see below) also act as wine merchants, and sell wine by the bottle, to take away.

A Few Good Addresses

Nicolas ... naturally. Besides the everyday wines on which the success of the business is built, Nicolas has an exceptional stock of Grands Crus and old vintages. Further details are in the catalogue, which can be obtained from any one of the 367 branches in Paris and the provinces, or by writing to the company's head office (2 Rue de Valmy, 94220 Charenton; tel. (1) 43 75 92 00).

Hédiard: Worth knowing about, not only for its Paris branches but also for the provincial branches and subsidiaries. (2 Bis Passage de la Madeleine, 75008 Paris; tel. (1) 43 04 51 92).

Around Paris (by district)

Legrand One of the best cellars in Paris. Everything about this cellar is exceptional. The staff have a vast store of information, and are generous and courteous in sharing it with the customers. (11 Rue de la Banque, 75002 Paris; tel. (1) 42 60 07 12).

Jean-Baptiste Besse Though it may look like the Old Curiosity Shop, this place has some excellent wines, and miracles have been known to occur when Jean-Baptiste goes down into the cellar ... (48 Rue de la Montagne-Ste-Geneviève, 75005 Paris; tel. (1) 43 25 35 80).

Steven Spurrier les Caves de la Madeleine One of those Englishmen who knows more about French wine than the French. Good selection, including decent, inexpensive labels. (25 Rue Royale, 75008 Paris; tel. (1) 42 65 92 40).

Peter Thustrup – Vins Rares et de Collection Another foreigner who has made his mark in the capital. Peter came to France from Sweden in 1979, and it is incredible to think that he has established such a superb cellar in so short a time. Exceptional. (3 Rue Laugier, 75017 Paris; tel. (1) 47 66 58 15).

Les Caves Georges Duboeuf The name Duboeuf signifies Beaujolais, and good Beaujolais at that. There are also excellent wines from other areas in stock, notably from Alsace, Burgundy and Bordeaux, as well as from the Loire. (9 Rue Marboeuf, 75008 Paris; tel. (1) 47 20 71 33).

Fauchon This deluxe grocery stocks an enormous variety of top-quality wines, from every appellation imaginable. (26 Place de la Madeleine, 75008 Paris; tel. (1) 40 73 11 90).

... and also

Gambrinus (13 Rue des Blancs Manteaux, 75004 Paris; tel. (1) 48 87 81 92). *Melvieux* (69 Rue du Rocher, 75008 Paris; tel. (1) 42 93 07 68). *La Carte des Vins* (8 Bis Bld Richard-Lenoir, 75011 Paris; tel. (1) 43 38 74 99). *La Cave des Gobelins* (56 Av. Des Gobelins, 75013 Paris; tel. (1) 43 31 66 79). *La Cave des Grands Vins* (144 Bld Montparnasse, 75014 Paris; tel. (1) 43 20 89 38). *La Vieille Cave* (131 Rue Lamarck, 75018 Paris; tel. (1) 46 27 52 39). *Ma Cave* (105 Rue de Belleville, 75019 Paris; tel. (1) 42 08 62 95). *Pétrissans* (30 Bis. Av. Niel, 75017 Paris; tel. (1) 42 77 83 84).

In the Suburbs

Les Toques Gourmandes Four Parisian restaurateurs, Alain Dutournier of 'Le Trou Gascon', Bernard Fournier of 'Le Petit Colombier', Jean-Pierre Morot-Gaudry and Henri Faugeron select excellent wines sold by mail order. (29 Bis Route de Versailles, 78560 Port-Marly; tel. (1) 49 16 11 73).

Mannevy A very good selection of wines, particularly strong on Bordeaux and Burgundy. (50 Bld Richard Wallace, 92800 Puteaux; tel. (1) 45 06 07 75).

Aux Caves Royales (6 Rue Royale, 78000 Versailles; tel. (1) 49 50 14 10).

Claude Constant (5 Bld de la Liberte, 94770 Le Perreux; tel. (1) 43 24 20 61).

In the Provinces

Réserve et Sélection (119 Rue du Dessous-des-Berges, 75013 Paris; tel. (1) 45 83 65 19); *Arnaud Dewavrin-Divinord* (10 Rue Morice, 92110 Clichy; tel. (1) 47 30 30 56; 3 Rue Robert-de-Flers, 75015 Paris; tel. (1) 45 79 57 72; *La Cave des Paquebots* (5 Rue Anatole-France, 92300 Levallois-Perret; tel. (1) 47 57 03 50; *Centre de Distribution des Vins de Propriété* (13 Bld Ney, 75018 Paris; tel. (1) 42 09 61 50).

WINE-BUYERS' CLUBS

Wine clubs are able to offer their members intelligent advice on choosing wines by employing the services of some of the most reputable experts from the wine and restaurant trades. It is the perfect system for people who want to have good-quality wines delivered direct to their homes. Two of the biggest names in this area are the *Savour Club* (44 Av. de Chatou, 92500 Reuil-Malmaison; tel. 47 51 03 20), created fifteen years ago, and now has more than 150000 members; and the *Club Français du Vin* (Ch. de Lancié, BP 2, Lancié, 69821 Belleville Cédex; tel. 64 66 45 85). Other clubs include the *Compagnie Bourgignonne des Oenophiles* (18 Rue Ste-Anne, 21000 Dijon; tel. 80 30 10 01); and *Les Grands Petits Crus* (15 Av. Victor-Hugo, 75116 Paris; tel. (1) 45 02 18 00).

Another area of the wine business is served by the new *Villésime* chain. 'Villésime' is not strictly speaking a club. It functions in much the same way as Interflora: you simply choose a wine that is stocked in any of the hundred-odd branches, which is then sent – along with a 'winogramme' bearing your chosen message – to whomever you please. If the local branch in the recipient's area does not have exactly the right wine in stock, one of similar quality and characteristics will be sent instead. (18 Rue Emeric-David, 13100 Aix-en-Provence; tel. 42 38 04 73).

A CELLAR IN YOUR OWN HOME

Nowadays the traditional vaulted cellar is beyond the reach of the majority of city-dwellers. Happily, viable alternatives do exist. For example it is possible to buy cabinets of varying degrees of sophistication that enable you to keep wines at the right temperature and humidity. Alternatively, it is possible to construct a cellar complete with all the necessary apparatus under your garage or in the garden. Finally, if you are very lucky you may be able to leave your wines to mature by renting a section of someone else's cellar.

Wine Cabinets

Eurocave Models for laying down 140, 200 or 250 bottles; also compartments for 65, 120, 170 and 210 bottles at room temperature and for chilling. Also models for restaurants. (BP 43 Rue François-Delaplace, 59610 Fourmies; tel. 27 60 38 55).

Idéal Cave: Société Eurodic Twelve models for 50–260 bottles. (5 Rue du Général-Clergerie, 75116 Paris; tel. (1) 47 04 61 55).

Caves Bacchus A specialist in cabinets for professionals, Bacchus has just launched a range for the public. Capacities for 50–60 and 200–250 bottles. (106 Av. Philippe-Auguste, 75011 Paris, tel. (1) 43 72 00 55).

Stone Cellars

Caves Harnois Round cellars, oval cellars, stepped cellars. The price varies according to the depth, size and type of soil. (BP 18, 91540 Mennecy; tel. 64 99 77 80).
Caves Henri Tradaire Similar to the companies already mentioned, except the cellars are the traditional type, with straight stairs. (22 Rue de la Folie-Méricourt, 75011, Paris).

WINE BARS

Real 'regulars' never like to see the address of 'their' bistro blazoned across the pages of a guide like this. This is the kind of information, they feel, that should only be tendered – at the right moment – to a dear friend. This friend will then in his turn be able to feel, as he leans on the bar, that he is in fact an old chum of the patron, himself an enthusiastic and loquacious son of Bacchus.

In Paris and other large cities the fashion for wine bars ('bistros à vin'), which first began to appear in the 1950s, is relatively recent. Since then whole chains have sprung up, and the more ambitous now have branches in the suburbs and in the provinces. The shop-sign is no guarantee you will get the warm welcome enjoyed by the people of Alsace in their 'winstubs', or by the Lyonnais in their 'bouchons', but cheerful service is the norm. Classic or original wines, typical of their kind and of excellent quality, are served by the glass and accompanied by food of the region, usually charcuterie and cheeses, but sometimes more elaborate dishes. It is worth noting that the provinces are not well served in this area of the wine trade; people living in the provinces often have the immense advantage of being able to discover wines for themselves – at source. Some bistros sell wines to take away. Every year in a ceremony in Paris one of them is awarded the 'Coupe du Meilleur Pôt' (of Beaujolais, of course!)

Around Paris (by district)

Le Bar de l'Entracte Not far from the Palais-Royal, it serves good estate-bottled wines, and, notably, an excellent Cahors. (47 Rue de Montpensier, 75001 Paris; tel. (1) 42 97 57 76).
Le Bar du Caveau Managed by an enthusiast who serves very good Beaujolais and Bordeaux, as well as good-quality lesser wines that deserve to be better known. (17 Place Dauphine, 75001 Paris; tel. (1) 43 54 45 95).
Le Beaujolais-St-Honoré Beaujolais, of course, but also Côtes du Rhône, St-Emilion, Cahors and many Loire wines. (24 Rue du Louvre, 75001 Paris; tel. (1) 42 60 89 79).
La Taverne Henry IV One of the best bistros in Paris, Robert Cointepas likes Loire wines, but also serves Beaujolais and a very good Jurançon Demi-Sec. Excellent charcuterie and very good cheeses. (13 Place du Pont-Neuf, 75001 Paris; tel. (1) 43 54 27 90).
Willi's Wine Bar There are other Willi's in Paris (one of which is at 18 Rue des Halles), but this one has a splendid selection of northern Côtes du Rhône and good red and white Bordeaux. Good food. (13 Rue des Petits-Champs, 75001 Paris; tel. (1) 42 61 05 09).
Le Gourmet's Modern and very attractive; some German wines. (26 Place Dauphine, 75001 Paris; tel. (1) 43 26 72 93).
Chez Gus-Le Cirque du Vin Halfway between a typical bistro and a wine bar. A sommelier who used to work at the 'Tour d'Argent' matches wines and food with

great skill. Loire wines a speciality.(157 Rue Montmartre, 75002 Paris; tel. (1) 42 36 68 40).

Le Duc de Richelieu A meeting place for journalists who appreciate the patron's Beaujolais. (110 Rue de Richelieu, 75002 Paris; tel. (1) 47 42 01 62).

L'Entre-Deux-Verres Loïc de Rocquefeuil, who is from Bordeaux, likes to share his taste for the wines of his native region. (48 Rue Ste-Anne, 75002 Paris; tel. (1) 42 96 42 26).

Le Jeroboam Owned by Nicolas, the wine company. An impressive wine list, with something for everyone. (8 Rue de Monsigny, 75002 Paris; tel. (1) 42 62 21 71).

Au Franc-Pinot The restaurant is in the basement, but on the ground floor you can drink very good wines by the glass, accompanied by tasty snacks. Friendly. (1 Quai de Bourbon, 75004 Paris; tel. (1) 43 29 46 98).

La Tartine Worth visiting for its atmosphere as a traditional bistro, and for its large selection of wines. (24 Rue de Rivoli, 75004 Paris; tel. (1) 42 72 76 84).

Le Café de la Nouvelle Mairie Yet another pearl! Wines from the Loire, Beaujolais – nothing but the best. The outside of the café is very unexceptional, but the warm welcome and the quality of the wines take over once you are inside. (19 Rue de Fossés-St-Jacques, 75005, Paris; tel. (1) 43 31 22 38).

Millésimes Cheerfully ruddy-faced patron, who seems to drink as much as all his clients put together! To speak to the perennial Chico Selsa is a must. The snacks that accompany the wine are generally good. (7 Rue Lobineau, 75006 Paris; tel. (1) 46 34 22 15).

Le Petit Bacchus Well known in Parisian wine circles, Jean-Marie Picard offers a good selection of wines from all over France. On Saturdays you can meet wine producers. (13 Rue du Cherche-Midi, 75006 Paris; tel. (1) 45 44 01 07).

La Sancerre (22 Av. Rapp, 75007 Paris; tel. (1) 45 51 75 91).

Le Sauvignon One of the original bistros. Henri Vergne won the 'coupe du meilleur pôt' in 1961 – proof enough, if it were needed, of his long-standing love of wine. The décor is dated, and there are some attractive, rather risqué engravings. All the wines are good. (80 Rue des Sts-Pères, 75007 Paris, tel. (1) 45 48 49 01).

Ma Bourgogne Without spending too much, it is possible to drink most Beaujolais and some Burgundies here, especially those from around Châlon. (133 Bld Haussmann, 75008 Paris; tel. (1) 45 63 50 61).

Le Blue Fox Bar Good choice from almost every region of France. Next door to Steven Spurrier's 'Caves de la Madeleine'. (Cité Berryer, 25 Rue Royale, 75008 Paris; tel. (1) 42 65 10 72).

La Boutique des Vins Excellent wines and good food. Prices are, unfortunately, high. (31–33 Rue de l'Arcade, 75008 Paris; tel. (1) 42 65 27 27).

L'Ecluse Nothing but Bordeaux, but the very best. (64 Rue François 1er, 75008 Paris; tel. (1) 47 20 77 09; 15 Place de la Madeleine, 75008 Paris; tel. (1) 42 65 34 69; 15 Quai des Grands-Augustins, 75006 Paris; tel. (1) 46 33 58 74; 2 Rue du Général-Henrion-Berthier, 92300 Neuilly; tel. (1) 42 65 34 69; Rue Mondétour, 75001 Paris; tel. (1) 47 03 30 73); and the *Comptoir de l'Écluse* has a larger selection of wines. Trendy, good food, high prices. (2 Rue Christine, 75006 Paris; tel. (1) 43 29 01 76).

Le Val d'Or Considering the neighbourhood, the prices are quite reasonable. (28 Av. Franklin-Roosevelt, 75008 Paris; tel. (1) 43 59 95 81).

La Cave Drouot Some very good wines from the south-west, plus some excellent Beaujolais and Loire wines. (8 Rue Drouot, 75009 Paris; tel. (1) 47 70 83 38).

Jacques Melac The man from Aveyron with the splendiferous moustache now has a very mixed clientèle frequenting his old-fashioned bistro. (42 Rue Léon-Frot, 75011 Paris; tel. (1) 43 70 83 38).

La Royale Specializing in Loire wines, notably Chinons. (80 Rue de l'Amiral-

Mouchez, 75015 Paris; tel. (1) 45 88 38 09).
Le Père Tranquille If you manage to find the place, it is well worth going inside. A wide range of Loire wines and an interesting menu. (30 Av. du Maine, 75015 Paris; tel. 42 22 88 12).
Le Pain et le Vin Opened two years ago by the 'four Musketeers' from the 'Toques Gourmandes', its regulars would not think of going anywhere else. Every wine in France, give or take a few . . . (1 Rue d'Armaille, 75017 Paris; tel. (1) 47 63 88 29).
Aux Négociants The perfect bistro, with a patron who spends his time digging out unknown wines (Loire, Burgundy, Côtes-du-Rhône, Bordelais . . .). (27 Rue Lambert, 75018 Paris; tel. (1) 46 06 15 11).

. . . and a few more

Le Bar du Sommelier (3 Rue de Castiglione, 75001 Paris; tel. (1) 42 60 37 80); *Le Rubis* (10 Rue du Marché-St-Honoré, 75001 Paris; tel. (1) 42 61 03 34); *La Cloche des Halles* (28 Rue Coquillère, 75001 Paris; tel. (1) 42 36 93 89); *La Gaité Bar* (7 Rue Papin, 75003 Paris; tel. (1) 42 72 79 45); *Les Vignerons* (18 Rue du Pot-de-Fer, 75005 Paris; tel. (1) 47 07 29 99); *Le Beverly* (9 Rue de l'Ancienne-Comédie, 75006 Paris; tel. (1) 43 26 78 48); *Le Chai de l'Abbaye* (26 Rue de Buci, 75006 Paris; tel. (1) 43 26 68 26); *Le Café Parisien* (15 Rue d'Assas, 75006 Paris; tel. (1) 45 44 41 44); *Le Mâconnais* (10 Rue du Bac, 75007 Paris; tel. (1) 42 61 21 89); *Vin sur Vin* (20 Rue de Montessuy, 75007 Paris; tel. (1) 47 05 14 20); *Le Bistrot du Sommelier* (97 Bld Haussmann, 75008 Paris; tel. (1) 42 65 24 85); *L'Oenothèque* (20 Rue St-Lazare, 75009 Paris; tel. (1) 48 78 08 76); *La Devinière* (70 Rue Alexandre, 75011 Paris; tel. (1) 43 73 22 97); *Le Limonaire* (88 Rue de Charenton, 75012 Paris; tel. (1) 43 43 49 14); *Le Rallye* (6 Rue Daguerre, 75014 Paris; tel. (1) 43 22 57 05); *Les Caves Solignac* (9 Rue Decrès, 75014 Paris; tel. (1) 45 45 58 59); *Les Caves Angevines* (2 Place Léon-Dubel, 75016 Paris; tel. (1) 42 88 88 93); *Le Winstub* (11 Av. de la Grande-Armée, 75017 Paris; tel. (1) 45 00 12 31).

In the Suburbs

J.-P. Chastang (8 Rue Aristide-Briand, 92160 Antony; tel. (1) 46 66 01 14); *Chez Serge* (7 Bld Jean-Jaurès, 93400 St-Ouen; tel. (1) 42 54 06 42); *La Tassée d'Argent* (21 Av. Gabriel-Péri, 94100 St-Maur; tel. (1) 48 88 00 14).

In the Provinces

Le Bistro d'Avignon (place de l'Horloge, 84000 Avignon; tel. 90 86 06 45); *Le Bistro de la Promenade* (7 Promenade des Anglais, 06000 Nice; tel. 93 81 63 48); *Le Bistro de Bordeaux* (Rue Pillier-de-Tutelle, 33000 Bordeaux; tel. 41 86 07 71); *La Vinothèque* (Rue Roé, 49000 Angers; tel. 41 86 07 71).

We should not forget the 'winstubs' of Alsace, such as:
Winstub du Sommelier (51 Grande-Rue, Bergheim; tel. 89 73 69 99); *Chez Yvonne* (10 Rue du Sanglier, 67000 Strasbourg; tel. 88 32 84 15); *Pfifferbrieder* (Place du Marché-aux-Cochons-de-Lait, 67000 Strasbourg; tel. 88 32 14 73); *Le St-Sépulcre* (15 Rue des Orfèvres, 67000 Strasbourg; tel. 88 32 39 97); *S'Parisser Stewele* (4 Pl. Jeanne-d'Arc, 68000 Colmar; tel. 89 41 42 33).

And there are several Lyonnais 'bouchons' worth visiting, such as:
Le Mitonné (26 Rue Tronchet, 69006 Lyon; tel. 78 89 36 71); *Chez Silvain* (4 Rue Tupin, 69002 Lyon; tel. 78 42 11 98); *Café des Fédérations* (8 Rue Major-Martin, 69001 Lyon; tel. 78 28 26 00); *Dussaud* (12 Rue Pizay, 69001 Lyon; tel. 78 28 10 94).

TOP CELLARS IN RESTAURANTS

If you lack the confidence and expertise to plunge straight into the search for good wine on your own, there is no better way to learn the ropes than by eating at the best restaurants; their cellars are often superb, and chefs and sommeliers alike are becoming more and more knowledgeable. The best of them will often recommend very reasonably priced wines, and many offer a 'menu-dégustation' specifically designed as an introduction to the fascinating and skilful art of marrying wines and dishes to create a harmonious meal (see the discussion between André Vedel and Alain Dutournier at the beginning of this guide).

A list of restaurants where the quality of the food is on par with that of the wine is printed below. It does not claim to be exhaustive, and you will obviously want to add your own suggestions and discoveries to it, but it will hopefully prove useful as a rough guide.

Paris

Auberge Pyrénées-Cévennes – Chez Philippe Some very good, fruity Beaujolais, good Brouilly and Chiroubles, but also some very old Bordeaux and Bourgognes. (106 Rue de la Folie-Méricourt, 75011 Paris; tel. (1) 43 57 33 78).

La Barrière de Clichy Claude Verger, assisted by Robert Turlan, is as choosy about his excellent Bordeaux and Burgundies as he is about his chefs. (1 Rue de Paris, 75017 Paris; tel. (1) 47 37 05 18).

Le Beauvilliers The menu is short, but the 70000 bottles in the cellar are marvellous: Ch. Palmer (Margaux) 1929; Ch. Yquem 1936, 1937; Bonnes-Mares et Richebourg 1930, 1936; many St-Emilions. (52 Rue Lamarck, 75018 Paris; tel. (1) 42 54 19 50).

Le Bistrot de Paris – Michel Oliver. Class always shines through. A passion for good wine, and especially good Bordeaux, runs in the family. Michel Oliver has selected 40000 quite reasonably priced bottles! (33 Rue de Lille, 75007 Paris; tel. (1) 42 61 16 83).

Au Comte de Gascogne – Claudine and Gérard Vérane. With its 1380 entries, the wine list looks very much like a telephone directory. 100000 bottles in all, amongst them eighty different estate-bottled vintages, and a collection of Armagnacs from 1893–1953.

Le Crillon – Jean-Paul Bonnin. The restaurant likes to introduce its customers to the Jura's Vin Jaune (either as an apéritif, or with foie gras, oysters and morels). All the most important labels are represented, both of Bourgogne and of Bordeaux (10 Place de la Concorde, 75008 Paris; tel. (1) 42 65 24 24).

Henri Faugeron A restaurant does not have to be old to be good: the cellar is relatively youthful, and it is growing all the time. There are about thirty youngish wines, all reasonably priced. (52 Rue de Longchamps, 75016 Paris; tel. (1) 47 04 24 53).

Le Grand Véfour The great Raymond Oliver used to favour his native Bordeaux (very old vintages). The selection remains strict, but also includes some white Châteauneuf-du-Pape and the famous Château-Grillet. (17 Rue de Beaujolais, 75001 Paris; tel. (1) 42 96 56 27).

Jamin Jamin was clever in buying several real gems: Chambertin 1943, La Tour 1933 and 1934, Lafite 1933, Pétrus 1934, Yquem 1934 and 1945. Joël Robuchon carries on the good work. (32 Rue de Longchamps, 75016 Paris; tel. (1) 47 27 12 27).

Joséphine, Chez Dumonet This solo navigator, now a fully paid-up member of the International Wine Academy, had two great loves: good food and good wine. The cellar is full of priceless treasures: Romaneé-Conti 1919, Bordeaux Rouges 1919, 1921, 1928, 1929, 1934, 1935, 1947, 1949, through to 1983, Margaux 1929 and so

on, and so forth ... (117 Rue du Cherche-Midi, 75006 Paris; tel. (1) 45 48 52 40).
Lasserre More than 180 000 bottles selected with care by R. Lasserre and his
sommeliers. Including 1928, 1929, 1934, 1937 ...(17 Av. F-D-Roosevelt, 75008
Paris; tel. (1) 43 59 53 59).
Laurent Some collectors' vintages, 1928, 1929, 1945, 1947, 1949, 1961, all on the
world's most beautiful avenue, the Champs-Elysées. (41 Av. Gabriel, 75008
Paris; tel. (1) 42 25 00 39).
Lenôtre: Le Pré Carelan Jean-Luc Pouteau, world champion sommelier, super-
vizes a varied cellar. Wines cost from 80–4500 francs. Excellent selection at
100–150 francs. (Route de Suresnes, Bois de Boulogne, 75016 Paris; tel.
(1) 45 24 55 58) and *Pavillon Elysée* (10 Av. des Champs-Elysées, 75008 Paris; tel.
(1) 42 65 86 10).
Lucas Carton – Alain Senderens. The great wines complement the splendid food
(1929, 1945, 1947, 1953, 1955). Also champagnes from 1911 (must be ordered two
weeks in advance), plus a selection from 80–1500 francs. (2 Place de la
Madeleine, 75008 Paris; tel. (1) 42 65 22 90).
La Marée The sadly missed Marcel Trompier passed on his passion for good wine
to his son Éric. Great Bordeaux (1957, 1959, 1961) and sublime Burgundies.
(1959–1982). (1 Rue Daru, 75008 Paris; tel. (1) 47 63 52 42).
Morot-Gaudry For a happy combination between wine and food this is the tops,
although prices are not quite so elevated. Old vintage Burgundies and Bordeaux.
(1926, 1928, 1929, 1934, 1945). (8 Rue de la Cavalerie, 75015 Paris; tel.
(1) 45 67 06 85).
Chez Pauline Stocks every cru, although Beaujolais and Burgundy are predominant. (5 Rue Villedo, 75001 Paris; tel. (1) 42 96 20 70).
Le Petit Colombier 'Président' Bernard Founier is setting an example by trying to
keep prices down. Estate-bottled wines, Bordeaux Premiers Crus, Burgundy and
Côtes du Rhône. (42 Rue des Acacias, 75017 Paris; tel. (1) 43 80 28 54).
Le Récamier Martin Cantegrit worships wine with wisdom and wit: Burgundies
are the stars here. (4 Rue Récamier, 75007 Paris; tel. (1) 42 22 51 75).
Le Relais Louis XIII In the cellar, are 67 000 bottles, offering a wide choice, with
a bias towards Bordelais. (91 Rue du Pont-de-Lodi, 75006 Paris; tel.
(1) 43 26 75 96).
Le Ritz – Restaurant l'Espadon The greatest domaines, the greatest vintages,
(1928, 1929, 1945, 1947 in Bordeaux; 1961 and 1969 in Burgundy), plus the
selection of Cognacs and Armagnacs started at the turn of the century by M. Ritz.
(15 Pl. Vendôme, 75001 Paris, tel. (1) 42 60 38 30).
Michel Rostang In the air-conditioned cellar visible from the restaurant, Savoie
wines have pride of place, as do some great Bordeaux. (1934, 1953, 1955) Wine
list with notes. (20 Rue Rennequin, 75017 Paris; tel. (1) 47 63 40 77).
Taillevent By common consent, one of the very best cellars in France. (15 Rue
Lamennais, 75008 Paris; tel. (1) 45 63 39 94).
Tan-Dinh Proof enough that great wines and foreign dishes can combine to make
an excellent meal. (60 Rue de Verneuil, 75007 Paris; tel. (1) 45 44 04 84).
La Tour d'Argent Every great vintage is displayed in this wine museum created by
'Monsieur' Claude Terrail for the pleasure of his delighted clientèle. (15 Quai de
la Tournelle, 75005 Paris; tel. (1) 43 54 23 31).
Au Trou Gascon Indefatigable in his search for something special, Alain
Dutournier offers extremely good vintage Armagnacs both here and at his other
establishment in the Rue de Castiglione. (40 Rue Taine, 75012 Paris; tel.
(1) 43 44 34 26).
Les Vieux Métiers de France Bordeaux holds centre-stage, but without completely
stealing the scene from the Burgundies, the Sancerre and various white wines.
(13 Bld A-Blanqui, 75013 Paris; tel. (1) 45 88 90 03).

In the Suburbs

Le Vivarois Madame Peyrot supervises a very good cellar, which is dominated by wines from the Rhône valley. (192 Av. Victor-Hugo, 750167 Paris; tel. (1) 45 04 04 31).

Le Camélia A very grand, handwritten wine list will help you to choose from Guy Delaveyne's carefully balanced selection. Margaux, St-Emilion, Pauillac, Graves, etc. All good years. (Quai G-Clemenceau, 78380 Bougival; tel. 39 69 03 02).

Le Coq Hardi The cellars carved into the hillside at Louveciennes have been drawing the faithful since 1806. Finances permitting, you will have the chance to sample Musigny 1919, Romanée Conti 1899 and 1940 and Paulillac 1806. Prices are from ˜70–8000 francs. (16 Quai Rennequin-Sualem, 78380 Bougival; tel. 39 69 01 43).

Le Duc d'Enghein A prestigious list, very strong on Bordeaux and Burgundy. (3 Av. de Ceinture, 95880 Enghien, tel. 34 12 90 00).

La Vieille Fontaine Although this is a young cellar, old vintages are to be found (Haut-Brion 1933, Margaux 1934, Corton 1934, etc.) Côtes du Rhône and Côtes de Provence are also given pride of place. (8 Av. Gretry, 786000 Maisons-Laffite, tel. 39 62 01 78).

In the Provinces

Aux Armes de France Every type of wine is kept by *M.* and *Mme.* Gaertner. Emphasis is on the wines of Alsace, but there are also plenty of Bordeaux and Burgundies. Cellar of 40 000 bottles. (8 Av. Gretry, 78600 Maisons-Laffite, tel. 39 62 01 78).

Auberge de l'Ill The cellar built up by the Haeberlin brothers has made the Auberge's reputation. All the best Alsace wines are represented, but Burgundies are not forgotten (68150 Illhaeusern; tel. 89 71 83 23).

Auberge de Kochersberg The Cellar contains Burgundies, Champagnes, Alsaces, Bordeaux, and foreign wines. Oldest vintage: Pauillac 1877. (Landersheim, 67700 Saverne; tel. 88 69 91 58).

Jean Bardet This is the favourite cellar of Gérard Depardieu and Jean Carmet. Specializes in Loire wines, as well as local wines. (36000 Chateauroux; tel. 54 34 82 69).

Georges Blanc The air-conditioned cellar serves as a kind of museum, exhibiting over 90 000 bottles, amongst them Ch. Yquem 1870, 1949, 1957. Attention is also given to local wines. Wine can be taken away or mailed. (01540 Vonnas; tel. 74 50 00 10).

Paul Bocuse 'Because the Saône is prone to flooding, I am obliged to stock up with Grands Crus'. That's Paul's excuse for having more than 25 000 bottles in his cellar, including some of his own Beaujolais from his vineyards at Lettra. (69660 Collonges-au-Mont-d'Or, tel. 78 22 01 40).

La Bonne Auberge This restaurant gives preference to white Burgundy and red Bordeaux, but there are also Provençal wines on the list! (N7, Quartier de la Brague, 06600 Antibes; tel. 93 33 36 65).

Boyer-Crayères Let the fun begin – mention almost any champagne you can think of and you will find it here. And let us not forget some great Bordeaux, too. Rare vintages: 1928, 1947. (64 Bld Henry-Vasnier, 51100 Reims; tel. 26 82 80 80).

Buerehiesel Four hundred listed wines (Alsaces, Burgundies, Bordeaux, Côtes-du-Rhône, Loire), with a few rare ones: Alsace 1928, 1934, Bordeaux 1947, Burgundies 1947, 1949. (4 Parc de l'Orangerie, 67000 Strasbourg; tel. 88 61 62 24).

Café de Paris – Pierre Laporte The biggest and best collection of magnums and jeroboams of Bordeaux. Speciality: Médoc. Oldest vintage: 1924. A very pretty list of 1450 wines. (5 Place Bellevue, 64200 Biarritz; tel. 59 24 19 53).

Le Chabichou Young regional wines. (Av. Foch, 83900 St-Tropez; tel. 94 97 00 04).

Michel Chabran Côtes du Rhône, Hermitage (1962, 1966, 1969), Châteauneuf-du-Pape (1972), Côte Rôtie (1971). (Pont-de-l'Isère, 26600 Tain-l'Hermitage; tel. 75 84 60 09).

Chanzy Voted best cellar in 1979 by the Ordre Mondial des Gourmets-Dégustateurs; a choice of 1000 wines, with a stock of more than 120000. Bias towards St-Emilion. Oldest vintage: 1875. (8 Rue Chanzy, 62000 Arras; tel. 21 71 02 02).

Alain Chapel A great centre for wine pilgrims. Some exceptional wines (Cas d'Estournel 1928, Riche-Bourg 1931, Pommard 1947), as well as wines of the region. (St-André-de-Corcy, 01390 Mionnay; tel. 78 91 82 02).

Hôtel de la Cloche His cellar has its roots in his native Burgundy: with its Gevrey-Chambertin, Volnay, Savigny and Pommard 1923. (Jean-Pierre Billoux new address 14 Place Darcy, 21000 Dijon; tel. 80 30 12 32).

La Côte-St-Jacques Jacqueline Lormais keeps watch over the treasures of the cellar. Bordeaux (1928, 1934), Romanée-Conti (1940), but all the Burgundies are there, with a very good selection of Chablis. (14 Fg. de Paris, 89300 Joigny; tel. 86 62 09 70).

Le Crocodile Emile Jung is personally responsible for this first-class cellar, which specializes in Alsatian wines, (1943, 1959, 1967) with a marked preference for Riesling and Tokay. (10 Rue de l'Outre, 67000 Strasbourg; tel. 88 32 13 02).

Darroze Large selection of Bordeaux, exceptional collection of Armagnacs. (19 Rue Castellane, 31000 Toulouse; tel. 61 62 34 70).

Dubern – La Réserve Mme Elourens and her assistants have picked the flower of Bordeaux production to please their clientèle. (42 Allées de Tourny, 33000 Bordeaux; tel. 56 07 13 28).

Le Flambard A very eclectic list! German, Italian and Californian wines shoulder-to-shoulder with fine vintage Bordeaux (1928). The list of St-Emilions is full of grands crus and vintages. (79 Rue d'Angleterre, 59800 Lille; tel. 20 51 00 06).

Hôtel de France – André Daguin. André Daguin is a food expert from Gascony, and he loves the wines of his region: Madiran, Colombard, Pacherenc; rare vintages: 1924, 1929, 1952. (2 Place de Paris, 32000 Auch; tel. 62 05 00 44).

Hôtel de la Gare More than 500 wines (125 of them Bordeaux) of which seventy are less than 100 francs a bottle, 3000 bottles of primeurs. (2 Route du Languedoc, 48130 Aumont-Aubrac; tel. 66 42 80 07).

Les Prés et les Sources d'Eugénie – Michel Guérard. Michel Guérard has been fascinated by wine for a long time, and is awaiting the first harvest of his own Côte-de-Gascogne. Speciality: Bordeaux, with more than 200 types. (Eugénie-les-Bains, 40320 Géaune; tel. 58 51 19 01).

Hiély-Lucullus All the most important wines of the Rhône valley. (55 Rue de la République, 84000 Avignon; tel. 90 86 17 07).

l'Huitrière The specialities of the house mean that the cellar favours white wines – Burgundies and wines of the Loire region. Among the red wines, Bordeaux is the most important. (3 Rue des Chats-Bossus, 59800 Lille; tel. 20 55 43 41).

Le Moulin du Kaegy An Alsacien born and bred offers old vintage Rieslings and Gewürztraminer, but there is room on the list for Bordeaux and Burgundies as well. (Steinbrunn-le-Bas, 68100 Mulhouse; tel. 89 81 30 34).

Lameloise Heaven for lovers of great Burgundies. (36 Place d'Armes, 71150 Chagny; tel. 85 87 08 85).

Léon de Lyon – Jean-Paul Lacombe. Plenty of Beaujolais, with Chirouble the star of the cellar; Bordeaux (1928), Burgundy (1945). (1 Rue Pleney, 69001 Lyon; tel. 78 28 11 33).

La Côte-d'Or – Bernard Loiseau. Run by the first winner of the Grand Prix Hachette des Cuisiniers de France, this restaurant specializes in Burgundy. Meursault, Chambertin and Volnay. (2 Rue d'Argentine, 21210 Saulieu; tel. 80 64 07 66).

Lou Mazuc Good primeurs from good years, but there are no really old vintages as yet. (12210 Laguiole; tel. 65 44 32 24).

Le Négresco – Jacques Maximin. The list will please even the most choosy of clients' white Burgundy, Bordeaux. Old vintages, plus the excellent and little-known local wine, Bellet. (37 Promenade des Anglais, 06000 Nice; tel. 93 88 39 51).

L'Oasis Louis Outhier offers a classic wine list, where fine vintage Bordeaux and Burgundy are to be found alongside the wines of Provence. (Rue Jean-Honoré-Carle, 06210 Mandelieu-la-Napoule; tel. 93 49 95 52).

L'Oustau de Baumanière A wealth of good wines courtesy of Raymond Thuillier and J-A Chariel. Among the 90 000 bottles, some great Côtes-du-Rhône and old Bordeaux (1870, 1877, 1893). (Rue Jean-Honoré-Carle, 06210 Mandelieu-la-Napoule; tel. 93 49 95 52).

Hôtel de Paris An extraordinary range of old Vins Jaunes, Arbois and old brandies. (9 Rue de l'Hôtel-de-Ville, 39600 Arbois; tel. 84 66 05 67).

Restaurant de Paris – *Loïc Martin*. Loïc loves the wines of Anjou (his favourite discovery: Coteau du Layon) Also stocks white Burgundies, Bordeaux Rouge. (52 Bis Rue Esquermoise, 59800 Lille; tel. 20 55 29 41).

Jacques Pic A real ambassador of Rhône valley wines. (285 Av. Victor-Hugo, 26000 Valence; tel. 75 44 15 32).

La Pyramide – *Chez Point* About fifty champagnes, plus some Condrieu, Ch.-Grillet; old Bordeaux (Ch. Lafite-Rothschild 1806). (14 Bld Fernand-Point, 38200 Vienne; tel. 74 53 01 96).

Jean Ramet Excellent Bordeaux, presented with wisdom and care. (7–8 Place Jean-Jaurès, 33000 Bordeaux; tel. 56 44 12 51).

Alain Raye 15 000 bottles. Savoie, Côtes du Rhône, Gewürztraminer (1974) Noble grapes, Yquem, Pétrus (1975), best Cuvée Champagnes (8 Place Charles-Albert, 73200 Albertville; tel. 79 32 00 50).

Le Relais St-Jean Wines from every area: Loire, country wines, Bordeaux (Graves). (1 Cité Bartissol, 66000 Perpignan; tel. 68 51 22 25).

Le Réverbère Wines which, if he had any sense, Claude Giraud would never part with: vintage Sauternes, Meursault 1941, 1954, 1963; Clos de Vougeot 1933; Pommard 1947, 1952. And, if you must, he will find you something from Languedoc-Roussillon. (4 Place des Jacobins, 11100 Narbonne; tel. 68 32 29 18).

Royal Gray Particularly keen on wines from Provence and the Rhône valley, but there is also a splendid list of Bordeaux (Latour 1943, Haut-Brion 1955, Sauternes 1940) and Burgundies (Pommard 1949, Bâtard-Montrachet 1945). (Hotel Gray d'Albion, 38 Rue des Serbes, 06400 Cannes; tel. 93 68 54 54).

St-James – J-M Amat. A marvellous cellar for Bordeaux. Exhaustive, interesting. (Place Camille-Hostein. Bouliac, 33270 Floirac; tel. 56 20 52 19).

Schillinger More than 35 000 bottles (Alsace, Bordeaux, Bordelais) Collectors' item: Alsace 1834. (16 Rue Stanislas, 68000 Colmar; tel. 89 41 43 17).

Trois-Gros A family concern, Jean-Baptiste and Jean, the father-and-son team, laid the foundations of a cellarful of great Burgundies (1929, 1947, 1959) Rich in Côtes du Rhône and Bordeaux, too. House champagne and a light Côte Roannaise by the jug. (Place de la Gare, 43200 Roanne; tel. 77 71 66 97).

Vanel Wine list with a preface by Antoine Blondin ('nothing but scribbles and crossings-out'). Excellent value for money. (22 Rue Maurice-Fonvielle, 31000 Toulouse; tel. 61 21 51 82).

Le Moulin de Mougins – Roger Vergé. Good years of all the top wines. American and Italian wines, but above all old vintages (1918–28). Good Bordelais (Ch. Yquem 1893). Plus Burgundies, Loire wines, wines from Alsace, Beaujolais, etc. In the cellar there are 15000 bottles including of course, the sunny local wines. (06250 Mougins; tel. 93 75 78 24).

INDEX OF APPELLATIONS

INDEX OF WINES

695

711

INDEX OF PRODUCERS, SHIPPERS AND COOPERATIVES

INDEX OF PLACES

Notes

Notes

Notes